Ats
REF
297.03

Ref. DS 37
.E523 1989

THE ENCYCLOPAEDIA OF ISLAM

NEW EDITION

ENCYCLOPÉDIE DE L'ISLAM

NOUVELLE ÉDITION

INDEX
to Volumes / des Tomes
I-V
and to the Supplement, Fascicules /
et du Supplément, Livraisons
1-6

COMPILED BY / ÉTABLI PAR
H. & J. D. PEARSON
EDITED BY / PUBLIÉ PAR
E. VAN DONZEL

D1245523

Nyack College Library

E. J. BRILL
LEIDEN • NEW YORK • KØBENHAVEN • KÖLN
ÉDITIONS G.-P. MAISONNEUVE & LAROSE S.A.
PARIS
1989

18446

Published on the recommendation of the International Council for Philosophy and Humanistic Studies.

Publié sur la recommandation du Conseil International de Philosophie et de Sciences Humaines.

The preparation of this Index of the Encyclopaedia of Islam was made possible in part through grants from the Research Tools Program of the National Endowment for the Humanities, an independent Federal Agency of the United States Government.

Library of Congress Cataloging-in-Publication Data

The Encyclopaedia of Islam / compiled by H. & J. D. Pearson = Encyclopédie de l' Islam / établi par H. & J. D. Pearson.—New ed. / edited by E. van Donzel = Nouvelle éd. / publié par E. van Donzel.
p. cm.
Index to v. 1-<5 >; and to Supplements 1-<6 >
ISBN 90-04-08849-0
1. Encyclopaedia of Islam—Indexes. 2. Islam—Indexes. 3. Islamic countries—Indexes. I. Pearson, J. D. (James Douglas), 1911- . II. Pearson, H. (Hilda) III. Donzel, E. J. van. IV. Title: Encyclopédie de l'Islam.
DS35.53.E533E53 1989
909'.097671—dc 88-38591
CIP

ISBN 90 04 08849 0

© *Copyright 1989 by E. J. Brill, Leiden, The Netherlands*

All rights reserved. No part of this book may be reproduced or translated in any form, by print, photoprint, microfilm, microfiche or any other means without written permission from the publisher

PRINTED IN THE NETHERLANDS BY E. J. BRILL

PREFACE TO THE FIRST EDITION

It is obvious that the contents of a publication such as the *Encyclopaedia of Islam* are by far much richer than might appear from the entries alone. The Editors therefore are pleased to put the wealth of information, contained already in the first three volumes of the second edition, at the disposal of the Islamologist, the Arabic, Persian and Turkish scholar, but also of the more general geographer, historian and sociologist.

The publication of this Index of over 18,000 entries has only been possible thanks to the intelligence, devotion and unfailing energy of Mrs. Hilda Pearson, who prepared, arranged and checked the cards. Her work was difficult and painstaking. The spellings are sometimes inconsistent and use different languages; the same person can have numerous names and titles, which can have changed during his lifetime and be spelt in a variety of ways; many people and places have identical names, and printing errors invariably creep into the *Encyclopaedia*, sometimes in dates given. In eliminating these disparities and in solving many other problems, constant help and encouragement was received from Professor J. D. Pearson of SOAS, London, whose collaboration proved to be essential.

The original invitation was to include only "persons, places, institutions and notions", but the Editors are grateful to Professor and Mrs. Pearson for having widened the scope of the Index to include other aspects which they felt would prove useful without, however, adding too much unnecessary weight to it.

The present publication is not designed as a complete and all-embracing index, which – apart from being an even more laborious and lengthy task – would have produced a mass of unwieldy information. It is rather an attempt to assist the researcher into the Muslim world in finding information which might be of use to him in his studies. Consequently, in cases where this world came into contact with others, e.g. with Europeans, entries have been made mainly from the Muslim point of view, and Europeans only appear when their impact on the Muslim world seems to warrant their inclusion, e.g. during the Arab conquest in Spain.

The alphabetical sequence and the spelling in general follow that adopted in the *Encyclopaedia*. If in doubt, the Arabic "a" tends to be used in favour of the Turkish "e", e.g. Aḥmad, Aḥmed. The article "al" is ignored in the sequence, and persons well-known in the form "Ibn" are placed therein, e.g. Ibn Sīna, Ibn Rushd. Titles such as "Mullā, shaykh, Mīrzā" and "al-Ẓāhir, Ḳuṭb al-Dīn", etc. do not appear before the name, except, for instance, in the case of the Ayyūbid rulers who are known by their title *al-Malik*.

Books do not appear under their titles unless they are written anonymously; they can be found under the author's names. Words which do not appear in the singular form may possibly be found under the plural form if this is in more general use.

In order to make the *Encyclopaedia* more accessible to a wider public, English and French references to the terms used in the articles have been inserted.

The Editors plan to publish a second Index of this kind after the completion of Volume V, into which will be incorporated the present one as well as the one to the Supplement to the first three Volumes. A cumulative index to the whole work is planned after the second edition of the *Encyclopaedia of Islam* and its Supplements will be completed. By having a dual Index printed, for both the English and the French editions, the Editors

have tried to put within the reach of all those interested this contribution to the study of the Muslim world.

Since a work covering so many fields can only reach perfection through collaboration, users are invited to send in their corrections.

E. VAN DONZEL

PREFACE TO THE SECOND, CUMULATIVE EDITION

The second edition of the Index, into which the first edition of 1979 is incorporated, covers Volumes I-V, and Fascicules 1-6 of the Supplement.

By far the greater part of the work was again done by Mrs. Hilda Pearson, with the assistance of Professor J. D. Pearson. The fascicules of the Supplement were indexed by the Editors of the *Encyclopaedia*.

In the process, many corrections have been made, but users are still invited to send in any further corrections of their own.

PRÉFACE DE LA PREMIÈRE ÉDITION

Il est évident que le contenu d'une publication telle que l'*Encyclopédie de l'Islam* est de beaucoup plus riche que ne le laissent paraître les seules vedettes. Aussi les Rédacteurs sont-ils heureux de mettre à la disposition des Islamologues, des chercheurs dans le domaine de l'arabe, du persan et du turc, mais aussi des géographes, des historiens et des sociologues la mine de renseignements déjà contenus dans les trois premiers volumes de la deuxième édition.

La publication de cet Index contenant plus de 18 000 noms n'a pu être réalisée que par l'intelligence, le dévouement et l'énergie inlassable de Mme Hilda Pearson, qui a préparé, classé et contrôlé les fiches. Son travail était difficile et ingrat. L'orthographe fondée parfois sur des langues différentes, n'est pas toujours consistante; le même personnage peut avoir plusieurs noms et titres différents, qui parfois même changent au cours de sa vie et sont alors écrits de diverses manières; beaucoup de personnes ou de lieux ont des noms identiques; d'autre part, des fautes d'impression se sont glissées dans l'*Encyclopédie*, quelquefois même dans les dates. L'élimination de ces disparités et la solution de nombre d'autres problèmes n'ont été possibles qu'avec l'aide et l'encouragement du Professeur J. D. Pearson, de la SOAS de Londres, dont la collaboration a été essentielle.

Mme Pearson avait été invitée à inclure «des personnages, des lieux, des institutions et des notions», mais les Éditeurs sont reconnaissants aux compilateurs d'avoir élargi l'objectif de l'Index dans la mesure qui leur a paru utile, sans pourtant l'alourdir démesurément.

Cette publication n'a pas pour but de présenter un index absolument complet. La tâche aurait été encore plus laborieuse et prolongée et aurait produit une masse d'informations peu maniable. Elle tend plutôt à aider le chercheur à trouver des renseignements qui peuvent lui être utiles dans ses recherches. Ainsi, dans le cas où le monde musulman est entré en contact avec d'autres, par exemple l'Europe, la décision d'introduire un nom ou une notion a presque toujours été prise en partant du point de vue islamique, les Européens ne figurant que dans la mesure où leur influence sur le monde musulman semble justifier leur insertion, comme par exemple pendant la conquête arabe en Espagne.

L'ordre alphabétique et l'orthographe en général suivent ceux qui ont été adoptés dans l'*Encyclopédie*. En cas de doute, le «a» arabe a tendance à être préféré au «e» turc, par exemple Aḥmad, Aḥmed. Dans l'ordre alphabétique, l'article «al» est négligé, et les personnages bien connus sous la forme «Ibn», se trouvent sous ce nom, comme par exemple Ibn Sīnā, Ibn Rus̲h̲d. Des titres comme «Mulla, S̲h̲ayk̲h̲, Mīrzā», et «al-Ẓāhir, Ḳuṭb al-dīn» etc. ne se trouvent pas devant le nom, sauf, par exemple, dans le cas des Ayyūbides, connus par leur titre *al-Malik*.

Les livres n'apparaissent sous leurs titres que quand ils sont anonymes; on les trouve sous le nom des auteurs. Des mots qui ne figurent pas au singulier peuvent être cherchés sous la forme du pluriel, si ce dernier est plus commun.

Afin de rendre l'*Encyclopédie* plus accessible, on a inséré des renvois en anglais et en français aux termes employés dans les articles.

Les Rédacteurs envisagent la publication, après l'achèvement du volume V,

d'un deuxième Index de ce genre dans lequel sera incorporé le présent Index ainsi que celui du Supplément aux trois premiers volumes. Un Index cumulatif de l'ouvrage entier est envisagé après l'achèvement de la deuxième édition de l'*Encyclopédie de l'Islam* et de ses Suppléments. En publiant un Index double pour les deux éditions anglaise et française, les Éditeurs cherchent à mettre à la portée de tout chercheur cette contribution aux études du monde musulman.

Comme un ouvrage qui couvre tant de sujets ne peut arriver à la perfection que par collaboration, les usagers sont invités à envoyer leurs corrections.

E. VAN DONZEL

PRÉFACE DE LA DEUXIÈME ÉDITION CUMULATIVE

La deuxième édition de l'Index, dans lequel la première édition de 1979 a été incorporée, couvre les Tomes I-V, et les Livraisons 1-6 du Supplément.

De nouveau, la grande majorité du travail a été faite par Mme Hilda Pearson, avec l'aide du Professeur J.D. Pearson. L'indexage des fascicules du Supplément a été fait par la Rédaction.

Au cours du travail, beaucoup de corrections ont été introduites, mais les usagers sont toujours invités à envoyer les leurs.

SYMBOLS USED

Small roman numerals denote the English version, and large roman numerals the French one. Bold type indicates the main article.

An arrow denotes: 'see', an 'a' denotes the first column on a page, a 'b' the second column and 's' the Supplement.

SYMBOLES EMPLOYÉS

Les petits chiffres romains renvoient à l'édition anglaise, les grands chiffres romains à l'édition française. Les gros caractères indiquent l'article principal.

Une flèche veut dire: «voir», tandis que les lettres a et b indiquent les colonnes et la lettre S le Supplément..

A

Aʿara ii, 246b — II, 253b
Aaron → Hārūn
Aaron b. Elijah (the Younger/le Jeune) iv, 605b — IV, 630a
Aaron b. Jeshuah → Hārūn b. al-Faradj
Aaron b. Joseph (the Elder/l'Ancien) iv, 605b, 607a — IV, 630a, 631b
al-Aʿazz i, 440a — I, 452b
Āb → Taʾrīkh
Āb-i Diz v, 830a, 867b — V, 836a, 874a
Āb-i Gargar v, 867a, b — V, 873b, 874a
ʿAbāʾ → Kisāʾ
Abā al-Khayl, Āl i, 1313a — I, 1353a
Abā 'l-Ḳiʿdān → Abḳayḳ
Abā Yazmū al-Muṣʿabī iii, 96b, 97a — III, 99a, 100a
ʿAbābda i, **1a**, 1172a — I, **1a**, 1207a
Abad i, **2a**; v, 95a — I, **2a**; V, 97b
Ābādah i, **2b** — I, **2b**
Ābādān → Abbādān
Ābādeh → Ābādah
ʿAbādila → ʿAbdalī
ʿAbādila → Dhawū ʿAbd Allāh
Abāḍites → Ibāḍiyya
Abʿādiyya → Ibʿādiyya
Abāʿir s, 117b — S, 116b
Abāḳā Khān i, 1110a, 1188b, 1295a; ii, 606b, 607b; iii, 106a, 1122a, 1125a; iv, 30b, 31a, 88a, 620b, 817a, 1167b; v, 162a, 827a — I, 1143b, 1223b, 1335a; II, 621b, 622b; III, 108a, 1149b, 1153a; IV, 32b, 33b, 92a, 645a, 850a, 1200a; V, 160a, 833a
Aban, Ramdan iv, 362b — IV, 378b
Abān → Taʾrīkh
Abān b. ʿAbd Allāh al-Marwānī s, 153a — S, 153a
Abān b. ʿAbd al-Ḥamīd al-Lāḥiḳī i, **2b**, 108a, 587a, 1216b; iii, 73a, 309a, 878b; iv, 54b, 504a, 822b — I, **2b**, 111a, 606a, 1253a; III, 75b, 318b, 903a; IV, 57b, 526a, 855b
Abān b. Ṣadaḳa i, 1034a — I, 1065b
Abān b. ʿUthmān b. ʿAffān i, **2b**; s, 230b — I, **3a**; S, 230b
Abān b. ʿUthmān b. Yaḥyā i, 3a — I, 3a
Abandon a Dieu → Islām
Abanūs i, **3a** — I, **3a**
Abarḳubādh i, **3a** — I, **3b**
Abarḳūh i, **3b** — I, **3b**
Abarshahr i, **3b** — I, **3b**
Abas i, 637b; ii, 679b — I, 658a; II, 696b
Abaskūn i, **3b** — I, **4a**
Abatteur → Djazzār
Ābāza i, **4a**, 1189a, 1190a — I, **4a**, 1224b, 1225a
Ābāza Ahmed Pasha v, 257a, b — V, 255a
Ābāza Ḥasan Pasha i, **4a**; iii, 88a, 318a, 1001b, 1248b; iv, 843b, 885a; v, 33a, b, 258a, b, 729a — I, **4b**; III, 90b, 327b, 1026b, 1281a; IV, 876b, 917b; V, 34a, b, 256a, 734a
Ābāza Meḥmed Pasha i, **4a**; ii, 712b, 724a, 1090b; iii, 1248a; iv, 869b, 970a, 971b — I, **4a**; II, 731a, 742b, 1116a; III, 1280b; IV, 903a, 1002a, 1003b, 1004a
Abāza Muḥammad Katkhudā s, 44a — S, 44b
Ābāza Muḥammad Pasha i, **4b** — I, **4b**
Abb → Ibb
ʿAbba → Libās
Abbā Djifār ii, 545b — II, 558b
ʿAbbād (Banū) → ʿAbbādid(e)s
ʿAbbād b. Djulanda i, 451a — I, 464a
ʿAbbād b. Muḥammad → al-Muʿtadid b. ʿAbbād
ʿAbbād b. Sulaymān al-Ṣaymarī i, **4b**; ii, 570a; iv, 985b; v, 576b, 806a; s, 226b, 391b — I, **5a**; 584b; IV, 1018a; V, 581a, 811b; S, 226b, 392a
ʿAbbād b. Ziyād i, **5a**; iii, 882a; iv, 536a — I, **5a**; III, 906a; IV, 559a
ʿAbbādān i, **5a**, 927b; iv, 6a, 7b, 674b, 906a, 1171b; v, 65b, 81a; s, 32a, 48b, 57a, 291a — I, **5a**, 955b; IV, 6b, 8b, 702a, 939a, 1205a; V, 67b, 83a; S, 32b, 49a, 57b, 290b
al-ʿAbbādī, Abū ʿĀṣim i, **5b** — I, **5b**
ʿAbbādid(e)s i, **5b**, 862a, 1338b; v, 632b — I, **5b**, 886b, 1379a; V, 636b
ʿAbbās, Banū iv, 361a, b, 478a — IV, 377a, b, 499a
ʿAbbās I, Shāh i, **7b**, 15a, 95a, 190a, 228b, 240b, 267b, 553b, 625b, 643a, 685b, 701a, 707b, 904a, 942b, 1013a, 1066a, 1067a, 1068a, 1117a; ii, 16b, 104a, 283a, 976a, 1083b; iii, 157b, 210b, 214a, 348a,b, 1101b, 1190a; iv, 36a, 50a, 98a, 103a, 695a, 976b, 1041a, 1044a; v, 245a, 371a, 457b, 493a, 663b, 829b, 908b, 1113b; s, 63a, 94b, 139a, b, 140a, b, 238a, 239a, 274b, 275a, 308a — I, **7b**, 15a, 98a, 194b, 235b, 248a, 275b, 571b, 646b, 663b, 706a, 722b, 728b, 931b, 971b, 1044b, 1098a, 1099a, 1100a, 1151a; II, 17a, 106b, 801b, 998a, 1108b; III, 161a, 216b, 220a, 359a, b, 1128b, 1219b; IV, 38b, 53a, 102b, 107b, 723a, 1009a, 1072a, 1075b; V, 243a, 372a, 460b, 496a, 668b, 835b, 914b, 1110a; S, 63b, 94a, 138b, 139a, b, 140b, 238a, 239a, 274b, 308a
ʿAbbās II, Shāh i, 228b, 243a, 1068a; iii, 1102b; iv, 977a; v, 493b, 869a, 1089b, 1114a; s, 139a, 276a — I, 235b, 252a, 1100b; III, 1129b; IV, 1009b; V, 496b, 875b, 1086b, 1110a; S, 138b, 275b
ʿAbbās III, Shāh ii, 310b — II, 319b
ʿAbbās b. ʿAbd al-Muṭṭalib i, **8b**, 15a, 80a, 152b; ii, 726a; iii, 328a; iv, 320a; s, 92b — I, **9a**, 15a, 82b, 157a; II, 744b; III, 338a; IV, 334b; S, 92b
ʿAbbās b. Abi 'l-Futūḥ i, **9a**, 196b, 198b; ii, 318a — I, **9a**, 202a, 204a; II, 327a
al-ʿAbbās b. Aḥmad b. Ṭūlūn i, 250b; v, 49a; s, **1a** — I, 258a; V, 50b; S, **1a**
ʿAbbās b. al-Aḥnaf i, **9b**, 587a, 1081b; ii, 1031b; iii, 1202b, 1262a; iv, 489a — I, **10a**, 606a, 1114a; II, 1055b; III, 1233a, 1294b; IV, 510a
al-ʿAbbās b. ʿAlī b. Abī Ṭālib iii, 609b, 610a, 611a; v, 823a; s, 95a — III, 630b, 631a, b; V, 829a; S, 94b
al-ʿAbbās b. ʿAmr al-Ghanawī i, **11a** — I, **11a**
al-ʿAbbās b. Djaʿfar s, 326b — S, 326a
al-ʿAbbās b. al-Faḍl iv, 733a — IV, 762b
ʿAbbās b. Firnās i, **11a**, 83a; ii, 1038a — I, **11a**, 85b; II, 1062a
al-ʿAbbās b. al-Ḥasan al-Djardjarāʾī → al-Djardjarāʾī
al-ʿAbbās b. al-Ḥusayn al-Shīrāzī i, **11b**; ii, 827a; iii, 730a — I, **11b**; II, 846b; III, 752b
al-ʿAbbās b. al-Maʾmūn i, **11b** — I, **11b**
al-ʿAbbās b. Mirdās al-Sulamī i, **12a**, 343b; ii, 1023b — I, **12a**, 354a; II, 1047a
al-ʿAbbās b. Muḥammad b. ʿAlī i, **12b**; iv, 871a — I, **12b**; IV, 904a
ʿAbbās b. Nāṣiḥ al-Thaḳafī i, **12b** — I, **12b**
ʿAbbās Āḳā Ṣarrāf s, 365a — S, 365a
ʿAbbās b. Shīth ii, 1100a — II, 1126a
al-ʿAbbās b. al-Walīd i, **12b**, 57b, 1244a; ii, 715a — I, **12b**, 59a, 1281b; II, 733b
ʿAbbās Efendī → ʿAbd al-Bahāʾ
ʿAbbās Ḥilmī I i, **13a**, 396a, 815a; ii, 149a, 423b; iv, 775b — I, **13a**, 407b, 838b; II, 153b, 434b; IV, 807a
ʿAbbās Ḥilmī II i, **13a**, 817b; iii, 515a; s, 39b, 123a, 300a — I, **13b**, 840b; III, 532b; S, 39b, 122a, 300a
ʿAbbās Khān s, 327b — S, 327a
ʿAbbās Ḳulī Khān Ādamiyyat s, 291a — S, 290b
ʿAbbās Ḳulī Khān Lārīdjānī v, 664a — V, 669a
ʿAbbās Mīrzā i, **13b**, 15a, 626a; ii, 839a, 952a; iii, 1103b, 1109a; iv, 163b, 391b, 392a, b, 462a, 861b,

1047b; v, 919a — I, **14a,** 15a, 646b; II, 858b, 974a; III, 1130b, 1136b; IV, 170b, 408b, 409a, 482b, 895a, 1078b; V, 924b
ʿAbbās Mīrzā Mulk-ārā iv, 393b — IV, 410a
ʿAbbās Sarwānī s, **1b** — S, **1b**
ʿAbbās al-S͟hihābī ii, 444a, 636a — II, 455b, 652a
ʿAbbāsa bint al-Mahdī i, **14b** — I, **14b**
ʿAbbāsa bint Aḥmad b. Ṭūlūn i, 14b — I, 14b
ʿAbbāsa bint al-Mahdī i, **14a,** 1034b; s, 263a — I, **14a,** 1066a; S, 262b
ʿAbbāsābād i, **14b** — I, **15a**
ʿAbbāsī → Sikka
al-ʿAbbāsī, Muḥammad al-Mahdī s, 411b — S, 411b
ʿAbbāsid(e)s i, **15a,** 33a, 34a, 43a, 59a, 102a, 103b, 124b, 125a, 141a, 149a, 381a, 386b, 402b, 530a, 550b, 1352a; ii, 74b, 168b, 281a, 551b, 951a; iii, 265a, 984b; iv, 15b-17b, 44b-45b, 939a; v, 326a, 347b, 620b, 736a, 1233a; s, 31b — I, **15a,** 34a, b, 44a, 61a, 105a, 106b, 128a, b, 145a, 153b, 392a, 397b, 414a, 546a, 568a, 1391a; II, 76a, 173b, 289b, 565a, 973a; III, 272b, 1009a; IV, 17a-19a, 47b-48b, 972a; V, 325b, 348b, 624b, 741b, 1223b; S, 31b
- administration ii, 78a, 143a, 144a, 304b, 305a, 324a, 890b; iv, 755a, b, 939a-943a, 973b — II, 79b, 146b, 148a, 313a, b, 333b, 911a; IV, 785b, 786a, 972a-976a, 1006a
- art, architecture i, 561a, 616a; ii, 745b, 1054b; v, 216b — I, 578a, 636b; II, 764a, 1079a; V, 214a
- histories/histoires i, 118a; iii, 899b, 925b; v, 488a — I, 121b; III, 923b, 950a; V, 491a
al-ʿAbbāsiyya → Ṭubna
ʿAbbāsiyya (Cairo/Caire) s, 208b — S, 208a
al-ʿAbbāsiyya (Ifrīḳiya) i, **24a,** 248a, 815b; iv, 829a; s, 144a — I, **24b,** 255b, 838b; IV, 862a; S, 144a
ʿAbbāsiyya (military academy/académie militaire) s, 5b — S, 4b
Abbotābād iii, 336a — III, 346b
Abbreviations s, **2a**
ʿAbbūd, Ibrāhīm v, 1064b — V, 1062a
ʿAbd, ʿabīd i, **24b,** 47a, 371a, 490b, 1060a; ii, 133b, 858b, 1079b, 1081a; iii, 3a, 277a, 345b; iv, 82b-83a, 282b, 567a, 738a, 1116a; v, 58a, 358b, 359a, 856b, 942a, 1248b — I, **25a,**48b, 381b, 505b, 1091b; II, 137a, 878b, 1104b, 1106a; III, 3b, 285a, 356a; IV, 86b-87a, 295a, 589b, 767b, 1193b; V, 59b, 359b, 360a, 863b, 946a, 1239a
ʿAbd al-Aḥad Abu Aḥmad Sirhindī s, 313a — S, 312b
ʿAbd al-Aḥad K͟hān i, 1296a — I, 1335b
ʿAbd al-ʿĀl i, 280b — I, 289a
ʿAbd al-ʿAlī al-Lak͟hnawī → Baḥr al-ʿUlūm
ʿAbd Allāh, A.H. v, 190a — V, 187b
ʿAbd Allāh, King/le roi → ʿAbd Allāh b. al-Ḥusayn
ʿAbd Allāh, Mawlāy → ʿAbd Allāh b. Ismāʿīl
ʿAbd Allāh I (Ag͟hlabid(e)) i, 248a, 250a; iii, 982a — I, 256a, 258a; III, 1006b
ʿAbd Allāh II (Ag͟hlabid(e)) i, 250b, 986b; iii, 982b — I, 258b, 1017a; III, 1007a
ʿAbd Allāh II (ʿAbd al-Wādid) iv, 1156b — V, 1188b
ʿAbd Allāh (Umayyad(e)) → ʿAbd Allāh b. Muḥammad b. ʿAbd al-Raḥmān
ʿAbd Allāh b. al-ʿAbbās i, **40a,** 55b, 107a, 567b; ii, 219b, 359b, 416a, 480b, 888b, 1071a; iii, 235b, 241a, 242a, 370b, 608b, 649a, 1081b; iv, 767b; v, 406b; s, 311a, b, 358a — I, **41a,** 57b, 110a, 585b; II, 226b, 369b, 427a, 492b, 909b, 1095b; III, 242b, 248a, 249a, 382a, 629a, 670a, 1108b; IV, 798a; V, 408a; S, 311a, 358a
ʿAbd Allāh b. ʿAbbō i, 1343a — I, 1383b
ʿAbd Allāh b. ʿAbd al-ʿAzīz b. ʿAbd al-Ḥaḳḳ v, 60b, 61a — V, 62b
ʿAbd Allāh b. ʿAbd al-ʿAzīz b. Musāʿad i, 1313a — I, 1353a
ʿAbd Allāh b. ʿAbd al-Ḥakam → Ibn ʿAbd al-Ḥakam, ʿAbd Allāh
ʿAbd Allāh b. ʿAbd al-Ḳādir i, **41b** — I, **42b**
ʿAbd Allāh b. ʿAbd al-Malik b. Marwān i, **42a**; v, 500a — I, **43b**; v, 503a
ʿAbd Allāh b. ʿAbd al-Muʾmin i, 160b; iii, 138b; s, 113b — I, 165a; III, 141b; S, 113a
ʿAbd Allāh b. ʿAbd al-Muṭṭalib i, **42b,** 80a, 438b — I, **43b,** 82b, 450b
ʿAbd Allāh b. ʿAbd al-Raḥmān I iii, 74a, 495a; iv, 254b, 672b — III, 76b, 512a; IV, 265b, 700a
ʿAbd Allāh b. ʿAbd al-Raḥmān b. Abī Bakr ii, 730a — II, 748b
ʿAbd Allāh b. ʿAbd al-Ẓāhir → Ibn ʿAbd al-Ẓāhir
ʿAbd Allāh b. Abī Bakr i, 109b, 110a, 738a — I, 112b, 113a, 760a
ʿAbd Allāh b. Abī Bakr al-Miyānad͟jī i, 840a, 841a; s, **2b, 104b** — I, 863a, 864b; S, **2a, 104a**
ʿAbd Allāh b. Abi 'l-D͟jawād i, 249b — I, 257b
ʿAbd Allāh b. Abī Isḥāḳ i, **42b;** iii, 1262a — I, **44a,** III, 1295a
ʿAbd Allāh b. Abī Sabḥ s, 221b — S, 221b
ʿAbd Allāh b. Aḥmad b. Ḥanbal i, 273b; iii, 158b; s, 16a — I, 281b; III, 162a; S, 16a
ʿAbd Allāh b. Aḥmad b. K͟halīfa iv, 953a — IV, 985b
ʿAbd Allāh b. ʿAlawī al-Haddād i, 829b — I, 852b
ʿAbd Allāh b. ʿAlī i, 16a, 17a, **43a,** 103a, 108b, 773a; ii, 281a; iii, 292b, 398a, 991a — I, 16b, 17b, **44a,** 106a, 111b, 796a; II, 289b; III, 301b, 410b, 1015b
ʿAbd Allāh b. ʿAlī al-ʿAbs͟hamī s, 26a — S, 26b
ʿAbd Allāh b. ʿAlī b. Nāṣir, Sayyid iv, 886b, 887a — IV, 919a, b
ʿAbd Allāh b. ʿAlī al-ʿUyūnī iv, 664a — IV, 690b
ʿAbd Allāh b. al-Amīn s, 116b — S, 116a
ʿAbd Allāh b. ʿĀmir i, **43b,** 47b, 107a, 304a, 441a, 695b, 1130a; ii, 811b; iii, 304a; iv, 14b, 220a; v, 56b — I, **44b,** 49a, 110a, 313b, 453b, 716b, 1164a; II, 831a; III, 313a; IV, 15b, 16a, 229b; V, 58a, b
ʿAbd Allāh b. ʿAmr al-Kindī i, 48b; iv, 837b, 838a — I, 50a; IV, 870b, 871a
ʿAbd Allāh b. Asad → al-Yāfiʿī
ʿAbd Allāh b. Barrī → Ibn Barrī, Abū Muḥammad
ʿAbd Allāh b. Budayl iv, 99b; v, 354b — IV, 104a; V, 356a
ʿAbd Allāh b. Bulayhid v, 998b — V, 994a
ʿAbd Allāh b. Buluggīn i, **43b,** 251a, 600a; ii, 1013a, 1016b — I, **45a,** 258b, 620a; II, 1036b, 1040a
ʿAbd Allāh b. D͟jabala b. Ḥayyān iii, 1151a — III, 1179a
ʿAbd Allāh b. D͟jaʿfar b. Abī Ṭālib i, **44a;** ii, 372b; iii, 608b, 819b, 889b; s, 92b — I, **45b;** II, 382b; III, 629b, 843b, 913b; S, 92b
ʿAbd Allāh b. D͟jaḥs͟h i, **44b**; v, 316a — I, **45b**; V, 315b
ʿAbd Allāh b. D͟jalwī Āl Saʿūd i, 1313a — I, 1353a
ʿAbd Allāh b. D͟jarīr al-Bad͟jalī iv, 1106b — IV, 1138a
ʿAbd Allāh b. D͟judʿān i, **44b,** 115b; iii, 389b, 739a; iv, 821a; s, 247a, 380b — I, **45b,** 118b; III, 401b, 762a; IV, 854a; S, 247a, 380b
ʿAbd Allāh b. Fayṣal ii, 176b — II, 182a
ʿAbd Allāh b. Fayṣal b. ʿAbd al-ʿAztz Āl Suʿūd s, 305b — S, 305b
ʿAbd Allāh b. Fūdī v, 222b — V, 220a
ʿAbd Allāh b. G͟haṭafān, Banū s, 225b — S, 225b
ʿAbd Allāh b. al-Ḥaḍramī → Ibn al-Ḥaḍramī
ʿAbd Allāh b. Ḥamdān ii, 453a; iii, 126b; v, 451b — II, 464b; III, 129a; V, 454a
ʿAbd Allāh b. Hammām b. al-Salūlī i, **45a** — I, **46a**
ʿAbd Allāh b. Ḥamza → al-Manṣūr biʾllāh
ʿAbd Allāh b. Ḥanẓala i, **45a,** 50a, 55a; iii, 226b, 227a; v, 997a — I, **46b,** 51b, 57a; III, 233b, 234a; V, 992a
ʿAbd Allāh b. Ḥarb → ʿAbd Allāh b. ʿAmr al-Kindī
ʿAbd Allāh b. al-Ḥārit͟h s, 233a — S, 232b

ʿAbd Allāh b. al-Ḥasan b. al-Ḥasan (ʿAlid(e)) i, **45b;** iii, 615b, 786b, 984a — I, **46b;** III, 636b, 809b, 1008b
ʿAbd Allāh b. Ḥātim iii, 125b — III, 128a
ʿAbd Allāh b. Ḥaydara i, 345a — I, 355b
ʿAbd Allāh b. Hilāl al-Ḥimyarī al-Kūfī i, **45b** — I, **47a**
ʿAbd Allāh b. Ḥumayd b. Ḳaḥṭaba v, 855b — V, 862b
ʿAbd Allāh b. Ḥumayyid al-Sālimī i, 736a; s, 356a — I, 758a; S, 356a
ʿAbd Allāh b. al-Ḥusayn i, **46a,** 447b; ii, 662b; iii, 264b, 605a, 606b, 1065b, 1066a; iv, 262a; v, 337b, 1053b, 1054b; s, 70a, 301a — I, **47a,** 460b; II, 679a; III, 272a, 626b, 627a, 1092b, 1093a; IV, 273b; V, 338a, 1050b, 1051b; S, 70b, 301a
ʿAbd Allāh b. ʿIbāḍ i, 810a; iii, 648a, 651b; s, 337b — I, 833a; III, 669b, 672b; S, 337b
ʿAbd Allāh b. Ibrāhīm al-Aghlab → ʿAbd Allāh I/II (Aghlabid(e))
ʿAbd Allāh b. Ibrāhim b. Shāhrukh i, 91a, 135a, 147b, 227b; iii, 989b — I, 93b, 139a, 152a, 234b; III, 1014a
ʿAbd Allāh b. Ibrāhīm al-Mismaʿī → al-Mismaʿī
ʿAbd Allāh b. Ibrāhīm al-Nadjdī iii, 677b — III, 699b
ʿAbd Allāh b. Idrīs al-Djaʿfarī i, 784a — I, 807a
ʿAbd Allāh b. Iskandar i, **46b,** 1295b; ii, 45a, 446a — I, **47b,** 1335a; II, 45b, 457b
ʿAbd Allāh b. Ismāʿīl i, **47a,** 356a; ii, 510b, 820a; v, 1192a — I, **48b,** 367a; II, 523a, 839b; V, 1182a
ʿAbd Allāh b. ʿItbān iv, 99b — IV, 103b
ʿAbd Allāh b. Ḳaḥṭān ii, 854a; iv, 199b — II, 874a; IV, 208a
ʿAbd Allāh b. Ḳāsim al-Fihrī i, 1309b; iii, 496a — I, 1350a; III, 513a
ʿAbd Allāh b. Ḳāsim al-Ẓāhirī i, 600a — I, 619b
ʿAbd Allāh b. Khālid b. Asīd s, 26a — S, 26a
ʿAbd Allāh b. Khaṭal iv, 821a — IV, 854a
ʿAbd Allāh b. Khurdhādhbah iv, 645b — IV, 672a
ʿAbd Allāh b. Khāzim al-Sulamī i, 3b, **47b,** 86a, 1293a — I, 4a, **49a,** 88b, 1332b
ʿAbd Allāh b. Lahīʿa s, 87b — S, 87b
ʿAbd Allāh b. Maḥfūf al-Munadjdjim iv, 1130a — IV, 1161b
ʿAbd Allāh b. Maḥmūd al-Shāshī i, 147a — I, 151b
ʿAbd Allāh b. Mālik iv, 1127a — IV, 1158b
ʿAbd Allāh b. Marwān i, 16a; ii, 906b — I, 16b; II, 92a
ʿAbd Allāh b. Masʿūd → Ibn Masʿūd
ʿAbd Allāh b. Masʿūd al-Tudjībī iii, 653b — III, 675a
ʿAbd Allāh b. Maymūn i, **48a;** ii, 170a, 301a, 850b, 851b; iii, 1072a — I, **49b;** II, 175a, 309a, 870b, 871b; III, 1099a
ʿAbd Allāh b. Mazdalī ii, 1013a — II, 1037a
ʿAbd Allāh b. Muʿāwiya i, **48b,** 53b; ii, 441a; iii, 1266a; iv, 44b, 99b, 837a, 838a; v, 63b; s, 233a — I, **50a,** 55a; II, 452b; III, 1298b; IV, 47a, 104a, 870a, 871a; V, 65b; S, 232b
ʿAbd Allāh b. al-Mubārak → Ibn Mubārak
ʿAbd Allāh b. Muḥammad → Makka
ʿAbd Allāh b. Muḥammad b. ʿAbd al-Laṭīf iii, 1065a — III, 1091b
ʿAbd Allāh b. Muḥammad b. Lubb s, 80a — S, 80a
ʿAbd Allāh b. Muḥammad b. ʿAbd al-Raḥmān al-Marwānī i, **49a,** 83b, 85b, 634a; iv, 665b; s, 153a — I, **50b,** 86a, 88a, 654b; IV, 692b; S, 153a
ʿAbd Allāh b. Muḥammad b. ʿAbd al-Salām → Abdullahi Sikka
ʿAbd Allāh b. Muḥammad b. ʿAbd al-Wahhāb iii, 678b — III, 700b
ʿAbd Allāh b. Muḥammad b. Maslama → Ibn al-Afṭas
ʿAbd Allāh b. Muḥammad b. Saʿd i, 1083a — I, 1115b
ʿAbd Allāh b. Muḥammad Āl Muʿammar ii, 321a — II, 330b
ʿAbd Allāh b. Muḥammad Fūdī ii, 942a, 1145a; iii, 276b — II, 963b, 1172a; III, 284b
ʿAbd Allāh b. Muḥammad al-Kātib i, 1309a; iv, 830a — I, 1349b; IV, 863a
ʿAbd Allāh b. Muḥammad Ḳuṭb Shāhī s, 302a — S, 301b
ʿAbd Allāh b. Muḥammad al-Māzandarānī ii, 81a; iv, 1035a — II, 82b; IV, 1066b
ʿAbd Allāh b. Muḥammad al-Taʿāʾishī (Khalīfa) i, **49b,** 765a, 962a; ii, 124a; iv, 687a, 952b, 953a; v, 268a, 1249a, 1249b-1251b — I, **50b,** 788a, 991b; II, 127a; IV, 715b, 985a, b; V, 265b, 1239b, 1240b-1242a, b
ʿAbd Allāh b. al-Muḳaffaʿ → Ibn al-Muḳaffaʿ
ʿAbd Allāh b. Mūsā b. Nuṣayr i, **50a** — I, **51b**
ʿAbd Allāh b. Muslim i, 1033b — I, 1065a
ʿAbd Allāh b. al-Muʿtazz → Ibn al-Muʿtazz
ʿAbd Allāh b. Muṭīʿ i, 45a, **50a;** iii, 226b, 227b — I, 46b, **51b;** III, 233b, 234a
ʿAbd Allāh b. Nawf i, 850b — I, 874a
ʿAbd Allāh b. Rabīʿ iii, 650b — III, 672a
ʿAbd Allāh b. Rabīʿa b. Riyāḥ al-Hilālī s, 92b — S, 92b
ʿAbd Allāh b. al-Rand ii, 463b; iv, 415b; v, 1181b — II, 475a; IV, 433b; V, 1171b
ʿAbd Allāh b. Rashīd → Rashīd, Āl
ʿAbd Allāh b. Rawāḥa i, **50b,** 968b; ii, 372a; iii, 354a; iv, 835b, 1187b; v, 398b — I, **52a,** 998b; II, 382b; III, 365a; IV, 868b, 1220a; V, 400a
ʿAbd Allāh b. Sabaʾ i, **51a,** 382b; ii, 1094a; iii, 1164a — I, **52b,** 393b; II, 1119b; III, 1192b
ʿAbd Allāh b. Saʿd i, **51b,** 115a, 451b, 966a, 1029a, 1157b; ii, 131a, 327b, 525b, 615a; iv, 825b; v, 90b — I, **53a,** 118a, 464b, 996a, 1060b, 1192a; II, 134b, 337a, 538b, 630b; IV, 858b; V, 93a
ʿAbd Allāh b. Salām i, **52a,** 1020b; ii, 363a; iii, 1232b; iv, 212a, 824b — I, **53b,** 1052a; II, 373a; III, 1264b; IV, 221b, 857b
ʿAbd Allāh b. Ṣāliḥ s, 397a — S, 397a
ʿAbd Allāh b. Sālim Āl Ṣabaḥ v, 575a — V, 579b
ʿAbd Allāh I b. Saʿūd ii, 321a; iii, 362b, 999a — II, 330b; III, 374a, 1024a
ʿAbd Allāh b. Shaykh i, 781b — I, 804b
ʿAbd Allāh b. Sinān iv, 117a — IV, 122a
ʿAbd Allāh b. Ṭāhir i, **52b,** 99b, 121b, 154a, 157b, 241a, 619a, 685a, 789b; ii, 524a; iii, 1083a; iv, 17a, 20b, 531a, 646a, b; v, 57b, 872b, 923a; s, 15a — I, **54a,** 102a, 125a, 158a, 162a, 248b, 637b, 706a, 812b; II, 537a; III, 1109b; IV, 18b, 22a, 554a, 672b, 673a; V, 59b, 878b, 928b; S, 15a
ʿAbd Allāh b. Ṭarīf iii, 659b — III, 680b
ʿAbd Allāh b. Thawr → Abū Fudayk
ʿAbd Allāh b. Ubayy b. Salūl i, **53a,** 307b, 514b, 1283a; iv, 824b, 1187b; v, 996b; s, 133b — I, **54b,** 317b, 530a, 1322b; IV, 857b, 1220a; V, 991b; S, 133a
ʿAbd Allāh b. ʿUfayṣān iv, 751a — IV, 781b
ʿAbd Allāh b. ʿUmar b. ʿAbd al-ʿAzīz i, 49a, **53b,** 257b; ii, 90a, 744b; v, 731a — I, 50a, **55a,** 265b; II, 92a, 763a; V, 736a
ʿAbd Allāh b. ʿUmar al-ʿArdjī → al-ʿArdjī
ʿAbd Allāh b. ʿUmar b. al-Khaṭṭāb i, 40a, 50b, **53b,** 382b; iii, 65a — I, 41b, 51b, **55b,** 393b; III, 67b
ʿAbd Allāh b. ʿUmāra s, 223a — S, 223a
ʿAbd Allāh b. Unays al-Djuhanī iii, 540b; v, 315b — III, 559b; V, 315a
ʿAbd Allāh b. ʿUthmān ii, 737a — II, 755b
ʿAbd Allāh b. Wahb al-Ḳurashī → Ibn Wahb
ʿAbd Allāh b. Wahb al-Rāsibī i, **54b;** iii, 235a; iv, 1074b, 1075a — I, **56a;** III, 242a; IV, 1106b
ʿAbd Allāh b. Yaḥyā al-Kindī → Ṭālib al-Haḳḳ
ʿAbd Allāh b. Yāsīn i, 762a, 864a, 1044b, 1176a; ii, 527a, 1121b; v, 653b, 654a, b; s, 27a — I, 785a, 888a, 1076a, 1211a; II, 540a, 1148a; V, 657b, 658b; S, 27a
ʿAbd Allāh b. Yazīd (Ibāḍī) s, 225b — S, 225b
ʿAbd Allāh b. al-Ziʿbarā s, 91a — S, 90b

ʿAbd Allāh b. al-Zubayr i, 41a, 45a, 50b, **54b,** 76b, 77a, 107a, 113b, 115a, 148b, 443b, 453b, 482a, 550a, 704a, 713b, 784b, 810a; ii, 89b, 197a, 360a, 415a; iii, 40a, 226b, 270b, 607b, 608b, 620b, 970a, 1254b; iv, 319a, 493a, 938a, 1075b; v, 997a, 1231a, 1232a; s, 26a, 230b, 311a, b, 357b — I, 42a, 46a, 52a, **56b,** 78b, 79a, 110a, 116b, 118a, 153a, 456a, 466b, 496a, 567b, 725b, 735b, 807b, 833a; II, 91a, 203b, 370a, 425b; III, 41b, 233b, 278b, 628b, 629b, 641a, 994b, 1287b; IV, 333a, b, 514a, 971a, 1107a; V, 992a, 1221b, 1222b; S, 26b, 230b, 311a, b, 357b
ʿAbd Allāh Abū Dj̲ābir b. ʿAbd Allāh s, 230a — S, 230a
ʿAbd Allāh Abuʾl-Dj̲imāl, Sīdī v, 51a — V, 52b
ʿAbd Allāh Āl Kh̲alīfa ii, 108b — II, 111a
ʿAbd Allāh Āl Th̲ānī ii, 177b — II, 183a
ʿAbd Allāh al-Aydarus i, 781a — I, 804a
ʿAbd Allāh al-Balʿamī → al-Balʿamī
Abd Allāh al-Balansī → ʿAbd Allāh b. ʿAbd al-Raḥmān I
ʿAbd Allāh al-Bayyāsī i, 1150b; ii, 516a — I, 1184b; II, 528b
ʿAbd Allāh Bey s, 268a — S, 267b
ʿAbd Allāh Bosnevī i, 1271b — I, 1310b
ʿAbd Allāh Dj̲ammāʿ al-Ḳāsimī iv, 892b — IV, 925b
ʿAbd Allāh Dj̲ewdet → Dj̲ewdet
ʿAbd Allāh al-Gh̲ālib biʾllāh (Saʿdid(e)) i, **55b,** 245a, 859b, 1224b; ii, 619b; s, 377b — I, **57b,** 252b, 883b, 1261a; II, 635a; S, 377b
ʿAbd Allāh al-Ḥas s, 248a — S, 248b
ʿAbd Allāh Ilāhī, Mollā s, 51b — S, 52a
ʿAbd Allāh al-Kātib → ʿAbd Allāh b. Muḥammad
ʿAbd Allāh Kh̲ān → Ḥasan ʿAlī Bārha
ʿAbd Allāh Kh̲ān (1855) s, 46a — S, 46b
ʿAbd Allāh Kh̲ān (Gh̲azīpūr) s, 325b — S, 325a
ʿAbd Allāh Kh̲ān (Kh̲īwa, 1920) iv, 1065b — IV, 1097a
ʿAbd Allāh Kh̲ān Brahoi i, 1005b — I, 1036b
ʿAbd Allāh Kh̲ān b. Iskandar (Sh̲aybānid(e)) s, 340a, b — S, 339b, 340a
ʿAbd Allāh Kh̲ān Rohilla iii, 60a, b — III, 62b, 63a
ʿAbd Allāh Ḳuṭb al-Mulk → Ḥasan ʿAlī Bārha
ʿAbd Allāh Ḳuṭb Sh̲āh iii, 318b, 319a, 427a; v, 549b — III, 328a, 330a, 440b; V, 554b
ʿAbd Allāh Marwārīd iii, 490b — III, 507b
ʿAbd Allāh Mīrzā i, 91a, 227b; s, 51a — I, 93b, 234b; S, 51b
ʿAbd Allāh Niyāzī Sirhindī ii, 500a, b; iii, 492b — II, 512b, 513a; III, 509b
ʿAbd Allāh Suhrawardī s, 10b, 11a — S, 10a
ʿAbd Allāh Sulṭānpūrī v, 1235b; s, **3a** — V, 1226a; S, **2a**
ʿAbd Allāh Pas̲h̲a → Fikrī
ʿAbd Allāh Pas̲h̲a i, 1078b; ii, 210a, 636a — I, 1111a; II, 216b, 652a
ʿAbd Allāh Pas̲h̲a Muḥsin-Zāde Čelebi i, **56a,** 292a; iii, 132b — I, **58a,** 301a; III, 135a
ʿAbd Allāh al-Riḍā → ʿAbd Allāh al-Sh̲aykh̲ al-Ṣāliḥ
ʿAbd Allāh Saʿd i, 765a; ii, 351b — I, 788a; II, 361b
ʿAbd Allāh Sari → Sari ʿAbd Allāh Efendī
ʿAbd Allāh Sh̲aṭṭārī, Sh̲aykh̲ i, 1284a — I, 1323b
ʿAbd Allāh al-Sh̲aykh̲ al-Ṣāliḥ iii, 262b — III, 270a
ʿAbd al-ʿAllām Fayẓ Kh̲ān Og̲h̲lu iv, 505a — IV, 527a
ʿAbd ʿAmr → ʿAbd al-Raḥmān b. ʿAwf
ʿAbd al-As̲h̲hal i, 771b — I, 794b
ʿAbd al-ʿAzīz (Banū ʿAbbās) iv, 478a — IV, 499a
ʿAbd al-ʿAzīz (Gh̲alzay) i, 229a; iii, 603b — I, 236a; III, 624b
ʿAbd al-ʿAzīz (Mamlūk) ii, 781b — II, 800a
ʿAbd al-ʿAzīz I (Marīnid(e)) → Abū Farīs ʿAbd al-ʿAzīz I
ʿAbd al-ʿAzīz (Ottoman) i, **56b,** 285b, 286b, 397b, 836b, 948a; ii, 49a, 935b; iii, 250a, 621b; iv, 876a; s, 281b — I, **58a,** 294a, 295a, 408b, 860a, 977b; II, 50a, 957b; III, 257a, 642a; IV, 909a; S, 281b
ʿAbd al-ʿAzīz, Mawlāy → ʿAbd al-ʿAzīz b. al-Ḥasan
ʿAbd al-ʿAzīz b. ʿAbd al-Ḥakk v, 60a — V, 62a
ʿAbd al-ʿAzīz b. ʿAbd al-Ḳādir b. Gh̲aybī i, 67a — I, 68b
ʿAbd al-ʿAzīz b. ʿAbd al-Raḥmān b. Abī ʿĀmir i, 446a, 985b — I, 459a, 1016a
ʿAbd al-ʿAzīz b. Abī Dulaf ii, 623b; iv, 100a — II, 639a; IV, 104a
ʿAbd al-ʿAzīz b. Dj̲aʿfar → Gh̲ulām al-Kh̲allāl
ʿAbd al-ʿAzīz b. Fayṣal al-Dawīsh → ʿUzayyiz b. Fayṣal
ʿAbd al-ʿAzīz b. al-Ḥādjdj Ibrāhīm i, **57a** — I, **58b**
ʿAbd al-ʿAzīz b. al-Ḥadj̲dj̲ādj̲ i, **57a;** iii, 990b — I, **59a;** III, 1015a
ʿAbd al-ʿAzīz b. al-Ḥasan i, **57b,** 357a, 1281b; ii, 820a; iii, 62a, 240a, 562a; v, 890a, 1193a, b; s, 114a — I, **59b,** 368a, 1320b; II, 839b; III, 64b, 247a, 581b; V, 896b, 1183a, b; S, 113b
ʿAbd al-ʿAzīz b. Ḥātim i, 1041a; ii, 679a — I, 1072b; II, 696a
ʿAbd al-ʿAzīz b. Marwān i, 42b, **58a,** 76b, 77b, 148b, 1242b; ii, 327b, 427b, 788a, 958a; iii, 271b, 572a, 819b; v, 552a, b; s, 273a — I, 43b, **60a,** 78b, 80a, 153a, 1280a; II, 337a, 438b, 807a, 980b; III, 279a, 591b, 843b; V, 557a, b; S, 273a
ʿAbd al-ʿAzīz b. Muḥammad b. al-Nuʿmān ii, 169b; iii, 78b, 79a — II, 174b; III, 81a, b
ʿAbd al-ʿAzīz b. Muḥammad b. Saʿūd i, 554a; ii, 321a, 492b; iii, 678b; iv, 925a, b — I, 571b; 330b, 504b; III, 700a; IV, 958a, b
ʿAbd al-ʿAzīz b. Muḥammad al-Fis̲h̲tālī i, **58a,** 289a — I, **60a,** 298a
ʿAbd al-ʿAzīz b. Mūsā b. Nuṣayr i, 50a, **58b,** 608b, 1054b, 1338b; ii, 485b. 1009a, 1012b; iii, 587b; iv, 115a, 672b; v, 367b — I, 51b, **60b,** 628a, 1086b, 1378b; II, 497b, 1032b, 1036a; III, 607b; IV, 120a, 700a; V, 368b
ʿAbd al-ʿAzīz b. Sh̲uʿayb i, 121b; iii, 1084b, 1085a — I, 125a; III, 1111b, 1112a
ʿAbd al-ʿAzīz b. Yūsuf s, **4a** — S, **3b**
ʿAbd al-ʿAzīz b. al-Walīd i, **58b** — I, **60b**
ʿAbd al-ʿAzīz al-Ahwānī ii, 743b; v, 605b, 608b — II, 762a; V, 609b, 612b
ʿAbd al-ʿAzīz Āl Saʿūd i, 39a, 233b, 443b, 555b, 709b, 762a, 885b, 958a, 1299a, 1313a; ii, 77a, 108b, 175b, 176b, 354a, 569a, 573a, 626a, 660a; iii, 238a, 263b, 326b, 361b, 365a, 643b, 1062a, 1064b, 1066a, b; iv, 680b, 703b, 765b, 925b, 1073a; v, 63a, 574b, 575a, 998a, 999a; s, **3b,** 4b, 293b, 305b — I, 40a, 241a, 456b, 572b, 731a, 785a, 911b, 987a, 1339a, 1353a; II, 78b, 111a, 181a, 182a, 363b, 583a, 587a, 641b, 676b; III, 245a, 271b, 337a, 372b, 376b, 665a, 1088b, 1091a, 1092b, 1093a; IV, 708b, 732a, 796a, 958b, 1104b; V, 64b, 579a, b, 993b, 994a; S, **2b,** 3b, 293a, 305b
ʿAbd al-ʿAzīz al-Bakrī i, 6a, 155b; ii, 1009a — I, 6a, 159b; II, 1032b
ʿAbd al-ʿAzīz al-Bawandī ii, 436a — II, 447b
ʿAbd al-ʿAzīz al-Dabbāg̲h̲ i, 277b; v, 647b — I, 286a; V, 651b
ʿAbd al-Azīz al-Dihlawī, Sh̲āh i, **59a,** 1193a; ii, 254b — I, **60b,** 1228a; II, 261b
ʿAbd al-ʿAzīz Efendi Ḳara Čelebizāde → Ḳara Čelebizāde
ʿAbd al-Azīz Fahmī iii, 516a, 518b — III, 533b, 536a
ʿAbd al-ʿAzīz Kh̲ān i, 1295b; ii, 446a — I, 1335b; II, 458a
ʿAbd al-ʿAzīz al-Manṣūr → ʿAbd al-ʿAzīz b. ʿAbd al-Raḥmān
ʿAbd al-Bahāʾ i, 915b, 916b, 917a, 918a; s, 77a — I,

943b, 944a, b, 945b; S, 76b
ʿAbd al-Bāḳī, Maḥmūd → Bāḳī
ʿAbd al-Bāḳī (Farangī Maḥall) s, 4b, 292a — S, 3b, 292a
ʿAbd al-Bāḳī b. ʿAlī b. Muḥammad s, 122b — S, 122a
ʿAbd al-Bāḳī al-Fārūḳī → al-Fārūḳī
ʿAbd al-Bāḳī al-Ḥanbalī iii, 677b — III, 699b
ʿAbd al-Bāḳī Nahāwandī i, 857a — I, 880b
ʿAbd al-Bāḳī Nakshbandī → Bāḳī biʾllāh
ʿAbd al-Bārī, Ḳiyām al-Dīn Muḥammad s, **4b**, 74a, b, 292a, b, 293b, 360b — S, **3b**, 74b, 75a, 292a, 293a, 360b
ʿAbd al-Barr b. ʿAnbasa iv, 346b — IV, 361a
ʿAbd al-Dār, Banū iv, 320a; v, 581a, b — IV, 334b; V, 586a, b
ʿAbd al-Djabbār, Shaykh ii, 964a — II, 986a
ʿAbd al-Djabbār b. ʿAbd al-Raḥmān al-Azdī i, **59a** — I, **61a**
ʿAbd al-Djabbār b. Aḥmad i, **59b**, 343a; iii, 832a, 905b, 1019a, 1023a, 1071b, 1072a, 1144a, 1165b, 1171a; iv, 615b, 985b; v, 96a, 97a, 237a, 240a, 833b; s, 13a, b, 14a, 25a, b, 31b, 225b, 343a, b, 346a, 348a, 392a, 393a — I, **61b**, 353b; III, 856a, 929b, 1045a, 1049a, 1098b, 1172b, 1194b, 1200a; IV, 640a, 1018a; V, 98a, 99b, 235a, 238a, 839b; S, 13b, 14a, 25b, 32a, 225b, 342b, 343a, 348a, 392b, 393a
ʿAbd al-Djabbār b. al-Ḥusayn b. Muʿayya s, 19a — S, 19a
ʿAbd al-Djabbār b. Ḳays al-Murādī iii, 653b — III, 675a
ʿAbd al-Djalīl b. ʿAbd al-Malik ii, 402a — II, 412b
ʿAbd al-Djalīl Abu ʾl-Maḥāsin → al-Dihistānī
ʿAbd al-Fattāḥ ʿAmr s, 301a — S, 301a
ʿAbd al-Fattāḥ Fūmanī i, **60a**, — I, **61b**
ʿAbd al-Ghaffār b. ʿAbd al-Karīm → al-Ḳazwīnī
ʿAbd al-Ghaffār al-Akhras → al-Akhras
ʿAbd al-Ghaffār al-Dasūḳī → al-Dasūḳī, Ibrāhīm b. Ibrāhīm
ʿAbd al-Ghaffār al-Ḥimṣī iv, 115b — IV, 120b
ʿAbd al-Ghaffār Khān v, 251a — V, 249a
ʿAbd al-Ghāfir (Ghaffār) b. Husayn al-Kādjgharī iv, 699a — IV, 727a
ʿAbd al-Ghanī b. Ismāʿīl al-Nābulusī i, **60a**, 596a, 795b, 1109b, 1235b; ii, 900a; iii, 935a; iv, 1006b — I, **62a**, 615b, 819a, 1143a, 1272b; II, 921a; III, 959b; IV, 1038b
ʿAbd al-Ghanī b. Saʿīd al-Miṣrī s, 38a — S, 38a
ʿAbd al-Ghanī al-Maḳdisī → al-Maḳdisī, ʿAbd al-Ghanī
ʿAbd al-Hādī, Banū iv, 834b — IV, 867b
ʿAbd al-Ḥāfiẓ → al-Ḥāfiẓ, ʿAbd
ʿAbd al-Ḥakam, Banū → Ibn ʿAbd al-Ḥakam
ʿAbd al-Ḥakīm ʿĀmir s, 5b, 8b, 9a — S, 4b, 8a, b
ʿAbd al-Hakīm al-Siyālkōtī → al-Siyālkōtī
ʿAbd al-Ḥaḳḳ, Shaykh s, 10b — S, 10a
ʿAbd al-Ḥaḳḳ b. ʿAbd al-ʿAzīz b. Khurāsān iii, 137b; v, 60a — III, 140b; V, 61b, 62a
ʿAbd al-Ḥaḳḳ b. Faḍl-i Ḥaḳḳ ii, 735b, 736b — II, 754a, 755a
ʿAbd al-Ḥaḳḳ b. Sayf al-Dīn al-Dihlawī i, **60b**, 702b, 957a; ii, 296b — I, **62b**, 724a, 986b; II, 304b
ʿAbd al-Ḥaḳḳ Abū Muḥammad → Marīnid(e)s
ʿAbd al-Ḥaḳḳ Ḥāmid i, **61a**, 1302a; ii, 692b; iii, 1199b; iv, 1153a; s, 149b — I, **63a**, 1342a; II, 709b; III, 1229b; IV, 1185a; S, 150a
ʿAbd al-Ḥaḳḳ al-Ishbīlī s, 389b — S, 389b
ʿAbd al-Ḥaḳḳ Mollā i, 61a, 921a; iv, 1153a — I, 63a, 948b; IV, 1185a
ʿAbd al-Ḥaḳḳ Muḥaddith i, 260a; iii, 430a, 435a — I, 268a; III, 444a, 449a
ʿAbd al-Ḥalīm Maḥmūd s, 224b — S, 225a
ʿAbd al-Ḥalīm Pasha iii, 515a — III, 532b
ʿAbd al-Ḥamīd I i, **62b**, 481b, 1004a; ii, 209b, 534a; iv, 946a; v, 314a; s, 401b — I, **64a**, 496a, 1035a; II, 216a, 547a; IV, 978b; V, 313b; S, 402a
ʿAbd al-Ḥamīd II i, **63b**, 286b, 289b, 294b, 298b, 431a, 657a, 736a, 776a, 948a, 958a, 1090a; ii, 104b, 289a, 354b, 418b, 430b, 474b, 489b, 513b, 532a, 533b, 642a, 682a, 878b; iii, 357b, 364a, 993a, 994a, 1199a, 1257b; iv, 168b, 681b, 872a, 876b, 946a; v, 61b, 905a, 949a, 1035a; s, 100b, 161b, 179a, 211b, 282b, 296b, 330b, 359b — I, **65b**, 295a, 298b, 303b, 307b, 443a, 678a, 758a, 799b, 977b, 987a, 1122b; II, 107a, 297a, 364b, 429b, 441b, 486b, 502a, 526b, 545a, 546b, 658a, 699a, 898b; III, 368b, 375b, 1018a, 1019a, 1229b, 1290b; IV, 176a, 709b, 905b, 909b, 979a; V, 63a, 911b, 952b, 1031b; S, 99b, 161b, 180a, 211b, 282b, 296a, 330a, 359b
ʿAbd al-Ḥamīd b. Bādīs → Ibn Bādīs
ʿAbd al-Ḥamīd b. Yaḥyā b. Saʿd i, **65b**, 588a; ii, 304b; iii, 494b, 1242b, 1263a; iv, 755b — I, **67b**, 607a; II, 313a; III, 511b, 1274b, 1296a; IV, 786a
ʿAbd al-Ḥamīd Efendi ii, 878b — II, 898b
ʿAbd al-Ḥamīd Khān iv, 711a — IV, 739b
ʿAbd al-Ḥamīd Lāhawrī i, **66a** — I, **68a**
ʿAbd al-Ḥayy, Mawlawī iv, 196a; s, 4b — IV, 204b; S, 3b
ʿAbd al-Ḥayy, Shaykh s, 312a — S, 312a
ʿAbd al-Hayy al-Lakhnawī i, **66a**, 282b; iii, 164a; s, 292b, 293a — I, **68a**, 291a; III, 167b; S, 292b
ʿAbd al-Ḥusayn Hazhīr ii, 882b — II, 903a
ʿAbd al-Ḥusayn, Mīrzā iv, 979a — IV, 1011b
ʿAbd al-Ilāh ii, 827b; iii, 264a — II, 892b; III, 271b
ʿAbd al-Kaʿba → ʿAbd al-Raḥmān b. Abī Bakr; ʿAbd al-Raḥmān b. ʿAwf; ʿAbd al-Raḥmān b. Samura
ʿAbdelkader → ʿAbd al-Ḳādir
ʿAbd el-Kader → ʿAbd al-Ḳādir b. Muḥyī al-Dīn
ʿAbd al-Ḳādir (Fundj) ii, 944a — II, 966a
ʿAbd al-Ḳādir b. Burhān Shāh iii, 625b, 1161a — III, 646b, 1189a
ʿAbd al-Ḳādir b. Ghaybī i, **66b**; ii, 1074a — I, **68b**; II, 1098b
ʿAbd al-Ḳādir b. Muḥyī al-Dīn al-Ḥasanī i, **67a**, 85a, 357a, 369a, 789a, 1177b, 1197b, 1247a; ii, 160b, 173a, 288b; iii, 561b, 806b; iv, 362a, 383a; v, 1160b, 1192b; s, 296a — I, **69a**, 87b, 367b, 380a, 812b, 1212b, 1232b, 1285a; II, 165b, 178a, 296b; III, 581a, 829b; IV, 378a, 400a; V, 1150a, 1182b; S, 296a
ʿAbd al-Ḳādir al-ʿAydarūs i, 255b, 594b, 781a; iv, 449b — I, 263b, 614a, 804b; IV, 469b
ʿAbd al-Ḳādir Badāʾūnī → Badāʾūnī
ʿAbd al-Ḳādir al-Baghdādī i, **68a**, 712b; s, 388a, 407b — I, **70a**, 734a; S, 388b, 407b
ʿAbd al-Ḳādir Dihlawī i, **68b**; ii, 735b; iv, 196a — I, **70b**; II, 754a; IV, 204b
ʿAbd al-Ḳādir al-Djīlānī (Djīlī) i, **69a**, 91b, 137b, 595b, 1173a; ii, 535b; iii, 160b, 842b; iv, 380a-383a, 1134a; v, 475a, 1201a; s, 182b, 223b, 323b — I, **70b**, 94b, 141b, 615a, 1208a; II, 549a; III, 164a, 866b; IV, 396b-399b, 1165b; V, 478a, 1191a; S, 182b, 223b, 323a
ʿAbd al-Ḳādir al-Fāsī → al-Fāsī, ʿAbd al-Ḳādir
ʿAbd al-Ḳādir al-Gīlānī → ʿAbd al-Ḳādir al-Djīlānī
ʿAbd al-Ḳādir al-Ḳurashī i, **70b**; s, 191b — I, **72b**; S, 193a
ʿAbd al-Ḳādir al-Maghribī ii, 451b; iv, 159a — II, 463b; IV, 166a
ʿAbd al-Ḳādir Sirhindī, Mawlānā s, 3a — S, 2b
ʿAbd al-Ḳāhir b. Ṭāhir al-Baghdādī → al-Baghdādī
ʿAbd al-Ḳāhir al-Djurdjānī → al-Djurdj anī
ʿAbd al-Karīm, Mīr i, 254a — I, 261b
ʿAbd al-Karīm b. ʿAdjarrad → Ibn ʿAdjarrad
ʿAbd al-Karīm b. ʿAli Pérez i, 405a — I, 416b
ʿAbd al-Karīm b. Mughīth s, 92a — S, 92a

ʿAbd al-Karīm Bukhārī i, **71a** — I, **73a**
ʿAbd al-Karīm al-Djazārī, Banū iii, 961a — III, 986a
ʿAbd al-Karīm al-Djīlī i, **71a,** 596a; iii, 329a, 709a, 1240b; v, 525b — I, **73a,** 615b; III, 339a, 731a, 1272b; V, 529b
ʿAbd al-Karīm Kashmīrī i, **71b** — I, **73b**
ʿAbd al-Karīm al-Khalīl iii, 519b, 1259a — III, 537b, 1291b
ʿAbd al-Karīm Khān (Ḳarakhānid) iii, 1113b; iv, 698b; v, 856b — III, 1141a; IV, 727a; V, 863a
ʿAbd al-Karīm Khān (Noghay) i, 721b — I, 743b
ʿAbd al-Karīm Khān b. Shāhrukh v, 29a — V, 30a
ʿAbd al-Karīm Lāhurī ii, 55a — II, 56a
ʿAbd al-Karīm Munshī i, **72a** — I, **74a**
ʿAbd al-Ḳays i, **72b,** 529a, 545a, 942a; iv, 764a; v, 346a; s, 24b — I, **74b,** 545a, 562a, 971a; IV, 794b; V, 347a; S, 25a
ʿAbd al-Khāliḳ Ḥassūna s, 240b — S, 241a
ʿAbd al-Khāliḳ b. Abi'l-Ṭalḥ al-Shihābī iii, 124b — III, 127a
ʿAbd al-Ḳuddūs, Iḥsān v, 190a — V, 187b
ʿAbd al-Ḳuddūs al-Anṣārī v, 1005b — V, 1001a
ʿAbd al-Ḳuddūs Gangōhī, Shaykh ii, 54b, 55a, 56a — II, 55b, 56a, b
ʿAbd al-Laṭīf al-Baghdādī i, **74a,** 595a; iii, 877a, 956b; v, 862a, 1129b, 1130a; s, 115b, 408a — I, **76b,** 614a; III, 901a, 981a; V, 869a, 1125b, 1126a; S, 115a, 408a
ʿAbd al-Laṭīf Čelebī → Laṭīfī
ʿAbd al-Laṭīf Ḳastamunilī → Laṭīfī
ʿAbd al-Laṭīf Khān (Ḳazān) iv, 849a — IV, 882a
ʿAbd al-Laṭīf Khān (Samarḳand) i, 46b — I, 48a
ʿAbd al-Laṭīf Mīrzā i, 91a, 227b — I, 93b, 234a
ʿAbd al-Madān iii, 223a, b — III, 229b, 230a
ʿAbd al-Madjīd I (Abdülmecid) i, 37a, **74b,** 216b, 284b, 298a, 776a; 1226a; ii, 49a, 613a, 801a, 912a, 935a; iv, 143a — I, 38a, **77a,** 223a, 293b, 307b, 799a, 1262b; II, 50a, 628a, 820a, 933b, 957a; IV, 149a
ʿAbd al-Madjīd II (Abdülmecid) i, **75b,** ii, 119b; iv, 946b — I, **77b,** II, 122b; IV, 979b
ʿAbd al-Madjīd (Fāṭimid(e)) → al-Ḥāfiẓ
ʿAbd al-Madjīd Salīm s, 208b — S, 208b
ʿAbd al-Malik I (Sāmānid(e)) i, 421b, 984b; iii, 46b; v, 325a, 1162b; s, 230b, 357b, 358a — I, 433b, 1015a; III, 48b; V, 324b, 1152a; S, 230b, 357b, 358a
ʿAbd al-Malik II iii, 196b — III, 201a
ʿAbd al-Malik b. Abī ʿĀmir i, **75b,** 446a, 494b, 1040b; iii, 495b, 819a; iv, 632b — I, **77b,** 459a, 509b, 1072a; III, 512b, 842b; IV, 657b
ʿAbd al-Malik b. Aḥmad II b. Hūd → ʿImād al-Dawla b. Hūd
ʿAbd al-Malik b. ʿAttāsh → Ibn ʿAttāsh
ʿAbd al-Malik b. Bishr b. Marwān, Amīr s, 52a — S, 52b
ʿAbd al-Malik b. Ḥabīb iv, 87a, b — IV, 91a, b
ʿAbd al-Malik b. Hishām → Ibn Hishām, ʿAbd al-Malik
ʿAbd al-Malik b. Ḳaṭan al-Fihrī i, **76a,** 991a; iv, 494b, 672b, 805a — I, **78a,** 1021b; IV, 515b, 700a, 837b
ʿAbd al-Malik b. Makkī iv, 338a — IV, 352a
ʿAbd al-Malik b. al-Manṣūr → (a) ʿAbd al-Malik b. Abī ʿĀmir (b) ʿAbd al-Malik al-Muẓaffar
ʿAbd al-Malik b. Marwān i, 2b, 45a, 47b, 55b, 58a, **76a,** 120a, 142a, 148b, 320b, 453b, 482a, 550a, 610a, 710b, 1038a, 1143b, 1242b, 1293a, 1349a; ii, 117b, 297b, 319b, 324a, 360a, 456b, 480a, 768b, 911a; iii, 40a, 648b, 717a; iv, 654b, 929b; s, 103b, 311a, b — I, 3a, 46a, 49a, 57a, 60a, **78b,** 123b, 146b, 153a, 330a, 466b, 496a, 567b, 613a, 732a, 1069b, 1178a, 1280a, 1332b, 1389a; II, 120a, 305b, 328b, 333b, 370a, 468b, 492a, 787a, 932b; III, 41b, 670a, 739a; IV, 681a, 962b; S, 103a, 310b, 311a, b
ʿAbd al-Malik b. Mughīth i, 608b; ii, 485b; v, 1121a — I, 628a; II, 497b; V, 1117b
ʿAbd al-Malik b. Muḥammad b. Djahwar ii, 389a — II, 399b
ʿAbd al-Malik b. Muḥammad al-Shaykh al-Mahdī i, 55b, 288b — I, 57b, 297b
ʿAbd al-Malik b. Mūsā b. Nuṣayr i, 50a — I, 51b
ʿAbd al-Malik b. Nūḥ → ʿAbd al-Malik I
ʿAbd al-Malik b. Ṣāliḥ b. ʿAlī i, **77b,** 761b — I, **80a,** 784a
ʿAbd al-Malik b. Zuhr → Ibn Zuhr
ʿAbd al-Malik al-Muẓaffar (d./m. 1008) → ʿAbd al-Malik b. Abī ʿĀmir
ʿAbd al-Malik al-Muẓaffar (d./m. 1065) i, 446a, 985b; ii, 1012a — I, 459a, 1016b; II, 1035b
ʿAbd Manāf, Banū i, 681a; iv, 320a; v, 435a, 581a — I, 702a; IV, 334b; V, 436b, 586a
ʿAbd al-Masīḥ → Ibn Buḳayla
ʿAbd al-Matīn Khān ii, 317a — II, 326b
ʿAbd al-Muʾmin b. ʿAbd Allāh Khān i, 8a, 46b, 1001b; s, 340b — I, 8a, 48a, 1032b; S, 340a
ʿAbd al-Muʾmin b. ʿAlī b. ʿAlwī (Muʾminid(e)) i, **78a,** 680a, 1044b, 1129b, 1148b, 1176a, 1205b; ii, 145b, 307b, 331b, 352b, 353a, 459a, 516a, 537a, 818b, 1009a; iii, 138b, 207b, 386b, 470b, 910a, 958b, 978b; iv, 415b, 479b, 827b, 943b; v, 61a, 379a, 626a, 1189b, 1245b; s, 113b, 376b — I, **80a,** 700b, 1076a, 1163b, 1183a, 1211a, 1241a; II, 149b, 316b, 341a, 362b, 471a, 529a, 550b, 838a, 1033a; III, 141b, 213a, 399a, 486b, 934a, 983a, 1003a; IV, 434a, 501a, 860b, 976b; V, 62b, 379b, 630a, 1179b, 1236a; S, 113a, 376b
ʿAbd al-Munʿim Ayyūb II i, 1280b — I, 1320a
ʿAbd al-Muṭṭalib b. Hāshim i, 42b, **80a,** 115b, 136b, 851a; iii, 203b, 260a, 1093a; iv, 260a, 264a, 270b — I, 43b, **82a,** 118b, 140b, 875a; III, 208b, 267b, 1120a; IV, 271b, 275b, 282b
ʿAbd al-Nabī b. Aḥmad Sirhindī s, 313a — S, 312b
ʿAbd al-Nabī b. ʿAlī ii, 517a; v, 1244b, 1245a — II, 530a; V, 1235a, b
ʿAbd al-Nāṣir, Djamāl ii, 649a, 674a; iii, 518a, 1069b, 1259a; iv, 125a, b, 719a, 781a, 783b; v, 1061b; s, **5a,** 70a, 306a — II, 665a, 691a; III, 536a, 1096a, 1291b; IV, 130b, 131a, 748a, 812b, 815a; V, 1058b; S, **4a,** 70b, 305b
ʿAbd al-Nāṣir Ḥusayn → ʿAbd al-Nāṣir, Djamāl
ʿAbd Rabbih al-Kabīr i, 810b; iv, 753a — I, 834a; IV, 783b
ʿAbd al-Raḥīm b. Aḥmad i, 402b — I, 414a
ʿAbd al-Raḥīm b. Aḥmad b. Ḥadjdjūn v, 386b — V, 387b
ʿAbd al-Raḥīm b. ʿAlī → al-Ḳāḍī al-Fāḍil
ʿAbd al-Raḥīm b. Ilyās ii, 857a; iii, 80a — II, 877a; III, 82b
ʿAbd al-Raḥīm b. Muḥammad → Ibn Nubāta
ʿAbd al-Raḥīm al-ʿAbbāsī i, 1109b — I, 1143a
ʿAbd al-Raḥīm Khān Khānān i, **80b,** 431a, 628a, 1136a, b, 1331a; ii, 597b; iii, 457b; iv, 1018a, 1127b — I, **82b,** 443b, 648b, 1170b, 1171a, 1371b; II, 612b; III, 473b; IV, 1050a, 1159a
ʿAbd al-Raḥīm al-Mutawakkil ʿalā ʾllāh iv, 673a — IV, 700b
ʿAbd al-Raḥmān, Sharīf (Pontianak) s, 150b — S, 150b
ʿAbd al-Raḥmān I al-Dākhil (Marwānid(e)) i, **81b,** 86b, 493b, 497b, 618b, 1079b; ii, 1009a; iii, 12a, 702a; iv, 665b; v, 510b, 1160a, 1164b; s, 82a — I, **84a,** 89a, 508b, 512b, 637b, 1112a; II, 1032b; III, 12b, 724a; IV, 692b; V, 514a, 1149b, 1154b; S, 81b
ʿAbd al-Raḥmān II al-Mutawassiṭ (Marwānid(e)) i, 11a, **82b,** 121b, 494a, 498a, 864b, 1012a, 1319b; ii, 515b, 1009a, 1038a; iii, 74a, 816a; iv, 672b, 822a; v, 510b, 1118b, 1119b — I, 11a, **85a,** 125a, 509a, 513a,

888b, 1043a, 1360a; II, 528b, 1032b, 1062a; III, 76b, 839b; IV, 700a, 855a; V, 514a, 1115a, 1116b
ʿAbd al-Raḥmān III al-Nāṣir (Marwānid(e)) i, **83b,** 439b, 494a, 498a, 628b, 658a, 864b, 997a, 1012a, 1092a, 1150a, 1326a, 1343a; ii, 297b, 525a, 821b, 915b, 1009a; iii, 46a, 1042a; iv, 254b, 632b, 943a; v, 510b, 625b, 777b, 1008b; s, 80a, 153a — I, **85b,** 452a, 509a, 513a, 649a, 679a, 889a, 1027b, 1043a, 1124b, 1184b, 1366b, 1383b; II, 305b, 538a, 841a, 937a, 1032b; III, 48a, 1068a; IV, 265b, 657b, 976a; V, 514b, 629b, 783b, 1004a; S, 80a, 153a
ʿAbd al-Raḥmān IV al-Murtaḍā (Marwānid(e)) i, **84a;** ii, 1012b; iii, 147a, 496a, 791a — I, **86b;** II, 1036a; III, 150b, 513a, 814b
ʿAbd al-Raḥmān V al-Mustaẓhir (Marwānid(e)) i, **84a;** iii, 791a, 938b — I, **86b;** III, 814b, 963b
ʿAbd al-Raḥmān, Mawlāy → ʿAbd al-Raḥmān b. Hishām
ʿAbd al-Raḥmān b. ʿAbbās b. Rabīʿa iii, 716b, 717b — III, 739a, 740a
ʿAbd al-Raḥmān b. ʿAbd Allāh → Ibn ʿAbd al-Ḥakam, Abuʾl-Ḳāsim
ʿAbd al-Raḥmān b. Abī ʿĀmir i, 76a, **84a,** 446a, 494b; iii, 495b, 739b, 746b, 819a; v, 743b, 1239a, b — I, 78a, **86b,** 459a, 509b; III, 512b, 762b, 769b, 842b; V, 749a, 1230a
ʿAbd al-Raḥmān b. Abī Bakr i, 109b, 110a, 145b; ii, 625b; s, 351b — I, 112b, 113a, 150a; II, 641a; S, 351b
ʿAbd al-Raḥmān b. Abī Nuʿaym i, 143a — I, 147a
ʿAbd al-Raḥmān b. ʿAlī → Ibn al-Daybaʿ
ʿAbd al-Raḥmān b. ʿAlī b. Bā Ḥassān iii, 270a — III, 278a
ʿAbd al-Raḥmān b. al-Ashʿath → Ibn al-Ashʿath
ʿAbd al-Raḥmān b. ʿAwf i, **84b,** 382a, 687a; ii, 366a, 625a, 846a; iii, 209b, 586b; iv, 521b; v, 110b; s, 89b — I, **87a,** 393a, 708a; II, 376a, 640b, 865b; III, 215b, 607a; IV, 544a; V, 1106b; S, 89b
ʿAbd al-Raḥmān b. al-Ḍaḥḥāk ii, 90a — II, 91b
ʿAbd al-Raḥmān b. Djābir b. ʿAbd Allāh s, 231a — S, 230b
ʿAbd al-Raḥmān b. Fayṣal (1889) iv, 925b — IV, 958b
ʿAbd al-Raḥmān b. Fayṣal b. ʿAbd al-ʿAzīz Āl Suʿūd s, 305b — S, 305b
ʿAbd al-Raḥmān b. Ḥabīb al-Fihrī → ʿAbd al-Raḥmān al-Fihrī
ʿAbd al-Raḥmān b. Ḥabīb al-Ṣiḳlabī i, 86b — I, 89a
ʿAbd al-Raḥmān b. al-Ḥakam s, 10a — S, 9b
ʿAbd al-Raḥmān b. Ḥassān b. Thābit s, **9b** — S, **9a**
ʿAbd al-Raḥmān b. Hishām (ʿAlawī) i, 67b, **84b,** 315b, 356b, 357a, 1224b, 1346b; ii, 117a, 160a, 173a, 510b, 823a; iii, 806a; iv, 634a — I, 69b, **87a,** 325a, 367b, 1261b, 1387a; II, 119b, 165a, 178a, 523a, 842b; III, 829b; IV, 660a
ʿAbd al-Raḥmān b. Ḥusayn iv, 1073a — IV, 1104b
ʿAbd al-Raḥmān b. ʿĪsā i, 387b; iv, 1094a — I, 398b; IV, 1125a
ʿAbd al-Raḥmān b. ʿĪsā al-Murshidī i, 867b — I, 891b
ʿAbd al-Raḥmān b. Isḥāḳ b. Haytham i, 214a — I, 220b
ʿAbd al-Raḥmān b. Kaʿb al-Aṣamm i, 266b — I, 274b
ʿAbd al-Raḥmān b. al-Ḳāsim → Ibn al-Ḳāsim
ʿAbd al-Raḥmān b. Kaysān s, 88b, 90b — S, 88b, 90a
ʿAbd al-Raḥmān b. Khālid b. al-Walīd i, **85a,** 449b; iv. 928b — I, **87b,** 462a; IV, 961b
ʿAbd al-Raḥmān b. Mahdī i, 272b — I, 281a
ʿAbd al-Raḥmān b. Mahdī (Sudan/Soudan) v, 1252b — V, 1243b
ʿAbd al-Raḥmān b. al-Manṣūr → ʿAbd al-Raḥmān b. Abī ʿĀmir
ʿAbd al-Raḥmān b. Marwān b. Yūnus i, **85b,** 494a, 1092a, 1339a; ii, 1009a — I, **88a,** 509a, 1124b, 1379a; II, 1032b
ʿAbd al-Raḥmān b. Mishkam al-Khawlānī iv, 1135a — IV, 1166b
ʿAbd al-Raḥmān b. Muʿāwiya → ʿAbd al-Raḥmān I
ʿAbd al-Raḥmān b. Muḥammad b. al-Ashʿath → Ibn al-Ashʿath
ʿAbd al-Raḥmān b. Muḥammad b. ʿAlī al-Barḳī s, 127a — S, 126b
ʿAbd al-Raḥmān b. Muṣṭafā al-ʿAydarūsī i, 280b, 782a — I, 289b, 805a
ʿAbd al-Raḥmān b. Nāṣir s, 401b — S, 402a
ʿAbd al-Raḥmān b. Rabīʿa → al-Bāhilī
ʿAbd al-Raḥmān b. Rustam i, 125a, 134b, 1175b; iii, 297a, 654a, b, 655a, 1041b; iv, 827a; v, 696a — I, 128b, 138a, 1210b; III, 306b, 675b, 676a, 1067b; IV, 860a; V, 701a
ʿAbd al-Raḥmān b. Samura i, 47b, **86a,** 1001a, 1344a; iv, 14b, 356b; v, 57a — I, 49a, **88a,** 1031b, 1384b; IV, 15b, 16a, 372a; V, 58b
ʿAbd al-Raḥmān b. Sulaymān al-Ahdal i, 255b, 782a — I, 263b, 805a
ʿAbd al-Raḥmān b. ʿUdays v, 318b — V, 318a
ʿAbd al-Raḥmān b. Umm al-Ḥakam iii, 970a — III, 994b
ʿAbd al-Raḥmān ʿAbdī Pasha → ʿAbdī Pasha
ʿAbd al-Raḥmān al-ʿAmr iv, 961a — IV, 993a
ʿAbd al-Raḥmān ʿAzzām Pasha s, 240b — S, 240b
ʿAbd al-Raḥmān al-Fāsī → al-Fāsī, ʿAbd al-Raḥmān
ʿAbd al-Raḥmān al-Fihrī i, 81b, **86a;** iii, 654a; iv, 336b — I, 84a, **88b;** III, 675a; IV, 351a
ʿAbd al-Raḥmān al-Ghāfiḳī i, **86b,** 493a, 988b — I, **89a,** 508a, 1019a
ʿAbd al-Raḥmān Ghāzī s, 280a — S, 280a
ʿAbd al-Raḥmān Harawī ii, 433b — II, 445a
ʿAbd al-Raḥmān Kahyā → ʿAbd al-Raḥman Katkhudā
ʿAbd al-Raḥmān Ḳaramānī i, 1235a — I, 1272a
ʿAbd al-Raḥmān Katkhudā (Kiḥya) i, 815a; iv, 438a, 439b, 852b, 853a — I, 838a; IV, 457b, 459a, 885b, 886a
ʿAbd al-Raḥmān Khān (Barakzay) i, **87a,** 223b, 224b, 232a, 796b; ii, 1001b; iv, 411a; v, 1079a; s, 237b, 368a — I, **89b,** 230a, 231a, 239a, 820a; II, 1024b; IV, 429a; V, 1076b; S, 237b, 367b
ʿAbd al-Raḥmān Khān (Noghay) i, 721b — I, 743b
ʿAbd al-Raḥmān al-Nadjūmī i, 49b, 765a; v, 1250a, b — I, 51a, 788a; V, 1241a
ʿAbd al-Raḥmān al-Nāṣir → ʿAbd al-Raḥmān III
ʿAbd al-Raḥmān Pasha (d./m. 1684) i, 905a, 1284b — I, 932a, 1324a
ʿAbd al-Raḥmān Pasha Bābān i, 845a — I, 868b
ʿAbd al-Raḥmān al-Rashīd ii, 123a — II, 126a
ʿAbd al-Raḥmān Rushdī Pāshā i, 1299b — I, 1339b
ʿAbd al-Raḥmān Sanchuelo → ʿAbd al-Raḥmān Ibn Abī ʿĀmir
ʿAbd al-Raḥmān Sheref i, 1089b; iv, 297b — I, 1122a; IV, 310b
ʿAbd al-Raḥmān al-Ṣūfī i, **86b;** ii, 300a; s, 251a — I, **89a;** II, 308a; S, 251a
ʿAbd al-Raḥmān al-Sūr i, 63b — I, 65b
ʿAbd al-Rashīd b. Maḥmūd i, 1130b, 1344b; ii, 1052a — I, 1165a, 1385a; II, 1076a
ʿAbd al-Rashīd b. Ṣāliḥ al-Bākuwī i, 967a — I, 997a
ʿAbd al-Rashīd Daylamī iv, 1128a — IV, 1159b
ʿAbd al-Rashīd Khān ii, 622b; iii, 317a — II, 638a; III, 326b
ʿAbd al-Rashīd al-Tattawī i, **88a,** iv, 526a — I, **90b,** 549a
ʿAbd al-Raʾūf al-Sinkilī i, **88a,** 742a; iii, 1220a, 1233b; v, 433a, 525b — I, **90b,** 764a; III, 1251a, 1265b; V, 435b, 529b
ʿAbd al-Rāziḳ, ʿAlī iii, 1168b; iv, 161a, 906b, 947a; s,

121b – III, 1197b; IV, 168a, 939b, 980a; S, 121a
ʿAbd al-Rāziḳ, Muṣṭafā i, 820a – I, 843a
ʿAbd al-Razzāḳ, wazīr i, 1192a – I, 1227a
ʿAbd al-Razzāḳ (Ṣufrī) iii, 1036a – III, 1062a
ʿAbd al-Razzāḳ b. ʿAbd al-Ḳādir iv, 380b, 381a – IV, 397a, b
ʿAbd al-Razzāḳ b. Ḥammām al-Ṣanʿānī v, 1162a – V, 1151b
ʿAbd al-Razzāḳ b. Ḥasanwayh iii, 258a – III, 265a
ʿAbd al-Razzāḳ of/de Bānsa s, 292b, 293a – S, 292b, 293a
ʿAbd al-Razzāḳ al-Kas͟hānī i, **88b**, 347a, 351a – I, **91a**, 357b, 362a
ʿAbd al-Razzāḳ al-Lāhidjī → Lāhidjī
ʿAbd al-Razzāḳ al-Samarḳandī i, **90b**; iii, 58a; s, 51a – I, **93b**; III, 60b; S, 51b
ʿAbd al-Res͟hīd ʿIsmet Allāh s, 82a – S, 82a
ʿAbd al-Saʿīd Mir ʿĀlim → Mir ʿĀlim
ʿAbd al-Salām II i, 1072a – I, 1104a
ʿAbd al-Salām, al-Ḥādjdj iii, 395b – III, 408a
ʿAbd al-Salām b. Aḥmad → lbn G͟hānim
ʿAbd al-Salām b. Mas͟hīs͟h al-Ḥasanī i, **91a**, 353a; v, 1201a; s, 350b – I. **94a**, 363b; V, 1191b; S, 350b
ʿAbd al-Salām b. Muḥammad al-Fāsī s, **10a** – S, **9b**
ʿAbd al-Salām ʿĀrif → ʿĀrif, ʿAbd al-Salām
ʿAbd al-Salām K͟hundjī, S͟hayk͟h v, 671a – V, 676b
ʿAbd al-Salām Yazbak ʿAmād ii, 444a – II, 455b
ʿAbd al-Ṣamad b. al-Muʿad͟hd͟hal → Ibn al-Muʿad͟hd͟hal
ʿAbd al-Ṣamad lbn K͟hazar v, 1179b – V, 1169b
ʿAbd al-Ṣamad al-Palimbānī i, **92a**; ii, 183a; iii, 1233b – I, **94b**; II, 189a; III, 1265b
ʿAbd S͟hams (tribe/tribu) i, 9a, 55b, 136b, 151a; v, 435a; s, 103b – I, 9a, 57a, 140b, 155a; V, 437a; S, 102b
ʿAbd al-ʿUzza → ʿAbd al-Raḥmān b. Abī Bakr; Abū Lahab b. ʿAbd al-Muṭṭalib
ʿAbd al-Wādid(e)s i, **92a**, 129b, 168a, 367a, 1176b, 1205b; iii, 67b, 68b, 499a, 832a, 833b; v, 531a, 1180a, b, 1190a; s, 113a, 144b, 376b – I, **95a**, 133b, 172b, 378a, 1211b, 1241b; III, 70a, 71a, 516a, 855b, 857b; V, 535a, 1170a, b, 1180a; S, 112b, 144b, 377a
ʿAbd al-Wahhāb (Ṭāhirid(e)) i, 181b – I, 186b
ʿAbd al-Wahhāb, Mawlānā s, 360b – S, 360b
ʿAbd al-Wahhāb, Muḥammad, b. Ḥasanayn al-Ḥiṣāfī s, 371a – S, 371a
ʿAbd al-Wahhāb b. ʿAbd al-Raḥmān b. Rustam (Imām) i, 250a; ii, 441b; iii, 297b, 651a, 655a, 1041b; iv, 415b, 919b – I, 256a; II, 453a; III, 307a, 672a, 676a, 1067b; IV, 433b, 952b
ʿAbd al-Wahhāb b. Abi 'l-Faradj iii, 161a – III, 164b
ʿAbd al-Wahhāb b. Buk͟ht i, 1103a, b; ii, 234b, 236a – I, 1136a, b; II, 241b, 242b
ʿAbd al-Wahhāb b. Faḍl Allāh ii, 732a – II, 750b
ʿAbd al-Wahhāb b. Muḥammad b. G͟hālib b. Numayr al-Anṣārī s, 15b – S, 15b
ʿAbd al-Wahhāb b. Yūsuf s, 11a – S, 10b
ʿAbd al-Wahhāb Buk͟hārī, S͟hayk͟h s, **10b** – S, **10a**
ʿAbd al-Wahhāb al-Hamadānī i, 234a – I, 241a
ʿAbd al-Wahhāb al-Makkī iv, 338a – IV, 352b
ʿAbd al-Wahhāb al-Subkī → al-Subkī, Tādj al-Dīn
ʿAbd al-Wahhāb al-Sumādiḥī al-Tudjībī s, **11a** – S, **10b**
ʿAbd al-Wāḥid II al-Ras͟hīd iii, 338a, 705a, 921b, 1055a; v, 48b – III, 348a, 727a, 946a, 1081b; V, 50a
ʿAbd al-Wāḥid (Almohad(e)) s, 389a – S, 389b
ʿAbd al-Wāḥid b. Ayman s, 357b – S, 357b
ʿAbd al-Wāḥid b. Sulaymān b. ʿAbd al-Malik iii, 878a; v, 1156a – III, 902a; V, 1145b
ʿAbd al-Wāḥid b. Yazīd al-Hawwārī iii, 169b, 297b, 1040b – III, 173a, 306b, 1066b
ʿAbd al-Wāḥid al-Hās͟himī s, 400b – S, 401a
ʿAbd al-Wāḥid al-Liḥyānī → Abu Darba al-Liḥyānī
ʿAbd al-Wāḥid al-Marrākus͟hī i, **94a**, 389b, ii, 72a; v, 1160b; s, 388a – I, **97a**, 400b; II, 73b; V, 1150a; S, 388b
ʿAbd al-Wāsiʿ Djabalī b. ʿAbd al-Djāmiʿ i, **94b** – I, 97a
ʿAbd al-Wāsiʿ al-Niẓāmī i, 91a – I, 93b
ʿAbd Yag͟hūt͟h b. Ṣalāt iii, 223a – III, 230a
ʿAbd al-Ẓāhir, Banū ii, 305b – II, 314a
ʿAbda b. al-Ṭabīb iv, 833a, 998b – IV, 866a, 1031a
Abdāl i, **94b**; s, 168b – I, **97b**; S, 169a
Abdāl Mūsā iv, 811b – IV, 844b
Abdāl, S͟hayk͟h → Bābā Walī
Abdālān-i Rūm i, 1162a; iv, 473b – I, 1196b; IV, 494b
Abdālī (Durrānī) i, 72b, **95a**, 229a, b, 295a; ii, 628b; iii, 177b, 604a; iv, 537b – I, 74b, 97b, **98a**, 235b, 236a, 304b; II, 644b, III, 182a, 624b; IV, 560b
ʿAbdalī, ʿAbdiliyyūn i, **95b**, 345a – I, **98a**, 355b
ʿAbdallāb ii, 351b, 944a; iv, 892b – II, 361a, 965b; IV, 925b
Abdallah → ʿAbd Allāh
ʿAbdallāhī → ʿAbdullāhi
ʿAbdān i, **95b**; ii, 851a; iii, 123b; iv, 198a, b, 660b – I, **98b**; II, 871a, III, 126a; IV, 206b, 207a, 687a
al-ʿAbdarī i, **96a**, 602b; iii, 736b – I, **98b**, 622a, III, 759a
al-ʿAbdarī Abū ʿAbd Allāh b. al-Ḥādjdj → lbn al-Ḥādjdj
Ābdast → Wuḍūʾ
Abdelkader → ʿAbd al-Ḳādir b. Muḥyī al-dīn al-Ḥasanī
ʿAbdī i, **96b** – I, **99b**
al-ʿAbdī → Abu 'l-Hud͟hayl; Djaʿfar b. al-Sammāk; al-Walīd
ʿAbdīʾ, Mawlawī ʿAbd Allāh v, 611a – V, 615a
ʿAbdī Čelebi Čiwi-zade ii, 56b – II, 57b
ʿAbdī Efendi i, **97a** – I, **99b**
ʿAbdī Pas͟ha i, **97a**; iv, 438a, 569a – I, **99b**; IV, 457b, 591b
Abdication → Tanāzul
ʿAbdīn (palace) s, 301a – S, 300b
Abdjad i, **97a** – I, **100a**
Abdjar b. Djābir i, 964a – I, 993b
Abdul Kadiri ii, 1146a – II, 1173b
Abdullah → ʿAbd Allāh
Abdullahi Ba Demba ii, 960, 1132b – II, 982a, 1159a
Abdullahi dan Fodio → ʿAbd Allāh b. Muḥammad Fūdī
Abdullahi Sikka iv, 550a – IV, 574a
ʿAbdullāhi al-Taʿāʾis͟hī → ʿAbd Allāh b. Muḥammad al-Taʿāʾis͟hī
Abéché → Abes͟hr
Ābeh → Āwa
Abeilles → Naḥl
Abel → Hābīl
Abencerages → al-Sarrādj, Banū
Abenguefith → lbn Wāfid
Abenragel → lbn Abī ʾl-Ridjāl
Abes͟hr (Abeche) i, **98a**; s, 164a, 165b – I, **100b**; S, 164a, 165b
Abhā i, **98a**, 707b, 709b – I, **101a**, 729a, 731a
Abhar i, **98b**; s, 22a – I, **101b**; S, 22b
al-Abharī i, **98b**, 321a; ii, 949a; iii, 805a; iv, 92a; s, 414a – I, **101b**, 331a; II, 970b; III, 828b; IV, 96a; S, 414b
Abhay Singh i, 1053a; iii, 1010b – I, 1084b; III, 1035b
al-Abī ii, 590b – II, 605a
Abi 'l-ʿĀfiya, Banū ii, 979a – II, 1001a
Abi 'l-Ḥasan, Banū → Kalbid(e)s
Āb-i Istāda (lake/lac) s, 329b – S, 329a

Abi 'l-Shawārib, Banū iii, 691a; s, 386a — III, 713a; S, 386b
Abīb → Taʾrīkh
ʿAbīd → ʿAbd; Makhzan
ʿĀbid, Banu 'l- iv, 416a; v, 379a — IV, 434a; V, 379b
al-ʿAbīd, wādī s, 223b — S, 223b
ʿAbīd b. al-Abraṣ i, **99a,** 1241b; iii, 1177b; s, 272b — I, **101b,** 1279a; III, 1206b; S, 272a
ʿAbīd b. Sharya → Ibn Sharya
ʿAbīd al-Bukhārī i, 47a, 356a; v, 1191b, 1192a — I, 48b, 367a; V, 1181b, 1182a
ʿAbīdā b. Hilāl i, 811a; iv, 753a; v, 378a — I, 834a; IV, 783b; V, 379a
ʿĀbidīn Pasha iii, 1117a; s, 63a — III, 1144b; S, 63b
ʿĀbidiyya iv, 668a — IV, 695b
Abidjan ii, 63a — II, 64a
Ābiḳ → ʿAbd
Ābinūs → Abanūs
Ābish Khātūn ii, 812a; iv, 975b, 1046b, 1047a — II, 831a; IV, 1008a, 1078a, b
Abīward (Bāward) i, **99b** — I, **102a**
al-Abīwardī, Abu 'l-Muẓaffar Muḥammad i, **100a**; s, 326b — I, **102b**; S, 326a
Abjuration → Murtadd
Abkarib Asʿad → Asʿad Kāmil
Abkarius → Iskandar Agha
Abḳayḳ (Buḳayḳ) i, **100a** — I, **103a**
Abkhāz i, **100b,** 1189b; iv, 351a; v, 488a, b, 496a — I, **103a,** 1224b; IV, 366a; V, 490b, 491b, 499a
ʿAbla i, 518b, 521b — I, 534a, 537a
al-Ablaḳ → Samawʾal
al-Ablaḳ al-Asadī i, 659b — I, 680b
Ablution → Ghusl, Tayammum, Wuḍūʾ
al-Abnāʾ i, **102a**; v, 1111a; s, 115b, 116a — I, **104b**; V, 1107a; S, 115a, b
Abnāʾ al-Atrāk i, 102a — I, 105a
Abnāʾ al-dawla i, 102a; v, 57b — I, 105a; V, 59a
Abnā-yi sipāhīyān i, 102a — I, 105a
Abnūs → Abanūs
Abomey ii, 93b, 94a — II, 95b, 96a
Abou Chabakeh, Elias → Abū Shabaka, Ilyās
Aboukir → Abūḳīr
Abraha i, **102a,** 144b, 549a; ii, 895a; iv, 318b — I, **105a,** 149a, 566a; II, 916a; IV, 332b
Abraham → Ibrāhīm al-Khalīl
Abrash al-Kalbī iii, 494b — III, 511b
Abreuvoir → Māʾ
Abréviations S, **12a**
Abricot → Mishmish
Abrogation → Nāsikh wa-Mansūkh
ʿAbs, Banū i, 518b, 521b; ii, 71b, 873b, 1023a; iv, 1144a; s, 177a — I, 534a, 537a; II, 73a, 893b, 1046b; IV, 1175b; S, 178a
al-Abshīhī → al-Ibshīhī
Absolution → Kaffāra
Abstinence → Istibrāʾ, Tabattul
Abtariyya iii, 244a; s, 129b — III, 251a; S, 129a
Abū → Kunya
Abu 'l-ʿAbbās, amīr → Aḥmad II (Ḥafṣid(e))
Abu 'l-ʿAbbās b. Wāsil s, 119a — S, 118b
Abu 'l-ʿAbbās Aḥmad (Ḥafṣid(e)) → Aḥmad I, II
Abu 'l-ʿAbbās Aḥmad (Ḥusaynid Sharīf/Sharīf Ḥusaynide) s, 112b — S, 112a
Abū 'l-ʿAbbās Aḥmad (Marīnid(e)) i, 167b; iii, 836a — I, 172b; III, 860a
Abu 'l-ʿAbbās Aḥmad b. ʿAbd Allāh → Abū Maḥallī al-Sidjilmāssī
Abu 'l-ʿAbbās Aḥmad b. al-ʿArūs → Ibn ʿArūs
Abu 'l-ʿAbbās al-Aʿmā → al-Aʿmā al-Tuṭīlī
Abū 'l-ʿAbbās al-Īrānshahrī i, 1031b — I, 1063a
Abu 'l-ʿAbbās al-Ḳaṣṣāb i, 146a; iv, 1057b — I, 150b; IV, 1089a
Abu 'l-ʿAbbās al-Maghribī ii, 528a — II, 541a
Abu 'l-ʿAbbās Muḥammad b. al-Aghlab → Muḥammad I (Aghlabid(e))
Abu 'l-ʿAbbās al-Nabātī i, 214b; iii, 737a; s, 114b — I, 220b; III, 759b; S, 114a
Abū 'l-ʿAbbās al-Saffāḥ (ʿAbbāsid(e)) i, 12b, 16a, 17a, 42b, 43a, 45b, **103a,** 107b, 116b, 149a, 485a, 895a, 1033b; ii, 178a, 324a; iii, 265b, 988b; iv, 446b, 729a; v, 1233a; s, 31b, 198b — I, 12b, 16b, 17b, 43b, 44a, 46b, **106a,** 110b, 120a, 153a, 499b, 922a, 1065a; II, 183b, 333b; III, 273a, 1013a; IV, 466b, 758a; V, 1223b; S, 31b, 198b
Abu 'l-ʿAbbās Ṣuʿlūk s, 356b — S, 356a
Abū ʿAbd al-ʿĀl → Aḥmad al-Badawī
Abū ʿAbd Allāh b. Djarāda iii, 730b, 766a; s, 30a — III, 753b, 789a; S, 30a
Abū ʿAbd Allāh b. Mandah → Ibn Manda
Abū ʿAbd Allāh b. Muʿādh → Ibn Muʿādh
Abū ʿAbd Allāh b. Muḥsin al-Bashīr iii, 207b — III, 213a
Abū ʿAbd Allāh al-Baṣrī al-Djuʿal iii, 832a,b; s, **12b** — III, 856a; S, **13a**
Abū ʿAbd Allāh al-Dāmaghānī s, 29b — S, 29b
Abū ʿAbd Allāh al-Djayhānī → al-Djayhānī
Abū ʿAbd Allāh Ḥusayn iii, 128b — III, 131b
Abū ʿAbd Allāh al-Ḥuṣrī i, 146a — I, 150a
Abū ʿAbd Allāh al-Māhānī → al-Māhānī
Abū ʿAbd Allāh al-Mahdī li-Dīn Allāh s, 363a, b — S, 363a
Abū ʿAbd Allāh Muḥammad, amīr iii, 68b, 826a,b — III, 10b, 850a
Abū ʿAbd Allāh Muḥammad I → al-Mustanṣir
Abū ʿAbd Allāh Muḥammad II → Abū ʿAṣīda
Abū ʿAbd Allāh Muḥammad III → al-Muntaṣir
Abū ʿAbd Allāh Muḥammad V i, 678a; iii, 69a; iv, 1156a — I, 698b; III, 71b; IV, 1188a
Abū ʿAbd Allāh Muḥammad Ibn ʿAbd al-Munʿim → Ibn ʿAbd al-Munʿim
Abū ʿAbd Allāh Muḥammad b. al-ʿAbbās s, 403a — S, 403b
Abū ʿAbd Allāh Muḥammad b. Aḥmad Djayhānī iv, 22a — IV, 24a
Abū ʿAbd Allāh Muḥammad b. ʿAlī al-ʿAlawī s, 19a, 401a — S, 19a, 401b
Abū ʿAbd Allāh Muḥammad b. ʿAnbasa i, 159a — I, 163b
Abū ʿAbd Allāh Muḥammad b. Bakr al-Nafūsī ii, 141a; iii, 95b — II, 145a; III, 98a
Abū ʿAbd Allāh Muḥammad b. Ḥamawiya al-Djuwaynī i, 765b — I, 788b
Abū ʿAbd Allāh Muḥammad b. al-Ḥasan s, 13a, b — S, 13a, b
Abū ʿAbd Allāh Muḥammad b. Ibrāhīm b. al-Sarrādj → Ibn al-Sarrādj
Abū ʿAbd Allāh Muḥammad b. Khālid al-Barkī s, 127b — S, 126b
Abū ʿAbd Allāh Muḥammad b. Muḥammad b. Yūsuf al-Sarrādj → Ibn al-Sarrādj
Abū ʿAbd Allāh Muḥammad Ādarrāḳ s, 40a — S, 40b
Abū ʿAbd Allāh Muḥammad al-Andalusī i, 56a — I, 57b
Abū ʿAbd Allāh Muḥammad al-Fāsī → Ibn al-Ḥādjdj
Abū ʿAbd Allāh Muḥammad al-Gharnāṭī → Ibn al-Sarrādj
Abū ʿAbd Allāh Muḥammad al-Ḥādjdj s, 223b — S, 224a
Abū ʿAbd Allāh Muḥammad al-Ḥasan → al-Ḥasan
Abū ʿAbd Allāh Muḥammad al-Hazmīrī iii, 339a,b — III, 349a,b
Abū ʿAbd Allāh Muḥammad al-Mālaḳī → Ibn al-Sarrādj

Abū ʿAbd Allāh Muḥammad al-Masnāwī s, 223b — S, 223b
Abū ʿAbd Allāh al-Ṣaymarī s, 25a — S, 25b
Abū ʿAbd Allāh al-Shīʿī i, **103b,** 249a, 863b, 1175b; ii, 98a, 852a, b; iii, 655b; iv, 198a, 361a; v, 540b, 1242b, 1243a — I, **106b,** 257a, 888a, 1210b; II, 100a, 872a,b; III, 677a; IV, 206b, 377a; V, 545a, 1233b
Abū ʿAbd Allāh al-Tamīmī iv, 1134a — IV, 1165b
Abū ʿAbd Allāh Yaʿḳūb b. Dāʾūd i, **103b,** 157b; ii, 870a; v, 1238b — I, **106b,** 162a; II, 890a; V, 1229a
Abu ʿAdnān s, 20a — S, 20b
Abū Aḥmad ʿAbd al-Salām ii, 127b; v, 928b — II, 130b; V, 933b
Abū Aḥmad al-ʿAskarī → al-ʿAskarī
Abū Aḥmad al-Mūsawī iv, 378a — IV, 394b
Abū 'l-ʿAlāʾ b. Karnīb i, 159a — I, 163b
Abū 'l-ʿAlāʾ al-Maʿarrī → al-Maʿarrī
Abu 'l-ʿAlāʾ Mawdūdī ii, 437a; iii, 433b — II, 448b; III, 447b
Abu 'l-ʿAlāʾ al-Rabaʿī → Ṣāʿid al-Baghdādī
Abū ʿAlī b. Khalāṣ s, 111b — S, 111a
Abū ʿAlī b. Marwān ii, 344a; iii, 128b; v, 453a — II, 353b; III, 131b; V, 455b
Abū ʿAlī b. Muḥammad b. Sūrī ii, 1099b, 1100a — II, 1125b, 1126a
Abū ʿAlī b. al-Samḥ s, 25a — S, 25b
Abū ʿAlī b. ʿUthmān II, Abū Saʿīd s, 112b — S, 112a
Abū ʿAlī b. al-Walīd s, 30a — S, 30a
Abū ʿAlī Aḥmad b. Muḥammad b. al-Muẓaffar s, 386b — S, 387a
Abū ʿAlī al-Baghdādī → al-Ḳālī, Abū ʿAlī
Abū ʿAlī al-Balʿamī → al-Balʿamī
Abū ʿAlī al-Baṣīr s, 25a — S, 25a
Abū ʿAlī Čaghānī iv, 22b-23a, 100b; v, 76a; s, 125b — IV, 24b, 104b; V, 78b; S, 124b
Abū ʿAlī al-Farmadhī ii, 1038b; iii, 103a; iv, 1058a; s, **14b** — II, 1063a; III, 105b; IV, 1089a; S, **14b**
Abū ʿAlī al-Ḥākim → Muḥammad b. Aḥmad Abu 'l-Shalaʿlaʿ
Abū ʿAlī al-Ḥasan b. ʿAlī al-Djīlī i, 1237a; ii, 496a — I, 1274b; II, 508b
Abū ʿAlī al-Ḥasan b. Ismāʿīl b. Ḥammād (Ibn Dirham) s, **385a** — S, **385b**
Abū ʿAlī Ḥusayn b. Abī 'l-Ḥusayn i, 688a; iii, 255a — I, 709a; III, 262b
Abū ʿAlī al-Ḥusaynī ii, 125b; v, 1126b — II, 129a; V, 1122b
Abū ʿAlī Ḳalandar Pānīpatī i, **104b**; iv, 666a — I, **107b**; IV, 693a
Abū ʿAlī al-Ḳālī → al-Ḳālī
Abū ʿAlī Muḥammad b. Ilyās ii, 1b; iii, 1156b; v, 158a, b, 352b — II, 1b; III, 1185a; V, 157b, 353b
Abū ʿAlī Muḥammad al-Balkhī ii, 918b — II, 940a
Abū ʿAlī al-Ṣadafī iv, 290a — IV, 302b
Abū ʿAlī Ṣāliḥ b. ʿAbd al-Ḥalīm v, 1157a — V, 1146b
Abū ʿAlī Shatrandj iii, 355b — III, 366b
Abū ʿAlī al-Sindī i, 162b — I, 167a
Abū ʿAlī Simdjūrī v, 624b — V, 628b
Abū ʿAlī Ṭāhir al-Mazdaḳānī ii, 282a — II, 290a
Abū ʿAlī Ṭarsūsī i, 146b — I, 150b
Abu ʿAlī al-Yūsī → al-Yūsī
Abū ʿAlī Zāhir i, 146a — I, 150a
Abū 'l-ʿĀliya al-Riyāḥī i, **104b** — I, **107b**
Abu 'l-ʿAmaythal s, **15a** — S, **15a**
Abū ʿAmmār ʿAbd al-Kāfī al-Wardjlānī iii, 96b; s, **15a** — III, 99a; S, **15b**
Abū ʿAmmār al-Aʿmā i, 163a, 164a; iii, 95b, 659b — I, 167b, 168a, b; III, 98a, 680b
ʿAbū ʿAmr ʿAbbād b. Muḥammad → al-Muʿtaḍid b. ʿAbbād
Abū ʿAmr b. al-ʿAlāʾ al-Māzinī → al-Māzinī
Abū ʿAmr al-Iṣṭakhrī iii, 823b — III, 847a
Abū ʿAmr al-Mughāzilī i, 159a — I, 163b
Abū ʿAmr al-Shaybānī iv, 524b; s, **15b**, 394b — IV, 547a; S, **16a**, 395a
Abū ʿAmr Zabbān b. al-ʿAlāʾ i, 42b, 104b, **105a,** 158a, 167a, 717b; iii, 136a, 742a; iv, 249a; v, 805a; s, 24b — I, 44a, 107b, **108a,** 162b, 172a, 739a; III, 139a, 764b; IV, 259b; V, 811a; S, 24b
Abū ʿAmr al-Zāhid s, 37b — S, 38a
Abū ʿAmra Kaysān → Kaysān
Abu 'l-ʿAnbas al-Ṣaymarī iv, 1099b; s, **16a** — IV, 1130b; S, **16b**
Abu 'l-ʿArab Muḥammad al-Tamīmī i, 24a, **106a** — I, 25a, **109a**
Abū ʿArīsh i, **106b**; v, 808a; s, 30a — I, **109b**; V, 814a; S, 30b
Abū ʿArūba i, **106b** — I, **109b**
Abu 'l-Asad al-Ḥimmānī s, **17b** — S, **17b**
Abū ʿAṣīda iii, 67b — III, 70a
Abū ʿĀṣim al-Nabīl iii, 25a; s, **17b** — III, 26a; S, **18a**
Abu 'l-Aswad al-Duʾalī (Dīlī) i, **106b,** 565a, 566b, 1297b; iii, 173a; iv, 731b; v, 116b — I, **110a,** 583b, 584b, 1337b; III, 176b; IV, 761a; V, 119a
Abū 'l-Aswār Shāwur i, 638a, 660b; ii, 680b; iv, 347b, 348a, 815a — I, 659a, 681b; II, 697a; IV, 362b, 848a
Abū ʿAṭāʾ al-Sindī i, **107a** — I, **110a**
Abu 'l-ʿAtāhiya i, **107b,** 569b, 587a, 751b, 1081b; iii, 618a, 996a, 1019b, 1262b; s, 122b, 304a — I, **110b,** 588a, 606a, 774a, 1114a; III, 638b, 1021a, 1045a, 1295b; S, 122a, 303b
Abu 'l-ʿAtāhiya (Yaman) s, 335a — S, 334b
Abu 'l-Aʿwar al-Sulamī i, **108a**; s, 221b — I, **111a**; S, 221b
Abū ʿAwn al-Khurasānī i, 16a, **108b**; iv, 447b — I, 16b, **111b**; IV, 467b
Abu 'l-ʿAynāʾ i, **108b,** 1082b; iii, 672b; s, 25a — I, **XIV,** 1114b; III, 694a; S, 25a
Abu 'l-ʿAysh Aḥmad iii, 1036b — III, 1062b
Abū Ayyūb al-Anṣārī i, **108b,** 312b; iv, 270b; v, 533a — I, **111b,** 322b; IV, 282b; V, 537a
Abū Ayyūb al-Madīnī ii, 1011b; iii, 682a, 698b — II, 1035a; III, 704a, 720b
Abu 'l-ʿAzāʾim s, **18a** — S, **18a**
Abū Baghla iv, 362a — IV, 378a
Abū Baḥr Ṣakhr → al-Aḥnaf b. Ḳays
Abu 'l-Baḳā, Shaykh i, 841b — I, 864b
Abu 'l-Baḳāʾ b. Abī Zakariyyāʾ iii, 67b; v, 531a — III, 70a; V, 535a
Abu Bakari b. Mwengo s, 351b — S, 351b
Abū Bakr (al-Ṣiddīḳ) i, **109b,** 114b, 127b, 158b, 381b, 382a, 443b, 549b, 697a, 1113b; ii, 601a, 725a, 842b, 844a, 845b; iii, 33a, 64a, b; iv, 927b, 937a; v, 404b, 777a; s, 89b, 129b, 130a, 343a — I, **112b,** 118a, 131a, 163a, 392b, 456a, 567a, 718a, 1147a; II, 616a, 743b, 862a, 864a, 865a; III, 35a, 66b, 67a; IV, 960b, 970a; V, 406a, 783a; S, 89a, 128b, 129a, 343a
Abū Bakr (Ḥafsid(e)) → Abū Yaḥyā Abū Bakr
Abū Bakr (Salghūrid(e)) → Abū Bakr b. Saʿd b. Zangī
Abū Bakr, Sayf al-Dīn ii, 285b — II, 293b
Abū Bakr b. ʿAbd Allāh → lbn Abī 'l-Dunyā
Abū Bakr b. ʿAbd al-ʿAzīz i, 446a, 986a — I, 459a, 1016b
Abū Bakr b. ʿAbd al-Ṣamad → ʿAbd al-Ṣamad
Abū Bakr b. ʿAbd al-Raḥmān ʿUbayd Allāh s, 311b — S, 311a
Abū Bakr b. Abī 'l-Ḳāsim al-Ahdal i, 255b — I, 263b
Abū Bakr b. Abī Saʿīd i, 852b — I, 876a
Abū Bakr b. Abī Shayba → lbn Abī Shayba
Abū Bakr b. Aḥmad → lbn Ḳāḍī Shuhba
Abū Bakr b. Aḥmad b. Muḥammad b. Zayd Ṭūsī i, 423b — I, 435b
Abū Bakr b. ʿAlī al-Ḥamawī → Ibn Ḥidjdja

Abū Bakr b. ʿAlī al-Ṣinhādjī → al-Baydhāk
Abū Bakr b. al-ʿArabī → Ibn al-ʿArabī
Abū Bakr b. ʿAyyāsh i,707a — I, 728a
Abū Bakr b. Bahrām al-Dimashkī i, 698a; ii, 589a — I, 719a; II, 604a
Abū Bakr b. Eldiguz → Abū Bakr b. Pahlawān
Abū Bakr b. Ḥammād iv, 662b — IV, 689a
Abū Bakr b. Ibrāhīm al-Sahrawī → lbn Tifalwīt
Abū Bakr b. Ismāʿil b. ʿAbd al-Hakk v, 60b — V, 62b
Abū Bakr b. Kīrān s, 390b — S, 391a
Abū Bakr b. al-Khamīs s, 382a — S, 382a
Abū Bakr b. Kuṭb al-Yaman i, 255b — I, 263b
Abū Bakr b. al-Makbūl al-Zaylaʿī v, 807b — V, 813a
Abū Bakr b. Mudjāhid → lbn Mudjāhid, Aḥmad
Abū Bakr b. al-Mughīra al-Makhzūmī s, **311a** — S, **310b**
Abū Bakr b. Muḥammad, Shaykh s, 223a — S, 223a
Abū Bakr b. Muḥammad, Sultan i, 286b; iii, 4a — I, 295b; III, 4a
Abū Bakr b. Pahlawān Muḥammad i, 300b; iii, 1111b, 1112a; iv, 349a — I, 310a; III, 1139a, b; IV, 364a
Abū Bakr b. Saʿd b. Zangī i, 434a, 942b; iv, 498a, 764b; v, 671a — I, 446b, 971a; IV, 519b, 795a; V, 676a
Abū Bakr b. Shāhūya iv, 664b — IV, 691b
Abū Bakr b. ʿUmar al Lamtūnī → al-Lamtūnī
Abū Bakr b. Zahr iv, 1007b — IV, 1039b
Abū Bakr b. Zayd al-Djirāʿī i, 759a — I, 781b
Abū Bakr b. Ẓafar Khān ii, 1077a — II, 1102a
Abu Bakr al-Ādjurrī → al-Ādjurrī
Abu Bakr Aḥmad b. ʿAlī b. Thābit → al-Khaṭīb al-Baghdādī
Abū Bakr al-Aṣamm → al-Aṣamm
Abū Bakr al-ʿAydarūs i, 181b, 781a; iv, 450a — I, 186b, 804a; IV, 470a
Abū Bakr al-Bayṭār → lbn al-Mundhir
Abū Bakr Dughlat → Abū Bakr Mīrzā b. Sāniz
Abū Bakr Hishām → Hishām III
Abū Bakr al-Kaffāl i, 146a — I, 150a
Abū Bakr al-Katīʿī i, 273b; iii, 158b — I, 282a; III, 162a
Abū Bakr al-Khallāl → al-Khallāl
Abū Bakr al-Kharāʾiṭī → al-Kharāʾiṭī
Abū Bakr al-Khwārizmī → al-Khwārizmī
Abū Bakr al-Marwazī i, 274a, b, 1039a; iii, 159a — I, 282b, 283a, 1070b; III, 162b
Abū Bakr al-Mayūrkī iii, 712b, 732a — III, 735a, 754b
Abū Bakr Mīrāz (Tīmūrid(e)) iv, 586a, b — IV, 609a
Abu Bakr Mīrzā b. Sāniz ii, 622a; iv, 699a — II, 637b; IV, 727b
Abū Bakr Muḥammad b. Ayyūb → al-Malik al-ʿĀdil I
Abū Bakr Muḥammad b. Hāshim iii, 111a; iv, 936b — III, 113b; IV, 969b
Abū Bakr Muḥammad al-Mādharāʾī v, 953b — V, 957a
Abū Bakr al-Rāzī → al-Rāzī
Abū Bakr Sayf al-Dīn b. Kāmil → al-Malik al-ʿĀdil II
Abū Bakr al-Shāshī i, 126b; s, 194b, 384a — I, 130a; S, 193b, 384b
Abū Bakr al-Sidjistānī iii, 158b — III, 162a
Abū Bakr Wafāʾī i, 966a — I, 996a
Abū Bakr Yaʿkūb b. Nāṣir al-Dīn iv, 1127b — IV, 1159a
Abū Bakr al-Zubaydī → al-Zubaydī
Abū Bakra i, **111a**; s, 354b — I, **114b**; S, 354b
Abū Barāʾ i, 1232b — I, 1269a
Abu 'l-Barakāt al-ʿAlawī al-Zaydī s, **19a** — S, **19a**
Abu 'l-Barakāt Hibat Allāh al-Baghdādī i, **111b;** ii, 774a; iv, 306a; s, 273b — I, **114b;** II, 792b; IV, 319b; S, 273a
Abu 'l-Barakāt Muḥammad al-Balāfikī → lbn al-Ḥādjdj
Abū Barākish i, 131b; s, **19a** — I, 135a; S, **19b**
Abū Baṭṭa → al-Irdjānī
Abu 'l-Bayḍāʾ al-Riyāḥī s, 20a, 73b — S, 20b, 73b
Abū Bayhas al-Hayṣam b. Djābir i, **113a** — I, **116b**
Abū Bilal → Mirdās b. Udayya
Abu Bishr Mattā b. Yūnus → Mattā b. Yūnus
Abū Burda → al-Ashʿarī
Abū Dabbūs i, 1176b — I, 1211b
Abū Dahbal al-Djumaḥī i,**113b** —I, **116b**
Abū Ḍabī → Abū Ẓabī
Abū Ḍamḍam i, **113b** — I, **116b**
Abū Ḍarba al-Liḥyānī iii, 67b; iv, 338a; v, 1247a — III, 70a; IV, 352b; V, 1237b
Abu 'l-Dardāʾ i, **113b,** 959b — I, **117a,** 989a
Abū Dāʾūd al-Bakrī i, 141b, 1001a — I, 145b, 1032a
Abū Dāʾūd al-Sidjistānī i, **114a;** iii, 24a, 158b; s, 232b — I, **117b;** III, 25a, 162a; S, 232b
Abū Dāwūd Muḥammad b. Aḥmad s, 125b — S, 124b
Abū Dāwūdid(e)s → Bānīdjūrid(e)s
Abū Dhabī → Abū Ẓabī
Abu 'l Dhahab → Muḥammad Abu 'l-Dhahab
Abu 'l-Dhahab, Muḥammad Bey i, 391b, 392a, 1033a; iii, 992a, iv, 853a; s, **20b**, 44a — I, 403a, 1064b; III, 1016b, IV, 886a; S, **20b**, 44b
Abū Dharr al-Ghifārī i, **114b,** 266b, 382a, 549b; ii, 846b — I, **118a,** 274b, 393a, 567a; II, 866b
Abū Dharr al-Harawī i, 864b — I, 889a
Abu 'l-Dhawwād Muḥammad s, 119a — S, 118b
Abū Dhuʾayb al-Hudhalī i, **115a;** iii, 273a; iv, 252a — I, **118a;** III, 281a; IV, 263a
Abu 'l-Ḍiyā Tewfīk → Ebüzziya Tevfik
Abū Djad → Abdjad
Abū Djaʿfar b. Aḥmad b. ʿAbd Allāh iii, 9a — III, 9b
Abū Djaʿfar Aḥmad b. Abī ʿAbd Allāh Muḥammad al-Barkī s, 127b — S, 126b
Abū Djaʿfar Aḥmad b. ʿAṭiyya ii, 1014a — II, 1037b
Abū Djaʿfar lbn Saʿīd iii, 66a — III, 68b
Abū Djaʿfar Aḥmad b. Muḥammad al-Barkī → al-Barkī
Abū Djaʿfar al-Andalūsī → al-Ruʿaynī
Abū Djaʿfar al-Ḥadhdhāʾ iii, 823b — III, 847a
Abū Djaʿfar Ḥamdīn → ʿAlī b. Aḍḥā
Abū Djaʿfar al-Hāshimī i, 1040a; iii, 160a, 699b, 700a, 766b — I, 1071b; III, 163b, 722a, 789b
Abū Djaʿfar al-Khāzin → al-Khāzin
Abū Djaʿfar al-Manṣūr → al-Manṣūr (ʿAbbāsid(e)
Abū Djaʿfar Muḥammad s, 357a — S, 357a
Abū Djaʿfar Muḥammad b. ʿAbd Kān → lbn ʿAbd Kān
Abū Djaʿfar Muḥammad b. al-Zubayr → lbn al-Zubayr
Abū Djaʿfar al-Ruʾāsī → al-Ruʾāsī
Abū Djaʿfar al-Ṭūsī → al-Ṭūsī
Abū Djaʿfar Ustādh-Hurmuz → Ustādh-Hurmuz
Abū Djahl i, **115a,** 136b, 151a, 868a; ii, 843b; iii, 152b — I, **118b,** 140b, 155b, 892a; II, 863a; III, 156a
Abū 'l-Djarūd → al-Djārūdiyya
Abū 'l-Djārūd Ziyād b. al-Mundhir ii, 485a; s, 48b — II, 497b; S, 49a
Abū 'l-Djaysh Mudjāhid → Mudjāhid al-Āmirī
Abū Djisrā i, 865b — I, 890a
Abū Djubayla → Djabala b. al-Ḥārith
Abu 'l-Djūd Muḥammad b. al-Layth iv, 1182b — IV, 1215b
Abū Djummayza ii, 124a; iv, 953a; v, 1250b — II, 127a; IV, 985b; V, 1241a
Abu 'l-Djunayd → Abū Nukhayla

Abū Du'ād al-Iyādī i, **115b**; iv, 289a, 919a — I, **119a**; IV, 302a, 952a
Abū Dulaf (Sāmarrā) i, 621a, 624a — I, 641a, 643b
Abū Dulaf, Mis'ar b. Muhalhil i, **116a**, 570b, 967a; iii, 106a; s, 363a — I, **119a**, 589a, 996b; III, 108b; S, 362b
Abū Dulaf al-Ḳāsim al-'Idjlī → al-Ḳāsim b. 'Isā
Abū Dulāma Zand b. al-Djawn i, **116b**, 909b; iv, 1003b — I, **120a**, 937a; IV, 1036a
Abu 'l-Dunyā Abu 'l Ḥasan 'Alī i, **117a** — I, **120a**
Abū Duwād → Abū Du'ād
Abu 'l-Faḍā'il → Ḥamdānid(e)s
Abu 'l-Faḍā'il al-Sayyid Rukn al-Dīn → al-Astarābādhī, Rukn al-Dīn
Abu 'l-Faḍl b. Idrīs Bidlīsī → Bidlīsī
Abu 'l-Faḍl b. Mubārak → Abu 'l-Faḍl 'Allāmī
Abū Faḍl b. al-Naḥwī → lbn al-Naḥwī
Abu 'l-Faḍl al-'Abbās b. 'Īsā iv, 683b — IV, 711b
Abu 'l-Faḍl al-'Abbās al-Shīrāzī → al-'Abbās b. al-Ḥusayn
Abu 'l-Faḍl 'Allāmī i, **117a**, 297a, 1331a; ii, 296a, 380a, 871a, b; iii, 423b; iv, 704a,759b, 1127b; s, 3b, 142b, 280a, 325a, 410b — I, **120b**, 306b, 1371b; II, 304a, 390b, 891a, b; III, 437b; IV, 732b, 790a, 1159a; S, 2b, 142a, 279b, 325a, 411a
Abu l'-Faḍl Dja'far al-Dimashḳī s, 42b — S, 43a
Abu 'l-Faḍl Dja'far al-Thā'ir fi 'llāh iii, 255a; s, 363a — III, 262b; S, 363a
Abu 'l-Faḍl Djamāl al-Dīn Muḥammad → Djamāl Ḳarshī
Abu 'l-Faḍl al-Djārūdī i, 515b — I, 531a
Abu 'l-Faḍl Ismā'īl → Ismā'īl, Abu 'l-Faḍl
Abu 'l-Faḍl 'Iyāḍ → 'Iyāḍ
Abu 'l-Faḍl Muḥammad → lbn al-'Amīd
Abu 'l-Faḍl Muḥammad al-Baghdādī v, 929b — V, 934b
Abu 'l-Faḍl Mūsā al-Iznīḳī → al-Iznīḳī
Abu 'l-Faḍl Raydān → Raydān al-Saḳlabī
Abu 'l-Faradj → Babbaghā'; lbn al-Djawzī; lbn al-'Ibrī; lbn al-Nadīm; lbn al-Ṭayyib; al-Shīrāzī
Abu 'l-Faradj b. Mas'ūd Rūnī iv, 61b; s, **21a** — IV, 64b; s, **21a**
Abu 'l-Faradj b. al-Ṭayyib → Ibn al-Ṭayyib
Abu 'l-Faradj Furḳān → Jeshuah b. Judah
Abu 'l-Faradj Hārūn → Hārūn b. al-Faradj
Abu 'l-Faradj al-Iṣbahānī (Iṣfahānī) i, 10a, **118a**, 590a, 1354a; iii, 928a; v, 936b; s, 24a, 35b, 64a, 116b, 183a, 310b, 311b, 401a, 409a — I, 10a, **121b**, 609b, 1393a; III, 952b; V, 940b; S, 24a, 35b, 64b, 116a, 184b, 310b, 311a, 401b, 409a
Abu 'l-Faradj Muḥammad Fasāndjus → lbn Fasāndjus
Abu 'l-Faradj Muḥammad al-Wa'wā iv, 1005b — IV, 1038a
Abu 'l-Faradj Sidjzī s, 21a — S, 21a
Abu 'l-Faraḥ (Bārha) s, 126b — S, 125b
Abū Fāris b. Abī Isḥāḳ iii, 67a — III, 69b
Abū Fāris 'Abd al-'Azīz al-Mutawakkil (Ḥafsid(e)) i, 93a, 448b, 1225a, 1247a; ii, 459a; iii, **68b**, 778a, 843b; iv, 416a, 739b; v, 531a; s, 399a — I, 95b, 461a, 1261b, 1284b; II, 471a; III, **71a**, 801b, 867b; IV, 434a, 769b; V, 535a; S, 399b
Abu Fāris 'Abd al-'Azīz I iii, 832a, 836a — III, 855b, 859b
Abū Farrādj → Aḥmad al-Badawī
Abu 'l-Fatḥ → lbn al-'Amid; lbn al-Furāt; al-Muẓaffar
Abu 'l-Fatḥ b. Abi 'l-Shawk i, 512b — I, 528a
Abu 'l-Fatḥ al-Balaṭī → al-Balaṭī
Abu 'l-Fatḥ Beg Bayāndur ii, 174a; s, 280b — II, 179a; S, 280b
Abu 'l-Fatḥ al-Bustī → al-Bustī
Abu 'l-Fatḥ al-Daylamī, al-Nāṣir li-Dīn Allāh s, **22a** — S, **22b**
Abu 'l-Fatḥ al-Ḥarrānī iii, 766b — III, 789b
Abu 'l-Fatḥ al-Ḥulwānī iii, 766b — III, 789b
Abu 'l-Fatḥ al-Ḥusaynī s, 383a — S, 383a
Abu 'l-Fatḥ Ibrāhīm → Ibrāhīm b. Shāhrukh
Abu 'l-Fatḥ al-Iskandarī → al-Hamadhānī
Abu 'l-Fatḥ Khān Bakhtiyārī iv, 104a, b — IV, 109a
Abu 'l-Fatḥ Muḥammad b. 'Annāz → Muḥammad b. 'Annāz
Abu 'l-Fatḥ Naṣr b. Ibrāhīm v, 330a — V, 330a
Abu 'l-Fatḥ al-Yaftalī i, 852a — I, 876a
Abu 'l-Fawāris i, 131b — I, 135b
Abu 'l-Fayyāḍ Sawwār s, 35b — S, 35b
Abu 'l-Fayd ii, 446a — II, 458a
Abu 'l-Fidā i, **118b**, 595a, 804b; ii, 585a; iii, 120a, 900b, 966b; iv, 485a; v, 925a, 1011b — I, **122a**, 614b, 828b; II, 599b; III, 122b, 924b, 991a; IV, 506a; V, 930b, 1007a
Abū Firās al-Ḥamdānī i, **119b**, 592a, 1249b; iii, 129b, 398a, 825a; iv, 55b; v, 647b — I, **122b**, 611b, 1287b; III, 132a, 410b, 849a; IV, 58b; V, 651b
Abu 'l-Fityān → Aḥmad al-Badawī
Abū Fudayk 'Abd Allāh b. Thawr i, **120a**, 550a, 942a; iv, 764a, 1076a — I, **123b**, 567b, 971a; IV, 794b, 1107b
Abu Fuṭrus → Nahr Abī Fuṭrus
Abū 'l-Futūh al-Ḥasan i, 552a; iii, 262b — I, 569b; III, 270a
Abu 'l-Futūh al-Rāzī i, **120a** — I, **123b**
Abu 'l-Futūḥ Yūsuf → Buluggīn b. Zīrī
Abu 'l-Futūḥ Yūsuf b. 'Abd Allāh iv, 497a — IV, 518a
Abu 'l-Ghanā'im Sa'd ii, 827a — II, 847a
Abū Ghānim Bishr b. Ghānim al-Khurāsānī i, **120b**, iii, 653b, 656b — I, **124a**; III, 674b, 678a
Abū Ghānim Naṣr iv, 494a, 661a — IV, 515a, 687b
Abu 'l-Gharānik → Muḥammad II (Aghlabid(e))
Abu 'l-Ghayth b. 'Abda iv, 662a — IV, 689a
Abu 'l-Ghāzī Bahādur Khān i, **120b**, 607b, 45a; ii, 1109b; iv, 1064a; v, 24a, 273b; s, 97b, 168b, 228a, 245b, 280b, 419b, 420a — I, **124a**, 627b, 45b; II, 1135b; IV, 1096a; V, 24b, 271b; S, 96b, 97a, 168b, 228a, 245b, 280b, 420a
Abū Ghufayl i, 1044a — I, 1076a
Abū Ghosh, Banū v, 334a — V, 334b
Abū Ghubshān v, 78a — V, 80a
Abū Ḥadīd, Muḥammad Farīd Wadjdī i, 598a; s, 244b — I, 617b; S, 244b
Abu 'l-Ḥadjdjādj b. al-Shaykh s, 381b — S, 382a
Abu 'l-Ḥadjdjādj Yūsuf b. Abi 'l-Ḳāsim → Ibn al-Sarrādj
Abu 'l-Ḥadjdjādj Yūsuf b. al-Sarrādj → Ibn al-Sarrādj
Abū Ḥafṣ al-Ḥaddād → Malāmatiyya (Nīshāpūr)
Abu Ḥafṣ al-Shiṭrandjī → al-Shiṭrandjī
Abu Ḥafṣ Sughdī iv, 55a, 525b — IV, 57b, 548a
Abū Ḥafṣ al-'Ukbarī v, 10a — V, 10b
Abū Ḥafṣ 'Umar I iii, 67a — III, 69b
Abū Ḥafṣ 'Umar b. Djamī' i, **121a** — I, **124b**
Abū Ḥafṣ 'Umar al-Ballūṭī i, 83a, **121b**, 1249a; ii, 744b; iii, 1083a — I, 85b, **125a**, 1287a; II, 763a; III, 1109b
Abū Ḥafṣ 'Umar b. al-Ḥādjdj iv, 116a — IV, 121a
Abū Ḥafṣ 'Umar al-Hintātī (Īntī) i, 78b, 79a, b, **121b**, 161a; ii, 526b; iii, 66a, 461b — I, 80b, 81b, 82a, **125a**, 165b; II, 539b; III, 68b, 478a
Abū Ḥāḳa, Aḥmad iii, 112a — III, 114b
Abu 'l-Hakam b. al-Mughīra → Abū Djahl
Abū Ḥala al-Tamīmī iv, 898b — IV, 931a
Abū Ḥāmid al-Gharnāṭī i, **122a**, 203b, 204a, 593b, 602b; v, 1012a, 1016a, 1018a — I, **125b**, 209b, 210a, 613a, 622a; V, 1008, 1011b, 1012a, 1013b

Abū Ḥāmid al-Isfarāʾinī ii, 136a; v, 345a — II, 139b; V, 346a
Abū Ḥāmid al-Marw al-Rūdhī i, 126b — I, 130a
Abū Ḥammū I i, 93a, 94a, **122b**; v, 1180a — I, 95b, 96b, **126a**; V, 1170a
Abū Ḥammū II i, 93a, **122b**, 155a; ii, 979a; iii, 826b, 831b, 832a — I, 95b, **126a**, 159b; II, 1001b; III, 850b, 855b
Abū Ḥamza → al-Mukhtār b. ʿAwf
Abū Ḥamza Madjmaʿ b. Samʿān al-Ḥāʾik s, 341b — S, 341a
Abū Ḥanīfa al-Dīnawarī → al-Dīnawarī
Abū Ḥanīfa al-Nuʿmān (Fāṭimid(e)) → al-Nuʿmān
Abū Ḥanīfa al-Nuʿmān b. Thābit i, 70b, **123a**, 164a, 481b, 692a, 730b, 904a; ii, 489a, 1022a; iii, 512a, 687b, 984b; iv, 855b; v, 239b, 731b; s, 232b, 303b, 304a, 401a — I, 72b, **126b**, 169a, 495b, 713a, 752b, 913b; II, 501a, 1046a; III, 529b, 709a, 1009a; IV, 889a; V, 237b, 737a; S, 232b, 303b, 401b
- doctrine i, 164b, 332b; ii, 116a, 832a; iii, 162b, 209b, 1164b — I, 169b, 343a; II, 118b, 851b; III, 166a, 215b, 1193a
Abū Ḥanẓala → Abū Sufyān b. Ḥarb b. Umayya
Abū Ḥarb (Kākūyid(e)) iv, 465b — IV, 486b
Abū Ḥarb b. Manučihr v, 662a — V, 667b
Abū Ḥarb al-Mubarḳaʾ v, 326b — V, 326b
Abu 'l-Ḥārith Muḥammad b. Farīghūn ii, 799a — II, 817b
Abu 'l-Ḥasan al-Aḥmar s, **22b** — S, **22b**
Abu 'l-Ḥasan ʿAlī → ʿAzafī
Abu 'l-Ḥasan b. Bahlūl al-Ṭirhānī i, 737b — I, 759a
Abu 'l-Ḥasan al-Akhfash i, 167b, 321b — I, 172b, 331b
Abu 'l-Ḥasan ʿAlī (Ḥamdānid(e)) iii, 130b — III, 133a
Abu 'l-Ḥasan ʿAlī (Marīnid(e)) i, 93a, **124b**, 129b, 138a, 155a, 496a, 506b, 634a, 1149a, 1339b; ii, 146a, 525a, 822b; iii, 67b, 68a, 135a, 867b; iv, 828a; v, 531a, 1190a; s, 45b, 376b, 377a — I, 95b, **128a**, 133b, 142a, 159a, 510b, 521b, 655a, 1183a, 1379b; II, 150a, 538a, 842a; III, 70a, b, 137b, 890b; IV, 861a; V, 535a, 1180a; S, 46a, 376b, 377a
Abu 'l-Ḥasan ʿAlī b. ʿAbd Allāh s, 343a — S, 342b
Abu 'l-Ḥasan ʿAlī b. Abī Fāris iii, 69a — III, 71b
Abu 'l-Ḥasan ʿAlī b. Kaʿb al-Anṣārī s, 13b — S, 14a
Abu 'l-Ḥasan ʿAlī b. Khalaf al-Zayyāt s, 390b — S, 391a
Abu 'l-Ḥasan ʿAlī b. al-Khalīl iv, 1004a — IV, 1036b
Abu 'l-Ḥasan ʿAlī b. Muḥammad al-Ṣūfī al-Muzayyin s, 350a — S, 350a
Abu 'l-Ḥasan ʿAlī b. Saʿd (Naṣrid(e)) → Ibn al-Sarrādj
Abū 'l-Ḥasan ʿAlī al-Ḥuṣrī → al-Ḥuṣrī
Abu 'l-Ḥasan ʿAlī al-Maghribī → al-Maghribī
Abu 'l-Ḥasan ʿAlī al-Shādhilī → al-Shādh ilī
Abu 'l-Ḥasan al-Anṣārī s, **23a** — S, **23a**
Abu 'l-Ḥasan Ardistānī s, 23b — S, 23b
Abu 'l-Ḥasan al-Battī s, **23a** — S, **23a**
Abu 'l-Ḥasan Djīlwa, Mīrzā s, **23b** — S, **23b**
Abu 'l-Ḥasan al-Karkhī s, 12b, 13a, 14a — S, 13a, b, 14a
Abu 'l-Ḥasan Kharaḳānī → Kharaḳānī
Abū 'l-Ḥasan (Tānā) Ḳuṭb Shāh i, 120a; ii, 180b; iii, 427a; v, 549b — I, 1246a; II, 186b; III, 441a; V, 554b
Abu 'l-Ḥasan Muḥammad b. Ibrāhīm b. Sīmdjūr → Sīmdjūr, Banū
Abu 'l-Ḥasan al-Maghribī s, **24a** — S, **24a**
Abu 'l-Ḥasan al-Rabaʿī → al-Rabaʿī
Abu 'l-Ḥasan al-Rummānī → Rummānī
Abu 'l-Ḥasan Shāh iv, 201b — IV, 210b
Abu 'l-Ḥasan al-Samlālī i, 355b — I, 366b
Abu 'l-Ḥasan Shīrāzī → al-Shīrāzī, Abu 'l-Ḥasan
Abu 'l-Ḥasan al-Tamgrūtī i, 593b — I, 613a
Abu 'l-Ḥasanāt Muḥammad → ʿAbd al-Ḥayy
Abū Ḥāshid b. Yaḥyā b. Abī Ḥāshid s, 22b — S, 22b
Abū Hāshim (Sharīf) → Makka
Abū Hāshim b. al-Djubbāʾī i, 4b, 411a; ii, 218b, **570a;** iii, 171b, 832a, 1143a, 1165b; v, 702a; s, 12b, 13b, 25b, 32a, 226b, 343b, 346b, 348a — I, 5a, 423a; II, 225a, **584b;** III, 175b, 856a, 1171b, 1194b; V, 707a; S, 13a, 14a, 25b, 32a, 226b, 343b, 346a, 348a
Abū Hāshim ʿAbd Allāh b, Muhaammad b. al-Ḥanafiyya i, 15a, 48b, **124b**, 402a; ii, 441a; iii, 265a, 574a, 1265b; iv, 837a; s, 357b — I, 15b, 50a, **128a**, 412b; II, 452b; III, 272b, 594a, 1298b; IV, 870a; S, 357b
Abū Hāshim al-Bāwardī iv, 797a, 800b — IV, 829b, 833a
Abū Ḥassūn ʿAlī al-Bādisī i, 859b, 860a; ii, 819b — I, 883b, 884a; II, 839a
Abū Ḥātim Aḥmad → ʿAzafī
Abū Ḥātim ʿAnbasa b. Isḥāḳ ii, 72a — II, 73b
Abū Ḥātim al-Malzūzī i, **125a;** iii, 297a, 654b — I, **128b;** III, 306a, 676a
Abū Ḥātim al-Rāzī i, **125a**, 160b, 694a; iii, 158b; iv, 661b — I, **129a**, 165a, 715a; III, 162a; IV, 688b
Abū Ḥātim al-Sidjistānī i, **125b**, 158b, 167b, 718b; iii, 641b, 844b — I, **129a**, 163a, 172b, 740; III, 662b, 868b
Abū Ḥātim al-Warsinānī v, 167a — V, 164b
Abū Ḥātim Yaʿḳūb b. Ḥabīb → al-Ibāḍiyya
Abū Ḥātim Yūsuf b. Muḥammad → Rustumids
Abū Ḥātim al-Zuṭṭī iv, 661a — IV, 687b
Abu 'l-Hawl s, 408a — S, 408a
Abu 'l-Hawl (Hōl) i, **125b** — I, **129a**
Abu 'l-Haydjāʾ ʿAbd Allāh b. Ḥamdān → ʿAbd Allāh b. Ḥamdān
Abu 'l-Haydjāʾ Hadhbānī v, 454a, 455a — V, 457a, b
Abu 'l-Haydjāʾ al-Ḥamdānī iii, 130b; s, 94a — III, 133a; S, 93b
Abu 'l-Haydjāʾ al-Rawwādī ii, 680a — II, 697a
Abū Ḥayyā al-Numayrī s, **24a** — S, **24b**
Abū Ḥayyān al-Gharnāṭī i, **126a**, 445b, 593a, 602b; iii, 698b, 801a, 861b — I, **129b**, 458b, 612b, 622a; III, 720b, 824b, 885b
Abū Ḥayyān al-Tawḥīdī i, **126b**, 130a, 151b, 159a, 176a, 427a, 590a, 1354a; ii, 387b, 766b, 774b; iii, 355a, 672b, 754b, 1071b, 1263b; v, 320a; s, 13a, b, 72b, 88b, 119b, 289b, 389b, 398b — I, **130a**, 134a, 156a, 163b, 180b, 439a, 609a, 1393a; II, 397b, 785a, 793a; III, 366a, 694a, 777b, 1098a, 1296a; V, 319a; S, 13b, 73a, 88b, 119a, 289b, 390a, 398b
Abū 'l-Ḥazm Djahwar ii, 389a; iii, 496a, 786a, 973b — II, 399b; III, 513a, 809b, 998a
Abū Hiffān, ʿAbd Allāh b. Aḥmad al-Mihzamī iv, 1005a, s, **24b** — IV, 1037b; S, **25a**
Abū Hilāl al-ʿAskarī → a-ʿAskarī
Abū Ḥimāra → Bū Ḥmāra
Abu 'l-Hindī al-Riyāḥī iv, 1004 — IV, 1036a, b
Abū Hubayra b. Rabīʿa b. Riyāḥ al-Hilālī s, 92b — S, 92b
Abu 'l-Hudā i, 63b; ii, 418b, 419a; v, 949a — I, 65b; II, 429b; V, 953a
Abu 'l-Hudhayl al-ʿAllāf i, 2a, 4b, 10a, **127b**, 204b, 713b; ii, 449b; iii, 63b, 172a, 1143a, 1266a; v, 384a, 576b; s, 88b, 225b, 226a, 227a, 392a, 393b — I, 2a, 5a, 10a, **131a**, 210b, 735a; II, 461a; III, 66a, 175b, 1171b, 1299a; V, 385a, 581a; S, 88b, 225b, 226a, 227a, 392b, 394a
Abū Ḥulmān al-Fārisī iii, 570b — III, 590a
Abū Hurayra al-Dawsī al-Yamānī i, 52a, **129a**, 266b, 714a; iii, 242b; v, 1010a; s, 230b, 311a, b — I, 54a, **132b**, 274b, 736a; III, 249b; V, 1005b; S, 230b, 310b,

311a
Abū Hurayra al-Rāwandī iv, 838a — IV, 871a
Abū Ḥusayn, Banū → Kalbid(e)s
Abu 'l-Ḥusayn b. Abī Yaʿlā i, 274a, b, 1039a; iii, 766b; iv, 990a — I, 282b, 1070b; III, 789b; IV, 1022b
Abu 'l-Ḥusayn b. Samʿun iii, 159b; v, 10a — III, 163a; V, 10b
Abu 'l-Ḥusayn Aḥmad b. al-Uṭrūsh i, 688a; iii, 255a; s, 356b — I, 709a; III, 262b; S, 356b
Abu 'l-Ḥusayn al-Baṣrī iii, 1023b, 1025b, 1144a; s, 14a, **25a** — III, 1049a, 1051b, 1172b; S, 14a, **25b**
Abū 'l-Ḥusayn al Ṣālihī iv, 986a — IV, 1018b
Abū Ḥuzāba, al-Walīd b. Ḥunayfa s, **26a** — S, **26a**
Abu 'l-Ibar, Abu 'l-ʿAbbās Muḥammad s, 16b, **26a** — S, 17a, **27b**
Abū Ibrāhīm Aḥmad b. Muḥammad i, 24a, 248b, 250b, 621a; iii, 287b; iv, 829b — I, 25a, 256b, 258a, 641b; III, 296a; IV, 862a, b
Abū Ibrāhīm Isḥāḳ al-Fārābī → al-Fārābī
Abū ʿIḳāl al-Aghlab i, 248b, 250b; iv, 415b — I, 256a, 258a; IV, 433b
ABŪ ʿIkrima iv, 446a — IV, 466a
Abū ʿIkrisha → Ḥādjib b. Zurāra
Abū ʿImrān Faḍl b. al-Djarrah ii, 484b — II, 497a
Abū ʿImrān al-Fāsī s, **26b** — S, **26b**
Abū ʿImrān Mūsā al-Ḥasan v, 247b — V, 245a
Abū ʿInān Fāris i, 93a, 124b, **129b,** 155a; ii, 822a, 979a; iii, 68a, 462a, 736a, 756a, 826a, 867a; iv, 635a, 729b; v, 531a, 626b, 1190a — I, 95b, 128a, **133b,** 159b; II, 841b, 1001b; III, 70b, 478a, 758b, 779a, 849b, 890b; IV, 661b, 758b; V, 535a, 630b, 1180a
Abū ʿInāniyya (Madrasa) s, 223b — S, 223b
Abu 'l-ʿIrmās → Abū Nukhayla
Abū ʿĪsā al-Iṣfahānī i, **130a**; iv, 96a, 603b, 604b, 606b — I, **133b**; IV, 100a, 628a, 629a, 631a
Abū ʿĪsā Muḥammad al-Warrāḳ i, **130a;** 905a; iv, 1132a — I, **133b;** III, 929a; IV, 1163b
Abū Isḥāḳ I (Ḥafṣid(e)) iii, 48b, 67a — III, 50b, 69b
Abū Isḥāḳ II (Ḥafsıd(e)) iii, 68a, 867a — III, 70b, 891a
Abū Isḥāḳ → al-Shāṭibī
Abū Isḥāḳ b. al-Rashīd i, 439b — I, 452a
Abū Isḥāk Čishtī ii, 50b — II, 51a
Abū Isḥāḳ Djamāl al-Dīn Īndjū iii, 1022a, 1208b; iv, 102b, 498b, 909b; v, 163a; s, 415a — III, 1048a, 1239a; IV, 107a, 520a, 942b; V, 161a; S, 415a
Abū Isḥāḳ al-Fārisī → al-Iṣṭakhrī
Abū Isḥāḳ al-Fārisī, Ibrāhīm b. ʿAlī s, **27b** — S, **27b**
Abū Isḥāḳ al-Ḥuṣrī → al-Ḥuṣrī
Abū Isḥāḳ Ibrāhīm b. Abī ʿAbd Allāh b. al-Sarrādj → Ibn al-Sarrādj
Abū Isḥāḳ Ibrāhīm b. Alp-Takīn i, 421b — I, 433b
Abū Isḥāḳ Ibrāhīm al-Adjdābī → al-Adjdābī
Abū Isḥāḳ Ibrāhīm al-Harawī i, 162b — I, 167a
Abū Isḥāḳ Ibrāhīm al-Ṣābīʾ → al-Ṣābīʾ
Abū Isḥāḳ al-Ilbīrī i, **130b,** 602a — I, **134a,** 621b
Abū Isḥāḳ Ismāʿīl b. al-Ḳāsim → Abu 'l-Atāhiya
Abū Isḥāḳ al-Kāzarūnī → al-Kāzarūnī
Abū Isḥāḳ Muḥammad b. Maʿmūn → al-Muʿtasim
Abū Kabīr al-Hudhalī i, **130b** — I, **134b**
Abū Kabrayn → Bū Ḳabrīn
Abū 'l-Kalām Āzād → Āzād
Abū Ḳalammas → Ḳalammas
Abū Ḳalamūn i, **131a** — I, **135a**
Abū Kalb → Sikka
Abū Kālīdjār i, **131b,** 512b, 1355a, b; ii, 194a, 391a, 856a, 962a; iii, 860a; iv, 294b, 379a, 457b, 911b — I, **135b,** 528a, 1394a, 1395a; II, 200a, 401b, 876a, 984a; III, 884a; IV, 307b, 395b, 477b, 944b
Abū Kālīdjār Garshāsp → Garshāsp
Abu 'l-Kamāl Tamīn b. Zīrī v, 1177b — V, 1167b
Abū Karib → Ibn Karib
Abū Kāmil Shudjāʿ b. Aslam i, **132b;** ii, 361b — I, **136a;** II, 371b
Abu 'l-Kāmil Tamīm i, 1044b; iii, 1043a — I, 1076a; III, 1069a
Abū Kālīdjār Abū Karib Budayr b. Abī Ṣakhr s, 357b — S, 357b
Abu 'l-Ḳāsim i, **133b** — I, **137b**
Abu 'l-Ḳāsim b. Abi 'l-Zinad s, 380b — S, 380b
Abu 'l-Ḳāsim b. Manda → Ibn Manda, ʿAbd al-Raḥmān
Abu 'l-Ḳāsim b. Maḥfūẓ iv, 810b — IV, 843b
Abu 'l-Ḳāsim b. ʿUbayd Allāh al-Mahdī i, 207b; iii, 297b; v, 1175a, 1243b — I, 213b; III, 306b; V, 1165a, 1234a, b
Abu 'l-Ḳāsim b. Yūsuf b. al-Sarrādj → Ibn al-Sarrādj
Abu 'l-Ḳāsim ʿAbd al-ʿAzīz b. Yūsuf s, 398a — S, 398b
Abi 'l-Ḳāsim Anūdjūr (Unūdjūr) → Unūdjūr
Abu 'l-Ḳāsim ʿĀrif iv, 71a — IV, 75a
Abu 'l-Ḳāsim Bābur i, 91a, 147b, 701a; iii, 603a; iv, 523b — I, 93b, 152a, 722a; III, 623b; IV, 546a
Abu 'l-Ḳāsim al-Barrādī → al-Barrādī
Abu 'l-Ḳāsim Bishr-i Yāsīn i, 146a — I, 150a
Abu 'l-Ḳāsim Djaʿfar b. al-Uṭrūsh i, 688a; iii, 255a; s, 356b — I, 709a; III, 262a; S, 356b
Abu 'l-Ḳāsim al-Djardjarāʾī → al- Djardjarāʾī
Abu 'l-Ḳāsim Farāhānī → Ḳāʾim-Maḳām, Abū l'-Ḳāsim
Abu 'l-Ḳāsim al-Fazarī → al-Fazarī
Abu 'l-Ḳāsim al-Ḥakkār → ʿAbd al-ʿAzīz b. Yūsuf
Abu 'l-Ḳāsim al-Ḥusayn al-Maghribī → al-Maghribī
Abu 'l-Ḳāsim al-Kaʿbī al-Balkhī → al-Balkhī
Abu 'l-Ḳāsim Ḳāʾimmaḳām (Irān) s, 70b — S, 71a
Abu 'l-Ḳāsim Khalaf → al-Zahrāwī
Abu 'l-Ḳāsim al-Ḳushayrī → al-Ḳushayrī
Abu 'l-Ḳāsim al-Madjrīṭī → al-Madjrīṭī
Abu 'l-Ḳāsim al-Mudlidjī i, 127a — I, 130b
Abu 'l-Ḳāsim Muḥammad b. Yaḥyā → ʿAzafī
Abu 'l-Ḳāsim Muḥammad al-ʿIrāḳī v, 112a; s, 270a — V, 114b; S, 269b
Abu 'l-Ḳāsim Shaykh al-Raʾīs iv, 164b — IV, 171b
Abu 'l-Ḳāsim al-Wāsānī → al-Wāsānī
Abu 'l-Ḳāsim Yazīd b. Makhlad iii, 95a, b, 656a; s, 48b — III, 97b, 98a, 677b; S, 49a
Abu 'l-Ḳāsim al-Zayyānī → al-Zayyānī
Abū Ḳays b. al-Aslat i, 771b — I, 794b
Abū Khālid ʿAbd al-ʿAzīz i, 148b — I, 153a
Abū Khālid Yazīd al-Wāsiṭī ii, 485a; s, 48b — II, 497b; S, 49a
Abu Khalīfa al-Djumaḥī → al-Faḍl b. al-Ḥubāb
Abu 'l-Khaṣīb i, **133b** — I, **137b**
Abu 'l-Khaṭṭāb al-Asadī i, **134a,** 1156a; iv, 203a, 1132a — I, **137b,** 1190b; IV, 212a, 1163b
Abu 'l-Khaṭṭāb al-Kalwadhānī → al-Kalwadhānī
Abu 'l-Khaṭṭāb al-Maʿāfirī i, **134a,** 1099a, 1175a; ii, 374b; iii, 296a, 297a, 654a, 1040b; iv, 827a; v, 696a — I, **138a,** 1132a, 1210b; II, 385a; III, 305b, 306a, 675b, 1066b; IV, 860a; V, 700b
Abu 'l-Khaṭṭār i, **134b,** 490a; ii, 1012b; iii, 601b; iv, 494b, 672b — I, **138b,** 504b; II, 1036a; III 622b; IV, 515b, 700a
Abu 'l-Khayr i, 827b; s, 354b — I, 850b; S, 354b
Abu 'l-Khayr Ḥammād al-Dabbās i, 69a — I, 71a
Abu 'l-Khayr al-Ḥusayn al-Baghdādī i, 1236b — I, 1274a
Abu 'l-Khayr al-Ishbīlī i, **135b;** ii, 901b — I, **139b;** II, 922b
Abū 'l-Khayr Khān s, 51a — S, 51b
Abu 'l-Khayr Özbeg i, 46b, **135a,** 147b, 148a; ii, 44b — I, 47b, **138b,** 152a; II, 45b
Abu 'l-Khayrāt b. Ibrāhīm ii, 124a — II, 127a

Abū Khaythama iii, 678a — III, 708b
Abū Khazar Yaghlā b. Zaltāf iii, 95a, b, 656a — III, 97b, 98a, 677b
Abū Khāzim b. Abi Yaʿlā iii, 766b — III, 789b
Abū Khāzim Ibn al-Farrāʾ iii, 766b — III, 789b
Abū Khirāsh Khuwaylid i, **136a** — I, **140a**
Abuḳraṭ(īs) → Buḳrāṭ
Abū Ḳubays i, **136a,** 178a — I, **140a,** 183a
Abū Kudāma Yazīd b. Fandīn al-Īfranī iii, 1041b — III, 1067b
Abū Ḳuḥāfa (ʿUthmān) b. ʿĀmir i, 109b, 110a — I, 112b, 113a
Abū Kuraib → Ibn Karib
Abū Ḳuraysh i, 1298a — I, 1338a
Abū Ḳurrā al-Īfranī al-Maghīlī i, 367a, 1175b; iii, 1040b, 1041a; v, 1164b — I, 378a, 1210b; III, 1066b, 1067a; V, 1154b
Abū Ḳurra, Theodore i, **136b** — I, **140b**
Abū Lahab i, 9a, 80a, 115b, **136b,** 152b; iii, 366b — I, 9a, 82b, 118b, **140b,** 157a; III, 378a
Abū Layla → al-Hārith b. ʿAbd al-ʿAzīz; Sulaymān Pasha Misrāklī
Abū Layla Isḥāḳ b. Muḥammad s, 103a — S, 102b
Abu ʾl-Layth Naṣr → al-Ḥāfiẓ al-Samarḳandī
Abu ʾl-Layth al-Samarḳandī i, 123b, **137a;** ii, 98b; iii, 163a — I, 127a, **141a;** II, 100b; III, 166b
Abū Layth al-Siḳillī iv, 118a — IV, 123a
Abū Likaylik ii, 944b — II, 966b
Abū Lubāba i, 266b — I, 274b
Abū Luʾluʾa iii, 586b — III, 607a
Abu ʾl-Maʿālī (Mughal) s, 324b — S, 324a
Abu ʾl-Maʿālī ʿAbd al-Malik → al-Djuwaynī
Abu ʾl-Maʿālī b. Sayyid Mubārak (Bayhaḳī) s, 132a — S, 131a
Abu ʾl-Maʿālī Muḥammad b. ʿUbayd Allāh i, **137a** — I, **141a**
Abu ʾl-Maʿālī Naṣr Allāh iv, 704a — IV, 732b
Abu ʾl-Maʿālī Saʿd al-Dawla → Saʿd al-Dawla Sharīf
Abu ʾl-Maʿālī Sharīf I → Saʿd al-Dawla Sharīf
Abu ʾl-Maʿālī Sharīf II iii, 130b — III, 133a
Abū Māḍī, Īliyyā v, 1254b, 1255a, b; s, **27b** — V, 1245b, 1246a, b; S, **28a**
Abū Madyan, Hawwārī → Boumedienne
Abū Madyan, Muḥammad ii, 123b — II, 126b
Abū Madyan Shuʿayb al-Andalusī i, 91b, **137b,** 141a, 159b, 1205a; ii, 100b, 183a; iii, 339a, 701b, 800a, 844a, 866a; iv, 1006b; s, 403a — I, 94a, **141b,** 145a, 164a, 1241a; II, 102b, 189a; III, 349a, 723b, 823b, 868a, 890a; IV, 1038b; S, 403a
Abu ʾl-Maghrāʾ b. Mūsā b. Zurāra iv, 89a, b, 90a — IV, 93a, b, 94a
Abū Maḥallī al-Sidjilmāssī s, **28b** — S, **28b**
Abu ʾl-Maḥāsin b. Taghrībirdī i, **138a,** 595a; ii, 782a, 954a; iii, 188b, 775b; iv, 294b; s, 386b, 389a — I, **142a,** 614b; II, 800b, 976a; III, 193a, 798b; IV, 308a; S, 386b, 389a
Abu ʾl-Makārim b. Muḥammad al-Abharī v, 930a — V, 934b
Abu ʾl-Makārim, Tādj al-Dīn ii, 333b — II, 343b
Abū Makhrama → Makhrama, Bā
Abu ʾl-Malīḥ b. Mammati → Ibn Mammatī
Abu ʾl-Manadjdja, Baḥr iv, 514b, 515a — IV, 537a
Abū Manṣūr → al-Thaʿālibī
Abū Manṣūr b. Bahāʾ al-Dawla s, 119a — S, 118b
Abū Manṣūr b. Yūsuf iii, 699b, 766a; s, **29b,** 192a — III, 721b, 789a; S, **29b,** 193a
Abū Manṣūr al-Azdī i, 515b — I, 531a
Abū Manṣūr Farāmurz iii, 471b; iv, 101a, 465b — III, 488a; IV, 105a, b, 486b
Abū Manṣūr Ilyās al-Nafūsī i, **139a;** ii, 369a; iv, 920a — I, **143a;** II, 379a; IV, 953a
Abū Manṣūr Kumrī s, 271b — S, 271b
Abū Manṣūr al-Maʿmarī (Muʿammarī) iv, 63b — IV, 67a
Abū Manṣūr Muḥammad b. ʿAbd al-Razzāḳ ii, 918b — II, 940a
Abū Manṣūr Muḥammad b. ʿAlī ii, 127b; v, 928b — II, 130b; V, 933b
Abū Marwān, Sīdī i, 512a — I, 527b
Abū Marwān ʿAbd al-Malik b. ʿAbd al-ʿAzīz s, 81b — S, 81a
Abū Marwān b. Ḥayyān → Ibn Ḥayyān
Abū Marwān b. Razīn s, 81b — S, 81a
Abū Maʿshar Djaʿfar b. Muḥammad al-Balkhī i, **139a,** 589b; iii, 463b, 1072b, 1136b, 1137a; iv, 1182b; v, 130b, 297a, 950a; s, 17a — I, **143b,** 608b; III, 480a, 1099a, 1164b, 1165a; IV, 1215b; V, 133b, 296b, 954a; S, 17a
Abū Maʿshar Nadjīḥ al-Sindī i, **140a** — I, **144a**
Abū Maslama i, 755a — I, 778a
Abū Midfaʿ → Sikka
Abū Miḥdjan Nuṣayb b. Rabāḥ → Nuṣayb
Abū Miḥdjan al-Thaḳafī i, **140a;** iii, 850b; iv, 385b, 1002a — I, **144a;** III, 874b; IV, 402b, 1031b
Abū Mikhnaf i, **140b;** iii, 608a, 610a; v, 947b — I, **144b;** III, 628b, 631a; V, 951b
Abū Mismār, al-Sharīf Ḥammūd s, **30a** — S, **30b**
Abu ʾl-Muʿaskar al-Ḥusayn b. Maʿdān iii, 906a — III, 930b
Abu ʾl-Muʾayyad Balkhī ii, 918b — II, 940a
Abū Mudar Ziyādat Allāh → Ziyādat Allāh III
Abū Mudjālid al-Baghdādī iv, 1162a — IV, 1194a
Abu ʾl-Mughīra b. Ḥazm → Ibn Ḥazm
Abu ʾl-Mughīra ʿAmr b. Sharaḥīl al-ʿAnsī iv, 370a — IV, 386b
Abu ʾl-Mughīth al-Rāfiḳī i, 153b — I, 157b
Abu ʾl-Muhādjir Dīnār ii, 525b; iv, 826a; v, 518a — II, 538b; IV, 859a; V, 521b
Abū Muḥammad b. Abī Hafṣ ii, 1007b, 1008a — II, 1031b
Abū Muḥammad b. Baraka i, **140b;** iii, 731b — I, **144b;** III, 754b
Abū Muḥammad b. Djiyār al-Djayyānī ii, 516a — II, 529a
Abū Muḥammad ʿAbd Allāh b. ʿAbd al-Muʾmin iii, 386b; v, 61a — III, 399a; V, 62b
Abū Muḥammad ʿAbd Allāh b. ʿAbd al-Wāḥid iii, 66a — III, 68b
Abū Muḥammad ʿAbd Allāh b. Barrī → Ibn Barrī
Abū Muḥammad ʿAbd Allāh b. Manṣūr → Ibn Ṣulayḥa
Abū Muḥammad ʿAbd Allāh b. ʿUmar i, 766a, b — I, 789a, b
Abū Muḥammad ʿAbd al-Wahhāb b. Aḥmad → Ādarrāḳ
Abū Muḥammad Djaʿfar al-Sarrādj i, 69a, 516a — I, 71a, 531b
Abū Muḥammad Ḳāsim → ʿAzafī
Abū Muḥammad al-Rāzī ii, 462a; iii, 158b — II, 474a; III, 162b
Abū Muḥammad Ṣāliḥ b. Yanṣāran i, **141a;** iii, 339a — I, **145a;** III, 349a
Abū Muḥammad al-Tamīmī iii, 766b — III, 789b
Abū Muḥammad Wīslān b. Yaʿḳūb iii, 95b — III, 98a
Abū Muḥammad Ziyādat Allāh → Ziyādat Allāh I
Abū Muḥammad al-Zubayr b. ʿUmar ii, 1013b — II, 1037a
Abū Muḥriz i, 685a — I, 706a
Abu ʾl-Mulūk → Bāwand
Abu ʾl-Munadjdjā iv, 663b — IV, 690a
Abū Mūsā (island, île) i, 535b; iv, 778a, b; s, 417b, 418a — I, 552a; IV, 809b, 810a; S, 418a
Abū Mūsā al-Ashʿarī → al-Ashʿarī

Abū Mūsā al-Dabīlī → al-Dabīlī
Abū Mūsā ʿĪsā b. Ādam → ʿĪsā b. Ādam
Abū Mūsā ʿĪsā b. Ṣabīḥ → al-Murdār
Abū Mūsā al-Kharrāz iv, 801a — IV, 833a
Abū Muṣʿab Muḥammad b. Ayyūb → Muḥammad b. Ayyūb
Abū Muslim al-Khurasānī i, 15b, 16a, 16b, 43a, 49a, 103a, 116b, **141a,** 149a, 755a, 1293a; ii, 78a, 86b, 110a, 505a, 739b, 966b; iii, 802b, 988a; iv, 15b, 16a, 45a, 411b, 446b, 718a, 838a; v, 57a, b, 63b, 64a, 69a, 618a, 855a — I, 16a, 16b, 17a, 44b, 50b, 106a, 120a, **145a,** 153a, 778a, 1332b; II, 79b, 88b, 112b, 518a, 758a, 988b; III, 826a, 1012b; IV, 17a, b, 48a, 429b, 466b, 747a, 870b; V, 59a, 65b, 71a, 622a, 861b
Abū Muslim b. Ḥammād iv, 662b — IV, 689a
Abu 'l-Muṭāʿ Dhu 'l-Ḳarnayn iii, 128b — III, 131b
Abu 'l-Muṭahhar al-Azdī i, 133b; iii, 368a, 1264a; s, **31a** — I, 137b; III, 379b, 1297a; S, **31a**
Abu 'l-Muṭarrif b. ʿAmīra → Ibn ʿAmīra
Abu 'l-Muʾthir al-Bahlawī i, **141b** — I, **145b**
Abū Muṭīʿ al-Balkhī i, 124a — I, 127b
Abu 'l-Muẓaffar, amīr iii, 799a — III, 822b
Abu 'l-Muẓaffar b. Yūnus iii, 751b — III, 774b
Abu 'l-Muẓaffar Ḥamdān s, 36a — S, 36b
Abū Naḍḍāra i, **141b,** 597a; ii, 466b — I, **146a,** 616b; II, 478a
Abū Nadjāḥ b. Ḳannāʾ i, 440a — I, 452b
Abu 'l-Nadjīb → ʿAmʿaḳ
Abu 'l-Nadjm → Badr b. Ḥasanwayh
Abu 'l-Nadjm al-ʿIdjlī i, **142a,** 207b; s, 259a — I, **146a,** 214a; S, 258b
Abū Nahshal b. Ḥumayd al-Ṭūsī i, 154a, 1289b; iii, 573a — I, 158a, 1329a; III, 593a
Abū Naṣr Aḥmad al-Farīghūnī ii, 799b — II, 818a
Abū Naṣr Aḥnad al-Munāzī → al-Munāzī
Abū Naṣr Manṣūr b. ʿAlī → Ibn ʿIrāḳ
Abū Naṣr al-Miṣrī s, 267a — S, 266b
Abū Naṣr Muḥammad Shār ii, 1011a — II, 1034b
Abū Naṣr Mushkān i, 1130b; iv, 758b — I, 1164b; IV, 788b
Abū Naṣr Sābūr → Sābūr b. Ardashīr
Abū Naṣr Shāh-Fīrūz s, 118b — S, 118a
Abū Nuʿaym al-Faḍl b. Dukayn al-Mulāʾī i, **143a** — I, **147a**
Abū Nuʿaym al-Iṣfahānī i, **142b;** ii, 359b; iv, 212a; v, 1234b, 1235a — I, **146b;** II, 369b; IV, 221b; V, 1225a, b
Abū Nukhayla al-Ḥimmānī s, **31a** — S, **31b**
Abū Nuḳṭa s, 30b — S, 30b
Abū Numayy I, Muḥammad i, 21a, 553a; iii, 262b — I, 22a, 570b; III, 270a
Abū Numayy II, Muḥammad i, 1032b; ii, 517b, 572a, 788a; iii, 262b; v, 18a — I, 1064a; II, 530b, 586b, 806b; III, 270a; V, 18b
Abū Nūr b. Abī Ḳurra iii, 1043b — III, 1069b
Abū Nuwās i, 2b, 10b, 14a, 108a, 116b, 118b, **143b,** 150b, 158b, 196b, 438a, 587b, 751b, 1081b; ii, 437b, 591b, 1032a; iii, 156b, 328a, 618a, b, 745b, 1202b, 1262b; iv, 54b, 252a, 919a, 1004a, b, 1008b; v, 133a, 778b; s, 25a, 58b, 253a, 352b — I, 2b, 10b, 14a, 111a, 120a, 122a, **147b,** 155a, 163a, 202a, 450b, 606b, 774a, 1114a; II, 449a, 606a, 1056a; III, 159b, 338a, 638b, 639a, 768b, 1233a, 1295b; IV, 57b, 263a, 952a, 1036a, b, 1041a; V, 135b, 184b; S, 25a, 59a, 252b, 352b
Abu 'l-Rabīʿ (Marīnid(e)) s, 112b — S, 112a
Abu 'l-Rabīʿ b. Sālim → al-Kalāʿī
Abū Rakwa Walīd b. Hishām ii, 858b; iii, 78b, 79b — II, 878a; III, 81a, 82a
Abū Rashīd al-Nīsābūrī s, **31b**, 345a, 346a, 393a — S, **32a**, 345a, 346a, 393b
Abu 'l-Rawāʾīn iv, 94a — IV, 98a
Abu 'l-Rayḥān al-Bīrūnī → al-Bīrūnī
Abū Ridjāʾ Muḥammad Zamān Khān ii, 500b — II, 513a
Abū Righāl i, **144b** — I, **149a**
Abū Riyāḥ iv, 837a — IV, 870a
Abū Riyāsh al-Ḳaysī v, 374b; s, **32a** — V, 375a; S, **32b**
Abū Ruḳayba → Bourguiba
Abu 'l-Saʿādāt Muḥammad → al-Nāṣir Abu 'l-Saʿādāt
Abu 'l-Ṣabbāh b. Yaḥyā al-Yaḥṣubī iv, 115a — IV, 120b
Abū Saʿd al-Ḥasan b. Hamdūn iii, 784a — III, 807b
Abū Saʿd al-Makhzūmī s, 32b — S, 32b
Abū Saʿd al-Mubārak al-Mukharrimī i, 69a — I, 71a
Abu 'l-Sādj Dīwdād b. Dīwdast i, **145a** — I, **149b**
Abū Safyān i, **145b** — I, **150a**
Abū Sahl Dūnash b. Tāmīm iv, 304a — IV, 318a
Abū Sahl al-Harawī s, 38a — S, 38a
Abū Sahl al-Kūhī s, 412b — S, 412b
Abū Saʿīd (Marīnid(e)) i, 859b; ii, 146a, 822a, 979a; s, 45b — I, 883b; II, 150a, 841b, 1001b; S, 46a
Abū Saʿīd b. Abi 'l-Khayr i, **145b,** 162b; iii, 103a; iv, 63b, 1025b, 1057b — I, **150a,** 167a; III, 105b; IV, 67a, 1057b, 1088b
Abū Saʿīd b. al-Aʿrābī i, 114b — I, 117b
Abū Saʿīd b. Ḳarā Yūsuf iv, 587b — IV, 611a
Abū Saʿīd b. Tīmūr i, 135a, **147b,** 227b, 311b, 852b; iii, 603a, 1100b; iv, 34a, 588a; s, 50b, 51a — I, 139a, **151b,** 234b, 321a, 876a; III, 623b, 1127b; IV, 36b, 611b; S, 51b
Abū Saʿīd Abak i, 1332a, b; ii, 282a; iii, 399a — I, 1372b, 1373a; II, 290b; III, 411b
Abū Saʿīd al-Aflaḥ → al-Aflaḥ b. ʿAbd al-Wahhāb
Abū Saʿīd Bahadur → Abū Saʿid al-Ilkhān
Abū Saʿīd al-Bayhaḳī i, 60a — I, 61b
Abū Saʿīd al-Djannābī → al-Djannābī
Abū Saʿīd, al-Ilkhān i, 91a, 510b, 764b, 908b, 1011a; ii, 68a, 401a, 706a; iii, 57b, 1122b; iv, 860a; s, 363b, 415a — I, 93b, 526a, 787b, 936a, 1042a; II, 69a, 411b, 724a; III, 60a, 1150b; IV, 893a; S, 363a, 415a
Abū Saʿīd al-Iṣṭakhrī ii, 1099a — II, 1124b
Abū Saʿīd al-Ḳarmāṭī → al-Djannābī
Abū Saʿīd Khalafa al-Badjī → Sayyidī Abū Saʿīd
Abū Saʿīd Khalīfa b. Farḥūn iv, 1130a — IV, 1161b
Abū Sāʿīd al-Kharrāz → al-Kharrāz
Abū Saʿīd al-Khaṭṭābī → al-Khaṭṭābī
Abū Saʿīd al-Marwazī i, 153b — I, 158a
Abū Saʿīd Sandjar al-Djāwulī → ʿAlam al-Dīn Sandjar
Abū Saʿīd al-Sīrāfī → al-Sīrāfī
Abū Saʿīd ʿUthmān I (ʿAbd al-Wādid(e)) i, 93a; iii, 833a — I, 96a; III, 857a
Abū Saʿīd ʿUthmān II (ʿAbd al-Wādid(e)) i, 93a; iii, 867a — I, 96a; III, 890b
Abū Saʿīd ʿUthmān (Marīnid(e)) → ʿUthmān II (Marīnid(e))
Abū Saʿīd ʿUthmān b. ʿAbd al-Muʾmin ii, 1013b, 1014a, iii, 66a, 755a, 772a — II, 1037b; III, 68b, 778a, 795a
Abū Saʿīd-zāde Feyḍ Allāh Efendi i, 394a — I, 405a
Abū Saʿīd Zayd i, 1310a — I, 1350a
Abū Ṣakhr al-Hudhalī i, **148b** — I, **153a**
Abū Salama al-Khallāl i, 15b, 16a, 16b, 103b, **149a,** 1293a; iii, 988a — I, 16a, 16b, 17a, 106b, **153a,** 1332b; III, 1012b
Abū Ṣāliḥ Mufliḥ iii, 161a, 735a — III, 164b, 757b
Abū Sālim ʿAlī (Marīnid(e)) iii, 826a, 867a — III, 850a, 891a
Abu 'l-Salt Umayya i, **149a** — I, **153b**
Abu 'l-Sarāyā → al-Sarī b. Manṣūr
Abu 'l-Sarāyā al-Ḥamdānī → Ḥamdānid(e)s
Abu 'l-Sarāyā al-Shaybānī i, **149b,** 402b; iii, 243b, 950b; iv, 17a — I, **153b;** 414a, III, 250b, 975b; IV,

18a
Abu 'l-Ṣaydā' Ṣāliḥ b. Ṭārif iii, 224a; iv 15b, 44b — III, 231a; IV, 16b, 47a
Abū Sayyāra, ʿUmayla b. al-Aʿzal s, **33a** — S, **33b**
Abū Sekkine i, 910b — I, 938a
Abū Seray → Ḳarḳīsiyā
Abū Shabaka, Ilyās s, **33b** — S, **33b**
Abū Shādī, Aḥmad Zakī i, 598b; s, **34a** — I, 618b; S, **34a**
Abū Shaḥma s, 230a — S, 230a
Abū Shakūr Balkhī iv, 63a; s, 35a — IV, 66b; S, 35a
Abū Shākir al-Dayṣānī i, 48b; iii, 496b — I, 49b; III, 513b
Abu 'l-Shalaʿlaʿ Muḥammad → Muḥammad b. Aḥmad
Abū Shāma i, **150a,** 1314b; iii, 268a, 693b, 753a, 934a, 1158a — I, **154a,** 1355a; III, 275b, 715b, 776a, 958b, 1186b.
Abu 'l-Shamaḳmaḳ i, **150a;** iii, 966a — I, **154b;** III, 990b
Abū Shamir al-Ḥanafī s, 88b — S, 88b
Abu 'l-Shawk Fāris i, 512b; iii, 258b, 571b; v, 453b, 454a — I, 528a; III, 266a, 591b; V, 456b
Abu 'l-Shibl ʿĀṣim al-Burdjūmī iv, 1005a — IV, 1037b
Abu 'l-Shīṣ al-Khuzāʿī i, **150b**; iv, 1004b; s, 33a — I, **154b**; IV, 1037a; S, 33a
Abū Shuʿayb (island/île) → Lār (island/île)
Abū Shuʿayb Ayyūb al-Sinhādjī i, 159b, 809b; iii, 339a — I, 164a, 832b; III, 349a
Abū Shudjāʿ Aḥmad b. Ḥasan i, **150b,** 867b; iii, 817a — I, **155a,** 891b; III, 841a
Abū Shudjāʿ Bādh b. Dustāk → Bādh
Abū Shudjāʿ Rudhrawārī ii, 384b; iii, 258b; s, 398a — II, 394b; III, 256b; S, 398b
Abū Shudjāʿ Shīrawayh iii, 105b — III, 108a
Abū Shurāʿa s, **35a** — S, **35b**
Abu Simbil → Abū Sinbil
Abū Sinbil s, **35b** — S, **35b**
Abū Ṣufra iv, 1056b — IV, 1087b
Abū Sufyān b. Ḥarb b. Umayya i, 9a, 115b, **151a,** 381b, 868a, 1283b; ii, 375b, 843b, 1020b; iii, 455a; s, 103b, 133b, 350a — I, 9a, 119a, **155a,** 392b, 892a, 1323a; II, 386a, 863b, 1044a; III, 471a; S, 103a, 133a, 350a
Abū Sufyān Maḥbūb b. al-Raḥīl → Maḥbūb b. al-Raḥīl
Abū Sulaymān Dā'ūd b. Ibrāhīm al-Thalātī i, 121b — I, 125a
Abū Sulaymān al-Manṭiḳī i, 127a, **151b,** 235b; ii, 359a; s, 13b, 398b — I, 130b, **156a,** 243a; II, 369a; S. 13b, 398b
Abū Sulaymān Muḥammad b. Maʿshar → al-Maḳdisī, Abū Sulaymān
Abu 'l-Surrī → Sahl b. Maṣlīaḥ
Abu 'l-Surūr al-Mufarridj → Ibn al-Sarrādj
Abu 'l-Suʿūd i, **152a,** 1235a; ii, 32b, 56b, 687a; iii, 163b; iv, 375a, 376a, 557a, 560a, 881b; v, 682a — I, **156a,** 1272a; II, 33a, 57b, 704b; III, 167a; IV, 391b, 392b, 581a, 582b, 914a; V, 687b
Abu 'l-Suʿūd, ʿAbd Allāh ii, 466b — II, 478a
Abū Taghlib (Ḥamdānid(e)) i, 211b, 824b, 954b; ii, 344a, 483a; iii, 127b, 128a, b, 246a, 841a; iv, 663b, 1084a; s, **36a** — I, 218a, 847a, 984a; II, 353b, 495a; III, 130b, 131a, 253a, 864b; IV, 690a, 1115b; S, **36a**
Abū Ṭāhir b. ʿAlī Atābeg v, 826b — V, 832b
Abū Ṭāhir b. ʿAwf iv, 137a — IV, 142b
Abū Ṭāhir Ibrāhīm al-Hamdānī iii, 128a,b — III, 130b, 131b
Abū Ṭāhir Saʿīd i, 147a — I, 151b
Abū Ṭāhir Sulaymān al-Karmaṭī → al-Djannābī
Abu 'l-Ṭāhir Tamīm → Tamīm b. Yūsuf
Abū Ṭāhir Ṭarsūsī i, **152b**; iv, 63b, 445a — I, **157a**; IV, 67a, 465a
Abū Ṭāḳa → Sikka
Abū Ṭālib i, 9a, 80a, 118b, **152b,** 381b — I, 9a, 82b, 122a, **157a,** 392b
Abū Ṭālib ʿAbd Allāh → ʿAzafī
Abū Ṭālib al-Akhīr s, 363a — S, 363a
Abū Ṭāib b. al-Ḥusayn s, 407b — S, 407b
Abū Ṭālib b. Muḥammad Khudābanda i, 8b; iii, 157b — I, 8b; III, 161a
Abū Ṭālib Iṣfahānī s, 290a — S, 290a
Abū Ṭālib Fanduruskī iii, 114b — III, 116b
Abū Ṭālib Kalīm → Kalīm
Abū Ṭālib Khān i, **153a;** iii, 1046a — I, **157b;** III, 1072a
Abū Ṭālib al-Makkī i, **153a,** 274a, 351a; iii, 570b; iv, 470a, 486b — I, **157a,** 282b, 362a; III, 590b; IV, 491a, 507b
Abū Ṭālib al-Nāṭiḳ s, 335b — S, 335a
Abū Ṭālūt iv, 1076a — IV, 1107b
Abu 'l-Ṭamaḥān al-Ḳaynī i, 115b; iv, 820a; s, **37a** — I, 119a; IV, 853a; S, **37b**
Abū Tammām Ḥabīb b. Aws i, 53a, 118b, **153a,** 331a, 386b, 449b, 592a, 822a, 857b, 1114b, 1289a, 1290a; ii, 248b; iii, 110b, 111b, 879a; v, 935a; s, 15a, 26a, 32b, 33a, 277b — I, 54b, 122a, **157b,** 341b, 397b, 462b, 611a, 845a, 881b, 1148a, 1328b, 1329b; II, 256a; III, 113a, 114a, 903b; V, 939a; S, 15b, 26b, 32b, 33a, 277a
Abū Tāshufīn I i, 122b, **155a** — I, 126a, **159a**
Abū Tāshufīn II i, 122b, 123a, **155a;** iii, 832a — I, 126a, b, **159a;** III, 855b
Abū Tāyih (Tawāyihī) → ʿAwda b. Ḥarb
Abū Ṭayyib → al-Mutanabbī; al-Ṭabarī
Abu 'l-Ṭayyib al-Lughawī iii, 665a; s, **37b**, 361b — III, 686b; S, **38a**, 361a
Abu 'l-Ṭayyib Muḥammad al-Numayrī iv, 1005b — IV, 1037b
Abū Ṭayyiba (cupper) s, 304a — S, 303b
Abū Thābit (ʿAbd al-Wādid) i, 93a; iii, 867a; s, 377a — I, 95b; III, 890b; S, 377a
Abū Thābit ʿĀmir v, 48b; s, 103a — V, 50a; S, 102b
Abu 'l-Thanā' Maḥmūd b. Ādjā i, 1109b — I, 1143a
Abū Thumāma iv, 472a — IV, 493a
Abū Thawr i, **155a** — I, **159b**
Abū Ṭulayḥ → Abuklea
Abū Turāb → ʿAlī b. Abī Ṭālib
Abū Turāb al-Athīrī s, 29b — S, 29b
Abū Turāb Ḥaydar al-Din ʿKāmil' iv, 544b — IV, 568a
Abū Turāb Mīrzā → Ismāʿīl III (Safawid(e))
Abū ʿUbayd al-Bakrī i, 96a, **155b,** 345a, 488a, 511b, 600b, 862b; ii, 584b; iii, 991b; iv, 339a; v, 1011a, 1017b; s, 304b, 376b — I, 99a, **159b,** 355b, 503a, 527a, 620a, 886b; II, 599a; III, 1016a; IV, 353a, b; V, 1006b, 1013b; S, 304a, 376b
Abū ʿUbayd al-Ḳāsim b. Sallām i, 156a, **157b,** 158b, 718b; iv, 547b; v, 175a; s, 15b, 317b — I, 160a, **161b,** 163a, 740a; IV, 571b; V, 172a; S, 16a, 317b
Abū ʿUbayd Allāh i, 103b, **157b,** 1033b — I, 106b, **162a,** 1065a
Abū ʿUbayd al-Thaḳafī ii, 555a — II, 569a
Abū ʿUbayda ʿĀmir al-Djarrah i, 110a, **158b,** 460b, 970b, 996a, 1137b, 1139a, 1215b; ii, 279b, 280a; iii, 397b; v, 923a — I, 113a, **163a,** 474a, 1000b, 1026b, 1172a, 1173b, 1251b; II, 288a; III, 410a; V, 928b
Abū ʿUbayda al-Djanāwanī → al-Djanāwanī
Abū ʿUbayda Maʿmar b. al-Muthannā i, 105b, 108b, 125b, 143b, **158a,** 167b, 588b, 717b, 718b, 794a; ii, 241a; iv, 1077a; s, 15b, 73b, 177a — I, 108b, 129a, 147b, **162a,** 172a, 607b, 739a, 817a; II, 248a; IV, 1109a; S, 16a, 74a, 178a
Abū Ubayda Muslim al-Tamīmī i, 120b, 134a; iii,

649b, 650b, 651b, 654a, 658a — I, 124a, 138a; III, 671a, b, 672b, 675b, 679b
Abu 'l-ʿUlāʾ b. ʿAbd al-Muʾmin ii, 1072a — II, 1096b
Abu 'l-ʿUlāʾ Idrīs → Idrīs al-Maʾmūn
Abū ʿUmar b. Yūsuf iii, 101a, 692a — III, 103b, 714a
Abū ʿUmar Inālū ii, 1013a — II, 1037a
Abū ʿUmar Tāshufīn iii, 867a — III, 890b
Abū Umayma → Ismāʿīl Ṣabrī
Abū Usāma al-Harawī s, **38a** — S, **38a**
Abū ʿUtba → Abū Lahab b. ʿAbd al-Muṭṭalib
Abū ʿUthmān Saʿīd b. Hāshim iii, 111a; iv, 936b — III, 113b; IV, 969b
Abū ʿUthmān Saʿīd b. Muḥammad b. al-Ḥaddād i, 249b — I, 257b
Abū ʿUthmān Saʿīd al-Dimashḳī i, 1223b, 1340a; ii, 948b — I, 1259b, 1380b; II, 970b
Abū ʿUzaiyyiz → Ḳatāda b. Idrīs
Abu 'l-Wafā, Shaykh iv, 230b — IV, 240b
Abu 'l-Wafāʾ b. al-ʿAḳīl → Ibn al-ʿAḳīl
Abu 'l-Wafāʾ al-Būzadjānī i, 127a, **159a,** 1354a; iii, 1140a; s, 398b, 412a, b, 413b, 414a — I, 130b, **163b,** 1393a; III, 1168a; S, 398b, 412a, 413a, b, 414a
Abu 'l-Walīd b. al-Aḥmar i, 352a — I, 363a
Abu 'l-Walīd al-Azraḳī → al-Azraḳī
Abu 'l-Walīd al-Bādjī → Bādjī
Abu 'l-Walīd Ḳurṭubī → Ibn Rushd, al-Djadd
Abu 'l-Walīd Muḥammad b. Aḥmad b. Abī Duʿād i, 271b — I, 279b
Abu 'l-Walīd Muḥammad b. Djahwar → Ibn Djahwar, Abu 'l-Walīd
Abu 'l-Ward b. al-Kawthar i, 43a; iv, 493b — I, 44a; IV, 514b
Abū Yaʿazzā al-Hazmīrī i, 137b, **159b**; s, 38b— I, 141b, **164a**; S, 29a
Abū Yaddās b. Dūnās iii, 1043b — III, 1069b
Abū Yaḥyā Abū Bakr I al-Shahīd iii, 67b — III, 70a
Abū Yaḥyā Abū Bakr II iii, 49a, 67b; iv, 416a; v, 531a — III, 50b, 70a; IV, 434a; V, 535a
Abū Yaḥyā al-Marwazī i, 159a — I, 163b
Abū Yaḥyā Zakariyyāʾ → Ibn al-Liḥyānī
Abū Yaḥyā Zakariyyāʾ → al-Irdjānī
Abū Yaknī iii, 138a — III, 141a
Abū Yaʿḳūb al-Aḳṭaʿ iii, 100a — III, 102b
Abū Yaʿḳūb Ḳādī al-Khandak i, 816a — I, 839b
Abū Yaʿḳūb al-Khuraymī i, **159b**; s, 25a— I, **164a**; S, 25a
Abū Yaʿḳūb al-Sidjzī (Sidjistānī) i, **160a;** iii, 328b; iv, 199a, 508b, 662b; s, 52b — I, **164b;** III, 338b; IV, 207b, 530b, 689a; S, 53a
Abū Yaʿḳub al-Sūsī iv, 990b — IV, 1023a
Abū Yaʿḳūb Yūsuf s, 112b — S, 112a
Abū Yaʿḳūb Yūsuf I b. ʿAbd al-Muʾmin (Almohad(e)) i, **160b,** 1288a, 1339b; ii, 352b, 525a, 744b, 1014a; iii, 771b, 910a, 957a; iv, 116a; s, 307a — I, **165a,** 1327b, 1379b; II, 362b, 538a, 763a, 1037b; III, 749b, 934a, 981b; IV, 121a; S, 306b
Abū Yaʿḳūb Yūsuf (Marīnid(e)) i, 92b; iii, 470b; s, 377a — I, 95b; III, 487a; S, 377a
Abū Yaʿḳūb Yūsuf b. Abū Saʿīd iv, 664a — IV, 691a
Abū Yaʿḳūb Yūsuf b. Ibrāhīm al-Wardjlānī s, 15b — S, 16a
Abū Yaʿḳūb Yūsif b. Nūḥ → Yūsuf b. Nūḥ
Abū Yaʿḳūb Yūsuf al-Bādisī i, 860a — I, 884a
Abū Yaʿḳūb Yūsuf al-Baṣir → Yūsuf al-Baṣīr
Abū Yasār ʿAbd Allāh al-Thaḳafī iv, 371a — IV, 387b
Abu 'l-Yakẓān Muḥammad b. Aflaḥ i, 139a — I, 143a
Abu Yaʿla b. al-Farrāʾ → Ibn al-Farrāʾ
Abū Yaʿzā iii, 339a, 800b — III, 349a, b, 823b
Abū Yazīd al-Bisṭāmī i, **162a,** 1168a; ii, 32a; iv, 321a, 1057b — I, **166b,** 1202b; II, 32b; IV, 335b, 1089a
Abū Yazīd al-Nukkārī i, **163a,** 699b, 770b, 863a, 1238a; ii, 852b, 977a; iii, 95b, 297b, 656a, 657b, 659b, 1040b, 1042a; iv, 459b, 479a, 740b, 827b; v, 696a, 1175a, b, 1246a, b; s, 236b, 306b — I, **167b,** 720b, 793b, 887a, 1275b; II, 872b, 999b; III, 98a 306b, 677a, 678b, 680b, 1066b, 1068a; IV, 480a, 501a, 770a, 860b; V, 701a, 1165a, b, 1237a; S, 236b, 306a
Abū Yazīd al-Sulamī → Yazīd b. Usayd al-Sulamī
Abu l'-Yumn al-ʿUlaymī → Mudjīr al-Dīn
Abū Yūsuf (Almohad(e)) → Abū Yaʿḳūb Yūsuf I
Abū Yūsuf Yaʿḳūb (Marīnid(e)) i, 1058a; ii, 819a, 822a, b; s, 112a, 113b — I, 1089a; II, 838b, 841b, 842a; S, 111b, 113a
Abū Yūsuf Yaʿḳūb (Rustumid(e)) iii, 655b — III, 677a
Abū Yūsuf Yaʿḳūb b. Ibrāhīm i, 28a, 123a, 124a, **164a,** 588b, 773a; ii, 231b, 890b; iii, 162b, 512b; iv, 949a — I, 29a, 126b, 127b, **168b,** 281a, 607b, 796a; II, 238b, 911a; III, 166a, 529b; IV, 981b
Abū Yūsuf Yaʿḳūb al-Ḳirḳisānī (Ḳarḳasānī) iv, 605a — IV, 629a
Abū Yūsuf Yaʿḳūb al-Manṣūr i, 137b, **165a,** 495b, 499b, 533b, 604b, 605b, 634a, 1224b; ii, 307b, 331b, 510a, 525a, 1007b; iii, 748b, 910b, 978b; iv, 118a, 461a, 614a, 729b; s, 274a — I, 141b, **169b,** 510b, 514b, 549b, 624b, 625a, 654b, 1261a; II, 316b, 341a, 522b, 538a, 1031a; III, 771b, 934b, 1003a; IV, 123a, 434a, 639a, 758b; S, 273b
Abū Zaʿbal s, **38a** — S, **38a**
Abū Ẓabī i, **166a,** 539b, 1313b, 1314a; ii, 557b, 619a; iv, 751b, 778a; v, 1058b; s, 42a, 416b — I, **171a,** 556b, 1354a; II, 571b, 634b; IV, 781b, 809b; V, 1055b; S, 42b, 417a
Abu 'l-Zādjir Ismāʿīl → Ismāʿīl b. Ziyād al-Nafūsī
Abū Ẓafar → Bāhadur Shāh II
Abū Zakariyyāʾ b. Khaldūn → Ibn Khaldūn
Abū Zakariyyāʾ al-Djanāwunī i, **166b,** 1028a — I, **171b,** 1059b
Abū Zakariyyāʾ al-Farrāʾ → al-Farrāʾ
Abū Zakariyyāʾ al-Maghribī ii, 198a; v, 924b, 926b — II, 204b; V, 930a, 932a
Abū Zakariyyāʾ Yaḥyā b. al-Khayr al-Wardjlānī i, 125a, **167a;** ii, 141a; iii, 95a; s, 15b — I, 128b, **171b;** II, 144b; III, 97b; S, 15b
Abū Zakariyyāʾ Yaḥyā I i, 121b, 605b; ii, 1008a, 1014b; iii, 66a, 296b, 338a, 461b, 673a; iv, 337b; v, 1150a; s, 111b — I, 125a, 625a; II, 1031b, 1038a; III, 68b, 305b, 348a, 478a, 694b; IV, 352a; V, 1140b; S, 111a
Abū Zakariyyāʾ Yaḥyā II → al-Wāthiḳ
Abū Zakariyyāʾ Yaḥyā III iii, 67a; iv, 338a — III, 69b; IV, 352b
Abū Zakariyyāʾ Yaḥyā IV iii, 69a — III, 71b
Abū Zakariyyāʾ al-Ẓamāmī iv, 661a — IV, 687b
Abū Zayd → al-Balkhī
Abū Zayd (Banū Hilāl) i, **167b;** iii, 387a, b — I, **172a;** III, 399b, 400a
Abū Zayd b. Yūsuf al-Ḥardānī iii, 231a — III, 237b
Abū Zayd ʿAbd al-Raḥmān → ʿAzafī
Abū Zayd ʿAbd al-Raḥmān b. Igit → Ibn Igit
Abū Zayd ʿAbd al-Raḥmān b. Maʿlā iii, 96a — III, 99a
Abū Zayd ʿAbd al-Raḥman al-Hazmīrī iii, 339a, b, 731a — III, 349a, b, 754a
Abū Zayd al-Anṣārī, Saʿīd b. Aws i, 108b, 125b, 143b, **167b,** 717b, 1098a; s, 38b, 73b, 317b — I, 129a, 147b, **172a,** 739a, 1131a; S, 39a, 74a, 317a
Abū Zayd al-Fāzārī iv, 541a — IV, 564a
Abū Zayd al-Ḥasan al-Sīrāfī ii, 583b; s, 56a — II, 598a; S, 56b
Abū Zayd al-Ḳurashī s, **38b** — S, **38b**
Abū Zayd al-Naḥwī s, 286b — S, 286a
Abū Zayd al-Sarūdjī → al-Ḥarīrī
Abū Zayd al-Sīrāfī → Akhbār al-Ṣīn waʾl-Hind

Abū Zayyān I (ʿAbd al-Wādid(e)) i, **167b**; v, 1180a — I, **172b**; V, 1170a
Abū Zayyān II i, **167b** — I, **172b**
Abū Zayyān III i, **168a** — I, **172b**
Abū Zayyān Muḥammad → Muḥammad IV (Marīnid(e))
Abu 'l-Zift al-Ḥasan iii, 616a — III, 636b
Abū 'l-Zinād iii, 494b; s, 380a — III, 511b; S, 380b
Abū Ẓiyā Tewfīḳ Bey → Tewfīḳ Bey
Abū Ziyād b. Salmā iv, 54a — IV, 57a
Abū Zunbūr al-Mādharāʾī v, 953a, b — V, 957a
Abū Zurʿa s, **39a** — S, **39a**
Abuʿam → Tāfīlālt
Abubacer → Ibn Ṭufayl
Abubakar Atiku iv, 550b — IV, 574b
Abubakar Imam iii, 282b — III, 291b
Abūdhiyye i, 730b — I, 753a
Abūḳīr i, **168a** — I, **172b**
Abuklea i, **168b** — I, **173b**
Abulcasis → al-Zahrāwī
Abulelizor, Albuleizor → Ibn Zuhr, Abu 'l-ʿAlāʾ
Abulpharagius Benattibus → Ibn al-Ṭayyib
Abumeron → Ibn Zuhr
Ābūn i, 288b — I, 295b
Ābunūs → Abanūs
al-ʿAbūr → Nudjūm
Aburdja, Mudjīr al-Dīn s, 105b — S, 105a
Abūshahr → Būshahr
Abushiri revolt/révolte iv, 889a — IV, 922a
Abushḳa → ʿAlī Shīr Nawāʾī
Abūṣīr → Būṣīr
al-Abwāʾ i, **169a;** iii, 362b; s, 312a — I, **173b;** III, 374a; S, 311b
Abwāb → Darband
Abyaḍ v, 700a, 705b — V, 705a, 710b
Abyaḍ, Georges s, **39b** — S, **39b**
Abyan i, **169a,** 538a; s, 338a — I, **173b,** 555a; S, 337b
Abyār s, 40a — S, 40a
al-Abyārī, Shaykh ʿAbd al-Hādī s, **40a** — S, **40a**
Abyssinia(e) → al-Ḥabash
Abyssinia(e)ns → Ḥabasha
al-Abzārī → ʿAmīd al-Dīn
Academy, Académie → Madjmaʿ ʿilmī
Ačalpur → Eličpur
Accession to the Throne/au Trône → Bayʿa, Khilāfa
Accident → ʿAraḍ
Accountancy → Muḥāsaba
Accra ii, 1003b — II, 1027a
Acemî oğlan → ʿAdjamī oghlān
Achat → Bayʿ
Acheh → Atjeh
Achehnese → Malay
Achir → Ashīr
Acier → Fūlādh
Acknowledgement → Iḳrār
Açores → al-Djazāʾir al-Khālidāt
Acquisition → Kasb
Acre → ʿAkkā
Acridoids/Acridiens → Djarād
Acrobat(e) → Djānbāz
Act(e), Action → ʿAmal, Fiʿl
Acte (Droit) → ʿAḳd
ʿĀd i, **169a,** 257a, iii, 537b, 1270a; iv, 820b; v, 497b, 811a — I, **174a,** 265a; III, 556a, 1303a; IV, 853b; V, 500b, 817a
Adāʾ i, **169b** — I, **174b**
ʿĀda i, **170a,** 173a, 277a, 741b, 744b, 746b, 980b, 1179a; ii, 22b, 890b; iv, 154b-156a — I, **174b,** 178a, 285b, 763b, 766b, 769a, 1011a, 1214a; II, 23a, 911b; IV, 161a-162a
ʿAdā iv, 272b — IV, 284b
Ada Ḳalʿe i, **174b** — I, **179b**
Ada Pāzārī i, **175a** — I, **180a**
Adab i, 23a, 66a, 133b, **175b,** 326a, 328b, 345b, 588a; ii, 951b; iii, 884b, 893a, 1262a; iv, 510a; s, 93b — I, 22b, 68a, 137b, **180a,** 336a, 338b, 356b, 607a; II, 973b; III, 908b, 917a, 1295a; IV, 532a; S, 93a
ʿAdad → Ḥisāb
Adage → Mathal
Adal i, **176b,** 763b, 1172b; iii, 3b, 4a — I, **181a,** 786b, 1207b; III, 3b, 4a
ʿAdāla → ʿAdl
ʿAdalī ii, 120b — II, 123a
Adalya → Antalya
Ādam i, **176b**; iv, 947b; v, 210a — I, **181b**; IV, 980a; V, 207b
Ādam, Mawlānā s, 353a — S, 353a
Adam, sultan of/de Banjarmasin s, 150b — S, 150b
ʿAdam i, **178b**; v, 578b — I, **183b**; V, 583a
Adama → Modibbo Adama
Adamiyyat, Ḥusayn Ruknzāda iv, 72b; v, 198b — IV, 76b; V, 196a
Adamawa i, **179a;** ii, 9b, 10b, 941b, 942b — I, **183b;** 9b, 10b, 963b, 964a
ʿAdan i, 106b, 169a, **180b,** 536a, 539a, 552a, 554b, 781a, 976a; ii, 469a, 675a, 737a; iii, 881b; iv, 519a, 746a, 901b, 1188b; v, 71a, 1059b, 1244b; s, 338a — I, 109b, 173b, **185b,** 552a, 556a, 570a, 572a, 804a, 1006b; II, 480b, 692a, 755b; III, 905b; IV, 541b, 775b, 934b, 1221b; V, 73a, 1056b, 1235a, b; S, 337b
Adana i, **182a**; v, 558a; s, 138b — I, **187a**; V, 563a; S, 138a
Adār → Adhār
Adareñña → Harari
Adārisa → Idrīsid(e)s
Ādarrāḳ s, **40a,** 399b — S, **40b,** 400a
Adāt → Naḥw
ʿĀdat → ʿĀda
al-ʿAdawī s, 40b — S, 41a
ʿAdawiyya i, 195a — I, 201a
al-ʿAḍaym i, **184a** — I, **189b**
Aḍḍād i, **184b**; v, 705a — I, **189b**; V, 710b
Addax → Mahāt
ʿAḍēm → al-ʿAḍaym
Aden → ʿAdan
Adfū i, **186a** — I, **191b**
al-Adfūwī i, 186b — I, 192a
Aḍḥāʾ → ʿĪd al-aḍḥāʾ
ʿAdhāb i, **186b** — I, **192a**
ʿAdhāb al-Ḳabr i, **186b**; iv, 667b; v, 236b — I, **192a**; IV, 694b; V, 234b
Adham Khān i, 1155a — I, 1189b
Adham Naḳīb s, 301b — S, 301b
Adhamiyya → Ibrāhīm b. Adham
Adhān i, **187b;** ii, 432b, 593b; iv, 181a — I, **193a;** II, 444a, 608a; IV, 188b
Ādhār → Taʾrīkh
Ādharbāydjān i, 8a, 13b, **188b,** 300b, 420b, 639a, 642b, 644a, 660a, 731b, 1052a, 1107b; ii, 680b, 903b; iii, 530a, 1099b; iv, 3a, 19b-20a, 347b, 392a; v, 496b, 497a, 729b, 730a, 1213b; s, 23b, 47a, 70b, 71b, 116a, 135a, 147b, 170a, 239b, 274b, 282a, 326a, 366a, 378a — I, 8a, 14a, **194a,** 310a, 432b, 659b, 663a, 664b, 680b, 753b, 1083b, 1141a; II, 697b, 924b; III, 1126b; IV, 3a-b, 21a-b, 362a, b, 409a; V, 499b, 500a, 734b, 735a, 1203a; S, 24a, 47b, 71b, 72a, 115b, 134b, 147b, 170a, 239b, 274b, 282a, 325b, 365b, 378b
Ādharbāydjān (S.S.R./U.R.S.S.) → Azerbaydjān
Adhargūn i, **191b** — I, **197a**
Ādharī (Azerī) i, 191a, **192a,** 756a, 1072b; ii, 89a, 938b; iv, 351a, 627b, 732a; v, 8a; s, 415b — I, 196b, **197b,** 778b, 1104b; II, 90b, 960b; IV, 366a, 652a, 761b; V, 8a; S, 416a

Adharyūn → Adhargūn
ʿAdhaym (river/rivière) v, 442a — V, 444b
ʿAdhīr iv, 217a — IV, 226b
ʿAdhrāʾ → Nudjūm
Adhriʿāt i, **194a** — I, **200a**
Adhruḥ i, 55a, 108b, **194b,** 384a, b, 451b; ii, 535a; iv, 938a; s, 230a — I, 56b, 111b, **200a,** 395a, b, 464b; II, 548b; IV, 971a; S, 230a
Adhur-Walāsh iv, 644b — IV, 671a
al-Adhwāʾ i, **194b** — I, **200b**
ʿAdī, Banū iii, 386a, b; v, 1183a — III, 398b, 399a; V, 1173a
ʿAdī, Banū (village) s, 40b — S, 41a
ʿAdī b. ʿAmr, Banū v, 78b, 79a — V, 81a
ʿAdī b. Arṭāt iv, 291a; s, **41a** — IV, 304a; S, **41a**
ʿAdī b. Ḥātim i, **195a;** iii, 241a, 274b; v, 499b — I, **200b,** III, 248a, 282b; V, 502b
ʿAdī b. Musāfir al-Hakkārī i, **195a;** v, 209a, 475b, 644a — I, **201a;** V, 206b, 478b, 648b
ʿAdī b. Naṣr b. Rabīʿa i, 450b — I, 463b
ʿAdī b. al-Riḳāʿ i, **196a,** 436a; ii, 480a — I, **201b,** 448b; II, 492a
ʿAdī b. Zayd i, 115b, **196a,** 565a, 584b; iii, 462b, 1261a; iv, 1002a — I, 119a, **201b,** 583a, 603b; III, 479a, 1294a; IV, 1031b
Ādi Granth iii, 456b — III, 472b
Adīb Isḥāḳ → Isḥāḳ, Adīb
Adīb al-Mamālik → Amīrī
Adīb Pīshāwarī s, **41a** — S, **41b**
al-ʿĀḍid li-Dīn Allāh i, **196b,** 797a; ii, 318a, 856b, 857a — I, **202a,** 820b; II, 327a, 876b, 877a
Adighe i, 1000a; ii, 21b, 22a — I, 1031a; II, 22a, b
al-ʿĀdil, al-Malik I, Sayf al-Dīn i, **197b,** 665a, 798b, 799b, 800a, b, 803b, 996a, 1316b; ii, 283b, 284a, 347b; iii, 87b, 228b, 504a; iv, 430a, 483b, 520a, 568a, 609a, 613b — I, **203a,** 684b, 822a, 823a, 824a, b, 828a, 1026b, 1356b; II, 292a, 357b; III, 89b, 235b, 521a; IV, 448b, 504b, 543a, 590a, 634a, 638a
al-ʿĀdil, al-Malik II i, 198b, 766a, b — I, 204a, 789a
ʿĀdil, Amīr ii, 401b; iv, 584b — II, 412a; IV, 608a
al-ʿĀdil b. al-Salār i, 9a, **198b;** ii, 318a, 856b; iii, 868a; iv, 137a — I, 9a, **204a;** II, 327a, 876b; III, 892b; IV, 142b
ʿĀdil Bey Isfendiyār-oghlu iv, 108b — IV, 113b
ʿĀdil Girāy ii, 88a — II, 89b
ʿĀdil Girāy Khān i, 311a; ii, 1113b; v, 140a — I, 320b; II, 1140a; V, 142b
ʿĀdil Khān I ii, 814b — II, 834a
ʿĀdil Khān II ii, 814b — II, 834a
ʿĀdil Khān III ii, 815a, 1127b; iii, 422a — II, 834a, 1154a; III, 435b
ʿĀdil Khān IV ii, 815a — II, 834b
ʿĀdil Pasha i, 920a — I, 948a
ʿĀdil-Shāhs i, **199a,** 1048a, 1202b, 1203a, 1323a; ii, 220a, 1135a; iii, 425a, 426a, 447b, 1161a — I, **204b,** 1079b, 1238a, 1239a, 1363b; II, 227a, 1162a; III, 439a, 440a, 462b, 1189b
ʿĀdil Shāh Afshār i, 246b; iii, 177b; iv, 104a — I, 254b; III, 182a; IV, 109a
ʿĀdila Khātūn i, **199a** — I, **204b**
ʿĀdilabād i, 1322a; ii, 257b, 258a; iii, 481b — I, 1362b; II, 264a, 265a; III, 498a
ʿĀdilī → Baysonghor
Adīnā Beg Khān i, 296a; iii, 1158b; v, 598b — I, 305a; III, 1187a; V, 602b
Adivar, Adnan Bey i, 836b; iv, 933b, 934a, b; s, **41b** — I, 859b; IV, 966b, 967a, b; S, **42a**
Adiyaman i, **199b** — I, **205b**
ʿAdj i, **200a,** 501a — I, **205b,** 516a
Adjaʾ wa-Salmā i, **203a,** 536b; s, 304b — I, **209a,** 553a; S, 304a
ʿAdjāʾib i, 122a, 157a, **203b;** ii, 77a, 583b, 586b — I, 125b, 161a, **209a;** II, 78b, 598a, 601a
Adjal i, **204a** — I, **210a**
ʿAdjala i, **205a** — I, **211a**
ʿAdjam i, **206a;** iii, 212b; iv, 338b — I, **212a;** III, 218b; IV, 353a
ʿAdjamī oghlān i, **206b,** 1004a, 1256b, 1278a; ii, 986a, 996b, 1087a; iv, 242b — I, **212b,** 1034b, 1249b, 1317a; II, 1008b, 1019b, 1112b; IV, 253b
al-ʿAdjamiyya → Aljamía
ʿAdjārida i, **207a** — I, **213a**
Adjaristān i, 468b, 1108b — I, 482b, 1141b
al-Adjdābī, Abū Isḥāḳ i, **207a** — I, **213b**
Adjdābiya i, **207a;** v, 695b; s, 380b — I, **213b;** V, 700b; S, 380b
Adjdir s, 377b — S, 378a
al-ʿAdjdjādj, Abu 'l-Shaʿthāʾ i, 142a, **207b,** 1154b, 1310b; iii, 1262a; s, 31b — I, 146b, **214a,** 1188b, 1350b; III, 1294b; S, 31b
ʿAdjīb s, 22a — S, 22b
ʿAdjīb al-Māndjilak ii, 944a; iv, 893a — II, 966a; IV, 925b
ʿAdjību b. ʿUmar Tal i, 297a — I, 306b
Adjil al-Yawir, Shaykh s, 101b — S, 101a
ʿAdjilān Beg b. Ḳarasī iv, 628a — IV, 653a
Adjīt b. Djaswant i, 769a — I, 792a
ʿAdjlān b. Rumaytha i, 553a — I, 570b
ʿAdjlān al-Hamdānī s, 400b — S, 401a
ʿAdjlūn i, **208a;** s, 391a — I, **214a;** S, 391b
ʿAdjmān s, **42a,** 416b — S, **42b,** 417a
Adjmēr i, **208a;** ii, 50a, 274b; iii, 441a; v, 1218b, 1219b; s, 5a, 55b, 293b, 353b, 420b — I, **214b;** II, 51a, 282b; III, 455b; V, 1208b, 1210a; S, 4a, 56a, 293a, 353a, 421a
Adjnādayn i, **208b;** v, 323b, 800a; s, 37a — I, **215a;** V, 323a, 806a; S, 37b
Adjōdhān s, 73b, 353a — S, 74a, 353a
Adjr i, **209a;** iii, 1017a — I, **215a;** III, 1042b
Adjūdānbāshī s, 108b, 290b — S, 108a, 290a
Ādjurr i, 1226b; v, 346b, 585b — I, 1264a; V, 347b, 590b, 591a
al-Ādjurrī, Abū Bakr iii, 159a, 735a; s, 83a — III, 162b, 757b; S, 82b
Ādjurrūmiyya → Ibn Ādjurrūm
ʿAdjūz i, 792b; iii, 71b — I, 816a; III, 73b
al-ʿAdjūz al-Djurashiyya → Asmāʾ bint ʿUmays
Adjwad b. Zāmil al-Djabrī i, 553a, 942b; ii, 159b, 176a; iv, 764b; s, 234a — I, 571a, 971b; II, 164b, 181b; IV, 795a; S, 234a
Adjwaf → Taṣrīf
ʿAdl i, **209a,** 334b, 410a, 415b; ii, 834a; iii, 1143b — I, **215b,** 344b, 422a, 427b; II, 854a; III, 1172a
ʿAdlī i, **210a** — I, **216a**
Administration → Dīwān; Idāra
A(d)miral → Ḳapudan
ʿAdn → Djanna
ʿAdnān i, **210a,** 544b; iv, 448a — I, **216b,** 561b; IV, 467b
Adrar i, **210b**; v, 654a — I, **216b**; V, 658a
Adrār n-Deren i, 748a — I, 770b
Adrar Ifoghas i, 210b, iii, 1038b — I, 216b; III, 1064b
Adrar Tmar i, 210b, 733b — I, 217a, 755b
Adrianople → Edirne
Adriatic/Adriatique → Baḥr Adriyas
ʿAḍud al-Dawla (Būyid(e)) i, 87a, 151b, **211b,** 381a, 824a, 899b, 900a, 955a, 1005b, 1223b, 1350b, 1353a, 1354a, 1355b; ii, 127a, 144b, 344a, 487a, 748b, 802b, 812a, 856a, 893b, 905a, 925b; iii, 128a, 258a, 344b, 671a, 703a, 704a, 730a, 823b, 1157a, 1176a; iv, 24a, 222a, 358a, 675a, 859b, 975a; v, 153a, 158b, 229b, 353a, 452b, 867b, 873a, 896b, 1125a; s, 4a, 36b, 94a, b, 118a, 119a, 127a, 263b, 304b, 390a — I, 89b, 156a, **217b,** 392a, 847a, 926b, 984a, 1036b, 1260a, 1390b,

1392a, 1393a, 1394b; II, 130b, 148a, 353b, 499a, 767a, 821b, 831a, 875b, 914b, 926a, 947b; III, 131a, 265a, 355a, 629b, 725b, 726a, 753a, 847a, 1185b, 1204b; IV, 25b, 232a, 373b, 702b, 892b, 1007b; V, 154b, 157b, 227a, 353b, 455a, 874a, 879b, 903a, 1121b; S, 3b, 37a, 93b, 117b, 118b, 126a, 263b, 304b, 390b
ʿAḍud al-Dīn → al-Īdjī
ʿAḍūd al-Dīn Muḥammad b. ʿAbd Allāh i, **212b**; iii, 891b — I, **219a**; III, 915b
ʿAḍudī Hospital/l' hôpital i, 900a, 901a, 1223b, 1224a — I, 927a, 928a, 1260a, b
Adultery/Adultère → Zināʾ
Adventurer → Ḳazaḳ
al-ʿAdwa s, 305a — S, 304b
ʿAdwān iii, 363b; s, 33a — III, 375a; S, 33b
Adwiya i, **212b**, 1056a, 1057a; v, 251b — I, **219a**, 1087b, 1088b; V, 249b
Aegean Sea i, 464a; v, 505b, 506a, b
Aesthetics → ʿIlm al-Djamāl
Afʿa i, **214b** — I, **221a**
Āfāḳī iv, 908a — IV, 941a
Afʿaluhū taʿālā i, 343a, 412b — I, 353b, 424a
Afāmiya i, **215a**; iv, 919b — I, **221b**; IV, 952b
ʿAfar (Somali(e)) ii, 113b, 535b; iii, 1053a; v, 522a, 524a — II, 116a, 549a; III, 1079a; V, 525b, 527b
ʿAfar (Umān) → al-ʿIfār
ʿAfārīt → ʿIfrīt
Afāriḳa iv, 338b, 339a, b — IV, 353a, b, 354a
Afāwīh s, **42a** — S, **42b**
al-Afḍal → Rasūlid(e)s
al-Afḍal b. Ṣalāḥ al-Dīn i, 197b, 198a, **215a**, 732a, 798b, 1017a; ii, 283b; iii, 724a, 876b; iv, 376b — I, 203b, **221b**, 754a, 822a, 1048b; II, 291b; III, 747a, 900b; IV, 393a
al-Afḍal b. Badr al-Djamālī i, 149a, **215a**, 440a, 711a, 870b, 1091b; ii, 127a, 305a, 329a, 855b, 856b, 858a, 861b; iii, 545b, 932a; v, 328a; s, 408a — I, 203b, **221b**, 452b, 732b, 894b, 1124a; II, 130a, 313b, 338b, 875b, 876b, 878a, 881b; III, 564b, 956b; V, 328a; S, 408a
Afḍal al-Dawla iii, 322b — III, 332a
Afḍal al-Dīn Turka s, **43b** — S, **44a**
Afḍal Khān (Bīdjāpūr) i, 199b, 1204a — I, 205a, 1240a
Afḍal Khān Barakzay i, 87a, 232a; ii, 638a — I, 89b. 239a; II, 654a
al-Afḍal Kutayfāt i, **216a**; ii, 857b; iii, 54b; iv, 200a — I, **222b**; II, 877b; III, 56b; IV, 209a
al-Afḍal Muḥammad b. Abi 'l-Fidāʾ i, 119a; iii, 120a, 900b — I, 122a; III, 123a, 924b
Afḍal-i Ṣadr, Khwādja → Afḍal al-Dīn Turka
ʿAfdja i, 540b — I, 557b
Afendopolo, Caleb iv, 605b — IV, 630a
Āferīn → Taʾrīkh
ʿAffān Abū ʿUthmān s, 103b — S, 103a
ʿAffān b. Muslim iv, 683a — IV, 711b
Affermage → Ḳabāla; Muḳāṭaʿa
Afghan/Afghane i, **216-221**, 1068a; iv, 1b, 37a-b; v, 72a, 461a, 782a; s, 1b, 142a, 143b, 147a, 206b, 312a, 325a — I, **223-227**, 1100b; IV, 1b, 39b; V, 74a, 464a, 788b; S, 1b, 141b, 143a, 147a, 206a, 312a, 325a
- literature/littérature i, 220b, 221a, 1123a; v, 72a — I, 227a, b, 1157a; V, 74a
- wars/guerres 1st: i, 72a, 962a; iv, 1143a; v, 102a, 580a; 2nd: i, 87b, 238a; v, 580b; 3rd: i, 238b; ii, 30b — Ière: I, 74a, 991b; IV, 1174b; V, 104b, 585a; 2ème: I, 90a, 245b; V, 585a; 3ème: I, 246a; II, 31a
al-Afghānī → Djamāl al-Dīn
Afghānī, ʿAlī Muḥammad iv, 73b — IV, 77a
Afghānistān i, **221a**, 853a, 676a; iii, 13a; iv, 535b; v, 501a; s, 214b, 237a, 329b, 332b, 367a — I, **227b**, 876b, 693a; III, 13b; IV, 558b; V, 504a; S, 214a, 237a, 329a, 322b, 366b
- demography/démographie s, 214b — S, 214a
- ethnography/ethnographie i, 95a, 216-220, 224a, b; v, 245b — I, 98a, 223-226, 230b, 231a; V, 243a
- geography/géographie i, 71a, 221-223 — I, 73a, 227-230
- history/histoire i, 39a, 77a, 87a, b, 225b-233a, 295b; ii, 3a, 638a, 657a, 1100b; iii, 13a; iv, 357b, 917b; s, 270a — I, 40a, 79b, 89b, 90a, 232b-240a, 304b; II, 3a, 654a, 673b, 1126b; III, 13b; IV, 373a, 950b; S, 270a
- institutions ii, 426a; iii, 13b; v, 1079a — II, 437a; III, 14a; V, 1076a
- languages/langues i, 220a, b, 225a — I, 226b, 227a, 231b, 232a
- religion i, 225b, 1123-4 — I, 232a, 1157-8
ʿAfīf al-Dīn al-Tilimsānī → al-Tilimsānī
al-ʿAfīfī, ʿAbd al-Wahhāb s, **44a**, 408a — S, **44b**, 408b
al-ʿAfīfiyya s, 44a — S, 44b
Afkal i, 74a; iv, 421b — I, 76a; IV, 439b
Afkhāz → Abkhāz
al-Aflādj i, **233a**, 538b, 546b; ii, 175b — I, **240a**, 555a, 564a; II, 180b
Aflaḥ b. ʿAbd al-Wahhāb iii, 657a, 659b, 1041b — III, 678a, 680b, 1067b
Aflaḥ (Marzūḳ) b. Yasār → Abū ʿAṭāʾ al-Sindī
Aflaḥ al-Nāshib ii, 495a — II, 507b
ʿAflaḳ, Michel iv, 125a, b, 126a, 783a — IV, 130b, 131a, b, 814b
Aflākī, Shams al-Dīn Aḥmad i, **234a**; s, 83b — I, **241a**; S, 83a
Aflāṭūn i, **234a**, 350a, 631a; ii, 493a, 779b; iv, 329a — I, **241a**, 360b, 651b; II, 505b, 798a; IV, 343b
Aflīmūn iv, 406a; s, **44b** — IV, 423b; S, **45a**
ʿAfrāʾ iii, 1038a — III, 1063b
al-Afrād i, 95a; ii, 789b — I, 97b; II, 808b
Āfrāg i, **236a** — I, **243b**
Āfrāg (al-Manṣūra) s, **45b** — S, **45b**
Afrāgha → Ifrāgha
Afrāʾīm b. al-Zaffān iii, 906b — III, 930b
Afrandj i, 1075b — I, 1107b
Afrāsiyāb i, **236b**, 1087a; iii, 1257a; iv, 813b, 816a — I, **244a**, 1119b; III, 1289b; IV, 846a, 848b
Afrāsiyāb II, Muẓaffar al-Dīn v, 827a — V, 833b
Afrāsiyāb (Tūrānian/Touranien) i, **236a**, 1072b; iii, 112b, 813b, 816a — I, **243b**, 1105; III, 115a, 846a, 848b
Afrāsiyāb b. Kiyā Ḥasan i, 237a — I, 244a
Afrāsiyāb b. Yūsufshāh iii, 337a, b; v, 827a — III, 347a, b; V, 833a
Afrāsiyābid(e)s i, **237a** — I, **244a**
Afrīdī i, 217a, 219b, **237b**, 769a; ii, 1066a; iv, 1143a — I, 223b, 226a, **245a**, 792a; II, 1090b; IV, 1174b
Afrīdūn → Farīdūn
Afrīdūn b. Farīburz iv, 348a — IV, 362b
Afrīghid(e)s iv, 753b, 754a, 1062a, 1063b, 1065b — IV, 784a, b, 1093b, 1095a, 1097a
Āfrīghūnid(e) → Farīghūnid
ʿAfrīn i, **239a** — I, **246b**
ʿAfrīt → ʿIfrīt
ʿAfṣ i, **239a** — I, **246b**
Afsāna v, 204b — V, 202a
Afsantīn i, **239b** — I, **247a**
Afshār i, **239b**; ii, 75b; iii, 1100a, 1102b, 1107a, 1109b; v, 154a, 825a; s, 71a, 147b — I, **247a**; II, 77a; III, 1127a, 1129b, 1134b, 1136b; V, 155a, 831a, b; S, 71b, 147b
Afshīn i, 52b, 145a, 154a, **241a**, 637a, 844a, 1072b, 1104a; iii, 471a; iv, 20b, 646a, 647a, 718b; v, 856a; s, 116a — I, 54b, 149b, 158b, **248b**, 658a, 867b, 1104b, 1137b; III, 487b; IV, 22a, 672b, 673b, 747a; V, 862b; S, 115b
Afsūn i, **241b** — I, **249a**

Afsūs (Afsōs) i, **241b** — I, **249a**
Afṣūs (Ephesus/Ephèse) → Aya Solūk
Afṭasid(e)s i, 6a, **242a,** 1092a, 1338b; iii, 680b — I, 6a, **249b,** 1124b, 1379a; III, 702b
al-Afwah al-Awdī i, **242b** — I, **250a**
Afyūn i, **243a;** ii, 904b — I, **251b;** II, 925b
Afyūn Ḳarā Ḥiṣār i, **243b**; iv, 578a; s, 268b, 348b — I, **250b**; IV, 601b; S, 268a, 348b
al-Afzārī, Asʿad b. Naṣr → ʿAmīd al-Dīn al-Abzārī al-Anṣārī
Aga → Agha
Agadès i, 307a — I, 316b
Agadir i, **244b** — I, **252a**
Agadir-Ighir i, 56a, **244b,** 357b, 1321a; iii, 62b — I, 58a, **252b,** 368a, 1361b; III, 65a
Āgāh Efendi iv, 875b, 876b — IV, 908b, 909b
Agāh Efendī → Čapanzāde Agāh Efendī
Āgahī s, **46a** — S, **46a**
Agarsif → Garsīf
Agau i, 1163a; v, 522a — I, 1197b; V, 525b
Agdāl i, 85a, **245b,** 1346b; s, 114a — I, 87b, **253a,** 1387a; S, 113b
Āgehī i, **245b** — I, **253a**
Agēl → ʿUḳayl
Agha i, 35b, **245b,** 368a, 1256a; ii, 1121a; v, 472b — I, 36b, **253b,** 379a, 1294b; II, 1147a; V, 475a
Agha-bakhsh i, 262b — I, 270b
Agha bölükleri ii, 61b — II, 62b
Aghā Furṣat Shīrāzī iv, 789a — IV, 820b
Āghā Ḥashar Kashmīrī i, 1166a; s, **46b** — 1200b; S, **47a**
Agha Ḥusayn Pasha → Ḥusayn Pasha, Agha
Agha Khān i, **246a;** ii, 140a; v, 942b — I, **254a;** II, 144a; V, 946a
Agha Khān I i, 246a, b; iv, 201b; v, 27a — I, 254a; IV, 210b; V, 27b
Agha Khān II i, 246b — I, 254a
Agha Khān III i, 1196b; iii, 532b — I, 1231b; III, 551a
Agha Khān IV ii, 129a; iv, 201b — II, 132b; IV, 210b
Aghā Khān Kirmānī iv, 70b, 72a, 397b, 788b — IV, 74b, 76a, 415a, 820b
Āghā Khān Maḥallatī i, 1008b; v, 164b, **1221b** — I, 1039b; V, 162b, **1212a**
Āghā Khān Nūrī iii, 554b; iv, 394a, 978b; s, 71a — III, 573b; IV, 411a, 1011a; s, 71b
Āghā Mīr → Sayyid Muḥammad Khān
Āghā Mīrak i, 1211b, 1213a — I, 1247b, 1249b
Āghā Mīrzā Furṣat Shīrāzī iv, 397b — IV, 415a
Āghā Muḥammad Shāh → Aghā Ḥashar Kashmīrī
Āghā Muḥammad Shāh Ḳādjār i, 230a, b, **246b,** 701b, 720b, 1008b; ii, 335b, 812a, 838b; iii, 106a, 1103a; iv, 38a-b, 390a, b, 391a, 638a, 855b, 978b, 1091b; v, 156a, 164b, 495a, 663b, 825b, 835a; s, 94b, 336a, 405b — I, 237a, b, **254a,** 722b, 742a, 1039b; II, 345a, 831b, 858a; III, 108b, 1130b; IV, 40b, 407a, b, 408a, 664a, 888b, 1011a, 1123a; V, 162a, 498a, 669a, 831b, 841b; S, 94a, 335b, 406a
Āghā Sayyid ʿAlī i, 833a — I, 856a
Āghā Sayyid Djamāl ii, 651a — II, 667a
Āghā Sayyid Ḥusayn i, 833b — I, 856b
Aghač i, **247a** — I, **254b**
Aghānī → Awghānī
al-Aghānī → Abu 'l-Faradj al-Iṣfahānī
Aghaoghlu, Aḥmed s, **47a** — S, **47b**
Aghāthūdhīmūn i, **247a;** v, 111b — I, **254b;** V, 114a
al-Aghlab al-ʿIdjlī i, **247b;** iii, 1262a — I, **255a;** III, 1294b
al-Aghlab al-Tamīmī i, 250a; iii, 981b, 1041b — I, 257b; III, 1006a, 1067b
Aghlabid(e)s i, 18a, 24a, 104a, **247b,** 439b, 532b, 862b, 986a, 1148b, 1175b, 1246b, 1319a, 1346a; ii, 145b; iii, 655b; v, 220b; s, 103a, 120b, 144b — I, 18b, 24b, 107a, **255b,** 452a, 549a, 887a, 1017a, 1183a, 1210b, 1284b, 1359b, 1386b; II, 149b; III, 676b; V, 218a; S, 102b, 120a, 144a
Āghmāt i, 7b, **250b**; v, 654b, 1178b — I, 7b, **258b**; V, 658b, 1168b
Aghrī i, **251a,** 1117b — I, **259a,** 1151a
Aghrī Dagh i, **251b**; v, 441a, 465a — I, **259a**; V, 443b, 467b
Aghsartʿan → Akhsitān
al-Aghwāt → Laghouat
al-Aghzāz → Ghuzz
Agnon, Samuel s, 61b — S, 62a
Āgra i, **252b,** 757b, 1323a, 1324a, 1347b; ii, 271a; iii, 449b, 450a, 575b; v, 1135a, 1217a, 1218b, 1219a; s, 10b, 142b — I, **260a,** 780a, 1363b, 1364b, 1388a; II, 279a; III, 465a, 595b; V, 1130b, 1206b, 1207a, 1208b, 1209a; S, 10a, 142a
Agriculture → Filāḥa
Agrigento/-e → Djirdjent
Agronomie → Filāḥa
Aguedal → Āgdāl
Agung, Sultan of/de Mataram ii, 390b; iii, 1221b; s, 150b — II, 400b; III, 1252b; S, 150b
Aḥābīsh i, 24b, 891b; iii, 7b — I, 25b, 918a; III, 8a
Āḥād → Khabar al-Wāḥid
Aḥadī v, 686b — V, 691b
Aḥādīth → Ḥadīth
Aḥadiyya → Allāh, Waḥda
Ahaggar i, **254b,** 433b; iii, 298a — I, **262b,** 445b; III, 307b
Ahangarān ii, 1096b, 1099b; s, 411a — II, 1122b, 1125b; S, 411a
Ahar s, 116a — S, 115b
ʿAhd i, **255a,** 429b, 439b, 1143b; ii, 164b, 302b, 303a; iii, 396b; iv, 14b, 938b — I, **263a,** 441b, 452a, 1178a; II, 169b, 311a, b; III, 409a; IV, 15b, 971b
al-Aḥdab → Ibrāhīm al-Aḥdab
al-Ahdal i, **255b** — I, **263b**
Aḥdāth i, **256a,** 687a, 1332b; ii, 963a; v, 329b — I, **264a,** 708a, 1373a; II, 985a; V, 329b
ʿAhdnāme ii, 116a; iii, 1179b — II, 118b; III, 1208b
Āhī i, **257a** — I, **264b**
Aḥiḳar → al-Ḥayḳar
al-Aḥḳāf i, 169a, **257a** — I, 174a, **265a**
Aḥkām i, **257a;** iii, 551b; iv, 151b — I, **265a;** III, 570a; IV, 157b
Ahl i, **257b,** 700b; iv, 785b — I, **265b,** 721b; IV, 817a
Ahl al-ʿabāʾ i, 258a — I, 266a
Ahl al-ahwāʾ i, **257b** — I, **265b**
Ahl al-Ayyām v, 349a, b — V, 350a
Ahl Bārikalla v, 891b — V, 898a
Ahl al-bayt i, **257b,** 957b; ii, 169b, 843b — I, **265b,** 987a; II, 174b, 863b
Ahl al-buyūtāt i, **258b** — I, **266b**
Ahl al-dār i, **258b** — I, **266b**
Ahl al-dhikr i, 264a — I, 272b
Ahl al-dhimma i, **258b,** 338a, 855b; ii, 126b, 127b, 131b, 142b, 154a, 211a, 324a, 341b, 487b, 559b, 565a, 657b, 1075b; iii, 233b, 1180a, 1187a; iv, 240b; v, 179a, 736b — I, **266b,** 348b, 879a; II, 129b, 131a, 134b, 146b, 158b, 217b, 333b, 351b, 500a, 573b, 579a, 674a, 1100b; III, 240b, 1209a, 1216b; IV, 251a; V, 176b, 741b
Ahl al-farḍ → Mīrāth
Ahl al-ḥadīth i, **258b,** 692a, 1242a; ii, 889a; iii, 163a, 269b, 512b; s, 293a — I, **266b,** 713a, 1280a; II, 909b; III, 166b, 277b, 530a; S, 292b
Ahl-i ḥadīth i, **259a** — I, **267a**
Ahl-i ḥaḳḳ i, **260a,** 840a, 841b; ii, 96a, 850a, 1140b; iv, 49a, 187b; v, 475b, 823a — I, **268a,** 863b, 865a; II, 98a. 870a, 1167a; IV, 52a,196a; V, 478b, 829a

Ahl al-ḥall waʾl-ʿaḳd i, **263b** — I, **272a**
Ahl al-ithbāt iii, 1144a — III, 1172b
Ahl al-kahf → Aṣḥāb al-kahf
Ahl al-kalām → Ahl al-naẓar
Ahl al-ḳibla i, **264a** — I, **272a**
Ahl al-kisāʾ i, **264a;** ii, 844a — I, **272a;** II, 863b
Ahl al-kitāb i, **264a;** ii, 1065b; iv, 408a, b — I, **272a;** II, 1090a; IV, 426a
Ahl al-madar i, 608b — I, 628b
Ahl al-naẓar i, **266a** — I, **274a**
Ahl al-raʾy → Aṣḥāb al-raʾy
Ahl al-Saḳīfa → Saḳīfa
Ahl Shamʿa i, 767a — I, 790a
Ahl al-ṣuffa i, 114a, 129a, **266a** — I, 117a, 133a, **274a**
Ahl al-sunna i, **267a,** 694a, 1039b; ii, 412a; iii, 248a, 846a; iv, 142a — I, **275a,** 715b, 1071a; II, 423a; III, 255a, 870a; IV, 148a
Ahl al-wabar i, 608b — I, 628b
Ahlī iv, 67a — IV, 70b
Ahl-i wāris i, **267a** — I, **275a**
Aḥlāf → Ḥilf
Ahliyya i, 818a — I, 841a
Aḥmad (Aghlabid(e)) → Abū Ibrāhīm Aḥmad
Aḥmad, Sultan of/de Brunei s, 152a — S, 152a
Aḥmad (Bahmani) → Aḥmad Shāh
Aḥmad (Djalāyirid(e)) → Aḥmad b. Uways
Aḥmad I (Ḥafṣid(e)) iii, 68a; iv, 416a — III, 70b; IV, 434a
Aḥmad II (Ḥafsid(e)) iii, 68b, 826b, 827b, 831b; v, 531a — III, 70b, 71a, 850a, b, 851a, 855b; V, 535a
Aḥmad III (Ḥafṣid(e)) iii, 69b — III, 71b
Aḥmad I (Hūdid(e)) i, 499a, 865a, 1040b; ii, 112a; iii, 542a; iv, 478a; v, 683a — I, 514a, 889a, 1072a; II, 114b; III, 561a; IV, 499a; V, 688a
Aḥmad II (Hūdid(e)) i, 495b; iii, 542b; s, 383a — I, 510a; III, 561b; S, 383b
Aḥmad III (Hūdid(e)) i, 1083a; ii, 1013b; iii, 543a — I, 1115b; II, 1037a; III, 561b
Aḥmad (Ilkhānid(e)) → Aḥmad Takūdār
Aḥmad I (Ḳarakhānid(e)) → Aḥmad Khān b. Khiḍr
Aḥmad I (Ottoman) i, **267b,** 510b, 954b, 1226a, 1267a; ii, 208b, 543a, 684a; iii, 1185a; v, 18a, b, 272a; s, 257b, 330b — I, **275b,** 526b, 983b, 1262b, 1305b; II, 215a, 556b, 701a; III, 1214b; V, 19a, 270a; S, 257a, 330a
— mosque (Istanbul) iv, 233a — IV, 243b
Aḥmad II (Ottoman) ii, **268a;** v, 262a — I, **276a;** V, 260a
Aḥmad III (Ottoman) i, **268b,** 394b, 395a, 776a, 836b, 1076b; ii, 212b, 684a; iii, 1002a; iv, 874a, 969b; v, 18b, 19a, 641b, 642b, 643b — I, **276b,** 406a, 799a, 859b, 1108b; II, 219a, 701a; III, 1027a; IV, 907b, 1001b; V, 19a, b, 645b, 646b, 647b
Aḥmad (Muḥammad) i, **267a** — I, **275a**
Aḥmad, Shaykh i, 1072a; v, 467a — I, 1104a; V, 470a
Aḥmad b. al-ʿAbbās b. ʿĪsā b. Shaykh iv, 90b — IV, 94b
Aḥmad b. ʿAbd Allāh (ʿAbd al-Wādid(e))→ Abū Zayyān III
Aḥmad b. ʿAbd Allāh, Sulṭān ii, 737a — II, 755b
Aḥmad b. ʿAbd Allāh al-Dilāʾī s, 223b — S, 223b
Aḥmad b. ʿAbd Allāh al-Khudjistānī i, 452b; iii, 245a; v, 47a, 48a — I, 465b; III, 252a; V, 48b, 49a
Aḥmad b. ʿAbd Allāh Maʿn al-Andalusī iv, 380a — IV, 396b
Aḥmad b. ʿAbd al-ʿAzīz b. Abī Dulaf i, 452b; ii, 301a, 623b; iv, 100a — I, 465b; II, 309a, 639a; IV, 104b
Aḥmad b. ʿAbd al-ʿAzīz al-Khurāsānī iii, 138b; v, 60b — III, 141a; V, 62a
Aḥmad b. ʿAbd al-Raḥīm → Abū Zurʿa
Aḥmad b. ʿAbd al-Raḥmān al-Djazāʾirī ii, 183a — II, 189a
Aḥmad b. Abi ʾl-ʿAzāʾim s, 18b — S, 18b
Aḥmad b. Abī Bakr → Muḥtādjid(e)s
Aḥmad b. Abī Duʾād i, 153b, **271a,** 273a; ii, 385b; iii, 707a, 974b, 994b; iv, 289b, 718b; v, 647a; s, 17b, 25a, 90b — I, 158a, **279b,** 281a; II, 396a; III, 729a, 999a, 1019b; IV, 302b, 747b; V, 651a; S, 18a, 25a, 90a
Aḥmad b. Abi ʾl-Ḳāsim al-Ṣawmaʿī i, 159b — I, 164a
Aḥmad b. Abī Khālid al-Aḥwal i, 241a, **271b** — I, 248b, **280a**
Aḥmad b. Abī Mismār s, 30b — S, 31a
Aḥmad b. Abi ʾl-Saʿīd iv, 632b — IV, 657b
Aḥmad b. Abī Saʿīd b. Tīmūr s, 51a — S, 51b
Aḥmad b. Abī Ṭāhir Ṭayfūr → Ibn Abī Ṭāhir
Aḥmad b. Abī ʿUmāra → Ibn Abī ʿUmāra
Aḥmad b. al-Aghlab i, 249b, 250b — I, 257b, 258a
Aḥmad b. Aḥmad al-Gīlānī i, 776b — I, 799b
Aḥmad b. ʿAlī (Rayy) i, 125b; iv, 661b — I, 129a; IV, 688b
Aḥmad b. ʿAlī, Mai i, 1260a — I, 1298a
Aḥmad b. ʿAlī b. Khayrān ii, 127b — II, 130b
Aḥmad b. ʿAlī b. Thābit → al-Khaṭīb al-Baghdādī
Aḥmad b. ʿAlī al-Ḥāshimī ii, 276a — II, 284a
Aḥmad b. ʿAlī, Sayyid, Karkiyā v, 603b — V, 607b
Aḥmad b. ʿAlī al-Ikhshīd iv, 418b — IV, 436b
Aḥmad b. ʿAlī Zunbul iv, 1130a — IV, 1161b
Aḥmad b. ʿAmr al-Sulamī i, 697a — I, 718b
Aḥmad b. al-Aṭrābulusī iii, 660a — III, 681a
Aḥmad b. Aṭṭāsh i, 353a; iii, 725a; iv, 101b, 102a — I, 363b; III, 748a; IV, 106a, b
Aḥmad b. al-ʿAynī s, 38a — S, 38b
Aḥmad b. Bā Ḥmād s, 114a — S, 113b
Aḥmad b. Baṣo iv, 118a — IV, 123a
Aḥmad b. Bāyazīd II i, 396a, 1120b; iv, 1159a; v, 677b — I, 407b, 1154a, b; IV, 1191a; V, 682b
Aḥmad b. Buwayh → Muʿizz al-Dawla Aḥmad
Aḥmad b. Djābir → Aḥmad Āl Djābir
Aḥmad b. Djaʿfar, Amīr s, 125b — S, 124b
Aḥmad b. Djaʿfar al-Kattānī → Muḥammad b. Djaʿfar al-Kattānī
Aḥmad b. Faḍlān → Ibn Faḍlān
Aḥmad b. Faradj → Ibn Faradj al-Djayyānī
Aḥmad b. Farīghūn ii, 798b — II, 817b
Aḥmad b. al-Furāt → Ibn al-Furāt, Aḥmad
Aḥmad b. Ghālib ii, 517b — II, 530b
Aḥmad b. Ḥābiṭ i, **272a** — I, **280a**
Aḥmad b. al-Ḥādjdj s, 403b — S, 404a
Aḥmad b. Ḥanbal i, 114a, 155a, 259a, 271a, **272b,** 589b, 694b, 1242a, 1244b, 1245b; ii, 182b, 294b, 889b, 890a, 1093a; iii, 24a, 158a, 1266a; iv, 142a, 469b, 470a, 735a; v, 426a, 731b; s, 16a, 392a — I, 117b, 159b, 267a, 279b, **280b,** 608b, 715b, 1280a, 1282b, 1283b; II, 188b, 302a, 910b, 1118b; III, 25a, 161b, 1299a; IV, 148a, 490b, 491a, 764b; V, 428b, 737a; S, 16b, 392b
Aḥmad b. Ḥarb iv, 668a — IV, 695a
Aḥmad b. al-Ḥasan, al-Mahdī li-Dīn Allāh, Imām i, 554a; v, **1241b** — I, 571b; V, **1233a**
Aḥmad b. Ḥasan al-Kalbī iv, 496b — IV, 518a
Aḥmad b. al-Ḥusayn, al-Mahdī li-Dīn Allāh, Imām v, **1241a** — V, **1231b**
Aḥmad b. al-Ḥusayn al-Muʾayyad bi-ʾllāh s, 363a — S, 363a
Aḥmad b. Ḥusayn, Sulṭān ii, 737a — II, 755b
Aḥmad b. Ibrāhīm b. Ḥamdūn → Ibn Ḥamdūn
Aḥmad b. Ibrāhīm al-Uḳlīdisī → al-Uḳlīdisī
Aḥmad b. Idrīs i, **277b,** 709b; s, 278b — I, **286a,** 731a; S, 278b
Aḥmad b. ʿImrān iii, 125b — III, 128a
Aḥmad b. ʿĪsā, ʿAmūd al-Dīn i, 277b — I, 286b
Aḥmad b. ʿĪsā b. Muḥammad b. ʿAlī i, **277b,** 551b — I, **286a,** 569a
Aḥmad b. ʿIsā b. Shaykh i, 145a; iv, 90a, b — I, 149b;

IV, 94a, b
Aḥmad b. ʿIsā b. Zayd s, **48a** — S, **48b**
Aḥmad b. Isḥāḳ, Khwādja Pīr s, 84b — S, 84a
Aḥmad b. Isḥāḳ al-Khārakī iv, 1004a — IV, 1036b
Aḥmad b. Ismāʿīl (Rasūlid(e)) i, 553a; iv, 642b — I, 570b; IV, 668b
Aḥmad b. Ismāʿīl (Samānid(e)) ii, 1082a; iii, 254b, 757b; iv, 22a, b — II, 1107b; III, 261b, 780b; IV, 23b, 24a
Aḥmad b. al-Ḳāḍī ii, 537b; iv, 361b, 1155b, 1156a — II, 550b; IV, 377a, 1187b, 1188b
Aḥmad b. Ḳāsim s, 132b — S, 132a
Aḥmad b. Kayghulugh iv, 100a — IV, 104b
Aḥmad b. Khālid → Aḥmad al-Nāṣirī
Aḥmad b. Khalīfa i, 942b; iv, 751a, 953a — I, 971b; IV, 781b, 985b
Aḥmad b. al-Khaṣīb, Abū ʿAlī → Ibn al-Khaṣīb
Aḥmad b. al-Khaṣīb al-Djardjarāʾī → al-Djardjarāʾī
Aḥmad b. Khiḍrōya i, 162b — I, 167a
Aḥmad b. Mādjid al-Nadjdjī → Ibn Mādjid
Aḥmad b. Maḥmūd iii, 1116a — III, 1143b
Aḥmad b. Makkī iv, 338a — IV, 352a
Aḥmad b. Maʿn ii, 635a — II, 651a
Aḥmad b. Marwān → Naṣr al-Dawla b. Marwān
Aḥmad b. Marzūḳ → Ibn Marzūḳ
Aḥmad b. al-Muʿadhdhal → Ibn al-Muʿadhdhal
Aḥmad b. Muʿāwiya → Ibn al-Ḳiṭṭ
Aḥmad b. al-Mubārak b. al-Walīd s, 62a — S, 62b
Aḥmad b. Muḥammad (Maḥmūd) s, **49a** — S, **49b**
Aḥmad b. Muḥammad (Sharwān-Shāh) iv, 346a, 347a — IV, 361a, b
Aḥmad b. Muḥammad b. ʿAbd al-Ṣamad i, **278a** — I, **286b**
Aḥmad b. Muḥammad b. Ilyās s, 80a — S, 80a
Aḥmad b. Muḥammad b. Khalaf i, 116a — I, 119b
Aḥmad b. Muḥammad b. Khayrāt ii, 517b — II, 530b
Aḥmad b. Muḥammad Ādarrāḳ → Ādarrāḳ
Aḥmad b. Muḥammad al-Aghlab → Abū Ibrāhīm Aḥmad
Aḥmad b. Muḥammad al-Barḳī → al-Barḳī
Aḥmad b. Muḥammad al-Ḥabūḍī s, 338b — S, 338a
Aḥmad b. Muḥammad ʿIrfān → Aḥmad Brēlwī
Aḥmad b. Muḥammad al-Manṣūr → Aḥmad al-Manṣūr
Aḥmad b. Muḥsin i, 1133a — I, 1167b
Aḥmad b. Mūsā b. Aḥmad al-Bukhārī → Bā Aḥmad
Aḥmad b. Mūsā b. Shākir s, 412a — S, 412a
Aḥmad b. Mūsā al-Samlālī → Ḥmad u-Mūsā
Aḥmad b. Nāṣīr i, 290a — I, 299a
Aḥmad b. Naṣr (Samānid(e)) s, 357a — S, 357a
Aḥmad b. Rusta → Ibn Rusta
Aḥmad b. Ṣadaḳa iv, 929a — IV, 962a
Aḥmad b. Sahl b. Ḥāshim i, **278a** — I, **286b**
Aḥmad b. Saʿīd → Bū Saʿīd, Āl
Aḥmad b. Saʿīd (d/m 961) i, 600a — I, 619b
Aḥmad b. Saʿīd (d/m 1783) i, 554a, 1098a, 1281b — I, 572a, 1131b, 1321a
Aḥmad b. Sālim v, 596b — V, 600a, b
Aḥmad b. Shādgeldi i, 432a, 1117b, 1118a — I, 444a, 1151b, 1152a
Aḥmad b. Sharḳāwī al-Khalifī s, 40b — S, 41a
Aḥmad b. Sulaymān, Imām i, 552b; v, 954a — I, 570a; V, 958a
Aḥmad b. Taymiyya → Ibn Taymiyya, Aḥmad
Aḥmad b. Ṭūlūn i, 139a, 205a, **278a,** 341a, 517a, 551a, 621a, 990a, b, 1224a; ii, 36b, 129b, 130a, 281b, 305a, 328a, 958b, 1080b; iii, 86a, 398a, 745b, 880a; iv, 134a, 655a, 841b; v, 49a, 91a, b, 327a, 624a; s, 120b — I, 143a, 211a, **287a,** 351b, 532b, 568b, 641b, 1021a, 1260b; II, 37b, 133a, 289b, 313b, 337b, 980b, 1105b; III, 88a, 410b, 768b, 904a; IV, 139b, 681a, 874b; V, 50b, 93b, 326b, 628a; S, 120a
Aḥmad b. ʿUbayd Allāh b. al-Khaṣīb → al-Khaṣībī, Aḥmad b. ʿUbayd Allāh
Aḥmad b. ʿUḳba al-Ḥaḍramī s, 208a — S, 208a
Aḥmad b. Uways i, 903b, 1051a, 1119a; ii, 401b; iv, 33b, 584b, 586a, b — I, 930b, 1082b, 1152b; II, 412a; IV, 36a, 608a, b, 609a
Aḥmad b. Yaḥyā, Imām (1948) i, 555a — I, 572b
Aḥmad b. Yaḥyā b. al-Murtaḍā, al-Mahdī li-Dīn Allāh v, **1241a** — V, **1232a**
Aḥmad b. Yaḥyā al-Yaḥṣubī → Tādj al-Dawla (Labla)
Aḥmad b. Yūsuf i, **279a** — I, **288a**
Aḥmad b. Yūsuf, Sīdī i, 374b, 1300b; iv, 481b — I, 385a, 1340b; IV, 502b
Aḥmad b. Yūsuf al-Akḥal iv, 497a — IV, 518b
Aḥmad b. Yūsuf al-Miṣrī → Ibn al-Dāya
Aḥmad b. Zayn al-Ḥabshī i, 829b — I, 852b
Aḥmad b. Zaynī Daḥlān → Daḥlān
Aḥmad ʿAbd al-Ḥaḳḳ, Shāh ii, 54a, 56a; s, 293a — II, 55a, 56b; S, 293a
Aḥmad Abu 'l-Fatḥ s, 6a — S, 5a
Aḥmad Agha Ḳara ʿOthmān-oghlu iv, 593a — IV, 617a
Aḥmad al-Aḥṣāʾī → al-Aḥṣāʾī
Aḥmad Āl Djābir Āl Ṣabāḥ iii, 1066a; v, 575a; s, 50a — III, 1092b; V, 579b; S, 50b
Aḥmad ʿAlī, Ḳāḍī v, 1252a, b — V, 1242b, 1243a
Aḥmad ʿAlī Khān i, 1196a, 1197a — I, 1231b, 1232a
Aḥmad ʿAlī Khān, Nawwāb iv, 666b; v, 779b — IV, 693b; V, 785b
Aḥmad Allāh, Mawlawī ii, 870b — II, 890b
Aḥmad Amīn i, **279b**; iv, 159b — I, **288a**; IV, 166a
Aḥmad al-ʿArabī v, 1005a — V, 1001a
Aḥmad al-Aʿradj ii, 527b; v, 119a — II, 540b; V, 1181a
Aḥmad Ashraf, Shāh s, 74a — S, 74b
Aḥmad Bā Djābir al-Ḥaḍramī i, 781b — I, 804b
Aḥmad Bābā i, 96b, **279b,** 289a, 594b; iii, 763b, 844a; iv, 476b — I, 99a, **288b,** 298a, 614a; III, 786b, 868a; IV, 497b
Aḥmad al-Badawī i, **280a,** 404a, 1127a; ii, 1009b; iii, 90b; — I, **289a,** 415b, 1161a; II, 1033b; III, 93a
Aḥmad Bakr b. Mūsā ii, 123a — II, 126a
Aḥmad Barēlawī → Aḥmad Brēlwī
Aḥmad Beg (Ḳarāmān-oghlu) → Fakhr al-Dīn Aḥmad
Aḥmad Bey (1790-1805) → Aḥmad Ḳaramānlī
Aḥmad Bey (Algeria/-e) v, 532a — V, 536a
Aḥmad Bey (Bosniak/Bosniaque) iv, 723a — IV, 752a
Aḥmad Bey (1837-55) i, 37a, **281b;** ii, 461b; iii, 94b, 561b, 636a, 684a, 720b — I, 38a, **290a;** II, 473a; III, 97a, 581a, 657b, 705b, 743a
Aḥmad Bey (1919-42) iii, 636b — III, 658a
Aḥmad Bīdjān → Bīdjān
Aḥmad Brēlwī i, **282a,** 432b; ii, 140a, 254b, 316b, 437a; iii, 119b, 335b, 431a; iv, 196a, b, 625b, 626a — I, **291a,** 445a; II, 144a, 262a, 326a, 448b; III, 122a, 345b, 445a; IV, 204b, 205a, 650b, 651a
Aḥmad al-Burnusī Zarrūḳ ii, 293a — II, 301a
Aḥmad Bushnāḳ Pasha i, 904b, 905a — I, 932a
Aḥmad Čelebi Fenārīzāde ii, 879a — II, 899b
Aḥmad Dghughī s, 53a — S, 53b
Aḥmad al-Dhahabī i, 47a, 356a — I, 48b, 367a
Aḥmad Djaʿfar Shīrāzī i, 1255a — I, 1293a
Aḥmad Djalāʾir → Aḥmad b. Uways
Aḥmad-i Djām i, **283a** — I, **291b**
Aḥmad Djayzān i, 1032b; ii, 517b — I, 1064a; II, 530a
Aḥmad Djazzār → Djazzār Pasha
Aḥmad Djewdet Pasha i, **284b,** 397a, 505a; ii, 474b,

702b, 935a; iii, 250a, b, 993a; iv, 168b, 872a; v, 837a, 1083a, 1084b — I, **293a,** 408b, 520b; II, 486b, 720b, 956b; III, 257b, 1017b; IV, 175b, 905b; V, 843b, 1080b, 1081b
Aḥmad Emīn Yalman ii, 475a, b — II, 487b
Aḥmad Evrenos-oghlu ii, 721a — II, 739b
Aḥmad Faḍīl iv, 687a — IV, 715b
Aḥmad Fahmī Abu 'l-Khayr s, 263a — S, 262b
Aḥmad Faḳīh s, **50a** — S, **51a**
Aḥmad al-Faḳīh al-Bābānī i, 845a — I, 868a
Aḥmad Fanākatī iv, 1020a — IV, 1052a
Aḥmad Fāris al-Shidyāk → Fāris al-Shidyāḳ
Aḥmad Fuʾād b. Fārūḳ s, 299b, 301b — S, 299a, 301b
Aḥmad Ghulām Khalīl → Ghulām Khalīl
Aḥmad Göwde i, 312a, 1082b; ii, 184a — I, 321b, 1115a; II, 190a
Aḥmad Grāñ b. Ibrāhīm i, **286b,** 932b, 1172b; ii, 91a; iii, 4a, 176a — I, **295b,** 961a, 1207b; II, 93a; III, 4a, 180a
Aḥmad al-Ḥārithī al-Dilāʾī s, 223b — S, 223b
Aḥmad Ḥasanayn Pasha s, 299b, 300 a, b — S, 299b, 300a
Aḥmad al-Hība (Hayba) v, 890b, 891a; s, **47b** — V, 897a; S, **48a**
Aḥmad Ḥikmet i, **287a;** iii, 260b — I, **295b;** III, 267b
Aḥmad Ḥusayn iv, 125a — IV, 130b
Aḥmad Ḥusayn (Miṣr al-Fatāt) s, 5b — S, 4b
Aḥmad Ibrāhīm al-Ghāzī → Aḥmad Grāñ
Aḥmad Iḥsān i, **287a;** ii, 474b — I, **296a;** II, 486b
Aḥmad ʿIzzet Pasha al-Fārūkī i, 330b — I, 340b
Aḥmad ʿIzzet Pasha Furgaç → ʿIzzet Pasha (Furgaç)
Aḥmad al-Kabīr, Sīdī i, 1300b — I, 1340b
Aḥmad-i Ḳarāḥiṣārī iv, 1125a, b — IV, 1157a
Aḥmad Ḳaramānlî iv, 617b, 618a; s, 243b — IV, 642b; S, 243b
Aḥmad Katkhudā Mustaḥfiẓān Kharpūṭlū iv, 438a — IV, 457b
Aḥmad Khān, Sayyid iii, 44b — III, 46a, b
Aḥmad Khān, Sir Sayyid i, 38b, **287b,** 403b, 443a, 505b, 827b; ii, 27b, 97a, 426b, 549b; iii, 93b, 358b, 431a, b, 433a, 458a, 1204b; iv, 170a, b; v, 202a; s, 74a, 106b, 107b, 247a — I, 39b, **96b,** 415a, 455b, 521a, 850b; II, 28a, 99a, 437a, 563a; III, 96a, 370a, 445a, b, 447a, 474a, 1235a; IV, 177b; V, 199b; S, 74b, 105b, 107a, 247a
Aḥmad Khān b. Ḥasan (Hārūn) iii, 1114b; iv, 581a — III, 1141b; IV, 604b
Aḥmad Khān b. Hūlāgū → Aḥmad Takūdār
Aḥmad Khān b. Khiḍr iii, 1114b, 1115b — III, 1142a, 1143a
Aḥmad Khān b. Muḥammad Zamān Khān → Aḥmad Shāh Durrānī
Aḥmad Khān Bangash ii, 808b; iii, 60a, 1158b — II, 827b; III, 62b, 1187a
Aḥmad Khān ʿAlāʾ al-Dawla, Mīrzā s, 365a — S, 365a
Aḥmad Khān Nāṣir al-Dawla, Mīrzā s, 23b — S, 24a
Aḥmad Khān Sūr → Sikandar Shāh Sūr
Aḥmad Khān Ūsmī ii, 87a — II, 88b
Aḥmad al-Khaṣībī iv, 424a — IV, 442a
Aḥmad Khattū Maghribī i, 1329b; ii, 1125b; v, **1209b**; s, 10b — I, 1370a; II, 1153a; V, **1200b**; S, 10a
Aḥmad Köprülü → Köprülü
Aḥmad al-Ḳushāshī i, 88a — I, 90b
Aḥmad Māhir s, 58a — S, 58b
Aḥmad Makhdūm Dānish s, 290a — S, 290a
Aḥmad al-Maʿḳūr ii, 122b — II, 125b
Aḥmad Maniklī Pasha iv, 686b — IV, 714b
Aḥmad al-Manṣūr al-Dhahabī (Saʿdid(e)) i, 58b, 279, **288b,** 1347a; ii, 134a, 308a, 510a, 819b; iii, 70a, 339b, 814a, 1047a; iv, 635a, b; v, 1119a; s, 28b, 223a — I, 60a, 288b, **297b,** 1387b; II, 137a, 317a, 522b, 839a; III, 72b, 349b, 837b, 1073a; IV, 661b; V, 1181a; S, 29a, 223a
Aḥmad Midḥat i, **289a,** 975a; ii, 473b, 474a, b; iii, 357b, 375a, 622a, 630a, 1200a; iv, 602a, 682a, 930a, 931b; v, 194a, 195b; s, 64b — I, **298a,** 1005b; II, 485b, 486a, b; III, 368b, 387a, 643a, 651a, 1230a; IV, 626b, 710a, 963a, 964b; V, 191a, 192b; S, 65a
Aḥmad Mukhtār Pasha iv, 201a; v, 314a; s, 64b — IV, 210a; V, 314a; S, 64b
Aḥmad al-Muḳtadir → Aḥmad I (Hūdid(e))
Aḥmad Mumtāz Pasha iv, 687a — IV, 715a
Aḥmad Mürshidī i, 1202a — I, 1238a
Aḥmad Mūsā iii, 1127a, b — III, 1155a, b
Aḥmad Nadā ii, 900b — II, 921a
Aḥmad al-Naḥḥās i, 321b — I, 331b
Aḥmad al-Nāṣir b. al-Ḥādī s, 335b — S, 335a
Aḥmad al-Nāṣir b. Yaḥyā al-Hādī iii, 124b — III, 127b
Aḥmad al-Nāṣirī al-Salāwī i, **290a,** 315b; v, 1209b; s, 395a, b — I, **299a,** 325a; V, 1200a; S, 395b, 396a
Aḥmad Nayrīzī iv, 1123b — IV, 1155b
Aḥmad Niyāzī → Niyāzī Bey
Aḥmad Niẓām Shāh i, 295a, 303a; ii, 814b, 1084b; iii, 15b, 1159b; s, 246a — I, 304a, 312b; II, 834a, 1110a; III, 16b, 1188a; S, 246a
Aḥmad Pasha → Djazzār; Hersek-zāde; Kücük; Miḳdād
Aḥmad Pasha, Ḳara i, **291b;** ii, 704a; v, 67a — I, **300b;** II, 722a; V, 68a
Aḥmad Pasha (Ṣūfī) s, 49b — S, 50a
Aḥmad Pasha b. Ḥasan Pasha i, 270a, **291a,** 905a; iii, 106a, 252a, 1257b — I, 278b, **300a,** 932b; III, 108b, 259a, 1290a
Aḥmad Pasha Abū Widān ii, 123b; iv, 686b — II, 126b; IV, 714b
Aḥmad Pasha Bonneval i, **291b,** 395b, 1064b; ii, 511b; iii, 203b, 253a; iv, 738b; v, 52b — I, **300b,** 407a, 1096b; II, 524a; III, 209a, 260a; IV, 768a; V, 54a
Aḥmad Pasha Bursalî i, **292a** — I, **301a**
Aḥmad Pasha Čapan-oghlu ii, 207b — II, 214a
Aḥmad Pasha Djalīlī ii, 402a — II, 413a
Aḥmad Pasha Djenābī i, 511a — I, 526b
Aḥmad Pasha Ekmekdjizāde s, 330b — S, 330a
Aḥmad Pasha Gedik i, **292b,** 354b, 767b; ii, 337b, 530a; iii, 341b; iv, 656a, 868b, 892a; v, 726a, 764a — I, **301b,** 365b, 790b; II, 347b, 543a; III, 352a; IV, 682b, 902a, 924b; V, 731a, 769b
Aḥmad Pasha Hezārpāre iii, 318a, 983b; v, 272b — III, 327b, 1008a; V, 270b
Aḥmad Pasha Khāʾin i, **293a;** iii, 998a — I, **302a;** III, 1023a
Aḥmad Pasha Küčük s, **49a** — S, **49b**
Aḥmad Rafīḳ Altînay i, **293b** — I, **302b**
Aḥmad al-Raḳḳī i, 758b — I, 781b
Aḥmad Rāsîm i, 287b, **293b**; v, 196a; s, 64b — I, 296a, **303a**; V, 193a; S, 65a
Aḥmad Rasmī i, 294b; iii, 157a — I, **303b;** III, 161a
Aḥmad al-Rāzī → al-Rāzī
Aḥmad Riḍwān iv, 129a — IV, 134b
Aḥmad al-Rīfī Pasha i, 47b — I, 48b
Aḥmad Rîza (Riḍā) ii, 430b, 474b; iv, 285a — II, 442a, 486b; IV, 297b
Aḥmad Ṣaʿlūk iv, 100a — IV, 104b
Aḥmad Shāh i, **295a,** 1193a, 1329b — I, **304a,** 1228b, 1370a
Aḥmad Shāh I Wali (Bahmanī) i, 923b, 924a, 925a, b, 1200a, b, 1323a; ii, 981a, 1115a, 1125b; iii, 15a, 417b, 420b, 638b; iv, 961b; v, 1215b — I, 951b, 952a, 953a, b, 1235b, 1236a, 1363b; II, 1003b, 1141a, 1153a; III, 15b, 431a, 434a, 659b; IV, 994a; V, 1205a
Aḥmad Shāh II, ʿAlāʾ al-Dīn (Bahmanī) i, 923b; ii, 814b; iii, 421a, 577a; iv, 962a — I, 951b; II, 834a; III,

434b, 597a; IV, 994a
Aḥmad Shāh III (Bahmanī) i, 923b — I, 951b
Aḥmad Shāh I (Gudjarāt) i, 295a, 299b, 506b; ii, 11a, 1125a; iii, 418b, 445a, 638a, 1010a — I, 304a, 308b, 522a; II, 11a, 1151b; III, 432a, 459b, 659b, 1035b
Aḥmad Shāh II (Gudjarāt) i, 295a; ii, 1125b — I, 304a; II, 1153a
Aḥmad Shāh III (Gudjarāt) ii, 1129a — II, 1155b
Aḥmad Shāh (Nizam) → Aḥmad Nizam Shāh
Aḥmad Shāh, ʿAlāʾ al-Dīn (Atjèh) i, 743b — I, 766a
Aḥmad Shāh Bahādur i, **295a;** iii, 60a, 1158b — I, **304a;** III, 62b, 1187a
Aḥmad Shāh Durrānī (Abdālī) i, 72b, 95b, 218b, 226b, 229b, 230a, 238a, **295a,** 432b, 454b, 970b, 1001b, 1005b, 1020a; ii, 488b, 628b, 1049b, 1131b; iii, 60b, 335b, 427b, 1158b; iv, 390a, 537b, 709b; v, 29a, 102a, 598b, 1079a — I, 74b, 98a, 224b, 233a, 236b, 237a, 245a, **304b,** 445a, 467b, 1000a, 1032a, 1036b, 1051b; II, 501a, 644b, 1074a, 1158a; III, 63a, 346a, 441b, 1187a; IV, 407a, 560b, 738a; V, 30a, 104a, 602b, 1076b
Aḥmad Shāh Gaṇesh, Shams al-Dīn i, 295a; iii, 419a — I, 304a; III, 432b
Aḥmad Shāh Ḳādjār ii, 652b; iv, 392a, 398b; v, 61b; s, 342a — II, 668b; IV, 408b, 415b; V, 63a; S, 342a
Aḥmad al-Shahīd Bā Faḍl ii, 730a — II, 748b
Aḥmad Shahīd, Sayyid ii, 54b — II, 55b
Aḥmad Shams al-Din al-Marmarāwī iv, 992a, b — IV, 1024b, 1025a
Aḥmad Sharīf (Sanūsī) i, 277b, 1071a; v, 758a — I, 286a, 1103a; V, 763b
Aḥmad al-Shaykh i, **297a;** ii, 567b; iii, 39b — I, **306a;** II, 582a; III, 41a
Aḥmad Shihābī ii, 444a, 635b — II, 455b, 651b
Aḥmad Ṣidddīḳ, Shaykh ii, 1078a — II, 1103a
Aḥmad al-Sidjzī i, 725a; s, 412b — I, 747b; S, 413a
Aḥmad Sirhindī, Shaykh i, **297a,** 347a, 957a, 1022b; ii, 30a, 55a, 296b, 380b, 871b, 1144a; iii, 430a, 432b, 435b; s, 313a — I, **306b,** 357b, 986b, 1054a; II, 30b, 56a, 304b, 391a, 891b, 1171a; III, 444a, 446b, 449b; S, 312b
Aḥmad Sūdī → Sūdī, Aḥmad
Aḥmad Tāʾib → ʿUthmān-zāde
Ahmad Takūdār i, 903a; ii, 606b, 607b; iii, 1122a; iv, 31a, 620b, 817b, 975b; v, 827a — I, 930a; II, 621b, 622b; III, 1150a; IV, 33b, 645b, 850a, 1008a; V, 833a
Aḥmad Ṭūsūn → Ṭūsūn b. Muḥammad ʿAlī
Aḥmad Wafīḳ Pasha i, 61b, 63b, 285b, **298a,** 473b; iii, 249b; iv, 791a — I, 63b, 65b, 294b, **307a,** 485b; III, 256b; IV, 822b
Aḥmad Wāṣif → Wāṣif
Aḥmad Wehbī → Pīr Meḥmed Wehbī Khayyāṭ
Aḥmad Yādgār s, 1b — S, 1b
Aḥmad Yasawī i, **298b,** 1162a; iii, 76b, 1115a, 1116a; v, 264a, 859a; s, 51a — I, **308a,** 1196b; III, 79a, 1142b, 1143b; V, 262a, 866a; S, 51b
Aḥmad Yuknakī, Adīb i, **299a** — I, **308b**
Aḥmad Zarrūḳ → Zarrūḳ, Aḥmad
Aḥmad Zekī Welīdī → Togan, Zekī
Aḥmad Ziwar Pasha ii, 934b; iii, 516b — II, 956a; III, 534b
Aḥmad Zog → Zog, King
Aḥmadābād i, **299b;** ii, 1125b; iii, 16a, 445a, b; v, 1210a; s, 10b, 23b, 70b, 335b — I, **308b;** II, 1153a; III, 16b, 459b, 460b; V, 1200b; S, 10a, 23b, 71a, 335a
Aḥmadī → Sikka
Aḥmadī (town/ville) s, **50a** — S, **50b**
Aḥmad-i Rūmī s, **49b** — s, **50a**
Aḥmadī, Tādj al-Dīn Ibrāhīm b. Khiḍr i, **299b,** 325a; ii, 98a; iii, 115a; iv, 128b — I, **309a,** 335a; II, 100b; III, 117b; IV, 134a
Aḥmadīl b. Ibrāhīm b. Wahsūdān al-Kurdī i, 300a; v, 454a — I, 309b; V, 456b
Aḥmadīlīs i, 190a, **300a;** iii, 1112a — I, 194b, **309b;** III, 1139a
Aḥmadiyya i, 225b, **301a;** ii, 58b, 63b, 129a, 535b, 538b, 1004a; iii, 411b, 433b, 1228b; iv, 84b, 890a, 891a, 951a; s, 248b, 278b — I, 232b, **310b;** II, 59b, 64b, 132b, 549a, 552a, 1027a; III, 424b, 447b, 1260b; IV, 88b, 922b, 923b, 983b; S, 248b, 278b
Aḥmadiyya (Derw(v)ish) i, 281a; ii, 164b — I, 289b; II, 170a
al-Aḥmadiyya (Khalwatiyya) iv, 992a, 993a — IV, 1024b, 1025b
Aḥmadnagar (Bombay) i, 81a, **303a;** ii, 99b, 158b; iii, 15b, 425b, 426b, 626a; iv, 202a; s, 246a — I, 83b, **312b;** II, 101b, 163b; III, 16a, 439b, 440a, 646b; IV, 210b; S, 246b
Aḥmadnagar (Gudjarāt) ii, 1125a; iii, 625b — II, 1151b, III, 646b
Aḥmadnagar (Uttar Pradesh) → Farrūkhābād
Aḥmadu Aḥmadu II i, 303b; ii, 941b; iii, 39a — I, 313a; II, 963b; III, 40b
Aḥmadu III i, 303b; ii, 941b — I, 313a; II, 963b
Ahmadū Bamba Mbacké ii, 63b, 568a — II, 64b, 582a
Aḥmadu Bello, Sir → Bello, Alhaji Aḥmadu
Aḥmadu Lobbo, Seku i, **303a;** ii, 251b, 252a, 941b; iii, 38b; v, 394b — I, **312b;** 259a, b, 963b; III, 40b; V, 395b
Aḥmadu Sheykhu → Aḥmad al-Shaykh
Aḥmadzay Khāns v, 102a — V, 104a
Aḥmar (colour/couleur) v, 700b, 706b — V, 705b, 711b
Aḥmar (Uḥaymir) i, 169b; iii, 1270a — I, 174a; III, 1303a
al-Aḥmar → Abu 'l-Ḥasan al-Aḥmar
Aḥmar, Banu 'l- → Naṣrid(e)s
Aḥmed → Aḥmad
Aḥmed Bahāʾī Abū Adîvar s, 41b — S, 42a
Aḥmed Khalīl → Fîndîkoghlu
al-Aḥnaf b. Ḳays i, **303b,** 343b, 1001a; ii, 415a, b; iii, 391b, 583a, 782a; iv, 14b; v, 56b — I, **313a,** 354a, 1031b; II, 426a, b; III, 404a, 603b, 805b; IV, 15b; V, 58a
Ahoms i, 719b — I, 741a
Aḥrām → Ḥaram
al-Aḥrām ii, 403b, 466b, 472a — II, 414b, 478a, 484a
Aḥrār, Khwādja ʿUbayd Allāh i, 147b, 148a, 849a; iv, 113a; v, 859a; s, **50b,** 121b — I, 152a, b, 872b; IV, 118a; V, 866a; S, **51a,** 121a
Aḥrār al-Dustūriyyīn s, 18a — S, 18b
Aḥrārs v, 803a — V, 809a
Aḥruf → Ḳirāʾa
Ahrun b Aʿyān al-Ḳass i, 213a; s, **52a** — I, 219b; S, **52b**
al-Aḥsāʾ → al-Ḥasā; Hufhūf
al-Aḥsāʾī, Shaykh Aḥmad i, **304b,** 596a; iv, 51a, 854b; s, 305a — I, **314a,** 615b; IV, 54a, 887b; S, 305a
Aḥsan → Djalāl al-Dīn
Aḥsan Mārahrawī ii, 84a — II, 86a
Aḥsanābād → Gulbarga
al-Ahtam iv, 832a, b — IV, 865a, b
Ahura Mazda iv, 11b-12a — IV, 12b-13a
Ahvāz → al-Ahwāz
Aḥwāḍ → Ḥawḍ
Aḥwāl → Ḥāl
al-Ahwānī, ʿAbd al-ʿAzīz → ʿAbd al-ʿAzīz al-Ahwānī
al-Aḥwaṣ al-Anṣārī i, 10b, **305a;** ii, 91a, 428b, 1029b; iii, 2b; iv, 1002a; s, 10a — I, 10b, **314b;** II, 92b, 439b, 1053a; III, 2b; IV, 1031b; S, 9b
al-Ahwāz i, 145a, 211b, **305b,** 695a, 1046b; ii, 383a; iii, 244b; iv, 6a, 7b, 675b; v, 80a, b, 81b, 867b; s, 35a, 118b, 119a — I, 149b, 218a, **315a,** 716b, 1078a; II,

393a; III, 251b; IV, 6b, 8b, 703a; V, 82b, 83b, 874a; S, 35b, 118a, b
- university/université ii, 426a — II, 437a
Aḥzāb → Ḥizb
Ai... → Ay...
ʿĀʾiḍ, Āl i, 555a, 709b — I, 572b, 731a
ʿĀʾiḍ b. Marʿī al-Mughaydī i, 709b — I, 731a
Aigle → ʿUḳāb
ʿĀʾila i, **305b,** 700a — I, **315b,** 721b
Āʾīn i, **306b** — I, **316a**
Āʾīn-nāma i, 306b; iii, 884a — I, 316a; III, 908a
Aïr i, **307a** — I, **316b**
ʿĀʾisha bint Abī Bakr i, 107a, 109b, 110a, **307b,** 383a, 1048a; ii, 414a, 415b, 416a, 845b, 1059a; iii, 64a, 65a, 242b, 359b; v, 616a; s, 133a, 230a, 311a — I, 110a, 112b, 113a, **317a,** 394a, 1080a; II, 425a, 426b, 427a, 865a, 1083b; III, 66b, 67b, 249b, 371a; V, 620a; S, 132b, 230a, 311a
ʿĀʾisha bint ʿImrān → ʿĀʾisha al-Mannūbiyya
ʿĀʾisha bint Muʿāwiya b. al-Mughīra i, 76a; s, 103b — I, 78b; S, 103a
ʿĀʾisha bint Ṭalḥa i, **308b** — I, **318a**
ʿĀʾisha bint Yūsuf al-Bāʿūnī i, 1109b — I, 1143a
ʿĀʾisha Ḳandīsha s, 52b, 351a — S, 53a, 351a
ʿĀʾisha Khatun (Sulṭān) iv, 230b — IV, 240b
ʿĀʾisha al-Mannūbiyya i, **308b** — I, **318a**
ʿAʾisha al-Taymūriyya i, 597b — I, 617a
Aïssaoua → ʿĪsāwa
Aït Aḥmad iv, 363a — IV, 379a
Ajarafe → al-Sharaf
Ajjer ii, 875a, 992a, 1022a — II, 895b, 1015a, 1046a
Aḳ Agha ii, 1088a, 1089b — II, 1113b, 1115a
Aḳ Deniz → Baḥr al-Rūm
Aḳ Ḥiṣār i, **309a**; v, 284b — I, **319a**; V, 283a
Aḳ Ḥisārī i, **309b** — I, **319b**
Aḳ Kirmān i, **310a,** 1119b, 1252b; iv, 239a — I, **320a,** 1153a, b, 1290b; IV, 249b
Aḳ Ḳoyunlū i, 148b, 190a, 240a, 292b, **311a,** 639b, 666b, 861a, 903b, 1067a, 1117a, 1128b, 1133b, 1234a, 1328a; ii, 20b, 174a, 344b, 348a, 614a, 711b; iii, 198b, 315b, 507a, 1100b, 1257a; iv, 34a-35a, 267b, 475a; v, 54a, 457a, 492a; s, 208a, 227b, 419b — I, 152b, 194b, 247b, 302a, **320b,** 660b, 687a, 885a, 930b, 1099a, 1150b, 1162b, 1167b, 1270b, 1368b; II, 21a, 179a, 354a, 357b, 629a, 730a; III, 203a, 325a, 524b, 1127b, 1289b; IV, 36b, 37a, 279b, 496a; V, 55b, 459b, 495a; S, 208a, 227b, 419b
Aḳ Masdjid i, **312a** — I, **322a**
Aḳ Sarāy (Anatolia(e)) i, **312a**; iv, 578b — I, **322a**; IV, 602a
Aḳ Sarāy i, **312b**; s, 59a, 146a — I, **322a**; S, 59b, 146a
Aḳ Shams al-Dīn i, 109a, **312b,** 777a, 869b; iii, 43b, 131a — I, 112a, **322a,** 800a, 893b; III, 45a, 133b
Aḳ Shehr i, **313a** — I, **322b**
Aḳ Ṣū (river/rivière) i, 184a, **313b,** 454b — I, 189b, **323a,** 467b
Aḳ Ṣu (town/ville) i, **313b** — I, **323a**
Aḳ Ṣu (village) i, **314a** — I, **323b**
Āḳ Sunḳur i, **314a,** 1117a — I, **324a,** 1150b
Āḳ Sunḳur, Ḳāsim al-Dawla i, **314a**; iii, 86b — I, **324**; III, 89a
Aḳ-Sunḳur al-ʿĀdilī al-Sāḳī iv, 484a — IV, 505a
Āḳ Sunḳur al-Ahmadīlī i, 300b — I, 310a
Āḳ Sunḳur al-Bursuḳī i, 300a, **314a,** 664a, 1337a; iii, 87a, 1118b; iv, 201a; v, 921b — I, 309b, **324a,** 684a, 1377a; III, 89a, 1146a; IV, 219b; V, 927a
Āḳā → Āghā
Āḳā Khān Kirmānī, Mirza ʿAbd al-Ḥusayn s, **53a,** 76b — S, **53b,** 76b
Āḳa Nadjafī, Muḥammad Taḳī Iṣfahānī v, 1087b; s, **54a** — V, 1085a; S, **54b**
Āḳā Ṣādiḳ, Ḥādjdjī s, 53a — S, 53b
al-ʿAḳaba i, 9a, 50b, **314b**; iii, 36a; v, 995b; s, 198b, 230a — I, 9a, 52a, **324b**; III, 37b; V, 991a; S, 198b, 230a
ʿAḳaba, Gulf of/Golfe de s, 8b — S, 8a
al-ʿAḳaba (Jordan(ie))i, 64b, **314b,** 534a, 548b, 783b — I, 66b, **324b,** 550a, 565b, 807a
ʿAḳabat al-Nisāʾ i, **315a** — I, **325a**
Āḳāʾī iv, 51b — IV, 54a
ʿAḳāʾid → ʿAḳīda
Akagündüz s, **55a** — S, **55b**
ʿAḳāl → ʿImāma
Akanṣūs i, **315a**; iii, 948b — I, **325a**; III, 973b
ʿAḳār s, **55a** — S, **55b**
ʿAkārib → ʿAḳrabī
ʿAḳarḳūf i, **315b** — I, **325b**
al-ʿAkawwak i, **315b**; iv, 718b; s, 17b — I, **325b**; IV, 747a; S, 17b
Akbar I (Mughal) i, 8b, 80b, 117a, b, 208b, 228b, 229a, 238a, 252b, 253a, **316a,** 417b, 710b, 733a, 856b, 864b, 1069a, 1135a, b, 1136a, b, 1194a, 1323a, 1324a, 1331a, 1347b; ii, 50a, 121a, 155b, 156b, 162a, 271b, 272a, 296a, 336b, 379b, 503b, 814a, 840a, 973b, 1048a, 1085a, 1122b, 1129a, 1131a, 1144a; iii, 201b, 245b, 318b, 348a, 423b, 430a, 449b, 482b; iv, 219a, 523b, 709a, 1104a, 1159b; v, 598a, b, 599b, 635a, 686a, 689b, 1135b, 1217a; s, 1b, 3a, b, 107b, 126b, 132a, 142b, 167a, 176b, 210b, 237b, 242b, 258a, 259b, 292a, 312a, 313a, 324b, 366b, 378a, 410b — I, 8b, 82b, 120b, 121a, 214b, 235b, 236a, 245a, 260b, 261a, **326a,** 429b, 731b, 755a, 880a, 888b, 1101a, 1169b, 1170a, b, 1229a, 1364b, 1371b, 1387b; II, 51a, 124a, 160b, 161a, 167a, 280a, 304a, 346a, 390a, 516a, 833b, 860a, 995b, 1072b, 1110b, 1149a, 1156a, 1158a, 1171a; III, 206b, 252b, 328a, 358b, 437a, 444a, 465a, 499b; IV, 228b, 546a, 737a, b, 1135b, 1191b; V, 602a, 603b, 639a, 691a, 694b, 1135b, 1207a; S, 1b, 2b, 107a, 125b, 131a, 142a, 167a, 177b, 210a, 237a, 242a, 257b, 259b, 291b, 312a, b, 324a, 366a, 378a, 411a
- literature/littérature i, 807b, 1123b; ii, 871a, 895a, 910a, 922a; iii, 457a — I, 831a, 1157b; II, 891a, 916a, 931b, 943b; III, 473a
Akbar II ii, 221b — II, 228b
Akbar b. Awrangzīb i, 769a; s, **55b** — I, 792a; S, **56a**
Akbar, Sayyid Ḥusayn Allāhābādī i, **317b**; iii, 358b — I, **327a**; III, 370a
Akbar Shāh iv, 1102b — IV, 1133b
Aḳbugha ʿAbd al-Wāḥid i, 814b — I, 838a
Aḳča i, 530b; s, 281a — I, 546b; S, 281a
Akçaabat s, 283b — S, 283a
Aḳčaḥisār i, 656a; iv, 139a — I, 676b; IV, 144b
Aḳče i, **317b**; ii, 118a, 119a, b; v, 974a — I, **327b**; II, 121a, b, 122a; V, 976a
Aḳče Kodja i, 468b — I, 482b
Akčuraoghlu Yūsuf iv, 791a — IV, 823a
ʿAḳd i, **318a**; ii, 303a, b; iii, 1091b — I, **328a**; II, 311b, 312a; III, 1118a
Akdariyya i, **320a** — I, **330a**
al-Akfānī i, 220b; iii, 1088a — I, 1257a; III, 1114b
Akh → ʿĀʾila, Ikhwān, Muʾakhāt
Ākhāl Tekke i, **320b** — I, **330b**
Akhalčikh → Akhiskha
Akhalkhalaki i, 643a; v, 495a, b — I, 664a; V, 498a, b
Akharnar → Nudjūm
Akh(w)āsh v, 153b — V, 155a
Akhaweyn i, 323a — I, 333a
Akhbār → Khabar, Taʾrīkh
Akhbār al-ʿAbbās iv, 446a — IV, 466a
Akhbār Madjmūʿa i, **320b,** 600b — I, **330b,** 620a
Akhbār al-Ṣīn wa ʾl-Hind i, 991b; ii, 583b; iv, 648a; s, **55b** — I, 1022a; II, 598a; IV, 674b; S, **56a**
al-Akhbārī, Muḥammad al-Nīsābūrī iv, 703b; s, 57a

— IV, 732a; S, 57b
Akhbāriyya iv, 50a, 51a; s, **56b**, 95b, 103b, 134b — IV, 53a, b; S, **57a**, 95a, 103a, 134a
Akhbāriyyūn i, 793b; iii, 588b — I, 817a; III, 608b
Akhḍar i, **321a**; v, 700b, 706a — I, **331a**; V, 705b, 711a
Akhḍar, Djabal i, 207b, 1048b, 1049a, b; v, 759b, 760a — I, 213b, 1080a, b, 1081a; V, 765b, 766a
al-Akhḍarī, Abū Zayd i, **321a**, 1019b — I, **331a**, 1051a
al-Akhfash i, **321a**; s, 22b, 361b — I, **331a**; S, 23a, 361a
al-Akhfash al-Akbar i, 321b — I, 331a
al-Akhfash al-Aṣghar i, 321b — I, 331b
al-Akhfash al-Awsaṭ i, 321b; iii, 758a; s, 317b — I, 331b; III, 781a; S, 317b
Akhī i, **321b**, 347b, 468a, 510a, 510b; ii, 966b, 967b; iv, 621a, b; v, 254a — I, **331b**, 358a, 482a, 526a; II, 988b, 989b; IV, 646a, b; V, 251b
Akhī Baba i, 323a, **323b**; ii, 968a; v, 173a — I, 333a, 333b; II, 990b; V, 170b
Akhī Čelebi iii, 340a — III, 350a
Akhī Ewrān i, 323a, **324a**, 510b; ii, 968a, 1138a; v, 173a — I, 333a, 333b, **334a**, 526a; II, 990a, 1165a; V, 170b
Akhī Faradj Zandjānī i, 322a; ii, 966b — I, 332a; II, 988b
Akhī Khazzām b. Ghālib iv, 215a, 216a — IV, 224b, 225b
Akhī Sirādj ii, 51b; v, 639a — II, 52b; V, 643a
Ākhir → al-Asmāʾ al-Ḥusnā
Akhīdjūk i, 323b, **325a**; ii, 401a, 967a — I, 333b, **335a**; III, 412a, 989a
Ākhir-i Čārshamba → Ṣafar
Ākhira i, **325a** — I, **335a**
Akhiskha i, 4a, **325a** — I, 4a, **335b**
Akhī-zāde i, 323a; v, 272b — I, 333a; V, 270a
Akhīzāde ʿAbdülḥalīm Efendi i, 732b; iv, 900b — I, 754b; IV, 933b
Akhlāḳ i, **325b** — I, **335b**
Akhlāṭ (Khilāṭ) i, **329a**, 627a, 639a, 799a, 1206b; ii, 393a; iv, 354b, 817b; v, 455a — I, **339a**, 647b, 659b, 822b, 1242b; II, 403b; IV, 370a, 850b; V, 457b
Akhmīm i, **330a**, 1038b — I, **340a**, 1070b
al-Akhnas b. Sharīḳ i, 891a — I, 918a
Akhnif ii, 1116a — II, 1142a
Akhnūkh → Idrīs
al-Akhras i, **330a** — I, **340b**
Akhsatān b. Manučihr b. Afridūn iv, 348b, 915a — IV, 363a, 948a
al-Akhshabān i, 136a — I, 140a
Akhshām → Ṣalāt
Akhsīkath i, **330b**; ii, 791a; s, 406b — I, **340b**; II, 810a; S, 406b
Akhsitān b. Gagik v, 489a, b — V, 492a, b
al-Akhṭal i, **331a**, 586a, 1241a; ii, 480a, 789a; iii, 354a; iv, 315b, 744b, 819a, 1002b, 1008b; s, 10a, 394a, b — I, **341a**, 605a, 1278b; II, 492a, 807b; III, 365a; IV, 329b, 774b, 852a, 1035a, 1041a; S, 9b, 394b, 395a
Akhtarī i, **331b**; iv, 365a — I, **342a**; IV, 381a
Akhū Muḥsin i, 95b, 96a, 403a — I, 98b, 414b
Ākhūnd i, **331b** — I, **342a**
Akhund Bābā ii, 316b — II, 326a
Akhund Darwīza → Darwīza
Ākhūnd-zāda, Fatḥ ʿAlī i, **331b**; ii, 217a; iii, 358a; iv, 73b; v, 919b; s, 53b, 76b, 109a, 290b — I, **342a**; II, 223b; III, 369b; IV, 77b; V, 925a; S, 54a, 76b, 108a, 290a
Akhūr → Amīr Ākhūr
Akhūremīrizāde Ḥāshimī iii, 153b — III, 157a
Akhwakh i, 504a; iv, 631a — I, 519b; IV, 656a
Akhyār iv, 259b — IV, 271a
ʿAḳīda i, 121a, 195a, 310a, **332b**; iv, 279b — I, 124b, 201a, 319b, **342b**; IV, 291b
ʿĀkif Pasha → Muḥammad ʿĀkif Pasha
ʿAḳīḳ i, **336a** — I, **346b**
al-ʿAḳīḳ i, **336b**; iii, 121b; s, 199b — I, **347a**; III, 124b; S, 199b
ʿAḳīḳ al-Yamāma (Tamra) i, 336b — I, 347b
ʿAḳīḳ Dhāt ʿIrḳ i, 336b — I, 347a
ʿAḳīḳa i, **337a**; iv, 488a — I, **347b**; IV, 509a
ʿĀḳil i, 993b; ii, 633a — I, 1024a; II, 649a
ʿAḳīl b. Abī Ṭālib i, **337b** — I, **348a**
ʿAḳīl b. Djābir b. ʿAbd Allāh s, 231a — S, 230b
ʿAḳīl Khān Rāzī, Mīr Muḥammad s, 57b — S, 58a
Āḳil al-Murār → Ḥudjr Āḳil al-Murār
ʿĀḳila i, **337b**; ii, 342a; iv, 334b — I, **348b**; II, 352a; IV, 349a
Aḳindjī i, **340a**, 1302b; ii, 611b — I, **350b**, 1342b; II, 626b
Akīra iii, 215b — III, 222a
Aḳiṭ ii, 1057b — II, 1082a
ʿAkk i, **340b** — I, **351a**
ʿAkkā i, 216a, **341a**, 946b, 1078a, b; ii, 63b, 129b; iii, 188a, 325a, b, 473a, 474b; iv, 485b, 965a; v, 594a, 595a; s, 20b, 120b, 121a, 162b, 205a, b, 268a, b — I, 222b, **351b**, 976a, 1110b; II, 65a, 133a; III, 192b, 335a, b, 489b, 491a; IV, 506a, 997a; V, 598a, 598b; S, 21a, 120a, b, 162b, 205a, b, 268a
al-ʿAḳḳad, ʿAbbās Maḥmūd i, 598a; iii, 1207b; iv, 85b, 159b; v, 189a; s, **57b** — I, 617b; III, 1238a; IV, 89b, 166b; V, 186b; S, **58a**
Akkār s, **58b** — S, **59a**
ʿAkkāsbāshī s, 109b — S, 109a
Akkerman → Aḳ Kirmān
ʿAḳl i, **341b**, 1116a; iv, 157a, 487a, b — I, **352a**, 1149b; IV, 163b, 508a
al-ʿAḳl al-awwal i, 89b — I, 92a
ʿAḳl faʿʿāl i, 415a; ii, 493b — I, 427a; II, 506a
Akli i, 36b — I, 37b
ʿAḳliyyāt i, **342b**; iv, 469b — I, **353a**; IV, 490a
Aklub iv, 1106a — IV, 1137b
Akmal al-Dīn al-Bābartī i, 299b — I, 309a
Aḳmesdjid iv, 500a — IV, 521b, 522a
Aḳnūm-i ʿadjam iv, 526a — IV, 548b
al-Aḳraʿ b. Ḥābis i, **343a**, 1247b; ii, 608b; iii, 169a; v, 109a — I, **353b**, 1285b; II, 623b; III, 172b; V, 111b
ʿAḳrab i, **343b** — I, **354a**
ʿAḳrabāʾ i, **344a**, 628b; ii, 569a — I, **354b**, 649b; II, 583b
Aḳrābādhīn i, **344a** — I, **354b**
ʿAḳrabī i, **345a** — I, **355b**
al-Akrād iii, 1096b — III, 1123b
Akritai ii, 1044a — II, 1068a
ʿAks → Balāgha
al-Aḳṣā → Masdjid al-Aḳṣā
Aḳsarā → Aḳ Sarāy
al-Aḳsarāʾī, ʿĪsā b. Ismāʿīl iii, 181a — III, 185b
Aḳsarayī → Djamāl a-Dīn
al-Aḳsarāyī, Karīm al-Dīn s, **59a** — S, **59b**
Aḳshehirli → Ḥasan Fehmī
Akstafa s, 146a — S, 146a
Aḳsu s, 98a — S, 97b
Aksūm ii, 895b; iii, 9a, b, 10a — II, 916b; III, 9b, 10a, b
Aḳṭāʿ v, 152a — V, 154a
al-Aḳṭaʿ → Abū Yaʿḳūb; ʿAmr b. ʿUbayd Allāh
Aḳtaw ii, 612b — II, 627b
Aḳṭāy i, 944b — I, 973b
Aktham b. Ṣayfī i, **345a** — I, **355b**
al-ʿAḳūla iv, 556a — IV, 580a
Aḳūnīṭun s, **59b** — S, **59b**
Aḳūr → Athūr
Akūsha ii, 141b, 142a — II, 145b, 146a
al-Aḳwās → Arkūsh
Al- → Taʿrīf
Āl (clan) i, 258b, **345b**, 700b — I, 266b, **356a**, 721b

Āl, followed by a family name, see under that name/suivi d'un nom de famille, voir sous le nom de cette famille
Āl (demon/démon) i, **345b** — I, **356a**
Āl → Sarāb
Āl-i Aḥmad, Sayyid Djalāl iv, 73b; v, 200b; s, **60a**, 135b — IV, 77a; V, 197b; S, **60b**, 135a
Āla i, **345b** — I, **356a**
al-ʿAlā, Djabal iii, 208b — III, 214a
al-ʿAlāʾ b. al-Ḥaḍramī i, 942a; ii, 811b; iv, 220a, 764a, 832b — I, 971a; II, 831a; IV, 229b, 794b, 865b
al-ʿAlāʾ b. Mughīth al-Djudhāmī i, 82a, 862a; iv, 665b — I, 84b, 886a; IV, 692b
Ala Dagh i, **346a** — I, **356b**
ʿAlāʾ al-Dawla (Kākūyid(e)) → ʿAlāʾ al-Dawla Muḥammad b. Dushmanziyār
ʿAlāʾ al-Dawla (Timūrid(e)) i, 147b — I, 152a
ʿAlāʾ al-Dawla b. Sulaymān Beg i, 324a; ii, 240a; iv, 553a — I, 334a; II, 246b; IV, 576b
ʿAlāʾ al-Dawla ʿAlī b. Farāmurz → ʿAlī b. Farāmurz
ʿAlāʾ al-Dawla Ata-Khān iv, 466b — IV, 487a
ʿAlāʾ al-Dawla Farāmarz b. ʿAlī i, 113a — I, 116a
ʿAlāʾ al-Dawla Ḥasan Bāwandī v, 662a — V, 667b
ʿAlāʾ al-Dawla Muḥammad b. Dushmanziyār i, 132a, 512b; iii, 331a, 942b; iv, 100b, 465a, b, 466b, 1103b — I, 136a, 528a; III, 341a, 967a; IV, 105a, 465b, 486a, 487a, 1134b
ʿAlāʾ al-Dawla al-Simnānī i, 88b, **346b**, 702b; v, 301a; s, 122a — I, 91a, **357a**, 723b; V, 300b; S, 121b
ʿAlāʾ al-Dīn → Djahān-sūz; Djuwaynī; Ghūrid(e)s; Ḳayḳubād I; Khwārizmshāhs; Saldjūḳs
ʿAlāʾ al-Dīn Aḥmad Bahmanī → Aḥmad Shāh II
ʿAlāʾ al-Dīn ʿĀlam → ʿĀlam Shāh
ʿAlāʾ al-Dīn ʿAlī, al Manṣūr ii, 159a — II, 164a
ʿAlāʾ al-Dīn ʿAlī b. Faḍl Allāh ii, 732b; iii, 758b — II, 751a; III, 781b
ʿAlāʾ al- Dīn ʿAlī b. Yūsuf Bālī ii, 879b — II, 899b
ʿAlāʾ al-Dīn ʿAlī Eretna i, 432a; ii, 706a — I, 444a; II, 724a
ʿAlāʾ al-Dīn ʿAlī Karamanoghlu i, 394a, 1118a; iv, 622b, 623a; v, 680a — I, 405b, 1151b; IV, 647b, 648a; V, 685b
ʿAlāʾ al-Dīn Aydughdī al-Ruknī iv, 960a — IV, 992a
ʿAlāʾ al-Dīn Beg i, **348a** — I, **358b**
ʿAlāʾ al-Dīn Fīrūz → Fīrūz Shāh (Bengal(e))
ʿAlāʾ al-Dīn Ḥasan Bahman Shāh i, 923b, 924b, 1200a; ii, 51b, 99b, 180a, 270a, 1124b — I, 951b, 952a, 1235a; II, 52b, 101b, 185b, 278a, 1151a
ʿAlāʾ al-Dīn Ḥusayn → Djahān-Sūz; Ḥusayn Shāh
ʿAlāʾ al-Dīn ʿImād Shāh i, 914b; iii, 425a, 1159b, 1160a — I, 942a; III, 439a, 1188a, b
ʿAlāʾ al-Din Ḳara Sonḳor i, 300b; iii, 1112a — I, 310a; III, 1139a
ʿAlāʾ (Ḍiyāʾ) al-Dīn Muḥammad ii, 1101b, 1103a — II, 1127b, 1129a
ʿAlāʾ al-Dīn Muḥammad → Muḥammad III (Ismāʿīlī)
ʿAlāʾ al-Dīn Muḥammad Khaldjī → Khaldjīs; Muḥammad Shāh I (Dihlī)
ʿAlā al-Dīn Muḥammad Khwārizmshāh i, 4a, 1001b, 1010a, 1311a; ii, 43a, 329b, 393b, 571a, 606a, 752a, 894a, 1101b; iii, 114a, 195b, 196b, 197a, 198a; iv, 502b, 583a, 1067b; v, 662b; s, 246a — I, 4a, 1032a, 1041a, 1351b; II, 43b, 403a, 404a, 585b, 621a, 770a, 914b, 1127b; III, 116b, 200b, 201b, 203a; IV, 524b, 606b, 1099b; V, 667b; S, 246a
ʿAlāʾ al-Dīn Pasha → ʿAlāʾ al-Dīn Beg
ʿAlāʾ al-Dīn Riʿāyat Shāh al-Ḳahhār i, 743a; iii, 1220a — I, 765b; III, 1250b
ʿAlāʾ al-Dīn (Sihālī) i, 936b; s, 292a — I, 965b; S, 291a
ʿAlāʾ al-Dīn Tekish → Tekesh
Ala Shehir i, **346a** — I, **356b**
Ālā Singh i, 1022b, 1194b; ii, 488b; iii, 485a — I, 1054a, 1229b; II, 501a; III, 502b
ʿAlā-yi Tabrīzī, ʿAbd Allāh iv, 1045b, 1047b — IV, 1077a, 1079a
Ālaba wa 'l-ḳilāʿ i, **348b** — I, **359a**
Alaca ii, 62b — II, 64a
Alačik iv, 1150b — IV, 1182b
Aladdin i, 359a, b — I, 370a
Aladja i, **348b** — I, **359a**
Aladja Dagh i, **348b** — I, **359a**
Aladja Ḥiṣār i, **348b** — I, **359a**
Alaham, Banū s, 145a — S, 144b
Alahort → al-Ḥurr b. ʿAbd al-Raḥmān al-Thaḳafī
al-ʿAlāʾī s, 251b — S, 251b
ʿAlāʾī, shaykh ii, 500a; iii, 492b — II, 512b; III, 509b
Alain → Alān
ʿAlāʾiyya → Alanya
ʿAlāḳa → Nisba
ʿAlam i, **349a;** iii, 197a — I, **359b;** III, 201b
ʿĀlam i, **349b** — I, **360a**
ʿĀlam, poet/poète iii, 457b — III, 473b
ʿAlam, Queen/la reine i, 552b; v, 1244a — I, 570a; V, 1235a
ʿAlam al-Dīn, Āl ii, 749b, 751a; iv, 834b— II, 768a, 769b; Iv, 867a, b
ʿAlam al-Dīn Ḳayṣar i, 780b; iii, 967a — I, 804a; III, 991b
ʿAlam al-Dīn al-Sakhāwī i, 150a — I, 154b
ʿAlam al-Dīn Sandjar al-Djāwulī iv, 960a; v, 628a — IV, 992b; V, 632a
ʿĀlam al-djabarūt i, 89b, 350b — I, 92a, 361b
ʿĀlam al-ghayb i, 351a — I, 361b
ʿAlam Khān → ʿAyn al-Mulk Multānī
ʿAlam Khān Fārūkī (I) → ʿĀdil Khān III
ʿĀlam Khān Fārūkī (II) ii, 814b — II, 834a
ʿĀlam Khān Lodī i, 848a; ii, 271a, 1129a; iii, 420b — I, 871b; II, 279a, 1155b; III, 434a
ʿĀlam al-ḳudra i, 89b — I, 92a
ʿĀlam al-malakūt i, 350b — I, 361b
ʿĀlam al-mithal i, 350b — I, 361b
ʿĀlam al-mulk i, 351a — I, 361b
ʿĀlam Shāh i, 855b, 856a; ii, 270b; iii, 418a; v, 783b — I, 879b, 880a; II, 279a; III, 431b; V, 789b
ʿĀlam al-shahāda i, 89b — I, 92a
al-Aʿlam al-Shantamarī → al-Shantamarī
ʿAlāma i, **352a;** ii, 302a, 303a, 307b, 331b — I, **362b;** II, 310b, 311a, 316b, 341a
Alamak → Nudjūm
Alamayn iii, 36a; s, 300b — III, 37b; S, 300b
Alambic → al-Anbīḳ
ʿAlamdār i, 1135a — I, 1169a
ʿĀlamgīr I → Awrangzīb
ʿĀlamgīr II iii, 1158b — III, 1187a
al-ʿAlamī i, **352a** — I, **363a**
al-ʿAlamī, ʿAbd al-Ḳādir → Ḳaddūr al-ʿAlamī
al-ʿAlamī, Muḥammad b. al-Ṭayyib i, **352b** — I, **363a**
ʿĀlamiyān, Mīrzā iv, 1039b, 1044b — IV, 1071b, 1076a
Alamūt i, **352b,** 688b, 1359b; ii, 191a, 192a, 194a; iii, 253b, 254a, 501b; iv, 199b, 201b, 202a, 859b; v, 656b; s, 356b — I, **363b,** 709a, 1399b; II, 197a, 198a, 200a; III, 261a, 519a; IV, 208b, 210b, 211a, 892b; V, 660b; S, 356b
Alān i, **354a,** 837a; ii, 86a; iv, 344a, 345a, b, 349a, b; v, 288a — I, **365a,** 860; II, 87b; IV, 358b, 359b, 360a, 363b, 364b; V, 286b
Alangu, Tahir s, **61b** — S, **61b**
Alanya i, **354b,** 476b; iv, 817b — I, **365b,** 490b; IV, 850b
Alarcos → al-Arak
Alas i, 740a — I, 762a
Alashehir ii, 989b; iii, 211b — II, 1012a; III, 217b

Alasonia s, 55a — S, 55b
Ālāt → Āla
Alava → Ālaba wa 'l-ḳilā'
'Alawī ('Adan) i, **355a** — I, **366a**
'Alawī, Bā → Bā 'Alawī
'Alawī, Buzurg iv, 73a; v, 199b, 200a — IV, 77a; V, 197a, b
'Alawids, Alawites → 'Alawīs; Nuṣayrīs
'Alawīs, 'Alawiyya i, 47a, 315b, **355a,** 689a, 1058a, 1149a; ii, 134a, 146a, 308a, 823a; iii, 256b, 536a, 973a; iv, 634a; v, 592a, 656a; s, 48a, 336b, 339a — I, 48b, 325a, **366a,** 710a, 1090a, 1183a; II, 137b, 150a, 316b, 842b; III, 263b, 554b, 997b; IV, 660a; V, 595b, 660a; S, 48b, 336a, 338b
'Alawiyya (Mamlūks) iii, 992a — III, 1017a
Alay i, **358a** — I, **369a**
'Alāyā → 'Alanya
al-'Alāyilī, 'Abd Allāh iv, 783a — IV, 814b
Alay-beyi-zāde → Muḥammad Emīn b. Ḥadjdji Meḥmed
Albacete → al-Basīṭ
Albaicin → Gharnāṭa
Albania(e) → Arnawutluḳ
Albanian/Albanais i, 650a; v, 276b — I, 670a; V, 274b
Albarracin → Razīn, Banū
Albarrana i, 1320b — I, 1360b
Albatenius, Albategni → al-Battānī
Albistān → Elbistan
Alboacen/Albohazen → (Abu 'l-Ḥasan) Ibn Abī 'l-Ridjāl al-Ḳayrawānī
Albohali → al-Khayyāt, Abū 'Alī
Albouzème → al-Ḥusayma
Albū Muḥammad → Bū Muḥammad, Āl
Albubather → Ibn al-Khaṣīb, Abū Bakr
Albucasis → al-Zahrāwī
Albufera i, 985b, 1288a — I, 1016a, 1327b
Albumasar → Abū Ma'shar al-Balkhī
Albuquerque, Alfonso de i, 181b, 553b, 1038b; iii, 585a; s, 234b — I, 186b, 571a, 1070a; III, 605a; S, 234a
Alburz i, **358b**; iv, 1a, 4b-5a, 6b, 9b, 400b; v, 657b; s, 309a — I, **369a**; IV, 1a, 5a-b, 7a, 10b, 418a; V, 663a; S, 308b
Alcabitius → al-Ḳabīṣī, 'Abd al-'Azīz Abu 'l-Ṣaḳr
Alcacer do Sal → Ḳaṣr Abī Dānis
Alcala → al-Ḳal'a
Alcantara → al-Ḳanṭara
Alcaraz s, 143a — S, 143a
Alcazar i, **358b** — I, **369b**
Alcazarquivir → al-Ḳaṣr al-Kabīr
Alchemy/Alchimie → al-Kīmiyā'
Alcira → Djazīrat Shuḳr
Alcohol/Alcool → al-Kuḥl
Alcolea → al-Ḳulay'a
Alcoran → al-Ḳur'ān
Alcove → al-Kubba
Aldamov → 'Alibek Aldamov
Aldebaran → Nudjūm
Aledo → Alīṭ
Alekper → 'Alī Akbar
Alembic → al-Anbīḳ
'Alemdār Muṣṭafā Pasha v, 1083a, 1084a — V, 1080b, 1081b
Aleppo/Alep → Ḥalab
Alessio → Lesh
Ālev yazîsî iv, 1126b — IV, 1158a
Alexander of Aphrodisias/Alexandre d'Aphrodise → al-Iskandar al-Afrūdīsī
Alexander the Great/Alexandre le Grand → al-Iskandar
Alexander of Damascus/Alexandre de Damas → al-Iskandar al-Dimashḳī
Alexander romance → Iskandar-nāma
Alexandretta/Alexandrette → Hatay; Iskandarūn
Alexandria/Alexandrie → al-Iskandariyya
Alexandropolis → Dede Aghač
Alf layla wa-layla i, 144b, **358b,** 359a, 574b, 595b, 1127a; ii, 356b, 547b; iii, 81a, 281b, 371a, 1050a; v, 951a — I, 148b, **369b,** 370a, 593a, 615a, 1161a; II, 366a, 561a; III, 83b, 290a, 383a, 1076b; V, 955a
Alfa → Ḥalfā'
Alfarabius → al-Fārābī
Alfard → Nudjūm
Alfraganus → al-Farghānī
Alfonso → Alfūnsho
Alfūnsho i, **364b** — I, **375b**
Alfūnsho (the Warrior/le Batailleur); i, 390a, 495b, 1150a; ii, 526b, 1007a, 1013a; iii, 543a, 771a; s, 81a, 397b — I, 401a, 510a, 1184b; II, 539b, 1030b, 1037a; III, 561b, 794b; S, 80b, 398a
Alfūnsho III i, 85b, 1338b; ii, 1009a, b; iii, 842a; v, 498b, 1107b; s, 92a — I, 88a, 1378b; II, 1032b, 1033a; III, 865b; V, 501b, 1103b; S, 92a
Alfūnsho V iv, 139b, 730a — IV, 145b, 759a
Alfūnsho VI i, 6b, 7a, 43b, 242b, 390a, 495a; ii, 243b, 1013a; iii, 706a; v, 392b, 498b, 1107b — I, 6b, 7a, 45a, 250a, 401a, 510a; II, 250b, 1036b; III, 728a; V, 393a, 501b, 1103b
Alfūnsho VII i, 1083a, 1150a; ii, 1009b, 1013b; iii, 771b; v, 498b — I, 1115b, 1184b; II, 1033a, 1037b; III, 794b; V, 501b
Alfūnsho VIII i, 161b, 165b, 495b, 605b, 1150a; iii, 1055a; iv, 482b; v, 392b — I, 166a, 170b, 510b, 625a, 1184b; III, 1081a; IV, 503b; V, 393a
Alfūnsho XI ii, 525a — II, 538b
Algarve → Gharb al-Andalus
Algazel → al-Ghazālī
Algebra/Algèbre → al-Djabr wa 'l-Muḳābala
Algeciras → al-Djazīra al-Khaḍrā'
Algedi → Nudjūm
Alger → al-Djazā'ir
Algeria i, **364b,** 661a, 1321a; ii, 172b; iii, 297b, 385a; iv, 1155b; v, 696a; s, 215b
- demography s 215b
- geography i, 364b-366b
- history i, 37a, 85a, 356a, 366b-370b; iii, 524b, 561b, 562b, 564a, 727b, 1003b; iv, 362b
- institutions i, 373a, 374a, 413a, 978a; ii, 425b; iii, 524b, 727b, 1003b; v, 916a
- languages, literature i, 374a-379b; ii, 469a; iii, 727b
- population i, 171a, 370b-373a, 1177a, b; v, 1164b
Algérie I, **375b,** 682a, 1361b; II, 178a; III, 307a, 397b; IV, 1187b; V, 701a; S, 215a
- démographie S, 215a
- géographie I, 375b-377b
- histoire I, 37b, 87a, 367a, 377b-384a; III, 542b, 581a, 582a, 583b, 750a, 1028b; IV, 378b
- institutions I, 384a, 384b, 423b, 1008b; II, 436a; III, 542b, 750a, 1028b; V, 921b
- langues, littérature I, 384b-390b; II, 481a; III, 750a
- population I, 176a, 1212a, b; V, 1154a
Algeziras → al-Djazīra al-Khaḍrā'
Algiers → al-Djazā'ir
Algol → Nudjūm
Algomaiza → Nudjūm
Algorithmus i, **379b**; iv, 1070b — I, **390b**; IV, 1102a
Alhabor → Nudjūm
Alhagiag bin Thalmus → Ibn Ṭumlūs
Alhaiot → Nudjūm
Alhama → al-Ḥamma
Alhambra → Gharnāṭa
Alhazen → Ibn al-Haytham
Alhichante i, 405a — I, 416b

Alhidade → Asṭurlāb
Alhucemas → al-Khuzāmā
ʿAlī I b. Muḥammad (Idrīsid(e)) iii, 1035b; s, 103a — III, 1061b; S, 102b
ʿAlī II b. ʿUmar (Idrīsid(e)) iii, 1035b, 1036a; s, 103a — III, 1061b; S, 102b
Alī, Mai of/de Bornū i, 1259b — I, 1298a
ʿAlī, Muṣṭafā b. Aḥmad Čelebī i, **380a;** ii, 895a; iii, 1200b; iv, 704a; s, 83a — I, **391a;** II, 916a; III, 1230b; IV, 732b; S, 83a
ʿAlī b. al-ʿAbbās al-Madjūsī i, **381a;** ii, 60a, 481b; iv, 330a; s, 52b, 271b — I, **391b;** II, 61a, 494a; IV, 344a; S, 53a, 271b
ʿAlī b. ʿAbd Allāh Sharīf iii, 605b — III, 626a
ʿAlī b. ʿAbd Allāh b. al-ʿAbbās i, **381a;** iii, 574a — I, **392a;** III, 594a
ʿAlī b. ʿAbd Allāh (dāʿī) s, 407a — S, 407a
ʿAlī b. ʿAbd Allāh al-Ṭūsī i, 718b; s, 394b — I, 740a; S, 395a
ʿAlī b. ʿAbd al-ʿAzīz Umm al-Walad-zāde iv, 471b — IV, 492b
ʿAlī b. ʿAbd al-Muʾmin i, 160b — I, 165a
ʿAlī b. ʿAbd al-Raḥmān iii, 81a — III, 83a
ʿAlī b. ʿAbd al-Raḥmān b. Hudhayl al-Andalusī i, 1149b — I, 1184a
ʿAlī b. ʿAbd al-Raḥmān al-Djamal ii, 160a — II, 165a
ʿAlī b. Abī Bakr i, 593b — I, 613a
ʿAlī b. Abi ʾl-Faradj al-Baṣrī iii, 111b — III, 113b
ʿAlī b. Abi ʾl-Gharāt i, 1214b — I, 1251a
ʿAlī b. Abī Ḥafs Iṣfahānī s, 35a — S, 35a
ʿAlī b. Abi ʾl-Ḥusayn al-Kalbī iv, 496b — IV, 517b
ʿAlī b. Abī Ṭālib i, 44a, 152b, 181b, 212b, 260b, 337b, **381b,** 400b, 549b, 765a; ii, 218a, 414a, 625b, 725a, 726a, 842b, 846a, 848a, 993a; iii, 33a, 241a, 583b, 887a, 1254b, 1265a; iv, 277b, 836b, 1035a, 1074b, 1140a; v, 406b, 499a, 777a, 996b; s, 89b, 92b, 94a, 119a, 130a, 157a, 270a, 351b, 357b, 358b, 401a — I, 45b, 157a, 186b, 218b, 268b, 348a, **392a,** 412a, 567a, 787b; II, 225a, 425a, 641a, 743b, 744b, 862a, 866a, 868a, 1016a; III, 35a, 248a, 603b, 911a, 1287a, 1298a; IV, 289b, 869b, 1067a, 1106a, 1171b; V, 408a, 502a, 783a, 992a; S, 89b, 92b, 118b, 129a, 157a, 269b, 351b, 357b, 358b, 401b
- antagonist(e)s i, 52a, 54a, 108a, 308a, 1343b; iii, 235a, 583a, 887a — I, 53b, 56a, 111b, 317b, 1384a; III, 242a, 603b, 911a
- doctrines i, 263a, 275b; ii, 889a, 961a, 1098b; iii, 1163b — I, 271a, 284b; II, 909b, 983b, 1124b; III, 1192a
- supporters/partisans i, 51a, 107a, 109a, 117a, 195a, 431b, 704a; ii, 480b; iii, 123b, 235a, 583a — I, 52b, 110a, 111b, 120a, 200b, 443b, 725b; II, 492b; III, 126a, 242a, 603b
ʿAlī b. Abī Zayd ii, 490a — II, 502b
ʿAlī b. Aḍḥā al-Hamdānī ii, 1013b; iii, 850a, b — II, 1037a; III, 874a
ʿAlī b. Afrāsiyāb → ʿAlī Pasha
ʿAlī b. Aḥmad b. Abī Saʿīd i, 1019a — I, 1050b
ʿAlī b. Aḥmad al-Ḍayf ii, 484a — II, 496a
ʿAlī b. Aḥmad al-Ḥabbāl ii, 137a — II, 140b
ʿAlī b. ʿAsākir → Ibn ʿAsākir
ʿAlī b. Burhān Niẓām Shāh iii, 1161a — III, 1189b
ʿAlī b. Buwayh → ʿImād al-Dawla ʿAlī
ʿAlī b. Dāʾūd i, 103b — I, 106b
ʿAlī b. Djabala → al-ʿAkawwak
ʿAlī b. Djahm i, 153b, 154a, **386a**; iv, 491a — I, 157b, 158b, **397b**; IV, 512a
ʿAlī b. Dūstī i, 347b — I, 358a
ʿAlī b. al-Faḍl al-Djayshānī i, 551b; iv, 198a, b, 661a; s, 335a — I, 569a; IV, 206b, 207a, 687b; S, 334b
ʿAlī b. Farāmurz iv, 466a, b — IV, 487a, b
ʿAlī b. al-Furāt → Ibn al-Furāt, ʿAlī
ʿAlī b. Ghadhāhum iv, 338b, 403b — IV, 352b, 421a
ʿAlī b. Ghāniya i, 165a, 1150a; ii, 463b, 1007a; iv, 337b, 614a, b — I, 170a, 1184b; II, 475a, 1030b; IV, 352a, 639a
ʿAlī b. al-Ḥaddād iv, 381a — IV, 397b
ʿAlī b. Ḥamdūn iv, 459a — IV, 479b
ʿAlī b. Ḥamdush s, 53a — S, 53b
ʿAlī b. Hammūd iii, 147a, 743a, 786a — III, 150a, 766a, 809b
ʿAlī b. Ḥamūd i, 1283a — I, 1321b
ʿAlī b. Ḥamza al-Iṣfahānī i, 154b; iii, 156b — I, 158b; III, 160a
ʿAlī b. Ḥanẓala b. Abī Sālim s, **61b** — S, **62a**
ʿAlī b. al-Ḥasan b. al-Muslima → Ibn al-Muslima
ʿAlī b. Ḥasan Bughra Khān s, 176b — S, 177b
ʿAlī b. al-Ḥasan al-Kalbī iv, 496b — IV, 518a
ʿAlī b. al-Ḥasan al-Mubārak → Abu ʾl-Ḥasan al-Aḥmar
ʿAlī b. Ḥātim → al-Ḥāmidī, ʿAlī b. Ḥātim
ʿAlī b. Haydar iii, 316a; iv, 34b — III, 325b; IV, 36b
ʿAlī b. Ḥazm → Ibn Ḥazm, ʿAlī
ʿAlī b. Ḥirzihim → Ibn Ḥirzihim, ʿAlī
ʿAli b. Hishām i, 400a; s, 116b, 252b — I, 411b; S, 116a, 252b
ʿAlī b. Hudhayfa b. Māniʿ iv, 87b — IV, 92a
ʿAlī b. Ḥusayn → Sīdī Raʾīs
ʿAlī b. al-Ḥusayn (Kilwa) v, 106b, 1157b — V, 108b, 1147b
ʿAlī b. Ḥusayn Zayn al-ʿĀbidīn → Zayn al-ʿĀbidīn
ʿAlī b. al-Ḥusayn b. ʿAbd al-ʿAlī al-Karakī → al-Muḥakkiḳ al-Thānī
ʿAlī b. al-Ḥusayn b. ʿAlī (Hāshimid(e)) ii, 572b; iii, 263b, 606b, 1067a — II, 587a; III, 271b, 627a, 1093b
ʿAlī b. al-Ḥusayn b. ʿAlī b. Abī Ṭālib iii, 227b, 610a, b — III, 234a, 630b, 631b
ʿAlī b. Ḥusayn b. Ḥusayn b. ʿAlī al-Ḳurashī s, **62a** — S, **62b**
ʿAlī b. Ḥusayn b. Idrīs (dāʿī muṭlaḳ) s, 358b — S, 358b
ʿAlī b. Ḥusayn al-Ḳurashī s, 62a — S, 62b
ʿAlī b. al-Ikhshid iv, 418a — IV, 436b
ʿAlī b. ʿĪsā b. al-Djarrāḥ i, **386b,** 1046b, 1223b; ii, 79b, 195a, 197b, 325a, b, 383a, 388b, 453a, 1080b; iii, 100b, 133a, 153a, 619b, 692a, 739a, 886b, 949a; v, 319b, 953a; s, 199a, 400b, 402a — I, **397b,** 1078a, 1259b; II, 81a, 201b, 204a, 334b, 335a, 393a, 399a, 464b, 1105b; III, 103a, 136a, 156b, 640b, 714a, 761b, 910b, 974a; V, 319a, 957a; S, 199a, 401a, 402b
ʿAlī b. ʿĪsā b. Māhān → Ibn Māhān
ʿAlī b. ʿĪsā b. Maymūn iv, 383b — IV, 400b
ʿAlī b. ʿĪsā al-Kaḥḥāl i, **388a,** 449a, 785b — I, **399a,** 461b, 808b
ʿAlī b. al-Ḳāḍī al-Nuʿmān i, 816a — I, 839a
ʿAlī b. Ḳara ʿUthmān i, 311b, 312a — I, 321b
ʿAlī b. al-Karmānī iii, 988b — III, 1013a
ʿAlī b. Khalīl iv, 221b — IV, 231a
ʿAlī b. Khashram i, 1244a — I, 1282a
ʿAlī b. Khurshīd i, 688a — I, 709a
ʿAlī b. Mahdī → Mahdid(e)s
ʿAlī b. Masʿūd I ii, 1051b — II, 1076a
ʿAlī b. Maʿṣūm → ʿAlī Khān
ʿAlī b. Maymūn i, **388b**; v, 625a — I, **399b**; V, 629a
ʿAlī b. Mazyad i, 684a; s, 119a — I, 704b; S, 118b
ʿAlī b. Mudjāhid al-ʿĀmirī i, 1055a; ii, 112a; iii, 542b, 773a — I, 1086b; II, 114b; III, 561a, 796b
ʿAlī b. Mudjaththil al-Mughaydī i, 709b — I, 731a
ʿAlī b. Muḥammad → Ṣulayḥid(e)s
ʿAlī II b. Muḥammad → ʿAlī ʿĀdil-Shāh II
ʿAlī b. Muḥammad b. Djaʿfar al-Ḳarashī s, **62a** — S, **62a**
ʿAlī b. Muḥammad b. Idrīs → ʿAlī I
ʿAlī b. Muḥammad b. Tawba i, 130b — I, 134a

ʿAlī b. Muḥammad al-Ṣulayḥī i, 181b; ii, 517a; iii, 862b — I, 186b; II, 530a; III, 886b
ʿAlī b. Muḥammad al-Tūnisī al-Iyādī s, **62b** — S, **63a**
ʿAlī b. Muḥammad b. al-Walīd iv, 200b; s, 61b — IV, 209b; S, 62a
ʿAlī b. Muḥammad al-Zandjī i, **388b,** 551a, 942a, 1096a; s, 49a — I, **400a,** 569a, 971a, 1129a; S, 49b
ʿAlī b. Muḳarrab i, 74a — I, 76a
ʿAlī b. Mūsā iii, 1114a — III, 1141a
ʿAlī b. Mūsā al-Riḍā → ʿAlī al-Riḍā
ʿAlī b. Nāṣir Abu 'l-Ḥārithī s, 355b — S, 355b
ʿAlī b. Rabah b. Djanbulāt ii, 443b — II, 455b
ʿAlī b. Rabban al-Ṭabarī → al-Ṭabarī
ʿAlī b. Ṣāliḥ → Wāsiʿ ʿAlīsī
ʿAlī b. Salmān al-Dāʿī iv, 78a — IV, 82a
ʿAlī b. Sayyid Muḥammad b. ʿAlī i, 277b — I, 286a
ʿAlī b. al-Shāh al-Fārisī → Bahnūd b. Saḥwān
ʿAlī b. Shams al-Dīn i, 60a, **389a** — I, 62a, **400b**
ʿAlī b. Sulaymān al-ʿAnṭakī s, 38a — S, 38a
ʿAlī b. Sulaymān al-Damnātī ii, 109b — II, 112a
ʿAlī b. ʿUbayd Allāh b. Abī Rāfiʿ iii, 1151a — III, 1179a
ʿAlī b. ʿUbayd Allāh b. al-Ḥasan iii, 951a — III, 975b
ʿAlī b. ʿUmar, amīr iii, 47a — III, 49a
ʿAlī b. ʿUmar al-Shādhilī i, 781a; iv, 449b, 450a, b, 741a — I, 804b; IV, 469b, 470a, b, 771a
ʿAlī b. ʿUmar b. Idrīs → ʿAlī II
ʿAlī b. ʿUmrān iv, 100b — IV, 104b
ʿAlī b. Wafā iv, 283b — IV, 295b
ʿAlī b. Wahsūdān ii, 191b, 192a; iv, 100a; s, 356b — II, 197b, 198a; IV, 104b; S, 356b
ʿAlī b. Waṣīf iv, 662b — IV, 689a
ʿAlī b. Yaḥyā b. Tamīm i, 149a; ii, 459a — I, 153b; II, 471a
ʿAlī b. Yaḥyā al-Munadjdjim ii, 127a; iv, 111a, 1005a; v, 1125a; s, 17b, 25a — II, 130a; IV, 116a, 1037b; V, 1121b; S, 18a, 25a
ʿAlī b. Yaḥyā al-Ṣūfī iv, 1125b — IV, 1157a
ʿAlī b. Yakhlaf al-Nafūsī iii, 657a — III, 678b
ʿAlī b. Yūsuf b. Tāshufīn i, 78b, **389a,** 495b, 499b, 1347a; ii, 818b, 821b, 838a, 1007a, 1013a; iii, 542b, 712b, 771a, 959a, 977b; iv, 633a; s, 397b — I, 81a, **400b,** 510a, 514b, 1387b; II, 838a, 841a, 857b, 1030b, 1036b; III, 561b, 735a, 794b, 983b, 1002b; IV, 659a; S, 398a
ʿAlī b. Yūsuf al-Tūnisī s, 62b — S, 63a
ʿAlī b. Ẓāfir → Ibn Ẓāfir
ʿAlī b. al-Zandjī v, 352b — V, 353b
ʿAlī ʿAbd al-Raḥmān al-Ḥusaynī s, 18a — S, 18b
ʿAlī ʿAbd al-Rāziḳ → ʿAbd al-Rāziḳ
ʿAlī Abū ʿAbbās Sarwānī → ʿAbbās Sarwānī
ʿAlī ʿAdil-Shāh I i, 199a, 1047a, 1202b, 1203b, 1323b; iii,426a, 1161a; v, 938a — I, 205a, 1079a, 1238a, 1239a, 1364a; III, 440a, 1189b; V, 942a
ʿAlī ʿAdil-Shāh II i, 199b; ii, 120b; iii, 119a, 426b — I, 205a; II, 123b; III, 121b, 440b
ʿAbī Agha, Shaykh iv, 322b; v, 296b — IV, 337a; V, 288a
ʿAlī al-Akbar → ʿAlī b. al-Ḥusayn b. ʿAlī
ʿAlī Akbar Dihkhudā iv, 71a — IV, 74b
ʿAlī Akbar Ḳawām al-Mulk s, 336a — S, 335b
ʿAlī Akbar Khiṭāʾī i, **390b;** ii, 588a — I, **402a;** II, 602b
ʿAlī Akbar Ṣābir i, 194a; iii, 358a — I, 199b; III, 369b
ʿAlī al-Aʿlā iii, 600b — III, 621a
ʿAlī al-Amīn s, 399a — S, 399a
ʿAlī Amīrī i, **391a** — I, **402a**
ʿAlī al-ʿArabī Ilyās i, 776b — I, 800a
ʿAlī al-Aʿradj i, 47b — I, 48b
ʿAlī al-Asʿad, Pasha s, 162b — S, 162b
ʿAlī al-Armanī i, 638b; ii, 235a — I, 659a; II, 242a
ʿAlī Aṣghar Khān Atābak ii, 418a, 435a, 652a; iv, 394a, 979b; s, 365a — II, 429a, 446b, 668b; IV, 411a, 1012a; S, 365a
ʿAlī ʿAzīz Efendi Giridli i, **391a;** iii, 375a — I, **402a;** III, 386b
Ali Baba i, 359a, 362b — I, 370a, 373a
ʿAlī Barīd Shāh i, 1047a, 1200a, b; iii, 426a; v, 1215b — I, 1079a, 1235b, 1236a; III, 439b; V, 1205b
ʿAlī Beg (Turkman/Turkmène) i, 243b; ii, 204b — I, 251a; II, 211a
ʿAlī Beg b. ʿAlāʾ al-Dīn (Ḳarāmānid(e)) iv, 623a, b — IV, 648a, b
ʿAlī Beg b. Shah-suvār ii, 240a — II, 247a
ʿAlī Beg Hersek-zāde iii, 342a — III, 352a
ʿAlī Beg Ḳarāmān-oghlu iv, 620a — IV, 644b
ʿAlī Beg al-Kabīr → ʿAlī Bey
ʿAlī Ber → Sonni ʿAlī
ʿAlī Bey i, **391b,** 728b; ii, 233b; iii, 158a, 300a; iv, 723a, 852b, 853a; s, 20b, 268a — I, **402b,** 750b; II, 240b; III, 161b, 309a; IV, 752a, 885b, 886a; S, 20b, 267b
ʿAlī Bey (Ḥusaynid(e) (1735-56) iii, 605a, 635b — III, 625b, 657a
ʿAlī Bey (Ḥusaynid(e) (1759-82) iii, 636a — III, 657a
ʿAlī Bey (Ḥusaynid(e) (1882-1902) iii, 636b — III, 658a
ʿAlī Bey al-ʿAbbāsī i, **392a** — I, **403b**
ʿAlī Bey Eretnaoghlu → ʿAlāʾ al-Dīn ʿAlī
ʿAlī Bey Evrenos-zāde ii, 703a, 721a — II, 721a, 739b
ʿAlī Bey Ḳaramanoghlu → ʿAlāʾ al-Dīn ʿAlī Ḳaramanoghlu
ʿAlī Bey Mikhāl-oghlu i, 340b — I, 351a
ʿAlī al-Biblāwī s, 123a — S, 122b
ʿAlī Burghul (Bulghūr) ii, 460a; iv, 617b — II, 471b; IV, 642b
ʿAlī Čelebī → ʿAlī, Muṣṭafā b. Aḥmad Čelebī; Ḳinalizāde ʿAlī
ʿAlī Dede al-Bosnawī i, 759a — I, 782a
ʿAlī Diara iii, 39a — III, 41a
ʿAlī Dīnār ii, 124a, 125a — II, 127a, 128a
ʿAlī Djāh iii, 322a — III, 331b
ʿAlī Djamālī → Djamālī
ʿAlī Djanbulāṭ (d. 1778) ii, 443b — II, 455b
ʿĀlī Efendi → ʿĀlī ʿAzīz
ʿAlī Ekber → ʿAlī Akbar
ʿAlī Emīrī s, **63a** — S, **63a**
Ali Fethi (Okyar) → Okyar
ʿAlī Fuʿād Cebesoy ii, 700b — II, 718a
ʿAlī al-Hādī → al-ʿAskarī, Abu 'l-Ḥasan ʿAlī
ʿAlī Ḥāfiẓ v, 1005b — V, 1001a
ʿAlī Ḥakīm-Ilāhī, Āḳā s, 24a — S, 24a
ʿAlī al-Hamādanī i, 347b, **392b,** 1004b; ii, 967a; iv, 708a; v, 301a; s, 364b — I, 358a, **403b,** 1035b; II, 989a; IV, 736b; V, 300b; S, 364b
ʿAlī Ḥarfūsh ii, 750a — II, 768a
ʿAlī Ḥazīn, Shaykh → Ḥazīn
ʿAlī-Ilāhīs i, 225b, 260a, **392b;** ii, 106b — I, 232a, 268b, **404a;** II, 109a
ʿAlī Ḳarabāsh i, 965b; iv, 991b — I, 995b; IV, 1024a
ʿAlī al-Ḳārī i, 1235b; ii, 500b; iii, 29a, 711a; v, 1235a, b — I, 1272b; II, 513a; III, 30a, 733b; V, 1225b, 1226a
ʿAlī Ḳarīb iii, 47a — III, 48b
ʿAlī al-Kassār ii, 39b — II, 40b
ʿAlī Kemāl Bey ii, 474b; iii, 595a; iv, 636a — II, 486b; III, 615b; IV, 662a
ʿAlī Khwādja (Djand) s, 246a — S, 246a
ʿAlī Khān → Mahdī ʿAlī Khān; Sayyid ʿAlī Khān
ʿAlī Khān b. Agha i, 246b — I, 254a
ʿAlī Khān b. Dawlat Khān ii, 47b — II, 48b
ʿAlī Khān al-Madanī i, **392b** — I, **404a**
ʿAlī Khān Ẓahīr al-Dawla → Ẓahīr al-Dawla
ʿAlī Khān Zangana, Shaykh v, 169b — V, 167a
ʿAlī Khūrshīd ii, 828a — II, 847b
ʿAlī Khwishāwand → ʿAlī Ḳarīb

ʿAlī Kiyā i, 237b; v, 603a — I, 244b; V, 607a
ʿAlī Kolen ii, 977a — II, 999b
ʿAlī Kücük, Zayn al-Dīn i, 1160b; ii, 347b; iv, 76a — I, 1195a; II, 357b; IV, 80a
ʿAlī Ḳulī Khān (Barēlī) i, 1042b — I, 1074a
ʿAlī Ḳulī Khān Afshār → ʿĀdil Shāh Afshār
ʿAlī Ḳulī Khān Istadjlū (Shīr Afkan) ii, 380b; s, 366b — II, 390b; S, 366a
ʿAlī Ḳulī Khān Khān-i Zamān ii, 498b; s, 325a — II, 511a; S, 325a
ʿAlī Ḳulī Khān Shāmlū i, 7b — I, 7b
ʿAlī Ḳulī Ṣafarov → Ṣafarov, ʿAlī Ḳulī
ʿAlī Kurdī of/de Ḳazwīn, Mawlānā s, 51b — S, 52a
ʿAlī al-Ḳūshdjī i, **393a**, 776b; ii, 588a — I, **404b**, 799b; II, 602b
ʿAlī Māhir s, 6b, 300a, 301b — S, 5b, 299b, 301a
ʿAlī Mardān i, **393b** — I, **404b**
ʿAlī Mardān Khaldjī i, **393b** — I, **404b**
ʿAlī Mardān Khān i, 228b, 1347b; iv, 666a; v, 886a; s, **63a** — I, 235b, 1388a; IV, 693a; V, 892a; S, **63b**
ʿAlī Mardān Khān Bakhtiyarī i, **393b**; ii, 311a; iii, 1103a; iv, 104b, 639b; v, 825b — I, **405a**; II, 320a; III, 1130a; IV, 109a, 666a; V, 831b
ʿAlī Mardān Khān Faylī v, 825a — V, 831a
ʿAlī Mardān Khān Shāmlū i, 393b — I, 405a
ʿAlī Mubārak ii, 167a; v, 908b, 909a — II, 172b; V, 914b
ʿAlī al-Mudjāhid i, 181b, 440b — I, 186b, 453b
ʿAlī Mughāyat Shāh i, 742b; ii, 1220a — I, 765a; III, 1250b
ʿAlī Muḥammad b. Aḥmad al-Balkhī ii, 918b — II, 940a
ʿAlī Muḥammad Khān i, 1042b; iii, 59b, 60a — I, 1074a; III, 62a, b
ʿAlī Muḥammad Mukhliṣ i, 1123b — I, 1157b
ʿAlī Muḥammad Shīrāzī → Bāb, ʿAlī Muḥammad
ʿAlī Murād Mamīwand Khān v, 825a, b — V, 831b
ʿAlī Murād Mīr iv, 1160a — IV, 1192a
ʿAlī Mushtāḳ, Mīr Sayyid v, 834b — V, 840b
ʿAlī al-Muttaḳī → al-Muttaḳī al-Hindī
ʿAlī al-Naḳī → al-ʿAskarī, Abu 'l-Ḥasan ʿAlī
ʿAlī Pasha → Djanbulāt-oghlū; Djānīkli; Ferah; Ḥādjdji; Kemānkesh; Muʾadhdhinzāde
ʿAlī Pasha (Baghdād) i, 199a, 905a — I, 204b, 932b
ʿAlī Pasha (Ḥusaynid(e)) → ʿAlī Bey
ʿAlī Pasha Afrāsiyāb i, 236b, 1087a — I, 244a, 1119b
ʿAlī Pasha ʿArabadji i, 268a, **394a**, 558a — I, 276b, **405a**, 575b
ʿAlī Pasha Čāndārlî-zāde i, **394a**, 1303a; ii, 444b, 611a — I, **405b**, 1342b; II, 456b, 626a
ʿAlī Pasha Čorlulu i, 56a, 268b, 269a, **394b**; ii, 1091a; iv, 233b — I, 58a, 276b, 277a, **405b**; II, 1116b; IV, 244a
ʿAlī Pasha Dāmād i, 268b, 269a, **395a**; iii, 1002a; iv, 969a — I, 276b, 277b, **406a**; III, 1027a; IV, 1001b
ʿAlī Pasha Güzeldje i, **395a**; iv, 572a — I, **406b**; IV, 594b
ʿAlī Pasha Ḥakīm-oghlu i, 174b, **395b**, 1018a, 1267b; iv, 437b, 544a, 861b; s, 268a — I, 179b, **407a**, 1049b, 1306b; IV, 457b, 567b, 894b; S, 267b
ʿAlī Pasha Ḳaramānlî iv, 617b, 618a — IV, 642a, b
ʿAlī Pasha Khādim i, **396a**, 1120b, 1207b; iv, 231a, 1093a; v, 269a, b — I, **407a**, 1154a, 1243b; IV, 241a, 1124a; V, 267a
ʿAlī Pasha Mubārak i, 168a, **396a**, 596b; ii, 131b, 892a; v, 22b, 909a; s, 369a — I, 173a, **407b**, 616a; II, 135a, 913a; V, 23b, 914b; S, 369a
ʿAlī Pasha Muḥammad Amīn i, 298b, **396b**; ii, 642a, 934b, 996b; iii, 357a, 1187b, 1188a — I, 307b, **408a**; II, 658a, 956b, 1019b; III, 368b, 1217b, 1218a
ʿAlī Pasha Rizvanbegowič → Riḍwān Begovič
Alī Pasha Semiz i, 291b, **398a**, 843b — I, 300b, **409b**, 866b
ʿAlī Pasha Silāḥdār iii, 628b — III, 649a, b
ʿAlī Pasha Sürmeli i, 268a, **398a** — I, 276b, **409b**
ʿAlī Pasha Tepedelenli i, **398b**, 653a, 657a; ii, 708b; iii, 91a, 628a; iv, 588b, 589a, 656b; v, 727b, 773b — I, **409b**, 673b, 677b; II, 727a; III, 93b, 648a; IV, 612a, b, 683a; V, 732b, 779b
Āli Rādjās iv, 547a — IV, 570b
ʿAlī Razmārā s, 158a — S, 158b
ʿAlī Reʾis b. Ḥüseyn → Kātib-i Rūmī
ʿAlī al-Riḍā i, **399b**, 402b, 551a, 1250a; ii, 248b, 731b; iii, 1169b; iv, 17a, 45b; v, 59a; s, 127b — I, **411a**, 414a, 568b, 1288a; II, 256a, 750a; III, 1198b; IV, 18b, 48a; V, 60b; S, 126b
ʿAlī Riḍā b. Ḥādjdjī Ibrāhīm Khān s, 336a — S, 335b
ʿAlī Riḍā-i ʿAbbāsī i, **400b**; iv, 1124a — I, **412a**; IV, 1155b
ʿAlī Riḍā Pasha ii, 813a; iv, 296b — II, 832b; IV, 309b
ʿAlī Shāfiḳ Özdemir v, 145a — V, 147b
ʿAlī Shāh → ʿAlī ʿAdil-Shāh; ʿAlī Barīd Shāh; Agha Khān II; Wādjid ʿAlī Shāh;
ʿAlī Shāh (wazīr) i, 627a; iii, 1122b — I, 648a; III, 1150a, b
ʿĀlī Shāh Čak s, 131b, 167a — S, 131a, 167a
ʿAlī Shahīd Pīr i, 1203b — I, 1239a
ʿAlī Shaʿrāwī iii, 516a — III, 533b
ʿAlī al-Sharīf, Mawlāy s, 114a — S, 113b
ʿAlī Sharmarke i, 1172b — I, 1207b
ʿAlī Shēr Ḳāniʿ → Ḳāniʿ
ʿAlī Shīr Khān i, 1004b — I, 1035b
ʿAlī Shīr Navāʾī → Navāʾī
ʿAlī Shukr Beg i, 1135a — I, 1169b
ʿAlī Suʿāwī ii, 473b, 474a — II, 486a
ʿAlī al-Ṭawīl i, 161b — I, 166a
ʿAlī Tegīn i, 424b, 662a; ii, 4b; iii, 1114a; v, 76a — I, 436b, 682b; II, 4b; III, 1141b; V, 78b
ʿAlī Wāsiʿ → Wāsi ʿAlīsi
ʿAlī Werdī Khān i, **400b**; ii, 371a — I, **412a**; II, 381a
ʿAlī Yūsuf, Shaykh ii, 466b; iii, 516a; s, 121b — II, 478b; III, 533b; S, 121a
ʿAlī al-Zaḳḳāḳ → al-Zaḳḳāḳ
ʿAlī Zayn al-ʿAbidīn i, 781b — I, 805a
ʿAlī-ābād iv, 1015a — IV, 1047a
ʿAli bek Aldamov ii, 18a — II, 18b
Alicante → Laḳant
Alidada(e) → Asṭurlāb
ʿAlid(e)s i, 45b, 48b, 73b, 103a, b, 125b, 143a, 149a, 290b, **400b**, 550b, 688a, 713a, 1035b, 1352a; ii, 168b, 191a, 192b, 851b; iii, 22a, 242a, 616a, 753a, 984b; iv, 88b; v, 1238b — I, 46b, 50a, 75b, 106a, b, 129a, 147a, 153a, 299b, **412a**, 568a, 709a, 734b, 1067a, 1391a; II, 174a, 197a, 198b, 871b; III, 23a, 249a, 636b, 776a, 1009a; IV, 92b; V, 1229a
Alif → Hidjāʾ
Aligaṛh i, 288a, **403a**, 1300a; ii, 97a, 132b; v, 283a; s, 4b, 106b, 247a — I, 297a, **414b**, 1340a; II, 99a, 136a; V, 281a; S, 4a, 105b, 247b
- movement/mouvement d'- iii, 433a; iv, 793a; s, 74a, 107b, 247a — III, 447a; IV, 825a; S, 74b, 107a, 247b
- university/université ii, 426b — II, 437a
ʿAlīkozāy ii, 629a — II, 645a
Alilat → al-Lāt
ʿĀlim → ʿUlamāʾ
ʿĀlim, Mīr i, 1296a; ii, 700b — I, 1335b; II, 718b
ʿĀlima i, **403b**; ii, 1029b, 1048b — I, **415b**; II, 1053a, 1072b
Alimentation → Ghidhāʾ
ʿĀlimiyya i, 818a — I, 841a
Alimtu i, 419a — I, 430b
ʿAlim Allāh, Shaykh s, 247a — S, 247a
ʿĀlim Khān (Khōḳand) iv, 631b; v, 29b — IV, 656b;

V, 30a, b
Alimentation → Ghidhā'
Aliments → Ghidhā'
ʿAlīnagar ii, 7a — II, 7a
Alindjaḳ i, **404a**; v. 491b — I, **416a**; V, 494a
Alip-manash → Alpamïsh
Alīsaʿ b. Ukhṭūb i, **404a** — I, **416a**
ʿAlīshānzāde Ismāʿīl Ḥaḳḳi → Ismāʿīl Ḥaḳḳī Pasha
Alīṭ i, 7a, 43b; iii, 904b; iv, 672b — I, 7b, 45a; III, 929a; IV, 700a
ʿAlītigin s, 176b — S, 177b
Aliwāl Khān i, 1209b — I, 1245b
ʿAlīwiyya ii, 224b — II, 231b
ʿAliyya Bohorās i, 1255a — I, 1293a
ʿAlīzāy ii, 629a — II, 644b
Aljamía i, **404b,** 502b; iv, 317a; s, 81a, 397a — I, **416a,** 517b; IV, 331a; S, 81a, 397b
Aljarafe → al-Sharaf
ʿAlḳa → ʿUḳūba
Alkali/Alcali → al-Ḳily
ʿAlḳama b. ʿAbada al-Tamīmī i, **405b;** iii, 1177b; iv, 998b, 1087b — I, **417a;** III, 1206b; IV, 1031a, 1118b
ʿAlḳama b. ʿUlātha i, 441b, 442a, 690a — I, 454b, 455a, 711a
al-ʿAlḳamī i, **405b** — I, **417b**
Alkanna → al-Ḥinnā'
Alḳās Mīrzā i, **406a** — I, **417b**
Alkendi → al-Ḳindī, Abū Yūsuf Yaʿḳūb
All-India Muslim League v, 779b, 780a, 1080b; s, 4b — V, 785b, 786a, 1078a; S, 3b
ʿAllāf b. Ḥassān ii, 484a, b — II, 496b
Allāh i, 275a, 333a, 349b, **406a,** 773b, 776a; ii, 96a, 220b, 396a, 449a, 493b, 518a, 554a, 593b, 772b, 898b; iii, 28b, 82b, 497a, 870b, 917b, 1093b, 1196a; v, 3b, 411b — I, 283b, 343b, 360a, **418a,** 796b, 819b; II, 98a, 227a, 406b, 460b, 505b, 513a, 567b, 608a, 791a, 919b; III, 30a, 85a, 514a, 894b, 941b, 1120b, 1226b; V, 4a, 413a
al-Allaḥ b. ʿAbd al-Wahhāb iii, 655a — III, 676a
Allāh Akbar → Takbīr
Allāh Ḳulī Beg iv, 808a — IV, 840b
Allāh Ḳulī Khān ii, 973b — II, 996a
Allān Ḳulī Khān (Khīwa) iv, 1065a; s, 46a, 228a — IV, 1096b; S, 46b, 228b
Allāh Wirdī Khān ii, 1091b — II, 1117a
Allāh Yār Thānī → Murtaḍā Ḥusayn
Allāhābād i, **417b;** ii, 426a; v, 1218b; s, 325b — I, **429b;** II, 437a; V, 1208b; S, 325a
Allāhdād, Mawalānā s, 74a — S, 74a
Allāhumma i, **418a** — I, **429b**
Allāhwardī Khān i, 8a; iii, 585b; v, 672b, 825a — I, 8a; III, 605b; V, 677b, 831a
ʿAllāḳa ii, 483b; iii, 77a — II, 495b; III, 79b
al-ʿAllāḳī, Wādī i, **418a;** ii, 214a; iv, 567b, 965b, 967a — I, **430a;** II, 220b; IV, 590a, 969b
ʿAllāl al-Fāsī s, **63b** — S, **64a**
ʿAllaliyyīn s, 350b — S, 350b
ʿAllama Kamāl al-Dīn ii, 54a — II, 55a
ʿAllāma-i Ḥillī → al-Ḥillī, Djamāl al-Dīn Ḥasan
ʿAllāmī → Abu 'l-Faḍl ʿAllāmī
ʿAllāmī, Shaykh → Abū 'l-Faḍl ʿAllāmī
Allān → Alān
ʿAllawayh al-Aʿsar i, 160a; s, 17b, **64a** — I, 164b; S, 17b, **64b**
Allemands II, 716b, 717a; III, 1215a; IV, 43a, 921b, 922a
Allusion → Ishāra
ʿAllūya → ʿAllawayh
ʿAlma → ʿĀlima
Alma Ata i, **418b** — I, **430a**
Alma-dagh → Elma-dagh
Almada, almaden → al-Maʿdin
Almadia → Safīna
Almagest → Baṭlamiyūs
Almalïgh i, **418b;** iii, 1120b; v, 858b; s, 240a — I, **430a;** III, 1148a; V, 865b; S, 240a
Almanac(h) → Anwā': Ta'rīkh
Almani Omar ii, 960a — II, 982b
Almanzor → al-Manṣūr bi'llāh
Almās i, **419a;** v, 353b, 550a, 965a — I, **431a;** V, 354b, 555a, 969b
Almās Beg Ulugh Khān → Ulugh Khān
Almee → ʿĀlima
Almeria → al-Mariyya
Almicantarat → Muḳanṭarāt
Almodovar → al-Mudawwar
Almogávares i, **419b** — I, **431b**
Almohad(e)s → al-Muwaḥḥidūn
Almoravid(e)s → al-Murābiṭūn
Almuñecar → al-Munakkab
Alōr s, 163a — S, 162b
Alp i, **419b** — I, **431b**
Alp Arghūn Shams al-Dīn iii, 1100a; v, 826b — III, 1127a; V, 833a
Alp Arslān i, 329a, **420a,** 465b, 507b, 510a, 660b, 731a, 1041b, 1051b. 1336b; ii, 5a, 340a, 347b, 856a; iii, 86b, 196a, 197a, 471b, 1098b; iv, 27a, 291b, 347b, 348a, 458a, 807b, 840a; v, 388a, 489a; s, 14b, 65a, 245b — I, 339b, **432a,** 479b, 523a, 525b, 681b, 753a, 1073a, 1083a, b, 1376b; II, 5a, 350a, 357a, 876a; III, 88b, 200b, 202a, 488a, 1125b; IV, 29a-b, 304b, 362b, 363a, 478b, 840a, 873a; V, 389a, 492a; S, 15a, 65b, 245b
Alp Khān ii, 695a, 1124a; iv, 419a; s, 105b — II, 712b, 1150b; IV, 437b; S, 104b
Alp Khān → Hūshang Shāh Ghūrī
Alp Ḳush Kūn-i Khar i, 865b — I, 890a
Alp Yörük → Ḥusām al-Dīn Alp Yörük
Alpamïsh i, **421b;** iii, 116a — I, **433b;** III, 118b
Alpetragius → al-Biṭrūdjī
Alphabet → al-Hidja', Ḥurūf-; Muʿdjam
Alpharas → Nudjūm
Alphonso → Alfūnsho
Alpï b. Timurtash i, 664b; iii, 1119a, b — I, 684b; III, 1146b, 1147a
Alp Takīn i, 226b, **421b,** 823b, 824a, 984b; ii, 483a, 854a, 1049a; iii, 46b, 246a, 841a; iv, 24a, 663b — I, 233b, **433a,** 846b, 847a, 1015a; II, 495a, 874a, 1073a; III, 48b, 253a, 864b; IV, 26a, 690a
Alptakīn Bakdjur iii, 398a — III, 410b
Alpuente → al-Bunt
Alpujarras → al-Busharrāt
Alruccaba → Rukba
Alsh i, **422b,** 492a; s, 144b — I, **434b,** 507a; S, 144a
Altai(ï) i, **422b** — I, **434b**
Altaians i, **423a;** iii, 115a
Altair → Nudjūm
Altaïs I, **434b;** III, 117b
Altamġa ii, 14b, 157b — II, 14b, 162a
Altamish → Iltutmish
Altan Debter ii, 41a, 571a — II, 42a, 585b
ʿAlth i, **423a** — I, **435a**
Altï bölük iii, 191b, 192b — III, 196a, 197a
Alti ok ii, 430a, 596b — II, 441a, 611a
Altï Parmak i, **423b** — I, **435a**
Alti Shahr i, **423b** — I, **435b**
Altïlïk → Sikka
Altïn i, **423b** — I, **435b**
Altïn Köprü i, **424a** — I, **435b**
Altïn Ordu i, **424a;** iv, 280b — I, **436a;** IV, 292b
Altïntash, (Anatolia(e)) i, **424a** — I, **436a**
Altïntash, Tādj al-Dīn i, 431b — I, 444a
Alṭūniya → Malik Alṭūniya
Altūntāsh, Abū Saʿīd i, 278a, **424b;** iv, 1066b; s, 176b — I, 286b, **436b;** IV, 1098b; S, 177b

Aludel → al-ʿUthāl
Alughu Khān i, 1188a; ii, 3a, b; v, 38b — I, 1223a; II, 3a, b; V, 40a
ʿAlūk → al-Djinn
Alum (alun) → Shabb
Alus, Sermed Mukhtār s, **64b** — S, **64b**
al-Ālūsī i, **425a** — I, **437a**
ʿAlwa i, **425b** — I, **437b**
ʿAlwa bint Zurayḳa i, 1289b — I, 1329a
Alwāḥ → Lawḥ
Alwand b. Yūsuf b. Uzun Ḥasan i, 311b, 312a; ii, 937a; iv, 186b, 1048b — I, 321a, b; II, 959a; IV, 194b, 1080a
Alwand Kūh i, **426a** — I, **438a**
Alwar i, **426b** — I, **438b**
Ama → ʿAbd
al-Aʿmā al-Tuṭīlī i, **426b,** 595b, 602a; iii, 729b — I, **438b,** 615a, 621b; III, 752a
Amad i, 1078a — I, 1110b
ʿAmādiya i, **426b**; v, 460a— I, **438b**; V, 463a
Amādjūr i, 278b; iv, 89b — I, 287a; IV, 93b
Amadov Ḥamā Allāh Ḥaydara → Ḥamā Allāh
Amadu Sēku → Aḥmad al-Shaykh
ʿAmʿaḳ, Shihāb al-Dīn Bukhārī s, **64b** — S, **65a**
ʿAmal i, 171a, **427a;** ii, 898a — I, 175b, **439a;** II, 919a
ʿAmal al-yad ii, 481b — II, 493b
ʿAmala iii, 1106a, b — III, 1133a, b
ʿAmāla i, 439a — I, 451b
Amālī → Tadrīs
ʿAmālīḳ i, **429a;** ii, 917a; iii, 1270a; v, 994b — I, **441a;** II, 938b; III, 1303a; V, 989b
Amalric I ii, 318a, b — II, 327b
Amān i, **429a;** ii, 248a, 303b; iii, 197b, 547a, 1179b, 1181b, 1182a — I, **441b;** II, 255b, 311b; III, 202b, 566a, 1208b, 1210b, 1211a
Amān, Mīr i, **430b;** iii, 376a; v, 201b — I, **442b;** III, 388a; V, 199a
Amān Allāh Ḥusaynī ii, 910a; v, 1214b — II, 931b; V, 1204a
Amān Allāh Khān i, 232b, 626b — I, 239b, 647a
Amān Allāh Khān, King/le roi i, 232b, 626b; ii, 531b, 657a, 658b; v, 37a, 1079a, b; s, **65b**, 237b — I, 239b, 647a; II, 544b, 673b, 675a; V, 38a, 1076b, 1077a; S, **66a**, 237b
Amān al-Mulk ii, 30b, 317a — II, 31a, 326a
Amānat i, **430b** — I, **443a**
Amanos ii, 982a; v, 810b — II, 1004b; V, 816b
Amantnāg iv, 177b — IV, 186a
Amar Singh iii, 485b — III, 502b
ʿAmāra i, **431a**; s, 179a — I, **443a**; s, 180a
ʿAmāra Dūnḳas ii, 943b, 944a; iv, 892b — II, 965b, 966a; IV, 925b
ʿAmārāt i, 483a — I, 497b
Amarkot i, **431a** — I, **443b**
al-Aʿmash, Sulaymān i, 104b, **431b;** ii, 293a; iii, 843a; iv, 1112b — I, 107b, **443b;** II, 301a; III, 867a; IV, 1144b
Amasya i, 12b, **431b;** iii, 215a; iv, 576b, 1159a — I, 13a, **444a;** III, 221a; IV, 599b, 1191a
Amasyalî Meḥmed Efendi → Memek Čelebi
Amazigh i, 1173a — I, 1208a
Amazzal i, 171b — I, 176a
Ambāla i, **432b,** 1348a; s, 203a — I, **444b,** 1388b; S, 202b
Ambassador/Ambassadeur → Elči, Rasūl
Amber/ambre jaune → Kahrubā; Kārim
Ambergris/ambre gris → ʿAnbar
Ambon i, **433a** — I, **445a**
ʿAmd ii, 341a; iv, 767a, b, 768b, 769b — II, 351a; IV, 797b, 798a, 799a, 800a
ʿAmda Ṣeyōn (Sion) i, 176b; ii, 175a; iii, 3b — I, 181a; II, 180b; III, 3b; IV, 797b, 798a, 799a, 800a
al-Amdjad Bahrāmshāh → Bahrām Shāh
Âme → Nafs
Āmeddji i, **433a;** ii, 339a — I, **445b;** II, 348b
Ameer ʿAlī → Amīr ʿAlī
Amengku Rat I s, 201a — S, 201a
Aménokal i, **433b** — I, **445b**
America, emigrants/Amérique, émigrants ii, 403b, 404a; v, 1253a — II, 414b, 415a; V, 1244a
Amghar i, **433b** — I, **446a**
Āmid → Diyār Bakr
Āmid ii, 344b, 345a, b, 346a, 393a; iii, 1197b — II, 354a, b, 355b, 403b; III, 1227b
ʿAmīd i, **434a** — I, **446a**
ʿAmīd al-Dawla Ibn Djahir ii, 384a, b — II, 394b, 395a
ʿAmīd al-Dīn al-Abzārī al-Anṣārī i, **434a** — I, **446b**
ʿAmīd al-Mulk al-Kundurī → al-Kundurī
Amīd Tūlakī Sūnāmī s, **66b** — S, **67a**
al-Āmidi (d. 991) i, 154a, b — I, 158b, 159a
al-ʿAmīdī, Abū Saʿd Muḥammad b. Aḥmad s, 362a — S, 361b
al-Āmidī, ʿAlī i, **434b;** iii, 1025a, b — I, **446b;** III, 1051a, b
al-ʿAmīdī, Rukn al-Dīn i, **434b** — I, **446b**
ʿAmīḳ (lake/lac) s, 239a — S, 239a
ʿAmil, ʿawāmil i, **436a** — I, **448a**
ʿAmil, ʿummāl i, 19b, **435a,** 1255a; ii, 118b, 328a; iii, 284a, b; iv, 941a — I, 20a, **447a,** 1293; II, 121b, 337b; III, 292b, 293b; IV, 974a
ʿĀmila i, **436a;** ii, 573b; v, 632a — I, **448b;** II, 588a; V, 636a
al-ʿAmilī, Bahāʾ al-Dīn i, **436b;** ii, 761a; iv, 725b; v, 872b, 873b; s, 308b — I, **448b;** II, 779b; IV, 754b; V, 878b, 879b; S, 308a
al-ʿĀmilī, al-Ḥurr → al-Ḥurr al-ʿĀmilī; Thaʿlaba b. Salāma
al-ʿĀmilī, Shahīd al-Awwal Muḥammad b. Makkī s, 56b — S, 57a
al-ʿĀmilī, Shahīd al-Thānī Zayn al-Dīn s, 56b — S, 57a
al-Amīn → Abū Ḳubays
Amīn, āmēn i, **436b** — I, **449a**
Amīn, umanā i, **437a,** 633a, 975b, ii, 105a — I, **449a,** 654a, 1006a; II, 107a
Amīn, Ḳāsim → Ḳāsim Amīn
al-Amīn, Muḥammad i, 18a, 77b, 143b, 160a, **437a,** 897a, 899b, 1034b, 1036a; ii, 235a, 730b, 731a; iii, 231b, 274a, 360a, 618a; iv, 17a, 1091a; s, 22b, 116b — I, 18b, 80a, 147b, 164b, **449b,** 924a, 926b, 1066a, 1067b; II, 241b, 749b, 750a; III, 238a, 282a, 371b, 638b; IV, 18a, 1122a; S, 23a, 116a
Amīn Arslān iii, 593a II, 613b
al-Amīn Bey i, 1110b; iii, 637a; s, 11a — I, 1144a; III, 658a; S, 10b
Amīn al-Dawla b. Muḥammad Ḥusayn Khān iv, 104b, 105a, 476a — IV, 109b, 497a
Amīn al-ḥukm i, 437a — I, 449a
Amīn al-Ḥusaynī ii, 913b; iv, 961a; v, 336b, 337a; s, **67a** — II, 934b; IV, 993b; V, 337b; S, **67b**
Amīn Pasha Djalīlī ii, 402a — II, 413a
Amīn Pasha Fikrī ii, 892a — II, 913a
Amīn al-Sayyād s, 209a — S, 208b
Amīn Taḳī al-Dīn s, 159b — S, 159b
Amīna i, **438a** — I, **450b**
Amīndjī b. Djalāl b. Ḥasan s, **70b** — S, **71a**
Āmina bint Wahb i, 42b, 169a, **438a;** iii, 362b — I, 43b, 173b, **450b;** III, 374a
Amīr i, 19b, **438b,** ii, 507b; iii, 45b; iv, 941b, 942a; v, 686a, 1251b — I, 20a, **451a;** II, 520a; III, 47b; IV, 974b, 975a; V, 691a, 1242b
ʿĀmir s, 81b — S, 81b
ʿĀmir I i, **440b;** iii, 746a — I, **453b;** III, 769a

ʿĀmir II i, **441a;** ii, 730a; iii, 746a; v, 807b — I, **453b;** II, 748b; III, 769a; V, 813a
ʿĀmir, Banū i, 1a, **440b;** ii, 252b, 709a; iii, 6a, 7b; v, 522a, 583b; s, 177a — I, 1a, **453a;** II, 260a, 728a; III, 6a, 7b; V, 525b, 588b; S, 178a
ʿĀmir (ʿAbd Allāh, ʿAlī) Abu 'l-Fazārī s, 306a — S, 306a
ʿĀmir (D̲j̲aʿda) i, 446a; ii, 365b — I, 459a; II, 375b
al-Āmir bi-Aḥkām Allāh i, 215b, **440a,** 814b, 1091b; ii, 170b, 857b, 858a, b; iii, 54b; iv, 944a — I, 222a, **452b,** 837b, 1124a; II, 175b, 877b, 878a; III, 56b; IV, 976b
ʿĀmir b. ʿAbd al-Ḳays al-ʿAnbarī i, **441a,** 960a — I, **453b,** 989b
ʿĀmir b. ʿAbd al-Wahhāb → ʿĀmir II
ʿĀmir b. Dāwud iv, 901b — IV, 934b
ʿĀmir b. Ḍubāra i, 49a; iii, 802b; iv, 99b, 447a — I, 50b; III, 826a; IV, 104a, 467a
ʿĀmir b. Fuhayra i, 110a; iii, 366b — I, 113a; III, 378b
ʿĀmir b. Kurayz s, 267b — S, 267a
ʿĀmir b. Luʾayy, Banū iii, 819b — III, 843a
ʿĀmir b. Rabīʿa b. ʿUḳayl s, 234a — S, 234a
ʿĀmir b. Ṣaʿṣaʿa i, **441a,** 544b; ii, 72a, 353b, 895b, 1023a; iii, 168b; v, 101b, 526a, 583b, 640b, 954a; s, 178a — I, **453b,** 562a; II, 73a, 363b, 916b, 1047a; III, 172b; V, 103b, 529b, 589a, 644b, 958a; S, 179a
ʿĀmir b. S̲h̲ahr iii, 123a — III, 126a
ʿĀmir b. Ṭāhir → ʿĀmir I
ʿĀmir b. al-Ṭufayl i, 441b, **442a,** 690a, 1232b; iii, 136b; iv, 1106a — I, 454a, **455a,** 711a, 1269a; III, 139a; IV, 1137b
Amīr Āk̲h̲ūr i, **442b**; iv, 217b — I, **455b**; IV, 227a
Amīr ʿAlī, Sayyid i, 38b, **442b;** iii, 431b, 532b; iv, 170b; s, 73b — I, 39b, **455b;** III, 445b, 551a; IV, 178a; S, 74a
Amīr-i Amīrān iii, 87a — III, 89b
Amīr Barīd i, 1047a, 1200a; ii, 1135a; iii, 425b, 1159b, 1160a, b — I, 1078b, 1235b; II, 1162a; III, 439b, 1188a, b, 1189a
Amīr Bas̲h̲kurt i, 1075b — I, 1107b
Amīr Dād i, **443b** — I, **456a**
Amīr Doladay iv, 586a, b — IV, 608b, 609a
Amīr al-Ḥād̲j̲d̲j̲ i, **443b**; iv, 679a — I, **456a**; IV, 706b
Amīr Ḥamza → Sīrat al-Amīr Ḥamza
Amīr Ḥasan Sid̲j̲zī ii, 55b; iv, 32b — II, 56b; IV, 34b
ʿAmīr al-Hintātī iii, 462a — III, 478a
Amīr Ḥusayn i, 441a; ii, 322a, 1127b; iv, 32b — I, 453b; II, 331b, 1154a; IV, 34b
al-Amīr al-Kabīr i, **444a**; v, 792b — I, **456b**; V, 798b
al-Amīr al-Kabīr, Muḥammad s, 411a — S, 411b
Amīr Kabīr → Taḳī K̲h̲ān, Mīrzā
Amīr Karōṛ i, 217b — I, 224a
Amīr K̲h̲ān i, 282b, **444a,** 1195b; ii, 567a — I, 291a, **456b,** 1230b; II, 581b
Amīr K̲h̲ān Turkmān iii, 157b — III, 161a
Amīr K̲h̲usraw Dārāʾī iv, 704a — IV, 732b
Amīr K̲h̲usraw Dihlawī i, **444a,** 1212b, 1329a; ii, 56b, 504a, 794a; iii, 249a, 439a, 453a, 456b, 492a; iv, 66b, 759b, 1010a, 1136a; v, 937b, 1104b; s, 46b, 105a, 124a — I, **457a,** 1249a, 1369b; II 57b, 517a, 813a; III, 256a, 453a, 468b, 472a, 509a; IV, 70a, 789b, 1042a, 1167b; V, 941b, 1100b; S, 47a, 104b, 123b
Amīr Kiyāʾīs s, 363b — S, 363a
Amīr Mad̲j̲lis i, **445a** — I, **457b**
Amīr Masʿūd → Masʿūd b. Maḥmūd
Amir Mentes̲h̲e i, 728b — I, 806a
Amīr Mīnāʾī v, 959a, 960b, 962a — V, 963a, 965a, 966a
Amīr Muḥammad Zamān iv, 475b — IV, 496b
Amīr Muʿizzī iii, 356a — III, 367a
Amir al-Mulk ii, 30b — II, 31a
Amir Mukarram Lārid̲j̲ānī v, 664a, b — V, 669b
Amīr al-muʾminīn i, 21b, 79b, 83b, **445a;** ii, 676a — I, 22a, 82a, 86a, **458a;** II, 693a
Amīr al-muslimīn i, 79b, **445b** — I, 82a, **458b**
Amīr Niẓām, Ḥasan ʿAlī K̲h̲ān s, **71a** — S, **71b**
ʿĀmir Rabīʿa i, 942a, b; iv, 664a, b — I, 971a; IV, 690b, 691b
Amīr Rūḥānī iii, 1155b — III, 1184a
Amīr-i Ṣadah i, 1200a — I, 1235a
al-Amīr al-Ṣag̲h̲īr, Muḥammad s, 411a — S, 411b
Amīr S̲h̲āh Ḳāsim Bēglār iii, 1030a — III, 1056a
Amīr silāḥ i, **445b** — I, **458b**
Amīr al-umarāʾ i, 19a, 20a, b, **446a,** 899b, 1040a; ii, 507b; v, 622a — I, 20a, 21a, **458b,** 926b, 1071b; II, 520a; V, 626a
Amīr Yas̲h̲bak ii, 172b — II, 178a
Amīra Ḳubād i, 1066b — I, 1098b
Amīrān i, 195b — I, 201b
Amīrān-i Ṣadah ii, 99b, 218b, 1124a — II, 101b, 225b, 1150b
Amīrāns̲h̲āh b. Ḳāwurd i, 827a — I, 850a
Amīrg̲h̲aniyya → Mīrg̲h̲āniyya
ʿĀmirī i, **446a** — I, **459a**
al-ʿĀmirī → Muḥammad b. Yūsuf
al-ʿĀmirī, Muḥammad b. Yūsuf i, 235b; ii, 949a; s, **72b** — I, 243a; II, 971a; S, **72b**
ʿAmīrī, Muhammad Ṣādiḳ Adīb al-Mamālik iv, 71a; s, **73a** — IV, 74b, S, **73b**
Amīr-i Aʿẓam Sangsarī v, 664a — V, 669b
Amīr-i Niẓām → Taḳī K̲h̲ān, Mīrzā
ʿĀmirid(e)s i, 76a, 84b, **446a;** iii, 495b, 743a — I, 78a, 86b, **459a;** III, 512b, 766a
Āmiriyya iii, 54b; iv, 200b, 201a — III, 56b; IV, 209a, b
al-ʿAmḳ i, **446b**; s, 243a — I, **459a**; S, 243a
ʿAmlūḳ i, 429a — I, 441a
ʿAmm iv, 916b — IV, 949b
ʿĀmma i, 900a, 902a; v, 605b — I, 927a, 929a; V, 609b
al-ʿAmma waʾl-K̲h̲āṣṣa → al-K̲h̲āṣṣa
ʿAmmān i, **447a,** 975b — I, **460a,** 1006a
Amman, Mir → Amōn, Mīr
ʿAmmār, Banū i, **448a;** ii, 353b, 568b — I, **461a;** II, 363a, 582b
ʿAmmār b. ʿAmr iv, 1003b — IV, 1036a
ʿAmmār b. Yāsir, Abuʾl-Yaḳẓān i, **448b,** 704b; ii, 846a; iii, 29b, 241a, 874a; s, 354b — I, **461b,** 726a; II, 866a; III, 31a, 248a, 898a; S, 354b
ʿAmmār b. Yazīd → K̲h̲idās̲h̲
ʿAmmār al-Mawṣilī i, **448b,** 785b — I, **461b,** 805b
ʿAmmāra bint Ḥamza ii, 372a, — II, 382a
ʿAmmāriyya i, 371b, **449a** — I, 382a, **462a**
Ammī → Mūsā b. ʿĪsā
ʿAmmūn, Iskandar s, 159b — S, 159b
ʿAmmūriya i, 154a, **449a;** ii, 237a — I, 158a, **462a;** II, 243b
Amoḳḳrān iv, 478b — IV, 499b
Amorium → ʿAmmūriya
Amour → ʿIs̲h̲k; Maḥabba
Amr i, 414b, **449b,** 1170a — I, 426b, **462b,** 1205a
ʿAmr b. ʿAbd al-Mālik al-Warrak iv, 1005a — IV, 1037a
ʿAmr b. Abī ʿAmr al-S̲h̲aybānī s, 16a — S, 16a
ʿAmr b. Abī Ṣayfī iv, 821a — IV, 854a
ʿAmr b. Abī Sufyān i, 151a — I, 155b
ʿAmr b. ʿAdī i, **450b**; v, 633a — I, **463b**; V, 637a
ʿAmr b. al-Ahtam i, **450b** — I, **463b**
ʿAmr b. al-ʿĀṣ i, 111a, 207a, 208b, 383b, 384a, **451a,** 531b, 659b, 812b, 932a, 966a, 1049a, 1098a, 1343b; ii, 306a, 327b, 372a, 625b, 910b, 957b, 1024b, 1056a; iii, 540b, 587a, 889b, 975b; iv, 132b, 424a, 514a, 841b, 1103b; v, 90b, 318a, 799b; s, 157a, 267b — I, 114a, 213b, 215a, 394b, 395a, **464a,** 547b, 680b, 835b, 960b,

996a, 1080b, 1131a, 1384a; II, 314b, 337a, 382a, 641a, 932a, 980a, 1048b, 1080b; III, 559b, 607a, 913b, 1000a; IV, 138a, 442b, 536b, 874b, 1134b; V, 93a, 317b, 805b; S, 157a, 267a
ʿAmr b. ʿAwf i, 771b — I, 794b
ʿAmr b. Bakr al-Tamīmī iii, 887a, b — III, 911a, b
ʿAmr b. Bāna (Bānata) → Ibn Bāna
ʿAmr b. Djamīl s, 326b — S, 326a
ʿAmr b. al-Djamūḥ s, 230a — S, 230a
ʿAmr b. al-Djuʿayd iv, 421a — IV, 439b
ʿAmr b. al-Ḥadjdjādj al-Zubaydī iii, 609b, 610b — III, 630a, 631a
ʿAmr b. Ḥazm iv, 927b — IV, 960b
ʿAmr b. Hind i, **451b,** 772a; iii, 226b; v, 633b, 640a — I, **464b,** 795a; III, 229a; V, 637b, 644b
ʿAmr b. Ḥurayth al-Makhzūmī i, 1242b — I, 1280b
ʿAmr b. Ḳamīʾa i, **452a,** 963b; iii, 1177b, 1178a — I, **465a,** 993a; III, 1206b, 1207a
ʿAmr b. Kirkira s, 20b, **73b** — S, 20b, **73b**
ʿAmr b. Kulthūm i, **452a;** iii, 222b; iv, 998a; v, 633b — I, **465a;** III, 229a; IV, 1030b; V, 637b
ʿAmr b. al-Layth i, 278a, **452b,** 1001a, 1294a; ii, 191b, 553b, 812a, 1048b; iii, 344b, 1202a; iv, 21a, b, 22a, 100a, 188b, 266a, 975a; v, 158a; s, 125b — I, 286b, **465b,** 1032a, 1333b; II, 197b, 567b, 831a, 1073a; III, 355a, 1232b; IV, 22b, 23a, b, 104b, 197a, 278a, 1007a; V, 157b; S, 124b
ʿAmr b. Luḥayy i, **453a;** ii, 572a; iii, 537a; iv, 91b, 421b; v, 76b, 77a, b, 692a — I, **466a;** II, 586a; III, 555b; IV, 95b, 440a; V, 79a, b, 697a
ʿAmr b. Maʿdīkarib i, **453a** — I, **466a**
ʿAmr b. Masʿada i, 279b, **453b** — I, 288a, **466b**
ʿAmr b. al-Nuʿmān i, 53a, 771b, 1283a; iv, 1187b; v, 995a — I, 546, 794b, 1322b; IV, 1220a; V, 990b
ʿAmr b. Saʿīd al-Ashdak i, 58a, 76b, **453b;** ii, 360b; iii, 226b, 271a, 608b — I, 60a, 79a, **466b;** II, 370a; III, 233b, 278b, 629b
ʿAmr b. Sālim al-Tudjībī i, 250b; v, 78a, b — I, 258a; V, 80b, 81a
ʿAmr b. Shimr s, 233a — S, 232b
ʿAmr b. Sufyān → Abu 'l-Aʿwar al-Sulamī
ʿAmr b. ʿUbayd i, 274a, **454a;** iii, 985a, 1142b; iv, 370b — I, 282a, **467a;** III, 1009b, 1171a; IV, 387a
ʿAmr b. ʿUbayd Allāh al-Aḳṭaʿ i, 1103a, b; ii, 234b, 237a, b — I, 1136a, 1137a; II, 241b, 243b, 244b
ʿAmr b. ʿUmayr b. ʿAwf s, 355a — S, 354b
ʿAmr b. Umm Iyās i, 1241b — I, 1279b
ʿAmr b. al-Zubayr i, 55a, 453b; iii, 970a — I, 56b, 466b; III, 994b
ʿAmr al-Ḍāʾīʿ → ʿAmr b. Ḳamīʾa
Amr al-Ḳays b. ʿAmr i, 526a — I, 542a
ʿAmr Makkī iii, 100a, 102a — III, 102b, 104b
ʿAmr Muzayḳiyāʾ i, 771a — I, 794a
Amram → ʿImrān
Amradtī s, 297b — S, 279b
al-ʿAmrī → Muḥammad b. ʿUthmān
Amritsar i, **454a,** 1348a; s, 242a — I, **467a,** 1388a; S, 242a
Amrōhā s, **73b** — S, **74a**
Amrōhāʿī, Maṣḥafī s, 74a — S, 74b
ʿAmrūn iv, 289b — IV, 302b
ʿAmrūs b. Fatḥ i, 120b — I, 124a
ʿAmrūs b. Yūsuf iii, 74a; s, 82a — III, 76b; S, 81b
ʿAms → Nuṣayrīs
Amū Daryā i, 222a, b, 313b, **454b,** 459b, 607a; 607a; ii, 1a, 2a; iv, 502b, 1060b; v, 24a, 388b, 581b, 868a; s, 125a, 281a — I, 228b, 229a, 323a, **467b,** 473a, 627a; II, 1a, 2a; IV, 524b, 1092a; V, 24b, 389b, 586b, 874b; S, 124b, 281a
ʿAmūd i, **457b** — I, **470b**
al-ʿAmūdī, Āl ii, 173b — II, 179a
ʿAmūdja-zāde → Ḥusayn Pasha, ʿAmūdja-zāde
Āmul, Māzandarān i, 237a, **459a;** ii, 746a; iv, 644a, 646b; s, 298a, 363b — I, 244b, **472a;** II, 764b; IV, 670b, 673a; S, 297b, 363b
Āmul, Turkmen S.S.R./turkmène R.S.S. i, **459b,** iii, 255a; iv, 583b; s, 228a, 281a, 335a, 356b, 357a — I, **472b;** III, 262a; IV, 607a; S, 228a, 281a, 334b, 356b
Amulets/Amulettes → Ḥamāʾil
Amulī → Awliyā Allāh; Karīm al-Dīn
al-Āmulī → Ḥaydar-i Āmulī
ʿAmūr i, 371b, 460b — I, 382b, 473b
ʿAmūr, Djabal i, **460a** — I, **473b**
Amurath → Murād
Āmūya → Āmul, Turkmenistan
ʿAmwās i, **460b** — I, **474a**
Āna → Sikka
ʿĀna i, **461a** — I, **474a**
Anadolu i, 292b, 322b, **461b;** ii, 8a, 83b, 966b; iii, 211a, 215b; v, 291b, 881a, 978a, 979a, 1144b — I, 302a, 332b, **475a;** II, 8a, 85a, 988b; III, 217a, 221b; V, 291a, b, 887b, 1137a
Anadolu (eyālet) i, **480b,** 1160a; ii, 32b, 722a — I, **494b,** 1194b; II, 33a, 741a
Anadolu Ḥiṣārí i, **481a,** 1251b, 1318a; iii, 483a — I, **495a,** 1289b, 1358b; III, 500a
Anadolu Kavaghî i, 481a, 1252a — I, 495a, 1290a
Anāhīd → Zuhara
Anahilwada → Anhalwāra
ʿAnāḳ i, **481a** — I, **495b**
Anakkaza i, 1258a — I, 1296a
Analogy, reasoning by-/Analogie, raisonnement par- → Ḳiyās
Anamur i, **481a** — I, **495b**
ʿĀnān b. David i, 481b; iv, 604a, b, 606a — I, 495b; IV, 628a, 629a, 630b
Anand Ram Mukhlis iv, 1127b, 1128a — IV, 1159a, b
Ananda b. Mangalay b. Ḳūbīlay iv, 553b — IV, 577b
ʿAnāniyya i, **481b;** iv, 604a — I, **495b;** IV, 628a
Anapa i, 63a, **481b;** ii, 25b — I, 65a, **496a;** II, 26a
Anārkalī ii, 380a — II, 390a
Anas b. Abī Unās iii, 224b — III, 231b
Anas b. Mālik i, 52a, 431b, **482a;** iii, 40b, 586b, 947b; iv, 899a — I, 54a, 443b, **496a;** III, 42a, 606b, 972b; IV, 931b
Anas b. Mudrik iv, 1106a — IV, 1137b
ʿĀnāt s, 130a — S, 129b
Anathema/Anathème → Liʿān
Anatolia/Anatolie → Anadolu
Anatomy/Anatomie → Tashrīḥ
Anavarza i, 790a — I, 813b
Anaw i, 701a — I, 722a
ʿAnaza (spear/lance) i, **482a,** 1215a — I, **496b,** 1251b
ʿAnaza (tribe/tribu) i, **482b,** 528b, 545a, 873b, 1093b; ii, 184b; iii, 293a, 1253b — I, **496b,** 544b, 562a, 897b, 1126a; II, 190b; III, 302a, 1286a
Anazarba → ʿAyn Zarba
ʿAnazeh i, 1277a — I, 1316a
al-Anbābī, Muḥammad i, 819b, 1019b — I, 842b, 1051a
Anbāduḳlīs i, 235b, **483b;** iii, 869a — I, 243a, **498a;** III, 893a
ʿAnbar i, **484a,** 837b — I, **498b,** 860b
al-Anbār i, 17a, **484b,** 1073b; ii, 195a, 946b; iv, 911b — I, 17b, **499a,** 1105b; II, 201a, 968b; IV, 944a, b
ʿAnbar, Banū 'l- → Tamīm
al-Anbārī → ʿĀmir b. ʿAbd al-Ḳays
al-Anbārī, Abū Bakr Muḥammad b. al-Ḳāsim i, 185a, **485b** — I, 190a, **500a**
al-Anbārī, Abu 'l-Barakāt i, **485b;** iii, 550b, 706b, 934b; v, 242b — I, **500a;** III, 569b, 728b, 959a; V, 240b
al-Anbārī, Abū Muḥammad i, **486a** — I, **500b**

Anbarköy s, 330a — S, 329b
ʿAnbasa al-Aʿwar iv, 346b — IV, 361a
Anbāt iv, 547b — IV, 571b
al-Anbīḳ i, **486a** — I, **500b**
Anbiya v, 651b, 652b — V, 656a, 657a
Ancyra → Anḳara
al-Andalīsh i, 486b — I, 501a
al-Andalus i, 58b, 75b, 76a, 79b, 82a, 85b, 86b, 121b, 134b, 162a, 165b, 242a, 390a, 427b, **486b,** 1046a, 1148a, 1319b; ii, 129b, 130a, 331a, 601b; iii, 220a, 1055a; v, 877a, 1118b, 1119a, 1149b; s, 103a — I, 60b, 77b, 78a, 81b, 84b, 88a, 89a, 125a, 138b, 166b, 170b, 249b, 401a, 440a, **501a,** 1078a, 1182b, 1360a; II, 132b, 133b, 341a, 616b; III, 226b, 1081a; V, 882b, 1115a, b, 1140b; S, 102b
- agriculture i, **491b;** ii, 901a; v, 878a — I, **506b;** II, 922a; V, 883b
- governors/gouverneurs i, **493a,** b; iii, 46a, 587b, 702a — I, **508a,** b; III, 48a, 607b, 724a
- history/histoire i, 44a, 320b; ii, 72a; iii, 762b, 789b, 805b, 848a; iv, 494b, 1156b — I, 45a, 330b; II, 73b; III, 785b, 812b, 829a, 872a; IV, 515b, 1188b
- literature and culture/littérature et culture i, 404b, **497a-503b,** 599a; ii, 729a, 988a; iii, 70a, b, 657b, 702a, 771b; iv, 1006b-1008a; v, 218b, 744b, 1128a — I, 416b, **512a-519a,** 619a; II, 747b, 1010b; III, 72b, 679a, 724a, 795a; IV, 1039a-1040a; V, 216a, 749b, 1124b
- in North Africa/en Afrique du Nord i, 92b, **496a;** ii, 161a; v, 1190b — I, 95b, **511a;** II, 166a; V, 1180b
ʿAndam i, 961b — I, 991a
Andaman isles/îles iii, 407a — III, 419b
Andarāb i, **504a** — I, **519a**
Andarāba s, 125b — S, 124b
Andarūn → Enderūn
Anday, Melih Cevdet iv, 545a — IV, 568b
Andi i, **504a,** 756a; ii, 86b, 88b — I, **519b,** 778b; II, 88a, 90b
Andidjān i, **504b,** 847b; ii, 791b, 792a; v, 461a — I, **520a,** 871a; II, 810b, 811a; V, 464a
ʿAndjar → ʿAyn al-Djarr
Andjudān iv, 201b — IV, 210b
Andjuman i, **505a,** xvi; ii, 429b, 433a, 434a, b; iv, 39b, 789b — I, **520b;** II, 440b, 444b, 445a, b; IV, 42a, 821a
Andjuman-i adab-i Irān i, 505a — I, 520b
Andjuman-i āthār-i millī i, 505a — I, 520b
Andjüman-i Dānish i, 284b, 505a; ii, 532a; v, 904a — I, 293b, 520b; II, 545a; V, 910a
Andjuman-i Ḥimāyat-i Islām i, 506a — I, 521a
Andjuman-i Khuddām-i Kaʿba s, 4b, **74a,** 293b — S, 3b, **74b,** 293a
Andjuman-i Makhfī ii, 434b — II, 445b
Andjuman-i millī i, 505a; ii, 435b — I, 520b; II, 447a
Andjuman-i Shuʿarāʾ i, 1302a — I, 1342a
Andjuman-i Tablīghāt-i Islāmī iv, 166b — IV, 174a
Andjuman-i Taraḳḳi-i Urdū i, 505b — I, 521a
Andkhūy i, **506a,** 530b; s, 281a — I, **521b,** 546b; S, 281a
Andrea Doria iv, 1156b, 1157b — IV, 1188b, 1189b
Andrinople → Edirne
Âne → Ḥimār
Aneiza → ʿUnayza
al-Anf, Banū iv, 201a — IV, 209b, 210a
Anfā i, **506a** — I, **521b**
Angels/Anges → Malāʾika
Anglo-Persian Oil Company iv, 790a — IV, 821b
Angohrān s, 129a — S, 128a
Angora → Anḳara
Angres s, 246b — S, 246b
Anhalwāra i, **506b;** ii, 1123b, 1124a — I, **522a;** II, 1149b, 1150a, b
Ānī i, 421a, **507a;** 637b, 638a, 639a; iv, 347b, 670a; v, 452a — I, 432b, **522b,** 658b, 659a, b; IV, 362b, 697a, b; V, 454b
Animals/Animaux → Ḥayawān
Anīs, Mīr Bābar ʿAlī i, **508b;** ii, 73b; iii, 119b; s, **74b,** 358b — I, **524a;** II, 74b; III, 122a; S, **75a,** 358b
ʿĀnis i, 993b — I, 1024a
ʿAnḳāʾ i, **509a;** iii, 169a; iv, 928a — I, **524b;** III, 173a; IV, 961a
ʿAnkabūt i, **509a** — I, **524b**
Anḳad v, 389b — V, 390b
Anḳara i, **509b,** 974b; s, 47b, 318a — I, **525a,** 1004b; S, 48a, 318a
- university/université ii, 425b — II, 436b
Anḳārawī → Ismāʿīl Anḳārawī
al-Ankubarda (Lombardy/Lombardie) → Īṭaliya
Anmār i, 73a, 865a — I, 75a, 889b
Anna → Sikka
al-ʿAnnāba i, **511b;** iv, 359b; s, 103a, 156a — I, **527a;** IV, 375a; S, 102b, 156b
Annal(e)s → Taʾrīkh
Annam iii, 1210b, 1211a — III, 1241a, b
ʿAnnāzid(e)s i, **512a;** iii, 258b; v, 453b — I, **527b;** III, 265b; 456b
Anniyya i, **513b** — I, **529a;** V, 456b
Anṣāb → Nuṣb
Ansar (Sudan/Soudan) v, 1249a, b, 1251a, 1252b — V, 1240a, b, 1241b, 1243b
al-Anṣār i, 45a, 55a, 110a, 305a, **514a,** 545a, 771a, 990b; ii, 728b; iii, 226b, 285b; iv, 1187a; v, 435a, 995a, 996b; s, 10a — I, 46b, 57a, 113a, 314b, **529b,** 562a, 794a, 1021b; II, 747a; III, 233b, 294a; IV, 1220a; V, 437b, 990a, 991b, S, 9b
Anṣār ṭarīḳa iii, 524a — III, 542a
ʿAnsāra i, **515a** — I, **530b**
al-Anṣārī → ʿAbd al-Ḳuddūs; Abū Zayd; al-Awsī; Zakāriyyāʾ
al-Anṣārī s, 125a — S, 124a
al-Anṣārī, Abu 'l-Ḳāsim Sulaymān b. Nāṣir s, 346b — S, 346b
al-Anṣārī al-Harawī i, 69b, 417a, **515b,** 936b; iii, 84a, 161a, 177b, 821b, 1148b; iv, 63b, 473a, 697a, 1057b; s, 292a — I, 71b, 428b, **531a,** 965b; III, 86a, 164b, 181b, 845b, 1176b; IV, 67a, 494a, 725b, 1089a; S, 291b
al-Anṣārī al-Ḥusayn b. Yaḥyā s, 82a — S, 81b
Anṣārī, Muḥammad Amīn s, 74a, 75a — S, 74b, 75b
Anṣārī, Shaykh Ḥusayn s, 75a — S, 75b
Anṣārī, Shaykh Murtaḍā v, 1087b; s, **75a** — V, 1085a; S, **75b**
al-ʿAnsī → Abu 'l-Mughīra; ʿUmar b. Hāniʾ
al-Anṭākī, Dāʾūd i, **516a,** 594a; iv, 1134a; s, 40b — I, **531b,** 613b; IV, 1165b; S, 40b
al-Anṭāki, Yaḥyā b. Saʿīd i, **516a;** iii, 81b — I, **531b;** III, 83b
Anṭākiya i, 182b, 466a, **516b,** 761b, 1125b; iii, 12b; v, 437a, 921b — I, 187b, 480a, **532a,** 784b, 1159b; III, 13a; V, 439b, 927a
Antalaotra i, 522a — I, 538a
Antalya i, 476b, **517b;** iv, 816b — I, 490b, **533a;** IV, 849a
Antambaok, Antambahwaka i, 522a — I, 538a
ʿAntar, Sīrat i, **518a,** 521b; ii, 236b, 238b; iii, 111b; v, 951b — I, **533b,** 537b; II, 243a, 245a; III, 114a; V, 955a
ʿAntara b. Shaddād i, 25a, **521a;** s, 38b, 178b — I, 26a, **537a;** S, 39a, 179b
ʿAntarī i, **522a** — I, **537b**
Anṭartūs → Ṭartūs
Antel → Djelāl, Ṣadreddīn
Antelope → Hahāt
Antemuru i, **522a** — I, **538a**
Antep → ʿAyntāb

Anthropoid(e) → Ķird
Antinomianism/antinomien → Ibāḥa
Antioch/Antioche → Anṭāķiya
Antioch in Pisidia/Antioche en Pisidie i, 12b — I, 13a
Antonym(e)s → Aḍḍād
Anṭūn Faraḥ → Faraḥ Anṭūn
Anūdjūr → Unūdjūr
Anūsha b. Abi 'l-Ghāzī iv, 754a; s, 281a, 420a — IV, 784b; S, 281a, 420a
Anūsharwān i, **522b** — I, **538b**
Anūsharwān (Chosroës) → Kisrā
Anūshirwān, Khusraw → Kisrā
Anūshirwān b. Kābūs iv, 100b — IV, 105a
Anūshirwān b. Khālid i, **522b;** iii, 221a, 327b, 1158a; iv, 265a — I, **538b;** III, 228a, 337b, 1186b; IV, 277a
Anūshirwān b. Ṭughrilbeg v, 388a — V, 389a
Anūshirwān al-Īlkhān ii, 47a — II, 48a
Anūshtekin → Anūshtigin
Anūshtigin al-Duzbarī ii, 484a — II, 496a
Anūshtigin Gharcha'ī ii, 1011a, 1082a; iv, 1064a, 1067a; s, 279a — II, 1034b, 1107a; IV, 1095b, 1098b; S, 279a
Anūshtigin Shīrgīr i, 1359b — I, 1399b
Anwā' i, **523a**; iv, 518b; s, 380b — I, **538b**; IV, 541a; S, 380b
Anwar ii, 222a — II, 228b
Anwār al-Dīn i, 62a — I, 645b
Anwār al-Ḥaķķ s, 293a — S, 293a
Anwār Ķāhira iv, 120a — IV, 125b
Anwār-i Suhaylī → Kalīla wa Dimna
Anwarī i, **524a,** 1301a; ii, 1034a; iii, 1115a; s, 21b, 65a, 240a — I, **540a,** 1341a; II, 1058a; III, 1142a; S, 21b, 65b, 240a
Anwarī, al-Ḥādjdj Sa'dullah → Enwerī
'Anz b. Wā'il i, 709a — I, 729b
Anzarūt s, **77b** — S, **77b**
Anzali → Enzeli
Aouguerout s, 328b — S, 328a
Apamea/Apamée → Afāmiya
Apanage → Iķṭā'; Tīmār
Ape → Ķird
Apiculture → Naḥl
Apolaffar i, 1166a; iv, 275a — I, 1201a; IV, 287a
Apollonius → Balīnūs
Apologue → Mathal
Apology/Apologie → Madḥ
Apostasy/Apostasie-Apostat(e) → Murtadd
Appel à la prière → Adhān
Apricot → Mishmish
Aprīdīs → Afrīdī
'Ār iii, 396a; s, 53a, **78a**, 191a — III, 408b; S, 53b, **78a**, 192a
al-'Āra i, **524b** — I, **540a**
al-'Arab i, **524b-533b;** iii, 1098a — I, **540b-550a;** III, 1125a
'Arab, Djazīrat al- i, 102b, **533b**; s, 213b— I, 105b, **550a**; S, 213b
- administration i, **539a,** 976a — I, **555b,** 1006a
- demography/démographie s, 213b — S, 213b
- ethnography/ethnographie i, 39a, 436a, **543b,** 872a — I, 40a, 448b, **560b,** 896b
- flora and/et fauna i, **540a — I, 556b**
- geography/géographie i, 156a, **534b,** 1230a, b; iii, 124a — I, 160b, **551a,** 1266b, 1267a, b; III, 127a
- history/histoire i, **547a-555a;** 773a, 881a — I, **564b-572b;** III, 796a, 905a
'Arab, Malik ii, 110b — II, 113a
al-'Arab al-'āriba i, 544a, 563b; iv, 448b — I, 561b, 581b; IV, 468b
al-'Arab al-bā'ida i, 544a, 563b; iv, 448b — I, 561b, 581b; IV, 468b
Arab Bank for Economic Development in Africa s, 241a
Arab Fund for Economic and Social Development s, 241a
Arab Institute for the Guarantee of Investments s, 241a
Arab League → Djāmi'a al-'Arabiyya
Arab Legion i, 46a; iii, 264b, 1258b
'Arab Muḥammad Khān i, 120b; v, 24a — I, 124a; V, 24b
'Arab al-musta'riba i, 563b, 873b — I, 581b, 897b
Arab Revolt i, 46a; ii, 289a, 872a; iii, 263b, 643b
Arab Socialist Union s, 8a, 9a
Arab Union → al-Ittiḥād al-'arabī
'Araba i, 205b, **556b**; v, 659a — I, 211b, **574b**; V, 663b
'Araba, Wādī i, **558b**; s, 117a— I, **576a**; S, 116b
Arababnī, Arabaynī i, 176b; iii, 3b — I, 181a; III, 3b
Arabesque i, 498b, 501a, **558b;** ii, 557a, 777b, 864a; iii, 219b; v, 232b, 991a — I, 513b, 516a, **576b;** II, 571a, 796a, 884a; III, 226a; V, 230b, 986a
'Arabfaķīh i, **561a** — I, **579a**
'Arabī Dafa' Allāh i, 1157a; v, 1251a — I, 1191a; V, 1242a
al-'Arabī al-Fāsī i, 428a — I, 440a
'Arābī Pasha → 'Urābī Pasha
Arabia → 'Arab, Djazīrat al-
Arabian Nights → Alf layla wa-layla
Arabic language → 'Arabiyya
Arabic writing → Khaṭṭ
Arabie → 'Arab, Djazīrat al-
Arabie séoudite I, 40a, b, 550a, b, 555b, 1354a; II, 571b, 676b; III, 374a; S, 417b
- institutions II, 435b; V, 1053b
'Arabistān i, **561b;** iii, 1102a; iv, 1171b; v, 80b, 81a — I, **579a;** III, 1129a; IV, 1204b; V, 82b, 83a
'Arabiyya i, 157b, 501b, **561b;** ii, 167a, 280a, 306b; 468b, 472a, 490b; iii, 1216a, 1259a; v, 185b, 605b, 804a, 914a, 915b, 1091b, 1093a, 1203a, 1207a — I, 162a, 516b, **579a;** II, 172b, 288b, 315b, 480b, 484a, 502b; III, 1247a, 1292a; V, 183a, 609b, 810a, 919b, 921a, 1088b, 1090a, 1193b, 1197b
al-'Arabiyya (Ṭarīķa) s, 411a — S, 411b
al-'Arabiyya, Djazīrat i, 535b, **603a** — I, 552a, **622b**
'Arabkīr i, **603a** — I, **622b**
'Arabshāhid(e)s ii, 45a; iv, 1064b, 1068a — II, 45b; IV, 1096a, 1100a
'Arād i, 128b, **603b** — I, 132a, **623a**
A'radj ii, 918a — II, 939a
al-A'rāf i, **603b** — I, **623b**
'Arafa, 'Arafāt i, 43b, **604a;** iii, 31b, 35b; s, 33a — I, 44b, **623b;** III, 33a, 37a; S, 33b
'Arafa, Mawlāy → Muḥammad b. 'Arafa
'Arafa, Sīdī iii, 69a; iv, 828a — III, 71b; IV, 861a
Araghūn s, **80a** — S, **79b**
Araignée → 'Ankabūt
al-Arā'ish i, 356a, **604b**; v, 1245b; s, 29a— I, 367a, **624a**; V, 1236a; S, 29a
al-Arak i, 165b, **605b** — I, 170b, **625a**
Arāk → Sulṭānābād
Arāk (Iran) s, 342a — S, 341b
Arakan i, **606a,** 1333a; ii, 32a — I, **625b,** 1272b; II, 32b
Arak'el of/de Tabrīz s, 275a — S, 274b
Araķiyya iv, 382b — IV, 399a
Aral sea i, 456a, **606b**; s, 169a, 244b— I, 469a, **626b**; S, 169a, 244b
Aram ii, 278a — II, 286b
Ārām Shāh ii, 267a; iii, 416a, 1155a; s, 360a — II, 275b; III, 429a, 1183b; S, 359b
Aramaic v, 229a — V, 226b
Arar → Harar
Ararat → Aghrî Dagh

Aras, Araxes → al-Rass
Arat, Reshīd Raḥmetī s, **82a** – S, **82a**
Arayabnī → Arababnī
Arbāᶜ i, 371b – I, 382b
Arbāb → Rabb
Arbad → Irbid
Arbalète → Ḳaws
ᶜArbān i, **608a** – I, **628a**
Arbaᶜūn Ḥadīthan s, **82b** – S, **82b**
Arbela → Irbid
Arbeles → Irbil
al-ᶜArbī (Larbi) Bakkūsh s, 387a – S, 387a
Arbil v, 455b, 456a – V, 458a, b
ᶜArbīlī, Ibrāhīm ii, 471a – II, 483a
Arbira → Irbil
Arbūna i, **608b;** iii, 495a; v, 1121a – I, **628a;** III, 512a; V, 1117b
Arc (arme) → Ḳaws
Arc-en-ciel → Ḳaws Ḳuzaḥ
Archery/Archerie → Ḳaws
Archidona → Urdjudhūna
Architecture i, 457b, **608b;** ii, 288a, 340b, 557a; iii, 142, 143, 228b, 1123b, 1267a; iv, 236a, b; v, 12a, 1136a – I, 470b, **628b;** II, 296a, 350a, 571a; III, 146, 147, 235b, 1151b, 1300a; IV, 246b; V, 11a, 1131b
- al-Andalus i, **497b;** ii, 1014b-1019a – I, **512b;** II, 1038a-1042b
- India, Indonesia/Inde, Indonésie ii, 598a, 1103b; iii, 148a, 440b, 1227b – II, 613a, 1129b; III, 151a, 454b, 1259a
Archives → Wathīḳa
Arči i, **624b,** 756a; ii, 88b – I, **645a,** 778b; II, 90b
Arcos → Arkūsh
Arcot i, **624b;** iii, 320a – I, **645a;** III, 331a
Arḍ i, 625a; ii, 93a, 900b – I, 645b; II, 94b, 921b
ᶜArḍ → Istiᶜrād
ᶜArḍ ḥal i, **625a** – I, **646a**
Ardabb → Kayl
Ardabīl i, **625a,** 837a; ii, 88a, 598b; iv, 7b, 49a, 1170a; v, 244a; s, 139a, 140a – I, **646a,** 860b; II, 89b, 613b; IV, 8b, 51b, 1203a; V, 241b; S, 138b, 139b
Ardahān i, 468b, **626a,** 643b – I, 482b, **646b,** 664a
Ardakān i, **626a;** s, 342a – I, **646b;** S, 341b
Ardalān i, **626b;** v, 170a – I, **647a;** V, 167b
Ardashāt i, 645b – I, 666a
Ardashīr (Bāwandid(e)) → Ḥusām al-Dawla
Ardashīr I i, 2b, 305b, 528a, 548b, **626b,** 1341b; ii, 16b, 135b, 925b; iii, 112b, 113a, 394a; iv, 809b – I, 2b, 315a, 544a, 566a, **647a,** 1381b; II, 16b, 139a, 947a; III, 115a, b, 406b; IV, 842a
Ardashīr II i, 626b – I, 647a
Ardashīr III i, 626b – I, 647a
Ardashīr Khurra → Fīrūzābād
Ardibehisht → Taᶜrīkh
Ardistān i, **626b;** iv, 99b; v, 1147b; s, 23b – I, **647b;** IV, 104a; V, 1139a; S, 23b
al-ᶜArdjī, ᶜAbd Allāh b. ᶜUmar i, 10b, 305a, **626b;** ii, 428b, 1011b, 1029b, 1030b – I, 10b, 314b, **647b;** II, 439b, 1035a, 1053a, 1054a
Ardjīsh i, **627a;** iv, 587a – I, **647b;** IV, 609b
Ardjīsh-Dagh → Erdjiyā s Daghī
Ardjun Singh ii, 380b; iii, 424a – II, 390b; III, 437b
Ardumusht s, 36a, 37a – S, 36b, 37a
Ardzrunī i, 637a, b – I, 658a
Areg (Reg) → ᶜIrḳ
Arenga ii, 309b, 315a – II, 318a, 324a
Areshgūl → Tafna
ᶜArfadja b. Harthama al-Bārikī ii, 811b – II, 831a
Argan i, **627b** – I, **648a**
Argent → Fiḍḍa
Arghana → Erghani
Arghen → Hargha
Arghiyān s, **83a** – S, **83a**
Arghun i, 148a, 227b, 228a, **627b;** iii, 420a, 632b – I, 152a, 234b, 235a, **648a;** III, 433b, 654a
Arghun Aḳa ii, 606a; iv, 30b – II, 621a; IV, 32b
Arghūn Khān i, 346b; ii, 606b, 607b; iii, 1122a; iv, 31a, 621a; v, 102b, 662b, 827a – I, 357a; II, 621b, 622b; III, 1150a; IV, 33b, 645b; V, 105a, 668a, 833a
Arghūn al-Nāṣirī iii, 954b – III, 979a
Arghūn Shāh (d. 1349) iii, 818a – III, 841b
Arghūn Shāh b. Kilidj Arslan II i, 431b – I, 444a
Argungu ii, 1146b – II, 1173b
Arguri i, 251b – I, 259b
Argyrocastro → Ergeri
ᶜArīb (singer/chanteur) iv, 821b – IV, 854b
ᶜArīb b. Saᶜd al-Kātib al-Ḳurṭubī i, 491b, 600a, **628a** – I, 506b, 620a, **649a**
ᶜĀrid iii, 196a, 197b; iv, 265a, 266a – III, 200b, 202b; IV, 276b, 278a
al-ᶜĀrid i, 72b, 126b, **628b** – I, 74b, 130b, **649a**
ᶜĀriḍ-i mamālik v, 685b – V, 690b
al-ᶜĀriḍ → Ibn Saᶜdān
al-ᶜArīḍa ii, 78b – II, 80a
ᶜArīḍa, Nasīb v, 1254b, 1255a, b – V, 1245b, 1246a, b
ᶜArīf i, 438b, **629a;** iv, 532a – I, 451a, **649b;** IV, 555a
ᶜĀrif → Djalāl al-Dīn; Muḥammad
ᶜĀrif, ᶜAbd al-Raḥmān v, 469a – V, 471b, 472a
ᶜĀrif, ᶜAbd al-Salām iii, 1259a; iv, 719a; v, 468b, 469a – III, 1292a; IV, 748a; V, 471a, b
ᶜĀrif, Abu l'-Ḳāsim iv, 789b – IV, 821b
ᶜĀrif, Amīr → ᶜĀrif Čelebī
ᶜĀrif, Mīrzā Abu l-Ḳāsim s, **83b** – S, **83b**
ᶜĀrif al-ᶜĀrif s, 67b – S, 68a
ᶜĀrif Čelebī s, **83b** – S, **83a**
ᶜĀrif Hikmet (calligraphy/-ie) iv, 1126b – IV, 1158a
ᶜArif Hikmet Bey i, 71a, **630a;** v, 263b, 1005a – I, 73a, **651a;** V, 261b, 1000b
ᶜĀrif Ḥikmet Hersekli → Hersekli
ᶜĀrif Pasha iv, 876b – IV, 909b
ᶜĀrif al-Shihābī iii, 519a, b – III, 537a, b
ᶜĀrif, Ulu → ᶜĀrif Čelebī
ᶜĀrifī, Mawlānā Maḥmūd iv, 67a; s, **84a** – IV, 70b; S, **84a**
Arîgh Böke i, 1188a; ii, 3a, 45b; iv, 811b; v, 38b, 300a – I, 1223a; II, 3a, 46b; IV, 844b; V, 40a, 299b
Arīn → Ḳubbat al-Arḍ
al-ᶜArīsh i, **630b** – I, **651a**
Aristotle, Theology of i, 349b, 416b, 449b, 514a, 631a; ii, 554b, 949a; iii, 644a, 942b; v, 701a, 842a
Aristote, Théologie d'- I, 360b, 428a, 462b, 529b, 651b; II, 568b, 971a; III, 665b, 967b; V, 706a, 848b
Arisṭūṭālīs i, 178b, 235b, 342a, 349b, 350a, 419b, 513b, **630b,** 736b, 795b, 1083b, 1155b, 1340a; ii, 101b, 249a, 358b, 493a, 550a, 740a, 765a, 770a, 779b, 948b; iii, 21b, 29b, 301b, 509a, 596b, 915b, 942b, 1130a – I, 183b, 243a, 352b, 360b, 431a, 529a, **651b,** 758b, 819a, 1116a, 1190a, 1380b; II, 103b, 256a, 368b, 505b, 563b, 758b, 783b, 788b, 798a, 970b; III, 22b, 31b, 310b, 526b, 617a, 939b, 967b, 1158a
Arithmetic/Arithmétique → ᶜIlm al-ḥisāb
Arithmomancy/-ie → Ḥisāb al-Djummal
Ariyaruk ii, 336a – II, 345b
ᶜAriyya i, **633a** – I, **654a**
Arḳa → ᶜIrḳa
Arkalī Khān i, 1036a; iv, 920b, 921a – I, 1067b; IV, 953b, 954a
al-Arḳam i, **633b – I, 654a**
Arkān → Rukn
Ārkāt → Arcot
Arkush i, 6a, **633b** – I, 6a, **654b**
Armenia/Arménie → Armīniya
Armenian/Arménien (language/langue) iv, 350b,

351b; v, 1a — IV, 365b, 366b; V, 1a
Armenians/Arméniens i, 470b, 638b, 666a; ii, 65b; iii, 214b; iv, 8a, 99a, 240b, 241b, 476a, 485b; v, 1a, 136b, 462b, s, 274b, 275a, b — I, 484b, 659a, 686b; II, 66b; III, 220b; IV, 8b-9a, 103a, 251a, b, 252a, 497a, 506b; V, 1a, 139b, 465b, S, 274b
Armīniya i, 10a, 18a, 64b, 77a, 465a, 470a, **634a,** 660a, 1052a; ii, 37a, 678b; iii, 12b; iv, 89b, 90a, 344b, 345b, 347b; v, 292a; s, 225b, 365a — I, 10a, 18b, 66b, 79b, 478b, 484a, **655a,** 680b, 1084a; II, 37b, 695b; III, 13a; IV, 93b, 94a, 359a, 360b, 362a; V, 292a; S, 225b, 365a
Arm(e)s → Silāḥ
Armiyā → Irmiyā
Armoise → Afsantīn
Armour/Armure → Silāḥ
Army → Djaysh, Lashkar, Ordu, etc
Arnab s, **84b** — S, **84a**
Arnawutluḳ i, **650a,** 1090b, 1118b, 1162a; ii, 184a, 721a; iv, 342b, 1173b; v, 265a, 284b; s, 149b — I, **670a,** 1123a, 1152a, 1196b; II, 190a, 739b; IV, 357a, 1206b; V, 262b, 283a; S, 149b
Arnedo → Arnīṭ
Arnīṭ i, **658a** — I, **678b**
ʿArnūn → Ḳalʿat al-Shaḳīf
Arpentage → Misāḥa
Aror → Arūr
Arba i, **658a** — I, **679a**
Arpa Khān ii, 45b, 401a; iii, 1208a — II, 46b, 411b; III, 1239a
Arpalīḳ i, **658a** — I, **679a**
Arrabal iii, 74a — III, 76b
ʿArrāda i, 556b, **658b;** iii, 469b, 470a, 482a — I, 574b, **679b;** III, 486a, b, 499a
Arradjān i, **659a**; s, 119a — I, **679b**; S, 118b
al-Arradjānī, Abū Bakr Aḥmad i, **659b**; iv, 863b; s, 326b — I, **680a**; IV, 897a; S, 326a
ʿArrāf i, **659b**; iv, 421b — I, **680a**; IV, 440a
Arrān i, 639a, 642a, **660a,** 1041a; ii, 975b; iii, 1110b; iv, 344b, 345b, 347b, 573a — I, 659b, 662b, **680b,** 1072b; II, 998a; III, 1138a; IV, 359a, b, 360b, 362b, 595b
Arrapkha v, 144a, 145a — V, 146b, 147b
Arrow → Nabl; Nushshāb
Arsak i, 99b — I, 102a
Arsenal → Dār al-Ṣināʿa; Bārūd
Arsenius iii, 79a — III, 81b
Arsh ii, 340b, 341b — II, 350b, 351a
ʿArsh → Kursī
ʿArsh i, **661a**; iv, 362a — I, **681b**; IV, 377b
Arshakid(e)s i, 188b — I, 194a
Arshashdib → Arči
Arshgūl i, **661b**; s, 376b — I, **682a**; S, 377a
Arshīn → Dhirāʿ
al-Arsiyya iv, 1174b — IV, 1207b
Arslan i, **661b** — I, **682b**
Arslān, Shakīb iii, 524b, 525a; iv, 159a; v, 794b; s, 159b — III, 542b, 543a; IV, 166a; V, 800b; S, 159b
Arslān b. Aḳ Sunḳur → Arslān Abīhī
Arslan b. Saldjūḳ i, **661b,** 1292a; ii, 4a, b, 1108b; iii, 1114a — I, **682b,** 1331b; II, 4b, 1134b; III, 1141b
Arslan b. Toghrul iii, 1110b — III, 1137b
Arslān Abīhī i, 300b; ii, 764b — I, 310a; II, 783a
Arslan Arghūn i, **662a,** 1051b, 1331b; iv, 1067a — I, **683a,** 1083a, b, 1372b; IV, 1098b
Arslan Baba i, 298b — I, 308a
Arslan Beg b. Balangirī → Khāṣṣ Beg Arslan
Arslan-beg i, 101a — I, 104a
Arslan Isrāʾīl → Arslan b. Saldjūk
Arslan Khān (Ḳarlūḳ) iii, 1115a, 1120a; iv, 808b — III, 1142b, 1148a; IV, 841a
Arslan Khān Aḥmad → Aḥmad Khān b. Ḥasan
Arslan Khān Muḥammad b. ʿAlī v, 45b; s, 245b — V, 47a; S, 245b
Arslān Khātūn iv, 26b, 466a — IV, 28b, 487a
Arslan Shāh b. Kirmān Shāh iv, 466a; v, 159b — IV, 487a; V, 158b
Arslān Shāh b. Masʿūd (Ghaznawid(e)) i, 217b, 940a; ii, 893b, 1052a — I, 224a, 968b; II, 914b, 1076b
Arslān Shāh b. Masʿūd (Zangid(e)) → Zangid(e)s
Arslan Shāh b. Toghrul Shāh i, 940b; iii, 197b; v, 160a — I, 969a; III, 202b; V, 158b
Arslanlī → Sikka
Arsūf i, **662b** — I, **683b**
Art i, 662b — I, 683b → Fann
Artena → Eretna
Artillery/Artillerie → Bārūd, Top
Artsruni, Ashot iv, 89b — IV, 93b
Artsruni, Gagik iv, 90a — IV, 94a
Artuḳ i, 662b; ii, 384b; v, 328a — I, 683b; II, 395a; V, 328a
Artuḳ Arslān iii, 1119b — III, 1147a
Artuḳ Inaḳ s, 420a — S, 420a
Artuḳid(e)s i, 466b, 467a, 639a, **662b;** ii, 344a, 613b; iii, 507a, 1099a, 1118a, 1197b; iv, 464b; v, 454b; s, 266b — I, 480a, b, 659b, **683b;** II, 354a, 629a; III, 524a, 1126a, 1145b, 1228a; IV, 485a; V, 457a; S, 266a
Artvin i, **667b;** ii, 62a — I, **688a;** II, 63b
ʿArūba → Taʾrīkh
ʿArūḍ i, **667b;** ii, 159b, 834b; iii, 672a; iv, 57a, 326b, 714b, 1187b — I, **688a;** II, 164b, 854a; III, 693b; IV, 60a, 340b, 743a, 1220b
Arūḍī → Niẓāmī Arūḍī
ʿArūdj (Barbarossa) i, 367b, 368a, **677b;** ii, 520a, 537b, 839b; iv, 361a, b, 1155b; v, 504a; s, 80b — I, 378b, **698b;** II, 533a, 550b, 859a; IV, 377a, 1187b; V, 507a; S, 80a
Arūr i, **679a**; v, 817a — I, **699b**; V, 823a
ʿArūs → ʿUrs
ʿArūs, Banū i, 604b — I, 624b
ʿArūs resmi i, **679a;** ii, 147a — I, **700a;** II, 151a
ʿArūsiyya i, **679b**; iii, 713b; s, 93a — I, **700a;** III, 735b; S, 92b
Arwād i, 935b; iii, 475a; s, 120b — I, 964b; III, 491b; S, 120a
Arwāḥ iv, 330b — IV, 345a
Arwand-rūd → Shaṭṭ al-ʿArab
Arya Damar iii, 1219a — III, 1250a
Āryabhaṭa i, 133a; iii, 1136a — I, 136b; III, 1164b
Arzachel → al-Zarḳālī
Arzan i, **679b**; ii, 712a — I, **700a;** II, 730b
Arzan al-Rūm → Erzurum
Ārzāw i, **680a** — I, **700b**
Arzila → Aṣīla
Ārzū, Khān i, **680a**; iv, 526b — I, **701a**; IV, 549a
Ās → Alān
Ās s, **87a** — S, **87a**
al-ʿĀs(ī) (Abu l'-K-) → Aʿyāṣ
ʿAṣā i, **680b**; iv, 377b — I, **701a**; IV, 394a
ʿAṣaba i, 30b, 681a; iv, 595b, 916b — I, 31b, 701b; IV, 619b, 949b
ʿAsabāt i, 320a — I, 330a
Aṣābih i, 95b — I, 98a
ʿAṣabiyya i, **681a;** ii, 962b; iii, 830b; iv, 46a — I, 701b, II, 984b; III, 854a; IV, 48b
al-Asad (lion) i, **681a** — I, **702a**
Asad (tribe/tribu) i, **684b;** ii, 71b; iv, 820a; v, 348a; s, 19b, 20a, 304b — I, **705b;** II, 73a; IV, 853a; V, 349a; S, 19b, 20a, 304a
Asad → Minṭaḳat al-Burūdj; Nudjūm
Asad, Banū i, 99a, 528a, b, **683a,** 1241a, 1358b; iii, 1177a — I, 101b, 544a, b, **704a,** 1279a, 1398b; III, 1206a
Asad b. ʿAbd Allāh al-Ḳasrī i, **684b,** 760a, 1001a, 1033a, 1293a; ii, 1010b; iii, 223b, 493b; iv, 54b, 926b;

v, 2a, b, 47b, 76a, 856a — I, **705b,** 782b, 1032a, 1065a, 1332b; II, 1034a; III, 230b, 510b; IV, 57b, 959b; V, 2a, b, 49a, 78a, 862b
Asʿad b. Abī Yaʿfur (Yuʿfir) iv, 661a; s, 335a — IV, 688a; S, 334b
Asad b. al-Furāt i, 248b, 249b, 250a, **685a;** iii, 817a; iv, 733a, 829b; v, 1159b — I, 256a, 257a, 258a, **706a;** III, 840b; IV, 762b, 862b; V, 1149a
al-Asʿad lbn Mammātī → lbn Mammātī
Asad b. Mūsā b. Ibrāhīm s, **87b** — S, **87b**
Asʿad b. Shihāb iii, 125b — III, 128a
Asʿad Abū Ḳarib al-Ḥimyarī iv, 318b — IV, 332b
Asad Allāh Iṣfahānī i, **685b** — I, **706a**
Asad al-Dawla i, **685b** — I, **706b**
Asʿad Efendī → Esʿad Efendī
Asʿad Kāmil, Tubbaʿ i, 548b; iii, 540b; v, 895a — I, 566a; III, 559a; V, 901b
Asad al-Dīn → Shirkūh
Asad al-Dīn Muḥammad b. al-Ḥasan v, 1241a — V, 1231b
Asad al-Ḳasrī → Asad b. ʿAbd Allāh
Asad Khān ii, 379b — II, 389b
Asad Khān Lārī iii, 1160b — III, 1189a
Asʿad al-Luḳaymī i, 60b — I, 62b
Asʿad Pasha al-ʿAẓm ii, 287b, 288a; iii, 120b; v, 925b — II, 295b, 296a; III, 123a; V, 931a
Asʿad al-Shidyāk ii, 801a — II, 819b
Asadābādh i, **685b** — I, **706b**
Asadābādī, Sayyid Djamāl al-Dīn s, 53b, 290b — S, 54a, 290a
Asadī (dynasty/dynastie) iii, 399b — III, 411b
al-Asadī, Abu 'l-Rūḥ ʿĪsā b. ʿAlī b. Ḥassān s, 392b — S, 393a
Asadī Ṭūsī i, **685b;** ii, 439b; iv, 61b, 62b, 525b, 1123b — I, **706b;** II, 451a; IV, 65a, 66a, 548a, 1155a
Āṣaf → ʿImād al-Mulk
Āṣāf b. Barakhyā i, **686a,** 775a — I, **707a,** 798a
Āṣaf al-Dawla (Ḳādjār) iv, 393a, b — IV, 410a
Āṣaf al-Dawla (Lucknow) i, 153a, 757a, b, 813b, 1095a; ii, 265a, 499a, 870b; iii, 1163a; v, 635a, 636a; s, 358b, 359a — I, 157b, 779b, 780a, 836b, 1128a; II, 273a, 511b, 890b; III, 1191b; V, 639a, 640b; S, 358b, 359a
Āṣāf-Djāh i, **686a,** 1015b, 1170a; ii, 99b; iii, 318b — I, **707a,** 1047a, 1205a; II, 101b; III, 328a
Āṣaf Djāh I, Niẓām al-Mulk i, 710a, 1026a, 1170a, 1193a, 1200a, 1201b, 1330b, 1331a; ii, 99b, 981b; iii, 318b, 320a, 427b; iv, 1023b; s, 280a — I, 731b, 1057b, 1205a, 1228b, 1235b, 1237a, 1371a, b, 1372a; II, 101b, 1004a; III, 328a, 330b, 441a; IV, 1055b; S, 279b
Āṣaf Djāh VII → ʿUthmān ʿAlī Khān
Āṣaf Khān (d./m. 1554) ii, 1129a — II, 1155b
Āsaf Khān, Abu 'l-Ḥasan i, **686a,** 1347b; ii, 381a, 813b; iv, 1020a; v, 601a — I, **707a,** 1388a; II, 391a, 832b; IV, 1052a; V, 604b
al-Āṣafī al-Ulughkhānī → al- Ulughkhānī
al-ʿAṣāʾib i, 95a — I, 97b
Aṣāʾil i, 541a — I, 558a
ʿAsākir, Banū ii, 283a; iii, 713b — II, 291b; III, 736a
al-Aṣamm i, **686b** — I, **707b**
al-Aṣamm, Abū Bakr (Egypt/Egypte) s, 90b — S, 90a
al-Aṣamm, Abū Bakr iii, 1166a — III, 1194b
al-Aṣamm, Abū Bakr ʿAbd al-Raḥmān s, **88b,** 226b — S, **88a,** 226b
al-Aṣamm, Muḥammad i, 142b, **686b** — I, 146b, **707b**
al-Aṣamm → Muḥammad b. ʿUmar; Sufyān b. al-Abrad
Asar Kale → ʿAmmūriya
ʿAṣar al-ʿUḳaylī s, 394a — S, 394b
Asardūn s, 132a — S, 131b
Asās → Ismāʿīliyya
ʿAsas i, **687a;** iv, 103b — I, **707b;** IV, 108a
Asas al-Sunna → Asad b. Mūsā b. Ibrāhīm
Asāṭīr al-Awwalīn iii, 369a; s, **90b** — III, 381a; S, **90b**
Asāwira iv, 44a — IV, 46b
Aṣba → Iṣbaʿ
Aṣbagh b. al-ʿAbbās s, 382a — S, 382a
al-Aṣbagh al-Kalbī i, 84b; ii, 625a; iv, 493b, 494a — I, 87a; II, 640b; IV, 515a
Asben → Aïr
Ascalon → ʿĀsḳlān
Aṣfar i, **687b;** v, 700b, 706b — I, **708b;** V, 705b, 711b
al-Aṣfar ('l-Muntafiḳ) iv, 663b — IV, 690b
Aṣfar, Banū 'l- i, 688a — I, 709a
Asfār b. Kurdūya s, 398a — S, 398b
Asfār b. Shīrawayhī (Shīrōya) i, **688a;** ii, 192a; iii, 255a; iv, 23a, 661b, 859b; s, 357a — I, **709a;** II, 198a; III, 262a; IV, 24b, 688b, 892b; S, 357a
Āṣfī i, 141a, **688b** — I, 145a, **709b**
Asfizār → Sabzawār
al-Aʿshā i, **689b** — I, **710b**
al-Aʿshā, Maymūn b. Ḳays i, 196a, 442b, **689b;** 963b, 1081b; iv, 1002a, 1008b; s, 197b — I, 202a, 455a, **710b,** 993a, 1113b; IV, 1031b, 1041a; S, 197b
Aʿshā Bāhila i, 689b, 920b — I, 710b, 949a
Aʿshā Hamdān i, **690b;** ii, 190b; iii, 123a, 354a, 716b — I, **711a;** II, 196b; III, 126a, 365a, 738b
Aṣḥāb → Ṣaḥāba
Ashʿab i, **690b** — I, **711b**
Aṣḥāb Abi 'l-Sādj i, 145b — I, 149b
Aṣḥāb al-arbāʿ i, 687a — I, 708a
Aṣḥāb al-barīd i, 1045b — I, 1077a
Aṣḥāb al-dalīl ii, 527b — II, 540b
Aṣḥāb al-farāʾiḍ i, 320a — I, 330a
Aṣḥāb al-ḥadīth → Ahl al-ḥadīth
Aṣḥāb al-kahf i, **691a,** 998a; iv, 724a — I, **712a,** 1028b; IV, 753a
Aṣḥāb al-rass i, 509a, **692a;** iii, 169a — I, 524b, **713a;** III, 172b
Aṣḥāb al-raʾy i, **692a;** ii, 889a — I, **713a;** II, 910a
Aṣḥāb al-saṭḥ i, 280b — I, 289a
Aṣḥāb al-shadjara s, 131a — S, 130b
Aṣḥāb al-shūrā i, 275b — I, 284a
Aṣḥāb al-ukhdūd i, 692a, **692b** — I, 713a, **713b**
al-Ashadjdj al-Muʿammar → Abu 'l-Dunyā
Ashāḳabāsh iv, 387b, 389a, 390b — IV, 404a, 406a, 407a
Ashām i, **692b;** iv, 460b — I, **714a;** IV, 480b
Aʿshār → ʿUshr
al-ʿAshara al-Mubashshara i, **693a** — I, **714a**
al-Ashʿarī i, 1154a; ii, 740b — I, 1188a; II, 759a
al-Ashʿarī, Abū Burda i, **693b** — I, **714b**
al-Ashʿarī, Abu 'l-Ḥasan i, 129a, 204b, 275a, 589b, **694a,** 958b, 1039a; ii, 412a, 449b, 554a, 569b, 570a, 931a; iii, 767a, 1037b, 1063a, 1144a, b, 1164b, 1170b, 1173b; iv, 271b, 470a; v, 526b; s, 347a, 392a — I, 132b, 210b, 283b, 609a, **715a,** 988a, 1070b; II, 422b, 461a, 568a, 584a, b, 952b; III, 790a, 1063a, 1089b, 1172b, 1193a, 1196b, 1202a; IV, 284a, 491a; V, 530b; S, 347a, 392b
al-Ashʿarī, Abū Mūsā i, 304a, 383b, 384a, 693b, **695a,** 704a; ii, 414b, 415b, 811b, 1120a; iii, 1015b; iv, 13b, 99b, 220a; v, 406b, 451a, 499b; s, 89b — I, 313b, 394b, 395a, 714b, **716a,** 725b; II, 425a, 426a, 831a, 1146a; III, 1041a; IV, 14b, 103b, 229b; V, 407b, 453b, 502b; S, 89b
Ashʿarīyya i, 179a, 333a, b, 334a, 335a, 410b, 411a, b, 412a, b, 413a, 415b, **696a,** 714a, 958b; ii, 102b, 365a, 449b, 493b, 605a, 608a, 618a, 833b, iii, 171b, 330a, 465b, 767a, 1072b, 1144b, 1146a; iv, 107b, 108a, 172b, 183a, 365b, 366a, 469a, 616a, 692a, 693a; v, 527a; s, 30a, 343b, 346b — I, 183b, 343b, 344a, 345b, 422a, b, 423b, 424b, 425a, 427b, **717a,** 735b, 988a; II,

104b, 375a, 461b, 506a, 620a, 623a, 633b, 853a; III, 175b, 340a, 482a, 790a, 1099a, 1172b, 1174b; IV, 112b, 113a, 180a, 191a, 381b, 382a, 490a, 640b, 720b, 721a; V, 531a; S, 30a, 343b, 346a
al-Ash^c^ath b. Dja^c^far al-Khuzā^c^ī s, 33a — S, 33a
al-Ash^c^ath b. Ḳays i, 42b, 625b, **696b,** 864a; ii, 198b; iii, 242b, 715a, 888b; v, 119b; s, 337b — I, 43b, 646a, **718a,** 888a; II, 204b; III, 249b, 737b, 912b; V, 122a; S, 337a
al-Ashdaḳ → ^c^Amr b. Sa^c^īd al-Ashdaḳ
al-Ashdja^c^ b. ^c^Amr al-Sulamī i, **697a** — I, **718a**
^c^Āshiḳ i, 193b, **697b;** ii, 990b; iii, 374a; iv, 706a; v, 275a — I, 199a, **718b;** II, 1013b; III, 386a; IV, 734b; V, 273b
^c^Āshiḳ, Muḥammad i, **697b;** ii, 588a; v, 982a; s, 330b — I, **718b;** II, 602a; V, 978b; S, 330a
^c^Āshiḳ Čelebi i, **698a**; iv, 1137a; v, 116a, 693a; s, 83a — I, **719a**; IV, 1169a; V, 118b, 698a; S, 83a
^c^Ashiḳ Pasha i, 419b, **698b;** iii, 375a; v, 173a — I, 431b, **719b;** III, 387a; V, 170b
^c^Āshik Weysel s, **91a** — S, **91a**
^c^Āshiḳ-pasha-zāde i, **699a;** ii, 1044b; iii, 23a — I, **720a;** II, 1069a; III, 24a
^c^Ashiklu iv, 577b — IV, 601a
Ashīr i, **699a,** 1319b; ii, 114b; iv, 459a — I, **720b,** 1359b; II, 117b; IV, 479b
^c^Āshir Efendi ii, 474a — II, 486a
^c^Ashīra i, **700a;** iv, 334a, b, 595a; v, 472a — I, **721b;** IV, 348b, 349a, 619a; V, 474b
Ashk iii, 376a — III, 387b
^c^Ashḳābād i, 320b, **700b** — I, 330b, **722a**
Ashkara i, 1190a — I, 1225a
Ashḳīlūla, Banū iv, 729b — IV, 758b
Ashkūdja → Darghin
al-Ashmūnayn → Ushmūnayn
Ashnās s, 106a — S, 105b
Ashot → Ashūṭ
Ashraf (Čūbānid(e)) → Malik Ashraf
Ashrāf → Sharīf
al-Ashraf, al-Malik (Ayyūbid(e)) i, 198a, 329a, 434b, 780b, 799a, b. 940b, 971a; ii, 284a, 347b; iii, 504a; iv, 502b, 817b — I, 203b, 339b, 446b, 803b, 822b, 969a, 1001a; II, 292a, 357b; III, 521a; IV, 543a, b, 850b
Ashraf, Māzandarān i, 8b, **701a**; s, 140b — I, 8b, **722b**; S, 140b
Ashrāf (faction) iii, 88a; v, 349b — III, 90b; V, 350b
Ashrāf (India/Inde) iii, 411a — III, 423b
Ashrāf (Sudan/Soudan) i, 49b, 765a; ii, 124a; v, 1250a, b — I, 50b, 788a; II, 127a; V, 1240b, 1241b
Ashraf b. ^c^Abd al-^c^Azīz i, 229b, 270a, 291a; iii, 604b; v, 461a — I, 236b, 278b, 300a; III, 625a; V, 464a
Ashraf ^c^Alī Thānawī i, **701b;** iii, 433b, 1174a, b — I, **723a;** III, 447b, 1203a, b
Ashraf ^c^Alī Khān i, **702a** — I, **723a**
Ashraf al-Dīn Gīlānī iv, 71a, s, **91b** — IV, 74b; S, **91b**
Ashraf Djahāngīr al-Simnānī i, **702b,** 859a; ii, 51b, 392a, 1115a — I, **723b,** 883a; II, 52b, 402b, 1141a
Ashraf Khān iv, 1127b — IV, 1159a
al-Ashraf Mūsā b. Ibrāhīm iii, 399b, 989b — III, 412a, 1014b
Ashraf-oghlu Rūmī iii, 43b — III, 45a
Ashraf Oghullarî i, **702b,** 1256b; iv, 621a — I, **724a,** 1295a; IV, 646a, b
Ashraf Rumī, ^c^Abd Allāh i, 704a — I, 725a
Ashrafī → Sikka
Ashrafiyya i, **704a**; v, 73a — I, **725a**; V, 75a
Ashrafiyya madrasa v, 1143a, b, 1144a — V, 1136a, b
Ashras b. ^c^Abd Allāh al-Sulamī ii, 600b; iii, 493b — II, 615b; III, 510b
al-^c^Ashshāb i, **704a** — I, **725a**
al-Ashtar, Malik i, 382b, **704a;** ii, 89b, 416a; iii, 1265a; iv, 1035a; v, 499b, 954a — I, 393b, **725b;** II, 91a, 427a; III, 1298a; IV, 1067a; V, 502b, 958a
Ashtarkhānid(e)s → Djānid(e)s
Ashturḳa s, **92a** — S, **91b**
Ashur → Athūr
^c^Āshūrā^3^ i, 265a, **705a,** 823b, 1352a; iii, 635a; s, 190a — I, 273a, **726a,** 846b, 1391b; III, 656a; S, 191b
Ashūṭ I i, 507a, 637a; v, 488b — I, 522b, 657b; V, 491b
Ashūṭ II i, 507a, 637b; ii, 679b — I, 522b, 658a; II, 696b
Ashūṭ III i, 507a, 637b; ii, 680a; iv, 670a — I, 522b, 658b; II, 697a; IV, 697a
Ashūṭ IV, 638a — I, 658b
Ashūṭ Msaker i, 507a — I, 522b
al-^c^Āṣī i, 239a, **706a;** ii, 555b, 556a; s, 243a — I, 246b, **727a;** II, 569b, 570a; S, 243a
Āṣif al-Dawla iv, 105a — IV, 109b
Aṣīla i, **706a**; v, 1118b — I, **727b**; V, 1115a
Asile → Bast; Bīmāristān
al-Aṣīlī iv, 341a — IV, 355b
^c^Āṣim Aḥmad i, **707a,** 1327b; ii, 536b; v, 951b — I, **728b,** 1368a; II, 366a; V, 955b
^c^Āsîm, Nedjīb iv, 791a — IV, 823a
^c^Āṣim b. ^c^Abd Allāh al-Hilālī ii, 601a; iii, 223b, 1202a — II, 615b; III, 230b, 1232a
^c^Āṣim b. Abi 'l-Nadjdjūd i, **706b;** iii, 63a; v, 127b, 128a — I, **728a;** III, 65b; V, 130b
^c^Āṣim b. Djamīl al-Yazdadjūmī ii, 1095b — II, 1121a
^c^Āṣim b. Thābit al-Anṣārī v, 40b, 41a — V, 41b, 42a
^c^Āṣim al-Aḥwal i, 104b — I, 107b
Asim Degel iv, 550b — IV, 574a
^c^Āṣîm Efendi Ismā^c^īl → Čelebi-zāde
^c^Āṣim al-Sadrātī iii, 654a, b — III, 675b, 676a
^c^Asīr, Arabia(e) i, 98a, 106b, 539a, **707b,** 811b, 881b; v, 391b; s, 3b, 30a, 278b — I, 101a, 109b, 555b, **729a,** 834b, 907a; V, 392a; S, 3a, 30b, 278b
Asīr, Djalāl al-Dīn i, **707b**; iv, 69a — I, **728b**; IV, 72b
Asīrgarh i, **710a;** ii, 815b; iv, 1023a — I, **731b;** II, 835a; IV, 1055a
Asīrī s, 109b — S, 109a
Āsitāna → Istanbul
Asiuṭ → Asyuṭ
Āsiya i, **710b;** ii, 848a, 917b — I, **731b;** II, 868a, 938b
Ask ii, 106b; v, 660b, 661a, 664a — II, 108b; V, 666a, b, 669a
^c^Āsḳalān i, 9b, **710b,** 946b; ii, 911a, 912a, 1056a; iv, 958b; v, 331a; s, 121a — I, 9b, **732a,** 975b; II, 932b, 933b, 1081a; IV, 992a; V, 331a; S, 120b
al-^c^Āsḳalānī → Ibn Ḥadjar
^c^Askar, ^c^asker ii, 507a, 511a; iv, 266a, 1144a; v, 685a — II, 519b, 523b; IV, 277b, 1176a; V, 690a
al-^c^Askar → Sāmarrā
al-^c^Askar (al-Fusṭāṭ) ii, 958b, 959a — II, 980b, 981a
^c^Askar Khān Afshār Arūmī s, 290a — S, 290a
^c^Askar Mukram i, **711b**; s, 12b, 37b — I, **733a**; S, 13a, 38a
^c^Askarī i, **712a;** ii, 147a; iv, 231b, 242a, b, 563a, 564a — I, **733b;** II, 151b; IV, 242a, 253a, 585a, 586b
al-^c^Askarī, Abū Aḥmad i, **712b**; s, 38a — I, **734a**; S, 38a
al-^c^Askarī, Abu 'l-Ḥasan ^c^Alī i, **713a;** iii, 246b; s, 95a, 127b — I, **734b;** III, 253b; S, 94b, 127a
al-^c^Askarī, Abū Hilāl i, 590b, **712b,** 759a, 857b; ii, 386a; iv, 249a — I, 609b, **734a,** 781b, 881b; II, 396b; IV, 260a
al-^c^Askarī, al-Ḥasan → al-Ḥasan al-^c^Askarī
^c^Askarī b. Bābur i, 228b, 1135b; iii, 575b, 576a; iv, 523b — I, 235a, 1170a; III, 595a, 596a; IV, 546a
^c^Askerī → ^c^Askarī
Askia Muḥammad ii, 977b — II, 1000a
Aṣl → Uṣūl
al-Asla^c^ b. ^c^Abd Allāh al-^c^Absī s, 177b — S, 178b

al-Aṣlaḥ i, **713b** — I, **735a**
Aslam, Banū v, 78b — V, 80b
Aslam, Em v, 204a, b — V, 201b, 202a
Asmāʾ bint Abī Bakr i, 109b, 110a, **713b**; s, 311a — 112b, 113a, **735b**; S, 311a
Asmāʾ bint Mukharriba i, 115b; iii, 169a — I, 118b; III, 172b
Asmāʾ bint al-Nuʿmān iii, 64b — III, 67a
Asmāʾ bint ʿUmays i, 44a, 109b, 400b;ii, 372a, 844b, 846a; iv, 1106b; S, **92b**, 172a — I, 45b, 112b, 412a; II, 382a, 864b, 866a; IV, 1138a; S, **92a**; 173a
al-Asmāʾ al-Ḥusnā i, 408a, **714a**; ii, 753a — I, 420a, **735b**; II, 771b
al-Aṣmaʿī i, 105b, 108b, 115a, b, 125b, 158a, 167b, 338a, 520b, 521b, 588b, **717b**, 772a, 921a, 1241a; ii, 952b; iii, 136a; iv, 249a; s, 15b, 17b, 20a, 33a, 128b, 277a, 317b, 394b — I, 108b, 118b, 119a, 129a, 162b, 172a, 349a, 536a, 537b, 607b, **739a**, 795a, 949a, 1279a; II, 974b; III, 139a; IV, 260a; S, 16a, 18a, 20b, 33b, 127b, 276b, 317b, 395a
al-Aṣmaʿiyyāt → al-Aṣmaʿī
al-Asmar, ʿAbd al-Salām al-Faytūrī s, **93a** — S, **92b**
Asper → Aḳče
ʿAṣr i, **719a** — I, **740b**
Asrāfīl → Isrāfīl
Āṣṣ → Alān
Assab i, **719a**; ii, 113a — I, **740b**; II, 115b
ʿAssāf al-Naṣrānī iii, 951b — III, 976a
al-ʿAssāl, Awlād → lbn al-ʿAssāl
al-ʿAssālī (mosque/mosquée) s, 49b — S, 50a
al-ʿAssāliyya iv, 992a — IV, 1024b
Assam i, **719a** — I, **741a**
ʿAṣṣār, Muḥammad i, **720a**; iv, 67a — I, **741b**; IV, 70b
ʿAssās i, 687b — I, 708b
Assassins → Nizārīs; al-Ḥashīshiyya
Assenid(e)s i, 1302a — I, 1342a
Assiout → Asyūṭ
Assistance publique → Khayr
Association → Andjumān; Djamʿiyya
Assuan → Uswān
Assyrians/Assyriens iv, 8a; v, 68a — IV, 9a; V, 70a
Astarābādh i, **720a**; ii, 1141a; iii, 212b, 1102a; iv, 389a, b, 390a, b, 855b; s, 139b, 356b, 357a, 363b, 380a — I, **741b**; II, 1168a; III, 218b, 1129a; IV, 406a, b, 407a, 888b; S, 139a, 356b, 363b, 380a
al-Astarābādhī i, **720b** — I, **742b**
al-Astarābādhī, Raḍī al-Dīn i, **721a**; iii, 781a, 861b — I, **742b**; III, 804b, 885b
al-Astarābādī, Mīrzā Muḥammad b. ʿAlī s, 56b — S, 57a
al-Astarābādī, Mullā Muḥammad Amīn b. Muḥammad Sharīf s, 56b, 57a — S, 57a, b
al-Astarābādhī, Rukn al-Dīn i, **721a** — I, **743a**
Asṭarlāb → Asṭurlāb
Astarte v, 692a, b — V, 697a, b
Astorga → Ashturḳa
Astrakhān i, **721b**, 1108a; ii, 44a, 179a; iv, 280b, 576a; v, 138a, b; s, 318a — I, **743a**, 1141a; II, 45a, 184b; IV, 292b, 599a; V, 140b, 141a; S, 318a
Astrakhānid(e)s → Djānids
Astrolabe → Asṭurlāb
Astrology/Astrologie → Nudjūm, Aḥkām al-
Astronomy/Astronomie → Baṭlamiyūs; Ghanam; ʿIlm al-hayʾa
Asṭurlāb i, **722b**; iii, 808b, 924a, 928b, 1136b; v, 46a — I, **744a**; III, 832a, 948b, 953a, 1165a; V, 47b
al-Asṭurlābī → al-Badīʿ
Aswad v, 700a, 705b — V, 705a, 710b
al-Aswad b. al-Mundhir ii, 71b — II, 73a
al-Aswad b. Yaʿfur i, **728b**; iv, 998b; s, 256a, 394b — I, **750a**; IV, 1031a; S, 255b, 395a
al-Aswad al-ʿAnsī i, 110b, **728a**, 738a; iii, 223b; iv, 1135b; s, 116a — I, 113b, **749b**, 759b; III, 230a; IV, 1167a; S, 115b
Aswan → Uswān
al-Aṣyaʿ al-Kalbī → al-Aṣbagh al-Kalbī
Asylum → Bast, Bīmāristān
Asyūṭ i, **728b**; ii, **424a**; v, 515a; s, 5a, 40b, 121b — I, **750b**; II, 434b; V, 519a; S, 4a, 41a, 121a
Ata i, **729a** — I, **751a**
ʿAṭāʾ i, **729a**; ii, 360a — I, **751a**; II, 370a
ʿAṭāʾ b. Abī Rabāḥ i, 123a, **730a**; ii, 538b, 886b, 888b; s, 232b, 386b — I, 126b, **752b**; II, 552a, 907a, 909a; S, 232b, 386b
ʿAṭāʾ b. Yaʿḳūb → Nakūk
ʿAtāʾ b. Yasār al-Hilālī iv, 369a — IV, 385b
ʿAṭāʾ Allāh Efendi i, 1235a; iv, 322b — I, 1272a; IV, 337a
ʿAṭāʾ Allāh Efendi, Shānī-zāde → Shānī-zāde
ʿAṭāʾ Allāh ʿOthmān-oghlu iv, 593a — IV, 617a
ʿAṭāʾ Bey, Meḥmed i, **730b** — I, **752a**
ʿAṭāʾ Bey, Ṭayyārzāde i, **730b** — I, **752a**
ʿAṭāʾ Ilāhī iii, 1107b — III, 1134b
ʿAṭāʾ, Khwādja s, 105b — S, 105a
ʿAṭāʾ Malik Djuwaynī → al-Djuwaynī
ʿAṭāʾ, Meḥmed s, 96a — S, 95b
ʿAtāba i, **730b** — I, **752b**
Atabak i, 3b, 20b, 639a, **731a**, 1081a, 1276b; iii, 1016a; iv, 26a, 32a, 466b; v, 826a, 828a — I, 3b, 21b, 659b, **753a**, 1106a, 1316a; III, 1041b; IV, 28a, 34a, 487a; V, 832b, 834a
Atābak al-ʿAsākir i, **732b**; v, 73a — I, **754b**; V, 75a
ʿAtabāt s, **94a**, 104a — S, **93b**, 103b
Atabeg → Atabak
Atabia ii, 1003b — II, 1026b
Atač, Nūr Allāh s, **96a**, 98b — S, **95b**, 98a
ʿAṭāʾī i, **732b** — I, **754b**
Aṭak i, **733a**; iv, 1102a, 1159b — I, **755a**; IV, 1133a, 1191b
Ātāk i, 99b; iii, 1108a — I, 102a; III, 1135b
Atalīḳ i, 733b; s, **96b** — I, 755b; S, **96a**
ʿAtama i, **733b** — I, **755b**
Atar i, **733b**; v, 654a — I, **755b**; V, 658a
Ātāsh Bahrām v, 1113a, 1114b — V, 1109a, b, 1110b
Ātash-begi i, 260b, 261b — I, 268b, 269b
al-Ātāsī, M. Hāshim iv, 138a — IV, 144a
Atatürk i, 75b, 470b, 511a, 641b, **734a**, 777a, 783a, 1255b;ii, 104b, 392a, 430b, 432a, 466b,475b, 497b, 531b,595b, 630a, 644b, 700a, 701b, 712b; iii, 526b, 622a; iv, 124a, 169a, 297b, 611b, 873a, 934a, b, 935b, 946b; v, 906a, 1099b; s, 41b, 63a, 98a, 282a, 329a — I, 77b, 484b, 527a, 662a, **756a**, 800a, 806a,1294a; II, 107a, 402b, 442a, 443a, 478a, b, 510a, 544b, 610a, 646a, 660b, 718a, 719b, 731a; III, 545a, 642b; IV, 129a, 176b, 311a, 636a, 906b, 967a, b, 968b, 979a; V, 911b, 1095a; S, 42a, 63b, 97b, 282a, 328b
Ātāy → Čay
Atay, Fāliḥ Rîfḳī s, **98a** — S, **97b**
Atbāʿ al-Tābiʿīn iv, 149a — IV, 155b
Atbara i, **735a**, 1172a, 1239b; iv, 686a; v, 1251b — I, **757a**, 1207b, 1277b; IV, 714a; V, 1242a
Atbedj → Athbadj
Ātbēgī → Atabak
Atčeken iv, 624b — IV, 649b
Atchin, Atcheh → Atjeh
ʿAteiba → ʿUtayba
Atek i, **735a** — I, **757a**
Ātesh → Mādjūs
Āteshizāde Memi Shāh ii, 1042b — II, 1067a
ʿAṭf i, **735b** — I, **757b**
Aṭfar → Djabala b. al-Ḥārith
Aṭfīḥ i, **735b** — I, **757b**
Aṭfiyāsh, Muḥammad i, **736a** — I, **758a**
Athāfit s, 22a, 335a — S, 22b, 334b

Athar i, **736a,** 1199a — I, **758a,** 1234b
al-Āthār al-ʿUlwiyya i, **736b;** iii, 30a — I, **758b;** III, 31b
Athāth v, 1158a; s, **99a** — V, 1148a; S, **98a**
Athbādj i, 533a, 1246b; iii, 138a, 386a; iv, 479a; v, 1179a; s, 62b — I, 549b, 1284b; III, 140b, 398b; IV, 501a; V, 1169a; S, 63a
Athens/Athènes → Atīna
Athīr, Banū iii, 723b, 961a — III, 746a, 985b
Athīr-i Akhsikatī iv, 62a — IV, 65a
ʿAthlīth i, **737b** — I, **759b**
ʿAthr i, **737b** — I, **759b**
ʿAththar → ʿAthr
ʿAththarī i, 969a, b — I, 999a, b
Athūr s, **100a** — S, **99b**
ʿĀṭif Efendi iii, 590a — III, 610a
ʿAtīḳ i, 30b, 109b; ii, 1090b — I, 31b, 112b; II, 1116a
ʿĀtika bint Muʿāwiya i, 113b — I, 116b
ʿĀtika bint Zayd i, **738a** — I, **760a**
Atīl i, 721b, **738a**; iv, 280a, 1173a, 1176a, 1177b, 1178b; v, 1013b — I, 743b, **760a**; IV, 292b, 1206b, 1209b, 1211a, 1212a; V, 1009a
Atīna i, **738b** — I, **760b**
ʿAtīra i, **739b**; s, 221b — I, **761b**; S, 221b
Ātish, Khwādja Ḥaydar ʿAlī ii, 84b; s, **102a** — II, 86a; S, **101b**
ʿAṭiyya, Banū iii, 642b — III, 664a
ʿAṭiyya b. al-Aswad al-Ḥanafī iv, 534b — IV, 558a
Atjèh i, 88a, 92a, **739b;** iii, 1218b, 1220a, 1233a; v, 21b; s, 199b — I, 90b, 94b, **761b;** III, 1249b, 1250b, 1265a; V, 22a; S, 199b
-war/la guerre d'- (1873-1904) i, 743b; iii, 1223a, 1228b — I, 766a; III, 1254a, 1260a
al-ʿAtk i, 538b, **747b** — I, 555a, **770a**
Atlagić Meḥmed Pasha v, 775a — V, 781a
Atlamīsh iv, 586a — IV, 608b
Atlantic Ocean/l'Atlantique → al-Baḥr al-Muḥīṭ
Atlas i, 364b, 460a, **748a**; v, 1184b, 1186b — I, 375b, 473b, **770b**; V, 1174b, 1176b
Atom/Atome → Djuzʾ
Aṭrābulus → Ṭarābulus
al-Aṭrābulusī → Aḥmad b. al-Ḥusayn
al-Atrash → al-Mādharāʾī
Atrek i, **749b** — I, **772a**
Atsīz b. Anūshtigin i, **750a;** ii, 603a; iii, 196b; iv, 29a, 1067a; v, 311b; s, 245b — I, **772b;** II, 618a; III, 201a; IV, 31b, 1099a; V, 311a; S, 245b
Atsīz b. Uvak i, **750b,** 870a; ii, 282a, 856b, 911b; iii, 160a; v, 328a — I, **773a,** 894b; II, 290a, 876a, 932b; III, 163a; V, 328a
ʿAttāb b. Asīd i, **751a** — I, **773b**
ʿAttāb b. Warḳāʾ i, 810b — I, 833b
al-ʿAttābī i, **751a,** 857b — I, **773b,** 881a
al-ʿAṭṭār i, **751b**; iv, 95b; s, 42b — I, **774a**; IV, 99b; S, 43a
al-ʿAṭṭār → Dāwūd b. ʿAbd al-Raḥmān
ʿAṭṭār, Farīd al-Dīn i, 146a, **752b;** ii, 98b, 1041b, 1138a; iii, 373a; iv, 62a, 63a, 65a, 402a — I, 150a, **775a;** II, 101a, 1066a, 1165a; III, 385a; IV, 65b, 66b, 68b, 419b
al-ʿAṭṭār, Ḥasan b. Muḥammad i, **755a,** 819b; ii, 356b — I, **777b,** 842b; II, 366a
al-ʿAṭṭār, Hāshim iv, 775b — IV, 806b
ʿAṭṭār, Khwādja Ḥasan s, 50b — S, 51b
ʿAṭṭāsh, ʿAbd al-Malik → Ibn ʿAṭṭāsh
Attock → Atak
Attribute/Attribut → Ḥāl; Ṣifa
Au-delà → Ākhira
Aurès → Awrās
Ausa → al-Khāliṣa
Auspicious and Inauspicious → Saʿd
Austria/Autriche i, 269b; iii, 193a, 253b, 480a, 997a, 1001a, 1186a; iv, 657a, b; v, 259b, 262a — I, 277b; III, 197b, 260b, 497a, 1022a, 1026a, 1215b; IV, 683b, 684a; V, 257a, 260a
Author → Muʾallif
Automata → Ḥiyal
Autourserie → Bayzara
Autruches, les → al-Naʿāʾim
Avanias/avanies iii, 1181a, b — III, 1210b
Avar i, 504a, 624b, **755a,** 998b; ii, 86a, b, 141b, 251a; iii, 157a; iv, 342b, 343a, 344b, 351a, 571b, 631b, 1172a; v, 55b, 81b, 579b — I, 519b, 645a, **777b,** 1029a; II, 88a, 145a, 258b; III, 160b; IV, 357a, b, 359a, 366a, 594a, 656a, 1205b; V, 57a, 83b, 584a
Avarice → Bukhl
Avaristān ii, 86a — II, 87b
Avempace → Ibn Bādjdja
Avenetan, Avennathan → Ibn al-Haytham
Avennasar → al-Fārābī
Avenzoar → Ibn Zuhr, Abū Marwān
Averroes → Ibn Rushd
Avesta i, 236a; iii, 112b; iv, 11a; v, 1110a — I, 243b; III, 115a; IV, 12a; V, 1106a
Avetis Sulṭān-Zāda s, 365b — S, 365b
Aveu → Iḳrār
Avicenna/Avicenne → Ibn Sīnā
Avram Camondo → Camondo
Avroman → Hawrāmān
Āwa i, **756b** — I, **779a**
ʿAwaḍ b. Ṣāliḥ i, 767a — I, 790a
Awadh i, 153a, **756b,** 809a, 1330a; ii, 808b, 870b; iv, 276b, 908a; v, 635a, 1033b, 1240a; s, 76b, 95a, 102b, 247a, 292a, 312b, 358b, 360a — I, 157b, **779a,** 832b, 1371a; II, 827b, 890b; IV, 289a, 941a; V, 639a, 1029b, 1230b; S, 76b, 94a, 101b, 247a, 291b, 312b, 358b, 360a
- Nawwāb of/d'- i, 856a, 1330a; ii, 808b, 870b; iii, 61a, 451a, 1163a — I, 879b, 1370b; II, 827b, 890b; III, 63b, 466b, 1191b
Awadh Panč iii, 395a — III, 370a
Awadhī iii, 456b — III, 472b
Awādhila → ʿAwdhila
Āwadj → Āwa
Awāʿil i, **758a,** 772b — I, **780b,** 795b
Awākhir i, 759a — I, 782a
Awʿāl iv, 984a — IV, 1016a
ʿAwāliḳ → ʿAwlaḳī
ʿAwālim → ʿĀlima
ʿAwāmil → ʿAmil
ʿAwāmir, al- i, **759b** — I, **782a**
ʿAwāmm → ʿĀmma
ʿAwāna b. al-Ḥakam al-Kalbī i, 760a; v, 947b — I, 782b; V, 951a
Awang Alak Betatar s, 151b — S, 152a
Awar → Avar
al-Aʿwar → Abū Yaʿḳūb al-Khuraymī
al-Awāradj ii, 78b — II, 80a
ʿAwāriḍ i, **760a;** ii, 147a; iv, 234b — I, **783a;** II, 151a; IV, 244b
Awārik i, 1239b — I, 1277a
ʿAwāṣim i, 145a, 239a, 465b, 517a, **761a,** 909b, 996a, 1292b; ii, 36a; s, 243a, b — I, 149b, 246b, 479a, 532b, **783b,** 937b, 1026b, 1332a; II, 36b; S, 243a, b
al-Awāzim i, 546a, **762a;** iii, 642a, 1068a — I, 563b, **784b;** III, 663b, 1094b
ʿAwda b. Ḥarb Abū Tāyih iii, 643a — III, 664b
Awdaghost i, **762a;** 1002a; iii, 288b, 657a; v, 653a — I, **785a;** II, 1025b; III, 297b, 678a; V, 657a
ʿAwdhalī i, **762b;** ii, 675b — I, **785b;** II, 692a
ʿAwdhila → ʿAwdhalī
Awdj → Nudjūm
Awdjila i, **763a,** 1049a, b — I, **758b,** 1081a, b
ʿAwf b. ʿAṭiyya iv, 998a — IV, 1030b
ʿAwf b. Badr al-Fazārī s, 177b — S, 178b

ʿAwf, Djabal i, 208a — I, 214a
Awfāt i, 176b, **763b;** iii, 3b, 5b — I, 181a, **786b;** III, 3b, 5b
ʿAwfī, Muḥammad i, 94b, **764a,** 780a, 1131a; iii, 373a, 1155b; v, 385b; s, 21a, 22a, 416a — I, 97a, **786b,** 803a, 1156b; III, 385a, 1184a; V, 386b; S, 21a, 22a, 416b
Awghānī i, 218a — I, 224b
al-Awḥad b. al-ʿĀdil i, 198a, 329a, 799a — I, 203b, 339b, 822b
Awḥad al-Dīn ʿAbd al-Wāḥid ii, 330a — II, 340a
Awḥad al-Zamān → Abu 'l-Barakāt
Awḥadī iii, 635a — III, 656b
Awḥadī, Rukn al-Dīn i, **764b**; iv, 67b — I, **787a**; IV, 71a
Awḳāf → Waḳf
Awḳāt → Waḳt
ʿAwl i, 320a, **764b** — I, 330a, **787b**
Awlād → name of ancestor/le nom de l'ancêtre
Awlād al-Balad i, **765a**; v, 1250a, 1251b — I, **788a**; V, 1240b, 1241a, 1242b
Awlād bu Ghanem s, 144b — S, 144b
Awlād bu Sbaa s, 144b — S, 144b
Awlād Khalīfa iv, 382b — IV, 399b
Awlād al-nās i, 102a, **765a,** 1060a; iii, 99b; iv, 552b — I, 105a, **788a,** 1091b; III, 102a' IV, 576a
Awlād al-Shaykh i, **765b,** 802b — I, **788b,** 826a
Awlād Sulaymān s, 164a, b — S, 164a, b
ʿAwlaḳī i, **766b;** ii, 675b — I, **789b;** II, 692a
Āwlīl ii, 1121b — II, 1148a
Awliyāʾ → Walī (Saint)
Awliyā Allāh Āmulī i, 871b; iii, 810b — I, 896a; III, 833b
Awliyā ata i, **767a** — I, **790a**
Awliyar, Shaykh iv, 723b — IV, 752b
Awlonya i, 656a, **767b** — I, 676b, **790b**
ʿAwn, Āl iii, 263a, 605b — III, 270b, 626a
ʿAwn Allāh Kāẓimī → al-Kāẓimī, Meḥmed
ʿAwn b. Djaʿfar b. Abī Ṭālib s, 92b — S, 92b
ʿAwn al-Rafīḳ ii, 91a — II, 93a
ʿAwnī → Muḥammad II
Awraba i, 1037a; iii, 1031b; v, 517b, 518a; s, **102b** — I, 1068b; III, 1057b; V, 521b; S, **102a**
Awrangābād i, **768a;** ii, 55a, 99b; iii, 450b — I, **791a;** II, 56a, 101b; III, 466b
Awrangābād Sayyid i, **768a** — I, **791a**
Awrangzīb i, 199b, 218a, 229a, 253a, 432b, 624b, **768a,** 954a, 1069a, 1161a, 1166a, 1193b, 1202b, 1210a, 1219a, 1300a, 1329b, 1331a; ii, 99b, 121a, 132a, 134b, 162a, 379a, 488b, 504a, 558a, 566b, 1049b; iii, 199a, 200b, 202a, 308b, 424b, 427a, 430a, 450b, 453b, 492b; iv, 93a, 286b, 514a, 914b, 1128a; v, 47b, 598b, 1135b, 1259a; s, 55b, 57b, 126b, 142b, 246b, 258a, b, 292a, 410b, 420b — I, 205a, 224b, 235b, 260b, 445a, 645b, **791a,** 983b, 1101a, 1196a, 1200b, 1228b, 1238a, 1246a, 1255a, 1340a, 1370b, 1371b; II, 101b, 124a, 135b, 138a, 167a, 389a, 500b, 517a, 572a, 581a, 1074a; III, 204a, 205b, 207b, 328a, 438a, 441a, 444a, 466a, 469b, 509b; IV, 97b, 299a, 536a, 947b, 1159b; V, 48b, 602a, 1131a, 1250a; S, 56a, 58a, 125b, 142a, 246b, 257b, 258a, 291b, 411a, 420b, 421a
Awrangzīb Khān → Bādshāh Khān
Awrās i, 170a, 171b, 366a, 367a, 748b, **770a,** 1037a; iv, 383a, 459b; v, 696a; s, 103a — I, 175a, 176a, 377a, b, 771a, **793a,** 1068b; IV, 400a, 480a; V, 701a; S, 102b
Awrigha i, 1049a — I, 1081a
Awrupa tudjdjārī i, 1171b — I, 1206b
al-Aws i, 514a, 544b, **771a,** 1283a; iii, 812a; iv, 835b, 1187a; v, 995a; s, 229b, 230a — I, 529b, 561b, **794a,** 1322b; III, 835b; IV, 868b, 1220a; V, 990a, b; S, 229b, 230a
Aws b. Ḥadjar i, **772a** — I, **795a**
Aws b. Ḥāritha b. Laʾm i, 1241a — I, 1279a
Awsan iv, 746a — IV, 776a
Awshār → Afshār
al-Awsī al-Anṣarī, ʿUmar b. Ibrāhīm iii, 181a — III, 185b
al-Awtād i, 95a, **772a** — I, 97b, **795a**
al-ʿAwwāʾ → Nudjūm
ʿAwwād, Tawfīḳ Yūsuf v, 189b, 190b — V, 186b, 187b
Awwal i, **772a** — I, **795a**
al-ʿAwwām b. al-Zadjdjādj iv, 764b — IV, 794b
al-ʿAwwām b. ʿAbd al-ʿAzīz al-Badjalī i, 134b — I, 138b
al-Awzāʿī i, 164b, **772b,** 1137b; ii, 489a, 889b, 1026b; s, 384b — I, 169a, **795b,** 1172a; II, 501a, 910a, 1050b; S, 385a
Awzān al-shiʿr i, 671a — I, 691b
Āya, āyāt i, **773b**; iv, 616a; v, 422a — I, **796b**; IV, 641a; V, 424a
Aya Mavra → Levkas
Aya Sofya i, 75a, **774a**; iv, 225a, b, 226a — I, 77a, **797a**; IV, 234b, 235b, 236a
Aya Solūk i, **777b** — I, **800b**
Aya Stefanos → Yeshilköy
Aʿyān i, 657a, **778a,** 1304a; ii, 33b, 640b, 724a; iii, 1187b — I, 677b, **801b,** 1344a; II, 34a, 657a, 742b; III, 1217a
ʿAyān Kāzarūnī, Shaykh s, 51b, S,52a
Aʿyāṣ s, **103b** — S, **102b**
Ayās i, **778b,** 946b; ii, 38a; iii, 475a — I, **802a,** 975b; II, 39a; III, 491b
Ayās Pasha i, 293b, **779a;** ii, 203b — I, 302b, **802a;** II, 210a
Āyāt → Āya
Āyāt Allāh Kāshānī → Kāshānī
Āyatullāh (Ayatollah) s, **103b** — S, **103a**
Ayāz, Abu 'l-Nadjm i, **780a** — I, **803a**
Ayāz, Amīr i, **780a** — I, **803b**
Aybak, ʿIzz al-Dīn al-Muʿaẓẓamī i, **780b;** ii, 284a; iv, 210a, 484b; v, 571a, 627b, 821a; s, 250a — I, **803b;** II, 292a; IV, 219b, 505b; V, 575b, 631b, 827a; S, 250a
Aybak, ʿIzz al-Dīn (d. 1251) → ʿIzz al-Dīn Aybak
Aybak Ḳuṭb al-Dīn → Ḳuṭb al-Dīn Aybak
Aybar, Mehmet Ali iv, 124b — IV, 130a
Aybeg → Aybak
ʿAydarūs i, **780b** — I, **804a**
ʿAydarūs b. ʿAlī i, 767a — I, 790a
ʿAydarūs b. ʿUmar al-Ḥabshī i, 782a — I, 805b
Aydemir, Colonel Talât iii, 204a — III, 209b
ʿAydhāb i, **782b,** 1158a; ii, 130b; v, 514b, 519a — I, **805b,** 1192b; II, 134a; V, 518a, 522b
Aydimur → ʿIzz al-Dīn Aydimur
Aydîn i, 467b, **782b,** 1234b; v, 505b, 506a, 557b — I, 481b, **806a,** 1271b; V, 509a, b, 562b
Aydîn-oghlu i, 346a, 778a, **783a,** 807a; ii, 599a — I, 356b, 801a, **806b,** 830a; II, 613b
Aydin Reʾīs iv, 1156a, b — IV, 1188a, b
Aydoghu b. Kushdoghan → Shumla
ʿAyhala b. Kaʿb → al-Aswad al-ʿAnsī
ʿĀyid, Āl i, 98b — I, 101a
ʿĀyisha Kargīli Diz → Ṭāḳ
al-Ayka → Madyan
Aykaç, Fāḍîl Aḥmed iii, 357b — III, 368b
Ayḳash i, 97b — I, 100a
Ayla i, 558b, 783b — I, 576a, **807a**
Aylūl → Taʾrīkh
Aymak i, **784a**; s, 367a — I, **807b**; S, 367a
Aymal Khān i, 970b — I, 1000a
Aymān → Ḳasam
al-Ayman ii, 173b — II, 178b
Ayman b. Khuraym i, **784b**; s, 273a — I, **807b**; S, 273a
ʿAyn → Hidjaʾ
ʿAyn (eye/l'œil) i, **785a**; iv, 954a — I, **808b**; IV, 986b
ʿAyn (evil eye/mauvais oeil) i, **786a**; iv, 1009a — I,

809a; IV, 1041b
ʿAyn, aʿyān (sight/la vue) i, **784b;** ii, 486b — I, **808a;** II, 499a
ʿAyn, ʿuyūn (spring water/source d'eau) i, 538b, 1232a — I, 555b, 1269a
ʿAyn Dārā iv, 834b — IV, 867b
ʿAyn al-Dawla ii, 650b, 651a — II, 666b, 667b
ʿAyn Dilfa i, **786b** — I, **810a**
ʿAyn Djālūt i, 21b, **786b,** 1125a; ii, 284b; iii, 184a; v, 571b — I, 22a, **810a,** 1158b; II, 292b; III, 188a; V, 576a
ʿAyn al-Djarr i, **787b**; s, 229b — I, **811a**; S, 229b
ʿAyn al-Ḳuḍāt i, 840a, 841a; s, 4b — I, 863a, 864b; S, 3b
ʿAyn al-Ḳuḍāt al-Hamadhānī → ʿAbd Allāh b. Abī Bakr al-Miyānadjī
ʿAyn al-Mulk Māhrū s, 105b — S, 105a
ʿAyn al-Mulk Multānī i, 764a; ii, 12b, 218b; iii, 405b; iv, 759a, 922a; v, 635a; s, **105a** — I, 787a; II, 12b, 225a; III, 416a; IV, 789b, 955a; V, 639a; S, **104b**
ʿAyn Mūsā i, **788a** — I, **811a**
ʿAyn Shams i, **788a;** ii, 424a — I, **811b;** II, 434b
ʿAyn al-Tamr i, **788b** — I, **812a**
ʿAyn Temushent i, **789a** — I, **812b**
ʿAyn al-Warda i, **789a** — I, **812b**
ʿAyn Warḳa s, 159b — S, 159b
ʿAyn Yashir i, 699b — I, 712a
ʿAyn Zarba i, **789a;** ii, 37b — I, **812b;** II, 38a
Ayna Čashnegīr, Sayf al-Dīn i, 510a — I, 525b
Aynabakhtī i, **790a**; iv, 882a; v, 504a; s, 80b — I, **813b**; IV, 914b; V, 507b; S, 80b
Aynāl → Īnāl
Aynalu (tribe/tribu) iv, 9b — IV, 10a
ʿAynayn → al-Djubayl
ʿAynayn, Āl Bū iv, 751b — IV, 781b
ʿAynī s, 109b — S, 109a
al-ʿAynī, Abū Muḥammad i, 138a, 595a, **790b,** 1128a; iii, 488b; iv, 966b; v, 489b — I, 142a, 614b, **814a,** 1162a; III, 505b; IV, 998b; V, 492b
ʿAynī, Ḥasan Efendi i, **790b** — I, **813b**
ʿAyniyya i, 51a; ii, 1094b; v, 889b, 892a — I, 52b; II, 1120b; V, 896a, 898a
ʿAynṭāb i, 262a, **791a;** ii, 206 — I, 270a, **814b;** II, 21a
ʿAynṭūra s, 33b — S, 33b
al-Aysar ii, 173b — II, 178b
ʿAyshe → ʿĀʾisha
Ayt Idrasen s, 113b — S, 113a
Ayt Isḥāk s, 223a — S, 223a
Ayt Mūsā s, 113b — S, 112b
Ayt Yūsī s, 113b — S, 113a
Aytak, Ikhtiyar al-Dīn ii, 253a — II, 260b
Aytākh al-Turkī s, **106a** — S, **105b**
Ayth Zekrī s, 403b — S, 403b
Aytimish al-Badjasī ii, 781b — II, 800a
Ayüke Khān i, 1076a — I, 1108b
Aywalïk i, **792a** — I, **815b**
Aywān → Iwān
Aywaz i, **792a** — I, **815b**
Ayyām al-ʿAdjūz i, **792b** — I, **816a**
Ayyām al-ʿArab i, 566a, **793a** — I, 584b, **816b**
Ayyār → Taʾrīkh
ʿAyyār, ʿayyārūn i, 256b, **794a,** 900a, b, 902a, b, 955a, 1355b; ii, 961b, 962a, 1043b; iv, 445a — I, 264b, **817b,** 927a, b, 929a, b, 984a, 1394b; II, 983b, 984a, 1068a; IV, 465a
ʿAyyāsh b. Lahīʿa i, 153b — I, 157b
ʿAyyāsh b. Nadjāh → Zabīd
al-ʿAyyāshī, Abu 'l-Naṣr Muḥammad i, **794b**; iv, 711b — I, **818a**; IV, 740a, b
al-ʿAyyāshī, Abū Sālim ʿAbd Allāh i, **795a;** ii, 161a; iii, 736b — I, **818a;** II, 166a; III, 759a
Ayyil i, **795a** — I, **818b**
Ayyūb i, **795b;** 242a — I, **819a;** II, 249a
Ayyūb, Rashīd v, 1254b, 1255a, b — V, 1245b, 1246a, b
Ayyūb (of Edessa/d'Édesse) i, 213a — I, 219a
Ayyūb b. Abi Yazīd al-Nukkārī i, 163b; iii, 1042a — I, 168a; III, 1068a
Ayyūb b. Ḥabīb al-Lakhmī i, 58b; iv, 477b — I, 60b; IV, 498b
Ayyūb b. al-Raḳḳī iv, 92a — IV, 96a
Ayyūb b. Shādhī b. Marwān i, 796b — I, 820a
Ayyūb b. Tamīm b. al-Muʿizz iii, 788a — III, 811b
Ayyūb Anṣārī s, 292a — S, 291b
Ayyūb Khan (d/m 1914) i, 232a, **796b**; iv, 537b — I, 239a, **819b**; IV, 561a
Ayyūb Khān (d/m 1974) iii, 533b, 565b, 566a; v, 1081b — III, 552a, 585a, b; IV, 1079a
Ayyūb Ṣabrī Pasha i, **796b** — I, **820a**
Ayyūb al-Sakhtiyānī iv, 370b — IV, 387a
Ayyūbid Art/Ayyūbide, Art → Supplement/Supplément
Ayyūbid(e)s i, 197b, 215a, 435b, 439b, 552b, 666b, **796b,** 814b, 816a, 1125a, 1206b, 1276b, 1316b; ii, 65a, 283b, 305b, 329b, 344b, 506a, 858a; iii, 120b, 228b, 473a, 507a; iv, 429b, 816b, 817b; v, 454b, 627b, 739a, 1245a; s, 154a, 338a, 387b, 396a — I, 203a, 221b, 448a, 452a, 570a, 687a, **820a,** 837b, 839b, 1159a, 1242b, 1316a, 1356b; II, 66b, 291b, 314a, 339a, 354a, 519a, 878a; III, 123a, 235b, 489b, 524b; IV, 448b, 849b, 850b; V, 457b, 631b, 744a, 1235b; S, 154b, 337b, 388a, 396a
- literature/littérature iii, 753a, 967a — III, 776a, 991b
al-ʿAyyūḳ → Nudjūm
ʿAyyūḳī iv, 57b, 62b — IV, 61a, 66a
ʿAzāʾ iv, 488a — IV, 509b
ʿAzab i, **807a**; iv, 230b, 723a — I, **830a**; IV, 241a, 752a
Āzād, Abu 'l-Kalām iii, 431b; iv, 170b; v, 7a, b; s, 4b, **106a**, 247b — III, 445b; IV, 178a; V, 7b, 8a; S, 3b, **105b**, 247b
Āzād, Muḥammad Ḥusayn i, **807b;** ii, 222a; iii, 93b; s, 74b, **107a** — I, **830b;** II, 229a; III, 96a; S, 75b, **106b**
Āzād Bilgrāmī i, **808a,** 1219b — I, **831a,** 1255b
Āzād Khān i, 190a; iii, 1103a; iv, 390a, 639b — I, 196a; III, 1130a; IV, 407a, 666a
Āzādī s, **107b** — S, **107a**
ʿAzafī, Banu'l- iv, 355b; s, 45b, **111b** — IV, 371a; S, 46a, **110b**
Azahari, Shaykh A.M. s, 152a, b — S, 152b
Azaḳ i, **808b** — I, **831b**
Azal → Ḳidam
Azalay i, **808b,** 1222a; ii, 368a, b — I, **832a,** 1258a; II, 378a, b
Azalī i, **809a** — I, **832a**
Azaliyya ii, 95b — II, 97b
Aʿẓam-i Humāyūn iv, 908a — IV, 941a
Aʿẓam Khān I (Rādjpūt) i, 809a; iv, 1018b — I, 832b; IV, 1050b
Aʿẓam Khān II (Rādjpūt) i, 809a — I, 832b
Aʿẓam Khān (Mālwa) v, 1a — V, 1b
Aʿẓam Khān Bārakzay → Muḥammad Aʿzam b. Dūst Muḥammad
Aʿẓam Shāh (Bengal(e)) ii, 216b; v, 638a — II, 223a; V, 642b
Aʿẓam Shāh (Mughal) → Muḥammad Aʿẓam b. Awrangzīb
Aʿẓamgarh i, **809a;** iii, 433a — I, **832a;** III, 447b
ʿAẓamiyya (Ṭarīḳa) → Abu 'l-ʿAzāʾim
Azammūr i, **809b** — I, **832b**
Āzar i, **810a;** iii, 980a — I, **833a;** III, 1004b
Azar Kaywan v, 1114a — V, 1110a
Azarbāydjān → Adharbaydjān; Azerbaydjān
Azāriḳa i, 77a, **810a;** iii, 40b, 657b; iv, 15a, 44b, 99b,

269a, 752b, 1075b; v, 157b — I, 79a, **833a;** III, 42a, 679a; IV, 16a, 47a, 104a, 281a, 783a, 1107b; V, 157a
Azarquîel → al-Zarḳālī
ʿAzāz i, 239a; v, 106a — I, 246b; V, 108a
ʿAzāzīl i, **811a** — I, **834b**
Azd i, 304a, 529b, 544b, 548b, **811b,** 1140b; iii, 223a, 782a; v, 77a; s, 222b — I, 313b, 545b, 565b, 566a, **834b,** 1175a; III, 230a, 805b; V, 79a; S, 223a
Azda bint al-Ḥārith b. Kalada s, 354b — S, 354b
Azdadja i, 1037a — I, 1068b
al-Azdī s, **113a**, 384a — S, **112b**, 384b
al-Azdī → Abu 'l-Muṭahhar; Abū Manṣūr; ʿIsā b. Rayʿān; Yazīd b. Ḥātim
al-Azdī, Abū Muḥammad Yūsuf (Ḳāḍī) s, 284a — S, 284a
al-Azdī, Abū Zakariyyāʾ i, **813a** — I, **836b**
al-Azdī, Ismāʿīl b. Isḥaḳ s, **113a** — S, **112b**
al-Azdī, Muḥammad b. al-Muʿallāʾ s, 394b — S, 395a
Azemmūr → Azammūr
Azerbaydjān, S.S.R./U.R.S.S. i, 191b, ii, 595a; iii, 530a; v, 1213b — I, 197a; II, 609b; III, 548b; V, 1203a
Azerī → Adharī
Aẓfarī i, **813b** — I, **836b**
al-Azhar i, **813b;** ii, 495a, 854a, 863a; iii, 841a, 986b; iv, 144a, 444a, 907b; v, 910b, 1124a; s, 18a, 40b, 121b, 132b, 262b, 408a, 411a — I, **837a;** II, 507b, 873b, 883a; III, 865a, 1011a; IV, 150a, 464a, 940a; V, 916b, 1120b; S, 18a, 41a, 121a, 132a, 262a, 408b, 411b
al-Azharī, Abū Mansūr Muḥammad i, 719a, **822a**; iv, 524b; s, 20a, 38a, 250b — I, 740b, **845a**; IV, 547a; S, 20a, 38a, 250b
al-Azharī, Aḥmad i, 821b — I, 844b
al-Azharī, Ibrāhīm i, 821b — I, 844b
al-Azharī, Ismāʿīl iii, 524a — III, 542a
al-Azharī, Khālīd i, 821b, 1314b — I, 844b, 1355a
ʿAzīb, ʿazl i, 661a — I, 682a
al-ʿAẓīm → al-ʿAḍaym
ʿAẓīm Allāh Khān i, **822a** — I, **845a**
ʿAẓīm al-Shān i, 914a, 1025b; ii, 7a, 379a, 810a — I, 941b, 1057a; II, 7a, 389b, 829a
ʿAzīma i, **822b;** ii, 545a — I, **846a;** II, 558b
ʿAẓīmābād → Bānkīpūr
Azimech → Nudjūm
al-Aẓīmī i, **823a** — I, **846a**
Azimut → al-Samt
al-ʿĀzir → Lazarus/Lazare
ʿAzīz iii, 25b — III, 26b
ʿAzīz ʿAlī al-Maṣrī s, 299b — S, 299b
al-ʿAzīz (Ayyūbid(e)) → al-ʿAzīz ʿUthmān
al-ʿAzīz (Hammādid(e)) iii, 138b — III, 141a
ʿAzīz b. Ardashīr Astarābādī i, 1328a — I, 1369a
al-ʿAzīz b. Djalāl al-Dawla i, 132a; ii, 391a; iii, 1201b — I, 136a; II, 401b; III, 1232a
ʿAzīz Efendī → ʿAlī ʿAzīz Giridlī
ʿAzīz Miṣr i, **825b** — I, **848b**
al-ʿAzīz biʾllāh Nizār (Fāṭimid(e)) i, 533a, 788a, 814b, 816a, **823a,** 1153b, 1218a; ii, 854a, 855a, 860a; iii, 76b, 128b, 130a, 246a, 385b; iv, 663b — I, 549a, 811b, 837b, 839a, **846a,** 1188a, 1254b; II, 874a, 875a, 879b; III, 79a, 131b, 132b, 253a, 398a; IV, 690a, b
ʿAzīz al-Dawla, Abū Shudjāʿ v, 929b, 933a, b, — V, 934b, 937a, b
ʿAzīz Ḍiyāʾ al-Dīn b. Zāhid v, 1005b — V, 1001a
ʿAzīz Khammār s, 73b — S, 74a
ʿAzīz Pasha ʿIzzat s, 300a — S, 299b
al-ʿAzīz ʿUthmān (Ayyūbid(e)) i, 173b, 197b, 198a, 798b, 1214b; ii, 283b; iv, 376b, 613b — I, 177a, 203b, 822a, 1250b; II, 292a; IV, 393a, 638a
ʿAzīza bint al-Ghiṭrīf b. ʿAṭāʾ s, 326b — S, 326a
ʿAzīza ʿUthmāna iii, 605a — III, 626a
ʿAzīzī i, **825b** — I, **848b**
ʿAzīzī → Ḳaračelebi-zāde
ʿAzl i, **826a** — I, **849a**
al-ʿAzm, Ibrāhīm v, 591b, 925b — V, 595b, 930b
ʿAzmī Gedizī v, 952a — V, 955b
ʿAzmī-zade, Muṣṭafā → Ḥāletī
Azores/Açores → al-Djazāʾir al-Khālidāt
Azougui → Atar
Azov, Sea of/Mer d'- → Baḥr Māyuṭis
ʿAzrāʾīl → ʿIzrāʾīl
Azrak v, 700a, 706a — V, 705b, 711a
al-Azraḳī s, 271b, 272a — S, 271b
al-Azraḳī, Abu 'l-Walīd i, 591a, 609a, **826b;** ii, 757b — I, 610b, 628b, **849b;** II, 775b
Azraḳī, Zayn al-Dīn i, **827a**; iv, 61b — I, **850a**; IV, 65a
Azraḳī Kurds → Zraḳī
Azraḳites → Azāriḳa
Azrū s, **113** — S, **112b**
Azuel → Abū Muḥammad al-Zubayr
Azulejo → Khazaf
Āzurda, Ṣadr al-Dīn i, **827b;** ii, 736a — I, **850a;** II, 754b
ʿAzūrī, Nadjīb iii, 519a — III, 537a
ʿAzza → Kuthayyir
ʿAzza i, 1049a — I, 1081a
ʿAzza al-Maylā i, **828a;** ii, 1073b; iii, 812a; iv, 821b — I, **851a;** II, 1098b; III, 835b; IV, 854b
ʿAzzāba iii, 95a, 96a — III, 97b, 98b
ʿAzzān b. Ḳays i, 554b, 1283a; iv, 1085a; s, 355b, 356a — I, 572a, 1321b; IV, 1116a; S, 355b
ʿAzzān b. Tamīm i, 813a — I, 836a

B

Bāʾ → Hidjāʾ
Bāʾ → Mawāzīn
Bā i, **828a** — I, **851a**
Bā ʿAbbād i, **828b** — I, **851b**
Bā Aḥmad i, 57b, 357a; ii, 820a; iii, 562b; v, 1193a; s, **114a**, 336b — I, 59b, 368a; II, 839b; III, 581b; V, 1183a; S, **113b**, 336a
Bā ʿAlawī i, 277b, 780b, **828b**; iv, 885b, 887b — I, 286b, 804a, **851b**; IV, 918b, 920a
Bā Faḍl → Faḍl, Bā
Bā Faḳīh → Faḳīh, Bā
Bā Ḥassān → Ḥassān, Bā
Bā Hmād → Bā Aḥmad
Bā Hurmuz → Hurmuz, Bā
Bā Kathīr → Kathīr, Bā
Bā Kāzim → Kāzim, Bā
Ba Lobbo i, 303b; ii, 914b; iii, 39b — I, 313a; II, 963b; III, 41a
Bā Madhḥidj → al-Suwaynī, Saʿd b. ʿĀlī
Bā Makhrama → Makhrama, Bā
Bā Ṣurra ii, 173b — II, 179a
Baalbek → Baʿlabakk
Bāb i, **832b;** ii, 97b; iv, 39a, 51b, 70b, 854b — I, **855b;** II, 99b; IV, 41b, 54a, 74b, 887b
Bāb (gate/porte) i, **830a**; v, 989b — I, **853a**; V, 984b
al-Bāb (Buṭnān) i, 1349a, 1357b, 1358a — I, 1389b, 1398a
Bāb, ʿAlī Muḥammad i, **833a,** 1030b; iv, 696a — I, **856a,** 1062a; IV, 724a
Bāb Abraz s, 384a — S, 384b
Bāb al-Abwāb i, 32a, **835b**; iv, 342a, 1173a — I, 33a, **858b**; IV, 356b, 1206b
Bāb-i ʿĀlī i, **836a**; iv, 568a, 1126a — I, **859b**; IV, 590b, 1158a
Bāb Allāh (Dimashḳ) s, 49a — S, 50a
Bāb Allān → Bāb al-Lān

Bāb Aylān s, 124b — S, 382b
Bā al-Azadj s, 192b — S, 194a
Bāb al-Dhahab i, 896a, 897a — I, 922b, 924a
Bāb al-Djīsa s, 126a — S, 125a
Bāb al-Ghadr iv, 685a — IV, 713a
Bāb al-Ḥadīd ii, 115b — II, 118a
Bāb-i Humāyūn i, **836b**; iv, 568a — I, **860a**; IV, 590b
Bāb al-Lān i, **837a**; iv, 342b — I, **860a**; IV, 357a
Bāb al-Mandab i, **837b,** 932a — I, **860b,** 960b
Bāb-i Mashīkhat i, **837b** — I, **861a**
Bāb-i Serʿaskerī i, **838a;** ii, 513a — I, **861a;** II, 525b
Bāb al-Ṭāḳ i, 897a, 898b, 900a, b; s, 192b, 194a, 381a — I, 923b, 925b, 927a; S, 193b, 381a
Bāb Zuwayla (al-Ḳāhira) s, 408a — S, 408a
Baba i, **838b** — I, **861b**
Bābā b. Ḥamā Allāh iii, 108a — III, 110b
Bābā Ādam i, 1168a; ii, 216a — I, 1202b; II, 223a
Bābā Afḍal i, **838b** — I, **862a**
Baba ʿAlī b. Ṣāliḥ b. Ḳuṭb al-Dīn ii, 989b — II, 1012b
Baba ʿAlī Mest-i ʿAdjemī iv, 1137a — IV, 1169a
Bābā Alī Nadjdjār s, 423b — S, 423b
Bābā Ardalān i, 626b — I, 647a
Bābā Ayyūb ii, 29b — II, 30a
Bābā Beg i, **839b** — I, **862b**
Bābā Dāghī → Babadaghī
Bābā Fighānī → Fighānī
Bābā Ghor iii, 16a — III, 17a
Bābā Girāy i, 838b — I, 861b
Baba Ḥasan → Ḥasan Baba
Bābā Ḥātim → Sālār Khalīl
Bābā Isḥāḳ i, 689b, 843b, 1161b; ii, 989a — I, 719b, 867a, 1196b; II, 1012a
Bābā Ismāʿīl Kubrawī s, 353b, 423b — S, 353b, 423b
Baba Khān → Fatḥ ʿAlī Shāh
Bābā Khoshīn i, 262b, 841b; v, 823a — I, 271a, 865a; V, 829a
Bābā Nūr al-Dīn Rishī s, **114a** — S, **113b**
Bābā Ratan → Ratan
Bābā Sāhib → Bhāskar Rāo
Bābā Ṭāhir i, 262b, **839b;** iii, 106a; iv, 62a — I, 270b, **862b;** III, 108a; IV, 65b
Baba Toma iv, 352a — IV, 367a
Bābā ʿUthmān s, 353b — S, 353b
Bābā Walī i, 506a; iii, 245b — I, 521b; III, 252b
Babadaghī i, **842b;** ii, 612a, 613a — I, **865b;** II, 627a, 628a
Babadjān b. Pinchas, Solomon iv, 310b — IV, 324b
Babaeski i, **843a** — I, **866b**
Bābāʾī i, 698b, 838b, **843b**; iv, 817a — I, 719b, 861b, **866b**; IV, 849b
Bābāʾī b. Farhād iv, 310a — IV, 323b
Bābāʾī b. Luṭf iv, 310a — IV, 323b
Bābak i, 52b, 153b, 154a, 241a, 625b, 660b, **844a,** 1072b; ii, 228a, 623b, 893a; iii, 274b, 471a; iv, 17a, 344b, 646a; v, 64b, 856a; s, 116a — I, 54a, 158a, b, 248b, 646a, 681b, **867a,** 1104b; II, 235a, 639a, 914a; III, 282a, 487b; IV, 18b, 359b, 672b; V, 66a, 862b; S, 115b
Bābalyūn i, **844b** — I, **867b**
Bābān i, **845a**; v, 460b — I, **868a**; V, 463a
Babba Zaki iv, 549a — IV, 572b
Bābar → Bābur
al-Bābartī → Akmal al-Dīn
Babatu ii, 1003b — II, 1027a
al-Babāwī → Shams al-Dīn Muḥammad
Babbaghāʾ i, **845b** — I, **868b**
al-Babbaghā, Abu 'l-Faradj i, 120a, **845b;** ii, 198a; s, 119b — I, 123a, **868b;** II, 204b; S, 119a
Bābil i, **846a** — I, **869a**
Bābīs i, 304b, 833a, **846b,** 1099b; v, 102a, 502a; S, 53b, 54b, 71a, 77a — I, 314a, 856a, **870a,** 1132b; V, 104a, 505a; S, 53b, 55a, 72a, 76b
Babor, Djebel iv, 359a, 360b, 361a — IV, 374b, 376a, 377a
Bābūnadj s, **114b** — S, **114a**
Bābur i, 218a, 227b, 228a, 252b, 627b, **847b,** 864b, 970a, 1069a, 1139b, 1192b, 1212a, 1323b, 1347b, ii, 29a, 47b, 120b, 264b, 271a, 792a, 973a, 978a, 1049b, 1122b, 1144a; iii, 199b, 200b, 202a, 317a, 422b, 448b, 492b, 995b; iv, 186b, 357a, 410a, 536b, 914b, 1021b; v, 36b, 45b, 250b, 649a, 687a, 885a, 1135a; s, 1b, 312a, 313a, 324b, 325a, 329b, 331b — I, 224b, 234b, 260b, 648b, **870b,** 888b, 1000a, 1101a, 1174a, 1228a, 1248a, 1364b, 1387b; II, 29b, 48a, 123b, 272b, 279a, 810b, 995b, 1000b, 1074a, 1149a, 1171a; III, 204b, 205b, 207a, 326b, 436a, 464a, 509b, 1020b; IV, 194b, 372b, 428a, 560a, 947b, 1053b; V, 38a, 47a, 248b, 653b, 692a, 891a, 1130b; S, 1b, 312a, 313a, 324a, b, 329a, 331a
Bābur Mīrzā → Abu 'l-Ḳāsim Bābur
Bābur-nāma i, 80b, 607a, 848b; ii, 909b — I, 83a, 627a, 872a; II, 931a
Babylon, Egypt/Babylone d'Égypte → Bābalyūn
Babylon (Mesopotamia/Mésopotamie) → Bābil
Bačča-i Saḳaw i, 232b; ii, 658b; v, 1079a; s, 66b — I, 239b; II, 675a; V, 1076b; S, 67a
Bāčkām → Badjkam
Backergunge → Bāḳargandj
Bactria/Bactriane i, 226a; v, 229a — I, 232b; V, 226b
Bactromancy/Bactromancie → Istiḳsām
Bād-i Hawā i, 656b, **850a;** ii, 147a — I, 677a, **873b;** II, 151a
Bād-i Ṣad-u-bīst rūz iv, 4b — IV, 4b
Badāʾ i, 265b, **850a** — I, 273b, **873b**
Badajoz → Baṭalyaws
Badakhshān i, 46b, 87a, 223b, **851b;** ii, 43a; iii, 575a; iv, 202b, 205b; s, 50b, 125a, b, 258b, 367b — I, 48a, 89b, 230a, **875a;** II, 43b; III, 595a; IV, 211b, 215a; S, 51b, 124a, b, 258a, 367a
Badakhshānī, Shams al-Dīn s, 73b — S, 74a
Badakhshī ii, 31b — II, 32a
Badal i, 760b, **855a;** ii, 147a — I, 783b, **878b;** II, 151a
Badal → Abdāl and/et Naḥw
Badan ii, 555a — II, 568b
Badan Singh i, 1193a — I, 1228a
Bādarāya → Badrā
Badāʾūn i, **855b;** ii, 274b; iii, 441b; iv, 749b; v, 1135a; s, 73b, 74a — I, **879b;** II, 282b; III, 455b; IV, 779b; V, 1130b; S, 74a, b
Badāʾūnī i, **856a,** 1136a, b; ii, 871a; s, 21a, 117b, 206b, 378a — I, **880a,** 1170b, 1171a; II, 891a; S, 21a, 117a, 206a, 378b
Badawī → Aḥmād al-Badawī
al-Badawiyya → Aḥmad al-Badawī
Badawlat → Yaʿḳūb Beg (Kāshghar)
Bādghīs i, **857a;** 253a; v, 47a; s, 367b — I, **881a;** II, 260a; V, 48b; S, 367a
Bādgīr v, 1148b; s, **115a** — V, 1139b; S, **114b**
Bādh i, 329a, 637b; ii, 344a; iii, 128b; v, 452b, 453a — I, 339b, 658b; II, 353b; III, 131b; V, 455a, b
Bādhām, Bādhān i, 102a, 728a; s, **115b** — I, 105a, 750a; S, **115a**
Bādhān Fayrūz i, 625b — I, 646a
Badhandūn → Bozanti
al-Badhdh i, 844a; s, **116a** — I, 867b; S, **115b**
Badhl al-Kubrā iv, 821b; s, 116b — IV, 854b; S, 116a
Badīʿ i, 587b, 592a, **857b,** 981b; iii, 663b, 665a, 799b; iv, 248b; v, 319a, 321b, 898a, 900a — I, 606b, 611b, **881a,** 1012a; III, 658a, 686b, 823a; IV, 259b; V, 318b, 321a, 904b, 906b
al-Badīʿ → Marrākush
Badī (Fundj) ii, 944a, b — II, 966a, b
Badīʿ, Ḥasan iv, 72b, v, 198a — IV, 76b; V, 195b
al-Badīʿ al-Asṭurlābī i, **858b;** iii, 780b — I, **882a;** III,

804a
Badīʿ al-Dīn Shāh Madār i, 702b, **858b**; s, 385b – I, 724a, **882b**; S, 358b
Badīʿ al- Zamān → al-Hamadhānī
Badīʿ al-Zamān b. Ḥusayn Bayḳarā i, 627b; iii, 603a; iv, 1020b – I, 648a; III, 623b; IV, 1052b
Badīʿ al-Zamān b. Shāhrūkh i, 853a – I, 876b
Badīʿ al-Zamān Mīrzā i, 406a – I, 418a
Badia y Leblich → ʿAlī Bey al-ʿAbbāsī
Badīha → Irtidjāl
Badīʿiyya i, 982b – I, 1013a
Badīl → Abdāl
Bādīnān → Bahdīnān
Bādis i, **859b** – I, **883a**
Bādīs b. Ḥabūs i, 6a, 130b, 1310a; ii, 1012b, 1015a; iii, 147b – I, 6b, 134a, 1350a; II, 1036b, 1038b; III, 150b → Zīrids of Spain/Zīrides d'Espagne
Bādīs b. al-Manṣūr i, **860a;** iii, 137a; iv, 479a; v, 1179a, 1182a, b – I, **884a;** III, 139b; IV, 501a; V, 1169a, 1172a, b
al-Bādisī s, 377b – S, 377b
al-Bādisī, ʿAbd al-Ḥaḳḳ i, 596a, **860a** – I, 615b, **884a**
al- Bādisī, Abū Ḥassan ʿAlī → Abū Ḥassan ʿAlī
al-Bādisī, Abū Yaʿḳūb Yūsuf → Abū Yaʿḳūb Yūsuf al-Bādisī
Bādiyya s, **116b** – S, **116a**
Bādj i, **860b;** ii, 147a; iii, 489b – I, **884b;** II, 151a; III, 506a
Bādj i, **862a** – I, **886a**
Bādja (al-Andalus) i, **862a,** 1092a; ii, 1009a – I, **886a,** 1124b; II, 1032b
Bādja (Ifrīḳiya) i, 163b, **862b**; v, 51b, 733a – I, 168a, **886b**; V, 53a, 738a
Bādja al-Ḳadīma i, 863a – I, 887b
Bādjaddā i, **863b** – I, **887b**
Bādjalān i, **863b** – I, **887b**
al-Badjalī → al-ʿAwamm b. ʿAbd al-ʿAzīz; Budayl b. Ṭahfa; Djarīr b. ʿAbd Allāh
al-Badjalī, al-Ḥasan b. ʿAlī b. Warsand i, **863b**; s, 402b – I, **888a**; S, 403a
Badjaliyya i, 863b; s, 402b – I, 888a; S, 402b
Badjalushka i, 1062b; iii, 477a – I, 1094b; III, 493b
Badjanāk → Pečeneg
al-Bādjarbaḳī ii, 377a – II, 387b
Bādjarmā i, **864a** – I, **888a**
Bādjarwān i, **864a** – I, **888a**
al-Badjasī → Aytimish
Bādjat al-Zayt i, 862a, 863a – I, 886b, 887a
Badjāwa → Bedja
Bādjawr i, 864a – I, 888b
Badjdjāna i, **864b** – I, **888b**
al-Bādjī, Abu'l-Walīd i, **864b;** iii, 542b – I, **889a;** III, 561a
Bādjī Rāō i, 710a, 1053a, 1195a; iii, 320a – I, 731b, 1084b, 1230b; III, 330b
Badjīla i, **865a**; iv, 925b, 1105b; v, 617a; s, 37b – I, **889b**; IV, 958b, 1137a; V, 621a; S, 37b
Badjimzā i, **865b** – I, **890a**
Bādjisrā i, **865b** – I, **890a**
Badjkam i, **866a,** 1040a, 1046b; iii, 127a, 345a, 902b – I, **890a,** 1071b, 1078b; III, 130a, 355b, 926b
Bādjūrān → Ṣārlīya, Shabak
Bādjūrī, Ibrāhīm b. Muḥammad i, 151a, 413a, 819b, **867b;** ii, 451a, 727b; iv, 173a, 693b, 1108a – I, 155a, 1425a, 842b, **891b,** 1355a; II, 463a, 746a; IV, 180b, 721b, 1139b
Badlīs → Bidlīs
Badr, Āl i, 759b – I, 782a
Badr (battle of/bataille de) i, **867b;** ii, 950b; v, 1162a; s, 44b, 230a, 351b – I, **892a;** II, 972b; V, 1152a; S, 44b, 230a, 351b
Badr (Mawlā) s, 82a – S, 81b
Badr b. ʿAmmar al-Asadī → Badr al-Kharshanī
Badr b. Hasanwayh i, 512b, 1030b; ii, 749a; iii, 244b, 258a, b; iv, 294a; v, 229b, 452b, 1124b; s, 118b, 119a – I, 528a, 1062a; II, 767b; III, 251b, 265a, b; IV, 307b; V, 227b, 455a, 1121a; S, 118a, b
Badr b. Hilāl i, 513a – I, 528b
Badr b. Muhalhil i, 513a – I, 528b
Badr Abū Ṭuwayriḳ i, 553b – I, 571a
Badr al-Dawla Sulaymān i, 663b, 983a – I, 685b, 1014a
Badr al-Dīn Awliyā i, 606b – I, 626a
Badr al-Dīn b. Djamāʿa → Ibn Djamāʿa
Badr al-Dīn b. Ḳāḍī Samāwnā i, 312b, **869a;** ii, 599b – I, 322b, **893a;** II, 614a
Badr al-Dīn Ibrāhīm (Ḳarāmān-oghlu) iv, 621b, 622a – IV, 646b, 647a
Badr al-Dīn Ibrāhīm b. Khuteni iv, 620a – IV, 644b
Badr al-Dīn Khurāsānī ii, 81a; s, 157b – II, 82b; S, 158a
Badr al-Dīn Luʾluʾ → Luʾluʾ
Badr al-Dīn Muḥammad I, II, III → Faḍl Allāh, Banū
Badr al-Dīn Muḥammad al-Hamdānī iv, 1188b – IV, 1221b
Badr al-Djamālī i, 638b, 832a, **869b,** 926b, 1228a, 1316a; ii, 484b, 857b, 863b; iii, 253b; iv, 424b, 568a; v, 91b, 328a, 514b; s, 390a – I, 659a, 855b, **894a,** 954b, 1264b, 1356b; II, 497a, 877b, 883a; III, 261a; IV, 443a, 590a; V, 94a, 328a, 518a; S, 390b
Badr al-Ḥammāmī iv, 100a – IV, 104b
Badr al-Kabīr iv, 494a – IV, 515a
Badr Khān Djazīri v, 462a, b – V, 465a
Badr al-Kharshanī i, **870b** – I, **894b**
Badr al-Muʿtaḍidī Abu ʾl-Nadjm i, 11a, 1223a; ii, 1080a; s, **117b** – I, 11a, 1259b; II, 1105a; S, **117a**
Badr-i Čāčī s, **117b** – S, **117a**
Badra i, **870b** – I, **895a**
Badrān b. Ṣadaḳa iv, 911b – IV, 944b
al-Badrī ii, 900b -II, 921a
Badrkhānī i, **871a** – I, **895a**
Bādshāh Khān ii, 317a – II, 326b
Bādūrayā i, **871b,** 899b; v, 566b – I, **895b,** 926b; V, 571a
Bādūsbānid(e)s i, **871b;** iii, 255a; iv, 808a; v, 663a, b; s, 297b, 298a – I, **896a;** III, 262b; IV, 840b; V, 668b; S, 297a, b
Badw i, 14b, **872a,** 1049b, 1149b, 1230a, 1239b, 1288b; ii, 92b, 174b, 342b, 455a, 1005b, 1055a, 1059b; iii, 190b, 1261b; iv, 960b, 961a; v, 334a – I, 15a, **896b,** 1081a, 1184a, 1266b, 1277a, 1328a; II, 94b, 180a, 352a, 467a, 1029a, 1079b, 1084a; III, 195a, 1294b; IV, 992b, 993a; V, 334b
- language/langue v, 1205b, 1206a, b – V, 1195b, 1196b, 1197a
Baena → Bayyāna
Baeza → Bayyāsa
Bafilo → Kubafolo
Bafur i, 211a – I, 217a
Bagauda iii, 275b; iv, 548b, 551a – III, 283b; IV, 572a, 574b
Bāgerhāt ii, 486b; iii, 444a – II, 498b; III, 459a
Baggāra → Baḳḳāra
Bāgh → Bustān
al-Baghawī i, **893a;** ii, 382a; iii, 24b – I, **919b;** II, 392a; III, 25b
Bāghāya iv, 422b – IV, 441a
Baghbūr → Faghfūr
Bāghče Sarāy i, **893a;** ii, 1113a; v, 138a, 140b – I, **919b;** II, 1139a; V, 140b, 143b
Baghdād i, 8a, 17a, 18a, b, 19a, 21a, 291a, 438a, 576a, 616a, 866b, **894b,** 975a, b. 1038a; ii, 128b, 184b, 391a, 579b, 964a; iii, 702b, 1255a, 1256b, 1258a; iv, 20a,

215a, 652b; v, 33a, b, 458a, 928b; s, 13a, b, 15b, 33a, 95a, 102a, 113a, 182b, 191b, 192a, 199a, 225b, 267b — I, 8a, 17b, 19a, 20a, 21b, 300a, 450a, 595a, 636b, 890b, **921a,** 1005b, 1006a, 1069b; II, 132a, 190b, 401b, 594a, 986a; III, 724b, 1287b, 1289a, 1290b; IV, 21b, 224b, 678b; V, 34a, 35a, 460b, 933b; S, 13a, 14a, 16a, 33a, 94a, 101b, 112b, 182b, 193a, 199a, 225b, 267a
- commerce i, 905b, 907a; ii, 745b; iii, 218a, 1252b — I, 932b, 934b; II, 764a; III, 224b, 1285a
- history/histoire i, 1309b; iii, 692b, 756a, 897a — I, 1349b, III, 715a, 779a, 921a
- institutions i, 212b, 899a, 900a, 902a, 903a, 906b, 1223a; ii, 127a; iii, 140a, 159b, 160b; v, 1127a, 1148a — I, 218b, 926a, 927a, 929a, 930a, 934a, 1259b; II, 130b; III, 142b, 163a, 164a; V, 1123a, b, 1139a
- monuments i, 11b, 52b, 616b, 831a, 832b, 896a-904b, 1354a; iii, 1268a; iv, 378a — I, 11b, 54b, 636b, 854a, 855b, 922b-932a, 1393a; III, 1301a; IV, 394b
- university/université ii, 424b — II, 435b
Ba<u>gh</u>dād <u>Kh</u>ātūn i, **908b;** ii, 68a, 980b — I, **936a;** II, 69a, 1003a
Ba<u>gh</u>dād Yolu i, 475a — I, 489a
al-Ba<u>gh</u>dādī → ʿAbd al-Ḳādir; ʿAbd al-Latīf; Abu 'l-<u>Kh</u>ayr al-Ḥusayn; al-<u>Kh</u>aṭīb; Bahāʿ al-Dīn; Ma<u>dj</u>d al-Dīn
al-Ba<u>gh</u>dādī, ʿAbd al-Ḳāhir i, **909a;** ii, 96a, 296a; iii, 1140a; iv, 183a-b, 667b — I, **936b;** II, 98a, 303b; III, 1168a; IV, 191a, 694b
Ba<u>gh</u>ir iv, 327a — IV, 341b
Bā<u>gh</u>istān s, 50b — S, 51a
Ba<u>gh</u>l i, **909a**; iv, 1146a — I, **936b**; IV, 1178a
Ba<u>gh</u>lī → Dirham
Ba<u>gh</u>r → Mārid
Ba<u>gh</u>rās i, 239a, **909b,** 1134a — I, 246b, **937a,** 1168b
Bagirmi (Ba<u>gh</u>irmi) i, **910a**; v, 278b, 357b; s, 164a, b— I, **937b**; V, 276b, 359a; S, 164a, b
Bagrat III v, 489a — V, 492a
Bagrat IV iv, 346b; v, 489a — IV, 361a; V, 492a
Bagrat V v, 491a — V, 494a
Bagratid(e)s i, 100b, 101a, 466a, 507a, 637b, 638a; iv, 346b, 347b, 669b; v, 488b, 489a, 496a — I, 103b, 479b, 522b, 658a, b; IV, 361a, 362a, 697a; V, 491b, 492a, 499a
Baguette → Ḳaḍīb
Bagulal i, 504a — I, 519b
Bagzāda iii, 292a — III, 301a
Bāh i, **910b;** ii, 552a — I, **938a;** II, 566a
Bahāʾ Allāh i, 833b, 834b, 846b, 847a, **911a,** 916a; iii, 325b; iv, 51b, 696a; v, 698b, 1172b; s, 77a — I, 856b, 857b, 870a, 870b, **938b,** 944a; III, 335b; IV, 54b, 724a; V, 703b, 1162b; S, 76b
Bahāʾ al-Dawla wa-Ḍiyāʾ al-Milla, Abu Naṣr Fīrūz i, 512a, 899b, 1354a; ii, 348b, 749a; iii, 219b, 244b, 258b, 388a, 671b; iv, 378a; v, 348a, 1028a; s, 4b, **118a** — I, 528a, 926b, 1393b; II, 358a, 767b; III, 225b, 251b, 265b, 400a, 693a; IV, 394b; V, 349a, 1024a; S, 3b, **117b**
Bahāʾ al-Dīn al-ʿĀmilī → al-ʿĀmilī
Bahāʾ al-Dīn Ba<u>gh</u>dādī iii, 1243a — III, 1275a
Bahāʾ al-Dīn Mar<u>gh</u>īnānī ii, 3b — II, 3b
Bahāʾ al-Dīn Muḥammad b. <u>Dj</u>uwaynī ii, 607b; iv, 102a — II, 622b; IV, 106b
Bahāʾ al-Dīn Sām (Bamiyān) i, 1001b; ii, 1101b, 1103a — I, 1032a; II, 1127b, 1129a
Bahāʾ al-Dīn Sām I ii, 382a, 928b, 1096b, 1100b — II, 392b, 950a, 1122a, 1126b
Bahāʾ al-Dīn Sām II ii, 1103a — II, 1129a
Bahāʾ al-Dīn <u>Sh</u>ākir iv, 285a, 872b — IV, 297b, 906a
Bahāʾ al-Dīn Walad ii, 393b — II, 404a
Bahā al-Dīn Zakariyyāʾ Ṣuhrawardī i, **912a;** iii, 635a, 1269a; v, 26a; s, 10b, 353b — I, **939b;** III, 656b, 1302a; V, 27a; S, 10a, 353b
Bahāʾ al-Dīn Zuhayr i, 570b, 595b, **912b;** ii, 1032b; iii, 875b — I, 589b, 614b, **940a;** II, 1056b; III, 899b
Bahāʾ al-Ḥaḳḳ → Bahāʾ al-Dīn Zakariyyā
Bāhā Lāl Dās Bayrāgī ii, 134b — II, 138a
al-Bahāʾ Zuhayr → Bahāʾ al-Dīn Zuhayr
Bahādur i, **913a** — I, **940b**
Bahādūr Gīlānī ii, 1127b; v, 1258a — II, 1154a; V, 1249a
Bahādur Girāy I iv, 178b — IV, 185b
Bahādur <u>Kh</u>ān II ii, 185b — II, 191b
Bahādur <u>Sh</u>āh → Niẓām <u>Sh</u>āh
Bahādur <u>Sh</u>āh I i, 781b, **913b,** 1012b, 1068b, 1195a, 1210a; ii, 30a, 558a; iii, 427a; iv, 507b, 598b — I, 805a, **941a,** 1043b, 1101a, 1230b, 1246a; II, 30b, 572a; III, 441a; IV, 529b, 602a
Bahādur <u>Sh</u>āh II i, **914a,** 953b, 1012b; ii, 221b — I, **942a,** 983a, 1043b; II, 228b
Bahādur <u>Sh</u>āh Fārūkī ii, 815b — II, 835a
Bahādur <u>Sh</u>āh Gu<u>dj</u>arātī i, **914b,** 1193b; ii, 322b, 815a, 1128b; iii, 16a, 199b, 421b, 422a, 425b, 575b, 1160a; s, 335b — I, **942a,** 1228b; II, 332a, 834a, 1155a; III, 16b, 205a, 435a, b, 439b, 595a, 1188b; S, 335a
Bahāedidn <u>Sh</u>ākir → Bahāʾ al-Dīn <u>Sh</u>ākir
al-Bahāʾī → al-ʿĀmilī
Bahāʾī Meḥmed Efendi i, **915a** — I, **943a**
Bahāʾīs i, 263b, 833a, 847a, **915b;** iii, 325b; iv, 39a, 51b — I, 272a, 856a, 870b, **943b;** III, 335b; IV, 41b, 54b
Baḥammou s, 328a — S, 327b
Bahār s, 327a — S, 326b
Bāhar iv, 1127b — IV, 1159a
Bahār → Kayl
Bahār, Muḥammad Taḳī i, **918b;** iv, 71a, b; s, 110a, 334a — I, **946b;** IV, 74b-75a, 75b; S, 109b, 333b
Bahār, Rāy Tēkčand iv, 526b — IV, 549a
Bahār <u>Kh</u>ān Noḥānī s, 203a — S, 203a
Bahār-i Dāne<u>sh</u> → ʿInāyat Allāh Ḳanbū
Bahāristān → <u>Dj</u>āmī
Bahārlū i, **919a;** iii, 1109b; iv, 9b; v, 668b — I, **947a;** III, 1136b; IV, 10a; V, 672b
Bahasa Indonesia iii, 1215b, 1217a, 1213a — III, 1246b, 1248a, 1263a
Bahā<u>sh</u>ima s, 25b — S, 25b
Bahāwal <u>Kh</u>ān I i, 919b; ii, 186a — I, 947b; II, 192a
Bahāwal <u>Kh</u>ān II ii, 186a — II, 192a
Bahāwal <u>Kh</u>ān III ii, 186b — II, 192b
Bahāwal <u>Kh</u>ān IV ii, 187a — II, 193a
Bahāwal <u>Kh</u>ān V ii, 187a — II, 193a
Bahāwalpūr i, **919b;** ii, 185b, 186a, 669a — I, **947b;** II, 191b, 192a, 685b
Bahčekent iv, 590a — IV, 613b
Baḥdal i, **919b** — I, **947b**
Bahdīnān i, 427a, **920a**; v, 460a — I, 439a, **948a**; V, 463a
Bah<u>dj</u>at <u>Kh</u>ān ii, 12b — II, 13a
Bah<u>dj</u>at Muṣṭafā Efendi i, 707a, **921a;** ii, 356b — I, 728b, **948a;** II, 366a
Baḥḥāra i, 929a — I, 957b
Bāhila i, **920b,** 1096b; v, 541a; s, 243a — I, **948b,** 1129a, b; V, 545b; S, 243a
al-Bāhilī, ʿAbd al-Raḥmān i, **921b**; iv, 343b, 1173b — I, **949a**; IV, 358a, 1206b
al-Bāhilī, Abū Naṣr Aḥmad i, 717b, 718b, **921b** — I, 739a, 740a, **949b**
al-Bāhilī, al-Ḥusayn → al-Ḥusayn al-<u>Kh</u>alīʿ
al-Bāhilī, Salmān → Salmān b. Rabīʿa
Baḥīra → Buḥayra
Baḥīra (monk/moine) i, **922a** — I, **949b**
Baḥīrā i, **922a,** 1276b — I, **950a,** 1315b

Bahishī → Djanna
Bāhithat al-Bādiya → Nāṣif, Malik Ḥifnī
Bāhiya (palace) s, 114a — S, 113b
al-Bahlawī → Abu 'l-Muʿthir
Bahlūl i, **923a** — I, **951a**
Bahlūl b. Marzūḳ s, 82a — S, 81b
Bahlūl Lōdī i, 218a, 1322a; ii, 47b, 48b, 270, 498b, 1131a, 1144a; iii, 418a, 419b, 420a, 485a, 632a, 633b; iv, 276b; v, 31b, 598a, 783a, b; s, 1b, 10b, 203a — I, 224b, 1362b; II, 48a, 49b, 279a, 511a, 1158a, 1171a; III, 431b, 433a, b, 502a, 653a, 654b; IV, 288b; V, 32b, 602a, 789a, b; S, 1b, 10a, 202b
Bahlūl Pasha i, 923b — I, 951a
Bahmaʾī iii, 1107a — III, 1134a
Bahman → Taʾrīkh
Bahman b. Isfandiyār iv, 809b — IV, 842a
Bahman b. Kayūmarth iv, 808a; v, 663a — IV, 840b; V, 668b
Bahman Mīrzā iv, 393a, b, 398a — IV, 410a, 415a
Bahman Shāh → ʿAlāʾ al-Dīn Ḥasan Bahman
Bahmandīz iii, 501b; iv, 815b; v, 229a — III, 518b; IV, 848b; V, 227a
Bahmanīs i, 768a, **923b,** 1047a, 1170a, 1200a, b, 1203b; ii, 99b, 120b, 158b, 180a; iii, 15a, 114a, 420b, 446b; iv, 514a; v, 1a, 1258a; s, 280a — I, 791a, **951b,** 1078b, 1205a, 1236a, b, 1239a; II, 101b, 123b, 163b, 185b; III, 15b, 116b, 434a, 461b; IV, 536a; V, 1a, 1249a; S, 279b
Bahmanyār, Abu 'l-Ḥasan i, **926a** — I, **954a**
Bāḥmīn (Bohemians) s, 170b — S, 171a
al-Bahnasā i, **926a** — I, **954a**
Bahnasiyya i, 945a — I, 974a
Bahnūd b. Saḥwān iv, 503b — IV, 525b
Baḥr → ʿArūḍ
Baḥr i, **926b**; v, 949b — I, **954b**; V, 953b
al-Baḥr al-Abyaḍ → Baḥr al-Rūm
Baḥr Adriyas i, 927a, 935b — I, 955a, 964a
al-Baḥr al-Aḥmar → Baḥr al-Ḳulzum
al-Baḥr al-Aswad → Baḥr Bunṭus, Ḳara Deniz
Baḥr Āzāk → Baḥr Māyuṭis
Baḥr al-Banāt i, 927a — I, 955a
Baḥr Bunṭus i, **927a,** 935b; iv, 575a; v, 313a — I, **955a,** 964a; IV, 598a; V, 312b
Baḥr al-Dardūs iv, 514b — IV, 537a
Baḥr al-Djabal i, 929a — I, 957a
Baḥr Fāris i, **927b,** 930a; ii, 577b; iii, 1251b; iv, 500b; v, 66a, 507a, 572a; s, 222b — I, **955b,** 958a; II, 592a; III, 1284a; IV, 522a; V, 68a, 510b, 577a; S, 222b
Baḥr al-Ghazāl i, **929a,** 1156b; v, 1248b, 1249b, 1250b — I, **957a,** 1191a; V, 1239a, 1240a, 1241b
Baḥr al-Hind i, **930a;** ii, 584a; iii, 856b; v, 940b — I, **958a;** II, 598b; III, 880b; V, 944a
Baḥr al-Khazar i, 3b, 191a, **931a**; iv, 1b; s, 245b — I, 4a, 196b, **959b**; IV, 1b; S, 245b
Baḥr al-Khazar, provinces iv, 6b-7a, 19a — IV, 7a-b, 20a-b
Baḥr Khwarizm → Aral
Baḥr al-Ḳulzum i, **931b**; iii, 856b; iv, 686b; v, 367b — I, **960a**; III, 880b; IV, 714b; V, 368b
Baḥr Lūṭ i, **933a** — I, **961b**
Baḥr al-Maghrib → Baḥr al-Rūm
Baḥr Māyuṭis i, **933b**; iv, 576b — I, **962b**; IV, 599b
al-Baḥr al-Muḥīṭ i, **934a** — I, **962b**
al-Baḥr al-Muẓlim → al-Baḥr al-Muḥīṭ
Baḥr al-Nīl → al-Nīl
Baḥr Nīṭas → Baḥr Bunṭus
Baḥr al-Rūm i, **934b**, 936b; ii, 577b; v, 503a — I, **963b,** 965a; II, 592a; V, 506a
al-Baḥr al-Shāmī → Baḥr al-Rūm
Baḥr Tīrān i, 935b — I, 964a
Baḥr al-ʿUlūm, ʿAbd al-ʿAlī al-Lakhnawī i, **936b;** ii, 104a; s, 292b, 293a, b — I, **965b;** II, 106b; S, 292a, 293a, b
Baḥr al-ʿUlūm, Sayyid Mahdī s, 135a — S, 134b
Baḥr al-Warank i, 934a, 935b — I, 962b, 964b
Baḥr al-Zandj i, 484a, **937b** — I, 498b, **966b**
Baḥr al-Ẓulma (Ẓulumāt) → al-Baḥr al-Muḥīṭ
Baḥra i, 1288a — I, 1327b
Bahrāʾ i, **938a** — I, **967a**
Bahrāič s, 280a — S, 280a
Bahrāidj → Djawnpur
Baḥrain → al-Baḥrayn
Baḥrak, Djamāl al-Dīn i, **938a** — I, **967a**
Bahrām i, **938b**; v, 1113b — I, **967b**; V, 1110a
Bahrām (d./m. 1140) i, 638b, **939a;** ii, 858a; iii, 55a — I, 659b, **968a;** II, 878a; III, 57a
Bahrām I-IV i, 938b; v, 169a — I, 967b; V, 166b
Bahrām V Gūr i, 226a, 568b, 939a; iv, 53a; v, 816b — I, 232b, 587a, 967b, 968a; IV, 55b; V, 823a
Bahrām b. Lashkarsitān iv, 807a — IV, 839b
Bahram Čubīn i, 939a; iii, 113a, 584b — I, 967b, 968a; III, 115b, 604b
Bahrām al-Ismāʿīlī i, 1017a — I, 1048b
Bahrām Khān Māzandarānī ii, 814a — II, 833b
Bahrām-Lam → Ibrāhīm Inal
Bahrām Pasha i, 920a — I, 948a
Bahrām Shāh, Muʿizz al-Dīn ii, 267b, 609a, 973a — II, 276a, 624b, 995a
Bahrām Shāh b. Masʿūd i, 94b, 217b, 227a, **940a;** ii, 382a, 1052a, 1100b; v, 159b, 501a — I, 97a, 224a, 233b, **968b;** II, 392b, 1076b, 1126b; V, 158b, 504b
Bahrām Shāh b. Tughrul Shāh i, **940b**; v, 160a — I, **969a**; V, 158b
Bahrām Shāh al-Malik al-Amdjad i, 803b, **940b,** 971a — I, 826b, **969a,** 1001a
al-Baḥrānī → Muḥammad b. ʿAlī
al-Baḥrānī, ʿAbd ʿAlī b. Aḥmad al-Dirāzī s, 57a — S, 57b
Al-Baḥrānī, ʿAbd Allāh b. Ḥādjdj Ṣāliḥ al-Samāhīdjī s, 57b — S, 57b
al-Baḥrānī, Yūsuf b. Aḥmad iii, 1152a; s, 57a — III, 1180a; S, 57b
al-Baḥrayn (Baḥrain) i, **940b**; iv, 664a, 751b, 764a, 953a, 1130b; v, 1057b; s, 234b, 318a, 417a — I, **969b**; IV, 690b, 691a, 782a, 794b, 985b, 1162a; V, 1054b; S, 234b, 317b, 417a
al-Baḥrayn i, 19a, 55a, 72b, 73a, b, 120a, 233b, 535b, 540a, 553b, **941a,** 976a; ii, 108b, 177a, 452b — I, 19b, 57a, 75a, b, 123b, 241a, 552a, 556b, 571a, **969b,** 1006b; II, 111a, 183a, 464b
Baḥri Mamlūks → Mamlūks
Baḥriyya (navy/marine) i, **945b**; s, **119b** — **I, 974b**; S, **119a**
Baḥriyya (oasis) i, **945a** — I, **974a**
al-Baḥriyya (regiment/régiment) i, 804a, **944b**; iv, 424b, 428a, 430a; v, 571a, b; s, 392b — I, 828b, **973b**; IV, 443a, 446b, 448b; V, 576a; S, 392b
Baḥriyye vekāleti i, 948b — I, 978a
Bahrūr → Bhakkar
Baḥshal i, **949a** — I, **978a**
Bahshamiyya ii, 570a — II, 584b
Baḥth i, **949a** — I, **978a**
Bahū Bēgum ii, 870b — II, 890b
Bahū (Bao) s, 242a — S, 242a
Bahurasīr → al-Madāʾin
Bahūṣiyya i, 375b — I, 386b
al-Bahūtī al-Miṣrī i, **949a**; iii, 162a — I, **978b;** III, 165b
Bahw i, **949b** — I, **979a**
Baḥya ibn Paḳūda iv, 487a — IV, 507b
Baikal i, **950b** — I, **979b**
Bail → Kirāʾ
Bailo → Bālyōs
Bain → Ḥammām

al-Baʿīth i, 950b – I, 980a
Bajazet → Bāyazīd
Baḳāʾ wa-Fanāʾ i, 951a; iii, 546a; iv, 1083b, 1163a –
I, 980a; III, 565a; IV, 1114b, 1195a
Baḵʿa → Buḵʿa
al-Baḵʿa → al-Biḵāʿ
Baḵāʾī i, 1104a – I, 1137b
Bākalamūn → Abū Ḳalamūn
Baḳar i, 951b – I, 980b
Bāḳar, Āghā i, 952a – I, 981a
Baḳar, ʿĪd → Bayram; ʿĪd
Bāḳargandj i, 951b – I, 981a
Baḳāriṭṭa (Buḳraṭūn) → Buḳrāṭ
Bakāwalī iii, 376b – III, 388b
Baḳāyā i, 1145a – I, 1179b
Bākbāk i, 278b; iii, 955b – I, 287a; III, 980a
Bakdjūr i, 824b; ii, 483a; iii, 129b, 841a; v, 1211a –
I, 847b; II, 495b; III, 132b, 864b; V, 1201a
Bākhamrā i, 952a – I, 981b
Bākharz i, 952a – I, 981b
al-Bākharzī, Abu 'l-Ḥasan i, 952b, 1132a; s, 31a – I,
981b, 1166b; S, 31a
al-Bākharzī, Sayf al-Dīn i, 347b; v, 301a – I, 358a;
V, 300a
Bakhīt, Shaykh i, 821a – I, 844a
Bakhīt al-Muṭīʿī al-Ḥanafī s, 121b – S, 121a
al-Baḵhrāʾ i, 57b, 952b; s, 117a – I, 59a, 982a; S, 116b
Bakhshī i, 953a; iv, 268b, 269a, 757b; v, 686b – I,
982a; IV, 280b, 281a, 788a; V, 691b
Bakhshī Aḥmad Khān iii, 61b – III, 64a
Bakhshīsh i, 953a – I, 982b
al-Bakhshiyya iv, 992a – IV, 1024b
Bakht Girāy ii, 1114a – II, 1140a
Bakht Khān i, 953b; ii, 809a – I, 982b; II, 828a
Bakhtanaṣṣar → Bukht-naṣar
Bakhtāwar Khān i, 954a – I, 983a
Bakhtī i, 954b – I, 983b
Bakhtī, amīr v, 1179a – V, 1169a
Bakhtigān i, 954b – I, 983b
Bakhtīshūʿ → Bukhtīshūʿ
Bakhtiyār, ʿIzz al-Dawla i, 11b, 211b, 954b, 1350b; ii,
748b; iii, 46b, 128a, 246a, 258a, 704a, 730a, 1176a,
1201b; iv, 24a, 208b, 293b; s, 13a, 36a, 118b, 398a –
I, 11b, 217b, 984a, 1309b; II, 767a; III, 48b, 130b,
253a, 265a, 726a, 752b, 1204b, 1232a; IV, 25b, 218a,
306b; S, 13b, 36b, 118a, 398b
Bakhtiyār → Muḥammad; Ḳuṭb al-Dīn
Bakhtiyār-nāma i, 955a; iii, 373a, 377a – I, 984b;
III, 384b, 389a
Bakhtiyārī i, 955b; iii, 1102a, b, 1103a, 1105a, 1110a;
iv, 5b, 8a, 9a, 98b, 706a; v, 664a, 822a, 824a, 825a,
826a, 829b, 830a; s, 142b, 146a, 147b, 365b – I, 985a;
III, 1129a, b, 1130a, 1132b, 1137a; IV, 6a, 8b, 9b,
103a, 134b; V, 669b, 828b, 830a, 831a, 832a, 836a; S,
142a, 145b, 147b, 365b
al-Baḳīʿ s, 311b – S, 311a
Bāḳī, Maḥmūd ʿAbd al- i, 292b, 956a; ii, 221a; iv,
1137b; s, 324a – I, 301b, 985; II, 227b; IV, 1169b;
S, 323b
Baḳī b. Makhlad i, 600a, 956b; iii, 692b – I, 619b,
986a; III, 714b
Bāḳī bi'llāh, Khwādja i, 957a; iii, 432b; s, 121b – I,
986b; III, 446b; S, 121a
Baḳīʿ al-Gharḳad i, 957b – I, 987a
Baḳī Khān Čela Ḳalmāḳ ii, 1085a – II, 1110a
Bāḳī Muḥmmad (calligraphe(r)) iv, 1127b – IV,
1159a
Bāḳī Muḥammad Khān i, 8a; ii, 44b, 446a – I, 8a;
II, 45b, 457b
Bāḳīkhanlī, Bāḳīkhānov i, 193b, 958a – I, 199b,
987b
Bakīl → Ḥāshid wa-Bakīl

al-Bāḳillānī i, 212a, 413a, 696b, 858a, 958b; ii, 294a,
570b, 765a, 774b; iii, 544a, 1020a, 1063a, 1144b; iv,
108a, 183a, 272a, 378b, 470b, 616a, 949a; v, 426b; s,
26b, 343b, 345a, 346b – I, 218b, 425a, 717b, 881b,
988a; II, 302a, 584b, 783b, 793a; III, 562b, 1045b,
1089b, 1173a; IV, 112b, 113a, 191a, 284a, 395a, 491b,
640b, 982a; V, 429a; S, 27a, 343b, 344b, 346a
al-Bāḳir → Muḥammad b. ʿAlī al-Bāḳir
Bakir b. Māhān iii, 988a – III, 1012b
Bāḳir Khān Khurāskānī iv, 104b, 391a – IV, 109a,
408a
Baḳḳ → Ḳaml
Baḳḳ iv, 522a – IV, 544b
Baḳish iii, 1106b – III, 1134a
al-Baḳḳa i, 100a – I, 103a
Bakkāʾ i, 959a – I, 988b
al-Bakkāʾī, Aḥmad v, 394a – V, 395a
al-Bakkāʾi, Ziyād iii, 801a – III, 824a
Baḳḳāl i, 961a – I, 990b
Baḳḳam i, 961b – I, 991a
Bakkār i, 961b – I, 991a
Baḳḳāra i, 49b, 962a; ii, 122a, 124a; v, 266b, 1249a,
1250a, 1251b – I, 50b, 51a, 991b; II, 125a, 127a; V,
264b, 1240a, 1241a, 1242b
Baḳliyya i, 962b; iv, 661a – I, 992a; IV, 687b
al-Bakr, Aḥmad Ḥasan v, 469a – V, 472a
Bakr, Banū i, 526b, 527a, 529b, 962b, 1339a; ii, 71b;
iii, 222b; v, 116b, 346a, 362a – I, 542b, 543a, 545b,
992b, 1379b; II, 73a; III, 229a; V, 119a, 347a, 363a
Bakr b. ʿAbd al-ʿAzīz b. Abī Dulaf iii, 126a, 619a; iv,
718b – III, 129a, 639b; IV, 747b
Bakr b. ʿAbd Manāt v, 78a, b, 79a – V, 80a, b, 81a
Bakr b. Ḥassād (Ḥammād) al-Bāhirī iii, 889b – III,
913b
Bakr b. Khāridja iv, 1003b – IV, 1036a
Bakr b. al-Naṭṭāḥ, Abu 'l-Wāʾil s, 122a – S, 121b
Bakr b. Wāʾil i, 545a, 962b; ii, 241a, 343b; iii, 166b,
1254a; iv, 321b; s, 122a – I, 562a, 992b; II, 247a,
353b; III, 170a, 1287a; IV, 336a; S, 121b
Bakr Beg i, 845a – I, 868a
Bakr Ṣidḳī ii, 1045a; iii, 1258b – II, 1069b; III,
1291a
Bakr Sūbāshī i, 904a, 962b; iii, 1257a – I, 931b,
992a; III, 1290a
al-Bakrī → ʿAbd al-ʿAzīz; Abū ʿUbayd
al-Bakrī → Bakriyya; Ṣiddīḳī
al-Bakrī, Abu 'l-Ḥasan i, 964b; ii, 159a – I, 994b; II,
164a
al-Bakrī, Ibn Abi 'l-Surūr i, 965a – I, 995a
al-Bakrī, Muḥammad i, 965b; iv, 451b, 505b – I,
995a; IV, 471b, 527a
al-Bakrī, Muḥammad Ṭawfīḳ b. ʿAlī s, 122b, 132b
– S, 122a, 132a
al-Bakrī, Muṣṭafā Kamāl al-Dīn i, 60a, b, 956b; iv,
991b, 992a; s, 44a – I, 62a, b, 995b; IV, 1024b; S, 44b
al-Bakrī, Shaykh → Shaykh al-Bakrī
Bakriyya i, 966a – I, 996a
al-Bakriyya i, 966a; s, 122b – I, 995b; S, 122a
Bakt i, 32a, 966a – I, 33a, 996a
Baktāsh al-Fakhrī, Badr al-Dīn iv, 485a – IV, 506a
Bākū i, 191b, 966b; iii, 530b; iv, 348a; s, 73a, 136a,
365a, b – I, 197a, 996b; III, 548b; IV, 363a; S, 73b,
135b, 365a
Baʿḳūba i, 967b – I, 997b
Bākūm i, 609a – I, 628b
Bakumpai s, 151a – S, 151a
Bākusāyā i, 870b, 968a – I, 895a, 998a
Baʿl i, 491b, 968a – I, 506b, 998a
Bal-Fakīh → Fakīh, Bal-
Bālā i, 969b – I, 999b
Baʿla v, 692b – V, 697b
Bālā-ghāt i, 970a – I, 1000a

Bālā Ḥiṣār i, **970a;** ii, 978a, 1119a — I, **1000a;** II, 1000b, 1145a
Bālā Pīr → Ghāzī Miyān
Balābādh → Balāwāt
Baʿlabakk i, 940b, **970b,** 1051a, 1214b — I, 969a, **1000b,** 1083a, 1250b
Balaban iv, 140a — IV, 146a
Balabān Zaynī, Sayf al-Dīn iv, 483b — IV, 504b
Balad ʿAns s, 22b — S, 22b
al-Balādhurī i, 591a, 635b, 760a, **971b;** ii, 131b; iii, 608a; iv, 275a, 342b — I, 610b, 656b, 782b, **1001b;** II, 135a; III, 628b; IV, 287b, 357a
Baladiyya i, **972b** — I, **1002b**
Balāgh iv, 203b — IV, 212b
Balăgha i, 858a, **981b,** 1114a, b, 1116a; ii, 824a — I, 881b, **1012a,** 1147b, 1148a, 1149b; II, 843b
Balak, Nŭr al-Dawla i, 664b, 732a, **983a,** 1025a; ii, 110b; iii, 87a; iv, 1084a; v, 106a — I, 684a, 754a, **1013b,** 1056b; II, 113a; III, 89a; IV, 1115b; V, 108a
Bālaḳ b. Ṣāfūn → ʿŪdj b. ʿAnāḳ
Balakhsh i, 851b — I, 875a
Bālakī i, 1031a — I, 1062b
Balaklava i, **983b** — I, **1014a**
Balʿam i, **984a** — I, **1014b**
Balʿamī i, 421b, **984a;** iv, 504a; s, 265b, 297b — I, 433b, **1015a;** IV, 526a; S, 265b, 297b
Bāl-ʿanbar → Tamīm
Balance → al-Ḳarasṭūn; Minṭaḳat al-Burūdj; Mīzān
Balandjar i, 921b, **985a;** iv, 343b, 344a, 1173a — I, 949b, **1015b;** IV, 358a, b, 1206b
Balansiya i, 446b, 495a, **985a,** 1288a; iii, 673a; iv, 468a; s, 143a — I, 459a, 510a, **1016a,** 1327b; III, 694b; IV, 489a; S, 143a
Bālāpur s, 280a — S, 279b
Balarm i, 250b, **986a;** ii, 115a, 864a; iv, 497a, 979b — I, 258b, **1017a;** II, 117b, 883b; IV, 518b, 1012a
Balāsāghūn i, **987a;** iii, 1114b; iv, 581a, 582a; v, 858a; s, 240a — I, **1017b;** III, 1141b; IV, 604b; 605b; V, 865a; S, 240a
Balāt i, 950a, **987b** — I, 979b, **1018a**
Balāt, Caria i, **987b** — I, **1018b**
Balaṭ (Balad) s, 123b — S, 123a
Balāt (road/voie) i, **988a** — I, **1018b**
Balāṭ al-Shuhadāʾ i, 86b, 493a, 988a, **988b** — I, 89a, 508a, 1018b, **1019a**
al-Balaṭī, Abu 'l-Fatḥ ʿUthman s, **123b** — S, **123a**
Balāṭunus i, **989b** — I, **1020a**
Balawī, Banū → Baliyy
Balāwāt i, **989b** — I, **1020b**
Balawhar → Bilawhar wa Yūdāsaf
al-Balawī i, 96b, **990a;** iii, 745b — I, 99a, **1020b;** III, 768b
Bālāy Miyān → Ghāzī Miyān
Balayeur → Kannās
Baʿlbak → Baʿlabakk
Balban, Ghiyāth al-Dīn Ulugh Khān i, 217b, 1036a; ii, 12b, 120a, 260b, 268a, 272b, 973a, 1084a, 143b; iii, 168a, 416a, 441b, 492a; iv, 749b, 818a; v, 629b, 638a, 685a, 1135a; s, 66b, 73b, **124a** — I, 1067b; II, 12b, 123a, 269a, 276a, 281a, 995a, 1109b, 1171a; III, 171b, 429a, 456a, 509a; IV, 779b, 851a; V, 633b, 642a, 690b, 1130b; S, 67a, 74a, **123a**
Baldj b. Bishr i, 76a, 82a, 134b, 490a, **990b;** 524b; iii, 494a; iv, 494b; v, 367a — I, 78b, 84b, 138b, 504b, **1021a;** II, 538a; III, 511a; IV, 515b, V, 368a
Baldwin I i, 216a, 341a, 440a, 630b, 662b, 664b, 784a
Baldwin II i, 983a; v, 53a, 922a
Baldwin III i, 711a, 1017a; ii, 555b
Baldwin IV ii, 555b
Balearic Isles/Baléares → Mayurḳa
Balewa, Abubakar Tafawa iii, 282b; iv, 774a — III, 291a; IV, 805a
Bālfurūsh → Bārfurūsh
Balharā i, **991a;** ii, 352a — I, **1022a;** II, 362a
Bal-ḥārith → Ḥārith b. Kaʿb
Bāli (al-Ḥabash) i, 176b, **991b;** iii, 6a — I, 181a, **1022b;** III, 6b
Bali (Indonesia/Indonésie) iii, 1213b, 1214b, 1219b, 1223a; v, 785a — III, 1244b, 1245a, 1250a, 1254a; V, 791b
Balī → Baliyy
Baʿlī i, 969b — I, 999b
al-Baʿlī, ʿAbd al-Raḥmān iii, 162a — III, 165b
Bali Bey i, 1163b; ii, 201b — I, 1198b; II, 208a
Baliabadra i, **992a** — I, **1022b**
Bāligh i, **993a** — I, **1024a**
Balîḳ i, 610b; ii, 971b — I, 626a; II, 993b
Bālik i, **993b** — I, **1024b**
Bālikesrī i, **993b;** iv, 628b — I, **1024b;** IV, 653b
Balîkhane i, 1279a — I, 1318a
Bālîm Sulṭān i, 1162a — I, 1196b
Balīnūs (of Perge/de Perga) → al-Nadjdjār
Balīnūs (of Tyane/de Tyane) i, 737a, **994a,** b; ii, 93b, 359a; iii, 464a; v, 111b; s, 270a — I, 759a, **1025a,** b; II, 95a, 368b; III, 480a; V, 114a; S, 269b
Bālis i, **995b** — I, **1026b**
al-Bālisī → Muḥammad b. Musallam
Bālish i, **996b** — I, **1027a**
Bālish i, **997a** — I, **1027b**
Baliyy i, 990a; iii, 363b; v, 317b, 318a, b — I, 1020b; III, 375a; V, 317a, b, 318a
Baliyya i, **997b** — I, **1028a**
al-Balḳāʾ i, **997b,** 1149a; s, 117a — I, **1028b,** 1183b; S, 116b
Balkā Khaldjī iii, 1155b — III, 1184a
Balkā-takīn i, 226b — I, 233b
Balkan i, 468a, **998a;** ii, 33b; iv, 297a — I, 482a, **1029a;** II, 34a; IV, 310a
Balkar i, **1000a;** ii, 23a; iv, 325a, 596b — I, **1031a;** II, 24a; IV, 339b, 620b
Balḳayn → Ḳayn
Balkh i, 8a, 17b, 46b, 147b, 223b, 296a, 662a, 684b, 768b, **1000b,** 1033a; ii, 4b, 43a, 201a; iii, 134b; iv, 809b; s, 97a, 125b, 227b, 326a, 340b, 416b, 419b — I, 8a, 18b, 48a, 152a, 230a, 305a, 683a, 705b, 791b, **1031b,** 1064b; II, 4b, 44a, 207b; III, 137a; IV, 842a; S, 96b, 124b, 227b, 325b, 340a, 416b, 419b
Balkha(r) iv, 323a — IV, 357b
Balkhān i, **1002a;** s, 280b — I, **1032b;** S, 280b
Balkhash i, **1002a** — I, **1033a**
al-Balkhī → Abū Maʿshar; Abū Muṭīʿ
al-Balkhī, Abu 'l-Ḳāsim i, **1002b;** iii, 979b; iv, 1162b; v, 702a; s, 14b, 335b — I, **1033b;** III, 1004a; IV, 1194b; V, 707a; S, 14b, 335a
al-Balkhī, Abū Zayd Aḥmad i, **1003a;** ii, 579b, 581a; iii, 57b, 787b, 1077b; iv, 223a, 1079a; s, 72b, 265a, 266a, 386b — I, **1033b;** II, 594a, 596a; III, 60a, 810b, 1104b; IV, 232b, 1110b; S, 72b, 264b, 265b, 387a
Balkis → Bilḳīs
Balkuwārā → Sāmarrā
Ballā, Sīdī, Abū Muḥammad Ibn ʿAzzūz s, **124b** — S, **382b**
Ballabh Rāyʾ, Rādja i, 952a — I, 981a
Ballahara → Balharā
al-Ballūtīn → Abū Ḥafṣ ʿUmar; Mundhir b. Saʿīd
Balōč → Baluč
Balshas, Balshiči i, 653b — I, 674a
Bālta Līmānī i, **1003b** — I, **1034b**
Baltadjî i, **1003b — I, 1034b**
Baltadjî Muḥammad Pasha → Muḥammad Pasha
Bālṭa-oghlū Sulaymān Beg i, 1003b — I, 1034b
Baltic Sea → Baḥr al-Warank
Baltistān i, **1004b;** s, 242a, 423b — I, **1035b;** S, 242a,

423b
Balūč, Baluchis i, 211b, 225a, 546a, **1005a,** 1354b; iii, 633b, 1098a, 1107b — I, 217b, 231b, 563b, **1035b.** 1393b; III, 655a, 1124b, 1134b
Balūčī i, 225a, 1005a, 1006-7; iv, 10b; v, 153a, 673b, 674b; s, 143b, 147a, 270b, 331b, 332a, b — I, 231b, 1036a, 1037-8; IV, 11a; V, 154a, 678b, 679b; S, 143a, 147a, 270a, 331a, 331b
Balūčistān i, **1005a;** ii, 669a, 1083b; iv, 3b, 8a, 364a; v, 101b, 520b, 580b; s, 71b, 222a, 270b, 329b — I, **1036a;** II, 658b, 1109a; IV, 3b, 8b, 380a; V, 103b, 524a, 585a; S, 72a, 222a, 270a, 329a
Balwant Singh i, 1166a — I, 1200b; IV, 3b, 8b, 380a; V, 103b, 524a, 585a; S, 72a, 222a, 270a, 329a
Balyā b. Malkān iv, 904b — IV, 937a
Balyemez i, **1007b,** 1062b — I, **1038b,** 1094b
Bālyōs i, **1008a;** ii, 60b — I, **1039a;** II, 61b
Balyūnash s, **124b** — S, **124a**
Bam i, **1008a;** iii, 502a; iv, 1052a; v, 148b, 149b, 151a; s, 127a, 327a — I, **1039b;** III, 519a; IV, 1083b; V, 150b, 151b, 153a; S, 126a, 326b
Bamako i, **1008b** — I, **1040a**
Bambara i, 297a, 1009a; ii, 252a; iii, 39b; iv, 314a; s, 295b — I, 306a, 1040b; II, 259b; III, 41a; IV, 328a; S, 295a
Bāmiyān i, **1009a;** ii, 1101a; s, 367a, b — I, **1040b;** II, 1127a; S, 367a, b
Bampūr i, **1010a** — I, **1041b**
Bān i, **1010b** — I, **1041b**
Banādir iv, 885b, 886a — IV, 918a, b
Banākat i, **1010b** — I, **1042a**
Banākitī i, **1011a** — I, **1042a**
Banāras → Benares
Bānās, Nahr i, 1029b — I, 1061a
Banat → Temesvar
Banāt Ḳayn iv, 493b — IV, 514b
Banāt Naʿsh → Nudjūm
Bānat Suʿād i, **1011b**; iv, 316a, b — I, **1042b**; IV, 330b
Banbalūna i, 83b, **1011b,** 1079b; v, 1119a — I, 86a, **1043a,** 1111b; V, 1115b
Band i, **1012a**; v, 862b, 867-9 — I, **1043a**; V, 869b, 873b-875b
Band-i Amīr i, 212b, 1012a; v, 867b — I, 218b, 1043b; V, 874a
Band-i Ḳīr iv, 675b; v, 867b — IV, 703b; V, 874a
Band-i Mīzān v, 867a, b — V, 873b
Bāndā i, **1012b** — I, **1043b**
Banda Bayrāgī i, 432b, 914a, 1022b; ii, 28b, 380b — I, 445a, 941b, 1054a; II, 29a, 390b
Banda islands/-, îles de i, **1012b** — I, **1044a**
Banda Nawāz → Sayyid Muḥammad
Bandanīdjīn i, 968a — I, 998a
Bandar i, **1013a** — I, **1044a**
Bandar b. Fayṣal b. ʿAbd al-ʿAzīz Āl Suʿūd s, 305b — S, 305b
Bandar ʿAbbās i, 928a, **1013a,** 1172b, 1282a, 1283a; iii, 585a; iv, 1170b; v, 148a, 151b, 152a, 183b, 673a, 674a — I, 956a, **1044a,** 1207b, 1321a, b; III, 605a; IV, 1203b; V, 150b, 153a, 154a, 181a, 678a, 679b
Bandar Kung → Kung
Bandar Linga → Linga
Bandar Nādiriyya → Būshahr
Bandar Pahlawī i, **1013b**; iv, 7a — I, **1045a**; IV, 7b
Bandar Seri Begawan (Bandar Brunei) s, 151b — S, 151b
Bandar Shāpūr i, 1342a — I, 1382a
Bandar Tawayih (Tawwāhī) i, 180b — I, 186a
Bandayr ii, 620b, 621a — II, 636a, b
Bandirma i, **1014a** — I, **1045b**
Bandj, bang i, **1014b;** ii, 1068b; iii, 266b — I, **1045b;** II, 1093b; III, 274a
Bandjarmasin i, **1014b**; s, 150a, b, 151a, 199b — I, **1046a**; S, 150b, 151a, 199b
Bandjī b. Nahārān Shansabānī ii, 1099b — II, 1125a
Bandjūtekīn → Magūtakīn
Bangāla i, 400b, 606a, **1015a;** ii, 183b, 751b, 1092a; iii, 14b, 419a, 422a, 427b, 444a, 533a, 631b; iv, 210b; s, 247a — I, 412a, 625b, **1046a;** II, 189a, 770a, 1118a; III, 15b, 432b, 436a, 441b, 458b, 551b, 652b; IV, 220a; S, 247a
Bangalore v, 1259b, 1260a, b — V, 1250a, b, 1251a, b
Banganapalle i, **1015b** — I, **1046b**
Bangash i, 218b, 219a; ii, 808a; v, 250b — I, 224b, 225b; II, 827b; V, 248b
Bangka i, **1015b** — I, **1047a**
Bangla → Fayḍābād
Bangladesh v, 1082a — V, 1079b
Banhā i, **1015b** — I, **1047a**
Bani (Annam) iii, 1210b, 1212a — III, 1241a, 1242b
Banī Suwayf i, **1016a** — I, **1047b**
al-Bānīdjūrī → Dāwūd b. ʿAbbās
Bānīdjūrid(e)s i, 504a; v, 76a; s, **125a** — I, 519a; V, 78a; S, **124a**
Banīḳa i, **1016a** — I, **1047b**
Bāniyās (Balanea) i, **1016b** — I, **1048a**
Baniyās (Paneas) i, **1017a**; iv, 200a; s, 204b — I, **1048a**; IV, 208b, 209a; S, 204b
Bāniyās, Nahr → Bānās
Banjaluka i, **1017b,** 1263b, 1265b, 1266b, 1270b — I, **1048b,** 1302a, 1304a, 1305a, 1309b
Banking → Djahbadh and Ṣayrafī
Bānkīpūr i, **1018a** — I, **1049b**
Bannā᾽ → Binā᾽
al-Bannā᾽, Aḥmad → al-Dimyāṭī
al-Bannā᾽, Ḥasan i, **1018b;** ii, 429b; iii, 518a, 1068b, 1070a — I, **1049b;** II, 440b; III, 535b, 1095b, 1096b
Bannā᾽ī, Kamāl al-Dīn i, **1019a;** ii, 208a — I, **1050a;** II, 215a
al-Bannānī i, **1019b**; s, 405a — I, **1050b**; S, 405a
Bannū i, **1020a**; v, 251a, 501a; s, 329b — I, **1051a**; V, 249a, 504a; S, 329a
Bannʿučīs i, 1020a — I, 1051a
Banque → Djahbadh et Ṣayrafī
Bantam, Bantem iii, 1219b, 1223b; s, 199b, 201a, 202a, 374b — III, 1250a, 1255a; S, 199b, 201a, b, 374b
Banū, followed by the name of the eponymous ancestor of a tribe, see under the name of that ancestor
-, suivi du nom de l'ancêtre éponyme d'une tribu, voir sous le nom de cet ancêtre
Banu 'l-Afṭas → Afṭasid(e)s
Banū Isrāʾīl i, 264b, **1020a** — I, 272b, **1051b**
Banū Maslama → Afṭasid(e)s
Bañuelo ii, 1015a — II, 1038b
Banūr i, **1022a;** ii, 28b; s, 1b — I, **1053b;** II, 29a; S, 1b
al-Banūrī, Ādam i, **1022b** — I, **1054a**
Banya i, 700a — I, 721a
Banyan v, 807b — V, 813b
Banyar i, **1023a** — I, **1055a**
Bānyās → Baniyās
Banzart i, **1023b**; s, 145a — I, **1055a**; S, 144b
Bā᾽olī i, **1024a**; v, 884b, 888b — I, **1055b**; V, 890b, 894b
Bāonī i, **1024b** — I, **1056a**
Bar Bahlūl → Abu 'l-Ḥasan b. Bahlūl
Bar Dīṣān → Ibn Dayṣan
Bar Hebraeus → Ibn al-ʿIbrī
al-Bāra i, 145b, **1024b** — I, 150a, **1056a**
al-Barā᾽ b. ʿĀzib i, 98b, **1025a**; iv, 858b — I, 101b, **1056b**; IV, 891b
al-Barā᾽ b. Maʿrūr i, **1025a,** 1241b; v, 82b — I, **1057a,**

1279b; V, 84b
Bāra Sayyids i, **1025b** — I, **1057a**
Bārā Wafāt i, **1026a** — I, **1057b**
Barāʾa i, 207a, 811a, **1026b;** ii, 78b, 79b, 308a — I, 213a, 834a, **1058a,** II, 80a, 81a, 317a
Baraba i, **1028a** — I, **1059b**
Barābra i, **1028b** — I, **1060a**
Baradā i, **1029a;** ii, 1105a — I, **1060b;** II, 1131a
Baradā (Djayhūn) i, **1030a** — I, **1061b**
Baradān i, **1030a** — I, **1061b**
Barādūst i, **1030b** — I, **1062a**
Barāghīth i, 1049b — I, 1081a
Baraghwāṭa → Barghawāṭa
Barāhima i, 173a, **1031a,** 1092b; ii, 166b; iii, 905a; v, 550a; s, 93a — I, 177b, **1062b,** 1125a; II, 171b; III, 929a; V, 554b; S, 92b
Barahūt → Barhūt
Barak i, 1233b — I, 1270a
Baraḳ Baba i, **1031b;** ii, 1085b — I, **1063a;** II, 1111a
Baraḳ Ḥādjib → Burāk Ḥādjib
Baraḳ Khāns → Būraḳ Khān
Baraka i, **1032a;** iii, 305b; v, 745a — I, **1063b;** III, 315a; V, 750b
Baraka (ṣūfī) s, 3a — S, 2a
Baraka Khān (Mamluk(e)) → al-Saʿīd Baraka Khān
Baraka Khān (Mongol) → Berke Khān
Barakai i, 1190a — I, 1225a
Barakāt I-IV (Makka) i, **1032a;** ii, 517b; iv, 552b — I, **1064a;** II, 530a; IV, 576b
Barakāt b. Mūsā iv, 514a, 552a, 553a — IV, 536b, 576a, 577a
Bārakzay i, 87a, 95b, 231a; ii, 628b, 629a; s, 65b — I, 89b, 98a, 238a; II, 644b, 645a; S, 66a
Baramendana Keita ii, 1132a — II, 1158b
al-Barāmika i, 2b, 10a, 14a, 17b, 107b, 143b, 160a, 271b, 364a, 751b, 897a, **1033a**; ii, 40b, 78a, 305a, 576b; iii, 231a; iv, 221b, 447a, 756a; s, 130a, 225b — I, 2b, 10a, 14a, 18a, 111a, 147b, 164b, 280a, 375a, 773b, 924a, **1064b**; II, 41b, 79b, 313b, 591a; III, 238a; IV, 231a, 466b, 786b; S, 129b, 225b
Bārāmūla s, 167a — S, 167a
Baran → Bulandshahr
al-Barandjār i, 1305b — I, 1345b
Barānī, Bārānlu → Ḳarā Ḳoyunlu
Baranī, Ḍiyāʾ al-Dīn i, **1036a;** iv, 210b; s, 105a, b, 409a, b — I, **1067b**; IV, 220a; S, 104b, 105a, 409b
al-Barānis i, **1037a,** 1349b; s, 102b — I, **1068b,** 1390a; S, 102a
Baranta i, **1037b** — I, **1069a**
Barār → Berār
Barāthā i, **1038a,** 1040a; s, 400b — I, **1069b,** 1071b; S, 401a
Barawa i, **1038a** — I, **1069b**
Barāz (banda) iv, 16a; v, 64a — IV, 17b; V, 66a
Barbā i, **1038b** — I, **1070a**
Barbād (Bārbud) iv, 53b, 730b — IV, 56b, 759b
al-Barbahārī, al-Ḥasan b. ʿAlī i, 277a, **1039a;** iii, 159a, 734b; iv, 172b, 470a — I, 286a, **1070b;** III, 162b, 757b; IV, 180a, 490b
Bārbak Shāh b. Bahlūl Lōdī ii, 47b, 270b, 498b; iii, 420a, 632a, 633b — II, 48a, 279a, 511a; III, 433b, 653b, 655a
Bārbak Shāh Ilyās iii, 14b; s, 203a — III, 15b; S, 202b
Barbarī, Barābira → Barābra
Barbarīs → Hazāras
Barbarossa → ʿArūdj; Khayr al-Dīn
Barbary → al-Maghrib
Barbashturu i, 83b, **1040b**; v, 1119b; s, 152b — I, 86a, **1072a**; V, 1116a; S, 152b
Barbat → ʿŪd
Barbe → Saḳal
Barber/Barbier → Čelebi; Ḥallāḳ
Barberousse → ʿArūdj; Khayr al-Dīn
Barcelona/Barcelone → Barshalūna
Barčlīgh-kent s, 246a — S, 246a
Bard Sīr (valley/vallée)
Bardalla, Abu ʿAbd Allāh Muḥammad s, **125b** — S, **125a**
Bardas Sclerus i, 212a — I, 218b
Bardasīr → Kirmān
Bardesanes → Ibn Dayṣān
Bardhaʿa i, 660a, b, **1040b**; iv, 346b; v, 397a — I, 681a, **1072b**; IV, 361b; V, 398a
Bardjalūna → Barshalūna
Bardjawān, Abu 'l-Futūḥ i, **1041b;** ii, 858a; iii, 77a; iv, 1091b — I, **1073a;** II, 878a; III, 79b; IV, 1122b
Bārdjīk iv, 1173b — IV, 1207a
Bardo → Tunisia/Tunisie
Bardsīr v, 150b, 152a, b — V, 152b, 154a
Bardsīrī → Āḳā Khān Kirmānī
Bareilly, Barēlī i, **1042b;** iii, 60b, 61b; s, 73b, 420b — I, **1074a;** III, 63a, 64a; S, 74a, 421a
Bārfurūshī, Nadīm iv, 1035a — IV, 1067a
Barghash b. Saʿīd b. Sulṭān i, 37b, **1043b,** 1282b; v, 1030b, 1031a; s, 355b — I, 38b, **1075a,** 1321b; V, 1026b, 1027a; S, 355b
Barghawāṭa i, 157a, **1043b;** ii, 275b, 1008b; v, 654b, 1160a, 1189a, 1199b — I, 161a, **1075b;** II, 284a, 1032a; V, 658b, 1150a, 1179a, 1189b
Bārgīn-farākh → Ḳarā-köl
Bārgīr iv, 219a, b — IV, 229a
Barghūth → Ḳaml
Bārha Sayyids s, **126a** — S, **125b**
Barhebraeus → Ibn al-ʿIbrī
Barhūt i, **1045a** — I, **1076b**
Bari iv, 275a — IV, 287a
Bārī Bēgam iii, 336a — III, 346a
Bariba ii, 94a; iv, 538b; v, 281a — II, 96a; IV, 561b; V, 279a, b
Barīd i, **1045a,** 1039b; ii, 487a, 969b; iii, 109b, 182a; iv, 215b; v, 1142b — I, **1077a,** 1126a; II, 499a, 991b; III, 112a, 186a; IV, 225a; V, 1135b
Barīd Shāhīs i, **1047a,** 1200a, b, 1201a; iii, 421b, 425a, b, 447a — I, **1078b,** 1236a, b; III, 435a, 438b, 439b, 462a
al-Barīdī, Abū ʿAbd Allāh i, 866a, b, 867a, **1046b;** ii, 454a; iii, 127b — I, 890b, 891a, **1078a;** II, 465b; III, 130a
al-Barīdī, Abu 'l-Ḥusayn i, 1046b, 1047a — I, 1078b
al-Barīdī, Abu 'l-Ḳāsim i, 1047a; iii, 1175b — I, 1078b; III, 1204b
al-Barīdī, Abū Yūsuf i, 1046b, 1047a — I, 1078a, b
Bāridjān → Bāriz
Bāriḥ i, **1048a** — I, **1079b**
al-Bāriḥ iv, 290b — IV, 303b
Bārimmā → Ḥamrīn, Djabal
Barīra i, **1048a** — I, **1080a**
'Barisal Guns' i, 952a — I, 981a
Barito (river) s, 150b — S, 150b
Bariyya iv, 980b — IV, 1013a
Bāriz, Djabal s, **127a** — S, **126a**
al-Bārizī, Kamāl al-Dīn iii, 799b; iv, 642a — III, 823a; IV, 668b
Barḳa i, **1048b,** 1169a; ii, 160b, 161b; iii, 296b; v, 694b, 695b, 758a, 760a; s, 1a — I, **1080a;** 1204a; II, 165b, 166b; III, 305b; V, 699b, 700b, 763b, 765b; S, 1a
Barḳa (Ḳumm) s, 127a — S, 126b
Barḳaʿīd i, **1050a** — I, **1082a**
al-Barkat ii, 1022b — II, 1046a, b
al-Barḳī s, **127a,** 266a — S, **126b,** 265b
Barḳiyya ii, 318a, b, 858b — II, 327a, b, 878b
Barḳūḳ (Mamlūk) i, 14b, 138a, 816b, 869a, **1050a,**

1109a, 1138a; ii, 24a, 105b, 239b, 285b, 330a, 337b; iii, 48b, 185a, 187a, 188a, 190a, 299b, 756b, 799b, 1198a; iv, 432b, 642a; v, 628a, 1141a — I, 15a, 142a, 839b, 893a, **1082a,** 1142b, 1172b; II, 24b, 108a, 246a, 293b, 339b, 347b; III, 50b, 189a, 191a, 192b, 194b, 309a, 779b, 823a, 1228a; IV, 451b, 668a; V, 632a, 1134a
Barḳūt i, 950b — I, 979b
Barkyārūḳ b. Malikshāh (Saldjūḳ) i, 314a, 353a, 466a, 513a, 664a, 731a, 780a, **1051b,** 1070b, 1336b; ii, 282a, 384b; iii, 196a; iv, 28b, 101b, 102a; v, 437a; s, 279a, 382b, 384a — I, 324a, 363b, 480a, 529a, 684a, 753a, 803b, **1083a,** 1103a, 1377a; II, 290a, 395a; III, 201a; IV, 30b, 106a, b; V, 439b; S, 279a, 382b, 384a
Barlaam and/et Josaphat → Bilawhar wa Yūdāsaf
Barlās, Banū v, 182a — V, 179b
Barmak i, 1001a, 1033a, b — I, 1031b, 1065a
al-Barmakī → Djaʿfar b. Yaḥyā
Barmakid(e)s → Barāmika
Barniḳ → Benghāzī
Barōda i, **1053a** — I, **1084b**
Bārōghil ii, 29a — II, 29b
Barr al-Djazāʿir → Algeria/Algérie
al-Barrāḍ b. Ḳays al-Kinānī ii, 883b; iii, 285b; v, 116b — II, 904a; III, 294b; V, 119a
al-Barrādī i, 120b, 167a, **1053a;** ii, 140b; iii, 235b — I, 124a, 171b, **1085a;** II, 144b; III, 242a
Barrage (irrigation) → Band
Barrāḥ ii, 103a — II, 105a
Barrāk b. Ghurayr Āl Ḥumayd → Barrāk b. ʿUrayʿir
Barrāk b. ʿUrayʿir Āl Ḥamīd iv, 765a, 925a — IV, 795b, 958a
Barrāz al-Massūfī ii, 1009b; iii, 771b; iv, 116a; v, 586b — II, 1033a; III, 794b; IV, 121a; V, 591b
Bārs Ṭūghān iv, 911b — IV, 944b
Barṣawmā al-Zāmir, Isḥāḳ s, **128a** — S, **127b**
Barsbāy, Sultan i, 138a, 354b, 945b, 1032b, **1053b;** ii, 6a, 286a; iii, 20a, 99b, 186a, 190a, 923a, 1198a; iv, 133b, 267b, 433b, 642a, 643a; v, 304a; s, 39a, 43b, 273b — I, 142a, 365b, 974b, 1064a, **1085b;** II, 6a, 294a; III, 21a, 102a, 190b, 194a, 947b, 1228a; IV, 139a, 279b, 452b, 668b, 669b; V, 303b; S, 39b, 43b, 273b
Bārsbīk → Bārdjīk
Barshalūna i, 75b, **1054b;** ii, 485b — I, 78a, **1086b;** II, 497b
Barshawīsh → Nudjūm
Barṣīṣā i, **1055a** — I, **1086b**
Barskhān iv, 213a — IV, 222b
Barsṭoghan ii, 391a — II, 401b
Bartāʾīl ii, 486b — II, 498b
Bartang i, 853b, 854a — I, 877a, b
Bārūd i, **1055b;** iii, 191a; v, 687a, 979a — I, **1087a;** III, 195b; V, 692a
al-Bārūdī, Maḥmūd Sāmī i, 597b, **1069b;** s, 132b — I, 617a, **1101b;** S, 132a
Barūdjird (Burudjird) i, **1070b;** v, 828b, 829a, b; s, 75a, 157b, 384a — I, **1102b;** V, 835a, 836a; S, 75b, 158a, 384b
al-Bārūnī, ʿAbd Allāh i, 1070b — I, 1103a
al-Bārūnī, Sulaymān i, **1070b;** ii, 595a — I, **1103a;** II, 609b
Barwānī → Ibrā
Barzakh i, 940b, **1071b,** 1093a; ii, 581b; iv, 120b — I, 969b, **1103b,** 1125b; II, 596a; IV, 125b
Bārzān i, **1072a;** v, 467b — I, **1104a;** V, 470a
Barzand i, **1072a** — I, **1104b**
Bārzānī → Muṣṭafā Bārzānī
Barzbān, Prince/le prince ii, 85b — II, 87b
Barzikanī iii, 258a — III, 265a, b
Barzū-nāma i, **1072b** — I, **1104b**
Barzūya i, **1073a** — I, **1105a**
Basadar s, 145a — S, 145a
al-Basāsīrī i, 20b, 513a, 900b, **1073a,** 1355a; ii, 348b, 856a; iii, 159b, 891b, 1255b; iv, 26b, 457b, 458a, 911b; v, 73b; s, 29b — I, 21a, 528b, 927b, **1105b,** 1394a; II, 358a, 876a; III, 163a, 915b, 1288a; IV, 28b, 478a, 944b; V, 75b; S, 29b
Basawpyv i, 606a — I, 625b
Basbās s, **128b** — S, **127b**
Bāshā → Pasha
Bashdefterdār → Daftardār
Bashdjirt i, **1075a,** 1305a; ii, 995b; v, 1011b, 1012a, 1019a, b, 1020b — I, **1107a,** 1345b; II, 1018b; V, 1007b, 1015a, b, 1016b
Bashî-bozuḳ i, **1077b;** v, 35b — I, **1109b;** V, 36b
al-Bashīr b. al-Mundhir iii, 652a — III, 673b
Bashīr b. Saʿd i, **1077b** — I, **1109b**
Bashīr Čelebi i, **1078a** — I, **1110a**
Bāshīr Ibrāhīmī → Ibrāhīmī
Bashīr Ḳāsim Malḥam ii, 636a — II, 652b
Bashīr Kizlar-aghasî iii, 253a — III, 260a
Bashīr Shihāb I b. Ḥusayn ii, 635a — II, 651a
Bashīr Shihāb II i, **1078a,** 1138a, 1281a; ii, 444a, 635b; iii, 999b; v, 792b; s, 159b, 162b — I, **1110b,** 1172b, 1320a; II, 455b, 651b; III, 1024b; V, 799a; S, 159b, 162b
Bashīr al-Wansharīsī iii, 959b — III, 984a
Bashirā iv, 1019b — IV, 1051b
Bashkard, Bashākard, Bashkardia v, 352b; s, **129a** — V, 353b; S, **128a**
Bashkirs → Bashdjirt
al-Bashkunish i, 82a, 1011b, **1079b;** v, 1121a — I, 84b, 1043a, **1111b;** V, 1117b
Bashkurt → Bashdjirt
Bashḳut, Djewād Fehmī s, **129b** — S, **128b**
Bashlîk, Bashluk iv, 706a — IV, 734b
Bashmaḳ → al-Naʿl al-Sharīf
Bashmaḳlîk i, **1079b** — I, **1112a**
Bashmuḥāsaba → Māliyya
Bashshār b. Burd i, 10a, 143b, 331b, 587b, 857b, **1080a;** ii, 551b, 1031b; iii, 135b, 1019b, 1262b; iv, 54b, 1003b; s, 58b — I, 10a, 148a, 341b, 606b, 881a, **1112a;** II, 565b, 1055b; III, 138b, 1045a, 1295b; IV, 57b, 1036a; S, 59a
Bashshār b. Muslim iii, 41b — III, 43b
Bashshār al-Shaʿīrī i, **1082a** — I, **1114b**
Bāshūra i, 831a — I, 854a
Bashyāčī, Elijah iv, 605b, 606a, 607b — IV, 630a, b, 632a
Bashwakīl → Başvekil
Basil I i, 182b — I, 187b
Basil II i, 638a; ii, 855a; iii, 77a, 130b; v, 820b — I, 658b; II, 875a; III, 79b, 133a; V, 826b
Baṣinnā iv, 654a — IV, 680b
al-Baṣīr, Abū ʿAlī i, **1082a;** v, 118a — I, **1114b;** V, 120b
Baṣīrī (tribe/tribu) i, **1082b;** iv, 9b; v, 668b — I, **1115a;** IV, 10a; V, 672b
Bāsirī iii, 1106b, 1107a — III, 1133b
al-Basīt i, 1083a — I, 1115b
Basīṭ → ʿArūḍ
Basīṭ wa murakkab i, **1083b** — I, **1116a**
Baskets → Ḥalfāʾ
Basmačîs i, 1077a, **1084a;** ii, 366b, 700b; iv, 792b — I, 1109a, **1116b;** II, 376b, 718b; IV, 824b
Basmala i, **1084a;** ii, 303a; iii, 122b; v, 411b — I, **1116b;** II, 311a; III, 125a; V, 412b
Basmil i, 1240a — I, 1278a
Basques → al-Bashkunish
al-Baṣra i, 40b, 62b, 76b, 86a, 131b, 236b, 389a, 529b, 549b, 695a, 810b, 907a, **1085a;** ii, 385a, 391a, 414b; iii, 1254b, 1257a; iv, 640a; v, 57a, 646a, 950b; s, 12b,

15b, 17b, 18b, 20a, 24a, 26a, 27b, 31a, 32a, 35a, 41a, 88b, 113a, 119a, 122a, 179a, 198b, 225b, 243a, 284b, 352a, 354b, 384b, 385a, 389b — I, 41b, 64b, 78b, 88b, 135b, 244a, 400a, 545b, 567a, 716b, 833b, 934a, **1117b;** 395b, 401b, 425b; III, 1287a, 1289b; IV, 666a; V, 58b, 650a, 954b; S, 13a, 16a, 18a, 20b, 24b, 26a, 27b, 31b, 32b, 35b, 41a, 88b, 112b, 118b, 121b, 180a, 198b, 225b, 243a, 284b, 352a, 354b, 385a, b, 390a
- commerce i, 1086a, 1087a, b; ii, 130b; iii, 1252b — I, 1118b, 1119b, 1120a; II, 134a; III, 1285a
- monuments i, 610a; iii, 1268a — I, 629b, 630b; III, 1301a
- school of/l'école de i, 4b, 569b, 587b, 717b — I, 5a, 588a, 606b, 739a
al-Baṣra (Marocco/Maroc) i, **1087b;** iii, 149a — I, **1120a;** III, 152a
al-Baṣrī → ʿAlī b. Abi 'l-Faradj
al-Baṣrī, ʿAbd al-Djalīl s, 162b — S, 162b
Bassorah → al-Baṣra
Bast i, **1088a;** iii, 1170a; iv, 51a — I, **1120b;** III, 1199a; IV, 54a
Basṭ i, **1088b;** iii, 361a; iv, 326a — I, **1121a;** III, 372b; IV, 340b
Basta i, **1089a;** s, 144b — I, **1121b;** S, 144b
al-Basūs i, 565a, **1089a;** v, 362a; s, 234b — I, 583a, **1121b;** V, 363a; S, 234a
Başvekalet Arşivi i, 626a, **1089b;** ii, 82b, 128a — I, 646b, **1122a;** II, 84a, 131a
Başvekil i, **1091a** — I, **1123b**
al-Baṭāḥira i, **1091a** — I, **1123b**
al-Baṭāʾiḥ → al-Baṭīḥa
al-Baṭāʾiḥī, al-Maʾmūn i, 440a, **1091b;** ii, 127a, 130a, 858a, 859b; iv, 429a — I, 452b, **1124a;** II, 130a, 133a, 878a, 879a; IV, 447b
al-Baṭāʾihī, Muḥammad → Muḥammad al-Baṭāʾihī
Batak iii, 1214b, 1220a, 1225b — III, 1245a, 1250b, 1257a
Baṭalyaws i, 6a, 161a, **1092a;** iii, 498b — I, 6a, 165b, **1124b;** III, 515b
al-Baṭalyawsī i, 602a, **1092b;** ii, 838a; iv, 1007b; v, 929b — I, 622a, **1125a;** II, 857b; IV, 1039b; V, 934b
Batavia i, 980b; ii, 390b; iii, 1221b — I, 1011a; II, 400b; III, 1252b
Bateau → Baḥriyya; Safīna
Bath → Ḥammām
Baʿth (resurrection/résurrection) i, **1092b** — I, **1125a**
Baʿth → Nabīʾ
Baʿth party/partie iv, 125a, b, 126a; v, 486a, b, 1048b; s, 7b — IV, 130b, 131a, b; V, 471a, 1045a; S, 7a
Batha s, 166a — S, 166a
al-Bathaniyya i, **1093a;** iii, 293a — I, **1126a;** III, 302a
Baṭḥarī i, 1091a — I, 1123b
Báthory ii, 704a — II, 722a
al-Baṭīḥa i, **1093b;** iii, 1175b; v, 865a; s, 118b, 119a, 243a — I, **1126b;** III, 1204b; V, 871b; S, 118a, b, 243a
Bāṭil → Fāsid wa bāṭil
Bāṭin i, 1039a, 1099a, b; ii, 97b, 169a; iii, 662a; iv, 203a, b — I, 1070b, 1132a, b; II, 99b, 174b; III, 683b; IV, 212a, b
al-Bāṭin i, **1097b** — I, **1130b**
al-Bāṭina i, 536b, 541a, **1098a** — I, 553a, 558a, **1131a**
Bāṭina Yāl Saʿd s, 355b — S, 355b
Bāṭiniyya i, 256b, 839a, **1098b,** 1332b; ii, 169a, 282a, 733b, 734a, 1040b, 1094b; iv, 25b, 28b-29a, 47a, 101b-102a — I, 264a, 862a, **1131b,** 1373a; II, 174b, 290a, 752a, b, 1064b, 1120b; IV, 27b, 31a, 49b-50a, 106a-b
al-Bātiya → Nudjūm
Batjan i, **1100a** — I, **1133a**
Baṭlamiyūs i, **1100a;** ii, 357b, 577b, 578a, 763a; iii, 788b, 906b, 1135b, 1136b; iv, 517b, 1182b; v, 762a — I, **1133a;** II, 367a, 592a, b, 781b; III, 811b, 931a, 1163b, 1164b; IV, 540a, 1216a; V, 768a
Batman → Wazn
Baṭn i, **1102a** — I, **1135b**
Baṭn al-Agharr s, 198b — S, 198b
Baton → ʿAṣā
Baṭrīḳ → Biṭrīḳ
Batriyya, Butriyya iii, 244a, 1166a; s, 48b, **129b** — III, 251a, 1195a; S, 49a, **128b**
Batrūn i, **1102b** — I, **1135b**
al-Batt s, 23a — S, 23a
Baṭṭāl v, 332b — V, 332b
al-Baṭṭāl, ʿAbd Allāh i, 243b, **1102b;** iii, 493b — I, 250b, **1136a;** III, 510b
al-Baṭṭāl, Sayyid i, **1103b;** ii, 110a, 234b, 237b; iii, 115a; iv, 845b; v, 951b — I, **1137a;** II, 112b, 241b, 244b; III, 117a; IV, 878b; V, 955a
Baṭṭāl b. ʿAbd Allāh s, 223a — S, 223a
Baṭṭāl Husayṅ Pasha ii, 25b, 207b — II, 26a, 214a
al-Battānī i, 589b, 727a, **1104b;** iii, 228a, 1137a; v, 84b; s, 412b, 413b — I, 608b, 749a, **1137b;** III, 235a, 1165a; V, 86b; S, 413a, b
al-Battī → Abu 'l-Ḥasan al-Battī
Bātū Khān i, 135a, 467a, **1105a,** 1106b, 1187b, 1308a; ii, 3a, 44a, 571b; iv, 849a; v, 491a; s, 203b — I, 139a, 481a, **1138a,** 1139b, 1222b, 1348b; II, 3a, 45a, 586a; IV, 882a; V, 494a; S, 203a
Batuʾid(e)s i, 1105a, b, **1106b,** 1308a; ii, 315b, 1112a; iii, 1121b; iv, 349b, 1064a; v, 136b, 137a; s, 203b — I, 1138a, b, **1139b,** 1348a; II, 324b, 1138a; III, 1149a; IV, 364b, 1095b; V, 139a, b; S, 203a
Batumi i, 468b, **1108a** — I, 482b, **1141b**
Baʿūḍ iv, 522a — IV, 544b
Baudouin I I, 222b, 351b, 452b, 651a, 683b, 684a, 807a
Baudouin II I, 1013b; V, 54b, 927b
Baudouin III I, 732b, 1048b; II, 569a
Baudouin IV II, 569a, b
al-Bāʿūnī i, **1109a** — I, **1142b**
Bāvī iii, 1107a — III, 1134a
Bawānātī, Muḥammad Bāḳir iv, 70b — IV, 74b
Bāwand i, 237a, 872a, **1110a;** iii, 254b, 810a; iv, 207b, 645b; s, 298a, 309a, 356b, 416a — I, 244a, 896a, **1143a;** III, 262a, 833b; IV, 217a, 672a; S, 297b, 308b, 356b, 416a
al-Bawandī, Shaykh → ʿAbd al-ʿAzīz al-Bawandī
Bāward → Abīward
Bawāzīdj i, **1110b** — I, **1144a**
Bāwiyān v, 896a — V, 902b
Bawraḳ (Būraḳ) s, **130b** — S, **129b**
Baxar s, 325a — S, 324b
Bay (Bey) i, **1110b;** ii, 146b, 638b — I, **1144a;** II, 150b, 654b
Bayʿ i, **1111a** — I, **1144b**
al-Bayʿa i, 1111a, **1113a;** ii, 302b, 308a; iv, 943b, 944a — I, 1144a, **1146b;** II, 311a, 317a; IV, 976a, 977a
Bayān i, **1114a;** v, 898a, 899b — I, **1147b;** V, 904a, 906a
Bayān b. Samʿān al-Tamīmī i, **1116b;** ii, 1094b; iv, 837a — I, **1150b;** II, 1120a; IV, 870a
Bayān al-adyān ii, 74a — II, 75a
Bayānā iii, 441b — III, 455b, 456a
Bayāndur, Abu 'l-Fatḥ Beg → Abu 'l-Fatḥ Bayāndur
Bayāniyya iii, 1256b; iv, 837a — III, 1298b; IV, 870a
Bayar, Celâl ii, 204a, 432b, 596a; iii, 527a — II, 210b, 444a, 611a; III, 545a
Bayās → Payas
al-Bayāsī, Yūsuf b. Muḥammad iii, 111a — III, 113b
Bayāt i, **1117a;** iii, 1101b, 1102b, 1108a; iv, 387a; v, 828a, b — I, **1150b;** III, 1128b, 1130a, 1135a; IV, 404a; V, 834a, b

Bayᶜat al-ḥarb i, 314b; v, 995b — I, 324b; V, 991a
Bayᶜat al-nisāʾ i, 314b; v, 995b — I, 324b; V, 990b
Bayᶜat al-riḍwān s, 131a — S, 130a
Bāyazīd I i, 21b, 313a, 346a, 394a, 432a, 468a, 481a, 510b, 517b, 640a, 783b, 842b, 947b, 988a, 999a, **1117b,** 1251b, 1263a, 1303a, 1334a; ii, 11b, 239b, 292a, 611a, 684a, 697a, 722a, 984a, 989b, 990a, 1086a; iii, 1183a, 1248a; iv, 586a, 600b, 623a; v, 539a, 677a; s, 314b — I, 22a, 323a, 356b, 405b, 444a, 482a, 495a, 526a, 533b, 661a, 806b, 866a, 976b, 1018b, 1029b, **1151a,** 1289b, 1301b, 1343a, 1374a; II, 11b, 246a, 300a, 626b, 701a, 714b, 741a, 1006b, 1012b, 1111b; III, 1212a, 1280b; IV, 608b, 625a, 648a; V, 543b, 682a; S, 314b
Bāyazīd II i, 293a, 310b, 432a,510b, 842b, 1061a, **1119a,** 1207b, 1225b, 1253a; ii, 26a, 62a, 118b, 291b, 420b, 529a, 530a, 612a, 685a, 715a, 879a, 1087b; iii, 213a, 341a; iv, 92a, 230b, 291b, 463a, 565a, 1159a; v, 269a, 589b, 677b — I, 302a, 320a, 444a, 526b, 866a, 1093a, **1153a,** 1243b, 1262a, 1291a; II, 26b, 63a, 121a, 299b, 431a, 542a, 543a, 627a, 702b, 733b, 899b, 1113a; III, 219a, 351a; IV, 96a, 240b, 304b, 483b, 587b, 1191a; V, 267a, 593b, 682b
Bāyazīd i, **1117b** — I, **1151a**
Bāyazīd b. Uways al-Djalāyir i, 1117b; ii, 4016 — I, 1151a; II, 412a
Bāyazīd Anṣārī i, 220a, 225b, 238a, **1121b;**iii, 430a, 575b — I, 226b, 227a, 232b, 245a, **1155a;** III, 444a, 595a
Bāyazīd al-Bisṭāmī → Abū Yazīd al-Bisṭāmī
Bāyazīd Ḳān Kararānī ii, 183b — II, 189a
Bāyazīd Kötürüm iv, 108b — IV, 113b
Bāyazīd Sarwānī → ᶜAbbās Sarwānī
Baybars I (Mamlūk) i, 21a, 280b, 354a, 517a, 553a, 662b, 711a, 786b, 804b, 945b, 946a, 966b, 989b, 1017a, 1046a, **1124b,** 1126b, 1127b, 1188a; ii, 38a, 170b, 285a, 568b, 693b, 966a; iii, 20a, 48a, 109b, 184b, 189a, 399b, 402b, 473a, 504b, 506a, 679a, 832b, 1121a; iv, 87b, 216b, 402b, 431a, 432b, 483b, 484b, 609a, 655a, 842b, 843a, 944b; v, 571b, 801b; s, 391a — I, 22a, 289a, 364b, 532b, 570b, 683b, 732b, 810a, 828b, 974b, 975a, 996b, 1020a, 1048b, 1077b, **1158b,** 1160b, 1162a, 1223b; II, 38b, 176a, 293a, 582b, 711a, 988a;III, 21a, 50a, 112a, 189a, 193b, 412a, 415a, 490a, 521b, 523a, 701a, 856b, 1148b; IV, 92a, 226a, 420a, 450a, 451b, 504b, 505b, 634a, 681b, 875b, 876a, 977b; V, 576a, 807b; S, 391b
Baybars II (Mamlūk) i, **1126b,** 1325a; iii, 952a; iv, 429a, 433b — I, **1160b,** 1365b; III, 977a; IV, 447b, 452b
Baybars, Sīrat i, **1126b** — I, **1160b**
Baybars al-Djāshenkīr (Čāshnegīr) → Baybars II
Baybars al-Manṣūrī i, **1127b**; s, 388b — I, **1162a**; S, 389a
Bāybūrd i, **1128a;** ii, 223b — I, **1162b;** II, 230b
al-Bayḍā i, **1128b** — I, **1163a**
Baydaḳ → Shaṭrandj
Baydarā, amīr iv, 964b, 965b; v, 595a — IV, 997a, b; V, 598b
Baydamūr iii, 818a — III, 841b
al-Bayḍāwī, ᶜAbd Allāh i, **1129a;** ii, 95b; iv, 912b — I, **1163a;** II, 97b; IV, 945b
al-Baydhaḳ i, 78a, 122a, 389a, **1129b;**iii, 958b; v, 1209a — I, 80b, 125b, 400b, **1163b;** III, 983a; V, 1199b
Baydju Noyon i, 467a; ii, 38a, 712a; iv, 814a, 843a; v, 271b — I, 481a; II, 38b, 730b; IV, 846b, 876a; V, 269b
Baydu i, **1129b;** ii, 982a; iii, 1122b; v, 162b, 553b — I, **1164a;** II, 1004b; III, 1150a; V, 160b, 558b
Bayero ii, 1146b — II, 1173b
Bāyezīd → Bāyazīd
Bayhaḳ i, **1130a,** 1131b; s, 343a — I, **1164a,** 1166a; S, 342b
al-Bayhaḳī → Abū Saᶜīd
Bayhaḳī Sayyids s, **131b**, 329a — S, **130b**, 328b
al-Bayhaḳī, Abū Bakr Aḥmad i, **1130a;** iii, 24b; v, 1126b — I, **1164b;** III, 25b; V, 1123a
al-Bayhaḳī, Abū Djaᶜfar Aḥmad s, 289b — S, 289b
al-Bayhaḳī, Abu 'l-Faḍl Muḥammad i, **1130b;** ii, 336a, 1053a; v, 1224b; s, 245b — I, **1164b;** II, 345b, 1077b; V, 1215a; S, 245b
al-Bayhaḳī, Abu 'l-Ḥasan ᶜAlī i, 594b, **1131b**; s, 245b — I, 614a, **1165b**; S, 245b
al-Bayhaḳī, Aḥmad s, 354a — S, 354a
Bahyaḳī, Djaᶜfarak iv, 525b — IV, 548b
al-Bayhaḳī, Ibrāhīm i, 759a, **1132a** — I, 781b, **1166b**
Bayhaḳī, Sayyid Muḥammad s, 423b — S, 423b
al-Bayhaḳī, Zayd b. al-Ḥasan s, 236a — S, 236a
Bayḥān (wadi) i, **1132b;** iii, 208a; iv, 746a, b; s, 337a — I, **1166b,** III, 213b; IV, 776a, b; S, 336b
Bayḥān al-Kaṣāb i, **1133a;** ii, 675b; iv, 681a — I, **1167a;** II, 692a; IV, 709a
Bayhasiyya i, 113a; iii, 661a — I, 116b; III, 682b
Bayîndîr (tribe/tribu) i, 311a, **1133b;** ii, 200b; iii, 1100b; iv, 463a — I, 321a, **1168a;** II, 207a; III, 1127b; IV, 483b
Bāyirāt iv, 1036a — IV, 1068a
Bāyḳarā i, **1133b**; iv, 33a — I, **1168a**; IV, 35a
Bāyḳarā, Sultan Ḥusayn Mīrzā s, 423a — S, 423b
Bāykbāk → Bākbāk
Baylaḳān i, **1134a** — I, **1168b**
al-Baylamān → Madjlis
Baylān i, **1134a** — I, **1168b**
Baynūn i, **1134b** — I, **1169a**
Bayraḳ → ᶜAlam
Bayraḳdār i, **1134b**; iv, 679a — I, **1169a**; IV, 706b
Bayrām i, 817a; iii, 1007b — I, 840b; III, 1033a
Bayram, Muḥammad i, 597a — I, 616a
Bayram ᶜAlī i, **1135a** — I, **1169b**
Bayram ᶜAlī Khān i, **1135a** — I, **1169b**
Bayrām Beg i, 1067a — I, 1099a
Bayram Khān, Muḥammad i, 80b, 316a, **1135a,** 1194b; ii, 156a; iii, 423b; iv, 1020a; v, 629b; s, 312a — I, 82b, 326a, **1169b,** 1229b; II, 161a; III, 437a; IV, 1052a; V, 633b; S, 312a
Bayrām Khwadja iii, 1100b; iv, 584a — III, 1127b; IV, 608a
Bayram Pasha iii, 357a; iv, 573b — III, 368a; IV, 596b
Bayram al-Tūnusī v, 1160b — V, 1150a
Bayrām-i Walī → Hādjdji Bayrām
Bayrāmiyya i, 312b, 313a, 423b, 511a, **1137a,** 1235a; iii, 43a; s, 283a — I, 322a, 435a, 526b, **1171b,** 1272a; III, 45a; S, 282b
Bayrānwand v, 617a — V, 621a
Bayrūt i, **1137a;** ii, 129b, 635b — I, **1171b;** II, 133a, 651b
- institutions ii, 424a — II, 435a
Baysān i, **1138b** — I, **1173a**
Bāysongh or, Ghiyāth al-Dīn i, **1139a;** ii, 919b, 1076a; iv, 1123a, 1124a — I, **1173b;** II, 941a, 1101a; IV, 1155a, 1155b
Bāysonghor b. Maḥmūd i, **1139b**; I, **1174a**
Bāysonghor b. Yaᶜḳūb i, 312a, **1139b** — I, 3216, **1174a**
Bāysonḳor, Muḥammad b. s, 43b, 84a — S, 44a, 84a
Bāysunkur → Bāysonghor
Bayt i, **1139b;** ii, 113b; iv, 1146b, 1148a — I, **1174a;** II, 116a; IV, 1178a, 1179b
Bayt, abyāt i, 668a — I, 688b
Bayt Djibrīn i, **1140a;** ii, 911b; s, 204b — I, **1174b;** II, 933a; S, 204b
Bayt al-Faḳīh i, **1140b**; s, 30b — I, **1175a**; S, 30b

Bayt al-ḥikma i, 589a, 899a, **1141a;** iii, 872a; v, 1125a — I, 608a, 926a, **1175b;** III, 896b; V, 1121b
al-Bayt al-ḥarām i, 1139b — I, 1174a
Bayt Ḳayʿāl i, 759b — I, 782b
Bayt Laḥm i, **1141a** — I, **1175b**
Bayt al-Maḳdis → al-Ḳuds
Bayt al-māl i, 729b, **1141b;** ii, 144b, 325a; v, 1251b, 1252a; s, 200a — I, 751b, **1176a;** II, 148b, 334b; V, 1242b, 1243a; S, 200b
al-Bayt al-Muḳaddas → al-Ḳuds
Bayt Rās i, **1149a;** s, 117a — I, **1183b;** S, 116b
Bath Shaʿar →Bayt
Bayt al-ṭirāz iii, 344b; iv, 216b — III, 355a; IV, 225b
Bayṭār i, **1149b** — I, **1184a**
al-Bayṭār, Ṣalāḥ al-Dīn iv, 161b — IV, 168b
Bāytūz i, 1348b; v, 691a — I, 1388b; V, 695b
Bayundur → Bayîndîr
Bayyāna i, **1150a** — I, **1184a**
Bayyāsa i, **1150a** — I, **1184b**
al-Bayyāsī iv, 116a — IV, 121b
Bayyina i, **1150b** — I, **1185a**
Bayyūmiyya i, 281a, **1151b** — I, 289b, **1186a**
Bayzara i, **1152a;** iv, 745a — I, **1186a;** IV, 774b
Bāz Bahādur i, **1155a;** ii, 815a; iii, 421b, 453b — I, **1189b;** II, 834b; III, 435a, 469b
Baza → Basta
Bāzabdā iv, 639a — IV, 665b
Bāzahr i, **1155b;** v, 672a, 1229a — I, **1190a;** V, 677b, 1219a
Bāzār → Sūḳ
Bāzargān → Tidjāra
Bāzargān, Mahdī iv, 166a — IV, 173a
al-Bazdawī b. Aḥmad al-Nasafī s, 132a, 225b — S, **131a**, 225b
Bazh → Bādj
Bazīgh b. Mūsā i, **1156a;** iv, 1132b — I, **1190b;** IV, 1164a
Bāzinḳir i, **1156b** — I, **1190b**
Bazirgan i, **1157a** — I, **1191b**
Bazmān, Kūh-i iv, 3b — IV, 3b
Bazm-i Ṣūfiyya-yi Hind s, 4b, 293b — S, 4a, 293a
Bāzūkiyyūn i, **1157a;** iii, 1108b; iv, 1029b; v, 459a — I, **1191b;** III, 1136a; IV, 1061b; V, 461b
Bāzyār i, 1152b, 1153a — I, 1187a, b
al-Bazzār i, 273b — I, 282a
Bazzāz → Bezzāz
al-Bazzāz, ʿAbd al-Raḥmān iv, 782b, 783a — IV, 814a, b
Bazzāzistān → Ḳayṣariyya
Beard → Saḳal
Beaufort, Castle/Château → Ḳalʿat al-Shaḳīf
Beč i, **1157b** — I, **1191b**
Bécharré → Bsharra
Bečkem → Badjkam
Bedding → Mafrūshāt
Bedel → Badal
Bédel → Bīdil
Bedestān → Bezzāzistān
Bedj → Beč
Bedja i, 1a, 782b, **1157b,** 1172a, 1239b; iii, 5b; iv, 686a, b, 687a; v, 99a, 368b; s, 243b — I, 1a, 805b, **1192a,** 1207a, 1277b; III, 5b; IV, 714a, b, 715a; V, 101b, 369a; S, 243b
- language/langue v, 521b, 523a — V, 525b, 527a
Bēdjwān i, 863b — I, 887b
Bedouins → Badw; Marʿa; al-Marʾa
Bedrî Rahmî Eyuboğlu → Eyyūboghlu, Bedrī Raḥmī
Beersheba → Bīr al-Sabʿ
Beg, Bey i, **1159a;** ii, 507b; v, 629b — I, **1193b;** II, 520a; V, 633b
Bēgam Ṣāḥib ii, 378b — II, 389a
Bēgam Sulṭān ii, 922a — II 943a
Begdili i, **1159b;** iii, 1100a — I, **1194a;** III, 1127a
Bēglār iii, 1030a — III, 1055b
Beglerbegi i, 368a, 468b, 978a, **1159b,** 1191a; ii, 146a, 201b, 722a, 723b — I, 379a, 489b, 1008b, **1194a,** 1226a; II, 150a, 207b, 740b, 742a
Begteginid(e)s i, **1160b;** ii, 347b; v, 144b — I, **1195a;** II, 357b; V, 147a
Begtimur → Shāh-i Arman
Begum i, 1159a, **1161a** — I, 1193b, **1195b**
Bēḥān → Bayḥān
Behāristān → Djāmī
Behdīn v, 1113a, b, 1114a — V, 1109b, 1110b
Beḥera → Buḥayra
Behesnī → Besni
Behisht → Djanna
Behistūn → Bīsutūn
Behman → Bahman
Behnesā → Bahnasā
Behrām → Bahrām
Behrasīr v, 945a, 946a — V, 949a, b
Behzād → Bihzād
Beirut → Bayrūt
el-Beizāʾ → al-Bayḍāʾ
Béja → Badja
Bekaa → al-Biḳāʿ
Bekār odalarî iv, 236a — IV, 246b
Bekbulatovič, Simeon → Sāyin Bulāt
Bekči iv, 234b — IV, 245a
Bekrī Muṣṭafā Agha i, **1161b;** iii, 375a — I, **1196a;** III, 387a
Bektāsh al-Fākhirī i, 571a — I, 590a
Bektāsh Walī → Ḥādjdjī Bektāsh
Bektāshiyya i, 309b, 653a, 768a, 844a, **1161b;** ii, 202b, 292a, 968a; iii, 600b, 662b; iv, 168a, 811b, 951b; v, 283b, 285a; s, 95b — I, 319a, 673b, 791a, 867a, **1196a;** II, 209a, 300a, 990a; III, 621a, 684a; IV, 175b, 844b, 984a; V, 281b, 283b; S, 95a
Bēla → Las Bēla
Belalcázar → Ghāfiḳ
Belediye → Baladiyya
Beledjik → Bīredjik
Bēlen → Baylān
Belesh → Bālish
Belette, la → lbn ʿIrs
Beleyn i, **1163a** — I, **1197b**
Belgrade i, 268a, 269b, 293a, 656a, **1163a;** iv, 239a, 969b; v, 262a, 263a — I, 276b, 277b, 302a, 676b, **1197b;** IV, 249b, 1001b; V, 259b, 261a
Belhūba, Belhīt → Abu 'l-Hawl
Belief in God → ʿAḳīda, Īmān, Iʿtiḳād
Bélier → Minṭaḳat al-Burūdj; Silāḥ
Belīgh, Ismāʿīl i, **1165b** — I, **1200a**
Belīgh, Meḥmed Emīn i, **1165b** — I, **1200a**
Belitung → Billiton
Belkasem Krim → Ibn al-Ḳāsim Karīm
Bello, Alhaji Aḥmadu iii, 282b; iv, 549b, 550a, 774a — III, 291a; IV, 573b, 805a
Belomancy/Bélomancie → Istiḳsām
Béloutchistan/Beluchistan → Balūčistan
Ben-ʿamma iii, 389a — III, 401b
Ben Ayed ii, 460a — II, 471b
Ben Badīs → lbn Bādīs
Ben Bella, Aḥmad iii, 564a; v, 1070b — III, 583b; V, 1068a
Ben Cheneb (Shneb) → lbn Abī Shanab
Ben Ganah i, 1247a — I, 1285a
Ben Ghedahem → Ibn Ghidhāhum
Ben Sedira iii, 689b, 690b — III, 711a, 712b
Benares/Bénarès i, **1165b;** s, 47a — I, **1200b;** S, 47a
Benavent i, **1166a** — I, **1201a**
Benavert i, **1166b** — I, **1201a**

Bender → Bandar
Bender, Bessarabia/Bessarabie i, **1166b** — I, **1201b**
Benediction/Bénédiction → Baraka
Beng → Bandj
Bengal/Bengale → Bangāla
Bengali i, **1167a** — I, **1201b**
Benghāzī i, 1049a, 1050a, **1169a**; v, 759b, 760a; s, 164b — I, 1081a, b, **1204a**; V, 765b, 766b; S, 164b
Beni Amer → Āmīr, Banū
Benī Mellāl s, **132a** — S, **131b**
Benī Menāser → Manāṣīr, Banū
Beni-Saf s, 376b — S, 376b
Beni Suef → Bani Suwayf
Benia → Banya
Benjamin → Binyāmīn
Benjamin b. Mishal iv, 310a — IV, 324a
Benlāk → Bennāk
Bennāk i, **1169b;** ii, 32b — I, **1204b;** II, 33a
Benue, river/Benué, rivière i, 179a — I, 184a
Beograd → Belgrade
Berār i, 924b, **1170a;** ii, 815b, 981b; iii, 425a, 1159a; v, 1a; s, 279b, 280a — I, 952b, **1205a;** II, 834b, 1003b; III, 439a, 1187b; V, 1b; S, 279b
Berāt i, **1170a;** ii, 32b, 119a; iii, 1180b, 1187a — I, **1205a;** II, 33a, 121b; III, 1209b, 1216b
Berātlî i, **1171b** — I, **1206b**
Berber (language)/Berbère (langue) i, 171a, 374b, 379a, 568b, 573b, 578b, 763a, 770a, 792a, 889a, 1044b, 1177a 1180-5; ii, 109b, 460a, 591b, 873b, 992b; iv, 307b, 1149a; v, 754b, 760a, 1206a; s, 397a — I, 175b, 385a, 390a, 587a, 592b, 597a, 786a, 793a, 815a, 915b, 1076b, 1212a, 1215-20; II, 112a, 472a, 606a, 894a, 1015b; IV, 321a, 1181a; V, 760b, 766a, 1196b; S, 397b
- territory/territoire i, **1171b**; v, 1249b — I, **1206b**; V, 1240b
Berberā i, **1172b** — I, **1207b**
Berberi i, **1173a** — I, **1222a**
Berbers/Berbères i, 32a, 47b, 79b, 86b, 92a, 125a, 163b, 167b, 171a, 207b, 244b, 245a, 254b, 355b, 367a, 374b, 379a, 532b, 699a, 770a, 990b,, 1043b, 1049a, b, 1071b, **1173a,** 1238a, 1246b, 1321a; ii, 57b, 992b; iii, 494a, 982b; iv, 75a-b, 307b, 339a, 359a, 415a, b, 562a; v, 517b, 744a, 1156b, 1160a, 1187a; s, 145a, 153a, 376b — I, 32b, 48b, 82a, 88b, 95a, 128b, 168a, 172b, 175b, 213b, 252a, b, 262b, 366b, 377b, 385a, 390a, 548b, 720b, 793a, 1021b, 1075b, 1081a, b, 1103b, **1208a,** 1275b, 1284b, 1361b; II, 58b, 1015b; III, 511a, 1007a; IV, 79a-b, 321a, 353b, 374b, 433b, 584a; V, 521a, b, 749b, 1146b, 1149b, 1177a; S, 144b, 153a, 376b
- in al-Andalus/en Andalousie i, 5b, 6a, b, 76a, 82a, b, 490b, 494a, b, 1176a, 1249a; ii, 505a, 541b; iii, 12a, 147a, 495b, 1043b; v, 1239b — I, 6a, b, 78b, 84a, 85a, 505a, 508b, 509b, 1211a, 1287a; II, 517b, 555a; III, 12b, 150a, 512b, 1069b; V, 1230a, b
- ethnography/ethnographie i, 370b, 1037a, **1173a,** 1349b; iii, 295b, 1039a; iv, 360b, 511b; v, 1196b — I, 381b, 1068b, **1208a,** 1390a; III, 305a, 1065a; IV, 376a, 533b; V, 1186b
- religion i, **1178a;** ii, 1079a; iii, 134b — I, **1213a;** II, 1104a; III, 137b
Berdī Beg Khān i, 325a, 1107b; ii, 401a — I, 335a, 1141a; II, 412a
Berdi Khodja iv, 584a, b; s, 280b — IV, 608a; S, 280b
Bergama i, **1187a**; iv, 628a; s, 137b — I, **1222a**; IV, 653a; S, 137a
Berger → Čūpān
Berger, le (astronomie) S, 321a
Bergi → Birge
Berke Khān i, 1106a, b, **1187b;** ii, 44a; iii, 185a, 679a; iv, 30b, 349b; v, 301a — I, 1139a, 1140a, **1222b;** II, 45a; III, 189a, 701a; IV, 32b, 364b; V, 300a
Béroia, Bérrhoia → Karaferye
Besermyans i, **1188b** — I, **1223b**
Beshike i, **1189a** — I, **1224a**
Beshiktash ii, 1042b; iv, 233a; v, 905a, 949a — II, 1067a; IV, 243a; V, 911b, 952b
Beshlik ii, 28b — II, 28b
Beshparmak i, **1189a** — I, **1224a**
Besika Bay/Baie de - → Beshike
Beskesek-Abaza i, **1189a** — I, **1224b**
Besleney ii, 21b, 22a — II, 22b, 23a
Besni i, **1190b** — I, **1225b**
Bessarabia/Bessarabie → Budjāk
Bestiary/Bestiaire → Ḥayawān
Bēt → Bayt
Bétail → Baḳar
Bétail, petit → Ghanam
Betelgeuze → Nudjūm
Bethlehem/Bethléem → Bayt Laḥm
Bey → Bay/Beg
Beyatlî → Yaḥyā Kemāl Beyatlî
Beyhan, Princess/la princesse ii, 999a — II, 1022a
Beylerbeyi → Beglerbegi
Beylik i, 368a, **1191a;** ii, 338b — I, 379a, **1226a;** II, 348b
Beyoghlu i, 973a, b; iii, 1181a; s, 314a, 315b — I, 1003a, b; III, 1210a; S, 314a, 315b
Beyond, The → Ākhira
Beyrouth → Beirut
Beyshehir i, 703a, 703b, **1191b**; iv, 620b, 622a, 623a; s, 137a — I, 724a, 724b, **1226b**; IV, 645b, 647a, 648a; S, 136b
Bežeta ii, 251a; iv, 571b — II, 258b; IV, 594a
Bezistān → Ḳayṣariyya
Bezm-i ʿĀlem → Walide Sultān
Bezoar → Bāzahr
Bezzāz v, 559b, 560a — V, 564b
Bezzāzistān iii, 212b, 213a; iv, 226b, 227a, b; v, 559b — III, 218b, 219a; IV, 236b, 237a, b; V, 564b
Bhagwān Dās iv, 709a — IV, 737b
Bhagwanis i, 173a — I, 177b
Bhagwant Rāy i, 1330a — I, 1371a
Bhakkar i, **1192a;** iii, 633a — I, **1227a;** III, 654a
Bhakti ii, 51b; iii, 435b, 456b — II, 52b; III, 450a, 472a
Bharatpūr i, **1192b**; s, 358b — I, **1228a**; S, 358b
Bharoč i, **1193a;** ii, 1129a; iii, 444b; s, 358b — I, **1228a;** II, 1155b; III, 459b; S, 358a
Bhāskar Rāo ii, 220a — II, 227a
Bhāskara i, 133a — I, 136b
Bhattā-Shāh s, 327b — S, 327a
Bhaṭṭi i, **1193b;** iii, 225b — I, **1229a;** III, 232a
Bhattinda i, **1193b** — I, **1229a**
Bhawāni Rām ii, 219a — II, 225b
Bhīls iv, 1023b — IV, 1055b
Bhīm-Dēv s, 242a — S, 242a
Bhitāʾī, Shāh ʿAbd al-Laṭīf i, **1194b** — I, **1230a**
Bhōdja, Rādja i, 1197a; ii, 218b, 219b — I, 1232a; II, 225a, 226a
Bhōdjpur iii, 638b — III, 660a
Bhōpāl (State/État) i, **1195a** — I, **1230b**
Bhōpāl (City/Ville) i, **1196b** — I, **1232a**
Bhutto, Zulfiqar Ali v, 1081b — V, 1079a, b
Biʿa → Kanīsa
Bībān i, **1197a** — I, **1232b**
Bībī i, **1197b** — I, **1233a**
Bībī Aḳā Malik → al-Djawnpūrī
Bībī Djamāl ii, 49b — II, 50b
Bībī Khwunza iii, 632a — III, 653a
al-Biblāwī, ʿAlī b. Muḥammad s, **132b** — S, **132a**
Bible i, 118a, 564b; iii, 1205a; iv, 303a, 308b, 312a — I, 121b, 582b; III, 1235b; IV, 316b, 322b,

326a → Indjīl; Tawrat; Zabūr
Bibliography/Bibliographie i, 59a, 68a, 120b, 167a, 213a, 280a, 302b, 478a, 575a, 594b, 645b, 816b, **1197b**, 1248a; iv, 761b – I, 61a, 70a, 124a, 171b, 219b, 288b, 312a, 492b, 594a, 614a, 666a, 840a, **1233a**, 1286a; IV, 792a
Bibliomancy/Bibliomancie → Ḳurʿa
Bibliothèque → Khizāna; Maktaba
Bîčaḳdjî-zāde Mustafā Čelebī i, 775b, 799a
Bidʿ →al-Dawḥa (Ḳaṭar)
Bidʿa i, 277a, 1039a, **1199a**; iv, 141b – I, 286a, 1070b, **1234b**; IV, 147b
Bīdar i, 924a, 925a, b, 1047a, b, **1199b**, 1323a; iii, 425b, 447a; v, 295b, 888b, 1135a, 1215a, b – I, 952a, 953a, b, 1079a, **1235a**, 1363b; III, 439b, 462a; V, 295b, 895a, 1130b, 1205a
Bidʿat ii, 147a – II, 151a
Bīdil, Mīrzā i, **1201a**; ii, 865b – I, **1236b**; II, 885b
Bīdjān, Aḥmed i, **1202a**; ii, 587b; iii, 43b – I, **1237b**; II, 602a; III, 45a
Bidjanagar → Vidjayanagara
Bīdjāpūr i, 199a, 768b, 769a, 913b, 924b, 1015b, **1202b**, 1323b; iii, 15a, 287b, 288a, 425a, b; v, 884b, 888b, 1259a, b; s, 246b – I, 204b, 791b, 792a, 941a, 952b, 1046b, **1238a**, 1364a; III, 16a, 296b, 297a, 438b, 439b; V, 890b, 895a, 1250a, b; S, 246b
- monuments i, 1203b, 1204b; iii, 446b, 447b; v, 295a, 1216a – I, 1239a, 1240a; III, 461b, 462b; V, 295a, 1205b
Bidjār s, 142a, b – S, 142a
Bidjay Rāy i, 1194a – I, 1229b
Bidjāya (Bougie) i, 155a, 165a, 678a, **1204b**; ii, 130a, 747b, 863b; iii, 67a, b, 138a, b, 500a; iv, 359b, 360b, 361b, 479b; v, 531a; s, 113b – I, 159a, 170a, 699a, **1240b**; II, 133b, 766a, 883b; III, 69b, 70a, 141a, b, 517a; IV, 375a, 376a, 377b, 501a; V, 535a; S, 113a
Bīdjbehāra s, 114a – S, 113b
Bidjnawr i, 288a, **1206a**; s, 73b, 74a – I, 296b, **1241b**; S, 74a
Bidlīs i, **1206a**; v, 457a, 458b, 459a – I, **1242a**; V, 459b, 461a, b
Bidlīsī, Abu ʾl-Faḍl i, 1208a; iv, 704b – I, 1244a; IV, 733a
Bidlīsī, Idrīs i, **1207b**; ii, 1136b; v, 457a, b, 481b – I, **1243b**; II, 1163a; V, 460a, b, 484b
Bidlīsī, Sharaf Khān i, 1207a, **1208b**; v, 458a, b, 481b – I, 1242b, **1244b**; V, 460b, 461b, 484b
Bidpay → Kalīla wa-dimna
Bīdrī i, 1201a – I, 1236b
Biga s, 330a – S, 329b
Bīgha i, **1209a** – I, **1245a**
Bīgha → Misāḥa
Bighāʾ ii, 551a, b; v, 778a; s, **133a** – II, 564b, 565b; V, 784a; S, **132b**
Bihādhīn → Muḥammad Iʿtimāzāda
Bihʾāfrid b. Farwardīn i, **1209a**; iv, 44b, 910a; v, 1111b – I, **1245a**; IV, 47b, 943a; V, 1107b
Biḥamad Khānī s, 353a – S, 353a
Bihār i, **1209b**; iii, 423b; v, 783b; s, 167a, 203a, 325b – I, **1245b**; III, 437a; V, 790a; S, 167a, 202b, 325a
Bihār-i Dānish → ʿInāyat Allāh Ḳanbū
al-Bihārī, Muḥibb Allāh i, 937a, b, **1210a**; iii, 435a – I, 966a, **1246a**; III, 449b
Bihāristān → Djāmī
Bihbihān i, 659a; iii, 1107a; v, 876a; s, 134b – I, 680a; III, 1134a; V, 882a; S, 134a
Bihbihānī, Sayyid ʿAbd Allāh s, 104a, 365b – S, 103b, 365a
al-Bihbihānī, ʿAbd al-Ḥusayn s, 135a – S, 134b
al-Bihbihānī, Muḥammad ʿAlī s, 135a – S, 134b
al-Bihbihānī, Muḥammad Bāḳir s, 57a, **134b** – S, 57b, **134a**
Bihbūd Khān iv, 390a – IV, 406b
Bihisht → Djanna
Bihishtī i, **1210b**; iv, 129a; v, 1105b – I, **1246b**; IV, 134b; V, 1101b
Bihḳubādh i, 789a, **1210b** – I, 812b, **1246b**
Bihrangī, Ṣamad v, 200b; s, **135a** – V, 198a; S, **134b**
Bihrūz (Saldjuk) i, 797a – I, 820a
Bihrūz, Amīr i, **1211a** – I, **1247a**
Bihrūz Khān i, **1211a** – I, **1247a**
Bihzād, Kamāl al-Dīn i, 205b, **1211a**; s, 138b, 139a, b – I, 211b, **1247a**; S, 138a, b, 139a
al-Biḳāʿ i, 787b, **1214a**; ii, 750a; v, 790a, 739b; s, 154a, 250a – I, 811a, **1250a**; II, 768a; V, 796a, 799b; S, 154a, 250a
Bikbāshī → Biñbashî
Bikfayā s, 27b – S, 28a
Bikramadjit Singh iii, 995b – III, 1020a
Bikrami i, 1239a – I, 1277a
Biḳratīs → Buḳrāt
Bīḳrid i, 1066b – I, 1098b
Bi-lā Kayf i, 333b, 412a – I, 344a, 424a
Bilād al-Djarīd → Djarīd
Bilād al-Islām iv, 173a – IV, 180b
Bilād al-Sūdān i, 156b; ii, 121b, 137a – I, 161a; II, 124b, 140b
Bilād-i thalātha i, **1214b** – I, **1250b**
Bilād al-Zandj iii, 653a – III, 674b
Bilāl b. Abī Burda al-Ashʿarī i, 694a; ii, 232a, 245a; iii, 155a, 650a; iv, 919a, 926b – I, 715a; II, 239a, 252a; III, 158b, 671b; IV, 952a, 959b
Bilāl b. Djarīr al-Muḥammadī i, **1214b** – I, **1251a**
Bilāl b. al-Ḥārith i, 336b – I, 347a
Bilāl b. Rabāḥ i, 24b, 110a, 188a, 482a, 1141b, **1215a**; ii, 846b – I, 25b, 113a, 193b, 496b, 1176a, **1251a**; II, 866a
Bīlāwar v, 460b – V, 463b
Bilawhar wa-Yūdāsaf i, 2b, **1215b**; iv, 63a – I, 2b, **1251b**; IV, 66a-b
Bīlbak al-Khāzindār i, 816b – I, 839b
al-Bilbālī, Makhlūf b. ʿAlī iv, 550a – IV, 573b
Bilbās i, **1217b** – I, **1254a**
Bilbays i, **1218a**; s, 159a – I, **1254a**; S, 159a
Bile → Bīredjik
Bileam → Balʿam
Biledjik i, **1218b**; iii, 215a; s, 282a – I, **1254b**; III, 221a; S, 282a
Bilgā Takīn (Bilgetegin) i, 421b; ii, 978a; s, 284b – I, 433b; II, 1000b; S, 284b
Bilgrām i, **1218b** – I, **1255a**
Bilgrāmī → Ghulām Nabī
Bilgrāmī, ʿAbd al-Djalīl i, 808a, **1219a** – I, 831a, **1255b**
Bilgrāmī, Sayyid ʿAlī i, **1219b** – I, **1255b**
Bilḳīs i, 262a, **1219b**; ii, 218a; iii, 541b – I, 270a, **1256a**; II, 224b; III, 560b
Billawr i, **1220b**; v, 965a – I, **1256b**; V, 969b
Billiton i, **1221a** – I, **1257b**
Billūr Köshk i, **1221a**; iii, 375a – I, **1257b**; III, 387a
Bilma i, **1221b** – I, **1258a**
Bilmedje i, **1222a** – I, **1258b**
Bilmen, Ömer Nasuhî iii, 163b – III, 167a
Bilyānī s, 36a – S, 36a
Bilyar i, 1306b – I, 1347a
Bīmāristān i, 899a, **1222b**; ii, 283b, 1015b, 1120a; iii, 195b; iv, 485b; v, 1006a; s, 273b, 274a, 381a – I, 926a, **1259a**; II, 291b, 1039b, 1146b; III, 200a; IV, 506b; V, 1001b; S, 273a, b, 381b
al-Bimāristān al-ʿAḍudī s, 29b – S, 30a
Bīmārkhāne v, 1145a – V, 1137a
Bināʾ i, **1226a** – I, **1262b**
Biñbashî i, **1229a** – I, **1265b**
Bingöl i, **1229a** – I, **1266a**

Bingöl Dagh i, **1229a** – I, **1266a**
Binn s, **135b** – S, **135b**
Bint al-Khuss → Hind bint al-Khuss
Binyāmīn i, 261a, 262a, **1229b** – I, 269a, 270a, **1266b**
Biʾr i, 538b, **1230a**; s, 318b – I, 555a, **1266b**; S, 318a
Biʾr ʿAlālī s, 165a – S, 165a
Biʾr Ahmad i, 345a – I, 355b
Biʾr Maʿūna i, 442b, **1232b**; v, 41a – I, 455a, **1269a**; V, 42a
Biʾr Maymūn i, **1232b** – I, **1269b**
Biʾr muʿaṭṭala i, 181a – I, 186a
Bīr al-Sabʿ i, **1233a** – I, **1269b**
Bīr Singh Dēva i, 117b; ii, 380a – I, 121a; II, 390b
al-Bīra i, **1233a**, b – I, **1270a**, b
Biraima iv, 352a – IV, 367a
Bīrbal → Radja Bīrbal
Bīrbal Kāčrū s, 332a, 333a – S, 332a
Birdhawn iv, 1146a – IV, 1177b
Bīrdjand i, **1233a**; iv, 4a-b; V, 355a, b – I, **1270a**; IV, 4b; V, 356b, 357a
Birdjās ii, 954a, 955a; iv, 265b – II, 976a, 977a; IV, 277b
Bīredjik i, **1233b** – I, **1270b**
Birge i, **1234b** – I, **1271b**
Birgewī, Birgili i, 332b, **1235a**; iv, 560a – I, 343a, **1272a**; IV, 582b
Bîrghos → Lüleburgaz
Birkat Ḳārūn iv, 673b – IV, 701a
Birmali Sala Pate ii, 942a – II, 964a
Birmanie I, 625b, **1272b**
Birnin-Katsina iv, 773b – IV, 804b
Birr i, **1235b** – I, **1273a**
Birs i, **1235b** – I, **1273a**
Bīrūn i, **1236a**; ii, 15a, 1089a – I, **1273b**; II, 15b, 1114b
al-Bīrūnī, Abū Rayḥān i, 87a, 119a, 213a, 419a, 455b, 591b, 725a, 726b, 1014b, 1031a, b, 1131a, 1220b, **1236a**; ii, 584a; iii, 9a, 30b, 113b, 405a, 406a, 459a, 858a, 1206b; iv, 358b, 707a, 754a, 1061a, 1063a; v, 86a, b, 1025b; s, 56a, 59b, 249b, 251b, 253a, 327b, 363a, 413b – I, 89b, 122b, 219a, 220a, 431a, 468b, 610b, 747b, 748b, 1045b, 1062b, 1063a, 1165a, 1257a, **1273b**; II, 598b; III, 9b, 32a, 116a, 417b, 418b, 475a, 882a, 1237a; IV, 374a, 735b, 784b, 1092b, 1094b; V, 88a, b, 1021a; S, 56b, 60a, 250a, 252a, b, 327a, 362b, 414a
Birzāl, Banū i, **1238a**; iv, 254b, 665b – I, **1275b**; IV, 265b, 692b
al-Birzāli → Muhammad b. ʿAbd Allāh
al-Birzālī, ʿAlam al-Dīn i, **1238a**; ii, 522b; iv, 863b – I, **1276a**; II, 536a; IV, 897a
Bisāṭ v, 1158b; s, **136a** – V, 1148a; S, **135b**
Bisbarāy Karkarni i, **1239a** – I, **1276b**
Bisermini v, 1015a, 1019a – V, 1010b, 1014b
Bīsha i, 538a, b, **1239a** – I, 554b, **1277a**
Bīsharʿ i, **1239b** – I, **1277a**
Bishāra al-Khūrī s, 159b – S, 159b
Bishārīn i, 1b, 1172a, **1239b** – I, 1b, 1207a, **1277b**
Bishbalîk i, **1240a** – I, **1277b**
al-Bishr i, **1240b** – I, **1278b**
Bishr b. Abī Khāzim i, **1241a** – I, **1279a**
Bishr b. al-Barāʾ i, **1241b** – I, **1279b**
Bishr b. Ghiyāth al-Marīsī i, **1241b**; ii, 373a, 388a; iv, 1163b; s, 89a, 90a – I, **1279b**; II, 383b, 398b; IV, 1195b; S, 88b, 90a
Bishr b. Marwān i, **1242b**; ii, 788a; iii, 40b, 73a, 715a – I, **1280a**; II, 807a; III, 42a, 75b, 737b
Bishr b. al-Muʿtamir i, 454a, 587a, **1243a**; iii, 1143b, 1266a; s, 89b, 225b, 226a, b – I, 467a, 606a, **1281a**; III, 1171b, 1299a; S, 89b, 225b, 226a, b
Bishr b. Ṣafwān i, 50a; ii, 327b; iii, 169b – I, 51b; II, 337a; III, 173a
Bishr b. al-Walīd i, **1244a**; iii, 990b – I, **1281b**; III, 1015a
Bishr al-Ḥāfī i, **1244a**; s, 384b – I, **1282a**; S, 385a
Bishr-i Yāsīn → Abu ʾl-Kāsim
Bishtāsb iv, 809b – IV, 842a
Biskra i, **1246b**; v, 1181a – I, **1284a**; V, 1171a
Bismillāh → Basmala
Bisṭām i, **1247a**; s, 149a, 235a – I, **1285a**; S, 149a, 234b
Bisṭām b. Ḳays i, 343a, 963b, **1247b**, ii, 72a – I, 353b, 993a, **1285b**; II, 73a
Bisṭām b. ʿUmar al-Ḍabbī → al-Ḍabbī, Bisṭām
al-Bisṭāmī, ʿAbd al-Raḥmān i, **1248a**; ii, 376a – I, **1286a**; II, 386b
al- Bisṭāmī, Abū Yazīd → Abū Yazīd
al-Bisṭāmī, ʿAlā al-Din → Muṣannifak
Bīstī → Sikka
Bīsutūn i, **1248b**; v, 169a – I, **1286a**; V, 166b
Bīsutūn b. Djihāngīr b. Kāwūs iv, 808a – IV, 840b
Biswak s, 167a, b – S, 167a, b
al-Bīṭār, Ṣalāḥ al-Dīn iv, 125a – IV, 130b
Bitik, bitikči i, **1248b**; iv, 757a – I, **1286b**; IV, 787b
Bitlis → Bidlīs
Bitolja → Manastir/Monastir
Biṭrawsh i, **1249a**; ii, 744a; v, 510a – I, **1287a**; II, 762b; V, 513b
Biṭrīḳ i, 642b, **1249b**; v, 620a – I, 663a, **1287b**; V, 624a
al-Biṭrūdjī i, **1250a**; iii, 957a; iv, 518a – I, **1288a**; III, 982a; IV, 540b
Bitume(n) → Ḳaṭrān
Biyābānak i, **1250a** – I, **1288a**
Biya-pīsh → Gīlān-i Biyā Pas
Biyār, al-Biyār s, **149a** – S, **149a**
Biyārdjumand → Biyār
Bîyîḳlî ʿAlī Āghā i, 396a – I, 407a
Bîyîḳlî Meḥmed Pasha → Meḥmed Pasha Bîyîḳlî
Bizāʿā → Buzāʿā
Bīzabān → Dilsiz
Bizerta/Bizerte → Banzart
Black Sea → Baḥr Bunṭus; Ḳarā Deniz
Black Stone → al-Ḥadjar al-aswad
Blacksmith → Ḳayn
Blanchisseur → Ghassāl
Blazon/Blason → Rank
Blé, le → Ḳamḥ
Bleda → Midḥat Shükrü
Blessing → Baraka
Blida → Bulayda
Blood (guilt) → Dam
Blood-letter → Faṣṣād; Ḥadjdjām
Boabdil → Muḥammad XII (Naṣrid(e))
Boar, wild → Khinzīr
Boat → Baḥriyya; Safīna
Bobastro → Bubashtru
Bocskay, Stephen/Étienne i, 267b; ii, 704a – I, 275b; II, 722a
Bodrum i, 476b, **1250b** – I, 490b, **1288b**
Body → Djism
Boghā al-Kabīr → Bughā al-Kabīr
Boghā al-Sharābī → Bughā al-Sharābī
Boghā Tarkhān iii, 493b – III, 510b
Boghasî v, 560b, 561a – V, 565b, 566a
Boghaz → Boghaz-iči
Boghaz-iči i, **1251a**; v, 243a – I, **1289a**; V, 241a
Boghaz Kesen → Rūmeli Ḥiṣār
Boghazköy ii, 62b – II, 64a
Boghdān i, 4b, 310b, 1120a, **1252b**; v, 39b – I, 4b, 320a, 1153b, **1290b**; V, 40b
Bōgrā i, **1253b** – I, **1291b**
Bohemia → Čeh
Bohémond I ii, 37a, 110b – II, 37b, 113a

Bohémond II ii, 110b — II, 113a
Bohémond III ii, 37b; v, 591a — II, 38a; V, 594b
Bohémond IV ii, 37b; v, 591a — II, 38b; V, 595a
Bohémond VII iv, 485a — IV, 506a
Bohorās, Bohras i, 172a, **1254a;** ii, 170b; iii, 381a, 434a, b, 544b; iv, 199b, 888a; v, 942b; s, 70b — I, 176b, **1292a;** II, 175b; III, 393a, 448a, b, 563b; IV, 208a, 920b; V, 946a; S, 71a
Bohtān → Kurds/Kurdes
Bois → Khashab
Bokar Biro ii, 960b, 1132b — II, 982b, 1159b
Bokar Salif Tall iii, 108a — III, 110b
Bokhārā → Bukhārā
Bolēday Balūč s, 222a — S, 222a
Boleslav I → Čeh
Bölge i, 469b — I, 483b
Bolmats i, 755b — I, 778a
Bolōr iv, 409a — IV, 427a
Bolor Dagh → Pamir
Bolu i, **1255b**; s, 98b — I, **1293b**; S, 97b
Bölük i, 657a, 999b, **1256a,** 1278a; ii, 1098a, 1121a — I, 677b, 1030a, **1294a,** 1317a; II, 1124a, 1147a
Bölükbashî, Aḥmed Durmush s, 149b — S, 149b
Bölük-bashî, Rîdā Tewfîḳ i, **1256b**; iv, 933a; s, **149b** — I, **1294b**; IV, 966a; S, **149b**
Bolwadin i, **1256b**; s, 238b — I, **1294b**; S, 238b
Bombay City/la ville de- i, 979a, **1257a;** ii, 426a; s, 47a, 247a — I, 1009a, **1295a;** II, 437a; S, 47a, 247a
Bombay state/l'état de- i, **1257a** — I, **1295b**
Bondū → Senegal
Bône → al-ʿAnnāba
Bonneval, Comte de → Aḥmad Pasha Bonneval
Book, Bookbinding → Kitāb
Bookkeeping → Muḥāsaba
Booty → Fayʾ, Ghanīma
Bordj → Burdj
Bori ii, 278a — III, 286a
Böri Tigin → Ibrāhīm Tamghač Khān
Börk → Libās
Börklüdje Muṣṭafā i, 869b; ii, 599b — I, 893b; II, 614a
Borkov i, **1257b** — I, **1295b**
Borku s, 165a, 116a — S, 164b, 166a
Borneo/Bornéo i, 1258b; iii, 1213a, b, 1215b, 1225b; v, 309b, 539b; s, **150a** — I, 1297a; III, 1243b, 1244b, 1246a, 1257a; V, 309a, 544a; S, **150a**
Bornū i, 35a, **1259a;** iii, 276a; iv, 541a, b, 548b, 567a; v, 278b; s, 164a, b — I, 36a, **1297a;** III, 284a; IV, 564b, 565a, 572a, b, 589b; V, 276b; S, 163b, 164a
Borsippa → Birs
Börte Fudjin ii, 41b, 42a, 571a — II, 42b, 585b
Borusu i, 1290b, 1291a, b , 1330a, b, 1331a, b
Bosna i, 4a, 97a, 285a, 310a, 656b, 1018a, **1261a;** ii, 211b, 681b; v, 32a, 263b, 774a; s, 281b — I, 4b, 99b, 293b, 320a, 677a, 1049a, **1299a;** II, 218a, 698b; V, 33a, 261a, 780a; S, 281b
Bosna-sarāy → Sarajevo
Bosnia/Bosnie → Bosna
Bosphorus → Boghaz-iči
Boṣrā i, **1275b,** 1316a, b; v, 1138a, b, 1139a; s, 117a — I, **1314b,** 1356b, 1357b; V, 1132a, b, 1133a; S, 116b
Bostān Čelebī iv, 190a — IV, 198a
Bostāndjî i, **1277b**; iv, 1100b — I, **1316b**; IV, 1131a
Bostāndjî-bashî i, **1278b** — I, **1318a**
Bostānzāde (ʿulamā) i, **1279a** — I, **1318b**
Bostānzāde Meḥmed Efendi i, 1279b; iv, 884a — I, 1319a; IV, 917a
Böszörmeny v, 1015a, 1019a — V, 1010b, 1014b
Botaharī i, 575a — I, 593b
Botany/Botanique → Nabāt
Botlikh → Andī
Boṭṭīwa i, 680a — I, 701a
Bou Saada s, 134a — S, 133b
Bouazid i, 371b — I, 382b
Boucher → Djazzār
Bouclier → Turs
Bouddha → Budd
Boudhistes → Sumaniyya
Bougie → Bidjāya
Bouira → Sūḳ Ḥamza
Boumedienne, Houari iii, 564a; iv, 363a; v, 1071a — III, 583b; IV, 379a; V, 1068a
Bouquetin → Ayyil
Bourguiba, Ḥabīb ii, 470b, 639a; iii, 524a, 563b, 636b; v, 915a, 1068b, 1161a — II, 482b, 655b; III, 542a, b, 583a, 658a; V, 920b, 1066a, 1151a
Bourzey → Barzūya
Boussole → Maghnāṭīs
Bow (weapon) → Ḳaws
Bowl/Bol → Ḳadāḥ
Boy iii, 374a — III, 385b
Boyar i, 1253a, b — I, 1291a, b
Boyer Aḥmad iv, 5b — IV, 6a
Boynu-Yaralî Meḥmed Pasha v, 257a — V, 254b, 255a
Bozanti i, **1280a**; v, 257a, b — I, **1319a**; V, 255a, b
Bozdja-ada i, **1280b**; v, 257a, b — I, **1319b**; V, 255a, b
Bozo ii, 251b — II, 259a
Bozoḳ → Yozgat
Bozoḳlu Muṣṭafā Pasha i, 268a — I, 276b
Boztepe, Khalīl Nihād iii, 357b; s, 324b — III, 368b; S, 324a
Bradj-bhāshā ii, 491a, 871a; v, 644b — II, 503a, 891a; V, 648b
Brādost, Banū v, 460a — V, 462b
Brahima bi Saidu ii, 942a — II, 964a
Brahmagupta iii, 1136a — III, 1164a, b
Brahman(e)s → Barāhima
Brahōī i, 1005a, b; ii, 388a; iv, 10b, 364b; v, 102a, 684b; s, 222a — I, 1036a, b; II, 398a; IV, 11b, 380b; V, 104b, 690a; S, 222a
Brahūʾī →Brahōī
Brăila → Ibrail
Brass → Shabah
Brava → Barawa
Bread → Khubz
Brick →Labin
Bridge → Djisr; Ḳanṭara
Bridj i, 1193a — I, 1228a
Brigand → Djālālī; Fallāḳ; Ḳazaḳ; Liṣṣ; Ṭarīḳ
Brimstone → al-Kibrīt
Brique → Labin
British, Britanniques iv, 777b, 778a, 889b, 890a, b, 953b, 1056b, 1143a, 1172a; v, 102b, 251a, 574a, 580a, 1259a — IV, 809a, b, 922b, 923a, 986a, 1088a, 1174b, 1205a; V, 104b, 248b, 578b, 585a, 1250a
Broach → Bharūč
Broker → Dallāl
Broker → Dallāl, Simsār
Bronze → Ṣafr
Brousse → Bursa
Brunei s, 150a, **151b** — S, 150a, **151b**
Brusa → Bursa
Bryson → Tadbīr al-Manzil
Bryson iv, 691a — IV, 719b
Bsharrā i, **1280b** — I, **1320a**
Bteddīn i, **1281a** — I, 1320a
Bū → Kunya
Bū Alī, Banī ii, 440b — II, 452a
Bū ʿAlī Čaghānī → Abū ʿAlī Čaghānī
Bū ʿAlī Ḳalandar → Abū ʿAlī Ḳalandar
Bū ʿAmāma i, 369b, 1281b; ii, 885b — I, 380b, 1320b; II, 906a

Bū ʿAzza →Abū Yaʿazza
Bū Bakr b. Sālim, Shaykh s, 420b — S, 420b
Bū Bakr b. Shaykh, Āl s, 420b — S, 420b
Bū Dali ii, 538a — II, 551a
Bū Dhanayn, Āl s, 42a — S, 42b
Bū Falāḥ, Āl i, 1313b — I, 1353b
Bū Falāsā, Āl ii, 618b — II, 634a
Bū Ḥanak v, 531b, 532a — V, 536a
Bū Ḥasan, Āl →ʿArab, Djazīrat al-
Bū Ḥmāra i, 57b, 357a, **1281a;** ii, 620a, 820a, 1116a; iii, 62b; v, 1193a — I, 59b, 368a, **1320b;** II, 635b, 839b, 1142b; III, 65a; V, 1183a
Bū Ḳabrīn iv, 361a — IV, 376b
Bū Kamya v, 531b — V, 535b
Bū Khuraybān s, 42a — S, 42b
Bū Marwān, Sīdī s, 156a — S, 156b
Bū Muḥammad, Āl i, 431a, 1096a, b; s, 243a — I, 443a, 1129a, b; S, 243a
Bū Saʿāda s, 224a — S, 224a
Bū Saʿīd, Āl i, 539b, 554a, 1038b, **1281b**; iv, 887a, b,; V, 507b, 655b; s, 332b, 355b — I, 556a, 572a, 1070a, **1321a**; IV, 919b, 920a; V, 511a, 659b; S, 332a, 355b
Buʿāth i, **1283a**; iv, 1187b; v, 436a, 995a — I, **1322b**; IV, 1220a; V, 438b, 990b
Bubakar Sori ii, 942b — II, 964a
Bubashtru (Bobastro) s, **152b** — S, **152b**
Bučaḳ →Budjāḳ
Bučāḳčī v, 154b — V, 155b
Bucharest/Bucarest → Bükresh
Buda → Budīn
Budalāʾ i, 95a — I, 97b
Budapest → Budīn
Budayl b. Ṭahfa al-Badjalī ii, 188a, 488a — II, 194a, 500b
Budayl b. Warḳāʾ i, **1283b** — I, **1322b**
Budd i, **1283b** — I, **1323a**
Buddha → Budd
Buddhists → Sumaniyya
Buddūma iv, 540b — IV, 564a
Budha iv, 534b — IV, 557b
Budhiya → Budha
Budhan, Shaykh i, **1284a** — I, **1323b**
Būdhāsaf → Bilawhar wa-Yūdāsaf
Budīn i, 1164a, **1284b;** ii, 1133b, 1134a; iii, 998a; v, 1022a, b; s, 171a — I, 1198b, **1324a;** II, 1160b, 1161a; III, 1023a; V, 1018a, b; S, 171a
Budja → Bedja
Būdjādī i, 98a — I, 100b
Budjāḳ i, 1253b, **1286b** — I, 1291b, **1326a**
Budjatlî → Bushatlîs
Budjayr b. Aws al-Ṭāʾī s, 37b — S, 37b
Budjnūrd i, **1287a**; s, 235a — I, **1326b**; S, 234b
Budūḥ ii, 370a; s, **153a** — II, 380a; S, **153a**
Budukh → Shāh Dagh
Buduma s, 165a — S, 165a
Buffalo (Indian)/Buffle (Indien) → Djāmūs
Bugeaud, Général i, 67a, 369b; iv, 179a, 362a — I, 69a, 380a; IV, 186b, 378a
Bughā al-Kabīr i, 551a, 637a, 844a, **1287a;** ii, 1024a; iv, 345a, 1175a; v, 997a — I, 568b, 657b, 867b, **1327a;** II, 1047b; IV, 359b, 1208b; V, 992b
Bughā al-Sharābī i, **1287b;** ii, 679a, 1080a; iv, 88b, 89a; v, 488b — I, **1327a;** II, 696a, 1105a; IV, 92b, 93a; V, 491a
Bughāt iv, 771b — IV, 802b
Bughrā Khān b. Balban i, 444a; ii, 268a; iv, 818a, 920b; v, 685b; s, 124b — I, 457a; II, 276b; IV, 851a, 953b; V, 690b; S, 123b
Bughra Khān Hārūn b. Mūsā i, 987a; ii, 254a; iii, 1113b, 1114a — I, 1017b; II, 261a; III, 1141a
Bughračuḳ iv, 189b — IV, 197b
al-Bughtūri i, **1287b** — I, **1327a**
Bugi → Celebes
Buginese s, 151a — S, 151a
Bugtīs s, 332a — S, 331b
Buhār s, 292b — S, 292a
Buḥayra, Beḥera i, **1288a;** iii, 299b; iv, 134a; s, 244a, 268a — I, **1327b;** III, 309a; IV, 140a; S, 244a, 267b
al-Buhriy, Hemedi b. Abdallah s, 351b — S, 351b
al-Buḥayra al-Mayyita → Baḥr Lūṭ
al-Buḥayra al-Muntina → Baḥr Lūṭ
Buḥayrat Anṭākiyya i, 446b — I, 459b
Buḥayrat Khwarizm → Aral
Buḥayrat Māyuṭis → Baḥr Māyuṭis
Buḥayrat Nastarāwa → Burullus
Buḥayrat Yaghrā → Buḥayrat Anṭākiyya
Buhlūl i, **1288b** , **1328a**
Buhlūl, Shaykh iii, 455b — III, 471b
Buhlūl b. Rāshid i, 1289a — I, 1328b
Buhlūl Lōdi → Bahlūl Lōdī
al-Buḥturī i, 118b, 153b, 154a, 386b, 592a, **1289a;** iii, 111a, 573a, 693a; v, 935a; s, 16b, 25a, 26a, 277b — I, 122a, 158a, b, 397b, 611a, **1328b;** III, 113b, 593a, 715a; V, 938b; S, 16b, 25a, 26b, 277a
Buḥturid(e)s ii, 634b; iv, 834b — II, 650b; IV, 867b
Būḳ i, **1290b** — I, **1330a**
Būḳa i, **1292a**; s, **154a** — I, **1332a**; S, **154a**
Buḳa i, **1292a** — I, **1331b**
Buḳʿa i, 1292b; s, **154a** — I, 1332a; S, **154a**
Buḳa Temür → Tugha Temür
Būkalā i, **1292b;** iii, 290a — I, **1332a;** III, 299a
Būḳalamūn → Abū Ḳalamūn
Bukar Garbai i, 1260b; v, 359a — I, 1298b; V, 360a
Bukarest → Būkresh
al-Buḳayʿa i, **1292b**; s, 154a — I, **1332a**; S, 154a
Buḳayḳ → Abḳayḳ
Bukayr b. Māhān i, **1292b;** ii, 601a; iv, 446b, 837b; v, 2a, 3a — I, **1332b;** II, 616a; IV, 466b, 870b; V, 2a, 3a
Bukayr b. Wishāḥ i, 47b, **1293a** — I, 49a, **1332b**
Bukhār Khudāt i, 1293b, 1294a; s, 327a — I, 1333b; S, 326b
Bukhārā i, 320, 36a, 46b, 71a, 103a, 121a, 141b, 147b, 750a, 853a, **1293b;** ii, 2b, 43a, 446a, 932b, 1096a; iv, 188b, 189b, 310a; v, 28b, 541b, 853b, 856b, 858a, 859b, 966b, 1149a; s, 49a, 50b, 65a, 66a, 97a, 107a, 145a, 227b, 228a, 261a, 265a, 281a, 326b, 340a, 419b, 420a — I, 33a, 37a, 48a, 73a, 106a, 124b, 145b, 152a, 772b, 877a, **1333a;** II, 2b, 44a, 457b, 954a, 1122a; IV, 196b, 197b, 324a; V, 29a, 546a, 860b, 863b, 865a, 866b, 971a, 1140a; S, 49b, 51b, 65a, b, 66b, 96b, 106b, 145a, 227b, 228a, 260b, 264b, 281a, 326a, 339b, 419b, 420b
al-Bukhārī → Ṣalāḥ al-Dīn b. Mubārak
al-Bukhārī, Muḥammad b.ʿAbd al-Bāḳī i, **1296b** — I, **1336a**
al-Bukhārī, Muḥammad b. Ismāʿīl i, 791a, 808a, 892b, **1296b;** ii, 125b; iii, 24a, 27b, 512b, 778a, 803a, 862a, 909b, 948b; iv, 736b; s, 87b, 232b, 404b — I, 814b, 831b, 919a, **1336a;** II, 128b; III, 25b, 29a, 530a, 801b, 826b, 886a, 933b, 973a; IV, 766b; S, 87b, 232b, 404b
al-Bukhārī, Muḥammad ʿAlī Khān ii, 618a — II, 633b
Bukhārlîk i, **1297a** — I, **1337a**
Bukhl i, **1297b** — I, **1337a**
Bukht-Naṣar i, 846a, **1297b;** ii, 112b; iv, 809b — I, 869b, **1337b;** II, 115a; IV, 842a
Bukhtīshūʿ i, **1298a;** iii, 872b; iv, 649a; s, 379b — I, **1338a;** III, 896b; IV, 675b; S, 379b
Būḳīr → Abūḳīr
Bukovina/Bukovine → Khotin
Buḳrāṭ ii, 402b; iii, 897b; iv, 406b; s, **154b** — II, 413a; III, 921b; IV, 424a; S, **154b**

Bükresh i, 1298b — I, 1338b
Buķūm i, **1299a** — I, **1339a**
Būlāķ i, **1299b;** ii, 167a; iv, 425a, 442a, b — I, **1339a;** II, 172b; IV, 443b, 462a
Būlala iv, 541a; s, 164a — IV, 564b; S, 163b
Bulandshahr i, **1299b** — I, **1339b**
Būlātmūriyān iv, 860a — IV, 893b
Bulāy i, **1300b** — I, **1340a**
Bulayda i, **1300b** — I, **1340b**
Bulayday Maliki s, 332a — S, 331b
al-Bulayṭī → al-Balaṭī
Bulbul i, **1301a;** ii, 1133a — I, **1340b;** II, 1160a
Bulbul Shāh iv, 708a; s, **156a** — IV, 736b; S, **156a**
al-Buldadjī iii, 163b — III, 167a
Buldur → Burdur
Bulgaria/Bulgarie i, 394a, **1302a;** ii, 610b, 611a; v, 534a, 1014b — I, 405b, **1342a;** II, 625b, 626a; V, 538a, 1010a
Bulghar i, 998b, 1000a, 1075b, 1105a, **1304b;** ii, 21a, 69b, 202b, 853b, 1107b; iii, 759a; iv, 280a, 648b, 1173a; v, 1011a — I, 1029a, 1031a, 1107b, 1138b, **1344b;** II, 21a, 71a, 209a, 873a, 1133b; III, 782a; IV, 292b, 675a, 1206a; V, 1007a
Bulghār-dagh → Toros
al-Bulghārī → Sharaf al-Dīn Husām al-Dīn; Yaʿķūb b. Nuʿmān.
Bulghār-maʿden → Toros
Bulgur → Burghul
Bulkiah I, Sultan of/de Brunei s, 152a — S, 152a
Bulkiah, Sultan Sir Hassanal s, 152b — S, 152b
al-Bulķīnī, ʿAbd al-Raḥmān b. ʿUmar i, 138a, **1308b;** iii, 777b — I, 142a, **1349a;** III, 800b
al-Bulķīnī, Muḥammad b. Muḥammad i, **1309a** — I, **1349a**
al-Bulķīnī, Ṣāliḥ b. ʿUmar i, **1308b** — I, **1349a**
al-Bulķīnī, Siradj al-Dīn ʿUmar i, **1308b;** iii, 699a — I, **1348b;** III, 721a
Bullū s, 148a — S, 148a
Buluggīn b. Bādīs b. Ḥabūs b. Zīrī i, 491b — I, 506a
Buluggin b. Muḥammad iii, 137b — III, 140a
Buluggīn b. Zīrī i, 699b, 824a, 1044b, 1088a, **1309a;** ii, 520a, 821b, 854a; iii, 1036b, 1043a; v, 1010b, 1176a, b, 1177a — I, 720b, 847a, 1076a, 1120b, **1349a;** II, 533a, 841a, 874a; III, 1062b, 1068b; V, 1006a, 1166a, b, 1167a
Bulūgh → Bāligh
Būlūghān, amīr iv, 1047a — IV, 1078b
Buluķķīn → Banya
Buluwādīn → Bolwadin
Būna → al-ʿAnnāba
Bunān b. ʿAmr al-Ḍārib s, 284b — S, 284b
Bundahishn iv, 11a, 12a — IV, 12a, 13a
Bundār al-Iṣbahānī → Ibn Lizza
al-Bundārī i, 523a, **1309b;** iii, 918b; iii, 1158a — I, 538b, **1349b;** II, 940a; III, 1186b
Bunduķ, bunduķiyya i, 1059b; ii, 964b — I, 1091b; II, 986b
Bunduķdār → Baybars
Bunduķī → Sikka
al-Būnī, Abu 'l-Abbās ii, 376a; iii, 596a; iv, 1134a; v, 222b; s, 153a, **156a** — II, 386b; iii, 616b; IV, 1165b; V, 220a; S, 153a, **156b**
Bunīča ii, 151a, b — II, 155b, 156a
Bunn → Ķahwa
Buñsuz Ķarāmān-oghlu iv, 619b, 620a — IV, 644a
al-Bunt i, **1309b** — I, **1350a**
Bunyād-i Pahlavī iv, 41b — IV, 44a
Bunyāt i, 1294a — I, 1333b
Būr → Baʿl
Bura i, 1259b — I, 1297b
al-Burādiʿīm ʿAlī iii, 162a — III, 165b
al-Burāķ i, **1310a;** ii, 71a, 108a, 785b — I, **1350a;** II, 72a, 110a, 804b
al-Burāķ b. ʿAbd Allāh iii, 887a, b — III, 911a, b
Burāķ Ḥādjib i, **1311a;** ii, 393a; iv, 32a, 583b; v, 161b, 553a — I, **1351b;** II, 403b; IV, 34b, 607a; V, 159b, 558a
Burāķ Khān (Čaghatay) i, **1311b;** ii, 1b, 3b, 45a, 791b; iv, 811b; v, 39a — I, **1352a;** II, 1b, 3b, 46a, 810b; IV, 844b; V, 40a
Burāķ Khān i, 1076b — I, 1108b
Burāķ Reʾīs iv, 882a — IV, 914b
al-Burak al-Ṣarīmī (Ṣuraymī) s, **157a** — S, **157a**
Būrān i, 897b, **1312a;** ii, 731b; iii, 243b, 345b — I, 924a, b, **1352b;** II, 750a; III, 250b, 356a
Būrāniyya → Baķliyya
Burayda i, 873a, **1312b;** iv, 717a — I, 897b, **1352b;** IV, 746a
Burayda b. al-Ḥuṣayb i, **1313a;** v, 78b — I, **1353b;** V, 80b
Burayka ii, 454b — II, 466b
al-Buraymī i, 539b, **1313b;** s, 42a, 417b — I, 556b, **1353b;** S, 42b, 417b
Burd, Banū → Ibn Burd
Burda i, **1314b;** iii, 1232a; iv, 316a, 940a; v, 6b, 734a; s, 159a — I, **1354b;** III, 1264a; IV, 330b, 973a; V, 6b, 739b; S, 159a
Burdj i, 248b, **1315a;** iii, 475a — I, 256b, **1355a;** III, 491b
Burdj → Nudjūm
Burdj al-ruʾūs ii, 461a — II, 473a
Burdjā → Birdjās
al-Burdjamī i, 900b; ii, 962a — I, 927b; II, 984a
Burdjan i, 1305a — I, 1345a
Burdjīs → Mamlūks
Burdjiyya i, 1050b, **1324b;** iv, 486a — I, 1082a, **1365a;** IV, 507a
al-Burdjumī → al-Burdjamī
Burdur i, **1325a** — I, **1366a**
Burdwān s, 366b — S, 366a
Bure → Khirķa; Ṣūf
Burgas i, **1325b** — I, **1366b**
Burghaz, Būrghūs → Lüleburgaz
al-Burghāzī, Yaḥyā i, 323b, 324b; ii, 968a — I, 333a, 334b; II, 990a
Burghū i, 1291a — I, 1331a
Burghul ii, 1067a — II, 1091b
Burghush i, **1326a** — I, **1366b**
Burghūth → Muḥammad b. ʿĪsā
Burghūth (fleas/puces) iv, 522a — IV, 544b
Burghūthiyya i, **1326a** — **I, 1367a**
Burgos → Burghush
Burhāmiyya i, 281a — I, 289b
al-Burhān i, **1326b;** iii, 543b — I, **1367a;** III, 562b
Burhān i, 1056b, **1327b;** iv, 526a — I, 1088b, **1368a;** IV, 549a
Burhān, Āl-i i, 1295a, **1327b;** iii, 1115a; v, 858a — I, 1334b, **1368a;** III, 1142a; V, 865a
Burhān anna ii, 101b, 102a — II, 104a, b
Burhān al-Dīn, Ķāḍī Aḥmad i, 311b, 432a, 1117b, 1118a, **1327b;** ii, 706a; iv, 623a, 843a, 871a; s, 324a — I, 321a, 444a, 1151b, 1152a, **1368a;** II, 724a; IV, 647b, 876a, 904b; S, 323b
Burhān al-Dīn Gharīb, Mawlānā i, **1328b,** 1331a; ii, 48a, 51b, 55a, b, 816a; s, 352b — I, **1369b,** 1371b; II, 49a, 52b, 56a, b, 835b; S, 352b
Burhān al-Dīn Ķuṭb-i ʿĀlam i, **1329b;** ii, 1125b — I, **1370a;** II, 1153a
Burhān al-Din al-Marghīnānī → al-Marghīnānī
Burhān al-Dīn Muḥaķķiķ ii, 393b — II, 404a
Burhān al-Dīn Naṣr i, 283a — I, 292a
Burhān ʿImād Shāh iii, 425a, 1161a — III, 439a, 1189b
Burhān limā ii, 101b, 102a — II, 104a, b

Burhān al-Mulk i, 757a, **1330a;** ii, 870a; iv, 666a; v, 635a; s, 325b — I, 779b, **1370b;** II, 890a; IV, 693a; V, 639a; S, 325a
Burhān Nizām Shāh I i, 914b, 1069a; iii, 425b, 426a, 1160a, b — I, 942a, 1101a; III, 439b, 1188b, 1189a
Burhān Nizām Shāh II ii, 815a, 921b; iii, 426b — II, 834b, 943a; III, 440b
Burhāniyya ii, 166a — II, 171b
Burhānpūr i, **1330b;** ii, 816a; iii, 446b — I, **1371b;** II, 835b; III, 461b
al-Būrī s, 390b — S, 391a
Būrī → Tādj al-Mulūk
Būrī Takīn → Ibrāhīm Tamghač Khān
Buribars i, 662a, **1331b** — I, 683a, **1372b**
Būrid(e)s i, 216a, **1332a;** ii, 282a — I, 222b, **1372b;** II, 290a
al-Būrīnī, al-Ḥasan i, **1333a** — I, **1373b**
al-Burḳān i, 536b; s, 50a — I, 553a; S, 50b
Burke Sulṭān i, 135a — I, 139a
Bürklüdje Muṣṭafā → Dede Sulṭān
al-Burḳuʿ iv, 317b — IV, 331b
Burḳuʿ, Ḳaṣr s, **157a** — S, **157b**
Burma i, 606a, **1333a**
Burnous → Libās
Būrrūdh (river/rivière) s, 356b — S, 356a
Burnus i, 1037a, 1349b — I, 1068b, 1390a
Bursa i, 4a, 298a, 1225b, **1333b;** ii, 746b; iii, 210b, 211b, 212b, 214a, 215a, 216a; iv, 574a, 1159b; v, 32b, 651a; s, 170a, 282b — I, 4a, 307b, 1262a, **1374a;** II, 765a; III, 216b, 217b, 218b, 220a, 221a, 222a; IV, 597a, 1191b; V, 33b, 655a; S, 170b, 282b
Bursalî → Aḥmad Pasha
Bursalî, Djelīlī Ḥamid-zāde v, 1105b — V, 1101b
Bursalî Ṭāhir ii, 980b; iv, 284b — II, 1003a; IV, 296b
Bursiyya i, 1236a — I, 1273b
Bursuḳ i, 1052b, **1336a** — I, 1084a, **1376b**
Bursuḳ b. Bursuḳ i, 1336b, 1337a; iii, 1118b; v, 924b — I, 1377a; III, 1146a; V, 930a
al-Bursukī → Aḳ Sunḳur
al-Burt i, **1337a** — I, **1377b**
Burtās/Burdās i, 1305b, **1337b;** ii, 69b, 817a — I, 1345b, **1378a;** II, 71a, 836b
Burtuḳāl i, 58b, **1338b** — I, 60b, **1378b**
al-Burūdj → Nudjūm
Burūdjird → Barūdjird
Burūdjirdī, Ḥusayn Ṭabāṭabāʾī, Āyat Allāh iv, 165b; s, 104a, **157b** — IV, 172b; S, 103a, **157b**
Burūdjirdī, Shaykh Asad Allāh s, 75a — S, 75b
Buruḳlus i, 234b, **1339b;** ii, 765a, 929b; iii, 1129b; iv, 129b — I, 241b, **1380a;** II, 783b, 951b; III, 1158a; IV, 135b
Burullus i, **1340b** — I, **1381a**
Burundjîḳ s, 168b — S, 169a
Burushaski s, **158b** — S, **158b**
Burūsho s, 158b — S, 158b
Burzōē i, 1359a; iv, 503a, b — I, 1399a; IV, 525a, b
al-Burzulī, Abu ʾl-Ḳāsim i, **1341a** — I, **1381a**
Busard, Buse → Bayzara
Busayra → Ḳarḳīsiyā
Būshahr i, 928a, 1013b, **1341a;** iii, 1191a; iv, 851a — I, 956b, 1044b, **1381b;** III, 1221a; IV, 884a
Bushḥāḳ i, **1342a;** iii, 355b; iv, 66a; s, 415b — I, **1382b;** III, 366b; IV, 69b; S, 416a
Būshandj i, **1342b**; iv, 1073a — I, **1382b**; IV, 1105a
al-Bushārrāt i, **1343a** — I, **1383a**
Bushatlîs i, 653a, 657a; iv, 588a; v, 276b, 775a — I, 673b, 677b; IV, 612a; V, 274b, 781a
Būshīr → Būshahr
Būṣīr i, **1343a;** iii, 961b — I, **1383b;** III, 986a
Bushra iv, 459b — IV, 480a
al-Bushrawī, ʿAbd Allāh b. al-Ḥādjdj Muḥammad al-Tūnī s, 57a — S, 57b
Būṣīr iv, 774a; s, 159a — IV, 805a; S, 158b
al-Būṣīrī, Sharaf al-Dīn i, 595b, 821b, 1011b, 1070b, 1314b; iii, 720b; iv, 316a, 1134a; v, 958b; s, **158b**, 404b — I, 615a, 844b, 1042b, 1102b, 1354b; III, 743a; IV, 330b, 1165b; V, 962b; S, **158b**, 404b
Busr b. Abī Arṭāt i, 109a, 695b, **1343b;** ii, 481a; iii, 782a; v, 532b, 533a; s, 230b — I, 111b, 717a, **1384a;** II, 493a; III, 805b; V, 536b, 537a; S, 230b
Busr al-Ḥarīrī v, 593b — V, 597a
Buṣrā → Boṣrā
Bust i, **1344a;** ii, 1054a, 1100b; v, 230a, 690b, 691a — I, **1384a;** II, 1078b, 1126b; V, 228a, 695b, 696a
Bustān i, **1345b;** ii, 908b, 1019a; v, 888b — I, **1385b;** II, 929b, 1042b; V, 895a
Bustān Efendiʾ ii, 880b — II, 900b
al-Bustānī, Āl s, **159a** — S, **159a**
al-Bustānī, ʿAbd Allāh s, **159b** — S, **159b**
al-Bustānī, Buṭrus b. Būlus i, 596b; ii, 428b, 467a; iv, 525a; v, 794b; s, **159b** — I, 616a; II, 440a, 479a; IV, 547b; V, 800b; S, **159b**
al-Bustānī, Buṭrus b. Sulaymān s, **160a** — S, **160a**
al-Bustanī, Karam s, **160b** — S, **160b**
al-Bustānī, Saʿīd v, 188a — V, 185b
al-Bustānī, Salīm b. Buṭrus v, 188a; s, 160a, **161a** — V, 185a; S, 160a, **160b**
al-Bustānī, Sulaymān b. Khaṭṭār i, 597b; iii, 112a; s, **161b** — I, 617a; III, 114b; S, **161a**
al-Bustānī, Wadīʿ s, **162a** — S, **162a**
al-Bustānī, Yūsuf s, 159b — S, 159b
al-Bustānī b. Salīm s, **160b** — S, **160b**
al-Bustī, Abu 'l-Fatḥ i, **1348b**; iv, 61a — I, **1388b**; IV, 64b
al-Bustī, Abū Ḥātim v, 1126b — V, 1122b
But → Budd
Buṭāna iv, 686a, b — IV, 714a, b
Buṭayn → Nudjūm
Butin → Fayʾ; Ghanīma
al-Buṭlān ii, 829b, 836b — II, 849a, b, 856a
Buṭnān i, **1348b,** 1357b — I, **1389a,** 1398a
al-Butr i, **1349b** — I, **1389b**
Butriyya → Abtariyya
Buṭrus Karāma s, **162b** — S, **162b**
Buṭrus al-Tūlawī ii, 795a — II, 814a
al-Buwayb iv, 386a — IV, 403a
Buwayhid(e)s i, 19a, 20a, 131b, 211b, 434a, 439b, 512b, 551b, 696a, 866b, 899b, 1045b, 1073b, **1350a;** ii, 144a, 178b, 192b, 214b, 326a, 487a, 506a, 748b, 1050b; iii, 46b, 159a, 1201b, 1255b; iv, 18a, 19a, 23a, b, 46b, 100b, 208b, 221b, 266a, 293b; v, 621b, 622a, 824a; s, 12b, 23a, 56b, 118a, b, 119a, b, 192a, 267b, 363a — I, 20a, 21a, 135b, 217b, 446a, 452a, 528a, 569a, 717a, 891a, 926b, 1077b, 1105b, **1390a;** II, 148a, 184a, 198b, 221a, 335b, 499a, 518b, 767a, 1075a; III, 48b, 162b, 1232a, 1288a; IV, 19a-b, 20b, 25a, 49b, 104b, 217b, 231a, 278a, 307a; V, 626a, 830a; S, 13a, 23b, 57a, 117b, 118a, b, 193a, 267a, 363a
Buwayr Aḥmadī iii, 1107a — III, 1134a
Buxar i, **1357b** — I, **1397b**
Būyids → Buwayhid(e)s
Büyük Millet Medjlisi i, 734b; ii, 644a — I, 756a; II, 660b
Büyük Nutuk ii, 595b — II, 610b
Büyük Sulaymān Pasha → Sulaymān Pasha Büyük
Buyuruldu i, **1357b** — I, **1397b**
Buyūtāt ii, 335a — II, 345a
Buzāʿā i, 1349a, **1357b** — I, 1389b, **1398a**
Būz-Abeh i, **1358a**; iv, 498a — I, **1398a**; IV, 519b
Būzači (Boz Ḥādjî) s, 168b, 169a — S, 169a
Buzākha i, **1358b** — I, **1398b**
Būzān i, 1336b — I, 1376b
Buzan ii, 4a — II, 4a
Būzār → Ūzār

al-Būzdjānī → Abu 'l-Wafā'
Buzghāla Khāna ii, 116a — II, 118b
al-Būzīdī, Muḥammad iii, 696b, 697a, 700b — III, 718b, 719a, 723a
Buzurg/Khwādja s, 98a — S, 97b
Buzurg b. Shahriyār i, 203b, 204a, 570b, **1358b;** ii, 583b — I, 209b, 210a, 589a, **1398b;** II, 598a
Buzurgmihr i, **1358b**; iv, 53b, 503a, b — I, **1399a**; IV, 56b, 525a, b
Buzurg-ummīd, Kiya i, 353b, **1359b**; v, 656b — I, 364a, **1399b**; V, 660b
Buzyūn i, 645b; ii, 681a — I, 666a; II, 698a
Buzzard → Bayzara
Bwākher ii, 116b, 510b, 511a — II, 119b, 523a, b
Byblos → Djubayl
Byzantin(e)s i, 18a, 54b, 76b, 77a, 121b, 182b, 346a, 420b, 465b, 517a, 637b, 679b, 789b, 1128a, 1319a; ii, 14a, 345a, 347b, 456a, 712a, 853a, 855a; iii, 77a, 128b, 129b, 233b, 271a, 1083b; v, 124b — I, 18b, 56b, 78b, 79b, 125a, 187b, 356b, 432a, b, 479a, 532b, 658b, 700b, 813a, 1162b, 1359b; II, 14a, 354b, 357a, 468a, 730b, 873a, 875a; III, 79b, 131a, 132a, 240b, 279a, 1110b; V, 127a
Byzantion → Istanbul
Byzantium → Rūm
Bžedukh → Čerkes

C

Čaʿb → Kaʿb
Cabra → Ḳabra
Čāč s, 117b — S, 117a
Čač, Rāy iv, 364a, 534b — IV, 380a, 558a
Cachemire → Kashmīr
Cachet → Khātam
Čāčī, Badr al-Dīn Muḥammad → Badr-i Čāčī
Čač-nāma iii, 459a; s, **162a** — III, 475a; S, **162a**
Čad, Chad iv, 540a, b, 566b, s, **163b**, 218a — IV, 563b, 564a, 589a, S, **163b**, 217b
Cadeau → Ḥiba
Cádiz/Cadix → Ḳādis
Cadran solaire → Ṭawḳīt
Čādur v, 749b, 750a — V, 755a, 756a
Caesar/César → Ḳayṣar
Caesarea → Ḳaysariyya, Kayseri, Sharshal
Caffa → Kefe
Café → Ḳahwa
Čaghal-oghlu → Čighālazade Sinān Pasha
Čaghāniyān ii, **1a**; s, 50b, 386b — II, **1a**; S, 51b, 387a
Čaghān-khudāt ii, 1a — II, 1a
Čaghān-rūd ii, **2a** — II, **2a**
Čaghatāy Khān i, 418b, 1105b; ii, **2a**, 3a, 43a, 44a, 269a, 571b; iii, 198a, 1120a; iv, 584a — I, 430b, 1139a; II, **2a**, 3a, 44a, 45a, 277a, 586a; III, 203a, 1148a; IV, 607b
Čaghatay Khānate/Khānat de- i, 120b, 1295b, 1311b; ii, **3a**, 45b; iii, 1100a; iv, 274a, 587a; v, 858a, b; s, 96b, 98a, 227b, 240a, 246a — I, 124a, 1335a, 1352a; II, **3a**, 46b; III, 1127b; IV, 272a, 609b; V, 865a, b; S, 96a, 97a, 227b, 240a, 246a
- literature/littérature i, 813b; ii, 792a; iii, 317a; iv, 527a; v, 836a, 859b; s, 46a, b — I, 836b; II, 811a; III, 327a; IV, 550a; V, 842b, 866b; S, 46b
Čaghmīnī → al-Djaghmīnī
Čaghrī Beg Dā'ūd i, 662a, 1159a; ii, **4a**, 1108b; iii, 1114a; iv, 25a, 26b, 347b; v, 58a; s, 195a — I, 682b, 1193b; II, **4a**, 1134b; III, 1141b; IV, 26b, 28b, 362a; V, 60a; S, 195a
Čahār Aymāḳ i, 224b; ii, **5b** — I, 231a; II, **5b**
Čahār Bāgh s, 275a — S, 275a
Čahār darwīsh iii, 376a — III, 388a
Čahār-Lang i, 955b; iii, 1105a, b; v, 822b — I, 985a; III, 1132b; V, 828b
Čahār Maḥall iv, 98a, b; s, 147b — IV, 102a, b; S, 147b
Čahār Maḳāla → Niẓāmī ʿArūḍī Samarḳandī
Čahār martaba-i-ikhlās i, 117b — I, 121a
Čāhbār i, 1282a, 1283a — I, 1321a, b
Caïd → Ḳā'id
Čā'ildā, Shaykh s, 73b — S, 74a
Caïn → Hābīl wa Ḳābīl
Cairo/le Caire → al-Ḳāhira
Čaka (Tzachas) i, 466a; ii, 686b — I, 480a; II, 704a
Čaḳa b. Noghay i, 1302b; ii, 610b — I, 1342a; II, 625b
Čakarsaz i, 424b — I, 436b
Čakïrdjï-bashï ii, **6a**, 614b — II, **6a**, 629b
Čak(k) iii, 420a; iv, 709a; s, 131b, **167a**, 324b, 354a, 423b — III, 433b; IV, 737a, b; S, 131a, **167a**, 324a, 353b, 424a
Čak, Tādjī s, 423b — S, 424a
Čaka (Tzachas) v, 505a; s, 168b — V, 508b; S, 168b
Čākana iv, 177b — IV, 186a
Čakāwa Mandāta s, 325a — S, 324b
Čaḳmaḳ i, 138b, 281a, 1032b; ii, **6a**, 239b, 598b; iii, 187a, 1198a — I, 142b, 289b, 1064a; II, **6a**, 246b, 613b; III, 191b, 1228b
Čakmak Kavaklï ii, **6b**; iii, 527a — II, **6b**; III, 545a
Čakradeva s, 242a — S, 242a
Čākur, Mir i, 1005b — I, 1036b
Čala → Bukhārā
Calabash → Kashkūl
Calabria/Calabre → Ḳillawriya
Calame → Ḳalam (pen/plume)
Calatayud → Ḳalʿat Ayyūb
Calatrava → Ḳalʿat Rabāḥ
Calcul → Ḥisāb
Calcutta i, 979a; ii, **7a**, 426a; v, 201b; s, 106a, 247a — I, 1009a; II, **7a**, 437a; V, 199a; S, 105b, 247b
Čāldirān i, 1030b, 1066b; ii, **7b**; iv, 35a, 186b; v, 35a, 457a — I, 1062a, 1098b; II, **7b**; IV, 37b, 195a; V, 36a, 460a
Calebasse → Kashkūl
Calendar/Calendrier → Anwā', Ta'rīkh
Čalï Bey i, 947b — I, 976b
Calicut → Kalikat
Caliph/Calife → Khalīfa
Caliz → Khalisioi
Call to prayer → Adhān
Calligraphy/Calligraphie → Khaṭṭ
Calomnie → Ḳadhf
Čam ii, **8b**; iii, 1209a — II, **8b**; III, 1239b
Čamalal i, 504a — I, 519b
Cambay → Khambāyat
Cambodia/Cambodge → Khmer
Camel → al-Djamal; Ībil
Camel, Battle of the - → al-Djamal
Camel-driver → Djammāl
Caméléon → Ḥirbā'
Cameroon s, 218a — S, 218a
Cameroons/Cameroun ii, **9a** — II, **9a**
Camieniec → Kaminča
Čamishgezek v, 459a — V, 462a
Čamlïbel, Fārūḳ Nāfidh s, **167b**, 324b — S, **167b**, 324a
Camomil(l)e → Bābūnadj
Camondo, Avram s, **168a** — S, **168a**
Čampa v, 227a — V, 225a
Čāmpānēr ii, **10b**, 1127a; iii, 445b, 482a, 575b; v, 1216b — II, **11a**, 1153b; III, 460b, 498b, 595b; V, 1206b
Camphor/camphre → Kāfūr

Campiña → Kanbāniya
Č'an v, 713b, 714a – V, 719a
Čanaḳ-ḳal'e Boghazî i, 4b, 1252a; ii, **11a**, 209a; iv, 628b, 884b, 1169b; v, 259a – I, 4b, 1290a; II, **11b**, 215b; IV, 653b, 917b, 1202b; V, 257a
Čanaḳ Ḳal'esi ii, 11b – II, 11b
Canal → Ḳanāt; Mā'; Nahr
Canary Islands/Canaries, Iles → al-Djazā'ir al-Khālidāt
Cancer → Minṭaḳat al-Burūdj
Čandā Ṣāḥib → Ḥusayn Dūst Khān
Čandahār s, 332a – S, 332a
Čandarlî → Djandarlî
Čandar-oghlu → Isfendiyār-oghlu
Čānd-Bībī i, 81a, 303a, 1202b; iii, 15b, 426b, 626a – I, 83b, 312b, 1238a; III, 16a, 440b, 647a
Čandērī ii, **12b;** iii, 446a; v, 644b; s, 331b – II, **12b;** III, 461a; V, 648b; S, 331a
Candia/Candie → Ḳandiya; al-Khandaḳ
Candlesticks v, 987a
Čandrā Sēn i, 1300a – I, 1339b
Čandragiri iii, 148b – III, 152a
Cane (port) s, 337a – S, 336b
Canea → Ḥanya
Čanēsar, Malik Sinān al-Dīn iii, 1155b – III, 1183b
Canestrine → Ḳinnasrīn
Čanga Shāh v, 1113a, b – V, 1109b
Čangshi ii, 4a – II, 4a
Canik → Djānīk
Čankîrî ii, **13a**; v, 248a, 257a – II, **13b**; V, 245b, 254b
Cannabis → Hashīsh
Cannanore → Kannanur
Canne à sucre → Ḳaṣab al-sukkar
Cannelle → Dār Ṣīnī
Čannēy Khān ii, 185a – II, 191a
Cantemir → Ḳantimūr
Canton → Khānfū
Čao i, 903a; ii, **14a**, 982a; iv, 31a – I, 930a; **14b**, 1004b; IV, 33b
Capacity/Capacité → Istiṣā'a
Capacity, Measures of-/Capacité, Mesures de- → Makāyīl
Čapakčur → Bingöl
Čapan-oghlu → Derebey
Čapanoghlu Aḥmad → Aḥmad Pasha
Čapanoghlu Djalāl al-Dīn Pasha iii, 88b – III, 90b
Čapanoghullarî i, 469a; ii, 206b, 207a; iv, 843b – I, 483a; II, 213b; IV, 876b
Čapanzāde Agāh Efendi ii, 207b, 466a – II, 214a, 478a
Čapar ii, 3b, **14b**, 45b; s, 240a – II, 3b, **14b**, 46b; S, 240a
Čaparoghullarî → Derebey; Supplement/Supplément
Capitulations → Imtiyāzāt
Cappadocia/Cappadoce i, 12b; ii, 34b – I, 13a; II, 35b
Capsa → Ḳafsa
Caracul → Karakay
Čaras v, 885, 888b – V, 891b, 894b
Čarat Singh Djāt ii, 1131a – II, 1157b
Caravan/Caravane → Azalay; Kārwān
Caravanserai/Caravansérail → Funduḳ
Carcastillo → Ḳarḳastal
Čardaḳ ii, 61b – II, 63a
Čārdjūy → Āmul
Čārī (river/rivière) s, 327a – S, 326b
Čarkh v, 884b, 885a – V, 891a
Carlowicz → Ḳarlofča
Carmathians → Ḳarmaṭī
Carmona → Ḳarmūna
Carnatic → Karnatak
Carpenitze → Kerbenesh
Carpet → Bisāṭ; Ḳālī
Carré magique → Wafḳ
Čarshî iv, 227a, b, 228b – IV, 237a, b, 238b
Cart → Araba
Carthage/Carthagène → Ḳartadjanna
Carte, cartographie → Kharīṭa
Casablanca → Dār al-Bayḍā'; Anfā
Casbah → Ḳaṣaba (town/ville)
Casena → Katsina
Čāshna-gīr ii, **15a** – II, **15a**
Čashnagīr-bashî ii, **15a** – II, **15a**
Caspian Sea/Caspienne, mer → Baḥr al-Khazar
Castamina, Castemol → Ḳasṭamūnī
Castilla → Ḳasṭīliya
Castille → Ḳashtāla
Castillo del Hierro → Firrīsh
Castle → al-Ḳal'a; Ḳaṣr
Castriota, Georges → Iskender Beg
Castro Giovanni → Ḳaṣryānnih
Cat → Sinawr
Cata → Ḳaṭā
Čatāldja ii, **15b** – II, **15b**
Catania/Catane → Ṣiḳilliya
Categories/Catégories → Maḳūlāt
Čātgām → Chittagong
Čatr iii, 1115a – III, 1142b
Cattle → Baḳar
Caucasus/Caucase → Ḳabḳ
Cause → 'Illa
Čā'ūsh ii, **16a** – II, **16a**
Ča'ushbashî i, 625a; ii, 16a – I, 646a; II, 16b
Caution → Ḳabāla
Cavalier → Fāris; Furūsiyya
Cavalle → Ḳawāla
Čāwdor (Čawdîr) ii, 16a; s, 143b, **168b** – II, 16b; S, 143a, **168b**
Čawgān ii, **16b**, 954a, 1035b; v, 688a – II, **16b**, 976a, 1059b; V, 693a
Čawhān i, 256a; ii, 1122b; iii, 168a, 225a; iv, 1023a – I, 263a; II, 1148b; III, 171b, 232a; IV, 1055a
Čawlī → Fakhr al-Dawla; Mubāriz al-Dīn
Cawnpore → Kānpur
Čawth iii, 320a – III, 330b
Čawundur → Čawdor
Čay ii, **17b**, 904b; v, 1145b – II, **17b**, 925b; V, 1137a
Čāy-khāna s, **169a** – S, **169b**
Čaylak Tewfīḳ s, **170a** – S, **170b**
Cayor ii, 567b – II, 582a
Čeboksarî iv, 280b – IV, 293a
Čečens ii, **18a;** iii, 1235b, 1236a; iv, 351a – II, **18a;** III, 1267b, 1268a; IV, 366b
Cedar-oil → Ḳaṭrān
Cédréléon → Ḳaṭrān
Čegrei i, 1190a – I, 1225a
Čeh s, **170b** – S, **170b**
Čeke → Čaḳa
Celal Nuri Ileri → Ileri, Djelāl Nūrī
Celebes/Célèbes ii, 19a; iii, 1213a, 1214b, 1219b, 1220a, 1226a; s, 151a – II, 19a; III, 1243b, 1244a, 1245a, 1250b, 1251a, 1257a; S, 151a
Čelebī ii, **19a**, 394b – II, **19a**, 405a
Čelebi Efendi → Djalāl al-Din Rūmī; Muḥammad b. Aḥmad Ṭāhāzāde
Čelebi-zāde Ismā'īl 'Āṣim i, **19b**, 1076a – II, **20a**, 1101a
Čelebi zāde Efendi → Sa'īd Efendi
Celibacy, voluntary/Célibat volontaire → Tabattul
Čeltükdji → Kürekčis
Cemalettin Mahir → Kemal Tahir
Cemetery → Maḳbara
Čenāb s, 241b, 242a – S, 241b, 242a

Cenap Şehabettin → Djanāb Shihāb al-Dīn
Čendereli → Djandarlî
Čepni ii, **20b** — II, **20b**
Ceramics/Céramique → Fakhkhār; Khazaf
Cercina, Cercinitis → Ḳarḳana
Cereals/Céréales → Ḳamḥ
Čeremiss/Čeremisses ii, **20b** — II, **21a**
Cerigo → Čoka Adasî
Čerkes/Cerkesses i, 32b, 64b, 470b, 732b, 1000a, 1050b, 1189b; ii, **21a,** 172b, 458a, 781b; iii, 316a; iv, 345b, 350a, 351a, 569a, 597a; v, 139a, 288a — I, 33b, 66b, 484b, 754b, 1031a, 1082a, 1224b; II, **22a,** 177b, 470a, 800a; III, 325b; IV, 360a, 365a, 366a, 591b, 621a; V, 141b, 286a, b
Čerkes Edhem ii, **25b** — II, **21b**
Čerkes Ismāʿīl Pasha ii, 878b — II, 899a
Čerkes Meḥmed Pasha → Muḥammad Pasha Čerkes
Čerkes Meḥmed Tewfik ii, 25b, 26a — II, 21b
Čerkes Reshīd ii, 25b, 26a — II, 21b
Čerleshiyya iv, 991b — IV, 1024a
César → Ḳayṣar
Césarée → Ḳaysariyya, Ḳayseri, Sharshal
Česhme ii, **26a** — II, **26b**
Česhmī Meḥmed Efendi ii, 26b — II, 26b
Česhmīzāde, Muṣṭafā ii, **26b** — II, **26b**
Ceuta → Sabta
Cevat Rifat Atilhan s, 296b — S, 296b
Cevat Şakir Kabaağaçli → Haliḳarnas Balîḳčîsî
Ceylon/Ceylan i, 177b; ii, **26b,** 577a; v, 297a — I, 182b; II, **27a,** 591b; V, 296b
Čeyrek ii, **28b** — II, **28b**
Chaanba s, 328b — S, 328a
Chacal → Ibn Āwā
Chach → Čač
Chad →Čad
al-Chādirchī, Kāmil iv, 125a — IV, 130b
Chah → Shāh
Chair → Kursī
Chaire → Minbar
Cham → Čam; Ḥam
Chamanisme IV, 1207a
Chamba → Djāba
Chamberlain/Chambellan → Ḥādjib
Chameau → al-Djamal; Ībil
Chameau, bataille du - → al-Djamal
Chameleon → Ḥirbāʾ
Chamelier → Djammāl
Chamito-Sémitique → Ḥām et Sām
Champa → Ṣanf
Chamyl → Shāmil
Chandax → al-Khandaḳ
Chandeliers v, 982b
Chant → Ghināʾ
Chanteur, chanteuse → ʿĀlima; Ḳayna; Ghināʾ, Mughannī
Chanvre indien → Ḥashīsh
Charbon → Faḥm
Chariot, Charrette → ʿAraba
Charisma/Charisme → Baraka
Charity, Charité → Khayr
Charlemagne s, 82a — S, 81b
Charles V (Spain/Espagne) i, 1023b; ii, 520b; iii, 94b; iv, 1157a — I, 1055a; II, 533b; III, 97a; IV, 1189a
Charles XII (Sweden/Suède) i, 268b, 269a, 270b, 394b; ii, 204a, 291b; v, 263a — I, 277a, 279a, 406a; II, 210a, 299b; V, 260b
Charrue → Filāḥa; Miḥrāth
Chasse → Bayzara; Fahd; Kanṣ; Sayd; Ṭard
Chat → Sinawr
Čhat ii, **28b,** 29a — II, **29a,** b
Čhat-Banūrī (Čhatrāwdī) ii, 28b — II, 29a
Château → al-Ḳalʿa; Ḳaṣr
Châtiment → ʿAdhāb al-Ḳabr; Barzakh; ʿIḳāb; Ḳatl
Čhatr, Čhattar → Miẓalla
Čhatrīs iii, 442b, 445b — III, 457a, 460b
Chauhars i, 173a — I, 177b
Chaussure → Libās; Naʿl
Chechaouen → Shafshawan
Cheetah → Fahd
Chef (tête) → Kalāntar
Cheikh → Shaykh
Chélif v, 1173b, 1175a, 1179a, b, 1180a — V, 1163b, 1165a, 1169a, b, 1170a
Chemin de fer trans-iranien IV, 43a
Cheminée d'aération → Bādgīr
Chenab (Pandjāb) s, 361a — S, 360b
Cheng Ho v, 849b, 850a — V, 853b, 854a
Cherchell → Sharshāl
Chérif → Sharīf
Chess → Shaṭrandj
Cheval → Faras; Khayl
Chevalerie → Fāris; Furūsiyya; Futuwwa
Chevaliers de St.-Jean de Jérusalem I, 302b, 1153a, 1288b; II, 6a, 542b; III, 521b, 1031b; IV, 506a, 810a, b; V, 266b, 594b; S, 92a, 204a
Chevaliers Teutoniques → Dāwiyya et Isbitāriyya
Chèvre → Ghanam; Maʿz
Chicane → Čawgān
Chief (leader) → Kalāntar
Chien → Kalb
Chiffre → Ḥisāb
Chiffres → Ḥisāb
Chiisme → Shīʿa
Child → Ṣaghīr, Walad
Chimie → Kīmiyāʾ
China/Chine → al-Ṣīn
Chinchilla s, 144b — S, 144b
Chin-chi-pʾu v, 847a, b, 848a, b — V, 851b, 852a, b
Chinguetti → Shinḳīt
Chintz → Ḳalamkārī
Chionites i, 225b, 226a; iii, 303b — I, 232b, 233a; III, 312b
Chios/Chio → Saḳîz
Chirognomy/Chiromancie →al-Kaff, ʿIlm-
Chirurgien → Djarrāh
Chitral ii, **29a,** 317a; s, 158b — II, **29b,** 326a; S, 158b
Chittagong i, 606a, 1333a; ii, **31b**; iv, 177b — I, 625b, 1272b; II, **32b**; IV, 186a
Chivalry → Furūsiyya
Chleuh i, 1181b, 1182a, b, 1183a, b — I, 1216b, 1217a,b, 1218a, b
Chocim → Khotin
Chole (island/île) → Mafia
Cholera/Choléra → Ṭāʿūn
Chonae → Khōnās
Chorfa → Sharīf
Chosroës → Kisrā
Čhotī Begam ii, 83b — II, 85a
Chrétiens → Naṣārā
Christians → Naṣārā
Chronicles/Chroniques → Taʾrīkh
Chronogram/chronogramme → Ḥisāb al-djummal
Chronology/Chronologie → Taʾrīkh
Chum, Hajji s, 351b — S, 351b
Chundawand i, 172a — I, 177a
Church → Kanīsa
Chypre → Ḳubrus
el-Cid → al-Sīd
Ciel → Samāʾ
Čift-resmi i, 999a, 1169b; ii, **32a,** 146b, 907a; iv, 211a — I, 1030a, 1204b; II, **32b,** 150b, 928a; IV, 220b

Čiftelik i, 1264b, 1266a, b, 1268b, 1269a; ii, **32b,** 907a – I, 1303b, 1304b, 1305b, 1307b, 1308a; II, **33a,** 928a
Cigerdelen Parkani s, 171a – S, 171a
Čighālazāde Sinān Pasha i, 8a, 267b, 904a; ii, **33b;** iii, 1001a; s, 238b – I, 8a, 275b, 931a; II, **34b;** III, 1026a; S, 238b
Čihil Sutūn s, 257a, 259b, 325b – S, 256b, 259a, 325a
Čihilgānī s, 124a – S, 123a
Čihra iv, 268b – IV, 280b
Čiḥrāzād → Humāy
Čiḳma ii, 1086b, 1089b – II, 1111b, 1115a
Cilicia/Cilicie i, 184a; ii, **34b,** 65b – I, 189a; II, **35b,** 67a
Čilla i, 1122a; ii, 55b; iv, 991a – I, 1156a; II, 56b; IV, 1023b
Cimetière → Maḳbara
Čimkent ii, **39a** – II, **39b**
Čīn → al-Ṣīn
Cin → Djinn
Čīn-Kālān → Khānfū
Čīn Ḳilic Khān → Āṣaf Djāh I
Čīn-Temür ii, 606a; s, 246a – II, 621a; S, 246a
Cinema/Cinématographe ii, **39b** – II, **40a**
Čingāne ii, **40b** – II, **41a**
Čingiz Khān i, 121a, 227a, 418b, 879b, 1295a; ii, 2a, 38a, **41a,** 393a, 571a, 607a, 894a; iii, 198a, 472a; iv, 30a; v, 391b, 858a; s, 176b – I, 124b, 233b, 430b, 905a, 1335a; II, 2a, 38b, **42a,** 403a, 585b, 622a, 914b; III, 202b, 488b; IV, 32a; V, 392b, 865a; S, 177b
Čingizid(e)s ii, **44a**; iv, 723b; s, 97a – II, **44b**; IV, 752b; S, 96b
Čīnīōt (Cinyot) ii, **47a** – II, **48a**
Cinnamon → Dār Ṣīnī
Cinq → Khams(a)
Cintra → Shintara
Cipaye → Sīpāhī
Ciphers → Ḥisāb
Čirāgh ʿAlī iii, 431b; iv, 170b – III, 445b; IV, 177b
Čirāgh-i Dihlī ii, **47b,** 51a, 54a, 55a, b, 392a, 1114b; iii, 429b – II, **48b,** 52a, b, 56a, b, 402b, 1141a; III, 443b
Čirāghān ii, **49a** – II, **49b**
Circars → Sarkārs
Circassians/Circassiens → Čerkes
Circesium → Ḳarḳīsiyā
Circumcision/Circoncision → Khafḍ; Khitān
Čirmen ii, **49a** – II, **50a**
Cirta → Ḳusṭanṭīna
Čishtī, Muʿīn al-Dīn i, 72b, 208a, 912a, 1024a; ii, 48b, **49b,** 50b, 378b, 796b; iii, 429a; v, 546b; s, 5a, 293b, 353b – I, 74b, 214b, 940a, 1055b; II, 49b, **50b,** 51a, 389a, 815b; III, 443a; V, 551a; S, 4a, 293a, 353a
Čishtī, Shaykh Ibban s, 74a – S, 74a
Čishtī-Niẓāmī s, 293a, 360b – S, 293a, 360b
Čishtī-Ṣābirī → Ṣābiriyya
Čishtiyya i, 95a; ii, **50b,** 137b, 296b, 421a, 796b, 1115b; iii, 167b, 429a, 433a, 1174b; iv, 48a, 507a, 1026b; s, 5a, 312b, 313a, 353a – I, 98a; II, **51a,** 141b, 304b, 431b, 815b, 1141b; III, 171a, 443a, 447a, 1203a; IV, 50b, 529a, 1058b; S, 4a, 312b, 353a
Cistern/Citerne → Ḥawḍ; Istakhr
Citadel/Citadelle → Ḳaṣaba
Čitawr, Čitōr iii, 457a, 482b; s, 105a – III, 473a, 499b; S, 104b
Čitr → Ghāshiya
Čitrāl → Chitral
Citron → Muḥammadāt
Citrus → Muḥammadāt
Čittagong → Chittagong
Civet(te) → Zabād
Čiwi Ilyāsii, 50b – II, 57b
Čiwi-zāde ii, **56b** – II, **57b**
Cizrî, Melayê v, 482a – V, 484b
Claim → Dayn
Clan → Āl; Ḥayy
Claudias → Ḳalāwdhiya
Clef → Miftāḥ
Clepsydra/Clepsydre → Ḥiyal; Sāʿa
Cleromancie → Ḳurʿa
Climate/Climat → Iḳlīm; Manākh
Clive, Robert ii, 371b – II, 381b
Cloak → Khirḳa
Clothing → Libās
Clou de girofle → Ḳaranful
Clove → Ḳaranful
Coal → Faḥm
Coat of Mail → Silāḥ
Čōbān → Čūbān
Čoban Girāylar ii, 1113b – II, 1139b
Čōbān-Oghullarî s, **171b** – S, **172a**
Cock → Dīk
Coeur → Ḳalb
Coffee → Ḳahwa
Čoghondur i, 99b – I, 102b
Coiffeur → Ḥallāḳ
Coiffure → Libās
Coilom → Kūlam
Coïmbra/Coïmbre → Ḳulumriyya
Coinage → Sikka
Čoka → Ḳumāsh
Čoka Adasî ii, **57a** – II, **58a**
Cölemerik ii, **57a**; v, 456b – II, **58a**; V, 459a
Colomb-Béchar ii, **57b** – II, **58b**
Colombe, Colombophilie → Ḥamām
Colonia → Shābīn Ḳarā Ḥiṣār
Colonnes d'Hercule → Ḳādis
Colour → Lawn
Column/Colonne → ʿAmūd
Comania → Dasht-i Ḳīpčaḳ
Comans → Ḳipčak
Comes → Ḳūmis
Comité Union et Progrès → Ittiḥād we Teraḳḳī Djemʿiyyeti
Commensal → Nadīm
Commentary/Commentaire → Ḥāshiya; Sharḥ; Tafsīr
Commerce → Tidjāra
Commercial privileges → Imtiyāzāt
Commissionnaire → Dallāl, Simsār
Committee of Union and Progress → Ittiḥād we Teraḳḳī Djemʿiyyeti
Communications → Barīd, Tarīḳ, Ulaḳ etc.
Communism(e) → Shuyūʿiyya
Communist/Communiste iii, 528b, 532a, 534a, 1223b; v, 614b – III, 547a, 550b, 552b, 1255a; V, 618b
Community/Communauté → Djamāʿa; Umma
Comnenus, Alexis/Comnène, Alexis v, 103b, 505a, 712b – V, 105b, 106a, 508b, 717b
Comnenus, Isaac Ducas/Comnène, Isaac v, 302b – V, 302a
Comnenus, John/Comnène, Jean ii, 37a, 110b; v, 712b – II, 38a, 113a; V, 717b
Comnenus, Manuel/Comnène, Manuel i, 466b, 289b, 791b; ii, 37a, b, 111a, 715a; v, 104a – I, 480b, 813a, 815a; II, 38a, 113b, 733b; V, 106b
Comores → Ḳumr
Compagnie Anglaise des Indes Orientales I, 779b, 1009a, 1044b, 1205a, 1231a, 1381b; II, 124a, 129b, 347a, 381a, 612b, 754b, 830a, 1004a; III, 232b, 331b, 474a, 605b, 1220a, 1221a; V, 578a
Companions of the Prophet/Compagnons du Prophète → Muḥammad; Ṣaḥāba
Compass → Maghnāṭīs

Compensation money/Compensation pécuniaire → Diya
Comptabilité → Muḥāsaba
Compulsion in mariage → Djabr
Comput digital → Ḥisāb al-ʿAḳd
Conakry → Konakry
Concubine → Khāṣṣekī
Conduit d'eau → Ḳanāt
Congo ii, **58a**; iv, 749b, 750b – II, **59a**; IV, 780a, b
Congress/Congrès → Muʾtamar
Congrès national indien → Indian National Congress
Congress of Popular Forces/Congrès des Forces Populaires s, 8a – S, 7b
Conjugaison → Ṣarf
Conjunction/Conjonction → Ḳirān
Connaissance → ʿIlm
Constantina ii, 924a – II, 945b
Constantine III v, 492a, b – V, 495a, b
Constantine/Constantin → Ḳusṭanṭīna
Constantine the African/Constantin l'Africain i, 381a; ii, **59b**; s, 271b – I, 392a; II, **60b**; S, 271b
Constantine of Lampron/Constantin de Lampron ii, 37b, 38a – II, 38b
Constantinople → Istanbul; Ḳusṭanṭīniyya
Constanza → Köstendje
Constitution → Dustūr
Construction → Bināʾ
Consul ii, **60b** – II, **61b**
Conteurs → Ḳāṣṣ; Maddāḥ
Contract/Contrat → Aḳd; Baḳt; Bayʿ; Dhimma; Īdjār; Kirāʾ
Contrainte matrimoniale → Djabr
Conversion → Islām
Cooperations/Coopératives → Taʿāwun
Čopān → Čūbān
Čopan-ata ii, **61a,** 69b – II, **62b,** 70b
Copper → Maʿdin; Nuḥās
Coptic/Copte iii, 721b, 722a, 1205b; iv, 134b; v, 92b – III, 744a, b, 1236a; IV, 140a; V, 94b, 95a
Coptos → Ḳifṭ
Copts/Coptes → Ḳibṭī
Coq → Dīk
Cor → Būḳ
Coran → al-Ḳurʾān
Čorbadjî ii, **61b** – II, **62b**
Corbeau → Ghurāb
Cordova/Cordove → Ḳurtuba
Corduene v, 447b, 448a – V, 450a, b
Coré → Ḳārūn
Corea/Corée → al-Sīlā
Corfu/Corfou → Körfüz
Coria → Ḳūriya
Corinth/Corinthe → Kordos
Čorlu ii, **62a**; s, 282a – II, **63a**; S, 282a
Čorlulu ʿAlī Pasha → ʿAlī Pasha Čorlulu
Cormaghun iv, 349b, 670a – IV, 364a, 697b
Corne d'Or → Ghalaṭa; Istanbul; Takhtaḳalʿe
Cornelian/Cornaline → ʿAḳīḳ
Coromandel → Maʿbar
Coron → Koron
Corporation → Ṣinf
Corps → Djism
Corps de métier → Ṣinf
Corpse-washer → Ghassāl
Correspondence/Correspondance → Diplomatic/Diplomatique; Inshāʾ; Kātib; Risāla
Corsair(e) → Ḳurṣān
Corsica/Corse s, 120b – S, 120a
Čoruh (Corukh) ii, **62a** – II, **63b**
Čorum ii, **62a**; s, 394b – II, **63b**; S, 395a
Cos → Istanköy
Cosaques → Kazakh
Cosmetics → Khiḍāb
Cossacks → Kazakh
Costume → Libās
Côte d'Ivoire ii, **62b** – II, **64a**
Côte de l'or → Ghāna
Côte des Pirates → al-Sāḥil
Cotonou → Kotonou
Cotte de mailles → Silāḥ
Cotton/Coton → Ḳuṭn
Couchitique → Kūsh
Coudée → Dhirāʿ
Couleur → Lawn
Couleuvre → Ḥayya
Council of Arab Economic Unity s, 241a
Coupole → Ḳubba
Course en mer → Ḳurṣān
Courtier → Dallāl
Courtisan → Nadīm
Couscous → Kuskusū
Coussin → Mikhadda
Coutume → ʿĀda
Couvent → Dayr; Khānḳāh
Čowdors → Čawdors
Crac → Kerak
Crac des Chevaliers → Ḥiṣn al-Akrād
Črār s, 114b – S, 113b
Créance → Dayn
Creation/Création → Ḥudūth, Ibdāʿ, Khalḳ
Crécelle → Nāḳūs
Creed/Credo → ʿAḳīda; Iʿtiḳād
Crescent moon → Hilāl
Crete/Crète → Iḳrītish
Crieur public → Dallāl
Crimea/Crimée → Ḳîrîm
Criquet → Djarād
Cristal → Billawr
Crocodile → Timsāḥ
Croisades I, 203b, 222a, 351b, 480a, 532b, 535a, 570b, 683b, 732a, 759b, 801a, 806b, 807a, 822a, 823a, 937b, 1045b, 1048b, 1056b, 1077b, 1105a, 1135b, 1152b, 1159b, 1172a, 1173b, 1225b, 1254b, 1398a; II, 37b, **64b,** 133b, 168a, 876a, 933a, 1006a, 1080b; III, 89a, 301b, 334b, 489a, 491a, 521a, 1071a; IV, 304b, 504a, 506a, 875a, 991b; V, 105b, 302a, 330a, b, 806b, 929b; S, 204b
Croissant lunaire → Hilāl
Croja → Kroya
Crossbow → Ḳaws
Crow → Ghurāb
Croyance → ʿAḳīda, Iʿtiḳād
Crusades i, 197b, 198a, 215b, 341a, 466a, 517a, 519a, 552b, 662b, 710b, 737b, 778a, 783a, 784a, 798b, 799b, 910a, 1014a, 1017a, 1025a, 1045b, 1073a, 1102b, 1118b, 1125b, 1137b, 1139a, 1190b, 1218a, 1358a; ii, 37a, **63b,** 130a, 163a, 856a, 911b, 983b, 1056a; iii, 86b, 292b, 324b, 472b, 474b, 503b, 504a, 1045a; iv, 291b, 483a, 485a, 842a, 958b; v, 103b, 303a, 330a, b, 800b, 924a; s, 204b, 205a
Crystal → Billawr
Ctesiphon iii, 1254b; v, 945a, 946a; s, 298a – III, 1287a; V, 949a, 950a; S, 297b
Ču ii, **66b**; iv, 212b – II, **68a**; IV, 222a
Čūbak, Ṣādiḳ iv, 73a; v, 200a; s, 60a – IV, 77a; V, 197b; S, 60b
Čūbān, Prince/le prince- ii, 87a – II, 89a
Čūbān, Amīr i, 347a., 468a, 703a, 908b; ii, 68a, 69a; iii, 1122b; iv, 621b, 672a, 738a, 817b; v, 554b – I, 357b, 481b, 724b, 936a; II, 69a, 70b; III, 1150b; IV, 646b, 699b, 767b, 850b; V, 559a
Čūbānid(e)s ii, **67b,** 401a – II, **69a,** 411b
Cubit → Dhirāʿ

Čūčak Bēgam iii, 633b — III, 654b
Cuenca → Kūnka
Cuergour s, 145a — S, 144b
Čufut Ḳalʿe i, 893a, b — I, 919b, 920a
Čūhā-i Shāh Dawla ii, 1131b — II, 1158a
Cuir → Djild
Cuisine → Ṭabīkh
Cuivre → Maʿdin; Nuḥās
Čuka → Ḳumāsh
Čukhūr Saʿd i, 8a — I, 8a
Čukurova → Cilicia
Čulāḳ-Sūrkhay-Khān ii, 87b; v, 296b — II, 89b; V, 287b
Čulîm ii, **68b** — II, **69b**
Culture → Thaḳāfa
Cumans i, 1302a; ii, 610a — I, 1342a; II, 625a
Cümhuriyet → Djümhūriyyet
Cumin → Kammūn
Čūpān ii, **69a**; s, 319b, 321a — II, **70a**; S, 319a, 321a
Čūpān-ata → Čopan-ata
Čūpān, Amīr → Čūbān
Čūpānbegī → Ḳūbčūr
Cupper → Faṣṣād; Ḥadjdjām
Čūrāman Djāt i, 1193a; ii, 810b — I, 1228a; II, 829b
Cushion → Mikhadda
Custom → ʿĀda
Čuwash(es) i, 1307b, 1338a; ii, **69b**; iv, 281a, 608b — I, 1347b, 1378a; II, **70b**; IV, 293a, 633a
Cynegetics/Cynégétique → Ṭard, Ṭardiyya
Cyprus → Ḳubrus
Cyrenaïca/Cyrénaïque → Barḳa
Cyrillus b. Laḳlaḳ s, 396a — S, 396b
Cyrus → al-Muḳawḳis
Cythère → Čoka Adasî
Czechoslovakia → Čeh

D

Dāʾ al-Kalab iv, 490a, 491b — IV, 511a, 512b
al-Daʿʿār, Banū s, 338a — S, 337b
Daʾb → Adab
al-Dabarān → Nudjūm
Ḍabb ii, **70a**; s, 286b — II, **71a**; S, 286a
Dābba ii, **71a** — II, **72a**
Ḍabba ii, **71b** — II, **72b**
Ḍabba b. Muḥammad al-Asadī iv, 637b — IV, 663b
Dabbāba iii, 475a — III, 491b
Dabbāgh (tanner/tanneur) s, **172a** — S, **173a**
al-Dabbāgh, Abū Zayd ʿAbd al-Raḥmān s, **172b**, 395a — S, **173b**, 395a
al-Dabbās → Abu ʾl-Khayr Ḥammād
al-Ḍabbī, Abū Djaʿfar i, 602b; ii, **72a** — I, 622a; II, **73b**
al-Ḍabbī, Abū ʿIkrima → al-Mufaḍḍal
al-Ḍabbī, Bisṭām iii, 649b, 658b — III, 670b, 680a
al-Dabbī, al-Musayyab b. Zuhayr s, 327a — S, 326b
Dābiḳ ii, **72b**, 360b, 912a — II, **73b**, 370a, 933b
Dabīḳ ii, **72b** — II, **74a**
Dabīl → Dwīn
al-Dabīlī, Abū Mūsā i, 162b — I, 167a
Dabīr iv, 758b, 759a; S, **173a** — IV, 788b, 789a; S, **174a**
Dabīr, Salāmat ʿAlī i, 508b; ii, **73a**; iii, 119b; s, 74b — I, 524a; II, **74a**; III, 122a; S, 75a
Dabistān al-Madhāhib ii, **74a** — II, **75a**
Ḍābiṭ i, 975a; ii, **74a** — I, 1005a; II, **75b**
Ḍābita Khān i, 1206a; ii, 1092b; iii, 61a — I, 1242a; II, 1118a; III, 63b
Dābōē → Dābūya
Ḍabṭ ii, **74b** 155b, 156a — II, **75b**, 160a, 161a
Ḍabṭiyya ii, **74b**; iv, 611b — II, **75b**; IV, 636a
Dabuʿ s, **173b** — S, **174a**
Dabūsiyya s, **176b** — s, **177b**
Dābūya i, 871b; ii, **74b**; iv, 207b, 644a; v, 69a; s, 297b — I, 896a; II, **76a**; IV, 217a, 670b; V, 71a; S, 297a
Dābūyid(e)s s, 298a, b — S, 298a
Dacca → Ḍhākā
Dactylonomy/dactylonomie → Ḥisāb al-ʿAḳd
Ḍad ii, **75a** — II, **76a**
Dada → Dede
Dadaloghlu ii, **75b** — II, **76b**Dādhawayh i, 728a — I, 750a
Dād-Beg Ḥabashī s, 279a — S, 279a
Dādhburzmihr b. Farrukhān ii, 74b, 809a; s, 299a — II, 76a, 828b; S, 298b
Dadjādja ii, **76a** — II, **77a**
Dadjāʿima i, 526a — I, 542a
al-Dadjdjāl i, 932a; ii, **76a**, 486b; iv, 408b; v, 800a — I, 960b; II, **77b**, 498b; IV, 426a; V, 806a
Dādjū ii, 122a — II, 125a
Dādū, Pīr v, 26b — V, 27b
Daff → Duff
Ḍafīr ii, **77a** — II, **78b**
Dafn → Dhunūb, Dafn al-
Daftar i, 1090a, b; ii, **77b**, 82a, b, 147b, 563a; iv, 1047b — I, 1122b, 1124a; II, **78b**, 83b, 84a, 151b, 577a; IV, 1079a
Daftar-i Khāḳānī i, 999a; ii, **81b**, 147b — I, 1030a; II, **83b**, 151b
Daftardār i, 480b; ii, **83a**, 723b; iv, 560b — I, 495a; II, **84b**, 742a; IV, 583a
Dāgh, Mīrzā Khān ii, **83b**; iii, 119a; v 961b — II, **85a**; III, 121b; V, 966a
Dagh-Čufut ii, 86b, 88b, 89a — II, 88b, 90b
Dāgh u Taṣḥīḥa v, 685b, 686b; s, **176b** — V, 691a, b; S, **177b**
Dāghistān i, 504a, 755a, 756a, 958a; ii, **85a**, 206a, 746b; iii, 157a; iv, 343a, b, 350a, 846b; v, 55b, 246a, 382a, 617b, 618a, 729b; s, 143a — I, 519b, 777b, 778b, 987b; II, **86b**, 212b, 765a; III, 160b; IV, 357b, 365a, 879b; V, 57a, 243b, 383a, 621b, 622a, 734b; S, 143a
Ḍaghṭa i, 187a — I, 192b
Dagno iv, 139b — IV, 145a
Dahāḳīn iv, 13b, 14a — IV, 14b, 15a
Dāhār iv, 534b — IV, 558a
Dahdam → Lamlam
Dah sāla i, 317a — I, 327a
al-Ḍaḥḥāk → Zuhāk
Ḍaḥḥāḳ, Azhd ii, 106b, 1099a; v, 449a — II, 109a, 1125a; V, 451b
al-Ḍaḥḥāk b. Ḳays al-Fihrī i, 53b, 704b; ii, **89a**, 360a; iii, 270b, 687b — I, 55b, 725b; II, **91a**, 370a; III, 278b, 709a
al-Ḍaḥḥāk b. Ḳays al-Shaybānī ii, **90a**; iv, 1076a — II, **92a**; IV, 1108a
Daḥḥāk b. Muzāḥim v, 1123a — V, 1119b
Daḥḥūn, Banū iii, 12a — III, 12b
Ḍāḥik, Mīr s, 358b — S, 358b
Ḍāhir i, 762b — I, 785b
Dāhir of/de Sind s, 163a — S, 162a
Ḍāhir al-ʿUmar → Ẓāhir al-ʿUmar
Dāḥis ii, 873a, 1023a; s, 177a — II, 893b, 1046b; S, 178a
Dahistan → Dihistān
Ḍaḥiyya ii, 884a; iii, 54a — II, 904b; III, 56a
Dahlak ii, **90b**, 709b — II, **92b**, 728b
Daḥlān, Aḥmad b. Zaynī i, 66a; ii, **91a** — I, 68a; II, **93a**
al-Dahmāʾ s, 394a — S, 394b
al-Dahnāʾ i, 537a; ii, **91b** — I, 553b; II, **93b**
al-Dahnadj ii, **93a** — II, **95a**

Dahomey ii, **93b**; v, 279b— II, **95b**; V, 277b
Dahr ii, **94b** — II, **96b**
Dahriyya ii, **95a,** 770b; s, 89a — II, **97a,** 789a; S, 88b
Daḥshūr ii, **97b** — II, **99b**
Dāʿī i, 832b; ii, **97b** — I, 855b; II, **99b**
Dāʿī, Aḥmad b. Ibrāhīm ii, **98a;** iii, 1243a — II, **100a;** III, 1275a
Dāʿī al-muṭlaḳ i, 1255a; v, 1033a — I, 1293a; V, 1029a
Ḍaʿīf ii, 462b; iii, 25a — II, 474a; III, 26b
Dāʿī ʾl-duʿāt v, 1033a, 1125b — V, 1029a, 1122a
Dāira → Dawāʾir
Dāʾira ii, 621a — II, 636b
Dāʾira Saniyya s, **179a** — S, **180a**
Daḳahliyya ii, **99a** — II, **101a**
Dakanī, Walī v, 1106a — V, 1102a
Dakar S, **179a** — S, **180b**
Dakārna iv, 679b — IV, 707b
Dakhalieh → Daḳahliyya
Dakhan i, 81a, 117b, 923b; ii, **99a;** iii, 15a, 420b; v, 937a, 1214b, 1215a, b; s, 74b, 335b — I, 83b, 121a, 951b; II, **101a;** III, 15b, 434a; V, 940b, 1204a, 1205a; S, 75a, 335b
Da<u>kh</u>anī → Urdū
Da<u>kh</u>aw → ʿAlī Akbar Dih<u>kh</u>udā
Da<u>kh</u>īl ii, **100a;** iii, 1018a; iv, 412a — II, **1020a;** III, 1043b; IV, 430a
al-Dā<u>kh</u>il → ʿAbd al-Raḥmān I; al-Ḥasan
Dā<u>kh</u>la wa <u>Kh</u>ār<u>dj</u>a → al-Wāḥāt
Da<u>kh</u>ma v, 1114a, 1116a, b, — V, 1110a, 1112a, b,
Da<u>kh</u>nī iii, 458b; v, 550a — III, 474b; V, 555a
Dakibyza → Gebze
Daḳīḳī, Abū Manṣūr Muḥammad ii, **100a,** 918b, 1035b; iii, 113a; iv, 60b, 62b — II, **102a,** 939b, 1059b; III, 115b; IV, 64a, 65b
al-Daḳḳāḳ, Abū ʿAbd Allāh i, 137b; ii, **100b** — I, 141b; II, **102b**
al-Daḳḳāḳ, Abū ʿAli v, 526b — V, 530a, b
Dakkanī, Walī v, 961a — V, 965a
Dakrūnī → Dakārna
Daḳūḳā i, 184a, 512b; ii, **101a** — I, 189b, 1528a; II, **103a**
Dāl ii, **101a** — II, **103a**
al-Dalāl, Abū Zayd Nāḳid iv, 1087b; s, **183a** — IV, 1118b; S, **184b**
Dalāla i, 1115a; iv, 145b — I, 1148b; IV, 151b
Dalāṣ s, 159a — S, 158b
al-Dalāsīrī → al-Būṣīrī
Dālāy iv, 31b, 975b — IV, 34a, 1008a
Dalhama → <u>Dh</u>u ʾl-Himma
Ḍāliʿ i, 446a; ii, 675b — I, 459a; II, 692a
Dālī b. Aḥmad al-Maʿḳūr ii, 122b — II, 125b
Dalīl (guide) → Dallāl
Dalīl ii, **101b;** iii, 543b — II, **103b;** III, 562a
Dalīl Baḥr → Dālī b. Aḥmad al-Maʿḳūr
Dalīpgarh i, 1020a — I, 1051b
Dallāl ii, **102b;** v, 1004a, 1005a— II, **104b;** V, 1000a, b
Dalmatia/Dalmatie S, **183b** — S, **184b**
Daltāwa ii, **103a** — II, **105b**
Dalūka iii, 71b — III, 73b
Dalw i, 1230a, 1231b — I, 1267a, 1268b
al-Dalw → Minṭaḳat al-Burū<u>dj</u>; Nu<u>dj</u>ūm
Dām → Sikka
Dam (blood/sang) s, **188b,** 221b — S, **190a,** 221b
Dam (irrigation) → Band
Dāmād ii, **103b** — II, **105b**
al-Dāmād, Mīr ii, **103b;** s, 308b— II, **106a;** S, 308a
Dāmād Ferīd Pa<u>sh</u>a ii, **104b,** 431b, 533b, 630b; iii, 595a; iv, 873a, b — II, **107a,** 442b, 546b, 646a; III, 615b; IV, 906b, 907a
Dāmād Pa<u>sh</u>a → ʿAlī Pa<u>sh</u>a; Ḥasan Pa<u>sh</u>a; Ibrāhīm Pa<u>sh</u>a; Sinān Pa<u>sh</u>a
Dāmā<u>dj</u>ī i, 1053a — I, 1084b
al-Dāma<u>gh</u>ānī, Abū ʾl-Hasan ʿAlī s, **194a** — S, **193b**
al-Dāma<u>gh</u>ānī, Āl s, **191b** — S, **193a**
al-Damāmīnī, Muhammad b. ʿUmar iv, 135a — IV, 140b
al-Damāmīnī, Tā<u>dj</u> al-Dīn iv, 641a — IV, 667b
Ḍamān i, 1144a; ii, **105a;** iv, 323b, 324a, 326a, 404b, 1046a, — I, 1178b; II, **107a;** IV, 337b, 338b, 340a, 422a, 1077b
Damanhūr, Buḥayra i, 1288a, b; ii, **105b** — I, 1327b, 1328a; II, **108a**
Damanhūr al-<u>Sh</u>ahīd ii, 105b — II, 107b
Damascening → Maʿdin
Damascus/Damas → Dima<u>sh</u>ḳ
Damasquinage, Damasquinure → Maʿdin
Damāwand i, 358b; ii, **106a;** iv, 402; v, 89a, 657b, 659b, 660a; s, 298a — I, 369a; II, **108b;** IV, 419b; V, 91a, 663a, 665a, b; S, 297b
Damawiyya iv, 334b — IV, 349a
Damdam → Lamlam
Damēlī ii, 31a, 138b — II, 32a, 142a
Dām<u>gh</u>ān ii, **107a;** iv, 701b; v, 377b, 378a; s, 149a, 192a, 357a — II, **109b;** IV, 730a; V, 378a, b; S, 149a, 193a, 356b
Dām<u>gh</u>ānī, <u>Sh</u>ams al-Dīn ii, 1124b; iii, 14b; iv, 218b — II, 1151a; III, 15a; IV, 228a
Damietta/Damiette → Dimyat
Ḍamīr → Naḥw
al-Dāmir iv, 686b — IV, 714b
Damir Ḳapu → Dar-i Āhanīn
al-Damīrī i, 509a, 594b; ii, **107b;** iii, 306b, 307b, 313a; s, 392b — I, 524b, 613b; II, **109b;** III, 316a, 317a, 322b; S, 393a
Ḍamma iii, 172b — III, 176b
Ḍamma → Ḥaraka
al-Dammām ii, **108a,** 175b, 569a; iii, 238b — II, **110b,** 181a, 583a; III, 245b
Dammar, Banū i, 6a — I, 6a
Damnāt ii, **109a** — II, **111b**
al-Damnātī → ʿAlī b. Sulaymān
al-Damurdā<u>sh</u>ī, Aḥmad ii, **109b** — II, **112a**
Dānaḳ → Sikka
Danāḳil → Danḳalī
Danāḳla i, 765a; ii, 615a; v, 1248b — I, 788a; II, 630b; V, 1239a
Danānīr al-Barmakī i, 1036a; s, 116b — I, 1067b; S, 116a
Danaor s, 324b — S, 324a
Dance → Raḳṣ
Dandānḳān, Dandānaḳan s, **195a,** 245b — S, **195a,** 245b
al-Dandarāwī, Abu ʾl-ʿAbbās s, 279a — S, 278b
al-Dandarāwiyya s, 279a — S, 278b
Dāndē<u>sh</u> → <u>Kh</u>āndē<u>sh</u>
Danhā<u>dj</u>a iv, 729b — IV, 758b
al-Dānī, Abū ʿAmr ii, **109b,** 112a; iii, 753b; iv, 731b; v, 128a — II, **112a,** 114b; III, 776b; IV, 761a; V, 130b
al-Danī, Abū Bakr Muḥammad → Ibn al-Labbāna
Daniel → Dāniyāl
Dāni<u>sh</u>, Aḥmad s, 109b — S, 108b
Dāni<u>sh</u>gāh → <u>Dj</u>āmiʿa
Dāni<u>sh</u>kada i, 919a — I, 946b
Dāni<u>sh</u>mand Tigin i, 418b — I, 430b
Dāni<u>sh</u>mend, Malik Aḥmad <u>Gh</u>āzī i, 465b, 466a, b, 1103b, 1104a; ii, 37a, 110a, 1044a; iii, 115a — I, 479b, 480a, 1137a, b; II, 38a, 112b, 1068a; III, 117a
Dāni<u>sh</u>mendid(e)s i, 431b, 466b, 510a, 639a, 665a, 666a; ii, 13b, **110a;** iv, 627b, 737b; v, 103b, 106a; s, 154b — I, 444a, 480b, 525b, 659b, 684b, 686b; II, 13b, **112b;** IV, 652b, 767b; V, 106a, b; S, 154b
Dāniya ii, **111b;** v, 631b — II, **114a;** V, 635b

Dāniyāl ii, **112b,** 377a; iv, 654a – II, **115a,** 387a; IV, 680b
Dāniyāl b. Akbar i, 80b, 1331a; ii, **113a,** 851b, 871a; iv, 1017b – I, 83a, 1371b; II, **115b,** 835a, 891a; IV, 1049b
Dāniyāl b. Shaʿya i, 388b – I, 399b
Dāniyāl Beg (Mangit) i, 230b, 1295b; iv, 310a; s, 97a – I, 237b, 1335b; IV, 324a; S, 96b
Dāniyār b. Ḳāsim Khān iv, 723b – IV, 752b
Danḳalī i, 176b, 765a, 1028b; ii, **113a,** 351a; iii, 4a, 5b – I, 181a, 788a, 1060a; II, **115b,** 360b; III, 4a, 5b
Dann, dinān iv, 997b – IV, 1030a
Danse → Raḳṣ
Dār ii, **113b**; iv, 236a, b, 1015a, 1016b; v, 23a – II, **116a**; IV, 246b, 247a, 1047a, 1048b; V, 24a
Dar-i āhanīn ii, **115b** – II, **118a**
Dār al-ʿahd i, 1253a; ii, **116a** – I, 1291a; II, **118b**
Dar-i Alān → Bāb al-lān
Dār al-Baḥr s, 62b – S, 63a
al-Dār al-Bayḍāʾ i, 506a, 977b; ii, **116b,** 727a; s, 63b, 134a, 145a, 223b – I, 521b, 1008a; II, **119a,** 745; S, 64a, 133b, 144b, 223b
Dār al-ḍarb i, 24a, 1335b; ii, **117b,** 205b, 874b; iii, 41b; iv, 134b, 230b; v, 264b, 488b – I, 25a, 1375b; II, **120a,** 212a, 894b; III, 43a; IV, 140b, 241a; V, 262b, 491b
Dār al-djihād i, 1163b – I, 1198a
Dār Fartīt i, 929a, b – I, 957b, 958a
Dār al-funūn → Djāmiʿa
Dār Fūr i, 35a, 49b, 929a, b, 962a; ii, **121b,** 351a; v, 267a, 1248b, 1249b; s, 164a – I, 36a, 51a, 957b, 991b; II, **124b,** 361a; V, 264b, 265a, 1239a, 1240a; S, 164a
Dār al-Ḥadīth ii, **125b,** 283a; v, 1129a; s, **195a** – II, **128b,** 291b; V, 1125a; S, **195a**
Dār al-Hamara iii, 149a – III, 152a
Dār al-ḥarb i, 429b; ii, 116a, **126a,** 131b – I, 441b; II, 118b, **129b,** 135a
Dār al-ḥikma i, 816a, 1141a; ii, **126b,** 169b, 859b; iii, 78b; v, 1033a, 1125b – I, 839b, 1175b; II, **130a,** 175a, 879a; III, 81a; V, 1029a, 1122a
Dār al-ʿIlm i, 899a; ii, **127a,** 169b; iii, 78b; v, 1125a, b, 1126a, 1129a; s, 95b – I, 926a; II, **130a,** 175a; III, 81a; V, 1121b, 1122a, b, 1125a; S, 95a
Dār al-Imāra i, 899b, 900a, 901a; ii, 128b – I, 926b, 927a, 928a; II, 131b
Dār al-inshāʾ ii, 129b, 335b; iv, 757b, 759b – II, 132b, 345a; IV, 787b, 788a, 790a
Dār al-Islām ii, 116a, **127b,** 131b; iii, 546b; iv, 173a, b – II, 118b, **130b,** 134b; III, 565b; IV, 180b, 181a
Dār al-Ḳurʾān wa ʾl-Ḥadīth ii, 126a – II, 129a
Dār al-Maḥfūẓāt al-ʿUmūmiyya ii, **128a** – II, **131a**
Dār al-Mamlaka i, 901a, 1352b, 1354a – I, 928a, 1392a, 1393a
Dār al-Muʿallimīn i, 284b, 285b – I, 293b, 294a
Dār al-Muṣannifīn ii, 132b – II, 135b
Dār al-Nadwa ii, **128b** – II, **131b**
Dār Runga s, 164b – S, 164b
Dār al-Saʿāda → Saray
Dār al-Saʿāde Aghasî → Saray-aghasî
Dār al-Salām ii, **128b** – II, **132a**
Dar-es-Salaam ii, **128b**; v, 1031a – II, **132a**; V, 1027a
Dār al-Shifāʾ i, 1225b – I, 1262a
Dār al-Shifāʾ (Srīnagar) s, 353b – S, 353b
Dār al-Shifāʾ (Tihrān/Teheran) s, 23b – S, 23b
Dār al-Ṣināʿa ii, **129b;** iii, 271b; s, 120a – II, **132b;** III, 279b; S, 119b
Dār Sīnī s, **197a** – S, **197a**
Dār al-Siyāda iv, 48b – IV, 51a
Dār al-Ṣulḥ ii, **131a** – II, **134b**
Dār al-Tablīgh al-Islāmī iv, 166b – IV, 174a
Dār al-Taḳrib Baynaʾl-Madhāhib al-islāmīyya iv, 165b – IV, 172b
Dār al-Taḳrīb → Ikhtilāf
Dār Tāma ii, 123b – II, 126b
Dār al-Ṭibāʿa → Maṭbaʿa
Dār Ṭirāz → Ṭirāz
Dār al-ʿUlūm i, 817b, 818a, 819a, 820a; ii, **131b,** 205a; V, 909a, 910b; s, 18a, 262b – I, 840b, 841a; 842a, 843a; II, **135a,** 211b; V, 915a, 916b; S, 18a, 262a
Dār al-Wikāla iv, 136a – IV, 141b
Dāra (Abyssinia/Abyssinie) i, 176b – I, 181a
Darʿa → Adhriʿāt
Darʿa ii, **133b**; v, 1185a; s, 29a, 402b – II, **137a**; V, 1175a; S, 29a, 403a
Dārā, Dārāb ii, **132b**; iv, 809b – II, **136a**; 842a
Dārā Shukōh i, 229a, 768b, 769a, 781b, 1136a, 1166a; ii, 54b, **134a,** 378b; iii, 202a, b, 436a, 459a; iv, 69a; s, 308b – I, 235b, 791b, 792a, 805a, 1170b, 1200b; II, 55b, **137b,** 389a; III, 207b, 450b, 475b; IV, 73a; S, 308a
Dārāb Khān i, 81b – I, 83b
Dārābdjird i, 43b, 896b; ii, **135b** – I, 44b, 923a; II, **139a**
Dārābī, Ḥakīm ʿAbbās s, 308b – S, 308b
Darabukka ii, **135b** – II, **139a**
Ḍarāʾib i, 1144a; ii, 142b – I, 1178b; II, 146b
Darak s, **198a – S, 198a**
Darāk → Dawraḳ
Darakhsh i, 1233b – I, 1270a
al-Dāraḳuṭnī ii, **136a;** iii, 24b, 758a, 768b;s, 400b – II, **139b;** III, 25b, 781a, 791b; S, 401a
al-Darazī, Muḥammad ii, **136b,** 631b; iii, 80b, 154b – II, **140a,** 647b; III, 82b, 158a
Darb i, 672b – I, 693a
Darb → Madīna
Ḍarb → Dār al-Ḍarb; Sikka
Ḍarb (geomancy/géomancie) iv, 1128b – IV, 1160a
Darb Āl ʿAlī iii, 208a – III, 213b
Darb al-arbaʿīn ii, 122a, **137a** – II, 125a, **140b**
Darb al-Fīl i, 707b – I, 729a
Darb al-Kunhurī i, 748a – I, 770b
Darb Zubayda ii, 92a; s, **198b,** 304b – II, 94a; S, **198b,** 304b
Darband → Derbend
Darband-nāma ii, 141b – II, 145b
Darbkhāne → Dār al-ḍarb
Darbukka → Darabukka
Ḍarbzan (darbūzan) i, 1063a, 1066b – I, 1094b, 1098b
Darčīn s, 327a – S, 326b
Dard ii, **137b** – II, **141a**
Dard, Mīr s, 358b – S, 358b
Dardanelles → Čanaḳ-kalʿe Boghazî
Dardic and Kāfir Languages ii, **138a**; iv, 711b; v, 649a; s, 158b
Dardiques et Kāfires, Langues II, **142a**; IV, 740a; V, 653a; S, 158b
al-Dardīr i, 867b – I, 891b
Dardīriyya ii, **139b** – I, **143b**
Dardistān ii, **140a**; s, 167a – II, **143b**; S, 167a
al-Dardjīnī, Aḥmad i, 167a, 1053b; ii, **140b;** iii, 96b, 656b – I, 171b, 1085a; II, **144a;** III, 99a, 678a
Dargāh ii, **141b**; iv, 26a – II, **145a**; IV, 27b
Darghin i, 756a; ii, 86b, 89a, **141b**; iv, 846a, b; v, 285b – I, 778b; II, 88a, 90b, **145a**; IV, 879b, 880a; V, 283b
Darī ii, **142a**; iv, 55a – II, **146a**; IV, 58a
Darʿī, Moses iv, 605b – IV, 629b
Darial, Dariel → Bāb al-Lān
Ḍarība ii, **142b**; s, **199b** – II, **146a**; S, **199b**
Dārim iii, 49a; iv, 717a – III, 51a; IV, 746a
al-Dārimī, ʿAbdallāh ii, **159a;** iii, 24b – II, **164a;** III, 25b
al-Dārimī, Sufyān b. Mudjāshiʿ iv, 832b – IV, 865b
Dārin → Tārūt

Ḍarīr, Muṣṭafā ii, **159a** — II, **164a**
Darius, King/le roi → Dārā, Dārāb
Ḍariyya ii, **159b** — II, **164b**
al-Darʿiyya → al-Dirʿiyya
Darḳāwa i, 368b, 371a; ii, **160a,** 224a; iii, 261b, 696a, 701a, 968a; s, 371a — I, 379b, 382a; II, **165a,** 231a; III, 269a, 718b, 723a, 992b; S, 371a
Darna i, 1049a; ii, **160b** — I, 1081a; II, **165b**
Darōhar s, 163a — S, 163a
Daron → Dārūm
Darrābūn i, 687a — I, 708a
Darrās al-Fāsī iv, 341a; v, 1208b — IV, 355b; V, 1199a
Dar<u>sh</u>an ii, **162a** — II, **167a**
Darsim v, 465a — V, 468a
Dars-i Niẓāmī v, 1135b — V, 1131a
Dārū<u>gh</u>a ii, **162a;** iii, 491a; iv, 103b, 268b; s, 97a — II, **167a;** III, 508a; IV, 108a, 280b; S, 96b
Darūliyya → Eski<u>sh</u>ehir
al-Dārūm i, 1140a; ii, **163a** — I, 1174b; II, **168a**
Ḍarūra ii, **163b;** iii, 306b; iv, 692b — II, **168b;** III, 315b; IV, 720b
Darvī<u>sh</u> <u>Kh</u>usraw iv, 860b — IV, 894a
Darwī<u>sh</u> ii, **164a**; iv, 49b; s, 154a— II, **169a** IV, 52a; S, 154a
Darwī<u>sh</u> ʿAbdi iv, 1126a — IV, 1157b
Darwī<u>sh</u> ʿAlī <u>Kh</u>ān i, 722a — I, 743b
Darwī<u>sh</u> Muḥammad Naḳḳā<u>sh</u> i, 1211b — I, 1247b
Darwīza, A<u>kh</u>und i, 1121b, 1123a — I, 1155b, 1156b
Daryā ʿImād <u>Sh</u>āh iii, 425a, 1160b, 1161a — III, 439a, 1188b, 1189b
Daryā <u>Kh</u>ān Noḥānī ii, 1129a; v, 72a; s, **203a** — II, 1155b; V, 74a; S, **202b**
Daryā-begi ii, **165b** — II, **170b**
Daryā-yi <u>Sh</u>āhī → Urmiya
Dās, Rā<u>dj</u>ā <u>Bh</u>agwān s, 167a — S, 167a
Daskara ii, **165b** — II, **171a**
Dāsenī → Ṭasinī
Da<u>sh</u>i<u>sh</u>a v, 259a — V, 257a
Da<u>sh</u>takī, <u>Gh</u>iyā<u>th</u> al-Dīn iv, 610a — IV, 634b
Da<u>sh</u>tī, ʿAli iv, 73a; v, 199a — IV, 76b; V, 196a
Da<u>sh</u>t-i Kavīr iv, 2a; s, 149a — IV, 2a; S, 149a
Da<u>sh</u>t-i Kipčaḳ s, **203b** — S, **203a**
Da<u>sh</u>t-i Lūṭ iv, 2a-b, 4b; v, 147b, 352b — IV, 2a-b, 4b; V, 150a, 353b
Dasta<u>dj</u>ird ii, **166a** — II, **171b**
Dastān i, 422a; iii, 114b, 117a, 119a, 373a, 375b; v, 201b — I, 433b; III, 117a, 119b, 121b, 385a, 387b; V, 198b
Dāstā-i Ḳahramān → Ḳahramān-nāma
Dāstān-i Aḥmed Ḥarāmī iii, 375a — III, 386b
al-Dāstānī, <u>Sh</u>ay<u>kh</u> Abū ʿAbd Allāh i, 162b; iv, 1058a — I, 167a; IV, 1089a
Dastūr → Dustūr
Dastūr Dīnār iii, 15a — III, 16a
Dasūḳ s, 18a — S, 18a
al-Dasūḳī, Ibrāhīm b. ʿAbd al-ʿAzīz ii, **166a** — II, **171b**
al-Dasūḳī, Ibrāhīm b. Ibrāhīm ii, **167a** — II, **172b**
al-Dasūḳī, Ibrāhīm b. Muḥammad ii, **167b** — II, **172b**
Dātā Gan<u>dj</u> → Hu<u>dj</u>wīrī
Dates → Na<u>kh</u>la; Tamr
Da<u>th</u>īna ii, **167b,** 675b; iv, 746a, 747b — II, **173a,** 692a; IV, 776a, 777b
Dattes → Na<u>kh</u>la; Tamr
Dattū Sarwanī s, 313a — S, 312b
Dāʾūd, David → Dāwūd
Dāʾū-Potra → Bahāwalpūr
David ben Abraham al-Fāsī iv, 305b, 605a — IV, 319a, 629b
David b. al-Hītī iv, 605b — IV, 630a
Davitʿ i, 638a — I, 658b
Dawāʾ → Adwiya
Daʿwā ii, **170b** — II, **176a**
Daʿwa, daʿawāt i, 832b; ii, 97b, **168a**; iv, 203b; 815a — I, 855b; II, 99b, **173a**; IV, 212b; V, 521a
Daʿwa <u>dj</u>adīda iii, 254a — III, 261a
Dawā <u>Kh</u>ān → Duwā <u>Kh</u>ān
Dawādār ii, **172b** — II, **177b**
al-Ḍawāḥī i, 761a — I, 784a
Dawāʾir ii, **172b** — II, **178a**
Dawʿan ii, **173b** — II, **178b**
al-Dawānī, Muḥammad ii, **174a**; iv, 267b, 471b, 850b; v, 53b — II, **179a**; IV, 279b, 492b, 883b; V, 55a
Dawār ii, **174b**; s, 318b — II, **180a**; s, 318a
Dāwar → Zamīn-i Dāwar
Dāwar Ba<u>kh</u><u>sh</u> i, 686b; v, 74a — I, 707b; V, 76a
Dawārō i, 176b; ii, **175a;** iii, 3b — I, 181a; II, **180b;** III, 3b
Dawāsir i, 233b, 545b, 873b; ii, 108b, **175b**; v, 40a — I, 241a, 562b, 898a; II, 111a, **180b**; V, 41a
Dawāt v, 988b; s, **203b** — V, 984a; S, **203a**
Daʿwat al-<u>sh</u>ams ii, 370a — II, 380a
Dāwātdār iv, 759a — IV, 789a
Dawāwida i, 1247a — I, 1285a
Daʿwet ii, 314b — II, 323b
Dawḥa i, 536a — I, 552b
al-Dawḥa (Ḳaṭar) ii, **177a**; iv, 751a, b — II, **182b**; IV, 781b, 782a
Dawid b. Georgi La<u>sh</u>a v, 491a — V, 493b, 494a
Dawid b. Luarsab → Dāwūd <u>Kh</u>ān (Georgia/Géorgie)
Dawid II A<u>gh</u>ma<u>sh</u>enebeli v, 489b — V, 492a
Dawit I iii, 4a — III, 4a
Dāwiyya and/et Isbitāriyya i, 293b, 1119b, 1250b; ii, 6a, 529b; iii, 325b, 504a, 1006b; iv, 483b; v, 342b; s, **204b** — I, 302b, 1153a, 1288b; II, 6a, 542b; III, 325b; 521b, 1032a; IV, 483b; V, 342b; S, **204a**
Dawla ii, **177b**; iv, 293b; v, 621b, 623a — II, **183a**; IV, 306b; V, 625b, 627a
Dawlat-Begs s, 367b — S, 367a
Dawlat Čak s, 324b — S, 324a
Dawlat Girāy I ii, **178b**; v, 137a, 138a, b — II, **184b**; V, 139b, 141a
Dawlat Girāy II ii, 1047a; iv, 569a; v, 140b — II, 1071b; IV, 591a; V, 143a
Dawlat Girāy III i, 270b, 1287a — I, 279a, 1326b
Dawlat Ḳāḍī i, 606b — I, 626a
Dawlat <u>Kh</u>ān i, 809a — I, 832a
Dawlat <u>Kh</u>ān b. Shu<u>dj</u>āʿ i, 1155a — I, 1189b
Dawlat <u>Kh</u>ān Lōdī (d./m. 1414) i, 218a; iii, 417b, 485a; s, **206a** — I, 224b; III, 430b, 502a; S, **206a**
Dawlat <u>Kh</u>ān Lōdī (d./m. 1525) i, 848a; ii, 271a; iii, 420b, 995b; v, 598a — I, 871b; II, 224b; III, 434a, 1020a; V, 602a
Dawlat Rao Sindhiya i, 303a — I, 312b
Dawlat-<u>Sh</u>āh ii, **179a**; s, 65a, 84a, 415a — II, **185a**; S, 65b, 84a, 415a
Dawlatābād i, 1322b, 1329a; ii, 99b, **179b**; iv, 922b; v, 884a; s, 57b, 105a, b, 279b, 352b — I, 1363a, 1369b; II, 101b, **185a**; IV, 955b; V, 890b; S, 58a, 104b, 105a, 279b, 352b
— monuments i, 1323b; ii, **180a,** 442a — I, 1364a; II, **186a,** 456b
al-Dawlatābādī i, 702b, 859a; ii, **180b** — I, 724a, 883a; II, **186b**
Dawlatyār s, 367a — S, 368a
Dawr s, **206b** — S, **206a**
Dawraḳ ii, **181a**; v, 89a — II, **186b**; V, 91a
Daws i, **811b;** ii, 246b — I, **835a;** II, 253b
Dawsa ii, **181b** — II, **187a**
Dawsar ii, 354b — II, 364a
Dāwūd i, 261a; ii, **182a**; iv, 947b — I, 269a; II, **187b**;

IV, 980b
Dāwūd b. ʿAbbās al-Bānīdjūrī i, 1001a; s, 125a, b — I, 1032a; S, 124b
Dāwūd b. ʿAbd al-Raḥmān al-ʿAṭṭār i, 827a — I, 850a
Dāwūd b. Abī Dāwūd s, 125b — S, 124b
Dāwūd b. al-ʿĀḍid iv, 200b — IV, 209b
Dāwūd b. Abū Hind i, 104b — I, 107b
Dāwūd b. ʿAdjab Shāh i, 1254b; iv, 201a — I, 1292b; IV, 210a
Dāwūd b. ʿAlī b. ʿAbbās i, 43a; iv, 973b — I, 44a; IV, 1005b
Dāwūd b. Idrīs II iii, 1035b; iv, 632b — III, 1061b; IV, 657b
Dāwūd b. Khalaf al-Ẓāhirī i, 337a; ii, **182b,** 889b, 890a; v, 239b — I, 347b; II, **188a,** 910b; V, 237b
Dāwūd b. Ḳuṭb Shāh i, 1254b, 1255a; iv, 201a — I, 1292b, 1293a; IV, 210a
Dāwūd b. Marwān al-Raḳḳī → al-Muḳammiṣ
Dāwūd b. Muḥammad i, 300b — I, 309b
Dāwūd b. Suḳmān i, 664b, 983b; iii, 507a — I, 684b, 1014a; III, 524b
Dāwūd b. Sulaymān ii, 517a — II, 530a
Dāwūd b. Sulaymān (Kilwa) v, 106b, 1157b — V, 108b, 1147b
Dāwūd b. Yazīd b. Ḥātim s, 326b — S, 326a
Dāwūd al-Anṭāḳī → al-Anṭāḳī
Dāwūd Barakāt s, 159b — S, 159b
Dāwūd Burhān al-Dīn → Dāwūd b. Ḳuṭb Shāh
Dāwūd al-Faṭānī ii, **183a** — II, **188b**
Dāwūd Khākī, Bābā s, 167b — S, 167b
Dāwūd Khān (Carnatic/Carnatique) i, 624b — I, 645b
Dāwūd Khān (Fārūḳī) ii, 814b — II, 834a
Dāwūd Khān (Georgia/Géorgie) v, 493a — V, 495b, 496a
Dāwūd Khān (Gudjuratī) ii, 1125b — II, 1153a
Dāwūd Khān Kararānī ii, **183a;** ii, 202b, 423b — II, **189a;** III, 208a, 437a
Dāwūd Khān Kurayshī i, 1210a — I, 1246a
Dāwūd Khān (Rohilla) iii, 59b — III, 62a
Dāwūd Pasha (d./m. 1498) ii, **184a**; iv, 231a — II, **190a**; IV, 241b
Dāwūd Pasha (d./m. 1623) ii, **183b** — II, **189b**
Dāwūd Pāshā (d./m. 1851) i, 330b, 905b; ii, **184b,** 813a, 1257b; s, 75a — I, 340b, 993a; II, **190a,** 832a, 1290b; S, 75b
Dāwūd Pasha (d./m. 1875) ii, **184b,** 637a — II, **190b,** 653a
Dāwūd-Shāh Mengüček iv, 817b, 818b, 871a — IV, 850b, 851b, 904b
Dāwūd al-Ṭāʾī i, 124a — I, 127b
Dāwūdis i, 552b, 1255a; ii, 98a; iv, 201b — I, 570a, 1293a; II, 100a; IV, 210a
Dāwūdiyya → Ẓāhiriyya
Dāwūdpōtrās i, 230a; ii, **185a** — I, 237a; II, **191a**
al-Dawwānī i, 326b, 329a — I, 337a, 339a
Day → Layl and Nahār
Ḍayʿa i, 1145b; ii, **187b** — I, 1180a; II, **193b**
Dayak s, 150b, 151a — S, 151a
Dayā Bahādur ii, 219a — II, 225b
Dayānat Khān ii, 336b, 868b — II, 346a, 888b
Daybul ii, **188a;** iii, 441a; iv, 597b; s, 243a — II, **194a;** III, 455a; IV, 621b; S, 243a
Daydabān ii, **189a** — II, **195a**
Ḍayf ii, **189a;** iii, 1018a — II, **195a;** III, 1043b
Ḍayfa Khātūn iii, 87b — III, 89b
Dayi̊ i, 368a; ii, **189a** — I, 379a; II, **195a**
Daylam i, 20a; ii, **189b,** 732a, 1111a; iv, 19a, 345b, 346a, 1078a; s, 297b, 298a, 299a, 363a — I, 21a; II, **195b,** 750b, 1137a; IV, 20a-b, 360b, 1109b; S, 297a, b, 298b, 362b
Daylamān s, 335a — S, 334b
al-Daylamī, Abu 'l-Ḥasan iii, 823a — III, 846b
al-Daylamī, Abū Ṭāhir Ilyās s, 192b — S, 193b
Daylamī, Banu ʾl- s, 22b — S, 22b
Daylamites i, 190a, 688a, 839b, 1350a, 1354a, 1355b; ii, **190a**, 506a, 1082b, 1111b; iii, 197a, 671b, 1201b; iv, 208a, 465a, 859a; s, 118b, 309a, 356b — I, 195b, 709a, 863a, 1390a, 1393b, 1394b; II, **196a**, 518b, 1108a, 1137b; III, 202a, 693a, 1232a; IV, 217a, 485b, 892a; S, 118a, 309a, 356a
Dayn s, **207a** — S, **206b**
Dayr ii, **194b** — II, **200b**
Dayr ʿAbd al-Raḥmān ii, **195b** — II, **202a**
Dayr al-Aʿlā s, 36b — S, 36b
Dayr al-ʿĀḳūl ii, **196a** — II, **202a**
Dayr al-Aʿwar ii, **196b** — II, **202b**
Dayr al-Djamādjim i, 42b; ii, **196b,** 304b; iv, 289a, 495a, b; v, 639b — I, 43b; II, **203a,** 313a; IV, 302a, 516a, 517a; V, 644a
Dayr al-Djāthalīk ii, **197a** — II, **203a**
Dayr Kaʿb ii, **197b** — II, **203b**
Dayr al-Ḳamar s, 159a, 160b — S, 159a, 160b
Dayr Ḳunnā ii, **197b** — II, **203b**
Dayr Ḳurra ii, **197b** — II, **204a**
Dayr Murrān ii, **198a,** b — II, **204a,** b
Dayr Mūsa ii, **198b** — II, **204b**
Dayr al-Rummān ii, 198b — II, 205a
Dayr Samʿān ii, **198b;** iii, 130a — II, **204b;** III, 132b
Dayr al-Suryānī i, 201a, 624a; ii, 195b — I, 206b, 643b; II, 201b
Dayr al-Zōr ii, **198b**; iv, 655a — II, **205a**; IV, 681b
Dayrī, Banū v, 333a — V, 333a
Dayriyyāt iv, 1005a, b — IV, 1037b, 1038a
Dayrūṭ s, 132b — S, 132a
Daysam b. Ibrāhīm al-Kurdī i, 190a; ii, 680a; v, 451a — I, 194b; II, 697a; V, 454b
Dayṣāniyya ii, **199a**; v, 384b — II, **205a** V, 385b
Dayzan → al-Ḥaḍr
al-Ḍayzan b. Djabhala iii, 51a — III, 52b
Daza s, 165a — S, 165a
Dazā i, 1258a — I, 1296a
Dead Sea → Baḥr Lūt
Dēbal → Daybul
Debdou → Dubdū
Debt → Dayn
Deccan → Dakhan
Declamation → Shiʿr
Declension → Iʿrāb
Déclinaison → Iʿrāb
Decoration → Fann
Decree, Divine/Décret Divin → al-Ḳadāʾ wa ʾl-Ḳadar
Dedan i, 547b; v, 761b, 762a — I, 565a; V, 767b, 768a
Dede ii, **199b** — II, **206a**
Dede Aghač ii, **200a** — II, **206a**
Dede Ḳorḳut i, 311a, 419b; ii, 75b, **200a,** 1109a; iii, 374a — I, 321a, 431b; II, 77a, **206b,** 1135a; III, 385b
Dede Sulṭān i, 869b; ii, **200b** — I, 893b; II, **207a**
Dede ʿUmar Sikkīnī iii, 43b — III, 45a
Deed (juridical) → ʿAḳd
Default of Heirs → Mīrāth
Defter → Daftar
Defter Emini ii, **201a** — II, **207a**
Defterdār → Daftardār
Dehās ii, **201a** — II, **207a**
Dehhānī, Khodja ii, **201a** — II, **207b**
Dehkān → Dihḳan
Dehkhudā, ʿAlī Akbar s, **207b** — S, **207b**
Deir ez-Zor → Dayr al-Zōr
Deldoul s, 328b — S, 328a
Delhemme → Dhu 'l-himma
Delhi → Dihlī
Deli ii, **201a** — II, **207b**

Deli Birader → Ghazalī, Meḥmed
Deli Ḥasan Pasha ii, 208b; iv, 499a, 595a – II, 215a; IV, 520b, 619a
Deli Muṣṭafā i, 1278b – I, 1317b
Deli-Orman ii, **202a** – II, **208b**
Délit → Djarīma
Déluge → Nūḥ
Delvina ii, **203a** – II, **209b**
Demak s, 150b, 199b, 201a, 202a – S, 150b, 199b, 201a, b
Demavend → Damāwand
Demesne → Ḍayʿa
Demetrius/Démétrius i, 101a, 1132a – I, 104a, 1166a
Demir → Kemal Tahir
Demir Baba ii, 202b – II, 209a
Demir Khān b. Ḳarāmān iv, 622a – IV, 646b
Demir Khān b. Karasî iv, 628a – IV, 653a
Demir Kapî → Dar-i Āhanīn
Demirbāsh ii, **203b** – II, **210a**
al-Demirdāsh Bāshā, ʿAbd al-Raḥmān Muṣṭafā s, 208b – S, 208b
Demirdāshiyya i, 1152a; iv, 991b; s, **208a** – I, 1186a; IV, 1024a; S, **207b**
Demirtash → Timurtash
Demnat → Damnāt
Democracy/Démocratie → Djumhūriyya; Dustūr; Ḥurriyya; Shūrā
Demography/Démografie s, **209b** – S, **209a**
Demokrat Parti ii, **204a,** 569a, 645a; iv, 124b; v, 264a, 1038b – II, **210b,** 611a, 661b; IV, 129b; V, 261b, 1034b
Demon → Djinn; Shayṭān
Demotika → Dimetoḳa
Denau (Āmū Dāryā) s, 281a – S, 281a
Dendi ii, 94a – II, 96a
Deneb → Nudjūm
Denia → Dāniya
Deñizli ii, **204a** v, 557a, 588b; s, 44b, 138a – II, **210b**; V, 562a, 592b; S, 45a, 137b
Denkart iv, 11a – IV, 12a
Denktaş, Rauf v, 1078a – V, 1075b
Deoband ii, 55a, 132a, b, **205a,** 437a; v, 1135b; s, 66b, 74a, 292b, 293b – II, 56a, 135b, 136a, **211b,** 448b; V, 1131a; S, 67a, 74b, 292a, 293a
Deōgīri → Dawlatābād
Depālpur s, 105b – S, 105a
Deportation → Sürgün
Derʿa → Adhriʿāt
Dēra Fatḥ Khān ii, 205b; iii, 633b – II, 212a; III, 655a
Dēra Ghāzī Khān → Dēradjāt
Dēra Ismāʿīl Khān → Dēradjāt
Dēradjāt i, 1005b; ii, 185b, 186a, b, **205b**, 206a; iii, 633b; s, 329b, 331b, 332a – I, 1036b; II, 191b, 192a, b, **212a**; III, 655a; S, 329a, 331a, b
Derbend i, 32a, 835b, 921b, 1066b; ii, 85b, 87b, 88a, 115b, **206a** iv, 342b, 344a, b, 346a, 348a, b – I, 33a, 858b, 949a, 1098b; II, 87a, 89b, 90a, 118b, **212b**; IV, 357a, 358b, 359a, 361a, 362b, 363b
Derbouka → Darabukka
Derde Shay s, 165a, b, 166b – S, 165a, b, 166b
Derivation → Ishtiḳāḳ
Derdli, Ibrahim ii, **206b** – II, **212b**
Derdli Kātib ii, 202b – II, 209a
Derebey i, 469a; ii, **206b,** 446b – I, 483a; II, **213a,** 458b
Deren i, 748a – I, 770b
Dergāh → Dargāh
Derna → Darna
Dersim ii, **208a** – II, **214b**
Dervish/Derviche → Darwīsh
Derwīsh Ḥasan Pasha → Derwīsh Pasha (d./m. 1603)
Derwīsh Meḥmed Pasha (d./m. 1655) ii, **209a,** 339a; iii, 1248a – II, **215b,** 348b; III, 1280b
Derwīsh Meḥmed Pasha (d./m. 1777) ii, **209a** – II, **215b**
Derwīsh Meḥmed Pasha (d./m. 1837) i, 241a, 1078b; ii, **209b** – I, 248b, 1111a; II, **216a**
Derwīsh Meḥmed Ẓillī ii, 717b; v, 18a – II, 736a; V, 18b
Derwīsh Pasha (d./m. 1603) i, 1271a; ii, **208a** – I, 1310b; II, **214b**
Derwīsh Pasha (d./m. 1606) ii, **208b,** 287b; iv, 572b; v, 641a– II, **215a,** 295b; IV, 595a; V, 645a
Derwīsh Waḥdetī ii, 475a; iv, 283b – II, 487a; IV, 296a
Desert/Désert → Badw; Ṣaḥrāʾ
Déshérence → Mīrāth
Desk, Writing → Kitāba
Destān → Dastān
Destin, Destinée → al-Ḳaḍāʾ wa ʾl-Ḳadar
Destiny, Fate → al-Ḳaḍāʾ wa ʾl-Ḳadar
Destour ii, 639a; iii, 524a – II, 655a; III, 542a
Devagiri → Dawlatābād
Deval Devi ii, 269a, 695a, 1124a; iv, 922a – II, 277b 712b, 1150b; IV, 955a
Devarāya iii, 148a – III, 151a, b
Deve Boynu ii, **210a** – II, **216b**
Devedji ii, **210b** – II, **217a**
Develi Ḳara Ḥiṣār → Ḳara Ḥiṣār
Develŭ iv, 389a – IV, 406a
Devil → Iblīs; Shayṭān
Devise → Shiʿār
Devkot ii, 297a – II, 305a
Devshirme i, 36a, 206b, 268b, 269b, 656b, 712a, 807a, 999b; ii, **210b,** 1086a, 1087a; s, 269b – I, 36b. 212b, 276b, 278a, 677a, 733b, 830b, 1030a; II, **217a,** 1111b, 1112b; S, 269a
Dewa Emas Kayangan s, 151b – S, 152a
Dēwal → Daybul
Dewal Dewi → Deval Devi
Dewlet → Dawlat
Dewlet-berdi iii, 44a – III, 45b
Dey → Dayî
Deymer → Hüsnü, Shefīk
Dghughī → Sīdī Aḥmad Dghughī
Dghughiyyīn s, 350b – S, 350b
al-Dhabḥānī, Muḥammad b. Saʿīd iv, 449b – IV 469b
Dhabīḥa ii, **213a**; s, 221b – II, **219b**; S, 221b
Dhafār → Ẓufār
Dhahab ii, **214a,** 1002a, 1003a; v, 964a, 965b, 967a, 970a, 977a – II, **220b,** 1025a, 1026b; V, 968b, 969b, 972b, 976a
al-Dhahabī → Aḥmad al-Dhahabī; Aḥmad al-Manṣūr
al-Dhahabī, Shams al-Dīn i, 70a, 74b, 594b, 595a, 965a, 1238b; ii, 125b, **214b,** 522b, 523a; iii, 756a, 954b; s, 225b, 311b, 386b, 400a – I, 72a, 76b, 614a, b, 994b, 1276a; II, 128b, **221a,** 535b, 536a; III, 779a, 979a; S, 225b, 311b, 386b, 400b
Dhahabiyya → Kubrāwiyya
al-Dhahr → al-Ẓahr
Dhahran → Ẓahrān
Dhākā ii, 7a, **216a,** 426a – II, 7a, **222b,** 437a
Dhakāʾa ii, 213a – II, 220a
Dhakhīrat al-Iskandar i, 995a; iii, 463b, 464a – I, 1026a; III, 480a, b
Dhākir, Ḳāsîm Bey i, 193b; ii, **217a** – I, 199b; II, **223b**
Dhakwān b. ʿAmr al-Fuḳaymī ii, 998b – II, 1021b
Dhāl ii, **217b** – II, **224a**

Dhala → Ḍāliʿ
Dhalūl i, 541a — I, 558a
Dhamār ii, **218a**; s, 335a — II, **224b**; S, 334b
Dhamarmar s, 61b — S, 62a
al-Dhammiyya ii, **218a,** 570a — II, **225a,** 584b
Dhanab → Nudjūm
Dhanb iv, 1106b, 1109a — IV, 1138a, 1140b
Dhār ii, **218b,** 276b, 1124a; iii, 446a; s, 105a — II, **225a,** 285a, 1150b; III, 460b; S, 104b
Dharāʾiʿ i, 276a — I, 284b
Dharra ii, **219b** — II, **226b**
Dhārwār ii, **220a** — II, **226b**
Dhāt ii, **220a**; v, 1261a, 1262a — II, **227a**; V, 1252b, 1253a
Dhāt al-Himma → Dhu 'l-Himma
Dhāt al-Ṣawārī i, 51b, 936a; s, 120b, **221b** — I, 53a, 964b; S, 120a, **221b**
Dhātī i, 956a; ii, **220b,** 737b; iv, 1137b — I, 985b; II, **227b,** 756a; IV, 1169a
Dhawḳ ii, **221a,** 1041a — II, **228a,** 1065b
Dhawḳ, Muḥammad i, 807b, 914b, 1116a; ii, 83b, 84a, **221b;** iii, 1095a; iv, 716b; v, 960a, b, 961b; s, 107a — I, 831a, 942a, 1149b; II, 85b, **228b;** III, 1122a; IV, 745a; V, 964a, b, 965b; S, 106b
Dhawū ʿAbd Allāh iii, 263a — III, 270a
Dhawū 'l-Āḳāl i, 1247b — I, 1285b
Dhawū Barakāt iii, 263a — III, 270a
Dhawū Zayd iii, 263a — III, 270a
Dhawwāk → Čashnagīr
al-Dhiʾāb ii, **222b**; iv, 79a — II, **229b**; IV, 83a
Dhiʾb ii, **223a** — II, **230a**
Dhihnī, Bayburtlu ii, **223b** — II, **230b**
Dhikr i, 346b; ii, 55b, 160a, 164b, **223b,** 891b; iii, 1051a; iv, 94b, 487b, 992b; s, 313a — I, 357a; II, 56b, 165a, 169b, **230b,** 912a; III, 1077b; IV, 99a, 508b, 1025a; S, 313a
Dhikrīs, Zikrīs v, 1230b; s, **222a** — V, 1221a; S, **222a**
Dhimār → Dhamār
Dhimma i, 429b, 811a; ii, **227a**; iv, 1146b — I, 441b, 834a; II, **234a**; IV, 1178a
Dhimma ii, **231a** — II, **238a**
Dhimmī → Ahl al-Dhimma
Dhira i, 98b — I, 101a
Dhirāʿ ii, **231b** — II, **238b**
Dhiyāb b. Bādi iv, 893a — IV, 925b
Dhiyāb, Nadjīb ii, 471a — II, 483a
Dhiyān Singh i, 432b — I, 445a
Dhofar → Ẓufār
Dholkā iii, 445a — III, 460a
Dhū Bīn s, 22a — S, 22b
Dhū, dhī, dhā i, 194b, 195a; ii, **232b** — I, 200b; II, **239a**
Dhū 'l-Aktāf → Shāpūr II
Dhu 'l-Faḳār i, 742a; ii, **233a** — I, 764a; II, **239b**
Dhu 'l-Faḳār i, 903b; iii, 1257a — I, 931a; III, 1289b
Dhu 'l-Faḳār ʿAlī Khān iii, 61b — III, 64a
Dhu 'l-Faḳār Bahādur i, 1012b — I, 1044a
Dhu 'l-Faḳār Bey ii, 233b — II, 240a
Dhu 'l-Faḳāriyya ii, **233a**; iv, 723a, 852a — II, **240a** IV, 752a, 885a
Dhu 'l-Fiḳār Khān i, 295b, 1025b; ii, 379a, 810a — I, 304b, 1057b; II, 389b, 829a
Dhu 'l-Ḥidjdja iii, 31b, 33b — III, 33b, 35b → Taʾrīkh
Dhu 'l-Himma i, 1102b, 1103b, 1104a; ii, **233b** — I, 1136a, b, 1137a; II, **240b**
Dhū Ḥusā, Day of/Journée de s, 178a — S, 179a
Dhū ilāh iv, 421b — IV, 439b
Dhu 'l-Ḳaʿda → Taʾrīkh
Dhu 'l-Ḳadr i, 468a, b, 1190b; ii, 8a, **239a,** 724b; iii, 1105a; iv, 553a, 562b, 843a — I, 482a, 1225b; II, 8a, **246a,** 743b; III, 1132b; IV, 576b, 585a, 876a
Dhū Ḳār i, 690a, 964a; ii, **241a**; iv, 289a; v, 634a — I, 711a, 993b; II, **247a**; IV, 302a; V, 638a
Dhu 'l-Ḳarnayn → Iskandar
Dhu 'l-Ḳarnayn b. ʿAyn al-Dawla ii, 111a — II, 113b
Dhu 'l-Khalaṣa i, 865b; ii, **241b**; iv, 1106a — I, 889b; II, **248b**; IV, 1137b
Dhu 'l-Khimār → al-Aswad al-ʿAnsī
Dhu 'l-Kifl i, 404b; ii, **242a** — I, 416a; II, **249a**
Dhu 'l-lisānayn iv, 54b — IV, 57b
Dhū Marmar iv, 201a — IV, 209b
Dhu 'l-Marwa v, 316b — V, 316a
Dhu 'l-Nūn Abu 'l-Fayd ii, **242a** — II, **249a**
Dhu 'l-Nūn, Amīr ii, 111a — II, 113b
Dhū 'l-Nūn Beg Arghūn i, 627b; iv, 536b; v, 579b — I, 648a; IV, 560a; V, 584b
Dhu 'l-Nūn al-Miṣrī i, 274a, 718a; ii, **242a;** iii, 83b; iv, 990a — I, 282b, 739b; II, **249a;** III, 85b; IV, 1022b
Dhu 'l-Nūnid(e)s i, 7a, 202b; ii, **242b**; v, 392a — I, 7a, 208a; II, **249b**; V, 393a
Dhū Nuwās, Yūsuf Ashʿar i, 549a, 692b; ii, **243b**; v, 120b, 776b; s, 229b — I, 566a, 713b; II, **250b**; V, 123a, 782b; S, 229b
Dhū Raydān i, 548a, b — I, 565b, 566a
Dhu 'l-riyāsatayn iv, 51b — IV, 54b
Dhu 'l-Ruḳayba v, 526a — V, 529b, 530a
Dhu 'l-Rumma i, 586b; ii, 92b, **245a**; s, 42b — I, 605b; II, 94b, **252a**; S, 42b
Dhu 'l-Sharā ii, **246a**; iv, 321b; v, 1156b — II, **253a**; IV, 336a; V, 1146a
Dhu 'l-Yamīnayn Ṭāhir v, 57b — V, 59a
Dhū Yazan → Sayf
Dhuʾayb b. Mūsā iii, 134a; iv, 200b — III, 136b; IV, 209a
Dhubāb ii, **247b** — II, **254b**
Dhūbān, Shaykh s, 263a — S, 263a
Dhubbān iv, 96b — IV, 101a
Dhubyān, Banū ii, 71b, 873b, 1023a; s, 177a, 178a — II, 73a, 893b, 1046b; S, 178a, 179a
Dhufār → Ẓufār
Dhuhl b. Thaʿlaba i, 963a — I, 992b
Dhunnūnid(e)s → Dhu 'l-Nūnid(e)s
Dhunūb (sins, péchés) → Dhanb
al-Dhunūb, Dafn ii, **248a,** 303b ; iv, 407a — II, **255a,** 312a; IV, 424b
Dhurr → Ḳamḥ
Diable → Iblīs; Shayṭān
Dialect(e) → ʿArabiyya
Diamond/Diamant → Almās; Djawhar
Ḍibāb → ʿĀmir b. Ṣaʿṣaʿa
Dībādj → Ḳumāsh
al-Dībadjāt → Maldives
Dibbiyya s, 159a, b, 161b, 162a — S, 159a, b, 161a, 162a
al-Dibdiba ii, **248b** — II, **255b**
Diʿbil i, 154a, 1290a; ii, **248b**; iv, 929a; v, 375a; s, 32b, 35b — I, 158b, 1329b; II, **255b**; IV, 962a; V, 376a; S, 32b, 35b
Dibir i, 756a — I, 778b
Dibs, dbs ii, 1060b, 1062b, 1063b; iii, 400b — III, 1085a, 1087b, 1088a; III, 413a
al-Dibsī → Yaʿḳūb
Dictionary/Dictionnaire → Ḳāmūs; Farhang; Muʿdjam
Ḍīdān b. Fahhād → Ibn Ḥithlayn
Ḍidd i, 184b; ii, **249a** — I, 189b; II, **256a**
Dīdebān → Daydabān
Didja al-ʿAwrāʾ → Shaṭṭ al-ʿArab
Didjla i, 184a, 191a, 634b, 1094b, 1095a, b; ii, **249a;** iii, 1251a; iv, 654a, 675a; v, 442a, 645b, 646b, 864b, 945a; s, 37a — I, 189b, 196b, 655a, 1127b, 1128a, b; II, **256b;** III, 1283b; IV, 680b, 702b; V, 444b, 649b, 650b, 871b, 948b; S, 37a

Dido i, 756a; ii, 86b, 88b, **251a**; iv, 571b; v, 55b — I, 778b; II, 88a, 90b, **258b**; IV, 594a; V, 57a
Dienné i, 303a; ii, **251b** — I, 312b; II, **258b**
Dieu → Allāh
Dig (Bharatpur) s, 358b — S, 358b
Difrīgī → Diwrīgī
Digital Computation → Ḥisāb al-ʿAḳd
Diglal ii, **252b** — II, **260a**
Digue → Māʾ
Digurata → Ossetes
Dihak s, 127a — S, 126a
Dihātī → Muḥammad Masʿūd
Dihgāns i, 224a, b — I, 230b, 231a
Dih-i Naw → Djand
Dihistān ii, **253a**; s, 299a — II, **260a**; S, 298b
al-Dihistānī, ʿAbd al-Djalīl i, 1052b — I, 1084a
Dihḳan ii, **253b**; v, 853a, 854a — II, **261a**; V, 860a, 861a
Dihkhudā, ʿAlī Akbar iv, 72b, 527a — IV, 76b, 549b
Dihlawī, ʿAbd al-Ḥaḳḳ s, 353b — S, 353b
al-Dihlawī, Aḥmad Ḥasan s, 409a — S, 409b
al-Dihlawī, Nūr al-Ḥaḳḳ → Nūr al-Ḥaḳḳ al-Dihlawī
al-Dihlawī, Shāh ʿAbd al-ʿAzīz i, **59a,** 1193a; ii, 254b; s, 293a — I, **60b**; 1228a; II, 261b; S, 292b
al-Dihlawī, Shāh Walī Allāh i, 297b, 593a, 937a; ii, 138a, 205b, **254a,** 437a; iii, 324a, 358b, 430b, 432b, 435a, b; v, 833a; s, 126b, 292b — I, 306b, 612b, 965b; II, 141b, 211b, **261b,** 448b; III, 334a, 369b, 444b, 446b, 449a, b; V, 839b; S, 126a, 292b
Dihlī ii, 205a, **255b;** iii, 420a; v, 883b, 1135a; s, 57b, 66b, 74a, 102a, 247a, 353a, b, 358b — II, 211b, **263a;** III, 433b; V, 890a, 1130b; S, 58a, 67a, 74b, 101b, 247a, 353a, 358b
- history/histoire i, 230a, 914a, 953b; ii **255-9**; v, 6a — I, 237a, 942a, 983a; II, **263-7**; V, 6a
- monuments i, 1321b, 1324a, 1348a; ii, 254a, **259-66;** iii, 287b, 441a, 442a, b, 443a, 449a; iv, 268b; v, 1214b, 1219b — I, 1362a, 1364b, 1388b; II, 261b, **267-74;** III, 296b, 455b, 456b, 457a, b, 464b; IV, 280b; V, 1204b, 1210a
Dihlī Sultanate/Sultanat de- i, 34a, 1036a, 1321b; ii, 153b, **266b,** 336a, 1124a; iii, 198b, 201a, 416a, 417a, 420a; iv, 218a, 759a; v, 598a, 685a, 1214b; s, 117b, 124a, 203a, 206a, b, 258a, 284b, 359b, 409a — I, 34b, 1067b, 1362a; II, 158b, **274b,** 345b, 1150b; III, 203b, 206b, 429b, 430a, 433b; IV, 228a, 789b; V, 601b, 690b, 1204a, b; S, 117a, 123a, 202b, 206a, 257b, 284b, 359b, 409b
- art ii, **274a** — II, **282b**
Dihwārs i, 224a — I, 230b
Diḥya b. Khalīfa al-Kalbī ii, **274b,** 363b, 846a; iv, 492b, 839a — II, **283a,** 373b, 866a; IV, 514a, 872a
Dīk ii, **275a** — II, **283b**
al-Dīkdān s **222b** — S, **222b**
Dīk al-Djinn al-Ḥimṣī ii, **275b** — II, **284a**
Dike → Māʾ
Dikka ii, **276a** — II, **284b**
Dikwa i, 1260a, b; ii, 10b — I, 1298b; II, 10b
Ḍilʿ i, 536b — I, 553a
Dil Hersek iii, 341b — III, 352a
al-Dilāʾ v, 1191b; s, 29a, **223a** — V, 1181b; S, 29a, **223a**
Dilāla ii, 102b — II, 104b
Dilāʾiyyūn s, 223a — S, 223a
al-Dilam iv, 1072b, 1073a — IV, 1104a, b
Dilāwar Khān (d./m. 1405) ii, 218b, 219a, 270b, **276a,** 1125a; iii, 417a, 638a — II, 225b, 226a, 278b, **284b,** 1151b; III, 430b, 659a
Dilāwar Khān (Ḥabshī, 1492) iii, 15a — III, 16a
Dilāwar Khān (Ḥabshī, 1588) ii, 921b, 922a; iii, 15b, 426b — II, 943a; III, 16a, 440b
Dilāwar Khān Lōdī iii, 995b; iv, 1020a — III, 1020a; IV, 1052a
Dilāwar Pasha ii, **276b** — II, **285a**
Dilāzāks i, 218b — I, 224b
Dildār ʿAlī iii, 434a — III, 448b
Dilfān v, 617a — V, 621a, b
Dilshād Khātūn i, 908b; ii, 68a — I, 936a; II, 69b
Dilsiz ii, **277a** — II, **285b**
Dimashḳ i, 153b, 256a, 551b, 824a, 870a, 975a, b, 1029a, b, 1332a; ii, **277b,** 360a, 541a, 1105a, 1106a; iii, 714a, 931b, 958a; iv, 174b, 214b; v, 993a; s, 20b, 37a, 49a, 195a, b, 199a, 239a, 268a — I, 157b, 264a, 569a, 847a, 894b, 1005b, 1006a, 1061a, 1372b; II, **286a,** 369b, 554b, 1131a, 1132a; III, 736b, 956a, 982b; IV, 182b, 224a; V, 988a; S, 20b, 37b, 49b, 195a, b, 199a, 239a
- the Great Mosque/la grande mosquée i, 610b, 622a; ii, 280b, 281a, 282a, b, 286a, 956a, b; iii, 286b, 921a — I, 631b, 643a; II, 289a, b, 290a, b, 294a, 978a, b; III, 295b, 945b
- institutions i, 1224a; ii, 283a, b, 286a, 288a, b, 289a, 290a, 424a; iii, 139b; v, 1127a — I, 1260b; II, 291a, b, 294a, 296a, b, 297a, 298a, 453a; III, 142b; V, 1123b
- monuments i, 831a, 1316a; ii, 280b, 283a, 284b, 285a, 286a, 287b, 1106a; iii, 142a; v, 217b, 1139a, 1140a — I, 854a, 1356a; II, 288b, 291a, 292b, 293a, 294a, b, 295b, 1132a; III, 146a; V, 215a, 1133a, 1133b
Dimashḳ Khodja b. Sālim ii, 614a — II, 629a
al-Dimashḳī → Abū ʿUthmān; Ibn Isrāʾīl; Shams al-Dīn Muḥammad
al-Dimashḳī, Shams al-Dīn i, 594b; ii, **291a**; iv, 1081b, v, 1012b; s, 45a, 130b — I, 613b; II, **299a**; IV, 1113a; V, 1008a; S, 45b, 129b
Dimetoḳa ii, **291b** — II, **299b**
Dimitrash i, 808b — I, 832a
Dimlī → Zāzā
Dīmuḳrāt s, 154b — S, 155a
Dimyāṭ i, 946b; ii, 63b, 72b, **292a**; iv, 520b; v, 92a; s, 120b — I, 976a; II, 65a, 74a, **300a**; IV, 543a; V, 94b; S, 120a
al-Dimyāṭī al-Shāfiʿī ii, **292b** — II, **300b**
al-Dimyāṭī, al-Bannāʾ ii, **293a** — II, **301a**
al-Dimyāṭī, Nūr al-Dīn ii, **293a** — II, **301a**
Dīn ii, **293b**; iv, 171b, 174a; v, 621b, 622b, 623a, b, 629a; — II, **301b**; IV, 179a, 181b; V, 625b, 626b, 627a, b, 633a
Dīnādjpur ii, **297a** — II, **305a**
Dīnār ii, 120b, **297a,** 768b; v, 964a, 965b — II, 123a, **305a,** 787a; V, 968b, 969b
Dīnār, Malik ii, **299a,** 1109a; iii, 1099b; v, 160b — II, **307a,** 1135a; III, 1126b; V, 159a
Dīnār-Sārī s, 235a — S, 235a
Dīnawar ii, **299a**; iv, 13b; v, 169b; s, 17b — II, **307a**; IV, 14b; V, 167a; S, 17b
al-Dīnawarī, Abū Ḥanīfa Aḥmad i, 135b, 213a, b, 718b; ii, **300a**; v, 1025a; s, 42b, 128b, 249b, 277a, 314a — I, 139b, 219a, 220a, 740a; II, **308a**; V, 1021a; S, 42b, 128a, 250a, 276b, 313b
al-Dīnawarī, Abū Saʿīd Naṣr ii, **300b;** iii, 772a; s, 259a — II, **309a;** III, 795b; S, 258b
Dindān ii, **301a** — II, **309a**
Dinet, Alphonse s, **224a** — S, **224a**
Dīn-i ilāhī i, 317a; ii, **296a;** iii, 423b, 459a — I, 327a; II, **304a;** III, 437b, 475b
Dionysos → Aʿara
Diophantes iv, 600a — IV, 624a
Dioula ii, 63a; v, 252b — II, 64b; V, 250b
Dioscorides/Dioscoride → Diyusḳuridīs
Diplomacy → Elči; Muʿāhada; Safīr
Diplomatic ii, **301b**
Diplomatie → Elči; Muʿāhada; Safīr
Diplomatique II, **309b**
Dīr s, 132a — S, 131b

Dīr (India/Inde) i, 864a; ii, 30b, **316b** — I, 888b, II, 31a, **325b**
Dir (Somali(e)) ii, 317b — II, 327a
Dīrač → Drac
Ḍirār b. ʿAmr i, 333b; iii, 1037a, 1143a, 1166a; iv, 692b; s, 88b, 89a, **225b** — I, 344a; III, 1063a, 1171b, 1194b; IV, 720b; S, 88b, 89a, **225b**
Ḍirār b. Ḥusayn ii, 72a — II, 73a
Ḍirār b. al-Khaṭṭāb ii, **317b;** iii, 975b; iv, 775a — II, **326b;** III, 1000b; IV, 806b
Dire Dawa ii, **317b** — II, **326b**
Ḍirghām i, 197a; ii, **317b,** 856b — I, 202b; II, **327a,** 876b
Dirham ii, 119a, 121a, **319a,** 991b; iii, 1116a; iv, 248b; v, 855a, 964a, 965b — II, 121b, 124a, **328b,** 1016a; III, 1143b; IV, 259b; V, 862a, 968b, 970a
Dirham b. Naṣr b. Ṣāliḥ iv, 20b — IV, 22a
al-Dirʿiyya i, 628b; ii, 159b, **320b;** iii, 678b; iv, 925a, b, 1072b; v, 508a; s, 30b — I, 649b; II, 165b, **329b;** III, 700a; IV, 958a, b, 1104b; V, 511b; S, 30b
Dirlik ii, **322a** — II, **331b**
Dirridj ii, 135b — II, 139a
Dissolution → Faskh
Ditch → Khandaḳ
Diū ii, **322a** — II, **331b**
Divan → Dīwān
Divination → Kihāna
Divittār → Dawādār
Divorce → Ṭalāḳ
Dīw ii, **322b,** 1125a, 1128a, b; iv, 332a — II, **332a,** 1151a, 1155a, b; IV, 346b
Dīwān (administrative/administration) i, 19b, 279b, 316b, 382a, 729a, b, 801b, 905b, 1003b, 1141b, 1143a, 1145b; ii, 304b, 305b, **323a,** 360a, 505b; iv, 26a, 937b; v, 500b; s, 210a — I, 20a, 288a, 326b, 393a, 751b, 825a, 933a, 1034a, 1176a, 1177b, 1180a; II, 313a, 314a, **332b,** 370a, 518a; IV, 27b, 970b; V, 504a; S, 210a
Dīwān (poetic/poésie) i, 143b, 1070a; ii, **323a,** 999b — I, 147b, 1102a; II, **332b,** 1023a
Dīwān-i aḥkām-i ʿadliyye i, 56b, 285a — I, 58b, 293b
Dīwān-Begi s, 97a, **227b** — S, 96b, **227b**
Dīwān al-djaysh i, 1145b; ii, 326a, 328b, 330b, 331b; iv, 265a, 266a — I, 1180a; II, 335b, 338b, 340a, 341a; IV, 276b, 278a
Dīwān al-djund ii, 323b, 325b, 326a, 601b — II, 333a, 335a, b, 616b
Dīwān-i Ḥikmet i, 299a — I, 308a
Dīwān-i Humāyūn ii, **337b** — II, **347a**
Dīwān al-inshāʾ ii, 302b, 303b, 305a, b, 326a, b, 328a, b, 330a, 336a; iii, 1242b; iv, 758b, 759a, 1182a; s, 409a — II, 311a, 312a, 313a, 314a, 335b, 336a, 337b, 338a, 339b, 346a; III, 1274b; IV, 789a, b, 1215a; S, 409b
Dīwān al-madāris v, 908b, 909a — V, 914a, b, 915a
Dīwān al-muḳātila → Dīwān al-djaysh
Dīwān School s, 58a — S, 58a
Dīwān Sāwan Mal s, 332a — S, 331b
Diwān al-shiʿr i, 1035b — I, 1067a
Dīwān al-Shūrā → Madjlis al-Shūrā
Dīwānī i, 1145b; ii, 128a, 332b; iv, 1125b, 1127b — I, 1180a; II, 131a, 342a; IV, 1157b, 1159a
Dīwāniyya ii, **339b** — II, **349a**
Dīwānkhāne ii, 338b — II, 348a
Dīwdād → Abu 'l-Sādj
Diwrīgī ii, **340a** — II, **349b**
Ḍiyāʿ → Ḍayʿa
Diya i, 29a, 31b, 171b, 338a, 892a; ii, 228a, **340b**; iv, 766b; v, 180a — I, 30a, 32a, 176a, 348b, 918b; II, 235a, **350b**; IV, 797a; V, 177b
Ḍiyāʾ al-Dīn b. al-Athīr → Ibn al-Athīr
Ḍiyāʾ al-Dīn Muḥammad → ʿAlāʾ al-Dīn Muḥammad
Ḍiyā Gökalp → Gökalp, Ziya
Ḍiyāʾ al-Ḥaḳḳ → Zia ul-Haqq
Ḍiyāʾ al-Dīn, Sayyid iv, 398b — IV, 416a
Ḍiya Pasha → Ẓiya Pasha
Diyāb i, 167b — I, 172a
Ḍiyāfa → Ḍayf, Mihmān, Musāfir
Ḍiyāʾiyya s, 195b, 197a — S, 195b, 197a
Diyālā i, 184a; ii, **343a**; v, 442a — I, 189b; II, **352b**; V, 444b
Diyānat → Dayānat
Diyār Bakr i, 4b, 8a, 639a, 662b, 664a, 665b, 666a, 1054a; ii, 8a, **343b,** 384b, 523b, 707a; iii, 1197b; iv, 90b, 816b; v, 453a, 457b; s, 36b, 37a, 63a, 250a, 266b — I, 4b, 8a, 659b, 683b, 684a, 686a, 1085b; II, 8a, **353a,** 395a, 536b, 725a; III, 1227b; IV, 94b, 849b; V, 455b, 460a; S, 36b, 37a, 63a, 250a, 266a
Diyār Muḍar i, 11a, 119b, 804a; ii, **347a,** 523b — I, 11a, 123a, 828a; II, **357a,** 536b
Diyār Rabīʿa ii, 344a, **348a,** 523b; s, 37a — II, 353b, **357b,** 536b; S, 37a
al-Diyārbakrī, Ḥusayn ii, **349a** — II, **358b**
Diyusḳuridīs i, 3a, 213a, b; ii, **349a;** iii, 147b, 259a, 737b, 928a; iv, 254b; s, 43a, 59b, 78a, 114b — I, 3a, 219a, 220a; II, **359a;** III, 150b, 266a, 760a, 952b; IV, 266a; S, 43b, 60a, 77b, 114b
Diz (river/rivière) v, 81a, 887a — V, 83b, 893b
Dizai v, 471b, 473b — V, 474b, 476b
Dizfūl ii, **350a**; iv, 7b, 675a; v, 867b; s, 75a, b — II, **359b**; IV, 8b, 703a; V, 873b; S, 75b
Dizi-i Pisar-i ʿUmāra → al-Dīkdān
Diz-i Siyāh v, 63a, 831b — V, 65a, 837b
Dizmār iv, 1044a, b — IV, 1075b
al-Djaʿalī, Muḥammad v, 267a — V, 264b
Djaʿaliyyūn ii, **351a,** 944b; v, 1248b; s, 164a — II, **360b,** 966b; V, 1239a; S, 164a
Djaʿba iv, 799b, 800a — IV, 831b, 832a
Djabā → Bennāk
Djaba → Djebe
Djāba (Chamba) ii, **352a** — II, **361b**
Djabaev → Djambul Djabaev
Djabal → name of mountain/nom de la montagne
al-Djabal → al-Djibal
Djabal ʿĀmila i, 463a; iv, 484a — I, 448b; IV, 504b
Djabal ʿAmūr iv, 481b; s, 144b — IV, 502b; S, 144a
Djabal Bāriz v, 148a, 153b — V, 150b, 154b
Djabal Ḥamrīn s, 100a — S, 99b
Djabal-i Barakāt → Yarpūt
Djabal al-Ḥārith → Aghridāgh; Djudī
Djabal al-Ḳilāl i, 935b — I, 964b
Djabal Masār s, 22a — S, 22b
Djabal Mūsā s, 124b — S, 124a
Djabal Nafūsa i, 139a, 1186a; ii, 369a, 441b; iii, 657b, 927b; iv, 78a, 919b — I, 143a, 1221a; II, 379a, 453a; III, 678b, 952a; IV, 82a, 952b
Djabal al-Raḥma i, 604a; iii, 35b — I, 623b; III, 37a, b
Djabal Says s, 117a, b, **228b** — S, 116b, **228b**
Djabal Shammar i, 536b; iii, 326b; S, 3b, 304b, 407b — I, 553a; III, 336b; S, 2b, 304a, 407b
Djabal al-Sirādj ii, 817b — II, 837a
Djabal al-Summāḳ iv, 200a — IV, 208b
Djabal Taḳarbūst iv, 478b, 479a, b — IV, 499b, 501a, b
Djabal Ṭāriḳ i, 79b, 124b, 439a; ii, **352b** — I, 81b, 128a, 508a; II, **362a**
Djabal al-Ṭayr i, 535b — I, 551b
Djabal Thawr iii, 760a — III, 783a
Djabal Zarhūn s, 53a, 350b — S, 53b, 350b
Djabala (Nadjd) ii, **353b;** iii, 49a; v, 526a, 640a, b — II, **363a;** III, 51a; V, 529b, 644b
Djabala (Syria/Syrie) ii, **353a** — II, **363a**
Djabala b. al-Ayham i, 1339a; ii, 24b, **354a**; iv, 820b

— I, 1379a; II, 25a, **364a**; IV, 853b
Djabala b. al-Ḥārith iv, 556b; s, **229b** — IV, 580b; S, **229b**
Djabanyāna s, 11a — S, 10b
Djaʿbar, Ḳalʿat ii, **354a** — II, **364a**
Djaʿbar b. Sābik ii, 354b — II, 364a
Djabarites → Djabrids/Djabrites
Djabart (Djabara) i, 763b; ii, **355a,** 709a, 710a; iii, 5a, b; v, 522a — I, 786b; II, **364b,** 728a, 729a; III, 5a, 6a; V, 525b
al-Djabartī, ʿAbd al-Raḥmān i, 707a, 819b; ii, 109b, **355a**; s, 38b, 302a — I, 728b, 842b; II, 112a, **365a**; S, 38b, 302a
Djabarūt → ʿĀlam
Djabbāna v, 23a, 347a — V, 24a, 348a
al-Djabbār → Nudjūm
Djabbāra i, 942b; iv, 9b — I, 971b; IV, 10a
Djabbul ii, **357a** — II, **366b**
al-Djabbūl i, 1349a; ii, **357a;** iii, 85a — I, 1389a; II, **367a;** III, 87b
Djabbūya → Yabghu
Djābir, Banū s, 356a — S, 356a
Djābir b. ʿAbd Allāh al-Anṣārī s, 75a, 94a, **230a** — S, 75b, 93b, **230a**
Djābir b. Aflaḥ i, 1250a; ii, **357a**; s, 413b — I, 1288a; II, **367a**; S, 414a
Djābir b. Ḥayyān i, 131b, 235b, 247a, 995a, 1100b, 1156a; ii, **357a,** 370b, 375a, 949b; iii, 267a, 378a; v, 112a, 113a; s, 270a — I, 135a, 242b, 255a, 1025b, 1133b, 1190a; II, **367b,** 380b, 385b, 971b; III, 274b, 389b; V, 114b, 115b; S, 269b
Djābir b. Zayd ii, **359b;** iii, 648b, 649a, b, 652a — II, **369a;** III, 669b, 670a, 671a, 673b
Djābir al-Djuʿfī s, **232b** — S, **232a**
al-Djābiya ii, 280a, **360a**; s, 117a, 229b — II, 288b, **369b**; S, 116b, 229b
Djabr i, 371b; ii, 365a, 388b; s, **233a** — I, 382b; II, 375a, 399a; S, **233a**
al-Djabr wa 'l-Muḳābala ii, **360b**; iv, 1070a — II, **370b**; IV, 1102a
Djabr b. al-Ḳāsim ii, **362b** — II, **372b**
Djabrāʾīl ii, **362b,** 846a, 847a; v, 210a; s, 231a — II, **372b,** 866a, b, 867a; V, 207b; S, 231a
Djabrāʾīl b. Bahāʾ al-Din Djadja v, 172a, b — V, 169b, 170a
Djabrāʾīl b. Bukhtīshūʿ i, 1223a, 1298a — I, 1259b, 1338a
Djabrān Khālīl Djabrān i, 597a; ii, **364a,** 404a, 471b; v, 188b, 1254b, 1255a, b, 1256b — I, 616b; II, **373b,** 415a, 483b; V, 185b, 1245b, 1246a, b, 1247b
Djabrī Saʿdallāh → Saʿd Allāh Djabrī
Djabrids/Djabrites i, 942b; ii, 176a; iv, 764b; s, **234a** — I, 971b; II, 181b; IV, 795a; S, **234a**
Djabriyya i, 249b, 257b; ii, **365a;** iii, 1142b; iv, 271b — I, 257b, 265b; II, **375a;** III, 1171a; IV, 283b
Djabuk i, 983a — I, 1013b
Djaʿd b. Dirham → Ibn Dirham
Djaʿda i, 233b; ii, **365a**; iv, 745b — I, 240b; II, **375a** IV, 775b
Djaʿda b. Kaʿb → ʿĀmir b. Ṣaʿṣaʿa
Djadd, Banu 'l- iii, 748a — III, 771a
al-Djadd b. Ḳays s, 131a — S, 130b
Djaddibal s, 423b — S, 423b
Djadhīma al-Abrash i, 196b, 450b; ii, **365b**; iv, 820a; s, 272a — I, 202a, 463b; II, **375b**; IV, 853a; S, 272a
Djadhīma b. ʿĀmir ii, **365b**; s, 189b — II, **375b**; S, 190b
Djadhīma b. ʿAwf iv, 764a — IV, 794b
Djadhmā i, 1225a — I, 1261b
Djadīd ii, **366a,** 932b; iv, 792a, 848a — II, **376a,** 954a; IV, 824a, 881a
al-Djadīda i, 56a, 85a, 291a, 356b, 809b; ii, **366b** — I, 57b, 87b, 300a, 367a, 833a; II, **376b**
Djadīdīs → Nūristānīs
Djadīs → Ṭasm
Djādisiyya → al-Ḳādisiyya
Djadjarm s, 83a, **235a** — S, 83a, **234b**
al-Djādjarmī, Badr al-dīn b. ʿUmar s, **235b** — S, **235a**
al-Djādjarmī, Muḥammad b. Badr s, **235b** — S, **235b**
Djādū ii, **368a**; s, 15b — II, **378a**; S, 15b
Djādū ii, **368b** — II, **378b**
Djadwal ii, **370a** — II, **380a**
al-Djady → Nudjūm
Djāf i, 512b; ii, **370b,** 491a — I, 528a; II, **380b,** 503b
Djaʿfar (Ḳarmaṭī) iv, 663b — IV, 690a, b
Djaʿfar, Banū i, 441b, 442a; v, 489b — I, 454a, b; V, 492b
Djaʿfar, Mīr ii, **371a,** 1091b — II, **381a,** 1117a
Djaʿfar, Mullā s, 53a — S, 53b
Djaʿfar b. ʿAbd Allāh i, 1306b, 1307b — I, 1346b, 1347b
Djaʿfar b. ʿAbd al-Raḥmān v, 1009b — V, 1005a
Djaʿfar b. Abī Ṭālib i, 109b, 118b, 152b; ii, **372a;** iii, 1266a; v, 398b; s, 92b — I, 112b, 122a, 157a; II, **382a;** III, 1298b; V, 400a; S, 92b
Djaʿfar b. Abī Yaḥyā, Shams al-Dīn Abu ʾl-Faḍl s, **236a** — S, **236a**
Djaʿfar b. ʿAlī al-Andalusī i, 1044b, 1238a, 1309a; ii, **372b;** iii, 1042b; v, 1176a, b, 1177a, — I, 1076a, 1275b, 1349b; II, **383a;** III, 1068b; V, 1166a, b, 1167a
Djaʿfar b. ʿAlī (Tiflīs) iv, 346b, 347b; v, 489a, b — IV, 361a, 362a; V, 491b, 492a, b
Djaʿfar b. al-Faḍl b. al-Furāt → Ibn al-Furāt, Djaʿfar
Djaʿfar b. Fahardjis v, 451b — V, 454a
Djaʿfar b. al-Hādī s, 116b — S, 116a
Djaʿfar b. Ḥamza s, 223a — S, 223a
Djaʿfar b. Ḥarb ii, **373a;** iii, 1037a, 1266a; iv, 126b, 629b — II, **383a;** III, 1063a, 1299a; IV, 132a, 721a
Djaʿfar b. Hārūn iv, 645a — IV, 671b
Djaʿfar b. al-Ḥasan al-Uṭrūsh s, 356b, 357a — S, 356b, 357a
Djaʿfar b. Ḥinzāba iv, 419b — IV, 438a
Djaʿfar b. al-Ḳāsim al-ʿIyānī s, 22a — S, 22b
Djaʿfar b. Khiḍr → Kāshif al-Ghiṭāʾ
Djaʿfar b. Ḳudāma al-Kātib v, 319a, b — V, 318b, 319a
Djaʿfar b. Manṣūr al-Yaman ii, 861b; s, **236b** — II, 881b; S, **236b**
Djaʿfar b. Mubashshir ii, **373a;** iii, 1266a; s, 89a — II, **383a;** III, 1299a; S, 89a
Djaʿfar b. Muḥammad → Abū Maʿshar al-Balkhī
Djaʿfar b. Muḥammad (Kalbid(e)) iv, 497a — IV, 518a
Djaʿfar b. Muḥammad (Mūsāwid(e)) iii, 262b — III, 270a
Djaʿfar b. Muḥammad b. Aḥmad b. Hudhār s, 1a — S, 1a
Djaʿfar b. Muḥammad b. Ḥamdān al-Mawṣilī ii, 127a; v, 1125a — II, 130b; V, 1121b
Djaʿfar b. Muṣṭafā b. ʿAlī Zayn al-Ābidīn i, 781b — I, 805a
Djaʿfar b. al-Sammāk al-ʿAbdī iii, 649b — III, 671a
Djaʿfar b. Sulaymān iii, 876a, 878a — III, 900a, 902a
Djaʿfar b. Yaḥyā al-Barmakī i, 14a, 718a, 1034a, b, 1035b, 1045a, 1114b, 1298a; ii, 78a, 195a, 281b, 305a, 731a; iii, 233a — I, 14a, 739a, 1065b, 1066a, 1067a, 1077a, 1148a, 1338a; II, 79b, 201a, 289b, 313b, 749b; III, 239b
Djaʿfar b. Yūsuf iv, 497a — IV, 518b
Djaʿfar Beg ii, **373b** — II, **383b**
Djaʿfar Čelebi ii, **374a,** 839b — II, **384a,** 859a
Djaʿfar al-Falāḥ ii, 854a; iii, 246a — II, 874a; III,

253a
Djaʿfar Khān Gakkhaŕ iii, 336a — III, 346a
Djaʿfar Khān Zand iii, 1191a; iv, 104b, 391a; iv, 104b, 391a; v, 825b, 835a; s, 336a, 405b — III, 1221a; IV, 109a, 408a; V, 831b, 841a; S, 335b, 405b
Djaʿfar Ḳulī Khān iv, 104b, 391a — IV, 109a, 408a
Djaʿfar Pasha i, 183b — I, 188b
Djaʿfar al-Ṣādiḳ b. Muḥammad al-Bāḳir i, 48a, 134a, 402a, 402b, 1082a, 1116b, 1156a, 1245a; ii, 168b, 357b, 359a, **374a,** 377b, 761a, 857a; iii, 496b, 616b, 682b, 1061a, 1166b; iv, 114b, 1132a, b, 1134a; v, 1236b; s, 231b, 232b, 233a, 401a — I, 49b, 137b, 412b, 414a, 1114b, 1150b, 1190b, 1283a; II, 174a, 367b, 368b, s, 231b, 232b, 233a, 401a, **384b,** 387b, 779a, 877a; III, 513b, 637a, 704b, 1087b, 1195b; IV, 119b, 1163b, 1164a, 1165b; V, 1227a; S, 231b, 232b, 401b
Djaʿfar al-Ṣādiḳ b. ʿAlī Zayn al-ʿĀbidīn i, 781b — I, 805a
Djaʿfar Sharīf ii, **375a** — II, **385b**
Djaʿfar al-Ṭayyār → Djaʿfar b. Abī Ṭālib
Djaʿfar Zattallī iii, 358b — III, 369b
Djafāra v, 759b — V, 765b
Djaʿfarābād s, 246b — S, 246b
Djaʿfarī, Abū ʿAlī Muḥammad iv, 859b — IV, 892b
Djaʿfariyya ii, 375a; iv, 50b, 764a — II, 385a; IV, 53b, 794a
Djaff v, 471b — V, 474b
Djafr ii, **375b;** iii, 595b; iv, 1129a — II, **386a;** III, 616a; IV, 1160b
al-Djafura i, 537a — I, 553b; IV, 1160b
Djagat → Dwārkā
Djagat Singh iv, 543b — IV, 567a
Djaghatay → Čaghatay
al-Djaghbūb ii, **378a**; v, 759b, 760a; s, 165a — II, **388a**; V, 765b, 766a; S, 164b
al-Djaghmīnī, Maḥmūd ii, **378a** — II, **388b**
Djāghurī iii, 304a — III, 313b
Djāgīr ii, 155b, 156b, 158a, 272b, **378b**; s, 126b, 131b — II, 160a, 161b, 163a, 281a, **388b**; S, 125b, 130b
al-Djāh v, 543a — V, 547b
Djaḥādila iii, 363b, 541a — III, 375a, 560a
Djahan Khān Pōpalzaʾi ii, 186a — II, 192a
Djahān Shāh i, 914a; ii, 379a — I, 941b; II, 389b
Djahānābād v, 264b — V, 262b
Djahānārā Bēgam i, 253b, 1161a; ii, 50a, **378b,** 627b — I, 216b, 1195b; II, 51a, **389a,** 643b
Djahāndād Khān ii, 974a — II, 996a
Djahāndār Shāh (d./m. 1713) i, 241b, 914a, 1025b; ii, **379a,** 810a — I, 249a, 941b, 1057b; II, **389b,** 829a
Djahāndār Shāh (d./m. 1878) i, 853a — I, 876b
Djahāngīr (Mughal) i, 8b, 81a, 117b, 118a, 238a, 252b, 253a, 297b, 686a, 1331b, 1347b; ii, 54b, 121a, 157a, 162a, **379b,** 503b, 840a; iii, 424a, 434a, 450a, 492b; iv, 279a, 282a, 543a, 709a, 1017b; v, 598a, 600b, 1135b, 1214a; s, 1b, 142b, 167b, 258a, 259b, 313b, 366b — I, 8b, 83b, 121a, 245b, 260b, 261a, 306b, 707a, 1372a, 1387b; II, 55b, 124a, 162a, 167a, **390a,** 516a, 860a; III, 437b, 448a, 465b, 509b; IV, 291a, 294b, 566b, 737b, 1050a; V, 602a, 604b, 1131a, 1203b; S, 2a, 142a, b, 167b, 258a, 259a, 313a, 366a
Djahāngir Djalīlī iv, 72b — IV, 76b
Djahāngīr Muḥammad Khān i, 1195b, 1197a — I, 1231a, 1232a
Djahāniyān Djahān Gasht i, 702b — I, 723b
Djahannam i, 334b; ii, **381b** — I, 345a; II, **392a**
Djahānpanāh i, 1322b; ii, 258a, 259a; v, 888b, 1214b — I, 1363a; II, 264a, 266b; V, 894b, 1204b
Djahānshāh (Ḳara Ḳoyunlu) → Djihānshāh
Djahānshāh (Mughal) → Shāh Djahān
Djahān-Sūz, ʿAlāʾ al-Dīn Ḥusayn i, 940a; ii, **382a,** 1049b, 1052b, 1100b, 1103b; iii, 196a; v, 691a — I, 969a; II, **392b,** 1074a, 1077a, 1126b, 1129b; III, 200b; V, 696a
Djahān u Arghiyān s, 83b — S, 83a
Djahbadh i, 898b, 1144b; ii, 78b, 79b, 324b, 325a, **382b**; iv, 1032b — I, 925b, 1179a; II, 80a, 81a, 334a, b, **392b**; IV, 1064b
Djahdam b. ʿAbd Allāh iii, 986a — III, 1010b
al-Djaḥḥāf b. Ḥukaym i, 1241a — I, 1278b
Djāhidiyya → Khalwatiyya
Djāhil wa ʿĀḳil ii, 633a — II, 649a
Djāhiliyya i, 890a; ii, **383b,** 998b, 1073a; iii, 305b; iv, 998a; s, 33a, 189a — I, 916a; II, **393b,** 1021b, 1097b; III, 314b; IV, 1030b; S, 33a, 190a
Djaḥīm → Nār
Djahīr, Banū ii, 344a, **384a** — II, 354a, **394b**
al-Djāḥiẓ i, 10b, 105b, 127a, 176a, 214b, 266a, 271b, 316a, 585a, 588b, 717b, 857b, 1115a, 1243b, 1297b; ii, 95b, 300a, **385a,** 536b, 552a, 590b, 824a, 951b, 1097a; iii, 312a, 354b, 367b, 389b, 990a, 1143a, 1263a; iv, 490b, 822b, 949a; v, 113b, 778b, 1224a, 1225a, b; s, 13b, 24a, 25a, 35b, 45a, 73b, 85b, 88b, 124a, 263a, 273a, 286a, 294b, 316b, 318a, 392b, 402a — I, 10b, 108b, 131a, 180b, 221a, 274a, 279b, 325b, 604a, 608a, 739a, 881b, 1148b, 1281a, 1337b; II, 97b, 308a, **395a,** 550a, 565b, 605a, 843b, 973b, 1123a; III, 321b, 366a, 379a, 402a, 1014b, 1171b, 1296a; IV, 512a, 855b, 981b; V, 116a, 784b, 1214a, 1215b; S, 14a, 24b, 25a, 35b, 45b, 74a, 85a, 88b, 123a, 263a, 272b, 286a, 294b, 316b, 318a, 393a, 402b
Djahl iii, 391a — III, 403b
Djahlāwān ii, **387b** — II, **398a**
Djahm b. ʿAtiyya iv, 477a — IV, 466b
Djahm b. Ṣafwān i, 274a, 1242a; ii, **388a;** iii, 224a, 747b; s, 225b — I, 282a, 1279b; II, **398a;** III, 231a, 770b; S, 225b
Djahmiyya i, 124a, 275a, 976b, 333b, 334a, 335a, 410b; ii, 365a, **388a;** iii, 161b, 822a, 1143a, 1171a; iv, 469a, 1087a — I, 127b, 283b, 285a, 344a, b, 345a, 422b; II, 375a, **398b;** III, 165a, 846a, 1171a, 1200a; IV, 490a, 1118a
al-Djahrāʾ iv, 680b — IV, 708b
Djahriyya iv, 554b — IV, 578b
Djahrum v, 671b — V, 676b, 677a
al-Djahshiyārī i, 361a; ii, **388b;** iii, 371a; s, 48b — I, 372a; II, **399a;** III, 382b; S, 49a
Djahwarid(e)s i, 5b, 6a; ii, **389a** — I, 6a; II, **399b**
Djaḥẓa, Aḥmad b. Djaʿfar i, 1036a; ii, **389b** — I, 1067b; II, **400a**
Djai Singh i, 768b, 769a — I, 791b, 792a
Djāisī, Malik Muḥammad iv, 922a — IV, 955a
Djāʾiz i, 2a; ii, **389b** — I, 2b; II, **400a**
Djāʾiza → Ṣila
Djakam ii, 781b — II, 800a
Djakarta i, 980b; ii, **390a,** 426b; iii, 1214a — I, 1011a; II, **400b,** 437b; III, 1244b
Djakat → Zakāt
Djaḳmaḳ, Sultan → Čaḳmak
Djaʿl → Tazyīf
Djalāhima iv, 751a — IV, 781b
Djalāʾirid(e)s → Djalāyirids
Djalāl, ʿUthmān i, 597a — I, 616b
Djalāl al-Dawla ii, **390b** — II, **401a**
Djalāl al-Dawla, Abū Ṭāhir i, 131b, 512b, 1073a; ii, **391a,** 856a; iii, 860a; iv, 379a, 457a, b, 653a; s, 119a — I, 135b, 528a, 1105b; II, **401a,** 876a; III, 884a, b; IV, 395a, b, 477b, 679b; S, 118b
Djalāl al-Dīn b. Bayazīd Anṣārī i, 238a, 1123a — I, 245a, 1157a
Djalāl al-Dīn Aḥsan ii, **391b** — II, **402a**
Djalāl al-Dīn ʿĀrif ii, **391b** — II, **402a**
Djalāl al-Dīn al-Dawānī → al-Dawānī
Djalāl al-Dīn Fārūḳī ii, 54b — II, 55b
Djalāl al-Dīn Ḥasan → Ḥasan III (Ismāʿīlī)

Djalāl al-Dīn Ḥusayn al-Bukhārī i, 868b; ii, 186b, **392a;** iii, 434a; s, 10b — I, 893a; II, 192b, **402b;** III, 448a; S, 10a
Djalāl al-Dīn Ḳaratāy i, 732a; iv, 813b; v, 1145a — I, 754a; IV, 846b; V, 1137a
Djalal al-Dīn Khaldjī → Fīrūz Shāh II
Djalāl al-Dīn Khwārazm-shāh i, 190a, 227a, 301a, 329a, 353b, 508a, 665a, 799a, 919b, 1010a, 1206b, 1311a; ii, 2a, 43b, 188b, 267b, 284a, **392b,** 606a, 680b, 711b, 975b, 1049b, 1083a; iii, 196b, 197a, 1112a; iv, 30a, 102a, 349a, 817b, 1068a; v, 31b, 455a, 490b — I, 194b, 233b, 310a, 339b, 364b, 523a, 686a, 822b, 947a, 1041a, 1242b, 1351b; II, 2a, 44b, 194b, 275b, 292a, **403a,** 621a, 697b, 729b, 998a, 1074a, 1108b; III, 201b, 202a, 1139b; IV, 32a-b, 106b, 364a, 850b, 1099b; V, 32b, 458a, 493b
Djalāl al-Dīn Mangubirtī → Djalāl al-Dīn Khwārazm Shāh
Djalāl al-Dīn Muḥammad → Muḥammad Shāh Gaṇeśa
Djalāl al-Dīn Mīrzā s, 23b — S, 24a
Djalāl al-Dīn Pasha i, 1268a — I, 1307a
Djalāl al-Dīn Rūmī i, 109b, 234a, 347a, 698b, 752b, 753b, 780a, 843b, 916b, 1194b; ii, 221a, **393b;** iii, 429b, 602a, 711a; iv, 65a, 67a, 190a, 570a; v, 255a, 676b; s, 49b, 83b, 108a — I, 112b, 241a, 357b, 720a, 775a, 776a, 803a, 867a, 944b, 1230a; II, 228a, **404a;** III, 443b, 623a, 733b; IV, 68b, 70b, 198a, 592b; V, 253a, 682a; S, 50b, 83a, 107a
Djalāl al-Dīn Tabrīzī → Tabrīzī, Djalāl al-Dīn
Djalāl al-Dīn Ṭayyibshāh ii, 737a — II, 755b
Djalāl al-Dīn Thanesarī → Thanesarī, Djalāl al-Dīn
Djalāl Ḥusayn Čelebi ii, **397b** — II, **408a**
Djalāl Khān b. Shīr Shāh Sūrī (Bihār) ii, 271a — II, 279b
Djalāl Khān (Deccan) iii, 577a — III, 597a
Djalāl Khān Lōdī ii, 271a; iii, 420b, 995a — II, 279a; III, 434a, 1020a
Djalāl al-Mulk ʿAlī b. Muḥammad ii, 448a — II, 461a
Djalāl Nūrī → Ileri, Celāl Nūrī
Djalāl Redjāʾīzāde → RedjāʾīzādeB
Djalālābād ii, **397b**; iv, 409b; s, 66b, **237a** — II, **408a**; IV, 427a, b; S, 67a, **237a**
Djalālī i, 1334b; ii, 183b, 209a, 1046b; iii, 237b, 1002a, 1248b; iv, 499a, 594a, 843b; v, 258b, 270a, 677b; s, **238a** — I, 1374b; II, 189b, 215b, 1071a; III, 244b, 1027a, 1281a; IV, 520b, 618a, 876b; V, 256b, 267b, 682b; S, **238a**
Djalālī (calendar/calendrier) ii, **397b**; iv, 52a — II, **408a**; IV, 55a
Djalālzāde Muṣṭafā Čelebi ii, **400a;** iii, 998b; iv, 565b, 566a — II, **410b;** III, 1023b; IV, 588a
Djalālzāde Ṣāliḥ Čelebi ii, **400b** — II, **411a**
Djalaw Khān iv, 672a — IV, 699b
Djalāyīn s, 357a — S, 357a
Djalāyrid(e)s i, 66b, 190a, 311b, 508a, 861a, 903b, 1128b; ii, 348b, **401a;** iii, 1123a, 1256b; iv, 32a; v, 45b; s, 364a — I, 68b, 194b, 321a, 523b, 885a, 930b, 1162b; II, 358b, **411b;** III, 1150b, 1289a; IV, 34b; V, 47a; S, 363b
Djalī (calligraphy/calligraphie) iv, 1123a, b, 1125b, 1126a; v, 224a — IV, 1155a, b, 1157a, b; V, 222a
Djālī → Djawālī
Djalīḳiya s, 92a — S, 92a
Djalīlī ii, **402a** — II, **412b**
Djālīnūs i, 213a, 234a, 327a, b, 344b, 388a, 1198a; ii, 60a, 249a, **402b,** 765a, 771a, 780b, 929b; iii, 266b, 579a, 906b; iv, 129a, 329b, 330a, b, 406b; s, 154b, 271a, 379b — I, 219a, 241b, 337a, b, 355a, 399b, 1233b; II, 61a, 256a, **413a,** 783b, 789b, 799b, 951a; III, 274a, 599a, 931a; IV, 134b, 344a, b, 345a, 424a; S, 154b, 271a, 379b
Djāliya ii, **403b,** 470b — II, **414a,** 482b
Djaʿliyyīn i, 1a, 765a — I, 1a, 788a
Djallāb, djallāba i, 32b, 929a — I, 33a, 957b
Djallāb, Djallābiyya i, 1349b; ii, **404b** — I, 1390a; II, **415b**
Djallāba Hawwāra iii, 300a — III, 309b
Djāllandharī → Ḥafīz
Djalliḳiyya → Djillīḳiyya
Djālo i, 763a — I, 786a
Djālor ii, **405a;** iii, 441b — II, **416a;** III, 456a
Djalūlāʾ ii, **406a**; iv, 13b, 386a — II, **417a**; IV, 14b, 402b
Djālūt ii, **406a** — II, **417a**
Djālwand v, 617a — V, 621a
Djalwatiyya i, 1137a — I, 1171b
Djalwī b. Turkī Āl Saʿūd i, 1313a — I, 1353a
Djām ii, **406b**; v, 1148a — II, **417b**; V, 1139a
Djām ʿAlī Khān III v, 684b, 685a — V, 690a
Djamʿ, djamāʿa ii, **406b** — II, **417b**
Djām Firūz i, 627b; iii, 632b — I, 648b; III, 654a
Djām Mīr Khān I v, 684b — V, 690a
Djām Mīr Khān II v, 684b, 685a — V, 690a
Djām Nanda i, 627b; iii, 420a, 634a — I, 648a; III, 433b, 655a
Djamāʿa i, 171a, 276b, 373b, 770b, 1179b; ii, **411a,** 885b; iii, 98a; iv, 154b, 362a; v, 1198b — I, 176a, 285a, 384b, 793b, 1214b; II, **421b,** 906a; III, 100b; IV, 161a, 377b; V, 1189a
Djamāʿa, Banū iii, 749a — III, 772a
Djamāʿat i, 1278a; ii, 61b, 210b; iv, 238b, 239a — I, 1317a; II, 62b, 217a; IV, 249a, 250a
Djamāʿat al-Khilāfa al-Islāmiyya bi-Wādī al-Nīl s, 18b — S, 18b
Djamāʿat-i Islāmī iii, 433a — III, 447b
Djamādjim → Ḥumāḥim
Djāmakiyya ii, **413b** — II, **424b**
Djamal → Ibil
al-Djamal i, 43b, 55a, 308a, 383b, 448b, 704b; ii, **414a** — I, 44b, 56b, 317b, 394a, 461b, 725b; II, **424b**
Djamāl → ʿIlm al-djamāl
Djamāl al-ʿĀlam i, 743b — I, 766a
Djamāl al-Din b. Nubāta → Ibn Nubāta al-Miṣrī
Djamāl al-Dīn al-Afghānī i, 64b, 327a, 332a; ii, 97a, **416b,** 429a, 417a, 650a, 932b, 933b; iii, 250b, 514a, b, 1145b, 1149b, 1170a; iv, 112a, 159a, 162b, 164a, b, 397b, 720b, 946a; s, 76a, 106b, 244b, 248a, 296a — I, 66a, 337a, 342a; II, 99a, **427b,** 440b, 483a, 666b, 954a, 955a; III, 257b, 531b, 532a, 1174a, 1178a, 1199a; IV, 117a, 165b, 169a, 171a, b, 415a, 749a, 979a; S, 76a, 106a, 244b, 248a, 296a
Djamāl al-Dīn Aḳsarayī ii, **419b** — II, **430a**
Djamāl al-Dīn al-Ardistānī v, 53b — V, 55a
Djamāl al-Dīn Efendi ii, **420a** — II, **430b**
Djamāl al-Dīn Hānsawī → Hānsawī
Djamāl al-Dīn Ibrāhīm, Shaykh al-Islām iv, 1040b, 1046b — IV, 1072a, 1077b
Djamāl al-Dīn Iṣfahānī, Muḥammad b. ʿAbd al-Razzāḳ iv, 62a, 515b; s, **239b** — IV, 65b, 538a; S, **239b**
Djamāl al-Dīn al-Ḥillī → al-Ḥillī, Ḥasan b. Yūsuf
Djamal al-Dīn al-Iṣfahānī → al-Djawād al-Iṣfahānī
Djamāl al-Dīn Maḥmūd iii, 773b — III, 797a
Djamāl al-Dīn Muḥammad Būrī i, 1332a — I, 1372b
Djamāl al-Dīn Muḥammad b. Aḥmad b. ʿAbd Allāh ii, 730a — II, 748b
Djamāl al-Dīn al-Waṭwāṭ ii, 900a; v, 1227a — II, 921a; V, 1217a
Djamāl al-Dīn Yāḳūt ii, 1084a; iii, 14a — II, 1109b; III, 15a
Djamāl al-Ḥusaynī ii, 420a — II, 431a
Djamāl Karshī ii, 3b; v, 39a; s, **240a** — II, 3b; V, 40a; S, **240a**

Djamāl Khān iii, 426b — III, 440b
Djamāl Khān, Ḥadjdjī i, 231a, 295b — I, 238a, 304b
Djamāl al-Mulk i, 440a — I, 452b
Djamāl Pasha → Djemāl Pasha
Djamālī, ʿAlī ii, **420a** — II, **431a**
Djamālī, Ḥāmid ii, **420b** — II, **431b**
Djamālī Kambo, Shaykh s, 312a — S, 312a
al-Djamāliyya iv, 991b, 992a — IV, 1024a, b
Djamālzāda, Muḥammad ʿAli iv, 73a, 789b; v, 199a — IV, 77a, 821b; V, 196b
Djāmasp s, 297b — S, 297a
Djambi → Palembang
Djambi s, 201a — S, 201a
Djambul → Awliyā ata
Djambul Djabaev i, 767a; ii, **421a** — I, 790a; II, **432a**
Djamdār ii, **421b** — II, **432a**
Djāmiʿ → Masdjid
Djāmiʾ, Banū iv, 337a — IV, 351b
Djāmī, ʿAbd al-Raḥmān i, 88b, 146a, 347b, 753a, 1082b, 1211b; ii, **421b;** iii, 131b, 373a, 710b, 711a; iv, 64b, 66b, 650a, 1010a, 1073b; v, 482a, 650b, 1104b; s, 46b, 83a, 415a — I, 91a, 150a, 358a, 775b, 1115a, 1247b; II, **432b;** III, 134a, 385a, 733a, b; IV, 68a, 70a, 676b, 1042b, 1105a; V, 484b, 654b, 1100b; S, 47a, 82b, 415b
al-Djāmiʿ al-Azhar → al-Azhar
Djāmiʿ al-Miḳyās s, 38a — S, 38a
Djāmiʿa i, 56b; ii, **422b;** iii, 250b; iv, 70b; v, 365a, 904b, 919a — I, 58b; II, **433b;** III, 257b; IV, 74a-b; V, 366a, 910b, 924b
al-Djāmiʿa al-Ahliyya ii, 423b — II, 434b
al-Djāmiʿa al-ʿArabiyya i, 46a, 279b; iii, 264a; iv, 783a, 947a; s, **240a** — I, 47b, 288a; III, 271b; IV, 814b, 979b; S, **240a**
Djamia Millia Islamia ii, 426b — II, 437b
Djāmid → Naḥw and/et Ṭabīʿa
Djamīl, Ṭanburī → Ṭanburī Djamīl
Djamīl Nakhla al-Mudawwar ii, **428a** — II, **439a**
Djamīl al-ʿUdhrī i, 10b; ii, **427b,** 1031a; s, 42b — I, 10b; II, **438b,** 1055a; S, 42b
Djamīla (singer/chanteuse) ii, **428b,** 1011b; iii, 931b; iv, 821b — II, **439b,** 1035a; III, 956b; IV, 854b
Djamīla (Ḥamdānid(e)) s, 36b, 37a — S, 36b, 37a
Djamʿiyya ii, **428b,** 650b; iii, 514b; iv, 924a — II, **439b,** 666b; III, 532a; IV, 957a
Djamʿiyya al-Ḥiṣāfiyya al-Khayriyya s, 371a — S, 371a
al-Djamʿiyya al-Ḳaḥṭāniyya iii, 519b — III, 537b
al-Djamʿiyya al-tashrīʿiyya v, 1060b, 1064a — V, 1057b, 1061a
Djamʿiyyat al-ʿahd iii, 520b — III, 538a
Djamʿiyyat al-djāmiʿa al-ʿarabiyya iii, 520b — III, 538b
Djamʿiyyat al-iṣlāḥ al-shaʿbī iii, 521b, 522a — III, 539b, 540a
Djamʿiyyat ittiḥād Miṣr al-fatāt iii, 514b — III, 532a
Djamʿiyyat al-nahḍa iii, 519a — III, 537a
Djamʿiyyat-i ʿUlamāʾ-i Hind s, 4b, 106b — S, 3b, 105b
al-Djammāʿīlī, Taḳī al-Dīn iii, 867b — III, 891b
Djammāl s, **241b** — S, **241b**
al-Djammāz ii, **437b;** iii, 879a — II, **449a;** III, 903b
Djammū s, **241b** — S, **241b**
Djamnā ii, 255b, 265b, **437b**; s, 313a — II, 263a, 273b, **449a**; S, 312b
al-Djamra ii, **438a;** iii, 36a — II, **449b;** III, 37b
Djamshīd ii, **438b**; iv, 12a, 220b, 221a, 1104b — II, **450a**; IV, 13a, 230a, b, 1135b
Djamshīdī i, 224b, 857a; ii, 5b; iii, 1107b — I, 231a, 881a; II, 5b; III, 1135a
Djamuḳa ii, 42a, 571a — II, 43a, 585b
Djamunā v, 885b — V, 891b, 892a
Djāmūs s, **242b** — S, **242b**
Djān iv, 732b — IV, 762a
Djān ʿAlī Khān iv, 723b, 849b — IV, 752b, 882b
Djān b. Yār Muḥammad ii, 44b — II, 45b
Djān-i Djanān → Maẓhar
Djanāb Shihāb al-Dīn ii, **439b,** 474b; iii, 261b — II, **451a,** 486b; III, 268b
Djanāb-i Ṭāhira → Ḳurrat al-ʿAyn
al-Djanaba i, 1091b; ii, **440b;** iii, 270a — I, 1124a; II, **452a;** III, 278a
Djanāba ii, **440b** — II, **452a**
al-Djanad s, 337b — S, 337a
al-Djanadī i, 255b; ii, **441a** — I, 263b; II, **452b**
Djanāḥ al-Dawla Ḥusayn iii, 398b — III, 411a
al-Djanāḥiyya i, 49a; ii, **441a;** iii, 1266a; iv, 44b, 838a — I, 50b; II, **452b;** III, 1298b; IV, 47a, 871a
Djānavar, djanībar iii, 314 — III, 323b
Djanāwān, Ayyūb Muḥammad s, 15b — S, 15b
al-Djanāwanī, Abū ʿUbayda ii, 369a, **441b;** iii, 657b; iv, 919b — II, 379a, **453a;** III, 678b; IV, 952b
al-Djanāwunī → Abū Zakariyyāʾ
al-Djanāwunī, Abū Yaḥyā Tawfīḳ i, 1287b — I, 1327a
Djanāza ii, **441b** — II, **453b**
Djanb, Banū v, 954b — V, 958a, b
Djanbās Ḳalʿa i, 831a; iii, 502b — I, 854a; III, 519b
Djānbāz ii, **442b** — II, **454a**
Djānbāzān ii, **443a** — II, **454b**
Djānbeg Girāy i, 310b; iii, 252a — I, 320b; III, 259a
Djanbī i, 125a — I, 128b
al-Djanbīhī, Muḥammad b. ʿAbd al-Nabī s, **244a** — S, **244a**
Djānbirdi al-Ghazālī → al-Ghazālī
Djānbulāṭ i, 1078a; ii, **443b**; v, 106a, 793a — I, 1110b; II, **455a**; V, 108a, 799a
Djānbulāṭ, Shaykh Ḳāsim i, 1078a; ii, 444a, 636a — I, 1110b; II, 455b, 652a
Djanbulāṭ-oghlu ʿAlī Pasha i, 4a, 182b, 267b; ii, 443b, 635a, 750a; iii, 88a; iv, 499a; s, 239a — I, 4a, 188a, 276a; II, 455a, 651a, 768b; III, 90b; IV, 520b; S, 239a
Djand ii, 571b; iii, 472a; iv, 542b; v, 247a; s, **244b** — II, 585b; III, 488b; IV, 566a; V, 244b; S, **244b**
Djandaba b. al-Ḥārith ii, 234a — II, 241a
Djāndār ii, **444a**; v, 685a — II, **456a**; 690b
Djāndār, Anadolu i, 467b — I, 481b
Djandarlî i, 348a; ii, **444b**, 722a; iv, 292a; v, 1023b — I, 358b; II, **456a**, 740b; IV, 305a; V, 1019b
al-Djandī, Yaʿḳūb b. Shīrīn (Ḳāḍī) s, 246a — S, 246a
Djandjīra iii, 15b; s, **246a** — III, 16b; S, **246a**
Djandjis → Gangā
Djandōl ii, 317a — II, 326b
Djandūba → Djanbī
Djanfidā Khatūn → Supplement/Supplément
Djangalī ii, **445b**; v, 310b — II, **457a**; V, 310a
Djangī Yūsuf Dede iv, 190a — IV, 198b
Djānī Beg i, 46b — I, 47b
Djānī Beg al-ʿAzīzī i, 841a — I, 864b
Djānī Beg Özbeg iv, 391b — IV, 408b
Djānī Beg Tarkhān i, 80b — I, 83a
Djāni Bēgum i, 81a — I, 83b
Djānī Khān Ḳashḳāy iv, 706a — IV, 734b
Djānībak Ṣūfī i, 1054b; iii, 923a — I, 1086a; III, 947b
Djānibak al-Ẓāhirī v, 73a — V, 75a
Djānībeg Khān i, 325a, 808b, 1107b; ii, 401a — I, 335a, 831b, 1141a; II, 412a
Djānībek Girāy → Djānbeg Girāy
Djānid(e)s i, 1295b; ii, 44b, **446a**; v, 273b; s, 97a, 227b, 419b — I, 1335a; II, 45b, **457b**; V, 271b; S, 96b, 227b, 419b
Djānīk ii, **446b** — II, **458a**
Djānīkli ii, 207a, 446b — II, 213b, 458b

Djānīkli ʿAlī Pasha ii, 207b, **446b** – II, 214a, **458b**
Djānim al-Ashrafī v, 73a – V, 75a
Djān-Ḳalʿa s, 244b – S, 244b
Djānḳī ii, 334b; s, 163a – II, 344a; S, 163a
Djanna i, 334b; ii, **447a** – I, 345a; II, **459a**
Djannāba ii, **452a** – II, **464a**
al-Djannābī, Abū Muḥammad Muṣṭafā ii, **452b**; iv, 406a – II, **464a**; IV, 424a
al-Djannābī, Abū Saʿīd Ḥasan i, 11a, 73b, 551b; ii, **452b**; iv, 198a, 661a, 664a, 764a – I, 11a, 76a, 569a; II, **464a**; IV, 206b, 687b, 691a, 794b
al-Djannābī, Abū Ṭāhir i, 485a, 551b; ii, **452b;** iii, 236a, 238a; iv, 198b, 661b, 662a, b, 664a; s, 305a – I, 499b, 569a; II, **452b;** III, 243a, 245a; IV, 207a, 688b, 689b, 691a; S, 304b
al-Djannābī, Saʿīd ii, 452b; iv, 664a – II, 464b; IV, 691a
Djanpulāt → Djanbulāt
Djānū → ʿUthmān Ādam
Djanza → Gandja
Djār → Djiwār
al-Djār ii, **454b** – II, **466a**
Djara iv, 335b, 338b, 340a – IV, 350a, 352b, 354b
Djarād ii, **455a** – II, **466b**
Djarāda → al-Djarādatānⁱ
al-Djarādatānⁱ iv, 820b; s, **246b** – Iv, 853b; S, **246b**
Djarādjima i, 761a; ii, **456a** – I, 784a; II, **468a**
Djarash i, 208a; ii, **458a** – I, 214a; II, **469b**
Djarāwa iii, 1039b, 1041b; iv, 422b, 479a, b; v, 1174b – III, 1065b, 1067a; IV, 440b, 501a, b; V, 1164b
Djarba (Djerba) ii, **458a,** 461a; iv, 1156a; v, 503b; s, 15b, 80b – II, **470a,** 473a; IV, 1188a; V, 507a; S, 15b, 80b
al-Djarbāʾ ii, **461b** – II, **473a**
Djarbādhakān → Gulpāyagān
Djarbi ii, 459b – II, 471a
al-Djardjarāʾī, al-ʿAbbās b. al-Ḥasan ii, **461b;**iii, 619b, 767b, 892b – II, **473b;** III, 640a, 790b, 916b
al-Djardjarāʾī, Abu 'l-Ḳāsim ii, **462a;** iii, 79a – II, **473b;** III, 81b
al-Djardjarāʾī, Aḥmad b. al-Khaṣīb i, 1289b; ii, **461b;**iii, 835a, 1085a – I, 1329a; II, **473b;** III, 858b, 1112a
al-Djardjarāʾī, Muḥammad b. al-Faḍl ii, **461b** – II, **473b**
al-Djarh wa 'l-taʿdīl i, 1199b; ii, **462a** – I, 1234b; II, **473b**
Djārī → Khaṭṭ
Djarīb → Kayl
Djarīd → Djerīd
Djarīd, Bilād al- ii, **462b**; iv, 739b, 740a – II, **474b**; IV, 769a, b
Djarīda i, 279b, 287a, b, 288a, 289b, 871a, b; ii, 288b, 289b, 364a, 403b, 404a, 417b, 418a, 428a, 429a, **464b,** 596b; iv, 73; iv, 70b, 71a, b, 112a, 124a, 681b, 857a, 876a; v, 438a, 484b, 838b, 1254b, s, **247a** – I, 288a, 296a, b, 298b, 895b; II, 296b, 297a, 374a, 414a, b, 428a, b, 439a, 440a, **476a,** 611b; IV, 74a, b, 75b, 117a, 129a, b, 709b, 890a, 909a; V, 440b, 487b, 845a, 1245b; S, **247a**
Djarīda (military/militaire) ii, 78b, 79a, 80a – II, 80a, b, 81b
al-Djarīda i, 597b; ii, 466b; iii, 515b – I, 617a; II, 478b; III, 533b
Djarīma ii, **479b** – II, **491b**
Djarīr, Awlād ii, 509b – II, 522a
Djarīr b. ʿAbd Allāh al-Badjalī i, 865b; ii, 241b – I, 889b; II, 248b
Djarīr b. ʿAṭiyya i, 158b, 196a, 331a, 436b, 586a, 950b, 1080a; ii, 245b, **479b,** 788b; iii, 42a, 354a, 853b; s, 15a, 273a – I, 162b, 201b, 341b, 448b, 605a, 980a, 1112b; II, 252b, **492a,** 807b; III, 43b, 365a, 877b; S, 15b, 273a
Djarīr b. Ḥammād b. Zayd s, 384b – S, 385a
Djāriya → ʿAbd
Djāriya b. Ḳudāma ii, **480b;** iii, 782a – II, **492b;** III, 805b
Djarkh → Ḳaws
Djarr → Naḥw
Djarrāḥ ii, **481b** – II, **493b**
al-Djarrāḥ, Banū → Djarrāḥid(e)s
al-Djarrāḥ b. ʿAbd Allāh al-Ḥakamī i, 837a, 985a; ii, **482a;** iii, 493b; iv, 344a, 1173b – I, 860a, 1015b; II, **494a;** III, 510b; IV, 358b, 1207a
Djarrāḥid(e)s i, 386b, 784a; ii, 197b, **482b,** 854a; iii, 767b; v, 327b – I, 398a, 807a; II, 203b, **495a,** 874a; III, 790b; V, 327b
Djārsīf → Guercif
Djarūd iv, 532b – IV, 555b
al-Djārūd i, 73a, 942a – I, 75b, 971a
al-Djarūdiyya ii, **485a;** iii, 1166a; s, 129b, 130a, 400b – II, **497a;** III, 1195a; S, 129a, 401a
Djarūn → Bandar ʿAbbās
Djarunda i, 82a; ii, **485a** – I, 84b; II, **497b**
Djarwānid(e)s s, 234a – S, 234a
Djasad ii, 555a – II, 568b
Djāsak ii, **486a**; v, 675a – II, **498a**; V, 680b
Djasīm al-Dīn i, 1169a – I, 1204a
Djāsim b. Djābir iv, 751b –IV, 782a
Djāsim b. Muḥammad iv, 751b, 752a, 953b – IV, 782a, 986a
Djasrat b. Shaykhā v, 31b – V, 32b
al-Djaṣṣāṣ, Aḥmad ii, **486a** – II, **498a**
al-Djassāsa i, 932a; ii, **486b** – I, 960b; II, **498b**
Djassawr ii, **486b** – II, **498b**
Djastanid(e)s → Djustānid(e)s
Djāsūs ii, **486b;** iii, 181b – II, **499a;** III, 186a
Djaswant Rāo Holkar i, 444a – I, 456b
Djaswant Singh i, 768b, 769a; ii, 567a; iii, 202a – I, 791b, 792a; II, 581b; III, 207b
Djāt i, 224b, 253a, 1005a, 1193a; ii, **488a,** 504a, 797b, 928b, 1122a, 1131b; iii, 197b; iv, 364b; s, 163a – I, 231b, 261a, 1036a, 1228a; II, **500a,** 516b, 816b, 950b, 1148b, 1158b; III, 202b; IV, 380b; S, 163a → Zuṭṭ
Djāvuldur → Čāwdors
Djāwa → Djāwī
al-Djawād al-Iṣfahānī i, 604a, 1160b; ii, **489a** – I, 623b, 1195a; II, **501b**
Djawād Karbalāʾī s, 53a – S, 53b
Djawād Pasha ii, **489b** – II, **502a**
Djawāhir → Djawhar
al-Djawāʾib ii, 466a, 801a, 802a – II, 477b, 820a, 821a
Djawālī ii, 327a, 329a, **490a,** 561a – II, 336b, 338b, **502a,** 575a
al-Djawālīḳī i, 485b, 593a; ii, **490a;** iii, 733a; iv, 913a – I, 500a, 612a; II, **502b;** III, 755b; IV, 945b
Djāwān i, 941b – I, 970b
Djawān, Mīrzā Kāẓim ʿAlī ii, **490b**; v, 644b – II, **503a**; 648b
Djawān Mardi → Futuwwa
Djāwānī Kurd(e)s → Djāf
Djawānrūd ii, **491a** – II, **503b**
Djāwars s, **249b** – S, **249b**
Djawāsim → Ḳawāsim
al-Djawāzir i, 1096b – I, 1129b
al-Djawbarī, ʿAbd al-Raḥīm iii, 487b, 511a; s, 43a, **250a** – III, 504b, 528b; S, 43b, **250a**
Djawdhar ii, **491a,** 1080b – II, **503b,** 1106a
Djawdhar pasha i, 289a; ii, 977b – I, 298a; II, 1000a
Djawf i, 1313b; ii, **491b** – I, 1354a; II, **504a**
al-Djawf ii, **492a,** 624b – II, **504b,** 640a
Djawf b. Nāṣir i, 538a; ii, 492b; iv, 1074a – I, 555a; II, 504a; IV, 1106a

Djawf Kufra ii, **492b**; s, 164b, 165a — II, **505a**; s, 164b
Djawhar i, 128b, 784b; ii, 220a, **493a** — I, 132a, 808a; II, 226b, **505a**
Djawhar (jewel, jewelry/pierre précieuse) i, 1157b; ii, 1119b; iii, 30b; v, 965a; s, **250b** — I, 1192a; II, 1146a; III, 32a; V, 969b; S, **250b**
Djawhar, Āftābačī ii, **494a** — II, **506b**
Djawhar al-Ḳanḳabā'ī i, 814b — I, 838a
Djawhar al-Ṣiḳillī i, 814a, 824a; ii, **494b,** 853a, b, 860a, 1080b; iii, 246a, 768b, 785b, 1036b, 1042b; iv, 275b, 663b, 1091b; v, 1160a, 1176a — I, 837b, 847a; II, **507a,** 873a, b, 879b, 1106a; III, 253a, 791b, 808b, 1062b, 1068b; IV, 287b, 690b, 1122b; V, 1150a, 1166a
al-Djawharī ii, **495b,** 926b; iii, 733a, 738b; iv, 524b, 527b; s, 38b, 240a, 289a, b — II, **508a,** 948a; II, 755b, 761b; IV, 547a, 550a; S, 39a, 240a, 289a
al-Djawharī, al-ʿAbbās b. Saʿīd s, 411b, 412b, 414a — S, 412a, b, 414a
al-Djawharī, Maḥammad s, 395b — S, 396a
Djawharī, Ṭanṭāwī s, **262b** — S, **262a**
Djāwī ii, **497a** — II, **509b**
Djāwīd, Meḥmed ii, **497b,** 616a; iv, 285a, 297b — II, **510a,** 631b; IV, 297b, 310b
Djāwīdhān b. Sahl i, 844a; v, 64b — I, 867b; V, 66a
Djāwīdhān Khirad iv, 504b; s, **263a** — IV, 526b; S, **263a**
Djawkān → Čawgān
al-Djawl i, 536a — I, 552b
Djawlakiyya iv, 473a, b — IV, 494a, b
al-Djawlān ii, **498a**; s, 229b — II, **510b**; S, 229b
Djawn, Banu ʾl- v, 119a — V, 121b
Djawnā Khān → Muḥammad b. Tughluḳ
Djawnpūr ii, 270b, **498b,** 925a; iii, 419a, b, 420a, 442b, 444a, 632a, 1003a; iv, 276b; v, 783b, 889a, 1135a, 1216b; s, 206b, 325a — II, 278b, **510b,** 946b; II, 432b, 433b, 457a, 459a, 653a, 1028a; IV, 288b; V, 789b, 895b, 1130b, 1206b; S, 206a, 324b
al-Djawnpūrī, Maḥmūd i, 593a — I, 612b
al-Djawnpūrī, Sayyid Muḥammad ii, **499b**; v, 1230b — II, **512a**; V, 1221a
Djawshakānī, Niʿmat Allāh s, 139a — S, 138b
Djāwuliyya iv, 960a — IV, 992b
Djaww → Djawf
al-Djawwād Yūnus b. Mawdūd b. al-ʿĀdil i, 766b — I, 789a
al-Djawwānī ii, **501a** — II, **514a**
Djawz s, **264a** — S, **263b**
al-Djawzāʾ → Minṭaḳat al-Burūdj; Nudjūm
al-Djawzahar ii, **501b** — II, **514b**
Djay iv, 98b, 99b, 100a, 106a — IV, 103a, b, 104b, 110b
Djay Appā Sindhiyā iii, 60b — III, 62b
Djay Singh Sawāʾī I i, 1166a — I, 1200b
Djay Singh Sawāʾī II i, 1193a; ii, 503b, 504a; s, 411a — I, 1228a; II, 516b; S, 411a
Djāyasī → Malik Muḥammad Djāyasī
Djayb-i Humāyūn ii, **502b** — II, **515a**
Djayfar b. Djulanda i, 451a — I, 464a
Djayḥān ii, 35a, b, **502b** — II, 36a, **515b**
al-Djayhānī, Abū ʿAbd Allāh Aḥmad b. Muḥammad s, 245a, 256b — S, 245a, 265b
al-Djayhānī, Abū ʿAbd Allāh Muḥammad b. Aḥmad i, 434a; ii, 581a; iv, 847a, 1079b; s, **265a,** 376b — I, 446a; II, 595b; IV, 880a, 1111a; S, **264b,** 376b
al-Djayhānī, Abū ʿAlī Muḥammad b. Muḥammad i, 984b, 1003a; iv, 847a; s, **265a** — I, 1015a, 1034a; IV, 880a; S, **264b**
Djayḥūn → Baradā
Djayḥūn → Āmū Daryā
al-Djayla s, 356a — S, 356a
Djayn ii, **503a,** 1123b — II, **516a,** 1150a
Djaypāl, Rādjā ii, 1050b, 1123a; iii, 460b — II, 1075a, 1149a; III, 476b
Djaypūr ii, **503b**; s, 260a — II, **516b**; S, 260a
Djaysalmer s, 312b — S, 312a
Djaysh ii, **504a**; v, 685a — II, **517a**; V, 690a
Djayshān s, 335a — S, 334b
Djaysh b. Ṣamṣāma i, 1042a; ii, 483b; iii, 77a — I, 1073b; II, 495b; III, 79b
Djaysinh b. Dāhir ii, 600b — II, 615a
Djaysinha s, 163a — S, 163a
al-Djayṭālī ii, **515a;** iii, 95a, 97b — II, **528a;** III, 97b, 100a
Djayyān i, 1343a; ii, **515b;** iii, 498b — I, 1383b; II, **528b;** III, 515b
Djayyāsh b. Nadjāḥ → Nadjāḥ, Bā
Djayzān (Djāzān) i, 109a; ii, **516a** — I, 729b; II, **529a**
Djāz-Muryān s, 129a — S, 128a
Djazāʾ ii, **518a** — II, **531a**
Djazāʾilčī i, 238a — I, 245b
al-Djazāʾir i, 34b, 67b, 367b, 368b; ii, 115b, **519b;** iii, 251b, 606b; iv, 359b; s, 325b — I, 35b, 69b, 378a, 379b; II, 118a, **533a;** III, 258b, 627b; IV, 375b; S, 325a
- dey → Dayī
- university/université ii, 425b — II, 436a
al-Djazāʾir (tribes/tribus) → al-Djawāzir
Djazāʾir-i Baḥr-i Safīd ii, **521b** — II, **534b**
Djazāʾīr Ibn Khalfān → Khūriyā Mūriyā
al-Djazāʾir al-Khālidāt ii, **522a**; v, 755b — II, **535a**; V, 761b
Djazāʾir al-Saʿādāt ii, 522a — II, 535a
al-Djazāʿirī → Ḳaddūra al-Djazāʿirī
al-Djazāʾirī → Aḥmad b. ʿAbd al-Raḥmān
al-Djazāʿirī, ʿAlī b. Hilāl s, 380a — S, 380a
al-Djazāʾirī, Ṭāhir iii, 519a; iv, 159a — III, 536b; IV, 166a
Djazāʿirli Ḥasan → Djezāʿirli Ḥasan Pasha
al-Djazarī, Badī ʿal-Zamān v, 861b; s, **266b** — V, 868b; S, **266a**
al-Djazarī, Shams al-Dīn ii, **522b**; iv, 965a — II, **535b**; IV, 997a
al-Djazarī, Shams al-Milla wa ʾl-Dīn s, **267a,** 371b, 372b, 373a, b, 400a — S, **266b,** 371b, 372b, 373a, b, 400b
Djazīra ii, **523a** — II, **536a**
al-Djazīra i, 11b, 12b, 198a; ii, 64b, 249b, 344b, 347a, 348a, **523a;** iii, 933b, 1250b, 1252a; v, 453b, 457a, 458a; s, 101a, 266b — I, 12a, 12b, 203b; II, 65b, 256b, 354b, 357a, b, **536a;** III, 958a, 1283a, 1284b; V, 456a, 459b, 461a; S, 100b, 266a
al-Djazīra al-Khaḍrāʾ i, 6a, 12b, 58a, 1057b; ii, **524b**; v, 1119a — I, 6a, 12b, 59b, 1089a; II, **537b**; V, 1115b
Djazīrat al-ʿArab → ʿArab, Djazīrat al-
Djazīrat al-Khiḍr → Abbādān
Djazīrat Firʿawn i, 784a — I, 807b
Djazīrat ibn Kāwān → Kishm
Djazīrat ibn ʿUmar → Ibn ʿUmar, Djazīrat
Djazīrat Ḳays → Ḳays, Djazīrat
Djazīrat Sharīk ii, **525b** — II, **538b**
Djazīrat Shukr ii, **526a** — II, **539a**
Djazīrat Ṭarīf i, 7a, 493a — I, 7a, 507b
Djazm → Naḥw
al-Djazr v, 921a, b, 922a — V, 926b, 927a, b
al-Djazr wa ʾl-madd → Madd
Djazūla ii, **526b** — II, **539b**
al-Djazūlī, Abū Mūsā ʿIsā ii, **528a;** iii, 733a — II, **541a;** III, 755b
al-Djazūlī, Shaykh ii, **527a;** iii, 70a, 721b — II, **540a;** III, 72b, 743b
Djazūliyya i, 245a; ii, 528a; iii, 339b; iv, 93b, 380a; s, 223a — I, 252b; II, 541a; III, 349b; IV, 97b, 396b; S, 223a

Djazzār s, **267a** – S, **267a**
al-Djazzār Pasha, Aḥmad i, 341b, 1078; ii, 444a, 635b, 912a; iii, 325b; iv, 842b; s, **268a** – I, 352a, 1110b; II, 455b, 651b, 933b; III, 335b; IV, 875b; S, **267b**
Djebe i, 836a, 987a; ii, 43a – I, 859a, 1018a; II, 43b
Djebedji i, 807b, 1061b; s, **269b** – I, 830b, 1093a; S, **269a**
Djebel → Djabal
Djebeli, djebelü ii, **528b**, 1090a – II, **541b**, 1115b
Djeblé → Djabala
Djedda → Djudda
Djedīd → Djadīd
Djegar iv, 327a, b – IV, 341b, 342a
Djek → Shahdāgh
Djekermish i, 1052a – I, 1084a
Djelāl, Ṣadreddīn iv, 124a – IV, 129b
Djelal ed-Din Roumi → Djalāl al-Dīn Rūmī
Djelāl Sāhir s, 98a – S, 97b
Djelali → Djalālī
Djelālzāde → Djalālzāde Muṣṭafā Čelebi
Djem i, 293a, 510b, 1119a, b, 1334b; ii, **529a**; iii, 341a; iv, 463a, 738a – I, 302a, 526b, 1153a, 1374b; II, **542a**; III, 351a; IV, 483b, 768a
Djemāʿa → Djamāʿa
Djemāʿat → Djamāʿat
Djemāl Pasha ii, 289b, 431a, **531a**, 637b, 699b; iv, 284b, 872b, 906b; s, 98a – II, 297b, 442a, **544a**, 653b, 717b; IV, 297a, 906a, 939b; S, 97b
Djemalī Efendi → Djamālī, ʿAlī
Djemʿiyyet → Djamʿiyya
Djemʿiyyet-i ʿIlmiyye-i ʿOthmāniyye – ii, **532a** – II, **545a**
Djemshid → Djamshīd
Djenābī Aḥmad → Aḥmad Pasha Djenābī
Djenah, Shēkh i, 684a – I, 705a
Djenānī → ʿĀṣim, Aḥmad
Djenāze Ḥasan Pasha → Kahyā Ḥasan Pasha
Djendereli → Djandarlī
Djenné → Dienné
Djerāʾim ii, 147a – II, 151a
Djerba → Djarba
Djerīd ii, **532a**, 954a – II, **545b**, 976a
Djerīd, Bilād al- → Djarīd
Djerīde-i Ḥawādith ii, 465b – II, 477b
Djerime → Djarīma
Djewād Shākir → Halikarnas Balîkčîsî
Djewān Bakht i, 914a – I, 942a
Djewānshīr iv, 573a – IV, 595b, 596a
Djewdet, ʿAbd Allāh ii, 430b, 474b, 475a, **533a**, 1117a; iii, 393a; iv, 168b, 169a – II, 441b, 487a, **546a**, 1143a; III, 405b; IV, 176a
Djewdet, Aḥmed → Aḥmad Djewdet Pasha
Djewdet Pasha → Aḥmad Djewdet Pasha
Djezāʾirli Ghāzī Ḥasan Pasha i, 63a; ii, 26b, **533b**; iii, 992b; iv, 455b, 588b, 853a; v, 764a, 1248a – I, 65a; II, 26b, **547a**; III, 1017a; IV, 476a, 612a, 886a; V, 770a, 1238b
Djezzar → Djazzār
Djibāl i, 1350a; ii, **534b**; iv, 97b, 465a; v, 169a; s, 43b – I, 1390b; II, **547b**; IV, 101b, 486a; V, 166b; S, 44a
al-Djibāl i, 49a, 437b; ii, **534b** – I, 50b, 450a; II, **548a**
Djibāli s, 98a – S, 97b
Djibāliyya iii, 642a – III, 663b
Djibāya i, 533b; iv, 244b – I, 549b; IV, 255b
Djibbālī s, 339b – S, 339a
Djibrīl → Djabrāʾīl
Djibrān → Djabrān
Djibūtī (Djibouti) ii, **535b** – II, **548b**
Djich → Djaysh, III
al-Djidd wa 'l-hazl ii, **536a** – II, **549b**
Djidda → Djudda
Djidjelli ii, **537a**; iv, 361a, 362a – II, **550a**; IV, 377a, 378a
Djihād i, 7a, 31b, 179b, 250b, 276b, 314a, 445b, 664a; ii, 64a, 65a, 126a, 504b, **538a**; iii, 180a, 181b; iv, 772a, 796b; v, 1243b, 1250a – I, 7b, 32b, 184b, 258b, 285a, 324a, 458a, 684a; II, 65a, 66a, 129b, 517a, **551b**; III, 184a, 185b; IV, 803a, 828b; V, 1234b, 1241a
Djihādiyya i, 1157a; v, 267b, 1252a – I, 1191a; V, 265b, 1242b
Djihān-Pahlawān Muḥammad b. Eldigüz i, 300b; iii, 47b, 1110b, 1111a, b; s, 416a – I, 310a; III, 49a, 1137b, 1138b; S, 416b
Djihāngīr (Mughal) → Djahāngīr
Djihāngīr b. ʿAlī i, 311b, 312a – I, 321b
Djihāngīr b. ʿAzīz iv, 808a – IV, 840b
Djihāngīr b. Süleymān iv, 232a; v, 727a – IV, 242b; V, 732a
Djihānshāh (Ḳara Ḳoyunlu) i, 147b, 311b; iv, 34a, 102b, 587b, 588a – I, 152a, 321a; IV, 36b, 107a, 611a, b
Djihinnām i, 690a – I, 711a
Djikil iv, 213a – IV, 222b
Djīl Djīlān s, 298a – S, 297b
Djilāla, Djilālism(e) iv, 381b, 382b, 383a; s, 351a – IV, 398a, 399b; S, 351a
Djilālī b. Idrīs → Bū Ḥmāra
Djīlān s, 297b, 298a – S, 297a, b
Djilaw-dār iv, 218a – IV, 227b
Djilaw Khān ii, 68a – II, 69a
Djild ii, **540a** – II, **553a**
al-Djildaḳī, ʿIzz al-Dīn Aydamir iv, 1134a; V, 112a; S, **270a** – IV, 1165b; V, 114b; S, **269b**
al-Djīlī → ʿAbd al-Ḳādīr al-Djīlanī
al-Djīlī, Ḳuṭb al-Dīn → ʿAbd al-Karīm al-Djīlī
Djilliḳ ii, **541a**, 1021a; s, 117a – II, **554a**, 1045a; S, 116b
Djillīḳiyya ii, **541b**; v, 781b – II, **554b**; V, 787b
Djilwa ii, **542b** – II, **555b**
Djilwatiyya ii, **542b**; iii, 538b; iv, 191b – II, **555b**; III, 557a; IV, 199b
Djīm ii, **543b** – II, **556b**
Djimat ii, **545a** – II, **558b**
Djimmā ii, **545a** – II, **558b**
Djimrī i, 467a; ii, 204b, 989a – I, 481a; II, 211a, 1012a
Djināh, Muḥammad ʿAlī i, 1196b; ii, **545b**; iii, 532b, 1204b; iv, 299a; v, 780a – I, 1231b; II, **559a**; III, 551a, 1235a; IV, 312a; V, 786a
Djinās → Tadjnīs
Djināza → Djanāza
Djinbāwāy s, 244a – S, 244a
al-Djinbayhī/al-Djunbayhī → al-Djanbīhī
Djindji Khwādja → Ḥusayn Djindji
Djinn i, 187a; ii, 323a, 518b, **546b**; iii, 273b, 669a, 1050a; iv, 264b; v, 1101a, 1202a; s, 52b, 371a – I, 192a; II, 332b, 531b, **560a**; III, 281b, 690b, 1076a; IV, 276b; V, 1097a, 1192b; S, 53a, 370b
Djinnī iv, 643b – IV, 670a
Djins (genus/genre) ii, **550a** – II, **563b**
Djins (sex/sexe) ii, **550b** – II, **564a**
Djirab al-Doula ii, 178b – II, 184a
Djirāya ii, 413b – II, 424b
Djirdja → Girga
al-Djirdjāwī, ʿUthmān iv, 852b – IV, 885b
Djirdjent ii, **553a**; iv, 496b – II, **566b**; IV, 517b
Djirdji Zaydān → Zaydān
Djirdjīs ii, **553a** – II, **567a**
Djirga v, 1079a; s, **270a** – V, 1076b; S, **270a**
Djirm → Djism
Djirm, Badakhshān i, 851b – I, 875b
Djīruft i, 810b; ii, **553b**; iv, 4a; v, 148b, 149a, 150b; s, 129a – I, 834a; II, **567b**; IV, 4a; V, 150b, 151b, 152b; S, 128a

Djīsh → Gīsh
Djism ii, **553b** – II, **567b**
Djisr ii, **555a**, 716a; iv, 555a – II, **569a**, 734b; IV, 579a
Djisr Banāt Yaʿḳūb ii, **555a** – II, **569a**
Djisr al-Ḥadīd ii, **555b** – II, **569b**
Djisr Manbidj → Kalʿat Nadjm
Djisr al-Shughr ii, **556a**; iv, 1015a – II, **570a**; IV, 1047a
Djisr-i Muṣṭafā Pasha s, 149b – S, 149b
Djiṣṣ ii, **556b** – II, **570b**
Djītal → Sikka; Wazn
al-Djiṭālī → al-Djayṭālī
Djiti Shahr → Alti Shahr
al-Djiwāʾ i, 539b; ii, **557b** – I, 556b; II, **571a**
Djīwan ii, **558a** – II, **572a**
Djiwār i, 429b, 890b; ii, **558b**; iii, 1017b – I, 441b, 917b; II, **572b**; III, 1043a
Djīza (Gizeh) i, 125b; iii, 173b; s, 407b – I, 129a; III, 177a; S, 407b
Djīzān → Djayzān
al-Djīzī ii, **559a** – II, **573a**
Djizya i, 656a, b, 1090b, 1144a, 1146a; ii, 121a, 131a, 142b, 146b, 151b, 154a, 227a, 272a, 490a, **559a**; iii, 1181a; iv, 500a, 939a, 1033a, 1095a; v, 92b, 262b, 500b – I, 677a, b, 1123b, 1178b, 1180b; II, 124a, 134b, 146a, 150b, 156a, 158b, 234a, 280b, 502a, **573a**; III, 1210a; IV, 521b, 972a, 1064b, 1126a; V, 94b, 260a, 503b
Djoči Khān → Djuči, Khān
Djōdhpur ii, **567a** – II, **581a**
Djogdjakarta ii, 426b, 427a – II, 437b, 438a
Djohan Shāh, ʿAlāʾ al-Din i, 743b – I, 766a
Djolof ii, **567a** – II, **581b**
Djowān Mīr iv, 730b – IV, 759b
Djuanda Kartawidjaja ii, 666b – II, 683a
Djuʿaydī iii, 206a – III, 211b
Djuʿayl, Banū v, 318a – V, 317b
al- Djuba → al-Djawf
Djubar, Banū iv, 361a, b – IV, 377a
Djubayl ii, **568a**; v, 789a, 793a – II, **582b**; V, 796a, 799a
al-Djubayl ii, **568b** – II, **583a**
al-Djubayla i, 628b; ii, **569a** – I, 649b; II, **583b**
Djubba → Libās
al-Djubbāʾī, Abū ʿAlī Muḥammad i, 4b, 128b, 412a, 694a; ii, 449b, **569b**, 802b; iii, 465b, 1143a, 1165b; iv, 183a, 693a, 1162b, 1163a; s, 13b, 88b, 90b, 344a, b, 345b, 347a – I, 5a, 132b, 424a, 715a; II, 461b, **584a**, 821b; III, 481b, 1171b, 1194b; IV, 191a, 721a, 1194b, 1195a; S, 14a, 88b, 90a, 344a, b, 345b, 346b, 347a
al-Djubbāʾī, Abū Hāshim → Abū Hāshim b. al-Djubbāʾī
Djubn ii, 1057b – II, 1082a
Djubūr ii, **570b**; s, 101b – II, **585a**; S, 101a
Djuči, Khān i, 1105a, 1106b, 1187b, 1188a; ii, 2a, 43a, 44a, **571a**; s, 96b, 246a – I, 1138a, 1139b, 1222b, 1223a; II, 2a, 44a, 45, **585b**; S, 96a, 246a
Djučid(e)s s, 340a – S, 339b
Djudāla → Gudāla
Djudayʿ al-Kirmānī iii, 224a – III, 230b, 231a
Djudda i, 380b, 546b, 1032b, 1054b; ii, 91b, **571b**; iii, 11b, 362b, 760b, 1067a; v, 808a – I, 391b, 564a, 1064a, 1086a; II, 93a, **586a**; III, 12a, 373b, 783b, 1093b; V, 813b
Djudhām (tribe/tribu) i, 436a, 528b, 532a, 630b, 1140a; ii, **573b**; v, 594a, 632a, b, 897b – I, 448b, 544b, 548b, 651a, 1174b; II, **588a**; V, 597b, 636a, b, 903b
Djudhām (leprosy/lèpre) s, **270b** – S, **270b**
al-Djudhamī, Abū ʿAbd Allāh s, 381b – S, 382a
Djudhayma al-Abrash i, 788b – I, 812a
Djūdī iii, 324b – III, 334b
Djūdī, Djabal i, 251b; ii, **573b**; s, 36a – I, 259a; II, **588a**; S, 36b
Djūdī al-Mawrūrī ii, **574b** – II, **589a**
Djudjayn b. Thābit ii, 590b – II, 605b
Djūdjhar Singh Bundelā i, 768b – I, 791b
Djufayna iii, 586b – III, 607a
Djuʿfī ii, 1059b, 1061b – II, 1084a, 1086a
al-Djufra ii, **575a** – II, **589b**
Djughrāfiyā i, 1102a; ii, **575b**; iv, 1078a-1083a – I, 1135a; II, **590a**; IV, 1109b-1114b
Djugī ii, 41a – II, 42a
Djuḥā ii, **590b** – II, **605a**
al-Djuhanī → ʿAbd Allāh b. Unays; Maʿbad
Djuhayna → Ḳudāʿa
Djuhhāl → Djāhil
Djūkāndār ii, 17a – II, 17b
Djuke-Tau → Zhukotin
Djūlāmerg → Čölemerik
al-Djulandā, Banū i, 812b, 813a, 1098a; s, 222b, 223a – I, 835b, 836a, 1131a; S, 222b, 223a
al-Djulandā b. Masʿūd i, 550b; ii, **592b**; iii, 652a – I, 568a; II, **607a**; III, 673b
Djulbān iv, 552a, b – IV, 576a
Djulfā i, 8a, 643a; iv, 476a; s, **274b** – I, 8b, 663b; iv, 497a; S, **274b**
Djulfar → Raʾs al-Khaymā
Djullanār s, **277a** – S, **276b**
al-Djulūdī, ʿAbd al-ʿAzīz b. Yaḥyā iv, 927a – IV, 960a
Djulūs bakhshīshi i, 953b – I, 982b
Djumʿa ii, **592b** – II, **607a**
Djumʿa of/de Iṣfahān, Imām s, 169b – S, 169b
Djumādā → Taʾrīkh
Djumaḥ s, 284a – S, 284a
al-Djumaḥī → Abū Dahbal; Ibn Sallām
al-Djumaḥī, Saʿīd b. ʿAbd al-Raḥmān s, 225b – S, 225b
Djumayla i, 233b – I, 241a
Djumblāṭ → Djanbulāṭ
Djumhūr b. al-ʿIdjlī iv, 99b – IV, 104a
Djumhūriyya ii, **594a**, 644b – II, **608b**, 660b
al-Djumhūriyya al-ʿarabiyya al-muttaḥida ii, 649a, 674a; iii, 264b, 1259a; v, 1061a; s, 2b, 7b – II, 665a, 691a; III, 272a, 1291b; V, 1058b; S, 7b, 12b
Djümhūriyyet Khalḳ Fîrkasî i, 734b; ii, 432b, **595b**; iii, 526b; iv, 124b, 791b, 988a; v, 1038a – I, 756b; II, 443a, **610a**; III, 545a; IV, 129b, 823b, 1020b; V, 1034a
Djumla → Naḥw
al-Djummal i, 97b – I, 100a
Djūn Ghurbānī i, 99b – I, 102b
Djūnā Khān → Muḥammad b. Tughluḳ
Djūnāgaṙh (Kathiawar) ii, **597a**, 1127a; iii, 451a; s, 246b – II, **611b**, 1153b; III, 466b; S, 246b
Djunayd, Shaykh ii, **598b**; iii, 315b, 1006b – II, **613b**; III, 325a, 1032a
Djunayd (Aydînoghlu) i, 309a, 346a, 783b; ii, **599a** – I, 319a, 356b, 806b; II, **613b**
al-Djunayd, Abu ʾl-Ḳāsim i, 162a, 415b; ii, **600a**; iii, 823b; iv, 114b; s, 350a – I, 166b, 427b; II, **614b**; III, 847a; IV, 119b; S, 350a
al-Djunayd b. ʿAbd Allāh i, 1292b; ii, **600b**; iv, 708a – I, 1332b; II, **615a**; IV, 736b
Djunayd b. ʿAbd al-Raḥmān s, 252a – S, 252a
Djunayd b. Ibrāhīm → Ṣafawid(e)s
Djunayd Khān v, 24a, b – V, 25a
Djunaydib Akhū Banī Rawāḥa s, 177b – S, 178b
Djunaydiyya i, 868b – I, 892b
Djunbulāṭ → Djanbulāṭ
Djund i, 76a, 82a, 134b, 248a, 490a, b, 729b, 991a; ii, 505a, **601a**; v, 685a – I, 78b, 84b, 138b, 255b, 504b, 505b, 751b, 1020b; II, 517b, **616a**; V, 690a

Djund (province) v, 125a – V, 127b
Djundab b. Khāridja al-Ṭāʾī i, 1241b – I, 1279a
Djundaysābūr → Gondēshāpūr
Djundī → Ḥalḳa
Djundīsāpūr → Gondēshāpur
Djundub b. Djunāda → Abū Dharr
Djūnī iv, 743b – IV, 773b
Djūniyya s, 149b – S, 149b
Djunnar ii, **602a** – II, **616b**
Djunub ii, 440b – II, 452a
Djūr → Fīrūzābād
Djuradh s, **285b** – S, **285b**
Djurash s, 326b – S, 326a
Djurʾat ii, **602a** – II, **617a**
Djuraydj i, 1021b; ii, **602b** – I, 1053a; II, **617a**
Djurbadhāḳān → Gulpāyagān
Djurdjān → Gurgān
al-Djurdjānī, ʿAbd al-Ḳāhir i, 590b, 858a, 982a, 1115b; ii, 824b; iii, 834b, 1020a; iv, 250b, 251a, b, 864a; v, 899a, 900b, 1026a; s, **277a** – I, 609b, 882a, 1012b, 1149a; II, 844a; III, 858b, 1045b; IV, 261b, 262a, b, 897b; V, 905b, 906b, 1022a; S, **277a**
Djurdjanī, Abu ʾl-Ḳāsim s, 14b – S, 15a
al-Djurdjānī, ʿAlī b. ʿAbd al- ʿAzīz iv, 249b – IV, 260b
al-Djurdjānī, ʿAlī b. Muḥammad i, 342b, 343a, 351a, 714b, 715b, 1327a; ii, 294a, **602b,** 608a, 774a; iii, 330a, 664b, 1147b; iv, 123a, 272a – I, 353a, b, 362a, 736a, 737a, 1368a; II, 302a, **617b,** 623a, 792b; III, 340a, 686a, 1175b; IV, 128a, b, 284a
Djurdjānī, Fakhr al-Dīn → Gurgānī
al-Djurdjānī, Ismāʿīl b. al-Ḥusayn i, 213b; ii, **603a**; s, 271b – I, 220a; II, **617b**; S, 271b
al-Djurdjānī, Nūr al-Dīn ii, 603a – II, 617b
al-Djurdjāniyya → Gurgandj
Djurdjīs b. Djibrīl b. Bukhtīshūʾ i, 212b, 1298a – I, 219a, 1338a
Djurdjūma ii, 456a, 457b – II, 468a, 469a
Djurdjura i, 369b; ii, **603a**; iv, 359a, 360a, 361a, 362b – I, 380b; II, **618a**; IV, 374b, 376a, 377a, 378b
Djurhum (Djurham) i, 563a; ii, **603b;** iii, 389b, 739a; iv, 185a, 448b; v, 77a, b, 763a – I, 581a; II, **618b;** III, 402a, 762a; IV, 193a, 468b; V, 79a, b, 769a
Djurm ii, 479b, **604a** – II, 491b, **618b**
Djurmāghūn iv, 102a – IV, 106b
Djurmāʾīs v, 163a – V, 161a
Djurnal i, 64a – I, 66a
al-Djurr, Shukr Allāh v, 1256a, b – V, 1247a, b
al-Djurūmiyya v, 65a, 183a – V, 66b, 180b
al-Djurz i, 991b; ii, 352a – I, 1022a; II, 362a
Djurzan v, 488a – V, 490b, 491a
Djusham (Djishum) s, 343a – S, 342b
Djusham b. Muʿāwiya, Banū ii, 626b; v, 48b – II, 642b; V, 50a
Djushaysh iv, 1134b – IV, 1166b
Djusnas Abū Farrukhān s, 298b – S, 298a
Djustān b. Wahsūdān ii, 192a – II, 198a
Djustān I ii, 191a; v, 452a – II, 197a; V, 455a
Djustān II ii, 191a, b; iii, 245a – II, 197a, b; III, 252a
Djustānid(e)s ii, 191a, 193b; iii, 254b; v, 602b, 603a; s, 356b – II, 197a, 199b; III, 261b; V, 606b, 607a; S, 356b
Djusūr v, 862b – V, 869b
Djuwayn ii, **604b**; iv, 5a; s, 235a – II, **619b**; IV, 5b; S, 235a
al-Djuwaynī, ʿAbd Allāh ii, **605a**; iv, 149b; v, 526b – II, **620a**; IV, 155b; V, 530a
al-Djuwaynī, ʿAbd al-Malik i, 410b, 411a, 485a, 593a, 1130b; ii, 570b, **605a,** 1038b, 1040a; iii, 330a, 914a, 1019b, 1024b, 1145a; iv, 149b, 257b, 272a; s, 343b, 346b, 347a, b, 348a, 403a – I, 422b, 423a, 499b, 612a, 1164b; II, 585a, **620a,** 1063a, 1064a; III, 340a, 938a, 1045a, 1050a, 1173b; IV, 155b, 268b, 284a; S, 343b, 346a, 347a, b, 348a, 403b
Djuwaynī, ʿAlāʾ al-Dīn i, 902b; ii, **606a;** iii, 738a; iv, 865a; v, 311b; s, 94b – I, 930a; II, **621a;** III, 760b; IV, 898a; V, 311b; S, 94a
al-Djuwaynī, Bahāʾ al-dīn Muḥammad ii, 607b; s, 235b – II, 622b; S, 235a
Djuwayni, Shams al-Dīn ii, 334a, **607a;** iii, 572b, 1269a; iv, 620b; v, 868b; s, 235b – II, 343b, **622a;** III, 592b, 1302a; IV, 645a; V, 875a; S, 235a
al-Djuwaynī, Sharaf al-Din Harūn ii, 607b – II, 622b
Djuwayra → Abū Duʾād al-Iyādī
Djuwayriyya bint Abī Djahl i, 751a – I, 773b
Djuwayriyya bint al-Ḥārith v, 78b – V, 80b
Djūybārī s, 228a – S, 228a
Djuyum → Djuwayn
Djuyūsh-beg i, 300b – I, 309b
Djuzʾ (in poetry/en poésie) i, 669b; ii, **607b** – I, 690b; II, **623a** → ʿArūḍ, Ḳurʾān
Djuzʾ ii, 220a, **607b** – II, 226b, **623a**
Djūzdjān ii, 1b, **608b,** 798b; s, 125b, 367b, 376a, b, 386b – II, 1b, **623b,** 817b; S, 124b, 367a, 376a, b, 387a
al-Djūzdjānī iii, 331a, 941a, b – III, 341a, 966a, b
al-Djūzdjanī, Minhādj al-Dīn i, 1131a; ii, **609a,** 1099a; iii, 1155b – I, 1165b; II, **624a,** 1125a; III, 1184a
Djyūsh → Djīsh
Dnieper → Özi
Doʾāb ii, **609b,** 868a; s, 57b, 124a, 126a, 206b – II, **625a,** 888a; S, 58a, 123b, 125b, 206a
Dōʿān → Dawʿān
Dobʿa iii, 6a – III, 6a
Dobrotič ii, 611a, 971b – II, 626a, 993b
Dobrudja i, 1302a; ii, **610a,** 909a, 971b; v, 277b – I, 1342a; II, **625a,** 930a, 993b; V, 275b
Dōdāīs i, 1005b; s, 332a – I, 1036b; S, 331b
Ḍofār → Ẓafār
Dog → Kalb
Döger (Ghuzz) i, 666b; ii, **613b,** 1107b – I, 687a; II, **629a,** 1133b
Döger Sālim Beg iv, 584b, 586a – IV, 608a, b
Doghandjī ii, 614a – II, 629b
Dogma/Dogme → ʿAḳīda
Dōgrā iv, 709b; s, 241b – Iv, 738a; S, 242a
Doha → al-Dawḥa
Dokkali i, 210b – I, 216b
Doḳūz Khātūn iii, 569b, 1122a – III, 589a, 1149b
Dokuz ʿUmde ii, 596b – II, 611a
Dolma Baghče → Istanbul
Domain(e) → Ḍayʿa
Dōmbkī → Balūčistān
Dome/dôme → Ḳubba
Dome of the Rock/dôme du Rocher → Ḳubbat al-Ṣakhra; Masdjid al-Aḳṣā
Don expiatoire → Kaffāra
Donation/Don → Hiba
Donanma ii, **615a** – II, **630a**
Donbolī i, 1211a – I, 1247a → Kurd(e)s
Dongola i, 50a; ii, **615a**; s, 278b – I, 51a; II, **630b**; S, 278b
Donkey → Ḥimār
Dönme ii, **615b** – II, **631a**
Dönüm ii, 32b – II, 33b
Donza i, 1258a – I, 1296a
Door → Bā (Gate/Porte)
Dō-Rāha s, 420b – S, 420b
Dorylaion → Eskishehir
Dōsa → Dawsa
Dōst Muḥammad → Dūst Muḥammad
Dot, Douaire → Mahr

Douane → Gümrük
Douar → Dawār
Dougga v, 755b, 756b — V, 761b, 762b
Dove → Ḥamām
Dowry → Mahr
Draʿ → Darʿa
Draa → Darʿa
Drač ii, **616b** — II, **632a**
Drafsh-i Kāwiyān → Kāwa
Drāgal Hills s, 331b — S, 331b
Drag(o)man → Turdjumān
Dragon → Tinnīn
Dragut → Turghud ʿAlī Pasha
Drama → Masraḥiyya
Drapeau → ʿAlam, Shiʿār
Dravidian/Dravidienne iii, 412a — III, 425a
Dreams → al-Ruʾyā; Taʿbīr
Dress → Libās
Drīshak → Balūčistān
Droguiste → ʿAṭṭār
Droit → ʿĀda; ʿAmal; Fiḳh; Ḥuḳūḳ; Ḳānūn; Maḥkama; Sharīʿa; Siyāsa; Tashrīʿ; Uṣūl; etc.
Droit coutumier → ʿĀda; ʿUrf
Dromedary/Dromadaire → Ibil
Druggist → ʿAṭṭār
Drum → Darabukka; Ṭabl; Tunbur
Druzes/Druses → Durūz
Duʿāʾ ii, 302a, 314b, **617a**; iv, 715b; v, 74a, b, 621b, 956b, 960a — II, 310a, 324a, **632b**; IV, 744a; V, 76a, b, 625b, 960a, 964b
Duʾa Khān → Duwā Khān
Dualism/Dualisme → Khurramiyya; Thanawiyya; Zindīḳ
Dūʿan → Dawʿan
Dubai → Dubayy
Dubays I b. ʿAlī i, 684a, 1073b, 1074a, 1075a; iii, 390a; iv, 911a — I, 704b, 1105b, 1106a, 1107a; III, 402a; IV, 944a → Mazyadīs
Dubays II b. Ṣadaḳa i, 300b, 314a, 684a; iv, 493b, 911b — I, 309b, 324a, 705a; IV, 515a, 944b
Dubaytī → Rubāʿī
Dubayy i, 166b, 928b, 1313b; ii, **618b**; iv, 778a; s, 416b — I, 171a, 956b, 1354a; II, **634a**; IV, 809b; S, 417a
al-Dubb → Nudjūm
Dubbāṭ al-Aḥrār s, 6a — S, 5a
Dubdū ii, **619b** — II, **635a**
Dubrovnik → Ragusa
Duče Meḥmed Pasha i, 656b — I, 677b
Dūd Bandja ii, 124a — II, 127a
Dūd al-Ḳazz → Ḥarīr
Dūdāniyya → Dido
Dudekula v, 648b — V, 652b
Dūdhū Miyān i, 952a; ii, 784a — I, 981a; II, 803a
Dudjayl → Kārūn
Dudlebs (Dūlāba) s, 170b — S, 171a
Dūdū b. Ḥayda ii, 620a — II, 635b
Duero → Wādī Duwayro
Duff ii, **620a** — II, **635b**
Dūghlāt (Dūḳlāt) ii, 45b, **621b** — II, 46b, **637a**
Ḍuḥā ii, **622b** — II, **638a**
al-Duhaym b. Khalīl, Aḥmad s, 113a — S, 112b
Duhn → Khazaf
Duḳāḳ b. Tutush i, 664a, 731b, 1052a, 1332a; ii, 282a; iii, 398b — I, 683b, 753b, 1083b, 1372b; II, 290a; III, 411a
al-Dūkālī, ʿAbd al-Wāḥid s, 93a — S, 92b
Dukayn al-Rādjiz ii, **622b** — II, **638a**
Dukhān → Tütün
Dukchi Ishān iv, 113a — IV, 118b
Dukkāla ii, **623a** — II, **638b**
al-Dukkālī, Abū Shuʿayb iv, 159b — IV, 166b
Dükkān iv, 227b — IV, 237b
Duḳḳat al-bashāʾir iii, 189b — III, 193b
Ḍulāʿ, Djabal iv, 779b — IV, 811a
Dūlāb → Nāʿūra
Dūlāb (Daylam) iv, 725a — IV, 754a
Dulafid(e)s ii, **623a**; iv, 100a — II, **639a**; IV, 104a, b
Dūlandj ii, 68a — II, 69a
Dulat ii, 622b — II, 638a
Dulaym, Banū i, 461a; ii, **623b** — I, 474b; II, **639a**
Duldul ii, **624a** — II, **639b**
al-Dulfīn → Nudjūm
Dulghadir → Dhu ʾl-Ḳadr
Dulūk i, 791b; ii, **624a** — I, 815a; II, **639b**
Dūmat al-Djandal i, 55a, 384a, 525a, 882b, 969a; ii, **624b**; iv, 492b, 928a, b — I, 56b, 395a, 541a, 908a, 999a; II, **640a**; IV, 514a, 961a, b
Dumayr ii, 1021b — II, 1045a
Dumbulī ii, 193a; v, 460a — II, 199a; V, 462b
Dunama b. Aḥmad i, 1260a; v, 356a — I, 1298a; V, 357b
Dunama Dibbalemi iv, 567a — IV, 589b
al-Dunaydin iv, 416a — IV, 434a
Dunaysir ii, **626a**; v, 248a — II, **641b**; V, 246a
Dunbāwand → Damāwand
Dunbulī → Dumbulī
Dündar Beg → Falak al-Dīn Dündar
Dungan (Dōngan, Tungan) → Čīn
Dunghuzlum → Deñizli
Dungina → Ḳayalīḳ
Dunḳulā → Dongola
Dunyā i, 2a, 325a; ii, 295a, **626b** — I, 2b, 335a; II, 303a, **642a**
Duodécimains → Ithnā-ʿashariyya
Dupleix i, 625a — I, 645b
Dur Sharrukin v, 67b — V, 70a
Durač, Durrës → Drač
Dūrāh ii, 29a — II, 29b
Durand Agreement/l'accord de- i, 87b — I, 90a
Durand Line s, 66a, 270b — S, 66a, 270a
al-Duraybī, Āl i, 1312b — I, 1353a
Durayd s, 144b — S, 144b
Durayd b. al-Ṣimma ii, **626b**; iii, 578a; iv, 1027a — II, **642b**; III, 598a; IV, 1059a
Durazzo → Drač
Dūrbāsh ii, **627b** — II, **643a**
Durčaʾī, Sayyid Muḥammad Bāḳir s, 157b — S, 158a
Duress (law) → ʿIkrāh
Durgara → Dōgrā
Durkānī → Balūčistān
al-Durr i, 95b; ii, 557b, **628a**; iv, 764b; v, 572b, 675a, 819a — I, 98a; II, 571b, **643b**; IV, 795a; V, 577a, 680a, 825b
Durra (Djāriya) s, 122b — S, 122a
al-Durra al-Fākhira i, 351b — I, 362b
Durrānī i, 72b, 95a, 217b, 219b, 230a, b, 295a; ii, **628b**, 1001b; iii, 202a, 428a; iv, 357a, 537b; s, 66b, 270a, 332b — I, 74b, 98a, 224a, 226a, 237a, b, 304b; II, **644b**, 1024b; III, 207b, 441b; IV, 372b, 561a; S, 67a, 270a, 331b
al-Durrī iv, 646b, 647a — IV, 673a, b
Dürrī Meḥmed Efendi ii, 629a; iii, 604a, 1002b — II, 645a; III, 624b, 1027b
Dürrizāde ʿAbd Allāh Bey ii, 105a, **630a** — II, 107a, **646a**
Dürrīzāde Meḥmed Efendi ii, **629b** — II, **646a**
Dürrīzāde Muṣṭafā Efendi ii, **629b** — II, **645a**
Dürrīzāde Seyyid ʿAbd Allāh ii, **630a** — II, **645b**
Dürrīzāde Seyyid Meḥmed ʾĀrif ii, **629b** — II, **645b**
Dürrīzāde Seyyid Meḥmed ʿAtāʿ Allāh ii, **629b** — II, **645b**
Dursun b. ʿAdjilān Ḳarasī iv, 628a — IV, 653a
Dursun Meḥmed Pasha i, 174b — I, 179b
al-Durūʿ ii, **630b**; iii, 1004b — II, **646b**; III, 1030a

Durūn (Darūn) i, 320b – I, 330b
Durūz i, 68a, 483a, 552a, 571a, 1042a, 1078b, 1093b; II, 98a, 136b, **631b,** 749b, 1026b; iii, 21a, 76b, 293a; iv, 199a, 332a, 484a, 834b; v, 791b, 793b; s, 49a, b, 135b, 206b, 268b, 269a, 371a – I, 69b, 497b, 569b, 589b, 1074a, 1110b, 1126a; II, 100a, 140a, **647b,** 768a, 1050a; III, 22a, 79a, 302a; IV, 207b, 346b, 504b, 867b; V, 797b, 799b; S, 49b, 50a, 135b, 206b, 268b, 370b
Dusares → Dhu ʾl-Sharā
Dushan, Stephan i, 653b – I, 674a
Dushmanziyār → Kākawayhid(e)s
Dushmanziyārī iii, 1106b – III, 1134a
Dūst Bū Saʿd Dada i, 147b – I, 151b
Dūst Muḥammad Khān (d./m.1740) i, 1195a, 1197a – I, 1230b, 1232a
Dūst Muḥammad Khān (d./m.1863) i, 231a; ii, 417a, **637b**; iv, 537b; v, 48a; s, 237b, 367b – I, 238a; II, 428a, **653b**; IV, 561a; V, 49b; S, 237b, 367b
Dustūr i, 170a; ii, 79a, 151a, **638a;** iii, 186b – I, 174b; II, 80b, 155b, **654b;** III, 191a
Dutch i, 744b, 1341b; ii, 27b, 390b; iii, 566b, 1190a, 1221b; iv, 970b; v, 360b, 1155a, b
Duwā Khān i, 504b; ii, 3b, 14b, 45a, 268b; iv, 31b, 32a – I, 520a; II, 3b, 15a, 46a, 277a; IV, 33b, 34b
Duwaydār → Dawādār
Duwayḥ s, 278b – S, 278b
al-Duwayhī → Iṣṭifān al-Duwayhī
al-Duwayḥī, Ibrāhīm al-Rashīd s, **278b** – S, **278b**
Duwayḥis iv, 925a – IV, 958a
Duwayra iv, 1025b – IV, 1057b
Duyūn-i ʿUmūmiyye ii, **677a** – II, **694a**
Dūzakh → Djahannam
Düzmedje Muṣṭafā → Muṣṭafā Düzme
Dwārkā ii, **678a,** 1127a – II, **695a,** 1153b
Dwīn i, 636a, 638a, 645a, b; ii, **678a** – I, 656b, 658b, 665b, 666a; II, **695a**
Dyallo i, 303a – I, 312b
Dyeing → Sabbāgh
Dynasty/Dynastie → Dawla
Džabić, A.F. i, 1271b, 1274a; ii, **681b** – I, 1311a, 1313b; II, **698b**
Džambul Džabaev → Djambul Djabaev
Dzhek iv, 1029a; v, 284b – IV, 1061a; V, 282b

E

Eagle → ʿUkāb
East Africa ii, 682a
East India Company i, 757a, 979a, 1013a, 1170a, 1195b, 1341b; ii, 121a, 186b, 337a, 371a, 597b, 736a, 810b, 981b; iii, 226a, 322a, 458a, 585b, 1190a, 1191a; v, 573b
Eau → Māʾ
Eblis → Iblīs
Ebony/Ébène → Abanūs
Ebro/Èbre → Ibruh
Ebüzziya Tevfik i, 289b; ii, 474b, **682a** – I, 298b; II, 486b, **699a**
Échanson → Sāķī
Échecs → Shatrandj
Ecija → Istidjaʿ
Éclairage → Tanwīr
Éclipse → Kusūf
École → Kuttāb, Madrasa, Taʿlīm
Economic Life/Économie → Filāḥa; Māl; Ṣināʿa; Tadbīr al-Manzil; Tidjāra
Écritoire → Kitāba
Écriture → Khaṭṭ
Écrivain → Muʾallif
Ecstasy → Darwish; Dhikr; Shaṭḥ
Écurie → Iṣṭabl
Edebiyyāt-i Djedīde ii, **683a** – II, **700a**
Edessa/Edesse → al-Ruhā
Edi(c)t → Farmān
Edfu/Edfou → Adfū
Edhem, Čerkes → Čerkes Edhem
Edhem, Khalīl → Eldem, Khalīl
Edhem Pasha → Ibrāhīm
Edigü i, 1108a; ii, 44a, 1112a; iii, 117a – I, 1141a; II, 45a, 1138b; III, 119b
Edirne i, 269a, 398b, 999a, 1078a, 1279a, 1334a; ii, **683a;** iii, 352a; iv, 590a; s, 149b, 274a, 330b – I, 277a, 410a, 1029b, 1110a, 1318b, 1374b; II, **700a;** III, 363a; IV, 614a; S, 149b, 273b, 330a
- institutions i, 1225b; ii, 686a, 1133b – I, 1262a; II, 703a, b, 1160b
- monuments ii, 684a, b, 685a, b; iv, 592a, 722b, 1159a; v, 225a – II, 701b, 702a, b; IV, 616a, 751b, 1191a; V, 222b
Edirneli Naẓmī v, 264b – V, 262a
Edje Khalīl ii, 983b – II, 1006a
Edrei → Adhriʿāt
Edremit ii, **686b** – II, **703b**
ʿEdrūs → ʿAydarūs
Education/Éducation i, **687a** – I, **704a**
Edwardes, Herbert i, 1020a; ii, 186b – I, 1051a, b; II, 192b
Efe → Zeybek
Efendi i, 75a; ii, 19a, **687a** – I, 77a; II, 19b, **704a**
Eflāķ i, 340b, 1118b, 1298b; ii, 611b, **687b,** 688b, 703a, 915; iii, 1004a – I, 351a, 1152a, 1338b; II, 626b, **705a,** 721a, 936a; III, 1029a
Egalité → Kafāʾa
Egée, mer I, 477b; V, 509a, b, 510a
Egerdir → Eğridir
Eğin ii, **689a** – II, **706a**
Église → Kanīsa
Eğri ii, **689b** – II, **707a**
Eğri Dagh → Aghrī Dagh
Eğriboz ii, **691a**; v, 722b – II, **708b**; V, 778b
Eğridir ii, **691b** – II, **709a**
Egypt/Égypte → Miṣr
Ekbez s, 171b, 172a – S, 172a, b
Ekdālā iii, 634b – III, 655b
Ekinči b. Ķočķar iv, 1067a; v, 385b; s, **279b** – IV, 1099a; V, 387a; S, **279a**
Ekrem Bey i, 287b, 558a; ii, 440a, **692a;** iii, 357b; iv, 930b; v, 195b – I, 296a, 576a; II, 451b, **709b;** III, 368b; IV, 963b; V, 192b
Elam, Elamite v, 830b – V, 836b
Elath → Ayla
Elaziğ → Maʿmūrat al-ʿAzīz
Elbasan i, 652b, 655b; ii, **693a**; iv, 140a – I, 673a, 676a; II, **710a**; IV, 146a
Elbistān ii, 239a, b, 240a, **693a**; iv, 463a; v, 73b – II, 246a, b, **710b**; IV, 483b; V, 75b
Elburz → Alburz
Elche → Alsh
Elči ii, **694a**; iv, 31b – II, **711a**; IV, 34a
Eldem, Khalīl Edhem ii, **694b;** iii, 993b – II, **711b;** III, 1018a
Eldigüz, Eldigüzid(e)s → Ildeñiz, Ildeñizid(e)s
Electricity/Électricité → Kahrubā
Electuary/Électuaire → Adwiya
Elegy/Élégie → Marthiya
Elephant/Éléphant → ʿĀdj; Fīl
El-Erg → Djālo
Elesbaas i, 103a – I, 105b
Élevage → Ghanam; Ibil; Khayl
El-Gāʿda i, 460b – I, 473b

Elias Andrawus s, 301a — S, 300b
Eličpur → Gāwilgaṙh
Eličpur/Iličpur s, **279b** — S, **279b**
Elijah/Élie → Ilyās
Elisha/Élisée → Alīsaʿ
Elite/Élite → al-Khāṣṣa wa ʾl-ʿāmma
Elixir → al-Iksīr
Elkass mirza → Alkāṣ mīrzā
Ellipse → Halīladj
Ellora → Elurā
Elma Daghî ii, **694b,** 982a; v, 810a, b — II, **712a,** 1004b; V, 816a, b
Elmalî ii, **695a** — II, **712a**
Eloche → Alsh
Éloge → Madīḥ
Eloquence/Éloquence → Balāgha; Bayān; Faṣāḥa
Eltuzar Înaḳ s, 420a — S, 420a
Elurā ii, **695a** — II, **712b**
Elvira → Ilbīra
Elwān Čelebi i, 698b; ii, 62b — I, 719b; II, 63b
Elwend → Alwand
Émail → Mīnā
Emancipation → Taḥrīr
Emānet i, 1090b; ii, 147b, 695b — I, 1123a; II, 152a, 713a → Emīn
Emanet-i Muḳaddese ii, **695b** — II, **712b**
Embalming/Embaumement → Ḥināṭa
Emblem/Emblème → Shiʿār
Ememik → al-Yamāmī
Emerald/Émeraude → Djawhar; Zumurrud
Émerillon → Bayzara
Emesa/Émèse → Ḥims
Emigration/Émigration → Djāliya; Hidjra; Muhādjirūn
Emil iv, 581a — IV, 604b
Emīn ii, **695b** — II, **713a**
Emin, Mehmed → Yurdakul, Mehmed Emin
Emīn Pasha ii, 636b — II, 652b
Emīn Pasha (E.C. Schnitzer) ii, **696a**; v, 1250b — II, **713b**; V, 1241b
Emīne Sulṭān i, 394b; s, 282b — I, 406a; S, 282b
Emir → Amīr
Emīr Süleymān → Sulaymān Čelebi
Emīr Sulṭān ii, 103b, **697a**; s, 282b — II, 105b, **714b**; S, 282b
Émirats Arabes Unis → al-Imārāt al-ʿArabiyya al-Muttaḥida
Emniyyet-i ʿUmūmiyye ii, 74b — II, 75b
Empedocles/Empédocle → Anbāduḳlīs
Emr → Amr
Emrāh s, 91b — S, 91a
Emreli ii, **697b** — II, **715a**
Enamel → Mīnā
Enbaqom s, 396b — S, 396b
Encens → Lubān; Mibkhara
Enchantement → Siḥr
Enchères → Dallāl; Simsār
Encre → Midād
Encrier → Dawāt
Encyclopaedia/Encyclopédie → Mawsūʿa
Enderūn ii, **697b,** 1089a, 1091a; iv, 1097a — II, **715a,** 1114b, 1116b; IV, 1128a
Endive → Hindibāʾ
Endjümen → Andjuman
Enez → Enos
Enfant → Ṣaghīr; Walad
Enfer → Djahannam
Engürü → Ankara
Engürüs → Madjāristān; Ungurus
Enif → Nudjūm
Énigme → Bilmedje; Lughz
Enīs ʿAwnī → Akagündüz
Enīs Behīdj s, 168a — S, 168a
Enluminure → Kitāb
Enna → Ḳaṣryānnih
Ennayer → Innāyēr
Ennedi s, 165a, 166a — S, 165a, 166a
Enoch → Idrīs
Enos ii, **698a** — II, **715b**
Enseignement → Tadrīs; Djāmiʿa; Maʿārif;
Ensign/Enseigne → ʿAlam; Liwāʾ
Entente Libérale → Ḥürriyet we Iʿtilāf
Enterrement → Djanāza
Entrepôt → Funduḳ; Khān
Ents Behīdj s, 168a — S, 168a
Enwer Pasha i, 63b; ii, 431b, 531a, b, **698a**; iii, 1199b; iv, 284b, 285b, 297a, b; v, 537b — I, 65b; II, 442b, 544b, **716a;** III, 1229b; IV, 297a, 298a, 310a, 311a; V, 542a
Enwerī ii, **702b** — II, **720b**
Enzel → Inzāl
Enzeli → Bandar ʿAbbās
Épargne → Māl
Épée → Sayf
Épervier → Bayzara
Éphèbe → Liwāṭ
Ephesus/Éphèse → Aya Solūḳ
Ephthalites → Hayāṭila
Epic → Ḥamāsa; Malḥama
Épices → Afāwīh
Épices → Tawābil
Épicier → Baḳḳāl
Epigone/Épigone → al-Salaf wa ʾl-Khalaf
Epigram/Épigramme → Hidjāʾ
Epigraphy/Épigraphie → Kitābāt; Khaṭṭ; Naḳsh
Epithet/Épithète → Naʿt; Ṣifa
Épitre → Risāla
Épopée → Ḥamāsa
Equality → Kafāʾa
Equator/Équateur → Istiwāʾ; al-Khaṭṭ
Équitation → Furūsiyya; Khayl
Equity/Équité → Inṣāf
Erbakan, Necmettin iv, 791b — IV, 823b
Erbīl → Irbīl
Erciyas → Erdjiyas
Erdebīl → Ardabil
Erdel ii, **703a** — II, **720b**
Erden ʿAlī → ʿAlāʾ al-Dīn Beg
Erdjīsh → Ardjīsh
Erdjiyas Daghî ii, **705a**; iv, 845b — II, **723a**; IV, 878b
Ereğli ii, **705a**; iv, 575b, 621a — II, **723a**; IV, 598b, 646a
Erekle → Iraklî II
Eretna i, 432a, 510b; ii, 401a, **705b**; iv, 622b, 843a — I, 444a, 526a; II, 411b, **724a**; IV, 647b, 876a
Erg → Ṣaḥrāʾ
Erganí ii, **707a** — II, **725a**
Ergen, Özbeg Khān s, 246a — S, 246a
Ergene Khātūn → Orkîna Khātūn
Ergenekon ii, **707b** — II, **726a**
Ergin, Osman ii, **708a** — II, **726a**
Ergiri ii, **708b** — II, **726b**
Ergun, Saʿd al-Dīn Nüzhet s, **280a** — S, **280a**
Eritrea ii, **709a;** iii, 6a
Eriwan/Erivan → Rewān
Ermenak, Ermenek ii, **710a;** iii, 1006b; iv, 619a, 622a, b, — II, **727a;** III, 1032a; IV, 643b, 647a
Ermine → Farw
Erotic/Érotique (poésie) → Ghazal; Nasīb
Érotologie → Bāh; Djins
Error → Khaṭaʾ
Ersarî i, **224a**; v, 582a; s, 143b, 147a, **280b** — I, 231a; V, 587a; S, 143a, 147a, **280b**
Ersoy → Mehmet Akif Ersoy

Ertoghrul i, 329b, 340a; ii, **710b**, 715b – I, 340a, 350b; II, **727b**, 733b
Ertoghrul, Bursa i, 1218b; ii, 711a – I, 1254b; II, 727b
Ertoghrul b. Bāyazīd ii, 711a – II, 728a
Érythrée II, **728a;** III, 6a
Erzen → Arzan
Erzerum → Erzurūm
Erzindjān i, 639a, 1328a; ii, 33a, **711a**; iv, 817b – I, 659b, 1368b; II, 33b, **729b**; IV, 850b
Erzurūm i, 4a, 465a, 636a, 639a; ii, 210a, 425b, 711b, **712a,** 945b; iii, 212b, 214b; iv, 394b, 817b; v, 33b; s, 136a, 308a – I, 4a, 479a, 656b, 659b; II, 216b, 436b, 729b, **730a,** 967b; III, 218b, 221a; IV, 411b, 850b; V, 34b; S, 135b, 307b
Esᶜad Efendi, Aḥmed ii, **712b** – II, **731a**
Esᶜad Efendi, Meḥmed (d./m. 1625) ii, **713a**; iv, 900b – II, **731b**; IV, 933b
Esᶜad Efendi, Meḥmed (d./m. 1753) ii, **713b,** 931b; iv, 527b – II, **731b,** 953a; IV, 550b
Esᶜad Efendi, Meḥmed (d./m. 1778) ii, **713b** – II, **732a**
Esᶜad Efendi, Meḥmed (d./m. 1848) i, 630a; ii, 465b, **714a** – I, 651a; II, 477b, **732a**
Esᶜad Mukhliṣ Pasha ii, 636b – II, 652b
Esᶜad Pasha (d./m. 1932) iv, 873b – IV, 907a
Esᶜad Pasha, Sakîzlî Aḥmed s, **281b** – S, **281b**
Esāme → Yeni Čeri
Eschatology/Eschatologie → Ḳiyāma
Esclavage, Esclave → ᶜAbd
Esclavons → Saḳāliba
Esdras → Idrīs; ᶜUzayr
Esen Bugha I ii, 3b – II, 3b, 4a
Esen Bugha II i, 148a; ii, 45b; v, 859a – I, 152a; II, 46a; V, 866a
Esen Tayshi iv, 512a – IV, 534a
Esendal, Memdūḥ Shewket v, 194b, 197a; s, **282a** – V, 192a, 194b; S, **281b**
Eshām → Ashām
Eshkindji ii, 528b, **714b** – II, 541b, **733a**
Eshḳiyāᶜ iii, 317b – III, 327a
Eshref → Ashraf
Eshref, Meḥmed s, **282b** – S, **282a**
Eshref, Rüshen (Ünaydin) iv, 874b – IV, 908a
Eshref-i Rūmī → Eshrefoghlu
Eshrefiyye s, 282b – S, 282b
Eshrefoghlu ᶜAbd Allāh s, **282b** – S, **282b**
Eski Baba → Babaeski
Eski Ḳaplîdja iv, 570a – IV, 593a
Eski Ḳarā Ḥiṣār → Īsdje Ḳarā Ḥiṣār
Eski Sarāy → Sarāy
Eski Üdjüm s, 82a – S, 82a
Eskishehir ii, **715a** – II, **733b**
Eṣnāf → Ṣinf
Esne → Isnā
Esoterics/Ésotérisme → Ẓāhir
Espagne → al-Andalūs
Esparto-grass → Ḥalfāᶜ
Espionage/Espionnage → Djāsūs
Esprit de Corps → ᶜAṣabiyya
Esrār Dede ii, 999a; s, **283a** – II, 1022b; S, **283a**
Essence → Dhāt; Djawhar
Estate → Ḍayᶜa
Esthétique → ᶜIlm al-Djamal
Estrangelo iii, 963b – III, 988a
Eszék ii, **715b** – II, **734a**
Esztergom ii, **716a**; v, 641a, 1022a; s, 171a – II, **734b**; V, 645a, 1018a; S, 171a
Étable → Iṣṭabl
Étain → Ḳalᶜī
Etājā, Etaya → Itāwā
État → Dawla
Etawah → Itāwa
Étendard → Liwāᵓ
Eternity/Éternité → Abad; Ḳidam
Ethics, Ethology/Éthique, Éthologie → Akhlāḳ
Ethiopia/Éthiopie → al-Ḥabash
Ethiopians/ Éthiopiens → Ḥabasha
Éthique → Akhlāḳ
Etil → Itil (river/rivière)
Et-Meydani → Istanbul
Étoiles → Nudjūm
Être et Non-être → Wudjūd et ᶜAdam
Etymology/Étymologie → Ishtiḳāḳ
Euboea → Eğriboz
Euclid/Euclide → Uḳlīdish
Eugène of Savoy/-de Savoie i, 269b, 292a, 395a; iv, 969b – I, 277b, 301a, 406b; IV, 1001b
Eulogy/Eulogie → Madīḥ
Eunuch/Eunuque → Khādim; Khaṣi; Kîzlar aghasî
Euphemism(e)s v, 117b, 118a – V, 120a, b
Euphrates/Euphrate → al-Furāt
Eutychius → Saᶜīd b. Biṭrīḳ
Évangile → Indjīl
Eve/Ève → Ḥawwāᶜ
Éventail → Mirwāḥa
Ev-göčü iv, 239b – IV, 250a
Evidence → Bayyina
Evora → Yābura
Evran → Akhī Ewrān
Evrenos → Ewrenos
Ewer → Ibrīḳ
Ewliyā Čelebi i, 310b, 843a, 993a, 1076a; ii, 589b, **717b;** iii, 7a; iv, 185b; v, 726b, 816a; s, 171b, 187a, 208b, 315b, 330b – I, 320a, 866a, 1023b, 1108a; II, 604a, **736a;** III, 7b; IV, 193b; V, 732a, 822a; S, 171b, 188a, 208a, 315a, 330a
Ewrāḳ i, 109a – I, 1122b
Ewrenos Beg, Ghāzī ii **720a,** 722a; iv, 628b; v, 772a; s, 330a, b, 331a – II, **738b,** 740b; IV, 653b; V, 778a; S, 329b, 330a, b
Ewrenos-oghullarî i, 340b, 1118b; ii, **720b** – I, 351a, 1152a; II, **739b**
Exchange value → ᶜIwād
Excision → Khitān
Exegesis/Exégèse → Tafsīr
Execution → Ḳatl
Existence → Anniyya; Wudjūd
Exorcism/Exorcisme → Ruḳya
Expenditure → Nafaḳa
Expiation → Kaffāra
Expiatory offering → Kaffāra
Extra-territoriality/Exterritorialité → Imtiyāzāt
Eyālet i, 468b, 469a, 640b, 906b, 974a, 1263b; ii, **721b** – I, 482b, 483a, 661a, 934a, 1004b, 1302a; II, **740a**
Eylūl → Taᶜrīkh
Eymir (Eymür) ii, **724a** – II, **743a**
Eyvān → Īwān
Eyyūb iv, 226a, 233a, 238b, 244a; s, 315a – IV, 236a, 243a, 249a, 255a; S, 315a
Eyyūb Agha Ḳara ᶜOthmān-oghlu iv, 593b – IV, 617b
Eyyūb Ṣabrī iv, 284b – IV, 297a
Eyyūboghlu, Bedrī Raḥmī s, 283a – S, 283a
Eyyūboghlu, Ṣabāḥ al-Dīn Raḥmī s, **283b** – S, **283a**
Ezafe → Iḍāfa
Ezan adî iv, 181a – IV, 188b
Ēzānā iii, 10a – III, 10b
Ezbek iv, 462b, 463a – IV, 483b
Ezbekiyya iv, 442a, b – IV, 462a, b
Ezekiel/Ezéchiel → Ḥizḳīl
Ezelī → Azalī
Ezra → Idrīs; ᶜUzayr

F

Fāʿ ii, **725a** — II, **743a**
Fable → Ḥikāya; Ḳiṣṣa; Mathal
Faḍāʾil → Faḍīla
Fadak ii, **725a,** 844b — II **743b,**864a
Faḍāla ii, **727a** — II, **745b**
al-Faḍāli, Muḥammad i, 334a, 867b; ii, **727b** — I, 344a, 891b; II, **746a**
Fadʿān i, 483a — I, 497b
Faddān → Misāḥa
Fadhlaka ii, **727b** — II, **746a**
al-Fāḍil → al-Ḳāḍī al-Fāḍil
Fāḍil Bey, Ḥüseyn ii, **727b** — II, **746a**
Fāḍil Ḥüsnī Dağlarca s, 150a — S, 150a
Fāḍil Khān → al-Bihārī
Fāḍil Pasha, Muṣṭafā ii, 474a, 642a, 682a, **728a,** 935b; iii, 357a, 593a; iv, 875b, 876a — II, 486a, 658a, 699a, **746b,** 957b; III, 368b, 613b; IV, 909a
Fāḍil Yuldash i, 422a — I, 434a
Faḍīla i, 327b; ii, **728b**; v, 331b — I, 338a; II, **747a**; V, 331b
Fādiliyya v, 889b, 892a — V, 896a, 898a
Fadjīdj → Figuig
al-Fadjīdjī i, 1154a — I, 1188a
Fadjr → Ṣalāt
Fadjr-i Ātī → Fedjr-i Ātī
Faḍl iii, 1202b — III, 1233a
Faḍl, Āl iv, 87b — IV, 91b
Faḍl, Bā ii, **729b** — II, **748b**
Faḍl I ii, 680a — II, 697a
Faḍl, Muḥammad ii, 123b — II, 126b
al-Faḍl b. al-ʿAbbās i, 137a — I, 141a
Faḍl b. Abi Yazīd i, 164a — I, 168b
al-Faḍl b. Aḥmad al-Isfarāʾinī ii, **730a,** 919a; iv, 107b — II, **749a,** 940a; IV, 112a
Faḍl b. ʿAlī al-ʿAbdalī i, 95b; v, 602a, b — I, 98a; V, 606a, b
Faḍl-i ʿAlī Khān i, 809a — I, 832b
al-Faḍl b. Djaʿfar b. al-Furāt → Ibn al-Furāt, Abuʾl-Fatḥ
al-Faḍl b. al-Ḥubāb al-Djumāḥī s, **284a** — S, **284a**
al-Faḍl b. Ḳārin iv, 493b — IV, 515a
al-Faḍl b. Marwān ii, **730b**; iv, 929a — II, **749a**; IV, 962a
Faḍl b. Muḥammad b. Shaddādid iv, 1176b — IV, 1210a
Faḍl b. Nuʿayr, Āl iii, 400a — III, 412a
al-Faḍl b. al-Rabīʿ i, 107b, 143b, 437b, 438a, 1035a, 1298a; ii, **730b**; iii, 45b; iv, 17a; s, 48a, 304b — I, 110b, 148a, 449b, 450a, 1066b, 1338a; II, **749a;** III, 47b; IV, 18a; S, 49a, 304b
al-Faḍl b. Sahl i, 271b, 400a, 437b, 1035b; ii, **731a;** iii, 231b, 243b; v, 621a; s, 15a — I, 280a, 411b, 449b, 1067a; II, **749b;** III, 238a, 250b; V, 625a; S, 15b
al-Faḍl b. Ṣāliḥ i, 823b, 824a; ii, 483a; iii, 79b, 128b — I, 846b, 847a; II, 495a; III, 82a, 131a
al-Faḍl b. Shādhān iv, 660b, 661b; s, 89b — IV, 687a, 688a; S, 89b
al-Faḍl b. Yaḥyā al-Barmakī i, 241a, 1033b, 1034a, b; ii, 191a, 540b, **732a;** iii, 233a, b; iv, 356b, 419b, 631b, 1164a, 1174b; v, 855b — I, 248b, 1065a, b, 1066a; II, 197a, 554a, **750b;** III, 239b, 240a; IV, 372a, 438a, 656b, 1196a, 1208a; V, 862b
Faḍl al-Shāʿira, al-Yamāmiyya s, **284b** — S, **284a**
Faḍl Allāh, Aḥmad → Ibn Faḍl Allāh al-ʿUmarī
Faḍl Allāh, Banū i, 1046a; ii, 305b, **732a;** iii, 758b; iv, 509b — I, 1077b; II, 314a, **750b;** III, 781b; IV, 531b
Faḍl Allāh → Rashīd al-Dīn
Faḍl Allāh b. ʿĪsā Tashkandī iv, 505a — IV, 527a
Faḍl Allāh b. Muḥibb Allāh i, 1333a — I, 1373b
Faḍl Allāh b. Rabeh i, 1260a — I, 1298b
Faḍl Alīh b. Rūzbihān Khundjī iv, 1036b; v, 873a — IV, 1068a, b; V, 879a
Faḍl Allāh Balkhī → Iḳbāl Khān
Faḍl Allāh Dabbās iv, 966b — IV, 998b
Faḍl Allāh Djamālī → Djamālī
Faḍl Allāh Efendi iv, 194a — IV, 202a
Faḍl Allāh Ḥurūfī i, 1162a; ii, 685a, **733a,** 924a; iii, 600a, 601a — I, 1196b; II, 702b, **751b,** 945b; III, 620b, 621b
Faḍl al-Ḥaḳḳ iii, 533a — III, 551b
Faḍl al-Mawlā Muḥammad v, 1250b, 1251a — V, 1241b, 1242a
Faḍl-i Ḥaḳḳ i, 827b; ii, 104a, **735b,** 736a; iv, 196a, 197a — I, 850a; II, 106b, **754a, b**; IV, 204b, 205b
Faḍl-i Imām i, **736a** — II, **754b**
Faḍlawayh, Banū ii, **736b**; s, 326a — II, **755a**; S, 325b
Faḍlawayh b. ʿAlī i, 420a; ii, 736b; iii, 1097b; iv, 222a, 807b — I, 432a; II, 755a; III, 1124a; IV, 232a, 840a
Faḍlawī iii, 337a; v, 824b, 826b — III, 347a; V, 830b, 832b
Faḍlī (Fadhlī) ii, 675b, **737a** — II, 692a, **755b**
Faḍlī, Meḥmed i, 1301b; ii, **737b,** 1133a; v, 957b — I, 1341b; II, **756a,** 1160a; V, 961b
Faḍlūn b. Abi ʾl-Suvār iv, 773a — IV, 804a
Faḍlūn b. Minučihr iv, 670a — IV, 697b
Faḍlūn b. Shaddād iv, 346b; v, 489a — IV, 361a; V, 492a
Faḍlūya → Faḍlawayh b. ʿAlī
Fadu, Fadwa → Fidya
Faghfūr ii, **738a** — II, **756b**
Faghfūr (porcelain(e)) iii, 345b — III, 356b → Ṣīnī
Fahd ii, **738b** — II, **757a**
Fahd, Banū iii, 759b — III, 783a
Fahd b. ʿAbd al-ʿAzīz v, 1004a — V, 999b
Fahd b. Ibrāhīm iii, 77a, 78a — III, 79b, 80b
al-Fāhikī i, 1154a; ii, 740b — I, 1188a; II, 759a
Fahīm, Aḥmad → al-Fār
Faḥl ii, **743a** — II, **761b**
Fahm v, 965a, 967b — V, 969b
Fahm, Banū iii, 363b; s, 183a — III, 375a; S, 184b
Fahradj s, 127a — S, 126a
Fahrasa i, 70b, 96b, 1019b, 1092b; ii, **743b**; iii, 837b; s, 303a — I, 72b, 99a, 1050b, 1125a; II, **762a;** III, 861b; S, 302b
Faḥṣ al-Ballūṭ ii, **744a** — II, **762b**
Faïence → Kāshī
Fāʾik, amīr ii, 799a, — II, 818a
Fāʾiḳ, Saʿīd v, 195a — V, 192a
Fāʿil → ʿIlla
Fāʿil → Naḥw
Fair → Panāyir; Sūḳ
Faith → ʿAḳīda; Īmān
Fāʾiẓ ii, 148a — II, 152b
Fāʾiẓ bi-Naṣr Allāh i, 9b; ii, 857a; iv, 944a — I, 9b; II, 877a; IV, 977a
Faizullah Khodja → Khodjaev
Faḳāriyya → Dhu ʾl-Faḳāriyya
Faḳʿaṣ, Banū iv, 490b — IV, 511b
Fakhdh, Fakhidh i, 700a — I, 721b → ʿAshīra, Ḳabīla
Fākhita iv, 929b — IV, 962b
Fakhkh ii, **744b**; iii, 22a — II, **763a;** III, 23a
Fakhkhār i, 501a; ii, **745a;** iii, 1125b, 1267b; iv, 292a, 511b, 1164b; v, 942a — I, 516a; II, **763b;** III, 1153b, 1300b; IV, 305a, 533b, 1196b; V, 945b
Fakhr → Mufākhara
Fakhr al-Dawla Abū ʿAli iv, 859a — IV, 892b
Fakhr al-Dawla Abū Manṣūr Kūfī iv, 859a — IV, 892a

Fak̲h̲r al-Dawla ʿAlī i, 59b, 211b, 212a; ii, **748b;** iii, 258a, 671b; iv, 100b, 358a; s, 118b, 323a — I, 61b, 218a; II, **767a;** III, 265b, 693a; IV, 104b, 373b; S, 117b, 322b
Fak̲h̲r al-Dawla Čawlī i, 1012a; iii, 1097b; iv, 29a, 850b; v, 868a; s, 382b — I, 1043b; III, 1124a; IV, 31a, 883b; V, 874b; S, 383a
Fak̲h̲r al-Dawla Ḥasan b. S̲h̲āh Bāwand i, 237a, 1110a; s, 363b, 364a — I, 244a, 1143b; S, 363b
Fak̲h̲r al-Dawla Muḥammad b. D̲j̲ahīr i, 1206b; ii, 384a, b; v, 453a — I, 1242b; II, 394b, 395a; V, 455b
Fak̲h̲r al-Dīn I b. Maʿn ii, 634b, **749b**; iv, 483b — II, 650b, **768a**; IV, 504b
Fak̲h̲r al-Dīn II b. Maʿn i, 267b, 1138a; ii, 443b, 634b, **749b,** 912a; iii, 205b, 325a; iv, 834b; v, 792b; s, 49a, 159a — I, 276a, 1172b; II, 455a, 651a, **768a,** 933b; III, 211a, 335a; IV, 867b; V, 799a; S, 49b, 159a
Fak̲h̲r al-Dīn ʿAbd Allāh b. al-Hādī iii, 685a — III, 707a
Fak̲h̲r al-Dīn ʿAd̲j̲emī ii, 685a, 879a — II, 702b, 899b
Fak̲h̲r al-Dīn Aḥmad Ḳarāmān-og̲h̲lu iv, 622a, b — IV, 647a
Fak̲h̲r al-Dīn ʿAlī Ṣafī iv, 704a — IV, 732b
Fak̲h̲r al-Dīn ʿAlī Tabrīzī → Ṣāhib ʿAtāʾ
Fak̲h̲r al-Dīn Čis̲h̲tī → S̲h̲āh Fak̲h̲r al-Dīn
Fak̲h̲r al-Dīn Ibrāhīm b. Lukmān iii, 679b — III, 701b
Fak̲h̲r al-Dīn ʿIṣāmī ii, 153b; iii, 1155b; iv, **92b**; s, 105b — II, 158b; III, 1184a; IV, **96b**; S, 105a
Fak̲h̲r al-Dīn Kart iv, 672a — IV, 699b
Fak̲h̲r al-Dīn Mād̲j̲id iii, 774a — III, 797a
Fak̲h̲r al-Dīn Marʿas̲h̲ī, Sayyid v, 663a — V, 668a
Fak̲h̲r al-Dīn Masʿūd ii, 1100b, 1101a — II, 1126b, 1127a, b
Fak̲h̲r al-Dīn Mubāraks̲h̲āh ii, **751b** — II, **769b**
Fak̲h̲r al-Dīn Muḥammad b. Ḥasan b. ʿAllāma al-Ḥillī s, 364a — S, 363b
Fak̲h̲r al-Dīn Pīrīog̲h̲lu iv, 671a — IV, 698b
Fak̲h̲r al-Dīn al-Rāzī i, 113a, 342b, 411a, 594a, 1115b; ii, 393b, 449b, **751b,** 756b, 771a, 773b, 825b, 971a, 1025b; iii, 172a, 302a, b, 330a, 1020a, 1237b; iv, 120a, 183b, 251b, 367a, 406a, 669a; s, 25b, 90b, 343b, 396b — I, 116a, 353a, 423a, 613b, 1149a; II, 404a, 461b, **770a,** 784a, 789b, 792b, 845b, 938b, 1049a; III, 175b, 311b, 340a, 1045b, 1269b; IV, 125a, 191b, 262b, 383a, 423b, 696b; S, 25b, 26a, 90a, 343b, 397a
Fak̲h̲r al-Dīn Yūsuf b. al-S̲h̲ayk̲h̲ i, 711a, 766a — I, 732b, 789a
Fak̲h̲r al-Dīn Zāhid i, 868b — I, 892b
Fak̲h̲r-i Ḳawwās v, 1027a — V, 1023a
Fak̲h̲r-i Mudabbir Mubāraks̲h̲āh iii, 181a, 196a, 197a, 344a, 481b, 1155b, 1202a; iv, 267a; v, 546b, 688a; s, **284b** — III, 185b, 200b, 202a, 354b, 498b, 1184a, 1232b; IV, 279a; V, 551a, 693a; S, **284b**
Fak̲h̲r al-Mulk → ʿAmmār, Banū
Fak̲h̲r al-Mulk Muḥammad b. ʿAlī → Ibn K̲h̲alaf, Abū G̲h̲ālib
Fak̲h̲r al-Mulk b. Niẓām al-Mulk i, 1052b; ii, 1039b — I, 1084a; II, 1063b → Niẓāmid(e)s
Fak̲h̲r al-Mulk ʿAmmār i, 448a — I, 461a
Fak̲h̲rā → Fak̲h̲r al-Dīn Mubāraks̲h̲āh
Fak̲h̲rī ii, **755b** — II, **774a**
Fak̲h̲rī, S̲h̲ams al-Dīn Muḥammad ii, **755b**; iv, 526a, b — II, **774a**; IV, 548b, 549a
Fak̲h̲rī Pas̲h̲a v, 998a — V, 993a
Faḳīh i, 7a, 250a, 279b, 289a; ii, **756a**; v, 1124b, 1208a, 1248a — I, 7a, 258a, 288b, 298a; II, **774a**; V, 1121a, 1198b, 1239a
Faḳīh, Bā ii, **756a** — II, **774b**
Faḳīh, Bal ii, **756b** — II, **775a**
al-Fakīh, Ibrāhīm v, 190a — V, 187a
al-Fākihī, Muḥammad b. Isḥāḳ i, 591a, 827a; ii, **757a** — I, 610b, 850a; II, **775b**
Faḳīr ii, **757b**; v, 1124b, 1208a, 1248a — II, **776a**; V, 1121a, 1198b, 1239a
Faḳīr (well/puits) iv, 532b — IV, 555b
Faḳīr of/de Ipi s, **285a** — S, **285a**
Faḳīr Muḥammad K̲h̲ān ii, **758a** — II, **776a**
Faḳīr Muḥammad Lahorī i, 827b — I, 850b
Faḳīrī ii, **758a** — II, **776b**
Faḳḳara → Foggara
Faḳr iv, 94b — IV, 98b
Faḳr-i ʿad̲j̲am iv, 52a — IV, 54b
Fāl v, 670b, 671b, 672a — V, 676a, 677a
Faʿl ii, **758b** — II, **777a**
Fāl-nāma ii, **760b** — II, **779a**
Falad̲j̲ i, 233a, 539a, 1313b; iv, 531b — I, 240b, 555b, 1353b; IV, 554b
al-Falad̲j̲ → al-Aflād̲j̲
Falak ii, **761b** — II, **780a**
Falak ʿAlā-i Tabrīzī ii, 81a — II, 82b
Falak al-Dīn b. Aḳ Sunḳur i, 300b — I, 310a
Falak al-Dīn Dündar ii, 692a; iii, 132b; iv, 622a — II, 709a; III, 136a; IV, 646b
Falaḳa ii, **763b** — II, **782a**
al-Falakī, Maḥmūd Pas̲h̲a ii, **764a** — II, **782b**
Falakī S̲h̲irwānī ii, **764a**; iv, 62a, 348b; s, 333b — II, **782b**; IV, 65b, 363a; S, 333a
Falāsifa i, 351a, 414b, 415a; ii, **764b;** iii, 169b, 303a, 1146b, 1147b; iv, 366b, 469a, 794b; v, 237a, 238a, 702b — I, 362a, 426a, b; II, **783a;** III, 173b, 312a, 1174b, 1175b; IV, 382b, 490a, 827a; V, 235a, 236a, 707b
Falconry → Bayzara; Čakïrd̲j̲ï-bas̲h̲ï; Dog̲h̲and̲j̲ï
Fālid̲j̲ iii, 665b — III, 687a
Fallāh i, 1a, 575a — II, 1a, 594a → Filāḥa
Fallāḥiya → Dawraḳ
Fallāḳ ii, **767b**; iv, 954b — II, **786a**; IV, 987a
Fallāta ii, **767b** — II, **786a**
al-Fallātī, al-Ṭāhir b. Ibrāhīm iv, 773b — IV, 805a
Fallūd̲j̲a ii, **768a** — II, **786b**
al-Fallūd̲j̲a ii, **768a** — II, **786b**
Fallūd̲j̲a (Miṣr) s, 6a — S, 5a
Fals i, 203a; ii, **768a** — I, 209a; II, **786b**
Falsafa i, 414b, 415a, 427b; ii, 450a, 618a, 752b, 764b, **769b,** 898a; iii, 75a, 329b; iv, 615b, 794b, 986b; v, 1129b — I, 426a, b, 439b; II, 461b, 633b, 771a, 783a, **788a,** 919a; III, 77b, 339b; IV, 640a, 827a, 1019a; V, 1126a
Famagusta/Famagouste → Mag̲h̲os̲h̲a
Family/Famille → ʿĀʾila
Fan → Mirwāḥa
Fanāʾ → Baḳāʾ
Fanak ii, **775a;** iii, 809a — II, **794a;** III, 832a
Fanār → Fener, Manār
al-Fanārī, Aḥmad i, 99a — I, 101b
al-Fanārī, Muḥammad → al-Fenārī
Fanduruskī → Abū Ṭālib
Fānī → Navāʾī
Fann ii, **775b**; iv, 528a — II, **794b**; IV, 551a
Fannā K̲h̲usraw → ʿAḍud al-Dawla
Fāo → al-Fāʾū
Faʾr s, **285b** — S, **285a**
Farʿ → Furūʿ (tax/impot)
al-Fār, Aḥmad Fahīm iii, 368a — III, 379b
al-Faraʿ s, 335a — S, 334b
Fārāb ii, **778a**; s, 244b, 245a, 289a, b — II, **797a**; S, 244b, 245a, 289a
al-Fārābī, Abū Ibrāhīm Isḥāḳ ii, 496a — II, 508a
al-Fārābī, Abū Ibrāhīm Isḥāḳ b. Ibrāhīm s, **289a** — S, **288b**
al-Fārābī, Abū Naṣr i, 179a, 234b, 236a, 327b, 328a, 342a, b, 350b, 427a, 589a, 630b, 631b, 1102a; ii, 96a, 765b, 770b, **778b,** 949a; iii, 329b, 509b, 729a, 876b,

911b, 942b, 1148a; v, 113b, 702b; s, 289b, 408b — I, 183b, 241b, 243a, 337b, 338b, 352a, 353a, 361a, 439b, 608b, 651b, 652a, 1135a; II, 98a, 784a, 789a, **797a,** 971a; III, 339b, 527a, 751b, 900b, 935b, 967b, 1176a; V, 116a, 707b; s, 289b, 409a
Faradj, al-Malik al-Nāṣir b. Barḳūk (Mamlūk) i, 138a; ii, 24a, 285b, **781a;** iii, 187a, 189b, 190a, 774a, 827b; iv, 428a — I, 142a; II, 246b, 293b, **800a;** III, 191b, 194a,b, 797a, 851b; IV, 446b
Faradj b. Sālim iii, 754a — III, 777a
al-Faradj Baʿd al-Shidda → Nādira
Farāfra, Farāfira i, 945a; ii, **782a** — I, 974a; II, **801a**
Farāh ii, **782b**; s, 222a — II, **801a**; S, 222a
Faraḥ Anṭūn i, 597a; ii, **782b;** iii, 514b — I, 616b; II, **801b;** III, 532a
Faraḥābād i, 8b; ii, **783a** — I, 8b; II, **801b**
Farāhānī → Ḳāʾim-maḳām-i Farāhānī
Farāhānī, Mīrzā Ḥusayn Khān s, 109a — S, 108b
Farāʿiḍ ii, **783a** — II, **802a**
Farāʿiḍiyya i, 719b; ii, **783b,** 797b; iii, 433a — I, 741b; II, **802b,** 816b; III, 447a
Faramā i, 32a, 216a — I, 33a, 222b
Farāmarz, ʿImād al-Dawla → ʿImād al-Dawla
Farāmarz b. ʿAlī → ʿAlāʾ al-Dawla
Farāmurz (Kākūyid(e)) → Abū Manṣūr Farāmurz
Farāmūsh-khāna ii, 433b; s, **290a** — II, 445a; S, **289b**
Farangī Maḥall → Lakhnaw (monuments)
Farangt Maḥāll, Āl s, 4b, 5a, 74a, b, **292a,** 360b — S, 3b, 4a, 74b, 75a, **291b,** 360b
Faras ii, **784b;** iii, 314b, 890b; iv, 214a-219b; v, 689a, b — II, **803b;** III, 324a, 914b; IV, 223b-229a; V, 694a, b
Faras al-Māʾ s, **294a** — S, **293b**
Farasān i, 535a, 738a; ii, **787b** — I, 551b, 760a; II, **806b**
Farasnāma iv, 218b — IV, 228b
al-Farawī, Muḥammad b. Muḥ. b. ʿAlī s, 83a — S, 82b
al-Farazdaḳ i, 43a, 105a, 158b, 331a, 586a, 772a, 950b, 1248a; ii, 479b, **788a,** 998b; iii, 248a, 354a, 608b; iv, 819a; s, 24a, 31a, 273a — I, 44a, 108a, 162b, 341b, 605a, 795a, 980a, 1286a; II, 492a, **807a,** 1021b; III, 255a, 365a, 629b; IV, 852a; S, 24b, 31b, 273a
al-Fard → Nudjūm
Fard, afrād ii, **789b;** iii, 25b — II, **808b;** III, 26b
Farḍ, farīḍa ii, **790a;** iv, 141b — II, **809a;** IV, 147a
Farḍ ʿayn ii, 539a, 790a — II, 552b, 809a
Farḍ kifāya i, 1199a; ii, 539a, 790a — I, 1234b; II, 552b, 809a
al-Farfarūn → Farāfra
Farghānā i, 46b, 148a; ii, **790a;** iii, 1060b; iv, 632a; v, 29a, 31a, 45a, 966b; s, 51b, 97b, 327b, 406b — I, 48a, 152b; II, **809a;** III, 1087a; IV, 657a; V, 30a, 32a, 46b, 971a; S, 52a, 97a, 326a, 406b
al-Farghānī ii, **793a** — II, **812a**
al-Farghānī (Alfraganus) i, 589b; ii, 763a, **793a;** iii, 1137a — I, 608b; II, 781b, **811b;** III, 1165b
Farhād Khān iv, 808a; v, 663a — IV, 840b; V, 668b
Farhād Mīrzā (Ḳādjār) s, 95a — S, 94b
Farhād Mīrzā Muʿtamad al-Dawla s, 302a — S, 301b
Farhād Pasha → Ferhād Pasha
Farhād wa-Shīrīn ii, **793b**; iv, 601b, 730b; v, 650b — II, **812b**; IV, 625b, 759b; V, 654b
Farhang iv, 525b — IV, 548a
Farhangistān-i Irān i, 505a; v, 1095b, 1096a, b — I, 520b; V, 1092a, b, 1093a
Farḥāt, Djarmānūs i, 571b, 596b; ii, **795a** — I, 590a, 616a; II, **814a**
Farḥāt, Ilyās v, 1256b — V, 1247b
Farḥat b. Saʿīd i, 1247a — I, 1285a
Farḥāt ʿAbbās iii, 525a; iv, 784b — III, 543a; IV, 816b
Farḥat al-Mulk ii, 1124b — II, 1151a
Farīburz b. Garshāsp iv, 349a — IV, 364a
Farīburz b. Sallār iv, 348a, b; s, 326a — IV, 362b, 363a; S, 325b
Farīd (pearl/perle) s, 253a — S, 252b
Farīd Bukhārī, Shaykh s, 122a — S, 121b
Farīd al-Dīn → ʿAṭṭār
Fārīd al-Dīn Masʿūd Gandj-i Shakar ii, 51a, **796b;** iii, 167b, 429a, 435b, 456b; v, 546b, 611a; s, 73b, 353a — II, 52a, **815a;** III, 171a, 443a, 450a, 472b; V, 551a, b, 615a; S, 74a, 353a
Farīd Murtaḍā Khān Bukhārī, Shaykh iv, 543b — IV, 567a
Farīd Pasha → Dāmād Ferīd Pasha
Farīḍa → Farāʿiḍ, Farḍ
Farīda (queen/reine) → Ṣafīnāz
Farīdkōṭ ii, **797b** — II, **816a**
Farīdpur ii, **797b** — II, **816b**
Farīdūn ii, 106b, **798a;** iii, 105a; iv, 12a; v, 661a — II, 109a, **816b;** III, 107a; IV, 13a; V, 666b
Farīdūn → Ferīdūn Beg
Farīdūn, Djalāl al-Dīn → ʿĀrif Čelebī
Fārigh iv, 68a — IV, 71b
Farīghūnid(e)s ii, 608b, **798b**; s, 125b, 376a, 386b — II, 624a, **817b**; S, 124b, 376a, 387a
Farīḳ → Abū Sinbil
al-Fāriḳī, Shihāb al-Dīn iv, 642a — IV, 668a
Fāris ii, **800a** — II, **818b**
Fāris b. ʿĪsā iii, 103a — III, 105b
Fāris b. Muḥammad → Ḥusām al-Dīn Abū ʼl-Shawḳ
Fāris Nimr ii, 467a; v, 1090b — II, 479a; V, 1087b
Fāris al-Shidyāḳ i, 596b; ii, 464b, 466a, **800b,** 927a; iii, 665a; v, 1090a; s, 40a — I, 616a; II, 476a, 477b, **819b,** 948b; III, 687a; V, 1087b; S, 40b
al-Fārisī → Abū Ḥulmān; Kamāl al-Dīn; Salmān
al-Fārisī, ʿAbd al-Ghāfir s, 343a — S, 343a
al-Fārisī, Abū ʿAlī i, 87a; ii, **802b;** iii, 754b, 880b; iv, 182a; s, 13a, 19a, 277a, 361b — I, 89b; II, **821b;** III, 777b, 904b; IV, 190a; S, 13b, 19a, 277a, 361a
al-Fārisī, Muḥammad b. al-Ḥasan s, 277a — S, 277a
Fārisiyya → Īrān
al-Fārisiyya i, 535b; ii, **803a** — I, 552a; II, **821b**
Farja i, 705b — I, 726b
Fark → Faṣl
al-Farḳadānī → Nudjūm
Fārkat s, 51a — S, 51b
Fārmad s, 14b — S, 15a
al-Fārmadhī → Abū ʿAlī al-Fārmadhī
Farmān ii, 303b, 309a, **803a;** iii, 1189b; iv, 1131b — II, 312a, 317b, **822a;** III, 1219b; IV, 1163a
Farmān-Farmā iv, 105a — IV, 109b
Fārmāsūn → Māsūniyya
Farmāsūniyya s, **296a** — S, **295b**
Farming → Filāḥa
Farming of taxes → Bayt al-māl, Ḍarība, Iltizām, Muḳāṭaʿa
Farmūl ii, **806b** — II, 825b
Farouk → Fārūḳ
al-Farrāʾ ii, **806b**; v, 174a, 351a; s, 22b — II, **825b**; V, 171b, 351b; S, 23a
Farrān v, 41b, 42b — V, 42b, 44a
Farrāsh iv, 899a — IV, 931b
Farrukh-Hormizd i, 188b — I, 194a
Farrukh Khān Amīn al-Dawla s, 108b, 290b — S, 108a, 290a
Farrukh-Shāh → ʿIzz al-Dīn Farrukh-Shāh
Farrukhābād ii, **808a;** iii, 61a; s, 106b — II, **827a;** III, 63b; S, 106a
al-Farrukhān ii, 74b, **809a**; iv, 207b; s, **297b** — II, 76a, **828b**; IV, 217a; S, **297a**
Farrukhī, Muḥammad Ibrāhīm → Farrukhī Yazdī
Farrukhī Sīstānī i, 1301a; ii, **809b**; iv, 61a; s, 108a —

I, 1341a; II, **828b**; IV, 64b; S, 107a
Farrukhī Yazdī, Muḥammad iv, 71a, 789b; s, 110a — IV, 75a, 821b; S, 109b
Farrukhrū Parsay iv, 1152a — IV, 1184a
Farrukh-siyar i, 1025b, 1026a; ii, 7a, 121a, 379b, 567a, 808a, **810a;** iii, 427a; iv, 279b; s, 126b — I, 1057b; II, 7a, 124a, 389b, 581b, 827b, **829a;** III, 441a; IV, 292a; S, 125b
Farrukhyasār iii, 316a; iv, 350a — III, 325b; IV, 365a
Farrukhzād b. Maḥmūd ii, 5a, 1052a — II, 5a, 1076a
Fārs i, 2b, 8a, 43b, 49a, 131b, 132a, 211b, 212a, 659a, 695b, 731b, 954b, 1350a, 1356a, 1358a; ii, **811a;** iii, 1097a; iv, 19b, 774a, 1046b; v, 450b, 665b; s, 91a, 118b, 147b, 222b, 302a, 326a, 379b, 383b — I, 2b, 8a, 44b, 50b, 135b, 136a, 217b, 218b, 679b, 716b, 753b, 984a, 1390b, 1395a, 1398b; II, **830b;** III, 1124a; IV, 21a, 805b, 1078a; V, 453a, 670b; S, 90b, 117b, 147b, 223a, 301b, 325b, 379b, 384a
Farsakh (farsang) i, 247a; ii, **812b;** iii, 406a — I, 254b; II, **832a;** III, 418b
Farsh → Ḳālī
Farsh → Mafrūshāt
Fārsī ii, 142b — II, 146a → Īrān
Fārsistān → Irān
Fartanā iv, 821a — IV, 854a
Farthiyya iii, 660a — III, 681a
Fārūḳ → Anṣārī, Shaykh Murtaḍā
Fārūḳ, Day of/Journée de s, 178a — S, 179a
Fārūḳ, King/le roi ii, 648b; iii, 517a, 572a; v, 1062a; s, 5b, 6b, **299a** — II, 665a; III, 535a, 592a; V, 1059a; S, 5a, b, **299a**
al-Fārūk → ʿUmar b. al-Khaṭṭāb
al-Fārūḳī, ʿAbd al-Bāḳī i, 330b; ii, **813a** — I, 340b; II, **832a**
Fārūḳī, Kamāl iii, 1023b — III, 1049b
al-Fārūḳī, Mullā Maḥmūd ii, **813a** — II, **832b**
Fārūḳī, Rādjā → Malik Rādjā Fārūkī
Fārūḳid(e)s ii, **814a,** 1084b — II, **833b,** 1110a
Farw ii, **816b**; v, 752a, 857a — II, **836a**; V, 757b, 864a
Farwa(h) b. Musayk i, 728a; ii, 177b, 1096a; iv, 927b; v, 954a — I, 750a; II, 183b, 1122a; IV, 960b; V, 958a
Farwa b. Namfal iii, 1265b — III, 1298a
Farwān ii, **817b** — II, **837a**
Farwardīn → Taʾrīkh
Faryāb ii, **817b** — II, **837a**
Fāryāk → Fāris al-Shidyāḳ
Fās i, 35a, 47a, 70b, 86a, 92b, 355b, 687b, 977b, 1225a; ii, **818a,** 835a; iii, 62b, 149a, 694b, 814a; iv, 774b; v, 877a, 1178a, 1189a; s, 10a, 23a, 26b, 28b, 40a, 47b, 63b, 113b, 126a, 133b, 223b, 350b, 387b, 389a, 390b — I, 35b, 48b, 72b, 88b, 366b, 708b, 1008a, 1261b; II, **837b,** 854b; III, 65a, 152a, 717a, 837b; IV, 805b; V, 883a, 1168a, 1179a; S, 9b, 23a, 26b, 29a, 40b, 48a, 64a, 113a, 125a, 133a, 223b, 350b, 387b, 389b, 391a
- institutions i, 1224b; ii, 819a, 1822b; iii, 140a; v, 1190a, 1208a — I, 1261a; II, 839a, 842a; III, 142b; V, 1180a, 1198b
- monuments i, 85a, 499b, 1346b; ii, 818b, 821-823; iv, 632a; v, 1150a, b, 1151b, 1152a, 1153a — I, 87b, 514b, 1387a; II, 838a, 840-842; IV, 657a; V, 1140b, 1141a, b, 1142a, b
Fās al-Bālī ii, 819a, 822a, b, 823a — II, 838b, 841b, 842a, b
Fās al-Djadīd ii, 819a, 820b, 822a, b, 823a; iii, 499a — II, 838b, 840a, 841b, 842a, b; III, 516a
Fasā ii, **823b**; s, 302a — II, **843a**; S, 301b
Fasād → Fāsid, Kawn
Faṣāḥa i, 573b, 981b, 1114b; ii, **824a** — I, 592b, 1012a, 1148a; II, **843a**
Fasāʾī, Hādjdjī Mīrzā Ḥasan s, **302a** — S, **301b**
Fasāna → Afsāna
Fasandjus, Banū ii, **827a** — II, **846b**
al-Fasāsīrī → al-Basāsīrī
al-Fāshir (el-Fasher/el-Facher) ii, 122a, **827b** — II, 125a, **847a**
Fāshōda ii, **828a** — II, **847b**
al-Fāsī → Ibn Abī Zarʿ
Al-Fāsī, ʿAbd al-Kabīr (d./m. 1879) s, **303a** — S, **303a**
al-Fāsī, ʿAbd al-Ḳādir (d./m.. 1680) i, **70b**, 139a, 795a; s, **302b**, 325b — I, **72b**, 143a, 818b; S, **302b**, 325a
al-Fāsī, ʿAbd al-Raḥmān b. ʿAbd al-Ḳādir (d./m. 1685) s, **302b** — S, **302b**
al-Fāsī, ʿAbd al-Raḥmān b. Muḥammad (d./m. 1626) i, **86a**, 139a, 428a; s, **302b** — I, **88b**, 143a, 440a; S, **302a**
al-Fāsī, Abu ʿAbd Allāh Muḥammad (d./m. 1662) s, 404a — S, 405a
al-Fāsī, Abū ʿAbd Allāh Muḥammad (d./m. 1722) s, **303a**, 403b, 404b — S, **302b**, 404a, b
al-Fāsī, Abū ʿAbd Allāh Muḥammad (d./m. 1765) s, **303a** — S, **302b**
al-Fāsī, Abū ʿAbd Allāh Muḥammad (d./m. 1799) s, **303a** — S, **303a**
al-Fāsī, Abū Ḥafṣ ʿUmar (d./m. 1774) s, **303a** — S, **303a**
al-Fāsī, Abū Ḥāmid Muḥammad s, 404b — S, 404b
al-Fāsī, Abū Madyan Muḥammad (d./m. 1768) s, **303a** — S, **302b**
al-Fāsī, Abu ʾl-Maḥāsin (d./m. 1604) i, **238b**, v, 1029a; s, **302b** — I, **143a**; V, 1025a; S, **302a**
al-Fāsī, Abū Mālik ʿAbd al-Wāḥid (d./m. 1799) s, **303a** — S, **303a**
al-Fāsī, Aḥmad al-Ḥāfiẓ b. Abi ʾl-Maḥāsin (d./m. 1612) s, **302b** — S, **302b**
al-Fāsī, Āl s, **302a** — S, **302a**
al-Fāsī, ʿAllāl iv, 159b — IV, 166b
al-Fāsī, Muḥammad b. Muḥammad s, 371a — S, 371a
al-Fāsī, Muḥammad al-ʿArbī b. Abi ʾl-Maḥāsin (d./m. 1642) i, 139a; s, **302b** — I, 143a; S, **302b**
al-Fāsī, Muḥammad al-Mahdī (d./m. 1698) iii, 971b; s, **302b** — III, 996a; S, **302b**
al-Fāsī, Muḥammad al-Ṭāhir (d./m. 1868) s, **303a** — S, **303a**
al-Fāsī, Muḥammad al-Ṭayyib (d./m. 1701) ii, 1022a; s, **303a** — II, 1045b; S, **302b**
al-Fāsī, Sīdī ʿAbd al-Ḳādir s, 302b — S, 302a
al-Fāsī, Taḳī al-Dīn ii, **828b;** iii, 760a — II, **848a;** III, 783b
Fāsid wa-bāṭil i, 319a; ii, **829b** — I, 329a; II, **849a**
Faṣīḥ → Faṣāḥa
Faṣīh Dede ii, **833a** — II, **852b**
Fāsiḳ ii, **833a** — II, **853a**
Fāṣila ii, **834b** — II, **854a**
Faṣīla ii, **835a** — II, **854b**
al-Fāsiyyūn i, 70b, 138b, 139a; ii, **835a**; iv, 379b; s, 223b, 302a — I, 72b, 143a; II, **854b**; IV, 396a; S, 223b, 302a
Faskāt ū-Mzāl → Abū Ḥafs ʿUmar
Faskh ii, **836a;** iii, 1056b — II, **855b;** III, 1082b
Faṣl ii, **836b** — II, **856a**
Faṣl → Filāḥa, Mafṣūl
Faṣṣād s, **303b** — S, **303a**
Faste et néfaste → Saʿd
Fatā i, 256b; ii, **837a,** 961a, 1043b; iv, 705a — I, 264b; II, **856b,** 983a, 1068a; IV, 733b
Fatalism(e), fatalité → al-Ḳaḍā wa ʾl-ḳadar
al-Fatāwā al-ʿĀlamgīriyya i, 1331a; ii, 157b, 736a, **837a;** iii, 163b, 435a — I, 1372a; II, 162b, 754b, **857a;** III, 167a, 449b
Fate → al-Ḳaḍāʾ wa-ʾl-Ḳadar
Fatḥ → Ḥaraka
al-Fatḥ b. Khāḳān i, 1082b, 1289b; ii, 385b, **837b** — I, 1114b, 1329a; II, 396a, **857a**

al-Fatḥ b. Khāḳān al-Ishbīlī i, 602a; ii, **838a;** iii, 354b, 734a, 807b — I, 621b; II, **857b;** III, 365b, 756b, 831a
Fatḥ ʿAlī Akhund-zāda → Akhund-zāda, Mīrzā Fatḥ ʿAlī
Fatḥ ʿAlī Khān (Ḳuba) ii, 206a; v, 296b — II, 212b; V, 288a
Fatḥ ʿAlī Khān Dāghistānī iii, 604a; iv, 389b; v, 663b — III, 624b; IV, 406a, b; V, 669a
Fatḥ ʿAli Khān Develū iv, 391b, 392a, 597b — IV, 408b, 622a
Fatḥ ʿAlī Khān Tālpūr iii, 323b; iv, 1160a — III, 333b; IV, 1192a
Fatḥ ʿAlī Shāh Ḳādjār i, 13b, 246a, 304b, 682b, 1030b; ii, 335b, **838b,** 1083b; iii, 114a, 348b, 554a, 1103b, 1104a, 1191a; iv, 38b, 51a, 391a, b, 392a, b, 393a, 703b, 1040b; v, 371b, 750a, 1222a; s, 57a, 94b, 108b, 336a, 405b — I, 14a, 254a, 314a, 703a, 1062a; II, 345a, **858a,** 1109a; III, 116b, 359b, 573a, 1130b, 1131a, 1221a; IV, 41a, 54a, 407b, 408b, 409a, b, 732a, 1072a; V, 372a, 755b, 1212a; S, 57b, 94a, 108a, 335b
Fatḥ Allāh ʿImād al-Mulk ii, 981a; iii, 1159a — II, 1003b; III, 1187b
Fatḥ Allāh al-Shīrāzī, Mullā ii, 132a, 156b; s, 353b, 410b — II, 135b, 161b; S, 353b, 411a
Fatḥ Djang i, 231b — I, 238b
Fatḥ Girāy I ii, 1046b, 1113b — II, 1071a, 1139b
Fatḥ Girāy II iv, 569a — IV, 591b
Fatḥ Khān (Barakzay) i, 230b, 231a; ii, 637b — I, 237b, 238a; II, 653b
Fatḥ Khān (Dawūdpōtrā) ii, 187a — II, 192b
Fatḥ Khān (Gudjaratī) → Maḥmud I Begrā
Fatḥ Khān b. Malik ʿAnbar iii, 15b, 626a — III, 16b, 647a
Fatḥ Shāh Djalāl al-Dīn ii, 797b; iii, 14b; s, 131b — II, 816b; III, 15b; S, 131a
Fatḥa iii, 172b — III, 176b
Fatḥābād ii, 32a, 180a; iii, 442b; v, 1216b — II, 32b, 185b; III, 457a; v, 1206b
Fatḥnāme ii, **839b** — II, **859a**
Fatḥpūr Sīkrī i, 252b, 1024a, 1324a; ii, **840a;** iii, 287b, 449b; v, 1135b, 1218a; s, 378a — I, 260b, 1055b, 1364b; II, **860a;** III, 296b, 465a; V, 1131a, 1208a; S, 378a
Fātiḥ-Camii iv, 229a — IV, 239a
Fātiḥa ii, **841a**; v, 425a — II, **860b**; V, 427b
al-Fātik → Nadjāḥ, Banū
Fāṭima bint Abū Muslim v, 65a, b — V, 67a
Fāṭima bint ʿAmr b. Makhzūm i, 42b, 80a — I, 43b, 82b
Fāṭima bint Asad b. Hāshim i, 152b; ii, 850a — I, 157a; II, 870a
Fāṭima bint Barrī i, 280b — I, 289a
Fāṭima bint al-Ḥusayn s, 95a — S, 94b
Fāṭima bint Muḥammad i, 15a, 187a, 381b, 382a, 400b; ii, 725a, **841b**; iii, 1232a; s, 92b, 231a — I, 15b, 192b, 392b, 412a; II, 743b, **861a**; III, 1263b; S, 92b, 231a
Fāṭima bint Muḥammad IX (Naṣrid(e)) s, 399a — S, 399b
Fāṭima bint Muḥammad al-Fihrī iv, 632a — IV, 657b
Fāṭima bint ʿUmar b. Ḥafṣ iii, 694a — III, 716a
Fāṭima Khānîm s, 331a — S, 330b
Fāṭima Khātūn s, 83b — S, 83a
Fāṭima al-Maʿṣūma v, 370b, 371b — V, 371b, 372a
Fāṭima Lārā i, 841b — I, 865a
Fāṭima Sulṭān bint Aḥmad i, 269b, 395a; ii, 49a; iii, 1002a — I, 278a, 406a; II, 50a; III, 1027a
Fāṭima Sulṭān bint Selīm i, 291b — I, 300b
Fāṭimid(e)s i, 20a, 48b, 83b, 163a, 196b, 215b, 367a, 403a, 435b, 440a, 551b, 710b, 797b, 798a, 832b, 869b, 986a, 1074a, 1175b, 1354b; ii, 281b, 453b, 494b, 506a, **850a,** 911a; iii, 656a, 785a, 932a; iv, 198b, 200b, 204a, 378b, 458b; v, 327b, 620b, 623b, 738a, 1175b, 1243b; s, 120b, 236b, 254b, 256b, 326a, 338a, 389a, b — I, 21a, 49b, 86a, 167b, 202a, 222a, 378a, 414b, 448a, 452b, 569a, 732a, 820b, 821b, 855b, 894a, 1017a, 1106a, 1210b, 1394a; II, 290a, 465b, 507a, 518b, **870a,** 932b; III, 677a, 808b, 956b; IV, 207b, 209b, 213a, 395a, 479a; V, 327a, 624b, 627a, 743a, 1165b, 1234a; S, 120a, 236b, 254b, 256b, 325b, 337b, 389a, 390a
- administration i, 1148b; ii, 80a, 126b, 145b, 326a, 328a, **860a;** iii, 47b, 360a; iv, 943b, 1092a — I, 1183a; II, 81b, 130a, 149b, 335b, 337b, **879b;** III, 49b, 371b; IV, 976b, 1123a
- art, architecture i, 200b, 830a, 1319b; ii, 747a, 821b, **862b**; iv, 428b; v, 217a — I, 206b, 853a, 1183a; II, 765b, 841a, **882b**; IV, 447a; V, 214b
Fātin, Banū i, 1349b — I, 1390a
Faṭīn (Dāwūd) ii, **864b** — II, **884b**
Faṭma ʿAliyye Khanîm i, 286a — I, 295a
Fatra ii, **865a** — II, **884b**
Fattāḥī i, 257a; ii, **865a**; iv, 67a — I, 265a; II, **885a**; IV, 70b
al-Fattāl, al-Ḥasan b. ʿAbd al-Karīm s, 380a — S, 380a
Fatwā i, 40a, 399b; ii, 304a, 306a, **866a,** 890a — I, 41a, 411a; II, 312a, 314b, **866a,** 911a
al-Fāʾū v, 66a — V, 68a
Fauconnerie → Bayzara; Doghandjî
Faute → Khaṭīʾa
Fāʿw ii, **867b** — II, **887b**
Fawātiḥ al-suwwar v, **412a** — V, **413b**
Fawdj → Ḥarb, Lashkar
Fawdjdār ii, **868a**; s, 57b — II, **888a**; S, 58a
Fawrī, Aḥmad ii, **869a** — II, **889a**
Fawzī, Ḥusayn i, 598a — I, 617b
Fawzī al-Maʿlūf → Maʿlūf
Fawziyya, Princess(e) ii, 654b — II, 671a
Fayʾ i, 704a, 1142a, 1144a; ii, **869a**; iv, 973a, 1031a, 1141b — I, 725b, 1176b, 1178b; II, **889a**; IV, 1005a, 1062b, 1173b
Fayd, Ḥiṣn s, 198b, 199b, **304b** — S, 198b, 199b, **304a**
al-Fayḍ b. Abī Ṣāliḥ ii, **870a**; s, 17b — II, **890a**; S, 17b
Fayd b. Ḥām b. ʿAmalīḳ → Zayd al-Khayl al-Ṭāʾī
Fayḍ Allāh, Shaykh i, 1168a — I, 1203a
Fayḍ Allāh al-ʿAlamī i, 352b — I, 363a
Fayḍ Allāh Bey i, 1030b — I, 1062a
Fayḍ Allāh Efendi ii, 19b; iii, 627a; s, 63a — II, 20a; III, 649a; S, 63b
Fayḍ Allāh Khān iii, 60a, b, 61b — III, 62b, 63a, 64a
Fayḍ al-Kashī i, 596a — I, 615b
Fayḍ Muḥammad Khān i, 1195a, 1197a — I, 1230b, 1232a
Fayḍābād ii, 1a, **870a**; s, 74b, 102a, 358b — II, 1a, **890a**; S, 75a, 101b, 358b
Fayḍī i, 60b, 117a, 297a; ii, **870b;** iii, 376a, 423b; iv, 1010a — I, 62b, 120b, 306b; II, **890b;** III, 387b, 437b; IV, 1042b
Fayḍ-i Kāshānī s, **305a** — S, **305a**
al-Fayḍiyya iv, 992a — IV, 1024b
Faydj → Fuyūdj
Fayḍullāh → Fayḍ Allāh
Fāyiz, Awlād iv, 637b — IV, 664a
Faylaka island/île v, 573b, 574a — V, 578a, b
Faylasūf ii, **872a** — II, **892a**
Faylī iii, 1102b, 1106a; v, 823b, 829b — III, 1129b, 1133a; V, 829b, 835b
Fayoum → al-Fayyūm
Fayrūz → Fīrūz
Fayṣal I b. Sharīf Ḥusayn i, 46a, 684a; ii, 289b, 429b, 661a, **872a;** iii, 263b, 293a, 605b, 1258b; iv, 782b; v, 1044a, 1046b, 1091b; s, 67b — i, 47b, 705a; II, 297b,

18446

440b, 677b, **892b;** III, 271a, b, 302b, 626b, 1291a; IV, 814a; V, 1040b, 1043b, 1088b; S, 68a
Fayṣal II b. Ghāzī ii, 674b, **872b;** iii, 264a — II, 691b, **892b;** III, 271b
Fayṣal b. ʿAbd al-ʿAzīz Ibn Saʿūd i, 98b; iii, 1066a; iv, 261a; s, **305b** — I, 101b; III, 1092b; IV, 272b; S, **305b**
Fayṣal b. Ḥusayn → Fayṣal I
Fayṣal b. Saʿūd ii, 320b — II, 330a
Fayṣal b. Sulṭān al-Dawīsh iii, 1065b, 1066a, 1067a, b; iv, 681a; v, 575a, 998a, b — III, 1092a, b, 1093b, 1094a; IV, 708b; V, 579b, 993b
Fayṣal b. Turkī b. Saʿīd i, 98b, 554b; ii, 108b, 176b; iv, 751b, 765a, 1073a; s, 356a — I, 101a, 572a; II, 111a, 182a; IV, 782a, 795b, 1104b; S, 356a
Faytūriyya s, 93a — S, 92b
Fayyāḍ Beg iii, 1198b — III, 1228b
Fayyāḍī → Fayḍī
al-Fayyūm i, 1145a; ii, **872b;** iv, 774a; s, 379a — I, 1179a; II, **893a;** IV, 805a; S, 379b
al-Fayyūmī → Saʿadya al-Fayyūmī
Fayyumi, Nathanael iv, 304b — IV, 318a
Fayzabad → Fayḍābād
Fayẓī → Fayḍī
Fazāra, Banū ii, 122a, b, **873a,** 1023b; iv, 493b; v, 267a; s, 177a, b — II, 125a, b, **893b,** 1047a; IV, 514b; V, 264b; S, 178a, b
al-Fazārī iii, 1136a, b; iv, 517b — III, 1164b; IV, 540a
al-Fazārī → Ibrāhīm b. Muḥammad
al-Fazārī, Abu ʾl-Ḳāsim Muḥammad s, **306a** — S, **306a**
Fāzāz ii, **873b;** s, 113b — II, **894a;** S, 112b
Fāzil Ḥusayn Bey → Fāḍil Bey
Fazl, Fazlī → Faḍl, Faḍlī
Fazlullāh → Faḍl Allāh
Fāzūghlī ii, **874b** — II, **895a**
Fazyl → Fāḍil
Fazzān i, 35a, 39a; ii, **875a;** iii, 296b; iv, 542a; v, 759b; s, 163b, 164b — II, 36a, 40a; II, **895a;** III, 305b; IV, 565b; V, 765b; S, 163b, 164b
Feast → Kandūrī
Fedākārān-i Millet Djemʿiyyeti iv, 857a — IV, 890a
Fedala → Faḍāla
Fedjr-i Ātī ii, **877b;** iii, 261a — II, **898a;** III, 268a
Fedū → Fidya
Feeding → Ghidhāʾ
Fehīm, Süleymān i, 284b; ii, **878a** — I, 293a; II, **898a**
Fehīm, Undjuzāde Muṣṭafā ii, **878a** — II, **898a**
Fehīm-i Ḳadīm → Fehīm, Undjuzāde Muṣṭafā
Fehīm Pasha ii, **878a** — II, **898b**
Fehmī, Sheykh Ḥasan → Ḥasan Fehmī Efendi
Fehmī, Sheykh Muṣṭafā ii, **878b** — II, **898b**
Feisal → Fayṣal
Fellāgha → Fallāḳ
Fellani → Fulbe
Fellata → Fallāta
Felt → Keče, Libād
Femme → Marʾa
al-Fenārī, Meḥemmed i, 299b; ii, 602b, 879a; v, 681a — I, 309a; II, 617b, 899a; V, 686b
Fenārī-zāde ii, **879a** — II, **899a**
Fener ii, **879b;** iv, 241a — II, **900a;** IV, 252a
Fennec → Fanak
Fennel/fenouil → Basbās
Feodosia → Kefe
Fer → Ḥadīd
Fer → al-Ḥadīd
Ferah ʿAlī Pasha ii, 25a — II, 26a
Ferdī ii, 880a — II, 900b
Ferdinand I v, 367b — V, 368b
Ferdinand III i, 1150b; ii, 516a; iv, 355a, 665b — I, 1184b; II, 528b; IV, 370b, 692b
Ferdosi → Firdawsī
Ferghānā → Farghānā
Ferhād Pasha ii, 240a, **880b;** iii, 1001a; v, 493a; s, 238b — II, 247a, **900b;** III, 1026a; V, 496a; S, 238b
Ferhād u-Shīrīn → Farhād wa-Shīrīn
Ferhād Sokolović (Sokollu) i, 1017b, 1018a, 1263b; v, 775a — I, 1049a, 1302a; V, 781a
Ferhat → Farhat
Ferīd Pasha → Dāmād
Ferīdūn Beg i, 312b; ii, 56b, 128a, 589a, 839b, **881a;** iii, 1045b, 1243a; s, 330a — I, 322b; II, 57b, 131a, 603b, 859a, **901b;** III, 1071b, 1275a; S, 329b
Ferishte-oghlu i, 1162a — I, 1196b
Fermage de l'impôt → Bayt al-māl; Ḍarība; Iltizām; Muḳāṭaʿa
Fermān → Farmān
Ferme → Muzāraʿa
Fērōz → Fīrūz
Fērōzkōh → Fīrūzkūh
Fērōzshāh → Fīrūzshāh
Ferret → Ibn miḳraḍ
Fès → Fās
Festival → Bayram; ʿĪd
Fête → Bayram; ʿĪd
Fethiye i, 476b — I, 490b
Fetoua → Fatwā
Fetwa → Fatwā
Fetwākhāne i, 837b; ii, 867a — I, 861a; II, 887a
Feu → Nār
Feudality/Féodalité → Iḳṭāʿ
Feu d'artifice → Shenlik
Feu Grégeois → Barūd, Naft
Feudalism → Iḳtaʿ
Feutre → Keče, Libād
Fevrī → Fawrī
al-Fewet ii, 1022b — II, 1046b
Fewzī i, 1271a — I, 1310b
Feyḍ Allāh → Abū Saʿīd-zāde Feyḍ Allāh
Feyzioğlu, Turhan ii, 646a — II, 662b
Fez (headgear/coiffure) → Libās
Fez (town/ville) → Fās
Fezzān → Fazzān
Fibre → Ṣayd
Fichier de documentation berbère i, 1186a — I, 1221a
Fidāʾ iii, 183a; v, 647a; s, **306b** — III, 187b; V, 651a; S, **306b**
Fidāʾī (fidāwī) ii, **882a;** iii, 254a — II, **902b;** III, 261a
Fidāʾiyyān-i Islām ii, **882a;** iii, 529b; iv, 40b, 52a, 165a, 790a; s, 158a — II, **902b;** III, 548a; IV, 43a, 55a, 172b, 822a; S, 158a
Fidda ii, **883a,** 1139a; v, 964a, 965b, 966a, 967a, 970a, 977a — II, **903b,** 1166a; V, 968b, 970a, 973a, 976a
al-Fidjār ii, 627a, **883b;** iii, 285b, 389a; v, 3b, 434b — II, 642b, **904a;** III, 294b, 401b; V, 3b, 436b
Fidya ii, **884a** — II, **904b**
Fief → Djāgīr; Iḳṭāʿ; Tīmār
Fighānī, Bābā ii, **884a;** iv, 69a — II, **905a;** IV, 72b
Fighanī, Ramaḍān ii, **884b;** iii, 998a; iv, 715b — II, **904b;** III, 1023a; IV, 744a
Figs/Figues → Tīn
Figuig ii, **885a** — II, **905b**
Fiḥl → Faḥl
Fihr, Banū iv, 828b; s, 302a — IV, 861b; S, 302a
al-Fihrī → ʿAbd al-Raḥmān; al-Ḍaḥḥāk b. Kays
al-Fihrī, Abū Isḥāḳ ii, **885b** — II, **906a**
Fihrist i, 114b, 116a, 132b, 139b, 140b, 143a, 151b, 157b, 164b, 235b, 306b, 758b, 793b, 1237a; iii, 1263b — I, 117b, 119b, 136b, 143b, 144b, 147b, 156a, 162a, 169a, 243a, 316a, 781a, 817a, 1274b; III, 1296b
al-Fihrist i, 361a, 362b, 990a, 1197b; ii, 79a, 547a — I, 372a, 373b, 1020b, 1233a; II, 80b, 560b
Fiḳh i, 26a, 60b, 86a, 106a, 142b, 169b, 170a, 272b,

274a, 338a, 428a, 436b, 910b; ii, 605b, **886a,** 1069a; iii, 103b, 435a, 647a, 901a; iv, 204a; v, 1129b — I, 27a, 62b, 88b, 109a, 146b, 174b, 280b, 282b, 348b, 440a, 449a, 938a; II, 620b, **906b,** 1093b; III, 105b, 449a, 668a, 925b; IV, 213a, b; V, 1126a
Fiḳh Akbar I i, 187b, 332b, 335a; iv, 172a — I, 192b, 343a, 345b; IV, 179b
Fiḳh Akbar II i, 411a; ii, 294a; iv, 172a, 470b — I, 423a; II, 302a; IV, 179b, 491a
Fikr ii, **891b** — II, **912a**
Fikret, Tevfik → Tewfīk Fikret
Fikrī, ʿAbd Allāh Pasha ii, **892a** — II, **912b**
Fīl ii, **892b,** 1049b; iii, 201a, 345b; iv, 215a, 217b, 647b; v, 687a, 690a — II, **913a,** 1074a; III, 206a, 356b; IV, 224b, 227a, 674a; V, 692a, 694b
al-Fīl ii, **895a** — II, **916a**
Fiʿl ii, **895b**; v, 578a, b, 579a — II, **916b**; V, 582b, 583a, b
Fiʿl, afʿāl ii, **898a** — II, **919a**
Filāḥa ii, 32b, **899a;** iii, 964a — II, 33a, **920a;** III, 988b → Tafilalt
Filʾakovo s, 171a — S, 171a
Fīlālīs i, 355b, 403a; iii, 256b — I, 366b, 414b; III, 263b
Fīlān iv, 343a — IV, 357b
Filasṭīn i, 111a, 197b, 216a, 451a, 975b; ii, 854a, **910b;** iii, 523b; iv, 834b; v, 912a; s, 67b — I, 114a, 203b, 222b, 464a, 1005b; II, 874a, **932a;** III, 541b; IV, 867b; V, 917b; S, 68a
- literature/littérature ii, 468a — II, 480a
Filibe ii, **914a**; s, 328b, 330a — II, **935b**; S, 328a, 329b
Filīmūn ii, 916b — II, 938a
Filkhāna → Pīlkhāna
Fille, jeune → Ḳīz
Filori ii, **914b** — II, **936a**
Fils → Fals
Fils → Ibn, Walad
Fīn iv, 694b, 695b — IV, 723a, b
Finances → Bayt al-māl; Daftardār; Māl; Māliyya
Fîndîḳlî iv, 233a — IV, 243a
Fîndîḳlîlî Meḥmed v, 18b — V, 19a
Fîndîḳoghlu, Diyāʾ al-Dīn Fakhrī s, **308a** — S, **307b**
Findiriskī, Mīr Abū ʾl-Ḳāsim s, **308a** — S, **308a**
Fine → Djurm
Fine Arts → Fann
Finike s, 221b — S, 221b
Finkenstein, treaty of/traité de iv, 38b; v, 495b — IV, 41a; V, 498b
Finyāna, Fiñana ii, **915b** — II, **937a**
Firabr ii, **915b** — II, **937a**
Firandj → al-Ifrandj
Firāsa i, 146b; ii, **916a**; v, 100a, 235a — I, 150b; II, **937b**; V, 102b, 233a
Firʿawn ii, **917a;** iii, 1175a — II, **938b;** III, 1204a
Firaydan iv, 98a, b — IV, 102a, b
Firda → Furḍa
Firdaws ii, 448b, 451a — II, 460b, 463a → Djanna
Firdawsī i, 205b, 358b, 505a, 686a, 1072b, 1139b, 1309b, 1354a; ii, 132b, 740a, 794a, 798a, 894b, **918a,** 1050b; iii, 112b, 113a, 122a, 371a, 637b; iv, 62b; s, 108a — I, 211b, 369a, 520a, 706b, 1105a, 1174a, 1349b, 1393b; II, 136a, 758b, 812b, 816b, 915b, **939b,** 1075a; III, 115a, b, 124b, 383a, 659a; IV, 65b; S, 107a
Firdewsī ii, **921a** — II, **942b**
Firdousi → Firdawsī
Fire → Nār
Fireworks → Shenlik
Firīdun → Farīdūn
Firind v, 972a, b — V, 974b, 975a
Firishta → Malʾak
Firishta, Muḥaammad Ḳāsim i, 199a; ii, **921b**; s, 206b — I, 204b; II, **943a**; S, 206a
Firishte-oghlu ii, **923b** — II, **945a**
Firḳa → Ḥizb, al-Milal wa ʾl-niḥal, Tarīḳa
Firḳān al-Akhbār i, 260b, 261a, b, 263a — I, 268b, 269a, b, 271a
Firkovič, Abraham iv, 606a — IV, 630b
Firmān → Farmān
Firouz → Fīrūz
Firrīm iv, 644b; s, **309a** — IV, 671a; S, **308b**
Firrīsh ii, **924a** — II, **945b**
Fīrūhā s, 154b — S, 155a
Fīrūz iii, 1161b — III, 1190a
Fīruz (Sasānid(e)) i, 1094a; iv, 850b — I, 1127a; IV, 883b
Fīrūz b. Kabk s, 125b — S, 124b
Fīrūz Bey i, 340b, 1118b; ii, 611b, 688a — I, 350b, 1152a; II, 627a, 705a
Fīrūz al-Daylamī i, 728a; iv, 1134b; s, 116a — I, 750a; IV, 1166b; S, 115b
Fīrūz Ḥusayn iv, 571a — IV, 593b
Fīrūz Shāh Khaldjī → Khaldjīs
Fīrūz Shāh I (Muʿizzī) ii, 267b — II, 276a
Fīrūz Shāh II (Khaldjī) i, 444b, 855b, 1036a, 1202b; ii, 179b, 256b, 268a — I, 457a, 879b, 1067b, 1238a; II, 185a, 263b, 276b
Fīrūz Shāh III (Tughluḳ) i, 432b, 855b, 1036a, b, 1156b; ii, 48a, 120b, 270a, 392a, 814a, **924b,** 1047b, 1124b; iii, 202b, 416b, 434a; iv, 218b, 276a, 368a, 543a, 749b, 1019a; s, 73b, 105b, 238a, 325a, 409b — I, 44b, 879b, 1067b, 1068a, 1200b; II, 49a, 123b, 278a, 402b, 833b, **946a,** 1027a, 1151a; III, 208a, 430a, 448a; IV, 228a, 288b, 384a, 566b, 779b, 1051a; S, 74a, 105a, 238a, 324b, 409b
- administration ii, 154a, 336a, 566b, 924b, 1084b; iii, 492a — II, 158b, 346a, 580b, 946a, 1110a; III, 509a
- constructions i, 1322b; ii, 258a, 262a, b, 274b, 438a, 498b, 909b, 925a, 928b; iii, 225a, 442a, 485a; v, 549a, 884a, 885b, 1135a — I, 1363a; II, 264b, 270a, 271a, 283a, 449b, 511a, 931a, 946b, 950b; III, 232a, 456b, 502a; V, 553b, 890b, 891b, 1130b
Fīrūz Shāh (Baḥmanī) i, 1200a; ii, 1114b; iii, 15a, 417b — I, 1235b; II, 1141a; III, 15b, 431a
Fīrūz Shāh (Mughal) ii, 809a — II, 828a
Fīrūz Shāh, ʿAlāʾ al-Dīn (Bengal(e)) i, 1168a; v, 639a — I, 1203a; V, 643a
Fīrūz Shāh, Sayf al-Dīn (Bengal(e)) iii, 14b, 422a; v, 639a — III, 15b, 436a; V, 643a
Fīrūz Shāpūr i, 484b — I, 499a
Fīrūzābād (Adharbāydjān) iv, 989b — IV, 1022a
Fīrūzābād (Dihlī) i, 1322b; ii, 258a, 262b, 925a — I, 1363a; II, 264b, 271a, 946b
Fīrūzābād (Gūr) i, 43b; ii, **925b** — I, 44b; II, **947a**
al-Fīrūzābādī ii, 801b, **926a;** iii, 765a; iv, 524a, b — II, 820b, **947b;** III, 788a; IV, 546b, 547b
Fīrūzadj ii, **927b** — II, **949a**
al-Fīrūzādjiyya i, 866a — I, 890a
Fīrūzānid(e)s ii, **928a;** iii, 255a — II, **949b;** III, 262b
Fīrūzkūh (Harāt) ii, **928a,** 1096b, 1101a — II, **950a,** 1122b, 1127a
Fīrūzkūh (Ṭabaristān) ii, **928b**; s, 309b — II, **950a**; S, 309a
Fīrūzkūhī i, 224b; ii, 5b; iii, 1107b — I, 231a; II, 5b; III, 1135a
Fīrūzpūr ii, **928b** — II, **950a**
Fiscal Systems/Fiscalité → Bayt al-māl, Ḍarība etc.
Fish → Samak
Fisharakī, Sayyid Muḥammad s, 342a — S, 341b
Fishek → Shenlik
al-Fishtālī → ʿAbd al-ʿAzīz b. Muḥammad
Fisḳ → Fāsiḳ
Fīthāghūras i, 235b; ii, 765b, **929a** — I, 243a; II, 784a, **951a**
Fitna ii, **930b;** iii, 494b, 495b; v, 1109b — II, **952a;**

III, 511b, 512b; V, 1105a
Fiṭnat ii, 713b, **931b;** iii, 269a — II, 732a, **953a;** III, 277a
Fiṭr → ʿĪd al-fiṭr
Fiṭra ii, **931b** — II, **953b**
Fiṭrat, ʿAbd al-Raʾūf ii, **932a** — II, **954a**
Five → Khams(a)
Fityān → Fatā
Flag → Liwāʾ
Flax → Kattān
Fleas → Burghūth
Flèche → Ḳaws; Nabl; Nushshāb
Fleet → Usṭūl
Fleur → Nawriyya
Flood → Māʾ; Ṭūfān
Flores iii, 1219b — III, 1250b
Flori → Filori
Flower → Nawriyya
Flute → Nāy
Fly → Dhubāb
Foča i, 476a, 1270b; iii, 214b — I, 490b, 1309b; III, 220b
Fodié Sylla iii, 108a — III, 110b
Foggāra ii, 875b; iv, 529a, 532b — II, 896a; IV, 552a, 555b
Foi → Īmān
Foie → Kabid
Foire → Panayir, Sūḳ
Folie → Madjnūn
Folklore → Ḥikāya, Taḳālīd
Fomalhaut → Nudjūm
Fondouk → Funduḳ
Fontaine publique → Sabīl
Food → Ghidhāʾ; Ṭaʿām
Foreign Affairs → Khāridjiyya
Forests/Forêt → Ghāba
Forgeron → Kayn
Fornication → Zināʾ
Fortification → Burdj; Ḥiṣār; Ḥiṣn; Ḳalʿa; Sūr
Fortūn b. Mūsa iv, 713a — IV, 741b
Fortunate Islands → Djazāʾir al-Saʿādāt
Fossé → Khandaḳ
Fostat → al-Fusṭāt
Fou → Madjnūn
Fouad → Fuʾād
Foulbé → Fulbé
Fountain → Sabīl
Fourrure → Fanak; Farw
Fouta Djallon → Fūtā Djallon
Fowl → Dadjādja
Fraga → Ifragha
Frāmarz Shāh ii, 30a — II, 30b
Franc-Maçonnerie → Farāmūsh-Khāna; Farmāsūniyya; Māsūniyya
Français II, 476a, b; III, 1213a, 1220a; V, 920b, 1043b, 1065a, b, 1067b
Frankincense → Lubān; Mibkhara
Franks/Francs → al-Ifrandj
Frasa → Ifrāgha
Frashëri i, 650b — I, 671a
Frāsiyāb → Afrāsiyāb
Fraxinetum ii, **933b**, v, 503a — II, **955b**; V, 506b
Free Will → Ikhtiyār, Ḳadar
Freedom → Āzādī; Djumhuriyya; Ḥurriyya
Freemasonry → Farāmūsh-Khāna; Farmāsūniyya; Māsūniyya
French ii, 464b; iii, 1183b, 1190a; v, 915a, 1047a, 1068a, 1070a
Frères Musulmans → al-Ikhwān al-Muslimūn
Frieze → Khirḳa; Ṣūf
Frīsa iv, 95a — IV, 99b
Frolinat s, 166a, b — S, 166a, b
Front national (Iran) IV, 43b, 44a, b
Frontier/Frontière → ʿAwāṣim; Ghāzī; Murābiṭ; Ribāṭ; Thughūr
Frunze → Pičpek
Fuʾād al-Awwal (King/le roi) i, 13b; ii, **934a;** iii, 516a, 517a; v, 1061a; s, 18b, 299a — I, 13b; II, **956a;** III, 533b, 534b; V, 1058a; S, 18b, 299a
Fuʾād Pasha iv, 857a; v, 631a — IV, 890a; V, 635a
Fuʾād Pasha Kečedjizāde i, 284b, 286b, 397a, 397b; ii, 185a, 429a, 637a, **934b;** iii, 553a; iv, 295b, 460b; s, 281b — I, 293b, 295a, 408a, 408b; II, 190b, 440a, 653a, **956b;** III, 572a; IV, 308b, 481a; S, 281b
Fuat Köprülü → Köprülü
Fuḍayl b. ʿIyāḍ i, 274a, 284a, 1246a; ii, **936a** — I, 282b, 292b, 1283b; II, **958a**
Fuḍayl b. al-Zubayr al-Rassān ii, 485a — II, 497b
Fūdhandj s, **309b** — S, **309b**
al-Fudjayra ii, **936b**; s, 416b — II, **958b**; S, 417a
al-Fūdūdī i, 129b — I, 133b
al-Fuḍūl iii, 389b — III, 402a
Fuḍūlī, Muḥammad i, 956b; ii, 206b, **937a**; iv, 704b, 1137b; v, 1105b; s, 83a, 324a — I, 986a; II, 213a, **958b**; IV, 732b, 1169a; V, 1101b; S, 83a, 323b
Fughān → Ashraf ʿAlī Khān
al-Fujairah → al-Fudjayra
Fuḳahāʾ al-Madīna al-Sabʿa v, 997b; s, **310b** — V, 993a; S, **310a**
Fuḳarāʾ i, 1b, 483a — I, 2a, 497b
Fuḳaymī ii, 998b — II, 1021b
Fula ii, 939a, 940b, 942b — II, 961a, 962a, 964b
Fūlād Khān s, 335b — S, 335b
Fūlād b. Shansab ii, 1099a — II, 1125a
Fūlād-Sutūn i, 132a; iii, 1201a; v, 73b — I, 136a; III, 1231b; V, 75b
Fūlādh v, 971b, 978b — V, 974a, 977a
Fulani → Fulbe
Fulayḥ b. al-ʿAwrāʾ i, 118a; iii, 996a; s, 116b — I, 121b; III, 1021a; S, 116a
Fulaymūn → Aflīmūn
Fulbe i, 179a, 303a, 910b, 1259a, 1260a; ii, 9b, 10a, 94a, 251b, 767b, **939a,** 959b, 960b, 1132a, 1144b; iii, 276b, 646a; iv, 549a; s, 164a — I, 183b, 184a, 312b, 938a, 1297b, 1298a; II, 9b, 10a, 96a, 259a, 786a, **961a,** 981b, 982b, 1158b, 1172a; III, 284b, 667a; IV, 573a; S, 164a
Fulful b. Saʿīd i, 860a; v, 1176b, 1180b, 1182a — I, 884a; V, 1166b, 1170b, 1172a
Fulfulde → Fula
Fulk (king/roi) s, 204b — S, 204b
Fulūs → Fals
Fūman, Fūmin ii, 74b, **943b**; s, 298a — II, 76a, **965a**; S, 297b
Fūmanī → ʿAbd al-Fattāḥ Fūmanī
Fūmolutī, Aḥmad iv, 889a — IV, 921b
Fundj i, 425b, 1158a; ii, 252b, 615a, **943b**; iv, 686b, 891b; v, 267a — I, 437b, 1192b; II, 260a, 630b, **965b**; IV, 714b, 925b; V, 264b
Funduḳ ii, **945a**; iv, 135b, 136a, 1015a — II, **966b**; IV, 141a, b, 1047a
Funeral → Djanāza
Funeral obsequies/Funérailles → Djanāza
Fünfkirchen → Pécs
Fung → Fundj
Fur (skin/peau) → Fanak; Farw
Fūr, Fūrāwī ii, 122a, 123a; v, 1250b — II, 125a, 126a; V, 1241a
al-Fūrakī, Abū Bakr iii, 1165a — III, 1193b
al-Furāt i, 405b, 467b, 468a, 634b, 994a, 1094b, 1095a; ii, 250a, 686b, **945a;** iii, 1251a; iv, 482a; v, 441b, 864b; s, 37a — I, 417b, 481b, 482a, 655a, 1024b, 1127b, 1128a; II, 257a, 704a, **967a;** III, 1283b; IV, 502b; V, 444a, 871b; S, 37a

al-Furāt, Banū iii, 767b; iv, 189a; v, 953a — III, 790b; IV, 197b; V, 957a
Furḍa ii, **948a** — II, **970a**
Furdat al-ruʾūs ii, 149a, 948a — II, 153a, 970a
Furet, le → Ibn Miḳraḍ
Furfūriyūs i, 234b; ii, 550a, 780a, **948b,** 955a; iv, 92a — I, 241b; II, 563b, 798b, **970b,** 979b; IV, 96a
Furgač → ʿIzzet Pasha, Aḥmed
Furḳān ii, **949b** — II, **971b**
Furḳān b. Asad → Jeshuah b. Judah
Furḳān, Banū ii, 463a — II, 475a
Furn v, 41b, 42b — V, 42b, 43b
Furniture → Athāth
al-Furs ii, **950b** — II, **972b**
Fürstenspiegel → Siyāsa
Furūʿ (law/droit, doctrine) i, 257b, 277a; ii, 182b, 889b; iii, 162a, 182a — I, 265b, 285b; II, 188b, 910a; III, 165b, 186a
Furūʿ (poetic/poésie) i, 671a, b — I, 691b, 692b
Furūʿ (tax/impôt) i, 1144a; iv, 1041a — I, 1178b; IV, 1072b
Furūgh ii, **951b** — II, **974a**
Furūgh al-Dīn → Furūgh
Furūghī ii, **952a**; iv, 69b — II, **974a**; IV, 73b
Furūghī, Muḥammad ʿAli → Muḥammad ʿAli Furūghī
Furūḳ ii, 605a — II, 620a
Furūsiyya i, 520a; ii, **952b**; v, 688a, 689a, b — I, 536a; II, **974b**; V, 693a, 694a, b
Fusayfisāʾ i, 610b, 611b, 612a; ii, **955a**; iv, 1167b; v, 13b, 16b, 17a, 298b — I, 613a, 632a; II, **977b**; IV, 1200a; V, 14a, 17a, b, 298a
Fūshhandj → Būshandj
Fusṭāṭ (tent(e)) iv, 1147a — IV, 1179a
al-Fusṭāṭ i, 126a, 197a, 451b, 531b, 532a, 844b, 950b, 1346a; ii, 114b, 130a, 746a, **957b,** 1064b; iii, 79b, 675a; iv, 323b, 424a, b; s, 1a, 136b — I, 129b, 202b, 464b, 547b, 548a, 868a, 979b, 1386b; II, 117a, 133a, 764a, **979b,** 1089a; III, 81b, 696b; IV, 338a, 442b, 443a; S, 1a, 136a
- Djāmiʿ ʿAmr i, 610a, 619a, 624a, 814a; ii, 958a, 959a — I, 630a, 637b, 643b, 837b; II, 980a, 981a
Fuṣūṣ fi 'l-Ḥikma i, 414b; ii, 780a — I, 426b; II, 798b
Fūta v, 737b — V, 743a
Fūta Djallon ii, 941b, **959a,** 1131b — II, 963b, **981b,** 1158b
Fūthāghūras → Fīthāghūras
Futūḥāt → Ṭarābulus (al-Shaʾm)
al-Futūḥī, Tādj al-Dīn i, 949b — I, 978b
Futuwwa i, 21a, 256b, 277a, 321b, 322a, 520a, 794b, 900b; ii, 433a, **961a,** 1044a; iii, 671b, 1256a; iv, 705a — I, 21b, 264b, 285b, 331b, 332a, 536a, 817b, 927b; II, 444b, **983a,** 1068b; III, 693a, 1288b; IV, 733a
Fütüwwetnāme i, 323a; ii, 967b, 968a, b — I, 333a; II, 989b, 990a, 991a
Futyā → Fatwā
al-Fuwaṭī, Hishām → Hishām b. ʿAmr al-Fuwaṭī
al-Fuwaṭī, Kamāl al-Dīn → Ibn al-Fuwaṭī
Fuyūdj ii, **969b** — II, **991b**
Fuzūlī → Fuḍūlī
Fyzabad → Fayḍābād

G

Gă Ssuling → Ma Chung-ẏing
Gaban ii, **970a** — II, **992a**
Gabès → Ḳābis
Gabon ii, **970a** — II, **992a**
Gabr ii, **970b** — II, **993a**
Gabriel → Djabrāʾīl
Gadāʾī Kambō, Shaykh i, 1136a; s, **312a** — I, 1170b; S, **312a**
Gaddafi, Muʿammar → al-Ḳadhdhāfī
Gaeda i, 1258a — I, 1296a
Gāēkwār i, 1053a — I, 1084b
Gafsa → Ḳafṣa
Gafuri → Ghafūrī, Madjīd
Gagauz i, 1302b; ii, 610a, b, **971a**; iv, 600b, 814a — I, 1342a; II, 625a, 626a, **993a**; IV, 625a, 847a
Gage → Rahn
Gagik I i, 507b, 638a; ii, 680a -I, 522b, 658b; II, 697a
Gagik II i, 638a; ii, 680b; iv, 670a — I, 659a; II, 697b; IV, 697a
Gagik-Abas i, 638b — I, 659a
Gagik Ardzrunī i, 637a — I, 658a
Gāhanbārs ii, 398a — II, 408b
Gāikwār ii, 1129b — II, 1156b
Gain → Kasb
Gakkhaŕ ii, **972a,** 1131b, 1155b; v, 31b — II, **994b,** 1158a, 1184a; V, 32b
Galata → Ghalaṭa
Galata-Saray/Galata-Sérail → Ghalaṭa-Sarāyi̊
Gālbāghī v, 460b — V, 463a
Galen/Galien → Djālīnūs
Galena → al-Kuḥl
Galère → Safīna, Shāniya
Galicia/Galice → Djillīḳiya
Galla i, 176b; ii, 545a, b, **974a;** iii, 5b, 6a; iv, 888b; v, 522a, 524a — I, 181b; II, 558b, **996b;** III, 6a, b; IV, 921b; V, 525b, 527b
Galland, Jean Antoine i, 359a — I, 369b
Galley → Safīna, Shāniya
Gallipoli → Gelibolu
Gamasāb, Gamasiyāb → Karkha
Gambia/Gambie ii, **974b** — II, **997a**
Gambīrī ii, 138b — II, 142a
Gambling → Ḳimār; Maysir
Gambra → Bandar ʿAbbās
Games → Laʿib
Gamron (Gomron) → Bandar ʿAbbās
Ganāfa, Ganaveh → Djannāba
Gandamak s, 237b — S, 237a
Gandāpur ii, **975a** — II, **997b**
Gandāwa → Kandābīl
Gandhāra → Ḳandahār
Gandhi, M. K. i, 317b; v, 7b; s, 4b — I, 327b; V, 7b; S, 3b
Gandj ʿAlī Khān v, 164a — V, 161b
Gandja i, 8a, 191b, 660b, 1041b; ii, **975a**, iv, 1176b; v, 490a, 495b; s, 143a — I, 8a, 197a, 681b, 1073a; II, **997b**, IV, 1210a; V, 492b, 498b; S, 143a
Gandjābā → Ḳandābil
al-Gandjī, Muḥammad b. Yūsuf v, 1236b, 1237a — V, 1227a, b
Gandj-i-Shakar → Farīd al-Dīn Masʿūd
Gandjvar b. Isfandiyar s, 263b — S, 263a
Gando ii, 94a — II, 96a → Fulbe
Gandu iii, 277b — III, 285b
Gangā, Ganges/Gange ii, **976a** — II, **998b**
Gangōh s, 313a — S, 312b
Gangōhī, ʿAbd al-Ḳuddūs ii, 54b, 55a, 56a; s, **312b** — II, 55b, 56a, b; S, **312b**

Gangōhī, Rukn al-Dīn Muḥammad b. ʿAbd al-Ḳuddūs s, 313a — S, 312b
Ganja iii, 266b — III, 274b
Ganza → Gandja
Gao ii, **976b**; v, 222a; s, 295b — II, **999a**; V, 219b; S, 295a
Gāon sabhā i, 758a — I, 780b
Gaourang i, 910b — I, 938a
Garantie → Ḍamān, Kafāla, Rahn
Garde, gardien → Kapîdjî
Garden → Bustān
Gardīz ii, **978a** — II, **1000b**
Gardīzī ii, **978b**; v, 1001a; s, 136a, 245a, 266a, 326b — II, **1001a**; V, 1007a; S, 135b, 245a, 265b, 326a
Garĕbĕg → ʿĪd, Indonesia (Islam)
Garmādūz s, 116a — S, 115b
Garmrūdī, ʿAbd Allāh s, 290b — S, 290a
Garmsīr → Ḳîshlaḳ
Garrūs iii, 1102b, 1108b; s, 71a — III, 1129b, 1136a; S, 71b
Garrūsī, Amīr-i Niẓām s, 73a — S, 73b
Garshāsp b. ʿAlī iv, 466a, b — IV, 487a
Garshāsp b. Muḥammad iv, 466a — IV, 486b
Garshasp, ʿIzz al-Din v, 828a — V, 834b
Garsīf ii, **978b** — II, **1001a**
Gaspîralî (Gasprinski), Ismāʿīl i, 894a; ii, 366a, 474b, **979a**; iv, 630b; s, 47a, 123a — I, 920b; II, 376a, 487a, **1001b**; IV, 655b; S, 47b, 122b
Gasprinski → Gaspîralî
Gate, Gateway → Bāb
Gatha iv, 53a — IV, 56a
Gaṭṭāya iv, 95a — IV, 99a
Gāṭū, gaṭṭū iv, 743b — IV, 773b
Gaur iii, 444a, 634b; v, 638a — III, 459a, 655b; V, 642a
Gavras i, 664b, 983a — I, 684a, 1013b
Gāvur → Kāfir
Gawālior → Gwāliyar
Gāwān, Maḥmūd → Maḥmūd Gāwān
Gāwar-Bātī i, 225a; ii, 31a, 138b — I, 231b; II, 32a, 142a
Gāwbāra → Gīl Gawbarā
Gawhar Amān ii, 30a — II, 30b
Gawhar Amān b. Mulk Amān s, 327b — S, 327a
Gawhar Shād i, 147b, 148b — I, 152a, 152b
Gawhar-i Murād → Sāʿidī, Ghulām Ḥusayn
Gawhar-i Tādj ʿĀbida Sulṭān i, 1196b — I, 1232a
Gāwilgaŕh ii, **981a**; iv, 921a; s, 280a — II, **1003b**; IV, 954a; S, 279b
Gawr → Gaur
Gawur → Kāfir
Gāwur Daghlarî ii, **982a**; s, 171b — II, **1004b**; S, 172a
Gaykhātū i, 703a, 1129b; ii, 14a, **982a**, 1043a; iii, 284a, 1122a; iv, 31a, 621a; v, 162b, 553b, 827a — I, 724b, 1164a; II, 14b, **1004b**, 1067a; III, 293a, 1150a; IV, 33b, 645b; V, 160b, 558b, 833a
al-Gaylānī, Rashīd ʿĀlī → Rashīd ʿAlī
Gayō i, 740a — I, 762a → Atjeh
Gayomart iii, 1270a — III, 1303a
Gaza → Ghazza
Gazelle → Ghazāl
Gaziantep → ʿAyntāb
Gaz-i-ilāhī iv, 1055b; s, **313b** — IV, 1087a; S, **313a**
Gazūla, Gazūlī → Djazūla, Djazūlī
Geben → Gaban
Geber → Gabr, Madjūs
Geber → Djābir b. Aflaḥ
Gebze ii, **982b** — II, **1005a**
Gečid resmi ii, 147a — II, 151a
Gedaref → al-Ḳaḍārif
Gedi, Gede ii, **983a** — II, **1005b**
Gedik → Ṣinf
Gedik Aḥmed → Aḥmad Pasha Gedik
Gediz Čayî ii, **983a** — II, **1005bb**
Geg i, 650a, 651a — I, 670a, 671b → Arnawutluḳ
Gehenna/Géhenne → Djahannam
Geladjo i, 303a — I, 312b
Gelenbe s, 282b — S, 282a
Gelibolu i, 947b; ii, 11b, **983a**; iv, 571b; s, 41b, 149b — I, 976b; II, 11b, **1005b**; IV, 594b; S, 41b, 149b
Gemini, Twins/Gémeaux → Minṭaḳat al-Burūdj; Nudjūm
Gemlik ii, **987a** — II, **1010a**
Genāwah → Gnāwa
Genč ʿOthmān ii, 75b — II, 77a
Genç Spor Klübü iv, 138a — IV, 144a
Gendre (du Sultan) → Dāmād
Genealogy/Généalogie → Nasab
Generalife ii, 1019b — II, 1043a
Generosity/Générosité → Karam
Gênes IV, 287b, 599a; V, 303a
Genesis → Takwīn
Genghis Khan/Gengis Khan → Čingiz Khān
Genie/Génie → Djinn
Genil → Shanīl
Geniza ii, **987b**; v, 738b — II, **1010a**; V, 743b
Genoa iv, 275b, 576a; v, 304a
Genoese/Génois iv, 868a — IV, 901b
Genre → Djins
Geography/Géographie → Djughrāfiyā; Mamlaka
Geomancy/Géomancie → Khaṭṭ; Raml
Geometry/Géometrie → ʿIlm al-Handasa
George, Saint/Georges, Saint → Djirdjīs
Georgia/Géorgie → Abkhāz; Kurdj
Georgian/Géorgien iv, 351a, b; v, 490a-492a — IV, 366a, b; V, 492b-495a
Ger iv, 1151a — IV, 1182b
Gerasa → Djarash
Gerboise → Faʾr
Gerdek Resmi → ʿArūs Resmi
Germans ii, 699a; iii, 1185b; iv, 40b, 889a
Germiyan i, 243b, 467b; ii, 204b — I, 251a, 481b; II, 211a
Germiyān-oghullarî i, 346a, 510b, 1256b; ii, **989a**; v, 359b, 539a — I, 356b, 526a, 1295a; II, **1012a**; V, 360b, 543b
Gerona/Gérone → Djarunda
Gerri → Ḳerrī
Gessi Pasha s, 164b — S, 164b
Gesture/geste → Ishāra
Geṭna i, 733b — I, 755b
Gevherī, Meḥmed ii, **990a** — II, **1013a**
Geygellis ii, 40b — II, 41b
al-Ghāb ii, **990b** — II, **1013b**
Ghāba ii, **991a** — II, **1014a**
Ghaban iv, 1165b — IV, 1198a
al-Ghabrāʾ s, 177b, 178a — S, 178b, 179b
Ghaḍāʾirī iv, 61a — IV, 64b
Ghadāmes ii, 875a, 876b, **991b** — II, 895b, 897a, **1014b**
al-Ghaḍanfar → Abū Taghlib, Ḥamdanid(e)s
Ghaḍanfer Agha ii, 1088a — II, 1113b → Ḳapî Aghasî
Ghadār → Khazaf
Ghadīr Khumm i, 1025a, 1325b; ii, **993a** — I, 1056b, 1391b; II, **1015b**
al-Ghāḍirī ii, **994b** — II, **1017b**
Ghadjar ii, 40b — II, 41b
Ghaffārī, Aḥmad i, 423b; ii, **994b** — I, 435b; II, **1017b**
Ghaffūrī, ʿAlī iv, 166a — IV, 173b
Ghāfiḳ i, 1249a; ii, 744a, b; s, 313a — I, 1287a; II, 762b, 763a; S, 313b
al-Ghāfiḳī, Abū Djaʿfar Aḥmad i, 156a, 214a, 345a, 594b, 1156a; ii, 995a; iii, 737a; s, **313b**, 383a, 397a —

I, 160b, 220b, 355b, 613b, 1190b; II, 1018a; III, 760a; S, **313b**, 383b, 397b
al-Ghāfiḳī, Abu ʾl-Ḳāsim → al-Kabtawrī
al-Ghāfikī, Muḥammad i, 449a; ii, **995a** — I, 462a; II, **1018a**
Ghāfiḳī → ʿAbd al-Raḥmān al-Ghāfiḳī
Ghāfirī i, 545b; ii, 630b; iii, 403b; s, 355b, 356a — I, 562b; II, 646b; III, 415b; S, 355a, b
Ghafūrī, Medjīd ii, **995a** — II, **1018a**
Ghaghauz → Gagauz
Ghāʾib ii, **995b** — II, **1018b**
Ghāʿita → Ghayta
Ghalāfiḳa ii, **996a** — II, **1019a**
Ghalaṭa i, 973a, b; ii, 833a, 999a; iv, 225b, 228b, 231b, 239a, 240b, 244a, 1158b; v, 313a, 533b; s, 168a, **314a** — I, 1003a, b; II, 852b, 1022a; IV, 235a, 238b, 242a, 249b, 251a, 255a, 1191a; V, 312b, 537b; S, 168b, **314a**
Ghalaṭa-Sarāyi ii, **996b**; v, 904b — II, **1019b**; V, 910b
Ghalaṭāt-i Meshhūre ii, **997a** — II, **1020a**
Ghalča i, 225a; ii, **997b** — I, 231b; II, **1020b**
Ghaldan Khān iii, 1120b — III, 1148a
Ghaldjī → Ghalzay
Ghālī → Ghulāt
Ghālī, Rashīd v, 190a — V, 187a
Ghālib → Wahhābiyya
Ghālib, Ismāʿīl → Ismāʿīl Ghālib
Ghālib, Mīrzā Asad Allāh ii, 735b, **1000a,** 1036b; iii, 93b, 1095b; iv, 716b; v, 961b; s, 334a, 360b — II, 754a, **1023a,** 1060b; III, 96a, 1122a; IV, 745a; V, 966a; S, 333b, 360a
Ghālib, Sharīf i, 1299a; ii, 176b, 572b; v, 62b — I, 1339a; II, 182a, 587a; V, 64b
Ghālib b. ʿAbd al-Raḥmān ii, **997b;** iii, 31a, 74b, 1036b; v, 626a, 1008a — II, **1021a;** III, 32b, 77a, 1062b; V, 630a, 1004a
Ghālib b. ʿAlī b. Hilāl iii, 403b — III, 415b
Ghālib b. Ṣaʿṣaʿa ii, 788a, **998a** — II, 807a, **1021a**
Ghālib Dede, Shaykh ii, **999a;** iii, 90b; iv, 190b; s, 283a — II, **1022a;** III, 93a; IV, 198b; S, 283a
Ghālib Pasha → Meḥmed Saʿīd Ghālib Pasha
Ghaliya i, 1299a — I, 1339a
Ghallābakhshī ii, 155b, 156a, 157b — II, 160a, b, 162b
Ghalzay i, 88a, 95a, 217b, 219b, 229a, b, 1013b; ii, 812a, **1001a;** iii, 604b; iv, 537a, 917b; s, 66b, 237b, 329b, 367a — I, 90b, 98a, 224a, 226a, 235b, 236b, 1044b; II, 831b, **1024a;** III, 625a; IV, 560b, 950b; S, 67a, 237a, 329a, 368a
Ghamātiyyūn iii, 339a — III, 349a
Ghāmid ii, **1001b;** iii, 363b — II, **1024b;** III, 375a
Ghāna (Sūdān) ii, **1001b;** iii, 657a — II, **1025a;** III, 678b
Ghana i, 211a, 762a; ii, 94a, **1003a;** iii, 288b; v, 386b, 387a, 653b; s, 217b — I, 217a, 785a; II, 96a, **1026a;** III, 297b; V, 387b, 388b, 657b; S, 217a
Ghanam i, 876a; s, **316b** — I, 900b; S, **316a**
Ghanānand iii, 457b — III, 473b
Ghanī ii, **1004a,** — II, **1027b**
Ghanī b. Aʿṣur ii, **1004b** — II, **1028a**
Ghānim i, 359a — I, 370a
Ghānim, Khalīl → Khalīl Ghānim
Ghanīma i, 1142a, 1144a; ii, 146b, 154b, 504b, 869a, **1005a;** iii, 183a;iv, 1141b; v, 689b — I, 1176b, 1178b; II, 150b, 159b, 517b, 889a, **1028b;** III, 187a; IV, 1173a; V, 694b
Ghanīmat Kundjāhī, Muḥammad Akram ii, **1006b;** s, **322a** — II, **1030a** S, **321b**
Ghānimid(e)s ii, 517a; v, 333a — II, 530a; V, 333a
Ghāniya, Banū i, 92b, 161b, 165a, 367a, 533a, 798a, 1176a, 1205b; ii, 112a, 526a, **1007a;** iii, 1055b; iv, 337b, 416a, 479b; s, 80b — I, 95a, 166a, 169b, 378a, 549b, 821b, 1211a, 1241a; II, 114b, 539a, **1030b;** III, 1081b; IV, 352a, 434a, 501b; S, 80b
Ghanm, Banū i, 683b — I, 704b
Ghār s, 327a — S, 326b
Gharb (Morocco/Maroc) ii, **1008b;** iii, 300b; v, 1185b; s, 350b, 387b — II, **1032a;** III, 309b; V, 1175b; S, 350b, 387b
Gharb al-Andalus ii, **1009a** — II, **1032b**
al-Gharbiyya ii, **1009b**; s, 18a, 40a — II, **1033a**; S, 18a, 40a
Ghardāya ii, **1010a;** iii, 97b — II, **1033b;** III, 100a
Ghardjistān ii, **1010b**; s, 376b — II, **1034a**; S, 376b
Gharīb i, 157b, 275b; ii, **1011a;** iii, 25b — I, 162a, 284a; II, **1034b;** III, 26b
Gharībān ii, 921b, 1097b — II, 943a, 1123b
al-Gharībī, Muḥammad b. Sulayyim s, 355b — S, 355b
al-Gharīḍ ii, **1011b;** iii, 950a — II, **1035a;** III, 975a
Ghārim ii, **1011b** — II, **1035b**
Ghariyyān iii, 1064a — III, 1090b
Gharnāṭa i, 6a, 43b, 84a, 491b, 495b, 1057b; ii, **1012a;** iii, 135a, 220a, 836b, 1110a — I, 6b, 45a, 86b, 506a, 510b, 1089b; II, **1035b;** III, 137b, 226b, 860b, 1137b
- Alhambra → al-Ḥamra
- monuments i, 1225a, 1320b; ii, **1014b;** iii, 144a, 498b — I, 1261b, 1361a; II, **1038a;** III, 145b, 515b
al-Gharnāṭī → Abū Ḥāmid; Abu Ḥayyān; al-Ḥādjdj
Ghars → Kars
Ghars al-Dawla b. Shumla i, 240a — I, 247a
Ghars al-Dīn-zāde iii, 340a — III, 350a
Ghars al-Niʿma Muḥammad iii, 752b — III, 775b
Gharsiya b. Shandjuh s, 80b — S, 80b
Gharsiya b. Wanḳu i, 1079b — I, 1112a
Ghārūḳa s, **322b** — S, **322a**
Gharyān, ʿAbd al-Madjīd iv, 720b — IV, 749b
Ghaṣb ii, **1020a** — II, **1043b**
Ghāshiya ii, **1020a** — II, **1044a**
Ghaṣība ii, 321a — II, 330b
Ghasīl al-Malāʾika ii, **1020b** — II, **1044a**
Ghassāl s, **322b** — S, **322b**
Ghassān i, 1140b; ii, **1020b** — I, 1175a; II, **1044a**
Ghassān b. ʿAbbād i, 271b — I, 280a
Ghassān al-Kūfī ii, 1022a — II, 1046a
al-Ghassānī, Abū ʿAbd Allāh ii, **1021b**; s, 130b — II, **1045b**; S, 130a
Ghassānid(e)s i, 405b, 526a, 548b, 890a, 1249b; ii, 1020b; iii, 272b, 292b; iv, 492b, 839a, 1145a; v, 633b; s, 117a, 229b — I, 417a, 542a, 566a, 916b, 1287b; II, 1044a; III, 280a, 301b; IV, 514a, 872a, 1176b; V, 637b; S, 116a, 229b
Ghassāniyya ii, **1022a** — II, **1046a**
Ghāt ii, 875a, 876b, **1022a** — II, 895b, 897a, **1046a**
Ghaṭafān ii, 627a, **1023a;** iii, 285b; iv, 1139a, 1144a; s, 177a, 178a — II, 642b, **1046b;** III, 294b; IV, 1171a, 1175b; S, 178a, 179a
Ghaṭaṭ iv, 743b — IV, 773b
Ghātwāls ii, 868b — II, 888b
al-Ghawār ii, **1024a** — II, **1048a**
Ghawāzī → Ghāziya
al-Ghawr ii, **1024b** — II, **1048a**
al-Ghawrī, Sultan → Ḳānsūh al-Ghawrī
Ghawth v, 543b; s, **323b** — V, 548a; S, **323a**
al-Ghawth s, 37b — S, 37b
Ghawth Muḥammad Khān i, 1195b — I, 1230b
Ghawthī Dede ii, 833a — II, 852b
Ghawwāṣī iii, 376a — III, 388a
al-Ghayb ii, **1025a** — II, **1049a**
Ghayba ii, 996a, **1026a;** iii, 51b, 1167a; iv, 277b; v, 1236a — II, 1018b, **1049b;** III, 53a, 1195b; IV, 289b; V, 1226b
Ghaylān b. Muslim ii, **1026b;** iii, 1142b; iv, 271b, 370a, 371b — II, **1050a;** III, 1171a; IV, 283b, 386a,

388a
Ghaylān b. ʿUḳba → Dhu 'l-Rumma
Ghayn ii, **1026b** – II, **1050b**
Ghayr, ghayra iv, 272b, 273a – IV, 284b, 285a
Ghayr Mahdī → Muḥammad al-Djawnpūrī
Ghayṭa ii, **1027b** – II, **1051a**
Ghazal i, 10b, 107b, 586a, 592a, 677b; ii, **1028a**; iv, 57b, 62a, 65a, 714b; v, 836a; s, **323b** – I, 10b, 110b, 605a, 611b, 698a; II, **1051b**; IV, 60b-61a, 65b, 68b, 743a; V, 842b; S, **323a**
Ghazāl ii, **1036b**; iv, 649a – II, **1060b**; IV, 675b
al-Ghazāl, Yaḥyā i, 83a, 601a, 934b; ii, 516a, **1038a;** iii, 702a; v, 1119b – I, 85b, 620b, 963a; II, 592a, **1062a;** III, 724a; V, 1116b
al-Ghazālī, Abu 'l-Futūḥ s, 384a – S, 384b
al-Ghazālī, Abū Ḥāmid Muḥammad i, 25b, 92a, 274a, 326b, 327b, 333a, 347a, 350a, 351a, 390b, 411a, 412b, 414a, 416a, 427b, 513b, 593a, 595b, 696b, 714a, 715a, 826a, 839a, 1099b; ii, 96a, 144b, 225b, 451a, 605b, 765b, 767a, 773a, 834a, **1038b,** 1069b; iii, 254a, 512a, 544a, 683b, 712b, 915a, 958b, 1024b, 1029a, 1063b, 1148a, 1149a, 1168a, 1205b; iv, 25b, 149b, 257b, 279b, 487a, 697b, 895a; v, 54b, 329b; s, 2b, 15a, 153a, 293a, 305b – I, 26b, 94b, 282b, 336b, 338a, 343a, 357b, 361a, 362a, 401b, 422b, 424b, 425b, 426a, 428a, 439b, 529a, 612a, 615a, 717b, 735b, 736b, 849a, 862b, 1133a; II, 98a, 148b, 232b, 462b, 620b, 784a, 785a, 791b, **1062b,** 1094a; III, 261a, 529b, 563a, 705b, 735a, 939b, 983a, 1050a, 1055a, 1090a, 1176a, 1177a, 1197a, 1236a; IV, 27a, 155b, 268b, 291b, 508a, 726a, 928b; V, 56a, 329b; S, 2a, 15a, 153b, 292b, 305a
al-Ghazālī, Aḥmad ii, 1038b, **1041b**; iv, 64a-b; s, 2b – II, 1063a, **1066a**; IV, 67b; S, 2a
al-Ghazālī, Djānbirdi i, 779a; ii, 287a, **1042a;** iii, 88a, 400a – I, 802b; II, 294b, **1066a;** III, 90b, 412b
Ghazālī, Meḥmed ii, **1042a** – II, **1066b**
Ghāzān Khān i, 205b, 861a, 903a, 1011a, 1031b, 1126b, 1129b; ii, 47a, 285b, 311b, **1043a,** 1045b; iii, 189b, 198a, 284a, 399b, 490b, 951b, 1089b, 1099b, 1122b, 1124a, b; iv, 31a-b, 48b, 621a, 637b, 818a, 945a, 975b, 976a, 1038b, 1045b; v, 162b, 312a, 554b, 662b, 872b; s, 59a, 94b – I, 211b, 885a, 930a, 1042a, 1063a, 1160b, 1164a; II, 48a, 293b, 320b, **1067a,** 1069b; III, 194a, 203a, 293a, 412a, 507b, 976b, 1116a, 1126b, 1150a, 1152a, b; IV, 33b-34a, 51a, 646a, 664a, 851a, 978a, 1008a, b, 1070a, 1077a; V, 160b, 311b, 559a, 668a, 878b; S, 59b, 94a
Ghazan Khān (Hunza) iii, 581a – III, 601b
Ghāzāniyye iii, 1124b, 1125a – III, 1152b, 1153a
Ghazāt → Ghazw
Ghāzī i, 322b; ii, 505b, **1043b;** iii, 196a – I, 332b; II, 518a, **1068a;** III, 201a
Ghāzī, Amīr → Gümüshtegin
Ghāzī, King/le roi ii, 872b, **1045a;** iii, 264a, 1258b; v, 1044b – II, 892b, **1069b;** III, 271b, 1291a; V, 1041a
Ghāzī I (Artukid(e)) i, 665a – I, 686a
Ghāzī I (Zangid(e)) i, 1160b; ii, 489b, 1045a; iii, 327b – I, 1195a; II, 501b, 1069b; III, 337b
Ghāzī II (Zangid(e)) ii, 1045a – II, 1069b
Ghāzī b. Ṣalāḥ al-Dīn → al-Ẓāhir Ghāzī
Ghāzī Čelebī ii, **1045a**; v, 505b – II, **1069b**; V, 509a
Ghāzī 'l-Dīn Ḥaydar i, 757b; ii, **1045b**; v, 635a, 637a – I, 780a; II, **1070a**; V, 639a, 641a
Ghāzī 'l-Dīn Khān → Shihāb al-Dīn, Mīr; Muḥammad Panāh, Mīr; ʿImād al-Mulk
Ghāzī 'l-Dīn Khān iii, 320b – III, 331a
Ghāzī Evrenos Beg → Ewrenos
Ghāzī Girāy I ii, **1046a,** 1113b – II, **1070b,** 1139b
Ghāzī Girāy II ii, **1046a**; v, 138b – II, **1070b**; V, 141b
Ghāzī Girāy III ii, **1047a**; iv, 569a; v, 140b – II, **1071b**; IV, 591b; V, 143a
Ghāzī Khān Čak iv, 709a; s, 167a, **324b**, 335b – IV, 737b; S, 167a, **324a**, 353b
Ghāzī Khusrew-bey → Khosrew beg
Ghāzī Ḳirān b. Sulṭān Aḥmad i, 1030b – I, 1062a
Ghāzī-Ḳumuḳ → Ḳumiḳ
Ghāzī Malik → Ghiyāth al-Dīn Tughluḳ I
Ghāzi Meḥmed Pasha → Muḥammad Pasha Bushatlī
Ghāzī Miyān, Sālār Masʿūd i, 756b, 855b; ii, **1047b**; iv, 210b; s, 280a – I, 779a, 879b; II, **1071b**; IV, 220a; S, 280a
Ghāzī Muḥammad → Ḳāḍī Muḥammad
Ghāzīpūr s, 203a, **325a** – S, 202b, **324b**
Ghāziya i, 404a, 1036a; ii, **1048a** – I, 415b, 1067b; II, **1072b**
Ghāziyan i, 1014a – I, 1045a
Ghaziyya i, 528b – I, 544b
Ghazna i, 222b, 223a, 226b, 940a; ii, 382a, **1048b,** 1054a, 1103b; s, 66b, 329b – I, 229a, 233b, 968b; II, 392b, **1073a,** 1078b, 1129b; S, 67a, 329a
Ghaznawid(e)s i, 226b, 420a, 421b, 434a, 439b, 1130b, 1342b, 1344b; ii, 4b, 266b, 336a, 893b, **1050a,** 1083a, 1109a; iii, 47a, 197a, 415b, 438b, 471a; iv, 18b, 24a-25a, 61a, 189b, 208b, 217b, 266b, 357a, 696b, 758b; v, 58a, 597b, 691a, 956b; s, 21a, b, 119a, 242a, 284b, 333a, 386b – I, 233b, 432a, 433a, 446a, 452a, 1165a, 1383a, 1385a; II, 4b, 274b, 345b, 914b, **1074b,** 1108a, 1135a; III, 48b, 202a, 428b, 453a, 487b; IV, 20a, 26a-b, 64a, 197b, 218a, 227a, 278b, 372b, 724b, 788b; V, 60a, 601b, 696a, 960b; S, 21a, b, 118b, 242a, 284b, 332b, 387a
- art, architecture ii, 1053b, 1103b – II, 1078a, 1129b
Ghaznī s, 367a – S, 367b
Ghaznīn s, 41a – S, 41b
Ghaznīn Khan iv, 219a – IV, 228b
Ghazw, Ghazwa i, 885b, 892a; ii, 64a, b, 509b, 1043b, **1055a**; v, 768a, 1161b – I, 911b, 918b; II, 65a, b, 522a, 1068a, **1079b**; V, 774a, 1151a
Ghazza ii, **1056a;** iii, 187b; v, 801b; s, 20b, 326a – II, **1080b**; III, 192a; V, 807b; S, 20b, 325b
al-Ghazzāl, al-Malaḳī s, **325b** – S, **325a**
al-Ghazzālī → al-Ghazālī
Ghazzan Khān b. Ḳāsim Khān ii, 316b – II, 326a
al-Ghazzāwī, ʿAlī Bey iv, 852b – IV, 885b
al-Ghazzī, Abū Isḥāḳ s, **326a** – S, **325b**
al-Ghazzī, Nadjm al-Dīn i, 100a, 594b – I, 103a, 614a
Gheghāya iii, 207a – III, 212b
Gheraba i, 371b – I, 382b
Ghība → Pandjāb
Ghidhāʾ ii, **1057a;** iii, 79a; s, 318b – II, **1081b;** III, 81b; S, 318b
Ghifār, Banū ii, **1072b**; v, 116b – II, **1097a**; V, 119a
Ghīlān, Ḳāʾid iv, 729b – IV, 758b
Ghilmān → Ghulām
Ghilzay → Ghalzay
Ghināʾ ii, **1072b**; iv, 821a; v, 480b – II, **1097b**; IV, 854a; V, 483b
Ghirbāl ii, 620b, 1074a – II, 636a, 1098b
Ghirbīb b. ʿAbd Allāh ii, **1075b** – II, **1100a**
Ghirsh (Ghūrsh) → Sikka
Ghīta → Ghayta
al-Ghiṭrīfī, Muḥammad b. Aḥmad s, 326b – S, 326a
al-Ghiṭrīf b. ʿAṭāʾ v, 855a, b; s, **326b** – V, 862a, b; S, **326a**
Ghiyār ii, **1075b**; v, 736b, 744b – II, **1100b**; V, 741b, 750a
Ghiyāth (dāʿī) iv, 661b – IV, 688a
Ghiyāth b. Muḥammad s, 271b – S, 271b
Ghiyāth Beg i, 253b; ii, 380b – I, 261b; II, 390b
Ghiyāth-al-Dīn Aʿẓam Shāh → Aʿẓam Shāh
Ghiyāth al-Dīn Balban → Balban

Ghiyāth al-Dīn Djāmī s, 139a — S, 138b
Ghiyāth al-Dīn Girāy ii, 1112b — II, 1138b
Ghiyāth al-Dīn Maḥmūd → Maḥmūd Ghūrī; Maḥmūd III (Bengal(e))
Ghiyāth al-Dīn Muḥammad b. Ḥusayn ii, 733a, 735a — II, 751b, 753b
Ghiyāth al-Dīn Muḥammad b. Rashīd al-Dīn s, 415b — S, 415b
Ghiyāth al-Dīn Muḥammad b. Sām ii, 406b, 752a, 928b, 1101a, 1103a, b; iii, 177b; iv, 669a — II, 417b, 770a, 950a, 1127a, 1129b; III, 181b; IV, 696a
Ghiyāth al-Dīn Muḥammad Eretna i, 1327b; ii, 239a, 706a, 712b — I, 1368b; II, 246a, 724a, 730b
Ghiyāth al-Dīn Muḥammad al-Kurtī i, 764b, 908b; ii, 68a; iii, 1022a; iv, 672a — I, 787b, 936a; II, 69a; III, 1048a; IV, 699b
Ghiyāth al-Dīn Naḳḳāsh ii, **1076a** — II, **1100b**
Ghiyāth al-Din Pīr ʿAlī iv, 672a — IV, 699b
Ghiyāth al-Dīn Pīr-Shāh i, 1311a; ii, 393a — I, 1351b; II, 403b
Ghiyāth al-Din Shīrāzī iv, 1073b — IV, 1105a
Ghiyāth al-Dīn Tughluḳ I i, 104b, 444b, 1322a; ii, 120a, 154b, 257a, 262a, 269b, 274b, 922b, **1076a;** iii, 201a, 416b, 441b, 492a; iv, 921b, 924a; v, 885a; s, 105b, 409a — I, 107b, 457b, 1362b; II, 123a, 159b, 263b, 269b, 277b, 283a, 944a, **1101a;** III, 206a, 429b, 456a, 509a; IV, 954b, 956b; V, 891b; S, 105a, 409b
Ghiyāth al-Dīn Tughluḳ II ii, **1077a** — II, **1102a**
Ghiyāth al-Umma → Bahāʾ al-Dawla Fīrūz
Ghom → Ḳumm
Ghōr s, 367a — S, 367b
Ghōrband s, 367b — S, 367a
Ghōriya Khēls i, 218b — I, 224b
Ghourides → Ghūrides
Ghouristan → Ghūr
Ghubār iii, 468b, 1140a; iv, 1124a, 1125b — III, 485a, 1168b; IV, 1155b, 1157a
Ghubayrā s, **327a** — S, **326b**
Ghubba i, 535b, 536a — I, 552a
Ghubrīnī ii, **1077b** — II, **1102a**
Ghudiyyāt v, 267a — V, 265a
Ghudjduwān ii, **1077b — II, 1102b**
Ghudjduwānī ii, **1077b** — II, **1102b**
Ghufrān ii, **1078a** — II, **1103a**
Ghūl ii, **1078b**; s, 52b — II, **1103b**; S, 53a
Ghulām i, 7b, 8a, 1278a; ii, 507a, 551b, 837a, **1079b,** 1103a; iii, 195a; iv, 36a, 242a; v, 245a, 691b, 820a — I, 8a, b, 1317a; II, 519b, 565b, 856b, **1104b,** 1129a; III, 199b; IV, 38b, 253a; V, 243a, 696b, 826a
Ghulām Aḥmad i, 301a, 302b; iii, 433b — I, 310b, 312a; III, 447b → Aḥmadiyya
Ghulām ʿAlī → Āzād Bilgrāmī
Ghulām ʿAlī, Shāh iii, 433b — III, 447b
Ghulām Farīd v, 611a — V, 615a
Ghulam Ḥalim → ʿAbd al-ʿAzīz al-Dihlawī
Ghulām Haydar Khān ii, 638a — II, 654a
Ghulām Ḥusayn Khān Tabāṭabāʾī ii, **1091b** — II, **1117a**
Ghulām Ḥusayn "Salīm" ii, **1092a** — II, **1118a**
Ghulām Ḳadir Rohilla i, 813b; ii, **1092b;** iii, 428a — I, 836b; II, **1118a;** III, 442a
Ghulām al-Khallāl i, 274a, 274b; ii, **1093a;** iii, 158b, 735a; iv, 990a, 1083b; v, 10a — I, 282b, 283a; II, **1118b;** III, 162a, 757b; IV, 1022b, 1114b; V, 10a
Ghulām Muḥammad iii, 565a, b; iv, 710b — III, 584b, 585a; IV, 739b
Ghulām Muḥammad b. Tīpū Sulṭān ii, 7b — II, 7b
Ghulām Nabī Bilgrāmī iii, 457b — III, 473b
Ghulām Naḳshband Lakhnawī i, 1219a — I, 1255b
Ghulām Shāh Kalhōrā ii, 186a; iii, 323b; iv, 544b — II, 192a; III, 333b; IV, 568a
Ghulām Shāhīs i, 295b — I, 304b
Ghulām Thaʿlab ii, **1093a**; v, 608a; s, 361a — II, **1119a**; V, 611b; S, 361a
Ghulām Yaḥyā iii, 430b — III, 444b
Ghulāt i, 51a, 1098b; ii, **1093b;** iii, 662a — I, 52b, 1132a; II, **1119b;** III, 683a
Ghulayfiḳa → Ghalāfiḳa
Ghuldja → Ḳuldja
Ghumāra i, 161a; ii, **1095a**; v, 1204a, b — I, 165b; II, **1121a**; V, 1194b, 1195a
Ghumdān ii, **1096a** — II, **1121b**
Ghumīk ii, 85b; iv, 348a — II, 87b; IV, 362b
Ghundjār ii, **1096a** — II, **1122a**
Ghunm → Ghanīma
Ghūr ii, **1096b**; s, 376b — II, **1122b**; S, 376b
Ghurāb ii, **1096b** — II, **1122b**
Ghurāb → Safīna
al-Ghurāb → Nudjūm
Ghurabāʿ, Ghurebā ii, **1097b** — II, **1123b**
Ghurābiyya ii, **1098b** — II, **1124b**
Ghūrak, Prince/le prince i, 241a — I, 248b
al-Ghuraynī, ʿAbd al-Raḥmān b. Sulaymān s, 44a — S, 44b
Ghurbat → Ḳurbat
Ghurbet ṭāʾifesi ii, 1098b — II, 1124b
Ghūrī → Dilāwar Khān, Mālwā
al-Ghūrī (Mamlūk) → Ḳānsūh al-Ghawrī
Ghūrid(e)s i, 217b, 218a, 223b, 227a, 420a, 852a, 1010a, 1344b; ii, 266b, 382a, 894a, 1049b, 1052b, 1096b, **1099a;** iii, 197b, 415b, 471b; iv, 210a; v, 597b; s, 242a, 284b — I, 224a, b, 230a, 233b, 432a, 876a, 1041a, 1385a; II, 275a, 392b, 914b, 1074a, 1077a, 1122b, **1125a;** III, 202a, 428b, 488a; IV, 219b; V, 601b; S, 242a, 284b
Ghurūsh → Sikka
Ghusl ii, **1104a;** iii, 1053a; iv, 264b — II, **1130a;** III, 1079a; IV, 276b
Ghūṭa i, 1029b; ii, 278a, 290b, 541a, **1104b** — I, 1061a; II, 286a, 298b, 554b, **1131a**
Ghuzāt → Ghāzī
Ghuzāt al-baḥr i, 1205b; ii, 521a, 526a, 678a; iii, 627b — I, 1241b; II, 534a, 539a, 695a; III, 648a
al-Ghuzūlī, ʿAlāʾ al-Dīn i, 361b; ii, **1106b**; s, 115b — I, 372b; II, **1132b**; S, 115a
Ghuzz (Aghzāz) i, 181b, 1029a; ii, **1110a;** — I, 186b, 1060b; II, **1136a**
Ghuzz (Oghuz) i, 147b, 190a, 227a, 239b, 311a, 512b, 524a, 607b, 660b, 661b, 662a, 729a, 1001b, 1073b, 1133b, 1292a; ii, 20b, 200a, 613b, 724a, 971a, 1101b, **1106b;** iii, 1098b, 1115a; iv, 18b, 26a-b, 29b, 101a, 347a, 614a, 1176a; v, 58b, 59a, 126a, 160a, b, 453b, 855b; s, 168b, 195a, 244b, 280b, 333b — I, 151b, 194b, 233b, 247a, 321a, 528b, 540a, 627a, 681b, 682b, 683a, 751a, 1032a, 1106a, 1167b, 1331b; II, 20b, 206b, 629a, 743a, 993b, 1127b, **1132b;** III, 1125b, 1142a; IV, 20a, 28a, 31b, 105a, 362a, 638b, 1209b; V, 60a, b, 128b, 159a, 456a, 862a; S, 168b, 195a, 244b, 280b, 333b
Giafar → Djaʿfar
Giālpō i, 1004b — I, 1035b
Giaour → Gabr, Kāfir
Gibel → Djabala
Gibraltar → Djabal Ṭāriḳ
Gibran → Djabrān
Gičkīs s, 222a, 332a — S, 222a, 331b
Gift → Hiba
Gīl/Gīlī ii, 1111a; s, 356b, 363a — II, 1137a; S, 356a, b, 362b
Gīl Gawbarā ii, 74b; iv, 644b; s, 298a, 299a — II, 76a; IV, 671a; S, 297b, 298b
Gīlakī, Amīr i, 1250a — I, 1288a
Gīlān i, 8a, 46b, 60a, 91a, 389a, 1014a; ii, 189b, 190a, 445b, 903b, **1111a;** iii, 211a, 212a, 214b; v, 602b,

604a; s, 13a, 23b, 139b, 299a, 356b, 357a, 363a, 365b — I, 8a, 48a, 62a, 93b, 400b, 1045a; II, 195b, 196a, 457b, 924b, **1137a;** III, 216b, 218a, 221a; V, 606b, 608a; S, 13b, 24a, 139a, 298b, 356b, 356b, 362b, 365a
Gīlān Shāh iv, 815a — IV, 848a
Gīlānī i, 903b, 904a — I, 931a, b
al-Gīlānī → Aḥmad b. Aḥmad al-Gīlānī
Gīlān-i Biyā Pas iv, 475b; v, 602b, 603a — IV, 496b; V, 606b, 607a
al-Gildakī → al-Djildakī
Gilgamesh iv, 902b — IV, 935b
Gilgit ii, 30a, b, 1112a; iii, 581a; s, **327b** — II, 30a, 31b, 1138a; III, 601b; S, **327a**
Gilit iii, 1259b — III, 1292a
Gīlīz iii, 207a — III, 212b
Gimbri → Ḳonbur
Gindibu i, 524b — I, 540b
Ginukh ii, 251a — II, 258b → Dido
Giorgi III v, 490a — V, 493a
Giorgi V v, 491a — V, 494a
Giorgi VI v, 491b — V, 494a
Giorgi XI → Gurgīn Khān
Giorgi XII v, 495a — V, 498a
Gipsies → Čingāne; Djāmūs; Lūrī; Nūrī; Zuṭṭ
Giraffe/Girafe → Zarāfa
Giralda tower/Giralda, la i, 497b — I, 512b
Girāy i, 893a; ii, 44b, 1046a, **1112a;** iv, 499b; v, 137a — I, 919b; II, 45a, 1070b, **1138a;** IV, 521a; V, 139b
Girdhār Bahādur ii, 219a — II, 225b
Girdkūh iii, 501b — III, 518b
Giresün ii, **1114a** — II, **1140a**
Girgā ii, **1114a** — II, **1140b**
Girgenti → Djirdjent
Girishk ii, **1114b** — II, **1140b**
Girit → Iḳrītish
Girīz, girīzgāh iv, 715b — IV, 744a
Girl → Ḳîz
Gīsh i, 47a, 356a; ii, 146b, 509b, 510b — I, 48b, 366b; II, 150a, 522a, 523b
Gīsū Darāz, Muḥammad ii, 54a, 55a, 56a, **1114b;** iii, 418a, 429b, 434a, 436a; iv, 962a; s, 353a — II, 52b, 56a, b, **1140b;** III, 431a, 443b, 448a, 450a; IV, 994a; S, 353a
Gitans → Čingāne; Djāmūs; Lūrī; Nūrī; Zuṭṭ
Gîte d'étape → Manzil
Giwa i, 956a — I, 985a
Gižduvan → Ghudjduwān
Gīza, Gizeh → al-Ḳāhira
Gjinokastër → Ergiri
Glass → Zudjādj
Glāwa ii, **1116a** — II, **1142a**
Glāwī Madanī ii, 1116a; iii, 62a — II, 1142a; III, 64b
Glāwī Tihāmī ii, 1116b — II, 1142b
Globe, terrestrial/Globe terrestre → Kurrat al-Arḍ
Gloss/Glose → Ḥāshiyya
Gnāns iii, 1163b; iv, 206a — III, 1192a; IV, 215a
Gnāwa iv, 381b — IV, 398a
Gnosis/Gnose → Maʿrifa
Goa i, 924a, 978b; ii, 1128a; iii, 422a — I, 951b, 1009a; II, 1154b; III, 435b → Hind; Ṣindābūr
Goat → Ghanam; Maʿz
Gobān → Ḳobān
Göbek adî iv, 181a — IV, 188b
Gokalā Djāt iv, 177b — IV, 186a
God → Allāh
Godoberi i, 504a — I, 519b → Andi
Gog and/et Magog → Yādjūdj wa-mādjūdj
Gogo → Gao
Goḥa → Djuḥā
Gök Tepe ii, **1116b** — II, **1143a**
Gökalp, Ziyā/Ḍiyāʾ i, 327a; ii, 345b, 475b, **1117a;** iv, 123b, 169a, 791a; v, 264a, 271b; s, 47b, 150a, 167b — I, 337a; II, 355b, 487b, **1143a;** IV, 129a, 176a, 823a; V, 261b, 269a; S, 48a, 150a, 168a
Gökbürī, Muẓaffar al-Dīn i, 300b, 1160b, 1161a; iii, 228b — I, 310a, 1195a, b; III, 235a
Gökbüri → Muẓaffar al-Dīn Gökbüri
Gökčay → Gökče
Gökče Mūsā ii, 614a — II, 629a
Gökče-Tengiz ii, **1118a** — II, **1144a**
Göklän ii, **1118a;** iii, 1108a — II, **1144b;** III, 1135a
Göksu ii, **1118b** — II, **1144b**
Göksun ii, **1118b;** s, 239a — II, **1145a;** s, 239a
Golconda/Golconde → Golkonḍā
Gold → Dhahab
Gold Coast → Ghana
Golden Horde → Bātūid(e)s; Kipčaḳ; Sarāy
Golden Horn → Ghalaṭa; Istanbul; Takhtaḳalʿe
al-Golea → al-Ḳulayʿa
Goletta → Ḥalḳ al-wādi
Golfe Persique → Baḥr al-Fāris
Goliath → Djālūt
Golkonḍā i, 768b, 769b, 924a, 1323b; ii, 158b, **1118b;** iii, 318b, 426b, 448a; v, 549b — I, 791b, 792b, 951b, 1364a; II, 163b, **1145a;** III, 328a, 440b, 463a; V, 554a
Gombroon/Gombrun → Bandar ʿAbbās
Gomme, Gomme Arabique → Ṣamgh
Gondar i, 49b; iii, 7a — I, 51a; III, 7b
Gondēshāpūr i, 212b, 516b, 1223a; ii, 577a, **1119b;** iii, 872b; v, 919a; s, 354a — I, 219a, 532a, 1259b; II, 591b, **1146a;** III, 897a; V, 924b; S, 354a
Gönüllü ii, **1120b** — II, **1146b**
Gora, Abdallāh Suleymān v, 483a — V, 485b
Gōrgān → Gūrgān
Gördes ii, **1121a;** s, 136b, 138a, 282b — II, **1147b;** S, 136a, 137b, 282b
Gordon, Charles George i, 37b, 168b, 929b, 1156b, 1172a; ii, 351b, 696a; v, 70a, 1248b, 1249b — I, 38b, 173b, 957b, 1191a, 1207a; II, 361b, 713b; V, 72a, 1239a, 1240b
Gorein, Djabal iv, 478b, 479b — IV, 499b, 501b
Görele s, 283a — S, 283a
Gorgan → Gurgān
Göridje → Korča; Manastîr
Göridjeli Ḳočî Beg → Ḳočî Beg
Gorno- Badakhshān i, 853a — I, 877a
Gorwekht s, 285a — S, 285a
Gōsiōs s, 52a — S, 53a
Gospels → Indjīl
Goudron → Ḳaṭrān
Goule → Ghūl
La Goulette → Ḥalḳ al-Wādī
Goum → Gūm
Gourara (Gurāra) s, **328a** — S, **327b**
Goût → Dhawk
Government/Gouvernement → Dawla; Hukūma; Siyāsa; Sulṭān; etc.
Governor/Gouverneur → Amīr; Wālī
Govind Singh i, 913b; ii, 928b — I, 941b; II, 950b
Govindapur ii, 7a — II, 7a
Gövsa, Ibrāhīm ʿAlāʾ al-Dīn s, **328b** — S, **328a**
Goyum → Djuwayn
Gōzgān → Djuzdjān
Grabadin i, 345a — I, 355b
Grammar/Grammaire → Fiʿl; Naḥw; Taṣrīf
Gran → Esztergom
Grañ → Aḥmad Grañ
Granada → Gharnāṭa
Grande Horde, la I, 1141a; II, 45a; V, 140a, b
Great Horde i, 1108a; ii, 44a; v, 137a, b
Grèce, Grecs → (ancienne) Yūnān, (byzantine) Rūm, (ottomane) Mora
Greece, Greeks → (ancient) Yūnān, (byzantine)

Rūm, (ottoman) Mora
Greek Fire, Gregorian Fire → Bārūd; Naft
Grégeois (feu) → Bārūd; Naft
Grenade → Gharnāṭa
Grenades → Rummān
Grenadier, fleur de → Djullanār
Grenier → Agadir
Gresik s, 201b — S, 201b
Grocer → Baḳḳāl
Guadalajara → Wādi 'l-Ḥidjāra
Guadalquivir → al-Wādi 'l-Kabīr
Guadarrama → al-Sharrāt
Guadiana → Wādī Yāna
Guadix → Wādī Āsh
Guanche i, 1180b — I, 1215b
Guarantee → Amān; Ḍamān; Ḳabāla; Kafāla
Guard, guardian → Ḳapidjī
Guardafui ii, **1121b** — II, **1147b**
Gudāla ii, **1121b**; v, 653b — II, **1148a**; V, 658a
Gūdarz iv, 815b, 816a — IV, 848b
Gūdjar i, 224b; ii, **1122a,** 1123a; iii, 335b — I, 231b; II, **1148b,** 1149b; III, 345b
Gudjarāt i, 506b, 561b, 924a, 1053a, 1254b; ii, 11a, 814b, 816a, **1123a;** iii, 16a, 421b, 444b, 857a, 1010a; iv, 199b, 202b, 901b; v, 26b, 1117a, 1216b; s, 105a, 200a, 312a, 335b — I, 522a, 579a, 952a, 1084b, 1292b; II, 11a, 834a, 835b, **1149b;** III, 16b, 17a, 435b, 459a, 881a, 1035b; IV, 208a, 211b, 934b; V, 27a, 1113b, 1206b; S, 104b, 200a, 312a, 335a
Gudjarātī i, 1255a; ii, **1130b** — I, 1293a; II, **1157a**
Gudjarī, Gudjurī ii, 31a, 1122b — II, 32a, 1149a
Gūdjrāṅwāla ii, **1130b;** iii, 63a — II, **1157b;** III, 65b
Gudjrāt i, 80b; ii, **1131a** — I, 83a; II, **1158a**
Guèbres → Gabr
Guellala → Ḳallala
Guépard → Fahd
Guerara → Ḳarāra
Guergour s, 144b, — S, 144a
Guerre → Djihād, Ḥarb
Guerres russo-turques (1769-1774) I, 4b, 304a, 977a; III, 197b, 260a
- (1877-1878) II, 90a, 628b; III, 1017b
Guersif/Guercif → Garsīf
Guet → ʿAsas
Guezebida i, 1221b — I, 1258a
Guide → Zaʿīm
Guild(s) → Ṣinf
Guinea/Guinée ii, **1131b**; v, 252a — II, **1158b**; V, 250a
Guitar(e) → Kītāra
Gujarat, Gujerat → Gudjarāt
Gujarati, Guzarati → Gudjarātī
Guklān → Göklān
Gul ii, **1133a** — II, **1159b**
Gül ii, 1133b, 1134a — II, 1160b
Gul Khātūn s, **329a** — S, **328b**
Gulāb Sīngh ii, 30a, 140a; iii, 336a; iv, 709b; s, 242a — II, 30b, 144a; III, 346a; IV, 738a; S, 242a
Gulʿanbar → Shahrizūr
Gülbaba i, 1286a; ii, **1133b** — I, 1325b; II, **1160b**
Gulbadan Bēgam ii, **1134b** — II, **1161a**
Gulbāng ii, **1135a** — II, **1161b**
Gulbargā i, 924b, 925a, 1323a; ii, 54a, **1135a;** iii, 15a, 442a, 446b; v, 295b — I, 952b, 953a, 1363b; II, 52b, **1162a;** III, 16a, 456b, 461b; V, 295b
Gülek Boghaz ii, 1135b — II, 1162a
Gulia, Dimitri i, 101b — I, 104b
Gulistān ii, 839a, **1135b**; iv, 392b, 394b — II, 858b, **1162a**; IV, 409a, 411a
Gulistān i, 241b, 680a, 1212b — I, 249a, 701a, 1249a → Saʿdī
Gulistān, Treaty of/Traité de v, 495b, 657a — V, 498b, 661a
Gülkhāne i, 74b; ii, 147b, **1135b** — I, 77a; II, 152a, **1162b**
Gulkunda → Golkonḍā
Gülnūsh Sulṭān iv, 233b, 1100a — IV, 244a, 1131a
Gulpāyagān ii, **1135b** — II, **1162b**
Gulrukh bint Kāmrān iv, 523b — IV, 546a
Gulshanī, Ibrāhīm ii, 345b, **1136a;** iii, 393a; iv, 991b — II, 355b, **1162b;** III, 405b; IV, 1024a
Gulshanī Ṣarūkhānī ii, **1137b** — II, **1164b**
Gulshaniyya ii, 1137b — II, 1164b
Gülshehrī ii, **1138a**; v, 173a — II, **1164b**; V, 170b
Gulshīrī, Hūshang v, 201a — V, 198a
Gum, gum arabic → Samgh
Gūm ii, **1138b**; iv, 784b — II, **1165b**; IV, 816a
Gūmāl (Gomal) s, **329b** — S, **329a**
Gum-resin → Anzarūt
Gümrük i, 861b; ii, 147a — I, 886a; II, 151a → Maks
Gumukh → Kemākh
Gümüldjine s, **329b** — S, **329a**
Gümüshhāne, Gümüshkhāne i, 645b, 1128b; ii, **1139a**; v, 966a, 977a — I, 666a, 1162b; II, **1166a**; V, 970a
Gümüshtegin i, 731a; ii, **1139b** — I, 753a; II, **1166a**
Gümüshtegin, Amīr Ghāzī i, 466a, b, 664b, 983a, 1276b; ii, 110b, 1139b — I, 480a, 684a, 1013b, 1316a; II, 113a, 1166a
Gunabādī → Ḳāsimī; Sulṭān ʿAlī
Gunābādiyya iv, 51b — IV, 54b
Gunbadh → Ḳubba
Gunbadh-i Ḳābūs ii, **1139b,** 1141b; iv, 6b, 358a — II, **1166a,** 1168b; IV, 7a, 373b
Güneri Bey i, 703a; iv, 620b, 621a, b; v, 677a — I, 724a; IV, 645a, b, 646a; V, 682a
Gunpowder, Guns → Bārūd
Güntekin, Reşat Nuri → Reshād Nūrī
Gunzalī → Khunzal
Gūr → Fīrūzābād
Gūrān ii, **1139b;** iii, 292a, 1109a; v, 168b — II, **1166b;** III, 301a, 1136a; V, 166a
Gūran, Shaykh Abu ʾl-Fatḥ s, **331b** — S, **331a**
Gūrānī, Sharaf al-Dīn ii, **1140b** — II, **1167b**
Gūrānī language/langue i, 262b, 840a, 863b; ii, 1140a; iii, 1261a — I, 270b, 863b, 887b; II, 1167a; III, 1293b
Gurāra → Gourara
Gurčānī s, **331b** — S, **331a**
Gurdjistān → Kurdj
Gurdjü ʿAbd al-Nabī iv, 766a — IV, 796b
Gürdjü Meḥmed Pasha v, 257a — V, 255a
Gürdjü Muṣṭafā Pasha iv, 723a — IV, 752a
Gurgān i, 3b, 40a; ii, 253a, 746a, 1139b, **1141a;** iii, 501b; iv, 6b, 10a, 19a; s, 13a, 86b, 235a, 277a, 298a, 326b, 356b — I, 4a, 41b; II, 260b, 764b, 1166b, **1168a;** II, 519a; IV, 7a, 10b, 20b; S, 13b, 86b, 235a, 277a, 297b, 326a, 356b
Gurgandj i, 120b, 456a, b; ii, 2a, 43b, 571b, **1141b**; iv, 1061b, 1063b, 1064a, b, 1066a; v, 858a; s, 246a, 280b — I, 124a 469a, b; II, 2a, 44a, 586a, **1168b**; IV, 1093a, 1095a, b, 1096a, 1098a; V, 865a; S, 246a, 280b
Gurgānī → Djurdjānī
Gurgānī, Abu ʾl-Haytham iv, 60b — IV, 64a
Gurgānī, Fakhr al-Dīn ii, **1142b**; iv, 62b; s, 108a — II, **1169b**; IV, 66a; S, 107a
Gurgīn, King/le roi → Giorgi
Gurgīn Khān i, 229a; iii, 603b; v, 493b — I, 236a; III, 624b; V, 496b
Gurgīn Milād v, 661a, 670a — V, 666b, 675b
Gurieli i, 1108b — I, 1141b
Gūrjara-Pratīhāras → al-Djurz
Gūrkhān i, 987a, 1131a; ii, 791b, **1143a;** iii, 1114b;

iv, 581b, 582a — I, 1017b, 1351b; II, 810b, **1170b;** III, 1142a; IV, 605a, b
Gürpinar → Ḥusayn Raḥmī
Gürsel, General/général ii, 433a, 646a — II, 444a, 662a
Gurush ii, 119a, b — II, 122a
Gurz v, 691b — V, 696b
Guwākharz → Bākharz
Guwayn → Djuwayn
Gūyān → Djuwayn
Güyük Khān i, 1105b; ii, 3a, 45b — I, 1139a; II, 3a, 46b
Guyum iv, 9b — IV, 10a
Güzel Ḥiṣār → Aydîn
Güzeldje Hisar → Anadolu Ḥiṣārî
Gūzgān → Djūzdjān
Gwādar i, 1282a; v, 684b; s, **332a** — I, 1321a; V, 690a; S, **331b**
Gwāliyār ii, **1143b;** iii, 995b; v, 1216a; s, 331b — II, **1170b;** III, 1020a; V, 1206a; S, 331a
Gwandu ii, **1144b** — II, **1171b**
Gwāṭar Bay s, 332b — S, 332a
Gynécée → Ḥarīm
Gypaète → Humā
Gypsies → Čingāne; Lūlī; Nūrī; Zuṭṭ
Gypsum/Gypse → Djiṣṣ
Gyromancy → Raml

H

Hā' iii, **1a** — III, **1a**
Ḥā' iii, **2a** — III, **2a**
al-Habā'a, Day of/Journée de s, 177a, 178a, b — S, 178a, 179a, b
Ḥabāba i, 1149a; ii, 428b, 1011b; iii, **2b**; iv, 821b — I, 1183b; II, 439b, 1035a; III, **2b**; IV, 854b
Habar Awal i, 1173a — I, 1208a
Ḥabash i, 39a, 44a, b, 80a, 84b, 102b, 286b, 547b, 561a, 763b, 991b; ii, 91a, 535b, 545a; iii, **2b**; v, 116b, 1250a — I, 40a, 45b, 82b, 87a, 105a, 295b, 565a, 579a, 786b, 1022b; II, 93a, 548b, 558b; III, **3a**; V, 119a, 1241a
Ḥabash (musician/musicien) s, 64a, 183a — S, 64b, 184b
Ḥabash ʿAmīd ii, 2b, 3b — II, 2b, 3b
Ḥabash al-Ḥāsib al-Marwazī i, 159b; ii, 577a; iii, **8a,** 1137a; v, 85a; s, 413b — I, 164a; II, 591b; III, **8b,** 1165a; V, 87a; S, 413b
Ḥabasha i, 24b, 102a; ii, 244b, 940a; iii, **2b** — I, 25b, 105a; II, 251b, 962a; III, **3a**
Ḥabashat iii, **9a** — III, **9b**
Ḥabaṭ iii, **10b** — III, **11a** → Ḥawṭa
Ḥabawnā i, 538a — I, 554b
Ḥabba iii, **10b** — III, **11a**
Habba Khātūn s, **332a** — S, **332a**
al-Habbāl al-Miṣrī s, 390b — S, 391a
Ḥabbān iii, **11a** — III, **11b**
Habbāniyya, Lake/lac ii, 947b; iii, 1250b — II, 969b; III, 1283a
Ḥabbūs → Ḥabūs
Ḥabesh iii, **11a** — III, **12a**
Ḥabeshī Meḥmed Agha ii, 1088a; iii, 175b — II, 1113b; III, 179a
Ḥabīb b. ʿAbd al-Malik iii, **11b** — III, **12b**
Ḥabīb b. ʿAbd al-Raḥmān al-Fihrī i, 86b — I, 89a
Ḥabīb b. Abī ʿUbayda al-Fihrī i, 86a, 990b; v, 367a — I, 88b, 1021b; V, 368a
Ḥabīb b. Aws → Abū Tammām
Ḥabīb b. Maslama i, 325a, 635b, 636a, 660a, 1349a; ii, 276a, 456a, 678b; iii, **12b,** 20a; iv, 343b, 654b, 870b; v, 487b — I, 335b, 656b, 681a, 1389a; II, 284a, 468a, 695b; III, **13a,** 21a; IV, 358a, 681a, 904a; V, 490b
Ḥabīb b. Muẓāhir iii, 610a — III, 631a
Ḥabīb b. ʿUmar Tal i, 297a — I, 306a
Ḥabīb b. Yazīd b. al-Muhallab s, 41a — S, 41a
Habīb Allāh b. Khalīl Allāh iv, 961b, 962a — IV, 994a
Ḥabīb Allāh II → Bačča-i Saḳaw
Ḥabīb Allāh Khān i, 88a, 232a; iii, **13a**; v, 1079a; s, 65b, 237b — I, 90b, 239b; III, **13b**; V, 1076b; S, 66a, 237b
Ḥabīb Iṣfahānī iv, 72a — IV, 76a
Ḥabīb al-Nadjdjār i, 517a; iii, **12b** — I, 532b; III, **13a**
Ḥabīb al-Raḥmān v, 803a — V, 809a
Ḥabīb Ṣāliḥ b. Ḥabīb ʿAlawī v, 655b, 656a — V, 660a
Ḥabīb Shāh s, 167a, 324b — S, 167a, 324a
Ḥabība bint Khāridja i, 109b — I, 112b
Ḥabība Saldjūḳ-Khātūn i, 1328a — I, 1368b
Ḥabībī i, 193a — I, 199a
Ḥabībīs iii, 12a — III, 12b
Hābīl wa Ḳābīl i, 178a, 181a; iii, **13b**; iv, 724a — I, 183a, 186a; III, **14a**; IV, 753a
Hābil-oghlu i, 431b — I, 444a
Habillement → Kisā', Libās
Habitation → Bayt, Dār, Suknā
Ḥābiṭiyya → Aḥmad b. Ḥābiṭ
Habitude → ʿĀda
Ḥabla Rud iv, 1030a — IV, 1061b
Habous → Waḳf
Ḥabsān → Djadjīra
Habshī ii, 816a, 1084b, 1129a; iii, **14a,** 419a, 422a, 631b; v, 687b — II, 835b, 1110a, 1155b; III, **15a,** 432b, 436a, 652b; V, 692b
Ḥabsiyya s, **333a** — S, **332b**
Ḥabūḍa s, 338b — S, 338a
Ḥabūḍīs s, 338b — S, 338a
Ḥabūs i, 1146a — I, 1180b
Ḥabūs b. Ḥumayd iii, 688a — III, 709b
Ḥabūs b. Māksan ii, 516a, 1012b, 1015a; iv, 355a — II, 528b, 1036b, 1038b; IV, 370b
Ḥāč Ovasî → Mezö-Keresztes
Hacîlar s, 171b, 172a — S, 172a, b
Ḥadabas i, 536b — I, 553a
Ḥaḍāna iii, **16b** — III, **17b**
Hadanduwa i, 1158a,b; iv, 686b — I, 1192b, 1193a; IV, 714b
Ḥaḍārib i, 1157b, 1158a — I, 1192a,b
Ḥadath iii, **19b** — III, **20b**
al-Ḥadath i, 1190b; iii, **19b**; v, 1239a — I, 1225b; III, **20b**; V, 1229b
Hadāyā ii, 146a — II, 150a
Ḥadd i, 382a, 383a; ii, 632a; iii, **20a,** 204b; iv, 770b, 771b; v, 730b, 731b — I, 393a, 394a; II, 648a; III, **21a,** 210a; IV, 801b, 802b; V, 735b, 736b
Hadda s, 237a — S, 237a
Ḥaddād, ʿAbd al-Masīḥ v, 1254b, 1255a, b — V, 1245b, 1246a, b
Ḥaddād, Banū iv, 540b — IV, 564a
al-Ḥaddād, Nadjīb i, 597a — I, 616b
Ḥaddād, Nudra v, 1254b, 1255a, b — V, 1245b, 1246a, b
al-Ḥaddād, al-Ṭāhir iv, 161a; s, **334a** — IV, 168a; S, 333b
Haddūḳa, A.H. ben v, 191a — V, 188a
Hadendoa → Bedja
Ḥādha s, 198b — S, 198b
Hadhbānīs v, 451b, 453b — V, 454a, 456a
Ḥadhf → Naḥw
Ḥadhw iv, 412a — IV, 430a
al-Hādī ila 'l-Ḥaḳḳ (ʿAbbāsid(e)) i, 14a, 17b, 402b, 1034a, 1045b, 1298a; iii, 20a, **22a,** 29a, 231a, 232b, 617a, 742a, 996a; iv, 645a, 1164a; s, 22a, 326b — I,

14a, 18a, 414a, 1065b, 1077a, 1338a; III, 21a, **23a,** 30b, 238a, 239b, 637b, 764b, 1021a; IV, 671b, 1196a; S, 22b, 326a
al-Hādī ila ʾl-Ḥaḳḳ Yaḥyā (Zaydī) i, 551b; iii, 617b; v, 1241a; s, **334b**, 358a — I, 569a; III, 638a; V, 1231b; S, **334b**, 358a
Hādī Sabzawārī → Sabzawārī
al-Ḥadīd iii, **22b**; iv, 819b; v, 964b, 966a, 967b, 971a, 978a, 1166b — III, **23b**; IV, 852a; V, 969a, 970b, 973b, 1156a, b
Ḥadīḍ → Nudjūm
Ḥadīdī iii, **22b** — III, **23b**
al-Ḥāḍina iii, **23a** — III, **24a**
Ḥādir s, 48b — S, 49a
al-Ḥādira iii, **23a** — III, **24b**
Ḥadīth i, 25b, 258b, 326a, 410a, 566a, 589b, 1021a, b; ii, 71a, 125b, 448a, 729a, 889a; iii, **23b,** 369b, 435a; iv, 148a, b, 172a, 767b, 983b, 995a, 1107a, 1112a, 1135b; v, 1123b, 1132b, 1232a, b — I, 26b, 266b, 336a, 421b, 584b, 608b, 1052b, 1053a; II, 72a, 128b, 460a, 747b, 909b; III, **24b,** 381a, 449a; IV, 154a, b, 179b, 798a, 1016a, 1027b, 1138b, 1143b, 1167b; V, 1120a, 1128b, 1222b
- literature/littérature i, 59a, 60b, 106b, 158b, 273b; ii, 159a; iii, 927a — I, 61a, 62b, 109b, 163a, 281b; II, 164a; III, 951b
- scholars/spécialistes i, 104b, 129a, 143a, 272b, 275b, 485b, 791a, 1130a, 1296b; ii, 136a, 292b, 301a; iii, 82a, 821a, 848b, 860b, 874a — I, 107b, 133a, 147a, 280b, 284a, 500a, 814b, 1164b, 1336a; II, 139b, 300b, 309a; III, 84b, 844b, 872b, 884b, 898a
Ḥadīth Ḳudsī i, 88b; iii, **28b,** 101b; s, 83a — I, 91a; III, **30a,** 104a; S, 82b
Ḥadītha iv, 855b — IV, 888b
Ḥadīthat al-Furāt iii, **29b** — III, **31a**
Ḥadīthat al-Mawṣil iii, **29a** — III, **30b**
Ḥadīthat al-Nūra → Ḥadīthat al-Furāt
Hadiyya iii, 343a, 346b, 347b, 350a — III, 353a, 357a, 358a, 361a
Hadj → Ḥadjdj
Hadjar → al-Ḥasā
Hadjar (town/ville) iii, **29b** — III, **31a**
Ḥadjar (stone/pierre) iii, **29b**; iv, 1128b; v, 117b — III, **31a**; IV, 1160a; V, 120a
al-Hadjar, Djabal i, 536b — I, 552b
al-Ḥadjar al-Aswad i, 178a, 551b, 867a; ii, 453a; iv, 317a, b, 319a, b, 321b, 662a, b; v, 10a, 77b, 78a — I, 182b, 569a, 891b; II, 465a; IV, 331b, 332a, 333a, b, 335b, 688b, 689b; V, 10a, 79b, 80a
Ḥadjar Bādis i, 859b — I, 883b
Hadjar Ḥinū al-Zarīr iii, 208a; iv, 747a — III, 214a; IV, 777a
Ḥadjar al-Nasr iii, **30b** — III, **32a**
Hadjarayn iii, **31a** — III, **32b**
Ḥadjdj i, 178a, 443b; iii, **31b,** 927a, 1052b; iv, 320b, 322a; v, 424b, 897a, b, 1003a, 1004a — I, 182b, 456a; III, **33a,** 951b, 1078b; IV, 334b, 336b; V, 427a, 903b, 998b, 1000a
Hadjbūn al-Randāḥī, Abu ʾl-ʿAbbās s, 112a — S, 111a
Ḥādjdj(ī) iii, 38b — III, 40a
al-Ḥadjdj al-ʿArbī v, 596b — V, 600a, b
Ḥadjdj, Baʾl ii, 730a — II, 748b
al-Ḥādjdj al-Gharnāṭī ii, 901b — II, 922b
al-Ḥādjdj Ḥammūda iii, **38b** — III, **40a**
Ḥādjdj Muḥammad Ṭrīḳı iii, 247a — III, 254a
al-Ḥādjdj ʿUmar i, 297a, 303b; ii, 63a, 252b, 941b, 1132b; iii, **38b,** 107b, 289a — I, 306a, 313a; II, 64a, b, 259b, 963b, 1159a,b; III, **40a,** 110a, 298a
Ḥadjdjādj → Ḳutlugh Khāns
Ḥadjdjādj, Banū iv, 115b — IV, 120b
al-Ḥadjdjādj b. ʿAbd al-Malik b. Marwān ii, 280b, 304b, 480a; iii, 73a, 573b — II, 289a, 313a, 492a; III, 75b, 593a
Ḥadjdjādj b. Arṭāt i, 896b — I, 923a
Ḥadjdjādj b. Hurmuz i, 512b — I, 528a
Ḥadjādj b. Yūsuf b. Maṭar s, 411b — S, 412a
al-Ḥadjdjādj b. Yūsuf al-Ḥāsib iii, **43a,** 1136b, 1138b — III, **45a,** 1164b, 1166b
al-Ḥadjdjādj b. Yūsuf al-Thaḳafī i, 42b, 54a, 55b, 76b, 77b, 105a, 142a, 482a, 485, 550a, 690b, 714a, 810b, 1005b, 1094b; ii, 27a, 195b, 197a,b, 561b, 788b; iii, **39b,** 247b, 649a, 715a,b, 716a, 717a, 841b, 970a, 1255a, 1267a; iv, 15a, 99b, 319b, 531b, 724b, 753a, 1075b, 1076a; v, 541a, 735b, 947b; s, 230b, 243a, 354b — I, 43b, 56a, 57a, 79a, 79b, 108a, 146b, 496a, 499a, 567b, 711b, 735b, 833b, 1036a, 1127a; II, 27b, 202a, 203a, 204a, 574b, 807a; III, **41b,** 254b, 670b, 737b, 738a, 739a, b, 865b, 994b, 1287b, 1300a; IV, 16a-b, 104a, 333b, 554b, 753b, 783b, 1107b; V, 545b, 740b, 951b; S, 230b, 243a, 354b
Ḥadjdjām → Faṣṣād
Ḥadjdjī I, al-Muẓaffar ii, 24a; iii, 48a, 239b — II, 24b; III, 50a, 246b
Ḥadjdjī II i, 1050b, 1051a; ii, 159a — I, 1082a,b; II, 164a
Ḥādjdjī Aḥmad iv, 1082b — IV, 1114a
Ḥādjdjī ʿAlī-ḳulī Khān Bakhtīyarī s, 291a — S, 290b
Ḥādjdjī ʿAlī Pasha i, 268a, 394a — I, 276b, 405a
Ḥādjdjī Bayrām Walī i, 312b, 509b, 511a, 869a, 1137a, 1202a; ii, 542b; iii, **43a**; s, 282b — I, 322b, 525a, 526b, 893b, 1171b, 1237b; II, 556a; III, **45a**; S, 282b
Hādjdjī Beg → Riḍwān Begovič
Ḥādjdjī Bektāsh Walī i, 299a, 1161b, 1162a; ii, 20b; iii, 315a; iv, 811b — I, 308a, 1196a, 1197a; II, 20b; III, 324b; IV, 844b
Ḥādjdjī al-Dabīr s, **335b** — S, **335a**
Hādjdjī Dāwūd ii, 87b; v, 296b — II, 89b; V, 288a
Ḥādjdjī Girāy i, 1252b; ii, 44b, 1112b, 1113a; iii, **43b**; iv, 868b; v, 137a — I, 1290b; II, 45a, 1138b, 1139a; III, **45b**; IV, 902a; V, 140a
Ḥādjdjī Hāshim s, 336a — S, 335b
Ḥādjdjī Ibrāhīm Khān Kalāntar iii, 1106a; iv, 391b, 392a, 394a, 476a, 706a; v, 835a; s, **336a** — III, 1133b; IV, 408a, b, 410b, 497a, 734b; V, 841a, b; S, **335b**
Ḥādjdjī Ilbegi ii, 291b — II, 299b
Ḥādjdjī Ismāʿīl Agha i, 284b — I, 293a
Ḥādjdjī Ḳawām al-Dīn Shīrāzī s, 336a — S, 335b
Ḥādjdjī Khalīfa → Kātib Čelebi
Ḥādjdjī Maḥmūd ʿAlī s, 336a — S, 335b
Ḥādjdjī Mawlá iv, 922a — IV, 955a
Ḥādjdjī Mīrzā Āghāsī i, 833b; iii, 554b; iv, 393a, b, 394a, 395b, 978b; v, 876a, 1222a — I, 856b; III, 573b; IV, 410a, 411a, 412b, 1011a; V, 882a, 1212b
Ḥādjdjī Mīrzā ʿAlī Khān → Faḳīr of/de Ipi
Hādjdjī Muḥammad i, 1124a — I, 1158a
Ḥādjdjī Mullā Taḳi Barakānī i, 304b — I, 314a
Hādjdjī Nasīm Oghlu → Nasīm Oghlu
Ḥādjdjī Niʿmat Allāh → Niʿmat Allāh
Ḥādjdjī Pasha i, 299b; iii, **45a** — I, 309a; III, **46b**
Ḥādjdjī Shādgeldī i, 432a — I, 444a
Ḥādjdjī ʿUmar i, 1304a — I, 1344a
Ḥadjdjilu iv, 577b — IV, 601a
Hadji → Ḥādjdjī
Ḥādjib i, 5b, 94a; ii, 507b; iii, **45a,** 360a; iv, 421b; s, **336b** — I, 6a, 96b; II, 520a; III **47a,** 371b; IV, 439b; S, **336a**
Ḥādjib b. Zurāra ii, 354a; iii, **49a**; v, 640b — II, 363b; III, **51a**; V, 644b
Ḥādjib al-Tāʿī iii, 650b — III, 671b
Ḥadjiewad → Karagöz
al-Ḥādjir s, 198b — S, 198b
Hādjir, Banū iii, **49b** — III, **51b**

Ḥādjiz i, 940b — I, 969b
Ḥādjiz b. ʿAwf i, 812a — I, 835a
Ḥādjō Agha i, 871b — I, 895b
Ḥadjr i, 993b; iii, **50a** — I, 1024a; III, **52a**
Ḥadjr, Wādī s, 337a — S, 337a
Hadjw iii, 358b — III, 369b
Ḥaḍn i, 536a — I, 552b
al-Ḥaḍr i, 196b; iii, **50b** — I, 202a; III, **52b**
Ḥaḍra iii, **51a**; iv, 942a; s, 93a — III, **53a**; IV, 975a; S, 93a
al-Ḥadrabī i, 782b — I, 805b
Ḥaḍramawt i, 39b, 55a, 110b, 257a, 538a, 546b, 547b, 549b, 551b, 554a, 780b, 828b; iii, **51b**; s, **336b**, 420b — I, 40b, 57a, 113b, 265a, 555a, 563b, 565a, 567a, 569a, 571b, 804a, 851b; III, **53b**; S, **336b**, 420b
Ḥaḍramawt b. Ḥimyar s, 337a — S, 337a
Ḥaḍramī i, 553a, 553b; iii, 52a; iv, 886a — I, 571a; III, 54a; IV, 919a
Ḥaḍrat Bēgam i, 296a — I, 305a
Ḥaḍrat Maḥall, Bēgam i, 953b — I, 983a
Ḥaḍrat al-mallūk iv, 382b — IV, 399b
Ḥaḍrat Mīrzā Bashīr al-Dīn Maḥmūd Aḥmad i, 302a — I, 311a
Ḥaḍrat-i Rāz iv, 51b — IV, 54b
Ḥaḍūr Shuʿayb i, 536a; iii, **53a** — I, 552b; III, **55a**
Hady iii, **53b** — III, **55b**
Hadyā i, 176b; iii, 3b — I, 181a; III, 3b
Ḥafar al-Bāṭin → Bāṭin
Ḥaffār (Hafar) iv, 675a; v, 65b, 66a — IV, 702b; V, 67b
Ḥāfī i, 1246a — I, 1284a
al-Ḥāfī → Bishr
Hafik v, 248a — V, 246a
Ḥāfiẓ → Ḳurʾān
Ḥafiz Tanîsh v, 859b — V, 866b
al-Ḥāfiẓ (Fāṭimid(e)) i, 814b, 939b, 1215a; ii, 170b, 855a, 857b; iii, **54b**; iv, 200a, b— I, 837b, 968,b, 1251a; II, 175b, 875a, 877a; III, **56b**; IV, 209a
Ḥāfiẓ, ʿAbd al-(ʿAlawī) i, 58a, 357b, 1281b; ii, 820a, 1116a; iii, **62a**, 562b; v, 890b, 1193b; s, 47b — I, 59b, 368a, 1320b; II, 839b, 1142b; III, **64b**, 581b; V, 897a, 1183b; S, 48a
al-Ḥāfiẓ, Mawlāy → Ḥāfiz, ʿAbd al-
Ḥāfiẓ, Mullā s, 292a — S, 291b
Ḥāfiẓ, Shams al-Dīn i, 153a, 1301a; ii, 439b, 760b, 1034a; iii, **55a**; iv, 56b, 65b, 909b; v, 671a; s, 35a, 415a — I, 157b, 1341a; II, 451a, 779a, 1058a; III, **57b**; IV, 59b, 69a, 942b; V, 676b; S, 35a, 415a
Ḥāfiẓ ʿAbd Allāh i, 1023a — I, 1054b
Ḥāfiẓ-i Abrū i, 607a, 1131a; iii, **57b**, 574b; iv, 1082a — I, 627a, 1165b; III, **59b**, 594a; IV, 1113a
Ḥāfiẓ ʿAfīfī Pasha iii, 515b; s, 301a — III, 533a; S, 301a
Ḥāfiẓ Agha i, 289b — I, 298a
Ḥafiẓ Aḥmad, Mawlawī iv, 626a — IV 650b
Ḥāfiẓ Aḥmed Pasha i, 4a, 962b; ii, 635a, 750b; iii, **58a**; iv, 483b; v, 33a, 34a, b, 458a — I, 4a, 992a; II, 651a, 769a; III, **60b**; IV, 504b; V, 34a, 35a, b, 460b
Ḥāfiẓ al-Asad v, 1049a — V, 1045b
al-Ḥāfiẓ al-Dimashḳi → Ibn ʿAsākir
Ḥāfiẓ al-Dīn → al-Nasafī
Ḥafīz Djāllandharī iii, 119b — III, 122a
Ḥāfiẓ Djawnpūrī i, 1284a — I, 1323b
Ḥāfiz Ghulām Rasūl Shawḳ ii, 221b — II, 228b
Ḥāfiẓ Ibrāhīm i, 597b; iii, **59a**; iv, 159b, 967b; s, 57b — I, 617a; III, **61b**; IV, 166b, 999b; S, 58a
Hāfiz Ismāʿīl Haḳḳī ii, 637b, 698b, 699b — II, 653b, 716a, 717b
Ḥāfiẓ Muṣṭafā s, 282b — S, 282a
Ḥāfiẓ ʿOthmān iv, 1125a — IV, 1157a
Ḥāfiẓ Raḥmat Khān i, 1042b, 1043a; iii, **59b** — I, 1074b; III, **62a**
Ḥāfiẓ Ramaḍān iii, 515b — III, 533a
al-Ḥāfiẓ al-Samarḳandī i, 137a — I, 141a
Ḥāfiẓ Tanîsh s, 227b, 340a — S, 227b, 339b
Ḥāfiẓābād iii, **62b** — III, **65a**
Ḥāfiẓiyya iv, 200b — IV, 209a, b
Ḥafīẓ-uddīn iv, 505a — IV, 526b
al-Ḥafnāwī s, 403b — S, 403b
Ḥafrak iii, **63a** — III, **65b**
Ḥafṣ b. Sulaymān → Abū Salama
Ḥafs b. Sulaymān i, 707a; iii, **63a** — I, 728a; III, **65b**
Ḥafṣ al-Fard iii, **63b**; s, 88b, 225b — III, **66a**; S, 88b, 225b
Ḥafṣa bint al-Ḥādjdj iii, **66a** — III, **68b**
Ḥafṣa bint ʿUmar b. al-Khaṭṭāb i, 308a; ii, 414b; iii, **63b** — I, 317b; II, 425a; III, **66a**
Ḥafṣid(e)s i, 92b, 121b, 122b, 124b, 155a, 445b, 533a, 770b, 863a, 1027b, 1046a, 1148b, 1176b, 1205b, 1246b, 1341a; ii, 145a, 146a, 307b, 459b, 463b, 537a, 1077b; iii, 38b, **66a**; iv, 338a; v, 530b, 626a, b, 1190a, 1247a; s, 93a, b, 111b, 307b — I, 95b, 125a, 126a, 128a, 159a, 458a, 549b, 793b, 887a, 1059a, 1078a, 1183a, 1211b, 1241a, 1284b, 1381b; II, 149a, b, 316b, 471b, 475b, 550b, 1102b; III, 40a, **68b**; IV, 352b; V, 531a, 630a, 1180a, 1237b; S, 92b, 93a, 111a, 307a
Ḥafsiyya iii, 660a — III, 681a
Haft-Lang i, 955b; iii, 1105a,b; v, 825b — I, 985a; III, 1132b; V, 832a
Hagar iv, 184b, 185a — IV, 193a
Haggada iv, 307b, 308a — IV, 321b
Hagiography/Hagiographie → Manāḳib
Ḥāḥā iii, **69b** — III, **72a**
Ḥāḥiyyūn iii, 339a — III, 349a
Haifa → Ḥayfā
Ḥāʾik → Libās
Ḥāʾik s, **340b** — S, **340b**
al-Ḥāʾik, Muḥammad iii, **70a** — III, **72b**
Ḥāʾil → Ḥāyil
Ḥāʾir i, 535b, 613b; iii, **71a** — I, 552a, 633b; III, **73b**
Ḥāʾirī, ʿAbd al-Karīm Yazdī iv, 1028b; s, 157b, 158a, **342a** — IV, 1060b; S, 158a, **341b**
Ḥāʾiṭ al-ʿAdjūz iii, **71a** — III, **73b**
Ḥaḳāʾiḳ iii, **71b**, 134a — III, **74a**, 136b
Ḥaḳāḳiyya iv, 668a — IV, 695b
Ḥakam iii, **72a** — III, **74b**
al-Ḥakam I i, 11a, 12b; ii, 1038a; iii, **73b**; iv, 216b; s, 82a — I, 11a, 12b; II, 1062a; III, **76a**; IV, 226a; S, 81b
al-Ḥakam II i, 156b, 494a, 498b, 601b, 628a, 864b, 950a, 1088a, 1291a; ii, 956a, 957a; iii, 30b, 46a, **74b**, 762b; v, 71b, 511a, 1119a — I, 161a, 509a, 513b, 621a, 649a, 889a, 979a, 1120b, 1330b; II, 978a, 979a; III, 32b, 48a, **77a**, 785b; V, 73b, 514b, 1115b
al-Ḥakam b. ʿAbdal iii, **72b**; s, 52a — III, **75a**; S, 52b
al-Ḥakam b. Abi ʾl-ʿĀs ii, 811b — II, 831a
Hakam b. ʿAmr al-Ghifarī ii, 1072b — II, 1097a
al-Ḥakam b. Ḳanbar iii, **73a** — III, **75b**
Ḥakam b. Saʿd ii, 516b; iii, **73b** — II, 529b; III, **76a**
Ḥakam b. Saʿīd al-Ḳazzāz iii, 496a — III, 513a
al-Ḥakam b. ʿUtayba s, 129b — S, 129a
al-Ḥakam b. al-Walīd II iii, 990b — III, 1015a
al-Ḥakam Abū Marwān I s, 103b — S, 103a
al-Ḥakamī → Abū Nuwās; al-Djarrāḥ b. ʿAbd Allāh; ʿUmāra b. ʿAlī
Hakari → Ḥakkārī
Ḥakhām, Simon iv, 310b — IV, 324b
Ḥaḳīḳa iii, **75a**, 1240b; v, 1261a, 1262a — III, **77b**, 1272b; V, 1252b, 1253a
Ḥakīm → Ṭabīb
Hakīm, Mīrzā → Muḥammad Hakīm
al-Ḥakīm, Tawfīḳ i, 598a, 598b; v, 189a, b, 191b, 192b — I, 617b, 618a; V, 186b, 187a, 188b, 189b
al-Ḥākim bi-Amr Allāh (Fāṭimid(e)) i, 620a, 814b,

816a, 1029a, 1042a, 1141a, 1218a; ii, 125b, 126b, 127a, 136b, 169b, 229a, 232b, 483b, 495b, 631b, 854a, 855a, 857a, 859b, 911b; iii, **76b,** 130b, 154a; iv, 199a, 944a; v, 91b, 327b, 1125b; s, 136a, 267b, 323a — I, 640b, 837b, 839b, 1060b, 1073b, 1175b, 1254b; II, 129a, 130a,b, 140a, 174b, 236a, 239a, 496a, 508a, 647b, 874a, 875a, 877a, 879a, 932b; III, **79a,** 133a, 157b; IV, 207b, 977a; V, 94a, 327b, 1122a; S, 135b, 267a, 322b
al-Ḥākim I bi-Amr Allāh (ʿAbbāsid(e)) ii, 966a; iii, 679a; iv, 944b — II, 988a; III, 701a; IV, 977b
Ḥakīm b. Ḥizām i, 151b; iv, 898b — I, 155b; IV, 931b
Ḥakīm Ata i, 299a; iii, **76b** — I, 308a; III, **78b**
Ḥakim ʿAyn al-Mulk i, 856b, — I, 880a
Ḥakīm-Bashî → Hekīm -Dashî
al-Ḥākim al-Djushāmī s, 14b, 90b, **343a** — S, 14b, 90a, **342b**
Ḥakīm Idrīs → Bidlīsī, Idrīs
Ḥakim Maysarī iv, 63a — IV, 66b
al-Ḥākim al-Naysābūrī ii, 136a; iii, 25a, 27a, 28a, **82a** — II, 139b; III, 26a, 28b, 29b, **84b**
al-Ḥākim al-Shahīd iii, 163a — III, 166b
Ḥaḳīrī al-Ādharbāydjānī v, 1105b — V, 1101b
Ḥaḳḳ i, 60b, 275a; ii, 294b; iii, **82b** — I, 62b, 283b; II, 302b; III, **84b**
Ḥaḳḳ al-Dīn i, 763b — I, 786b
Hakkārī iii, **83a,** 1109a; v, 452b, 454b, 456b, 459b, 462b — III, **85b,** 1136b; V, 455a, 457a, 459a, 462b, 465a
al-Hakkārī, ʿAdī → ʿAdī b. Musāfir
al-Hakkārī, ʾAlāʿ al-Dīn ii, 966a; iii, 680a — II, 988a; III, 702a
al-Hakkārī, Ibn ʿAbd Allāh iv, 137a — IV, 143a
al-Ḥakkārī, ʿIsā iv, 613a — IV, 638a
Ḥaḳḳī → ʿAbd al-Ḥaḳḳ b. Sayf al-Dīn
Ḥaḳḳī → Ibrāhīm Ḥaḳḳī; Ismāʿīl Ḥaḳḳī
Haḳḳī, Yaḥyā v, 190b, 191a, 192a — V, 187b, 188b, 189a
Ḥāl (attribut(e)) s, **343b** — S, **343a**
Ḥāl (grammar, grammaire) → Naḥw
Ḥāl, aḥwāl (Ṣūfī) i, 411a, 603b, 1088b; ii, 570a; iii, **83b** — I, 423a, 623a, 1121a; II, 584b; III, **85b**
Ḥalab i, 256a, 824b, 983b; ii, 795a; iii, **85a,** 120a, 129a,b, 130b, 212b, 1118b; v, 561a, 923b, 925b, 1211a; s, 19a, 36a, 37b, 49a, 197a, 239a — I, 264a, 847b, 1014a; II, 814a; III, **87a,** 122b, 131b, 132a, 133a, 218b, 1146a; V, 566a, 929a, 931a, 1201a; S, 19a, 36b, 38a, 49b, 197a, 239a
- history of, l'histoire de- i, 823a; iii, 695b — I, 846a; III, 717b
- institutions i, 1224a; ii, 83b, 424a; iii, 89a, 139b — I, 1260b; II, 85a, 435a; III, 91b, 142b
- monuments i, 830a, 1317b; iii, 87a, b, 88a, b; v, 1139a — I, 853a, 1358b; III, 89b, 90a, b, 91a; V, 1133a
Ḥalabdja ii, 371a — II, 381a
al-Ḥalabī, Burhān al-Dīn iii, **90a,** 163b, 711a — III, **92b,** 167a, 733b
al-Ḥalabī, Nūr al-Dīn iii, **90b** — III, **93a**
Ḥalaḳat Dimashḳ al-saghīra iii, 519a — III, 536b
Ḥalāl wa Ḥarām → Sharīʿa
Halāward s, 125a — S, 124b
Ḥālet Efendi i, 399a, 399b; ii, 209b; iii, **90b,** 628b; iv, 295a — I, 410b, 411a; II, 216a; III, **93a,** 649b; IV, 308b
Haletī ʿAlī Aʿlā, Ḥasan iv, 991b — IV, 1024a
Ḥāletī, ʿAzmī-zāde Muṣṭafā i, 826a; iii, **91b** — I, 849a; III, **94a**
Halevi, Judah iv, 304b — IV, 318a
Halevi, Moses ben Joseph iv, 305a — IV, 318b
al-Ḥalf iv, 687b, 689a — IV, 715b, 717a
Ḥalfāʾ iii, **92a** — III, **94b**
Ḥalfāyat al-Mulūk iv, 893a — IV, 925b
Ḥālī → Bannāʾī
Ḥalī → Ḥaly
Ḥālī, Alṭāf Ḥusayn i, 807b; iii, **93b,** 119b, 433a; iv, 170b; v, 202a, 962a; s, 74b, 106a, 107a, b — I, 851a; III, **96a,** 122a, 447a; IV, 178a; V, 199b, 966a; S, 75b, 105b, 106b, 107a
Halide Edīb → Khālide Edīb
Haliḳarnas Balîḳcîsî v, 195a, 197a; s, **348b** — V, 192a, 194b; S, **348b**
Halil Kut → Khalīl Pasha
Halīladj iv, 357a; s, **349a** — IV, 372b; S, **349a**
Ḥalīm b. Muḥammad ʿAlī i, 142a; s, 296a — I, 146a; S, 296a
Ḥalīma iii, **94a** — III, **96b**
Ḥalīma bint Abī Dhuʾayb i, 957b; iii, **94a** — I, 987a; III, **96b**
Ḥalīmī, Luṭf Allāh iv, 526a — IV, 548b
Ḥalḳ Fîrkasî → Khalḳ Fîrkasî
Ḥalḳ al-Wādī i, 281b; iii, **94b**; s, 80b — I, 290b; III, **97a**; S, 80b
Ḥalḳa (councils, conseils) i, 817a; ii, 141a; iii, **95a**; v, 1129a, 1134a, 1158b — I, 840a; II, 145a; III, **97b**; V, 1125b, 1129b, 1148a
Ḥalḳa (soldiers, soldats) i, 765b, 947a; iii, **99a,** 185b — I, 788b, 976a; III, **101b,** 189b
Ḥalḳa (sūfism(e)) → Taṣawwuf
Ḥalḳa (tactic/tactique) iii, 187b — III, 192a
Halkevi → Khalḳevi
Halkevleri i, 734b; ii, 596b — I, 756b; II, 611b
Halkodalarî ii, 596b; iv, 988a — II, 611b; IV, 1020b
al-Ḥallādj i, 46a, 324b, 387b, 416a, 753a, 754a, 951a, 1128b; ii, 197b, 223b, 734a, 891b; iii, 83a, **99b,** 165b, 620a, 669b, 700a, 1207a; iv, 114b, 615b, 616b; v, 543b; s, 385b — I, 47a, 334b, 399a, 428a, 775b, 776b, 980a, 1163a; II, 204a, 230b, 752b, 912a; III, 85a, **102a,** 169a, 640b, 691a, 722a, 1237b; IV, 119b, 640a, 641a; V, 548a; S, 386a
Ḥallādjīn v, 559a — V, 564a
Ḥallādjiyya ii, 224b; iii, 103a, 823b — II, 231b; III, 105b, 847a
Ḥallāḳ s, **350a** — S, **350a**
al-Ḥallāniyya i, 535b; iii, 270a — I, 551b; III, 278a
Ḥālūmat al-ṭībāʿ al-tāmm iv, 260a — IV, 271b
Halvetiyye → Khalwatiyya
Ḥalwa → Ghidhāʾ
Ḥaly iii, **104b** — III, **106b**
Haly Abbas → ʿAli b. al-ʿAbbās
Halys (river, fleuve) → Kîzîl-Irmāk
Ḥām iii, **104b**; v, 521a, b — III, **107a**; V, 525a
Ḥamā(h) → Ḥamāt
Ḥamā Allāh Ḥaydara iii, 107a, b, 108a, 289a — III, 109b, 110a, b, 298a
al-Ḥamād i, 536b; iii, 1253a — I, 553a; III, 1285b
Ḥamad b. ʿĪsa iv, 954a — IV, 986a
Ḥamad ʿImrān i, 1239b — I, 1277b
Ḥamāda, Banū ii, 568b — II, 583a
al-Hamadanī → ʿAlī
Hamadhān i, 426a, 840a; iii, **105a,** 761b; iv, 3a, 7b, 13b, 465a; v, 171a; s, 2b, 84a, 118b, 142b — I, 438a, 863a; III, **107b,** 784b; IV, 3b, 8b, 14b, 486a; V, 168b; S, 2a, 83b, 142a
al-Hamadhānī, Abū Saʿd ʿAlī s, 119b — S, 119a
al-Hamadhānī, ʿAyn al-Ḳuḍāt → ʿAbd Allāh b. Abī Bakr al-Miyānadjī
al-Hamadhānī → Ibn al-Faḳīh; Yūsuf
al-Hamadhānī, Badīʿ al-Zamān i, 116a, 331b, 590b; ii, 246a; iii, **106a,** 368a, 373a, 764a, 1264a; iv, 1069b; v, 132b, 768b, 1010a; s, 17a, 31a — I, 119b, 341b, 610a; II, 253a; III, **108b,** 379b, 384b, 787b, 1297a; IV, 1101a; V, 135b, 774b, 1005b; S, 17b, 31a
Ḥamādisha/Ḥmādsha s, 53a, **350b** — S, 53b, **350b**

Ḥamadu → Aḥmadu
Ḥamāʾil → Siḥr; Tamāʾim; Ṭilasm
al-Ḥamal → Minṭaḳat al-Burūdj; Nudjūm
Ḥamal b. Badr al-Fazārī s, 177b, 178a — S, 178b, 179a
Ḥamāliyya, Hamallism(e) i, 1009a; ii, 63a, 94b; iii, **107a** — I, 1040a; II, 64b, 96b; III, **109b**
Ḥamāllāh, Shaykh → Ḥamā Allāh Ḥaydara
Ḥamām iii, **108b**; v, 924b — III, **111a**; V, 930a
Ḥamāma s, 144b — S, 144a, b
Ḥamāma b. al-Muʿizz b. ʿAṭiyya v, 1177b — V, 1167b
Hāmān iii, **110a**; iv, 673a — III, **112b**; IV, 700b
Hāmarz iii, **110b**, 586a — III, **113a**, 606a
Ḥamāsa i, 154b, 584b, 586a, 892a; iii, **110b**; s, 32b, **351a** — I, 159a, 603a, 605a, 918b; III, **113a**; S, 32b, **351a**
Hamasāla iv, 1045a — IV, 1076a
Ḥamāt i, 118b, 609b; iii, **119b**; v, 923a, 925a — I, 122a, 629b; III, **122a**; V, 928b, 930b
Hamawand iii, **121b** — III, **124a**
Ḥamawī → Saʿd al-Dīn Ḥamawī
al-Ḥamawī → Ibn Ḥidjdja; Yāḳūt
Ḥamawiya, Banū → Awlād al-Shaykh
al-Hamaysaʿ b. Ḥimyar iii, 124a — III, 127a
Ḥamḍ, Wādī al- i, 538a; iii, **121b** — I, 554b; III, **124a**
Ḥamd Allāh, Shaykh iv, 1125a — IV, 1156b
Ḥamd Allāh Mustawfī al-Ḳazwīnī i, 358b, 903a; iii, 114a, **122a**; iv, 859a, b, 863a, 1051b, 1052a, 1081b, 1082a; s, 235a, 382b — I, 369a, 930b; III, 116b, **124b**; IV, 892a, b, 896a, 1083a, b, 1113a; S, 234b, 383a
Ḥamdala iii, **122b** — III, **125a**
Ḥamdallāhi i, 303a; ii, 941b; iii, 39b — I, 312b; II, 963b; III, 41a
Hamdān i, 544b, 548a; iii, **123a**; v, 346a — I, 561b, 565b; III, **125b**; V, 347a
Ḥamdān b. Ḥamdūn iii, 126a; iv, 89b — III, 129a; IV, 93b
Ḥamdān b. Nāṣir al-Dawla iii, 127b, 128a — III, 130b, 131a
Ḥamdān Abū ʿAndja iv, 687a — IV, 715a
Ḥamdān Ḳarmaṭ iii, **123b**, 198a, b, 660b — III, **126a**, 206b, 207a, 687a
al-Hamdānī → ʿĪsā b. ʿUmar
al-Ḥamdānī, Abū Muḥammad (Ibn al-Ḥāʾik) i, 534a; iii, 123b, **124a**, 1077a; iv, 335a; v, 110b, 113b; s, 341b — I, 550b; III, 126a, **126b**, 1103b; IV, 350a; V, 113a, 116b; S, 341b
Ḥamdānid(e)s (Syria/Syrie) i, 19a, 119b, 215a, 439b, 637b, 679b, 824b, 1046b, 1354b; ii, 281b, 348b, 524a; iii, **126a**, 398a; iv, 23b-24a — I, 20a, 123a, 221b, 452a, 658b, 700b, 847b, 1078b, 1394a; II, 290a, 358a, 537a; III, **128b**, 410b; IV, 25b
Hamdānid(e)s (Yemen/Yémen) iii, **125a**, 259b; v, 820a, b; s, 62a — III, **128a**, 267a; V, 826b; S, 62b
al-Ḥamdawī, Abū ʿAlī Ismāʿīl s, **352a** — S, **352a**
Ḥamdī (d. 1911) iv, 806b — IV, 839a
Ḥamdī, Ḥamd Allāh iii, **131a** — III, **133b**
Ḥamdī Bey → ʿOthmān Ḥamdī Bey
Ḥamdīs b. ʿAbd-al-Raḥmān al-Kindī i, 248a — I, 255b
Ḥamdūn, Banū → Ibn Ḥamdūn
Ḥamdūn ibn al-Ḥādjdj → Ibn al-Ḥādjdj
Ḥamdūn al-Ḳassār iii, **132a** — III, **134b**
al-Ḥamdūnī → al-Ḥamdawī, Abū ʿAlī Ismāʿīl
Ḥāmī iii, **132a** — III, **135a**
Ḥāmī iii, 394b — III, 407a
Ḥāmī-i Āmidī iii, **132b** — III, **135a**
Ḥāmī 'l-Ḥaramayn → Khādim al-Ḥaramayn
Hamian i, 372a — I, 382b
Ḥamīd, Ḥamīd-oghullari̊ i, 467b, 468a; ii, 692a; iii, **132b**; iv, 210b — I, 481b, 482a; II, 709a; III, **135b**; IV, 220a
Ḥamīd, Sayyid s, 1b — S, 1b
Ḥāmid b. al-ʿAbbās i, 387a; iii, 100b, 101a, **133a**, 739a, 767b; iv, 100a; v, 737a — I, 398a; III, 103a, b, **136a**, 761b, 791a; IV, 104b; V, 742a
Ḥāmid b. Muḥammad al-Murdjibī → al-Murdjibī
Ḥāmid b. Mūsā al-Ḳayṣarī i, 869a; iii, 43b — I, 893b; III, 45a
Ḥāmid b. Saʿīd i, 1281b — I, 1321a
Ḥamīd Allāh Khān i, 1195b, 1196a, b — I, 1231a, b
Ḥamīd al-Anṣārī s, 247b — S, 247b
Ḥamīd al-Dawla Ḥātim iii, 125b — III, 128b
Ḥamīd al-Dīn b. ʿAmʿaḳ → Ḥamīdī b. ʿAmʿaḳ
Ḥamīd al-Dīn Ḳāḍī Nāgawrī s, **353a** — S, **353a**
Ḥamīd al-Dīn al-Kirmānī → al-Kirmānī, Ḥamīd al-Dīn
Ḥamīd al-Dīn Ṣūfī Nāgawrī Siwālī ii, 51a, 55b; s, **353b** — II, 52a, 56b; S, **353a**
Ḥāmid Efendi ii, 56b — II, 57b
Ḥamīd Ḳalandar i, 1329a; ii, 48b, 55b; s, 352b — I, 1369b; II, 49a, 56b; S, 352b
Ḥamīd Kashmīrī i, 72a — I, 74a
Ḥamīd Khān (Dihlī) (XVth c./XVᵉ s.) v, 783b — V, 789b
Ḥamīd Khān (Ḥabshī) iii, 15b; iv, 1018b — III, 16a; IV, 1050b
Ḥamīd Pasha → Khalīl Ḥamīd
Ḥamīda Bānū Begam i, 316a, 1135b; iii, 455b — I, 326a, 1170a; III, 471b
Ḥamīd-oghullari̊ → Ḥamīd
Ḥamīdābād → Isparta
Ḥāmidī iii, **133b** — III, **136a**
al-Ḥamidī, ʿAlī b. Ḥātim iii, 125b, **134a**; v, 954b; s, 62a — III, 128b, **137a**; V, 958a; S, 62a
Ḥamīdī, Ḥamīd al-Dīn iii, **134b** — III, **137a**
al-Ḥāmidī, Ḥātim b. Ibrāhīm iii, **134a** — III, **137a**
al-Ḥāmidī, Ibrāhīm b. al-Ḥusayn iii, 72a, **134a**; iv, 200b, 204b; v, 894a — III, 14b, **136b**; IV, 209a, 213b; V, 900b
Ḥamīdī b. ʿAmʿaḳ s, 65a — S, 65b
Ḥamīdiyya v, 462b — V, 465b
Ḥamīdīzāde Muṣṭafā Efendi → Muṣṭafā Efendi
Ḥamīdū i, 368b; ii, 538a — I, 379b; II, 551a
Ḥā-mīm al-Muftarī i, 1178b, 1186a; ii, 1095b; iii, **134b** — I, 1213b, 1221a; II, 1121a; III, **137b**
Hamīrat s, 42a — S, 42b
Hamitic iii, 105a — III, 107b
Ḥaml v, 21a — V, 21b
Ḥamladjī i, 1278a — I, 1317a, b
al-Ḥamma i, 492b; ii, 463a, 464a; iii, **135a** — I, 507a; II, 475a, 476a; III, **137b**
Ḥammād, Banū → Hammādid(e)s
Ḥammād b. Abī Ḥanīfa al-Nuʿmān i, 124a; iii, 512a — I, 127b; III, 529b
Ḥammād b. Abī Sulaymān i, 123a; ii, 888b; v, 239b — I, 126b; II, 909a; V, 237b
Ḥammād b. Buluggīn i, 860a; iii, 137a; iv, 479a — I, 884a; III, 139b, 140a; IV, 501a
Ḥammād b. Isḥāḳ iii, 820a; iv, 111a — III, 843b; IV, 116a
Ḥammād b. Isḥāḳ b. Ismāʿīl s, **384b** — S, **385a**
Ḥammād b. ʿUdayy s, 305a — S, 304b
Ḥammād b. Zayd b. Dirham s, **384b** — S, **385a**
Ḥammād b. al-Zibriḳān iii, 135b, 136a; iv, 1003b — III, 138b, 139a; IV, 1036a
Ḥammād ʿAdjrad i, 160a, 1080b; iii, **135a**, 136a; iv, 1003b — I, 164b, 1113a; III, **138a**, 139a; IV, 1036a
Ḥammād al-Barbarī iii, 233a — III, 240a
Ḥammād al-Rāwiya i, 718b; iii, 135b, **136a**, 641b, 1177b; iv, 316b, 919a, 1003b — I, 740a; III, **138b**, 662b, 1206b; IV, 330b, 952a, 1036a
Ḥammāda iii, **136b**; v, 1185a — III, **139b**; V, 1175a
Ḥammādid(e)s i, 79a, 165a, 533a, 699b, 860a, 1176a,

1204b, 1246b, 1319b; ii, 115a, 145b, 537a, 747b; iii, **137a,** 386a; iv, 478b; v, 59b, 60a, 1179a — I, 81b, 170a, 549b, 720b, 884a, 1211a, 1240b, 1284b, 1359b; II, 117b, 149b, 550b, 765b; III, **139b,** 398b; IV, 499b; V, 61b, 62a, 1169a
Ḥammāl iii, **139a** — III, **141b**
Ḥammām iii, **139b,** 148b; v, 13b, 14a, b, 16a — III, **142a,** 151b; V, 13b, 14b, 16a, b
Hammam Ali s, 101b — S, 101a
Ḥammām Bourguiba v, 52a — V, 53b
Ḥammam Ḳarā Ḥiṣār iv, 580b — IV, 604a
Ḥammām al-Ṣarakh iii, 141b, **146a**; s, 229a — III, 144b, **149a**; S, 229a
Ḥammāma b. Zīrī iii, 1043a — III, 1069a
Ḥammār, lake/lac- i, 1095b — I, 1128b
Ḥammu Ḳiyu s, 53a — S, 53b
Ḥammūda Bey (1631-59) ii, 459b; iv, 825b, 828a — II, 471b; IV, 858b, 861a
Ḥammūda Bey (1782-1814) iii, 94b, 636a; iv, 403a — III, 97a, 657a; IV, 420b
Ḥammūdid(e)s i, 403a, 495a; ii, 525a; iii, **147a,** 938b, 1037a; s, 398b — I, 414b, 509b; II, 538a; III, **150a,** 963b, 1062b; S, 399a
Hammūya, Muḥammad b. s, 3a — S, 2a
Ḥammūya, Saʿd al-Dīn-i s, 364b — S, 364a
Hāmōn iii, **147b** — III, **150b**
Ḥamrāʾ al-Asad s, 230a — S, 230a
Hampī iii, **147b,** 451a — III, **151a,** 466b
al-Ḥamrāʾ iii, **148b** — III, **152a**
al-Ḥamrāʾ, Gharnāṭa i, 459a, 495b, 497b, 500a, 682a, 1321a, 1347a; ii, 115a, 556b, 1012b, **1016b,** 1019a, b; iii, 973a; v, 219b — I, 472a, 510b, 512b, 515a, 703a, 1361a, 1387b; II, 117b, 570b, 1036a, **1040a,** 1042b, 1043a; III, 997b; V, 217a
Ḥamrīn, Djabal i, 184a; iii, **149a** — I, 189b; III, **152b**
Hamshin v, 713a — V, 718a
Ḥamūd b. Muḥammad Abū Mismār i, 709a; ii, 517b; v, 808a — I, 729b; II, 530b; V, 814a
Ḥamūda b. Murād ii, 189b — II, 195b
Ḥamūda Pasha → Ḥammūda Bey (1782-1814)
Ḥamūla iii, **149b** — III, **153a**
Hāmūn i, 222a; iii, **150a** — I, 229a; III, **153b**
Ḥamūya, Saʿd al-Dīn v, 301a — V, 300b
Hamza iii, **150a** — III, **153b**
Ḥamza, Amīr → Ḥamza b. ʿAbd al-Muṭṭalib
Ḥamza b. ʿAbd Allāh → Ḥamza b. ʿAbd al-Muṭṭalib
Ḥamza b. ʿAbd Allāh (Khāridjī) → Ḥamza b. Adrak
Ḥamza b. ʿAbd al-Muṭṭalib i, 80a, 115b; iii, 114b, **152b,** 455a, 1234b; iv, 896b, 994b, 1106b; v, 197b, 1161b; s, 92b, 103b — I, 82b, 119a; III, 116b, **156a,** 471a, 1266b; IV, 929a, 1027a, 1138a; V, 195a, 1151a; S, 92b, 103a
Ḥamza b. Adrak i, 207a; ii, 978a; iii, 153a, 233b; v, 158a — I, 213a; II, 1000b; III, 156b, 240a; V, 157a
Hamza b. ʿAlī b. Aḥmad ii, 136b, 632a; iii, 80b, **154a**; iv, 199a — II, 140a, 647b; III, 82b, **157b**; IV, 207b
Ḥamza b. Asad → Ibn al-Ḳalānisī
Ḥamza b. Bīḍ iii, **154b** — III, **158a**
Ḥamza b. Ḥabīb iii, **155a** — III, **158b**
Ḥamza b. Muḥammad al-Ḥanafi iii, 155b — III, 159a
Ḥamza b. ʿUmāra (ʿAmmāra) i, 1116b; iv, 837a; v, 433b — I, 1150b; IV, 869b; V, 436a
Ḥamza b. ʿUthmān i, 311b, 312a; iii, 156b — I, 321b; III, 160a
Ḥamza Beg iii, **156b** — III, **160a**
Ḥamza Beg (Imām) i, 755b; ii, 88b; iii, **157a** — I, 778a; II, 90a; III, **160b**
Ḥamza Fanṣūrī i, 742a; iii, **155b,** 1220a, 1233a — I, 764a; III, **159a,** 1251a, 1265a
Ḥamza Ḥāmid Pasha iii, **157a** — III, **160b**
Ḥamza al-Ḥarrānī iii, **155b** — III, **159a**
Ḥamza al-Iṣfahānī i, 144b; iii, **156a,** 371a; s, 382b — I, 148b; III, **159b,** 382b; S, 383a
Ḥamza Makhdūm s, **353b** — S, **353b**
Ḥamza Mīrzā iii, **157b**; iv, 861a — III, **161a**; IV, 894a
Ḥamza Pasha iii, **157b** — III, **161a**
Ḥamza Pasha Nishandjî iv, 566a — IV, 588a
Ḥamzat Tsadasa i, 756a — I, 778b
Ḥamzawī ii, 98a; iii, 153b; iv, 128b — II, 100b; III, 157a; IV, 134a
Ḥamzāwī, Rashād v, 190b — V, 187b
Ḥamzevī → Ḥamzawī
Ḥamziyya i, 207a; iii, 153a, 653b, 658b — I, 213a; III, 156b, 674b, 679b
Ḥanābila i, 272b, 696a, 900a, 949a, 1040a; ii, 388a; iii, **158a,** 677b, 699b, 731a, 752a, 766a, 784b; iv, 173a; v, 9b; s, 29b — I, 280b, 717a, 927a, 978b, 1071b; II, 398b; III, **161b,** 699a, 721b, 753b, 775a, 789a, 807b; IV, 180b; V, 10a; S, 29b
- doctrine i, 333b, 338b, 339a, 414a; ii, 411b; iii, 17a, 1144b, 1148a, 1149a, 1164b, 1171b; iv, 172b, 183b, 691a, 990a — I, 344a, 349a, b, 425b; II, 422b; III, 17b, 1173a, 1176b, 1177b, 1193a, 1200b; IV, 180a, 191b, 719a, 1022b
al-Ḥanafī, Aḥmad b. Muḥammad Rūmī s, 49b — S, 50a
Ḥanafī-Māturīdī iii, 1149b, 1171a, 1172b, 1173a; iv, 172a, 470a, b, 693b — III, 1177b, 1200a, 1201b, 1202a; IV, 179b, 491a, 721b
Hanafites → Ḥanafiyya
Ḥanafiyya i, 70b, 123a, 164a, 332b, 338a, b, 340a, 803a; ii, 829b; iii, 6b, 17a, 90a, **162b,** 350b, 756b, 848b, 1024b; iv, 404a, b, 690a; s, 23a — I, 72b, 126b, 168b, 343a, 349a, 350b, 826a; II, 849b; III, 6b, 17b, 92b, **166a,** 361b, 779b, 872b, 1050a; IV, 422a, b, 718a; S, 23b
Ḥanbal b. Hilāl i, 272b — I, 280b
Ḥanbalīs, Ḥanbalites → Ḥanābila
Ḥanbīl i, 689a — I, 710a
Hand → Yad
Handasa → ʿIlm al-handasa
Ḥandūs → Sikka
Handžič (al-Khāndjī) s, **354a** — S, **354a**
al-Ḥanfāʾ s, 177b — S, 178b
Hāniʾ b. Hāniʾ s, 298b — S, 298b
Hāniʾ b. ʿUrwa al-Murādī iii, **164b,** 609b — III, **168a,** 629b
Ḥanīf iii, **165a** — III, **168b**
Ḥanīfa b. Ludjaym, Banū i, 545a, b, 963a; ii, 569a; iii, **166b**; s, 122a, 178a — I, 562a, b, 992b; II, 583b; III, **170a**; S, 121b, 179a
Ḥanīfa, Wādī → Wādī Ḥanīfa
Ḥannā i, 359a — I, 370a
Hansaliyya iii, **167a** — III, **170b**
Hānsawī, Djamāl al-Dīn iii, **167b,** 168b; s, 67a — III, **171a,** 172a; S, 67b
Hanshīr i, 661a — I, 682a
Hānsī iii, **167b,** 225b — III, **171b**, 232a
Hānswī → Hānsawī
Ḥanūt iii, 404a — III, 416a
Ḥānya iii, 983b, 1086a, b; iv, 539b — III, 1008a, 1113a; IV, 563a
Ḥanẓala b. Abī ʿĀmir → Ghasīl al-Malāʾika
Ḥanẓala b. Abī Sufyān i, 151a; ii, 1020b — I, 155b; II, 1044a
Ḥanẓala b. Mālik, Banū iii, **168b**; v, 640a — III, **172b**; V, 644b
Ḥanẓala b. Ṣafwān iii, **169a** — III, **172b**
Ḥanẓala b. Ṣafwān al-Kalbī i, 86b, 509a; iii, **169a,** 494a; iv, 826a — I, 88b, 524b; III, **173a,** 511a; IV, 859a
Ḥanẓala b. al-Sharḳī i, 115b — I, 119a
Ḥanẓala b. Thaʿlaba iii, 1022b — III, 1048b

Ḥanẓala Bādghīsī iv, 55a — IV, 58a
Haoussa → Hausa
Haouz → Ḥawz
Ḥāra ii, 230a; iii, **169b** — II, 237a; III, **173b**
Harābī i, 1049b — I, 1081a
Ḥarāfīsh → Ḥarfūsh
Ḥaraka wa-Sukūn iii, **169b**; iv, 731b — III, **173b**; IV, 761a
Ḥarakta s, 144b — S, 144a, b
Haram (pyramid(e)) iii, **173a** — III, **177a**
Ḥarām iii, 307a; iv, 372b, 1149a — III, 316a; IV, 389a, 1180b
Ḥaram (enclos(ure)) i, 892b; iii, 294a,b, 1018a; iv, 37a, 322a; v, 810a, 1003a, 1201a — I, 919a; III, 303b, 1043b; IV, 39b, 336a; V, 815b, 816a, 999a, 1191b
al-Ḥaram al-Sharīf iii, **173b**; v, 341b, 343b, 344a, 1143b, 1144a — III, **177b**; V, 342b, 344b, 345a, 1136a, b
al-Ḥaramayn iii, **175a**; iv, 956b; s, 304b — III, **179a**; IV, 990a; S, 304b
Hārand s, 116a, 332a — S, 115b, 331b
Harangue → Khuṭba
Harar i, 976a; iii, 3b, 4b, **176a** — I, 1006b; III, 3b, 4b, **179b**
Ḥarari iii, 7b, 176a — III, 8a, 180a
Ḥaras → Ḳaṣr
al-Ḥarāsīs iii, **176a** — III, **180a**
Harāt i, 7b, 8a, 47b, 91a, 147b, 222b, 223a, 227b, 228b, 1067b; ii, 1101b; iii, **177a,** 471b, 603a; iv, 39a, 394b, 523b, 672a; v, 58b, 59a, b, 873a, 993a; s, 38a, 41a, 50b, 71a, 138b, 139b, 140a, 142a, 340a, 380a, 423b — I, 7b, 8a, 49a, 94a, 152a, 229a, 230a, 234b, 235b, 1100a; II, 1127b; III, **181a,** 488a, 624a; IV, 41a-b, 411b, 546b, 699b; V, 60b, 61a, 879a, 988a; S, 38a, 41b, 51a, 71b, 138a, 139a, b, 142a, 340a, 380a, 423b
Ḥarāṭīn → Ḥarṭānī
al-Harawī → al-Anṣārī al-Harawī
al-Harawī, Maḥmūd b. Muḥammad s, 406b — S, 406b
Harawī, Mīrzā → ʿAbd al-Raḥmān Harawī
al-Harawī, Muḥammad iv, 801a — IV, 833a
al-Harawī al-Mawṣilī, ʿAlī i, 89a; iii, 71b, **178a,** 181a, b, 511a; iv, 958b; v, 214b — I, 91b; III, 74a, **182a,** 185b, 186a, 528a; IV, 991b; V, 212a
Ḥarāz iii, **178b**; iv, 201a; s, 407a — III, **182b**; IV, 209b, 210a; S, 407a
Harāz (river/rivière) v, 659b, 660a — V, 665a
Ḥarāzem, Sīdī → Ibn Ḥirzihim
Ḥarb iii, **179b,** 363b, 1065b; v, 998a — III, **183b,** 375a, 1092a; V, 993b
Ḥarb (war/la guerre) iii, **180a**; v, 687a — III, **184a**; V, 692a
Ḥarb b. Umayya i, 1241b; ii, 883b; iii, **203a**; s, 103b — I, 1279a; II, 904a; III, **208b**; S, 103a
Ḥarb Akademisi iii, 204a — III, 209b
Ḥarba → ʿAnaza; ʿAṣā; Ḳaḍīb; Silāḥ
Ḥarbāʾ iii, **203b** — III, **209a**
Harbaḳa iv, 726a — IV, 755a
Ḥarbī i, 429b — I, 441b
al-Ḥarbī → Ibrāhīm
Harbin s, 82a — S, 82a
Ḥarbiyya iii, 1265b; iv, 837b — III, 1298b; IV, 870a
Ḥarbiye ii, 425b, 513b; iii, **203b**; v, 903b — II, 436b, 526b; III, **209a**; V, 909b
Hare → Arnab
Ḥareket Ordusu iii, **204a** — III, **209b**
Harem → Ḥarīm; Sarāy
Ḥarf i, 345b; iii, 172a, **204b,** 597b, 598a, b; iv, 867b — I, 356a; III, 176a, **210a,** 618a, b, 619a; IV, 900b
Ḥarfūsh (amīrs) i, 971a; iii, **205b** — I, 1001a; III, **211a**
Ḥarfūsh, ḥarāfīsh ii, 963a; iii, **206a** — II, 985a; III, **211b**
Hargeisa iii, **206b** — III, **212a**
Hargha iii, **207a** — III, **212b**
Hari Čand iii, 225a — III, 231b
Hari Čand, Diwān ii, 140a — II, 144a
Harī Rūd iii, **207b**; v, 872b, 873b; s, 367a — III, **213a**; V, 878b, 879b; S, 368a
Harī Singh (Kashmīr) iv, 710a — IV, 738b
Harī Singh Nalwa i, 970b; ii, 1131a; iii, 336a — I, 1000b; II, 1157b; III, 346a
Ḥarīb iii, **207b**; iv, 747a — III, **213b**; IV, 777a
Ḥārik → Ḥurrāḳ
Ḥārim i, 239a; iii, **208b** — I, 246b; III, **214a**
Ḥarīm i, 35b; ii, 114b; iii, **209a**; v, 871b, 1149a — I, 36b; II, 117a; III, **214b**; V, 877b, 1180b
Harim b. Ḥayyān i, 73b — I, 75b
Harim b. Sinān ii, 1023a — II, 1047a
Ḥarīmī v, 269b — V, 267b
Harīpur iii, 336a — III, 346a
Ḥarīr ii, 904b; iii, **209b,** 400b; iv, 135a, 339b, 676b; v, 39a, 604b; s, 340b — II, 925b; III, **215a,** 413a; IV, 140b, 353b, 704b; V, 40b, 608b; S, 340b
al-Ḥarīrī, Abū Muḥammad ʿAlī iii, 811b — III, 835a
al-Ḥarīrī, al-Ḳāsim i, 523a, 570b, 591a, 669b; iii, **221a,** 733a, 834b, 1264a; iv, 913a; v, 207b, 608b; s, 31a, 123b — I, 538b, 589a, 610a, 690b; III, **227b,** 755b, 858b, 1297a; IV, 945b; V, 205a, 612b; S, 31a, 122b
Ḥarīriyya iii, **222a** — III, **228b**
Ḥarīsh → Karkaddan
al-Ḥārith, Banū s, 335a — S, 334b
al-Ḥārith, Djabal i, 251b; ii, 574a — I, 259b; II, 588b
al-Ḥārith b. ʿAbd al-ʿAzīz b. Abī Dulaf ii, 623b — II, 639a
al-Ḥārith b. ʿAbd al-Muṭṭalib i, 80a — I, 82b
al-Ḥārith b. Abi ʾl-ʾAlāʾ Saʿīd al-Taghlibī → Abū Firās
al-Ḥārith b. Abī Rabīʿa ii, 196a — II, 202a
al-Ḥārith b. ʿAmr i, 526b; iii, 1177a; v, 118b — I, 542b; III, 1206a; V, 121a
al-Ḥārith b. Asad s, 125b — S, 124b
al-Ḥārith b. ʿAwf → al-Ḥārith b. Ẓālim
al-Ḥārith b. Badr al-Fazārī s, 177b — S, 179a
Ḥarīth b. Bazīʿ iv, 713a — IV, 741b
Ḥārith b. Djabala i, 102b, 405b, 548b, 1249b; ii, 1020b; iii, 94a, **222a**; iv, 726a, 1138a; v, 633a, b; s, 229b — I, 105b, 417a, 566a, 1287b; II, 1044b; III, 96b, **228b**; IV, 755a, 1170a; V, 637b; S, 229b
al-Ḥārith b. Ḥammām i, 115b — I, 119a
al-Ḥārith b. Ḥilliza al-Yashkurī iii, **222b**; s, 272b — III, **229a**; S, 272a
al-Ḥārith b. Hishām i, 115b; s, 32b — I, 118b; S, 33a
Ḥārith b. Kaʿb iii, **223a** — III, **229b**
al-Ḥārith b. Kalada al-Thaḳafī ii, 1120a; iv, 820b; s, 133b, **354a** — II, 1146b; IV, 853b; S, 133a, **354a**
al-Ḥārith b. Khālid al-Makhzūmī i, 308b — I, 318a
al-Ḥārith b. Ṣabīra s, 172a — S, 173a
al-Ḥārith b. Suraydj i, 530a, 684b; ii, 388a, 1026b; iii, **223b,** 471a, 1202a; iv, 44b, 370a; v, 57a, 76a, 854a — I, 546a, 705b; II, 398a, 1050b; III, **230b,** 487b, 1232a; IV, 47a, 386b; V, 59a, 78a, 861a
al-Ḥārith b. Talid al-Ḥaḍramī iii, 653b — III, 675a
al-Ḥārith b. Thaʿlaba s, 229b — S, 229b
al-Ḥārith b. Tirmāḥ s, 136a — S, 135b
al-Ḥārith b. Waʿla i, 690a — I, 711a
al-Ḥārith b. Ẓālim al-Murrī ii, 1023a, b; iii, 812a; s, 178a — II, 1047a; III, 835b; S, 179a
Ḥārith al-Muḥāsibī → al-Muḥāsibī
Ḥāritha, Āl i, 771b — I, 794b
Ḥāritha b. Badr al-Ghudānī iii, **224b,** 1261b; iv, 1002b — III, **231b,** 1294b; IV, 1035a
Ḥāritha b. al-Ḥadjdjādj → Abū Duʾād al-Iyādī

Ḥāri<u>th</u>a b. Ḳaṭan i, 969a — I, 999a
al-Ḥāri<u>th</u>a b. al-Nuʿmān ii, 843a — II, 863a
al-Ḥāri<u>th</u>ī, Muḥammad b. Ṭāhir s, 62a — S, 62b
al-Ḥari<u>th</u>ī, Ṣāliḥ b. ʿAlī s, **355a** — S, **355a**
al-Ḥāri<u>th</u>iyya iii, 659a, 1266a; iv, 837b, 838a; v, 63b, 945b — III, 680b, 1298b; IV, 870a, 871a; V, 65b, 949b
Hariyānā iii, 168a, **225a** — III, 171b, **231b**
Ḥarka ii, 509b; v, 1221a — II, 522a; V, 1211b
Harkarn iii, **225b** — III, **232b**
Harmas, Harmīs → Hirmis
Harnais, Harnachement → <u>Kh</u>ayl
Harness, Trappings → <u>Kh</u>ayl
Harp Okulu iii, 204a — III, 209b
Harpo(o)n → Ṣayd
Ḥarra i, 535a; iii, **226a,** 362a — I, 551b; III, **232b,** 373b
al-Ḥarra i, 50b, 55a; iii, **226a**; v, 997a — I, 51b, 57a; III, **233a**; V, 992b
Ḥarrān i, 16b, 106b, 119b, 136b; ii, 347b, 348a; iii, **227b,** 287a; v, 593b; s, 36b — I, 16b, 109b, 123a, 140b; II, 357b; III, **234b,** 295b; V, 597a; S, 36b
al-Ḥarrānī → Abu ʾl-Fatḥ; Ḥamza; Ibrahīm b. <u>Dh</u>akwān; ʿĪsa b. ʿAlī
Ḥarrānians, Ḥarrāniens → Ṣābiʾa
Harrar → Harar
Ḥarrat Rahaṭ s, 198b — S, 198b
Harsusī (language, la langue) i, 575a; iii, 176b — I, 593b; III, 180b
Ḥarsūsī (tribe, tribu) → al-Ḥarāsīs
Ḥarṭānī i, 371a; ii, 133b, 877a; iii, **230b**; v, 1197a; s, 328b — I, 381b; II, 137a, 897a; III, **237b**; V, 1187a; S, 328a
Har<u>th</u>ama b. ʿArfa<u>dj</u>a iii, 29a — III, 30b
Har<u>th</u>ama b. Aʿyan i, 149b, 437b; ii, 196b, 886a; iii, **231a,** 233a, 243b, 982a; iv, 16b — I, 154a, 450a; II, 202b, 906b; III, **238a,** 240a, 250b, 1006b; IV, 18a
Har<u>th</u>ama b. Naṣr s, 106a — S, 105b
Harūd → Harī Rūd
Harūn b. Altūntā<u>sh</u> i, 424b; iv, 1067a — I, 436b; IV, 1098b
Harūn b. al-Fara<u>dj</u> iv, 605a — IV, 629b
Hārūn b. <u>Gh</u>arīb i, 688b, 962b; iii, 126b — I, 709b, 992a; III, 129b
Hārūn b. ʿImrān iii, **231b** — III, **238b**
Hārūn b. <u>Kh</u>umarawayh iii, 745b — III, 768b
Hārūn b. al-Mahdī → Hārūn al-Ra<u>sh</u>īd
Harūn b. Mūsā ii, 892b — II, 913a
Harūn b. Sayf al-Dīn b. Muḥammad Faḍl ii, 123b — II, 126b
Hārūn b. Yaḥyā i, 775a, 1033b; iii, **232a,** 1044b — I, 798a, 1065a; III, **238b,** 1070b
Hārūn b. al-Yamanī al-Mu<u>kh</u>ālif iii, 659b — III, 680b
Hārūn Bu<u>gh</u>ra <u>Kh</u>ān → Bu<u>gh</u>ra <u>Kh</u>ān Hārūn
Hārūn al-Ra<u>sh</u>īd i, 14a, 18a, 107b, 118a, 144b, 164b, 247b, 364a, 437a, 485a, 510a, 550b, 697a, 1034a, 1035, 1298a; ii, 191a; iii, 22b, 231a, **232b,** 344b, 345b, 996a, 1044b; iv, 16b, 97b, 858b, 940b, 1164a; v, 174b, 533b, 1239a; s, 22b, 26a, 48a, 64a, 122a, 128a, 198b, 199a, 225b, 251b, 252a, 263a, 304a, 326b, 372a — I, 14a, 18b, 110b, 121b, 148b, 169a, 255b, 375a, 449b, 499b, 525b, 568a, 718b, 1065b, 1066b, 1338a; II, 197a; III, 23b, 238a, **239a,** 355a, 356a, 1021a, 1070b; IV, 17b-18a, 101b, 892a, 973b, 1196a; V, 172a, 537b, 1229b; S, 23a, 26b, 49a, 64b, 121b, 127b, 198b, 199a, 225b, 252a, 262b, 304a, 326a, 372a
- constructions i, 182b, 199b, 616b, 761a, 789b; ii, 36a, 1120a; iii, 228a, 235a — I, 187b, 205b, 637a, 784a, 812b; II, 36b, 1146b; III, 235a, 241b
Hārūn al-<u>Sh</u>ārī ii, 524a; iii, 126a, 619a — II, 537a; III, 129a, 639b
al-Hārūniyya iii, **234b** — III, **241b**
Ḥarūrā i, 40b; iii, **235a** — I, 41b; III, **242a**
Ḥarūrites i, 384a, 385b; iii, 235a; iv, 1074b — I, 395a, 396b; III, 242a; IV, 1106b
Harūsindān b. Tīrdā<u>dh</u> s, 357a — S, 357a
Hārūt wa-Mārūt i, 811b; iii, **236b** — I, 834b; III, **243b**
Ḥarz iv, 1038a — IV, 1069b
al-Ḥasā i, 72b, 100a, 538b, 539a; iii, **237b**; iv, 663b, 664a, b, 764b, 925a, b; v, 684a; s, 135b, 234a, 380a — I, 75a, 103a, 555a, 555b; III, **244a,** 567b; IV, 690a, b, 691b, 795a, 958a, b; V, 689a; S, 135b, 234a, 380a
Ḥasab wa-nasab i, 892b; iii, **238b** — I, 919a; III, **245b**
Ḥasab Allāh b. Muḥammad Faḍl ii, 123b — II, 126b
Ḥasan iii, 25a — III, 26b
al-Ḥasan I, Mawlāy (ʿAlawid(e)) i, 290b, 356b, 357a, 1281a; ii, 109a, 820a, 823a, 885b, 1116a; iii, **240a,** 256a, 536a, 562a; v, 890a, 1192b, 1193a; s, 114a — I, 299b, 367b, 368a, 1320b; II, 111b, 839b, 842b, 906a, 1142b; III, **247a,** 263b, 554b, 581b; V, 896b, 1182b, 1183a; S, 113b
al-Ḥasan II (ʿAlawid(e)) ii, 673b; iii, 564a; v, 1072b, 1073a, 1195a — II, 690a; III, 583a; V, 1070a, b, 1185a
Ḥasan I (Nizārī) → Ḥasan-i Ṣabbāḥ
Ḥasan II (Ismāʿīlī) i, 353b; iv, 28a, 200a, 205a — I, 364b; IV, 30a, 208b, 214a
Ḥasan III (Ismāʿīlī) i, 353b; iv, 205b, 860a — I, 364b; IV, 214b, 893a
al-Ḥasan, Abū ʿAbdallāh Muḥammad iii, 69a; iv, 1157a — III, 71b; IV, 1189a
Ḥasan, Bayhaḳī Sayyid s, 131b — S, 130b
al-Ḥasan, Mawlāy → al-Ḥasan (ʿAlawid(e)); al-Ḥasan, Abū Abdullāh
Ḥasan, Mīr <u>Gh</u>ulām s, **358b** — S, **358b**
Ḥasan, Mullā (Farangī Maḥall) s, 292a — S, 292a
Ḥasan, Nāṣir al-Dīn i, 765b, 1050b; iii, **239b,** 900b; iv, 431b, 960a; v, 1141a — I, 788b, 1082a; III, **246b,** 925a; IV, 450a, b, 992b; V, 1134a
Ḥasan, Pīr v, 27a — V, 27b
Ḥasan b. ʿAbd Allāh → Nāṣir al-Dawla Ḥasan
Ḥasan b. Abi ʾl-Ḥasan → Japheth al-Barḳamānī
al-Ḥasan b. Abī ʾl-Hay<u>dj</u>āʾ → Nāṣir al-Dawla Ḥasan
al-Ḥasan b. Abī Numayy II, <u>Sh</u>arīf ii, 517b; s, 234b — II, 530a; S, 234b
Ḥasan b. Aḥmad al-Karmaṭī v, 368b — V, 369b
Ḥasan b. ʿAdī i, 195b — I, 201a
Ḥaṣan b. Aḥmad Bahmanī iii, 577a — III, 597a
al-Ḥasan b. ʿAlī (Zīrid(e)) iii, 138b, 933a — III, 141b, 958a
al-Ḥasan b. ʿAlī → al-Ḥasan al-Utrū<u>sh</u>; Ibn Mākūlā; Niẓām al-Mulk
al Ḥasan b. ʿAlī b. Abi ʾl-Ḥusayn iv, 496b; v, 105b — IV, 517b, 518a; V, 107b
al-Ḥasan b. ʿAlī b. Abī Ṭālib i, 40b, 43b, 86a, 163b, 194b, 385a, 550a, 697a; ii, 843a, 848b; iii, **240b,** 607b, 889b; v, 945b; s, 401a — I, 41b, 44b, 88b, 168a, 200b, 396b, 567b, 718a; II, 863a, 868b; III, **247b,** 628a, 913a; V, 949b; S, 401b
Ḥasan b. ʿAlī al-Baṣrī → Japheth b. Eli
al-Ḥasan b. ʿAlī al-Kalbī i, 986b; ii, 853a — I, 1017a; II, 873a
al-Ḥasan b. ʿAlī al-Maʾmūnī i, 149b — I, 154a
Ḥasan b. ʿAlī <u>Sh</u>āmma ii, 167a — II, 172a
al-Ḥasan b. ʿAlī ʿUmar al-Marrāku<u>sh</u>ī i, 727a; ii, 586b; v, 1209b; s, 413b — I, 749a; II, 601a; V, 1200a; S, 414a
al-Ḥasan b. ʿAmmār i, 1042a; ii, 858b; iii, 76b, 77a; iv, 497a; v, 1160a — I, 1073b; II, 878b; III, 79a, b; IV, 518a; V, 1150a
Ḥasan b. al-Bāḳir iv, 859a — IV, 892b
Ḥasan b. Buwayh → Rukn al-Dawla Ḥasan

Ḥasan b. al-Faḍl iv, 637b — IV, 664a
Ḥasan b. Faraḥ b. Ḥawshab b. Zādān al-Kūfī → Manṣūr al-Yaman
Ḥasan b. Farīghūn ii, 799b — II, 818b
al-Ḥasan b. Fīrūzān ii, 928a — II, 949b
Ḥasan b. Gannūn (Djannūn) i, 1088a; iii, 30b, 74b, 1036b — I, 1120a; III, 32a, 77a, 1062b
Ḥasan b. al-Ḥāfiẓ i, 939b; iii, 55a — I, 968a; III, 57a
al-Ḥasan b. Hāniʾ → Abū Nuwās
Ḥasan b. Ḥārūn i, 866a — I, 890a
Ḥasan b. Ḥassūna iv, 686b — IV, 714b
al-Ḥasan b. Ḥayy → al-Ḥasan b. Ṣāliḥ b. Ḥayy
al-Ḥasan b. Hibat Allāh Ibn Asākir iii, 713b; iv, 201a — III, 736a; IV, 210a
al-Ḥasan b. al-Ḥusayn iv, 646b, 647a — IV, 673a, b
Ḥasan b. Ibrāhīm b. Sahl al-Tustarī ii, 858a — II, 878a
Ḥasan b. Idrīs (Dāʿī Muṭlaḳ) s, 358b — S, 358b
al-Ḥasan b. Ismāʿīl Āl Shibām al-Makramī iv, 201a — IV, 210a
Ḥasan b. Ḳaḥṭaba i, 16a, 103a, 449b; ii, 196b, 679a, 715a; iii, 802b; iv, 447a, b — I, 16b, 106a, 462b; II, 202b, 696a, 733b; III, 826a; IV, 466b, 467b
Ḥasan b. al-Ḳāsim (Ḥasanid(e)) i, 688a; ii, 191b, 192a, b; iii, 254b; s, **356a** — I, 709a; II, 197b, 198a, b; III, 262a; S, **356a**
Ḥasan b. Ḳāsim (Idrisid(e)) → Ḥasan b. Gannūn
al-Ḥasan b. Khālid al-Ḥāzimī, Sharīf s, 30b — S, 30b
al-Ḥasan b. al-Khaṣīb → Ibn al-Khaṣīb
Ḥasan b. Khayr al-Dīn → Ḥasan Pasha (Algiers/Alger)
al-Ḥasan b. Maḥbūb i, 758b — I, 781b
al-Ḥasan b. Makhlad → Ibn Makhlad
al-Ḥasan b. Marwān v, 453a — V, 455b
al-Ḥasan b. Muḥammad (ʿAlawid(e)) → al-Ḥasan I, II
al-Ḥasan b. Muḥammad (Buwayhid(e)) → al-Muhallabī
al-Ḥasan b. Muḥammad (Khayrātid(e) i, 709b — I, 731a
al-Ḥasan b. Muḥammad (Nizārī) → al-Ḥasan II, III
al-Ḥasan b. Muḥammad Āl ʿĀʾiḍ i, 709b — I, 731a
Ḥasan b. Muḥammad al-ʿAṭṭār → al-ʿAṭṭār
al-Ḥasan b. Muḥammad b. al-Ḥanafiyya v, 1026b; s, **357b** — V, 1022b; S, **357b**
Ḥasan b. Muḥammad Naẓẓām al-Nīsābūrī s, 413a — S, 413b
Ḥasan b. Nāmāwar ii, 194a — II, 200a
Ḥasan b. Nūḥ al-Hindī s, **358b** — S, **358a**
al-Ḥasan b. Rabāḥ s, 352a — S, 352a
Ḥasan b. al-Ṣabbāḥ → Ḥasan-i Ṣabbāḥ
al-Ḥasan b. Sahl i, 149b, 271b, 316a, 897b, 1298a, 1312a; ii, 731a, b; iii, **243b,** 345b, 951a, 987b; iv, 17a; s, 15a, 263b — I, 154a, 280a, 325b, 924a, 1338a, 1352b; II, 749b, 750a; III, **250b,** 356a, 975b, 1012a; IV, 18a; S, 15b, 263a
al-Ḥasan b. Ṣāliḥ b. Ḥayy iii, **244a**; s, 48a, 130a — III, **251a**; S, 48b, 129a
al-Ḥasan b. Sanbar (Shanbar) iv, 664a — IV, 691a
Ḥasan b. Sulaymān iii, 1114a — III, 1141b
al-Ḥasan b. Suwār i, 631b, 632a — I, 652b
Ḥasan b. Tīmūrtāsh → Ḥasan Küčük
al-Ḥasan b. ʿUbayd Allāh b. Tughdj iv, 663a — IV, 690a
Ḥasan b. Ustadh-Hurmuz iii, **244b** — III, **251b**
Ḥasan b. Wahb i, 153b — I, 158a
al-Ḥasan b. Yūsuf → al-Ḥillī
al-Ḥasan b. Zayd b. al-Ḥasan i, 45b; iii, **244b,** 786b — I, 46b; III, **251b,** 809b
al-Ḥasan b. Zayd b. Muḥammad i, 352b; ii, 191a; iii, **245a**; iv, 46b; v, 662a — I, 363b; II, 197a; III, **252a**; IV, 49b; V, 667a
Ḥasan b. Ziyād al-Luʾluʾī i, 124a; iii, 163a — I, 127b; III, 166b
Ḥasan Abdāl iii, **245a** — III, **252a**
al-Ḥasan Abū ʿAlī iii, **240a** — III, **247a**
Ḥasan Aghā i, 1247a; iii, **245b** — I, 1285a; III, **252b**
Ḥasan Agha (author, auteur) v, 261a — V, 259a
Ḥasan Agha (Aydînoghlu) ii, 599a — II, 614a
Ḥasan Akhmīnī i, 330a — I, 340b
Ḥasan al-Akhram iii, 80b, 154a — III, 82b, 157b
al-Ḥasan ʿalā dhikrihi ʾl-salām → Ḥasan II (Ismāʿīlī)
Ḥasan ʿAlī b. Djahānshāh i, 148a; iv, 588a — I, 152b; IV, 611b
Ḥasan ʿAlī Bārha i, 1025b, 1026a; ii, 379a, 810a; iv, 279b; s, 126b — I, 1057b; II, 389b, 829a; IV, 292a; S, 125b
Ḥasan ʿAlī Manṣūr iv, 42a — IV, 44b
Ḥasan ʿAlī Mīrzā iv, 313a, 393a — IV, 327a, 409b
Ḥasan ʿAlī Shāh → Agha KhānI
al-Ḥasan Amīrkā b. Abi ʾl-Faḍl al-Thāʾir s, 363a — S, 363a
al-Ḥasan al-Aʿṣam i, 551b; ii, 854a; iii, **246a**; iv, 663a, b; s, 36b — I, 569a; II, 874a; III, **253a**; IV, 690a; S, 36b
Ḥasan al-ʿAskarī iii, **246b**; s, 95a — III, **253b**; S, 94b
Ḥasan Baba iii, **247a,** 629a — III, **254a,** 650a
Ḥasan Balfiyya iv, 852a — IV, 885a
al-Ḥasan al-Bannāʾ → al-Bannāʾ
al-Ḥasan al-Baṣrī i, 105a, b, 454a, 718a, 1080b; ii, 293a, 729a, 891b; iii, **247b,** 682b, 947b, 948a; iv, 142a, 212a, 369a, 486a, 734a, b; v, 209b, 936a, 1231b; s, 230b, 323b, 350a, 358a — I, 108a, b, 467a, 739b, 1113a; II, 301a, 747b, 912b; III, **254b,** 704a, 972a, b; IV, 148a, 221b, 385a, 507a, 763b, 764a; V, 207a, 940a, 1222a; S, 230b, 323a, 350a, 358a
Ḥasan Bāwand → Fakhr al-Dawla Ḥasan
Ḥasan al-Bawwāb i, 195b — I, 201a
Ḥasan Bāyḳarā → Bāyḳarā
Ḥasan Bedr al-Dīn (Pasha) s, **359b** — S, **359a**
Ḥasan Bey al-Djuddāwī iii, 992a, b — III, 1017a
Ḥasan Bey-zāde iii, **248b** — III, **255b**
Ḥasan Bey Melikor Zerdabi → Zerdabi
Ḥasan Buzurg i, 903b, 908b; ii, 68a, b, 401a, 706a; iii, 1122b, 1208b — I, 930b, 936a; II, 69a, b, 411b, 724a; III, 1150b, 1239a
Ḥasan Čelebi → Ḳinalîzāde
al-Ḥasan al-Dākhil iii, 256b — III, 263b
Ḥasan Dihlawī iii, **249a** — III, **256a**
Ḥasan Djalāyir → Ḥasan Buzurg
Ḥasan al-Fārūḳī ii, 814b; iii, 638a — II, 834a; III, 659b
Ḥasan Fehmī iii, **251a**; iv, 284a — III, **258a**; IV, 296a
Ḥasan Fehmī Efendi iii, **250a**; iv, 168b — III, **257a**; IV, 176a
Ḥasan Fehmī Pasha ii, 473b; iii, **249b** — II, 485b; III, **256b**
Ḥasan Ghaznawī Ashraf s, 416b — S, 416b
Ḥasan al-Ikhnāʾī i, 280b — I, 289a
Ḥasan-ili s, 168b — S, 169a
Ḥasan ʿIzzet Pasha ii, 699b — II, 717b
Ḥasan Kabīr al-Dīn, Pīr iv, 202b; v, 26a — IV, 211b; V, 27a
Ḥasan Kāfī i, 310a, 1271b — I, 319b, 1310b
Ḥasan Karlugh i, 227a — I, 234a
Ḥasan Khān (Ḳarakhānid(e)) → Ḥasan b. Sulaymān
Ḥasan Khān Bāyburdī iv, 1044b — IV, 1076a
Ḥasan Khān Ḳāshḳāy iv, 706a — IV, 734b
Ḥasan el-Kheyūn i, 684a — I, 705a
Ḥasan Küčük ii, 68a, 401a, 706a; iii, 1122b, 1208b — II, 69b, 411b, 724a; III, 1150b, 1239a

Ḥasan Malik of/de Čadura s, 366a — S, 366a
al-Ḥasan Nāṣir al-Dawla, Amīr s, 36a — S, 36a
Ḥasan Nithārī s, 340a — S, 339b
Ḥasan Niẓāmī v, 546b; s, **359b** — V, 551a; S, **359b**
Ḥasan Pasha → Djezāʾirli Ghāzī; Kāhya; Khādim; Kücük; Ṣokollī; Tiryākī; Yemenli; Yemishdji;
Ḥasan Pasha (Algiers, Alger) iii, **251a**; iv, 1158a; v, 362a — III, **258a**; IV, 1190a; V, 363a
Ḥasan Pasha (Baghdād) i, 905a; iii, **252a,** 1257b — I, 932b; III, **259a,** 1290a
Ḥasan Pasha, Dāmād iii, **252b** — III, **259b**
Ḥasan Pasha, Sayyid iii, **253a**; iv, 233b — III, **260a**; IV, 244a
Ḥasan Pasha, Sherīf ii, 534a; iii, **253a** ; s, 331a — II, 547b; III, **260a**; S, 330b
Ḥasan Pasha Čataldjalî iii, **252a**; iv, 92a — III, **259a**; IV, 96a
Ḥasan Pasha Predojevič i, 1266a — I, 1305a
Ḥasan al-Ramnāḥ i, 1056a — I, 1087b
al-Ḥasan al-Rayyī s, 252b — S, 252b
Ḥasan-i Rūmlū iii, **253b** — III, **260b**
Ḥasan-i Ṣabbāḥ i, 215b, 352b, 353a,b, 1359b; ii, 98a, 194a, 858b; iii, **253b,** 544b, 725a; iv, 199b, 200a, 205a — I, 221b, 363b, 364a, 1399b; II, 100a, 200a, 878a; III, **260b,** 563b, 747b; IV, 208b, 214a
Ḥasan Ṣabrī iii, 515b; s, 300b — III, 533a; S, 300a
Ḥasan Shāh b. Gul Khātūn (Kashmīr) s, 131b, 242a, 329a, 423b — S, 130b, 242a, 328b, 423b
Ḥasan Shāh Bahmanī → ʿAlāʾ al-Dīn Ḥasan
Ḥasan Shāh Bahmanī (d./m. 1484) s, 353b — S, 353b
Ḥasan Shīrāzī, Mīrzā s, 54a — S, 54b
al-Ḥasan al-Uṭrūsh i, 688a, 1350b; ii, 191b; iii, **254a**; iv, 19a; v, 603a; s, 356b, 363a — I, 709a, 1391a; II, 197b; III, **261b**; IV, 20b; V, 607a; S, 356a, 362b
Ḥasanak iii, **255b** — III, **263a**
Ḥasanayn al-Ḥiṣāfī → al-Ḥisāfī
Ḥasanī iii, **256a** — III, **263b**
Ḥasanī, Ḥasaniyyūn i, 403a; ii, 572b; iii, **256b**; v, 1191b — I, 414b; II, 586b; III, **263b**; V, 1181b
Ḥasanī, Ibrāhīm al- v, 133a — V, 135b
al-Ḥasaniyya iii, 660a — III, 681a
Hasankeyf → Ḥiṣn Kayfā
Ḥasanwayh al-Barzikānī i, 211b; ii, 299b, 748b; iii, **258a,** 703b; v, 452b; s, 118b — I, 218a; II, 307b, 767a; III, **265a,** 725b; V, 455a; S, 118a
Ḥasanwayhid(e)s i, 1030b; iii, 258a; v, 824a — I, 1062a; III, 265a; V, 830a
Ḥasanzāde Meḥmed Efendi iv, 737a — IV, 766b
Hasard, jeux de → Ḳimār
Ḥasdāy b. Shaprūt ii, 349b; iii, **259a** — II, 359a; III, **266a**
Ḥashā iv, 272b, 273a — IV, 284b, 285a
Ḥasharāt al-arḍ iii, 307b — III, 317a
Ḥāshid wa-Bakīl iii, **259a**; v, 807b — III, **266b**; V, 813b
Hāshim, Abū Ibrāhīm Shīrāzī s, 405b — S, 405b
Hāshim, Aḥmed iii, **260a** — III, **267b**
Hāshim, Banū → Hāshimid(e)s; Hāshimiyya; Ḥidjāz; Makka
Hāshim, Shehu i, 1260a; v, 358b — I, 1298b; V, 359b
Hāshim b. ʿAbd al-ʿAzīz i, 85b — I, 88a
Hāshim b. ʿAbd Manāf i, 15a, 80a, 115b; ii, 1056a; iii, **260a,** 262b, 265a, 1093a; v, 41b — I, 15b, 82a, 118b; II, 1080b; III, **267a,** 270a, 272b, 1120a; V, 43a
Hāshim b. ʿUtba iii, **260a** — III, **267a**
Hāshim al-Atāsī v, 1047a — V, 1043b, 1044a
Hāshim Baba ii, 543b — II, 556b
Ḥāshim (Sayyid) b. Ḥasan (Bayhaḳī) s, 131b — S, 131a
Hāshim Khodjandī iv, 505a — IV, 527a
Hāshim Musabbaʿāwī ii, 123a; v, 267a — II, 126a; V, 265a
Hāshim Ushkūrī s, 23b — S, 24a
al-Hāshimī, Shaykh iii, **261b** — III, **269a**
Hāshimid(e)s (Bāb al-Abwāb) i, 835b; iv, 345a — I, 859a; IV, 359b
Hāshimid(e)s (Ḥidjāz, ʿIrāk, Urdunn i, 41a; iii, **263a,** 1065b, 1066b; s, 3b — I, 42a; III, **270b,** 1092a, 1093b; S, 3b
Hāshimid(e)s (Mecca, Mekke) i, 552a; iii, **262b** — I, 569b; III, **269b**
Hāshimiyya i, 15a, 17a, 258a; iii, **265a**; iv, 446a, 837a; v, 1b-2b — I, 15b, 17b, 266a; III, **272b**; IV, 466a, 870a; V, 1b-2b
Hāshimiyya (Djilwatiyya) ii, 543b — II, 556b
al-Hāshimiyya i, 17a, 895b; iii, **265b**; iv, 729a — I, 17b, 922a; III, **273a**; IV, 758a
al-Ḥashīr i, 233b — I, 240b
Ḥashīsh i, 1014b; iii, **266a** — I, 1045b; III, **273b**
al-Ḥashīshiyya i, 353a; ii, 170b, 882a; iii, **267b**; v, 922a — I, 364a; II, 176a, 902b; III, **275b**; V, 927b
Ḥāshiya i, 816b; iii, **268b** — I, 840a; III, **276b**
Ḥāshiya (entourage) → Ḳaṣr
Ḥashm-i Ḳalb iii, 199a — III, 204a
Ḥashmet iii, **269a,** 357a — III, **277a,** 368a
Ḥashr → Ḳiyāma
Hashtād-Sar s, 116a — S, 115b
al-Ḥashw i, 671b; iii, 269b — I, 692a; III, 277b
Ḥashwiyya i, 410b; iii, **269b,** 905b; iv, 470a — I, 422b; III, **277b,** 929b; IV, 491a
Ḥāsib → ʿIlm al-ḥisāb
Ḥāsik iii, **269b** — III, **277b**
al-Ḥāsikiyya i, 535b; iii, 270a — I, 551b; III, 277b
al-Ḥaṣkafī iii, 163b — III, 167a
Ḥasrat Mohānī v, 7a; s, **360a** — V, 7b; S, **359b**
Ḥāssa → Ḥiss
Ḥassān, Bā iii, **270a** — III, **278a**
al-Ḥassān b. al-Djarrāḥ ii, 482b; iii, 246a — II, 495a; III, 253a
Ḥassān b. Mālik al-Kalbī ii, 89b, 360a; iii, **270b**; iv, 493a, 929b — II, 91b, 370a; III, **278a**; IV, 514a, 962b
Ḥassān b. Mufarridj ii, 483b, 484a, 855b; iii, 80a; iv, 842a; v, 1211b — II, 496a,b, 875a; III, 82a; IV, 875a; V, 1201b
Ḥassān b. al-Nuʿmān i, 77b, 862b, 1023b; ii, 130a; iii, **271a**; iv, 336b, 415b, 422a, b, 423a, 739b, 829b — I, 79b, 886b, 1055a; II, 133b; III, **279a**; IV, 351a, 433b, 440b, 441a, b, 769b, 862b
Ḥassān b. Thābit i, 50b, 145a, 828b, 1149a; ii, 541a, 993b, 1020b; iii, **271b,** 354a, 975b; iv, 835b, 1002a; s, 9b — I, 52a, 149a, 851b, 1183b; II, 554a, 1016b, 1044b; III, **279b,** 365a, 1000a; IV, 868b, 1031b; S, 9a
Hassani → Ḥasanī
Hassū Taylī s, **361a** — S, **360b**
Ḥassūn, Rizḳ Allāh ii, 471a — II, 483a
Ḥassūna v, 352a — V, 353a
Ḥātam Khān i, 444b — I, 457a
Hatay i, 468b, 517a; iii, **273a**; iv, 138b — I, 482b, 532b; III, **281a**; IV, 144a
Hataylā Pir → Ghāzī Miyān
Hātī Khān ii, 973a — II, 995b
Ḥāṭib b. Abī Baltaʿa iv, 821a — IV, 854a
Hātif iii, **273a,** 668b — III, **281a,** 690a
Hātif, Aḥmad iii, **273b** — III, **281b**
Hātifī, ʿAbd Allāh iii, 114a, **274a**; iv, 1010a, 1073b; v, 1105a — III, 116b, **281b**; IV, 1042b, 1105a; V, 1100b
Ḥaṭīm → Kaʿba
Ḥātim, Banū s, 61b, 387b, 388a — S, 62a, 388a
Ḥātim b. Aḥmad al-Ḥātimī v, 954b; s, 263a — V, 958a; S, 236a
Ḥātim b. ʿAlī al-Zurayʿid v, 954b, 1244b — V, 958a, b, 1235a
Ḥātim b. al-Ghashīm al-Mughallasī iii, 125b — III, 128a

Ḥātim b. Harthama i, 844a; iii, 231b, **274a**; v, 297b — I, 867b; III, 238a, **282a**; V, 297a
Ḥatim b. al-Ḥumās iii, 125b — III, 128b
Ḥātim al-Ahdal i, 255b, 781a — I, 263b, 804b
Ḥātim al-Ṭāʾī i, 195a, 364a, 1241b; ii, 961a; iii, **274b,** 343a; iv, 705a; s, 234b — I, 200b, 375a, 1279b; II, 983b; III, **282b,** 353b; IV, 733a; S, 234a
al-Ḥātimī, Abū ʿAlī Muḥammad iv, 249b; s, **361a** — IV, 260a; S, **361a**
Ḥatimid(e)s s, 236a — S, 236a
Hatra → al-Ḥaḍr
Hatta ii, 663a, 664a, 665b — II, 679b, 680b, 682a
Ḥaṭṭin → Ḥiṭṭīn
Hausa i, 179b, 1259a; ii, 10a, 479a; iii, **275a**; iv, 773b — I, 184a, 1297b; II, 10a, 491b; III, **283a**; IV, 804b
— language, literature / langue, littérature i, 179b; ii, 479a; iii, 278b; iv, 567b; v, 222b — I, 184b; II, 491b; III, 287a; IV, 589b; V, 220a
Havāyī i, 1063a — I, 1095a
Ḥawāla iii, **283a**; iv, 405b — III, **292a**; IV, 423a
Ḥawāla ii, 147b; iii, **283b** — II, 151b; III, **292b**
Ḥawār i, 535b — I, 552a
Ḥawārī iii, **285a** — III, **294a**
Ḥawāshī → Ḥāshiya
Ḥawāshib → Ḥawshabī
al-Hawāshim → Hāshimid(e)s
Hawāwīr iii, 300a — III, 309b
Hawāzin i, 12a, 544b; ii, 627a, 883b; iii, **285b,** 578a; s, 177b — I, 12a, 562a; II, 642b, 904a; III, **294a,** 598a; S, 178a
Ḥawḍ (ḥadīth) ii, 461b; iii, **286a** — II, 473a; III, **295a**
Ḥawḍ iii, **286b**; v, 884a, 888a — III, **295b**; V, 890a, b, 894b
Ḥawḍ (Mauritania, Mauritanie) iii, **288b**; v, 890a, 892a — III, **297b**; V, 896a, b, 898b
Hawdha b. ʿAlī i, 689b, 690a, 964a; iii, 166b — I, 710b, 711a, 993b; III, 170b
Ḥawfī iii, **289b** — III, **298b**
Ḥāwī iii, **291a,** 335a — III, **300a,** 345b
Hāwī iii, **291a** — III, **300a**
Ḥawīza i, 1096a; iii, **291b**; v, 80b — I, 1129a; III, **300b**; V, 82b
Hawking → Bayzara
Hawr al-Hammār s, 243a — S, 243a
Ḥawra iii, **291b** — III, **300b**
Ḥawra → al-Dhiʾāb
Hawrāmān iii, **292a** — III, **301a**
Ḥawrān i, 1079a, 1093b, 1277a; ii, 1021a; iii, **292a** — I, 1111a, 1126a, 1316a; II, 1045a; III, **301a**
al-Hawsamī, Abū Djaʿfar s, 363a — S, 363a
Ḥawshabī iii, **293b** — III, **302b**
Ḥawṭa iii, **294a**; s, 420b — III, **303a**; S, 420b
al-Ḥawṭa iii, **294b** — III, **303b**
Ḥawwāʾ iii, **295a,** 330b — III, **304b,** 340b
Ḥawwāʿ → Ḥāwī; Ruḳya
al-Ḥawwāʾ → Nudjūm
Hawwāra i, 250a, 254b, 1049a; ii, 979a, 1114b; iii, 66b, **295b,** 653b; iv, 481b, 568a; v, 515b — I, 258a, 262b, 1081a; II, 1001b, 1140b; III, 69a, **305a,** 675a; IV, 502b, 590a; V, 519a
Ḥawwārīn → Ḥuwwārīn
Ḥawz iii, **300b**; s, 48a, 144b — III, **309b**; S, 48b, 144b
Hayākil i, 835a — I, 858a
Hayʾa (astronomy, astronomie) → ʿIlm al-hayʾa
Hayʾa iii, 301a — III, **310a**
Ḥayāt iii, **302a** — III, **311a**
Ḥayāt b. Mulāmis → Ḥaywa b. Mulāmis
Ḥayāt, Shaykh iii, 230a — III, 237a
Ḥayāt Allāh Khān ii, 973b — II, 996a
Ḥayāt Muḥammad Khān i, 1195a — I, 1230b
Ḥayātī iv, 129a — IV, 134b
Ḥayātī → ʿAbd al-Hayy, Shaykh
Ḥayʾat-i shūrā-i dawlat ii, 658a — II, 674b
Ḥayātī-zāde iii, **303a** — III, **312b**
Hayāṭila i, 226a, b, 852a, 857a; ii, 1a; iii, 177a, **303b,** 584b; iv, 356a, 536a, 1172a, 1173b; v, 56b, 57a, 76a, 354b; s, 327a — I, 232b, 233a, 875b, 881a; II, 1a; III, 181a, **312b,** 604b; IV, 371b, 559a, 1205b, 1207a; V, 58a, b, 78a, 356a; S, 326b
Ḥayawān iii, **304b,** 311b; v, 991b — III, **313b,** 321a; V, 986b
Haybat Khān Niyāzī s, 324b — S, 324a
Ḥayḍ iii, **315b** — III, **325a**
Ḥaydar iii, **315b** — III, **325a**
Ḥaydar (clan) s, 105b — S, 105a
Ḥaydar (general/général) s, 301a — S, 301a
Ḥaydar, Āl iv, 857a — IV, 890a
Ḥaydar, Amīr (Bukhārā) i, 1295b — I, 1335b
Ḥaydar, Ghāzi 'l-Dīn → Ghāzi 'l-Dīn
Ḥaydar, Malik al-ʿUlamāʾ Mullā s, 4b, 292b — S, 3b, 292a
Ḥaydar, Mīr i, 530b — I, 546b
Ḥaydar, Shaykh i, 923a; iii, **315b**; iv, 34a, b, 573a; v, 243b — I, 951a; III, **325a**; IV, 36b, 595b; V, 241b
Ḥaydar al-Afshīn → al-Afshīn
Ḥaydar b. ʿAlī iii, **316a** — III, **325b**
Ḥaydar b. Kāʾus → al-Afshīn
Ḥaydar ʿAlī Khān i, 296b, 625a, 1015b; iii, **316b,** 428a; iv, 547a; v, 1259a, b, 1260a — I, 305b, 645b, 1047a; III, **326a,** 442a; IV, 571a; V, 1250a, b, 1251b
Ḥaydar Beg i, 153a — I, 157b
Ḥaydar Dūghlāt, Mīrzā i, 1002a; ii, 621b; iii, **317a**; iv, 213b, 410a, 612a, 708b; s, 131b, 167a, 324b, 366a — I, 1033a; II, 637b; III, **326b**; IV, 223a, 428a, 637a, 737a; S, 131a, 167a, 324a, 366a
Ḥaydar Ḳuli Sulṭān i, 240a — I, 247b
Ḥaydar Khān ʿAmū Ughlī s, **365a** — S, **364b**
Ḥaydar Malik s, 332b, **366a** — S, 332a, **366a**
Ḥaydar Pasha iv, 828a — IV, 861a
Ḥaydar Shāh b. Zayn al-ʿĀbidīn (Kashmīr) s, 131b, 329a — S, 130b, 328b
Ḥaydar Shihāb ii, 443b, 635a; v, 792b — II, 455b, 651a, b; V, 799a
Ḥaydar-i Āmulī, Bahāʾ al-Dīn iv, 49b, 698a; s, **363b** — IV, 52a, 726b; S, **363b**
Ḥaydar-oghlu Meḥmed i, 4a; iii, **317b**; iv, 766a — I, 4b; III, **327a**; IV, 796b
Ḥaydara b. Mahdī i, 345a — I, 355b
Ḥaydarābād (Deccan) i, 924a, 1170a; ii, 99b, 426b, 1119a; iii, **318a**; iv, 219b; v, 550b; s, 4b, 47a, 280a — I, 951b, 1205a; II, 101b, 437b, 1145a; III, **328a**; IV, 229a; V, 555a; S, 3b, 47b, 279b
- institutions ii, 426b; iii, 318b, 322b — II, 437b; III, 328b, 332b
- monuments iii, 319a, 448a — III, 328b, 463a
- Niẓām of/de i, 1170a, 1202b; iii, 318b, 322a — I, 1205a, 1238b; III, 328a, 332a
Ḥaydarābād (Sind) iii, **323b** — III, **333b**
Ḥaydarān iii, **324b** — III, **334b**
Ḥaydarī, Ḥaydar Bakhsh iii, 376b — III, 388a
Ḥaydarīkhāna s, 336a — S, 335b
Ḥaydarīs iv, 99a, 860b — IV, 103b, 893b
Ḥaydariyya iv, 474a — IV, 495a
Haydut i, 1267a — I, 1305b
Ḥayfā i, 946b; iii, **324b,** 365a — I, 976a; III, **334b,** 376b
Ḥāyil, Ḥāʾil iii, **326b**; s, 3b, 305a — III, **336b**; S, 2b, 304b
al-Ḥayḳ, Hayākil i, 181a — I, 186a
Haykal ii, 555a — II, 569a
Haykal, M. Ḥusayn i, 597b, 598a; ii, 467a; iv, 173a; v, 188b, 189b; s, 6b, 58a — I, 617a, 617b; II, 478b; IV, 180b; V, 185b, 187a; S, 5b, 58b
Haykal al-Zahra i, 488b — I, 503b

al-Ḥaykār (Aḥiḳar) v, 811b, 812a, 813a — V, 817b, 818a, 819a
al-Ḥayma iii, **327a** — III, **337a**
Ḥayr → Ḥā'ir
Ḥayr al-waḥsh (wuḥūsh) i, 898a; iii, 312a — I, 925a; III, 321a
Ḥayra iv, 95a — IV, 99a
Ḥayratī iv, 68a — IV, 71b
Ḥayrīdj s, 337a — S, 337a
Ḥays s, **366b** — S, **366b**
al-Ḥays s, 30b — S, 30b
Ḥayṣa Bayṣa iii, **327b**, 819b — III, **337b**, 843a
al-Hayṣam al-Hamdānī iii, 233a — III, 240a
Hayṣamiyya iv, 668a — IV, 695b
Hayṭal → Hayāṭila
al-Haytham b. ʿAdī iii, 136a, **328a**; s, 38b — III, 139a, **338a**; S, 39a
al-Haytham b. al-Rabīʿ b. Zurāra → Abū Ḥayyā al-Numayrī
Haythūm → Hethum
Hayūlā iii, **328a** — III, **338b**
Haywa b. Mulāmis al-Ḥaḍramī iv, 115a — IV, 120b
Ḥayy i, 306a; iii, **330a** — I, 315b; III, **340b**
Ḥayy b. Yaḳẓān iii, **330b**, 944a, 957a, 974b — III, **341a**, 968b, 981b, 999a
Ḥayya iii, **344b**; iv, 95a — III, **334b**; IV, 99a
Ḥayya b. Turkī b. Djalwī s, 305b — S, 305b
Ḥayyān b. Djabala iv, 646b — IV, 673a
Ḥayyān b. Khalaf → Ibn Ḥayyān
Ḥayyān al-Sarrādj iv, 837a — IV, 870a
Hazadj → ʿArūḍ
Hazār Afsāna i, 361a, b; iii, 313b — I, 371b, 372b; III, 323a
Hazāra (Afghānistān) i, 88a, 224a, b, 229a, 857a, 1010a, 1173a; ii, 5b; iii, 335a, 1100b, 1107b; s, **367a**, b — I, 90b, 231a, 236a, 881a, 1041a, 1222a; II, 5b; III, 345b, 1127b, 1135a; S, **366b**, 367a
Hazāra (Pakistān) iii, **335b** — III, **345b**
Hazāradjāt s, **367a** — S, **367b**
Hazārasp i, 421a, 872a; ii, 194a; iii, **336b**; s, 228b, 420a — I, 433a, 896a; II, 200a; III, **346b**; S, 228b, 420a
Hazārasp, Malik iii, 337a, b; v, 826b — III, 347a,b; V, 832b
Hazāraspid(e)s iii, **336b**,; iv, 32a; v, 824b, 826b — III, **347a**, 1041b; IV, 34a; V, 830b, 832b
Hazārāt i, 139b — I, 143b
Hazārdjarīb s, 140b, 309b — S, 140b, 309a
Hazārfann → Ḥusayn Hezārfenn
Hazāristān i, 223b — I, 230a
Hazārnao i, 238b — I, 245b
Hazhīr → ʿAbd al-Ḥusayn
Ḥāzī i, 659b; iv, 421b — I, 680b; IV, 439b → Kāhin
Ḥāzim b. ʿAlī ii, 484b — II, 497a
Ḥāzim b. Muḥammad al-Ḳarṭādjannī iii, **337b**; iv, 672b — III, 348a; IV, 700a
Ḥāzim b. Zayd al-Djahḍamī s, 384b — S, 385a
Ḥazīn, Muḥammad b. Abī Ṭālib (Shaykh ʿAlī) i, 680b, 1166a, 1301a; iii, 313b, **338b**; iv, 69b; s, 108a — I, 701a, 1200b, 1341a; III, 323a, **348b**; IV, 73a; S, 107b
Hazīrān → Taʾrīkh
al-Hazmīrī → Abū ʿAbd Allāh Muḥammad; Abū Zayd ʿAbd al-Raḥmān; Abū Yaʿazzā; Abū Zayd
Hazmīriyyūn iii, **338b** — III, **349a**
Hazrat, Āl s, 66b — S, 67a
Hazzāʿ b. Muḥammad i, 1032b — I, 1064a
Headgear → Libās
Heart → Ḳalb
Heaven → Samāʾ
Hebron, Hébron → al-Khalīl
Hedgehog → Ḳunfudh
Hedjaz → al-Ḥidjāz
Ḥefeṣ ben Yaṣlīaḥ iv, 306a — IV, 320a
Hegira, Hégire → Hidjra
Hejar, ʿAbd al-Raḥmān v, 483a — V, 486a
Ḥekīm-Bashî iii, **339b** — III, **350a**
Ḥekīm-oghlu ʿAlī Pasha → ʿAlī Pasha Ḥakīm-oghlu
Heliopolis iv, 442b — IV, 462b
Hell → Djahannam
Hellènes → Yūnān
Hellestheaios i, 102b — I, 105a
Helm → Safīna
Helmand, Helmend → Hilmand
Hélouan → Ḥulwān
Ḥelvā v, 642a, b — V, 646b
Hemerology, hémérologie → Ikhtiyārāt
Hemp (Indian) → Ḥashīsh
Hēmū i, 316a, 1136a; ii, 271b; iii, 423a — I, 326a, 1170a; II, 279b; III, 437a
Henna, Henné → Ḥinnāʾ
Henoch → Idrīs
Hepatoscopy/hépatoscopie iv, 331b — IV, 346a
Hephthalites → Hayāṭila
Heraclea → Ereğli
Heraldry, Héraldique → Hilāl; Rank; Shiʿār
Herat → Harāt
Herātī iv, 10b — IV, 11b
Hercule(s) → Hirḳil
Hercules, Pillars of/Hercule, Colonnes d'- → Ḳādis
Hereafter → Ākhira
Hereke → Ḳālī
Heresy, Hérésie → Bidʿa; Ghulāt; Ilḥād; Takfīr; Zandaḳa
Hergan Kale → ʿAmmūriya
Herī Rūd → Harī Rūd
Hérisson → Ḳunfudh
Héritage → Mīrāth
Herīz s, 142b — S, 142a
Hermes, Hermès → Hirmis
Hersek → Bosna
Hersekli ʿĀrif Ḥikmat i, 1302a; iii, 1200b — I, 1342a; III, 1230b
Hersek-zāde Aḥmed Pasha i, 244a, 1264b; iii, **340b**; iv, 565a; v, 774b — I, 251a, 1303a; III, **351a**; IV, 587b; V, 780b
Herzegovina, Herzégovine → Bosna
Ḥesene i, 483a — I, 497b
Heshdek i, 1075b — I, 1107b
Hethum I i, 639b; ii, 37b, 38a — I, 660a; II, 38a, b
Heybeli Ada → Marmara
Heyʾet-i aʿyān ii, 643a — II, 659a
Heyʾet-i mebʿūthān ii, 643a — II, 659a
Hezārfenn → Ḥusayn Hezārfenn
Hezārghrad iii, **342a** — III, **352b**
Hezārpāre → Aḥmad Pasha
Hiba (gift/cadeau) iii, **342b**; iv, 217b — III, **353a**; IV, 227a
Hiba (gift *inter vivos*/donation entre vifs) iii, **350a** — III, **361a**
al-Hība → Aḥmad al-Hība
al-Hiba ii, 1116a — II, 1142b
Hibat Allāh b. ʿAlī → Ibn Mākūlā
Hibat Allāh b. Djamīʿ → Ibn Djamīʿ
Hibat Allāh b. al-Ḥusayn s, 267a, 372a — S, 266b, 372a
Hibat Allāh b. Mākūlā → Ibn Mākūlā, Hibat Allāh
Hibat Allāh b. Malkā → Abu 'l-Barakāt
Hibat Allāh b. Muḥammad iii, **351b**; v, 815a — III, **362b**; V, 821a
Ḥibr → Kitāba
Ḥibrī iii, **351b** — III, **362b**
Ḥidāʾ → Ḥudāʾ
Ḥidād → ʿIdda, Libās

al-Hidāya al-Islāmiyya iv, 907a — IV, 940a
ʿHidayatʾ → Riḍā Ḳulī Khān
Hidāyat (Borneo) s, 150b — S, 150b
Hidāyat, Ṣādiḳ iii, **352a**; iv, 73a, b; v, 199b — III, **363a**; IV, 77a, b; V, 197a
Ḥidhāʾ → Libās
Hidjāʾ i, 442b, 584b, 586a; iii, **352b**; iv, 56a; s, 394a — I, 455a, 603a, 605a; III, **363b**; IV, 59a; S, 394b
al-Hidjāʾ, Ḥurūf → Ḥurūf al-hidjāʾ
Ḥidjāb i, 306b; iii, **359a**; v, 740a — I, 316a; III, **370b**; V, 745a
Ḥidjāba → Ḥādjib
al-Hidjar iii, **361b,** 1064b — III, **372b,** 1091b
al-Hidjarī i, 602b; iii, 926a — I, 622a; III, 950b
al-Ḥidjāz i, 25a, 37a, 46a, 77a, 103a, 268b, 272b, 315a, 443b, 539a, 554b; ii, 572b, 660a, 1030a; iii, 34b, 263b, **362a,** 606a, 1066b; iv, 1002a; v, 519a, b, 1127b; s, 3a, b, 4b, 10a, 20a, 198b, 305b — I, 25b, 38a, 47a, 79a, 106a, 276b, 281a, 324b, 456b, 555b, 572b; II, 587a, 676b, 1053b; III, 36a, 271a, **373a,** 626b, 1093b; IV, 1031b; V, 522b, 523a, 1124a; S, 2b, 3a, b, 9b, 20a, 198b, 305b
- dialect, dialecte i, 573b, 574a — I, 592b
- railway, chemin-de-fer i, 64b, 315a; ii, 289a; iii, 34b, 293a, 326a, 363a, **364a,** 605b; v, 998a — I, 66a, 324b; II, 297a; III, 36a, 302a, 336a, 374b, **375b,** 626b; V, 993a, b
Ḥidjāzī, Muḥammad iv, 73a; v, 199a — IV, 76b; V, 196a
Ḥidjr iv, 317a, 319b — IV, 331b, 333b
al-Ḥidjr iii, **365b** — III, **377a**
Hidjra iii, **366a**; s, **368a** — III, **378a**; S, **368a**
Hidjra, hudjra → Hidjar
Hidjris v, 131b — V, 134a, b
Hidjwiyya iv, 715b — IV, 744b
Hidrellez → Khiḍr-ilyās
Hierarchy of Saints → Abdāl; Ikhwān al-Ṣafāʾ
Hieroglyph(e)s → Barbā
Hīfūḳraṭīs (Īfūḳraṭīs) → Buḳrāṭ
Ḥifẓ → Ḳirāʾa, Ḳurʾān
Ḥikāya iii, **367a**; v, 187a, 812a, 951b — III, **379a**; V, 184b, 818a, 955b
Hikayat prang sabi i, 92a — I, 94b
Ḥikma iii, **377b**; iv, 120a; s, 324a — III, **389a**; IV, 125a; S, 323b
Ḥikmat Abū Zayd iv, 1152a — IV, 1184a
Ḥikmat Sulaymān iii, 521b, 1258b — III, 539b, 1291a
Ḥikmet, Aḥmad → Aḥmad Ḥikmet
Ḥikr s, **368b** — S, **368a**
Ḥīla → Ḥiyal
Hilāl iii, **379a** — III, **390b**
al-Hilāl ii, 403b, 466b, 472b — II, 414a, 478b, 484b
Hilāl, Banū i, 93b, 167b, 367a, 374a, b, 441a, 532b, 533a, 770b, 863a, 1049a, 1176a, 1204b; ii, 526a; iii, 138a, 324b, **385b**; iv, 337a, 739b, 827b, 830b; v, 60a, 760a, 1182b, 1196b; s, 62b, 328a — I, 96a, 172a, 378a, 385a, b, 454a, 548b, 549a, 793b, 887a, 1081a, 1211a, 1240b; II, 539a; III, 140b, 334b, **398a**; IV, 351b, 769b, 860b, 863b; V, 61b, 766a, 1172b, 1187a; S, 63a, 327b
Hilāl b. Abī Hilāl al-Ḥimṣī s, 412a — S, 412a
Hilāl b. Aḥwāz al-Tamīmī iv, 535a — IV, 558a
Hilāl b. Badr i, 512b; iii, 258b — I, 528a; III, 266a
Hilāl b. Mardanīsh i, 161a; iii, 865a — I, 165b; III, 889a
Hilāl b. Umayya v, 730b — V, 736a
Hilāl al-Ṣābiʾ i, 1354a, 1356b; ii, 80a; iii, 46a, 344a, **387b,** 741b; v, 624b — I, 1393a, 1395b; II, 81b; III, 48a, 354b, **400a,** 764a; V, 628b
al-Hilālī, Abu ʾl-Abbās al-Sidjilmāssī s, **370a** — S, **370a**
Hilālī, Badr al-Dīn i, 1301b; iii, **388a**; s, 46b — I, 1341a; III, **400b**; S, 47a
Ḥilf iii, **388b**; v, 581a, b, 596b — III, **401a**; V, 586a, b, 600a
Ḥilf al-fuḍūl i, 44b, 110a; iii, **389a**; v, 435a — I, 46a, 113a; III, **401b**; V, 437a
Ḥilla iii, 578a — III, 598a
al-Ḥilla i, 684a; iii, **389b**; v, 34a; s, 179a, 326a — I, 705a; III, **402a**; V, 35a; S, 180a, 325b
al-Ḥillī, Djamāl al-Dīn Ḥasan (ʿAllāma) ii, 774a; iii, **390a,** 1152a; iv, 277b; s, 56b, 380a — II, 792b; III, **402b,** 1180a; IV, 290a; S, 57a, 380a
al-Ḥillī, Nadjm al-Dīn Djaʿfār iii, **390b** — III, **403a**
al-Hillī, Naṣīr al-Dīn al-Kāshānī s, 364a — S, 363b
al-Ḥillī, Ṣafī al-Dīn → Ṣafī al-Dīn al-Ḥillī
al-Ḥillī, Taḳī al-Dīn Ḥasan iii, 1152a — III, 1180a
Ḥilm ii, 536a; iii, **390b**; v, 435a — II, 549b; III, **403a**; V, 436b
Hilmand i, 222a; iii, **392a**; v, 690b, 868a; s, 367a — I, 228b; III, **404b**; V, 695b, 874b; S, 368a
Ḥilmī, Aḥmed Shehbenderzāde iii, **392b** — III, **405a**
Ḥilmī, Hüseyn → Ḥusayn Ḥilmī Pasha
Ḥilmî, Refîq v, 483b — V, 486b
Ḥilmī, Tunalî iii, **393a** — III, **405b**
Ḥilmī Efendi, Aḥmed iii, **392b** — III, **405a**
Ḥilmī Pasha → Ḥusayn; Kečiboynuzu Ibrāhīm
Ḥimā i, 442a; iii, 294b, **393a**; iv, 488a, 1143b; s, 304b — I, 454b; III, 303b, **405b**; IV, 509a, 1175b; S, 304a
Ḥimā Ḍariyya ii, 159b; s, 234b — II, 164b; S, 234a
Ḥimā Kulayb ii, 159b — II, 164b
Ḥimār iii, **393b** — III, **406a**
Himatnagar ii, 1125a; iii, 1010a — II, 1151b; III, 1035b
Ḥimāya i, 1144a; ii, 143b; iii, **394a** — I, 1178b; II, 147a; III, **406b**
Ḥimṣ i, 57b, 85a, 119b, 609b, 1125a; ii, 590b; iii, **397a,** 1118b; s, 154a, 162b — I, 59a, 87b, 123a, 629b, 1159a; II, 605a; III, **409a,** 1146a; S, 154a, 162b
- buildings, bâtiments iii, 401a, b, 402a — III, 413b, 414a, b
Ḥimṣ, battle of/bataille de iii, **402b** — III, **415a**
al-Ḥimsī → Dīk al-Djinn
Himū → Hēmū
Ḥimyar → Yaman
Ḥimyar (language, langue) i, 564a; iii, 124b — I, 582a; III, 127a
Ḥimyar, Banū i, 195a, 544b, 1259b; ii, 223a, 244a; iii, 52a; iv, 448a; v, 119a, 120b, 315a; s, 337b — I, 200b, 561b, 1297b; II, 229b, 251a; III, 54a; IV, 468a; V, 121b, 123a, 314b; S, 337a
al-Ḥimyarī → Ibn ʿAbd al-Munʿim; al-Sayyid al-Ḥimyarī; Nashwān b. Saʿīd;
Hinā, Banū iii, **403b**; s, 355a, b — III, **415b**; S, 355a, b
Ḥināṭa iii, **403b** — III, **416a**
Hināwī → Hinā; ʿUmān
Hind i, 91a, 172a, 177b, 287b, 295b, 435b, 978b, 1068b; ii, 119b, 336a, 566a, 1084a; iii, 198b, **404b,** 481a; iv, 170a-b; v, 562a, 888a; s, 21a, 219b — I, 93b, 176b, 182b, 296b, 304b, 448a, 1009a, 1100b; II, 122b, 345b, 580a, 1109a; III, 203b, **417a,** 498a; IV, 177b; V, 566b, 894a; S, 21a, 219b
- agriculture ii, 909a; iii, 407b, 410a; iv, 1055b; v, 883b — II, 930b; III, 420a, 423a; IV, 1087a; V, 889b
- architecture i, 830b, 1321b; v, 294b — I, 853b, 1362a; V, 294b
- ethnography/ethnographie iii, 409b — III, 422a
- geography/géographie ii, 576b; iii, 404b; v, 938b — II, 591a; III, 417a; V, 942a
- institutions ii, 426a, 437a; iii, 491b, 532a, 1204a; iv, 268a, b; v, 1080b, 1101a, 1134b — II, 437a, 448b; III,

508b, 550b, 1234b; IV, 280a, b; V, 1078a, 1096b, 1130a
- languages, literature/langues, littérature i, 808a; ii, 1092a; iii, 164a, 412a; v, 232a — I, 831a; II, 1117b; III, 167b, 425a; V, 229b
- music/musique iii, 452b — III, 468a
Hind bint Abī ʿUbayda iii, 984a — III, 1008b
Hind bint ʿAwf b. Zubayr s, 92b — S, 92a
Hind bint al-Khuss iii, **454b**; iv, 472a — III, **470b**; IV, 493a
Hind bint ʿUtba iii, 152b, **455a**; iv, 332a — III, 156a, **471a**; IV, 346b
Hindāl b. Bābur i, 228b; iii, **455b**, 575a, b — I, 235a; III, **471a**, 595a, b
Hindī iii, 1b, 413b, **456a**, 460b — III, 1b, 426b, **472a**, 477a
Hindī, Sabk-i → Sabk-i Hindī
Hindibāʾ s, **370b** — S, **370a**
Hindiyya ii, 339b — II, 349b
Hindū i, 756b; iii, **458b**; iv, 794a — I, 779a; III, **474b**; IV, 826b
Hindū-Kush i, 221b, 223a, 1009b; ii, 29a; iii, **459b**; iv, 409b, 410b — I, 228a, 229b, 1040b; II, 29b; III, **476a**; IV, 427a, 428b
Hindū-Shāhīs iii, **460b**; v, 649a — III, **476b**; V, 653a
Hindūstān → Hind
Hindustānī i, 1167a; iii, **460b**; v, 644b — I, 1202a; III, **476b**; V, 648b
Hindustānī Beg → Gūran, Shaykh
Hinglādj → Las-bēla
Hinn s, **371a** — S, **370b**
Ḥinnāʾ iii, **461a**; v, 1b — III, **477a**; V, 1b
Ḥinṭa → Ḳamḥ
Hintāta iii, **461b** — III, **478a**
al-Hintātī → ʿAmīr al-Hintātī
Hippocrates, Hippocrate → Buḳrāṭ
Hippodrome → Maydān
Hippology, Hippologie → Bayṭār; Faras; Furūsiyya
Hippopotamus/Hippopotame → Faras al-Māʾ
Ḥirāʾ, Ḥarāʾ iii, **462a** — III, **478b**
al-Ḥīra i. 450b, 451b, 452a, 526a, 564b, 610a, 890a; iii, **462b**, 1254a; iv, 13b, 14a, 998b; v, 119a, 632a, b, 634a, b; s, 91a, 272b — I, 463b, 464b, 465a, 542a, 582b, 630a, 916b; III, **478b**, 1287a; IV, 14b, 15a, 1031a; V, 121b, 636a, b, 638a, b; S, 90b, 272a
Hiraḳla → Eregli
Ḥirār → Ḥarra
Ḥirbāʾ iii, **463a** — III, **479b**
Ḥirfa → Ṣinf
Hirḳil iv, 383b — IV, 400a
Hirmis i, 247a; iii, **463b**; iv, 120b; v, 111b; s, 270a, 407b — I, 255a; III, **479b**; IV, 126a; V, 114a; S, 269b, 408a
Ḥirth s, 355a, b — S, 355a
Ḥirz → Tamāʾim
Ḥisāb iii, **465a**; v, 224b — III, **481a**; V, 222a
Ḥisāb → ʿIlm al-ḥisāb; Muḥāsaba
Ḥisāb al-ʿaḳd iii, **466a** — III, **482b**
Ḥisāb al-djummal iii, **468a**; v, 224b — III, **484a**; V, 222a
Ḥisāb al-ghubār iii, **468b** — III, **485a**
Ḥisāb al-nīm iii, 468b — III, 484b
al-Ḥiṣāfī, Ḥasanayn s, 18a, **371a** — S, 18b, **371a**
al-Ḥiṣāfiyya al-Shādhiliyya s, 371a — S, 371a
Ḥiṣār (fortress, forteresse) iii, **483a** — III, **499b**
Ḥiṣār (Mā warāʾ al-Nahr) iii, **483a** — III, **500a**
Ḥiṣār (siege, siège) iii, **469a**; iv, 798b — III, **485b**; IV, 830b
Hisar, Abdülhak Şinasi iii, 260a, **484a**; v, 197a — III, 267b, **501a**; V, 194b
Ḥiṣār-Fīrūza ii, 134a; iii, 168a, 225b, 442b, **484b**; v, 884a, 855b; s, 206b — II, 137b; III, 171b, 232a, 457a, **501b**; V, 890b, 891b; S, 206a
Ḥiṣar-i Muḥammad → Narwar
Ḥisba i, 972b, 1335a; ii, 1064a; iii, 140a, **485b**, 489a, 491b, 681a, 960b; iv, 245a, 1161b — I, 1002b, 1375b; II, 1088b; III, 143a, **503a**, 505b, 508b, 702b, 985a; IV, 256a, 1193b
Hishām, Mawlāy ii, 510b — II, 523a
Hishām I, al-Riḍā i, 493b, 494a, 497b; iii, **495a**; s, 92a — I, 508b, 512b; III, **512a**; S, 92a
Hishām II, al-Muʾayyad biʾllāh i, 6a, 75b, 84b, 494a,b; ii, 389a; iii, 46a, 74b, 147a, 220a, **495b**, 746b, 755b; v, 1239a, b; s,183a — I, 6a, 76b, 86b, 509a,b; II, 399b; III, 48a, 77a, 150a, 226b, **512b**, 769b, 778b; V, 1230a, b; S, 184b
Hishām III al-Muʿtadd biʾllāh i, 1309b; iii, **496a**, 542a, 938b — I, 1350a; III, **513a**, 561a, 963b
Hishām b. ʿAbd al-Malik (Umayyad(e)) i, 142a, 613a,b, 1102b, 1292b; ii, 85b, 117b, 327b, 600b, 1026b; iii, **493a**, 747b; iv, 726a, 727a; v, 16b; s, 10a, 31b, 251b, 252a — I, 146b, 633a,b, 1136a, 1332a; II, 87a, 120a, 337a, 615a, 1050b; III, **510a**, 770b; IV, 755a, 756a; V, 17a; S, 9b, 31b, 251b, 252a
Hisham b. ʿAbd Manāf iv, 839a — IV, 872a
Hishām b. ʿAmr al-Taghlibī iv, 535a, 536a, 708a — IV, 558a, 559b, 736b
Hishām b. ʿAbd al-Djabbār iii, 819a — III, 843a
Hishām b. ʿAmr al-Fuwaṭī i, 4b; iii, **496b**, 1266a; s, 89a, 226b — I, 5a; III, **513b**, 1299a; S, 89a, 226b
Hishām b. al-Ḥakam i, 128a, 850a; ii, 374b, 554a; iii, **496b**, 1037a, 1063a; iv, 182b, 271b, 692b, 1132a; v, 384b; s, 89a, 225b, 392a, 393b — I, 131b, 873b; II, 385a, 567b; III, **513b**, 1063a, 1089b; IV, 190b, 283b, 721a, 1163b; V, 385b; S, 88b, 225b, 392b, 394a
Hishām b. Ḳubayb b. Rusaḥ iii, 125b — III, 128b
Hishām b. Muḥammad al-Kalbī → al-Kalbī
Hishām b. ʿUrwa iii, 810b — III, 834a
al-Hishamī (musician/musicien) s, 64a, 183a — S, 64b, 184b
Ḥishna, Banū v, 317b — V, 317a
Ḥiṣn iii, **498a**; iv, 1139b — III, **515a**; IV, 1171a
Ḥiṣn al-Akrād i, 1292b; iii, **503a**; s, 204b — I, 1332a; III, **520b**; S, 204b
Ḥiṣn Daī s, 132a — S, 131b
Ḥisn Dikbāya → al-Dīkdān
Ḥisn Ibn ʿUmāra → al-Dīkdān
Ḥisn al-Faradj i, 165b — I, 170a
Ḥiṣn al-Ghurāb iii, **506a** — III, **523a**
Ḥiṣn Kayfā i, 664b, 665a, 666b, 804b, 1067a, 1068a; ii, 344b; iii, **506b**; v, 459a; s, 250a — I, 684b, 686a, 687a, 828b, 1099a, 1100a; II, 354a; III, **524a**; V, 462a; S, 250a
Ḥiṣn al-Mahdī iv, 674b — IV, 702a, b
Ḥiṣn Manṣūr → Adiyaman
Ḥiṣn al-Ṭāḳ iii, 502a — III, 519a
Ḥiṣn Ziyād → Kharpūt
Ḥiss iii, **509a** — III, **526a**
Ḥiṣṣa, Ḥiṣṣe → Tīmār, Waḳf
Hissar → Ḥiṣār
Histoire secrète des Mongols II, 42a, 44b, 585b
Historian/Historien; Historiography/Historiographie; History/Histoire iii, 509b — III, 527a
Hīt ii, 947a; iii, **510a** — II, 969a; III, **527a**
Hitti, Philip v, 1255b, 1257a — V, 1246b, 1248a
Ḥiṭṭīn i, 798a, 946b; iii, **510b**; s, 205b — I, 821a, 975b; III, **528a**; S, 205a
Ḥiyāḍ → Ḥawḍ
Ḥiyal iii, 159b, **510b**; iv, 253b; s, **371b** — III, 163a, **528a**; IV, 265a; S, **371a**
Ḥizām b. Ghālib iv, 215a — IV, 224b
Ḥizb, aḥzāb ii, 224a; iii, **513a** — II, 231a; III, **530b**
Ḥizb (political, politique) ii, 429b; iii, **514a** — II,

440b; III, **531b**
Ḥizb al-aḥrār al-dustūriyyīn iii, 518a – III, 536a
Ḥizb al-istiḳlāl al-ʿarabī iii, 521a, 522a – III, 538b, 540a
Ḥizb al-lāmarkaziyya iii, 520a – III, 537b
Ḥizb al-umma iii, 515b – III, 533b
al-Ḥizb al-waṭanī iii, 515a; iv, 784b; s, 5b – III, 532b; IV, 816a; S, 4b
Ḥizḳīl i, 404b; ii, 242a; iii, **535a** – I, 416a; II, 249a; III, **554a**
Hizzān, Banū i, 482b – I, 497a
Hlivne → Livno
Ḥmad u-Mūsā i, 35a; ii, 527a; iii, **535b**; v, 132b – I, 35b; II, 540a; III, **554a**; V, 135b
Ḥmād<u>sh</u>a → Ḥamādi<u>sh</u>a
Ḥnay<u>sh</u>iyya iv, 95a – IV, 99a
Hōbyōt s, 339b – S, 339a
Hoca → <u>Kh</u>ʷā<u>dj</u>a
Hochow v, 847b, 848a, 851b – V, 851b, 852a, 855b
Hodh → Ḥawḍ
Ho<u>dj</u>a Aḥmed Sulṭān i, 1076b – I, 1108b
Hodna → Ḥuḍna
Hoesein Djajadiningrat s, **374b** – S, **374b**
Hofuf → al-Hufūf
Ḥogariyya → Ḥu<u>dj</u>riyya
Hoggar → Ahaggar
Holiness → Ḳadāsa
Hollandais I, 766b, 1381b; II, 27b, 28a, 400b, 401a; III, 586a, 1219b, 1252b; IV, 1002b; V, 361b, 1145a
Holy Places iii, 536a
Holy War → <u>D</u>jihād
Homiletics, Homélie → Waʿẓ
Homme → Insān
Homonym(e) → Aḍḍād
Homosexuality/-é → Liwāṭ
Homs → Ḥimṣ
Honaz → <u>Kh</u>ōnās
Hongrie I, 275b, 300b, 409b, 719a, 1107b, 1198b; II, 576b, 734b; III, 1026a; IV, 615a, b; V, 374a, **1006b**
Honour, Honneur → ʿIrḍ; Mufā<u>kh</u>ara
Hoopoe → Hudhud
Hôpital → Bīmāristān; Dār al-<u>Sh</u>ifāʾ
Hor → <u>Kh</u>awr
Horde iii, **536a** – III, **555a**
Horde Blanche I, 1140a; II, 45a,b
Horde d'Or → Bātūʾides; Ḳipčaḳ; Sarāy
Horloge → Sāʿa
Hormuz → Hurmuz
Hormuzd Arda<u>sh</u>īr → al-Ahwāz
Horn → Būḳ
Horology → Sāʿa
Horoscope → Ṭāliʿ
Horse → Faras; <u>Kh</u>ayl
Horseman → Fāris
Horsemanship → Furūsiyya
Horticulture → Būstān
Ho<u>sh</u>ang<u>sh</u>āh <u>Gh</u>ōrī → <u>Gh</u>ūrid(e)s
Hospital → Bīmāristān; Dār al-<u>Sh</u>ifāʾ
Hospitallers/Hospitaliers → Dāwiyya and/et Īsbitāriyya
Hospitality, Hospitalité → Da<u>kh</u>īl; Ḍayf; <u>D</u>jiwār; I<u>dj</u>āra
Hostelry → Funduḳ; <u>Kh</u>ān
Hōt → Balūčistān
Hôtellerie → Funduḳ; <u>Kh</u>ān
Hotin → <u>Kh</u>otin
Houri → Ḥūr
House → Dār
Household → <u>Kh</u>āne
Hsin-chiao iv, 554b – IV, 578a, b
Hsining v, 848a – V, 852a
Hubal iii, **536b**; iv, 263b, 264a, 320a, 321a; v, 77b – III, **555b**; IV, 275b, 334a, 336a; V, 79b
Hubayra b. Abī Wahb iii, 975b – III, 1000a
Hubay<u>sh</u>, Muḥammad s, 411a – S, 411b
Ḥubay<u>sh</u> b. al-Ḥasan al-Dima<u>sh</u>ḳī s, **375b** – S, **375b**
Ḥubay<u>sh</u> b. Muba<u>shsh</u>ir ii, 373b – II, 383b
Ḥubb → ʿI<u>sh</u>ḳ
Ḥubbā ii, 551b – II, 565a
Hubbu ii, 960a, 1132b – II, 982b, 1159a
Ḥubus → Waḳf
al-Ḥubūs iii, **537a** – III, **556a**
Hūd i, 169a, 828b, 1045a; iii, **537b**; iv, 448b; v, 421a – I, 174a, 851b, 1076b; III, **556a**; IV, 468b; V, 423a
Hūd, Banū → Hūdid(e)s
Ḥudāʾ ii, 1028b, 1073a; iii, 667b – II, 1052a, 1097b; III, 689b
Hudā ii, 294a – II, 302a
Hudā <u>Sh</u>aʿrāwī Pa<u>sh</u>a, Madame iii, 360a; v, 740a – III, 371b; V, 745b
Hūdāʿī, ʿAziz Maḥmūd ii, 542b, 543a; iii, **538a**; iv, 191b, 972a – II, 555b, 556b; III, **557a**; IV, 199b, 1004a
al-Huḍaybī, Ḥasan iii, 518a, 1069a, b; iv, 160a – III, 535b, 1096a; IV, 166b
al-Ḥudaybiya iii, **539a**; iv, 320a; s, 131a – III, **557b**; IV, 334a; S, 130a
al-Ḥudayda i, 709b; iii, **539b**; s, 30b – I, 731a; III, **558a**; S, 30b
al-Ḥuḍayn of/de Ūḳ s, 326b – S, 326a
al-Ḥuḍayn b. al-Mun<u>dh</u>ir iii, **540a** – III, **558b**
Ḥuḍayr b. Simāk i, 771b, 1283a; iv, 1187b; v, 995a – I, 794b, 1322b; IV, 1220a; V, 990b
Hu<u>dh</u>alī i, 115a; iii, 540b – I, 118b; III, 559b
al-Hu<u>dh</u>alī → Abū <u>Dh</u>uʾayb; Abū Kabīr; Abū Ṣa<u>kh</u>r; Saʿīd b. Masʿūd
Ḥu<u>dh</u>ayfa b. ʿAbd b. Fuḳaym b. ʿAdī → al-Ḳalammas
Ḥu<u>dh</u>ayfa b. Badr al-Fazārī ii, 873a, 1023a; s, 177a, b, 178a – II, 893b, 1046b; S, 178a, b, 179a
Hu<u>dh</u>ayfa b. al-Yamān i, 190a, 448b; iii, 512a, 1059b; v, 945b – I, 194b, 461b; III, 529b, 1086a; V, 949a
Hu<u>dh</u>ayl i, 149a, 545a; iii, 363b, **540a**; v, 763a – I, 153a, 562a; III, 375a, **559a**; V, 769a
Hudhud iii, **541b** – III, **560a**
Hūdid(e)s i, 1040b; iii, **542a,** 849b; v, 683a; s, 80b, 81a, 381b – I, 1072a; III, **560b,** 873b; V, 688a; S, 80b, 81a, 382a
Ḥu<u>dj</u>arīyya i, 866a; ii, 507a, 1080a,b; iii, 545b, 902b; iv, 1091b, 1092a – I, 890b; II, 519b, 1105b; III, 564b, 926b; IV, 1122b, 1123a
al-Ḥu<u>dj</u>ariyya (Yaman) v, 895a – V, 901a
al-Ḥu<u>dj</u>āwī, Mūsā i, 949b; iii, 162a – I, 978b; III, 165b
Ḥu<u>dj</u>aylān b. Ḥamad iv, 717b – IV, 746a
Ḥu<u>dj</u><u>dj</u>a (literary, littéraire) iii, **543b** – III, **562a**
Ḥu<u>dj</u><u>dj</u>a i, 832b; ii, 97b, 98a; iii, 254a, **544b**; iv, 203b – I, 855b; II, 99b, 100a; III, 261a, **563b**; IV, 212b
Ḥu<u>dj</u><u>dj</u>ā<u>dj</u> iii, 339a – III, 349a
Ḥu<u>dj</u><u>dj</u>at i, 283b; s, 157b – I, 292a; S, 158a
Ḥu<u>dj</u>r b. ʿAdī al-Kindī i, 693b; ii, 89b; iii, 242a, **545a,** 1265b; v, 349a, 499b – I, 714b; II, 91a; III, 249a, **564a,** 1298a; V, 349b, 502b
Ḥu<u>dj</u>r b. al-Ḥāri<u>th</u> i, 99a, 527a, 683b; ii, 785a; iii, 1177a; v, 118b – I, 101b, 543a, 704a; II, 804a; III, 1206a; V, 121a
Ḥu<u>dj</u>r Ākil al-Murār i, 526b, 548b; v, 118b, 119a – I, 542b, 566a; V, 121a, b
Ḥu<u>dj</u>ra iii, **545b** – III, **564b**
Ḥu<u>dj</u>riyya iii, **545b** – III, **564b**
al-Ḥu<u>dj</u>wīrī, ʿAlī i, 794b; ii, 55a; iii, 84a,b, 435b, **546a,** 570b; iv, 616b, 697a – I, 818a; II, 56a; III, 86b, 87a, 449b, **565a,** 590a; IV, 641a, 725b
Hudna ii, 131a, 303a; iii, **546b** – II, 134b, 311b; III,

565b
Ḥudna i, 749a; iii, **547b**; iv, 478b; s, 144b — I, 771b; III, **566b**; IV, 499b; S, 144b
Ḥudūd iii, **548a** — III, **567a**
Hudūd al-ʿĀlam i, 5a, 967a; ii, 581a, 799b; iii, 406a; iv, 223b, 342a, 1079b; v, 107b, 1011a; s, **376a** — I, 5b, 996b; II, 595b, 818b; III, 418b; IV, 233a, 356b, 1111a; V, 109b, 1007a; S, **376a**
Ḥudūd al-dīn ii, 170a — II, 175a
Ḥudūth v, 96a, b — V, 98a, b
Ḥudūth al-ʿālam iii, **548a** — III, **567a**
Huelva → Walba
Huesca(r) → Washḳa
Huete → Wabdha
Ḥufāsh iii, **548b** — III, **567b**
al-Hufūf iii, 237b, **548b**; iv, 925b; s, 234b — III, 244a, **567b**; IV, 958b; S, 234b
Huile → Zayt
al-Ḥukamāʾ i, 95a — I, 97b
Ḥukaym b. Djabala ii, 415a; iii, 583a — II, 425b; III, 603a
Ḥukm i, 257a, 1170b; ii, 273a, 294a; iii, 306b, **549a**; v, 241b — I, 265a, 1205b; II, 281b, 302a; III, 315b, **568a**; V, 239b
Hukōm i, 742b, 746b — I, 764b, 769a
Ḥuḳūḳ iii, **551b** — III, **570b**
Ḥüküm → Ḥukm
Ḥukūma i, 384a; iii, **551b** — I, 395a; III, **570b**
Ḥükūmet i, 469a — I, 482b
Ḥulā (ornaments, ornements) → Libās
al-Ḥūla (lake/lac) iii, **568b** — III, **588b**
Ḥūla (town/ville) iii, **568b** — III, **588b**
Hūlāgū (Īl-Khān) i, 21a, 190a, 329b, 353b, 665a, 787a, 902b, 1086b, 1188a, 1314b; ii, 47a, 194a, 204b, 284b, 376b, 606a, 966a, 1056b; iii, 208b, **569a,** 1121a; iv, 30b, 349b, 482a, 521a; v, 455b, 491a, 598a, 826b — I, 21b, 194b, 340a, 364b, 686a, 810a, 930a, 1119a, 1223a, 1354b; II, 48a, 200a, 211a, 292b, 387a, 621a, 987b, 1081a; III, 214b, **589a,** 1148b; IV, 32b, 364b, 503a, 544a; V, 458a, 494a, 601b, 833a
Hūlāgū (Lahore) iii, **569b** — III, **589b**
al-Ḥulal al-Mawshiyya iii, **570a** — III, **589b**
Ḥulm → Taʿbīr al-Ruʾyā
Ḥulmāniyya iii, **570b** — III, 590a
Hulu Sungai s, 150b — S, 150b
Ḥulūl iii, 102b, **570b**; iv, 283a — III, 104b, **590b**; IV, 295b
Ḥulwān (Irāḳ) iii, **571b**; v, 89b, 460b; s, 122b, 273a — III, **591a**; V, 92a, 463b; S, 122a, 273a
Ḥulwān (Miṣr) iii, **572a** — III, **591b**
Ḥulwān (donative, don) → Inʿām; Māl al-bayʿa; Pīshkash
Ḥulwān (tax, impôt) ii, 148b — II, 152b
al-Ḥulwānī, Abu 'l-Fatḥ → Abu 'l-Fatḥ al-Ḥulwānī
Humā iii, **572a** — III, **592a**
Humā (poet/poète) iv, 70a — IV, 73b
Ḥumāḥim i, 181a — I, 186a
Humai iv, 567a — IV, 589b
Humām, Nāṣir al-Dīn ii, 318a — II, 327b
Ḥumām b. Yūsuf i, 1029a; iii, 300a; iv, 723a — I, 1060b; III, 309a; IV, 752a
Humām al-Dīn b. ʾAlāʿ Tabrīzī iii, **572b** — III, **592b**
al-Ḥumās b. Ḳubayb iii, 125b — III, 128b
Humāy iii, 572b; iv, 809b — III, 592a; IV, 842a
Ḥumayd, Āl iv, 765a; s, 355b — IV, 795b; S, 355a
Ḥumayd, Banū i, 862b — I, 887a
Ḥumayd b. ʿAbd al-Hamīd al-Tūsī i, 316a; iii, **573a** — I, 325b; III, **592b**
Ḥumayd b. Ḥurayth al-Kalbī ii, 1023b; iv, 493a — II, 1047b; IV, 514b
Ḥumayd b. Maḥmūd ii, 484b — II, 497a
Ḥumayd b. Thawr al-Hilālī iii, **573a**; iv, 744b — III, **593a**; IV, 774b
Ḥumayd al-Arḳaṭ i, 1297b; iii, **573b** — I, 1337b; III, **593a**
Ḥumayda, Amīr iii, 952b — III, 977a
Ḥumayḍa b. Muḥammad i, 1032b — I, 1064a
al-Ḥumaydī, Abū ʿAbd Allāh i, 94b; ii, 72a; iii, **573b,** 790b — I, 97a; II, 73b; III, **593b**
al-Ḥumayma iii, **574a** — III, **594a**
Ḥumaynī i, 782a — I, 805b
Humāyūn iii, 572b, **574a** — III, 592a, **594a**
Humāyūn, Nāṣir al-Dīn (Mughal) i, 80b, 228b, 252b, 316a, 413a, 628a, 852b, 914b, 962a, 970a, 1135b, 1192a, 1218b, 1323b; ii, 120b, 155a, 259a, 264b, 271a, b, 494a, 498b, 973a; iii, 199b, 348a, 422b, 423a, 449a, 455b, 485a, 492b, **575a,** 633a; iv, 475a, 523b, 533b, 537a, 1022a; v, 598a, 1217a; s, 3a, 312a, 313a, b, 325a — I, 82b, 235a, 260b, 326a, 443b, 648b, 876b, 942b, 991b, 1000a, 1169b, 1227b, 1255a, 1364a; II, 123b, 160a, 265b, 272b, 279b, 506b, 511a, 995b; III, 204b, 358b, 436a, 437a, 464a, 471b, 502a, 509b, **595a,** 654a; IV, 496a, 546a, 557a, 560a, 1054a; V, 602a, 1206b; S, 2b, 312a, 313a, 324b
Humāyūn Shāh Bahmanī iii, 421a, b, **577a** — III, 434b, 435a, **597a**
Humāyūn-nāma iv, 505a — IV, 527a
Ḥumrān b. Abān i, 441a — I, 453b
Ḥumrīn → Ḥamrīn, Djabal
Ḥums iii, **577b** — III, **597b**
Ḥumūd b. ʿAzzān s, 355b — S, 355b
Hūn i, 120a — I, 123a
Ḥunayn (Makka) i, 9a, 12a; iii, 500a, **578a** — I, 9a, 12a; III, 517a, **598a**
Hunayn (seaport/port) s, **376b** — S, **376b**
Ḥunayn b. Isḥāḳ i, 213a, 234a, 235a, 236a, 327a, 570a, 589a, 631b, 785b, 1014b, 1149b; ii, 60a, 300b, 349b, 358b, 402b; iii, **578b,** 977a; iv, 110a, 254b; v, 133b, 701b; s, 52b, 375b — I, 219a, 241b, 242a, 243a, 337a, 588b, 608b, 652a, 808b, 1045b, 1184a; II, 61a, 309a, 359a, 368b, 413a; III, **598b,** 1001b; IV, 115a, 266a; V, 136a, 706b; S, 53a, 375b
Hungary i, 267b, 291b, 398a, 698a, 1075b, 1163b; ii, 562b, 716a; iii, 1001a; iv, 591b; v, 373a, **1010b**
Huns → Hayāṭila
Hunting → Bayzara; Fahd; Ṣayd; Ṭard
Hunting songs → Tardiyya
Hunza and/et Nagir iii, **581a**; s, 158b, 367b — III, **601a**; S, 158b, 367b
Huppe, la → Hudhud
Ḥūr ii, 447b, 449a; iii, **581b** — II, 459b, 460b; III, **601b**
Ḥūrānī, Akram iv, 125a — IV, 130b
Ḥurayḍa s, 337b — S, 337a
Ḥurayfish al-Makkī iv, 1006b — IV, 1038b
Ḥuraymilā iii, **582b** — III, **602b**
Hurayriyya iv, 838a — IV, 871a
al-Hūrīnī, Naṣr i, 596b — I, 616a
Ḥurḳūs b. Zuhayr ii, 415a; iii, **582b** — II, 426a, III, **603a**
Hurmuz iii, **583b** — III, **604a**
Hurmuz I-V iii, 584a, b — III, 604b
Hurmuz (Hormuz) i, 8a, 535b, 553a, 928a, 942b, 1013a; iii, **584b,** 1121b; iv, 500b, 764b; v, 149a, 150b, 183a, 671b, 673a, 675b; s, 115a, 129a, 234b — I, 8b, 552a, 570b, 956a, 971b, 1044b; III, **604b,** 1149a; IV, 522a, 795a; V, 151b, 152b, 180b, 676b, 677a, 678a, 680b; S, 114b, 128a, 234a
Hurmuz, Bā iii, **586a** — III, **606a**
al-Hurmuzān iii, 582b, **586a**; iv, 97a — III, 603a, **606a**; IV, 101b
Ḥurr iii, **587b** — III, **607b**
al-Ḥurr b. ʿAbd al-Raḥmān al-Thaḳafī iii, **587b**; v, 510a; s, 81b — III, **607b**; V, 513b; S, 81b

al-Ḥurr b. Yazīd iii, **588a,** 609a — III, **608a,** 630a
al-Ḥurr b. Yūsuf ii, 328a — II, 337b
al-Ḥurr al-ʿĀmilī iii, **588a,** 1152a; iv, 165b; s, 57a — III, **608b,** 1180a; IV, 172b; S, 57b
Ḥurr Riyā b. Yazīd iv, 638a — IV, 664a
Ḥurrāk iv, 456b — IV, 476b
Hurra-yi Khuttalī s, 125b — S, 125a
Ḥurriyya iii, **589a,** 1062b, 1063b — III, **609a,** 1089a, 1090a
Ḥürriyet we Iʿtilāf Fîrkasî ii, 104b; iii, 520a, **594b** — II, 107a; III, 538a, **615a**
Ḥurūb al-ṣalībiyya ii, 64a — II, 65a
Ḥurūf, ʿIlm al- ii, 376b, 734b; iii, **595b** — II, 386b, 753a; III, **616a**
Ḥurūf al-hidjāʾ iii, 205a, **596b** — III, 210b, **617b**
Ḥurūf muḳaṭṭaʿāt ii, 104b — II, 106b
Ḥurūf al-ʿulwiyya iv, 203a — IV, 212a
Ḥurūf al-zimām ii, 332b — II, 342a
Ḥurūfī → Faḍl Allāh
Ḥurūfiyya i, 193a, 260a, 720b, 1099b, 1162a, 1248a; ii, 733a, 924a, 1095a; iii, **600a**; iv, 48b, 721b; v, 823a — I, 199a, 268a, 742a, 1132b, 1196b, 1286a; II, 751b, 945b, 1120b; III, **620b**; IV, 51b, 750b; V, 829a
Ḥusām, Fakhr al-Dīn ii, 318a — II, 327b
al-Ḥusām b. Ḍirār → Abu ʾl-Khaṭṭār
Huṣam al-Dawla → Malik b. ʿAlī al-Barānī
Ḥusām al-Dawla Ardashīr b. Ḥasan iii, 810a; v, 662b — III, 833b; V, 667b
Ḥusām al-Dawla Ardashīr b. Kīnakhwār i, 1110a — I, 1143b
Ḥusām al-Dawla Shahriyār (Bāwandid(e)) s, 363b — S, 363a
Ḥusām al-Dawla Tāsh ii, 748b, 749a; iv, 358a — II, 767a; IV, 373b
Ḥusām al-Dīn → Timurtash
Ḥusām al-Dīn, (Ḳapūdān) ii, 26b — II, 26b
Ḥusām al-Dīn b. Abī ʿAlī iii, 967a — III, 991b
Ḥusām al-Dīn b. ʿAlī Shīr ii, 989a — II, 1012a
Ḥusām al-Dīn Abu ʾl-Shawḳ → Abu ʾl-Shawḳ Fāris
Ḥusām al-Dīn Alp Yürük iv, 738a — IV, 767b
Ḥusām al-Dīn Čelebi ii, 19a, 394b, 395a; iii, **602a** — II, 19b, 405a, b; III, **623a**
Ḥusām al-Dīn Khān ii, 1124a — II, 1150b
Ḥusām al-Dīn Luʾluʾ → Luʾluʿ
Ḥusām Girāy i, 310b — I, 320b
Ḥusām Khān v, 783a, b — V, 789b
Ḥusām Khān (Gudjarāt) s, 335b — S, 335b
Ḥusāmzāda Muṣṭafā Efendi iii, 1243a — III, 1275a
al-Ḥusayma v, 80a; s, **377a** — V, 82a; S, **377a**
Ḥusayn, Admiral/Amiral → Amīr Ḥusayn
Ḥusayn, King/le roi (Hidjāz) → al-Ḥusayn b. ʿAlī, Sharīf
Ḥusayn, King of Jordan/roi de Jordanie ii, 674b; iii, 264b; s, 7b, 9a — II, 691b; III, 272a; S, 6b, 8b
Ḥusayn I (Djalāyirid(e)) i, 66b; ii, 401b; iv, 584b — I, 68b; II, 412a; IV, 608a
Ḥusayn II (Djalāyirid(e)) ii, 401b; — II, 412b
Ḥusayn I (Ṣafawid(e)) i, 1068a; ii, 87b; iii, 348b, **603b,** 1102b, 1190b; iv, 37a, 104a, 1043b, 1092b; v, 493b, 494a, 1087a — I, 1100b; II, 89b; III, 359b, **624a,** 1129b, 1220a; IV, 39b, 108b, 1075a, 1123b; V, 496b, 497a, 1084b
Ḥusayn, Mullā i, 833a, 846b; v, 664a — I, 856a, 870a; V, 669a
al-Ḥusayn b. ʿAbd Allāh → Ibn Sīnā
Ḥusayn b. ʿAbd al-Raḥmān al-Ahdal → Ibn al-Ahdal
Ḥusayn b. ʿAbd al-Wahhāb ii, 845b, 849a — II, 865b, 869a
Ḥusayn b. Abi Bakr al-ʿAydarūs i, 782a — I, 805b
al-Ḥusayn b. Aḥmad → Abū ʿAbd Allāh al-Shīʿī; Ibn Khālawayh
Ḥusayn b. Aḥmad al-Shahīd ii, 730a — II, 748b
al-Ḥusayn b. ʿAlī → Ibn Mākūlā; al-Maghribī; al-Ṭughrāʾī
Ḥusayn b. ʿAlī (Ḥusaynid(e)) i, 1110b; iii, **604b,** 635b; iv, 828b — I, 1144a; III, **625b,** 657a; IV, 861b
al-Ḥusayn b. ʿAlī (Khayratīd(e)) ii, 518a — II, 530b
al-Ḥusayn b. ʿAlī, Ṣāḥib Fakhkh i, 402b, 551a; ii, 745a; iii, **615b** — I, 414a, 568b; II, 763b; III, **636b**
al-Ḥusayn b. ʿAlī, Sharīf i, 39a, 98b, 555a, 709b; ii, 289b, 429b, 531b, 572b; iii, 263a, b, 363b, **605a,** 1065b, 1066b; iv, 782b, 947a; v, 62b, 63a, 998a, 1055a, b; s, 3b, 4b, 293b — I, 40a, 101a, 572b, 731a; II, 297b, 440b, 544b, 587a; III, 270b, 271a, 375a, **626a,** 1092a, 1093a; IV, 814a, 979b; V, 64b, 993a, b, 1051b, 1052a; S, 3a, b, 293a
al-Ḥusayn b. ʿAlī b. Abī Ṭālib i, 44b, 55a, 113b, 385a, 430b, 508b, 550a, 711a; ii, 843a, 848b, 912a; iii, 119b, 164b, 242a, 588a, **607a**; iv, 637a; s, 94a, 128a, 352a, 401a — I, 45b, 56b, 116b, 396b, 443a, 524a, 567b, 732b; II, 863a, 868b, 933b; III, 122a, 168a, 249a, 608a, **628a**; IV, 663b; S, 93b, 127a, 352a, 401b
Ḥusayn b. ʿAlī b. ʿAlī b. Muḥammad b. Djaʿfar al-Ḳurashī s, **62a** — S, **62b**
Ḥusayn b. ʿAlī b. Ḥanzala → ʿAlī b. Ḥanzala
al-Ḥusayn b. ʿAlī b. ʿĪsā i, 437b — I, 450a
Ḥusayn b. ʿAlī b. Luhrasp i, 237b — I, 244b
al-Ḥusayn b. ʿAlī al-Marwazī (amīr) i, 278a, 1003a; iv, 661b — I, 286b, 1034a; IV, 688a
Ḥusayn b. ʿAlī Pasha i, 236b, 554a, 1087a — I, 244a, 571b, 1119b
Ḥusayn b. Amīn al-Ṣayyād s, 209a — S, 208b
Ḥusayn b. Bayḳara i, 148a, 227b, 228a, 627b, 847b, 920a, 1082b; ii, 334a; iii, 177b, **603a**; iv, 34a, 48b, 536b; v, 59a, 389a — I, 152a, 234b, 648a, 871a, 948a, 1115a; II, 343b; III, 181b, **623b**; IV, 36b, 51b, 560a; V, 60b, 389b
al-Ḥusayn b. Dadjn s, 81b — S, 81b
al-Ḥusayn b. al-Ḍaḥḥāk iii, **617b**; iv, 1003a, 1004a, b; s, 25a — III, **638b**; IV, 1035b, 1036a, 1037a; S, 25a
al-Ḥusayn b. Djaʿfar s, 352a — S, 352a
Ḥusayn b. Djanbulāt ii, 443b — II, 455a
al-Ḥusayn b. Djawhar ii, 495b; iii, 79a, b; v, 623b — II, 508a; III, 81b, 82a; V, 627b
al-Ḥusayn b. al-Faḍl al-Badjalī s, 392a — S, 392b
Ḥusayn b. Fakhr al-Dīn ii, 635a, 751a — II, 651a, 769b
Ḥusayn b. Ḥamdān iii, 126a, **619a**; iv, 493b, 494a — III, 129a, **639b**; IV, 515a
Ḥusayn b. Ḥamza iii, 156a — III, 159a
al-Ḥusayn b. al-Ḥusayn iii, **606b** — III, **627b**
al-Ḥusayn b. Ibrāhīm al-Natīli ii, 349b — II, 359a
al-Ḥusayn b. ʿImrān b. Shāhīn i, 212a; iii, 1176a — I, 218a; III, 1204b
al-Ḥusayn b. al-Ḳāsim i, 387b; ii, 178a; iii, 768a; iv, 1094a — I, 398b; II, 184a; III, 791b; IV, 1125a
al-Ḥusayn b. al-Ḳāsim al-ʿIyānī v, 1237b — V, 1228a
Ḥusayn b. Manṣūr b. Bayḳara → Ḥusayn Bayḳara
al-Ḥusayn b. Mansūr → al-Ḥallādj
al-Ḥusayn b. Muḥammad → al-Rāghib al-Iṣfahānī
al-Ḥusayn b. Muḥammad al-Marw al-Rūdhī i, 893a — I, 919b
Ḥusayn b. Numayr al-Sakūnī i, 55a, 810a; iii, **620b**; v, 119b — I, 57a, 833a; III, **641a**; V, 122b
al-Ḥuṣayn b. al-Ruḳād iii, 153a — III, 156b
Ḥusayn b. Saʿīd (Djabrid(e)) s, 234b — S, 234b
Ḥusayn b. Saʿīd b. Ḥamdān iii, 127b, 129a; v, 923b — III, 130a, 131b; V, 929a
Ḥusayn b. Salāma i, 181b; ii, 517a — I, 186b; II, 530a
Ḥusayn b. al-Ṣiddīḳ al-Ahdal i, 255b, 781a — I, 263b, 804a
Ḥusayn b. Ṭāhir al-Ṭāʾī iv, 188b — IV, 196b
al-Ḥusayn b. ʿUmar (Ibn Dirham) s, **386a** — S, **386b**

Ḥusayn b. Uways → Ḥusayn I (D̲j̲alāyirid(e))
al-Ḥusayn b. Ẓāhir al-Wazzān iii, 79a — III, 81b
Ḥusayn b. Zikrawayh iii, 619a; iv, 494a, 660b — III, 639b; IV, 515a, 687a
Ḥusayn Abū Muḥammad → Nāṣir al-Dawla Ḥusayn
Ḥusayn Aḥmad Madanī iii, 432a — III, 446a
al-Ḥusayn al-Ahwāzī iii, 123b — III, 126a
Ḥusayn Ak̲h̲lāṭī i, 869a — I, 893b
Ḥusayn ʿAlā ii, 882b — II, 903a
Ḥusayn ʿAlī Farmān-farmā ii, 804a; iv, 392b, 393a — II, 823a; IV, 409a, b
Ḥusayn ʿAlī K̲h̲ān Bārha i, 1015b, 1025b, 1026a, 1219b, 1330a, b; ii, 379b, 810a; iv, 279b, 507b; s, 126b — I, 1047a, 1057b, 1255b, 1370b, 1371a; II, 389b, 829a; IV, 292a, 529b; S, 125b
Ḥusayn ʿAlī Mīrzā ii, 812b; iii, 1106b, 1107a — II, 831b; III, 113b, 1134a
Ḥusayn ʿAlī Nūrī, Mīrzā → Bahāʾ Allāh
al-Ḥusayn al-Aṣg̲h̲ar i, 552a — I, 569b
Ḥusayn ʿAwnī → Akagündüz
Ḥusayn ʿAwni Pas̲h̲a i, 285b; iii, **621a** — I, 294a; III, **641b**
Ḥusayn Bādkūbaʾi, Sayyid s, 23b — S, 24a
Ḥusayn Beg b. Tay Bug̲h̲a iv, 584a, b — IV, 608a
Ḥusayn Bey (Egypt, Égypte) ii, 321b — II, 331a
Ḥusayn Bey (Tunis) iii, 636a; iv, 828b — III, 657a; IV, 861b
Ḥusayn D̲j̲ahānsūz → D̲j̲ahānsūz
Ḥusayn D̲j̲āhid (Yalçîn) i, 287b; ii, 474b, 475a, b, 497b; iii, **621b**; iv, 872b; s, 98a — I, 296a; II, 486b, 487a, 488a, 510a; III, **642a**; IV, 906a; S, 97b
Ḥusayn Djajadiningrat → Hoesein Djajadiningrat
Ḥusayn D̲j̲ind̲j̲i K̲h̲od̲j̲a iii, **623a,** 983a; iv, 720a — III, **643b,** 1007b; IV, 748b
Ḥusayn Dūst K̲h̲ān i, 625a — I, 645b
Ḥusayn Fahmī Ṣādiḳ s, 299b — S, 299a
Ḥusayn Hezārfenn ii, 110a; iii, **623b** — II, 112b; III, **644a**
Ḥusayn Ḥilmī Pas̲h̲a iii, **624a**; iv, 123b — III, **645a**; IV, 128b
Ḥusayn Ḳāʾinī iv, 199b — IV, 208b
Ḥusayn Kāmil i, 13b; iii, **624b**; s, 40b — I, 13b; III, **645b**; S, 41a
Ḥusayn-Ḳapudan Gradaščevič i, 1268b — I, 1307a
Ḥusayn al-K̲h̲alīʿ → al-Ḥusayn b. al-Ḍaḥḥāk
Ḥusayn K̲h̲alīfa Pas̲h̲a i, 2a, 1172a — I, 2a, 1207a
Ḥusayn K̲h̲ān (Āgra) i, 856b — I, 880a
Ḥusayn K̲h̲ān (Ḳaytāḳī) ii, 87a; v, 296b — II, 88b; V, 287b
Ḥusayn K̲h̲ān b. Mansūr Beg v, 829b — V, 835b
Ḥusayn K̲h̲ān Ād̲j̲ūdān-bās̲h̲ī i, 833b — I, 856b
Ḥusayn K̲h̲ān Mus̲h̲īr al-Dawla ii, 649b; iii, 555a; iv, 397b, 398a, 787a; v, 1086a — II, 666a; III, 574a; IV, 415a, b, 819a; V, 1083a
Ḥusayn K̲h̲armīl iii, 471b — III, 488b
Ḥusayn Kiyā i, 237b — I, 244b
Ḥusayn Ḳulī K̲h̲ān i, 1068a — I, 1100b
Ḥusayn Ḳulī K̲h̲ān Ḳād̲j̲ār iv, 104b, 391a, 392a — IV, 109b, 407b, 408b
Ḥusayn Ḳulī Mīrzā ii, 838b — II, 858a
Ḥusayn al-Kurdī i, 1032b; ii, 572a; iv, 552b — I, 1064a; II, 586b; IV, 576b
Ḥusayn Lawāsānī, Malik Sultān v, 663a, b — V, 668b
al-Ḥusayn al-Mahdī, Imām s, 22a — S, 22b
Ḥusayn Mīrzā, Sultan s, 423b — S, 423b
al-Ḥusayn al-Nāṣir s, 363a, b — S, 363a, b
Ḥusayn Niẓām S̲h̲āh I iii, 426a, **625b,** 1160b — III, 440a, **646b,** 1189a
Ḥusayn Niẓām S̲h̲āh II ii, 921b; iii, 626a — II, 943a; III, 647a
Ḥusayn Niẓām S̲h̲āh III iii, 626a — III, 647a
Ḥusayn Nūrī Ṭabarsī iii, 588b — III, 608b
Ḥusayn Pas̲h̲a → Ṣilaḥdār
Ḥusayn Pas̲h̲a, Ag̲h̲a iii, **628a,** 999b; v, 36a — III, **649a,** 1024b; V, 37a
Ḥusayn Pas̲h̲a, ʿAmūd̲j̲a-zāde i, 481a; iii, **626b**; iv, 233b, 657b — I, 495a; III, **648b**; IV, 244a, 684a
Ḥusayn Pas̲h̲a, Deli i, 904b; iii, **626a**; v, 258b — I, 932a; III, **647a**; V, 256b
Ḥusayn Pas̲h̲a, Ḥād̲j̲d̲j̲ ii, 402a — II, 412b
Ḥusayn Pas̲h̲a, Küčük i, 948a; ii, 534b; iii, **627a**; v, 35b — I, 977a; II, 547b; III, **647b**; V, 36b
Ḥusayn Pas̲h̲a Mezzomorto iii, **629a** — III, **650a**
Ḥusayn Pas̲h̲a, S̲h̲arīf v, 808b — V, 814a
Ḥusayn Raḥmī iii, 357b, 375a, 593a, **630a**; s, 64b — III, 368b, 387a, 613a, **651a**; S, 65a
al-Ḥusayn al-Rayyī s, 252b — S, 252b
Ḥusayn Rus̲h̲dī Pas̲h̲a iii, 625a — III, 646a
Ḥusayn Ṣāḥib al-S̲h̲āma iii, 398a — III, 410b
Ḥusayn S̲h̲āh, ʿAlāʾ al-Dīn i, 719b, 1015a; ii, 32a; iii, 14b, 422a, **631b,** 632a, 634b — I, 741a, 1046b; II, 32b; III, 15b, 436a, **625b,** 653b, 655b
Ḥusayn S̲h̲āh Arg̲h̲ūn i, 627b, 962a; iii, 575b, **632b,** 634a — I, 648b, 991b; III, 595b, **654a,** 655a
Ḥusayn S̲h̲ān Čak s, 167a, 325a, 366b — S, 167a, 324b, 366a
Ḥusayn S̲h̲āh Čakk → Kas̲h̲mīr
Ḥusayn S̲h̲āh Langāh I i, 1005b; ii, 47a; iii, **633b** — I, 1036b; II, 48a; III, **654b**
Ḥusayn S̲h̲āh Langāh II iii, 633a, **634a** — III, 654a, **655a**
Ḥusayn S̲h̲āh S̲h̲arḳī ii, 270b, 271a, 498b; iii, 419b, 420b, 453b, 631b, **632a**; iv, 1136a; v, 783b — II, 279a, 511a; III, 433a, 434a, 469a, 652b, **653a**; IV, 1167b; V, 789b
Ḥusayn Sirrī iii, 515b; s, 300b — III, 533a; S, 300a
Ḥusayn Sirrī ʿĀmir (general/général) s, 301a — S, 301a
Ḥusayn-i Tabrīzī i, 777a — I, 800a
Ḥusayn Wafā ii, 433b — II, 445a
Ḥusayn Wāʿiẓ → Kās̲h̲ifī
Ḥusaynābād iii, **634b,** 1163a — III, **655b,** 1191b
Ḥusaynī Dālān iii, **634b** — III, **656a**
Ḥusaynī Sādāt Amīr iii, **635a,** iv, 474a — III, **656a**; IV, 494b
al-Ḥusaynī, Ṣadr al-Dīn s, **378a** — S, **378b**
Husaynid(e)s i, 402a, 403a, 552a — I, 412b, 414b, 569b
Ḥusaynid(e)s (Tunisia/Tunisie) i, 281b, 863a, 1111a; ii, 463b; iii, 605a, **635b** — I, 290a, 887a, 1144a; II, 475b; III, 625b, **657a**
Ḥusaynīs iii, 523b; s, 67a — III, 541b; S, 67b
Ḥusayniya-yi Irs̲h̲ād iv, 167a — IV, 174a
al-Ḥusayniyya → al-Ḥasaniyya
al-Ḥusayniyya (Mawālī) → K̲h̲as̲h̲abiyya
Ḥusayniyya (Zaydī) v, 1237b — V, 1228a
Ḥusayn-zāde ʿAlī s, 47a — S, 47b
Husband → Ḳayyim
Hüseyin Cahid → Ḥusayn D̲j̲āhid
Ḥüseyin Raʾūf iv, 297b — IV, 310b
Ḥüseyn Ag̲h̲a Ḳara ʿOt̲h̲mān-og̲h̲lu iv, 593b — IV, 617a, b
Ḥüseyn Beg Ḥamīdog̲h̲lu ii, 692a; iii, 133b — II, 709a; III, 135b
Ḥüseyn Pas̲h̲a (beglerbeg) iv, 594b — IV, 618b
Ḥūs̲h̲ iii, **637b**; s, 381b — III, **658b**; S, 382a
Hūs̲h̲ang iii, **637b**; iv, 445a; v, 377b; s, 263a, b — III, **658b**; IV, 464b; V, 378b; S, 263a
Hus̲h̲ang b. Dilāwar K̲h̲ān → Hus̲h̲ang S̲h̲āh G̲h̲ūrī
Hus̲h̲ang S̲h̲āh G̲h̲ūrī i, 924a; ii, 218b, 270b, 276b, 814b, 1125a; iii, 418a, **638a,** 1003a; iv, 219a, 513a; v, 1a — I, 952a; II, 225b, 278b, 285a, 833b, 1151b; III,

431b, **659a,** 1028a; IV, 228b, 535a; V, 1a
Hushaym b. Bashīr al-Sulamī i, 272b; iv, 149a — I, 281a; IV, 155b
Ḥusn al-Ghurāb iii, 52a, b — III, 54a, b
Ḥusn al-Khātima iii, 1246a — III, 1278b
Ḥusn al-maḳṭaʿ iii, 1246a — III, 1278b
Ḥusn al-maṭlaʿ iii, 1006a — III, 1031b
Ḥusnī al-ʿArabī, Maḥmūd iv, 125a — IV, 130a
Ḥüanü, Shefīḳ iv, 124a — IV, 129a, b
Ḥusnī al-Zaʿīm → al-Zaʿīm
Hüsnümansur → Adiyaman
Husrev → Khusrev
al-Ḥuṣrī → Abū ʿAbd Allāh
al-Ḥuṣrī, Abū Isḥāḳ i, 591a; iii, **639a**; s, 62b — I, 610a; III, **660a**; S, 63a
al-Ḥuṣrī, Abū 'l-Ḥasan ʿAlī iii, **640a** — III, **661b**
al-Ḥuṣrī, Sāṭiʿ iv, 783a — IV, 814b
Ḥussāb i, 1145b — I, 1180a
Hut → Sukna
al-Ḥūt → Nudjūm; Yūnus; Zīdj
al-Ḥuṭam b. Ḍubayʿa iv, 764a — IV, 794b
al-Ḥuṭayʾa i, 1297b; iii, 136b, 272a, 354a, **641a,** 941a — I, 1337b; III, 139a, 280a, 365b, **662a,** 965b
Hutaym i, 528b, 546a; iii, **641b** — I, 544b, 563b; III, **663a**
Huwa Huwa iii, **642b** — III, **663b**
Huwala i, 941b, 942b; iv, 777b — I, 970b, 971b; IV, 808b
al-Huwaydira → al-Ḥādira
al-Ḥuwayrith b. Nuḳayẓ b. Wahb ii, 842b — II, 862a
al-Ḥuwayṭāt i, 315a; ii, 626a; iii, **642b**; iv, 335a — I, 324b; II, 641b; III, **664a**; IV, 349b
al-Ḥuwayyiṭ → Fadak
Ḥuwayza → Ḥawīza
al-Ḥuwayzī, ʿAbd ʿAlī b. Djumʿa al-ʿArūsī s, 57a — S, 57b
Huwiyya iii, **644a** — III, **665a**
Ḥuwwārīn iii, **645b** — III, **666b**
Hvar, island of/île de s, 185a — S, 186a
Hyderabad → Ḥaydarābād
Hydraulics/Hydraulique → Māʾ
Hydromancy/ie → Istinzāl; Maʾ
Hyena/hyène → Ḍabuʿ
Hymn/hymne → Ilāhī; Nashīd
Hyperbole → Mubālagha
Hypocrisy/Hypocrisie → Munāfiḳ, Riyāʾ
Hypostasis/Hypostase → Imāma, Tanāsukh

I

Iatromancy/Iatromancie → Firāsa; Istikhāra
Ibād → Naṣārā
ʿIbād Allāh Beg ii, 83b — II, 85b
Ibadan iii, **646a** — III, **667a**
ʿIbādāt i, 277a; iii, **647a**; iv, 154b — I, 285b; III, **668a**; IV, 161a
ʿIbādat Khāna s, **378a** — S, **378a**
al-Ibāḍīyya i, 57a, 120b, 121a, 125a, 134a, 139a, 140b, 141b, 166b, 167a, 171b, 188b, 249b, 250b, 371a, 736a, 759b, 770b, 810a, 813a, 1028a, 1043b, 1053b, 1175a; ii, 129a, 140b, 170a, 359b, 368b, 592b, 1010a; iii, 95a, **648a,** 924b, 927b, 1168a; iv, 78a, 1076a, 1077a; v, 697b, 997a, 1230a; s, 15a, 88b, 90a, 225b, 337b, 338a, 355a, b — I, 58b, 124a, b, 128b, 138a, 143a, 145a, b, 171b, 176a, 194a, 257b, 258b, 382a, 758a, 782b, 793b, 833b, 836a, 1059b, 1075a, 1058a, 1210b; II, 132b, 144b, 175b, 369b, 378b, 607a, 1033b; III, 97b, **669a,** 949a, 951b, 1196b; IV, 82a, 1108a, b; V, 702b, 992b, 1220b; S, 15b, 88b, 89b, 225b, 337b, 355a, b
Ibʿādiyya (Abʿādiyya) s, **379a** — S, **379a**
Ibāḥa (I) iii, **660b** — III, **682a**
Ibāḥa (II) ii, 136b; iii, **662a**; iv, 997a — II, 140a; III, **683a**; IV, 1029b
Ibāḥatiya ii, 1031a; iii, 434a, **663a** — II, 1055a; III, 448a, **684b**
Ibāḥiyya → Ibāḥa (II)
Ibak, Prince ii, 45a — II, 46a
ʿIbāra iv, 114a, b — IV, 119b
Ibb iii, **663b**; s, 236a — III, **685a**; S, 236a
Ibdāʿ iii, **663b**; iv, 986b, 987a — III, **685a**; IV, 1019a, b
Ibdāl iii, **665a** — III, **686b**
Ibex → Ayyil
Ibil i, 541a, 880b, 882a; ii, 1055a; iii, 32b, **665b**; iv, 676b, 677a — I, 558a, 906a, 907b; II, 1079b; III, 34a, **687a**; IV, 704b
Ibkishtīn s, 159a, 161b — S, 159a, 161a
Iblīs i, 45b, 71b, 177a, b, 181a, 262a, 796a, 811b, 1093a; ii, 547a; iii, **668a**; s, 136a — I, 47a, 73b, 181b, 182b, 186a, 270a, 819b, 834b, 1125b; II, 560a; III, **690a**; S, 135b
Ibn iii, **669b** — III, **691b**
Ibn ʿAbbād → ʿAbbādids; al-Muʿtamid; Muḥammad b. Ismāʿīl
Ibn ʿAbbād (Ṣiḳilliyya) → Benavert
Ibn ʿAbbād al-Rundī iii, **670b,** 720a, 722b; s, 404b — III, **692a,** 742a, 745a; S, 404b
Ibn ʿAbbād al-Ṣāḥib i, 59b, 119b, 126b, 590b, 712b, 1352b, 1354a; ii, 570a, 749a, b; iii, 487a, **671a,** 677a, 704a, 764b; iv, 61a, 524b, 862b, 1069b; v, 1028b; s, 4a, 13a, b, 24a, 38a, 118b, 124a, 393a — I, 61b, 123a, 130b, 610a, 734a, 1392a, 1393a; II, 584b, 767a, b; III, 504a, **692b,** 698b, 726b, 787b; IV, 64a, 547a, 895b, 1101a; V, 1024b; S, 3b, 13b, 24a, 38a, 118a, 123a, 393b
Ibn ʿAbbādī s, 416b — S, 416b
Ibn al-ʿAbbār, Abū ʿAbd Allāh i, 594b, 602b; ii, 308a; iii, 66b, **673a,** 704b, 762b, 803b, 904a; iv, 468a; s, 382a, 388a — I, 614a, 622a; II, 316b; III, 69a, **694b,** 727a, 785b, 827a, 928a; IV, 489a; S, 382a, 388b
Ibn al-Abbār, Abū Djaʿfar Aḥmad iii, **673b** — III, **695b**
Ibn ʿAbbās → ʿAbd Allāh b. al-ʿAbbās
Ibn ʿAbd Allāh → Ism
Ibn ʿAbd al-Barr i, 108a, 600a; iii, **674a**; s, 26b — I, 111a, 619b; III, **695b**; S, 27a
Ibn ʿAbd al-Hādī → Yūsuf b. ʿAbd al-Hādī
Ibn ʿAbd al-Ḥakam iii, **674b** — III, **696a**
Ibn ʿAbd al-Ḥakam, ʿAbd Allāh iii, **674b** — III, **696a**
Ibn ʿAbd al-Ḥakam, Abu 'l-Ḳāsim iii, **674b,** 775a, 1047b; s, 88a — III, **696a,** 798b, 1074a; S, 87b
Ibn ʿAbd al-Ḥaḳḳ i, 903a — I, 930a
Ibn ʿAbd Kān, Abū Djaʿfar ii, 305a, 328a — II, 313b, 337b
Ibn ʿAbd al-Karīm al-Ragrāgī ii, 1007b — II, 1031a
Ibn ʿAbd al-Malik al-Marrākushī iii, **675a**; s, 397a — III, **696b**; S, 397a
Ibn ʿAbd al-Munʿim al-Ḥimyarī i, 156b, 488a; iii, **675b,** 1033a; s, 171a — I, 160b, 503a; III, **697a,** 1059a; S, 171a
Ibn ʿAbd Rabbih i, 590a, 600b, 601a, 667b; ii, 246a; iii, **676b**; iv, 1188a; s, 16b — I, 609b, 620a, 620b, 688b; II, 253a; III, **698a**; IV, 1220b; S, 16b
Ibn ʿAbd al-Raʾūf i, 157a; iii, 486b — I, 161b; III, 503b
Ibn ʿAbd al-Salām al-Marrākushī iv, 1134a — IV, 1165b
Ibn ʿAbd al-Ṣamad iii, **677a** — III, **699a**
Ibn ʿAbd al-Wahhāb i, 554a, 593a, 942b; ii, 176b, 320b, 321a, 569a; iii, 162a, 295a, 582b, **677b**; iv, 717b, 925a — I, 571b, 612b, 971b; II, 182a, 330a, b, 583b;

III, 165b, 304a, 602b, **699a**; IV, 746a, 958a
Ibn ʿAbd al-Ẓāhir, Fatḥ al-Dīn iii, 679b, 680a — III, 701b, 702a
Ibn ʿAbd al-Ẓāhir, Muḥyi ʾl-Dīn iii, **679a**; iv, 464b, 965a — III, **701a**; IV, 485a, 997b
Ibn ʿAbdal → al-Ḥakam b. ʿAbdal
Ibn ʿAbdūn, Abū Muḥammad i, 591a, 602a; iii, **680b** — I, 610a, 621b; III, **702a**
Ibn ʿAbdūn al-Ishbīlī i, 156a, 157a, 390b, 1148b; iii, 486b, **681a** — I, 160b, 161b, 401b, 1183a; III, 503b, **702b**
Ibn ʿAbdūs → al-Djahshiyārī
Ibn ʿAbdūs, Aḥmad iii, **681b,** 973b, 974a — III, **703a,** 998a, b
Ibn ʿAbdūs, Muḥammad iii, **681a** — III, **703a**
Ibn Abī ʿĀmir → al-Manṣūr biʾllāh
Ibn Abi ʾl-Ashʿath s, 271b, **379b** — S, 271a, **379b**
Ibn Abī ʿAṣrūn i, 766a; iii, 120b, **681b** — I, 788b; III, 123a, **703b**
Ibn Abī ʿAtīḳ iii, **682a** — III, **703b**
Ibn Abi ʾl-ʿAwdjāʾ i, 1081a; iii, **682b** — I, 1113a; III, **704a**
Ibn Abī ʿAwn iii, **683a** — III, **704b**
Ibn Abī ʿAzafa → ʿAzafī
Ibn Abi ʾl-ʿAzāḳir → Muḥammad b. ʿAlī al-Shalmaghānī
Ibn Abi ʾl-Baghl → Muḥammad b. Yaḥyā
Ibn Abi ʾl-Bayān i, 1224b; iii, **683a,** 749b; v, 251b — I, 1261a; III, **705a,** 772b; V, 249b
Ibn Abī Dabbūs iii, 67a; iv, 338a — III, 69b; IV, 352b
Ibn Abi ʾl-Dam iii, **683b,** 967a — III, **705a,** 991b
Ibn Abī Dāʾūd v, 406a, 804a — V, 407b, 809b
Ibn Abī Dīnār al-Ḳayrawānī iii, **683b** — III, **705b**
Ibn Abi ʾl-Ḍiyāf iii, **684a** — III, **705b**
Ibn Abī Djumʿa → Kuthayyir
Ibn Abī Djumhūr al-Aḥsāʾī s, **380a** — S, **380a**
Ibn Abī Duʾād → Aḥmad b. Abī Duʾād
Ibn Abi ʾl-Dumayna → al-Hamdānī
Ibn Abi ʾl-Dunyā i, 326a, 590a; iii, **684a,** 922b; iv, 212a — I, 336a, 609b; III, **706a,** 947a; IV, 221b
Ibn Abī Ghudda iv, 509b, 510b — IV, 531b, 532b
Ibn Abi ʾl-Ḥadīd iii, **684b**; s, 25b — III, **706b**; S, 25b
Ibn Abī Ḥadjala iii, **686a** — III, **707b**
Ibn Abī Ḥaṣīna iii, **686b**; v, 935a — III, **708a**; V, 939a
Ibn Abī Ḥātim al-Rāzī → Abū Muḥammad al-Rāzī
Ibn Abī Ḥudhayfa → Muḥammad b. Abī Ḥudhayfa
Ibn Abī Ḥuṣayna → Ibn Abī Ḥaṣīna
Ibn Abī Khālid s, 112a — S, 111a
Ibn Abi ʾl-Khayr → Abū Saʿīd b. Abi ʾl-Khayr
Ibn Abī Khaythama iii, **687a,** 803b — III, **708b,** 827a
Ibn Abī Khāzim → Bishr b. Abī Khāzim
Ibn Abī Ḳuḥāfa → Abū Ḳuḥafa b. ʿĀmir
Ibn Abī Laylā, Muḥammad i, 123b; ii, 232a; iii, **687a** — I, 127a; II, 239a; III, **709a**
Ibn Abī Laylā al-Akbar iii, **687a** — III, **709a**
Ibn Abi ʾl-Layth iv, 289b — IV, 302b
Ibn Abī Muslim → Yazīd b. Abī Muslim
Ibn Abi ʾl-Rabīʿ ii, 743b, 744a; iii, 741a — II, 762a, b; III, 763b
Ibn Abī Rabīʿa → ʿUmar b. Abī Rabīʿa
Ibn Abī Randaḳa al-Ṭurṭūshī i, 594a — I, 613a → al-Ṭurṭūshī
Ibn Abi ʾl-Ridjāl, Aḥmad iii, **688b** — III, **710a**
Ibn Abi ʾl-Ridjal, Abu ʾl-Ḥasan ʿAlī al-Ḳayrawānī iii, **688a,** 902b; iv, 830b — III, **709b,** 927a; IV, 863b
Ibn Abi ʾl-Sādj → Muḥammad b. Abi ʾl-Sadj
Ibn Abi ʾl-Ṣaḳr → Muḥammad b. ʿAlī b. ʿUmar
Ibn Abi ʾl-Ṣalt → Umayya b. Abi ʾl-Ṣalt
Ibn Abi ʾl-Samḥ → Mālik b. Abi ʾl-Samḥ
Ibn Abī Sarḥ → ʿAbd Allāh b. Saʿd
Ibn Abī Shanab iii, **689a** — III, **711a**
Ibn Abī Sharīf, Kamā al-Din v, 333a — V, 333b
Ibn Abi ʾl-Shawārib iii, **691a** — III, **713a**
Ibn Abī Shayba i, 758b; iii, **692a** — I, 781a; III, **714a**
Ibn Abi ʾl-Surūr → al-Bakrī
Ibn Abī Ṭāhir Ṭayfūr i, 108b, 591b, 751b, 1081a, 1082b; iii, **692b,** 757a, 820a; s, 122b — I, 610b, 774a, 1113b, 1114b; III, **714b,** 780a, 843b; S, 122a
Ibn Abī Ṭayyiʾ i, 150a, 823a; iii, **693b** — I, 154a, 846a; III, **715b**
Ibn Abī ʿUmāra, Aḥmad iii, 67a, 825b; iv, 338a, 416a, 828a — III, 69b, 849a; IV, 352a, 434a, 861a
Ibn Abī Usāma iii, 922b — III, 947a
Ibn Abī Uṣaybiʿa i, 213a, 214a, 235b, 247a, 571a, 594b, 803b; iii, 683a, **693b,** 737a; s, 25a, 45a, 154b, 290a, 313b, 379b, 391a, 397b — I, 219b, 220a, 243a, 255a, 589b, 614a, 826b; III, 705a, **715b,** 760a; S, 25b, 45b, 155a, 289b, 313b, 379b, 391a, 397b
Ibn Abī ʿUyayna iii, **694a** — III, **716a**
Ibn Abī ʿUyayna → Muḥammad b. Abī ʿUyayna
Ibn Abī Yaʿlā → Abu ʾl-Ḥusayn; Abū Khāzim
Ibn Abī Zamanayn iii, **694b** — III, **716b**
Ibn Abī Zarʿ i, 290b; ii, 145b; iii, **694b**; v, 652b, 653a, 1209a; s, 27a, 376b — I, 299b; II, 149b; III, **717a**; V, 657a, b, 1199b; S, 27a, 376b
Ibn Abi ʾl-Zawāʾid → Sulaymān b. Yaḥyā
Ibn Abī Zayd al-Ḳayrawānī i, 106a; iii, **695a**; iv, 341a, 830b; s, 395a — I, 109a; III, 717a; IV, 355b, 863a; S, 395a
Ibn Abi ʾl-Zinād s, 310b, **380a** — S, 310b, **380b**
Ibn ʿĀbidīn iii, 163b, **695b**; s, 172a — III, 167a, **717b**; S, 173a
Ibn al-Adamī iii, 1137a — III, 1165b
Ibn Adham → Ibrāhīm b. Adham
Ibn ʿAdhārī → Ibn ʿIdhārī
Ibn ʿAdī s, 400b — S, 401a
Ibn al-ʿAdīm, Kamāl al-Dīn i, 594b, 823a; iii, 693b, **695b**; v, 927b — I, 614a, 846a; III, 715b, **717b**; V, 932b
Ibn ʿAdjarrad, ʿAbd al-Karīm i, 207a — I, 213a
Ibn al-Adjdābī iii, **696a**; s, **380b** — III, **718a**; S, **380b**
Ibn ʿAdjība iii, 262a, **696a**; s, 390b — III, 269b, **718a**; S, 391a
Ibn ʿAdjlān ii, 1031b — II, 1055b
Ibn Ādjurrūm iii, **697a** — III, **719a**
Ibn al-ʿAdjūz → Alīsaʿ
Ibn al-ʿAfīf al-Tilimsānī i, 596a; iii, **697b** — I, 615b; III, **719b**
Ibn al-Afṭas i, 242a — I, 249b
Ibn al-Ahdal i, 255b; iii, 711a — I, 263b; III, 733a
Ibn al-Aḥmar (poets/poètes) iii, **697b**; v, 1209a; s, 112a — III, **719b**; V, 1199b; S, 111b
Ibn al-Aḥnaf → ʿAbbās b. al-Aḥnaf
Ibn al-Ahtam → ʿAmr b. al-Ahtam; Khālid b. Ṣafwān
Ibn ʿĀʾidh iii, **698a** — III, **720a**
Ibn ʿĀʾisha (Almoravid(e)) i, 389b, 1337b; ii, 526b; iv, 672b — I, 400b, 1377b; II, 539b; IV, 700a
Ibn ʿĀʾisha, Ibrāhīm b. Muḥammad iii, **698b** — III, **720b**
Ibn ʿĀʾisha, Muḥammad ii, 428b; iii, **698b** — II, 39b; III, **720b**
Ibn ʿĀʾisha, Muḥammad b. Ḥafṣ iii, 698b — III, 720b
Ibn ʿĀʾisha, ʿUbayd Allāh iii, 698b — III, 720b
Ibn al-Akfānī al-Asadī, al-Ḳaḍī s, **381a** — S, **381a**
Ibn al-Akfānī, Hibat Allāh b. Aḥmad iii, 930b; s, **381a** — III, 955a; S, **381a**
Ibn al-Akfānī, Muḥammad b. Ibrāhīm s, 45a, **381a** — S, 45b, **381b**
Ibn Akhī Ḥizām i, 1149b — I, 1184a
Ibn ʿAḳīl (d./m. 1071) iv, 215b — IV, 224b
Ibn ʿAḳīl, ʿAbd Allāh i, 126b, 1308b; iii, **698b,** 861b — I, 130a, 1348b; III, **720b,** 885b

Ibn ʿAḳīl, Abu 'l-Wafāʾ ʿAlī i, 69b, 273b, 276b; iii, 103a, 160a, **699a,** 751a, 843a; iv, 172b, 513b; v, 234b; s, 194b — I, 71b, 282a, 285a; III, 105b, 163b, **721a,** 774a, 866b; IV, 180a, 535b; V, 232b; S, 193b
Ibn ʿAḳnīn, Yosēf iv, 304b, 306a — IV, 318b, 319b
Ibn Aktham → Yaḥya b. Aktham
Ibn al-Aʿlam i, 87a — I, 89b
Ibn ʿAlīwa iii, **700b**; iv, 95b, 326b — III, **722b**; IV, 99b, 340b
Ibn ʿAlḳama, Abū Ghālib Tammām iii, **701b** — III, **724a**
Ibn ʿAlḳama, Tammām b. ʿĀmir i, 601a; iii, **702a** — I, 620b; III, **724a**
Ibn al-Alḳamī iii, 685a, **702a** - III, 706b, **724b**
Ibn al-ʿAllāf iii, **702b** — III, **724b**
Ibn Amādjūr iii, **702b** — III, **725a**
Ibn al-ʿAmīd, Abu 'l-Faḍl i, 212a, 434a, 590b, 1352b, 1354a; ii, 305a; iii, 258a, 671a, b, **703a,** 1242b; iv, 1182a; s, 72b, 124a, 263b — I, 218b, 446a, 610a, 1392a, 1393a; II, 313b; III, 265a, 692b, 693b, **725a,** 1274b; IV, 1215a; S, 72b, 123a, 263b
Ibn al-ʿAmīd, Abu 'l-Fatḥ ʿAlī i, 126b; iii, 258a, 671a, **704a,** 730a, 780b; v, 621a; s, 72b — I, 130b; III, 265a, 692b, **726a,** 753a, 803b; V, 625a; S, 72b
Ibn al-ʿAmīd → Ibn al-Kalānisī; al-Makīn
Ibn al-Amīn Maḥmūd Kemāl → Inal
Ibn ʿĀmir, Abū ʿUmar iii, **704b** — III, **726b**
Ibn ʿAmīra ii, 526b; iii, **704b** — II, 539b; III, **726b**
Ibn ʿAmmār → ʿAmmār, Banū; al-Ḥasan b. ʿAmmār; Ṭarābulus
Ibn ʿAmmār, Abu 'l-Abbās Aḥmad iii, **705a** — III, **727a**
Ibn ʿAmmār, Abū Bakr Muḥammad i, 6b, 7a, 602a; iii, 542b, **705b,** 904b, 963a — I, 6b, 7a, 621b; III, 561a, **727b,** 929a, 987b
Ibn ʿAmmār al-Kutāmī → al-Ḥasan b. ʿAmmār
Ibn ʿAmr al-Ribāṭī s, **381b** — S, **381b**
Ibn al-Anbārī → al-Anbārī, Abū Bakr Muḥammad
Ibn al-ʿArabī, Abū Bakr Muḥammad iii, **707a,** 798b; iv, 290a — III, **729b,** 821b; IV, 302b
Ibn al-Aʿrābī, Muḥammad b. Ziyād ii, 248a; iii, **706b**; iv, 111a; s, 38b, 122a — II, 255a; III, **728b**; IV, 116a; S, 39a, 121b
Ibn al-ʿArabī, Muḥyī al-Dīn i, 60a, 71a, b, 88b, 90a, 347a, 388b, 594a, 596a, 869a, 937a, 1092b, 1103a; ii, 296b, 376a, 377a, 450b; iii, 29a, 51b, 90a, 262a, 429b, **707b,** 798b, 871a, 910b, 952a, 1240a; iv, 49b, 114b, 813b; v, 166a, 433a, 544a, 614a, 1160b; s, 93b, 208b, 293a, 313a, 363b, 364a, b, 380a — I, 62a, 73a, b, 91a, 92b, 357b, 400a, 613b, 615a, 893b, 966a, 1125a, 1136a; II, 304b, 386b, 387b, 462a; III, 30a, 53a, 92b, 269b, 443b, **730a,** 821b, 895a, 934b, 976b, 1272a; IV, 52a, b, 119b, 846b; V, 163b, 435b, 548b, 618a, 1150a; S, 93a, 208a, 293a, 313a, 363b, 364a, 380b
Ibn ʿArabshāh i, 137a, 595a; iii, 309a, **711b**; iv, 506b — I, 141a, 614b; III, 318b, **734a**; IV, 528b
Ibn ʿArafa i, 1341a; iii, 68b, **712a,** 827b — I, 1381a; III, 71a, **734b,** 851a
Ibn Arfaʿ Raʾs v, 112a; s, 270a — V, 114b; S, 269b
Ibn Arfaʿ Rāsuh s, 23a — S, 23a
Ibn al-ʿArīf, Abu 'l-Abbās Aḥmad iii, **712a,** 732a, 816b — III, **734b,** 754b, 840a
Ibn al-ʿArīf, al-Ḥusayn iii, **713a** — III, **735b**
Ibn Arṭāṭ → Ibn Sayḥān
Ibn ʿArūs, Sīdī i, 679b; iii, 69a, **713b**; s, 93a — I, 700a; III, 71b, **735b**; S, 92b
Ibn ʿAsākir, Abu 'l-Ḳāsim ʿAlī i, 150a, 594b; ii, 126a, 283b, 993b; iii, **713b,** 767a — I, 154b, 614a; II, 129a, 291b, 1016b; III, **736a,** 790a
Ibn ʿAsākir, al-Ḳāsim ii, 126a; iii, 714b — II, 129a; III, 737a
Ibn al-Ashʿath → Ḥamdān Ḳarmaṭ
Ibn al-Ashʿath, ʿAbd al-Raḥmān i, 77a, 690b, 1086a, 1344b; ii, 197a; iii, 40b, 247b, **715a,** 841b; iv, 15a, 356b; v, 119b, 349a, 1231b; s, 26a, 358a — I, 79b, 711b, 1118a, 1384b; II, 203a; III, 42b, 254b, **737b,** 865b; IV, 16b, 372a; V, 122b, 350a, 1221b; S, 26b, 357b
Ibn al-Ashʿath, Muḥammad → Muḥammad b. al-Ashʿath al-Khuzāʿī
Ibn ʿĀshir iii, 670b, 701b, **719b**; s, 390b — III, 692a, 723b, **742a**; S, 391a
Ibn al-Ashtar → Ibrāhīm b. al-Ashtar
Ibn ʿĀshūr iii, **720a** — III, **742b**
Ibn Āshūr, Muḥammad al-Fāḍil iii, 720b; iv, 159b, 924b — III, 743a; IV, 166a, 957b
Ibn ʿĀshūr, Muḥammad al-Ṭāhir i, 1314b; iii, **720b**; iv, 159b — I, 1355a; III, **743a**; IV, 166a
Ibn ʿĀṣim i, 427b, 602a; iii, **720b,** 948b — I, 440a, 622a; III, **743a,** 973a
Ibn ʿAskar, Abū ʿAbd Allāh iii, **721a** — III, **743b**
Ibn ʿAskar, Muḥammad b. ʿAlī al-Ghassānī s, **381b** — S, **382a**
Ibn al-ʿAssāl iii, **721b,** 1205b; v, 92b; s, 396a, b — III, **744a,** 1236a; V, 95a; S, 396a, b
Ibn al-Aswad iii, 712b — III, 735a
Ibn ʿAṭāʾ Allāh al-Iskandarī i, 351b; ii, 225a, b; iii, 670b, **722b,** 952a; s, 387a, 404a, b — I, 362b; II, 231b, 232b; III, 692b, **745a,** 977a; S, 387b, 404a, b
Ibn Aʿtham al-Kūfī i, 984b; iii, **723a** — I, 1015b; III, **745b**
Ibn al-Athīr, Ḍiyāʾ al-Dīn ii, 826a; iii, 221b, 487a, **724a**; iv, 252a, 755b; s, 177b — II, 845b; III, 228a, 504a, **746b**; IV, 263a, 786a; S, 178b
Ibn al-Athīr, ʿIzz al-Dīn i, 594b, 595a, 683a, 794a, 1115b; iii, **724a**; v, 821a — I, 614a, b, 703b, 817b, 1149a; III, **746b**; V, 827a
Ibn al-Athīr, Madjd al-Dīn iii, **723b** — III, **746a**
Ibn ʿAṭiyya al-Muḥāribī ii, 744a — II, 762a
Ibn al-ʿAṭṭār al-Isrāʾīlī i, 344b — I, 355a
Ibn ʿAttāsh i, 353a; iii, 253b, **725a**; iv, 101b — I, 363b; III, 261a, **747b**; IV, 106a
Ibn Āwā iii, **725b** — III, **748a**
Ibn al-ʿAwdjāʾ i, 1081a — I, 1113a → Ibn Abi 'l-ʿAwdjāʾ
Ibn al-ʿAwsadjī i, 762b — I, 785b
Ibn al-ʿAwwām ii, 902a; iv, 1145b; s, 128b, 370b — II, 922b; IV, 1177a; S, 128a, 370b
Ibn Ayās → Ibn Iyās
Ibn al-ʿAydarūs → ʿAbd al-Ḳādir al-ʿAydarūs; Abū Bakr al-ʿAydarūs
Ibn al-Azraḳ iv, 348b — IV, 363b
Ibn ʿAzzūz, Sīdī Ballā s, **382a** — S, **382b**
Ibn Bābā al-Kāshānī → al-Ḳāshānī, ʿAbu 'l-ʿAbbās
Ibn Bābashādh → Ṭāhir b. Aḥmad b. Bābashād
Ibn Bābawayh, Bābūya i, 120a, 162b, 1216a, 1352a; ii, 848a; iii, 24b, **726b,** 1266a; iv, 182b; v, 363b, 370b; s, 23b — I, 123b, 167a, 1252b, 1391b; II, 867b; III, 25b, **749a,** 1299a; IV, 190b; V, 364b, 371b; S, 24a
Ibn Bābshādh i, 131b — I, 135b
Ibn Bādīs, ʿAbd al-Ḥamīd iii, **727a,** 1003b; iv, 146b, 147b, 151a, 159a, 784b; v, 597a — III, **750a,** 1028b; IV, 152b, 153b, 157b, 165b, 816b; V, 601a
Ibn Bādīs → Muʿizz b. Bādīs
Ibn Bādjdja i, 234b, 594a, 631b, 1250a; ii, 771a, 773b, 838a; iii, 302b, 542b, **728a,** 849b; v, 704a — I, 242a, 613b, 652b, 1288a; II, 789b, 792a, 857b; III, 312a, 561b, **750b,** 873b; V, 709a
Ibn Badrūn iii, 680b — III, 702b
Ibn al-Baghdādī ii, 362a — II, 371b
Ibn Bahdal → Ḥassān b. Mālik al-Kalbī
Ibn Bahlūl → Abu 'l-Ḥasan b. Bahlūl
Ibn Baḳī i, 595b, 602a; iii, **729b,** 851b — I, 615a, 621b; III, **752a,** 875b

Ibn al-Bāḳillānī → al-Bāḳillānī
Ibn Baḳiyya i, 11b; iii, 704a, **730a,** 780b; s, 398a — I, 11b; III, 726b, **752b,** 803b; S, 398b
Ibn Bākūya i, 147a — I, 151a
Ibn al-Baladī iii, **730b,** 950b — III, **753a,** 975a
Ibn Balʿām, Judah iv, 306a — IV, 319b
Ibn al-Balkhī iii, 1097a, b; s, **382b** — III, 1124a, b; S, **382b**
Ibn Bāna (Bānata) ii, 1074a; iii, **730b** — II, 1098b; III, **753a**
Ibn Bāna, ʿAmr s, 64a — S, 64b
Ibn al-Bannāʾ al-Baghdādī iii, **730b**; s, 30a — III, **753b**; S, 30a
Ibn al-Bannāʾ al-Marrākushī iii, 339a, **731a**; iv, 477a, 725a; v, 1209b — III, 349a, **753b**; IV, 498a, 754b; V, 1200a
Ibn Baraka → Abū Muḥammad b. Baraka
Ibn Barradjān iii, 712b, **732a,** 800b, 816b — III, 735a, **754b,** 823b, 840a
Ibn Barrī, Abu 'l-Ḥasan ʿAlī iii, **732b,** 733a — III, **755b,** 756a
Ibn Barri, Abū Muḥammad ii, 528a; iii, **733a** — II, 541a; III, **755b**
Ibn Bashkuwāl i, 156a, 594b, 602b, 1092b; iii, 673a, **733b,** 762b, 803b, 976a — I, 160a, 614a, 622a, 1125a; III, 694b, **756a,** 785b, 827a, 1000b
Ibn Baṣṣāl ii, 901a — II, 922a
Ibn Bassām (9th c./9e s.) iii, **734b** — III, **757a**
Ibn Bassām (d./m. 1147) i, 602a; ii, 838a; iii, 354b, **734a,** 789b, 807b, 934b — I, 621b; II, 857b; III, 365b, **756b,** 813a, 831a, 959b
Ibn Baṭṭa al-ʿUkbarī i, 1040a; iii, 159b, **734b**; iv, 172b, 183b, 469b; v, 10a; s, 17a, 362a — I, 1071b; III, 163a, **757b**; IV, 180a, 191b, 490b; V, 10b; S, 17a, 362a
Ibn Baṭṭūṭa i, 96b, 186b, 323a, 593b, 775a, 903a; ii, 391b, 586a; iii, **735b**; iv, 649a; v, 671a, 827a, 1126a; s, 73b, 203b, 210b, 295b — I, 99a, 191b, 333a, 613a, 798a, 930b; II, 402a, 600b; III, **758a**; IV, 675b; V, 676b, 833b, 1122a; S, 74a, 203a, 210a, 295a
Ibn al-Bawwāb i, 1354a; iii, **736b**; iv, 1122b — I, 1393a; III, **759b**; IV, 1154a
Ibn al-Bayṭār i, 156a, 214b, 516a, 594b, 704a; ii, 349b, 1068a; iii, 267a, 693b, **737a**; iv, 627a; s, 43a, 78a, 313b, 370b, 397a — I, 160b, 220b, 531b, 613b, 725a; II, 359a, 1092b; III, 274b, 715b, **759b**; IV, 652a; S, 43b, 77b, 313b, 370b, 397a
Ibn al-Bazzāz al-Ardabīlī s, **382b** — S, **383a**
Ibn Bībī al-Munadjdjima i, 1197b; iii, **737b** — I, 1233a; III, **760a**
Ibn Biklārish s, **383a** — S, **383b**
Ibn al-Birr iii, **738b,** 859b — III, **761a,** 884a
Ibn al-Birzālī → al-Birzālī
Ibn Bishr → ʿUthmān b. ʿAbd Allāh
Ibn Bishr i, 1312b; iii, 773a — I, 1353a; III, 796a
Ibn Bishrūn iii, 929a; v, 1109b — III, 953b; V, 1105b
Ibn al-Biṭrīḳ → Saʿīd b. al-Biṭrīḳ; Yaḥya b. al-Biṭrīḳ
Ibn Buhlūl iii, **739a** — III, **761b**
Ibn Buḳayla i, 927b; iii, **739a** — I, 955b; III, **762a**
Ibn Bukhtīshūʿ ii, 894b — II, 915b
Ibn Bulbul → Ismāʿīl b. Bulbul
Ibn Burd → Bashshār b. Burd
Ibn Burd al-Akbar iii, **739b** — III, **762b**
Ibn Burd al-Aṣghar iii, **740a** — III, **762b**
Ibn Burghūth → Muḥammad b. ʿUmar
Ibn Buṭlān i, 32b; iii, **740b,** 906b; v, 930b — I, 33b; III, **763a,** 931a; V, 935a
Ibn Crispīn, Moses iv, 305a — IV, 318b
Ibn Daʾb iii, **742a** — III, **764b**
Ibn al-Dabaythī → Ibn al-Dubaythī
Ibn Dabba → Yazīd b. Miḳsam
Ibn al-Ḍaḥḥāk → Ḥusayn b. al-Ḍaḥḥāk
Ibn Dāhir → Djaysinh b. Dāhir
Ibn Daḳīḳ al-ʿĪd s, **383b** — S, **384a**
Ibn al-Daḳḳāk → Ibn al-Zaḳḳāḳ
Ibn al-Dāmād → al-Dāmād
Ibn Danān, Saʿdyā iv, 305b — IV, 319b
Ibn Dāniyāl i, 570b, 595b; iii, **742a**; iv, 602b, 1136b — I, 589b, 615a; III, **765a**; IV, 627a, 1168a
Ibn Dāra → Ibn Sabʿīn
Ibn Darrādj i, 1094a — I, 1127a
Ibn Darrādj al-Ḳasṭallī i, 592b, 601b; iii, **742b** — I, 611b, 621a; III, **765b**
Ibn Darrādj al-Ṭufaylī → Ṭufaylī
Ibn Dārust s, 29b, **383b** — S, 29b, **384a**
Ibn al-Dawādārī iii, **744a** — III, **767a**
Ibn Dāwud, Abraham iv, 304b — IV, 318a
Ibn Dāwūd, Muḥammad ii, 183a, 1032b; iii, 100b, 102a, **744b,** 762b, 792b, 949a, b — II, 188b, 1056a; III, 103a, 104b, **767b,** 785b, 816a, 974a
Ibn al-Dāya i, 1101b, 1156a; ii, 305a; iii, **745b** — I, 1134b, 1109b; II, 313b; III, **768a**
Ibn al-Daybaʿ iii, **746a** — III, **769a**
Ibn Dayṣān i, 48a; ii, 199a, b — I, 49b; II, 205a, b
Ibn Dhakwān, ʿAbd Allāh iii, **746b** — III, **769b**
Ibn Dhakwān, Abu 'l-ʿAbbās Aḥmad iii, 739b, **746b** — III, 762b, **769b**
Ibn Dhakwān, Abū Bakr Muḥammad iii, **747a** — III, **769b**
Ibn Dhakwān, Abū Ḥātim Muḥammad iii, **747a** — III, **769b**
Ibn Dhi → al-Hamdānī
Ibn Diḥya (Daḥya) ii, 1038b; iii, 702a, **747a**; v, 1119b — II, 1062b; III, 724a, **770a**; V, 1116b
Ibn Dīnār → ʿĪsā b. Dīnār; Mālik b. Dīnār; Muḥammad b. Dīnār; Yazīd b. Dīnār
Ibn Dirham, al-Azdī s, **384a** — S, **384b**
Ibn Dirham, Djaʿd iii, **747b,** 1019a; iv, 926b — III, **770b,** 1045a; IV, 959b
Ibn Dirham ʿUmar b. Muḥammad s, **386a** — S, **386a**
Ibn Dirham Yaʿḳūb b. Ismāʿīl b. Ḥammād s, **384b** — S, **385a**
Ibn Dirham Yūsuf b. ʿUmar s, **386a** — S, **386b**
Ibn Dirham Yūsuf b. Yaʿḳūb b. Ismāʿīl b. Ḥammād s, **385a** — S, **385b**
Ibn al-Djadd, Abū ʿĀmir Aḥmad iii, **748a** — III, **771a**
Ibn al-Djadd, Abū Bakr Muḥammad iii, **748b** — III, **771a**
Ibn al-Djadd, Abu 'l-Ḥasan Yūsuf iii, **748a** — III, **771a**
Ibn al-Djadd, Abu 'l-Ḳāsim Muḥammad iii, **748a** — III, **771a**
Ibn Djaʿfar i, 141a; iii, **748b** — I, 145a; III, **771b**
Ibn Djahīr → Djahīr, Banū
Ibn Djahir, ʿAmīd al-Dawla → ʿAmīd al-Dawla
Ibn Djahir, Fakhr al-Dawla → Fakhr al-Dawla
Ibn al-Djahm → ʿAlī b. al-Djahm; Muḥammad b. al-Djahm
Ibn Djahwar, Abī Ḥazm → Abū 'l-Ḥazm Djahwar
Ibn Djahwar, Abu 'l-Walīd i, 155b; ii, 389a; iii, 789a, 974a — I, 160a; II, 399b; III, 812b, 998b
Ibn Djamāʿa iii, **748b**; v, 333a — III, **771b**; V, 333a
Ibn Djamāʿa, Badr al-Dīn i, 439b; iii, 711a, 748b, 952a; iv, 949b; v, 333a — I, 452a; III, 733a, 771b, 977a; IV, 982a; V, 333b
Ibn Djamāʿa, Burhān al-Dīn Ibrāhīm iii, 748b, 749a — III, 771b, 772a
Ibn Djamāʿa, ʿIzz al-Dīn iii, 699a, 748b — III, 721a, 771b
Ibn Djāmiʿ, ʿAbd al-Karīm s, 164a — S, 164a
Ibn Djāmiʿ, Abu 'l-Ḳāsim Ismāʿīl i, 118a; iii, **749b,** 996a; s, 26a, 116b — I, 121b; III, **772b,** 1021a; S, 26b, 116a
Ibn Djāmiʿ, Hibat Allāh → Ibn Djumayʾ Hibat

Allāh al-Isrāᶜīlī
Ibn Djanāḥ iii, **750a** — III, **773a**
Ibn Djarāda → Abū ᶜAbd Allāh b. Djarāda
Ibn al-Djarrāḥ i, 386b; ii, 197b; iii, 619b, **750a**; s, 24b, 284b — I, 397b; II, 203b; III, 640a, **773a**; S, 25a, 284b
Ibn Djarrāḥ → Djarrāḥid(e)s
Ibn al-Djaṣṣāṣ, Ḥusayn (Ḥasan) iii, **750b**; v, 49b — III, **773b**; V, 51a
Ibn al-Djaṣṣāṣ, Isḥāḳ iii, 750b — III, 773b
Ibn al-Djawālīḳī → al-Djawālīḳī
Ibn al-Djawzī, Abu 'l-Faradj i, 69b, 70a, 274b, 275b, 594a, 595a, 802b; ii, 590b, 964a; iii, 160b, 700a, 735a, **751a,** 752b, 803a; s, 16b, 408a — I, 71b, 72a, 283a, 284a, 613b, 614b, 825b; II, 605a, 986a; III, 164a, 722a, 758a, **774a,** 775a, 826b; S, 16b, 408a
Ibn al-Djawzī, Muḥyi al-Dīn iii, 161a, 752a — III, 164b, 774b
Ibn al-Djawzī, Sibṭ i, 150a, 595a; iii, 700b, **752b**; iv, 173a, 1099b; v, 1236b — I, 154b, 614b; III, 722b, **775a**; IV, 180b, 1130a; V, 1227a
Ibn al-Djazarī, Abu 'l-Khayr i, 594b; iii, **753a** — I, 614a; III, **776a**
Ibn al-Djazarī, Shams al-Dīn → al-Djazarī
Ibn Djazla i, 1057a; iii, **754a**; iv, 331a — I, 1088b; III, **776b**; IV, 345b
Ibn al-Djazzār i, 803b; ii, 60a; iii, **754a**; iv, 830b — I, 826b; II, 61a; III, **777a**; IV, 863b
Ibn al-Djillīkī → ᶜAbd al-Raḥmān b. Marwān
Ibn Djinnī i, 143b; ii, 774b, 802b; iii, **754b,** 934b, 1128b; iv, 122b, 123a, 182a; v, 242b, 804b, 840b; s, 19a — I, 148a; II, 793a, 821b; III, **777b,** 959a, 1156b; IV, 127b, 128a, b, 190a; V, 240a, 810b, 847a; S, 19a
Ibn Djubayr i, 330a, 593b, 602b, 901a; ii, 143a, 228b; iii, 736a, **755a**; v, 1160b; s, 205a — I, 340b, 613a, 622a, 928a; II, 147a, 235a; III, 759a, **777b**; V, 1150a; S, 204b
Ibn Djudᶜān → ᶜAbd Allāh b. Djudᶜān
Ibn Djuhayr → Ibn Djahīr
Ibn Djuldjul i, 214a, 600b; iii, **755b**; iv, 254b; s, 52b, 59b, 309b, 397a — I, 220b, 620a; III, **778b**; IV, 266a; S, 53a, 60a, 309b, 397a
Ibn Djumayᶜ Hibat Allāh al-Isrāʾīlī iii, 683a, **749b**; v, 251b; s, 386a — III, 705a, **772b**; V, 249b; S, 386b
Ibn al-Djumayyil → Ibn Diḥya
Ibn Djuraydj al-Makkī s, 18a, **386a** — S, 18a, **386b**
Ibn Djuzayy iii, 736a, 755a, **756a** — III, 758b, 778a, **779a**
Ibn Ḍubāra → ᶜĀmir b. Ḍubāra
Ibn al-Dubaythī iii, **756a** — III, **779a**
Ibn Duḳmāk iii, **756b** — III, **779b**
Ibn al-Dumayna iii, **756b** — III, **779b**
Ibn Durayd i, 125b, 564a, 590a; ii, 1093b; iii, 512a, **757a**; iv, 123a, 524b; v, 608a; s, 361a, 388a — I, 129a, 582a, 609b; II, 1119a; III, 529b, **780a**; IV, 128a, 547a; V, 612a; S, 361a, 388b
Ibn Durustawayh iii, **758a** — III, **781a**
Ibn Ezra, Moses iv, 307a — IV, 320b
Ibn Faḍl Allāh al-ᶜUmarī i, 214a, 595a, 607a, 1139a, 1149a; ii, 303a, 305b, 732b; iii, 7a, 71b, **758a,** 1242b; iv, 431b, 510a, 742b; s, 395b — I, 220b, 614a, 627a, 1173b, 1183a; II, 311a, b, 314a, 751a; III, 7a, 74a, **781b,** 1274b; IV, 450a, 532a, 772a; S, 396a
Ibn Faḍlān i, 1305a, 1306b, 1307a; ii, 1107b; iii, **759a**; iv, 753b, 1063b, 1066a; s, 265a, b — I, 1345a, 1346b, 1347a; II, 1133b; III, **782a**; IV, 784a, 1095a, 1097b; S, 264b, 265a
Ibn Fahd iii, **759b** — III, **782b**
Ibn Fahd, ᶜIzz al-Dīn ᶜAbd al-ᶜAzīz iii, **760b** — III, **783b**
Ibn Fahd, Muḥibb al-Dīn Djār Allāh iii, **760b** — III, **783b**
Ibn Fahd, Nadjm al-Dīn ᶜUmar iii, **760a** — III, **783b**
Ibn Fahd, Taḳi 'l-Dīn Muḥammad iii, **760a** — III, **783a**
Ibn al-Faḥḥām iii, **760b** — III, **784a**
Ibn al-Faḳīh i, 203b, 645b; ii, 580a, b; iii, 106a, **761b,** 1077b; iv, 131b, 1099a; s, 56a, 265a — I, 209b, 666a; II, 594b, 595a; III, 108a, **784b,** 1104a; IV, 137a, 1130a; S, 56b, 265a
Ibn al-Fallāḥī ii, 858a — II, 878a
Ibn al-Faraḍī i, 600b; iii, 733b, **762a,** 789b, 848a — I, 620a; III, 756a, **785b,** 813a, 872a
Ibn Faradj al-Djayyānī i, 601a; iii, 734a, **762b** — I, 620b; III, 756b, **785b**
Ibn Faraḥ al-Ishbīlī iii, **763a** — III, **786a**
Ibn Faraḥ al-Kurṭubī iii, 763a — III, 786a
Ibn Farḥūn i, 280a, 594b; iii, **763b** — I, 288b, 614a; III, **786b**
Ibn al-Fāriḍ i, 60a, 89a, 596a, 816a, 1333a; ii, 363b; iii, **763b**; iv, 1006b — I, 62a, 91b, 615b, 839a, 1373b; II, 373b; III, **786b**; IV, 1038b
Ibn Farīghūn, Shaᶜyā s, 376a, **386b** — S, 376a, **387a**
Ibn Fāris i, 345b, 568a; iii, 111a, 672a, **764a**; iv, 524b; s, 346a — I, 356a, 586b; III, 113b, 693b, **787a**; IV, 547a; S, 346a
Ibn al-Farrāʾ → al-Baghawī
Ibn al-Farrāʾ, Abū Yaᶜlā i, 273b, 435b, 1040a; iii, 159a, b, 512b, 699b, 730b, 735a, **765b,** 784b, 1165a; iv, 458b; s, 195a — I, 282a, 447b, 1017b; III, 162b, 163a, 530a, 721b, 753b, 757b, **788b,** 808a, 1193b; IV, 478b; S, 193b
Ibn Farrūkh v, 1159b — V, 1149a
Ibn Fasāndjus, Abu 'l-Faradj i, 11b; ii, 827a — I, 11b; II, 846b
Ibn Fāṭima ii, 586a — II, 600b
Ibn Firishte → Firishte-oghlu
Ibn Firnās → ᶜAbbās b. Firnās
Ibn al-Fūrak ii, 125b; iii, **766b** — II, 129a; III, **790a**
Ibn al-Furāt iii, **767a** — III, **790b**
Ibn al-Furāt, Abu 'l-ᶜAbbās Aḥmad i, 386b; iii, **767b** — I, 398a; III, **790b**
Ibn al-Furāt, Abu 'l-Faḍl Djaᶜfar ii, 136a, 495a; iii, **768b,** 840b; v, 953b — II, 139b, 507b; III, **791b,** 864b; V, 957b
Ibn al-Furāt, Abu 'l-Fatḥ al-Faḍl iii, 79a, **768a**; v, 953b — III, 81b, **791a**; V, 957b
Ibn al-Furāt, Abu 'l-Ḥasan ᶜAlī i, 386b, 835b; ii, 461b; iii, 100b, 133a, 619b, 739a, 750b, **767b,** 824a, 886b; iv, 265a, 1063b; v, 857a, 953a — I, 398a, 859a; II, 473b; III, 103a, 136a, 640a, b, 761b, 773b, **790b,** 848a, 910b; IV, 277a, 1094b; V, 864a, 957a
Ibn al-Furāt, Abu 'l-Khaṭṭāb Djaᶜfar iii, **768a** — III, **791a**
Ibn al-Furāt, Muḥammad iii, 693b, **768b** — III, 715b, **792a**
Ibn al-Fuwaṭī iii, **769a** — III, **792a**
Ibn Gabirol iii, **770a**; iv, 304a — III, **793a**; IV, 318a
Ibn Ghalbūn iii, **770b** — III, **794a**
Ibn Ghalbūn → Muḥammad b. Khalīl
Ibn Ghālib al-Gharnāṭī iii, **771b** — III, **795a**
Ibn Ghānim i, 1186a; iii, **772a** — I, 1221a; III, **795a**
Ibn Ghāniya → ᶜAlī b. Ghāniya; Yaḥyā b. Ghāniya
Ibn Ghannām iii, **772a** — III, **795b**
Ibn Ghannām, Shaykh iii, **772b** — III, **795b**
Ibn al-Gharābīlī → Ibn Ḳāsim al-Ghazzī
Ibn Gharsiya iii, **773a** — III, **796b**
Ibn al-Ghasīl → ᶜAbd Allāh b. Ḥanẓala
Ibn Ghāzī iii, **773b** — III, **796b**
Ibn Ghidhāhum s, **387a** — S, **387a**
Ibn Ghiyāth (Ghayyāth), Isaac iv, 306a — IV, 319b
Ibn Ghurāb iii, **773b,** 923a — III, **797a,** 947b
Ibn Giḳatilia, Moses iv, 306a — IV, 319b
Ibn al-Habbāriyya iii, 309a, 354b, **774a,** 799b, 1264b; iv, 504a, 506a; s, 26b — III, 318b, 365b, **797b,** 823a,

1297a; IV, 526a, 528a; S, 26b
Ibn al-Ḥabḥāb → ʿUbayd Allāh b. al-Ḥabḥāb
Ibn Ḥabīb i, 600a, 718b; iii, 272b, **775a** — I, 619b, 740a; III, 280b, **798a**
Ibn Ḥabīb, Muḥammad → Muḥammad b. Ḥabīb
Ibn Ḥabīb al-Dimashḳī i, 119a, 595a; iii, **775a** — I, 122b, 614b; III, **798b**
Ibn Ḥābiṭ → Aḥmad b. Ḥābiṭ
Ibn al-Ḥaddād iii, **775b** — III, **799a**
Ibn Ḥadjar al-ʿAsḳalānī i, 275b, 594b, 595a, 791a, 1297a; ii, 159a, 215a, 743b; iii, 25b, 730b, **776a,** 818b; iv, 142b, 642b; s, 88a, 388b — I, 284a, 614a, 614b, 814b, 1336b; II, 164a, 221b, 762a; III, 26b, 753b, **799a,** 842a; IV, 148a, 669a; S, 88a, 389a
Ibn Ḥadjar al-Haytamī iii, **778 b**; iv, 451a, 741b; v, 1235a — III, **802a**; IV, 471a, 771a; V, 1225b
Ibn al-Ḥādjdj al-ʿAbdarī iii, **779b**; iv, 957b — III, **803a**; IV, 991a
Ibn al-Ḥādjdj, Abu ʾl-ʿAbbās al-Ishbīlī iii, **779b** — III, **803a**
Ibn al-Ḥādjdj, Abu ʾl-ʿAbbās al-Sulamī iii, **780a** — III, **803a**
Ibn al-Ḥādjdj, Abū ʿAbd Allāh al-Sulamī iii, **780a** — III, **803a**
Ibn al-Ḥādjdj, Abu ʾl-Barakāt al-Balāfiḳī iii, **780a** — III, **803a**
Ibn al-Ḥādjdj, Abū Isḥāḳ Ibrāhīm iii, **780a** — III, **803a**
Ibn al-Ḥādjdj, Ḥamdūn s, **387b**, 390b — S, **387b**, 391a
Ibn al-Ḥādjdj, Muḥammad al-Ṭālib iv, 774b; s, 387b — IV, 805b; S, 388a
Ibn al-Ḥādjdj, Shīth b. Ibrāhīm al-Ḳiftī iii, **780a** — III, **803a**
Ibn al-Hadjdjādj i, 133b, 858b; ii, 552a, 1032b; iii, 354b, **780a,** 1264a; s, 26a, 398b — I, 137b, 882b; II, 565b, 1056b; III, 365b, **803b,** 1297a; S, 26b, 398b
Ibn Ḥadjdjādj al-Ishbīlī ii, 901b — II, 922b
Ibn al-Ḥādjib i, 721a; iii, **781a,** 861a; iv, 414b — I, 742b; III, **804a,** 885a; IV, 432b
Ibn Ḥādjib al-Nuʿmān iii, **781b** — III, **805a**
Ibn al-Ḥaḍramī ii, 480b; iii, **782a** — II, 493a; III, **805a**
Ibn Ḥafsh iv, 722b — IV, 751b
Ibn Ḥafṣūn → ʿUmar b. Ḥafṣūn
Ibn al-Ḥāʾik → al-Hamdānī
Ibn al-Hāʾim v, 333a — V, 333a
Ibn al-Ḥakīm al-Rundī iii, 833b, 834a, 909a — III, 857b, 933b
Ibn Ḥamādu iii, **782b** — III, **805b**
Ibn Ḥamāma → Bilāl b. Rabāḥ
Ibn Ḥamdīn, Abu ʾl-Ḳāsim Aḥmad iii, 850a, 851b, 958b — III, 874a, 875b, 983a
Ibn Ḥamdīn, Muḥammad iii, 849a, b; iv, 290a — III, 873a, b; IV, 302b
Ibn Ḥamdīs i, 592b, 602a, 1205a; ii, 1033a; iii, **782b**; iv, 1007a; v, 60b — I, 611b, 621b, 1241a; II, 1056b; III, **806a**; IV, 1039b; V, 62a
Ibn Ḥamdūn iii, **783b**; s, 17b — III, **807a**; S, 18a
Ibn Ḥamdūn, Abu ʾl-Maʿālī iii, **784a** — III, **807b**
Ibn Ḥāmid iii, 159a, b, 765b, **784b** — III, 162b, 163a, 789a, **807b**
Ibn Hammād → Ibn Hamādu
Ibn Ḥammūd iv, 733b — IV, 763a
Ibn Hamushk i, 161a; ii, 516a, 1014a; iii, 850b, 865a; iv, 116a, 665b — I, 165b; II, 528b, 1037b; III, 874b, 889a; IV, 121a, 692b
Ibn al-Ḥanafiyya → Muḥammad b. al-Ḥanafiyya
Ibn Ḥanbal → Aḥmad b. Ḥanbal
Ibn Hāniʾ al-Andalusī i, 60b, 592a; ii, 855b, 861b; iii, **785a**; iv, 496b; s, 62b — I, 62b, 611b; II, 875b, 881b; III, **808a**; IV, 518a; S, 63a
Ibn al-Ḥannāṭ iii, **786a** — III, **809b**
Ibn al-Ḥanẓaliyya → Abū Djahl
Ibn Ḥarb → ʿAbd Allāh b. ʿAmr; ʿAbd Allāh b. Sabaʾ
Ibn Ḥarb → Muḥammad b. al-Mughīra b. Ḥarb
Ibn Harma iii, **786b**; iv, 1004b; v, 1156a — III, **809b**; IV, 1036b; V, 1145b
Ibn al-Ḥasan al-Nubāhī → al-Nubāhī
Ibn Ḥatim Badr al-dīn s, **387b** — S, **388a**
Ibn Ḥawḳal i, 96a, 488a, 1003a, 1041a; ii, 577b, 581a, 582a, 1002a; iii, 131a, 405b, **786b**; iv, 223a, b, 1079a, 1081a; v, 555a; s, 94b, 244b, 376b— I, 98b, 502b, 1034a, 1073a; II, 592a, 596a, b, 1025a; III, 133b, 418a, **810a**; IV, 232b, 233a, b, 1110b, 1112a; V, 560a; S, 93b, 244b, 376b
Ibn Ḥawshab → Manṣūr al-Yaman
Ibn al-Ḥawwās ii, 553a; iii, **788a,** 956a; iv, 733b — II, 567a; III, **811a,** 980b; IV, 763a
Ibn al-Haytham i, 785b, 816a, 1102a; ii, 362a; iii, **788a,** 1135b; iv, 515b, 518a, 1059b; v, 397b, 536a, 703b, 1025b; s, 412a, 413a, 414a — I, 809a, 839b, 1135a; II, 372a; III, **811b,** 1163b; IV, 537b, 540b, 1090b; V, 398b, 540b, 708b, 1021a; S, 412a, 413a, 414b
Ibn al-Haythamī i, 593a; iii, 856a — I, 612a; III, 880a
Ibn al-Hayyabān iv, 270a — IV, 282a
Ibn Ḥayyān, Abū Marwān i, 82b, 155b, 600b, 1040b; iii, **789a**; v, 1119b — I, 85a, 160a, 620a, 1072a; III, **812b**; V, 1116a
Ibn Ḥayyawayh iii, 922b — III, 947a
Ibn Ḥayyūs iii, **790a** — III, **813b**
Ibn Ḥāzim → Muḥammad b. Ḥāzim
Ibn Ḥazm iii, **790a** — III, **813b**
Ibn Ḥazm, Abū Bakr iii, **790a** — III, **813b**
Ibn Hazm, Abu ʾl-Mughīra iii, **790b,** 901b, 938b — III, **814a,** 926a, 936b
Ibn Ḥazm, Abū Muḥammad b. ʿAlī i, 84a, 147a, 265b, 414a, 427b, 497a, 590a, 600a, 601b, 865a; ii, 96b, 765a; iii, 308a, 744b, **790b,** 870b, 901b, 1019b, 1024a; iv, 113b, 142a, 272a; v, 703b, 704a; s, 45a, 362b, 396b — I, 86b, 151a, 273b, 425b, 439b, 512a, 609a, 619b, 621a, 889a; II, 98b, 783b; III, 317a, 767b, **814a,** 894b, 926a, 1045a, 1050a; IV, 118b, 148a, 284a; V, 708b, 709a; S, 45b, 362b, 397a
Ibn Ḥazm, Abū Rāfiʿ al-Faḍl b. ʿAlī iii, **790b** — III, **813b**
Ibn Ḥazm, Abū ʿUmar Aḥmad b. Saʿīd iii, **790a** — III, **813b**
Ibn Ḥibbān i, 1348b; iii, **799a** — I, 1388b; III, **822a**
Ibn Hibintā iv, 810a — IV, 842b
Ibn Ḥidjdja al-Ḥamawī i, 595b, 982b; iii, **799b** — I, 614b, 1013a; III, **823a**
Ibn Hilāl al-Ṣābiʾ → Ghars al-Niʿma Muḥammad
Ibn Hindū i, 236a; iii, **800a**; s, 72b — I, 243b; III, **823a**; S, 73a
Ibn Ḥinzāba → Ibn al-Furāt, al-Faḍl
Ibn Ḥirzihim, ʿAlī i, 137b; iii, 732a, **800a** — I, 141b; III, 755a, **823b**
Ibn Hishām, ʿAbd al-Malik i, 158b; iii, 272b, **800b**; v, 41a, 1161b — I, 163a; III, 280b, **824a**; V, 42a, 1151b
Ibn Hishām, Djamāl al-Dīn i, 126b, 593a, 821b; iii, **801a**; iv, 414b; s, 404b — I, 130a, 612b, 844b; III, **824b**; IV, 432b; S, 404b
Ibn Hishām al-Lakhmī v, 608b, 609b; s, **388a** — V, 612b, 613b; S, **388b**
Ibn Ḥithlayn iii, 1067b, 1068a — III, 1094b
Ibn Hubal iii, **802a** — III, **825b**
Ibn Hubayra, ʿUmar iii, **802a,** 1157b — III, **825b,** 1186a
Ibn Hubayra, Yaḥyā i, 122b; iii, 160b, 751a, **802b,** 1157b; iv, 912a, 942b; v, 623a, 1016a — I, 126a; III, 164a, 774a, **826a,** 1186a; IV, 945a, 975b; V, 627a, 1011b

Ibn Hubayra, Yazīd b. ʿUmar i, 16a, 103a, 107b, 123a; iii, 266a, **802a,** 1255a; iv, 447b, 728b, 1132b — I, 16b, 106a, 110b, 126b; III, 273b, **825b,** 1287b; IV, 467a, b, 758a, 1164a
Ibn Ḥubaysh iii, **803b** — III, **826b**
Ibn Hūd → Hūdid(e)s
Ibn Hūd al-Māssī ii, 1009b — II, 1033a
Ibn Ḥudaydj → Muʿāwiya b. Ḥudaydj
Ibn Hudhayl i, 594a; ii, 786b; iii, **804a** — I, 613a; II, 805b; III, **827b**
Ibn al-Humām iii, 164a — III, 167a
Ibn Ḥumayd → Sulṭān b. Bidjād
Ibn Ḥumayd al-Makkī iii, 162b — III, 166a
Ibn Ḥusām iii, 114b — III, 116b
Ibn al-ʿIbrī i, 214a; iii, **804b**; iv, 482a; s, 314a — I, 220b; III, **828a**; IV, 503a; S, 313b
Ibn ʿIdhārī i, 157a; iii, 789b, **805b**; iv, 830a; v, 1209a; s, 389b — I, 161a; III, 813a, **828b**; IV, 863a; V, 1199b; S, 390a
Ibn Idrīs, Abu 'l-ʿAlāʾ iii, **806b** — III, **830a**
Ibn Idrīs, Muḥammad iii, **806a** — III, **829b**
Ibn al-Iflīlī iii, **806b** — III, **830a**
Ibn Igit i, 1249a; ii, 744b — I, 1287a; II, 763a
Ibn al-Ikhshīd iii, **807a**; s, 12b, 13a — III, **830b**; S, 13a, b
Ibn Ilyās s, 327a — S, 326b
Ibn al-ʿImād al-Ḥanbalī i, 594b; iii, 162a, **807b**; s, 267b, 381a — I, 614a; III, 165b, **830b**; S, 267a, 381b
Ibn al-Imām al-Shilbī iii, **807b** — III, **831a**
Ibn ʿInaba iii, **807b** — III, **831a**
Ibn ʿIrāḳ i, 1236a, b, 1237a; iii, **808b**; iv, 1182a, b — I, 1274a, b; III, **831b**; IV, 1215b
Ibn al-ʿIrāḳī → Abū Zurʿa
Ibn ʿIrs iii, **808b** — III, **832a**
Ibn ʿĪsā → ʿAlī b. ʿĪsā b. al-Djarrāḥ
Ibn ʿĪsā → Muḥammad b. ʿĪsā al-Ṣufyānī
Ibn ʿĪsā, Maḥammad iii, **809b** — III, **833a**
Ibn ʿĪsā b. Madjd al-Dīn i, 309b — I, 319b
Ibn-i Isfandiyār iii, **810a**; s, 357a — III, **833b**; S, 357a
Ibn Isḥāḳ i, 158b, 588a; iii, 23b, 272b, 800b, **810b,** 1205b; iv, 370a; v, 1161b, 1162b, 1163a; s, 87b, 358a — I, 163a, 607a; III, 25a, 280b, 824a, **834a,** 1236a; IV, 386b; V, 1151b, 1152a, b; S, 87b, 358a
Ibn Isrāʾīl al-Dimashḳī iii, **811b** — III, **835a**
Ibn al-Iṭnāba al-Khazradjī iii, **812a** — III, **835b**
Ibn Iyās i, 571a, 595a; iii, **812a** — I, 590a, 614b; III, **835b**
Ibn Kabar, Abu 'l-Barakāt s, **388b**, 396a — S, **389a,** 396a
Ibn al-Ḳabisī → al-Ḳābisī, Abu 'l-Ḥasan ʿAlī
Ibn Ḳabṭūrnu iii, **813b** — III, **837a**
Ibn al-Ḳaddāḥ iii, 922b — III, 946b
Ibn al-Ḳāḍī i, 96b; iii, **814a**; s, 223a — I, 99a; III, **837b**; S, 223a
Ibn al-Ḳāḍī (Kabyle) → Aḥmad b. al-Ḳāḍī
Ibn Ḳāḍī Samāwnā → Badr al-Dīn b. Ḳāḍī Samāwnā
Ibn Ḳāḍī Shuhba iii, **814b**; iv, 641b — III, **838a**; IV, 667b
Ibn Kaḍīb al-Bārī iii, 1241a — III, 1273a
Ibn Ḳādūs i, 440a — I, 452b
Ibn al-Ḳaʿḳāʿ al-Makhzūmī v, 997b — V, 993a
Ibn Kākūya → ʿAlāʾ al-Dawla Muḥammad b. Dushmanziyār
Ibn Ḳalāḳis iii, **814b** — III, **838a**
Ibn al-Ḳalānisī iii, **815a**; iv, 181a; s, 204b — III, **838b**; IV, 189a; S, 204a
Ibn al-Ḳalānisī (vizier/vizir) s, 197a — S, 197a
Ibn al-Kalbī → al-Kalbī, Hishām
Ibn Kamāl → Kemalpasha-zāde
Ibn Ḳamīʾa → ʿAmr b. Ḳamīʾa
Ibn Kammūna iii, **815b** — III, **839a**
Ibn Ḳanbar → al-Ḥakam b. Ḳanbar
Ibn Karategin iii, 703a — III, 725b
Ibn Karib i, 1116b; v, 433b — I, 1150b; V, 435b
Ibn al-Ḳāriḥ v, 933b, 934a; s, 37b — V, 937b, 938a; S, 38a
Ibn Karrām → Muḥammad b. Karrām
Ibn Ḳasī (Banū) iii, **815b** — III, **839b**
Ibn Ḳasī, Aḥmad i, 1339a; ii, 1009a, b; iii, 712b, 732a, **816a**; v, 586b — I, 1379b; II, 1033a; III, 755a, **839b**; V, 591b
Ibn Ḳāsim → Muḥammad b. Ḥāzim
Ibn al-Ḳāsim ii, 889b; iii, **817a** — II, 910a; III, **840b**
Ibn Ḳāsim al-Ghazzī i, 151a; iii, **817a** — I, 155a; III, **840b**
Ibn al-Ḳāsim Karīm iv, 362b, 363a — IV, 378b, 379a
Ibn Kathīr, ʿAbd Allāh iii, **817b** — III, **841a**
Ibn Kathīr, Ismāʿīl i, 273b, 595a; iii, 700a, **817b,** 927a, 954b; v, 571a — I, 282a, 614b; III, 722b, **841a,** 951b, 979a; V, 575b
Ibn al-Ḳaṭṭāʿ, ʿAlī iii, 738b, **818b,** 859b; iv, 497b — III, 761b, **842a,** 884a; IV, 519a
Ibn al-Ḳaṭṭāʿ, ʿĪsā iii, **819a** — III, **842b**
Ibn al-Ḳaṭṭān, Abu 'l-Ḳāsim iii, 327b, **819b**; s, 396b — III, 338a, **843a**; S, 397a
Ibn al Ḳaṭṭān the Elder/l'Ancien s, **389a** — S, **389b**
Ibn al-Ḳaṭṭān the Younger/le Jeune i, 78a, 389a; s, **389b** — I, 80b, 400b; S, **389b**
Ibn al-Kawwāʾ i, 382b — I, 393b
Ibn Ḳays al-Ruḳayyāt iii, 572a, **819b** — III, 592a, **843a**
Ibn Kaysān, Abu 'l-Ḥasan Muḥammad al-Naḥwī iii, **820a**; v, 1131a; s, **389b** — III, **844a**; V, 1127a; S, **390a**
Ibn al-Ḳaysarānī, Abū 'l-Faḍl iii, **821a** — III, **844b**
Ibn al-Ḳaysarānī, Sharaf al-Dīn iii, **821b** — III, **845a**
Ibn al-Kayyāl → al-Kayyāl
Ibn Ḳayyim al-Djawziyya i, 273b, 274b, 276a, 276b, 593a, 982b, 1114b, 1116b; ii, 449a; iii, 161b, 513a, 745a, **821b,** 952b, 953a, 1020a; iv, 151b, 1134a; v, 114a — I, 282a, 283a, 284b, 285a, 612b, 1013a, 1148a, 1150a; II, 461a; III, 165a, 530b, 768a, **845b,** 977a, b, 1045b; IV, 157b, 1165b; V, 116b
Ibn Khafādja i, 602a; ii, 526b; iii, **822b,** 849b, 971a; iv, 1007a — I, 621b; II, 539b; III, **846a,** 873b, 995b; IV, 1039b
Ibn Khafīf, Shaykh iii, 103a, **823a**; iv, 46a — III, 105b, **846b**; IV, 49a
Ibn Khafīf → Muḥammad b. Khafīf
Ibn Khāḳān, ʿAbd Allāh iii, **824b** — III, **848a**
Ibn Khāḳān, al-Fatḥ → al-Fatḥ b. Khāḳān
Ibn Khaḳān, Muḥammad iii, **824a** — III, **848a**
Ibn Khāḳān, ʿUbayd Allāh b. Yaḥyā i, 1082b; iii, **824a,** 844b, 879b, 880a; s, 25a — I, 1114b; III, **848a,** 868b, 904a; S, 25a
Ibn Khāḳān, Yaḥyā iii, **824a** — III, **847b**
Ibn Khalaf (Ibāḍī) iv, 920a; v, 623b — IV, 953a; V, 627b
Ibn Khalaf, Abū Ghālib Muḥammad b. ʿAlī s, 119a, b, **390a** — S, 118b, 119a, **390b**
Ibn Khalaf, Abū Shudjāʿ Muḥammad s, **390a** — S, **390b**
Ibn Khalaf, ʿAlī b. ʿAbd al-Wahhāb al-Kātib s, **390a, b** — S, **390b**
Ibn Khalās iii, 921b, 925a — III, 946a, 949b
Ibn Khālawayh i, 120a, 258b; iii, 124b, **824b,** 874b, 880b; v, 927b; s, 37b, 361b — I, 123a, 266b; III, 127b, **848a,** 898b, 904b; V, 933a; S, 38a, 361a
Ibn Khaldūn, ʿAbd al-Raḥmān i, 15a, 286b, 376b, 579b, 593b, 595a, 659b, 681a, 816b, 858a, 959a, 1116b; ii, 285b, 308a, 586b, 767a, 774b; iii, 68b, 711a, **825a,** 1147a; iv, 260a; v, 782a, 1160b; s, 87b, 102b, 308a, 377a, 396a — I, 15b, 295a, 387b, 598a, 613a, 614b, 680b, 701b, 839b, 882a, 988a, 1150a; II, 293b,

316b, 601a, 785b, 793b; III, 71a, 733a, **849a,** 1175a; IV, 271b; V, 788a, 1150a; S, 87b, 102a, 307b, 377a, 396b
Ibn Khaldūn, Yaḥyā i, 123a; iii, 826b, **831b** — I, 126b; III, 850a, **855a**
Ibn Khallād iii, **832a**; s, 12b, 32a — III, **856a**; S, 13a, 32a
Ibn Khallikān i, 72a, 594b, 669b, 1161a; ii, 285a; iii, 814a, **832b,** 934a; v, 481b; s, 25b, 400a — I, 74a, 614a, 690b, 1195b; II, 293a; III, 837b, **856a,** 958b; V, 484a; S, 25b, 400b
Ibn Khamīs iii, **833a** — III, **857a**
Ibn al-Khammār iii, 895a — III, 919b
Ibn al-Khashshāb, ʿAbd Allāh iii, 803a, **834a** — III, 826b, **858a**
Ibn al-Khashshāb, Abu 'l-Ḥasan i, 983b; iii, 87a — I, 1014a; III, 89a
Ibn al-Khaṣīb, Abū ʿAlī Aḥmad iii, **835a**; iv, 742b — III, **858b**; IV, 772a
Ibn al-Khaṣīb, Abū Bakr iii, **835a** — III, **859a**
Ibn al-Khaṣīb, Aḥmad → al-Djardjarāʾī
Ibn al-Khaṣīb, Aḥmad b. ʿUbayd Allāh → al-Khaṣībī
Ibn al-Khaṭīb, Lisān al-Dīn i, 594a, b, 602a; ii, 306a; iii, 756a, 826b, 827a, **835b,** 972b; v, 626a, 707b, 782a; s, 23a, 52b, 382a — I, 613a, 614a, 621b; II, 314b; III, 779a, 850a, b, **859b,** 997a; V, 630a, 712b, 788a; S, 23a, 53a, 382a
Ibn Khaṭīb Dārayyā i, 759a — I, 781b
Ibn Khātima iii, **837a**; v, 609a; s, 388b — III, **860b**; V, 613a; S, 389a
Ibn Khaṭṭāb → al-Khaṭṭābīl
Ibn Khaṭṭāb al-Hawwārī ii, 875b — II, 896a
Ibn Khayr al-Ishbīlī i, 156a, 1198a; ii, 743b; iii, 221a, **837b**; s, 88a — I, 160a, 1233a; II, 762a; III, 228a, **861b**; S, 87b
Ibn al-Khayyāṭ, Abū Bakr Muḥammad iii, **837b** — III, **861b**
Ibn al-Khayyāṭ, Abū al-Ḥasan ʿAlī iii, **838a** — III, **862a**
Ibn Khayyāṭ al-ʿUṣfurī iii, **838b** — III, **862a**
Ibn Khazar b. Ṣūlat iii, 1041b; v, 1175a, b, 1180b — III, 1067b; V, 1165a, b, 1170b
Ibn Khāzim → ʿAbd Allāh b. Khāzim
Ibn Khims al-Taghlibī s, 178a — S, 179a
Ibn Khurradādhbih i, 32a, 589b, 761b; ii, 579a, 580a; iii, **839a,** 1077b; v, 319b; s, 266a, 327a, 376b — I, 33a, 608b, 784b; II, 593b, 594b; III, **863a,** 1104b; V, 319a; S, 265b, 326b, 376b
Ibn Khuzayma, Abū Bakr iii, 799a — III, 822b
Ibn al-Ḳifṭī i, 213a, 235b, 247a, 631a, 803b; ii, 770a, 771b; iii, **840a**; s, 17a, 25b, 32b, 45a, 289a, 362a — I, 219b, 243a, 255a, 652a, 826b; II, 788b, 790a; III, **864a**; S, 17a, 26a, 32b, 45b, 289a, 362a
Ibn Killis i, 816a, 823b; ii, 127a, 169b, 483a, 857b, 859b, 860a; iii, 130a, 404b, **840b**; v, 623a, 1124a, 1125b — I, 839a, 846b; II, 130a, 174b, 495b, 877b, 879a, b; III, 132b, 417a, **864b**; V, 627a, 1120b, 1122a
Ibn Kīrān, Abū ʿAbd Allāh s, **390b** — S, **391a**
Ibn Kīrān, Muḥammad b. ʿAbd al-Madjīd s, 390b — S, 391a
Ibn al-Ḳirriya i, 1115a; iii, **841b** — I, 1148b; III, **865b**
Ibn al-Ḳiṭṭ iii, **842a** — III, **865b**
Ibn Ḳubṭūrna → Ibn Ḳabṭūrnu
Ibn Ḳudāma al-Maḳdisī i, 273b, 277a, 949b; iii, 159a, 161a, 677b, 700a, 735a, 752a, 766b, **842b**; iv, 212a; v, 10a; s, 322b — I, 282a, 285b, 978b; III, 162b, 164b, 699b, 722a, 758a, 775a, 789b, **866a**; IV, 221b; V, 10a; S, 322b
Ibn Ḳudwa iv, 669a — IV, 696b
Ibn al-Ḳuff, Amīn al-Dawla ii, 481b; s, 130b, 271b, **391a** — II, 494a; S, 130a, 271b, **391a**
Ibn Kullāb al-Baṣrī s, **391b** — S, **391b**
Ibn Kunāsa iii, **843a** — III, **867a**
Ibn Kundādjīk → Isḥāk; Muḥammad b. Isḥāḳ
Ibn Ḳunfudh al-Ḳusanṭīnī iii, 339a, 719b, 731b, **843b** — III, 349a, 742a, 754a, **867a**
ibn Kuraysh, Judah iv, 305a, b — IV, 319a
Ibn al-Kurdī ii, 633a — II, 648b
Ibn Ḳurhub ii, 853a; iv, 275b — II, 873a; IV, 287b
Ibn al-Kushayrī iii, 160a, 1266a — III, 16b, 1299a
Ibn Ḳutayba i, 10b, 131a, 307a, 326b, 589a, 758b, 1092b; ii, 249a, 300a, 865a; iii, 28a, 512a, **844b,** 1263b; iv, 212a, 718a; v, 1026b; s, 42b, 227a, 273a, 380b, 392b — I, 10b, 134b, 316b, 336b, 608a, 781b, 1125a; II, 256a, 308b, 885a; III, 29a, 529b, **868b,** 1296a; IV, 221b, 746b; V, 1022b; S, 42b, 227a, 272b, 381a, 393a
Ibn al-Ḳūṭiyya i, 600a; iii, 702a, 789b, 845b, **847b** — I, 619b; III, 724a, 813a, 869b, **871b**
Ibn Ḳutlūbughā i, 594b; iii, 164a, **848b** — I, 614a; III, 167b, **872b**
Ibn Ḳuzmān, ʿAbd al-Raḥmān iii, **849b** — III, **873a**
Ibn Ḳuzmān, al-Akbar iii, **849a** — III, **873a**
Ibn Ḳuzmān, ʿĪsā iii, **849a** — III, **873a**
Ibn Ḳuzmān, Muḥammad al-Aṣghar i, 501b, 570b, 595b, 602a; iii, **849b**; iv, 1007b; v, 744a, 1207a — I, 516b, 589b, 615a, 621b; III, **873b**; IV, 1040a; V, 749a, 1197b
Ibn Ḳuzmān, ʿUbayd Allāh iii, **849b** — III, **873b**
Ibn al-Labbād → ʿAbd al-Laṭīf al-Baghdādī
Ibn al-Labbād, Abū Muḥammad s, 393a — S, 393b
Ibn al-Labbān iii, 766b — III, 789b
Ibn al-Labbāna i, 602a; iii, 677b, **853a**; iv, 1007a — I, 621b; III, 699a, **877a**; IV, 1039b
Ibn Ladjaʾ iii, **853b — III, 877b**
Ibn Lahīʿa iii, **853b** — III, **877b**
Ibn Lankak iii, **854a**; v, 43b; s, 32a — III, **878a**; V, 44b; S, 32b
Ibn Lazza → Ibn Lizza
Ibn al-Liḥyānī iii, 67b — III, 70a
Ibn Lisān al-Ḥummara iii, **854a** — III, **878a**
Ibn Lizza (Lirra) iii, **854b** — III, **878b**
Ibn Luʾayy, Khālid iii, 1065b, 1066b, 1068a; v, 63a — III, 1092a, 1093b, 1095a; V, 64b
Ibn LuʾLuʾ s, 119b — S, 119a
Ibn al-Lunḳuh ii, 901b — II, 922b
Ibn Luyūn al-Tudjībī ii, 902a; iii, **855a** — II, 923a; III, **879a**
Ibn Māʾ al-Samāʾ iii, **855a** — III, **879a**
Ibn Maḍāʾ iii, **855b** — III, **879b**
Ibn Maʿdīkarib → ʿAmr b. Maʿdīkarib
Ibn Mādja ii, 108a; iii, 24a, 692b, **856a**; s, 232b — II, 110b; III, 25b, 714b, **880a**; S, 232b
Ibn Mādjid i, 553b, 932a; ii, 517b, 583a, 586a; iii, **856a**; iv, 1082b, 1083a; v, 941a, 1025a — I, 571a, 960b; II, 530b, 597b, 600b; III, **880a**; IV, 1114a; V, 944b, 1021a
Ibn al-Mādjishūn iv, 87a — IV, 91a
Ibn Mādjūr → Ibn Amādjūr
Ibn al-Maghāzilī iii, 367b — III, 379b
Ibn al-Maghribī → ʿAlī b. al-Ḥusayn al-Maghribī
Ibn Māhān, ʿAlī b. ʿĪsā i, 437b; iii, 233b, 234a, 345b, **859a,** 1202a; iv, 16b, 645a, 718b — I, 450a; III, 240b, 241a, 356a, **883b,** 1232b; IV, 18a, 671b, 747a
Ibn Maḥfūf → ʿAbd Allāh b. Maḥfūf
Ibn al-Māḥūz → ʿUbayd Allāh b. al-Māḥūz; Zubayr b. al-Māḥūz
Ibn Makhlad, al-Ḥasan ii, 197b; iii, **859b** — II, 203b; III, **883b**
Ibn Makhlad, Sāʿid iii, **859b** — III, **883b**
Ibn Makhlad, Sulaymān b. al-Ḥasan i, 387b; iii, **859b** — I, 398b; III, **883b**
Ibn Makkī (Ḳābis) ii, 515a — II, 528a

Ibn al-Makkī (musician/musicien) s, 64a – S, 64b
Ibn Makkī, Abū Ḥafṣ ʿUmar iii, 738b, **859b**; v, 608b; s, 388a – III, 761b, **884a**; V, 612b; S, 388b
Ibn al-Maklātī iii, 788a, 956a – III, 811b, 980b
Ibn Mākūlā, Abū ʿAbd Allāh iii, 766a – III, 789a
Ibn Mākūlā, ʿAlī iii, **860b**; iv, 718b – III, **884b**; IV, 747b
Ibn Mākūlā, al-Ḥasan b. ʿAlī iii, **860a**; iv, 718b – III, **884a**; IV, 747b
Ibn Mākūlā, Hibat Allāh iii, **860a**; iv, 718b – III, **884a**; IV, 747b
Ibn Malak → Firishte-oghlu
Ibn Mālik, Abū ʿAbd Allāh al-Djayyānī i, 126a, 602b; iii, 699a, **861a,** 966b; s, 404b – I, 130a, 622a; III, 721a, **885a,** 991a; S, 404b
Ibn Mālik, Badr al-Dīn v, 898a, 900b – V, 904b, 907a
Ibn Mālik al-Yamanī iii, **862b** – III, **886b**
Ibn Malka → Abu 'l-Barakāt
Ibn Malka, Judah iv, 305a – IV, 318b
Ibn Mammātī, Abu 'l-Malīh iii, **862b** – III, **886b**
Ibn Mammātī, al-Asʿad i, 800b, 801b; ii, 900a; iii, 734a, 747b, **862b,** 894b; iv, 135b, 613b, 1181b; v, 92a; s, 408a – I, 824a, 824b; II, 921a; III, 757a, 770a, **887a,** 918b; IV, 141a, 638a, b, 1215a; V, 94a; S, 408a
Ibn Mammātī, al-Muhadhdhab iii, **862b**; v, 92a – III, **886b**; V, 94a
Ibn al-Maʾmūn → al-Baṭāʾiḥī
Ibn Manda iii, **863a** – III, **887b**
Ibn Manda, ʿAbd al-Raḥmān iii, 161a, **863b** – III, 164b, **888a**
Ibn Manda(h), Abū ʿAbd Allāh i, 142b; iii, 161a, **863b** – I, 146b; III, 164b, **887b**
Ibn Manda, Yaḥyā iii, **864a** – III, **888a**
Ibn Manglī, Muḥammad al-Nāṣirī v, 1229b; s, 175b, **392b** – V, 1219b; S, 176b, **392b**
Ibn Mangudjak i, 664b; ii, 110b – I, 684a; II, 113a
Ibn Manẓūr i, 822a; iii, **864b**; iv, 524b – I, 845a; III, **888b**; IV, 547b
Ibn Mardanīsh i, 79b, 160b, 986a, 1288a, 1347a; ii, 115a, 516a, 526b, 1013b; iii, 850b, **864b**; iv, 116a; v, 392b – I, 81b, 165a, 1016b, 1327b, 1387b; II, 117b, 528b, 539b, 1037b; III, 847b, **889a**; IV, 121a; V, 393a
Ibn al-Māristāniyya iii, 161a, 803a – III, 164b, 826b
Ibn Marwān → Abū ʿAlī b. Marwān
Ibn Marwān, al-Djillīḳī v, 498b – V, 501b
Ibn Maryam iii, **865b** – III, **889b**
Ibn al-Marzubān → Muḥammad b. Khalaf
Ibn Marzūḳ, Aḥmad b. Muḥammad s, 403a – S, 403b
Ibn Marzūḳ, Muḥammad VI al-Ḥafīd i, 1314b; iii, 720b, **866a** – I, 1355a; III, 743a, **890a**
Ibn Marzūḳ, Shams al-Dīn Abū ʿAbd Allāh al-Tilimsānī iii, **865b** – III, **890a**
Ibn Marzūḳ, Shams al-Dīn Muḥammad IV iii, **866b**; v, 1160b, 1209a; s, 403a – III, **890b**; V, 1150a, 1199b; S, 403a
Ibn Masʿada → ʿAmr b. Masʿada
Ibn Maṣāl i, 9a, 198b; ii, 858b; iii, **868a** – I, 9b, 204a; II, 878b; III, **892a**
Ibn Masarra i, 484a, 497a, 600a; ii, 774b; iii, 712b, 785a, 842a, **868b** – I, 498a, 512a, 619b; II, 793a; III, 735a, 808b, 865b, **892b**
Ibn Māsawayh i, 589b, 785b, 1223a; iii, 578b, **872a**; s, 271b, 303b, 314a – I, 608b, 808b, 1259b; III, 599a, **896b**; S, 271a, 303b, 313b
Ibn Mashīsh → ʿAbd al-Salām b. Mashīsh
Ibn al-Māshiṭa iii, **873a** – III, **897b**
Ibn Māssa s, 249b, 314a – S, 249b, 313b
Ibn Maṣṣāla al-Ibāḍī iii, 655b, 659b – III, 677a, 681a
Ibn Masʿūd, ʿAbd Allāh i, 114b, 687a; ii, 888b; iii, 41b, 540b, **873b**; iv, 378a; v, 127a, 350b, 406a, 407a, 409b; s, 227a, 311b – I, 118a, 707b; II, 909a; III, 43a, 559b, **897b**; IV, 394b; V, 129b, 351a, 407b, 408a, 410b; S, 227a, 311a
Ibn Masʿūd al-Khushanī ii, 743b; s, 306a – II, 762a; S, 306a
Ibn Masʿūd al-Shīrāzī s, 271b – S, 271b
Ibn Maṭrūḥ iii, **875b** – III, **899b**
Ibn Mattawayh i, 59b, 343a; iv, 615b; S, **393a** – I, 61b, 353b; IV, 640a; S, **393a**
Ibn al-Mawlā iii, **876a** – III, **900a**
Ibn al-Mawṣilī ii, 962a – II, 984a
Ibn Maymūn i, 214b; iii, 267a, **876a**; iv, 304b, 306b; s, 52b – I, 221a; III, 274b, **900a**; IV, 318a, b, 320a; S, 53a
Ibn Mayyāda iii, **878a**; iv, 1003a – III, **902a**; IV, 1035b
Ibn Māza, Burhān al-Dīn iii, 163b – III, 167a
Ibn Mengüček → Ibn Mangudjak
Ibn Mīkāl iii, 757a, b – III, 780a, b
Ibn Miḳsam al-Naḥwī s, **393a** – S, **393b**
Ibn al-Miʿmār ii, 964a, 965a, 966a – II, 986a, 987a, 988a
Ibn Misdjaḥ iii, **878b** – III, **902b**
Ibn Miskawayh → Miskawayh
Ibn Miskīn iv, 134b – IV, 140a
Ibn Mītham al-Tammār s, **393b** – S, **394a**
Ibn Muʿādh s, 372a, 373b – S, 371b, 373b
Ibn al-Muʿadhdhal, ʿAbd al-Ṣamad iii, **878b**; s, 352a – III, **902b**; S, 352a
Ibn al-Muʿadhdhal, Aḥmad i, 1114b; iii, **879a** – I, 1148a; III, **903a**
Ibn al-Muʿallim → al-Mufīd
Ibn Muʿammar → Muḥammad b. Mushārī
Ibn Muʿayyā iii, 808a – III, 831a
Ibn al-Mubārak, ʿAbd Allāh i, 124a, 1244a; iii, 512b, **879b**; s, 87b, 386b – I, 127b, 1282a; III, 530a, **903b**; S, 87b, 386b
Ibn al-Mubārak al-Lamaṭī → al-Lamaṭī
Ibn al-Mudabbir, Aḥmad i, 278b; ii, 144a, 328a; iii, **879b**; v, 91a – I, 287a; II, 148a, 337b; III, **903b**; V, 93b
Ibn al-Mudabbir, Ibrāhīm iii, **879b,** 880a, 1242b; s, 35a, b – III, **903b,** 904a, 1274b; S, 35b
Ibn al-Mudjāhid, Aḥmad i, 105b; iii, 101a, 817b, **880b,** 936a; v, 127b, 128a, 408b, 409a – I, 108b; III, 103b, 841a, **904b,** 960b; V, 130a, b, 410a
Ibn al-Mudjāwir, Yūsuf b. al-Ḥusayn iii, **881b** – III, **905b**
Ibn al-Mudjāwir, Yūsuf b. Yaʿḳūb i, 571a; iii, **880b** – I, 589b; III, **904b**
Ibn Mufarrigh iii, 354a, 620b, **881b,** 1261b; iv, 536a – III, 365a, 641a, **906a,** 1294b; IV, 559a
Ibn Mufliḥ, Akmal al-Dīn iii, **882b** – III, **907a**
Ibn Mufliḥ, Burhān al-Dīn iii, 162a, **882b** – III, 165a, **907a**
Ibn Mufliḥ, Shams al-Dīn iii, **882b** – III, **906b**
Ibn Mughīth → ʿAbd al-Malik b. Mughīth
Ibn Muḥayṣin ii, 293a – II, 301a
Ibn Muḥriz i, 828a; iii, **883a**; s, 273a – I, 851a; III, **907a**; S, 273a
Ibn al-Muḳaddam ii, 283b – II, 291b
Ibn al-Muḳaffaʿ, ʿAbd Allāh i, 65b, 66a, 176a, 306b, 326b, 569b, 588a, 784b, 1216b; ii, 951a; iii, 113a, 313b, 372b, **883a,** 1019b, 1263a; iv, 92a, 503b, 504a, b, 755b, 948b, 1098a; s, 85b, 88b, 263b – I, 67b, 180b, 316a, 336b, 588a, 607a, 808a, 1252b; II, 973a; III, 115b, 323a, 384b, **907a,** 1045a, 1296a; IV, 96a, 525a, b, 526a, 786a, 981b, 1129a; S, 85b, 88b, 263a
Ibn al-Muḳaffaʿ, Severus iii, **885b** – III, **909b**
Ibn Mukarram → Ibn Manẓūr
Ibn Muḳashshir iii, 81a – III, 83b

Ibn Muḳbil al-ʿĀmirī s, **394a** — S, **394b**
Ibn Muḳla i, 387b, 866a, b, 1040a, 1046b; ii, 305a, 388b; iii, 127a, 345a, 736b, **886b,** 902b, 936a, 1157a; iv, 423b, 1094a, 1122b — I, 398b, 890a, b, 1071b, 1078a; II, 313b, 399a; III, 130a, 355b, 759b, **910b,** 926b, 960b, 1185b; IV, 442a, 1125a, 1154a
Ibn Mukram i, 132a — I, 136a; IV, 442a, 1125a, 1154a
Ibn Muldjam i, 385a; iii, **887a**; iv, 1075a; s, 157a — I, 396a; III, **911a**; IV, 1107a; S, 157a
Ibn Munādhir ii, 1011a; iii, **890a** — II, 1034b; III, **914a**
Ibn al-Munadjdjim → ʿAlī b. Yaḥyā; Yaḥyā b. ʿAlī
Ibn al-Mundhir iii, **890b**; iv, 216a — III, **914b**; IV, 225b
Ibn Munīr → al-Ṭarābulusī al-Raffāʾ
Ibn al-Munḳidh → Usāma; Munḳidh, Banū
Ibn al-Murābiʿ iii, **891a** — III, **915a**
Ibn al-Murtaḍā → Muḥammad b. Yaḥyā al-Murtaḍā
Ibn al-Murtaḍā s, 25b, 225b — S, 26a, 225b
Ibn Musāfir → Muḥammad b. Musāfir
Ibn al-Muslima i, 1073b, 1074b, 1356a; iii, 766a, 860b, **891a**; iv, 457b; v, 73b — I, 1105b, 1106b, 1395a; III, 789a, 885a, **915a**; IV, 478a; V, 75b
Ibn Muṭayr iii, **892a** — III, **916a**
Ibn al-Muʿtazz i, 144a, 386b, 446a, 590a, 592a, 857b, 971b, 981b, 1132a; ii, 197b, 1032b; iii, 100b, 619b, 702b, 750b, **892a,** 955b, 1020a; iv, 90a, b, 491a, 1004a, 1005a; v, 319a, b, 321b; s, 25a, 31b, 35a, 122b, 385a, b — I, 148b, 398a, 458b, 609b, 611a, 881b, 1001b, 1012a, 1166b; II, 204a, 1056b; III, 103a, 640a, 724b, 773a, **916a,** 980a, 1045b; IV, 94b, 512a, 1036a, 1037b; V, 318b, 321a; S, 25a, 32a, 35b, 122a, 386a
Ibn al-Muthannā iii, 1137a — III, 1165b
Ibn Muṭīʿ → ʿAbd Allāh b. Muṭīʿ
Ibn Muʿṭī, Abu 'l-Ḥusayn Yaḥyā ii, 528b; iii, **893b,** 966b — II, 541b; III, **917b,** 991a
Ibn al-Muwaḳḳit iii, **893b**; iv, 159b — III, **917b**; IV, 166b
Ibn Muyassar iii, **894a** — III, **918a**
Ibn Muzāḥim → Naṣr b. Muzāḥim
Ibn al-Muzawwiḳ → Ibn al-Sadīd
Ibn al-Nabīh iii, **894b**; iv, 1006a — III, **918b**; IV, 1038a
Ibn al-Nadīm i, 105a, 151b, 213a, 235a, 247b, 1081a, 1197b, 1354a; ii, 771b, 1093b; iii, 370b, **895a,** 1045a, 1151a; iv, 53b, 1119a; v, 207b; s, 45a, 88b, 127b, 225b, 371b, 372b — I, 108b, 156a, 219b, 242a, 255a, 1113b, 1233a, 1393a; II, 790a, 1119a; III, 382b, **919a,** 1071a, 1179b; IV, 56b, 1150b; V, 205a; S, 45b, 88b, 126b, 225b, 371b, 372a
Ibn al-Nadjdjār (d./m. 1245) iii, 756a, **896b** — III, 779a, **920b**
Ibn al-Nadjdjār (d./m. 1572) i, 949b — I, 978b
Ibn Nādjī s, 173a, **394b** — S, 173b, **395a**
Ibn al-Nafīs i, 713b; iii, 694a, **897a,** 944b — I, 735a; III, 716a, **921b,** 969b
Ibn al-Naḥḥās iii, **898b**; v, 121b — III, **922b**; V, 124a
Ibn al-Naḥwī iii, 800a, b; iv, 481a — III, 823b, 824a; IV, 502a
Ibn al-Nāḳid iii, 683a — III, 705a
Ibn Nāḳiyā iii, **899a** — III, **923a**
Ibn al-Naḳūr s, 195a — S, 193b
Ibn Nāṣir (al-Nāṣirī) s, **395a** — S, **395a**
Ibn Nāṣir, Aḥmad b. Maḥammad s, **395a** — S, **395b**
Ibn Nāṣir, al-Ḥusayn b. Muḥammad s, **395a** — S, **395b**
Ibn Nāṣir, Maḥammad b. Muḥammad s, **395a** — S, **395b**
Ibn al-Nāṣir, Muḥammad b. ʿAbd al-Salām (al-Kabīr) s, **395b** — S, **395b**
Ibn Nāṣir, Muḥammad (al-Makkī) s, **395a** — S, **395b**
Ibn Nāṣir al-Darʿī ii, 161a — II, 166a
Ibn Nasṭūrus → Isā b. Nasṭūrus
Ibn al-Naṭṭāḥ iii, **899a** — III, **923b**
Ibn al-Naẓar iii, **900a** — III, **924a**
Ibn Nāẓir al-Djaysh iv, 510a; s, 395b — IV, 532b; S, 396a
Ibn Nubāta al Fāriḳī iii, **900a**; v, 75b — III, **924a**; V, 77b
Ibn Nubāta al-Miṣrī i, 1154a; iii, 781a, 799b, **900a**; iv, 471b, 864a — I, 1188a; III, 804a, 823a, **924b**; IV, 492b, 897a
Ibn Nudjaym al-Miṣrī i, 27a, 593a; ii, 163b; iii, 163b, **901a** — I, 28a, 612b; II, 168b; III, 167a, **925a**
Ibn Nudjaym iii, **901a** — III, **925a**
Ibn Nūḥ → Muḥammad b. Nūḥ
Ibn al-Nuʿmān, Ḳāḍī → Muḥammad b. al-Nuʿmān
Ibn Paḳūdā, Baḥya iv, 303b, 304b — IV, 317b, 318a
Ibn Rabban → al-Ṭabarī
Ibn al-Rabīb iii, 790b, **901b** — III, 814a, **925b**
Ibn Radjab, ʿAbd al-Raḥmān iii, 161b, 700a, 803b, **901b,** 954b; iv, 990a — III, 165a, 722b, 826b, **926a,** 979a; IV, 1022b
Ibn al-Rāhib s, **396a** — S, **396a**
Ibn Rāhwayh, Isḥāḳ iii, 844b, 846a, **902a** — III, 868b, 870a, **926a**
Ibn Rāʾiḳ i, 19a, 20a, 446a, 866a, b, 870b, 1040a, 1046b; ii, 144a, 453b, 1080b; iii, 46a, 86a, 127b, 768b, 887a, **902b,** 1255b; iv, 215a — I, 20a, 20b, 458b, 890a, b, 894b, 1071b, 1078a; II, 148a, 465a, 1105b; III, 47b, 88a, 130a, 791b, 911a, **926b,** 1288a; IV, 224b
Ibn al-Raḳā ii, 389a — II, 399b
Ibn al-Raḳīḳ iii, **902b**; iv, 830b, 1007a — III, **927a**; IV, 863b, 1039a
Ibn al-Rakkāḍ i, 759b — I, 782b
Ibn al-Raḳḳāḳ → Ibn al-Zaḳḳāḳ
Ibn Rashīd → Rashīd, Āl
Ibn Rashīd, Muḥammad iii, 326b — III, 336b
Ibn Rashīḳ, Abū ʿAlī Ḥasan i, 858a; iii, 354b, 640a, 688a, **903a,** 936a; iv, 250a, 867a; s, 27a, 62b, 394b — I, 882a; III, 365b, 661a, 709b, **927b,** 960b; IV, 260b, 900b; S, 27a, 63a, 395a
Ibn Rashīḳ, Abū Muḥammad i, 6b; iii, 706a, **904b** — I, 7a; III, 728a, **928b**
Ibn Rawāḥa → ʿAbd Allāh b. Rawāḥa
Ibn al-Rāwandī i, 129a, 130a; 373b, 780b; iii, **905a,** 1019b; iv, 1162b; v, 120b; s, 12b, 14a, 225b — I, 132b, 133b; II, 383b, 799b; III, **929a,** 1045a; IV, 1194b; V, 123b; S, 13a, 14b, 225b
Ibn Razīḳ i, 1283a — I, 1322a
Ibn Razīn i, 1092b — I, 1125a
Ibn al-Razzāz al-Djazarī iii, 511a — III, 528b
Ibn al-Riḍā → Ḥasan al-ʿAskarī
Ibn Riḍwān iii, 740b, 741b, **906a,** 977a; s, 30a — III, 763b, 764a, **930a,** 1001b; S, 30a
Ibn Rizām i, 48a, 95b, 96a; iv, 662b — I, 49b, 98b; IV, 689b
Ibn Rubayʿān, ʿUmar ii, 354a; iii, 1068a — II, 363b; III, 1094b
Ibn Rūḥ iii, 133a, **907a** — III, 136a, **931b**
Ibn Ruhayb → Ḳiṭfīr
Ibn al-Rūmī i, 592a; iii, 354b, **907b,** 955b; iv, 1005a; s, 58b, 352b — I, 611a; III, 365b, **931b,** 980a; IV, 1037b; S, 59a, 352b
Ibn al-Rūmiyya s, 313b, **396b** — S, 313b, **397a**
Ibn Rushayd iii, **909a** — III, **933a**
Ibn Rushd (al-Ḥafīd) i, 162a, 179a, 209b, 214a, 234b, 327b, 342b, 350b, 415a, b, 594a, 630b, 982b, 1154b; ii, 96b, 765b, 766a, 771a, 773b; iii, 170a, 509b, 644b, 729a, 748b, **909b,** 978a, b, 1132a, 1149a; v, 704a, 843a; s, 397b — I, 166b, 183b, 215b, 220b, 241b, 337b, 353a, 361a, 427a, 613b, 651b, 1013a, 1188b; II, 98b,

784a, b, 789b, 792a; III, 173b, 527a, 666a, 751b, 771a, **934a**, 1002b, 1160a, 1177a; V, 709a, 849b; S, 398a
Ibn Rushd, al-Djadd s, **397b** — S, **398a**
Ibn Rusta, Aḥmad i, 100b, 775a; ii, 579b, 580a, b; iii, 232a, **920a** — I, 103b, 798a; II, 594b, 595a; III, 239a, **944b**
Ibn Rustam → ʿAbd al-Rahmān b. Rustam
Ibn Saʿāda iii, **921a** — III, **945a**
Ibn al Sāʿātī, Aḥmad iii, **921a** — III, **945b**
Ibn al-Sāʿātī, Riḍwān iii, **921a**, — III, **945b**
Ibn Sabaʾ → ʿAbd Allāh b. Sabaʾ
Ibn al-Ṣabbāgh s, 29b — S, 30a
Ibn Sabʿīn i, 594a, 772b; iii, **921b** — I, 613b, 795b; III, **945b**
Ibn Saʿd, Abū ʿAbd Allāh Muḥammad i, 140a, 591a, 694a; iii, 838b, **922a** — I, 144a, 610b, 715a; III, 862b, **946b**
Ibn Ṣadaḳa iii, 221a — III, 228a
Ibn Saʿdān, Abū ʿAbd Allāh al-Ḥusayn b. Aḥmad i, 127a, 159a; s, 119b, 361b, **398a** — I, 130b, 163b; S, 119a, 361a, **398b**
Ibn Ṣaddīḳ, Joseph iv, 304b — IV, 318a
Ibn al-Sadīd (d./m. 1430) iii, **923a** — III, **947a**
Ibn al-Sadīd (d./m. 1324) iii, **923a** — III, **947b**
Ibn Ṣadr al-Dīn al-Shirwānī i, 327a — I, 337a
Ibn Saʿdūn → Yaḥyā b. Saʿdūn
Ibn al-Ṣaffār iii, **924a**, 1137a — III, **948b**, 1165b
Ibn al-Ṣaghīr iii, **924b** — III, **949a**
Ibn Ṣaghīr al-Barbarī al-Maṣmūdī iv, 920a — IV, 953a
Ibn Ṣāḥib al-Ṣalāt iii, **924b** — III, **949a**
Ibn Sahl i, 602a; iii, **925a**, 1047a; iv, 1007b — I, 621b; III, **949b**, 1073a; IV, 1039b
Ibn Saḥnūn, Muḥammad iii, 681a; v, 503b — III, 703a; V, 507a
Ibn al-Sāʿī iii, **925b**; s, 284b — III, **950a**; S, 284a
Ibn Saʿīd → al-Mundhir b. Saʿīd
Ibn Sāʿid (Ḥawrān) iv, 552b — IV, 576b
Ibn Saʿīd, Abū Djaʿfar → Abū Djaʿfar Ibn Saʿīd
Ibn Saʿīd al-Maghribī i, 119a, 602a, 602b; iii, 807b, **926a**; iv, 1081a; v, 1012a, 1020b; s, 86a, 266a — I, 122b, 621b, 622a; III, 831a, **950b**; IV, 1112b; V, 1008a, 1016b; S, 86a, 265b
Ibn al-Ṣāʾigh iii, **926b** — III, **951a**
Ibn al-Ṣalaḥ ii, 462a; iii, 25b, 27a, 818b, **927a** — II, 474a; III, 26b, 28b, 842a, **951b**
Ibn Salām iii, **927a** — III, **951b**
Ibn al-Sal(l)ār → al-ʿĀdil b. al-Salār
Ibn Sālim iii, 570b — III, 590b
Ibn Sālim al-Kalāʿī → al-Kalāʿī, Abu 'l-Rabīʿ b. Sālim
Ibn Sallām → Abū ʿUbayd al-Ḳāsim b. Sallām
Ibn Sallām al-Djumaḥī iii, 272b, 353b, 698a, **927b**, 1177b; s, 284a — III, 280b, 365a, 720a, **952a**, 1206b; S, 284a
Ibn al-Ṣalt, Aḥmad b. Muḥammad s, 400b — S, 401a
Ibn al-Salʿūs iv, 964b — IV, 997a
Ibn Samadjūn i, 214a; iii, **928a**; s, 313b, 314a — I, 220b; III, **952b**; S, 313b
Ibn al-Samḥ i, 600b; iii, **928b**, 1137a; s, 25a — I, 620a; III, **953a**, 1165b; S, 25b
Ibn Sammāk iii, 570a — III, 589b
Ibn Samʿun → Abu 'l-Ḥusayn
Ibn Samura → ʿUbayd Allāh Ibn Samura
Ibn Sanāʾ al-Mulk i, 595b; ii, 1033a; iii, **929a** — I, 615a; II, 1057a; III, **953b**
Ibn al-Ṣāniʿ → Ibn Yaʿīsh, Muwaffaḳ al-Dīn
Ibn Sarābiyūn iii, **929b** — III, **954a**
Ibn Ṣārah s, 352b — S, 352b
Ibn al-Sarāya → Ṣafī al-Dīn al-Hillī
Ibn al-Sarrādj → Ibn al-Ḳiṭṭ
Ibn al-Sarrādj, Abū ʿAlī iii, 842a — III, 866a
Ibn al-Sarrādj, Āl s, **398b** — S, **399a**
Ibn al-Sarrādj, Muḥammad b. ʿAlī iii, **930a** — III, **954b**
Ibn al-Sarrādj, Muḥammad b. al-Sarī iii, **930a**, 1128a — III, **945b**, 1156b
Ibn al-Ṣarṣarī iii, 952a — III, 976b
Ibn Ṣaṣra, Ṣaṣarrā iii, **930b** — III, **955a**
Ibn Saʿūd → ʿAbd al-ʿAzīz Āl Saʿūd
Ibn al-Sawdāʾ → ʿAbd Allāh b. Sabaʾ
Ibn Sawda → Ibn Sūda
Ibn Sawwār i, 1086b; ii, 127a — I, 1118b; II, 130b
Ibn Sayāba → Ibrāhim b. Sayāba
Ibn Sayf II iii, 604a — III, 624b
Ibn Sayḥān iii, **931b**; iv, 1002a — III, **956a**; IV, 1031b
Ibn al-Ṣayrafī, Tādj al-Riʾāsa ii, 80a, 304b, 305a; iii, **932a**, 1242b — II, 81b, 313a, b; III, **956b**, 1274b
Ibn al-Ṣayrafī, Abū Bakr Yaḥyā i, 389b; iii, **932b** — I, 400b; III, **957a**
Ibn al-Sayyid i, 600a — I, 619b
Ibn Sayyid al-Nās iii, **932b** — III, **957a**
Ibn al-Shabbāṭ iv, 403a — IV, 420b
Ibn Shaddād, ʿAbd al-ʿAzīz iii, **933a** — III, **957b**
Ibn Shaddād, Bahāʾ al-Dīn iii, **933b** — III, **958a**
Ibn Shaddād, ʿIzz al-Dīn i, 946a; iii, **933b**, 938a — I, 975a; III, **958a**, 962b
Ibn Shaddād Yūsuf s, 197a — S, 197a
Ibn al-Shadjarī al-Baghdādī i, 485b, 1241a; iii, 111a, **934b** — I, 500a, 1279a; III, 113b, **959a**
Ibn Shahīd s, 111b, 112a — S, 111a
Ibn al-Shahīd iii, **934b** — III, **959b**
Ibn Shāhīn → Nissīm ben Yaʿḳob Ibn Shāhīn
Ibn Shāhīn al-Ẓāhirī iii, **935a** — III, **959b**
Ibn Shahrāsūb i, 120a; ii, 848a; iii, **935a**, 1151b — I, 123b; II, 867b; III, **960a**, 1180a
Ibn Shākir → al-Kutubī
Ibn Shaḳīshaḳa s, 197a — S, 197a
Ibn Shakrūn al-Miknāsī s, 40a, **399b** — S, 40b, **400a**
Ibn al-Shalmaghānī → Muḥammad b. ʿAlī al-Shalmaghānī
Ibn Shannabūdh i, 1039b; iii, **936a**; v, 127b, 409a; s, 386a, 393b — I, 1071a; III, **960b**; V, 130a, 410a; S, 386b, 394a
Ibn Sharaf, Abu 'l-Faḍl i, 602a; iii, **936b** — I, 621b; III, **961b**
Ibn Sharaf al-Ḳayrawānī iii, 903b, **936a**; iv, 830b; v, 43b; s, 27a, 62b, 394b — III, 927b, **960b**; IV, 863b; V, 44b; S, 27a, 63a, 395a
Ibn Sharāfī, Ṣafī al-Dīn v, 92a — V, 94b
Ibn al-Shārī s, 388b — S, 389a
Ibn al-Sharīf ii, 160a — II, 165b
Ibn Sharya iii, 370a, **937a**; iv, 211b — III, 382a, **961b**; IV, 221a
Ibn al-Shāṭir iii, 1137b; iv, 518a, 810a — III, 1165b; IV, 540b, 843a
Ibn al-Shaykh al-Balawī i, 602a — I, 622a
Ibn Shaykh Ḥiṭṭīn → al-Dimashḳī
Ibn Shaykh al-Salāmiya → Ibn al-Ṣāʾigh
Ibn Shibl iii, **937b**; iv, 1005b — III, **962a**; IV, 1038a
Ibn Shihāb i, 830a — I, 853a
Ibn Shihāb al-Zuhrī → al-Zuhrī
Ibn al-Shiḥna al-Ḥalabī i, 119a; iii, **938a** — I, 122b; III, **962b**
Ibn Shīth al-Kurashī ii, 329b — II, 339a
Ibn Shubruma iii, 687b, **938a** — III, 709a, **962b**
Ibn Shudjaʿ Farrukhshāh v, 76b — V, 78b
Ibn Shuhayd i, 591a, 601b; iii, 346b, 355a, 370b, 740a, 786a, 790a, b, **938b**; iv, 1007a; v, 114b, 778b; s, 250a — I, 610a, 621a; III, 357b, 366a, 382b, 763a, 809b, 813b, 814a, **963a**; IV, 1039a; V, 117a, 784b; S, 250a
Ibn Shukr i, 800b, 801b — I, 824a, b
Ibn al-Sīd al-Baṭalyawsī → al-Baṭalyawsī

Ibn Sīda i, 600a, 601a; ii, 300b; iii, **940a**; iv, 524b — I, 620a, 621a; II, 308b; III, **964b**; IV, 547a
Ibn Sīduh s, 317b — S, 317b
Ibn al-Sikkīt i, 772a, 1241a; ii, 300a; iii, 803a, **940b**; iv, 1027b; s, 15b, 394b — I, 795a, 1279a; II, 308a; III, 826b, **965a**; IV, 1059b; S, 16a, 395a
Ibn al-Simāṭ v, 1247b — V, 1238a
Ibn Sīnā i, 74b, 112a, b, 147a, 179a, 213b, 234b, 327b, 342a,b, 350b, 415a, 427a, 434b, 589a, 630b, 772b, 784b, 785b, 839a, 926a, 1084a, 1236a, 1327a, 1354a; ii, 96a, 221a, 378b, 450a, 481b, 550a, 764b, 765a; iii, 30a, 170a, 329b, 330b, 333b, 509b, 543b, 897b, 916a, **941a**, 974b, 1028a, 1130b; iv, 120a, 331a, 358b, 366b, 466b, 615b; v, 842b, 1261b, 1262b; s, 24a, 40b, 59b, 72b, 270a, 271b, 305b, 308a, 314a, 380a — I, 76b, 115a, b, 151b, 183b, 220a, 242a, 338a, 352a, 353a, 361a, 426b, 439b, 446b, 608b, 651b, 795b, 808a, 809a, 862a, 954a, 1116b, 1274a, 1367b, 1393a; II, 98a, 228a, 388b, 462a, 494a, 564a, 783a, 784a; III, 31b, 174a, 339b, 341a, 343b, 527a, 562b, 921b, 940a, **965b**, 999a, 1054a, 1159a; IV, 125a, 345b, 374a, 382b, 487a, 640a; V, 849a, 1252b, 1253b; S, 24a, 40b, 60a, 73a, 269b, 271a, b, 305a, 308a, 313b, 380b
Ibn Sīrīn ii, 300b; iii, **947b**; v, 1232a — II, 309a; III, **972a**; V, 1222a
Ibn al-Sitrī → Ibn al-Bawwāb
Ibn Sūda iii, **948a** — III, **973a**
Ibn Sūda, Abū ᶜAbd Allāh Muḥammad iii, **948b** — III, **973a**
Ibn Sūdūn i, 571a — I, 590a
Ibn al-Ṣuḳāᶜī al-Naṣrānī s, **400a** — S, **400b**
Ibn Sukkāra s, 352b — S, 352b
Ibn Ṣulayḥa ii, 353b — II, 363a
Ibn Sulaym al-Aswānī iii, **949a** — III, **973b**
Ibn Ṣumādiḥ → al-Muᶜtaṣim Ibn Ṣumādiḥ
Ibn Surāḳa i, 773a — I, 796b
Ibn Suraydj, Abu 'l-Abbās Aḥmad iii, 100b, **949a** — III, 103a, **974a**
Ibn Suraydj, ᶜUbayd Allāh i, 118a, 828a; ii, 428b, 1011b; iii, **950a**; iv, 315b — I, 121b, 851a; II, 439b, 1035a; III, **974b**; IV, 329b
Ibn al-Sūrī ii, 350a — II, 359b
Ibn Suᶜūd → ᶜAbd al-ᶜAzīz Āl Saᶜūd
Ibn Suwayṭ ii, 77a — II, 78b
Ibn al-Taᶜāwīdhī i, 212b; iii, 891b, **950a** — I, 219a; III, 915b, **975a**
Ibn Ṭabāṭabā i, 149b, 402b; iii, 243b, **950b** — I, 154a, 414a; III, 250b, **975b**
Ibn Tafrāgīn iii, 49a, 68a, 826a, 867a; v, 1151a, 1247a — III, 50b, 70a, 849b, 891a; V, 1141b, 1237b
Ibn Taghrībirdī → Abu ʾl-Maḥāsin
Ibn Ṭāhir → ᶜAbd Allāh b. Ṭāhir
Ibn Talḥa al-ᶜAdawī al-Rādjī ii, 376a; v, 1236b — II, 386b; V, 1227a
Ibn Ṭalūt iv, 459a — IV, 479b
Ibn al-Tammār → Ibn Mītham
Ibn Ṭarf → Sulaymān b. Ṭarf
Ibn Taymiyya, Aḥmad i, 69b, 195a, 266b, 272b, 273b, 274b, 275b, 276a,b, 277a, 333a, 411b, 425a, 553a, 593a, 696a, 827b, 959a, 1238b; ii, 51a, 230a, 285b, 294a, 295a, 411b, 752b, 931a, 966a; iii, 161b, 162a, 429b, 512b, 700a, 711a, 722b, 752a, 821b, **951a**, 1148b, 1171b, 1207a; iv, 142a, 149b, 257b, 258b, 366a, 381b, 469b; v, 426a; s, 354a — I, 71b, 201a, 274b, 280b, 282a, 283a, 284a, b, 285a, b, 343a, 423b, 437a, 570b, 612b, 717b, 850b, 988a, 1276a; II, 52a, 236b, 293b, 302a, 303a, 422b, 771a, 953a, 988a; III, 164b, 165b, 443b, 530a, 722b, 733a, 745a, 775a, 845b, **976a**, 1176b, 1200b, 1237b; IV, 148a, 155b, 269a, 270a, 382a, 398a, 490b; V, 428b; S, 354a
Ibn Taymiyya, Madjd al-Dīn iii, 161a, 951a, 953b — III, 164b, 976a, 978a
Ibn al-Tayyām → Tammām b. Ghālib
Ibn al-Tayyānī i, 600a — I, 620a
Ibn al-Ṭayyib al-Baṣrī → Abu ʾl-Ḥusayn
Ibn al-Ṭayyib al-ᶜIrāḳī i, 328a, 388a; ii, 780a, 929b, 948b; iii, 740b, **955a**, 1205b; s, 25a, 396b — I, 338a, 399a; II, 799a, 951b, 970b; III, 763b, **979b**, 1236a; S, 25b, 397a
Ibn Thawāba iii, **955a** — III, **979b**
Ibn al-Thumna iii, 782b, 788a, **956a** — III, 806a, 811b, **980b**
Ibn Tifalwīt iii, 542b, 728a, 849b — III, 561b, 750b, 873b
Ibn al-Ṭiḳṭaḳā i, 157b, 595b; iii, 702a, **956a** — I, 162a, 614b; III, 724b, **980b**
Ibn al-Tilmīdh i, 111b, 344b, 858b, 1224a,b; iii, **956b** — I, 115a, 355a, 882b, 1260b, 1261a; III, **981a**
Ibn Ṭūbī, Mūsā iv, 307a — IV, 320b
Ibn Ṭufayl i, 162a, 594a, 1250a; ii, 773b, 1039b; iii, 330b, 333a, 729a, 910a, 911b, **957a** — I, 166b, 613a, 1288a; II, 792a, 1063b; III, 341a, 343a, 751b, 934a, 935b, **981b**
Ibn Ṭūlūn → Aḥmad b. Ṭūlūn
Ibn Ṭūlūn, Shams al-Dīn i, 571a; iii, **957b**; iv, 1161b; s, 195b — I, 590a; III, **982a**; IV, 1193b; S, 195b
Ibn Tūmart i, 78a, 121b, 122a, 251a, 389b, 390a, 592b, 1129b, 1176a, 1186a, 1205a; ii, 307b; iii, 207a, **958b**; iv, 290a, 558a; v, 626a, 744b, 1160b, 1199b — I, 80a, 125a, b, 258b, 400b, 401b, 612a, 1163b, 1211a, 1221a, 1241a; II, 316b; III, 212b, **983a**; IV, 303a, 582a; V, 630a, 750a, 1150b, 1190a
Ibn Ṭumlūs iii, **960a** — III, **984b**
Ibn Turayk, Abu 'l-ʾAlāᶜ iii, 782a — III, 805a
Ibn al-Ṭuwayr i, 801b; iii, **960b**; iv, 1145b — I, 824b; III, **985a**; IV, 1177a
Ibn ᶜUbayya v, 333b — V, 333b
Ibn ᶜUdjayl i, 1140b — I, 1175a
Ibn Udhayna → ᶜUrwa b. Udhayna
Ibn ᶜUḳba → Mūsā b. ᶜUḳba
Ibn ᶜUḳda, al-Hamdānī s, **400b** — S, **401a**
Ibn al-Ukhuwwa iii, **960b**; s, 273b — III, **985a**; S, 273a
Ibn ᶜUkkāsha i, 6b — I, 6b
Ibn ᶜUlayya, Abū Isḥāḳ Ibrāhīm b. Ismāᶜīl s, 90a — S, 90a
Ibn ᶜUmar → ᶜAbd Allāh b. ᶜUmar; Yaᶜḳūb b. ᶜUmar al-Maghribī
Ibn ᶜUmar, Djazīrat iii, **960b**; v, 447b, 458b; s, 267a — III, **985a**; V, 450a, b, 461a; S, 266b
Ibn ᶜUmāra → al-Dīkdān
Ibn Umayl ii, 358a,b; iii, 464b, **961b**; v, 112a; s, 270a — II, 367b, 368b; III, 481a, **986a**; V, 114b; S, 269b
Ibn Umayya i, 1343a — I, 1383b
Ibn ᶜUnayn iii, **962a** — III, **986b**
Ibn ᶜUrayba v, 1247b — V, 1238a
Ibn ᶜUṣfūr iii, **962b** — III, **987a**
Ibn Ustādh-Hurmuz, Abū ᶜAlī al-Ḥasan s, 118b, 119a — S, 118a
Ibn ᶜUthmān al-Miknāsī s, 308a, **401a** — S, 307b, **401b**
Ibn ᶜUyayna → Sufyān b. ᶜUyayna
Ibn Wadᶜān s, 83a — S, 82b
Ibn Wāfid i, 345a, 600b; ii, 901a; iii, **962b**; s, 314a — I, 355b, 620a; II, 922a; III, **987a**; S, 313b
Ibn Wahb → ᶜAbd Allāh b. Sabaʾ
Ibn Wahb, ᶜAbd Allāh al-Ḳurashī iii, **963a**; iv, 87a — III, **987b**; IV, 91b
Ibn Wahb, Abu 'l-Ḥusayn s, **402a** — S, **402b**
Ibn Wahbūn iii, **963a** — III, **987b**
Ibn Wahhās → al-Khazradjī, Muwaffaḳ al-Dīn
Ibn Waḥshiyya i, 247a; ii, 358a, 455b, 900a; iii, **963b**; iv, 120b, 659a; v, 112a, 222b, 997a; s, 59b, 310a, 392b — I, 255a; II, 367b, 467b, 920b; III, **988a**; IV, 126a,

685b; V, 114b, 220a, 1029b; S, 60a, 309b, 393a
Ibn Waḳār, Joseph iv, 305a — IV, 318b
Ibn Walmiya iv, 337a, b, 339a — IV, 351b, 352a, 353a
Ibn al-Wannān i, 290b; iii, **965b**; s, 381b — I, 299b; III, **990a**; S, 382a
Ibn al-Wardī, Sirādj al-Dīn i, 594b; ii, 587b; iii, **966a**; iv, 1081b — I, 613b; II, 602a; III, **990b**; IV, 1112b
Ibn al-Wardī, Zayn al-Dīn i, 119a; iii, 772b, **966b**; iv, 471b; v, 548a — I, 122b; III, 795b, **991a**; IV, 492b; V, 552b
Ibn Warsand s, **402b** — S, **402b**
Ibn Wāṣil iii, 934a, **967a**; s, 204b, 205a — III, 958b, **991b**; S, 204a, b
Ibn Waththāb ii, 484b — II, 496b
Ibn Wazīr → Sidrāy b. Wazīr
Ibn al-Wazzān s, 398a — S, 398a
Ibn Yaʿīsh, Muwaffaḳ al-Dīn i, 571a; ii, 896a; iii, 551a, **968a** — I, 589b; II, 917a; III, 570a, **992b**
Ibn Yaʿīsh, Salomo(n) (d./m. 1603) iii, **967b** — III, **992a**
Ibn Yaʿīsh, Solomon (d./m. 1345) iii, **967b** — III, **992a**
Ibn Yāḳūt → Muḥammad b. Yāḳūt
Ibn Yalbaḳ iii, 46a; iv, 423b — III, 47b; IV, 442a
Ibn Yallas, Muḥammad iii, 261b, **968a** — III, 269a, **992b**
Ibn-i Yamīn iii, **968a**; iv, 66a — III, **992b**; IV, 69b
Ibn-i Yamīn Shiburghānī iii, 968b — III, 993a
Ibn Yāsīn → ʿAbd Allāh b. Yāsīn
Ibn Yūnus → Abu ʾl-Muẓaffar b. Yūnus
Ibn Yūnus (Yūnis), Abu 'l-Ḥasan ʿAlī ii, 584a; iii, 9a, **969b,** 1137a; iv, 810a, 1079a; v, 85a, b; s, 115b, 413b — II, 599a; III, 9b, **994a,** 1165a; IV, 843a, 1110b; V, 87b, 88a; S, 115a, 413b
Ibn Yūnus, Abū Saʿīd iii, **969b** — III, **994a**
Ibn al-Zabīr iii, **970a** — III, **994b**
Ibn al-Zadjdjādj i, 942a — I, 971a
Ibn Ẓafar iii, 309a, **970a**; iv, 506a — III, 318b, **995a**; IV, 528a
Ibn Ẓāfir iii, **970b** — III, **995a**
Ibn Zāghū, Aḥmad b. Muḥammad s, 403a — S, 403a
Ibn Zāghū, Muḥammad b. Aḥmad iv, 477a — IV, 498a
Ibn Zakī iii, 708a — III, 730b
Ibn al-Zaḳḳāḳ i, 602a; iii, 823a, **971a**; iv, 1007a — I, 621b; III, 846b, **995b**; IV, 1039b
Ibn Zakrawayh → Ḥusayn b. Zakrawayh; Yaḥyā b. Zakrawayh
Ibn Zakrī s, **402b** — S, **403a**
Ibn Zakrī al-Fāsī s, **403b** — S, **404a**
Ibn Zakrī al-Tilimsānī s, **402b** — S, **403a**
Ibn Zākūr iii, **971b** — III, **996a**
Ibn Zamraḳ i, 602a; iii, 836a, **972b** — I, 621b; III, 860a, **997a**
Ibn al-Zarḳala → al-Zarḳalī
Ibn Zarḳūn iii, 680b, 798b — III, 702b, 821b
Ibn Zawlāk → Ibn Zūlāk
Ibn Zaydān iii, **973a** — III, **997b**
Ibn Zaydūn i, 591a, 592b, 601b; ii, 1033a; iii, 681b, 706a, **973b**; v, 377a — I, 610a, 611b, 621b; II, 1056b; III, 703a, 728a, **998a**; V, 377b
Ibn Zaylā iii, **974b** — III, **999a**
Ibn al-Zayyāt, Muḥammad iii, **974b**; s, 106a — III, **999a**; S, 105b
Ibn al-Zayyāt al-Tādilī iii, **975a** — III, **999b**
Ibn al-Zibaʿrā iii, **975a** — III, **999b**
Ibn Ziyād → ʿUbayd Allāh b. Ziyād
Ibn Ziyād iii, 779a — III, 802b
Ibn al-Zubayr → ʿAbd Allāh; ʿAmr; Muṣʿab
Ibn al-Zubayr, Abu ʿAbd Allāh iii, **976b** — III, **1001a**
Ibn al-Zubayr, Abū Djaʿfar iii, 762b, **976a** — III, 785b, **1000b**
Ibn Zuhr iii, **976b**; iv, 289b; s, 392b — III, **1001a**; IV, 302b; S, 393a
Ibn Zuhr, Abu ʾl-ʿAlāʾ iii, 850a, **976b** — III, 873b, **1001a**
Ibn Zuhr, Abu Bakr Muḥammad iii, **978b** — III, **1003a**
Ibn Zuhr, Abū Marwān i, 162a; ii, 481b; iii, 910b, **977b** — I, 166b; II, 494a; III, 935a, **1002a**
Ibn Zuknūn i, 273b — I, 282a
Ibn Zūlāḳ iii, **979a** — III, **1003b**
Ibn Zumruk → Ibn Zamraḳ
Ibn Zurʿa iii, **979b**; s, 398b — III, **1004a**; S, 398b
Ibnou-Zekri → Ibn Zakrī
Ibo → Nigeria/Nigérie
ʿIbra iv, 557a, b, 1031b, 1038a — IV, 581b, 1063b, 1069b
Ibrā (ʿUmān) s, 355b, 356a — S, 355a, 356a
Ibrāḍism(e) iv, 739b — IV, 769b
Ibrāhīm i, 177a, 315b; ii, 280a, 1106a; iii, 37a, 165a, **980a**; iv, 184a, b, 318a, b, 956a, b, 959a-b; v, 20a, 421a, 423b, 550b; s, 317a — I, 182a, 325b; II, 288b, 1132a; III, 38b, 168b, **1004b**; IV, 192a, b, 332a, 333a, 989a, b, 988a-b; V, 20b, 423a, 425b, 555b; S, 316b
Ibrāhīm I (Aghlabid(e)) i, 24a, 247b, 248a, 250a; iii, 233a, **981b,** 1032a; iv, 827a — I, 24b, 255b, 257b; III, 240a, **1006a,** 1058a; IV, 860a
Ibrāhīm II (Aghlabid(e)) i, 24a, 248b, 249a, 250b, 619b; iii, 297b, **892b**; iv, 275b, 337a; v, 105a, 777b; s, 1a — I, 25a, 256a,b, 258a, 639b; III, 306b, **1006b**; IV, 287b, 351b; V, 107b, 783b; S, 1a
Ibrāhīm (Ghaznavid(e)) → Ibrāhīm b. Masʿūd
Ibrāhīm (Ottoman) iii, 623a, **983a**; iv, 884b; v, 272b — III, 643b, **1007b**; IV, 917b; V, 270b
Ibrāhīm (Umayyad(e)) i, 57b, 1244a — I, 59b, 1282a
Ibrāhīm, al-Malik al-Manṣūr → Ibrāhīm b. Shīrkūh
Ibrāhīm, Sultan, Dār Fūr → Ibrāhīm b. Muḥammad Ḥusayn
Ibrāhīm b. ʿAbd Allāh b. al-Ḥasan b. al-Ḥasan (ʿAlid(e)) i, 45b, 103b, 123a, 402b, 952a, 1080a; iii, 616a, **983b**; s, 48b, 130a — I, 46b, 106b, 126b, 414a, 981b, 1112b; III, 636b, **1008a**; S, 48b, 129a
Ibrāhīm b. ʿAbd al-Wāḥid iii, 843a — III, 866b
Ibrāhīm b. Abī Ḥātim Aḥmad al-ʿAzafī s, 112b — S, 112a
Ibrāhīm b. Abī Salama s, 62a — S, 62b
Ibrāhīm b. Abu 'l Khayr iv, 310a — IV, 324a
Ibrāhīm b. Adham i, 274a; ii, 36b; iii, 843a, **985b** — I, 282b; II, 37a; III, 867a, **1010a**
Ibrāhīm b. al-Ashʿar → Ibn al-Sarrādj
Ibrāhīm b. ʾAlāʾ al-Dawla b. Baysunghur i, 147b — I, 152a
Ibrāhīm b. ʿAlī → al-Shīrāzī
Ibrāhīm b. ʿAlī b. Ḥasan al-Saḳḳāʾ iii, 250a, **986b** — III, 257a, **1011a**
Ibrāhīm b. ʿAlī b. ʿĪsā i, 387b — I, 398b
Ibrāhīm b. al-Ashtar i, 50b, 76b; iii, 620b, **987a**; iv, 1186b — I, 52a, 78b, 79a; III, 641a, **1011b**; IV, 1219a
Ibrāhīm b. Ayyūb ii, 79b — II, 81a
Ibrāhīm b. Bughāmardī iv, 494a — IV, 515a
Ibrāhīm b. Dhakwān al-Ḥarrānī iii, **987b** — III, **1012a**
Ibrāhīm b. Djalāl al-Dīn Aḥsan iii, 225a — III, 232a
Ibrāhīm b. Djibrīl iv, 356b — IV, 372a
Ibrāhīm b. al-Ḥadjdjādj iv, 822a — IV, 855a
Ibrāhīm b. Ḥammād s, **385a** — S, **385b**
Ibrāhīm b. Hilāl → al-Ṣābīʾ
Ibrāhīm b. Ismāʿīl al-Aṭrash ii, 637a — II, 653a
Ibrāhīm b. Ismāʿīl b. Yasār iv, 190a — IV, 198a
Ibrāhīm b. Ḳarātakīn ii, 1110a — II, 1136a
Ibrāhīm b. Ḳays i, 1283a — I, 1321b
Ibrāhīm b. Khālid → Abū Thawr

Ibrāhīm b. al-Mahdī i, 272a, 1312b; ii, 731a, 1072a; iii, 745b, 767b, 872b, **987b,** 996b; iv, 17a, 940a; v, 69b; s, 64a — I, 280a, 1352b; II, 749b, 1097a; III, 768a,b, 790b, 896b, **1012a,** 1021a; IV, 18b, 973a; V, 71b; S, 64b
Ibrāhīm b. Mālik → Ibrāhīm b. al-Ashtar
Ibrāhīm b. al-Marzubān ii, 680a — II, 697a
Ibrāhīm b. Masʿūd ii, 5a, 1052a, 1100a; iv, 942b; v, 622b; s, 21a — II, 5a, 1076a, 1126a; IV, 957b; V, 626b; S, 21a
Ibrāhīm b. al-Mudabbir → Ibn al-Mudabbir
Ibrāhīm b. Muhādjir iv, 667b — IV, 694b
Ibrāhīm b. Muḥammad b. ʿAlī i, 15b, 16a, 141a; iii, **988a**; iv, 446b — I, 16a, b, 145a; III, **1012b**; IV, 466b
Ibrāhīm b. Muḥammad b. Fahd al-Makramī iv, 201a — IV, 210a
Ibrāhīm b. Muḥammad al-Fazārī ii, 36b — II, 37b
Ibrāhīm b. Muḥammad Ḥusayn i, 929b; ii, 123b — I, 957b; II, 126b
Ibrāhīm b. Muḥammad Ẓāfir al-Madanī v, 949a — V, 953a
Ibrāhīm b. Mūsā iii, 262b — III, 270a
Ibrāhīm b. Mūsā al-Kāẓim s, 95a — S, 94b
Ibrāhīm b. Muzayn i, 600a — I, 619b
Ibrāhīm b. Sahl → Ibn Sahl
Ibrāhīm b. Sayāba iii, **989a** — III, **1013b**
Ibrāhīm (Sayyid) b. Sayyid Muḥammad (Bayhaḳī) s, 131b — S, 131a
Ibrāhīm b. Shāhrukh iii, 337a, b, **989a**; iv, 221b — III, 347b, **1014a**; IV, 231a
Ibrāhīm b. Shīrkūh iii, 399b, **989b** — III, 412a, **1014a**
Ibrāhīm b. al-Sindī iii, **990a** — III, **1014b**
Ibrāhīm b. Sulaymān al-Shāmī → al-Shāmī
Ibrāhīm b. ʿUmar al-Biḳāʿī al-Shāfiʿī iv, 92a — IV, 96a
Ibrāhīm b. Yaʿḳūb al-Isrāʾīlī al-Ṭurṭūshī i, 157a; iii, **991a,** 1045a; v, 719a, 1012b, 1013a, 1014a; s, 170b — I, 161b; III, **1015b,** 1071a; V, 724b, 1008a, 1009a, 1010a; S, 171a
Ibrāhīm b. Yūsuf b. Tāshufīn ii, 838a; iii, 728a, 822b, 977b — II, 857b; III, 750b, 846a, 1002a
Ibrāhīm Adilshāh I i, 199a; iii, 15b, 426a, 626a, 1160b, 1161a; v, 1216a — I, 205a; III, 16a, 439b, 646b, 1189a,b; V, 1205b
Ibrāhīm Adilshāh II i, 199b, 781b, 1200a, 1202b, 1203a,b, 1204a; ii, 921b, 922a; iii, 15b, 426b, 453b; v, 1216a — I, 205a, 804b, 1235b, 1238a,b, 1239b; II, 943a; III, 16a, 440b, 469b; V, 1205b
Ibrāhīm Agha → Kečiboynuzu Ibrāhīm Pasha
Ibrāhīm Āghā Mustaḥfiẓān iv, 431a — IV, 450a
Ibrāhīm al-Aḥdab iii, **991b**; s, 40a, 161a — III, **1016b**; S, 40a, 160b
Ibrāhīm al-ʿAwwānī s, 172b — S, 173b
Ibrāhīm al-Bādjūrī → Bādjūrī
Ibrāhīm Bahādur b. Meḥmed i, 783b; ii, 599a — I, 806b; II, 613b
Ibrāhīm Beg iii, 483b — III, 500b
Ibrāhīm Beg Ḳarāmān-oghlu iv, 623b, 624a; v, 677a — IV, 648b; V, 682a
Ibrāhīm Bey (Tunis) iii, 605a; iv, 828b — III, 625b; IV, 861a
Ibrāhīm Bey Isfendiyār-oghlu iv, 108b — IV, 113b
Ibrāhīm Bey al-Kabīr iii, **992a**; iv, 853a — III, **1016b**; IV, 886a
Ibrāhīm al-Dasūḳī → al-Dasūḳī
Ibrāhīm Derwish Pasha ii, 878b; iii, **992b** — II, 899a; III, **1017b**
Ibrāhīm al-Djazzār i, 551a — I, 568b
Ibrāhīm Edhem Pasha i, 285b; iii, **993a** — I, 294b; III, **1017b**
Ibrāhīm Gulshenī → Gulshanī
Ibrāhīm Ḥaḳḳī Pasha ii, 533b; iii, **993b,** 1188b — II, 546b; III, **1018b,** 1218b
Ibrāhīm al-Ḥalabī → al-Ḥalabī
Ibrāhīm al-Ḥāmidī → al-Ḥāmidī
Ibrāhīm al-Ḥarbī i, 718a; iii, **994b**; s, 304b — I, 739b; III, **1019a**; S, 304a
Ibrāhīm al-Hāshimī, Sharīf iv, 919b — IV, 952b
Ibrāhīm b. Hilāl s, 370a — S, 370a
Ibrāhīm Ḥilmī Pasha → Keči boynuzu Ibrāhīm Ḥilmī
Ibrāhīm Ḥusayn Mīrzā iv, 666a — IV, 693a
Ibrāhīm al-Imām → Ibrāhīm b. Muḥammad b. ʿAlī
Ibrāhīm Ināl i, 420a, 512b, 1074a; ii, 5a; iii, 258b; iv, 26b, 466a, 807a; v, 388a, 454a, 489a — I, 432a, 528b, 1106a; II, 5a; III, 266a; IV, 28b, 486b, 839b; V, 389a, 456b, 492a
Ibrāhīm Kāhya → al-Ḳāzdughlī, Ibrāhīm
Ibrāhīm Karāma s, 162b — S, 162b
Ibrāhīm Ḳaṭārāghāsī iii, 88b — III, 90b
Ibrāhīm Katkhudā i, 391b — I, 402b
Ibrāhīm al-Khalīl → Ibrāhīm
Ibrāhīm Khalīl Khān iv, 573a — IV, 595b, 596a
Ibrāhīm Khān iii, **995a** — III, **1019b**
Ibrāhīm Khān (Ḳazān) iv, 849a — IV, 882a
Ibrāhīm Khān Avar i, 755b — I, 778a
Ibrahīm Khān Sūr ii, 271b — II, 279b
Ibrāhīm Khān, Ẓahīr al-Dawla v, 155b, 164b — V, 156a, 162a
Ibrāhīm Khān b. Aḥmad iv, 581b — IV, 604b
Ibrāhīm Khan Zangana v, 169b — V, 167a
Ibrāhīm-Khānzāde iii, 995a — III, 1019b
Ibrāhīm Ḳuṭb Shāh v, 550a — V, 555a
Ibrāhīm Lōdī i, 252b, 848a, 1068b; ii, 271a; iii, 168a, 420b, **995a**; v, 784a; s, 203a, 331b — I, 260b, 871b, 1101a; II, 279a; III, 172a, 434a, **1020a**; V, 790a; S, 202b, 331a
Ibrāhīm al-Mawṣilī i, 10b, 107b, 108a, 118a; iii, 749b, 989a, **996a**; iv, 822a; s, 17b, 64a, 116b, 128a, 183a — I, 10b, 110b, 111a, 121b; III, 772b, 1013b, **1020b**; IV, 855a; S, 18a, 64b, 116a, 127b, 184b
Ibrāhīm al-Māzinī s, 57b — S, 58a
Ibrāhīm Mīrzā i, 1212a — I, 1248a
Ibrāhīm al-Mūsawī s, 423a — S, 423b
Ibrāhīm Müteferriḳa i, 63b, 270a, 1271b; ii, 589b, 704b; iii, **996b**; v, 641b — I, 65a, 278a,b, 1310b; II, 604a, 722b; III, **1021b**; V, 645b
Ibrāhīm Naʿīm al-Dīn ii, 990b — II, 1013a
Ibrāhīm al-Nakhaʿī ii, 888a,b; iii, 512a; v, 350b, 731a, b — II, 908b, 909b; III, 529b; V, 351b, 736a, b
Ibrāhīm Pasha → Khodja; Shāḳshāḳī; Shayṭān
Ibrāhīm Pasha (Maḳbūl) i, 293b; ii, 400a, 722b, 884b, 1042b, 1136a; iii, **998a,** 1183b; iv, 333b, 1137b; v, 650a; s, 315b — I, 302b; II, 410b, 741a, 904b, 1067a, 1163b; III, **1023a,** 1213a; IV, 348a, 1169a; V, 654a; S, 315b
Ibrāhīm Pasha, Ḥādjdjī iv, 594b — IV, 618b
Ibrāhīm Pasha, Ḳarā iii, **1001b** — III, **1026b**
Ibrāhīm Pasha b. Khalīl Djandarlî ii, 445a — II, 457a
Ibrāhīm Pasha b. Muḥammad ʿAlī i, 182b, 244a, 341b, 399a, 975a, 1079a, 1134a, 1138a, 1234a; ii, 38b, 108b, 288a,b, 321a,b, 514a, 636a, 912a; iii, 89a, 300a, 326b, 400a, 628b, **999a**; iv, 130b, 609b, 717b, 765a, 925b; v, 36a, 322b, 335a, 539b, 1253b — I, 188a, 251a, 352a, 410a, 1005b, 1111b, 1168b, 1172b, 1271a; II, 39a, 111a, 296a,b, 330b, 331a, 526b, 652a, 933b; III, 91b, 309a, 336b, 412b, 649b, **1024a**; IV, 136a, 634a, 746a, 795b, 958b; V, 37a, 321b, 335b, 543b, 1244b
Ibrāhīm Pasha Dāmād i, 270b, 826b; ii, 20a, 34a, 49a, 103b, 634b; iii, 342b, **1000b**; iv, 233b — I, 279a, 849a; II, 20b, 35a, 50a, 105b, 651a; III, 352b, **1025b**; IV, 244a
Ibrāhīm Pasha Djandarlî ii, 444b, 721a; iv, 231a —

II, 456b, 739b; IV, 241a
Ibrāhīm Pāsha Katkhudā i, 68b — I, 70a
Ibrāhīm Pasha Millī v, 463a — V, 465b
Ibrāhīm Pasha Nevshehirli i, 269b, 270a, 836b, 1004b; ii, 20a; iii, 997b, **1002a**; iv, 969b; v, 641a, b, 642a, b, 643a, b — I, 277b, 278a, 859b, 1035a; II, 20a; III, 1022b, **1027a**; IV, 1001b; V, 645b, 646a, 647a, b
Ibrāhīm Pasha Ṭawīl i, 236b — I, 244a
Ibrāhīm Pečewī → Pečewī
Ibrāhīm Pūr-i Dāwūd iv, 71a — IV, 75a
Ibrāhīm al-Rashīd s, 279a — S, 278b
Ibrāhīm al-Ṣābiʾ s, 398b — S, 398b
Ibrāhīm al-Sadjīnī s, 44b — S, 44b
Ibrāhīm Sālār iii, 703b — III, 725b
Ibrāhīm Shāh Sharḳī i, 702b, 859a, 1300a; ii, 51b, 180b, 499a; iii, 14b, 419a, **1003a**; iv, 513a; s, 206b — I, 724a, 883a, 1340a; II, 52b, 186b, 511b; III, 15a, 432b, **1028a**; IV, 535a; S, 206a
Ibrāhīm al-Sharīf → Ibrāhīm Bey (Tunis)
Ibrāhīm Shāshī s, 50b — S, 51a
Ibrāhīm al-Shāṭibī iv, 381b — IV, 398b
Ibrāhīm Shināsī → Shināsī
Ibrāhīm Shīrāzī, Ḥādjdjī s, **405b — S, 405b**
Ibrahīm Sori Maudo ii, 942a, 960a, 1132a — II, 963b, 982a, 1159a
Ibrāhīm Tamghač Khān iii, 1114a,b, 1115b; iv, 200a — III, 1141b, 1142a, 1143a; IV, 209a
Ibrāhīm Temo ii, 430b — II, 441b
Ibrāhīm al-Yāzidjī → al-Yāzidjī
Ibrāhīm Yināl → Ibrāhīm Ināl
Ibrahima Mussu → Karamoko Alfa
Ibrāhīmī, Muḥammad al-Bashīr iii, **1003b**; iv, 159b — III, **1028b**; IV, 166a
Ibrahimu Dabo iv, 549a — IV, 573a
Ibrail iii, **1004a** — III, **1029a**
ʿIbrī → Yahūd
ʿIbrī iii, **1004b** — III, **1029b**
Ibrīḳ v, 989a; s, **406a** — V, 984b; S, **406a**
Ibrīm (Piromi) s, 35b — S, 36a
Ibrishīm, Ibrisīm → Ḥarīr
ʿIbriyyūn iii, 1004b — III, 1029b
Ibruh i, 487b, 489a; iii, **1005a** — I, 502a, 503b; III, **1030a**
al-Ibshīhī, Aḥmad iii, 1006a — III, 1031a
al-Ibshīhī, Bahā al-Dīn ii, 536b; iii, 392a, **1005a**; s, 350a — II, 549b; III, 404b, **1030b**; S, 350a
al-Ibshīhī, Shihāb al-Dīn iii, 1006a — III, 1031a
Ibshīr Muṣṭafā Pasha → Ipshir Muṣṭafā Pasha
Ibtidāʾ iii, **1006a**; iv, 152a, 264a — III, **1031a**; IV, 158b, 276a
Ibuḳrāṭ(īs) → Buḳrāṭ
Ichthyology/Ichtyologie → Samak
Ič-oghlanî i, 394a, 395a; ii, 1087b, 1088b; iii, **1006b** — I, 405b, 406b; II, 1113a, 1114a; III, **1031b**
Ičil ii, 34b; iii, **1006b**; iv, 617a — II, 35b; III, **1031b**; IV, 641b
Içoglan → Ič-oghlanî
Iconography, Iconographie → Ṣūra
ʿĪd iii, **1007a**; v, 477a — III, **1032b**; V, 479b
ʿĪd al-aḍḥā i, 1b; iii, **1007b** — I, 1b; III, **1033a**
ʿĪd al-fiṭr iii, **1008a**; v, 714b — III, **1033a**; V, 720a
ʿĪd al-ghadīr iv, 1110b — IV, 1142a
ʿĪd al-kabīr → ʿĪd al-aḍḥā
ʿĪd-i Ḳurbān iv, 103b — IV, 108b
al-ʿĪd, Muḥammad iv, 159b — IV, 166b
al-ʿIdāda → al-Asturlāb
Iʿdādiyye i, 285b — I, 294a
Iḍāfa → Nisba
Iḍāfa iii, **1008a** — III, **1033a**
Iḍam → Ḥamḍ, Wādī al-
Iʿdām → Ḳatl
Īdar ii, 1128a; iii, **1010a** — II, 1154b; III, **1035a**
ʿIdda i, 28a, 172b; iii, **1010b**; iv, 253b — I, 28b, 177b; III, **1036a**; IV, 265a
Iddī, Āl s, 269a — S, 268b
Iddighām → Idghām
Idfū → Adfū
Idghām iii, **1013a** — III, **1038b**
Idgish v, 254a — V, 251b
Idgü Bahādur Barlās v, 163b — V, 161a
Idhāʿa iii, **1014a** — III, **1039a**
Īdhadj (Māl-Amīr) iii, **1015b**; iv, 675b; v, 826b, 827a, 830b — III, **1041a**; IV, 703a; V, 832b, 833b, 836b
Idhkhir iv, 322a — IV, 336a
Idil → Itil (river/rivière)
Idhn i, 429b; iii, **1016a**, 1181b — I, 442a; III, **1041b**, 1210b
Idhnnāme i, 679a — I, 700a
Idibaʾil i, 525a — I, 541a
Īdjāb i, 1111b; iii, **1017a** — I, 1145a; III, **1042b**
Idjār, idjāra iii, **1017a**; v, 126b — III, **1042b**; V, 129a
Idjāra iii, **1017b** — III, **1043a**
Iʿdjāz i, 858a, 958b, 981b; iii, **1018a**; v, 426b, 427a — I, 881b, 988a, 1012a; III, **1044a**; V, 428b, 429a
Idjāza i, 66a, 90b, 96a, 142b, 319b, 817a; ii, 304a; iii, 27a, 491a, **1020b**; iv, 412b, 634a, 950b, 1125b; v, 1125a, 1132b — I, 68a, 93b, 99a, 146b, 329a, 840a; II, 312b; III, 28b, 508a, **1046b**; IV, 430b, 660b, 983a, 1157a; V, 1121b, 1128a
Idjāza → Ḥadjdj
Idjdhāb iv, 95a — IV, 99a
al-Īdjī, ʿAḍud al-Dīn i, 342b, 593a, 715a, 715b; ii, 608a, 774a; iii, **1022a**, 1176a; iv, 737a — I, 353a, 612a, 736b, 737a; II, 623a, 792b; III, **1047b**, 1205a; IV, 767a
Idjil i, 809a — I, 832a
ʿIdjl i, 963b, 964b; iii, **1022b** — I, 993b, 994a; III, **1048b**
ʿIdjl b. Ludjaym s, 122a — S, 121b
al-ʿIdjlī → Abu 'l-Nadjm; al-Aghlab; al-Ḳāsim b. ʿĪsā
al-ʿIdjlī, Abū Dulaf → al-Ḳāsim b. ʿĪsā
al-ʿIdjlī, Abū Manṣūr i, 1099a; ii, 1094a — I, 1132a; II, 1120a
al-Idjlī, Harūn b. Saʿīd ii, 377b; s, 130a — II, 387b; S, 129a
ʿIdjliyya s, 130a — S, 129a
Idjmāʿ i, 259b, 1199b; ii, 182b, 411b, 888b; iii, **1023a**, 1061b; iv, 154a; v, 239a — I, 267b, 1235a; II, 188a, 422a, 909a; III, **1048b**, 1088a; IV, 160b; V, 237a
Idjnāwn ii, 369a — II, 379a
Idjtihād i, 259b, 276a; iii, 954a, 1025b, **1026a**; iv, 152b-154a, 1101a; v, 241a — I, 267b, 284b; III, 978b, 1051a, **1052a**; IV, 159a-160a, 1132a; V, 239a
Idjtimāʿ → Istiḳbāl
Idjtimāʿ iv, 259a; v, 577b — IV, 270b; V, 582a
Iḍmār iii, **1027b** — III, **1053b**
Idol, Idolatry/Idole, Idolâtrie → Ṣanam, Wathaniyya
Idrāk iii, **1028a** — III, **1054a**
Idrākī Bēglārī iii, **1029b** — III, **1055b**
Idrīs (prophet/prophète) iii, **1030b** — III, **1056b**
Idrīs, Mawlāy → Idris II b. Idrīs
Idris, Suhayl v, 191b — V, 188b
Idrīs, Yūsuf v, 191a, b — V, 188b
Idrīs I (King, le roi) ii, 667b; iv, 262a; v, 697a, 1066a — II, 684a; IV, 274a; V, 701b, 1063b
Idrīs I b. ʿAbd Allāh i, 402b, 1037a, 1175b; ii, 745a, 818a, 874a; iii, 616b, 617a, **1031a**; v, 1175a, 1189a; s, 103a — I, 414a, 1068b, 1210b; II, 763b, 837b, 894a; III, 637b, **1057a**; V, 1165a, 1179a; S, 102b
Idrīs II b. Idrīs i, 1088a; ii, 818a, 874a; iii, **1031b**; v, 1189a, 1200a, 1201a; s, 103a — I, 1120a; II, 837b, 894a; III, **1057b**; V, 1179a, 1190a, 1191b; S, 102b

Idrīs b. Aḥmad al-Ḥabūḍī s, 338b — S, 338a
Idrīs b. ʿAlī → al-Sharīf Abū Muḥammad Idrīs
Idrīs b. Bā Ḥmād s, 114a — S, 113b
Idrīs b. al-Ḥasan, ʿImād al-Dīn s, **407a** — S, **407a**
Idrīs b. al-Ḥusayn, Sharīf s, **407b** — S, **407b**
Idrīs b. Muḥammad al-Arbāb ii, 944a — II, 966a
Idrīs Alooma (Alawōma) iv, 567b; s, 164a — IV, 589b; S, 163b
Idrīs Atuma i, 1259b — I, 1298a
Idrīs Bidlīsī → Bidlīsī
Idrīs al-Maʾmūn iii, 207b; iv, 116a, 117b — III, 213a; IV, 121b, 122b
Idrīs al-Sanūsī i, 1049b, 1071b; v, 758a, b — I, 1081b, 1103b; V, 764a
al-Idrīsī, Abū ʿAbd Allāh i, 157a, 168a, 214a, 488a, 594a, 602b, 1337b; ii, 578a, 582a, 585a; iii, 7a, 405a, **1032b**, 1077a; iv, 274b, 1080b; s, 92a, 171a, 376b — I, 161b, 172b, 220b, 503a, 613b, 622a, 1377b; II, 592b, 596b, 599b; III, 7a, 418a, **1058b**, 1103b; IV, 286b, 1111b; S, 91b, 171a, 376b
al-Idrīsī, Abū Djaʿfar s, 123b — S, 123a
al-Idrīsī, Djamāl al-Dīn s, **407b** — S, **407b**
al-Idrīsī, Muḥammad b. ʿAlī i, 98b, 277b, 709b; ii, 518a; v, 758a, 808b, 809a — I, 101a, 286a, 731a; II, 531a; V, 763b, 814b, 815a
Idrīsī, Idrīsiyya i, 98b, 277b, 555a, 709b — I, 101a, 286a, 572b, 731a
Idrīsid(e)s i, 156b, 403a, 1044a; ii, 145b, 818a, 821a, 853a, 1095b; iii, 30b, **1035b**; iv, 632a, b — I, 161a, 414b, 1076a; II, 149b, 837b, 840b, 872b, 1121b; III, 32a, **1061a**; IV, 657b
Idṭirār iii, **1037a** — III, **1063a**
Iduḳ Ḳut i, 1240a,b — I, 1278a
ʿIdwa s, 408a — S, 408b
al-ʿIdwī al-Ḥamzāwī, Ḥasan v, 1237a; s, **408a** — V, 1228a; S, **408b**
Ifāḍa iii, 32a,b, 36a — III, 34a, 37b
al-ʿIfār ii, 631b; iii, **1037b** — II, 647a; III, **1063b**
Ifāt → Awfāt
ʿIffat b. Aḥmad Āl Thunayyān s, 305b — S, 305b
Iflāk → Eflāk
al-Iflīlī → Ibn al-Iflīlī
Iflīmūn → Aflīmūn
Ifni iii, **1038a** — III, **1064a**
Ifoghas i, 210b; iii, **1038b** — I, 216b; III, **1064a**
ʿIfrād iii, 35a, 53b — III, 37a, 55b
Ifrāgha iii, **1038b** — III, **1064b**
Īfran, Banū i, 6a, 367a; iii, **1039a**; v, 1164b, 1175a, 1179a, 1245b — I, 6a, 378a; III, **1065a**; V, 1154b, 1165a, 1169a, 1236a
al-Ifrandj i, 9b, 82b, 197a, 198b, 216a, 639b, 664a, 784a, 798a, 804a, 932b, 946a, 983a, 1017a, 1025a, 1054b, 1125b, 1332a; ii, 63b, 282b, 292b, 318b, 912a; iii, 325a, 398b, 503b, **1044a**, 1118b; iv, 520b, 642a, 779a; v, 921b, 924b; s, 205a — I, 9b, 85a, 202b, 204b, 222a, 660a, 684a, 807a, 821b, 828a, 961a, 975b, 1013b, 1048b, 1056b, 1086b, 1159a, 1373a; II, 65a, 290b, 300b, 327b, 933b; III, 335a, 411a, 521a, **1070a**, 1146a; IV, 543a, 668b, 810b; V, 927a, 930a; S, 204b
al-Ifrānī i, 315b; iii, **1046b**; s, 28b — I, 325a; III, **1073a**; S, 29a
Ifrāṭ, Ifrāṭ fiʾl-Ṣifa → Mubālagha
Ifrīḳiya i, 50a, 79a, 86a, 92b, 104a, 124b, 134b, 156b, 166a, 247b, 248a, 532b, 1321a; ii, 331b, 852b, 998a; iii, 1032a, 1040b, **1047a**; iv, 175a, b, 176b, 177a; v, 503a, 723b, 877a; s, 1a, 62b, 306a — I, 51b, 81b, 88b, 95a, 107a, 128a, 138a, 161a, 170b, 255b, 549a, 1361a; II, 341a, 872a, 1021a; III, 1058a, 1066b, **1073b**; IV, 182b, 183a, 184b; V, 506b, 728b, 882b; S, 1a, 63a, 306a
— language, literature/langues, littérature i, 568b — I, 587a
ʿIfrīt iii, **1050a**; s, 52b — III, **1076a**; S, 53a
Ifruḳlus → Buruḳlus
Iftāʾ ii, 866a,b — II, 886a,b
Iftikhār al-Dīn Muḥammad al-Bukhārī iv, 860a — IV, 893a
Iftitāḥ ii, 301b, 302a — II, 310a
Igdir s, 168b, 169a — S, 169a
Igerwān s, 113b — S, 113a
Ighār i, 1144b; iii, **1051a**; iv, 1032a — I, 1179a; III, **1077a**; IV, 1064a
Igharghar iii, **1051a** — III, **1077a**
Ighlān s, 395a — S, 395b
Ighrāḳ, Ighrāḳ fiʾl-Ṣifa → Mubālagha
Ighrak, Sayf al-Dīn iv, 918a — IV, 951a
Igīlīz → Gīlīz
Igliwa → Glāwa
Īhām → Tawriya
Iḥdāth iii, 664b, **1051a** — III, 686a, **1077b**
Ihlīladj iv, 357a — IV, 372b
Iḥrām iii, 35a, 36b, **1052b**; v, 329a — III, 36b, 38a, **1078b**; V, 328b
Iḥṣān → Muḥṣan
Iḥsān, Aḥmad → Aḥmad Iḥsān
Iḥsān Allāh Khān ii, 445b; v, 310b — II, 457a; V, 310a
Iḥsās → Ḥiss
Iḥtisāb → Ḥisba
Iḥtishām al-Dawla s, 302a — S, 302a
Iḥyāʾ iii, **1053b** — III, **1079b**
Īḳāʿ s, **408b** — S, **409a**
ʿIḳāb iii, **1055a** — III, **1081a**
al-ʿIḳāb i, 495b; iii, **1055a** — I, 510b; III, **1081a**
Iḳāla i, 319b; iii, **1056b** — I, 329b; III, **1082b**
Iḳāma i, 188b; iii, **1057a** — I, 194a; III, **1083a**
Iḳbāl, Āl s, 338a — S, 337b
Iḳbāl, Muḥammad i, 327a; ii, 546b, 1036b; iii, 119b, 432a, **1057a**; iv, 170b; v, 601a — I, 337a; II, 560a, 1060b; III, 122a, 446a, **1083b**; IV, 178a; V, 605a
Iḳbāl-nāma iv, 127b, 128b — IV, 133b, 134a
Iḳbāl b. Sābiḳ-i Sīstānī i, 347b — I, 358a
Iḳbāl al-Dawla → ʿAlī b. Mudjāhid al-Āmirī
Iḳbāl Khān → Mallū Iḳbāl Khān
Iḳfāʾ → Ḳāfiya
Ikhlāṣ iii, **1059b** — III, **1086a**
Ikhlāṣī, Shaykh Meḥmed iv, 761a — IV, 791a
Ikhmīm → Akhmīm
al-Ikhnāʾī, Taḳī al-Dīn iii, 953a — III, 977b
al-Ikhshīd → Kāfūr; Muḥammad b. Tughdj
Ikhshīdid(e)s i, 435b, 439b, 551b, 1042a; ii, 130a, 281b; iii, 129a, 768b, 979a, **1060b**; iv, 418a; s, 120b — I, 448a, 452a, 569a, 1073b; II, 133a, 289b; III, 131b, 791b, 1003b, **1087a**; IV, 436b; S, 120a
Ikhtilādj iii, **1061a** — III, **1087a**
Ikhtilāf i, 155a; iii, 160b, **1061b** — I, 159b; III, 164a, **1088a**
Ikhtisān, Muḥammad Ṣadr ʿAlāʾ s, **409a** — S, **409b**
Ikhtiyār i, 413a; iii, 1037a, **1062b** — I, 424b; III, 1063a, **1089a**
Ikhtiyār al-Dīn Aytak → Aytak
Ikhtiyār al-Dīn Ghāzī Shāh ii, 751b — II, 770a
Ikhtiyār al-Dīn Muḥammad Khāldjī → Muḥammad Bakhtiyār
Ikhtiyār al-Dīn Munshī iv, 1124a — IV, 1156a
Ikhtiyār Heyʾeti i, 972b — I, 1002b
Ikhtiyārāt (anthologies) → Mukhtārāt
Ikhtiyārāt (hemerology, hémérologie) iii, **1063b**; iv, 518b — III, **1090b**; IV, 541a
Ikhtiyāriyya s, **409b** — S, **409b**
al-Ikhwān ii, 469a; iii, 361b, **1064a**; iv, 680b, 681a, 1133b; v, 574b, 998a, b; s, 3b — II, 480b; III, 373a, **1090b**; IV, 708b, 1165a; V, 579b, 993b, 994a; S, 2b
al-Ikhwān al-Muslimūn i, 416b, 1018b; ii, 429b,

882b; iii, 162b, 518a, 557b, **1068b**; iv, 161b, 206b; s, 6a, b, 7a, 300b — I, 428b, 1050a; II, 440b, 903a; III, 166a, 535b, 577a, **1095b**; IV, 168b, 216a; S, 5a, 6a, 300a, b
Ikhwān al-Ṣafāʾ i, 247a, 350b, 589b, 659b, 737a, 772a, 1156a; ii, 93a, 358b, 361b, 554b, 579a, 765b, 766a, 774b; iii, 21b, 134a, 171a, 301a, 313a, 329a, 1059b, **1071a**, 1130a, 1139a, 1171b, 1207a; iv, 367a, 548a, 663a; v, 703a; s, 321a, 414a — I, 255a, 361b, 609a, 680b, 759a, 795b, 1190a; II, 95a, 368b, 371b, 568b, 593b, 784a,b, 793a; III, 22b, 136b, 175a, 310a, 322b, 339a, 1086a, **1098a**, 1158a, 1167a, 1200b, 1237b; IV, 383a, 571b, 689b; V, 708a; S, 320b, 414a
Ikhwāniyyāt iv, 1005b — IV, 1037b
Iḳlāba iv, 1113a — IV, 1144b
al-Iklīl → Nudjūm
Iklīl al-Malik s, **410a** — S, **410a**
Ikindi dīwāni ii, 339a — II, 348b
Iklān → Akli
Iḳlīm i, 489b, 988a; iii, **1076b**; iv, 223a, 273b; v, 398a — I, 504b, 1019a; III, **1103b**; IV, 233a, 285b; V, 399a
Iḳna → Ḳunā
ʿIkrāh i, 319a; s, **410b** — I, 329a; S, **410b**
Īḳrār iii, 511b, **1078a** — III, 529a, **1105a**
ʿIkrima i, 690b; ii, 895b; iii, 653b, **1081b**; s, 232b, 386b — I, 711b; II, 916a; III, 675a, **1108b**; S, 232b, 386b
ʿIkrima b. Abī Djahl i, 115b, 151a, 812b — I, 119a, 155b, 835b
Iḳrītish i, 83a, 121b, 397b, 935b, 1249a; ii, 130a, 489b; iii, 621a, **1082a**; iv, 539a, 766a, 1054a, 1157b; v, 503a; s, 120b, 186a — I, 85b, 125a, 409a, 964b, 1287a; II, 133b, 502a; III, 641b, **1109a**; IV, 562a, 796b, 1085a, 1189b; V, 506b; S, 120a, 187a
al-Iḳrītishī iii, 1085b — III, 1112a
al-Iksīr iii, **1087b**; v, 113b — III, **1114a**; V, 116a
Iḳṭāʿ i, 533b, 802a, 1144a, b, 1146b, 1353a; ii, 187b, 508a; iii, **1088a**; iv, 18a, 26a, 32a, 323b, 975a, 1043b; v, 688a, 862b — I, 549b, 825a, 1178b, 1179a, 1180b, 1392b; II, 193b, 520b; III, **1115a**; IV, 19a-b, 28a, 34a, 337b, 1007b, 1075a; V, 693b, 869b
Iḳtibās iii, **1091b** — III, **1118a**
Iḳtidāʾ iv, 152a — IV, 158b
Iḳtiḍāb → Tadjnīs; Takhalluṣ
Iktisāb → Kasb
Iḳwāʾ → Ḳāfiya
Īl iii, **1092a** — III, **1118b**
Īl-Arslān iii, 1110b; iv, 29b, 658b, 1067b; s, 245b — III, 1138a; IV, 31b, 685b, 1099a; S, 245b
Īlāʾ → Ṭalāḳ
Īlāf iii, **1093a** — III, **1119b**
ʿIlāfī iv, 534b — IV, 558a
Ilāh iii, **1093b** — III, **1120a**
Ilāhābād → Allāhābād
Ilāhī iii, **1094a**; v, 275a — III, **1120b**; V, 273a
Ilāhī Bakhsh «Maʿrūf» iii, **1095a** — III, **1121b**
Ilāhī Era s, **410b** — S, **411a**
Ilāhiyyāt i, 343a, 415a; iii, 1147b — I, 353b, 426b; III, 1175b
Īlāḳ s, 411a — S, 411a
Ilak Khān → Ilek-Khāns
ʿIlal i, 671b, 672a — I, 692a, 692b
Īlāt iii, **1095b** — III, **1122b**
Ilbars I ii, 45a — II, 45b
Ilbarī s, 124a — S, 123a
Ilbīra i, 49a; ii, 1012a, 1014b; iii, **1110a**; iv, 739a — I, 50b; II, 1036a, 1038b; III, **1137b**; IV, 769a
al-Ilbīrī → Abū Isḥāḳ al-Ilbīrī
Ilče i, 469b; iii, 1092b — I, 483b; III, 1119a
Ilči → Elči
Īlčī, Mīrzā Abu 'l-Ḥasan Khān s, 108b, 290a — S, 108a, 290a
Ildeñiz, Eldigüz, Ildigiz i, 190a, 300b; iii, **1110b**, 1112a — I, 194b, 310a; III, **1137b**, 1139b
Ildeñizid(e)s, Eldigüzid(e)s, Ildigizid(e)s ii, 975b; iii, **1110b**; iv, 348b, 349a — II, 998a; III, **1138a**; IV, 363b, 364a
Ildjāʾ ii, 188a; iii, 1113a — II, 194a; III, 1140a
Île → Djazīra
Ilek-Khāns i, 236b, 421a, 987a, 1295a; ii, 1b, 4b, 791b, 893b, 1143b; iii, 345b, **1113a**; iv, 572b, 581a, 658b, 699a; v, 857b; s, 176b, 240a, 245b, 326a — I, 244a, 432b, 1017b, 1334b; II, 1b, 4b, 810b, 914b, 1170b; III, 356a, **1140a**; IV, 595b, 604b, 685a, 727a; V, 864a; S, 177b, 240a, 245b, 325b
Ileri, Djelāl Nūrī iii, **1117a** — III, **1144b**
Ileri, Sedād Nūrī iii, 1117a — III, 1144b
Ileri, Ṣubḥī Nūrī iii, 1117a — III, 1144b
Îles Fortunées → Djazāʾir al-Saʿādāt
Iletmish → Iltutmish
Ilgaz → Čankiri
Ilghāz → Muʿammā
Īlghāzī b. Artuḳ (Artuḳid(e)) i, 664a, 665b, 983a, 1337a; iii, 87a, **1118a**; v, 124b — I, 683b, 684a, 686b, 1013b, 1377a; III, 89a, **1145b**; V, 127a
Ilghāzī II b. Nadjm al-Dīn Alpī (Artuḳid(e)) iii, **1119a** — III, **1146b**
Ilḥād → Mulḥid
Ilhām iii, **1119b** — III, **1147a**
Ili iii, **1120a**; iv, 512b; v, 363b — III, **1147b**; IV, 534b; V, 364b
Iličpur → Eličpur
Īlīdja iii, **1120b** — III, **1148b**
Īliyā → al-Ḳuds
Ilḳās Mīrzā iv, 103a — IV, 107b
Īlkhānī → Taʾrīkh
Ilkhāns i, 227a, 329b, 346a, 467a, 468a, 470a, 510b, 666a, 703a, 861a, 872a, 902b, 1106b, 1128a; ii, 45a, 47a, 401a; iii, 122a, 473a, 569b, **1120b**, 1256a; iv, 31a, 48a-b, 349b; v, 58b, 455b, 677a; s, 59a, 64b, 126b, 235b, 383a, 409b — I, 234a, 339b, 356b, 481a,b, 484a, 526a, 687a, 724a, 885a, 896a, 930a, 1140a, 1162b; II, 46a, 48a, 411b; III, 124b, 489b, 589a, **1148b**, 1289a; IV, 33a, 51a, 364b; V, 60b, 458a, 682a; S, 59b, 65a, 125b, 235b, 383a
- administration i, 1159a; ii, 81a, 83a, 311a, 313a, 334a, 903a; iii, 47b, 284a, 348a, 1089a; iv, 559b, 757a, 1045a, 1046a, b — I, 1193b; II, 82b, 84b, 320a, 322a, 343b, 924a; III, 49b, 292b, 358b, 1116a; IV, 582a, 787b, 1076b, 1077b
- art/architecture iii, 1123b, 1127b; v, 1148a — III, 1151b, 1155b; V, 1139a
ʿIlla i, 1327a; iii, **1127b** — I, 1367b; III, **1156a**
Illā iv, 272b; v, 241b — IV, 284b; V, 239a
ʿIllaysh, Muḥammad b. Aḥmad s, **411a** — S, **411b**
ʿIlliyyūn iii, **1132b** — III, **1161a**
Illuminations → Kirāb, Taṣwīr
ʿIlm iii, **1133a**; v, 1123b — III, **1161a**; V, 1120a
ʿIlm al-aktāf → Katif
ʿIlm al-ʿazāʾim iv, 264b — IV, 276b
ʿIlm al-balāgha i, 982a,b — I, 1012b, 1013a
ʿIlm al-Dīn al-Anṣārī → Wazir Khān
ʿIlm al-djamāl iii, **1134a** — III, **1162a**
ʿIlm al-farāʾiḍ ii, 783b — II, 802a
ʿIlm al-handasa s, **411b** — S, **411b**
ʿIlm al-hayʾa i, 1100b; ii, 586b; iii, 302a, 703a, 789a, **1135a**; iv, 491b, 1059a, 1182b; v, 46a, b, 83a-87b, 397a, 542b, 547a — I, 1133b; II, 601a; III, 311a, 725a, 812b, **1163a**; IV, 513a, 1090b, 1216a; V, 47b, 48a, 85b, 90a, 354b, 398a, 547a, 551b
ʿIlm al-ḥisāb iii, **1138a**; iv, 1070a; v, 527b — III, **1166b**; IV, 1101b; V, 531a
ʿIlm al-ḥurūf → Ḥurūf
ʿIlm al-kaff → al-Kaff
ʿIlm al-kalām ii, 605b, 608a, 618a, 898b, 931a; iii,

543b, 664b, 1132a, **1141b**; iv, 366b — II, 620b, 623a, 633b, 919b, 953a; III, 562b, 686a, 1160a, **1170a**; IV, 382b
ʿIlm al-lugha v, 806a — V, 812a
ʿIlm al-ridjāl iii, **1150b** — III, **1179a**
ʿIlm al-tawḥīd i, 714a; iii, 1142a — I, 735b; III, 1170a
ʿIlmiyye iii, **1152a** — III, **1180b**
Ilsh → Alsh
Iltizām ii, 147b, 148a; iii, **1154a**; iv, 324a, 1096a; v, 93b; s, 238b — II, 152a,b; III, **1182b**; IV, 338b, 1127a; V, 95b; S, 238b
Iltizām (rhetoric, rhétorique) → Luzūm mā lā yalzam
Iltutmish b. Ēlam Khān i, 208b, 432b, 764a, 856a, 912b, 1192a, 1209b, 1218b; ii, 50a, 120a, 153b, 260a, 266b, 267a, b, 274b, 609a, 1084a, 1143b; iii, 416a, 441a, 492a, **1155a**; iv, 533b; v, 549a, 597b, 629b, 883b, 1134b; s, 124a, 284b, 353a, 360a — I, 214b, 444b, 787a, 880a, 940a, 1227a, 1245b, 1255a; II, 51a, 122b, 158b, 267b, 274b, 275b, 282b, 624a, 1109b, 1170b; III, 429a, 455b, 509a, **1183b**; IV, 556b; V, 553b, 601b, 633b, 890a, 1130a; S, 123a, 284b, 353a, 359b
Iltüzer Khān iv, 1065a, 1068a; v, 24a — IV, 1096b, 1100a; V, 25a
Ilyās i, 404b, 1214b; iii, **1156a**; iv, 903a; v, 5a — I, 416a, 1250b; III, **1184b**; IV, 935b; V, 5a
Ilyās b. Aḥmad iv, 859a — IV, 892b
Ilyās b. Ḥabīb i, 86b — I, 89a
Ilyas b. Ḥamīd iii, 132b — III, 135b
Ilyās b. Ilyasaʿ s, 356b — S, 356b
Ilyās b. Isḥāḳ iv, 698b — IV, 727a
Ilyās b. Manṣūr al-Nafūsī (Ibāḍī) s, 1a — S, 1a
Ilyās b. Yuḥannā i, 593b — I, 613a
Ilyās Beg (Mirākhor) v, 265a, b — V, 263a
Ilyās Khān s, 331b — S, 331a
Ilyās Pasha v, 267b — V, 265b
Ilyās Pasha (Anadolu) s, 49a — S, 49b
Ilyās Shāh i, 1015a, 1168a; ii, 751b; iii, 202b, 416b; v, 638a — I, 1046a, 1203a; II, 770a; III, 208a, 430a; V, 642b
Ilyas-oghlu ii, 207b — II, 214a
Ilyasaʿ iii, 1156b; v, 158b — III, 1185a; V, 157b
Ilyāsid(e)s iii, **1156b**; v, 158b — III, **1185a**; V, 157b
Īmāʾ → Ishāra
ʿImād al-Dawla ʿAlī i, 211b, 866b, 1046b, 1350a; ii, 178b; iii, 197a, **1157a**; iv, 23a, b, 100a, b, 222a — I, 217b, 890b, 1078b, 1390b; II, 184a; III, 202a, **1185b**; IV, 24b-25a, 104b, 232a
ʿImād al-Dawla b. Hūd iii, 542b, 728a — III, 561b, 750b
ʿImād al-Dawla Farāmarz iii, 1162a — III, 1190a
ʿImād al-Dawla Sāwtigin → Sāwtegin
ʿImād al-Dīn, Amīr (Astarābādh) s, 380a — S, 380a
ʿImād al-Dīn b. Arslān Shāh v, 454b — V, 457a
ʿImād al-Dīn b. Ṣalāḥ al-Dīn → al-Malik al-ʿAzīz ʿImād al-Dīn
ʿImād al-Dīn Abu 'l-Fatḥ ʿUmar b. ʿAlī i, 765b — I, 788b
ʿImād al-Dīn ʿAlī, Faḳīh-i Kirmānī iv, 1010a; s, **414b** — IV, 1042a; S, **415a**
ʿImād al-Dīn Ḥasan b. ʿAlī s, 83a — S, 82b
ʿImād al-Dīn Ismāʿīl → al-Ṣāliḥ ʿImād al-Dīn
ʿImād al-Dīn al-Kātib al-Iṣfahānī i, 150a, 523a, 594a, 595a, 801b, 1309b; iii, 222a, 834b, **1157b**; v, 528b; s, 123b, 205a, 326a, 378b — I, 154a, 538b, 613b, 614b, 825a, 1349b; III, 228b, 858a, **1186a**; V, 532b; S, 123a, 205a, 325b, 378b
ʿImād al-Dīn Rayḥān → Rayḥān
ʿImād al-Dīn ʿUmar al-Shaykh i, 766b — I, 789a
ʿImād al-Dīn Zankī → Zankī
ʿImād al-Mulk (Multān) iii, 634a; s, 335b — III, 655a; S, 335a
ʿImād al-Mulk, Fatḥ Allāh → Fatḥ Allāh
ʿImād al-Mulk, Ghāzī al-Dīn i, 296a, 1024b; iii, 61a, **1158a**; v, 598b — I, 305a, 1056a; III, 63b, **1186b**; V, 602b
ʿImād Shahī(de)s i, 1170a; ii, 981b; iii, 425a, 447a, **1159a**; s, 280a — I, 1205a; II, 1003b; III, 438b, 462a, **1187b**; S, 279b
ʿImādī (Shahriyārī) iii, **1161b**; s, **416a** — III, **1190a**; S, **416a**
ʿImād-i Ḥasanī-i Sayfī iv, 1124b — IV, 1156a
ʿImādiyya → ʿAmādiya
Image → Ṣūra
Imāla iii, **1162a** — III, **1190b**
Imām → Imāma, Masdjid
Imām aʿẓam → Khalīfa
Imām al-difāʿ i, 125a; iii, 658a — I, 128b; III, 679a
Imām al-Dīn i, 72b — I, 74b
Imām al-Ḥaramayn → al-Djuwaynī, ʿAbd al-Malik
Imām al-Hudā → Abu 'l-Layth al-Samarḳandī
Imām-bārā iii, **1163a**; v, 1033a — III, **1191b**; V, 1029b
Imām-ḳāʾim iv, 205a — IV, 214b
Imām Ḳulī Khān i, 8b, 120b; ii, 446a, 812a, 975b; iv, 387b, 399a; v, 493a, 673a; s, 340b — I, 8b, 124a; II, 458a, 831b, 998a; IV, 404a, 416b; V, 496a, 678a; S, 340a
Imām Shāh iii, **1163a**; iv, 202b; v, 26b — III, **1191b**; IV, 211b; V, 27a
Imām-Shāhīs → Sat-panthīs
Imām Yaḥyā iv, 296b — IV, 309b, 310a
Imāma i, 27a, 276b, 832b; ii, 660b, 931a, 1094a; iii, 547a, 954a, **1163b**; iv, 50a, 182b, 184a, 234b, 277b, 278b, 456b, 943b, 944a, 948a, 987b; v, 166b, 1236a; s, 327b — I, 28a, 285a, 855b; II, 677a, 953a, 1119b; III, 566a, 978b, **1192a**; IV, 52b, 190b, 192a, 245a, 289b, 290b, 477a, 976b, 977a, 981a, 1020a; V, 164a, 1226b; S, 327a
ʿImāma → Libās
Imām-i Khurd → Yaḥyā b. Zayd
Imāmīyya i, 393a, 445b, 850a; iii, 497a, 1166b; iv, 610a; v, 1236a, b; s, 25b — I, 404a, 458b, 873b; III, 514a, 1195b; IV, 634b, 1226b, 1227a; S, 26a
Imāmzāda iii, 1124a, **1169b**; iv, 702a — III, 1152a, **1198b**; IV, 730a
Īmān i, 276b, 335a, 1242a; ii, 294a; iii, **1170b**; iv, 171b, 172a, 173a, b — I, 285b, 345b, 1279b; II, 302a; III, **1199b**; IV, 179a, b, 180b, 181a
Imāra i, 1191a — I, 1226a
al-ʿImāra s, 243a — S, 243a
ʿImārat (edifice) v, 680b, 681a — V, 685b, 686a
al-Imārāt al-ʿArabīyya al-Muttaḥida iv, 778b; v, 1058a; s, 2b, 42a, **416b** — IV, 810a; V, 1055a; S, 12b, 42a, **417a**
Imārat al-nubuwwa → Nubuwwa
ʿImāret → Khayr; Waḳf
Imazighen i, 433b, 1143a — I, 446a, 1208a
al-Imbābī, Muḥammad s, 411b — S, 411b
Imbros → Imroz
Imdād Allāh al-Hindī al-Makkī i, 701b; ii, 54b; iii, **1174a** — I, 723a; II, 55b; III, **1203a**
Imdād Ḥusayn Khān Nāṣir Djang ii, 808b — II, 828a
Imdyazen i, 1186b — I, 1221b
Imeretie → Kurdj
Imeum i, 741b — I, 763b
Immolation → Dhabīḥa
Impeccability/Impeccabilité → ʿIṣma
Impiety, Impiété → Kāfir
Impôt → Bādj; Ḍarība; Djahbadh; Kharādj
Imprimerie → Maṭbaʿa
Improvisation → Irtidjāl
Imraʾ al-Ḳays → Imruʾ al-Ḳays

Imrālī → Emreli
ʿImrān i, 177a; iii, **1175a** — I, 182a; III, **1204a**
ʿImrān (Sind) iv, 535a — IV, 558a
ʿImrān b. al-Faḍl iii, 125b — III, 128a
ʿImrān b. Ḥiṭṭān iii, 889b, **1175a**; iv, 1077a; s, 284a — III, 913b, **1204a**; IV, 1109a; S, 284a
ʿImrān b. Muḥammad b. Sabaʾ i, 181b — I, 186b
ʿImrān b. Mukhallad i, 248a — I, 255b
ʿImrān b. Mūsā al-Barmakī i, 1036a — I, 1067b
ʿImrān b. Shāhīn i, 211b, 955a; iii, 730a, **1175b** — I, 218a, 984a; III, 753a, **1204b**
ʿImrānī (of Shīrāz) iv, 309b — IV, 323b
al-ʿImrānī i, 133a; iii, **1176a**— I, 137a; III, **1205a**
Imroz i, 1280b; iii, **1176a**; v, 763b, 764b — I, 1320a; III, **1205a**; V, 769b, 770a
Imruʾ al-Ḳays iii, **1176b** — III, **1205b**
Imruʾ (Marʾ) al-Ḳays i, 548b, 564b; v, 120a; — I, 566a, 582b; V, 123a
Imruʾal-Ḳays b. Ḥudjr i, 99a, 405b, 452a, 527a, 583b, 1152a; ii, 241b, 550b, 785a, 1028b; iii, **1177a**; iv, 263b, 839a; v, 119a, 633a; s, 38a, 58b, 259a — I, 101b, 417a, 465a, 543a, 602a, 1186b; II, 248b, 564b, 804a, 1052a; III, **1205b**; IV, 275b, 872a; V, 121b, 637a; S, 38a, 59a, 258b
Imtiyāzāt ii, 912b; iii, **1178b**; iv, 38b — II, 934a; III, **1207b**; IV, 41a
Imuhagh, Imushagh i, 255a, 1173a — I, 263a, 1208a
Imẓad iii, **1195b** — III, **1225b**
In shāʾ Allāh iii, **1196a** — III, **1226b**
ʿInab → Khamr
I̊naḳ iv, 1065a; v, 392a; s, **419a** — IV, 1096b; V, 392b; S, **419a**
Inaḳid(e)s s, 420a — S, 420a
Inal iii, **1199a** — III, **1229a**
Īnāl, Īnālid(e)s ii, 344a; iii, **1197b** — II, 354a; III, **1227b**
I̊nal, I̊nalčuḳ iii, **1198a** — III, **1228a**
Īnāl al-Adjrūd i, 352a; iii, **1198a** — I, 363a; III, **1228a**
Inālū → Abū ʿUmar Inālū
Inʿām iii, 347b, **1200b** — III, 358a, **1231a**
ʿInān iii, **1202b** — III, **1232b**
Inanč Khātūn iii, 1111b — III, 1139a
Inandj, Ḳiwām al-Dīn i, 300b; ii, 333b; iii, 1110b — I, 310a; II, 343a; III, 1137b
Īnānlū iv, 858b — IV, 891b
Iʿnāt → Luzūm mā lā yalzam
ʿĪnāt s, 337b, **420b** — S, 337a, **420b**
ʿInāya i, 90a, 415a; iii, **1203a** — I, 92b, 427a; III, **1233b**
ʿInāyat Allah (Afghānistān) s, 65b, 66b — S, 66a, 67a
ʿInāyat Allāh (India/Inde) s, 292b, 293b — S, 292b, 293b
ʿInāyat Allāh Kańbū iii, **1203b** — III, **1234a**
ʿInāyat Allāh Khān → al-Mashriḳī
ʿInāyat Khān (d./m. 1681) s, **420b** — S, **420b**
ʿInāyat Khan (d./m. 1682) s, **420b** — S, **421a**
ʿInāyat Khān b. Ḥāfiẓ Raḥmat iii, 61a — III, 63b
ʿInāyat Khān b. Ẓafar Aḥsan ii, 1004b — II, 1028a
Incense → Mibkhara; Lubān
Incest(e) → Nikāḥ; Zinā
Incubation → Istikhāra
Independence/Indépendance → Istiḳlāl
India, Inde → Hind
Indian Congress Party s, 106b — S, 105b
Indian Mutiny → Mutiny, Indian
Indian National Congress iii, **1204a**; s, 4b — III, **1234b**; S, 3b
Indian Ocean → Baḥr al-Hind; Baḥr al-Zandj
Indigo → Nīl
Indjīl i, 264a; iii, **1205a** — I, 272a; III, **1235b**
Indjili Čavush iii, 375a — III, 387a
Īndjū iii, 55b, **1208a**; iv, 31b, 975b, 1094a; s, 235b — III, 58a, **1238b**; IV, 34a, 1008a, 1125a; S, 235b
Īndju Shīrāzī, Ḥusayn iv, 526a — IV, 549a
Indjūid(e)s iv, 32a; v, 163a — IV, 34b; V, 161a
Indo-Aryan(languages), Indo-aryennes (langues) iii, 412b — III, 425b
Indochina, Indochine iii, **1208b** — III, **1239b**
Indonesia, Indonésie iii, 502b, **1213a**; iv, 175b; v, 940b; s, 220a — III, 520a, **1243b**; IV, 183a; V, 944a; S, 220b
— administration i, 980b; iii, 566a — I, 1010b; III, 586a
- ethnography/ethnographie iii, 1214b — III, 1245a
- geography/géographie iii, 1213a — III, 1243b
- history/histoire ii, 19a, 595a, 662b; iii, 534a, 1218-1230 — II, 19a, 610a, 679a; III, 552b, 1249-1262
- institutions ii, 426b — II, 437b
- languages, literature/langues, littératures i, 88a, 92a; iii, 1215a, 1230b; iv, 1128a; v, 205a, 226b, 227a, 228b — I, 90b, 94b; III, 1245b, 1262b; IV, 1159b; V, 202b, 224a, b, 226a
Indus i, 222a; iii, 408a; iv, 597b — I, 228b; III, 420b; IV, 621b
Industry, Industrie → Ṣināʿa
Inebakhtî → ʿAynabakhtî
Infallibility/Infaillibilité → ʿIṣma
Infiʿāl → Fiʿl
Infidel, Infidèle → Kāfir
Infini → Nihāya
Infisākh ii, 836a — II, 856a
Infiṣāl → Waṣl
Inflection → Ṣarf
Ingiliz Muṣṭafā ii, 511b — II, 524a
Ingush ii, 18a,b; iii, **1235b** — II, 18a,b; III, **1267b**
Inḥiṣār s, **421a** — S, **421a**
Inhumation → Djanāza
Inimitableness of the Ḳurʾān/Inimitabilité du Ḳurʾān → Iʿdjāz
Ink → Dawāt; Midād
Inkār iii, **1236b** — III, **1268b**
Inḳilāb → Thawra
al-Inḳilish v, 1012b, 1013a — V, 1008b
Inkiyānū iv, 1046b — IV, 1078a
Innāyir → Yinnāyir
Inniya v, 1262a, b, 1263b — V, 1253b, 1254b
Innovation → Bidʿa
Inönü → Işmet Inönü; Sultān Önü
Inos(z) → Enos
Inṣāf iii, **1236b** — III, **1268b**
Insān iii, **1237a** — III, **1269a**
al-Insān al-Kāmil i, 117b; iii, **1239a**; v, 543b — I, 121a; III, **1271a**; V, 548a
Inscriptions → Kitābāt
Insectivores → Faʾr
Inshāʾ i, 594a, 595a; ii, 306b; iii, **1241b**; iv, 705a, 760a — I, 613b, 614a; II, 315a; III, **1273b**; IV, 733a, 790b
Inshā Allāh Khān iii, 358b, 376b, 458a, **1244a**; v, 959a, 960b, 961b — III, 370a, 388b, 474a, **1276a**; V, 963a, 964b, 965b
Inshāṣ (Palace) s, 301a — S, 300b
Insignia, Insigne → Nishān, Rasm, Shiʿār, Wisām
Inspection of Troops/Inspection des troupes → Istiʿrāḍ; Dāgh u Taṣḥīḥa
Institut d'Egypte iii, **1245a** — III, **1277b**
Intitut des Hautes Études Marocaines s, **421b** — S, **421b**
Institut des Hautes Études de Tunis s, **422a** — S, **422b**
Instrument → Āla
Insult(e) → Shatm
Intellect → ʿAḳl

Intendant → Emīn
Intention → Niyya
Intercession → Shafāʿa
Intérêt → Māl; Ribā
Interpreter/Interprète → Turdjumān
Interrogation → Istifhām; Istiʿrāḍ
Intī → Hintāta
Intidāb → Mandate/Mandat
Intihāʾ iii, **1246a** — III, **1278a**
Intiḥār iii, **1246b** — III, **1278b**
Intiḳālī iv, 978a — IV, 1010b
Intronisation → Bayʿa
Invective → Hidjāʾ
Investiture → Bayʿa, Khilʿa, Taḳlīd
Inzāl → Waḳf
Inzāl s, **423a** — S, **423a**
Ipshīr Muṣṭafā Pasha i, 4b; iii, 318a, 983b, **1248a**; v, 257a — I, 4b; III, 327b, 1008a, **1280b**; V, 254b, 255a
Iʿrāb i, 566a, 569b, 570a, 576b; iii, 697a, **1248b**; v, 567b — I, 584a, 588a,b, 595a; III, 719a, **1281a**; V, 571b
Irāde i, 414b; iii, **1250a** — I, 426b; III, **1282b**
Iradj Khān i, 702a — I, 723a
Īradj Mīrzā iv, 71b; s, 84a — IV, 75b; S, 83b
ʿIrāfa iv, 421b — IV, 440a
ʿIrāḳ iii, **1250a**; iv, 719a; v, 912a; s, 179a, 198b, 259a — III, **1282b**; IV, 748a; V, 917b; S, 180a, 198b, 258b
— art, architecture i, 609b, 1226a; iii, **1266b**; v, 292b, 293a, 1148a, — I, 629b, 1264a; III, **1299a**; V, 292a, b, 1139a
— ethnography/ethnographie i, 39a, 872b; iii, **1253a**; v, 440a, 466b — I, 40a, 896b; III, **1285b**; V, 442b, 469b
— geography/géographie i, 431a, 461a; iii, **1250a**; iv, 1b; v, 146a, 864b, 886b — I, 443a, 474a; III, **1283a**; IV, 1b; V, 148b, 871b, 893a
— history/histoire i, 16a, 18b, 21a, 33a, 46a, 53b, 76b, 77a, 111a, 140b, 211b, 383a,b, 388b, 400a, 549b, 1087a, 1350b; ii, 579b, 872b; iii, 263b, 521a, 558a, 560b, 1066a,b, **1254a**; iv, 15a, 16b-17b, 261b — I, 16b, 19a, 21b, 34a, 47b, 55a, 78b, 79b, 114a, 144b, 217b, 394a,b, 400a, 411b, 567a, 1119a, 1390b; II, 594a, 892b; III, 271b, 539a, 577b, 580a, 1093a, **1286b**; IV, 16a, 17b-18b, 273a
— institutions ii, 424b; v, 1044a, 1093b — II, 435b; V, 1040b, 1090b
- languages, literature/langues, litérature i, 568b, 576a; ii, 468b; iii, **1259a** — I, 586b, 595a; II, 480b; III, **1292a**
— sects/sectes i, 15a; iii, **1265a** — I, 15b; III, **1297b**
ʿIrāḳ-i ʿAdjamī → Djibāl
al-ʿIrāḳī, ʿAbd al-Raḥīm iii, 817b, 927a — III, 841a, 951b
ʿIrāḳī, Fakhr al-Dīn iii, 635a, 710b, **1269a**; iv, 65b, 67b, 474a — III, 656b, 733a, **1302a**; IV, 69a, 71a, 494b
al-ʿIrāḳī, Sayyid Shams al-Dīn s, **423a** — S, **423b**
Irakli II v, 494b, 495a — V, 497b
Īraḳlīdis Abū Buḳrāṭ s, 154b — S, 155a
Iram i, 169b; iii, **1270a** — I, 174a; III, **1303a**
Iram Dhāt al ʿimād i, 169a, 181a; iii, 1270b — I, 174a, 186a; III, 1303b
Īrān i, 38a, 62b, 270a, 291a, 406a; ii, 966b, 1135b; iv, **1a-75a**, 163b, 785a; s, 129a, 214b, 332b — I, 39a, 64b, 278b, 300a, 418a; II, 988b, 1162a; IV, **1a-79a**, 170b, 817a; S, 128a, 214a, 332b
- administration i, 978a; ii, 150a, 308b, 332b, 514b, 649b, 1081b; iii, 194b, 213b, 347b, 554a; iv, 1034a; v, 1042a — I, 1008b; II, 154b, 317a, 342a, 527a, 665b, 1106b; III, 199a, 219b, 358a, 573a; IV, 1066a; V, 1038a
- art, architecture iii, 501b; iv, 288a, b; v, 292b — III, 518b; IV, 301a; V, 292a, b
- demography/démographie s, **214b** — S, **214a**
- ethnography/ethnographie i, 36a; iv, 7a-11a; v, 439b, 466a — I, 37a; IV, 8a-12a; V, 442a, 468b
- geography/géographie ii, 902b; iv, 1a-8a; v, 865a — II, 923b; IV, 1a-8a; V, 872a
- institutions ii, 426a, 433a; iii, 527b; v, 919a, 1094b — II, 437a, 444b; III, 546a; V, 924a, 1091b
- language, literature/langues, littérature i, 1132a; ii, 308b; iii, 355a, 372b; iv, 52b-75a, 308a, 714a; v, 228b — I, 1166a; II, 317a; III, 366a, 384b; IV, 55b-79a, 322a, 743a; V, 226b
- mythology/mythologie iv, 12a-13a — IV, 12a-14a
- sects/sectes iv, 43a-52b — IV, 45b-55b
Īrānī → Mughals
Īrānshahr s, 263b — S, 263a
al-Irānshahrī → Abu 'l-Abbās al-Irānshahrī
Iraten iv, **75a** — IV, 79a
Irbid iv, **75b** — IV, **79b**
Irbil i, 1160b; iii, 1268a; iv, **76a**; v, 145b — I, 1195b; III, 1301a; IV, **80a**; V, 148a
ʿIrḍ iv, **77a** — IV, **81a**
Irdānā Bī v, 29a — V, 30a
al-Irdjānī, Abū Yaḥyā Zakariyyāʾ ii, 369a; iii, 656a; iv, **78a** — II, 379a; III, 677a; IV, **82a**
ʿIrfān Pasha iv, 879a — IV, 911b
Irian Barat iii, 1213a,b, 1215a — III, 1243b, 1244b, 1246a
Irič iii, 442b — III, 457a
Iridj Shāhnawāz Khān i, 80b, 81b, 769a, 1331a — I, 83a, 83b, 792a, 1371b
al-ʿIrʿīr ii, 176a — II, 181b
ʿIrḳ, ʿurūḳ i, 537a; ii, 92a; iv, **78b** — I, 553b; II, 94a; IV, **82b**
ʿIrḳ → Ṣaḥrāʾ
ʿIrḳ al-Luʾluʾ → Ṣadaf
ʿIrk Subay i, 537b — I, 554a
ʿIrḳa iv, **79a** — IV, **83a**
Irmiyā iv, **79a**; v, 442b — IV, **83a**; V, 445a
Irōn → Ossets/Ossètes
Iron → al-Ḥadīd
Irrigation → Māʾ
Irrigation → Māʾ; Ḳanāt; Nahr; Riyy
Irsāliyye iv, **79b**, 435b; v, 35a — IV, **83b**, 454b; V, 36a
Irtidjāʿ → Radjʿiyya
Irtidjāl iv, **80b** — IV, **84b**
Irtifāʿ → Falak; ʿIlm al-Hayʾa
Irtysh s, 245a — S, 245a
Īrwānī, Muḥammad s, 76a — S, 76a
al-ʿĪṣ iii, 152b — III, 156a
al-ʿĪṣ, Umayya b. ʿAbd Shams s, 103b — S, 102b
ʿĪsā i, 177a, 265a, 272a, 1020b, 1141a; ii, 280a; iii, 1206a; iv, **81a**; v, 41a, 421a, 423b, 1231a — I, 182a, 273a, 280a, 1052a, 1175b; II, 288b; III, 1236b; IV, **85a**; V, 42b, 423a, 425b, 1221b
ʿĪsā, Āl iv, 87b, 88a — IV, 91b, 92a
ʿĪsā, Nahr i, 897a; iv, **86b**, 88b — I, 924a; IV, **90b**, 92b
ʿĪsā, al-Ẓāhir i, 666b — I, 687b
ʿĪsā b. Aḥmad al-Dawsarī v, 40a, b — V, 41a, b
ʿĪsā b. Aḥmad al-Rāzī i, 321a, 600b — I, 330b, 620a
ʿĪsā b. ʿAlī (ʿAbbāsid(e)) iii, 883a — III, 907b
ʿĪsā b. ʿAlī (physician/médecin) i, 388a — I, 399a
ʿĪsā b. ʿAlī b. ʿĪsā i, 387b; iii, 895a — I, 398b; III, 919a
ʿĪsā b. ʿAlī Āl Khalīfa iv, 953b — IV, 986a
ʿĪsā b. ʿAlī al-Ḥarrānī iv, 340b — IV, 355a
ʿĪsā b. Dīnār i, 600a; iv, **87a** — I, 619b; IV, **91a**
ʿĪsā b. Djaʿfar iii, 907b — III, 932a
ʿĪsā b. al-Haytham al-Ṣūfī iv, 1162a, b — IV, 1194a, b
ʿĪsā b. Idrīs II ii, 874a; iii, 1035b — II, 894a; III, 1061b
ʿĪsā b. Idrīs (Dulafid(e)) ii, 623a — II, 639a

ʿĪsā b. Ismāʿīl al-Aḳsarāʾī → al-Aḳsarāʾī
ʿĪsā b. K̲h̲alīd b. al-Walīd → Abū Saʿd al-Mak̲h̲zūmī
ʿĪsā b. Maʿḳil i, 1293a — I, 1332b
ʿĪsā b. Miskīn i, 249b — I, 257b
ʿĪsā b. Muḥammad b. Sulaymān i, 661b — I, 682a
ʿĪsā b. Muhannā iii, 403a; iv, **87b** — III, 415a; IV, **91b**
ʿĪsā b. Mūsā (ʿAbbāsid(e)) i, 96a, 134a, 618b, 952a, 1033b; iii, 984a; iv, **88a**; v, 1238a; s, 31b — I, 98b, 137b, 637b, 981b, 1065a; III, 1008b; IV, **92b**; V, 1229a; S, 31b
ʿĪsā b. Mūsā (Ḳarmaṭī) i, 96a, 962b; iv, 198b, 662a, b, 838a — I, 98b, 992a; IV, 207a, 688b, 689a, 871a
ʿĪsā b. Mūsā al-Nūs̲h̲arī v, 327a — V, 327a
ʿĪsā b. Nasṭūrus i, 823b, 824b; ii, 858a; iii, 77a — I, 846b, 847b; II, 878a; III, 79b
ʿĪsā b. Rayʿān al-Azdī iii, 655b; v, 696a — III, 676b; V, 701a
ʿĪsā b. Ṣāliḥ (ʿUmān) i, 1283a — I, 1321b
ʿĪsā b. Ṣāliḥ (S̲h̲arḳiyya Hināwī) s, 355b — S, 355a
ʿĪsā b. Ṣāliḥ (ʿUmān) s, 356a — S, 356a
ʿĪsā b. Salmān iv, 954a — IV, 986b
ʿĪsā b. al-S̲h̲ayk̲h̲ al-S̲h̲aybānī ii, 344a; iv, **88b** — II, 353b; IV, **92b**
ʿĪsā b. ʿUmar al-Hamdānī iv, 91a — IV, 95a
ʿĪsā b. ʿUmar al-T̲h̲aḳafī i, 42b; iv, **91a** — I, 44a; IV, **95a**
ʿĪsā b. ʿUt̲h̲mān b. Fūdī iii, 281b, 282a — III, 290a,b
ʿĪsā b. Yaḥyā i, 213a, 1236b — I, 219b, 1274a
ʿĪsā b. Yūsuf al-ʿIrāḳī iii, 1246b — III, 1279a
ʿĪsā b. Zakariyyāʾ ii, 140b — II, 144b
ʿĪsā b. Zayd b. ʿAlī s, 130a — S, 129a
ʿĪsā Aydinog̲h̲lu i, 778a, 783b — I, 801a, 806b
ʿĪsā al-Asadī iv, 745a; v, 9a; s, 175b — IV, 774b; V, 9b; S, 176b
ʿĪsā Beg b. Evenros ii, 721a; iv, 139b — II, 739b; IV, 145b
ʿĪsā Bey i, 1263a, 1264b — I, 1301b, 1303a
ʿĪsā Čelebi i, 510b; ii, 599a — I, 526b; II, 614a
ʿĪsā al-ʿĪsā ii, 468a — II, 480a
ʿĪsā Ḳāʾimmaḳām (Irān) s, 70b — S, 71a
ʿĪsā K̲h̲ān Iʿtimād al-Dawla iii, 554a — III, 573a
ʿĪsā K̲h̲ān Tark̲h̲ān → Muḥammad ʿĪsā Tark̲h̲ān
ʿĪsā al-Suktānī i, 428a — I, 440a
Isaac → Isḥāḳ
Isaac b. Abraham iv, 605b — IV, 630a
Isāf wa-Nāʾila iv, **91a**; s, 133a — IV, **95b**; S, 132b
Īsāg̲h̲ūd̲j̲ī iv, **92a** — IV, **96a**
Isaiah/Isaïe → S̲h̲aʿyā
Isakča iv, **92a** — IV, **96a**
ʿIṣāmī → Fak̲h̲r al-Dīn ʿIṣāmī
ʿIṣāmī, ʿIzz al-Dīn iv, 210b — IV, 220a
Īsar-dās iv, **93a** — IV, **97a**
ʿIsāwā, ʿĪsāwiyya i, 371a; iv, **93b**; s, 325b, 350b, 351a — I, 382a; IV, **97b**; S, 325b, 350b, 351a
ʿIsāwī → Naṣārā
al-ʿIsāwiyya (al-Iṣfahāniyya) i, 130a; iv, **96a** — I, 133b; IV, **100a**
Iṣbaʿ iv, **96b** — IV, **100b**
Iṣbahān → Iṣfahān
Isçehisar, Ischtschi Ḥiṣār → Īsd̲j̲e Ḳarā Ḥiṣār
Ischkeul (lake/lac) s, 243b — S, 243b
Isd̲j̲ālāt al-ʿadāla ii, 303b — II, 312a
Īsd̲j̲e Ḳarā Ḥiṣār iv, 578a — IV, 601b
Iṣfabad̲h̲ b. Sāwtigīn al-Turkumānī iv, 208a — IV, 217b
Iṣfahān i, 142b, 643a; ii, 335a; iv, **97a**, 131b, 977b, 979a; v, 874a; s, 23b, 43b, 54a, 75a, 95b, 140b, 141b, 142a, 157b, 169b, 257a, 274b, 275a, 308a, 326a, 336a, 363b, 365b, 380a, 384a — I, 146b, 663b; II, 345a; IV, **101b**, 137a, 1010a, 1011b; V, 880a; S, 23b, 44a, 54b, 75b, 95a, 140b, 141b, 142a, 158a, 169b, 256b, 274b, 275a, 308a, 325b, 335b, 363b, 365a, 380b, 384b
- history/histoire iii, 156a, 863b, 864a; iv, 7b, 37a, 97a-105b, 465a, b; v, 1157a — III, 159b, 887b, 888a; IV, 8a, 39b, 101b-110a, 486a, b; V, 1147a
- institutions ii, 426a; iii, 1124a; iv, 101b, 103a; s, 139a — II, 437a; III, 1152a; IV, 106a, 107b; S, 138b
- monuments i, 400b; iii, 1124b, 1125a; iv, 36b, 105b-107a, 1137a; v, 1148b, 1149a — I, 412a; III, 1152b, 1153a; IV, 39a, 110b-111b, 1132a; V, 1139b, 1140a
Iṣfahān b. Ḳarā Yūsuf iv, 587b, 588a — IV, 611a, b
al-Iṣfahānī → Abu ʾl-Farad̲j̲; Abū Nuʿaym; ʿAlī b. Ḥamza; D̲j̲amāl al-Din Muḥammad; al-D̲j̲awād; Ḥamza; Ibn Dāwūd; ʿImād al-Dīn; Rūkn al-Dīn
al-Iṣfahānī, Abū Mūsā Muḥammad iii, 821a — III, 845a
Iṣfahāū, Ḥād̲j̲d̲j̲ī Āḳā Nūr Allāh s, 342b — S, 342a
Iṣfahānī, Mīrzā Abū Ṭālib s, 108a — S, 107b
Iṣfahānī, Sayyid Abu ʾl-Ḥasan s, 158a, 342a — S, 158a, 341b
Iṣfahānī, S̲h̲ayk̲h̲ al-S̲h̲arīʿa s, 342a — S, 341b
Iṣfahāniyya → ʿĪsāwiyya
Isfandiyār K̲h̲ān i, 120b; s, 91a — I, 124a; S, 90b
Isfandiyār b. Ad̲h̲arbād iv, 662a — IV, 689a
Isfandiyār b. Bis̲h̲tāsb iv, 809b — IV, 842a
Isfandiyār K̲h̲ān v, 24a; s, 281a — V, 25a; S, 281a
al-Isfarāʾinī → Ṭāhīr b. Muḥammad
al-Isfarāʾinī, Abū Isḥāḳ Ibrāhīm iv, **107b**, 183a — IV, **112b**, 191a
al-Isfarāʾinī, Saʿd al-Dīn i, 827a — I, 850a
Isfarāyīn iv, **107a** — IV, **112a**
al-Isfarāyīnī → al-Isfarāʾinī
Isfendiyār Bey iv, 108b — IV, 113a
Isfendiyār og̲h̲lu i, 1256a; iv, **108b**, 737b, 738a — I, 1294a; IV, **113a**, 767b, 768a
Isfīd Diz → Kalʿa-yi Safīd
Isfīd̲j̲āb v, 856a — V, 863a
Isfinṭ → Afsantīn
ʿIs̲h̲āʾ → Ṣalāt
Isḥāḳ iii, 980a; iv, **109a**, 184a, b — III, 1004b; IV, **114a**, 192b
Isḥāḳ (Ḳarmaṭī) iv, 663b — IV, 690a, b
Isḥāḳ, Adīb ii, 417b, 429a, 466b, 467b; iv, **111b** — II, 428a, 440a, 478a, 479a; IV, **116b**
Isḥāḳ b. Abraham b. Ezra i, 111b — I, 115a
Isḥāḳ b. Ayāz ii, 322a — II, 331b
Isḥāḳ b. Ayyūb iv, 89b — IV, 93b
Isḥāḳ b. Aʿẓam K̲h̲ān i, 88a — I, 90b
Isḥāk b. G̲h̲āniya ii, 112a — II, 114b
Isḥāḳ b. Ḥunayn i, 234b, 589a, 631b, 784b, 1340a; ii, 362a; iii, 579a, 1045a, 1136b; iv, **110a**; s, 411b, 412a — I, 242a, 608b, 652a, 808a, 1380b; II, 372a; III, 599a, 1071a, 1165a; IV, **115a**; S, 412a
Isḥāḳ b. al-Ḥusayn iii, 1077a — III, 1103b
Isḥāḳ b. Ibrāhīm b. Wahb i, 982a, 1115a — I, 1012b, 1148b
Isḥāḳ b. Ibrāhīm Ḳarāmān-og̲h̲lu iv, 624a — IV, 649a
Isḥāḳ b. Ibrāhīm al-Mawṣilī i, 118a, 718a; ii, 246a, 1011b; iii, 698b, 730b, 989a, 996b; iv, **110b**, 822a; v, 319b; s, 64a, 128b, 183a — I, 121b, 739a; II, 253a, 1035a; III, 720b, 753a, 1013b, 1021a; IV, **115b**, 855a; V, 319a; S, 64b, 127b, 184b
Isḥāḳ b. Ibrāhīm al-Muṣʿabī i, 153b; s, 106a — I, 158a; S, 105b
Isḥāḳ b. ʿImrān ii, 60a; iv, 627a, 829b; s, 303b, 314a — II, 61a; IV, 651b, 862b; S, 303b, 313b
Isḥāḳ b. Ismāʿīl, amīr iv, 345a, 669b; v, 488a, b — IV, 359b, 697a; V, 491a, b
Isḥāḳ b. Ismāʿīl b. Ḥammād s, **384b** — S, **385a**
Isḥāḳ b. Kundād̲j̲īḳ i, 279a; ii, 524a; iv, 89b, 90a; v, 49a — I, 287b; II, 537a; IV, 93b, 94a; V, 50b
Isḥāḳ b. Maḥmas̲h̲ād̲h̲ iv, 668a, 669a — IV, 695b,

696a
Isḥāḳ b. Muḥammad b. Ghāniya ii, 1007a — II, 1030b
Isḥāk b. Murād iv, **111a** — IV, **116a**
Isḥāḳ b. Rāhwayh → Ibn Rāhwayh
Iṣḥāḳ b. Sulaymān al-Isrāʾīlī i, 785b; ii, 60a; iv, **111b**, 304a, 829b; S, 197b, 314a — I, 809a; II, 61a; IV, **116b**, 318a, 862b; S, 197b, 313b
Isḥāḳ b. Zayd b. al-Ḥārith al-Anṣārī i, 49a; ii, 441a; iv, 838a — I, 50b; II, 453a; IV, 871a
Isḥāḳ Barbarossa i, 678a,b — I, 698b, 699a
Isḥāḳ Efendi iv, **112b** — IV, **117b**
Isḥāḳ Khān Karaʾī iii, 1107b — III, 1135a
Iṣḥāḳ Khuttalānī i, 392b; v, 301a — I, 404a; V, 300b
Isḥāḳ al-Mawṣilī → Isḥak b. Ibrāhīm al-Mawṣilī
Isḥāḳ Pasha v, 494a, b — V, 497a
Isḥāḳ al-Raffāʾ iv, 797a, 800b — IV, 829b, 833a
Isḥāḳ Sükūtī ii, 474b; iii, 393a; iv, **113a** — II, 487a; III, 405b; IV, **118a**
Isḥāḳ al-Turk iv, 16b; v, 64a — IV, 17b; V, 65b
Isḥāḳiyya → Kazarūniyya
Isḥāḳiyya (Karrāmiyya) iv, 668a; v, 945b — IV, 695b; V, 949b
Ishakovič → Üsküb
Isḥāḳzāy ii, 629a — II, 644b
Ishān iv, **113a** — IV, **118a**
Ishʿār iii, 32b — III, 34a
Ishāra iv, **113b** — IV, **118b**
Ishbāʿ iv, 412a — IV, 430a
al-Ishbīlī → Abu ʾ-l-Khayr; al-Fatḥ b. Khāḳān; Ibn Khayr; al-Ruʿaynī
Ishbīliya i, 5b, 6b, 7a,b, 83a, 162a, 491a, 493a; iii, 681a; iv, **114b**; s, 388a — I, 5b, 6b, 7a,b, 85b, 166b, 506a, 508a; III, 702b; IV, **120a**; S, 388b
- constructions i, 499b, 501b, 1226b; iii, 498b; iv, 117a-118b — I, 514b, 516b, 1264a; III, 515b; IV, 122a-123b
Īshīk-āḳāsī iv, **118b** — IV, **123b**
Ishim Khān ii, 45a — II, 46a
ʿIshḳ i, 416a; ii, 552a; iii, 103a; iv, **118b** — I, 428a; II, 565b; III, 105b; IV, **124a**
Ishkāshim i, 853b — I, 877a
Ishkāshimī i, 225a, 854a — I, 231b, 877b
ʿIshkhan ii, 1118a — II, 1144b
ʿIshḳī, Mīzāda iv, 789b; s, 110a — IV, 821b; S, 109b
Ishḳodra i, 285a, 654a, 657a; iv, 588b; s, 281b, 359b — I, 293b, 674b, 677b; IV, 612a; S, 281b, 359b
Ishmael → Ismāʿīl
Ishmaelite v, 1014b, 1015b, 1019a — V, 1010b, 1011b, 1015a
Ishrāḳ ii, 774a; iv, 50b, **119b** — II, 792b; IV, 53b, **125a**
Ishrāḳ → al-Dāmād
Ishrāḳīyyūn i, 234b, 351a, 416b, 596a; iv, **120b** — I, 242a, 362a, 428a, 615a; IV, **125b**
Ishtib iv, **121b** — IV, **126b**
Ishtiḳāḳ (etymology/étymologie) iv, **122a** — IV, **127a**
Ishtiḳāḳ (rhetoric/rhetorique) → Tadjnīs
Ishtirāk → Tawriya
Ishtirākiyya iv, **123b** — IV, **128b**
Īshūrūni iv, 301b — IV, 315a
Īshwar-dās → Īsar-dās
al-Isʿirdī, Nūr al-Dīn Muḥammad iv, 1006a — IV, 1038a
al-Iskāfī, Abū Djaʿfar Muḥammad iv, **126b**; s, 13b — IV, **132a**; S, 14a
al-Iskāfī, Abu 'l-Faḍl Djaʿfar iv, **126b** — IV, **132a**
al-Iskāfī, Abū Isḥāḳ Muḥammad iv, **127a** — IV, **132b**
al-Iskāfī, Abu 'l-Ḳāsim Djaʿfar iv, 127a — IV, 132b
Iskandar (Ḳarā-ḳoyunlu) iv, 587a, b — IV, 609b, 611a
al-Iskandar, Dhu ʾl-Ḳarnayn i, 935a, 1101a, 1206b; ii, 112b, 133a, 278b; iii, 181a; iv, **127b**, 131a, 498a — I, 963b, 1134a, 1242a; II, 115a, 136b, 286b; III, 185a; IV, **133a**, 136b, 519b
Iskandar b. Kayūmarth iv, 808a; v, 663a — IV, 840b; V, 668b
Iskandar b. ʿUmar Shaykh i, 1342a — I, 1382b
al-Iskandar al-Afrūdīsī i, 342a; ii, 550a, 771a; iii, 728b; iv, **129a** — I, 352b; II, 563b, 789b; III, 751b; IV, **134b**
Iskandar Agha iv, **130b** — IV, **136a**
Iskandar Beg → Iskender Beg
Iskandar Beg Munshī iv, **130b** — IV, **136a**
al-Iskandar al-Dimashkī iv, 129a — IV, 134b
Iskandar Khān i, 46b, 970a; ii, 44b; s, 340a — I, 47b, 1000a; II, 45b; S, 339b
Iskandar Muda i, 743b; iii, 1220a; s, 199b, 200b — I, 765b; III, 1251a; S, 199b, 200b
Iskandar nāma i, 299b, 325a; iii, 113a; iv, 62b, **127b**, 902b, 904a — I, 309a, 335a; III, 115b; IV, 66a, **133a**, 935b, 937a
Iskandar Pāsha iv, 435b — IV, 455a
Iskandar-i Shaykhī i, 237a — I, 244b
Iskandar Thānī i, 743b — I, 765b
al-Iskandariyya (Egypt/Égypte) i, 13a, 32a, 121b, 396b, 531b, 947a, 976a, 1288a; ii, 65a; iii, 1082b, 1193b; iv, **132a**; s, 1a, 5a, 120b, 121b — I, 13a, 33a, 125a, 408a, 548a, 976a, 1006a, 1327b; II, 66a; III, 1109b, 1223b; IV, **137b**; S, 1a, 4a, 120a, 121a
- institutions ii, 424a; v, 92a — II, 434b; V, 94a
al-Iskandariyya (towns/villes) iv, **131a** — IV, **136b**
Iskandarūn i, 468b, 476b; ii, 35b; iv, **138a** — I, 482b, 490b; II, 36b; IV, **143b**
Iskandarūna iv, 131a — IV, 136b
Iskeče s, 330a — S, 330a
Iskender Beg i, 309b, 651b, 654b; ii, 721a; iv, **138b**, 574b; v, 724a, 725a — I, 319a, 672a, 675b; II, 739b; IV, **144b**, 597b; V, 729b, 730a
Iskender Čelebi i, 1083a; ii, 1042b; iii, 998b — I, 1115a; II, 1067a; III, 1023b
Iskender Pasha i, 268a; ii, 704b — I, 276a; II, 722a
Iṣlāḥ i, 383a; iv, **141a** — I, 394a; IV, **146b**
Islām ii, 294a; iv, 44a-52a, **171b** — II, 302a; IV, 46b-55a, **179a**
Islâm Ansiklopedisi s, 42a — S, 42a
Islām, encyclopaedias/encyclopédies → Mawsūʿa
Islām Girāy I iv, **178a** — IV, **185a**
Islām Girāy II ii, 1113b; iv, **178b** — II, 1139b; IV, **185a**
Islām Girāy III iv, **178b**; v, 139b, 719b — IV, **185b**; V, 142a, 724b
Islām Khān i, 719b; ii, 216b, 797b — I, 741a; II, 223a, 816b
Islām Khān Sarwānī s, 203a — S, 202b
Islām Shāh Sūrī i, 432b; ii, 259a, 271a,b; iii, 199b, 423a, 492b; s, 1b, 3a — I, 444b; II, 266a, 279a,b; III, 204b, 436b, 509b; S, 1b, 2b
Islāmābād (India) ii, 32a; iv, **177b** — II, 32b; IV, **186a**
Islāmābād (Pakistan) iv, **177b** — IV, **186a**
Īṣlitan iii, 1040a — III, 1066a
Islambol → Istanbul
Island → Djazīra
Isly iv, **179a** — IV, **186b**
Ism (name/nom) ii, 302a; iv, **179a**; v, 396a — II, 310b; IV, **187a**; V, 397a
Ism (in grammar/en grammaire) iv, **181b** — IV, **189a**
ʿIṣma iii, 1024a; iv, **182b** — III, 1049b; IV, **190b**
Ismaël → Ismāʿīl
Ismāʿīl iii, 980a; iv, **184a**, 318a; v, 1014b — III, 1004b;

IV, **192a**, 332a; V, 1010b
Ismāʿīl (Izmail, town/ville) iv, **185a** — IV, **193b**
Ismāʿīl, Imām → Ismāʿīl b. Djaʿfar al-Ṣādiḳ
Ismāʿīl I (Naṣrid(e)) i, 1057b — I, 1089b
Ismāʿīl I (Rasūlid(e)) ii, 926a; iv, 1188b — II, 947b; IV, 1221b
Ismāʿīl I Shāh (Ṣafawid(e)) i, 193b, 228a, 237b, 262b, 311b, 625b, 627b, 903b, 920a, 1019a, 1030b, 1087a, 1120a,b, 1211b; ii, 8a, 44b, 254b, 310b, 344b, 374a, 812a, 937a, 967a; iii, 114a, 177b, 274a, 316a, 585a, 1101a; iv, 34b, 49b, 102b, **186a**, 389a, 610a, 855a; v, 457a, 492b, 603b; s, 94b, 95a, 138b, 147b, 382b — I, 199a, 235a, 244b, 270b, 321a, 646b, 648b, 931a, 948a, 1050b, 1062a, 1099a, 1119a, 1154a, 1247b; II, 8a, 45b, 262a, 319b, 354a, 384a, 831b, 959a, 989a; III, 116b, 181b, 282a, 325b, 605b, 1128a; IV, 37a, 52b, 107b, **194a**, 404b, 634b, 888b; V, 459b, 495b, 607b; S, 94a, 94b, 138a, 147b, 383a
Ismāʿīl II (Ṣafawid(e)) i, 7b, 1208b; ii, 310b; iii, 157b; iv, **188a** — I, 7b, 1244b; II, 319b; III, 161a; IV, **196a**
Ismāʿīl III (Ṣafawid(e)) ii, 311a; iv, 104b, 390a, b, 639b — II, 319b; IV, 109a, 406b, 407a, 666a
Ismāʿīl I (Sāmānid(e)) → Ismāʿīl b. Aḥmad
Ismāʿīl II (Sāmānid(e)) → Ismāʿīl b. Nūḥ
Ismāʿīl, Abū 'l-Faḍl i, 1332a,b; ii, 282a; iii, 120a — I, 1372b, 1373a; II, 290a; III, 122b
Ismāʿīl, Mawlāy (ʿAlawid(e) i, 34b, 47a, 159b, 289a, 356a; ii, 17b, 173a, 367b, 510a, 819b, 823a, 1022a; iii, 231a, 499b, 1047a; iv, 214a; v, 49a, 53b, 1191b, 1245b; s, 40a, 113b, 114a, 125b, 126a, 132a, 223b, 399b — I, 35b, 48b, 164a, 298a, 366b; II, 17b, 178a, 377b, 523a, 839a, 842b, 1045b; III, 237b, 516b, 1073a; IV, 223b; V, 50a, 54b, 1181b, 1236b; S, 40b, 113a, b, 125a, 131b, 223b, 400a
Ismāʿīl b. ʿAbbād → Ibn ʿAbbād al-Ṣāḥib
Ismāʿīl b. ʿAbbād al-Muʿtadid i, 6a — I, 6b
Ismāʿīl b. ʿAbbās → Ismāʿīl I (Rasūlid(e))
Ismāʿīl b. ʿAbd al-Ḥaḳḳ v, 60a, b — V, 62a
Ismāʿīl b. ʿAbd al-Raḥmān b. Dhi 'l-Nūn ii, 243a — II, 250a
Ismāʿīl b. Abu 'l-Ḳāsim Djaʿfar b. al-Uṭrūsh i, 688a; iii, 255a — I, 688a; III, 262b
Ismāʿīl b. Abī Sahl al-Nawbakhtī i, 143b — I, 148a
Ismāʿīl b. Aḥmad (Sāmānid(e)) i, 278a, 452b, 984b, 1001a, 1294a; iv, 21b, 22a, **188b**, 658b; v, 58a, 853a, 856a — I, 286b, 465b, 1015a, 1032a, 1333b; IV, 23b, **196b**, 685a; V, 59b, 859b, 863a
Ismāʿīl b. ʿAlī b. ʿUthmān al-Thaḳafī s, 163a — S, 162b
Ismāʿīl b. Bulbul iii, 739a, 767b, 955a; iv, **189a** — III, 761b, 790b, 979b; IV, **197a**
Ismāʿīl b. Djaʿfar al-Ṣādiḳ i, 402b, 550b; ii, 851a; iv, 1133a; v, 1242b — I, 414b, 568b; II, 871a; IV, 1164b; V, 1233a
Ismāʿīl b. Djāmiʿ → Ibn Djāmiʿ, Ismāʿīl
Ismāʿīl b. Isḥāḳ b. Ismāʿīl b. Ḥammād s, **385a** — S, **385b**
Ismāʿīl b. Ismāʿīl b. Ḥammād s, **385a** — S, **385b**
Ismāʿīl b. al-Ḳāsim → Abu 'l-ʿAtāhiya
Ismāʿīl b. Māzin iii, 299b — III, 309a
Ismāʿīl b. Muḥammad al-Nīsābūrī iii, 738b — III, 761b
Ismāʿīl b. Mūsā b. Mūsā iv, 713a; v, 683a — IV, 741b; V, 688a
Ismāʿīl b. Mūsā al-Kāẓim s, 95a — S, 94b
Ismāʿīl b. Nūḥ iv, **189b**; v, 622b; s, 176b — IV, **197b**; V, 626b; S, 177b
Ismāʿīl b. Sebüktegin ii, 799a, 1050b; iv, **189b** — II, 818a, 1075a; IV, **197b**
Ismāʿīl b. Yāḳūtī i, 1051b, 1052a; iv, 28b — I, 1083a, b; IV, 30b
Ismāʿīl b. Yasār i, 206b; iv, 54a, **189b** — I, 212b; IV, 57a, **198a**
Ismāʿīl b. Yūsuf al-Baṣrī iv, 1004a — IV, 1036b
Ismāʿīl b. Yūsuf al-Ukhayḍir i, 551a — I, 568b
Ismāʿīl b. Ziyād al-Nafūsī iii, 654a; iv, 336b — III, 675a; IV, 351a
Ismāʿīl ʿAdil Shāh iii, 425b, 1160a — III, 439b, 1188b
Ismāʿīl Agha Ṣīmḳo ʿAbdoy i, 1030b; v, 466a — I, 1062a; V, 468b
Ismāʿīl Anḳārawī iii, 711a; iv, **190a** — III, 733b; IV, **198a**
Ismāʿīl ʿĀṣim Efendi → Čelebi-zade
Ismāʿīl al-Aṭrash ii, 636b, 637a — II, 653a
Ismāʿīl Bey (d./m. 1791) iii, 992a; iv, 853a — III, 1016b; IV, 886a
Ismāʿīl Bey (Serez) i, 778b, 1304a; ii, 640a — I, 801b, 1344a; II, 656b
Ismāʿīl Bey b. Īwāẓ Bey iv, 723a — IV, 752a
Ismāʿīl Bey Isfendiyār-oghlu iv, 108b — IV, 113b
Ismāʿīl Djānbulāt iv, 284b, 285b — IV, 296b, 298a
Ismāʿīl Gasprinski → Gaspirali̊
Ismāʿīl Bey Ḳutḳashi̊nli̊ ii, 217a — II, 223b
Ismāʿīl Ghālib iii, 993b; iv, **190b** — III, 1018a; IV, **198b**
Ismāʿīl Ḥaḳḳi ʿĀlīshān ii, 637b; iv, **191a** — II, 653b; IV, **199b**
Ismāʿīl Ḥaḳḳī Baltadji̊oghlu iv, 1126b — IV, 1158a
Ismāʿīl Ḥakkī al-Brūsawī ii, 475a, 542b; iv, **191a** — II, 487a, 556a; IV, **199b**
Ismāʿīl Haḳḳī Pasha, Ḥāfi̊z ii, 698b, 699b — II, 716a, 717b
Ismāʿīl Kāmil Pasha ii, 351b, 615b, 874b, 1110b — II, 361a, 630b, 895a, 1137a
Ismāʿīl Kemāl i, 657b; iv, 195b — I, 678a; IV, 203b
Ismāʿīl Khān ii, 45b — II, 46b
Ismāʿīl Khān Ḳashḳāy iv, 706a — IV, 734b
Ismāʿīl Khandān i, 424b; iv, 1067a — I, 436b; IV, 1098b
Ismāʿīl al-Khashshāb ii, 356b — II, 366a
Ismāʿīl al-Manṣūr → al-Manṣūr (Fāṭimid(e))
Ismāʿīl Mukh i, 923b; ii, 99b, 180a, 1124b — I, 951a; II, 101b, 185b, 1151a
Ismāʿīl al-Muntaṣir s, 245a — S, 245a
Ismāʿīl Pasha → Čerkes
Ismāʿīl Pasha b. al-ʿAẓm v, 925b — V, 930b
Ismāʿīl Pasha, Khedive i, 37b, 142a, 825b, 929a, 1069b; ii, 149b, 167a, 423b, 514a, 642a, 647a, 728a, 892a, 934a; iii, 4b, 360a, 593a, 1000a, 1193b; iv, **192a**, 441b, 442a; v, 4a, 909a, 1060a, 1248a; s, 40a, 179a, 296b, 299b, 379a, 408b — I, 38b, 146a, 848b, 957b, 1102a; II, 154a, 172b, 434b, 527a, 658a, 663b, 746b, 913a, 956a; III, 4b, 371a, 613b, 1025a, 1223b; IV, **200a**, 461b, 462a; V, 4a, 914b, 1057a, 1239a; S, 40a, 180a, 296a, 299a, 379a, 408b
Ismāʿīl Pasha b. Bahrām i, 920a — I, 948a
Ismāʿīl Pasha Ayyūb ii, 123b — II, 126b
Ismāʿīl Pasha Baghdādli̊ i, 905a — I, 932a
Ismāʿīl Pasha Nishāndji̊ iv, **193b**; v, 258b — IV, **201b**; V, 256b
Ismāʿīl Rūmī iv, 382a, b — IV, 398b, 399a
Ismāʿīl Ṣabrī iv, **194b** — IV, **202b**
Ismāʿīl Ṣabrī Pasha iv, **194b** — IV, **203a**
Ismāʿīl Ṣafā iv, **195a** — IV, **203b**
Ismāʿīl Shāh → Ismāʿīl I, II, III
Ismāʿīl Shahīd, Muḥammad ii, 735b; iii, 431a, 436a; iv, **196a** — II, 754a; III, 445a, 450b; IV, **204b**
Ismāʿīl Ṣidḳī ii, 934b; iii, 515b, 516a, 517a; iv, **197b**; s, 58a — II, 956a; III, 533a, 534a, 535a; IV, **206a**; S, 58b
Ismāʿīl al-Tamīmī ii, 633a — II, 649a
Ismāʿīlī (Shabānkāra) iii, 1097b — III, 1124b
Ismāʿīlīyya i, 20a, 48a, 95b, 103b, 125a, 134a, 160a, 216b, 225b, 353a, 402b, 550b, 551a, 832b, 872a,

1052b, 1254b, 1332b, 1350b, 1358a; ii, 168b, 194a, 301a, 375a, 453b, 631b, 859a; iii, 80a, 123b, 253b, 254a, 411b, 433b, 862b, 1155b; iv, 28a, 29b, 30b, 46b-47a, **198a**, 660b, 859b, 887b, 910a; v, 25b, 1033a; s, 95b, 206b, 248b, 358b, 407a, 411a — I, 21a, 49b, 98b, 106b, 129a, 138a, 164b, 223a, 232a, 363b, 414b, 568b, 569a, 855b, 896a, 1084a, 1292b, 1373a, 1391a, 1398a; II, 174a, 200a, 309a, 385a, 465b, 647b, 879a; III, 82b, 126a, 261a, 424b, 447b, 886b, 1184a; IV, 30a, 31b, 32b, 49b-50a, **206b**, 687a, 892b, 920b, 943b; V, 26b, 1029a; S, 95a, 206b, 248b, 358a, 407a, 411b
- doctrine i, 160b, 414b, 450a, 834b, 1098b, 1099b; ii, 97b, 136b, 848b, 1066a, 1070a; iii, 71b, 232a, 1071a, 1130a; iv, 183a, 203a; v, 167a, b, 1242b — I, 165a, 426a, 463a, 857b, 1131b, 1132b; II, 99b, 140a, 868b, 1091a, 1095a; III, 74a, 258b, 1098a, 1158b; IV, 190b, 212a; V, 164b, 165a, 1233b
Ismāʿīliyya (town/ville) iv, 193a, **206b**; s, 6a — IV, 201a, **215b**; S, 5b
ʿIṣmatiyya i, 903a — I, 930a
Işmet Inönü i, 734b, 1255b; ii, 6b, 26a, 432b, 595b, 596a; iii, 1199b; iv, 873b, 934a; s, 98b — I, 756b, 1294a; II, 6b, 21b, 443b, 610b, 611a; III, 1229b; IV, 907a, 967a; S, 98a
Isna iv, **206b** — IV, **216a**
Isnād i, 259a; ii, 302a; iii, 25a, 26a; iv, **207a**; v, 947a — I, 267a; II, 310b; III, 26a, 27b; IV, **216a**; V, 951a
Ispahbadh i, 1110a; iv, **207a**, 208b, 465a; v, 662a; s, 309a — I, 1143b; IV, **216b**, 217b, 486a; V, 667a; S, 309a
Ispahsālār iv, **208a** — IV, **217b**
Isparta iv, **210b** — IV, **220a**
Ispendje ii, 32a, 146b; iv, **211a**, 563a — II, 33a, 150b; IV, **220b**, 585b
Isperukh Khān i, 1305a — I, 1345a
Ispirīzāde Aḥmed Efendi v, 643b — V, 647b
Isrāʾ → Miʿrādj
Israel, Israël → Banū Isrāʾīl; Filasṭīn; Yaʿḳūb
Israel ha-Maʿărābī iv, 605b, 606a — IV, 630a, b
Isrāfīl i, 1093a; iv, **211a**; s, 256a — I, 1125b; IV, **220b**; S, 255b
al-Isrāʾīlī → Ibn al-ʿAṭṭār; Ibrāhīm b. Yaʿḳūb; Isḥāḳ b. Sulaymān
al-Isrāʾīlī, Abu 'l-Faḍl b. Abi 'l-Bayān i, 344b — I, 355a
Isrāʾīliyyāt iv, **211b** — IV, **221a**
I̊ssı̊k-kul iv, **212b** — IV, **222a**
Iṣṭabl iv, **213b**, 266a — IV, **233a**, 278a
Iṣṭakhr (town/ville) i, 43b, 1355b; ii, 925b; iv, **219b** — I, 44b, 1394b; II, 947a; IV, **229a**
Istakhr (cistern/citerne) v, 869b — V, 876a
al-Iṣṭakhrī → Abū ʿAmr; Abū Saʿīd
al-Istakhrī, Abū Isḥāḳ i, 133a, 488a, 835b, 1003a, 1354a; ii, 581a,b, 582a; iii, 405b, 787a; iv, 220a, **222b**, 1079a; v, 1012a; s, 327a — I, 137a, 502b, 858b, 1034a, 1393a; II, 596a,b; III, 418a, 810b; IV, 229b, **232b**, 1110b; V, 1007b; S, 326b
Istān → Ustān
Istanba → Abū Isḥāḳ Ibrāhīm al-Harawī
Istanbul i, 13b, 37a, 109a, 293b, 294a, 394a, 466b, 467a, 973a, 974b, 1334b; ii, 63b, 83b, 708b, 907b; iii, 216b; iv, **224a**; v, 694a, 882a; s, 53b, 67b — I, 13b, 38a, 112a, 302b, 303a, 405b, 480b, 481a, 1003a, 1004b, 1374b; II, 65a, 85a, 726b, 928b; III, 223a; IV, **233b**; V, 698b, 888a; S, 53b, 67b
- fires/incendies iv, 237a-238b — IV, 247b-248b
- institutions i, 1225b; ii, 425b; iii, 140a, 1137b; v, 366a — I, 1262a; II, 436b; III, 142b, 1166a; V, 367a
- monuments i, 774a, 830b, 1318a; iii, 143b; iv, 225b, 232a, 720a, 1159a; v, 67a, 243a, 261a, 533b — I, 797a, 853b, 1358b; III, 147a; IV, 235b, 242b, 749a, 1191a; V, 69a, 241a, 259a; 537b
- population iv, 238a-244b — IV, 248b-255a
- streets/rues iv, 235a-237a — IV, 245a-247a
Istanköy → On Iki Ada
Istār iv, **248b** — IV, **259b**
Istiʿāra iv, **248b** — IV, **259b**
Istibḍāʿ s, 133a — S, 132b
Istibdād i, 64a — I, 66a
Istibrāʾ i, 28a, 1027a; iv, **252b** — I, 29a, 1058b; IV, **263b**
Istibṣār, Kitāb al- ii, 874b; iv, **254a** — II, 894b; IV, **265a**
Istidja iv, **254a**, 355a — IV, **265b**, 370b
Istidlāl → Manṭiḳ
Istidlāl i, 1326b — I, 1367b
Istīfāʾ → Mustawfī
Istīfāʾ i, 1145b — I, 1180a
Iṣṭifan b. Basīl iv, **254b** — IV, **266a**
Iṣṭifān al-Duwayhī iv, **255a** — IV, **266a**
Istifhām iv, **255a** — IV, **266b**
Istiḥḍār iv, 264b — IV, 276b
Istiḥsān ii, 164a; iii, 1237a; iv, **255b** — II, 169a; III, 1268b; IV, **267a**
Istiḳbāl iv, **259a** — IV, **270b**
Istikhāra iv, **259b** — IV, **271a**
Istikhdām → Tawriyya
Istikhrādj ii, 78b — II, 80a
Istiḳlāl iv, **260b**; v, 1194b, 1195a — IV, **272a**; V, 1194b, 1195a
al-Istiḳrār ii, 79a — II, 80b
Istiḳsām iv, **263a** — IV, **275a**
Iṣṭilāḥat ii, 765b; v, 805b — II, 784a; V, 811b
Istimṭār iii, 305b; iv, 270a — III, 315a; IV, 282a
Istiʾnāf iv, **264a** — IV, **276a**
Istinbāt → Māʾ; Rifāya
Istindjāʾ iv, **264b** — IV, **276a**
Istinshāḳ iv, **264b** — IV, **276b**
Istinzāl iv, **264b** — IV, **276b**
Istiʿrāḍ i, 810a; ii, 507b; iv, **269a**, 1076b; v, 19b — I, 833a; II, 520a; IV, **281a**, 1108b; V, 20a
Istiʿrāḍ, ʿarḍ iv, **265a** — IV, **276b**
Istiṣḥāb i, 276a; iv, **269b** — I, 284b; IV, **281b**
Istishrāḳ → Mustashriḳūn
Istisḳāʾ i, 109a; ii, 617b; iv, **269b**; v, 736a, 1202a — I, 112a; II, 633a; IV, **282a**; V, 741a, 1192b
Istiṣlāḥ → Istiḥsān
Istiṭāʿa i, 413b; iv, **271a** — I, 425b; IV, **283b**
Istithḳāl iii, 1128b — III, 1157a
Istithnāʾ i, 276b; ii, 302a; iii, 1079b, 1196a; iv, **272b** — I, 285b; II, 310b; III, 1106b, 1226b; IV, **284b**
Istiwāʾ, Khaṭṭ al- iv, **273a** — IV, **285a**
Istōnī (Istolnī) Belghrād ii, 208b; iv, **273b** — II, 215a; IV, **286a**
Īṭāʾ iv, 413a — IV, 431a
Iṭāʿa → Ṭāʿa
ʿItāb b. Warḳa iv, 99b — IV, 104a
Iʿtāḳ → ʿAbd
Ītākh iii, 45b — III, 47b
Italie → Īṭaliya
Īṭaliya iv, **274b**; v, 758a — IV, **286b**; V, 763b
Italy → Īṭaliya
Iʿtarada iv, 269a — IV, 281a
Itāwa iv, **276a** — IV, **288a**
Itāwā iv, **276a** — IV, **288a**
Itāy al-Bārūd s, 244a — S, 244a
Itbāʿ → Muzāwadja
Iṭfīr → Ḳiṭfīr
Ithbāt iv, **277a** — IV, **289a**
Ithm iv, 1106b — IV, 1138a
Ithnā-ʿashariyya i, 134a, 765a, 1130a, 1142a, 1350b, 1352a; ii, 375a, 1093b; iii, 380a, 433b, 544b, 726b, 1021a, 1150b, 1166b; iv, 46b, 47b, 49b-50a, 186a, **277a**, 888a; s, 56b, 134b, 248b — I, 138a, 787b, 1164a,

1176b, 1391a,b; II, 385a, 1119b; III, 392a, 447b, 563b, 749a, 1047a, 1179a, 1195b; IV, 49b, 50a, 52b, 194b, **289a**, 921a; S, 57a, 134a, 248b
Iʿtibār iii, 26b — III, 27b
Iʿtibār Khān ii, 1085a; iii, 225b; iv, **279a** — II, 1110a; III, 232b; IV, **291a**
Iʿtiḳād iv, **279a** — IV, **291b**
Iʿtiḳād Khān iv, **279b**; s, 167b — IV, **292a**; S, 167b
Iʿtikāf iv, **280a** — IV, **292a**
Itil → Atil
Itil (river/rivière) iv, **280a**, 1175b — IV, **292b**, 1209a
Iʿtimād iii, 706a — III, 728a
Iʿtimād al-Dawla i, 253b; ii, 380b; iv, **281b**; v, 630a — I, 261b; II, 390b; IV, **294a**; V, 634a
Iʿtimād al-Dawla → Shafīʿ Mazandarānī
Iʿtimād al-Dawla (Ghiyāth Beg) iv, **282a**, 543b — IV, **294a**, 567a
Iʿtimād al-Dawla (Ibrāhīm Shīrāzī) s, 405b — S, 406a
Iʿtimād Khān ii, 1129a; s, 335b — II, 1155b; S, 335a
Iʿtimād al-Salṭana → Muḥammad Ḥasan Khān Ṣāniʿ al-Dawla
Iʿtimāzāda, Muḥammad iv, 73b — IV, 77a
Itinéraires → al-Masālik wa-l-mamālik
Iʿtiṣām al-Dīn, Shaykh iii, 1046a; s, 108a — III, 1072a; S, 107a
ʿItḳ → ʿAbd
ʿI̊tḳnāme iv, **282b** — IV, **295a**
Iṭlāḳāt ii, 303b, 306b — II, 312a, 315a
al-Iṭlāḳiyya iii, 284a — III, 292b
ʿIṭr → ʿAnbar; Misk, etc.
Ittibāʿ iv, 152a — IV, 158b
Ittiḥād iv, **282b** — IV, **295a**
al-Ittiḥād al-ʿarabī ii, 674b — II, 691b
Ittiḥād-i Islām ii, 445b — II, 457a
Ittiḥād-i Muḥammedī Djemʿiyyeti iv, **283b** — IV, **296a**
al-Ittiḥād al-Lubnānī iii, 519b — III, 537b
al-Ittiḥād al-Sūrī iii, 520b — III, 538b
Ittiḥād we Teraḳḳī Djemʿiyyeti i, 734a; ii, 430b, 643b, 698b; iii, 204a, 251a, 526a, 994a; iv, 283b, **284a**, 611b, 872a, b, 873a; v, 905b, 1036a; s, 41b, 47b, 149b — I, 756a; II, 441b, 660a, 716a; III, 209b, 258a, 544b, 1018b; IV, 296a, **296b**, 636a, 905b, 906a; V, 911a, 1032a; S, 42a, 47b, 149b
Ittiḥādiyya iii, 161b, 822a, 952a — III, 165a, 846a, 976b
Ittīṣāl → Ittiḥād
Ivanko → Yanko
Ivoire, Côte d' → Côte d'Ivoire
Ivory Coast → Côte d'Ivoire
Ivory/Ivoire → ʿĀdj
Iwā i, 919a — I, 947a
ʿIwaḍ iv, **286a** — IV, **298b**
ʿIwaḍ Wadjīh iv, **286b** — IV, **299a**
Īwān i, 950a, 1228b; ii, 114a, 115b; iv, **287a**, 1073b, 1137a, 1138b, 1141b, 1146b — I, 979b, 1265a; II, 116b, 118a; IV, **299b**, 1105a, 1132a, b, 1134b, 1138a
Iwāẓ (ʿIwāḍ) Bey ii, 233b — II, 240a
ʿIwāz (Iwāḍ) Khaldjī, Ghiyāth al-Dīn ii, 267b; iii, 1155a — II, 275b; III, 1183b
ʿIwāz Khaldjī, Ḥusayn al-Dīn i, 393b — I, 405a
Iya basi ii, 124b — II, 127b
Iyād (tribe/tribu) ii, 196b, 197b; iv, **289a**; v, 77a, b, 639b, 640a — II, 202b, 203a, b; IV, **301b**; V, 79b, 643b, 644a
ʿIyāḍ b. Ghānim i, 329a, 635b, 679b, 695a, 1206b; ii, 344b, 523b, 624a, 625b; iii, 20a, 228a; iv, 841b — I, 339b, 656b, 700b, 716b, 1242b; II, 354b, 536b, 639b, 641a; III, 21a, 234b; IV, 874b
ʿIyāḍ b. Mūsā al-Ḳāḍī i, 602b; ii, 743b; iii, 680b, 707b, 867b; iv, 183b, **289b**, 912b; v, 71b, 1208b; s, 27a — I, 622a; II, 762a; III, 702b, 729b, 891b; IV, 191b, **302b**, 945b; V, 73b, 1199a; S, 27b
Iyāḍ b. Sūd, Banū iv, 289b — IV, 302b
al-Iyādī s, 306a — S, 306a
ʿIyāfa ii, 760a; iv, **290b** — II, 778b; IV, **303a**
ʿIyāl Manṣūr iii, 49b — III, 51b
ʿIyāl Zāyid ii, 175b — II, 181a
Iyāla → Eyālet
ʿIyār → Sikka
ʿIyār-i Dānish → Kalīla wa-Dimna
Iyās b. Ḳabīsa i, 689b, 690a; ii, 241a; v, 634a — I, 710b, 711a; II, 248a; V, 638a
Iyās b. Muʿāwiya iv, **291a** — IV, **304a**
Izadyār b. Masʿūd i, 217b — I, 224a
Izâfet → Iḍāfa
Izār (garment/vêtement) iii, 1053a; v, 732b, 733a — III, 1079a; V, 738a, b
Izmail → Ismāʿīl (Izmail)
Izmīd v, 250a — V, 247b, 248a
Izmīr i, 464a, 476a, 783b, 1335b; ii, 599a, b; iii, 210b, 214b; v, 505a, 1170a; s, 44b, 67b — I, 477b, 490b, 806b, 1375b; II, 613b, 614b; III, 216b, 220b; V, 508b, 1160a; S, 45a, 68a
- institutions ii, 425b — II, 436b
Iznīḳ i, 477a; ii, 746b; iv, **291b**, 702a, 1169a, b; v, 103b; s, 204a, 330b — I, 491a; II, 765a; IV, **304b**, 730b, 1201b, 1202b; V, 105b; S, 203b, 330a
- monuments iv, 291b, 292a — IV, 304b, 305a
al-Iznīḳī, Abu 'l-Faḍl Mūsā i, 137a — I, 141a
al-Iznīḳī, Ḳuṭb al-Dīn iii, 711a; v, **547a** — III, 733b; V, **551b**
Izraʿ v, 593b — V, 597a
ʿIzrāʾīl iv, **292b**; v, 210a — IV, **305b**; V, 207b
ʿIzz al-Dawla iv, **293b** — IV, **306b**
ʿIzz al-Dawla Bakhtiyār → Bakhtiyār
ʿIzz al-Dawla al-Bakrī → ʿAbd al-ʿAzīz al-Bakrī
ʿIzz al-Dīn b. al-Athīr → Ibn al-Athīr
ʿIzz al-Dīn b. Djahāndār ii, 379b; iii, 200a — II, 389b; III, 205a
ʿIzz al-Dīn b. Shudjaʿ al-Dīn v, 828b, 829a — V, 834b, 835a
ʿIzz al-Dīn Aybak (Mamlūk) → Aybak, ʿIzz al-Dīn al-Muʿaẓẓamī
ʿIzz al-Dīn Aybak (d./m. 1257) i, 732a, 804a, 944b — I, 754a, 828b, 973b
ʿIzz al-Dīn Aydimur al-Ḥillī i, 814b — I, 837b
ʿIzz al-Dīn Farrukh-Shāh v, 1139b — V, 1133b
ʿIzz al-Dīn Ḥusayn ii, 1100a — II, 1126a
ʿIzz al-Dīn Kaykāwus → Kaykāʾūs I, II
ʿIzz al-Dīn Khān-i Ayāz s, 66b — S, 67a
ʿIzz al-Dīn Shīr iv, 586a — IV, 609a
ʿIzz al-Dīn al-Sulamī → al-Sulamī
ʿIzz al-Dīn Usāma i, 208a; iv, 779a — I, 214a; IV, 810b
ʿIzz al-Mulk i, 1052b — I, 1084a
ʿIzzat al-Dawla s, 70b — S, 71a
ʿIzzet ʿAbed Pasha i, 64a; iii, 364a — I, 66a; III, 375b
ʿIzzet Bey ii, 641a — II, 657a
ʿIzzet Efendi iv, 1126a — IV, 1158a
ʿIzzet Molla i, 558a; ii, 934b; iv, **295a**; v, 710b, 1083b — I, 576a; II, 956b; IV, **308a**; V, 715b, 1081a
ʿIzzet Muḥammad Pasha iii, 627b — III, 648a
ʿIzzet Pasha → Aḥmad ʿIzzet; Ḥasan ʿIzzet
ʿIzzet Pasha (Furgaç) iv, **296a** — IV, **309b**
ʿIzzī Süleymān Efendi iv, **298b** — IV, **311b**

J

Jackal → Ibn Āwā
Jacob → Isrāʾīl; Yaʿḳūb
Jacob b. Reuben iv, 605b — IV, 629b
Jacob b. Simeon iv, 605b — IV, 629b
Jacobites → Yaʿḳūbiyya
Jactance → Mufākhara
Jaén → Djayyān
Jaffa → Yāfā
Jain → Djayn
Jaipur s, 140b, 142b — S, 140b, 142a
Jajce i, 1018a, 1263b — I, 1049a, 1302a
Jakarta → Djakarta
Jamna, river/rivière → Djamna
Janina → Yaniya
Janissaries/Janissaires → Devshirme; Yeni Čeri
Japan/Japon → Yābān
Japanese/Japonais i, 746a; ii, 478b; iii, 1229b — I, 768a; II, 490b; III, 1261b
Japara s, 201a, b — S, 201a, b
Japhet → Yāfith
Japheth b. Eli iv, 305b, 605a — IV, 319b, 629b
Japheth al-Barḳamānī iv, 605b — IV, 629b
Jardins → Bustān
Jasmin(e) → Yāsamīn
Jassy → Yash
Jativa → Shātiba
Jawnpur → Djawnpur
Java i, 170b, 174a, 981a; ii, 352a, 497a; iii, 566b, 1213a, b, 1214b, 1218b, 1219b, 1222a, b, 1226a; iv, 1128a; v, 225b, 226b, 227b, 1154b — I, 175a, 178b, 1011b; II, 362a, 509b; III, 586a, 1243b, 1244b, 1249b, 1250a, 1253a, b, 1257b; IV, 1159b; V, 223a, 224a, 225a, 1144a
Jaxartes ii, 778a, 790a, 791a; → Sīr Daryā
Jbala v, 1200b, 1203b — V, 1190b, 1194a
Jean-Baptiste → Yaḥyā b. Zakariyyāʾ
Jehlam (river/fleuve) s, 156a — S, 156a
Jellābas → Djallāb
Jenghiz Khan → Čingiz Khān
Jerboa → Faʾr
Jeremiah → Irmiyya
Jerez → Sharīs
Jericho → Rīḥā
Jerusalem/Jérusalem → al-Ḳuds
Jeshuah b. Judah iv, 305a, 605a, 607a — IV, 319a, 629b, 631a
Jessore → Djassawr
Jesus/Jésus → ʿĪsā
Jethro → Shuʿayb
Jeûne → Ramaḍān; Ṣawm
Jeunes Turcs → Yeni Othmanlîlar
Jeux → Ḳimār; Laʿib; Maysir
Jewelry → Djawhar; Libās; Ṣiyāgha
Jews → Yahūd
Jimeno, Count/Comte i, 161a; iii, 771b — I, 165b; III, 794b
Jinnah → Djināh
Joaillerie → Djawhar; Libās; Ṣiyāgha
Job → Ayyūb
Jōʾēl, Rabbi iv, 505b — IV, 527b
John the Baptist → Yaḥyā b. Zakariyyāʾ
Johore s, 150b, 151b — S, 150b, 152a
Jonah/Jonas → Yūnus
Jordan/Jordanie → Urdunn
Jordan, river/Jourdain, rivière i, 1017a; ii, 555a — I, 1048a; II, 569a
Joscelin of Edessa/Josselin d'Édesse i, 664b, 983a — I, 684a, 1013b
Joseph → Yūsuf
Joseph b. Noah → Yūsuf b. Nūḥ
Joseph ha-Rōʾeh → Yūsuf al-Baṣīr
Joshua/Josué → Yūshaʿ
Joshua ben Judah → Jeshuah b. Judah
Jour → Layl et Nahār
Jourdain → al-Urdunn
Journal → Djarīda
Journals/Journaux → Periodicals/Périodiques, Ouvrages
Joyaux → Djawhar
Judaeo-Arabic, Judéo-arabe i, 574b; iv, **299a**; v, 206b — I, 593b; IV, **312b**; V, 204a
Judaeo-Berber/Judéo-Berbère iv, **307b** — IV, **321a**
Judaeo-Persian/Judéo-Persan iv, **308a** — IV, **322a**
Judah Hadassī iv, 605b — IV, 629b
Judge/Juge → Ḳāḍī
Judgment/Jugement → Ḥukm
Jugement dernier → Ḳiyāma
Juifs → Yahūd
Jujube → ʿUnnāb
Jumblat → Djānbulāt
Jurisprudence → Fiḳh
Jusquiame → Bandj
Justice → ʿAdl
Jute → Khaysh

K

Ḳāʿa ii, 114b; iv, 428b — II, 117a; IV, 447a
Ḳaʿādi → al-Djarādatān[i]
Ḳaʾan → Khāḳān
Ḳāʾānčīs iv, 30b — IV, 33a
Ḳaʾānī, Ḥabīb Allāh ii, 433b; iii, 373a; iv, 69b, **313a** — II, 445a; III, 385a; IV, 73b, **327a**
Kaarta iv, **313b** — IV, **327b**
Kaʿb, Banū i, 441a; iii, 1102b, 1107a;iv, **314b**, 740a, 765a; v, 81a — I, 454a; III, 1130a, 1134b; IV, **328b**, 770a, 795b; V, 83a
Kaʿb b. ʿAmr, Banū v, 78b, 79a — V, 81a
Kaʿb b. Asad v, 436a — V, 438b
Kaʿb b. al-Ashraf iv, **315a** — IV, **329a**
Kaʿb b. Djuʿayl al-Taghlabī iv, **315a** — IV, **329a**
Kaʿb b. Mālik i, 50b; iii, 272b, 354a, 975b; iv, **315b** — I, 52a; III, 280a, 365a, 1000a; IV, **329b**
Kaʿb b. Māma i, 115b — I, 119a
Kaʿb b. Zuhayr i, 1011b, 1314b; iv, **316a**, 510a; v, 6b, 734a, 958b — I, 1042b, 1354b; IV, **330a**, 532a; V, 6b, 739b, 962b
Kaʿb al-Aḥbār i, 926b; ii, 363; iii, 370a; iv, 212a, **316b**, 1135b; v, 324a, 1231b — I, 955a; II, 373b; III, 382a; IV, 221b, **330b**, 1167a; V, 323b, 1222a
Kaʿba i, 55b, 136a, 178a, 268a, 453a, 551b, 608b, 867a, 892b, 1054a; ii, 247a, 453a, 603b, 695b; iii, 33a, 40a, 101a, 980b; iv, 184a, b, 260a, **317a**; 926a; v, 77b, 78a, 434a, b, 435b, 520a, 990b — I, 57a, 140a, 182b, 276a, 466a, 569a, 628b, 891b, 919a, 1086a; II, 254b, 465a, 618b, 713a; III, 34b, 42a, 103b, 1005a; IV, 192b, 271b, **331a**, 959a; V, 79b, 80a, 436b, 438a, 523b, 985b
Ḳabā, ḳabāʾ v, 739b, 743b, 748a, b, 749a, b — V, 744b, 749a, 753b, 754a, b, 755a
al-Kaʿba al-Yamāniya ii, 241b — II, 248b
Kabābīr iii, 326a — III, 336a
Kabābīsh v, 267a, 268a — V, 264b, 266a
Ḳabača, Nāṣir al-Dīn → Nāṣir al-Dīn Ḳabača
Kabadian → Ḳubādhiyān
Ḳabādiyān ii, 1a, 2a — II, 1a, 2a
Ḳabadj Khātūn i, 1293b — I, 1333a
Kabāʾir iv, 1107b, 1108b — IV, 1139a, 1140a

Kabak → Kebek
Ḳabaḳbāzī → Laʿb
Kabakčî-oghlu Muṣṭafā ii, 713a; iv, **322b** — II, 731a; IV, **337a**
Ḳabāla(t) i, 1144a; ii, 145b; iv, **323a**, 1032a, 1040a — I, 1178b; II, 149b; IV, **337a**, 1064a, 1071b
Kabards i, 1000a, 1189b; ii, 21b, 22a, b; iii, 1235b; iv, **324b**, 596b; v, 288b — I, 1031a, 1224b; II, 22a, b, 23a; III, 1267b; IV, **339a**, 620b; V, 286b
Kabartāy (Kaberda) ii, 25a — II, 25b
al-Ḳabbāb iv, **325b** — IV, **339b**
Ḳabbān → Mīzān
Ḳabḍ (contraction) i, 1088b; iii, 361a; iv, 326a — I, 1121a; III, 372b; IV, 340b
Ḳabḍ (possession) iii, 350a; iv, **325b** — III, 361a; IV, **340a**
al-Kaʿbī i, 204b; ii, 518b; s, 32a, 225b — I, 201b; II, 531b; S, 32a, 225b
Kabid iv, **327a** — IV, **341a**
Ḳābiḍ iv, **333b**, v, 41b — IV, **348a**; V, 42b
Ḳabīḥa Umm al-Muʿtazz s, 252b — S, 252b
Ḳābīl → Hābīl wa-Ḳābīl
al-Ḳābil s, 355b — S, 355a
Ḳabil Khān iv, 760a — IV, 790a
Ḳabīla i, 700a; iv, **334a**, 362a — I, 721b; IV, **348b**, 377b
Kabīr i, 1166a; iii, 456b, 459b; v, 630b — I, 1200b; III, 472b, 475b; V, 634b
Kabīr Panthīs → Supplement
Ḳābis i, 950a; iv, **335b**; s, 11a, 334a — I, 979b; IV, **350a**; S, 10b, 334a
al-Ḳabīṣī, ʿAbd al-ʿAzīz Abu ʾl-Ṣaḳr iv, **340b** — IV, **355a**
al-Ḳābisī, Abu ʾl-Ḥasan ʿAlī iv, **341a**; s, 26b — IV, **355b**; S, 27a
Ḳabḳ i, 18a, 270b, 380a; iv, 324b, **341b**; v, 287b, 288b, 495b; s, 136a, 143a, 169a, 218b — I, 18b, 279a, 391a; IV, 339a, **356a**; V, 286a, 287a, 498b; S, 135b, 142b, 169a, 218b
Ḳablān al-Ḳāḍī al-Tanūkhī ii, 433b — II, 455b
Ḳabludja → Ḳaplîdja
Kabou iv, **351b** — IV, **367a**
Kaboul → Kābul
Ḳabr iv, **352a**; v, 214b — IV, **367a**; V, 212a
Ḳabr Hūd i, 1045a; iii, 538a; s, 337b — I, 1076b; III, 556b; S, 337a
Ḳabra iv, **355a** — IV, **370b**
Kabsh → Badw (IIa); Silāḥ; Yürük; Zakāt
Kabsha/Kubaysha s, 394a — S, 394b
al-Kabtawrī, Abu ʾl-Ḳāsim iv, **355b** — IV, **371a**
Kabudhān s, 130b — S, 129b
Kābul i, 72a, 86a, 87b, 222a, b, 223a, 226b, 238a, b, 970a, 1347b; iii, 576a; iv, 175a, **356a**; v, 649a; s, 41a, 63a, 66a, b, 122a, 237a, b, 270a, 285a — I, 74a, 88b, 90a, 228b, 229a, b, 233b, 245a, b, 1000a, 1388a; III, 596a; IV, 182b, **371b**; V, 653a; S, 41b, 63b, 66a, 67a, 121a, 237a, b, 270a, 285a
- University/Université ii, 426a — II, 437a
Ḳabūl → Bayʿ
Ḳabūl Aḥmad ii, 1046a — II, 1070a
Kābul-Shāhs iv, 208a, 356b — IV, 217b, 371b, 372a
Ḳabūla al-Hindī iii, 104b — III, 107a
Kābulistān iv, **357b** — IV, **373a**
Ḳābūs b. Muṣʿab ii, 917b — II, 939a
Ḳābūs b. Wushmagīr (Wushmgīr) b. Ziyār i, 211b, 591a, 1110a, 1236a; ii, 748b, 1139b; iv, **357b**; v, 1028a; s, 13a, 361b — I, 218a, 610a, 1143b, 1274a; II, 767a, 1166b; IV, **373b**; V, 1024a; S, 13b, 361b
Ḳābūs al-Lakhmid v, 633b — V, 637b
Ḳābūs-nāma iv, 815a — IV, 848a
Kabyle, language/langue i, 1184a, b; iv, 361a — I, 1219a, b; IV, 376b
Kabyles i, 371a, 371b, 372a, 374a, 1177b; ii, 537b, 603b; iii, 607a; iv, 360b-363a — I, 382a, 382b, 383a, 384b, 1212b; II, 551a, 618b; III, 627b; IV, 376a-379a
Kabylia/Kabylie i, 171a, 365a, 369b, 433b; ii, 603b; iv, 75b, **358b**; s, 190a — I, 176a, 376a, 380b, 446a; II, 618a; IV, 79b, **374a**; S, 191a
Kačawča s, 74a — S, 74b
Ḳačḳun ii, 147a — II, 151a
Kaččh v, 689b — V, 694b
Kaččh(ī) Gandāwa iv, **364a**, 534b — IV, **380a**, 557b
Ḳaḍāʾ (divine decree/décret divin) i, 89b, 90a, 413a, 413b; ii, 618a; iv, **364b** — I, 92b, 424b, 425a; II, 633b; IV, **380b**
Ḳaḍāʿ (religious duty/service religieux) i, 169b — I, 174b
Ḳaḍā (region/région) i, 469a — I, 482b, 483a
al-Ḳaḍāʾ wa ʾl-Ḳadar iv, **365a** — IV, **381a**
Ḳadāḥ v, 989b — V, 984b
Ḳadam v, 95b — V, 98a
Ḳadam Sharīf iv, **367b** — IV, **383b**
Ḳadar i, 89b, 90a, 407a, 408b, 413a, 413b, 958b; ii, 365a, 374b, 618a; iii, 659a, 870b; iv, **365a**; v, 3b — I, 92b, 419a, 420b, 424b, 425a, 988a; II, 375a, 385a, 633b; III, 680b, 894b; IV, **381a**, b; V, 4a
al-Ḳaḍārif iv, 686a, 687a — IV, 714a, 715a
Ḳadariyya i, 124a, 276b, 412b; iii, 248a, 494b, 990b, 1142b; iv, 366a, **368a**, 734b, 938a; v, 936a; s, 358a — I, 127b, 285a, 424a; III, 255a, 511b, 1015a, 1170b; IV, 382a, **384b**, 764a, 971a; V, 940a; S, 358a
Ḳadāsa iv, **372a** — IV, **388b**
Ḳaddāḥid(e)s i, 48b; ii, 851b — I, 50a; II, 871a
Ḳaddūr al-ʿAlamī iv, **372b** — IV, **389a**
Ḳaddūra al-Djazāʾirī iv, **373a** — IV, **389b**
Kadets iii, 530b, 531a — III, 549a, b
Ḳadhf i, 29b; iii, 20b; iv, **373a**; v, 730b — I, 30b; III, 21b; IV, **389b**; V, 735b
al-Ḳadhdhāfī, Muʿammar v, 758b, 1067a — V, 764b, 1064a
Ḳāḍī i, 491a, 741b; ii, 119a, 519b, 867a, 888a, 890b; iii, 487b, 492a, 1152b, 1153a; iv, 365a, **373b**, 941a; v, 631a, 1133a, b — I, 506a, 763b; II, 121b, 532b, 887a, 908b, 911a; III, 504b, 509a, 1180b, 1181b; IV, 381a, **390a**, 974a; V, 635a, 1128b, 1129a
Ḳāḍī b. Muḥammad b. Walmiya iv, 337a — IV, 351b
Ḳāḍī-ʿaskar i, 480b, 712a; iii, 1152b; iv, **375b**, 735b — I, 495a, 733b; III, 1180b; IV, **392a**, 765b
Ḳāḍi ʾl-djamāʿa iv, 374b — IV, 390b
al-Ḳāḍī al-Fāḍil i, 150a, 594a, 801b; ii, 127a, 305b, 329b; iii, 679b, 863a, 901a; iv, **376a**, 613b, 614b; s, 124a — I, 154a, 613a, 824b; II, 130a, 314a, 339a; III, 701a, 887a, 925a; IV, **392b**, 638a, 639a; S, 123a
al-Ḳāḍī al-Harawī → al-ʿAbbādī
Ḳāḍī-Khān iii, 163b; iv, **377a** — III, 167a; IV, **393b**
Ḳāḍi ʾl-Ḳuḍāt i, 164b; iv, 374a — I, 169a; IV, 390a, b
Ḳāḍī Meḥmed → Lālezārī, Shaykh Meḥmed
Ḳāḍī Muḥammad ii, 88b; iii, 157a; iv, **377a**; v, 466a, b, 1213a, b — II, 90a; III, 160b; IV, **393b**; V, 469a, 1202b, 1203a
al-Ḳāḍī Nuʿmān → Nuʿmān
al-Ḳāḍī al-Rashīd b. al-Zubayr s, 251b — S, 251b
al-Ḳāḍī al-Saʿīd → Ibn Sanāʾ al-Mulk
al-Ḳāḍī al-Tahartī → Ibn al-Rabīb
Ḳaḍīb iv, **377b**, 940a — IV, **394a**, 973a
Ḳadīm v, 96a, b — V, 98a, b
Ḳādimīs ii, 366b — II, 376b
Ḳadîn → Marʾa; Sarāy
al-Ḳādir → al-Asmāʾ al-ḥusnā
al-Ḳādir → Yaḥya al-Ḳādir
al-Ḳādir biʾllāh i, 1352b, 1353a, 1355a; iii, 159a, 255b, 256a, 735a, 860a; iv, **378a**, 940b, 942a; s, 14b, 118a, b, 119a, 253b, 361b — I, 1391b, 1392a, 1394a; III,

162b, 263a, 758a, 884a; IV, **394b**, 973b, 975a; S, 15a, 117b, 118a, 253b, 361b
Ḳādir Khān, Yūsuf i, 662a; ii, 4b; iii, 347b, 1114a; v, 38b — I, 683a; II, 4b; III, 358b, 1141b; V, 39b
Ḳādir Shāh iii, 421b, 422b, 426a; iv, 276b — III, 435a, 436b, 439b; IV, 288b
Ḳādirī, ʿAbd al-Madjīd s, 74a — S, 74b
al-Ḳādirī, Abū ʿAbd Allāh iv, **379a**; s, 404b — IV, **395b**; S, 404b
Ḳādīrī Celebi iv, 333b — IV, 348a
al-Ḳādirī al-Ḥasanī, Abu 'l-ʿAbbās iv, **379b** — IV, **396a**
al-Ḳādirī al-Ḥasanī, Abū ʿAbd Allāh iv, **380a** — IV, **396b**
al-Ḳādirī al-Ḥasanī, Abu 'l-Faḍāʾil → al-Ḳādirī al-Ḥasanī, Abu 'l-ʿAbbās
al-Ḳāḍirī al-Ḥasanī, Abu Muḥammad iv, **380a**, 382a, 1085a — IV, **396b**, 398b, 1116a
Ḳādiriyya i, 69a, 257b, 281a, 303a, 371a, 782a, 1009a, 1173a, 1260b; ii, 10a, 58b, 63b, 94b, 134b, 164a, 535b, 710a, 975a, 1003b, 1004a; iii, 103b, 160b, 176a, 646b; iv, **380b**, 549b, 951a; v, 287b, 393b, 475a; s, 5a, 182b, 282b, 283a, 293a, 303a, 322a — I, 70b, 265b, 289b, 313a, 382a, 805a, 1040a, 1208a, 1298b; II, 10a, 59b, 64b, 96b, 138a, 169b, 549a, 729a, 997b, 1026b, 1027a; III, 106a, 164a, 180a, 667b; IV, **397a**, 573b, 983b; V, 286a, 394b, 478a; S, 4a, 182b, 282b, 292b, 303a, 321b
Ḳādiriyya Bakkāya ii, 1132a — II, 1158b
Ḳādis iv, **383a** — IV, **400a**
al-Ḳādisiyya iv, **384a**; s, 198b — IV, **400b**; S, 198b
Ḳādisiyya (battle/bataille) ii, 893b; iii, 194b, 1254b; iv, 384b, 385a-386b, 775a; v, 634a — II, 914a; III, 199b, 1287a; IV, 401a, 401b-403a, 806b; V, 638a
Kadiwala sayyids v, 26b — V, 27b
Ḳādiyānī → Aḥmadiyya
Ḳādīzāde Aḥmed Shams al-Dīn v, 27b — V, 28b
Ḳāḍī-zāde ʿAlī i, 1284b — I, 1324a
Ḳāḍī-zāde Meḥmed Beg i, 293b — I, 302b
Ḳaḍī-zāde-i Rūmī i, 393a, 869a; iv, 702b — I, 404b, 893a; IV, 731a
Ḳādjār (dynasty/dynastie) i, 13b, 36a, 190b, 246b, 296a, 720b, 1250b; ii, 150a, b, 151a, 309a, 334b, 433b, 654b, 656a; iii, 554a, 1100a, 1101b, 1103b; iv, 38a, 51a, 294a, **387b**, 577b, 1052b; v, 371b, 461b, 630a; s, 70b, 71a, 104a, 257a, b, 260b, 302a, 336a, 405b — I, 14a, 37a, 196a, 254a, 305a, 742a, 1288b; II, 154b, 155a, b, 318a, 344a, 444b, 671a, 672b; III, 573a, 1127a, 1129a, 1130b; IV, 40b, 53b, 307a, **404a**, 601a, 1084a; V, 372a, 464b, 634b; S, 71a, b, 103b, 256b, 257b, 260b, 302a, 335b, 405b
Ḳādjār (tribe/tribu) iii, 1100a, 1101b, 1103b; iv, **387a** — III, 1127a, 1129a, 1130b; IV, **403b**
al-Kadjgharī → ʿAbd al-Ghāfir
Kadkhudā i, 978a; iv, 103b — I, 1008b; IV, 108a
Ḳadmūs iv, 200a — IV, 209a
Ḳadm-i Rasūl ii, 32a — II, 32b
Ḳadr → Ḳaḍā; Ramaḍān
Ḳadr Khān → Ḳādir Khān
Ḳadrī iii, 114a; iv, **399a** — III, 116b; IV, **416b**
Ḳadrī Bey ii, 657b; iv, 853a — II, 674a; IV, 886b
Ḳāf (mountains/montagnes) i, 926b; iii, 332a; iv, 342a, **400b** — I, 955a; III, 342a; IV, 356a, b, **418a**
al-Kāf iv, 402b — IV, 419b
Kāf(k) iv, **399a** — IV, **416b**
Ḳāf(ḳ) iv, **400a** — IV, **417a**
Kafa → Kefe
Kafāʾa iv, **404a**, 1161b — IV, **421b**, 1193b
al-Kafādjī i, 1056b — I, 1088a
Kafāla iv, **404b** — IV, **422a**
al-Kaff (ʿIlm-) iv, **405b** — IV, **423a**
Kaff → ʿArūḍ; Ḳuʿūd
Kaffa → Kefe
Kaffāra iv, **406b**, 688a, 768a — IV, **424a**, 716a, 798b
Kāfī → Ḥasan Kāfī
al-Kāfī Zaʿīm al-Ruʾasāʾ ii, 384b — II, 395a
Kafīl → Kafāla
Ḳāfila → Karwān; Tidjāra
Ḳāfilat al-Sūdān ii, 137b — II, 141a
Kāfir i, 224b, 225a; iv, **407b**, 410b; v, 649a — I, 231a, 231b; IV, **425a**, 428b; V, 653a
Kāfir (language/langue) ii, 138a, b; iv, 409b — II, 142a; IV, 427a
Kāfiristān i, 223b; ii, 140a; iv, **409a**; s, 237a, b — I, 230a; II, 143b; IV, **427a**; S, 237a
Kāfirkūb(āt) iv, 44b, **411a** — IV, 47a, **429a**
Kāfirnihān ii, 2a — II, 2a
Ḳāfiya iv, **411b**; v, 320b — IV, **429b**; V, 320a
al-Kāfiyadjī iv, **414b** — IV, **432b**
Kāfiyya v, 740a — V, 745b
Ḳafīz → Makāyīl
Kafr ʿAwaḍ Allāh Ḥidjāzī s, 262b — S, 262a
Kafr al-Ḥiṣāfa s, 371a — S, 371a
Ḳafsa i, 161b; iv, **414b**; v, 1181b — I, 166a; IV, **433a**; V, 1171b
Ḳafṭān v, 737b, 739b, 752a — V, 743a, 745a, 757b
Kaftar s, 127a — S, 126a
Kāfūr iv, **417b** — IV, **435b**
Kāfūr Hazārdīnārī i, 444b; ii, 12b, 179b, 269a, 272a, 1084b, 1085a, 1124a; iv, **419a**, 921b, 922a, 923b, 1023a; v, 938a, 1258b; s, 105a — I, 457b; II, 13a, 185a, 277a, 280b, 1109b, 1110b, 1150b; IV, **437a**, 954b, 955a, 956b, 1055a; V, 941b, 1249b; S, 104b
Kāfūr al-Ikhshīdī i, 34a, 1042a; ii, 793b, 1080b; iii, 768b, 840b; iv, **418a**, 673b, 1091b; v, 327a, b, 619a — I, 34b, 1073b; II, 812a, 1105b; III, 791b, 864b; IV, **436b**, 701a, 1122b; V, 327a, 623a
Kāghad ii, 311a; iv, **419b**, 742a, 1114b; v, 854b — II, 320a; IV, **437b**, 772a, 1146a; V, 861b
Kaghalgha → Ḳalghay
Kāghān iii, 335b — III, 345b
Ḳaghan → Khāḳān
al-Kahf → Aṣḥāb al-Kahf
al-Ḳaḥḥāl → ʿAlī b. ʿĪsā
Kāhin i, 585b, 659b; iv, **420b**; v, 235a, 420a, 422a, 1101a — I, 604a, 680b; IV, **438b**; V, 233a, 422a, 424a, 1097a
Kāhina i, 367a, 770b, 1175a; iii, 271a, 296a, 1039b; iv, **422a** — I, 378a, 793b, 1210a; III, 279a, 305a, 1065b; IV, **440b**
al-Ḳāhir biʾllāh i, 19a, 1039b; ii, 1080b; iii, 46a, 126b, 345a, 886b; iv, **423b**, 940a — I, 20a, 1071a; II, 1105b; III, 47b, 129b, 355b, 910b; IV, **442a**, 973a
Ḳāhir b. ʿAlī b. Ḳānit v, 926a — V, 931b
al-Ḳāhira i, 9a, 396b, 451b, 551b, 832a, 976a; ii, 128a, 495a, 854a, 958b; iii, 81a, 756b, 813a; iv, 215b, **424a**; v, 993a — I, 9b, 408a, 464b, 569b, 855b, 1006a; II, 131a, 507b, 873b, 980b; III, 83a, 779b, 836b; IV, 225a, **442b**; V, 988a
- fortifications iv, 428b, 429b, 430b, 436a; v, 92a — IV, 447a, 448b, 449b, 455b; V, 94b
- madrasas iv, 430a, 432a, 437a; v, 1125b, 1127b, 1140b, 1141a — IV, 449a, 451a, 456b; V, 1121b, 1124a, 1133b, 1134a
- modern city/ville moderne iv, 441b-444b — IV, 461b-464a
- monuments i, 620a, 621a-624, 813-821, 863a, b; iii, 81a, 190a; iv, 424a-428b, 438a, b, 439a, 440a — I, 640b, 641b-645, 837-844, 883a, b; III, 83a, 194b; IV, 442b-447a, 457b, 458a, 459a, b
- mosques/mosquées i, 620a, 814b; iv, 428b, 430a, 431a, 436b, 437b, 444b; v, 93a, 500b — I, 640b, 837b; IV, 447a, b, 449a, b, 455b, 457a, 464a; V, 95a, 503b
- population iv, 443a, b — IV, 463a, b
- tombs/tombes iv, 425a-428b, 429b, 430b, 434a —

IV, 443b-447a, 448a, 449a, b, 453a
- university/université i, 818a; ii, 132a, 424a; iv, 441b, 444a — I, 841a; II, 135a, 434b; IV, 461b, 464a
Kāhiya iv, 894b — IV, 927b
Ḳahḳaha iv, 188a — IV, 196a
Kahlān i, 544b; iv, 448a — I, 561b; IV, 468a
Kāhrabāʾ → Kahrubā
Ḳahramān-nāma i, 152b; iv, **444b** — I, 157a; IV, **464b**
Kahrubā iv, **445b** — IV, **465a**
Ḳahrūn b. Ghannūsh v, 59b — V, 61b
Ḳaḥṭaba b. Shabīb i, 16a, 16b, 108b, 141a, 1033b; iii, 988b; iv, 99b, **445b** — I, 16b, 17a, 111b, 145b, 1065a; III, 1013a; IV, 104a, **465b**
Ḳaḥṭān i, 544b, 545b, 873b; ii, 176a; iii, 363b, 1065b; iv, **447b**; s, 338a — I, 561b, 563a, 897b; II, 181b; III, 375a, 1092a; IV, **467b**; S, 337b
Ḳahwa i, 540a, 1140b; ii, 1063a; iii, 179a; iv, **449a**; v, 109b — I, 557a, 1175a; II, 1078b; III, 183a; IV, **469a**; V, 112a
Kaḥyā → Ketkhudā
Kaḥyā (Djenāze) Ḥasan Pasha iv, **455b** — IV, **476a**
Ḳāʿid i, 977a; ii, 507b; iv, **456a**; v, 1198b — I, 1007b; II, 520a; IV, **476a**; V, 1188b
al-Ḳāʾid b. Ḥammād iii, 137a; v, 623b, 1177b — III, 140a; V, 627b, 1167b
Ḳaïdes iv, 384b — IV, 401b
Ḳāʾif → Ḳiyāfa
al-Ḳāʾim bi-amr Allāh (ʿAbbāsid(e)) (1031-75) i, 132b, 420a, 461b, 1073b, 1074b, 1075a; ii, 384a; iii, 86b, 159b, 196a, 345b, 860b, 891a; iv, 26b, **457a**, 942a, b; v, 388b; s, 192a, b, 194a — I, 136a, 432a, 474b, 1105b, 1106b, 1107a; II, 394b; III, 88b, 163a, 200b, 356a, 885a, 915a; IV, 28b, **477b**, 975a; V, 389a; S, 193a, b
al-Ḳāʾim (ʿAbbāsid(e)) (1451-55) iii, 1198b — III, 1228b
al-Ḳāʾim (Fāṭimid(e)) i, 699b, 1355b; ii, 491a, 851a, 853a; iv, **458b**; v, 1243b, 1246b; s, 62b, 236b — I, 720b, 1395a; II, 503b, 871a, 872b; IV, **478b**; V, 1234a, b, 1237a; S, 63a, 236b
Ḳāʾim Āl Muḥammad (Mahdī) iv, 203b, 204a, **456b**; v, 1235b — IV, 212b, 213a, **477a**; V, 1226a, b
Ḳāʾim Khān iii, 60a — III, 62b
Ḳāʾim-maḳām ii, 444a; iv, **461b** — II, 455b; IV, **482a**
Ḳāʾim-maḳām-i Farāhānī, Abū ʾl-Ḳāsim iv, 70b, 394a, **462a**; s, 73a — IV, 74a, 410b, **482b**; S, 73b
Ḳāʾim-maḳām-i Farāhānī, ʿĪsā iv, **462a**; v, 919a — IV, **482b**; V, 924b
Ḳāïmāz i, 1160b — I, 1195a
Ḳāʾime i, 693a; iv, **460a** — I, 714a; IV, **480b**
Ḳāʾin v, 354b, 355a, b — V, 356a, b, 357a
Kairowan/Kairovan → Ḳayrawān
Kaisos → Ḳays b. Salama
Ḳāʾitbāy (mosque/mosquée) s, 44a — S, 44b
Ḳāʾitbāy (Mamlūk) i, 281a, 349a, 553a, 815a, 1060a, 1119b, 1190b, 1234a, 1281a, 1317b; ii, 166b, 286a, 529b, 530a; iii, 48b, 186b, 346a; iv, 133a, 429a, 432a, **462b**, 563a, 642b, 960a; v, 304a, 1143b; s, 208a, b — I, 289b, 360a, 571a, 838a, 1091b, 1153a, 1226a, 1270b, 1320a, 1358b; II, 172a, 294a, 542b, 543a; III, 50b, 190b, 357a; IV, 138b, 447b, 451a, **483a**, 585a, 669a, 992b; V, 303b, 1136a; S, 208a
Ḳāʾitbāy b. Muḥammad i, 1032b — I, 1064a
al-Ḳaʿḳāʿ iv, **463b** — IV, **484a**
al-Ḳaʿḳaʿ b. ʿAmr iv, **464a** — IV, **484b**
al-Ḳaʿḳāʿ b. Maʿbad al-Tamīmī iv, 463b — IV, 484b
Kākāʾī i, 262b — I, 271a
Kākawayhid(e)s i, 1356a; iv, **465a**; v, 824a — I, 1395a; IV, **485b**; V, 830a
Kʾakh ii, 22a — II, 22b
Kakheti v, 493a — V, 496a
Kakhtā iv, **464a** — IV, **485a**
Kāḳshāls iii, 423b — III, 437b
Ḳāḳūn iv, 842b — IV, 875b
Kākūyid(e)s → Kākawayhid(e)s
Ḳalʿa → Agadir; Burdj; Ḥiṣār; Ḥiṣn; Ḳaṣaba
Ḳalʿa i, 367a, 904a, b, 1319b; ii, 863b; iii, 137a — I, 378a, 931b, 932a, 1359b; II, 883b; III, 139b
al-Ḳalʿa (castle/château) iv, **467a** — IV, **488a**
al-Ḳalʿa (Ḥammād) → Ḳalʿat Banī Ḥammād
Kalā (island/île) → Kalah
al-Ḳalʿa al-Bayḍāʾ → Ḳalʿe-i Sefīd
Ḳalʿa Kuhrūd v, 662a — V, 667b
al-Kalābādhī iii, 84a, 102b; iv, **467a**, 616b, 696b — III, 86a, 105a; IV, **488a**, 641a, 725a
Kalaband (Ottoman(e)) → Nafy
Kalāfa ii, 105a — II, 107b
Ḳalafat ii, 61b — II, 62b
Kalah iv, **467b**, 502a — IV, **488a**, 524a
Kalāh-bār iv, 468a — IV, 488b
Ḳalaʿī (tin/étain) → Ḳalʿī
al-Kalāʿī → Khālid b. Maʿdān
al-Kalāʿī, Abu ʾl-Rabīʿ b. Sālim iii, 804a; iv, **468a** — III, 827a; IV; **489a**
Ḳalʿa-i Dukhtār iv, 288a; v, 657b — IV, 300b; V, 663a
Ḳalʿa-i Iṣṭakhr iv, 221b, 222a — IV, 231b
Ḳalʿa-i Sefīd → Ḳalʿe-i Sefīd
Ḳalʿa-i Sulṭāniyya → Ḳalʿe-i Sulṭaniyye
Ḳalʿa-yi Dabūs s, 176b — S, 177b
Kalām i, 60b, 113a, 333a, 342b, 409b, 410a, 414a, 415b, 694b; ii, 449a, 608a, 618a; iii, 103b, 171b; iv, 46a, **468b**, 508b, 985a — I, 62b, 116b, 343a, 353a, 421b, 425b, 427a, 715b; II, 461a, 623a, 633b; III, 105b, 175a; IV, 48b, **489b**, 530b, 1017b
Ḳalam (pen/plume) iv, **471a**, 472a — IV, **491b**, 492b
Ḳalam (secretariat) iv, **471b** — IV, **492b**
Kalām (theology/théologie) → ʿIlm al-Kalām
Ḳalam al-Ṣāliḥiyya iv, 822b — IV, 855a
Ḳalama i, 1231a — I, 1268a
Kalaman i, 98a — I, 100b
Ḳalamdan → Ḳalam; Kitāba
Ḳalamdār iv, 471b; v, 988b — IV, 492a; V, 984a
Ḳalamkārī iv, **471b** — IV, **492b**
al-Ḳalammas iv, **472a** — IV, **493a**
Ḳalān iv, 31a, 1050a, b — IV, 33a, 1081b, 1082a
Kalān, Mīrzā i, 853a — I, 876b
Ḳalandar iv, 58b, **472b**; s, 352b — IV, 62a, **493a**; S, 352b
Ḳalandar Bakhsh → Djurʾat
Ḳalandariyya i, 104b; ii, 165a, 395a; iv, **473a** — I, 107b; II, 170a, 405b; IV, **493b**
Ḳalandariyyāt → Ḳalandar
al-Ḳalānisī, Aḥmad b. ʿAbd al-Raḥmān s, 392a — S, 392b
al-Ḳalānisī, Muḥammad i, 344b — I, 355a
Ḳalānisiyya s, 197a — S, 197a
Ḳalansuwa iv, 940a — IV, 973a
Kalāntar iv, 103b, **474a**; v, 155b; s, 275b, 405b — IV, 108a, **495a**; V, 156a; S, 275a, 405b
Kalāntar, Mīrzā Muḥammad s, 405b — S, 405b
Kalār s, 335a — S, 334b
Kalaśa s, 242a — S, 242a
Kalaṣa ii, 31a, 138b — II, 31b, 142a
al-Ḳalaṣādī, ʿAlī iv, **476b**, 725b — IV, **497b**, 754b
Kalāt i, 39a, 99b, 230a, 1006a; iii, 564b; iv, 364b, 395a, 535a, 1059b; v, **101b**, 580a, 684b; s, 222a, 332a — I, 40a, 102b, 237a, 1037a; III, 584a; IV, 380b, 412a, 558a, 1091a; V, **103b**, 584b, 690a; S, 222a, 331b
Ḳalʿat Abī Ṭawīl → Ḳalʿat Banī Ḥammād
Ḳalʿat Abū Safyān i, 145b — I, 150a
Ḳalʿat Ayyūb iv, **477b** — IV, **498b**
Ḳalʿat al-Azraḳ i, 780b — I, 803b

Ḳalʿat Banī ʿAbbās iv, **478a** — IV, **499a**
Ḳalʿat Banī Ḥammād i, 367a, 1319b, ii, 863b; iii, 137a; iv, **478b**, 1166a — I, 378a, 1359b; II, 883b; III, 139b; IV, **499b**, 1198a
Ḳalʿat Dawsar, Ḳalʿat Djaʿbar → Djaʿbar
Ḳalʿat Ḥammād → Ḳalʿa
Ḳalʿat Huwwāra iv, **481b** — IV, **502b**
Ḳalʿat al-Muhaylba → Balāṭunus
Ḳalʿat Nadjm iv, **482a** — IV, **502b**
Ḳalʿat Rabāh iii, 1055a, b; iv, **482b** — III, 1081a, 1082a; IV, **503b**
Ḳalʿat al-Rūm → Rūm Ḳalʿesī
Ḳalʿat al-Shaḳīf iv, **482b** — IV, **503b**
Ḳalʿat Sharḳāt → Athūr
Ḳalaṭa → Ghalaṭa
Ḳalʿat-i Nādirī iv, 38a; v, 59a, **102b** — IV, 40b; V, 61a, **105a**
Ḳalāʾun → Ḳalāwūn
Ḳalāwdhiya iv, **484a** — IV, **505a**
Ḳalawriya → Ḳillawriya
Ḳalāwūn, al-Malik al-Manṣūr (Mamlūk) i, 200b, 944b, 971a, 1016b, 1102b, 1127b, 1138a, 1224a, 1324b; ii, 38a, 285a, 305b, 353b; iii, 99a, 186b, 189a, 399b, 402b, 403a, 474b, 679b, 775b, 832b; iv, 464b, **484a**; v, 591a, 628a, 1140b; s, 205b, 389a — I, 206b, 974a, 1001a, 1048a, 1135b, 1162a, 1172b, 1260b, 1365b; II, 38b, 293a, 314a, 363a; III, 101b, 191a, 193b, 412a, 415a, b, 491a, 701a, 798b, 856b; IV, 485a, **505a**; V, 595a, 632a, 1134a; S, 205b, 389a
Kalaybar s, 116a — S, 115b
Ḳalb iv, **486a** — IV, **507a**
Kalb iv, **489b** — IV, **510b**
Kalb, Banū i, 550a; ii, 90a; iii, 838a; iv, **492b**, 820a; v, 1232a; s, 178a — I, 568a; II, 91b; III, 862a; IV, **513b**, 852b; V, 1222b; S, 179a
Kalb ʿAlī Khān ii, 84a — II, 85b
Kalb-i ʿAlī Khān Afshār i, 240b — I, 247b
Kalb b. Wabara iv, **492b**, 496a, 834a — IV, **513b**, 517b, 867a
Kalbāsī, Ḥādjdj Muḥammad Ibrāhīm s, 76a, 135a — S, 76a, 134b
al-Kalbī, ʿAbbās b. Hishām iv, **496a** — IV, **517a**
al-Kalbī, Hishām b. Muḥammad i, 210a, 758b; iii, 608a, 1047b; iv, 91b, **495a**; v, 350b; s, 31b, 177a — I, 216b, 781b; III, 628b, 1074a; IV, 95b, **516b**; V, 351b; S, 31b, 178a
al-Kalbī, Muḥammad b. al-Sāʾib iv, **495a**; s, 90b — IV, **516a**; S, 90a
al-Kalbī, al-Sāʾib b. Bishr iv, 494b — IV, 516a
al-Kalbī, Sulaymān b. Yaḳẓān s, 82a — S, 81b
Kalbīs (Syria)/Kalbites (Syrie) iii, 619a; iv, 370b — III, 639b; IV, 386b
Kalbides (Sicily, Sicile) i, 920a, 986b; ii, 553a; iv, **496a**; v, 105b — I, 947b, 1017a; II, 567a; IV, **517b**; V, 107b
Ḳalʿe → Ḳalʿa
Ḳalʿe-i Isfīd → Ḳalʿe-i Sefīd
Ḳalʿe-i Sefīd iv, **497b** — IV, **519a**
Ḳalʿe-i Sulṭāniyye ii, 11b — II, 11b
Ḳalender → Ḳalandar
Ḳalenderī → Ḳalandarīyya
Ḳalender-oghlū Meḥmed Pasha i, 267b, 510b, 826b, 1162b, 1334b; iii, 91b; iv, **499a**; s, 239a — I, 276a, 526b, 849a, 1197a. 1347b; III, 94a; IV, **520b**; S, 239a
Ḳalghay ii, 1113b; iv, **499b** — II, 1139b; IV, **521a**
Ḳalhāt iv, **500b** — IV, **522a**
al-Ḳalhātī iii, 235b — III, 242a
Kalhōrā i, 229b, 230b; ii, 185a, b, 186a; iii, 323b; iv, 364b — I, 236b, 237b; II, 191a, b; III, 333b; IV, 380b
Kalhur v, 168b, 460b, 659a — V, 166a, 463b, 663b
Ḳalʿī iv, 467b, **502a**; v, 964b, 967b — IV, 488a, **523b**; V, 969a
Kāl-i Shūr s, 235a — S, 234b
Kali → Ḳāḍī
Ḳālī (carpet/tapis) → Bisāṭ
Ḳălī → Erzurūm
al-Ḳālī, Abū ʿAlī i, 156a, 590a, 600a; iii, 845a; iv, **501a** — I, 160a, 609b, 619b; III, 868b; IV, **522b**
Ḳalīb i, 538b — I, 555a
Kalīdar s, 83b — S, 83a
Kālif iv, **502b**; s, 281a — IV, **524b**; S, 281a
Kalikat → Supplement
Ḳālīḳalā → Erzurūm
Kalikātā → Calcutta
Kalīla wa-Dimna i, 2b, 326b, 524b, 756a; ii, 758a, 951b; iii, 309a, 313b, 372b, 377a, 863a, 883b; iv, **503a**, 704a; s, 85b — I, 2b, 336b, 540a, 778b; II, 776a, 973b; III, 318b, 323a, 384b, 389a, 887a, 907b; IV, **524b**, 732b; S, 85b
Ḳalīm Abū Ṭālib iv, **506b** — IV, **528b**
Kalīm Allāh → Mūsā
Kalīm-Allāh Bahmanī i, 923b, 1047a, 1200a — I, 951b, 1079a, 1235b
Kalīm Allāh Djahānābādī ii, 55a; iv, **507a** — II, 56a; IV, **529a**
Kalima iv, 83a, **508a** — IV, 87a, **530a**
Kalimantan → Borneo/Bornéo
Kalimantan i, 1258b; iii, 1213a, b, 1215b, 1225b — I, 1297a; III, 1243b, 1244b, 1246a, 1257a
Kalīmī → Yahūd
Kalinin → Porsī
Káliz → Khalisioi
Ḳalḳaliyyūn s, 302b — S, 302a
al-Ḳalḳashandī (nisba) iv, 511a — IV, 533a
al-Ḳalkashandī, Aḥmad i, 119a, 239b, 430a, 595a, 761b; ii, 301b, 305b, 328a, 487a; iii, 344b, 487a, 1242b; iv, **509a**, 742b, 1119a; v, 627a; s, 1a, 203b — I, 122b, 247a, 442a, 614a, 784a; II, 310a, 314a, 337b, 499b; III, 354b, 504a, 1275a; IV, **531a**, 772b, 1151a; V, 631a; S, 1a, 203a
Kalkhur iii, 1102b, 1109a — III, 1129b, 1136a
al-Kallāʾ i, 1086a — I, 1118b
Ḳallabāt i, 49b; iv, 686a, 687a — I, 51a; IV, 714a, 715a
Ḳallabāt Gondar i, 49b — I, 51a
Ḳallala iv, **511a** — IV, **533b**
Kalmuk i, 121a, 135a, 422a, 722a, 1002b, 1028a; ii, 21b, 25a, 39a, 47a; iii, 117a, 1120b; iv, 213b, **512a**, 584a; v, 134b; s, 169a, 281a, 419b — I, 124b, 139a, 434a, 743b, 1033a, 1059b; II, 22a, 25a, 39b, 48a; III, 119b, 1148a; IV, 223a, **534a**, 607b; V, 137b; S, 169a, 281a, 419b
Ḳalpak v, 751b — V, 757b
Kalpī iii, 443b, 638b; iv, **513a**; s, 206b — III, 458a, 659b; IV, **535a**; S, 206a
al-Ḳalshănī i, 863a — I, 887a
Ḳalūdiya → Ḳalawdhiya
Ḳalūniya iv, 578b — IV, 602a
Ḳālūsh s, 269a — S, 268b
Kalwādhā iv, **513a** — IV, **535b**
al-Kalwadhānī, Abū 'l-Khaṭṭāb iii, 160a, 766b; iv, **513b**; s, 193a — III, 163b, 789b; IV, **535b**; S, 194a
Ḳalyān, Ḳalyūn → Baḥriyya; Safīna
Kalyānī i, 1323b; iv, **513b** — I, 1364a; IV, **536a**
Kalyar s, 313a — S, 312b
Ḳalyūb iv, **514a**; s, 371a — IV, **536a**; S, 371a
al-Ḳalyūbī, Shihāb al-Dīn iv, **515a** — IV, **537a**
al-Ḳalyūbiyya s, 121b — S, 121a
Kām Bakhsh i, 913b, 1202b — I, 941b, 1238b
Ḳamaʿa b. Khindif v, 76b, 77a — V, 79a
Kamadjas i, 1258a — I, 1296b
Ḳamaḥ → Kemākh
Kamāl → Kemāl
Kamāl, Shaykh s, 361a — S, 361a
Kamāl al-Dīn b. Arslan Khān Maḥmūd

(Ḳarā-Khānid) s, 245b — S, 245b
Kamāl al-Dīn Aḥmad b. Ṣadr al-Dīn i, 766b — I, 789b
Kamāl al-Dīn al-Fārisī iii, 1137a, 1139a; iv, **515b**, 804b; v, 397b, 547a — III, 1165a, 1167b; IV, **537b**, 836b; V, 398b, 552b
Kamāl al-Dīn Gurg ii, 405b, 1124a — II, 416b, 1150b
Kamāl al-Dīn Ḥusayn Beg i, 1191b — I, 1227a
Kamāl al-Dīn Ibn al-ʿAdīm → Ibn al-ʿAdīm
Kamāl al-Dīn Ismāʿīl (Ismāʿīl-i Iṣfahānī) iv, 62a, **515b**; s, 235b, 239b — IV, 65b, **538a**; S, 235b, 239b
Kamāl al-Dīn Ḳazwīnī ii, 54a — II, 55a
Kamāl al-Dīn Marʿashī, Sayyid v, 663a — V, 668a
Kamāl al-Dīn Shīr ʿAlī → Bannāʾī
Kamāl Ismāʿīl-i Iṣfahānī → Kamāl al-Dīn Ismāʿīl
Kamāl Khān ii, 973b — II, 995b
Kamāl Khudjandī i, 1301a; iv, **516b** — I, 1341a; IV, **538b**
Kamāl al-Mulk b. ʿAbd al-Raḥīm iii, 1201a — III, 1231b
Kamāl Pasha-zāde → Kemāl pasha-zāde
al-Kamāliyya iv, 991b — IV, 1024b
Kaman i, 606b — I, 626a
Kamanča → Malāhī
Ḳamāniča iv, **516b**; v, 260b — IV, **539a**; V, 258b
al-Ḳamar iv, **517a** — IV, **539b**
Ḳamar (singer/chanteuse) iv, 822a — IV, 855a
Ḳamar al-Dīn Dūghlāt ii, 622a — II, 637b
Ḳamar al-Dīn Khān i, 295b; iii, 59b — I, 304b; III, 62a
Ḳamar al-Zamān i, 359a — I, 370a
Ḳamarān i, 535b, 539a; iv, **519a** — I, 551b, 556a; IV, **541b**
Ḳambar Dīwāna iii, 482b — III, 499b
Kamenetz Podolski → Ḳamāniča
Kāmgār iv, 1018b — IV, 1050b
Ḳamḥ ii, 904a, 1062b; iv, **519b** — II, 924b, 1087b; IV, **542a**
Kamieniec → Ḳamāniča
Kāmil → ʿArūḍ
al-Kāmil → Shaʿbān I
Kāmil, Muṣṭafā → Muṣṭafā Kāmil
Kāmil Ḥusayn iii, 1207b; iv, 85b — III, 1238a; IV, 89b
Kāmil al-Ḥusaynī s, 67a, 68a — S, 67b, 68b
Kāmil Pasha i, 286a; ii, 643b, 698b; iii, 520a, 595a, 605b, 624a; iv, 284a — I, 294b; II, 659b, 716b; III, 538a, 615b, 626a, 645a; IV, 296a
Kāmiliyya (Cairo/Caire) s, 197a — S, 197a
Kamīn iii, 202b — III, 208a
Ḳamīs v, 733b, 748b, 749b — V, 738b, 754a, 755a
Kamkh → Kemākh
Ḳaml iv, **521b** — IV, **544a**
al-Kammad iv, **522a** — IV, **545a**
Kammūn iv, **522a** — IV, **545a**
al-Kammūnī, Muḥammad iv, **523a** — IV, **546a**
Ḳammūniya → Ḳamūniya
Kāmrān b. Bābur i, 228b; ii, 973a; iii, 422b, 423a, 455b, 485a, 575a, b, 576a, 633b, 634a; iv, **523b**, 537a — I, 235a; II, 995b; III, 436b, 471b, 502a, 595a, b, 596a, 654b, 655b; IV, **546a**, 560a
Kāmrān Mīrzā iv, 393b — IV, 410b
Kāmrān Shāh Durrānī i, 230b; ii, 637b; iv, **523b** — I, 238a; II, 653b; IV, **546a**
Kāmrūp i, 719b; iv, **524a** — I, 741a; IV, **546b**
Ḳamṣar v, 869a — V, 875a
Ḳamūniya iv, 825b, 826b — IV, 858b, 859b
Ḳāmūs ii, 801b, 926b; iv, **524a**; v, 837a, 1093a — II, 820b, 948a; IV, **546b**; V, 843b, 1090a
Ḳān → Khān
Kān wa-kān iv, **528a**; v, 372b — IV, **551a**; V, 373b
Ḳanā → Ḳunā
Ḳanāʿat Shāh Atalīḳ s, 98a — S, 97a
Kānamī → Kānemī
Kanʿān iv, **528b**; v, 521b — IV, **551b**; V, 525a
Kanʿān Pasha → Kenʿān Pasha
Kanarese → Kannada
Ḳanāt ii, 875b; iv, 8b, **528b**, 600b; v, 866a, b, 875b, 878b, 968b, 1108b — II, 896a; IV, 9a, **551b**, 624b; V, 872b, 873a, 881b, 884b, 971b, 1104b
Kanāta → Kunta
al-Ḳanāṭir iv, 555b; s, 230a — IV, 579b; S, 230a
Ḳanāṭir Firʿawn iv, 556b — IV, 580b
Ḳanawāt iv, **533a** — IV, **556a**
Kanawdj ii, 808b; iv, 276a, **533b**; s, 21a, 312a — II, 827b; IV, 288a, **556b**; S, 21b, 312a
Ḳanbāniya iv, **534a**; v, 509b — IV, **557a**; V, 513b
Ḳanbar Beg iv, 749b — IV, 779b
Kanbāya → Khambāyat
Kanbāya iii, 444b — III, 459b
Kanbōh → Supplement
Kanchandas i, 173a — I, 177b
Ḳand → Sukkar
Ḳandābīl iv, 364a, **534a** — IV, 380a, **557b**
Ḳandahār i, 5a, 8b, 72a, 80b, 95b, 222b, 223a, 768b, 1323b; ii, 134b, 628b; iv, 37b, **535a**; s, 63a, 66b, 367b, 423b — I, 5a, 8b, 74a, 83a, 98a, 229a, 230a, 791b, 1364a; II, 137b, 644b; IV, 40a, **558b**; S, 63b, 67a, 367b, 423b
Ḳandahār, Ḳandhār (Deccan) iv, **538a**; v, 579b — IV, **561b**; V, 584b
Kandi iv, **538b** — IV, **561b**
Kandia Koulibali iii, 39a — III, 40b
Ḳandīl → Ḳindīl
Ḳandiya(e) iv, **539a**, 590b; v, 260a, 261a — IV, **562a**, 614b; V, 258a, 259a
Ḳandiya (al-Khandaḳ) → al-Khandaḳ
Kandj Pashā i, 1078b — I, 1110b
Kandūrī iv, **540a** — IV, **563b**
Kanem i, 1259b, 1260a; ii, 369a, 876a; iv, **540a**, 566b; s, 163b, 164a, 165a — I, 1297b, 1298a; II, 379a, 896a; IV, **563b**, 589a; S, 163a, b, 164b
Kanembu i, 1260a; iv, 540b, 566b; s, 163b — I, 1298b; IV, 564a, 589a; S, 163b
Kānemī (language/langue) ii, 441b; iii, 657b — II, 453a; III, 678b
al-Kānemī, Muḥammad al-Amīn i, 1260a; ii, 942a; iii, 38b; iv, 541a, **541b**, 567a; v, 357b; s, 164b — I, 1298a; II, 963b; III, 40b; IV, 564b, **565a**, 589b; V, 359a; S, 164a
Kanesh → Kültepe
Kangāwar → Kinkiwar
Kanglï s, 420a — S, 420a
Ḳanghli, Ḳanḳlï iv, **542a**; s, 97b — IV, **565b**; S, 97a
Kāngrā iv, **542b** — IV, **566b**
Kānī, Abū Bakr iv, **544a** — IV, **567b**
Ḳāniʿ, Mir ʿAlī Sher iv, **544b** — IV, **568a**
Kānī, Muṣṭafā iv, 795b, 796a — IV, 828a
Kanik, Orhan Veli iv, **545a** — IV, **568b**
Kanīsa iv, **545a** — IV, **569a**
Kanīsat al-Ghurāb i, 488b — I, 503a
Kanīsat al-Ḳiyāma iv, 545b — IV, 569a
Kanizsa, Kanizhe iv, **546b**, 878a — IV, **570a**, 910b
Kankarides → Kurd(e)s
Kankiwar → Kinkiwar
Kankūt ii, 155b, 156a — II, 160a, 161a
Kannada (language/langue) v, 1258b — V, 1249b
Kannanūr iv, **546b**; v, 587a — IV, **570b**; V, 661b
Kannās iv, **547b** — IV, **571a**
Kannawdj → Kanawdj
al-Kannī, Abu 'l-ʿAbbās s, 236a — S, 236a
Kano iii, 275b, 276a; iv, **548a**; v, 1165b — III, 283b, 284a; IV, **572a**; V, 1155a
Kānpur iv, **551b**; s, 360b — IV, **575a**; S, 360a

Ḳanṣ → Ṣayd
Ḳānṣawh Bey iv, 723a — IV, 752a
Ḳānṣawh al-Ghawrī (al-Ghūrī) (Mamlūk) i, 315a, 815a, 1032b, 1057b, 1059a, 1060a; ii, 72b, 286a, 955a, 1127b, 1136b; iii, 346b, 760b, 813a; iv, 435a, b, 451a, **552a**; s, 43b — I, 324b, 838a, 1064a, 1089b, 1091a, 1092a; II, 73b, 294a, 977a, 1154a, 1163b; III, 357a, 783b, 836b; IV, 454b, 471a, **575b**; S, 43b
Ḳansāwuḳ Beg ii, 25a — II, 25b
Kansu iv, **553a**; v, 845a, b, 846a, 848a, b, 850b — IV, **577a**; V, 857a, b, 852b, 855a
Ḳānṣūh al-Ghurī → Ḳānṣawh al-Ghawrī
Ḳanṭara ii, 555a, 716a; iv, **555a** — II, 569a, 734b; IV, **579a**
al-Ḳanṭara i, 424a; iv, 555b — I, 435b; IV, 579b
Ḳanṭarat Zaynab iv, 556a — IV, 580b
Ḳantimūr, Demetrius i, 269a, 271a — I, 277a, 279a
Ḳantimūr Pasha i, 310b, 1287a — I, 320b, 1326b
Ḳānūn i, 152a, 170a, 171a, 975b; ii, 79a, 81b, 147a, 519a; iv, **556b**, 946b — I, 156b, 174b, 176a, 1006a; II, 80b, 83a, 151a, 532a; IV, **580b**, 979a
Ḳānūn (music/musique) → Malāhī
Ḳānūn al-arāḍī ii, 900b; iv, 168b — II, 921b; IV, 175b
Ḳānūn-i esāsī (asāsī) i, 63b; ii, 640a, 642a, 651b, 659b, 662b — I, 65b; II, 656a, 658b, 668a, 676a, 679a
Ḳānūn al-Kharādj ii, 78b — II, 80a
Ḳānūn-nāme i, 268a, 656b, 861b, 862a, 1147b, 1169b; ii, 83a; iv, 557a, **562a** — I, 276a, 677a, 885b, 886a, 1182a, 1204b; II, 84b; IV, 581a, **584b**
Ḳānūn Ṣanʿāʾ iv, 741b — IV, 771a
Ḳānūn-i sipāhiyān i, 712a — I, 733b
Ḳānūn al-Siyāsatnāma iii, 556b — III, 575b
Ḳānūngo ii, 156b — II, 161a
Kanuri i, 179b, 809a, 1221b, 1259a, b; ii, 10b, 368b; iv, **566b** — I, 184a, 832a, 1258a, 1297a, b, 1298a; II, 10b, 378a; IV, **589a**
Kānwa s, 331b — S, 331a
Kanz, Banu 'l iv, **567b** — IV, **590a**
Ḳapan ii, 147a; iii, 489b; iv, 226b, 228b — II, 151a; III, 506b; IV, 236b, 238b
Ḳapî iv, **568a** — Iv, **590b**
Ḳapî-aghasî → Ḳapu Aghasî
Ḳapi Kahyasî → Sarāy
Ḳapî ḳullarî i, 35b, 102a, 206b, 1256b; ii, 1090b, 1097b, 1120b; iv, 242b, 243a, 568a; v, 249b; s, 269b — I, 36b, 105a, 212b, 1294b; II, 1116a, 1123b, 1147a; IV, 253a, b, 590b; V, 247b; S, 269a
Ḳapî Ḳulu → Ordu
Ḳapidjî iv, **568a** — IV, **590b**
Ḳaplan Girāy I iv, **568b** — IV, **591a**
Ḳaplan Girāy II iv, **569b** — IV, **592a**
Ḳaplan Muṣṭafā Pasha i, 905a — I, 932a
Ḳaplîdja iii, 1120b; iv, **569b** — III, 1148b; IV, **592a**
Ḳapu Aghasî → ii, 1088a; iv, **570b**, 1093a — II, 1113b; IV, **593a**, 1124a
Ḳapuča iv, **571b** — IV, **594a**
Ḳapudān i, 269b, 948b, 1209a, 1266a, b, 1267b, 1268b; ii, 165b, 521b; iv, **571b**, 970b, 1158a — I, 277b, 977b, 1245a, 1305a, b, 1306b, 1307b; II, 170b, 534b; IV, **594a**, 1002b, 1190a
Ḳarā iv, **572b** — IV, **595b**
Karā (province) s, 203a — S, 202b
al-Ḳarā i, 536a — I, 552b
Ḳarā-aghač s, 282b — S, 282b
Ḳarā Aḥmad → Aḥmad Pasha
Ḳarā Aḥmed Shātîroghlu s, 91b — S, 91a
Ḳarā Āmid → Diyār Bakr
Ḳarā Arslān Beg → Ḳāwurd b. Čaghrî Dāwūd
Ḳarāba iv, **595a** — IV, **619a**
Ḳarābādhīn → Aḳrābādhīn
Ḳarābāgh iv, 389a, **573a**; s, 47a, 139b, 143a — IV, 404b, **595b**; S, 47b, 139a, 142b, 143a
Ḳarā Bahādur s, 324b — S, 324a
al-Ḳarābāshiyya iv, 991b, 993a — IV, 1024a, 1025b
Ḳarā Bayat i, 1117a; iii, 1101a — I, 1151a; III, 1128b
al-Karābīsī, Abū ʿAli al-Ḥusayn iv, **596a** — IV, **620a**
al-Karābīsī, Aḥmad b. ʿUmar iv, **596a** — IV, **620a**
al-Karābīsī, Asʿad b. Muḥammad iv, **596b** — IV, **620b**
Ḳarā Bîyîk-oghlū i, 396a — I, 407b
Ḳarā Boghaz s, 281a — S, 280b
Ḳarā Boghdān → Boghdān
Ḳaračay i, 1000b; ii, 23a; iv, **596b**; v, 288a — I, 1031a; II, 24a; IV, **620b**; V, 286a, b
Karačelebi-zāde i, 915b; iv, 298b, **573a** — I, 943a; IV, 312a, **596a**
Karačī (Adharbāydjān) ii, 41a; v, 818a — II, 42a; V, 824a
Karāčī i, 1006a; ii, 426b; iv, **597a**; v, 356a, 1222b; s, 332b — I, 1037a; II, 437b; IV, **621a**; V, 357b, 1212b; S, 332a
Ḳaradagh iii, 992b; iv, **574a**, 589a, 1054a; v, 263a — III, 1017b; IV, **597a**, 612b, 1085b; V, 261a
Ḳarā Dāwūd Pasha → Dāwūd Pasha (d./m. 1623)
Ḳarā Deniz iv, **575a** — IV, **598a**
Karadeniz Ereğlisi ii, 705a — II, 723a
al-Karadj ii, 623b; s, 17b, 122b — II, 639a; S, 17b, 121b
Ḳaradja, amīr iii, 398b, 503b; iv, 210a — III, 411a, 521a; IV, 219b
Ḳaradja Beg i, 511a; ii, 239a, 985b — I, 526b; II, 246a, 1008a
Ḳaradja Dagh s, 116a — S, 115b
Ḳaradja Ḥiṣār iv, 580b — IV, 603b
Ḳaradja Shehir iv, 580b — IV, 603b
Ḳaradjaoghlan i, 677b; ii, 75b; s, 91b, 324a — I, 698b; II, 77a; S, 91a, 323b
al-Karadjī, Abū Bakr Muḥammad i, 133b; iv, **600a**, 703a; s, 119b, 390a — I, 137a; IV, **624a**, 731a; S, 119a, 390b
Ḳarā Evlī iii, 1100a — III, 1127a
Ḳarā Faḍlī → Faḍlī, Meḥmed
al-Ḳarāfa → al-Ḳāhira
al-Ḳarāfa (cemetery/cimetière) s, 156a — S, 156b
Karaferye iv, **600b** — IV, **624b**
Ḳaragöz i, 152a, 792b, 1161b; iv, **601a**, 1136b — I, 156b, 815b, 1196a; IV, **625a**, 1168a
Ḳaragözlü iii, 1102b, 1109a; iv, **577b** — III, 1129b, 1136a; IV, **600b**
Ḳarā Ḥasan iv, 1156a, b — IV, 1188a, b
Ḳarā Haydar-oghlu → Haydar-oghlu Meḥmed
Ḳarā Ḥiṣār iv, **578a** — IV, **601b**
Ḳarā Ḥiṣār Adalia → Ḳarā Ḥiṣār-i Teke
Ḳarā Ḥiṣār Develi iv, 843b — IV, 876b
Ḳarā Ḥiṣār-î Behrāmshāh (Bayrāmshāh) iv, 579b — IV, 602b
Ḳarā Ḥiṣār-î Demirdji iv, 579b — IV, 603a
Ḳarā Ḥiṣār-î Ṣāḥib → Afyūn Ḳarā Ḥiṣār
Ḳarā Ḥiṣār-î Sharḳī, Shabkhāne → Shābīn Ḳarā Ḥiṣār
Ḳarā Ḥiṣār-î Teke iv, 579b — IV, 603a
Ḳarā Hülegü ii, 3a — II, 3a
Ḳarāʿī iii, 1107b; v, 154b — III, 1135a; V, 155b
Ḳarā Ibrāhīm Pasha → Ibrāhīm Pasha, Ḳarā
Ḳarāʾīm → Karaites
Karaites, Ḳarāʾiyyūn iv, 305a, b, **603b**; v, 136b, 326b — IV, 319a, **627b**; V, 139a, 326a
Karak i, 804b; iv, **609a**; s, 391a — I, 828b; IV, **633b**; S, 391a
Ḳaraḳalpaḳ i, 1076b; ii, 971a; iii, 116b; iv, **610b**; s, 97b — I, 1108b; II, 993a; III, 119a; IV, **635a**; S, 97a
Karakay (Karakul) i, 1135a — I, 1169b
Ḳarā Kemāl iv, 285b — IV, 298a

Ḳarā Khalīl Djandarlî → Djandarlî
Ḳarā Khalīlzade iv, 506a — IV, 528a
Ḳarā Khān i, 767a — I, 790a
Karakh iv, 347a — IV, 362a
Ḳarākhān → Khayr Khān
Ḳarakhānid(e) (language/langue) iv, 700a — IV, 728a, b
Ḳarakhānid(e)s → Ilek-khāns
Ḳarā Khiṭāy i, 750a, 987a, 1001b, 1240a, 1295a, 1311a; ii, 43a, 67a, 607a, 1101b, 1109a; iii, 1114b; iv, 29a-30a, 32a, 542b, **580b**, 1067b; v, 38b, 134b — I, 772b, 1017b, 1032a, 1278a, 1334b, 1351b; II, 43b, 68b, 622a, 1127b, 1135a; III, 1141b; IV, 31b-32a, 34b, 566a, **604a**, 1099a, b; V, 39b, 137a
al-Karakī, Nūr al-Dīn ʿAlī iv, **610a** — IV, **634b**
Ḳarā Kirgiz → Kirgiz
Ḳarakol iv, **611a** — IV, **636a**
Ḳarā-Köl i, 1135a; iv, 213b, **583b**; s, 97a, 227b, 318a — I, 1169b; IV, 223a, **607a**; S, 96b, 228a, 318a
Karakol Djhemʿīyyetī iv, **611b** — IV, **636a**
Karak Nūḥ iv, **609b** — IV, **634b**
Ḳaraḳorum ii, 45b, 606b; iv, **612b** — II, 46b, 622a; IV, **637a**
Ḳaraḳorum Mts iv, **611b**; s, 158b — IV, **636b**; S, 158b
Karaköy s, 314b — S, 314a
Ḳarā Ḳoyunlu i, 190a, 311b, 508a, 666b, 903b, 919a; ii, 334a, 344b, 401b, 598b, 711b; iii, 1100b, 1256b; iv, 33b-34a, **584a**; v, 456b — I, 194b, 321a, 523b, 687a, 930b, 947a; II, 344a, 354a, 412a, 613b, 730a; III, 1127b, 1289a; IV, 36a, b, **607b**; V, 459b
Ḳarākul → Ḳarā-köl
Ḳaraḳum iv, **613a** — IV, **637b**
Ḳarākum iv, 542b, 613a — IV, 566a, 637b
Ḳarāḳūsh al-Asadī iii, 173b; iv, **613a** — III, 177a; IV, **638a**
Ḳarāḳūsh al-Ghuzzī i, 161b, 165a, 533a, 797b, 798a; ii, 575a, 875b, 1007b, 1008a, 1110a; iii, 173b; iv, 210a, 337b, 424b, **614a**, 739b — I, 166a, 170a, 549b, 821a, b; II, 589b, 896a, 1031a, 1031b, 1136a; III, 177a; IV, 219b, 352a, 443a, **638b**, 769b
Ḳarā Maḥmūd Pasha i, 657a; iv, **588a** — I, 677b; IV, **612a**
Karam → Supplement
al-Karam, Banū → Zurayʿid(e)s
Karam, Yūsuf → Yūsuf Karam
al-Karam b. Yām i, 181b — I, 186b
Karam Allāh Kurḳusāwī i, 929b; ii, 696b — I, 958a; II, 714a
Karāma iv, **615a** — IV, **639b**
Ḳaramān i, 354b, 468a; iv, **616b**, 621a; v, 881b — I, 365b, 481b; IV, **641b**, 645b; V, 887b
Karāmān (town/ville) iv, 616b — IV, 641b
Ḳaraman b. Nūra Sūfî i, 467a, 468a; iv, 619b, 620a — I, 481a, 482a; IV, 643b, 644a
Karamānī Meḥmed Pasha → Meḥmed Pasha Ḳaramānī
Ḳaramānī Meḥemmed Pasha ii, 529a — II, 542a
Ḳarāmānid(e)s → Ḳarāmān-oghullarî
Ḳaramānlî ii, 161b, 876a, 876b, 971b; iv, **617a** — II, 166b, 896a, 994a; IV, **641b**
Ḳaramānlī Aḥmad Bey iv, 617a — IV, 642a
Ḳarāmān-oghullarî i, 240b, 244a, 292b, 1117b, 1118a; ii, 103b, 239b, 529b, 607b, 692a, 705b, 710b; iii, 1006b; iv, **619a**, 843a; v, 254a, 677a, b, 1144b — I, 248a, 251a, 302a, 1151b; II, 105b, 246b, 542b, 622b, 709a, 723b, 727a; III, 1032a; IV, **643b**, 876b; V, 252a, 682a, b, 1137a
Karāmat ʿAlī Djawnpūrī i, 952a; iv, 170a, **625b** — I, 981a; IV, 177b, **650b**
Karamba ii, 1132b — II, 1159a
Ḳarāmīd → Khazaf
Ḳarāmiṭa i, 387a, 822a, 824a, 867a — I, 398a, 845a, 847a, 891b
Karāmiyya → Karrāmiyya
Karamoko Alfa ii, 960a, 1132a — II, 982a, 1159a
Ḳarā Muḥammad i, 311b, 1051a; iv, 584b — I, 321a, 1082b; IV, 608a
Ḳarā Murād Pasha iv, 766a — IV, 796b
Karamuk → Bolwadin
Ḳarā Mūsā i, 293b — I, 302b
Ḳarā Muṣṭafā Pasha → Kemānkesh Ḳarā Muṣṭafā
Ḳarā Muṣṭafā Pasha Firārī i, 236b — I, 244a
Ḳara Muṣṭafā Pasha Merzifonlū i, 948a, 1284b; ii, 522a, 572b; iv, **589b**; v, 261b, 272b, 720b — I, 977a, 1324a; II, 535a, 587a; IV, **613a**; V, 259a, 270b, 726a
Karandal → Ḳalandar
Ḳaranful iv, **626b** — IV, **651b**
Karaosmanoğlu/Ḳarā ʿOthmān-Oghlî → Ḳarā ʿUthmān-oghullarî
Ḳarapapakh iv, **627a** — IV, **652a**
Ḳarā Pīrī Beg Ḳādjār iv, 387b, 389a — IV, 404b
Ḳarār → Mūsīḳī
al-Ḳarār i, 897a — I, 924a
Ḳarāra iii, 97b — III, 100b
Ḳarasaḳal i, 1076b — I, 1108b
Ḳarasî i, 467b, 468a, 994a; ii, 686b; iv, **627b** — I, 481b, 482a, 1024b; II, 704a; IV, **652b**
Ḳarasî-eli i, 468b — I, 482b
Ḳarā Sonḳor i, 1358a; ii, 975b — I, 1398a, b; II, 998a
Karasta i, 1205b — I, 1241b
al-Ḳarasṭūn iv, **629a** — IV, **653b**
Ḳarā-ṣū → al-Furāt
Ḳaraṣū-Bāzār iv, **629b** — IV, **654b**
Ḳara-ṣū → Khāsa
Ḳarāsunḳur iv, 432b; v, 1142b — IV, 451b; V, 1135b
Ḳārat al-Kibrīt ii, 631a — II, 646b
Karata (Kirdî-kalal) i, 504a; iv, **630b** — I, 519b; IV, **655b**
Karataï i, 1338a — I, 1378a
Ḳarā Takīn → Ḳaratigin
Ḳaratāy → Djalāl al-Dīn
Ḳaratekin ii, 14a — II, 14a
Ḳaratigin iv, **631a**; s, 228a — IV, **656a**; S, 228a
Ḳaratigin Isfīdjābī i, 852a; ii, 1082a; s, 356b — I, 876a; II, 1107a; S, 356b
Ḳarātisa s, 42a — S, 42b
Ḳarā ʿUthmān-oghullarî i, 469a, 783a; ii, 206b, 207a; iv, **592b**; v, 1170b — I, 483a, 806a; II, 213a, b; IV, **616b**; V, 1160a
Ḳaravul → Karakol
Ḳarāvulān iv, 860a — IV, 893b
Ḳarā Wāṣif iv, 611b — IV, 636a
Ḳarawī (language/langue) i, 575a — I, 593b
al-Ḳarawī, al-Shāʿir v, 1256b — V, 1247b
al-Ḳarawiyyīn ii, 821-3; iv, **632a**; v, 1152a, 1190a, 1208a; s, 126a, 303a — II, 840-2; IV, **657a**; V, 1142a, 1180a, 1198b; S, 125a, 302b
Ḳaray, ḳaraylar iv, 608a — IV, 632b
Karay, Refīḳ Khālid iii, 357b; iv, **635b**, 812a; v, 194b, 196b; s, 96a, 98b — III, 369a; IV, **661b**, 845a; V, 192a, 193b; S, 95b, 98a
Ḳarā Yazīdjî (ʿAbd al-Ḥalīm) iv, 499a, **594a**, 843b; s, 238b — IV, 520b, **618a**, 876b; S, 238b
Ḳarā Yülüḳ ʿUthmān i, 311b, 1054a, 1328a; ii, 614a; iii, 186a, 190a; iv, 586b, 587a, b, 871a — I, 321a, 1085b, 1368b; II, 629a; III, 190b, 194a; IV, 609a, b, 611a, 904b
Ḳarā Yūsuf i, 311b, 666b, 791b, 1119a; ii, 401b, 614a; iv, 33b, 586a, b, 587a — I, 321a, 687b, 815a, 1152b; II, 412a, 629a; IV, 36a, 608b, 609a, b
Karak Nūḥ s, 380a — S, 380a
Karbalāʾ i, 1168b; ii, 938a; iii, 115a, 119b, 610a; iv, **637a**; v, 1033a; s, 74b, 75a, 94a, b, 134b, 231b — I, 1203b; II, 960a; III, 117b, 122a, 630b; IV, **663b**; V,

1029b; S, 75a, b, 93b, 94a, 134a, 231b
Karbalāʾī Ḳurbān s, 70b — S, 71a
Kārbān → Kārwān
Karbughā i, 517a, 1052a — I, 532b, 1084a
Ḳardā and/et Bāzabdā iv, **639a** — IV, **665b**
Kardagh iv, 76a — IV, 80a
Kardj → Kerč
Ḳardū, Karduchoi v, 447b, 448a, b — V, 450a, b
al-Kardūdī, Abū ʿAbd Allāh iv, **639a** — IV, **665b**
Karghawayh, Karghūyah i, 119b; iii, 129b; v, 923b — I, 123a; III, 132a; V, 929a
Kārgudhār iii, 1193a — III, 1222b
Ḳāriʾ → Ḳirāʾa; Ḳurʾān; Ḳurrāʾ
Ḳārī iv, 66a — IV, 69b
al-Ḳārī → ʿAlī
Ḳarība (singer/chanteuse) → Ḳurayba
Ḳarība (tax(e)) v, 259a — V, 257a
Karibīya → Kuraybiyya
Kārim iv, 640b — IV, 666b
Karīm al-Dīn al-Amulī iii, 952a — III, 977a
Karīm al-Dīn al-Kabīr → Ibn al-Sadīd
Karīm Khān (Nagar) s, 327b — S, 327a
Karīm Khān Zand i, 190a, 230a, 246b, 393b, 1341b; ii, 311a, 812a; iii, 1102b, 1103a, 1191a, 1257b; iv, 104b, 390a, b, **639b**, 695a, 1056b; v, 617a, 674a, 825b; s, 405b — I, 196a, 237a, 254b, 405a, 1382a; II, 319b, 831b; III, 1129b, 1130a, 1221a, 1290a; IV, 109a, 406b, 407a, **665b**, 723a, 1087b; V, 621a, 679a, 831b; S, 405b
Ḳarīm Shāh → Agha Khān IV
Karīm Thābit s, 301a — S, 300b
Kārimī i, 800a; ii, 144b; iii, 776b; iv, 136a, b, 137a, **640a**; v, 514b; s, 43a — I, 823b; II, 148b; III, 799b; IV, 141b, 142b, 143a, **666b**; V, 518a; S, 43b
Ḳārin i, 47b; iv, 644a — I, 49a; IV, 670b
Ḳarīn iv, **643b** — IV, **670a**
Ḳarīn (mountains/montagne) s, 298a — S, 297b
Ḳārin b. Shahriyār Bāwand i, 1110a; iv, 645b, 646b; s, 363b — I, 1143b; IV, 672a, 673a; S, 363a
Ḳārin b. Wandād-Hurmuzd iv, 645a — IV, 671b
Ḳārinid(e)s iv, 207b, **644a**; v, 661a; s, 298a, 309a — IV, 217a, **670b**; V, 666b; S, 297b, 308b
Karîshdîran Süleymān Beg iv, 225a — IV, 234b
Kāriyān v, 1110a, 1112a — V, 1106a, 1108a
Kārīz → Ḳanāt
Karkaddan iv, **647a** — IV, **673b**
Ḳarḳana iv, **650b** — IV, **676b**
Karkand → Karkaddan
Karkarn → Bisbarāy
Ḳarkashandī, Banū v, 333a — V, 333a
Ḳarḳastal s, 80a — S, 80a
Karkh i, 896a; iv, **652a**; s, 13a, 172a, 192b, 193a — I, 921b; IV, **678b**; S, 13b, 173a, 194a
Karkha (river/rivière) iii, 1251a; iv, **653b**, 675a; v, 830a, 867b — III, 1283b; IV, **680a**, 703a; V, 836a, 874a
Karkhāyā iv, 652b — IV, 679a
al-Karkhī → al-Karadjī
al-Karkhī, Abū ʿAlī Muḥammad s, 25b — S, 26a
al-Karkhī, Maʿrūf b. al-Fayzurān iv, 653a — IV, 679b
Karkhina → Kirkūk
Karkī s, 281a — S, 281a
Ḳarḳīsiyā iv, **654b**; s, 117a — IV, **681a**; S, 116b
Kārkiyā ii, 194a; v, 603a, b, 604a — II, 200a; V, 607a, b, 608a
Karkūr iv, **655b** — IV, **681b**
Karlî-Īli; Karlo-Īli iv, **656a**; v, 725b, 726a — IV, **682a**; V, 731a
Ḳarlofča iv, **657a**; v, 721a, 727b; s, 187a — IV, **683b**; V, 726a, 732b; S, 188b
Karlowitz → Ḳarlofča
Ḳarluḳ ii, 67a, 1107b; iii, 335b, 1113a, 1116b; iv, 188b, 213a, **658a**, 917a; v, 854b, 855b, 856a, 857a; s, 326b — II, 68a, 1133b; III, 345b, 1140b, 1144a; IV, 197a, 222b, **684b**, 950a; V, 861a, 862b, 863a, 864a; S, 326a
Karm iv, **659a** — IV, **685b**
Ḳarmāsīn → Kirmānshāh
Ḳarmaṭī i, 11a, 19a, 73b, 95b, 194b, 551a, 942a, 1086a, 1276b, 1354b; ii, 98a, 168b, 281b, 385a, 452b, 482b, 495b, 854a, 1070a; iii, 123b, 126b, 238a, 246a, 255b, 380b, 619a, 799a; iv, 22b, 198a, 494a, **660b**, 764a; v, 327a, 348a, 923a; s, 12b, 36b, 117b, 199a — I, 11a, 19b, 76a, 98b, 200a, 569a, 971a, 1118b, 1315b, 1394a; II, 100a, 174a, 289b, 368a, 464a, 495a, 508a, 874a, 1094b; III, 126a, 129b, 245a, 253a, 263a, 392b, 639b, 822b; IV, 24a, 206b, 515a, **687a**, 794b; V, 327a, 349a, 928b; S, 13a, 36b, 117a, 199a
Karmīniyya s, 176b — S, 177b
Karmisīn → Kirmānshāh
Ḳarmūna i, 6a, 1238a; iv, **665a** — I, 6a, 1275b; IV, **692a**
Ḳarn i, 1290b; iv, 825b — I, 1330a; IV, 858b
Karnāl iv, **665b** — IV, **692b**
Karnātak i, 624b; iii, 316b; iv, **666b** — I, 645b; III, 326a; IV, **693b**
Karōfī ii, 156b — II, 161a
Karpenésion, Karpenisi → Kerbenesh
Ḳarrād v, 132a, b — V, 135a, b
Karrāmiyya i, 187b, 411a, 714a; ii, 218b, 752a, 791a, 931b, 1103a; iii, 177b, 767a, 1145a, 1165a, 1173a; iv, 46a, 183b, 469a, **667a**, 1025b; v, 328b; s, 149a — I, 193a, 422b, 735b; II, 225a, 770b, 810a, 953a, 1129b; III, 181b, 790a, 1173a, 1193b, 1202a; IV, 48b, 191b, 490a, **694a**, 1057b; V, 328b; S, 149a
Karranāy i, 1291b — I, 1331a
Ḳarrī → Ḳerrī
Ḳarrīṭa i, 206a — I, 212a
Karrūṣa i, 206a — I, 212a
Kars i, 468b, 637b, 638a, 640a, 641b; iv, **669b** — I, 482b, 658b, 659a, 661a, 662a; IV, **696b**
Ḳarṣana → Ḳurṣān
Karsh → Kerč
Ḳarshi i, 1019a; ii, 4a; iv, **671b**; v, 858b — I, 1050b; II, 4a; IV, **699a**; V, 865b
Karshūnī iv, **671b** — IV, **699a**
Kart i, 227a, 1343a; iii, 177b, 1121b; iv, 32a, **672a**; v, 58b — I, 233b, 1383a; III, 181b, 1149a; IV, 34a, **699a**; V, 60b
Ḳarṭādjanna i, 51b, 77b; iii, 271a; iv, **672b**; v, 1188a — I, 53a, 79b; III, 279a; IV, **700a**; V, 1178a
al-Ḳarṭādjannī → Ḥāzim al-Ḳarṭādjannī
Ḳarṭas → Ḳirṭās
Ḳarṭasa ii, 105b — II, 108a
Kartli v, 494a — V, 497a
Kārūd → Ḳalʿa Kuhrūd
Karūkh iv, **673a** — IV, **700b**
Ḳārūn iv, **673a** — IV, **700b**
Kārūn (river/rivière) i, 8b; iii, 1251a; iv, 6a, 9a, 654a, **673b**; v, 65b, 80b, 867a, 869a — I, 8b; III, 1283b; IV, 6b, 9b, 680a, **701a**; V, 67b, 82b, 873b, 875b
Kārwa iii, 197b — III, 202a
Kārwān iv, **676a** — IV, **704a**
Ḳarwāsh b. al-Muḳallad i, 1073b; iii, 80b, 860a; iv, 378b, 911a; v, 896b; s, 119a — I, 1105b; III, 83a, 884b; IV, 395a, 944a; V, 903a; S, 118b
Ḳarwasha iv, **679b** — IV, **707b**
Ḳarya iv, **680a** — IV, **708a**
al-Ḳarya al-Ḥadītha → Djand
Ḳarya al-Suflā iv, **680b** — IV, **708b**
Ḳarya al-ʿUlyā iv, **680b** — IV, **708b**
Karyatayn s, 117a — S, 116a
Karzūbī iii, 1097b — III, 1124b

al-Ḳaṣāb iv, **681a** — IV, **709a**
Ḳaṣab iv, **682a** — IV, **710a**
Ḳaṣāb, Teodor iv, **681b** — IV, **709a**
Ḳaṣab al-Sukkar iv, **682b** — IV, **710b**
Ḳaṣaba (town/ville) i, 1320a; iii, 498b; iv, **684b**, 685b — I, 1360b; III, 515b; IV, **712b**, 713b
Ḳaṣaba (citadel (le)) i, 974b; iv, **685a**; v, 654b — I, 1005a; IV, **713a**; V, 658b
Ḳaṣaba b. Kus̲h̲ s, 132a — S, 131b
Kāsagarān Madrasa s, 23b — S, 23b
Ḳasak → Čerkes
Kasala i, 1158b; iv, **686a**; v, 1251a — I, 1193a; IV, **714a**; V, 1241b
Ḳasam iv, **687b**; v, 178b, 179b — IV, **715b**; V, 176a, 177a
Ḳasāma i, 1151a; ii, 342b; iv, 687b, **689b** — I, 1185b; II, 352a; IV, 715b, **717b**
Ḳāsān → Kās̲h̲ān
al-Kāsānī, ʿAlāʾ al-dīn iii, 163b; iv, **690a** — III, 166b; IV, **718a**
Kasap → Ḳaṣāb
Ḳaṣaṣ → Ḳiṣṣa
Kasb i, 413b, 414a, 696b; ii, 365a; iii, 1037b; iv, **690b** — I, 425b, 717b; II, 375a; III, 1063a; IV, **718b**
Kasbah → Ḳaṣaba (town/ville)
Kasf → Kusūf
Kas̲h̲ (S̲h̲ahr-i Sabz) iv, **694a**, 711b; v, 181a, 858b; s, 97b — IV, **722a**, 740a; V, 178b, 865b; S, 96b
Kas̲h̲ad al-D̲j̲uhanī v, 316a, b — V, 316a
Kas̲h̲af-Rūd s, 83a — S, 83a
Kas̲h̲ak (Kasak) → Čerkes
Kās̲h̲ān i, 11a; ii, 746a; iii, 144b, 1125b; iv, **694b**, 1040a, 1047b, 1167a; v, 171a, 370a; s, 71a, 75b, 139a, b, 141a, 142a — I, 11a; II, 764b; III, 147a, 1153b; IV, **722b**, 1071b, 1079a, 1199b; V, 168b, 371a; S, 71b, 75b, 138b, 139a, 141a, b, 142a
al-Kās̲h̲ānī i, 351a — I, 362a
al-Kās̲h̲ānī, ʿAbd al-Razzāk → ʿAbd al-Razzāk al-Kās̲h̲ānī
al-Ḳās̲h̲ānī, Abu ʾl-ʿAbbās Aḥmad iv, **696a** — IV, **724b**
Kās̲h̲ānī, Abū Ṭālib → Ḳalīm Abū Ṭālib
Kās̲h̲ānī, Āḳā Muẓaffar s, 308b — S, 308b
Kās̲h̲ānī, Āyātullāh Abu ʾl-Ḳāsim ii, 882b; iii, 529b; iv, 165a, **695b**, 790a — II, 903a; III, 548a; IV, 172b, **724a**, 822a
al-Kās̲h̲ānī, G̲h̲iyāt̲h̲ al-Dīn → al-Kās̲h̲ī, D̲j̲ams̲h̲īd
Kās̲h̲ānī, Ḥād̲j̲d̲j̲ī Mīrzā D̲j̲ānī iv, **696a** — IV, **724a**
Kās̲h̲ānī, ʿIzz al-Dīn Maḥmūd s, 415b — S, 415b
Kās̲h̲ānī, Maḳṣūd s, 139a — S, 138b
al-Kās̲h̲ānī, Mulla Muḥsin Fayd s, 57a — S, 57b
Kas̲h̲f iv, **696b** — IV, **725a**
Kas̲h̲fahān ii, 556a — II, 570a
Kas̲h̲gān (river/rivière) v, 830a — V, 836a
Kas̲h̲g̲h̲āī → Ḳas̲h̲-ḳaʾī
Kās̲h̲g̲h̲ar i, 46b; iii, 1114a; iv, **698b**; v, 38a, b, 846a; s, 240a — I, 48a; III, 1141b; IV, 727a; V, 39a, b, 858a; S, 240a
al-Kās̲h̲g̲h̲arī, Maḥmūd iii, 115b, 1114a, 1116a; iv, 525a, 527a, **699b**, 1080b; s, 168b, 280b, 289b — III, 118a, 1141b, 1143b; IV, 547b, 549b, **727b**, 1111b; S, 168b, 280b, 289b
Kās̲h̲ī → Benares/Bénarès
Kās̲h̲ī iv, **701a**; v, 600a — IV, **729b**; V, 604a
al-Ḳās̲h̲ī, Abu ʾl-ʿAbbās Aḥmad → al-Ḳās̲h̲ānī
al-Kās̲h̲ī, D̲j̲ams̲h̲īd iii, 1137b, 1139b, 1140a; iv, **702b**, 725b, 726a — III, 1166a, 1167b, 1168a; IV, **730b**, 754b, 755a
Kās̲h̲if, Muḥammad S̲h̲arīf iv, **703a** — IV, **731b**
Kās̲h̲if al-G̲h̲iṭāʾ, S̲h̲ayk̲h̲ ʿAlī s, 75b — S, 76a
Kās̲h̲if al-G̲h̲iṭāʾ S̲h̲ayk̲h̲ D̲j̲aʿfar iv, **703b**; s, 57a — IV, **731b**; S, 57b
Kās̲h̲if al-G̲h̲iṭāʾ, S̲h̲ayk̲h̲ Mūsā s, 75a — S, 75b
Kās̲h̲ifī, Ḥusayn Wāʿiẓ i, 430b; iii, 274b, 351b, 372b, 490a; iv, 68a, 504b, **704a**, 1035a; s, 46b — I, 442b; III, 282b, 363a, 384b, 507a; IV, 71b, 526b, **732a**, 1067a; S, 47a
Kas̲h̲īnā, Kas̲h̲nā → Katsina
al-Kas̲h̲ināwī, Muḥammad iv, 773b — IV, 805a
Kas̲h̲īs̲h̲-Dag̲h̲ī → Ulu Dag̲h̲
Kās̲h̲-ḳaʿī, Ḳas̲h̲ḳāy ii, 925b; iii, 1105a, 1106a, 1110a; iv, 8a, 9a-b, **705b**; s, 142b, 146a, 147b — II, 947a; III, 1132a, 1133b, 1137a; IV, 8b, 9a, 10a, **734a**; S, 142a, 145b, 147b
Ḳāshḳār → Chitral
Kas̲h̲kas̲h̲a i, 709a — I, 729b
Kas̲h̲kūl iv, **706b** — IV, **735a**
Kas̲h̲mīr i, 71a, 231a, 392b, 856b; ii, 140a; iii, 317a, 420a; iv, **706b**; v, 588b; s, 63a, 114b, 131b, 156a, 167a, 241a, 242a, 324b, 327b, 332a, 333a, 366a, b, 423a, b — I, 73a, 238a, 403b, 880b; II, 144a; III, 326b, 433b; IV, **735a**; V, 592a; S, 63b, 113b, 130b, 156a, 167a, 241b, 242a, 324a, 327a, 332a, b, 366a, 423b
- monuments i, 1347b, 1348a; iii, 448a — I, 1388a, b; III, 463b
Kas̲h̲mīrī (language/langue) ii, 139a; iii, 413b; iv, 707a, **711b** — II, 142b; III, 426b; IV, 735b, **740a**
al-Kas̲h̲nāwī, Muḥammad iv, 773b — IV, 805a
Kas̲h̲s̲h̲āfa iii, 185a — III, 189a
al-Kas̲h̲s̲h̲ī, Abū ʿAmr i, 134a, 794b; iii, 1151a; iv, **711b** — I, 137b, 818a; III, 1179b; IV, **740a**
Ḳas̲h̲tāla iv, **712a**; v, 781b; s, 80b — IV, **740b**; V, 787b; S, 80a
Ḳaṣī, Banū i, 494a, 658a; iii, 815b; iv, 477b, **712b**; v, 683a; s, 80b, 82a — I, 509a, 679a; III, 839b; IV, 498b, **741**; V, 688a; S, 80b, 81b
Ḳāṣid → Safīr
Ḳaṣid Og̲h̲lu → Ḳāzdug̲h̲liyya
Ḳaṣīda i, 583b, 586a, 592a, 601b, 668a, 671b, 676b, 677a, 1290a; ii, 293a, 1028b; iii, 1178a; iv, 57a-b, 59a-b, 65a, **713b**; v, 930b, 956a, 957a, 958b, 963a — I, 602a, 605a, 611b, 621a, 688b, 692b, 697a, 698a, 1329b; II, 301a, 1052b; III, 1207a; IV, 60b, 62b, 68b, **742a**; V, 935a, 960a, 961a, 962a, 967a
Ḳaṣīdat al-burda i, 1011b — I, 1042b
al-Ḳaṣīm (Nad̲j̲d) i, 1312b, 1313a; iv, **717a**; s, 3b, 304b, 305a — I, 1352b, 1353a; IV, **745b**; S, 2b, 304a, b
Ḳāsim, ʿAbd al-Karīm iii, 1259a; iv, **719a**; v, 468a, 1213b — III, 1291b; IV, **747b**; V, 470b, 471a, 1203a
Ḳāsim, S.M. iv, 711a — IV, 739b
Ḳāsim b. Aḥmad I iv, **717a** — IV, **745b**
Ḳāsim b. Aḥmad b. Bāyazīd iv, **716b** — IV, **745b**
al-Ḳasīm b. ʿAlī b. ʿUmar s, 48b — S, 49a
Ḳāsim b. Aṣbag̲h̲ i, 600a, 1150a; iii, 845a; iv, **717b** — I, 619b, 1184b; III, 868b; IV, **746b**
Ḳāsim b. D̲j̲ihāngīr i, 311b — I, 321b
al-Kāsim b. D̲j̲iryāl al-Dimas̲h̲ḳī s, 267a — S, 266b
Ḳāsim b. Ḥammūd i, 6a; iii, 147a, 786a — I, 6b; 150a, b, 809b
Ḳāsim b. Ḥasan iii, 610b — III, 631b
al-Ḳāsim b. Ibrāhīm s, 48b, 335a — S, 49a, 334b
al-Ḳāsim b. Idrīs II i, 1088a; iii, 1035b — I, 1120a; III, 1061b
al-Ḳāsim b. ʿĪsā al-Id̲j̲lī i, 153b, 315b; ii, 623a; iv, **718a**; s, 17b, 122a — I, 158a, 325b; II, 639a; IV, **747a**; S, 17b, 121b
Ḳāsim b. Muḥammad (Katar) → D̲j̲āsim b. Muḥammad
al-Ḳāsim b. Muḥammad b. Abī Bakr s, **311b** — S, **311b**
al-Ḳāsim b. Muḥammad al-Muʾayyad v, 1242a — V, 1232b
al-Ḳāsim b. al-Ras̲h̲īd iv, 859a — IV, 892a

al-Ḳāsim b. ʿUbayd Allāh b. Wahb ii, 178a; iii, 767b, 892b, 908a; iv, 110a, 293b; v, 621b; s, 118a — II, 184a; III, 790b, 916b, 932b; IV, 115a, 306b; V, 625b; S, 117b
al-Ḳāsim b. ʿUmar iii, 651b — III, 672b
Ḳāsim b. ʿUmar, Amīr ii, 635b — II, 651b
al-Ḳāsim b. Yūsuf b. al-Ḳāsim iii, 309a — III, 318b
Ḳāsim Agha iv, **719b**; v, 257a — IV, **748b**; V, 255a
Ḳāsim ʿAlī i, 1211b, 1213a — I, 1247b, 1249b
Ḳāsim Alī, Mīr i, 1357b; ii, 1091b; iii, 61a — I, 1397b; II, 1117a; III, 63b
Ḳāsim Amīn i, 597a; ii, 423a; iii, 59a, 360a, 593a; iv, **720a**; s, 244b — I, 616b; II, 434a; III, 61b, 371a, 613b; IV, **749a**; S, 244b
Ḳāsim-i Anwar iv, 66a, **721a**, 1073b — IV, 69b, **750a**, 1105a
Ḳāsim Barīd i, 1047a, b, 1200a; iii, 15a, 421a — I, 1078b, 1079a, 1235b; III, 16a, 434b
Ḳāsim Beg ii, 529b; iv, 624a, b — II, 542b; IV, 649a
Ḳāsim Čelebi b. Bāyazīd iv, **716b** — IV, **745b**
Ḳasīm al-Dawla al-Bursuḳī → Āḳ Sunḳur al-Bursuḳī
Ḳāsim Djān, Munshī i, 72a — I, 74a
Ḳāsim Djānbulāt (Jumblat) → Djānbulāt
al-Ḳāsim Gannūn (Djannūn) iii, 1036b — III, 1062b
Ḳāsim Ghanī iii, 56b — III, 59a
Ḳāsim Khān (Mughal commander/général des Mughals) s, 167b — S, 167b
Ḳāsim Khān Mīr Baḥr (Afshar) i, 240a; iv, 709a; s, 132a — I, 247b; IV, 737b; S, 131a
Ḳāsim Khān (Tatar) i, 721b; iv, 723a, 849a — I, 743b; IV, 752a, 882a
Ḳāsim al-Khaṣāṣī → al-Khaṣāṣī
Ḳāsîm Pasha ii, 813a; s, 314b, 315b — II, 832a; S, 314a, 315b
Ḳāsim Pasha Djazarī iv, **722a** — IV, **751a**
Ḳāsim Pasha Ewliyā iv, **722a** — IV, **751a**
Ḳāsim Pasha Güzeldje iv, 233a, **722b** — IV, 243a, **751b**
Ḳāsim-Shāh iv, 201b — IV, 210b
al-Ḳāsim al-Wāthiḳ iii, 147b — III, 150b
Ḳāsim Yughayta ii, 330b — II, 340b
Ḳāsim Yūsuf → Ḳāsim Čelebi
al-Ḳāsimī, Djamā al-Dīn iv, 159a — IV, 166a
Ḳāsimī Gunabādī iii, 114a — III, 116b
al-Ḳāsimī, Shaykh Ṣaḳr b. Muḥammad s, 418a — S, 418a, b
al-Ḳāsimī, Shaykh Ṣaḳr b. Sulṭān s, 418a — S, 418b
Ḳāsimī tribes/tribus → Ḳawāsim
Ḳāsimiyya (Egypt(e)) ii, 233a;iii 300a; iv, **722b** — II, 240a; III, 309a; IV, **751b**
Ḳāsimiyya (Yemen) iii, 255a — III, 262a
Kasimov ii, 44b; iv, **723a**, 849a — II, 45a; IV, **752a**, 882a
al-Kasirḳī → Nūr al-Din ʿAbd al-Raḥmān al-Kasirḳī
Ḳāsiyūn, Djabal iv, **724a**; s, 197a — IV, **753a**; S, 197a
Kaskar iv, **724b** — IV, **753b**
Kasr (mathematic/mathématique) iv, **725a**, 731b — IV, **754a**, 760b
Ḳaṣr (palace/palais) iv, 236b — IV, 247a
Ḳaṣr ʿAbd al-Karīm → al-Ḳaṣr al-Kabīr
Ḳaṣr Abī Dānis ii, 1009b — II, 1033a
Ḳaṣr al-Abyaḍ → Khirbat al-Bayḍāʾ
Ḳaṣr Adjwad b. Zamīl s, 234b — S, 234a
Ḳaṣr al-Aghāliba → al-Abbāsiyya
Ḳaṣr al-ʿAynī s, 38a — S, 38b
Ḳaṣr Burḳuʿ s, 117a — S, 116b
Ḳaṣr Firʿawn → Walīlī
Ḳaṣr al-Ḥallābāt s, 117a — S, 116b
Ḳaṣr al-Ḥasanī i, 897b, 898a, 1312b; iii, 243b — I, 924a, b, 1352b; III, 250b
Ḳaṣr al- Ḥayr al-Gharbī i, 613a; ii, 557a, 1021a; iii, 71a, 141b, 310a, 494b; iv, **726a**; s, 117a — I, 633a; II, 571a, 1045a; III, 73b, 144b, 319b, 511b; IV, **755a**; S, 116b
Ḳaṣr al-Ḥayr al-Sharḳi i, 613a, 613b, 831a; iii, 71a, 494b; iv, **727b**, 1011b; s, 117a — I, 633b, 854a; III, 73b, 511b; IV, **756b**, 1045a; S, 116b
Ḳaṣr Hishām → Khirbat al-Mafdjar
Ḳaṣr Ibn Hubayra iii, 265b, 266a; iv, **728b** — III, 273b; IV, **758a**
al-Ḳaṣr al-Kabīr iv, **729a**; v, 1191a — IV, **758a**; V, 1181a
al-Ḳaṣr al-Ḳadīm → al-ʿAbbāsiyya
Ḳaṣr Kharāna → Kharāna
Ḳaṣr Kutāma → al-Ḳaṣr al-Kabīr
Ḳaṣr al-Luṣūṣ → Kinkiwar
Ḳaṣr al-Madjāz → al-Ḳaṣr al-Ṣaghīr
al-Ḳaṣr al-Ṣaghīr i, 56a, 706b; iv, **729b** — I, 57b, 728a; IV, **759a**
Ḳaṣr al-Shawḳ s, 44a — S, 44b
Ḳaṣr-i Shīrīn i, 624a, 1345b; ii, 793b, 794a; iv, **730b** — I, 643b, 1386a; II, 812b; IV, **759b**
Ḳaṣr Yānī → Kaṣryānnih
Kasra iii, 172b; iv, **731a** — III, 176b; IV, **760b**
Ḳaṣrān v, 661b — V, 667a
Kasrānī i, 1007b — I, 1038b
Kasrawī Tabrīzī, Aḥmad ii, 882b; iv, 166b, **732a**, 789b; v, 1097b, 1098a — II, 902b; IV, 173b, **761b**, 821b; V, 1093b, 1094a
Ḳaṣryānnih iv, **733a** — IV, **762b**
Ḳāṣṣ, Ḳaṣṣa iv, **733b**; v, 186a, b, 187a, 951a — IV, **763a**; V, 183a, b, 184a, 954b
Kassāh → Kannās
Kassala → Kasala
Kassām i, 824a, b; ii, 483a; iii, 128b, 841a; iv, **735b** — I, 847a, b; II, 495a; III, 131a, 864b; IV, **765a**
Ḳassām (rebel) s, 37a — S, 37b
Ḳaṣṣār → Ghassāl
al-Ḳaṣṣār, Abū ʿAbd Allāh iv, **736a** — IV, **766a**
Ḳaṣṣāra, Abu 'l-Ḥusayn ʿAlī iv, **736b** — IV, **766a**
al-Ḳaṣṣāṣīn s, 300b — S, 300b
Ḳaṣṣārī iii, 132a — III, 134b
al-Ḳasṭal s, 230a — S, 230a
al-Ḳasṭallānī, Aḥmad i, 1297a; iv, **736b** — I, 1336b; IV, **766a**
Ḳasṭallanī, Muṣṭafā iv, **737a** — IV, **766b**
Ḳasṭamonu → Ḳasṭamūnī
Ḳasṭamūnī iv, 108b, **737a**; v, 693b, 966b, 977b, 1145b; s, 274a — IV, 113a, **767a**; V, 698b, 970b, 977a, 1137b; S, 273b
Ḳasṭīlya (Castille) → Ḳashtāla
Ḳasṭīliya (Ilbīra) iv, **739a** — IV, **769a**
Ḳasṭīliya (Tunisia/Tunisie) ii, 462b, 463a; iv, **739b** — II, 474b, 475a; IV, **769a**
Kastoria → Kesriye
Kastriota, George → Iskender Beg
Ḳaṣūr ii, 929a — II, 950b
Ḳāt iv, **741a** — IV, **770b**
Ḳaṭʿ iv, **741b** — IV, **771b**
Ḳaṭʿ al-Ṭarīḳ → Ḳatl; Ṣuʿlūk
Ḳaṭā iv, **743a** — IV, **773a**
Ḳaṭā Sarāy iv, 579b — IV, 603a
Ḳaʿṭaba iv, **745b** — IV, **775a**
Ḳatabān i, 548a, 1132b; iii, 208a; iv, **746a** — I, 565b, 1166b; III, 213b; IV, **775b**
Ḳatāda b. Diʿāma i, 104b; iv, 370b, **748b**; v, 1232a — I, 107b; IV, 387a, **778b**; V, 1222a
Ḳatāda b. Idrīs i, 552b, 1032a; iii, 262b; iv, **748b** — I, 570b, 1064a; III, 270a; IV, **778b**
Ḳatāda b. Salāma al-Ḥanafī iv, 832a — IV, 865a
Ḳatādid(e)s iii, 262b, 881a — III, 270a, 905a
Katahr iv, **749a**; s, 73b, 206b — IV, **779b**; S, 74a, 206a

Ḳaṭāʾiʿ ii, 187b; iv, 323a, b, **754b**, 973a, 1031a; v, 23a, 347a – II, 193b; IV, 337b, 338a, **785a**, 1005b, 1063a; V, 24a, 348a
al-Ḳaṭāʾiʿ i, 279a; ii, 958b, 959a – I, 287b; II, 980b, 981a
Katak → Orissa
Kataman v, 21b – V, 22a
Ḳaṭāmi bint al-Shidjna iii, 887a, 888a – III, 911a, 912a
Katanga iv, **749b** – IV, **780a**
Ḳataniya → Ṣiḳiliyya
Ḳaṭar i, 536a, 539b, 941a, 944a; ii, 177a; iv, **750b**, 953b; v, 1058a; s, 417a, b – I, 552b, 556b, 969b, 971b; II, 182b; IV, **781a**, 985b; V, 1055a; S, 417a, b
Ḳaṭarī b. al-Fudjāʾa i, 686b, 810b; iii, 40b; iv, 207b, 269a, **752b**, 938a, 1075b; v, 157b – I, 707b, 833b; III, 42b; IV, 217a, 281b, **783a**, 971a, 1107b; V, 157a
Katbughā → Kitbughā
Kāth ii, 1142a; iv, **753b**, 1063b, 1064b, 1066b – II, 1169a; IV, **784a**, 1095a, 1096a, 1098a
Kathāwat s, 325a – S, 324b
Kathīr al-Nawwāʾ s, 129b – S, 129a
Kathīr b. Saʿd v, 2a, b – V, 2a, b
Kathīrī iii, 291b; iv, 10a; v, 184a; s, 337b, 338b – III, 300b; IV, 11a; V, 181b; S, 337a, 338a
Ḳāthiyāwār → Djunagaṛh
Katī ii, 31a, 138b; iv, 409b, 410b – II, 32a, 142a; IV, 427a, 428b
Kaʿti, Maḥmūd iv, **754a** – IV, **784b**
Ḳaṭīʿa → Ḳaṭāʾiʿ
Kātib i, 981b; ii, 324b; iii, 740a, 1242b; iv, **754b**; v, 1238b – I, 1012a; II, 334a; III, 762b, 1274b; IV, **785a**; V, 1229a
Kātib Čelebi i, 478b, 594b, 698a, 758a, 1198a; ii, 110a, 589a, 590a; iv, 168a, **760b**, 1082b; s, 171b, 289b – I, 492b, 614a, 719a, 781a, 1233a; II, 112b, 603b, 604b; IV, 175a, **791a**, 1114a; S, 171b, 289b
al-Kātib al-Iṣfahānī → ʿImād al-Dīn
Kātib al-sirr ii, 330a – II, 339b
al-Katība iv, 1141a, b – IV, 1173a, b
al-Kātibī, Nadjm al-Dīn Dabīrān iv, **762a** – IV, **792b**
Kātibī, Shams al-Dīn iv, **762b** – IV, **793a**
Kātibī Rūmi ii, 588b, 589b – II, 603a, 604a
Kātib-i Rūnī → Sīdī Reʾīs
Kātibzāde Meḥmed Refīʿ iv, 1126a – IV, 1157b
al-Ḳaṭīf i, 73a, 942b; iv, **763b**; s, 234a – I, 75a, 971a; IV, **794a**; S, 234a
Katif, ʿIlm al- iv, **763a** – IV, **793b**
Ḳaṭīfe iii, 216b, 217b – III, 223a, b
al-Ḳaṭīfī, al-Nadjaf Ibrāhīm iv, 610a – IV, 635a
al-Ḳaṭīʿī → Abū Bakr
al-Ḳaṭīʿī al-Baghdādī iii, 756a – III, 779a
Ḳatīl, Mīrzā iii, 1244b – III, 1276b
Katīn → Khātūn
Ḳaṭirān → Ḳaṭrān
Ḳātir iii, 1105b, 1106a – III, 1132b, 1133b
Ḳatirdji-oghlu Meḥmed Pasha i, 4b; iii, 317b; iv, **765b** – I, 4b; III, 327a; IV, **796a**
Ḳaṭʿiyya iv, 743a – IV, 772b
Katkhudā → Ketkhudā
Katkhudā Marzubān i, 955b – I, 984b
Katkhudā Pasha → Ibrāhīm Pasha
Ḳatl iv, **766b** – IV, **797a**
Kator → Kāfiristān
Katra Mīrānpūr iii, 61b – III, 64a
Katrabbul → Ḳuṭrabbul
Ḳaṭrān iv, **772b** – IV, **803b**
Ḳaṭrān, Ḥakīm iv, 61b, 525b, **773a** – IV, 65a, 548b, **804a**
Katsina iii, 275a, 276a; iv, **773b** – III, 283a, 284a; IV, **804b**
Kattān iv, **774a** – IV, **805a**
al-Kattānī, Āl iv, **774b** – IV, **805b**
al-Kattānī, Muḥammad b. Djaʿfar iv, 774b; v, 1209b; s, 350b, 404a, b – IV, 805b; V, 1200a; S, 350b, 404b
al-Ḳātūl iv, 384a – IV, 400b
Ḳaṭwān Steppe iv, 581b – IV, 604b, 605a
Katwar → Kāfiristān
Ḳarādh I iii, 571b – III, 591b
Kavafoğlu → Atač, Nūr Allāh
Kavaklî → Čakmak, Mustafa Fevzi
Kavala Shahīn → Shahīn Pasha
Kavas → Ḳawwās
Kāveh → Kāwah
Kavol ii, 41a – II, 42a
Ḳavuḳ v, 751a – V, 756b
Kāwa iv, 775a – IV, 806a
Ḳawad → Ḳiṣāṣ
Kawādh I s, 297b – S, 297a
al-Ḳawādhiyān ii, 577b – II, 592a
Kāwah iv, **775a** – IV, **806a**
al-Kawākibī, ʿAbd al-Raḥmān i, 597b; iii, 593b; iv, 143b, 144a, 145b, 151a, 159a, 162b, **775b**, 782b – I, 617a; III, 614a; IV, 149b, 150a, 151b, 157b, 165b, 169b, **806b**, 814a
Ḳawāla iv, **776a** – IV, **807a**
Ḳawām, Aḥmad i, 190b; ii, 653b; iii, 529a; v, 630b – I, 196a; II, 670a; III, 547b; V, 634b
Ḳawām al-Dīn Zawzanī iv, 1034b – IV, 1066b
Ḳawām al-Mulk iii, 1106a; v, 674b – III, 1133b; V, 679b
Kawār i, 1221b; iv, **777a** – I, 1258a; IV, **808a**
al-Ḳawāsim i, 928a, 1282a; ii, 619a; iv, 751a, **777b**; v, 70b, 183b, 507b, 508a, 765a; s, 42a – I, 956b, 1321a; II, 634b; IV, 781b, **808b**; V, 72b, 180b, 181a, 511a, b, 771a; S, 42b
al-Kawfanī → al-Abīwardī
Kawīr s, 61a – S, 61b
Kawkab → Nudjūm
Kawkab al-Hawāʾ iv, **778b**; v, 120b – IV, **810a**; V, 123a
Kawkabān iii, 134a; iv, **779a** – III, 137a; IV, **810b**
Kawkaw → Gao
Ḳawlīs i, 323a; v, 818b – I, 333a; V, 824b
Ḳawm iii, 411a; iv, **780b**, 785b – III, 424a; IV, **812a**, 817a
Ḳawm (military/militaire) → Gūm
al-Ḳawmā → al-Ḳūmā
Ḳawmiyya iv, **781a** – IV, **812b**
Kawn wa-fasād iv, **794b** – IV, **827a**
Kawōm → Ḳawm
al-Kawr i, 536a, b – I, 552b, 553a
Ḳawriya → Ḳūriya
Ḳaws ii, 506b; iii, 469b, 470a, 476a; iv, **795b** – II, 519b; III, 486a, b, 492b; IV, **828a**
Ḳaws Ḳuzaḥ iv, **803a** – IV, **835b**
Ḳawṣara iv, **805a** – IV, **837a**
al-Kawthar ii, 448b; iii, 286a; iv, **805b** – II, 460b; III, 295a; IV, **838a**
Ḳawuḳlu iv, **806a** – IV, **838b**
Ḳāwurd b. Čaghri Beg → Ḳāwurd Ḳarā Arslān
Ḳāwurd b. Čaghrî Beg Dāwūd i, 420a, 552a, 664b, 665a; iii, 195a, 507a, 1097b, 1098a; iv, 26b, 27b, 101a, **807a**; v, 158b, 353a; s, 127a – I, 432a, 569b, 684b; III, 199b, 524b, 1124a, 1125a; IV, 28b, 29b, 105b, **839b**; V, 158a, 353b; S, 126a
Kāwūs, Banū iv, **808a** – IV, **840b**
Kāwūs b. Kayūmarth iv, 808a; v, 663a – IV, 840b; V, 668b
Ḳawwās iv, **808b** – IV, **841a**
Kay Khusraw → Kaykhusraw
Kaya → Ketkhudā
Kayalars v, 582a – V, 587a

Ḳayalîḳ iv, **808b** — IV, **841a**
Kayānīd(e)s iv, 12b, **809a** — IV, 13a, **841b**
al-Kayd iv, **809b**, 1186a — IV, **842b**, 1219a
al-Ḳayd iii, 208a — III, 213b
Kaydaḳ → Ḳaytaḳ
Ḳaydū (Tīmūrid(e)) i, 1133b — I, 1168a
Ḳaydu Khān i, 504b, 1311b, 1312a; ii, 3a, 45a, b; iv, 808b, **811b**; v, 39a, 300a; s, 240a — I, 520a, 1352a, b; II, 3b, 46a, b; IV, 841b, **844a**; V, 40a, 299b; S, 240a
Ḳayghusuz Abdāl iv, **811b** — IV, **844b**
Kaygîlî, ʿOthmān Djemāl iv, **812a**; s, 64b — IV, **845a**; S, 65a
Ḳāyî iv, **812b** — IV, **845b**
Ḳayib Khān i, 1076b — I, 1108b
Ḳāyināt iv, 4a-b — IV, 4b
Kayîr Buḳu Khān s, 246a — S, 246a
Ḳayir Tigin → Ḳaratigin
Ḳayitbāy → Ḳāʾitbāy (Mamlūk)
Kaykāʾūs I (Saldjūḳid(e)) i, 313a, 336b, 467a, 510a; ii, 37b, 966b; iii, 708a; iv, 575b, **813b** — I, 323a, 343b, 480b, 525b; II, 38b, 988b; III, 730a; IV, 598b, **846a**
Kaykāʾūs II (Saldjūḳid(e)) i, 1188b, 1302b; ii, 204b, 610b, 971a; iv, 600b, **813b**; v, 104b, 254a, 286a — I, 1223b, 1342a; II, 210b, 625b, 993b; IV, 625a, **846b**; V, 106b, 252a, 284a
Kay Kāʾūs (Kayānid(e)) iv, 809a, **813a** — IV, 842a, **846a**
Kay Kāʾūs b. Iskandar iv, **815a**; s, 96b — IV, **847b**; S, 96a
Kay Khusraw (Kayānid(e)) i, 236b; iv, 809a, **815b** — I, 244a; IV, 842a, **848b**
Kaykhusraw I (Saldjūḳid(e)) i, 346a, 466b, 517b; ii, 111a; iii, 708a; iv, **816a**, 1061b — I, 356b, 480b, 533a; II, 113b; III, 730a; IV, **849a**, 1092b
Kaykhusraw II (Saldjūḳid(e)) i, 432a, 467a, 838b; ii, 38a; iv, **816b**; v, 271b, 286a, b — I, 444b, 480b, 861b; II, 38b; IV, **849b**; V, 269b, 284a, b
Kaykhusraw III (Saldjūḳid(e)) i, 703a; iv, 620b, **817a** — I, 724a; IV, 645a, b, **850a**
Kay Khusraw Īndjū iii, 1208a, b — III, 1239a
Kay Ḳubād (Kayānid(e)) iv, 809a — IV, 841b
Ḳayḳubād I ʿAlā al-Dīn (Saldjūḳid(e)) i, 329a, 354b, 355a, 424b, 467a, 510a, 665a, 799b, 1191b; ii, 38a, 444b, 692a, 710b, 711b; iii, 215b, 738a; iv, 521a, **817b**, 818b, 1084b; v, 255a, 285b — I, 339b, 365b, 366a, 436a, 480b, 525b, 686a, 822b, 1226b; II, 38b, 456a, 709a, 727a, 729b; III, 222a, 760b; IV, 543b, **850a**, 851b, 1115b; V, 253a, 284a
Kayḳubād II (Saldjūḳid(e)) iv, **818a** — IV, **851a**
Ḳayḳūbād III (Saldjūḳid(e)) ii, 201a; iv, **818a** — II, 207b; IV, **851a**
Ḳayḳubād, Muʿizz al-Dīn (Dihlī) ii, 256b, 268a; iv, **818a**, 920b; s, 73b — II, 263b, 276b; IV, **851a**, 953b; S, 74a
Kayḳubādiyya iv, **818b** — IV, **851b**
Ḳayl iv, **818b** — IV, **851b**
Kayl → Makāyīl
Ḳayla, Banū i, 514a, 771a; v, 995a — I, 529b, 794a; V, 990a
Kaylif → Kālif
Kay-Luhrāsb → Kayānid(e)s
Kaylūkarī s, 243b — S, 243b
Kaymak → Kīmāk
Ḳaymāz iii, 891b — III, 915b
Ḳaymaz Kāfūrī → Ṣārim al-Dīn
Ḳayn iv, **819a** — IV, **852a**
Ḳayn, Banuʾl- i, 684b; iv, **819b** — I, 705b; IV, **852b**
Ḳayna, Ḳaynāt i, 32b; ii, 551b, 1073b; iv, **820b**; s, 247a — I, 33b; II, 565a, 1098a; IV, **853a**; S, 247a
Ḳaynuḳāʿ, Banū i, 53a; iv, **824a**; v, 996a — I, 55a; IV, **857a**; V, 991b
Kayor, Kingdom of s, 179b — S, 180b
Kayra ii, 122a, b, 124b — II, 125a, b, 127b
al-Ḳayrawān i, 77b, 86b, 125a, 134b, 163b, 248a, 249a, 532b, 1175a; iii, 386a, 655a, 903b; iv, 479a, 532b, **824b**; v, 518a, 877b, 1159a; s, 26b, 62b, 103a, 144a, b, 145a, 172b, 274a, 303b, 306a, b, 394b — I, 79b, 89a, 128b, 138a, 168a, 255b, 257a, 548b, 1210a; III, 398b, 676a, 927b; IV, 501a, 555b, **857b**; V, 521b, 883b, 1149a; S, 27a, 63a, 102b, 144a, b, 173b, 273b, 303b, 306a, 395a
- constructions i, 457b, 624a, 1346a; ii, 863a, iii, 287b; iv, 825b, 828b-831b — I, 472a, 645a, 1386b; II, 883a; III, 296a; IV, 858b, 861b-864a
- great mosque/la grande mosquée i, 248b, 619b, 621a, 950a; ii, 746a; iii, 271b; iv, 829b, 1165b; v, 220b — I, 256a, 639a, 641b, 979a; II, 764a; III, 279b; IV, 862b, 1198a; V, 218a
al-Ḳayrawānī → Ibn Abī Zayd
al-Ḳays → Ḳaws Ḳuzaḥ
Ḳays (island/île) → Kīsh
Ḳays, Djazīrat i, 942b — I, 971a, b
Ḳays b. ʿAmr al-Nadjāshī s, 10a — S, 9b
Ḳays b. ʿĀṣim iv, **832a** — IV, **865a**
Ḳays b. al-Haytham al-Sulamī i, 47b, 1001a; iv, 14b — I, 49a, 1031b; IV, 15b, 16a
Ḳays b. al-Ḥusayn iii, 223b — III, 230a
Ḳays b. al-Imām Aḥmad i, 1282a; s, 355b — I, 1321a; S, 355b
Ḳays b. al-Khaṭīm iii, 941a; iv, **835b** — III, 965b; IV, **868b**
Ḳays b. Maʿdīkarib i, 689b, 696b; v, 119a — I, 7106, 718a; V, 122a
Ḳays b. al-Makshūḥ al-Murādī i, 110b, 728a; iv, 1134b — I, 113b, 750a; IV, 1166b
Ḳays b. Masʿūd al-Shaybānī i, 690a — I, 710b
Ḳays b. Muḥammad al-Ḥirāmī ii, 517b — II, 530b
Ḳays b. Saʿd i, 44a; iii, 241a, b, 242a — I, 45b; III, 248a, 249a
Ḳays b. Salāma b. al-Ḥārith i, 527a; iii, 1177b; v, 118b — I, 543a; III, 1206b; V, 121b
Ḳays b. Thaʿlaba i, 73a, 963b, 964a — I, 75b, 993b, 994a
Ḳays b. Zuhayr b. Djadhīma al-ʿAbsī i, 115b; ii, 873a, 1023a; s, 177a, b, 178a — I, 119a; II, 893b, 1046b; S, 178a, b, 179a
Ḳays ʿAbd al-Rashīd i, 218b — I, 225a
Ḳays ʿAylān i, 76b, 329a, 529b 532a, 544b, 643a, 1241b; ii, 89a, 327b; iii, 1255a; iv, 314b, 493a, 494b, **833b** — I, 78b, 339b, 545b, 548a, 562a, 663b, 1279a; II, 91a, 337a; III, 1287b; IV, 328b, 514a, 515b, **866b**
Ḳaysaba b. Kulthūm s, 37b — S, 37b
Kaysān iii, 820b — III, 844b
Kaysān, Abū ʿAmra iv, **836a**, b — IV, **869a**, b
Kaysāniyya i, 850b; ii, 1094b; iii, 1265b; iv, **836b**, 1086b; v, 350a, 433b, 552a, 1235b; s, 357b — I, 874a; II, 1120a; III, 1298b; IV, **869a**, 1117b; V, 350b, 435b, 557a, 1226a; S, 357b
Kayṣar iv, **839a** — IV, **871b**
Ḳayṣar, Banū i, 928a — I, 95a
Ḳayṣar Shāh b. Zamān i, 230b — I, 238a
al-Kaysarānī, Abu 'l-Faḍl b. Ṭāhir i, 100a; v, 330a — I, 103a; V, 330a
al-Ḳaysarī, Dāwūd b. Maḥmūd s, 364a, b — S, 364a
Ḳaysāriyya iv, **840a** — IV, **873a**
Ḳaysariyya (Caesarea) iii, 475b; iv, **841a** — III, 492a; IV, **874a**
Ḳayṣariyya (Kayseri) iv, 623b, **842b**; v, 1145a, b; s, 146a, 274a — IV, 648b, **876a**; V, 1137a, b; S, 146a, 273b
Ḳaysar-nāma s, 41a — S, 41b
Kayseri → Ḳayṣariyya
Ḳaysī ii, 635a; iii, 42b — II, 651a; III, 44a
Ḳaysīs s, 82a — S, 81b

Ḳaysūn i, 1190b — I, 1225b
Ḳayt al-Radjabī iv, 552a — IV, 576a
Ḳaytaḳ (Kaytagh) ii, 86b, 89a, 141b; iv, 345b, 350b, **846a**, 1176b — II, 88a, 90b, 145a; IV, 360a, 365b, **879b**, 1210a
Ḳaytās Bey i, 56a, 395a — I, 58a, 406b
Ḳāytbāy → Ḳā'itbāy
Kayūmarth, Shams al-Dīn ii, 268a; iv, 818b, 920b — II, 276b; IV, 851a, 953b
Kayūmarth b. Bīstutūn iv, 808a — IV, 840b
Kayūs b. Ḳubād i, 1110a — I, 1143b
Kayūsiyya i, 1110a — I, 1143b
al-Kayyāl, Aḥmad iv, **847a** — IV, **880a**
Ḳayyān iv, 822b — IV, 855b
Kayyarā s, 101b — S, 101a
Ḳayyim iv, **847b** — IV, **880b**
Ḳayyūm Nāṣirī iv, **848a** — IV, **881a**
Kāz → Ḳabḳ
Kaza → Ḳaḍā'
Kaza → Khāsa
Ḳazaghān iv, 32a — IV, 34b
Ḳazaḳ i, 120b, 135b, 268a, 418b, 481a, 722a, 1076b, 1077a, 1252a, 1287a; ii, 25a, 44b, 446a, 613a, 995b, 1066b; iii, 116b, 531b; iv, 40a, 178b-179a, 512b, 611a, **848a**; v, 134b, 135a; s, 169a — I, 124a, 139a, 276a, 430a, 495a, 743b, 1108b, 1109a, 1290a, 1326b; II, 25b, 45b, 458a, 628a, 1018a, 1091a; III, 119a, 550a; IV, 42b, 185b-186a, 534b, 635b, **881b**; V, 137b; S, 169a
Ḳazākhstān ii, 44b; v, 135b — II, 45b; V, 138a
Kazalinsk s, 244b — S, 244b
Ḳāzān i, 1075b, 1108a, 1308a; ii, 44b, 179a, 1113a; iv, 280b, 723b, **849a**; s, 82a, b, 96b — I, 1108a, 1141a, 1348a; II, 45a, 184b, 1139a; IV, 293a, 752b, **882a**; S, 82a, 96a
Ḳazan Khān ii, 4a — II, 4a
Kāzarān s, 73a — S, 73b
Kāzarūn i, 240a; iv, **850b** — I, 247b; IV, **883b**
al-Kazarūnī, Shaykh Abū Isḥāḳ i, 147a, 162b, 1129a, 1245b; iv, **851a**; v, 1112a — I, 151a, 167a, 1163a, 1283b; IV, **884b**; V, 1108b
Kazarūniyya iv, 46b, 851a — IV, 49a, 884a, b
Ḳāzbēgī → Sikka
Kazbek → Ḳabk
al-Ḳāzdughlī, Ibrāhīm Kahyā iv, 852a, b — IV, 885a, b
al-Ḳazdughlī, Muṣṭafā iv, 852a — IV, 885a
Ḳāzdughliyya ii, 233b; iv, **852a** — II, 240b; IV, **885a**
Kāzh → Kāth
Kazi-asker → Ḳāḍī ʿAskar
Ḳāzī-Ḳūmuḳ → Lak
Kazi Mulla → Ghāzī Muḥammad
al-Kāẓim → Mūsā al-Kāẓim
Kāzim, Bā i, 767a — I, 790a
Kāẓim Bey, Mīrzā s, 76a — S, 76a
Kāẓim Ḳadrī, Ḥusayn iv, **853a** — IV, **886b**
Kāẓîm Karabekir Pasha i, 641b; ii, 6b; iv, 671a, **853b** — I, 662a; II, 6b; IV, 698b, **887a**
Kāẓim Rashtī iv, 51a, **854a** — IV, 54a, **887b**
Kāẓimayn i, 903b; iv, **854b**; s, 57a, 77a, 94a, 95a — I, 931a; IV, **887b**; S, 57b, 76b, 93b, 94a
Kāẓimī → Sikka
al-Kāẓimī, ʿAbd al-Muḥsin iv, **856a** — IV, **889a**
al-Kāẓimī, ʿAbd al-Nabī b. ʿAlī iv, **856b** — IV, **889b**
al-Kāẓimī, Ḥaydar b. Ibrāhīm iv, **856b** — IV, **890a**
al-Kāẓimī, Meḥmed Sālim iv, **857a** — IV, **890a**
Kāẓimī, Murtaḍā Mushfiḳ iv, 72b; v, 198b — IV, 76b; V, 196a
Kāzimiyya → Kāzimayn
Kazimov → Ḳāsimov
Kazirūn → Kāzarūn
Ḳazwīn i, 8b, 688b; iv, 7b, **857b**; v, 875b; s, 43b, 83b, 84a, 139a, 336a, 423a — I, 8b, 709b; IV, 8b, **890b**; V, 881b; S, 44a, 83b, 138b, 335b, 423b
- monuments iv, 862b — IV, 895b
al-Ḳazwīnī, ʿAbd al-Djalīl s, 56b — S, 57a
al-Ḳazwīnī, Abū Ḥātim Maḥmūd iv, **863a** — IV, **896a**
Ḳazwīnī, Ḥamd Allāh → Ḥamd Allāh Mustawfī
al-Ḳazwīnī, Khaṭīb Dimashḳ i, 858a, 982b, 1116a; ii, 824a; iv, **863b**; v, 898a, b, 900b — I, 882a, 1013a, 1149b; II, 843a; IV, **896b**; V, 904a, b, 907a
al-Kazwīnī, Nadjm al-Dīn ʿAbd al-Ghaffār iv, 509b, **864b** — IV, 532a, **898a**
Ḳazwīnī, Sayyid Mahdī s, 135a — S, 134b
al-Ḳazwīnī, Zakariyyā i, 157a, 204a, 419b, 571a, 594b, 836a; ii, 587b; iii, 30a, 313a, 991b; iv, **865a**, 1081b; s, 128b — I, 161a, 209b, 431a, 589b, 613b, 859a; II, 602a; III, 31b, 322b, 1016a; IV, **898a**, 1112b; S, 128a
al-Ḳazzāz, Abū ʿAbd Allāh Muḥammad iv, **867a** — IV, **900b**
al-Ḳazzāz → Ḥakam b. Saʿīd
al-Ḳazzāz, Muḥammad b. ʿUbāda iii, 855b — III, 879b
Kebbawa ii, 1144b, 1146a — II, 1172a, 1173a
Kebek Khān ii, 4a, 14b, 45a; iv, 419a, 671b, 921b; v, 858b — II, 4a, 15a, 46a; IV, 437a, 699a, 954b; V, 865b
Kebra Nagast i, 1220a — I, 1256b
Keče → Libās
Kečedjīzāde → Fu'ād Pasha; ʿIzzet Mollā
Kechla i, 689a — I, 710a
Kēčī i, 1007a — I, 1038a
Kečiboynuzu Ibrāhīm Ḥilmī Pasha iv, 569b, **867b** — IV, 592a, **901a**
Kēdah iii, 1218a, 1219b; iv, 467b — III, 1249a, 1250b; IV, 488b
Kediri s, 202a — S, 201b
Kēdjuruns i, 740a — I, 762a
Kef, le → al-Kāf
Kefalia Shahīn → Shahīn Pasha
Kefe iii, 44a; iv, 576a, **868a**; v, 141a — III, 46a; IV, 599a, **901a**; V, 144a
Kel Ḥasan iv, 806b — IV, 839a
Kelāt → Kalāt
Keldibek iii, 117a — III, 119b
Kelek iv, **870a** — IV, **903b**
Kelesh-beg (Prince/le prince) i, 101a — I, 104a
Kelek i, 424a, 476a — I, 436a, 490a
Kēlvē-Māhīm → Māhīm
Kemākh iv, **870b** — IV, **904a**
Kemāl, ʿAlī iv, **871b** — IV, **905a**
Kemāl, Meḥmed Nāmîḳ i, 61b, 62a, 74b, 630b; ii, 430b, 473b, 474a, 682a, 692b, 878a, 1047a; iii, 592a; iv, **875a**; v, 1172b; s, 98a, 324b — I, 63b, 64a, 77a, 651a; II, 441b, 485b, 486a, 699a, 709b, 898b, 1071b; III, 612b; IV, **908b**; V, 1162b; S, 97b, 324a
Kemāl al-Dīn → Kamāl al-Dīn
Kemāl Pasha-zāde i, 89a, 698a, 1208a; ii, 552b, 997b, 1137a; iii, 164a, 596b, 708b; iv, 333b, **879b** — I, 91b, 719b, 1244a; II, 566b, 1020b, 1163b; III, 167b, 617a, 730b; IV, 348a, **912a**
Kemāl Re'īs ii, 588a; iv, **881b**; v, 506b — II, 602b; IV, **914b**; V, 509b
Kemal Tahir (Demir) iv, **882a**; v, 197a — IV, **915a**; V, 194a
Kemāl of/de Eğridir, Ḥādjdjī s, 50b — S, 51a
Kemāliye → Eğin
Kemānkesh ʿAlī Pasha iv, **884a** — IV, **917a**
Kemānkesh Ḳara Muṣṭafā Pasha ii, 804b; iii, 623a, 626b, 983a, 1001b; iv, 455b; v, 249a — II, 823b; III, 644a, 647a, 1007b, 1026b; IV, 476a; V, 246b
Kemkhā iii, 216b — III, 223a
Ḳenā → Ḳunā

Kenʿān Pasha iv, **884b**; v, 258a — IV, **917a**; V, 256a
Kenèh → Ḳunā
Kenesarî Khān v, 135b — V, 138a
Kenya, Kenia i, 38a; iv, **885a**; s, 248a, b — I, 39a; IV, **918a**; S, 248a, b
Kenz → Kanz, Banu ʾl-
al-Kerak → Karak
Kerasūn → Giresün
Kerbānsarāyî iv, 228a — IV, 238a
Kerbela → Karbalāʾ
Kerbenesh iv, **891b** — IV, **924a**
Kerboka i, 485a — I, 499b
Kerbughā → Karbughā
Kerč iv, **891b**; v, 141a — IV, **924a**; V, 143b
Keren i, 1163a — I, 1197b
Kerey → Giray
Kereyt, Kereit ii, 42a, b, 1112b — II, 42b, 43a, 1138b
Kerimba (islands/îles) iv, **892a** — IV, **925a**
Kerkenna → Ḳarḳana
Kerkha → Karkha
Kerkuk → Kirkūk
Kerkur → Karkūr
Kermān → Kirmān
Kermān Shāh → Kirmān Shāh
Kermiyān → Germiyān
Ḳerrī iv, **892b** — IV, **925b**
Kertch → Kerč
Kesh → Kash
Keskes → Kuskusu
Kesr-i mīzān ii, 83a — II, 85a
Kesriye iv, **893a** — IV, **926a**
Kestelī, Kestellī → Ḳasṭallanī, Muṣṭafa
Ketāma → Kutāma
Ketapang s, 150b — S, 150b
Kētehr → Katahr
Ketendji ʿÖmer Pasha-zade Meḥmed iii, 318a — III, 327b
Ketkhudā ii, 1121a; iii, 1180a; iv, 8b, 476a, **893b** — II, 1147a; III, 1209a; IV, 9a, 497a, **926b**
Ketkhudā Ḥasan Pasha → Kahyā Ḥasan Pasha
Key → Miftāḥ
Khāʾ iv, **894b** — IV, **927b**
Khabar (information) iii, 369a; iv, **895a**; v, 1103a — III, 381a; IV, **928b**; V, 1099a
Khabar (grammar/grammaire) iv, **895b** — IV, **928a**
Khabar al-wāḥid iv, **896a** — IV, **928b**
Khabbāb b. al-Aratt iv, **896b** — IV, **929a**
Khabbāz v, 41b, 42a — V, 42b, 43a
Khabīr al-Mulk, Ḥasan Khān s, 53b — S, 54a
Khabīr al-Mulk, Rūḥī Khān s, 53b — S, 54a
al-Khabīth, ʿAlī Muḥammad v, 451b — V, 454a
Khabn → ʿArūḍ
Khabrāʾ iv, **879b** — IV, **930a**
Khābūr (rivers/rivières) i, 608a; iv, 655a, **897b** — I, 628a; IV, 681b, **930b**
Khābūr al-Ḥasaniyaa iv, 898a; s, 37a — IV, 931a; S, 37a
Khabūshān → Ḳūčān
al-Khabūshānī i, 197a — I, 203a
al-Khaddām, ʿAbd Allāh b. Muḥammad iv, 515b — IV, 538a
Khaḍḍār i, 961a — I, 990b
Khaddāsh → Khidāsh
Khadīdja ii, 363b, 845b; iii, 152b; iv, **898b** — II, 373a, 865b; III, 156a; IV, **931a**
Khadīdja bint al-Ḥasan s, 95a — S, 94b
Khadīdja Begum iv, 391a — IV, 407b
Khadīdje Sulṭān bint Meḥemmed IV i, 96b; ii, 684b; iii, 216a, 252b — I, 99b; II, 701b; III, 222a, 259b
Khadidje Sulṭān Turkhān iii, 998a, b; iv, 1100a — III, 1023a, b; IV, 1131a
Khādim i, 33a; iv, **899a**, 1087a — I, 34a; IV, **931b**, 1118a
Khādim al-Ḥaramayn iv, **899b**, 946a — IV, **932b**, 978b
Khādim Ḥasan Pasha Ṣoḳollî iv, **900b**, 1093a — IV, **933b**, 1124a
Khādim Pasha → ʿAlī Pasha; Sinān Pasha; Sulaymān Pasha
Khādim Süleymān Pasha iv, 435b, **901a**, 1093a; v, 35a, 534b, 1022b — IV, 455a, **934a**, 1124a; V, 36b, 539a, 1018a
al-Khaḍir (al-Khiḍr) i, 117a, 347a, 1284a; ii, 1026a; iii, 1156a; iv, 674b, 810b, **902b**; v, 17b, 800b — I, 120a, 357b, 1323b; II, 1049b; III, 1184b; IV, 702a, 843a, **935a**; V, 18a, 806b
Khaḍīr, Banū i, 546a; iv, **905b** — I, 563a; IV, **938b**
al-Khaḍir, Djazīrat iv, **906a** — IV, **939a**
al-Khaḍir, Muḥammad b. al-Ḥusayn iv, **906a** — IV, **939a**
al-Khaḍir (Khiḍr) b. ʿAlī s, 263b — S, 263a
Khaḍiriyya i, 277b — I, 286a
Kh(w)ādja iv, **907a**; v, 26a — IV, **940a**; V, 27a
Kh(w)ādja ʿAbd Allāh Anṣārī Harawī i, 936b; s, 292a — I, 965b; S, 291b
Kh(w)adja Aḥrar → ʿUbayd Allāh Aḥrar
Kh(w)ādja ʿAlī ii, 350b — II, 360a
Kh(w)ādja Bāḳī biʾllāh → Bāḳī biʾllāh
Kh(w)ādja-i Djahān Aḥmad Ayāz i, 1036b, 1166a; ii, 814a; iii, 570a; iv, **907b** — I, 1068a, 1200b; II, 833b; III, 589b; IV, **940b**
Kh(w)ādjagān iv, 47b, 1092b — IV, 50b, 1123b
Kh(w)ādjagānlîḳ i, 433a; iv, 908b — I, 445b; IV, 941b, 942a
Kh(w)ādjagī, Mawlānā s, 122a — S, 121b
Kh(w)ādja-i Djahān Astarābādī iv, **908a** — IV, **941a**
Kh(w)ādja-i Djahān Aʿẓam-i Humāyūn iv, **908a** — IV, **941a**
Kh(w)ādja-i Djahān Dakhnī iv, **908a** — IV, **941a**
Kh(w)ādja-i Djahān Malik Sarwar iv, **907b** — IV, **940b**
Kh(w)ādja-i Djahān Nūr al-Dīn iv, **907b** — IV, **941a**
Kh(w)ādja-i Djahān Surūr iv, **907b** — IV, **941a**
Kh(w)ādja-i Djahān Turk iv, **908a** — IV, **941a**
Kh(w)ādjā Ghulām Farīd iv, 507b — IV, 529b
Kh(w)ādja Kamāl al-Dīn i, 302b — I, 312a
Kh(w)ādja Khiḍr iv, 905a, **908a** — IV, 938a, **941a**
Kh(w)ādja Muʿīn al-Dīn Ḥasan Sidjzī → Čishtī
Kh(w)ādja Shams al-Dīn v, 827a — V, 833a
Kh(w)ādja-zāde → Khōdja-zāde
Kh(w)ādjegān-i Dīwān-i Humāyūn iv, **908b** — IV, **941b**
Kh(w)adjū Kamāl al-Dīn Kirmānī i, 1301a; iv, 66a, b, **909b**, 1010a — I, 1340b; IV, 70a, **942b**, 1042a
Kh(w)āf iv, **910a**, 1073a; s, 57b, 420b — IV, **943a**, 1105a; S, 58a, 421a
Khafādja i, 528b; iv, **910b**; v, 348b; s, 119a — I, 544b; IV, **943b**; V, 349a; S, 118b
al-Khafādjī ii, 824b; iv, 250a — II, 844a; IV, 261a
al-Khafādjī, Shihāb al-Dīn al-Miṣrī i, 68a, 594a; iii, 222a; iv, **912a** — I, 70a, 613b; III, 228b; IV, **945a**
Khafāra ii, 143b; iii, 394a, 396b; iv, **913a** — II, 147a; III, 406b, 409a; IV, **945b**
Khafḍ (Khifāḍ) iv, **913a** — IV, **946a**
al-Kh(w)āfī, Abū Manṣūr ʿAbdallāh iv, 910a — IV, 943a
al-Kh(w)āfī, Faṣīḥ al-Dīn Aḥmad iv, 910b — IV, 943a
Kh(w)afī, Niẓām al-Dīn ʿAbd al-Raḥīm v, 872b, 873b — V, 878b, 879b
Kh(w)āfī Khān i, 769b; iv, **914a** — I, 792b; IV, **947a**
Khafīf → ʿArūḍ
Khafiyye i, 64a — I, 66a
Khaibar → Khaybar

Khāʾin Aḥmad → Aḥmad Pasha
Khāʾir Bey ii, 1042a; iv, 451a, 553a — II, 1066b; IV, 471a, 577a
Khāḳān iv, 343b, **915a**, 1010b, 1174a, 1176b, 1177a — IV, 358a, **948a**, 1042b, 1207a, 1209b, 1210b
Khāḳān → Fatḥ ʿAlī Shāh
Khāḳānī, Afḍal al-Dīn Ibrāhīm i, 677a, 680a; iv, 62a, 63b, 348b, **915a**; v, 619b; s, 108a, 239b, 333b — I, 698a, 701a; IV, 65b, 66b, 363a, b, **948a**; V, 623b; S, 107a, 240a, 333a
Khāḳānī Meḥmed Bey iv, **916a**; s, 83a — IV, **949a**; S, 83a
Khāḳānid(e)s → Shirwān Shāh
Khāksār (India/l'Inde) iv, **916b** — IV, **949b**
Khāksār (Iran) iv, 52a — IV, 54b
Khāl, akhwāl iv, **916b** — IV, **949b**
Khāl, Khayalān → Firāsa
Khalʿa → Khilʿa
Khalā iv, 272b, 273a — IV, 284b, 285a
Khaladj i, 99b, 217b; ii 1001a; iii, 1106b, 1108b; iv, 705b, **917a**; v, 369b — I, 102a, 224a; II, 1024b; III, 1134a, 1136a; IV, 734a, **950a**; V, 370a
Khaladjistān iv, 918a — IV, 951a
Khalaf i, 202a — I, 208a
Khalaf, Banū ʾl- ii, 463b — II, 475a
Khalaf b. ʿAbd al-Malik → Ibn Bashkuwāl
Khalaf b. Aḥmad i, 160a; ii, 1082a; iii, 471a, 502a — I, 164b; II, 1107a; III, 487b, 519b
Khalaf b. Ḥayyān al-Aḥmar, Abū Muḥriz i, 105b, 115b, 143b, 718b, 1081a; ii, 248b; iii, 136a; iv, **919a** — I, 108b, 119a, 147b, 740a, 1113b; II, 255b; III, 139a; IV, **952a**
Khalaf b. Hishām iii, 155b — III, 158b
Khalaf b. Mubārak al-Ḳuṣayyir iii, 403b — III, 415b
Khalaf b. Mulāʿib al-Ashhabī i, 215a; iii, 398b; iv, **919a** — I, 221b; III, 411a; IV, **952a**
Khalaf b. al-Samḥ i, 139a; ii, 441b; iii, 659b, 1040a; iv, 919b; v, 1230a — I, 143a; II, 453a; III, 681a, 1066a; IV, 952b; V, 1220b
Khalaf Allāh, Muḥammad Aḥmad i, 821a; ii, 452a; iv, 161b — I, 844a; II, 463b; IV, 168a
al-Khalafiyya iii, 659b, 1168a; iv, 47a, **919b** — III, 681a, 1197a; IV, 49b, **952b**
Khalandj iv, 1085b; v, 107b — IV, 1116b; V, 110a
al-Khalaṣa iv, 263b — IV, 275b
Khaldī v, 448a — V, 450b
Khaldjī Samarkandī, ʿAbd al-Salām s, 121b — S, 121a
Khaldjīs (Dihlī) i, 393b; ii, 268a, 1084a; iii, 441b; iv, 268b, 818b, 918a, **920b**; v, 688b; s, 124b, 280a, 352b, 353a, 409a — I, 405a; II, 276b, 1109b; III, 456a; IV, 280b, 851a, 951a, **953b**; V, 693b; S, 123b, 280a, 352b, 409b
Khaldjis (Mālwa) → Mālwa
Khaldūn, Banū iv, 115b; s, 111b — IV, 120b; S, 111a
al-Khaldūniyya (al-Djamʿiyya) iv, **924a** — IV, **957a**
Khalfūn, Amīr iv, 275a — IV, 287b
Khāliʿ Ḳasam i, 829a — I, 852a
Khālid, Banū i, 873b; ii, 77a, 108b; iii, 238a; iv, 765a, **925a**; v, 333a — I, 897b; II, 78b, 111a; III, 245a; IV, 795b, **958a**; V, 333a
Khālid b. ʿAbd Allāh al-Ḳasrī i, 207a, 684b, 865b, 1094b, 1116b, 1242b; ii, 36a; iii, 42a, 493b, 650a, 715a, 747b, 802b, 1255a; iv, 913b, **925b**; v, 347a, 374a; s, 232b — I, 213a, 705b, 889b, 1127a, 1150b, 1280b; II, 36b; III, 43b, 510b, 671b, 737b, 770b, 826a, 1287b; IV, 946a, **958b**; V, 347b, 375a; S, 232b
Khālid b. Abī Djaʿfar al-Barḳī s, 127b — S, 126b
Khālid b. Aḥmad al-Dhuhlī i, 1296b — I, 1336b
Khālid b. Asīd s, 267b, 386a — S, 267a, 386b
Khālid b. Barghash i, 1282b — I, 1321b
Khālid b. Barmak → al-Barāmika
Khālid b. Djaʿfar b. ʿĀmir ii, 1023a; iii, 812a — II, 1046b; III, 835b
Khālid b. Fayṣal b. ʿAbd al-ʿAzīz Āl Suʿūd s, 305b, 306a — S, 305b, 306a
Khālid b. Hamīd al-Zanātī v, 367a — V, 368a
Khālid b. Ibrāhīm, Abū Dāwūd v, 181b — V, 178b
Khālid b. Maʿdān al-Ṭāʾī iv, 446a; v, 19b — IV, 465b; V, 20a
Khālid b. Maʿdān b. Abī Kurayb al-Kalāʿī iv, 369a — IV, 385b
Khālid b. Manṣūr → Ibn Luʾayy
Khālid b. Muḥammad, Shaykh s, 418a — S, 418b
Khālid b. Ṣafwān b. al-Ahtam i, 1297b; iv, **927a**; v, 132a — I, 1337b; IV, **960a**; V, 135a
Khālid b. Saʿīd iv, **927a** — IV, **960a**
Khālid b. Shāhsuwār Bek i, 1157a — I, 1191b
Khālid b. Sinān al-ʿAbsī i, 509a; ii, 1024a; iii, 169a; iv, **928a** — I, 524b; II, 1048a; III, 172b; IV, **961a**
Khālid b. al-Walīd i, 110b, 111a, 145b, 208b, 484b, 549b, 788b, 964a, 1139a, 1215b, 1240b, 1343b, 1358b; ii, 279b, 366a, 625a, b, 1023b; iii, 85b, 223b, 397b, 578a, 739b, 1254b; iv, 13b, 289b, 407a, **928a**, 1106b; v, 458a; s, 230b — I, 113b, 114a, 150a, 215a, 499a, 567a, 812a, 994a, 1173b, 1251b, 1278b, 1384a, 1398b; II, 288a, 376a, 640b, 641a, 1047a; III, 88a, 230a, 410a, 598b, 762a, 1287a; IV, 14a-b, 302a, 424b, **961a**, 1138a; V, 461a; S, 230a
Khālid b. Yazīd b. Ḥātim iii, 694a — III, 716b
Khālid b. Yazīd b. Muʿāwiya ii, 360b; iii, 271a, 398a; iv, **929a**; s, 270a — II, 370a; III, 278b, 410a; IV, **962a**; S, 269b
Khālid b. Yazīd al-Kātib al-Tamīmī iv, **929a** — IV, **962a**
Khālid b. Yazīd b. Mazyad al-Shaybānī i, 154a; ii, 679a — I, 158a; II, 696a
Khālid Baghdādī al-Kurdī, Mawlanā v, 475a, 486a — V, 478a, 489a
Khālid al-Barmakī → al-Barāmika
Khālid Beklū i, 1157a — I, 1191b
Khālid Ḍiyā (Ziyā) i, 287b; iii, 260b; iv, **930a**; v, 194b, 195b — I, 296a; III, 267b; IV, **963a**; V, 191b, 192b
Khālid Fakhrī s, 168a — S, 168a
Khālid al-Ḳasrī → Khālid b. ʿAbd Allāh
Khālid al-Marwarrūdhī iv, 1182b — IV, 1215b
Khālid Muḥyī al-Dīn s, 6a — S, 5a
Khālid Pasha Ḳara ʿOthmān-oghlu iv, 593b — IV, 617b
al-Khālidāt → al-Djazāʾir al-Khālidāt
Khālide Edīb iii, 622b; iv, **933a**; v, 194b, 196a; s, 41b — III, 643a; IV, **966a**; V, 191b, 193b; S, 42a
al-Khālidī, Rūḥī iv, **936a** — IV, **969a**
al-Khālidiyyāni iv, **936b** — IV, **969b**
Khalīdj Amīr al-Muʾminīn i, 932a — I, 960b
al-Khalīdj al-Banādiḳī i, 935b — I, 964a
Khalīdj al-Ḳusṭantīniyya i, 927a, 935b — I, 955a, 964a
Khalīdj al-Nāṣirī i, 1299b — I, 1339a
Khalīfa iii, 344a; iv, **937a**, 1076b; v, 435a, b, 621a, 624a — III, 354b; IV, **970a**, 1108a; V, 437b, 625a, 628a
Khalīfa, Āl i, 233b, 540a, 554a, 942b; ii, 108b, 176b; iii, 23a; iv, 751a, **953a**; v, 508a, b, 573b — I, 241a, 556b, 572a, 917b; II, 111a, 181b; III, 24a; IV, 781a, **985b**; V, 511b, 512a, 578a
Khalīfa b. Abi ʾl-Maḥāsin i, 388b; iv, **954a** — I, 399b; IV, **986b**
Khalīfa b. ʿAskar ii, 767b; iv, **954b** — II, 786a; IV, **986b**
Khalīfa b. Bahrām s, 309a — S, 309a
Khalīfa b. Khayyāṭ → Ibn Khayyāṭ al-ʿUṣfurī
Khalīfa b. Muḥammad iv, 953a — IV, 985b
Khalīfa b. Shakhbūt i, 166b — I, 171a

Khalīfa b. Warrū v, 1182b — V, 1172b
Khalīfa Shāh Muḥammad iv, **954b** — IV, **987a**
Khalīfat al-Masīḥ i, 301b — I, 311a
Khāliḳ Abū Anīs s, 74b — S, 75a
al-Khalīl → Ibrāhīm
al-Khalīl (Hebron) ii, 911b; iv, **954b** — II, 933a; IV, **987a**
Khalīl, al-Malik al-Ashraf Ṣalāḥ al-Dīn (Mamlūk) i, 341b, 737b, 1127b, 1324b; ii, 912a, 966a; iii, 325a, 679b; iv, 485b, **964b**; v, 595a — I, 351b, 759b, 1162a, 1365b; II, 933b, 988a; III, 335a, 701a; IV, 506b, **996b**; V, 598b
al-Khalīl b. Aḥmad i, 11a, 106a, 587a, 588b, 668b, 669b, 670b, 674a, 675b; iii, 948b; iv, 412a, 524b, **962a**, 1187b; v, 711a, 806b; s, 73b, 289b, 408b — I, 11b, 109a, 606a, 607b, 688b, 690a, 691a, 695a, 696a; III, 973a; IV, 429b, 547a, **994a**, 1220b; V, 716a, 812b; S, 74a, 289a, 409a
Khalīl b. Alī Čandarlî → Ḳara
Khalīl b. Badr b. Shudjāʿ v, 828a — V, 834b
Khalīl b. Isḥāḳ b. Ward i, 163b; ii, 553a; iv, 459b, 979b — I, 168a; II, 566b; IV, 479b, 480a, 1012a
Khalīl b. Isḥāḳ al-Djundī i, 1019b; iii, 781b; iv, **964a** — I, 1051a; III, 805a; IV, **996a**
Khalīl b. Ismāʿīl v, 801b — V, 807b
Khalīl b. Ḳaradja ii, 239a — II, 246a
Khalīl b. Uzun Ḥasan iv, 1048b — IV, 1080a
Khalīl Allāh, Shāh imām (d./m. 1817) iv, 201b — IV, 210b
Khalīl Allāh b. Shāh Niʿmat Allāh Kirmānī (d./m. 1460) → Khalīl Allāh But-Shikan
Khalīl Allāh But-Shikan i, 1200b; iv, **961b, 965b** — I, 1236b; IV, **994a, 998a**
Khalīl Allāh Shīrvān-Shāh iv, 587b — IV, 611a
Khalīl Bahādur iv, 621a — IV, 645b
Khalīl Beg (Ḳarāmān-oghlu) iv, 621b, 622a, b — IV, 646a, 647a
Khalīl Bey iv, 828a, b — IV, 861a
Khalīl Edhem → Eldem
Khalīl Efendi-zāde iv, **966a** — IV, **998b**
Khalīl Ghaffa i, 600a — I, 619b
Khalīl Ghānim ii, 471a; iii, 593a; iv, **966b** — II, 483a; III, 613b; IV, **998b**
Khalīl Gibran → Djabrān Khalīl Djabrān
Khalīl Ḥamīd Pasha i, 63a, 1064b; ii, 534a, 629b; iv, 211a — I, 65a, 1096b; II, 547a, 645b; IV, 220a
Khalīl Ḥilmī s, 98a — S, 97b
Khalīl al-Khūrī ii, 466a — II, 477b
Khalīl Mīrzā i, 1211b — I, 1247a
Khalīl Mīrzā (Tīmūrid(e)) → Khalīl Sulṭān
Khalīl Muṭrān iv, **966b**; s, 34a — IV, **999a**; S, 34b
Khalīl Nūrī Efendi iv, 544a — IV, 567b
Khalīl Pasha Djandarlî ii, 445a, 721a; iv, **968b** — II, 456b, 739b; IV, **1000b** → Djandarlî
Khalīl Pasha Kut → Enwer Pasha
Khalīl Pasha Ḥādjdjī Arnawud iii, 1002a; iv, **969a** — III, 1027a; IV, **1001b**
Khalīl Pasha Ḳaisarīyyeli i, 4a, 268a; iv, **970a** — I, 4a, 276a; IV, **1002a**
Khalīl Sulṭān → Tīmūrids
Khalīl Yakhshī Beg i, 309a; ii, 599b — I, 319a; II, 614b
Khalīlī iv, **972b** — IV, **1004b**
al-Khalīlī (astronome(r)) v, 83b, 85a, 87a, b — V, 85b, 87a, 89b, 90a
al-Khalīlī, Imām Muḥammad b. ʿAbd Allāh s, 356a — S, 356a
Khāliṣ ii, 103a — II, 105b
Khāliṣa ii, 272b, 906b; iv, **972b**, 1035b; v, 688b — II, 281a, 927b; IV, **1005a**, 1067b; V, 693b
Khāliṣa (lady-in-waiting/dame de compagnie) s, 198b — S, 198b
al-Khāliṣa (citadel(le)) iv, **979b** — IV, **1012a**
Khāliṣī, Shaykh Mahdī s, 342a — S, 342a
Khalisioi v, 1015a, 1018b — V, 1011a, 1014a
Khalḳ iii, 663b, 664b; iv, **980a** — III, 685a, 686a, b; IV, **1012b**
Khalḳ Fîrḳasî i, 734b; ii, 432a, 595b — I, 756b; II, 443a, 610a
Khalḳevî iv, **988a**; v, 906b — IV, **1020b**; V, 912b
Khalkha iv, **988b** — IV, **1021a**
Khalkhāl iv, **989a** — IV, **1021b**
Khalkhālī, Muḥammad Ṣāliḥ s, 308b — S, 308b
Khallād b. ʿAmr b. al-Djamūḥ s, 230a — S, 230a
Khallād b. Khālid iii, 155b — III, 158b
al-Khallāl, Abū Bakr i, 274a, b; ii, 1093a; iii, 158b; iv, **989b** — I, 282b, 283a; II, 1118b; III, 162a; IV, **1022a**
Khallukh → Ḳarluḳ
Khalwa iii, 1011a; iv, 381b, 383a, **990a**, 992b; v, 23a, 1201a, b — III, 1036b; IV, 398a, b, 399b, **1022b**, 1025a; V, 23b, 1191a, 1192a
Khalwatīyya i, 95a, 965b, 1137a; ii, 164b, 203b, 224a, 542b, 1137b; iv, 721b, **991a**; s, 40b, 44a, 208a — I, 97b, 995b, 1171b; II, 169b, 209b, 231a, 556a, 1164b; IV, 750b, **1023b**; S, 41a, 44b, 207b
Khamāsa → Muzāraʿa
Khambāyat iii, 444b; iv, **993b**; s, 358b — III, 459b; IV, **1026a**; S, 358a
Khambhāt → Khambāyat
Khamīs iii, 182a — III, 186a, b
Khamīs (Thursday/Jeudi) iv, 994a, 1009a — IV, 1026b, 1041b
Khamīs Mushayṭ iv, **994a** — IV, **1026b**
Khamr ii, 1058b, 1059b, 1062a, 1069a; iii, 78b, 400b; iv, 135b, **994b** — II, 1083b, 1084b, 1086b, 1094a; III, 81a, 413a; IV, 141a, **1027a**
Khamrīyya i, 584b; iv, **998a** — I, 603b; IV, **1030b**
Khamsa (No.5) i, 786a; iv, **1009a** — I, 809b; IV, **1041b**
Khamsa (poem/poème) iv, **1009b**; v, 1104a — IV, **1041b**; V, 1100a
Khamsa, Khamseh (tribe/tribu) iii, 1106a, 1110a; iv, 9b; s, 146a, 147b — III, 1133b, 1137a; IV, 10a; S, 145b, 147b
Khamse → Wilāyāt-i Khamse
Khāmūsh, Ḳîzîl Arslan i, 301a; iii, 1112a — I, 310a; III, 1139b
Khān (title/titre) iii, 1113b; iv, **1010b**; v, 629b — III, 1140b; IV, **1042b**; V, 633b
Khān (staging-post/gîte d'étape) iv, 228a, b, 236a, 435a, 677b, **1010b**; v, 1124b — IV, 238a, b, 246b, 454b, 705a, **1043a**; V, 1121a
Khān Aḥmad (Ardalān) v, 33b, 34a — V, 34b, 35a
Khān Aḥmad Khān i, 1208b — I, 1244b
Khān Ātash i, 262b — I, 270b
Khān Baba → Bayram Khān
Khān Bahādur Khān i, 953b, 1043a — I, 983a, 1074b
Khan Balîḳ → Khānbalîḳ
Khān Begī Khānum i, 406a — I, 417b
Khān Djahān (d./m. 1459) → Khandjā ʿAlī
Khān-i Djahān iii, 1159a — III, 1187b
Khān-i Djahān Kokaltāsh ii, 488b — II, 500b
Khān Djahān Lōdī ii, 381a; iii, 424a; iv, **1017b** — II, 391a; III, 438a; IV, **1049b**
Khān Djahān Maḳbūl ii, 925a, 1084b; iv, **1019a** — II, 946b, 1109b; IV, **1051a**
Khān al-Khalīlī (al-Ḳāhira) s, 5a — S, 4b
Khān Khānān iv, 210b, **1019b**; v, 629b — IV, 220a, **1051b**; V, 633b
Khān Khānān Maḥmūd b. Fīrūz iv, 920b, 1019b — IV, 953b, 1052a
Khān Yakdas i, 1030b — I, 1062a
Khāna Pasha i, 845a — I, 868b
Khanagāh → Khanḳāh

Khānaḳah s, 49b — S, 50a
Khanāṣir → Khunāṣira
Khanāzir → Khinzīr
Khānbalîḳ iv, 420a, **1020a** — IV, 438b, **1052a**
Kh(w)and Mir ii, 500a — II, 512b
Khandaḳ (ditch/fossé) i, 121b; ii, 130a; iii, 1083a, 1084a, b, 1086b; iv, **1020b**; s, 351b — I, 125a; II, 133b; III, 1109b, 1111a, b, 1113a; IV, **1052b**; S, 351a
al-Khandaḳ →Ḳandiya
Khandaḳ Sābūr v, 634a — V, 638a
Khandaḳ Ṭāhir i, 897b — I, 924b
Kh(w)āndamīr i, 456a, 1211b, 1213a; iv, **1020b** — I, 469a, 1247b, 1249b; IV, **1052b**
Khande Rāo iii, 316b — III, 326a
Khāndēsh ii, 113a, 270b, 814a, 816a, 1125a; iii, 418b, 422a, 446b; iv, **1022a**; s, 335b — II, 115b, 278b, 833b, 835b, 1151b; III, 432a, 435b, 461b; IV, **1054b**; S, 335b
Khandjā ʿAlī ii, 486b; iii, 444a — II, 498b; III, 459a
Khandjara → Čankîrî
al-Khāndjī → Handžič
Khāne iv, 243a, b — IV, 254a, b
Khānfū iv, **1024a** — IV, **1056a**
Khān-i Djahān Maḳbūl iv, **1019a** — IV, **1051a**
Khāniḳīn iv, **1024b** — IV, **1056b**
Khān-i Shahīd → Muḥammad b. Balban
Khānḳāh iv, 433a, **1025a**; v, 1129b — IV, 452a, **1057a**; V, 1125b
Khānlar Khān Iʿtiṣām al-Mulk iv, 787a — IV, 819a
Khānlarī, Parwīz Nātil iv, 71b, 72a — IV, 75b
Khannāb s, 327a — S, 326b
Khannās i, 262a — I, 270a
al-Khansāʾ i, 12a; ii, 627a; iii, 941a; iv, **1027a** — I, 12a; II, 642b; III, 965b; IV, **1059a**
Khansā (Khinsā) iv, **1026b** — IV, **1058b**
Kh(w)ānsalār ii, 15a — II, 15a
Kh(w)ansārī, Aḳā Ḥusayn s, 308a — S, 308a
Kh(w)ānsārī, Muḥammad Bāḳir iv, **1027b** — IV, **1059b**
al-Kh(w)ānsarī, Muḥammad Riḍā al-Raḍawī s, 75a — S, 75b
Kh(w)ānsārī, Muḥammad Taḳī Mūsawī iv, **1028b**; s, 157b — IV, **1060a**; S, 158a
Khanuwā iii, 202a — III, 207a
Khān-zāda Bēgum iv, **1029a** — IV, **1060b**
Khanzīt iv, **1029a** — IV, **1060b**
Khaputs iv, **1029a**; v, 284b — IV, **1061a**; V, 282b
Kh(w)ār iv, **1029b** — IV, **1061a**
Kharābshahr iii, 501b — III, 519a
Kharādj i, 861b, 969a, 990b, 1143b; ii, 116a, 131a, 142b, 146b, 154a, 187b, 559b, 561b, 562b, 566a, 869b; iii, 1088a; iv, 14a, b, 15b, 323a, b, 755a, 939a, 974a, **1030b**; v, 872a — I, 885b, 999a, 1021a, 1178a; II, 118b, 134b, 146b, 150b, 159a, 193b, 573b, 575b, 576b, 580b, 890a; III, 1115a; IV, 15a, b, 16b, 337a, b, 785b, 972a, 1006a, **1062b**; V, 878a
al-Kharadjī, Abū Bakr Muḥammad iv, 529b, 530a — IV, 552b, 553a
Khārag, Khārak, Kharg ii, 812b; iv, **1056a**; V, 81a, 507 — II, 831b; IV, **1087b**; V, 83b, 511a
al-Kharāʾiṭ i, 1045b — I, 1077a
al-Kharāʾiṭī i, 326a; iii, 745a; iv, **1057a** — I, 336a; III, 768a; IV, **1088b**
Kharaḳānī → Abu ʾl-Ḥasan Kharaḳānī
Kharaḳānī, Abu ʾl-Ḥasan i, 147a, 515b, 780a; ii, 1078a; iv, **1051a**; s, 14b — I, 151b, 531a, 803b; II, 1102b; IV, 1088b; S, 15a
Khara-Khula iv, 512a — IV, 534a, b
al-Kharaḳī, Abū Bakr Muḥammad iv, **1059a** — IV, **1090b**
Khārān iv, **1059b**; v, 102b, 684b — IV, **1090b**; V, 104b, 690a
Kharāna iv, **1060a** — IV, **1091a**
Kh(w)ārazm i, 46b, 47a, 135a, 424b, 455b, 662b, 1131a; ii, 3a, 16a, 1141b; iii, 196a, 502a; iv, 753b, **1060b**; v, 24b, 542a, 857b; s, 168b, 169a, 245b, 279a, 289b, 420a — I, 48a, 139a, 436b, 469a, 683a, 1165a; II, 3a, 16b, 1168b; III, 200b, 519b; IV, 784a, **1092a**; V, 25a, 546b, 864b; S, 169a, 245b, 279a, 289a, 420a
Kh(w)ārazm-shāhs i, 20b, 21a, 227a, 424b, 732a, 750a, 804a, 1132a; ii, 606b, 1053a, 1101a, b; iii, 471b, 1115a, 1155a; iv, 29a-30a, 349a, b, 542b, 583a, 817b, 1063b, **1065b**; v, 38b, 331a, 1014a, 1015b, 1018b; s, 245b, 279a — I, 21b, 233b, 436b, 754a, 772b, 828a, 1166a; II, 621b, 1077b, 1127a, b; III, 488a, 1142b, 1183b; IV, 31b-32b, 364a, 566a, 606b, 850b, 1095a, **1097a**; V, 39b, 331b, 1009b, 1011a, 1014b; S, 245b, 279a
al-Kh(w)ārazmī, Abū ʿAbd Allāh Muḥammad iv, 1063a, **1068b**; s, 130b, 371b, 387a — IV, 1094b, **1100a**; S, 129b, 371b, 387a
al-Kh(w)ārazmī, Abū Bakr i, 590b; ii, 78b; iii, 6b, 106b; iv, 1063a, **1069b** — I, 610a; II, 80a; III, 7a, 108b; IV, 1094b, **1101a**
al-Kh(w)ārazmī, Abū Djaʿfar Muḥammad b. Mūsā i, 132b, 379b, 589b, 722b; ii, 360b, 577b, iii, 405a, 469a, 929b, 1137a, 1139a; iv, 1063a, **1070a**, 1078a, 1175b; s, 43a, 412b, 413b — I, 136b, 390b, 608b, 744b; II, 370b, 592a; III, 418a, 485a, 954a, 1165b, 1167b; IV, 1094b, **1101b**, 1110a, 1208b; S, 43a, 412b, 413b
al-Kh(w)ārazmī, Aḥmad b. Muḥammad b. Isḥāḳ s, 343a — S, 343a
Kh(w)ārazmian/Kh(w)arazmien (language/langue) iv, 1062b — IV, 1093b, 1094a
Kharbga iv, 1071b — IV, 1103b
Khārčīnī → Khārṣīnī
al-Khardj i, 538b; iv, **1072b** — I, 555a; IV, **1104a**
al-Khārdj → Khārag
Khardja → Muwashshaḥ
Khārdje, Khārga → al-Wāḥāt
Khardjird → Khargird
Khardjlîḳ ii, 714b — II, 733a
Kharfūsh → Ḥarfūsh
Kharg → Khārag
Kharga iv, 529a — IV, 552a
Khargird iv, **1073a**; v, 1137b, 1148b — IV, **1105a**; V, 1132a, 1139b
al-Khargūshī, al-Wāʿiẓ iv, **1074a** — IV, **1105b**
al-Khārid, Wādī i, 538a; iv, **1074a** — I, 554b; IV, **1105b**
Kharid i, 829b — I, 852b
Khāridja b. Ḥiṣn al-Fazārī i, 690a; ii, 1023b; iii, 23b — I, 711a; II, 1047a; III, 24b
Khāridja b. Ḥudhāfa i, 451b — I, 464b
Khāridja b. Zayd b. Thābit al-Anṣārī s, **311a** — S, **310b**
Khāridjites i, 16a, 40b, 49a, 54b, 55a, 77a, 113a, 120a, 158a, 163a, 207a, 248a, 332b, 367a, 384a, b, 445b, 451b, 550b, 686b, 810a, 942a, 972a, 1044a, 1110b, 1178b, 1242b; ii, 90a, 166a, 416a, 523b, 524a, 978a, 1095b; iii, 153a, 233b, 583b, 648a, 651a, b, 652a, 715b, 1164a, 1265a; iv, 15a, 20b, 415b, 673a, 753a, 827a, **1074b**; v, 499a, 855a, 945b, 1189a; s, 122b, 157a, 284a — I, 16b, 41b, 50b, 56a, 57a, 79a, 116b, 123b, 162b, 167b, 213a, 255b, 343a, 395a, b, 458b, 464b, 478a, 568a, 707b, 833a, 971a, 1002a, 1075b, 1144a, 1213b, 1280b; II, 92a, 171a, 426b, 536b, 537a, 1000b, 1121a; III, 156b, 240a, 603b, 669a, 672b, 673b, 737b, 1192b, 1298a; IV, 16a, 22a, 433b, 700b, 783b, 860a, **1106a**; V, 502a, 862a, 949b, 1179a; S, 122a, 157a, 284a
- doctrine i, 124a, 128b, 187b, 257b, 335a, 1027b; ii, 833b; iii, 19b, 235b, 658b, 661a, 1167b; iv, 938a, **1076a** — I, 127b, 132b, 193a, 265b, 345b, 1059a; II, 853a; III, 20b, 242a, 679b, 682b, 1196b; IV, 971a,

1108a
Kharīṭa, Khāriṭa iv, **1077b** — IV, **1109b**
Kh(w)ārizm(ī) → Kh(w)ārazmī)
Khark v, 878b, 879b, 880b — V, 884b, 885b, 886b
Kharkūshī → Khargūshī
al-Kh(w)ārizmī → Muḥammad b. Maḥmūd
Kharlukh → Ḳarluḳ
Kharm → ʿArūd
Kharpūt → Khart(a)pert
Kharrāna s, 229a — S, 229a
al-Kharrāz, Abū Saʿīd iv, **1083a** — IV, **1114b**
Kharrūba → Makāyīl
al Kharrūbī, Zakī al-Dīn iii, 776b; iv, 641b — III, 799b; IV, 668a
Kh(w)arshi ii, 251a — II, 258b
Khārṣīnī iv, **1084a** — IV, **1115a**
Khart(a)pert i, 665a, 983a; iii, 128a; iv, 1029a, **1084a**; s, 37a — I, 686a, 1013b; III, 131a; IV, 1061a, **1115a**; S, 37a
Kharṭūm i, 49b, 168b; v, **70a**, 1249b — I, 51a, 173b; V, **72a**, 1240b
- institutions i, 976a; ii, 424a — I, 1006a; II, 434b
Kharūṣ, Banū iv, **1084b** — IV, **1116a**
Khāṣ Pūlād-Khān ii, 88a — II, 89b
Khāsa (river/rivière) i, 184a; v, 441b — I, 189b; V, 444a
al-Khaṣāsī, Abu'l-Faḍl Ḳāsim iv, 379a, 380a, **1085a** — IV, 396a, b, **1116a**
Khashab iv, **1085a**; v, 108b, 655b — IV, **1116b**; V, 110b, 659b
al-Khashabāt iv, **1086a** — IV, **1117a**
Khashabiyya iii, 987a; iv, 411b, 836b, **1086a** — III, 1011b; IV, 429a, 869b, **1117b**
Khashkhāsh i, 934b; ii, 522b — I, 963a; II, 535b
Khashm i, 536b — I, 553a
Khasht → Khōst
Khāṣī iv, **1087a** — IV, **1118a**
al-Khaṣīb → Ibn al-Khaṣīb
al-Khaṣīb b. ʿAbd al-Ḥamīd i, 143b; iii, 835a — I, 147b; III, 858b
al-Khaṣībī, Abū ʿAlī Aḥmad → Ibn al Khaṣīb
al-Khaṣībī, Aḥmad b. ʿUbayd Allāh iii, 835a; iv, **1094a** — III, 858b; IV, **1124b**
al-Khāsir → Salm al-Khāsir
Khāṣṣ i, 850a, 1080a, ii, 83a, 103b; iv, 238b, 972b, **1094a** — I, 873b, 1112a; II, 84b, 105b; IV, 249a, 1005a, **1125a**
Khaṣṣ, Khāṣṣa (Iran) → Khāliṣa
Khāṣṣ Aḥmed Beg ii, 985b — II, 1008a
Khāṣṣ Beg Arslān i, 300b; iv, **1097a** — I, 310a; IV, **1128a**
Khaṣṣa niwīs iv, 759a — IV, 789a
Khāṣṣ Oda ii, 1088b, 1089b; iv, **1097a**; v, 18a, b, 938b — II, 1114a, 1115a; IV, **1128a**; V, 18b, 19a, 942b
Khāṣṣa i, 491a, 1099a; ii, 188a; iv, 36a, 972b, 976a, b, 977a, 1044a, 1094a — I, 506a, 1132a; II, 194a; IV, 38b, 1005a, 1009a, b, 1075a, 1125a
Khāṣṣa (occult(e)) iv, **1097b** — IV, **1128b**
Khāṣṣa ʿaskeri i, 1278b — I, 1317b
al-Khāṣṣa wa'l-ʿĀmma iv, **1098a**; v, 605b — IV, **1128b**; V, 609b
Khāṣṣadārs i, 238b; iv, 1143a — I, 246a; IV, 1175a
al-Khaṣṣāf i, 1113a; iii, 163a, 512b — I, 1146b; III, 166b, 530a
Khaṣṣakī i, 1225b — I, 1262a
Khāṣṣakī Muḥammad Pasha i, 904b — I, 932a
Khāṣṣakiyya iv, **1100a** — IV, **1130b**
Khāṣṣekī i, 1225b; iv, **1100a**; v, 66b — I, 1262a; IV, **1131a**; V, 68b
Khāṣṣköy iv, 242a, 1096b — IV, 252b, 1127b
Khaṭa' iv, 768b, 769b, **1100b** — IV, 799b, 800b, **1131b**
al-Khatādjī, Shihāb al-Dīn s, 362a — S, 361b
Khaṭāʾī → Ismāʿīl (Ṣafawid(e))
Khaṭak i, 218b; iv, **1102a**; v, 72a, 250b — I, 224b; IV, **1133a**; V, 74a, 248b
Khātam, Khātim ii, 306a, 307a, 311b, 315a; iv, **1102b**; s, 256b — II, 314b, 316a, 320b, 324b; IV, **1133b**; S, 256a
Khathʿam i, 442a, 811b, 812a; iv, **1105b** — I, 455a, 835a; IV, **1137a**
Khāthira, Day of/Journée de s, 177b — S, 179a
Khaṭīʾa iv, **1106b** — IV, **1138a**
Khaṭīb i, 981b; iv, **1109b**; v, 74a — I, 1012a; IV, **1141a**; V, 76a
al-Khaṭīb, Abū Bakr s, 195a — S, 193b
al-Khaṭīb al-Baghdādī i, 123b, 142b, 321b, 333a, 591b, 616b, 898a, 1309b; ii, 462a; iii, 27b, 512b, 735a, 754a, 860b; iv, **1111a**; v, 1129b; s, 32b, 323a, 326a, 361a — I, 127a, 146b, 331b, 343a, 610b, 636b, 925a, 1349b; II, 474a; III, 29a, 530a, 758a, 777a, 884b; IV, **1142b**; V, 1126a; S, 32b, 322b, 325b, 361a
Khaṭīb Dimashḳ → al-Ḳazwīnī
Khātim → Khātam
Khātima v, 960a — V, 964a
Khatlān → Khuttalān
al-Khatma, Khitma ii, 78b, 79b; iv, **1112b** — II, 80a, 81a; IV, **1144b**
Khatmiyya i, 277b, 1029a, 1158b; ii, 710a; iii, 523b; iv, 686b — I, 286a, 1060b, 1193a; II, 729a; III, 542a; IV, 715a
Khaṭṭ i, 1354a; ii, 311a, 777b; iv, **1113a**; v, 210b-233b passim, 379b, 992a — I, 1393b; II, 320a, 796a; IV, **1144b**; V, 208b-231b passim, 380a, 987a
Khaṭṭ (geomancy/géomancie) iv, **1128b** — IV, **1160a**
al-Khaṭṭ iv, **1130b** — IV, **1162a**
Khaṭṭ al-Istiwāʾ → Istiwāʾ
Khaṭṭ-i Humayūn/Khaṭṭ-i Sherīf i, 74b, 282a, 397a, 855a, 1090a; ii, 314a; iii, 553b; iv, **1131a**; v, 904b — I, 77a, 290b; 408b, 879a, 1122b; II, 323b; III, 572b; IV, **1162b**; V, 910b
Khaṭṭ-i muʿammāʾī iv, 1126b — IV, 1158a
Khaṭṭ-i shadjarī iv, 1126b — IV, 1158a
Khaṭṭ-i Sherīf → Khaṭṭ-i Humāyūn
Khaṭṭ-i sünbülī iv, 1126b — IV, 1158a
al-Khaṭṭābī, ʿAbd al-Karīm iii, 701a — III, 723a
al-Khaṭṭābī, Ḥamd b. Muḥammad iii, 1020a; iv, **1131b** — III, 1045b; IV, **1163a**
Khaṭṭābiyya i, 1082a; iv, 203a, **1132a** — I, 1114b; IV, 212a, **1163b**
al-Khaṭṭār (Ḳurzul) s, 177b — S, 178b
Khaṭṭāra iv, 532b — IV, 556a
Khatuḳāy ii, 25a — II, 25b
Khātūn iv, **1133a** — IV, **1164b**
Khātūnī s, 65a — S, 65b
Khāwa iii, 643a; iv, **1133a** — III 664a; IV, **1164b**
Khawand → Akhund
Khāwandagār i, 260b, 261b, 262a — I, 268b, 269b, 270a
Khawāridj → Khāridjites
Khawārizm(ī) → Kh(w)arazm(ī)
Khawarnaḳ i, 196b; iv, **1133b**; v, 633a — I, 202a; IV, **1165a**; V, 637a
Khawāṣṣ → Khāṣṣ, Khāṣṣa
Khawāṣṣ-i humāyūn iv, 1095a, b, 1096b — IV, 1125b, 1126b, 1127b
Khawāṣṣ al-Ḳurʾān iv, **1133b** — IV, **1165a**
Khawbar → Khōbar
Khawla i, 400b — I, 412a
Khawla bint Ḥakīm i, 307b — I, 317a
Khawlān, Banū i, 881b; iv, **1134a**; s, 22a — I, 907a; IV, **1165b**; S, 22b
al-Khawlānī, Abū Idrīs iv, **1135a**, 1136a — IV, **1167a**, b

al-Khawlānī, Abū Muslim iv, **1135b** — IV, **1167a**
Khawr i, 536a, 538b, 1094b, 1095a, b — I, 552b, 555b, 1127b, 1128a, b
Khawr Ḥasan v, 508a, b — V, 511b, 512a
Khayāl iii, 453b, 632b; iv, **1136a** — III, 469a, 653b; IV, **1167b**
Khayāl, Mīr Muḥammad Taḳī iv, **1136a** — IV, **1168a**
Khayāl al-ʿālam i, 89b — I, 92a
Khayāl al-ẓill iv, 602b, **1136b** — IV, 627a, **1168a**
Khayālī ii, 937a — II, 959a
Khayāli Bey iv, **1137a** — IV, **1168b**
Khaybar i, 9a, 435a; ii, 725a, 844b; iv, **1137b**; v, 250b; s, 351b — I, 9a, 447a; II, 744a, 864a; IV, **1169b**; V, 248a; S, 351b
Khaybar (Khyber) Pass i, 238a, b; iv, **1143a**; s, 329b — I, 245b, 246a; IV, **1174b**; S, 329a
Khaydāḳ → Ḳaytāḳ
Khaydhār → al-Afshīn
Khāyir Bey al-ʿAlāʾī i, 315a — I, 324b
Khāyir Bey al-Djarkasī s, 38a — S, 38b
al-Khayl iv, 495b, **1143a**; v, 75b — IV, 517a, **1175a**; V, 78a
Khayma iv, **1146b**; v, 444a — IV, **1178a**; V, 446b
Khayr iv, **1151a** — IV, **1183a**
al-Khayr b. Muḥammad b. al-Khayr v, 1176a, b, 1179a — V, 1166a, b, 1169a
al-Khayr b. Muḥammad Ibn Khazar iii, 1042b; v, 1175b — III, 1068a; V, 1165b
Khayr Allāh Efendi i, 61a; iv, **1153a** — I, 63a; IV, **1185a**
Khayr al-Bayān i, 1123a, b — I, 1157a
Khayr al-Dīn, Ustād iv, **1158b** — IV, **1190b**
Khayr al-Dīn Čandarlî → Djandarlî
Khayr al-Dīn Pasha Barbarossa i, 367b, 368a, 512a, 678a, 947b, 1023b, 1300b; ii, 189b, 353a, 520a, 522a, 537b, 722b, 839b; iii, 69a, 94b, 245b, 1086a; iv, 361a, b, 572a, 656b, 828a, **1155a**; v, 268b, 270b, 504a, 1010b; s, 80b — I, 378b, 527b, 698b, 699a, 977a, 1055a, 1340b; II, 195b, 362b, 533a, 535a, 550b, 741b, 859a; III, 71b, 97a, 252b, 1113a; IV, 377a, 594b, 683a, 861a, **1187b**; V, 266b, 268b, 507b, 1006a; S, 80a
Khayr al-Dīn Pasha al-Tūnusī i, 285b; ii, 436a; iii, 562a, 591b, 636b; iv, 924a, **1153b**; v, 949a — I, 294b; II, 447b; III, 581b, 612a, 657b; IV, 957a, **1185b**; V, 952b
Khayr al-Dīn Rāghib Pasha ii, 207b — II, 214a
Khayr Shāh, Sayyid iv, 1160b — IV, 1192b
Khayrābād (Indus) iv, **1159b** — IV, **1191b**
Khayrābād (Uttar Pradēsh) ii, 205a; iv, **1159b**; s, 420b — II, 211b; IV, **1191b**; S, 421a
Khayrān i, 84a; ii, 1012b; iii, 147a — I, 86b; II, 1036a; III, 150b
Khayrātid(e)s i, 709a, 709b; ii, 517b, 518a; s, 30a — I, 729b, 731a; II, 530b; S, 30b
al-Khayrī, Rāshid v, 204a — V, 201b
Khayriyye tudjdjārī i, 1171b — I, 1206b
Khayr Khān iii, 398b, 399a — III, 411a
Khayrpūr ii, 258b, 263b, 264a, 669a; iii, 443a; iv, **1159b** — II, 265b, 271b, 272a, 685b; III, 457b; IV, **1191b**
Khayrullāh Efendi i, 61a — I, 63a
al-Khayrūn iii, 155b — III, 158b
Khaysh iv, **1160b** — IV, **1192b**
Khayshan iv, 553b — IV, 577b
Khaywān s, 335a — S, 334b
Khayyāṭ iv, **1161a** — IV, **1193a**
al-Khayyāṭ, Abu 'l-Ḥusayn i, 129a; ii, 386b, 1026b; iii, 905b, 1144a; iv, **1162a**; s, 12b, 225b — I, 132b; II, 397a, 1050a; III, 929b, 1172a; IV, **1194a**; S, 13a, 225b
al-Khayyāṭ, Abū ʿAlī Yaḥyā iv, **1162a** — IV, **1194a**
al-Khayyāt, ʿUthmān v, 769a — V, 775a
al-Khayzurān bint ʿAṭāʾ al-Djuashiyya i, 633b, 1034a, 1035a, 1298a; iii, 22b, 231a, 232b; iv, **1164a**; v, 737b, 1239a; s, 326b — I, 654b, 1065b, 1066b, 1338a; III, 23b, 238a, 239a; IV, **1196a**; V, 743a, 1229b; S, 326a
Khazaf ii, 745a; iv, **1164b** — II, 763b; IV, **1196b**
Khazʿal Khan iv, **1171a** — IV, **1204b**
Khazāʾil (King, le roi) i, 525b — I, 541b
Khazāʿil i, 1096b; ii, 339b — I, 1129b; II, 349b
Khazar i, 18a, 100b, 625b, 660a, 835b, 837a, 864a, 921b, 931a, 985a, 1000a, 1305a, b, 1307a, b; ii, 85b, 86a, 482b, 1107b; iii, 234a, 759a; iv, 280a, 343a, b, 344a, b, 346b, 608b, 891b, **1172a**; v, 382a, 488a, 1013b; s, 106a, 297b — I, 18b, 103b, 646a, 681a, 858b, 860b, 888a, 949b, 959b, 1015b, 1031a, 1345a, b, 1347b, 1348a; II, 87a, b, 494b, 1133b; III, 241a, 782b; IV, 292b, 357b, 358a, b, 359a, 361b, 633a, 924b, **1205b**; V, 383a, 491a, 1009a; S, 105b, 297a
- language/langue iv, 1178b — IV, 1212a
Khazar, Banū v, 1174b, 1175a, 1176b, 1179b — V, 1164b, 1165a, 1176b, 1169b
Khazar b. Ḥafṣ b. Maghrāw v, 1174b — V, 1164b
Khazarān i, 738b; iv, 1176a, 1178a — I, 760a; IV, 1209b, 1211a
Khazaria iv, 1176b, 1177b — IV, 1209b, 1211a
Khāzim b. Khuzayma i, 550b; ii, 592b; iii, 652a — I, 568a; II, 607a; III, 673b
Khāzim b. Muḥammad iii, 501b — III, 518b
Khāzin ii, 304b; iv, **1181b** — II, 313a; IV, **1214b**
al-Khāzin, Abū Djaʿfar i, 1003a, 1100b; ii, 362a; iv, 629b, 1080a, **1182a**; s, 412a — I, 1034a, 1133b; II, 372a; IV, 654b, 1111a, **1215a**; S, 412a
Khazīne ii, 1088b; iv, **1183b** — II, 1114a; IV, **1216b**
Khazīne-i Enderūn i, 1147a; iv, 1183b, 1184a — I, 1181b; IV, 1216b, 1217a
Khazīne-i Ewrāḳ i, 75a, 1089b — I, 77a, 1122a
al-Khāzinī, Abu 'l-Fatḥ iii, 1137a; iv, **1186a** — III, 1165a; IV, **1218b**
al-Khāzir iv, 493a, **1186b** — IV, 514b, **1219a**
Khaznadār, Khāzindār iv, **1186b** — IV, **1219b**
Khaznadār, Muṣṭafā → Muṣṭafā Khaznadār
al-Khazradj i, 50b, 53b, 514a, 544b, 771a, 1283a; iii, 812a; iv, **1187a**; v, 995a; s, 229b, 230a — I, 52a, 55a, 529b, 561b, 794a, 1322b; III, 835b; IV, **1220a**; V, 990a, b; S, 229b, 230a
al-Khazradjī, Abū Dulaf s, 116a — S, 115b
al-Khazradjī, Ḍiyāʾ al-Dīn iv, **1187b** — IV, **1220b**
al-Khazradjī, Muwaffaḳ al-Dīn ii, 441a; iv, **1188b** — II, 452b; IV, **1221a**
al-Khazradjiyya → al-Khazradjī, Ḍiyāʾ al-Dīn
Khazrūn, Banū v, 1182a, b, 1183a — V, 1172a, b, 1173a
Khazrūn b. Fulful b. Khazar v, 1178a — V, 1168a
Khazrūn b. Saʿīd v, 1182b — V, 1172b
Khazz → Ḥarīr
Khazz iii, 209b — III, 215a
Khedive → Khidiw
Khedive Ismāʿīl → Ismāʿīl Pasha
Khēma → Khayma
Khemshil, Khemshin v, **1a** — V, **1a**
Khenafsa s, 328a — S, 327b
Khērla v, **1a**; s, 280a — V, **1a**; S, 279b
Khettara iv, 529a — IV, 552a
Kheyūn b. Djenāh i, 684a — I, 705a
Khibāʾ iv, 1147a — IV, 1178b
Khiḍāb v, **1b**; — V, **1b**
Khidāsh (Khaddāsh) i, 15b, 1293a; iv, 15b, 45a, 446a, 837b; v, **1b**, 63b — I, 16a, 1332b; IV, 17a, 47b, 466a, 870b; V, **1b**, 65b
Khidāsh b. Zuhayr al-Aṣghar v, **3b**; s, 394b — V, **3b**; S, 395a
Khidhlān i, 413b; v, **3b**, 833b — I, 425b; V, **4a**, 839b
Khiḍr → Khayr al-Dīn Pasha Barbarossa

Khidīw (Khedive) v, **4a** – V, 4a
Khidr iv, 1148a – IV, 1179b
al-Khiḍr → al-Khaḍir
Khiḍr Beg Aydînoghlu i, 778a, 783b; iii, 1183a; v, 506a – I, 801a, 806b; III, 1212a; V, 509b
Khîḍr Beg Čelebi iv, 225a; v, **4b** – IV, 234b; V, **4b**
al-Khiḍr Ḥusayn → al-Khaḍir, Muḥammad b. al-Ḥusayn
Khiḍr-Ilyās v, **5a** – V, **5a**
Khiḍr Khān b. Ibrāhīm iii, 1115b; s, 65a – III, 1143a; S, 65b
Khidr Khān of/de Multān s, 206b – S, 206a
Khiḍr Khān Sayyīd i, 444b; ii, 120b, 258b, 269a, 270b, 695a; iii, 417b, 418a, 485a; iv, 276b, 419a, 922b, 923b; v, **5b**, 598a, 782b, 783a; s, 73b – I, 457b; II, 123b, 265a, 277b, 278b, 712b; III, 430b, 431a, 502a; IV, 288b, 437b, 955a, 956b; V, **6a**, 601b, 789a; S, 74a
Khifāḍ → Khafḍ
Khilʿa i, 24a; iii, 215b, 344b, 346b; v, **6a**, 620a, 737a, 752a – I, 25a; III, 222a, 355a, 357a; V, **6b**, 624a, 742a, 757b
Khilāfa → Khalīfa
Khilāfat movement i, 443a; ii, 255a; iii, 1204b; iv, 793b; v, **7a**; s, 4b, 293b, 360a – I, 456a; II, 262a; III, 1235a; IV, 825b; V, **7b**; S, 3b, 293a, 360a
Khilāt → Akhlāt
Khildjī → Khaldjī
Khillaut, Khilut v, 7a – V, 7a
Khimar iv, 10b – IV, 11b
Khinalug v, **8a** – V, **8a**
Khindif i, 545a – I, 562a
Khinsā → Khansā
Khinzīr v, **8a** – V, **8b**
al-Khiraḳī, Abu 'l-Ḳāsim i, 277a; iii, 159a, b, 734b, 784b; v, **9b** – I, 285b; III, 162b, 163a, 757b, 808a; V, **10a**
Khirāsh b. Umayya s, 350a – S, 350a
Khirbat al-Bayḍāʾ v, **10a** – V, **10b**
Khirbat al-Mafdjar i, 613b; ii, 955b; iii, 71a, 142b, 310a, 494b; iv, 701b, 1164b; v, **10b**, 338a; s, 117a, 251a – I, 633b; II, 977b; III, 73b, 145a, 319a, 511b; IV, 730a, 1197a; V, **11a**, 338b; S, 116b, 251a
Khirbat al-Minya ii, 955b; v, **17a**; s, 117a, 229a – II, 978a; V, **17b**; S, 116b, 229a
Khirḳa iv, 474a; v, **17b**, 737a – IV, 495a; V, **18a**, 742a
Khirḳa-yî Saʿādet → Khirka-yî Sherīf
Khirḳa-yî Sherīf ii, 695b, 1088b; v, **18a**, 761b – II, 713a, 1114a; V, **18b**, 767b
Khirkat al-futuwwa v, 18a – V, 18b
Khirḳat al-irāda v, 18a – V, 18b
Khirḳat al-tabarruk v, 18a – V, 18b
Khirḳat al-taṣawwuf v, 18a – V, 18b
Khīrkhān b. Ḳarādja iii, 120a, 1118b – III, 122b, 1146a
Khirkī i, 768a; ii, 262b – I, 791a; II, 270b → Awrangābād
al-Khirrīt al-Nādjī v, **19b**, 451a – V, **20a**, 453b
Khiṣāʾ iv, 1087b, 1090b – IV, 1119a, 1121b
Khīsh ii, 905b – II, 926b
Khiṭa → Ḳarā Khiṭāy
Khiṭāʿī → ʿAlī Akbar
Khitān v, **20a**, 471a – V, **20b**, 473b
Khiṭaṭ v, **22b** – V, **23a**
Khiṭāy → Ḳarā Khiṭāy; al-Ṣīn
Khiṭba v, **22b** – V, **23b**
Khitma → Khatma
Khiṭṭa v, **23a** – V, **23b**
Khīwā i, 36a, 71a, 99b, 120b, 456a, 456b, 1296a; ii, 16a, 446a; iv, 611a, 1060b, 1064b, 1065a; v, **23b**, 859b; s, 46a, 66a, 73a, 419b, 420a – I, 37a, 73a, 102b, 124a, 469a, 469b, 1335b; II, 16b, 458a; IV, 635b, 1092a, 1096a, b; V, **24b**, 866b; S, 46a, 66b, 73b, 420a
Khīwa Khānate iv, 1065a; v, 24a, 392a; s, 97b, 169a, 228a, 281a – IV, 1096b; V, 24b, 392b; S, 96b, 169a, 228a, 281a
Khiyābānī, Shaykh Muḥammad iv, 789b; v, **24b**; s, 110a, 365b, 366a – IV, 821b; V, **25a**; S, 109b, 365a, b
Khiyāla → Khayl
Khiyām → Khayma
al-Khiyāmī, Muḥammad iii, 812a – III, 835a
Khiyār v, **25a** – V, **26a**
Khiyār (in theology/en théologie) → Ikhtiyār
Khiyār al-ruʾya v, 25b – V, 26a
Khiyār b. Sālim al-Ṭaʿī iii, 652a – III, 673b
Khiyār al-madjlis i, 1111b – I, 1145a
Khizāna i, 68a, 212b, 270a, 280a, 391a, 396b, 601a, 626a, 736a, 776a, 816b, 819a, 826b, 893b, 899a, 1018a, 1053a, 1139b, 1211b, 1272a, 1354a; ii, 7b, 126b, 127a, 132b, 290a, 714a, 837b, 871a, 885a; iii, 627a, 708b, 769a, 777b, 896a, 973a, 1200a, 1234b; – I, 70a, 218b, 278a, 288b, 402a, 407b, 621a, 646b, 758a, 799a, 840a, 842a, 849b, 920a, 926a, 1049b, 1085a, 1174a, 1247b, 1311a, 1393a; II, 7b, 130a, 135b, 298a, 732b, 857b, 891b, 905b; III, 649a, 731a, 792b, 800b, 920b, 997b, 1230b, 1266b → Maktaba
Khizānadār → Khāzindār
Khizānat al-ḥikma i, 1141a – I, 1175b
Khizānat al-kutub ii, 127a – II, 130a
Khizānat al-māl i, 1148a – I, 1182b
Khizāne-i ʿāmire → Khazīne
Khizr, Khizir → Khiḍr
Khloṭ → Khulṭ
Khmelnitsky, Boghdan iv, 178b, 179a – IV, 185b, 186a
Khmer → Ḳimār (Khmer)
Khnīfra s, 223a – S, 223a
Kho ii, 31a, b – II, 31b, 32a
Khōdja i, 36a, 172a, b, 246b, 552b, 1254a, 1333b; ii, 45b, 47b, 58b, 129a, 170b; iii, 381a, 434b, 545a; iv, 202b, 206a; v, **25b**, 942b; s, 332a – I, 37a, 176b, 177a, 254a, 570a, 1272b, 1292a; II, 46b, 48b, 59b, 132b, 176a; III, 393a, 448b, 563b; IV, 211b, 215a; V, **26b**, 946a; S, 331b
Khodja Čelebi → Abu 'l-Suʿūd
Khodja Čiwizāde → Muḥyi al-Dīn Shaykh Muḥammad
Khodja Dāwūd Pasha → Dāwūd Pasha (d./m. 1498)
Khodja Efendi Saʿd al-Dīn i, 826a, 956a; ii, 713a; iii, 91b, 248b; iv, 900b; v, **27a**, 682b – I, 849a, 985b; II, 731b; III, 94a, 255b; IV, 933b; V, **28a**, 687b
Khodja Eli → Ḳodja Eli
Khodja Ibrāhīm Pasha i, 395a – I, 406a
Khodja Kenʿān Pasha i, 843a; iv, 885a – I, 866a; IV, 917b
Khodja Muṣṭafā Pasha iii, 341b; iv, 231a, 882a – III, 351b; IV, 241b, 914b
Khodja Răghib Pasha → Rāghib Pasha
Khodja Sinān Pāshā i, 340b, 697b, 1298b, 1303b; ii, 34a, 287b, 688a, 880b; iii, 94b; v, 1023a – I, 351a, 719a, 1338b, 1343b; II, 34b, 295b, 705b, 901a; III, 97a; V, 1018b
Khodja Yūsuf Pasha i, 63a, 174b – I, 65a, 179b
Khodjaev v, **28a** – V, **29a**
Khodjand → Khudjand
Khōdjazāde iii, 1149a – III, 1177b
Khōī (Khuy) v, **28b**; s, 365b – V, **29b**; S, 365a
Khoḳand i, 71a, 504b, 1296a; ii, 45a, 67b, 440a, 792a; v, **29a**, 46a, 274a, 364a, 399b; s, 97b, 98a, 228b, 420a – I, 73a, 520a, 1335b; II, 46a, 68b, 458a, 811a; V, **30a**, 47a, 271b, 365a, 400b; S, 97a, 228b, 420b
Khokars ii, 972b, 1053a; v, **31a**, 598a – II, 995a, 1077b; V, **32a**, 601b
Khomayr → Khumayr

Khomeinī → Khumaynī
Khōnās i, 243b; ii, 204b – I, 251a; II, 211a
Khorāsān → Khurāsān
Khorkhut s, 245a – S, 245a
Khosham s, 363a – S, 362b
Khoshkadam → Khushkadam, al-Malik al-Ẓāhir
Khosraw → Anūshirwān; Amīr Khusraw; Khosrew; Khusraw; Kisrā; Parwīz
Khosrew Beg i, 1263b, 1270b, 1272a; ii, 201b; v, **31b**; s, 185a – I, 1302a, 1209b, 1311a; II, 208a; V, **33a**; S, 186a
Khosrew Pasha Deli (or Dīvāne) iv, 902a; v, **35a** – IV, 934b; V, **36a**
Khosrew Pasha, Meḥmed (d./m. 1855) v, **35b** – V, **36b**
Khōst v, **36b**, 1079b; s, 66a – V, **37b**, 1076b; S, 66b
Khotan iii, 1115b; v, **37a**; s, 98a – III, 1143a; V, **38a**; S, 97b
Khotin v, **39b**, 260b, 720a, 766a – V, **40b**, 258b, 725b, 772a
Khowár ii, 31a, 138b – II, 31b, 142a
Khoybūn i, 871a – I, 895b
al-Khubar v, **40a** – V, **41a**
Khubayb b. ʿAdī al-Anṣārī v, **40b** – V, **41b**
Khūbmesīḥīs iv, 333b; v, **41a** – IV, 348a; V, **42b**
al-Khubūb i, 1312b, 1313a – I, 1352b, 1353a
Khubz ii, 1058a; v, **41b** – II, 1082b; V, **42b**
al-Khubzaʾaruzzī, Abu ʾl-Ḳāsim v, 42a, **43a** – V, 43a, **44b**
Khudā Bakhsh i, 1018a; v, **43b** – I, 1049b; V, **45a**
Khudā-Yār Khān → Yār Muḥammad Khān
Khudābanda → Muḥammad Khudābanda; Uldjaytū Khudābanda
Khudādād i, 359a – I, 370a
Khudādād b. Miḥrāb Khān v, 521a – V, 524b
Khudāwand v, **44a** – V, **45b**
Khudāwand Khān iii, 1160a – III, 1188b
Khudāwand Muḥammad iv, 201b – IV, 210b
Khudāwendigār i, 468b; iv, 564a; v, **44b** – I, 482b; IV, 586a; V, **45b**
Khudāyār Khān v, 30a, b – V, 31a, b
Khudaybakhsh iv, 202b – IV, 211b
Khudāydād ii, 622a – II, 637b
Khudāynāma iii, 884a; iv, 11a, 809a – III, 908a; IV, 12a, 841b
Khūdjān → Ḳūčān
Khudjand(a) v, 30b, **45a**, 400a – V, 31b, **46b**, 401a
Khudjand, Āl-ī s, 239b – S, 239b
Khudjandī, Abu ʾl-Ḳāsim iv, 101b – IV, 106a
Khudjandī, Abū Maḥmūd v, **46a** – V, **47b**
a;-Khudjandī, Muʾayyad al-Dīn s, 364b – S, 364a
Khūdjī → Khūzī
Khudjistān v, **47a** – V, **48b**
al-Khudjistānī → Aḥmad b. ʿAbd Allāh; Muḥammad b. ʿAbd Allāh
Khugiyani s, 237b – S, 237a
Khuḳand → Khoḳand
Khulʿ → Ṭalāḳ
Khulayd ʿAynayn ii, 569a – II, 583a
al-Khuld i, 897a, b – I, 923b, 924a
Khuldābād i, 768a; v, **47a** – I, 791a; V, **48b**
Khulḳ → Akhlāḳ
Khulm v, **47b** – V, **49a**
Khulṭ v, **48b** – V, **49b**
Khumār Beg i, 852a – I, 875b
Khumārawayh b. Aḥmad b. Ṭūlūn (Ṭūlūnid(e)) i, 314b, 1290a; ii, 281b; iii, 745b, 750b; iv, 1090b; v, **49a**; s, 1a – I, 324b, 1329b; II, 289b; III, 768b, 773b; IV, 1121b; V, **50b**; S, 1a
Khumartāsh b. ʿAbd Allāh al-ʿImādī iv, 213b, 862b – IV, 211a, 895b
Khumaynī, Āyatollāh Ruḥollāh v, 372a; s, 95b, 104a, 342b – V, 372b; S, 95a, 103b, 342b
Khumayr v, **50b** – V, **52a**
Khumays b. Ḥudhāfa iii, 63b – III, 66a
Khumayyis, Āl ii, 631b – II, 647a
Khumbara i, 1063a; iii, 478b – I, 1095a; III, 495a
Khumbaradji i, 1062a; v, **52b** – I, 1093b; V, **54a**
Khumbaradjī Aḥmed Pasha → Aḥmad Pasha Bonneval
Khumm → Ghadīr al-Khumm
Khums i, 1085b, 1142a; ii, 146b, 156b, 869b – I, 1118a, 1176b; II, 150b, 160b, 889b
Khumurtāsh, amīr iii, 399a – III, 411b
Khumurtāsh al-Sulaymānī i, 732a – I, 754a
Khūnadj (Khūna) iv, 420a – IV, 438a
Khunāṣira v, **53a** – V, **54b**
Khunātha bint Bakkār v, **53b** – V, **54b**
Khundj v, 670b, 671a – V, 676a, b
Khundj-ū-Fāl v, 671b – V, 676b
Khundjī, Faḍl Allah v, **53b** – V, **55a**
Khunzal ii, 251a; v, **55b** – II, 258b; V, **57a**
Khūr iv, 6a – IV, 6b
Khurāfa iii, 369b – III, 381b
Khurāsān i, 3b, 16a, 18a, 19b, 43a, b, 52b, 59a, 77a, 99b, 108b, 141a, 147b, 149a, 228a, b, 230a, 246b, 278a, 296b, 437b, 529a, 684b, 964a, 1052a, 1293a, 1294a; ii, 4b, 43b, 1109a; iii, 163a; iv, 1051b; v, 2a, **55b**, 541a; 852b, 869a, 1238b; s, 14b, 15a, 24a, 31b, 38a, 57b, 66b, 72b, 83a, 84a, 139b, 140a, 142a, 149a, 195a, 204a, 235a, 259a, 263a, 265a, 266a, 281a, 299a, 326a, b, 363b, 420b – I, 3b, 16b, 19a, 20b, 44b, 54a, 61a, 79a, 102a, 111b, 145a, 151b, 153a, 235a, 237a, 254b, 286b, 306a, 450a, 545a, 705b, 994a, 1083b, 1332b, 1333b; II, 4b, 44a, 1135a; III, 166b; IV, 1083a; V, 2a, **57b**, 545b, 859a, 875a, 1229b; S, 15a, 24a, 31b, 38a, 58a, 67a, 72b, 83a, b, 139a, b, 142a, 149a, 195a, 203b, 234b, 258b, 263a, 264b, 265b, 281a, 298b, 325b, 326a, 363b, 421a
- administration ii, 505a, 561a; v, 56b – II, 518a, 574b; V, 58a
- ethnology/ethnologie iii, 1107b; iv, 20a; v, 56a, b – III, 1135a; IV, 21b; V, 57b, 58a
- history/histoire ii, 978b; iv, 15a-b; v, 56b-59b – II, 1001a; IV, 16a-b; V, 58a-61a
Khurāsān, Banū v, **59b** – V, **61b**
Khurāsānī → Badr al-Dīn
Khurāsānī, Ākhūnd Mullā v, **61a** –, V, **63a**
Khurāsānī, Muḥammad Kāẓim s, 76a, 95b – S, 76a, 95a
al-Khurayba v, 761b, 762a – V, 767b
al-Khuraymī → Abū Yaʿḳūb al-Khuraymī
Khūrī i, 1006b – I, 1037b
al-Khūrī, Fāris v, **62a** – V, **63b**
al-Khūrī, Rashīd Salīm → al-Ḳarawī, al-Shāʿir
al-Khūrī, Shukrī ii, 471b – II, 483b
Khūriyā-Mūriyā → Khūryān-Mūryān
al-Khurma v, **62b** – V, **64a**
Khurram, Prince/le prince i, 81a, 686a, 1331a; ii, 380b; iii, 424a – I, 83b, 707a, 1371b; II, 391a; III, 438a
Khurramābād v, **63a**, 830a, 831b – V, **65a**, 836a, 837b
Khurramdīnī → Khurramiyya
Khurramiyya i, 149b, 241a, 844a; iii, 234a; iv, 17a, 45a, 100a, 838b; v, **63b**, 243b, 823a – I, 153b, 248b, 867a; III, 241a; IV, 18b, 48a, 104a, 871b; V, **65a**, 241a, 829a
Khurramshahr i, 1342a; ii, 181a; iv, 6a; v, **65b**; s, 57a – I, 1382a; II, 187a; IV, 6b; V, **67b**; S, 57b
Khurrem Sulṭān i, 1225b; iii, 147b, 998b; iv, 232a, 1100a; v, **66a**, 333b, 720a, 802a – I, 1262a; III, 150b, 1023b; IV, 242a, b, 1131a; V, **68a**, 334a, 725b, 807b
Khursābād v, **67b** – V, **70a**

Kh(w)urshāh b. Muḥammad i, 354a — I, 364b
Khurshīd (Ṭabaristān) ii, 74b; iii, 501b; v, **68b**; s, 298b — II, 76a; III, 518b; V, **70b**; S, 298a
Khurshīd, K.H. iv, 711a — IV, 739b
Khurshīd Pasha i, 399a, b; ii, 637a; iii, 88b — I, 410b, 411a; II, 653a; III, 90b
Khurshīd Silūrzī i, 513b — I, 529a
Khurshīdī v, 828a — V, 834a
al-Khurṭūm → Kharṭūm
Khurūdj iv, 412a — IV, 430a
Khūryān-Mūryān i, 535b, 540a, 1282b; v, **70a** — I, 551b, 556b, 1321b; V, **72b**
Khusdār → Kalāt; Ḳuṣdār
al-Khushanī, Abū ʿAbd Allāh i, 600b; iii, 789b; v, **71a** — I, 620a; III, 813a; V, **73a**
al-Khushanī → Ibn Masʿūd
Khushḥāl Khān Khaṭak i, 218b, 221a; iv, 1102a; v, **72a** — I, 224b, 227b; IV, 1133b; V, **74a**
Khushḳadam, al-Malik al-Ẓāhir (Mamlūk) ii, 239b; iii, 1198b; iv, 960a; v, **73a**; s, 38a — II, 246b; III, 1228b; IV, 992b; V, **74b**; S, 38b
Khusraushāhī, Hādī iv, 167a — IV, 174a
Khusraw → Amīr Khusraw; Anūshirwān; Ghāzī Khusrew; Kisrā I, II
Khusraw, Mollā iii, 163b, 164a; v, **32b** — III, 167a, b; V, **33b**
Khusraw b. Djahangīr → Khusraw Sultān
Khusraw Beg i, 1139b — I, 1174a
Khusraw Fīrūz, al-Malik al-Raḥīm i, 132a, 513a, 1073b, 1352b, 1356a; ii, 192b; iv, 457b; v, **73b** — I, 136a, 528b, 1105b, 1106a, 1392a, 1395a; II, 199a; IV, 478a; V, **75b**
Khusraw Fīrūz (Djustānid) s, 357a — S, 356b
Khusraw Fīrūzān ii, 192a — II, 198a
Khusraw Khān Barwārī ii, 269a, 272a, 1076a, 1084a; iii, 416b; iv, 923b; s, 105b — II, 277b, 280b, 1101a, 1109b; III, 429b; IV, 956b; S, 105a
Khusraw Malik → Ghaznawid(e)s
Khusraw Mīrzā iv, 787a; s, 70b, 108b — IV, 819a; S, 71b, 108a
Khusraw Parvīv → Kisrā II
Khusraw Pasha Bosniak (d./m. 1632) i, 4a, 1159b, 1208b; ii, 1091a; iv, 971b; v, **32b**, 256b, 458a — I, 4b, 1194a, 1244b; II, 1116b; IV, 1004a; V, **33b**, 254b, 460b
Khusraw Pasha Dīvāne (or/ou Deli) → Khosrew Pasha Deli
Khusraw Shāh → Ghaznawid(e)s
Khusraw Shāh, Nāṣir al-Dīn → Khusraw Khān Barwārī
Khusraw Shāh b. Bahrām ii, 1052b — II, 1077a
Khusraw Sulṭān i, 686a; ii, 380a; iv, 282a; v, **74a** — I, 707a; II, 390b; IV, 294b; V, **76a**
Khusrawānī v, 185a — V, 182b
Khusrawī, Muḥammad Bāḳir iv, 72b; v, 198a — IV, 76b; V, 195b
Khusraw-zāde v, 609b — V, 613a
Khusūf → Kusūf
Khuṭba i, 20b, 132a, 261b; ii, 593a; iii, 35b; iv, 945a, 1110a; v, **74a** — I, 21a, 135b, 136a, 269b; II, 607b; III, 37a; IV, 977b, 1141b; V, **76a**
Khuttalān, Khuttal v, **75b**; s, 125a, b — V, **77b**; S, 124a, b
Khuttalī iv, 216a — IV, 225b
Khuwāra → Djand
al-Khuwārizmī → al-Kh(w)ārazmī
Khūy → Khōī
Khuzāʿa, Banū i, 453a, 1283b; v, **76b**, 434b — I, 466a, 1323a; V, **79a**, 436b
al-Khuzāʿī, Abū Muḥammad i, 827a — I, 850a
al-Khuzāʿī, Ḥamza b. Mālik s, 326b — S, 326a
al-Khuzāmā v, **80a**; s, 377a — V, **82a**; S, 377a
Khuzayma b. Khāzim v, 488a — V, 491a
Khuzayma b. Thābit al-Anṣārī v, 621a — V, 625a
Khuzdar → Ḳuṣdār
Khūzistān i, 3a, 131b, 239b, 240a, 305b, 437b, 528b, 561b, 659a, 695a, 866b, 1350a; ii, 903a; iii, 291b; iv, 6a, 42b; v, 65b, **80a**, 824a, 831a, 866b, 867a; s, 12b, 37b, 61a — I, 3b, 135b, 247a, b, 315a, 450a, 544b, 579a, 679b, 716b, 890b, 1390b; II, 923b; III, 300b; IV, 6b, 45a; V, 67b, **82a**, 830a, 837a, 873a, b; S, 13a, 38a, 61b
Khvarshî v, **81b** — V, **83b**
Khwadāy-nāmak → Khudāynāma
Khyber Pass → Khaybar
Kianghrī → Čankîrî
Kiari, Muḥammad al-Amīn i, 1260a — I, 1298b
Kiaya → Ketkhudā
Kibar v, 868b — V, 875a
Ḳibla i, 609b; ii, 213b; iv, 318a; v, **82a**, 323b, 1140b, 1141a, 1169a — I, 629b; II, 220b; IV, 332a; V, 84a, 323a, 1134a, 1158b
Ḳîbrîslî Meḥmed Emīn Pasha i, 397a — I, 408b
al-Kibrīt v, **88b**, 706b — V, **91a**, 712a
Ḳibṭ i, 435b, 471a, 532a, 803a, 1146b; ii, 229b, 330a, 560b, 958a; iii, 4a, 721b, 886a; v, **90a** — I, 448a, 485a, 548a, 826a, 1180b; II, 236b, 339b, 574b, 980b; III, 4a, 744a, 910a; V, **92b**
al-Ḳibṭī → Čingane
Ḳidāḥ iv, 488a — IV, 509a
Ḳidam v, **95a** — V, **97b**
Kidara i, 226a; iii, 303b — I, 232b; III, 313a
Ḳidjmas ii, 286a — II, 294a
Kifāyat Khān iv, 1128a — IV, 1159b
Ḳifṭ v, 90a, 92a, **99a**, 514a — V, 92b, 94a, **101a**, 517b
al-Ḳifṭī → Shīth b. Ibrāhīm
al-Ḳifṭī, ʿAlī b. Yūsuf → Ibn al-Ḳifṭī
al-Ḳifṭī, Yūsuf b. Ibrāhīm s, 289a — S, 289a
Kihāna ii, 322b; iv, 263b, 420b, 763a, 1128b; v, **99b** — II, 332a; IV, 275a, b, 438b, 793b, 1160a; V, **101b**
Kihsan v, 1148b — V, 1139b
Ḳîḳān, Kīkān → Kalāt
Kilā → Kalah
al-Ḳilāʿ → al-Ḳalʿa (castle/château)
Ḳilʿa Rāy Pithorā ii, 256a, b, 259a; v, 1214b — II, 263b, 264, 267a; V, 1204b
Kilāb b. Rabīʿa, Banū i, 441a, b, 442a; ii, 71b, 159b, 234a, 235a, 238a; v, **101b**, 459a, 923a — I, 454a, b; II, 73a, 164b, 240b, 242a, 244b; V, **103b**, 462a, 928b
Ḳilāba bint al-Ḥārith b. Kalada s, 355a — S, 354b
al-Kilāʿī, ʿAyyād (ʿAbbād; ʿImād) b. Naṣr iv, 403a — IV, 420b
al-Kīlānī, Rashīd ʿAlī → Rashīd ʿAlī
Kilār ii, 1088b — II, 1114a
Kilāt → Kalāt
Ḳîlburun v, **103a** — V, **105a**
Kili i, 1253a — I, 1291a
Kilī, Banū v, 459b — V, 462b
Kilia i, 1119b — I, 1153a, b
Ḳîlîçzāde Ḥaḳḳī iv, 169a — IV, 176a
Kilīd al-Baḥr → Čanaḳ-ḳalʿe Boghazî
Ḳîlîdj Alayi → Taḳlīd-i Sayf
Ḳîlîdj ʿAlī Beg v, 48a — V, 49b
Ḳîlîdj ʿAlī Pasha → ʿUlūdj ʿAlī
Ḳîlîdj Arslan I (Saldjūḳ) i, 466a, b, 664a, 732a; ii, 110a, b; v, **103b** — I, 480a, 684a, 754a; II, 112b, 113a; V, **105b**
Ḳîlîdj Arslan II (Saldjūḳ) i, 431b, 466b; ii, 111a; iv, 575b; v, **104a**, 254b — I, 444a, 480b; II, 113b; IV, 598b; V, **106a**, 252b
Ḳîlîdj Arslan III (Saldjūḳ) ii, 691b; v, **104b** — II, 709a; V, **106b**
Ḳîlîdj Arslan IV Rukn al-Dīn (Saldjūḳ) iv, 619b, 620a, 813b, 814a; v, **104b**, 254a — IV, 644a, b, 846b;

V, **106b**, 252a
Ḳîlîdj Bek i, 1157a – I, 1191b
Ḳilidjūrī v, 9a – V, 9b
Kilifi v, **105a** – V, **107a**
Ḳīlīḳiya → Cilicia/Cilicie
Killah → Kalah
Ḳillawriya iv, 496b; v, **105a** – IV, 518a; V, **107a**
Killigil ii, 701b, 702a – II, 719b
Killiz v, **105b** – V, **107b**
Kilmek Abiz i, 1076b – I, 1108b
Kilōgharī s, 352b – S, 352b
Kilwa iv, 886a, 892b; v, **106a**, 223b, 1157b – IV, 918b, 925a; V, **108b**, 221a, 1147b
al-Ḳily v, **107a** – V, **109a**
Kimäk v, **107b**, 126a; s, 245a – V, **109b**, 128b; S, 245a
Ḳimār i, 343a; v, **108b**, 616b, 768b – I, 353b; V, **111a**, 620b, 774b
Ḳimār (Khmer) ii, 9a; iii, 1208b; v, **108a**; 227a – II, 9a; III, 1239b; V, **110b**, 225a
al-Kīmiyāʾ iii, 965a; iv, 673b; v, **110a** – III, 989b; IV, 701a; V, **112b**
Kinā v, 515b, 519b – V, 519a, 523a
Kinabalu, Mount s, 150a – S, 150a
Kīnakhwāriyya i, 1110a; s, 363b – I, 1143b; S, 363b
Ḳinalîzāde ʿAlāʾ al-Dīn iv, 471b; v, **115a** – IV, 492b; V, **118a**
Ḳinalîzāde Ḥasan v, **116a** – V, **118b**
Kināna b. Khuzayma i, 545a; ii, 625a, 627a, 883b; iv, 334a; v, **116a** – I, 562a; II, 640b, 642b, 904a; IV, 348b; V, **118b**
Kināya v, **116b** – V, **119a**
Kinda i, 526b, 548b, 583b, 683b, 697a; ii, 354a; iii, 52b; v, 23a, **118a**; s, 326b, 337b – I, 542a, 566a, 602b, 704a, 718a; II, 363b; III, 54b; V, 24a, **121a**; S, 326a, 337a
al-Kindī, ʿAbd al-Masīḥ v, **120b** – V, **123a**
al-Kindī, Abū ʿUmar i, 153b; v, **121b** – I, 157b; V, **124a**
al-Kindī, Abū Yūsuf Yaʿḳūb i, 154a, 234b, 235a, 327b, 328a, 344b, 589a, 631a, 1003b, 1100b; ii, 376b, 578b, 765b, 771b, 872a; iii, 169b, 303a, 664a; iv, 332b, 418a, 763b, 795a; v, 113b, **122a**, 237b, 398b, 702b, 950a; s, 72b, 78a, 251b, 271b, 412a – I, 158a, 242a, b, 338a, b, 355a, 608b, 652a, 1034a, 1134a; II, 387a, 593a, 784a, 790b, 892a; III, 173b, 312a, 685b; IV, 347a, 436a, 793b, 827a, b; V, 116a, **124b**, 235b, 400a, 707b, 954a; S, 73a, 77b, 252a, 271a, 412a
Ḳindīl → Miṣbāḥ
Kinkiwar v, **123b**, 169a – V, **126a**, 166b
Ḳinnasrīn i, 761a; v, **124a**, 921a – I, 784a; V, **126b**, 926b
Kinship → Ḳarāba
Ḳinṭār → Makāyīl
Kiosque → Köshk
Ḳipčak i, 135a, 927a, 1075b, 1105a, 1188b; ii, 24a, 43a, 44b, 610a, 1108a, 1109a; iii, 1115a; iv, 32b, 349a, 350a, 527a, 542a, 892a; v, 30a, 108a, **125b**; s, 97b, 203b, 245b, 392b, 420a – I, 139a, 955b, 1107b, 1138b, 1223b; II, 24b, 44a, 45a, 625a, 1134a, 1135a; III, 1142b; IV, 35a, 363b, 364a, 365a, 549b, 565b, 924b; V, 31a, 110a, **128a**; S, 97a, 203a, 245b, 392b, 420a
Ḳipčak, Sayf al-Dīn ii, 285b – II, 293b
Ḳîr Shehir → Kîrshehir
Kirāʾ v, **126b** – V, **129a**
Ḳirāʾa → Tadrīs
Ḳirāʾa(t) i, 114a, 565b, 567b; ii, 293a; iii, 434b, 704b, 761a, 817b; iv, 822a; v, **127a**; s, 393b – I, 117a, 584a, 586a; II, 301a; III, 448b, 726b, 784a, 841a; IV, 855a; V, **129b**; S, 393b
Ḳirāḍ v, **129b** – V, **132a**
Ḳirān iii, 35a, 53b; iv, 259a; v, **130b** – III, 37a, 55b; IV, 271a; V, **133a**
Ḳīrāt → Makāyīl
Ḳīrāṭ iii, 10b – III, 11a
Ḳird v, **131a** – V, **133b**
Kirdi ii, 9b, 10a – II, 10a
Kirdî-Kalal → Ḳarata
Kîrdjalî i, 1304a – I, 1344a
Kiresun → Giresün
Ḳirghiz → Ḳirgiz
Ḳirgiz i, 224a, 853b, 1076b, 1077a; ii, 66b, 67b, 571a; iii, 116a, 117a; iv, 10a, 213b, 631b; v, **134a**, 247a – I, 231a, 877a, 1108b, 1109a; II, 68a, b, 585b; III, 118b, 119b; IV, 10b, 223a, 656b; V, **137a**, 244b
Kirid → Iḳrītish
Ḳîrîm i, 4b, 62b, 270b, 293a, 893a, 1108a, 1119b; ii, 24b, 25a, 1112a; iii, 44b; iv, 499b, 568b, 608a, 891b; v, **136a**, 719b; s, 96b – I, 4b, 64b, 279a, 302a, 919b, 1141a, 1153a; II, 25b, 26a, 1138a; III, 46a; IV, 521a, 591a, b, 632b, 924a; V, **138b**, 724b; S, 96a
- Khānate v, 141b-142a, 312b – V, 144b-145a, 312b
Ḳîrḳ Kilise/Kinise v, **143b** – V, **146a**
al-Ḳirḳisānī, Abū Yaʿḳūb Yūsuf iv, 306b – IV, 320a
Ḳîrḳlareli → Ḳîrḳ Kilise
Ḳîrḳ Wezīr → Shaykhzāde II
Kirkūk v, **144a** – V, **146b**
Ḳîrk-yir iii, 44b – III, 46b
Kirmān i, 8a, 86a, 131b, 132a, 211b, 420a, 731b, 830b, 1005a, 1311a, 1350a; ii, 299a, 746b, 1051a; iii, 1156b; iv, 14b, 19b, 391b, 807a, 1046b, 1170a; v, **147a**, 294a, 835a, 1114a, 1116a; s, 53a, 71b, 118b, 122b, 127a, 129a, 139b, 140b, 142a, 147b, 326a, 327a – I, 8a, 88b, 135b, 136a, 217b, 432a, 753b, 853b, 1036a, 1351b, 1390b; II, 307a, 764b, 1075b; III, 1185a; IV, 15b, 21a, 408a, 839b, 1078a, 1203a; V, **149b**, 294a, 841b, 1110a, 1112a; S, 53b, 72a, 117b, 122a, 126a, 128a, 139a, 140a, 142a, 147b, 325b, 326b
Kirmānī, Awḥad al-Dīn v, **166a** – V, **163b**
Kirmānī, Ḥādjdjī Karīm iv, 854b – IV, 887b
al-Kirmānī, Ḥamīd al-Dīn i, 450a; iii, 72a, 134a; iv, 204a; v, **166a** – I, 463a; III, 74b, 137a; IV, 213a; V, **164a**
Kirmānī, Kamāl al-Dīn → Kh(w)ādjū Kirmānī
Kirmānī, Mīrzā Āḳā Khān s, 109b – S, 108b
Kirmānshāh iv, 7b; v, **167b**; s, 73a, 84a, 135a, 142b – IV, 8b; V, **165b**; S, 73b, 83b, 134b, 142a
Kirmāsin → Kirmānshāh
Kirmāstī v, **171b** – V, **169a**
Ḳirmid v, 585b – V, 591a
Kirmīsīn → Ḳirmānshāh
Ḳirmiz i, 645b; ii, 681a – I, 666a; II, 698a
Kirovabad → Gandja
Ḳirsh → Sikka
Ḳîrshehir v, **172a** – V, **169b**
Ḳirṭās iv, 742a; v, **173b** – IV, 772a; V, **171a**
Ḳirwāsh → Ḳarwāsh
Kisāʾ → Libās
al-Kisāʾī, Abu 'l-Ḥasan ʿAlī b. Hamza ii, 806b, 807b; iii, 155a; v, **174a**, 351a; s, 22b, 128b – II, 826a, b; III, 158b; V, **171b**, 351b; S, 22b, 127b
al-Kisāʾī, Madjd al-Dīn iv, 60b; v, **175b** – IV, 64a; V, **172b**
al-Kisāʾī, Ṣāḥib Ḳiṣaṣ al-Anbiyāʾ iii, 306a; v, **176a**, 180b – III, 315a; V, **173b**, 178a
Kisakürek, Necip Fazil ii, 432b – II, 444a
Kisangani v, **176b** – V, **174a**
Ḳiṣāṣ ii, 341a; iv, 770a; v, **177a** – II, 350b; IV, 800b; V, **174b**
Ḳiṣaṣ → Ḳiṣṣa
Ḳiṣaṣ al-anbiyāʾ i, 169a; iv, 673b; v, 176a, **180a**, 186b, 193b, 197b, 205a – I, 174a; IV, 700b; V, 173b, **177b**, 184a, 190b, 194b, 202b
Kīsh (Ḳays, djabal) i, 552a, 942b, 1355a; iii, 881a; iv,

500b, **832a**; v, 670b, 671a; s, 222b — I, 569b, 971a, b, 1394b; III, 905a; IV, 522a, **865a**; V, 676a; S, 222b
Kīsh (Shahr-i Sabz) i, 1066b; iv, 694a, 711b; v, **181a**, 858b — I, 1098b; IV, 722a, 740a; V, **178b**, 865b
Ḳîshlāḳ iv, 1029b; v, **182b** — IV, 1061b; V, **180a**
Kishlū Khān iii, 202b; iv, 920b — III, 207b; IV, 953b
Kishm, Badakhshān i, 851b — I, 875b
Kishm island/île iii, 653a; iv, 777b; v, **183a**, 675a, b — III, 674b; IV, 809a; V, **180b**, 680b
Ḳishn v, **184a** — V, **181a**
Ḳishr iv, 452a — IV, 472a
Kishsh → Kash; Kish
Kishtwār s, 242a — S, 242a
Kishwar ii, 577a, 579b, 951b — II, 591b, 594a, 973b
Ḳisma, ḳismet v, **184a** — V, **181b**
Kisrā v, **184b** — V, **182a**
Kisrā (Ḳarmaṭī) iv, 663a, b — IV, 690a
Kisrā I Anūshirwān (Sāsānid(e)) i, 102a, 516b, 522b, 549a, 835b, 1094a; ii, 114a, 190b, 740a; iii, 304a; iv, 14a, 265a, 839a; v, 184b; s, 115b, 127a, 255b, 299a, 354b — I, 105a, 532b, 538b, 566a, 858b, 1127a; II, 116b, 196b, 758b; III, 313a; IV, 14b, 277a, 872a; V, 182a; S, 115a, 126a, 255b, 298b, 354a
Kisrā II Parwīz i, 510a, 996a, 1094a; ii, 793b; iii, 219a; iv, 730b, 1133b; v, 184b, 633b; s, 298b — I, 525b, 1026b, 1127a; II, 812b; III, 225b; IV, 759b, 1165a; V, 182b, 638a; S, 298a
Kisrawān s, 33b — S, 33b
al-Kisrawī, Abu 'l-Ḥasan ʿAlī v, **185b** — V, **182b**
Kissa → Khāsa
Ḳiṣṣa, Ḳiṣaṣ ii, 306a; iii, 369a, 374a; v, **185b**, 951a — II, 182a; III, 381a, 386a; V, **183a**, 955a
Ḳiṣṣa Čahār Darwīsh i, 430b; iii, 373a — I, 442b; III, 384b
Ḳisṭ → Makāyīl
al-Kīsumī, Abū Riḍā s, 363a — S, 363a
Kiswa ii, 541a; iv, 317b, 319b — II, 554b; IV, 331b, 333b
Ki-swahili → Swahili
Ḳiṭʿa → Muḳaṭṭaʿa
Kitāb i, 30a, 274a; ii, 214a, 302b; iii, 1127a; iv, 353b; v, **207a** — I, 31a, 282a; II, 221a, 310b; III, 1154b; IV, 368b; V, **204b**
Kitāb al-Aghānī i, 118a, 590a; ii, 551b, 1074a; iii, 1262b — I, 121b, 609b; II, 565a, 1098b; III, 1295b
Kitāb al-Aḥdjār i, 419a — I, 431a
Kitāb al-Ansāb i, 78a — I, 80b
Kitāb al-ʿAyn iv, 963a — IV, 995a
Kitāb al-Bayzara iii, 809a — III, 832b
Kitāb dhakhīrat al-Iskandar iv, 331b — IV, 346a
Kitāb al-Djilwa v, **208b** — V, **206a**
Kitāb al-Ghazawāt ʿArūdj wa Khayr al-Dīn i, 678a, b — I, 699a, b
Kitāb al-Ghundjā ii, 1004a — II, 1027b
Kitāb al-Ḥarb al-maʿshūḳ ii, 1066b, 1067a — II, 1091a, b
Kitāb al-Ḥarb wa ʾl-shadjāʿa iii, 181a — III, 185b
Kitāb al-ḥāwī iv, 215b; v, 865a — IV, 225a; V, 872a
Kitāb al-Ḥikāyāt al-ʿadjība wa ʾl-akhbār al-gharība iii, 369a — III, 380b
Kitāb al-Ḥiyal i, 1113a; iii, 511a — I, 1146b; III, 528a
Kitāb al-Iḍāḥ fī ʾl-Khayr al-Maḥḍ i, 1340a — I, 1380b
Kitāb al-Istibṣār → Istibṣār
Kitāb al-Maṣāyid was ʾl-maṭārid ii, 740b — II, 759a
Kitāb al-Nawādir Djuḥā ii, 590b, 591a — II, 605a, 606a
Kitāb-i Nawras iii, 453b — III, 469b
Kitāb-i Paykār iii, 113a — III, 115b
Kitāb al-Sakīsarān iii, 113a — III, 115a
Kitāb Shadjarat al-nihāl ii, 910a — II, 931b
Kitāb al-Shilḥa i, 1186a — I, 1221a
Kitāb al-Thālūdjiyā i, 1340a — I, 1380a
Kitāb al-Thamara i, 1156a — I, 1190b
Kitāb-Tīdjān iii, 370a — III, 382a
Kitāb al-ʿUyūn i, 1103a; iii, 754b — I, 1136a; III, 777b
Kitāba iv, 510a; v, 208a — IV, 532a; V, 205b
Kitābāt v, **210b**, 754b, 761b, 992b — V, **208a**, 760b, 767b, 988a
Kitābkhāna → Maktaba
Kitai → Ḳarā Khiṭāy
Kitāmiyya → Shādhiliyya
Ḳitarā → Ḳithāra
Kitbugha, al-Malik al-ʿĀdil (Mamlūk) i, 1126b, 1324b; ii, 285a; iv, 965b — I, 1160b, 1365b; II, 293b; IV, 998a
Kitbughā al-Manṣūrī iii, 954b; v, 595a — III, 979a; V, 598b
Kitbugha Noyon i, 786b — I, 810a
Kitchener, Lord i, 13b, 46a; ii, 828a — I, 13b, 47a; II, 848a
Kiṭfīr i, 825b; v, **233b** — I, 848b; V, **231b**
Ḳithāra v, **234a** — V, **232a**
al-Kitmān → al-Ibāḍiyya; Khāridjites; Taḳiyya
Ḳiṭmīr → Aṣḥāb al-Kahf, Kalb
Ḳiṭrān → Ḳaṭrān
Kivar → Kibar
Kiwām al-Dawla → Bahāʾ al-Dawla Fīrūz
Ḳiwām al-Din Shīrāzī iv, 910b, 1073b — IV, 943b, 1105a
Ḳiwāmī iv, 59b; s, 416b — IV, 62b; S, 416b
Kiyā → Afrāsiyābid(e)s
Kiyā Abu 'l-Faḍl (Thāʾirid(e)) s, 363a — S, 363a
al-Kiyā al-Harrāsī, Shams al-Islām v, **234b**; s, 347a — V, **232b**; S, 347a
Ḳiyāfa ii, 211a, 916a, b; v, **234b** — II, 217b, 937b, 938a; V, **233a**
al-Ḳiyāma i, 186b; iv, 47a, 205a, b; v, **235b** — I, 192a; IV, 50a, 214a, b; V, **233b**
Ḳiyān → Ḳayna
Ḳiyās i, 276a, 1199b, 1327a; ii, 102a, 182b; iii, 795a, 1025b, 1026a; iv, 153b, 256a; v, **238b** — I, 284b, 1235a, 1367b; II, 104b, 188a; III, 818b, 1051a, 1052a; IV, 160a, 267a; V, **236b**
Ḳiyāt s, 46a, 97b, 420a — S, 46a, 97a, 420a
Kiybad Çiftliği → Kayḳubadiyya
Ḳîz v, **242b** — V, **240b**
Kiẓāma iv, 532b — IV, 555b
Ḳizhduwān s, 246a — S, 246a
Ḳîzîl Ahmedlî → Isfendiyār Oghlu
Kîzîl Arslan Khāmūsh → Khāmūsh
Kîzîl Arslan ʿUthmān iii, 1111a, b, 1112a — III, 1138b, 1139b
Ḳîzîl-bāsh i, 1b, 224a, 262a, 1162a, 1229b; ii, 20b, 202b; iii, 253b, 316a, 1101a; iv, 34b, 35a, b, 36b, 186b, 188b; v, **243a**, 437b, 749a — I, 1b, 230b, 270a, 1196b, 1266a, II, 21a, 209a; III, 260b, 325b, 1128a; IV, 37a, b, 38a, 39a, 194b, 196b; V, **241a**, 440a, 754b
Ḳîzîl-elma (Kîzîl-alma) v, **245b** — V, **243b**
Ḳîzîl-Irmāḳ v, 172a, **246b** — V, 169b, **244a**
Ḳîzîl-Ḳum iv, 613a; v, **246b**; s, 244b — IV, 637b; V, **244b**; S, 244b
Kîzîl Orda i, 312a — I, 322a
Ḳîzîlrobāṭ ii, 406a — II, 417a
Kiziltepe v, 248a — V, 246a
Ḳizil-üzen v, **247a** — V, **245a**
Ḳîzîlyar s, 82a — S, 82a
Kizimkazi v, **247b** — V, **245a**
Kīzkānān → Kilāt
Kîzlar Aghasî i, 295a; iii, 175b; v, 243a — I, 304a; III, 179a; V, 240b
Klementi i, 652a, 656b — I, 672b, 677b
Klis v, 774b, 775a — V, 780b, 781a

Knight → Fāris
Knights Hospitallers → Knights of St. John
Knights of St. John i, 293b, 1119b, 1250b; ii, 6a, 529b; iii, 504a, 1006b; iv, 485a, 779a; v, 268b, 590b; s, 93b, 204b
Knights Templars → Dāwiyya and Isbitāriyya
Knights, Teutonic → Dāwiyya and Isbitāriyya
Ḳnīṭra iv, 556b – IV, 580b
Knowledge → ʿIlm
Kōbad → Ḳubādh
Ḳobān iv, 674b, 675a – IV, 702a, b
Köbeči → Ḳubači
Kōč → Ḳufč
Kocaeli → Kodja-eli
Kocha i, 719b – I, 741a
Ḳoč Ḥiṣār v, **247b** – V, **245b**
Kočī Beg i, 712a; iii, 983a; iv, 168a; v, **248b**, 266a – I, 733b; III, 1007b; IV, 175a; V, **246b**, 264a
Ḳočḳar (river/fleuve) iv, 212b – IV, 222a
Kodja → Khodja
Ḳodja-eli i, 468b; v, **250a** – I, 482b; V, **247b**
Ḳodja Ḥiṣār v, 248b – V, 246b
Kodok ii, 828a – II, 848a
Kogonia i, 101b – I, 104b
Kōhāt i, 238b; v, **250b** – I, 246a; V, **248a**
al-Kōhēn al-ʿAṭṭār v, **251a** – V, **249a**
al-Kōhīn → al-Kūhīn
Kohinoor → Kūh-i Nūr
Kōhistān → Kuhistān
Kohl → Kuḥl
Kōh-rud → Ḳuhrūd
Koil → Aligarh
Kökbürī → Gökbürī, Muẓaffar al-Dīn
Kokča → Badakhshān
Kokča, river/rivière i, 851b – I, 875b
Kökülü-oghlu ii, 207a – II, 213b
Ḳol i, 475a – I, 489a
Kolaba s, 246b – S, 246b
Kōlatirri Rādjās iv, 547a – IV, 570b
Koléa v, 362a – V, 363a
Ḳolonborna i, 1062b – I, 1094b
Ḳomač iii, 47b – III, 49a
Ḳōmis → Ḳūmis
Ḳomitadjīs i, 1304b – I, 1344b
Komoten → Gümüldjīne
Ḳomul v, 846a – V, 858a
Konakry v, **252a** – V, **250a**
al-Konawi → al-Ḳūnawī
Konboro ii, 251b – II, 259a
Kong ii, 63a; v, **252b** – II, 64b; V, **250b**
Ḳonghurtay iv, 620b – IV, 645b
Ḳongrat → Ḳungrat
Konkan iii, 426a; s, 246a – III, 440a; S, 246a
Ḳonḳīrat ii, 41b; v, 391b – II, 42b; V, 392b
Ḳonya i, 466b, 468a, 477b, 703a, 807a; ii, 202a, 746b; iv, 575b, 621a, b, 622a, 1167b; v, **253b**, 589a, 676b, 677b, 881a; s, 83b, 137a, 146a, 280b – I, 480b, 481b, 491b, 724b, 830a; II, 208a, 765a; IV, 598b, 645b, 646b, 1200b; V, **251a**, 593a, 681b, 682b, 887b; S, 83a, 136a, 146a, 280a
- monuments v, **254b**, 1145a, 1146a – V, **252b**, 1137a, b
Ḳonya (Ḳaramān) Ereğlisi ii, 705b – II, 723b
Kopak → Sikka
Köpek Khān → Kebek
Köpek, Saʿd al-Dīn iv, 816b; v, 285b – IV, 849b; V, 284a
Köprü → Vezīr Köprü
Köprü ḥaḳḳī ii, 147a – II, 151a
Köprü Ḥiṣārī v, **256a** – V, **254a**
Köprülü (viziers) i, 1064a; v, **256a** – I, 1096a; V, **254a**
Köprülü, Mehmed Fuad ii, 596a; v, **263b**; s, 82b – II, 611a; V, **261b**; S, 82a
Köprülü Aḥmed Pasha s, 171a – S, 171b
Köprülü Fāḍil Aḥmed Pāsha i, 68b, 1032b; ii, 635a, 833a; iii, 477a, 1086b; iv, 516b, 539a, 590a, 591a; v, 258b, **259a**, 720b, 766a – I, 70a, 1064a; II, 651a, 852b; III, 493b, 1113a; IV, 539a, 562a, 614a, b; V, 256b, **257a**, 726a, 772a
Koprülü Fāḍil Muṣṭafā Pasha i, 268a; iv, 193b, 194a, 233b; v, **261a** – I, 276b; IV, 202a, b, 244a; V, **259a**
Köprülü Meḥmed Pasha i, 4b; ii, 1090b; iii, 626b; iv, 233b, 589b, 720a; v, **256b** – I, 4b; II, 1116b; III, 647b; IV, 244a, 613a, 749a; V, **254b**
Köprülü Nuʿmān Pasha i, 268b, 269a, 395a; v, **262b** – I, 277a, 406a; V, **260b**
Ḳopuz → ʿŪd
Kōrā Djahānābād v, **264b** – V, **262b**
Korah → Ḳārūn
Koraltan, Refik ii, 596a – II, 611a
Korča v, **264b** – V, **262b**
Kordofān i, 35a; ii, 123a; v, **266b**, 1249a, b; s, 164a – I, 36a; II, 126a; V, **264a**, 1240a; S, 164a
Ḳordos v, **268b** – V, **266a**
Körfüz i, 395a; iv, 1157b; v, **268b**, 838a – I, 406b; IV, 1189b; V, **266b**, 844b
Körguz ii, 606a – II, 621a
Koritza → Korča
Ḳorḳmaz b. Fakhr al-Dīn Maʿn ii, 634b, 749b; iii, 205b – II, 651a, 768a; III, 211a
Ḳorḳud b. Bāyazīd i, 396a, 1120b; ii, 1042b; v, **269a** – I, 407b, 1154a; II, 1066b; V, **267a**
Ḳorḳud Dede → Dede Ḳorḳud
Köroghlu i, 792b; ii, 75b; iii, 117a, 374b; v, **270a**; s, 239a – I, 816a; II, 77a; III, 119b, 386b; V, **267b**; S, 239a
Ḳoron v, **270b** – V, **268a**
Ḳoryürek, Enīs Behīdj v, **271a** – V, **269a**
Kôs → Ḳūṣ
Köse Dagh v, **271b** – V, **269b**
Köse Mikhāl → Mīkhāloghlu
Köse Mūsā Pasha iv, 322b – IV, 337a
Kösem Wālide/Kösem Sulṭān iii, 623a, 983a; iv, 233b, 717a, 884b, 971b; v, **272a** – III, 643b, 1007b; IV, 244a, 745b, 917b, 1003b; V, **270a**
Ḳosh-begi v, **273a**; s, 97a, 419b – V, **271a**; S, 96b, 419b
Köshk v, **274a** – V, **272a**
Ḳoshma v, **274b** – V, **272b**
Ḳoshuḳ → Ḳoshma
Ḳoṣowa, Kosovo v, **275b** – V, **273b**
Kossaian v, 830b – V, 837a
Köstendil → Küstendil
Köstendje v, **277a** – V, **275a**
Kōt Kāṅgrā → Kāṅgrā
Kota kota v, **278a** – V, **276a**
Kota Waringin s, 150b – S, 150b
Koti iv, 1029b – IV, 1061b
Kotoko ii, 10a; iii, 98a; v, **278a** – II, 10a; III, 100b; V, **276a**
Kotonou v, **279a** – V, **277a**
Kotumble → Kudummul
Ḳotuz → Ḳuṭuz
Kōtwāl ii, 868a; iii, 199a, 493a; v, **279b**; s, 59a – II, 888a; III, 203b, 510a; V, **277b**; S, 59b
Kouandé v, **280b** – V, **278b**
Koulougli → Ḳul-oghlu
Koumis → Kumīs
Kounta → Kunta
Koweit → Kuwayt
Köy v, **281b** – V, **279b**
Köy enstitüleri v, **281b**; s, 283b – V, **279b**; S, 283b
Koyl v, **283a**; s, 331b – V, **281a**; S, 331a

Ḳoylu Ḥiṣār v, **283a** — V, **281a**
Ḳoyul Ḥiṣār v, **283b** — V, **281b**
Ḳoyun Baba v, **283b** — V, **281b**
Ḳoyunlū iv, 389a — IV, 406a
Kozak → Kazakh
Ḳōzān i, 285a, b; v, **283b** — I, 293b, 294b; V, **282a**
Ḳozan-oghullarï ii, 207a; v, **284a** — II, 213b; V, **282b**
Ḳožoñ v, 275b — V, 273b
Ḳrān → Sikka
Krawang s, 202a — S, 201b
Ḳrim → Ḳïrïm
Krishṇa iii, 457a — III, 473a
Krishna Deva Rāya i, 924a — I, 952a
Krishna Rādjā Wadiyar v, 1259a — V, 1250a
Ḳrïz iv, 1029a; v, **284b** — IV, 1061a; V, **282b**
Kroumir → Khumayr
Krujë iv, 139a, b, 140a; v, **284b** — IV, 144b, 145a, b, 146a; V, **282b**
Krushevats → Aladja Ḥisār
Ksar, Ksour → Ḳaṣr; Ḳaṣaba
Ḳsentīnī → al-Ḳusanṭīnī
Ḳṣība → Ḳaṣaba (town/ville)
Kuala Lumpur i, 980a; ii, 426b — I, 1010a; II, 437b
Ḳuʿaytīs i, 554b; s, 337b, 338b — I, 572a; S, 337a, 338b
Ḳuba → Ḳubba
Ḳubā ii, 791a — II, 810a
Ḳubači ii, 86b, 89a; iv, 1169a, 1170a; v, **285b** — II, 88a, 90b; IV, 1201b, 1203a; V, **283b**
Ḳubād b. Sulṭān Ḥusayn i, 920a — I, 948a
Ḳubādābād iv, 702a, 818a; v, **285b** — IV, 730b, 850b; V, **284a**
Ḳubādh b. Fīrūz i, 1041a, 1134a; ii, 78a, 253a; iii, 571b; s, 127a — I, 1072b, 1168b; II, 79a, 260b; III, 591b; S, 126a
Ḳubādh b. Yazīd iv, 347a — IV, 362a
Ḳubādh Firūz i, 1094a — I, 1127a
Ḳubādhiyān v, **286b** — V, **285a**
Ḳubādja → Nāṣir al-Dīn Ḳabača
Kubafolo v, **287a** — V, **285b**
Kuban i, 1305a — I, 1345a
Ḳuban (river/rivière) v, **287b** — V, **286a**
Ḳubāṭī iv, 774a — IV, 805a
Kubayh ii, 137b — II, 141a
Ḳubba (Ḳuba) v, **296a**; s, 143a — V, **287b**; S, 143a
Ḳubba (palace) s, 301a — S, 300b
Ḳubba (tent(e)) iv, 1147a — IV, 1179a
Ḳubba (tomb/tombeau) iv, 352b, 434a; v, 214b, **289a**, 1139b — IV, 367b, 453a; V, 212a, **288a**, 1133a
al-Ḳubba (Ḳubbat al-ʿAlam/al-Arḍ) v, **297a** — V, **296a**
Ḳubbat al-ʿĀlam → al-Ḳubba
Ḳubbat al-ʿArbaʿīn iv, 724a — IV, 753a
Ḳubbat al-hawāʾ iii, 274a; v, 297b — III, 282a; V, 297a
Ḳubbat al-Ṣakhra i, 77b; ii, 911a, 978a; iii, 174b, 381a; v, **298a** — I, 80a; II, 932b, 978a; III, 178b, 393b; V, **297b**
Ḳubbe wezīri v, **299b** — V, **299a**
Ḳūbčūr iii, 1099b; iv, 31a, 1042a, 1050a, 1051b; v, **299b** — III, 1126b; IV, 33a, 1073b, 1081b, 1083a; V, **299a**
Ḳubilāy Khān i, 1188a, 1311b; ii, 3a, 45b, 47a; iii, 472a; iv, 811b; v, 38b, 39a, **300a** — I, 1223a, 1352a; II, 3a, 46b; III, 488b; IV, 844b; V, 40a, **299b**
Ḳubilay Noyan iv, 583b — IV, 607a
Kubrā, Shaykh Aḥmad v, **300a** — V, **299b**
Kubrawiyya iv, 48a, 49a, 51b; v, 300a, 301a-b; s, 353b — IV, 50b, 52a, 54b; V, 299b, 300b; S, 353b
Ḳubrus i, 109a, 152a, 798b, 935b, 945b, 1054a; ii, 522a; iii, 186b, 189a, 1182b, 1198b; v, **301b**, 1077a, 1171a; s, 53a, 120b, 221b — I, 112a, 156b, 822a, 964b, 974b, 1085b; II, 535a; III, 190b, 193b, 1212a, 1228b; V, **301a**, 1074b, 1160b; S, 53b, 120a, 221b
Kubruslu → Ḳïbrïslï
Kubu i, 782a; v, **309b** — I, 805b; V, **309a**
Kūč → Ḳufč
Kučak → Wisāl
Kūčak Khān Djangalī, Mīrzā ii, 445b; iv, 398b, 789b; v, **310a**; s, 110a, 366a — II, 457a; IV, 416a, 821b; V, **309b**; S, 109b, 365b
Ḳūčān v, **311a**; s, 83a — V, **311a**; S, 83a
Kucha s, 136b — S, 136a
Küčlük i, 418b, 987b; ii, 42b, 43a, 791b; iii, 1114b; iv, 583a; v, 38b — I, 430b, 1018a; II, 43b, 810b; III, 1141b; IV, 606b; V, 39b
Küčük Aḥmad Pasha ii, 635a, 751a — II, 651a, 769b
Kücük ʿAlī-oghlu ii, 207b; s, 172b — II, 214a; S, 172b
Küčük Bālī Beg → Yaḥyā Pasha-zāde Küčük
Kücük Bostān i, 1279b — I, 1318b
Küčük Čelebi-zāde → Čelebi-zāde
Küčük Ḥasan Pasha i, 904b — I, 932a
Küčük Ḥusayn Pasha → Ḥusayn Pasha, Küčük
Küčük Ḳaynardja, Treaty of/Traité de i, 56b, 62b, 311a, 470b, 893b; ii, 26b, 60b, 688b; iii, 589b, 1186a; v, 141a, **312b**, 495a — I, 58a, 64b, 320b, 484b, 920a; II, 26b, 62a, 705b; III, 610a, 1216a; V, 143b, **312a**, 498a
Küčük Köy s, 330a — S, 329b
Küčük Meḥmed (Janissary/Janissaire) iv, 852a — IV, 885a
Küčük Meḥmed Khān i, 721b; ii, 44a — I, 743b; II, 45a
Küčük Muṣṭafā, Prince/le prince ii, 990a — II, 1013a
Küčük Saʿīd Pasha i, 285b; iii, 993b; v, **313b** — I, 294b; III, 1018a; V, **313b**
Küčük Suleymān Pasha i, 905b; iii, 91a — I, 933a; III, 93b
Küčük Sulṭān i, 1076a — I, 1108a,b
Ḳučum Khān ii, 45a; v, **314b** — II, 46a; V, **314a**
Küčümid(e)s i, 1076a — I, 1108a
Ḳuḍāʿa i, 1a, 545a, 563b, 962a; ii, 122a, 572a; iii, 363b; v, **315a** — I, 1a, 562a, 581b, 991b; II, 125a, 586a; III, 375a; V, **314b**
al-Ḳuḍāʿī, Yūsuf b. ʿAlī iii, 221a — III, 228a
Kūdakiyya v, 65a — V, 67a
Ḳudāma b. Djaʿfar i, 590b, 730a, 857b, 982a, b; ii, 579a, b, 580b; iii, 354b; iv, 249a; v, **318b**; s, 266a, 402a — I, 609b, 752a, 881b, 1012b, 1013a; II, 593b, 594b, 595a; III, 365b; IV, 260a; V, **318a**; S, 265b, 402b
Ḳudār al-Aḥmar → Aḥmar
Ḳudayd s, 312a — S, 311b
Ḳuddūs i, 847a — I, 870a
Ḳuddūs → Muḥammad ʿAlī Bārfurūshī
Kudjūr iv, 808a — IV, 840b
Ḳudra iv, 271b, 272b; v, 576a, b — IV, 283b, 284b; V, 580b, 581a
Kudrī iv, 743b — IV, 773a
al-Ḳuds i, 215b, 352a, 549b, 797b, 799b, 975b, 1310a; ii, 63b, 911b; iii, 1158a; v, 82b, 92a, **322a**, 1127b; s, 154a — I, 222a, 363a, 567a, 821a, 823a, 1005b, 1350b; II, 65a, 932b; III, 1186a; V, 84b, 94b, **321b**, 1123b; S, 154b
- monuments ii, 911a; iii, 174a,b; v, 327b, **339a-344a**, 1143a, b — II, 932b; III, 178a,b; V, 327a, **340a-345a**, 1135b, 1136a
- population v, 328b, 329a, 334a, 336a, b — V, 328a, b, 334a, 336b, 337a
al-Ḳuds → al Masdjid al-Aḳṣā
Ḳudsī → Bakïkhānlï
al-Ḳudsī, Abū Ḥāmid Muḥammad iii, 772b — III, 795b
Ḳudsī, Muḥammad Djān v, **344b** — V, **345b**

al-Ḳudsī, Nāẓim ii, 662a — II, 678b
Ḳudsiyya Bēgam i, 1195b, 1197a — I, 1231a, 1232b
Kudummul v, **345a** — V, **345b**
al-Ḳudūrī, Abu 'l-Ḥusayn/al-Ḥasan Aḥmad i, 310a, 791a; ii, 390a, 486a; iii, 163a; v, **345a**; s, 192a — I, 319b, 814a; II, 400b, 498b; III, 166b; V, **346a**; S, 193a
al-Kūfa i, 16a, 76b, 77a, 103a, 704a; ii, 196b, 415b, 453a; iii, 843a, 1252b, 1254b, 1255a; iv, 911a; v, 174a, **345b**, 945b; s, 15b, 16a, 19a, 48a, 198b, 225b, 230b, 304b, 357b, 358a, 389b, 393b, 400b, 401a — I, 16b, 78b, 79a, 106a, 725b; II, 203a, 426a, 465a; III, 867a, 1285a, 1287a,b; IV, 944a; V, 171b, **346b**, 949a; S, 16a, b, 19a, 48b, 198b, 225b, 230a, 304b, 357b, 390a, 393b, 401a, b
- ethnography/ethnographie i, 529b, 568a; v, 346a, b — I, 545b, 586b; V, 347a, b
- literature/littérature ii, 729a, 806b; iv, 1003a; v, 350b — II, 747b, 826a; IV, 1035b; V, 351a, b
- monuments i, 610a; v, 347a, b, 348b — I, 629b; V, 347b, 348a, 349b
Ḳufč i, 1005a, b, 1354b; iii, 1098a; iv, 807a — I, 1036a, b, 1393b; III, 1124b; IV, 839b
Kuffār → Kāfir (infidel/infidèle)
Kūfī iii, 820b, 846b — III, 844a, 870b
Kūfī, ʿAlī b. Ḥāmid b. Abī Bakr s, 163a — S, 162a
al-Kūfī, Muḥammad b. Sulaymān s, 335a — S, 335a
Kūfic ii, 67a, 91a, 260b, 372b, 709b; iv, 1121a, 1122a, 1123a, 1125a; v, 217a-221b **passim**, 229b-230b, 350b — II, 68a, 92b, 269a, 382b, 728b; IV, 1152b, 1154a, 1155a, 1156b; V, 214b-218b **passim**, 227b-228b, 351a
Ḳūfičīs → Ḳufṣ
Kufra ii, 492b; v, **351b**, 759b, 887a — II, 505a; V, **352b**, 765b, 893b
Ḳufṣ v, 152b, **352b**; s, 129a — V, 154a, **353a**; S, 128b
Kūg̲h̲ūn s, 327a — S, 326b
Kūhak → Čopan Ata
Kūhandil K̲h̲ān i, 231a, b; iv, 537b — I, 238a,b; IV, 561a
Kuḥaylat al-ʿAd̲j̲ūz ii, 785b — II, 804a
Kūh-Gīlū (Kūh-Gālū) iii, 1107a; iv, 5b, 9a; v, 822a, 824b, 829b, 830b — III, 1134a; IV, 6a, 9b; V, 828b, 831a, 835b, 836a, b
Kūh-Gīlūya v, 826b, 827a — V, 832b, 833a
Kūh-i Bābā i, 221b; v, **353a**; s, 367a — I, 228a; V, **354a**; S, 368a
Kuh-i Bāričī → Bāriz
Kūh-i Binālūd s, 83a — S, 83a
Kūh-i Hazār s, 127a — S, 126a
Kūh-i Iṣṭak̲h̲r iv, 221b — IV, 231b
Kūh-i Kalāt iv, 4a — IV, 4b
Kūh-i Ḳārin s, 309a — S, 309a
Kūh-i Lālazār s, 127a — S, 126a
Kūh-i Nūḥ → Ag̲h̲rī Dag̲h̲
Kūh-i-Nūr iii, 348a; v, **353b** — III, 358b; V, **354b**
Kūh-i Raḥmat iv, 221a — IV, 230b
Kūh-i Rang v, 830a — V, 836a
Kūh-i S̲h̲āh D̲j̲ahān s, 83a — S, 83a
Kūh-i Surk̲h̲ iv, 4a — IV, 4b
Kūh-i Taftān iv, 3b — IV, 3b
al-Kūhī, Abū Sahl V, **354b**; S, 119a
al-Kūhin v, **353b**; s, 390b — V, **355a**; S, 391a
al-Kūhīn al-ʿAṭṭār → al-Kōhēn al-ʿAṭṭār
Ḳūhistān i, 1233a; v, 56a, **354a**; s, 66b, 149a — I, 1270a; V, 57b, **355b**; S, 67a, 149a
Kūhistanī (language/langue) ii, 138b; v, 356a — II, 142b; V, 357b
al-Ḳuhistānī (d./m. 1543) iii, 163b — III, 167a
Kūhkamarī, Ḥusayn s, 76a — S, 76a
Kuḥl i, 1089a; v, **356a** — I, 1121b; V, **357b**
Kuhna-Abīward i, 99b — I, 102b
Kuhna-Ḳahḳaha i, 99b — I, 102b
Ḳuhrūd v, **357a**, 869a — V, **358b**, 875a
Kūhyār Bāwand iv, 645b, 646b, 647a — IV, 672a, 673a, b
Kū/īlkān ii, 791b — II, 810a
Kūka → Kūkawa
Kūkawa i, 1260a, b; v, **357b**; s, 164b — I, 1298b, 1299a; V, **359a**; S, 164b
Ḳuḳli Meḥmed Beg v, 724b — V, 729b
Kūko iv, 361a, b — IV, 377a, b
Ḳul ii, 25b, 147b; v, **359a**, 630a — II, 26a, 151b; V, **360a**, 634a
Ḳul Muṣṭafā Ḳayïkd̲j̲ï v, **359b** — V, **360b**
Ḳul-Bābā Kökältās̲h̲ s, 340a — S, 339b
Ḳula v, 615b — V, 619b
Ḳūla v, **359b** — V, **360b**
Kulāb → K̲h̲uttalān
Kulāčī ii, 975a; iv, 597a — II, 997b; IV, 621b
Kūlāh v, 751b — V, 757a
Kūlam v, **360a**, 937b — V, **361a**, 941a
al-Ḳulayʿa v, **361a** — V, **362a**
Kulayb b. Rabīʿa al-Tag̲h̲libī i, 1089a; ii, 159b; iii, 393a; v, **362a**; s, 234b — I, 1121b; II, 164b; III, 405b; V, **363a**; S, 234a
Kulayb Wāʾil i, 526b — I, 542b
al-Kulaynī, Abū D̲j̲aʿfar Muḥammad i, 1352a; iii, 726b, 1266a; v, **362b**; s, 56b, 103b — I, 1391b; III, 749a, 1299a; V, **364a**; S, 57a, 103a
Kulbarga → Gulbarga
Ḳuld̲j̲a iii, 1120b; v, **363b** — III, 1148a; V, **364b**
Külek Bog̲h̲az → Cilicia/Cilicie
Ḳulī K̲h̲ān Maḥram i, 80b, 117b — I, 83a, 121a
Ḳulī K̲h̲ān, Pads̲h̲ān s, 420b — S, 421a
Ḳulī Ḳutb al-Mulk ii, 922b, 1084b, 1118b, 1119a; iii, 15a, 421a; v, 549b, 1258a — II, 944a, 1110a, 1145a,b; III, 16a, 435a; V, 554a, 1249a
Ḳūlī S̲h̲āh i, 1120b; v, 677b — I, 1154a,b; V, 682b
al-Kulīnī, Abū D̲j̲aʿfar Muḥammad → Kulaynī
Kullābiyya iii, 1164b; iv, 469a; s, 392a — III, 1193b; IV, 490a; S, 392b
Ḳullar-āḳāsī iv, 36b; v, 359b — IV, 39a; V, 360b
Kulliyya ii, 423a; iv, 435b; v, **364b** — II, 434a; IV, 455a; V, **366a**
Kulliyyat al-ādāb i, 176a — I, 181a
Külliyye v, **366a** — V, **366b**
Ḳulluḳ-aḳčasï → Čift-resmi
Ḳul-og̲h̲lu i, 369a, 371a, 1119a; ii, 173a, 520b; iii, 340a; iv, 481b; v, **366b**, 1010b, 1247b — I, 380a, 381b, 1152b; II, 178b, 534a; III, 350b; IV, 502b; V, **367b**, 1006b, 1238a
Ḳulog̲h̲lu (poet/poète) v, **367a** — V, **367b**
Kulsāriʿ → Ḳuṭb al-Dīn
Kültepe s, 100b — S, 100a
Kult̲h̲ūm b. ʿIyāḍ al-Ḳus̲h̲ayrī i, 86b, 990b, 1175a; iii, 169b, 494a; v, **367a** — I, 88b, 1021a, 1210a; III, 173a, 511a; V, **368a**
Kültigin (prince/le prince) iv, 583b; v, 854a — IV, 607b; V, 860b
Ḳulumriya i, 390a, 1338b; v, **367a** — I, 401b, 1379a; V, **368a**
al-Ḳulzum i, 931a, 932a; ii, 129b; v, **367b** — I, 960a,b; II, 13a; V, **368b**
Ḳum → Ḳumm
Kuma (river/rivière) s, 169a — S, 169a
al-Ḳumā/al-Ḳawma v, **372b** — V, **373b**
Ḳumān ii, 202b; v, 126a, **373a** — II, 209a; V, 128b, **374a**
Ḳumās̲h̲ iii, 344b, 1126b; v, 151a, 216b, **373b**, 748a — III, 355a, 1154b; V, 153a, 214a, **374b**, 753b
Kumasi ii, 1003b — II, 1026b
Kumatgī iii, 287b — III, 296b
Kumayl b. Ziyād i, 89a — I, 91b
Kumayt b. Zayd al-Asadī i, 402a; ii, 1011a; v, **374a** —

I, 412b; II, 1034b; V, **375a**
Ḳumbara → Khumbara
Kumbaradjī → Khumbaradjî
Ḳumbi Ṣāliḥ → Kunbi Ṣāliḥ
Kumīdjīs ii, 1a; iv, 631b; v, 75b, **375b** — II, 1a; IV, 656b; V, 78a, **376a**
Ḳumîḳ → Ḳumuḳ
Kumîs iv, 998a; v, **375b** — IV, 1030b; V, **376b**
Ḳūmis (Comes) i, 491a; v, **376a** — I, 506a; V, **376b**
Ḳūmis (province) v, **377a**; s, 149a, 192a, 298a, 309b — V, **378a**; S, 149a, 193a, 297b, 309a
Ḳūmis b. Antunyān v, 376b — V, 377a
al-Ḳūmisī, Daniel iv, 604a, b — IV, 628a, b, 629a
Kūmiya v, **378b** — V, **379b**
Ḳumḳum v, 988a — V, 983b
Ḳumm i, 16b; iii, 1124b, 1169b; iv, 7b; v, 292b, 350a, **369a**; s, 56b, 104a, 127a, b, 139a, 157b, 158a, 305a, 342a — I, 17a; III, 1152b, 1198b; IV, 8b; V, 292a, 351a, **369b**; S, 57a, 103b, 126b, 138b, 158a, 305a, 342a
Ḳummī → Malik Ḳummī
Ḳum(m)ī, Ḥādjdjī Ākā Ḥusayn s, 158a, 342b — S, 158a, 342a
Ḳum(m)ī, Ḳādī Aḥmad v, **379a** — V, **379b**
al-Ḳum(m)ī, Saʿd b. ʿAbd Allāh iv, 661b — IV, 688a
al-Ḳum(m)ī, Sayyid Muḥsin b. Muḥammad al-Riḍawī s, 380a — S, 380a
Ḳum(m)ī, Sayyid Ṣadr al-Dīn s, 134b — S, 134a
al-Ḳummī, Ḥasan b. Muḥammad iii, 1169b — III, 1198b
Ḳumr i, 170a, 522a; v, **379b**, 939a, 940b — I, 175a, 538a; V, **380b**, 943a, 944b
al-Ḳūm-Rīshī, Shihāb al-Dīn iv, 810a — IV, 843a
Ḳumuḳ ii, 89a, 141b; v, **381b**, 617b — II, 90b, 145a; V, **382b**, 621b
- language, literature v, 382b, 383a, 617b — V, 383b, 384a, 621b
Kumūn v, **384a**; s, 226a — V, **385a**; S, 226a
Ḳumūsh i, 767a — I, 790a
Kumzārī i, 575a — I, 593b
Kun iv, 982b — IV, 1015a
Ḳūn, Banū v, 373a, **385a**; s, 279a — V, 374a, **386b**; S, 279a
Ḳunā v, **385b**, 1161a — V, **387a**, 1150b
Kunar iv, 409b, 411a — IV, 427a, 429a
Kunāsa v, 347a, b — V, 348a, b
al-Ḳūnawī, ʾAlāʿ al-Dīn i, 596a; iii, 953a — I, 615b; III, 977b
al-Ḳūnawī, Ṣadr al-Dīn → Ṣadr al-Dīn
Ḳunayṭira → Ḳanṭara
Kunāz, Banū iv, 568a — IV, 590a
Ḳunbi Ṣāliḥ ii, 1002a; v, **386b** — II, 1025a; V, **387b**
Kund-Sūlḳān s, 423a — S, 423b
Kundar (river/rivière) s, 329b — S, 329a
Kundjāh/Kandjāh ii, 1006b; s, 322a — II, 1030a; S, 321b
Kundjpura iv, 666b — IV, 693b
Kundur → Lubān
al-Kundurī, ʿAmīd al-Mulk i, 420a, 421a, 434a, 952b; ii, 192a, 605a; iii, 1148b, 1201a; iv, 458a; v, **387b**; s, 192a — I, 432a, 433a, 446a, 981b; II, 198a, 620a; III, 1176b, 1231b; IV, 478b; V, **389a**; S, 193a
Ḳunduz i, 853a; v, **388b** — I, 876b; V, **389b**
Ḳunfudh, Ḳunfadh v, **389b** — V, **390a**
al-Ḳunfudha v, **391a** — V, **391b**
Kung v, 673a, b, 765a — V, 678a, b, 771a
Ḳungrāt i, 422a, 607b; ii, 45a; iv, 610b, 1065a; v, 24a, 273b, **391b**; s, 97b, 169a, 420a — I, 434a, 627b; II, 46a; IV, 635b, 1096b; V, 24b, 271b, **392b**; S, 97a, 169a, 420a
Kūnī ḳadar iv, 203a — IV, 212a
Ḳūniya (Ḳamūniya) iv, 826b — IV, 859b
Ḳuniya (Ḳonya) → Ḳonya
Ḳūnka v, **392a**; s, 143a — V, **393a**; S, 143a
Ḳunṣul → Consul
Ḳunṣul, Ilyās v, 1257a — V, 1248a
Ḳunṣul, Zakī v, 1257a — V, 1248a
Kunta i, 809a; iv, 382a; v, **393a**, 889b, 1166a — I, 832a; IV, 399a; V, **393b**, 896a, 1155b
Ḳunūt v, **395a** — V, **396a**
Kunūz i, 1028b — I, 1060a
Kunya ii, 302a; iv, 179a; v, 116b, **395b** — II, 310b; IV, 187a; V, 119a, **396b**
Kuominchün horde v, 845a, b — V, 857a, b
Kur (river/rivière) i, 634b; v, **396b**, 866a, 867b — I, 655b; V, **397b**, 872b, 874a
Ḳurʾ, Ḳurūʾ iii, 1011a; iv, 253b — III, 1036b; IV, 264b
Kūr Galdwan ii, 828a — II, 847b
Kūra i, 489b; v, **397b** — I, 504a; V, **399a**
Ḳurʿa iv, 259b; v, **398a** — IV, 271a; V, **399a**
al-Kura (sphere/sphère) v, **397a** — V, **398a**
Ḳurakh v, 729b, 730a — V, 734b, 735a
Kuram (river/rivière) → Kurram
Ḳurama v, **399b** — V, **400b**
Ḳuraʿān i, 1258a — I, 1296a
Ḳurād b. Ḥanīfa iii, 49a — III, 51a
Kuraibiya → Kuraybiyya
Ḳurʾān i, 55a, 77b, 107a, 383b, 549a, 565b, 567b, 585b, 922b, 1084b, 1199b, 1242a, 1345b; ii, 126a, 388b, 728b, 834b, 841a, 949b; iii, 24a, 41b, 65a, 152a, 369a, 513b, 874b, 1127a; iv, 81a-84b, 146a, b, 469b, 902b, 980b-986b, 1133b; v, 127a, **400a** — I, 56b, 79b, 110a, 394b, 566b, 584a, 586a, 604b, 950b, 1117a, 1234b, 1279b, 1386a; II, 129b, 399a, 747a, 854a, 860b, 972a; III, 25a, 43a, 67b, 155b, 380b, 531a, 898b, 1155a; IV, 85b-88a, 152a, b, 490b, 935a, 1013a-1018b, 1165a; V, 129b, **401a**
- chronology(ie) v, **414b** — V, **416a**
- commentaries/commentaires i, 89a, 104b, 117a, 120a, 126a, 143a, 152a, 302a, 310a, 352b, 425a, 701b, 958b, 1129a; iii, 696b, 753b, 845b, 880b; iv, 495a, 508a, 704b, 705a, 734b; v, 512b, 513b — I, 91b, 107b, 120b, 123b, 130a, 147a, 156b, 311b, 319b, 363a, 437a, 723a, 988a, 1163a; III, 718b, 776b, 869a, 904b; IV, 516a, 530a, 733a, b, 764a; V, 516a, 517a
- history/histoire v, **404a**, 426a — V, **405b**, 428a
- interpretations/interprétations i, 24b, 38b, 90a, 128b, 158b, 204a, 257a, 264a, 267a, 272a, 275a, 325a, 338a, 561b, 603b, 691a, 788a, 935b, 968b, 1021a, 1026b, 1055a, 1071b, 1326b; ii, 71a, 95a, 128b, 219b, 383b, 447a, 549b, 617a, 626b, 869b, 917a, 949b, 950a, 1025a; iii, 172a, 359a, 465a, 543b, 661a, 795a, 797a, 912a, 1091b, 1172a, 1205a; iv, 1106b — I, 25a, 39b, 92b, 132b, 163a, 210a, 265a, 272a, 275a, 280a, 283b, 335a, 348b, 579b, 623b, 712a, 811a, 964a, 998a, 1052a, b, 1058a, 1087a, 1103b, 1367a; II, 72a, 97a, 132a, 226b, 394a, 459a, 563a, 632b, 642a, 889b, 938b, 972a, 1049a; III, 175b, 370b, 481a, 543b, 682a, 818a, 820b, 936b, 1118a, 1201a, 1235b; IV, 1138a
- language/langue v, **419a** — V, **420b**
- Muḥammad and/et v, **402b**, 415a, 1101a — V, **403b**, 416b, 1097a
- readings, readers/lectures, lecteurs v, **406a** — V, **407a**
- references/renvois i, 169a, 177a, 187a, 209a, 384a, 406-417, 448b, 453a, 514a, 680b, 714a, 773b, 795b, 850b, 922a, 940b, 1020a,b, 1032a, 1092b, 1150b, 1297b; ii, 168a, 182a, 214a, 223b, 293b, 363a, 447a, 536a, 551a, 576a, 848a, 1061a; iii, 13b, 53b, 165a, 209b, 235b, 295a, 302a, 377b, 379a, 537b, 668b, 980a, 1237a,b, 1239b; iv, 141a, 171b, 184a, b, 353b, 365b, 407a, b, 486b, 508b, 595a, 692a, 766b, 805b, 994b; v, 186a, 236a, b, 400b, 698a — I, 174a, 181b, 192b, 215a, 395a, 418-429, 461b, 466a, 529b, 701a, 735b, 796b,

819a, 874b, 949b, 969b, 1051b, 1063b, 1125b, 1185a, 1337a; II, 173a, 187b, 220b,230b, 301b, 373a, 459a, 549b, 564b, 590b, 867b, 1086a;III, 14b, 55b, 168b, 215a, 242b, 304b, 311a, b, 389b, 390b, 556a, 690a, 1004b, 1269a,b, 1271b; IV, 146b, 147a, 179a, 192a, b, 369a, 381b, 425a, b, 507a, 530b, 619a, 720a, 797a, 838a, 1027a; V, 183b, 234a, b, 402a, 703a
- scholars/savants i, 40a, 68b, 105a, 114a, 120a, 152a, 696a, 706b, 1129a; ii, 254a; iii, 155a, 753b, 880b, 936a, 1081b; iv, 1112b; v, 128a, 174a — I, 41a, 70b, 108a, 117a, 123b, 156a, 717a, 728a, 1163a; II, 261b; III, 158b, 776b, 904b, 960b, 1108b; IV, 1144b; V, 130b, 171b
- translations/traductions i, 68b, 88b, 404b; ii, 255a; iv, 891a, 1123a; v, **429a** — I, 70b, 91a, 416b, II, 262a; IV, 923b, 1155a; V, **431b**
al-Kūrānī, Ibrāhīm v, **432b**, 525b — V, **435a**, 529b
Kurānī, Shams al-Dīn → Gurānī
Kūrānkidj iv, 215a — IV, 224b
al-Ḳurashī → ʿAbd al-Ḳādir
al-Kurashī, Abu ʾl-Ḥasan → al-Kurshī
al-Ḳurashī, Djamāl iv, 525b — IV, 548b
Kurayb ii, 77b — II, 79a
Ḳurayba iv, 821a — IV, 854a
Kuraybiyya iii, 1265b; iv, 836b; v, **433b** — III, 1298b; IV, 869b; V, **435b**
al-Ḳurayniyya i, 628b — I, 649b
Ḳuraysh i, 80a, 382b, 545a, 549a, 565a, 890b, 891b, 1073b, 1074a, b, 1241b; ii, 128b, 348b, 627a, 883b; iii, 7b, 285b, 363b, 389a, 577b, 975b, 1093a; v, 116b, 316a, b, **434a**, 520a, b, 581a; s, 284a — I, 82b, 393b, 562a, 566b, 583a, 916b, 918a, 1105b, 1106a, b, 1279a; II, 131b, 358a, 642b, 904a; III, 8a, 294b, 374b, 401b, 597b, 1000a, 1120a; V, 119a, 316a, **436a**, 523b, 524a, 586a; S, 284a
Ḳuraysh b. Badrān → ʿUkayl, Banū
Ḳurayya i, 901a, b — I, 928a, b
Ḳurayyāt al-Milḥ v, **435b** — V, **438a**
Ḳurayẓa, Banū i, 381b; iv, 270a; v, **436a**, 996a — I, 392b; IV, 282a; V, **438b**, 991b
al-Ḳuraẓī → Muḥammad b. Kaʿb.
Ḳurba → Ḳarāba
Kurbāl v, 867b, 868a — V, 874a, b
Ḳurbān v, **436b** — V, **439a**
Ḳurbat ii, 40b; v, 818a, b — II, 41b; V, 824a, b
Kurbuḳa, Kür-Bugha v, **437a** — V, **439b**
Ḳūrčī v, **437a** — V, **439b**
Ḳurčībāshī iii, 1102a; iv, 36b; v, 437b, 630a — III, 1129a; IV, 39a; V, 440a, 634a
Kurd ʿAlī, Muḥammad Farīd i, 598a, 990a, b; ii, 290a; iv, 159a; v, **437b**, 1090b — I, 617b, 1020b, 1021a; II, 298a; IV, 166a; V, **440a**, 1088a
Kurd Hamza ii, 750a — II, 768b
Kurdes I, 194b, 201a, 259a, 484b, 485b, 488a, 527b, 528b, 593b, 664b, 772b, 820a, 895a, 948a, 1062a, 1104a 1242b, 1244b, 1326b, 1393b, 1395a; II, 58b, 190b, 214b, 1136b, 1166b; III, 85b, 265a, 986a, 1123a, b, 1129b, 1136a, 1286b; IV, 6a, 8b, 9b, 10b, 394a; V, 147b, 149a, 311b, **441a**, 621a, 828a, 1202b, 1203a, b; S, 118b
Kurdī (dog/chien) iv, 491a — IV, 512a
al-Kurdī, Muḥammad Amīn v, 475b, **486a** — V, 478b, **489a**
Kurdish/Kurde (language/langue) i, 840a, 871b, 1006b; ii, 1139b; iii, 1b, 1260b; iv, 351a, b; v, 208b, 209a, b, **479a**, 1105a — I, 863b, 895b, 1037b; II, 1166b; III, 1b, 1293b; IV, 366a, b; V, 206a, 207a, **482a**, 1101a
Kurdistān i, 8a, 62b, 845a; ii, 8a; iv, 3a-b, 19b; v, **438b**; s, 72a, b — I, 8a, 64b, 868a; II, 8a; IV, 3b, 21a; V, **441a**; S, 72a
- economy(ie) v, **472b** — V, **475b**
- history/histoire v, **447b** — V, **450a**
- inhabitants/habitants v, **444a**, 456a, b — V, **446b**, 459a
- folklore and literature/folklore et littérature v, **480b** — V, **483a**
- religion v, **474b** — V, **477b**
- society/société v, **470a** — V, **472b**
Kurdj (Georgia/Géorgie) i, 8a, 100b, 420b, 636a, 642a, 644b; ii, 162b; iii, 1112b; iv, 342b, 347b, 348b, 349a, b, 391b, 476a, 670a, 1174b; v, **486b** — I, 8a, 103a, 432b, 657a, 663a, 665a; II, 168a; III, 1140a; IV, 357a, 362a, 363b, 364a, 408a, 497a, 697b, 1207b; V, **489b**
- languages/langues iv, 350b; v, 486b — IV, 365b; V, 489b
Kurdjī Muḳaddam al-Burdjiyya i, 1325a — I, 1365b
Kurdoghlu Khizir Reis i, 743b — I, 765b
Kurds i, 190a, 195b, 251a, 470b, 471b, 474a, 512a, 513a, 575a,644a, 750a, 796b, 871a, 920a, 1030b, 1072a, 1207a, 1208b, 1287a, 1354b, 1356a; ii, 57a, 184b, 208a, 1110b, 1139b; iii, 83a, 258a, 961a, 1096b, 1102b, 1109a, 1254a; iv, 5b, 8a, 9a, 10a, 377b; v, 145a, 146b, 312a, **438b**, 617a, 822a, 1213a, b; s, 71b, 119a
Kurdufān → Kordofān
Kürekčis i, 760b; v, 880a, b — I, 783b; V, 886a, b
Ḳurḥ v, **497b** — V, **500b**
Ḳurhub b. Djābir al-Khuzāʿī v, **498a** — V, **501a**
Kūri iv, 540b — IV, 564a
Kuria Muria (islands/les îles-) → Khūryān-Mūryān
Ḳūrīltāy iv, 499b; v, **498a** — IV, 521b; V, **501a**
Kürin v, **498a**, 729b, 730a — V, **501b**, 734b, 735a
Kürin Khānate/Khanat de-) → Lezghhin
Ḳūriya v, **498b** — V, **501b**
Kurkī s, 421a — S, 420b
Ḳurḳūb v, **498b** — V, **501b**
Ḳurḳūra i, 325b — I, 335b
Kurr → Kur, river/rivière
Ḳurra iv, 521b — IV, 544b
Ḳurrāʾ v, 349b, 409a, **499a** — V, 350b, 410b, **502a**
Ḳurra, Banū ii, 741a; iii, 79b — II, 759b; III, 82a
Kurra, Muḥammad ii, 123a; v, 267a — II, 126a; V, 265a
Ḳurra b. Sharīk ii, 305a, 323b, 327b; iv, 742a, 1103b; v, **500a** — II, 313b, 333b, 337a; IV, 772a, 1134b; V, **503a**
Kurram (river/rivière) v, **501a**; s, 329b — V, **504a**; S, 329a
Ḳurrat al-ʿAyn Ṭāhira i, 834a, 846b, 847a; iv, 70b; v, **502a** — I, 857a, 870a, b; IV, 74b; V, **505a**
Ḳurṣān v, **502b** — V, **506a**
al-Kurshī, Abu ʾl-Ḥasan iv, 729a — IV, 758a
Kursī v, **509a** — V, **512b**
Ḳūrṣūl → Boghā Tarkhān
Kurt → Kart
Ḳurt Ḥasan b. Djunayd ii, 599b — II, 614b
al-Kurtī (wazīr) → Ghiyāth al-Dīn Muḥammad
al-Ḳurṭī i, 361b; ii, 238a — I, 372b; II, 245a
Ḳurṭuba i, 5b, 6b, 82a, 83a, 85b, 390b, 491b, 493a, 494b; iii, 74a, 140a, 496a, 762a; v, 318b, **509b**, 1008b, 1239b; s, 152b, 397b — I, 6a, 6b, 84b, 85b, 88a, 401b, 506a, 508a, 509b; III, 76b, 142b, 513a, 785b; V, 318a, **513a**, 1004b, 1230a, b; S, 152b, 398a
- great mosque/la grande mosquée i, 459a, 498b, 500b, 618b, 950a, 1228a, 1319b; ii, 956a, b; iii, 495a; v, 510b — I, 472a, 513b, 516a, 637b, 979b, 1264b, 1360a; II, 978a, b; III, 512a; V, 514a
Ḳurṭuba, Djibāl i, 488b — I, 503b
al-Ḳurṭubī → ʿArīb b. Saʿd; Ibn Faraḥ
al-Ḳurṭubī, Abu ʾl-ʿAbbās v, 512b — V, 516a
al-Ḳurṭubī, Abū ʿAbd Allāh v, **512b** — V, **516a**
al-Ḳurṭubī, Yaḥyā b. ʿUmar v, **513b** — V, **517b**
Ḳurūʾ → Ḳurʾ

Ḳūrū s, 165a — S, 164b
Kurūr i, 272a — I, 280b
Ḳūş v, 99b, **514a**, 519a; s, 383b — V, 101b, **517b**, 522b; S, 384a
Kūs owasî → Ḳoşowa'
Ḳusanṭīna → Ḳusṭanṭīna
al-Ḳusanṭīnī, Rashīd v, **515b** — V, **519b**
al-Kūsawī al-Djāmī i, 283a — I, 292a
Kusayla b. Lamzam i, 367a, 1175a; iii, 296a; iv, 336b, 827a; v, **517b**; s, 103a — I, 372b, 1210a; III, 305a; IV, 351a, 860a; V, **521a**; S, 102a
Ḳuṣayr (al-Ḥīra) i, 450b — I, 463b
Ḳuṣayr (port) v, 386a, **518b** — V, 387b, **522b**
al-Ḳuṣayr → Abū Zaʿbal
Ḳuṣayr ʿAmrā i, **612a**; iii, 141b, 146b, 310a; s, 117b, 251a — I, **632a**; III, 144b, 150a, 319a; S, 116b, 251a
Ḳuṣayy ii, 128b; iii, 260a, 975b; iv, 320a, 421b; v, 77b, 78a, 116b, 434b, **519b**, 581a, 692b — II, 131b; III, 267a, 1000a; IV, 334a, 440a; V, 80a, 119a, 436b, **523a**, 586a, 697b
Ḳuṣdār v, 102a, **520b** — V, 104a, **524a**
Kūsh v, **521a** — V, **524b**
Kushadasī i, 777b, 778a — I, 801a
al-Kushādjim i, 1153b; ii, 740b; iii, 809a; iv, 1005b; v, **525a**, 1229b; s, 175b, 203b — I, 1188a; II, 759a; III, 832b; IV, 1037b; V, **529a**, 1219b; S, 176b, 203a
Kushan i, 225b; s, 237a — I, 232b; S, 237a
al-Ḳushāshī, Ṣafī al-Dīn v, 433a, **525b** — V, 435a, **529a**
Ḳushayr i, 233b, 442a; v, **526a** — I, 240b, 454b; V, **529b**
al-Ḳushayrī, Abu ʾl-Ḳāsim i, 146b; ii, 125b, 605a; iii, 589a; iv, 697a; v, **526a**, s, 14b, 15a — I, 151a; II, 129a, 620a; III, 609b; IV, 725a; V, **530a**; S, 15a
al-Ḳushayrī, Abu 'l-Naṣr v, **527a** — V, **531a**
Ḳush-begi → Ḳosh-begi
Ḳushči v, 273a — V, 271a
Ḳūshdji ii, 774a — II, 793a
al-Ḳūshdjī → ʿAlī al-Ḳūshdjī
Kushitic → Kūsh
Ḳushtemür iii, 197a — III, 202a
al-Ḳushūrī → Naṣr
Kūshiyār b. Labbān iii, 1137a, 1139b; iv, 1071a; v, **527a** — III, 1165a, 1167b; IV, 1102b; V, **531a**
Kushterī, Shaykh iv, 601b — IV, 626a
Ḳūsira → Ḳawṣara
Kuskusū v, **527b** — V, **531b**
Ḳuşmān iv, 717a, b — IV, 746a, b
Ḳuss b. Sāʿida i, 585b; v, **528b** — I, 604a; V, **532b**
Ḳuṣṣās → Ḳāṣṣ, Ḳaṣṣa
Ḳusṭā b. Lūḳā i, 328a, 589a, 727a; ii, 771b, 900a; iii, 378a; iv, 329b, 600a; v, 397b, **529b**; s, 412a — I, 338a, 608b, 749a; II, 790a, 921a; III, 390a; IV, 344a, 624a; V, 398b, **533a**; S, 412b
Kustāndīl → Constantine III
Ḳusṭanṭīna i, 155a; v, **530a** — I, 159a; V, **533b**
Ḳusṭanṭīniyya iv, 224a; v, **532b** — IV, 234a; V, **536b**
Küstendil v, **534a** — V, **538a**
Ḳusṭūs al-Rūmī ii, 900a — II, 920b
Kusūf v, **535b** — V, **540a**
al-Ḳūṣūnī, Badr al-Dīn iv, 451b — IV, 471b
Kūt al-ʿAmāra v, **537a** — V, **541b**
Ḳuṣūr i, 1321b — I, 1361b
Ḳutadghu Bilig i, 299a, 677b; iv, 700a; v, **538a** — I, 308a, 698a; IV, 728b; V, **542b**
Kutāhiya (Kütahya) i, 182b; ii, 747a; iv, 1169b; v, **539a**; s, 49a, 359b — I, 188a; II, 765b; IV, 1202b; V, **543b**; S, 49b, 359a
Kutai v, **539b**; s, 151a — V, **544a**; S, 151a
Ḳutalmish → Ḳutlumush
Kutāma i, 104a, 249a, 367a, 1037a, 1042a, 1175b, 1177b, 1178b, 1309b; ii, 852b; iii, 77a; iv, 199a, 827b, 830a; v, **540a**; 1160a, 1243a — I, 107a, 257a, 378a, 1068b, 1073b, 1210b, 1212b, 1213b, 1350a; II, 872b; III, 79a; IV, 208a, 860b, 862b; V, **544b**, 1150a, 1233b
al-Kutamī, ʿAbd al-Karīm iv, 729a — IV, 758b
al-Ḳuṭāmī, ʿUmayr iv, 315b; v, **540b** — IV, 329b; V, **545a**
al-Kutāmī al-Fāsī, Abu 'l-Ḥasan ʿAlī → Ibn al-Ḳaṭṭān the Elder
Ḳutayba i, 920b — I, 949a
Ḳutayba b. Muslim i, 529b, 684b, 921a, 1001a, 1293b; ii, 1a, 601a, 790b; iii, 41a, 304a, 471a, 493b; iv, 1062a; v, 47b, 181a, 378a, **541a**, 853b, 854a, 1111a; s, 299a — I, 545b, 705b, 949a, 1032a, 1333b; II, 1a, 615b, 809b; III, 43a, 313a, 487b, 510b; IV, 1093b; V, 49a, 178b, 379a, **545b**, 860a, b, 1107a; S, 298b
Ḳutayba b. Tughshāda i, 1294a, b — I, 1333b, 1334a
Ḳuṭayfa s, 117a — S, 116a
Kutayfāt → al-Afḍal Kutayfāt
Kutayla bint ʿAbd al-ʿUzzā i, 109b — I, 112b
al-Kuṭb i, 95a, 280a; iv, 950a; v, **542b**; s, 323b — I, 97b, 289a; IV, 982b; V, **547a**; S, 323a → Abdāl
Ḳuṭb, Sayyid iii, 1069b, 1070a; iv, 160a, 166a — III, 1096b, 1097a; IV, 167a, 173a
Ḳuṭb ʿAlī, Shaykh iii, 456b — III, 472b
Ḳuṭb al-Awliyāʾ → ʿAbd al-Salām Khundjī
Ḳuṭb al-Dīn → Mawdūd b. Zangī; al-Nahrawālī
Ḳuṭb al-Dīn I (Ḳutlugh-Khān) → Ḳuṭb al-Dīn Khān b. Burāḳ
Ḳuṭb al-Dīn II (Ḳutlugh-Khān) → Shāh Djahān b. Suyurghatmish
Ḳutb al-Dīn (Bengal) s, 366b — S, 366a
Ḳuṭb al-Dīn, Malik iv, 672a — IV, 699b
Ḳuṭb al-Dīn, Mullă i, 936b; s, 292a, 293a — I, 965b; S, 291b, 293a
Ḳuṭb al-Dīn Aḥmad iii, 340a — III, 350a
Ḳuṭb al-Dīn Aybak i, 208b, 393b, 403b, 506b, 756b, 855b, 1209b, 1300a, 1321b; ii, 256a, 260a, 266b, 267a, 1084a, 1103a, 1123b; iii, 168a, 415b, 1155a; iv, 210a, 1127a; v, 283a, **546a**, 549a; s, 284b, 359b, 360a — I, 214b, 404b, 415a, 522a, 779a, 879b, 1245b, 1339b, 1362a; II, 263b, 267b, 274b, 275a, b, 1109a, 1129a, 1150a; III, 171b, 429a, 1183b; IV, 219b, 1158b; V, 281a, **550b**, 553b; S, 284b, 359b
Ḳuṭb al-Dīn Bakhtiyār Kākī ii, 796b; v, **546b**, 549a; s, 353a — II, 815b; V, **551a**, 554a; S, 353a
Ḳuṭb al-Dīn Ḥabash ʿAmīd → Ḥabash ʿAmīd
Ḳuṭb al-Dīn Ḥasan al-Ghūrī ii, 1100a — II, 1126a
Ḳuṭb al-Dīn al-Iznīḳī v, **547a** — V, **551b**
Ḳuṭb al-Dīn Khān b. Burāḳ v, 161b, 162a, 553b — V, 160a, 558a
Ḳuṭb al-Dīn Kulsāriʿ i, 731a — I, 753a
Ḳuṭb al-Dīn Mawdūd → Mawdūd b. Zangī
Ḳuṭb al-Dīn Mubārak → Khaldjīs
Ḳuṭb al-Dīn Mubārak → Mubārak Shāh I
Ḳuṭb al-Dīn Muḥammad (Ghūrid(e)) i, 940a; ii, 382a, 928a, 1096b, 1100b — I, 968b; II, 392b, 950a, 1122b, 1126a
Ḳuṭb al-Dīn Muḥammad b. Anūshtigin (Kh(w)ārazm-Shāh) iv, 1067a; s, 279a — IV, 1099a; S, 279a
Ḳuṭb al-Dīn al-Rāzī ii, 774a — II, 792b
Ḳuṭb al-Dīn Shīrāzī ii, 399a, b; iii, 1137b; iv, 1059b; v, **547a** — II, 409b, 410a; III, 1165b; IV, 1090b; V, **551b**
Ḳuṭb al-Dīn-zāde Muḥammad v, 547a, **548b** — V, 551b, **553a**
Ḳutb Khān Lōdī iii, 632a; iv, 513a — III, 653a; IV, 535a
Ḳuṭb Mīnār v, 546b, **548b** — V, 551a, b, **553a**
Ḳuṭb al-Mulk → Ḳulī Ḳuṭb al-Mulk
Ḳuṭb Shāhī i, 1048a; ii, 1119a; iii, 318b, 426a, 427a, 448a; v, **549b**; s, 302a — I, 1079b; II, 1145a; III, 328a,

440a, 441a, 463a; V, **554a**; S, 301b
Ḳuṭb al-Yaman al-Ahdal i, 255b — I, 263b
Ḳuṭba b. Arus → al-Ḥādira
Ḳuṭb-i ʿĀlam → Burhān al-Dīn
Kuṭbid(e)s ii, 517b — II, 530a
Kūthā v, 550b — V, 555a
Ḳutham b. al-ʿAbbās v, **551a** — V, **555b**
Kuthayyir b. ʿAbd al-Raḥmān i, 402a; ii, 1029b; iv, 836b, 1086b; v, 433b, **551b** — I, 412b; II, 1053a; IV, 869b, 1118a; V, 436a, **556b**
al-Kutla al-wataniyya iii, 522b — III, 540b
Kutlu Beg i, 311b — I, 321a
Ḳutlugh al-Aḥmadīlī i, 300b — I, 310a
Ḳuṭlugh Inanč b. Pahlawān iii, 1111b — III, 1139a
Ḳutlugh Khān (Djand) s, 246a — S, 246a
Ḳutlugh Khānid(e)s i, 1311a; v, 161b, **553a** — I, 1351b; V, 159b, 160a, **558a**
Ḳutlugh Murād Khān s, 46a, 420a — S, 46b, 420a
Ḳutlugh-Shāh Noyan v, **554a** — V, **559a**
Kutlugh Tīmūr iv, 1064a — IV, 1095b
Kutlughtakin i, 731b — I, 753b
Ḳutlumush i, 420a, 1074a; iii, 195b — I, 432a, 1106a; III, 200b
Ḳuṭn v, **554b** — V, **559b**
Ḳuṭr v, **566b** — V, **570b**
Ḳuṭrabbul iii, 774a; v, **566b** — III, 797b; V, **571a**
Ḳuṭrub v, **566b** — V, **571a**
Ḳuṭrub, Muḥammad v, **567a** — V, **571b**
Kuttāb → Kātib
Kuttāb (school/école) iv, 436a; v, **567b**, 909a, b, 911b, 1123a — IV, 455a, b; V, **572a**, 914b, 915b, 917a, 1119b
Kutub al-ḥidthān ii, 377a — II, 387a
al-Kutubī, Abū ʿAbd Allāh al-Dimashḳī v, **570b** — V, **575a**
al-Kutubiyya → Marrākush
Ḳutulmish iv, 220a — IV, 230a
Kutun ii, 904b, 1009b — II, 925b, 1033b
Kütüphane → Maktaba
Ḳuṭuz i, 786b, 1125a; ii, 284b; iii, 184b, 1121a; iv, 484b, 641a; v, **571a** — I, 810a, 1158b; II, 293a; III, 189a, 1148b; IV, 505b, 667a; V, **575b**
al-Kuʿūb → Kaʿb, Banū
Ḳuʿūd v, **572a** — V, **576b**
Ḳuwā iv, 330b — IV, 345a
Ḳuwādhiyān → Ḳubādhiyān
Kuwait → Kuwayt
Kuwayk, Banū iv, 137a — IV, 143a
al-Kuwayt i, 39b, 233b, 534a, 540a, 762a, 976a; ii, 176b, 469a, 673a; iii, 1066a, b; iv, 680b, 925a; v, **572a**, 1057a; s, 3b, 50a — I, 40b, 241a, 550b, 556b, 785a, 1006b; II, 182a, 480b, 690a; III, 1092b, 1093a; IV, 708b, 958a; V, **576b**, 1054a; S, 2b, 50b
- university/université ii, 425a — II, 435b
Ḳuwwa iv, 271b; v, **576a** — IV, 283b; V, **580b**
al-Ḳuwwatli → Shukrī
Kuybishev iv, 281a — IV, 293a
Ḳuyudju Murād Pasha → Murād Pasha
Kūz v, 989b
Ḳuzaḥ iv, 803a — IV, 835b
Ḳuzdār → Ḳuṣdār
Ḳuz-Ordu → Balāsāghūn
Kwanadi v, **579b** — V, **584a**
Kwaťta v, 102b, **579b** — V, 104b, **584b**
Kythera → Čoka Adasî

L

Laʿaḳat al-dam v, **581a**; s, 189b — V, **586**; S, 190b
Laâba → Arbāʾ
Laʿb → Laʿib
Labāb v, **581b** — V, **586b**
Labakī, Naʿʿūm ii, 471b — II, 483b
Laban ii, 1057b — II, 1082a
Labbai v, **582a** — V, **587a**
Labbayka → Talbiya
Labbès iv, 361a — IV, 377a
Labda s, 1a — S, 1a
Labībī v, **583a** — V, **588a**
Labīd b. Rabīʿa v, **583b**; s, 178b — V, **588b**; S, 179b
Labin v, **584b** — V, **590a**
Labla i, 6a; ii, 1009a; iii, 748b; v, **586a** — I, 6a; II, 1032b; III, 771b; V, **591a**
Labūʿ i, 73b — I, 75b
Laccadives i, 170b; iv, 547a, b; v, **587a**
Ladākh v, **588a**; s, 156a, 242a — V, **592a**; S, 156a, 242a
Lādhiḳ (Amasya) v, **589a** — V, **593a**
Lādhiḳ (Denizli) i, 204a; v, **589b** — I, 210b; V, **593b**
Lādhiḳ (Konya) v, **589a** — V, **593a**
al-Lādhiḳiyya v, **589b**; s, 133b — V, **593b**; S, 133a
Lādhū Shāh, Mawlānā s, 353a — S, 353a
Lādīḳ → Deñizli
Ladjāʾ v, **593a** — V, **596b**
Ladjāya s, 103a — S, 102b
Ladjdjūn v, **593b** — V, **597b**
Lādjīn, al-Malik al-Manṣūr i, 622b, 1126b, 1128a, 1325a; ii, 38a, 285a, 958b; iii, 286b, 951b; iv, 437b, 964b, 965b; v, **594b** — I, 643a, 1160b, 1162a, 1365b; II, 38b, 293a, 980b; III, 295b, 976a; IV, 457a, 997a, b; V, **598b**
Ladjnat al-fatwā i, 819b — I, 842b
Lafiyar Toga ii, 1146a — II, 1173b
Lafẓ v, 320b, 321b — V, 320a, b
La-Garde-Freinet → Fraxinetum
Laghîm, laghîmlar i, 1063a, 1064a; iii, 479b — I, 1095a, 1096a; III, 496a
Laghîmdjîlar i, 1062a — I, 1093b
Laghmān → Lamghān
Laghwāt, Banū v, 1181a — V, 1171a
Laḥad → Ḳabr
Lāhawr i, 1323a, 1324a, 1347b, 1348a; ii, 134b, 267b, 380a; iii, 450a; v, 31b, **597a**; s, 21a, 47a, 63a, 142b, 247a, 284b, 333a, 360a — I, 1363b, 1364b, 1388a, b; II, 137b, 275b, 390a; III, 465b; V, 32b, **601a**; S, 21a, 47b, 63b, 142a, 247a, 284b, 332b, 359b
- monuments v, 599b, 1217b, 1219b — V, 603a, 1207b, 1209b
- university/université ii, 426a; iv, 1127a, b — II, 437a; IV, 1158b, 1159a
Lāhawri → ʿAbd al-Ḥamīd
Laḥdj → Laḥidj
Lahdjat-i Sikandar Shāhī iii, 453b — III, 469a
al-Laḥdjī, Muslim s, 236a — S, 236a
Laḥ(i)dj i, 39b, 95b, 181a; ii, 192a, 193a, 675b; iii, 294a; v, **601b**, 604a; s, 338a — I, 40b, 98a, 186a; II, 198a, 199a, 692a; III, 303a; V, **605b**, 608b; S, 337b
Lāhīdjān ii, 192a, 193a; v, **602b**, 604b; s, 363a, b — II, 199a; V, **606b**, 608b; S, 363a
Lāhīdjī, ʿAbd al-Razzāḳ v, **605a** — V, **609a**
Lāhīdjī, Shams al-Dīn Muḥammad v, **604b**, 605b — V, **608b**, 609b
al-Lāḥiḳī → Abān b. ʿAbd al-Ḥamīd
Lahistan → Leh
Laḥn al-ʿāmma v, **605b**, 803b; s, 388b — V, **609b**, 809b; S, 388b

Lahndā v, **610a** — V, **614a**
Lahore → Lāhawr
Lāhūt wa-Nāsūt i, 351a; v, **611b** — I, 361b; V, **615b**
Lāhūtī, Abu 'l-Ḳāsim iv, 71a; v, **614b**; s, 110a — IV, 75a; V, **618b**; S, 109b
Laʿib v, 478b, **615a** — V, 481a, **619a**
al-Lāʾiḥa al-Asāsiyya ii, 647b — II, 663b
Laine → Ṣūf
Lāʾiṭ → Liwāṭ
Lait, le → Laban
Laiton → Shabah
Lak (Kurd(e)s) i, 755b, 756a; ii, 86b, 87a, 141b; iii, 1102b, 1109a; iv, 344a, 351a; v, 154b, **616b**, 822b, 825b — I, 778a, b; II, 88a, 89a, 145a; III, 1129b, 1136a; IV, 358b, 366a; V, 155b, **620b**, 828b, 831b
Laḳ (Caucasus/Caucase) v, **617b** — V, **621b**
Laḳab ii, 302a; iv, 180a, 293b, 294a; v, **618b** — II, 310b; IV, 188a, 306b, 307a; V, **622b**
al-Laḳānī, ʿAbd al-Salām iv, 613b — IV, 638b
Laḳant v, **631b** — V, **635b**
Lakay, Ibrāhīm ii, 701a — II, 718b
Lakhm ii, 573b; v, **632a** — II, 588a; V, **636a**
al-Lakhmī, Abu 'l-ʿAbbās → ʿAzafī, Banu 'l-
al-Lakhmī, Abu 'l-Ḳāsīm → ʿAzafī, Banu 'l-
al-Lakhmī, ʿAlī b. Rabāḥ s, 81b — S, 81b
al-Lakhmī, Muḥammad → ʿAzafī, Banu 'l-
al-Lakhmī al-Sabtī, Muḥammad b. ʿAlī s, 388b — S, 389a
Lakhmid(e)s i, 73a, 405b, 450b, 451b, 526a, 532a, 548b, 684b, 890a; ii, 1021a; iii, 462b, 1254a; iv, 1144b; v, 632a, **632b**; s, 229b — I, 75b, 417a, 463b, 464b, 542a, 548b, 566a, 705b, 916b; II, 1044b; III, 479a, 1286b; IV, 1176b; V, 636a, **636b**; S, 229b
Lakhnaw ii, 132a, b, 205a; iii, 451a; v, **634b**, 1033b; s, 74a, b, 102a, 106a, 247a, 292b — II, 135b, 211b; III, 466b; V, **638b**, 1029b; S, 74b, 75a, 101b, 105b, 247b, 292a
- monuments i, 66a; ii, 132a; v, 7a, **636a**, 1135b — I, 68a; II, 135b; V, 7b, **640a**, 1131a
Lakhnawtī i, 393b, 1015a; ii, 270a; v, **637b**; s, 124a — I, 405a, 1046b; II, 278a; V, **642a**; S, 123b
Laḳīṭ v, **639a** — V, **643a**
Laḳīṭ b. Mālik al-Ātikī i, 812b — I, 835b
Laḳīṭ b. Yaʿmur al-Iyādī iv, 289a; v, **639b** — IV, 302a; V, **643b**
Laḳīṭ b. Zurāra ii, 353b; iii, 168b; v, **640a**; s, 37b — II, 363b; III, 172b; V, **644b**; S, 37b
Laḳḳūt b. Yūsuf i, 251a — I, 258b
Lakshadweep → Laccadives/Laquedives
Lakshmaṇ Singh iii, 458a — III, 474a
Lakz → Lezgh
Lāl Kunwar ii, 379a — II, 389b
Lala iii, 340a; iv, 37a — III, 350a; IV, 39b
Lala Meḥmed Pasha i, 267b, 1284b; ii, 716b; iv, 499a; v, **640b** — I, 275b, 1324a; II, 735a; IV, 520b; V, **645a**
Lālā Muṣṭafā Pasha → Muṣṭafā Pasha Lala
Lāla Ratan Čand s, 126b — S, 125b
Lala Shahīn i, 1159b, 1302b; ii, 683b, 722a, 914a — I, 1194b, 1342b; II, 700b, 740b, 935b
Lāle v, 172b, 642a, 644a — V, 170a, 646a, 648a
Lāle dewrī i, 270a, 558a; iii, 1002b; v, **641a** — I, 278a, 575b; III, 1027b; V, **645a**
Lālezarī, Shaykh Meḥmed v, **644a** — V, **648a**
Lālezarī, Shaykh Meḥmed Ṭāhir v, **644a** — V, **648a**
Lālī → Shāh Sulṭān Muḥammad
Lālish v, **644a** — V, **648b**
Lalitpur v, **644b** — V, **648b**
Lālkōt ii, 256a, b, 259a — II, 263a, b, 267a
Lālla Khadīdja i, 371b — I, 382a
Lallūdjī Lāl ii, 491a; iii, 458a; v, **644b** — II, 503a; III, 474a; V, **648b**
Lām v, **644b** — V, **649a**
Lām, Banū i, 431a, 528b, 1096a, b; iii, 1107b; iv, 10a, 552b; v, 81a, **645b** — I, 443a, 544b, 1129a, b; III, 1134b; IV, 11a, 576b; V, 83a, **649b**
Lamak v, **646b** — V, **650b**
Lamak b. Mālik iv, 199b — IV, 208a
Lamasar → Lanbasar
Lamas-ṣū v, **647a**; s, 306b — V, **651a**; S, 306b
al-Lamaṭī, Abu 'l-ʿAbbās b. al-Mubārak v, **647b** — V, **651b**
al-Lamaṭī, Aḥmad al-Ḥabīb v, **647b** — V, **651b**
Lambadis v, **648a** — V, **652a**
Lamdiyya, Banū v, 1010b — V, 1006a
Lamech → Lamak
Lamentation → Niyāḥa
Lamghān iv, 409b, 411a; v, 649a, b — IV, 427a, 429a; V, 653a, b
Lamghānāt v, **648b**, 782a; s, 237a — V, **653a**, 788b; S, 237a
Lāmiʿī, Abuʾl-Ḥasan v, **649b** — V, **653b**
Lāmiʿī, Shaykh Maḥmūd ii, 869a; v, **649b** — II, 889a; V, **654a**
Lamine Bey → al-Amin Bey
Lamlam v, **651a** — V, **655b**
Lamp(e) → Sirādj
Lamṭ iii, 347a; v, **651b**, 1227b — III, 357b; V, **655b**, 1218a
Lamṭa v, 651b, **652a** — V, 655b, **656b**
Lamtūna i, 211a, 251a, 389b, 1176a, 1178b; ii, 1122a; v, **652b** — I, 217a, 258b, 400b, 1211a, 1213b; II, 1148a; V, **656b**
al-Lamtūnī, Abū Bakr b. ʿUmar i, 211a, 251a, 1176a; ii, 1002b, 1122a; iii, 288b; v, 653b, **654a** — I, 217a, 258b, 1211a; II, 1025b, 1148a; III, 297b; V, 657b, **658b**
Lamu v, **655a**, 963a — V, **659a**, 967b
al-Lān → Alān
Lanbasar iii, 501b; v, **656a** — III, 519a; V, **660b**
Land → Khāliṣa
Langāh, Ḥusayn Shah → Ḥusayn Shāh Langāh
Langar iv, 1073b — IV, 1105a
Langaŕ Khān Langāh iii, 634a — III, 655a
Language/langue → Lugha
Langue Arabe → ʿArabiyya
Lankabālūs iii, 407a — III, 419b
Lankar Čak → Čaks
Lankoran v, **656b** — V, **661a**
Laodicaea → Lādhiḳ, Lādhiḳiyya
Laos iii, 1208b — III, 1239b
Lapin → Arnab
Laquedives I, 175a; IV, 570b, 571a; V, **661b**
Lār (island/île) v, **674b** — V, **680a**
Lār, Lārīdjān v, **657a**, 670b — V, **663a**, 675b
Lār, Lāristān v, 604b, **665a** — V, 608b, **670b**
Larache → al-ʿArāʾish
Lārak → Djāsak
Lāranda i, 468a; iv, 621a, b, 624a; v, **676b**, 1145b — I, 481b; IV, 645b, 646b, 649a; V, **681b**, 1137b
al-Lārī → Muṣliḥ al-Dīn
Lārī (coin/monnaie) → Lārīn
al-Lārī, Muṣliḥ al-Dīn ii, 345b; v, **682a** — II, 355b; V, **687a**
al-Lārī, Muḥammad b. Ṣalāḥ v, **682a** — V, **687a**
Lârî, Yahuda iv, 309b — IV, 323b
Lārī Čelebi iii, 340a — III, 350a
Laribunder iv, 597b — IV, 621b
Laribus → al-Urbus
Lārida v, **682b** — V, **687b**
Lāridjan s, 357b — S, 356b
Larin ii, 120b; v, 672a, **683b** — II, 123b; V, 677a, **688b**
Larissa → Yenishehir
Lāriz v, 661a, 664b — V, 666b, 670a
Las Bēla v, **684a**; s, 222b — V, **689a**; S, 222b

Lascaris, Theodore iv, 816a, b — IV, 849a
Lāsh ii, 605a — II, 620a
Lāshārīs s, 332a — S, 331b
Lashgarniwīs iv, 757b — IV, 788a
Lāshīn, Maḥmud Ṭāhir v, 189a — V, 186a
Lashkar → ʿAskar Mukram
Lashkar (army/armée) v, **685a** — V, **690a**
Lashkarī iv, 100a — IV, 104b
Lashkarī, ʿAlī b. Mūsa iv, 347b, 773a — IV, 362b, 804a
Lashkar-i Bāzār i, 1345a; ii, 1054a, 1082b, 1083a; v, **690b** — I, 1385b; II, 1078b, 1107b, 1108a; V, **695b**
Lāshōn iv, 301b — IV, 315a
al-Lāt i, 151b; iv, 321b; v, **692a** — I, 155b; IV, 336a; V, **697a**
Latakia/Lataquié → al-Lādhiḳiyya
Latency/Latence → Kumūn
Laṭīfī, Čelebi v, 116a, **693a** — V, 118b, **698a**
Latitude and/et longitude → Djughrāfiya; Ḳubbat al-arḍ
Lavage → Ghusl
Laveur de morts → Ghassāl
Law → ʿĀda; ʿAmal; Fiḳh; Ḥuḳūḳ; Ḳānūn; Maḥkama; Sharīʿa; Siyāsa; Tashrīʿ; Uṣūl; etc.
Lawāta i, 207b, 440a, 1049a, 1174b, 1349b; iii, 1040a; v, **694b** — I, 213b, 452b, 1081a, 1209b, 1390a; III, 1066a; V, **699b**
al-Lawātī, Abū Muḥammad v, **697b** — V, **702a**
Lawei s, 150b — S, 150b
Lawḥ i, 911b; iv, 354a; v, **698a**; s, 231a — I, 939a; IV, 369b; V, **703a**; S, 230b
al-Lawḥ al-maḥfūz i, 90a; v, 698a; s, 93a — I, 92b; V, 703a; S, 93a
Lawn v, **698b** — V, **703b**
Lawsha v, **707b** — V, **712b**
Lawth iv, 690a — IV, 718a
Lâye s, 182b — S, 182b
Layl and/et Nahār v, **707b** — V, **712b**
Laylā b. Nuʿmān iii, 255a; iv, 23a, 1066a — III, 262a; IV, 24b, 1097b
Layla al-Akhyaliyya iv, 912a; v, **710a** — IV, 945a; V, **715a**
Laylā bint al-Djūdī ii, 625b — II, 641a
Laylā bint Masʿūd i, 400b — I, 412a
Laylā Khānîm (d./m. 1847) v, **710a** — V, **715a**
Laylā Khānîm (d./m. 1936) iii, 1117a; v, **710b** — III, 1144b; V, **715b**
Laylā ū Madjnūn → Madjnūn wa-Laylā
Laylat al-barāʾa i, 1027b — I, 1059a → Ramaḍān
Laylat al-Ḳadr iv, 280a — IV, 292a → Ramaḍān
Laylī ii, 191a — II, 197a
Laylī b. Nuʿmān → Laylā b. Nuʿmān
al-Layth i, 681a — I, 702a
al-Layth b. al-Muẓaffar iv, 963a; v, **711a** — IV, 995a; V, **716a**
al-Layth b. Saʿd v, **711b**; s, 87b — V, **716b**; S, 87b
Layth b. ʿAlī iii, 619b — III, 640a
Layth b. Kahlān iii, 856b, 857b — III, 880b, 881b
Lāyzān iv, 343a — IV, 357b
Laz i, 100b, 469b, 471b, 474b; iv, 350a, 351a, 576b; v, **712a** — I, 103b, 483b, 485b, 488b; IV, 365a, 366a, 599b; V, **717a**
Lazarus/Lazare v, **714b** — V, **719b**
Lazistān v, 712a, 713a, b — V, 717a, 718a, b
Lazz, Āl i, 759b — I, 782b
Lead (metal) → Khārṣīnī; Raṣāṣ
League of Arab States → Arab League
Lease → Kirāʾ
Leather → Djild
Lebanon → Lubnān
Lĕbaran v, **714b** — V, **720a**
Lebou/Lebu v, 694b, 753b — V, 699b, 759b
Lecteurs, lectures du Ḳurʾān → Ḳirāʾa; Ḳurrāʾ
Leff i, 1179b; v, **715a** — I, 1214b; V, **720a**
Lefḳosha v, **716a** — V, **721a**
Legacy/Legs → Mīrāth
Legend/Légende → Ḥikāya; Ḳiṣaṣ al-Anbiyāʾ; Ḳiṣṣa
Légion arabe, la I, 47b; III, 272a, 1291b
Legislation/Législation → Tashrīʿ
Leh (Poland/Pologne) v, **719a** — V, **724a**
Lēk → Lakz
Lekë Dukagjin i, 170b, 652a — I, 175a, 672b
Lemdiya → al-Madiyya
Lemnos → Limni
Lenkoran → Lankoran
Leninabad → Khudjand
Leo Africanus/Léon l'Africain iv, 339b; v, **723a** — IV, 354a; V, **728a**
Leo(n) I (Armenia) i, 182b; ii, 37a — I, 187b; II, 38a
Leo(n) II ii, 37b — II, 38a
Leo(n) III iv, 1174a — IV, 1207a
Leo(n) IV iv, 1174a — IV, 1207a
Leo(n) V i, 790a; ii, 38b — I, 813a; II, 39a
Leon, kingdom of/royaume de → Liyūn
Leopard → Fahd
Lepanto/Lépante → Aynabakhtî
Leprosy/Lèpre → Djūdhām
Lérida → Lārida
Lesh v, **724a** — V, **729a**
Leskofdjalî Ghālib ii, 878a; iii, 1200b; s, 324b — II, 898b; III, 1230b; S, 324a
Letter/Lettre → Barīd; Ḥarf; Risāla
Letur s, 143a — S, 143a
Leucas → Levkas
Levante → Sharḳ al-Andalus
Levend → Lewend
Levi b. Japheth iv, 605a — IV, 629b
Levice s, 171a — S, 171b
Levkas (island/île) iv, 656a; v, **725b** — IV, 682a; V, **730b**
Lévrier → Salūḳī
Lewend iii, 317b; v, 506b, **728a** — III, 327b; V, 510a, **733a**
Lexicography/Lexicographie → Ḳāmūs
Leylā Saz → Laylā Khānîm (d./m. 1936)
Lézard → Ḍabb
Lezgh ii, 86a, 89a; iii, 604a; iv, 343a; v, 494a, 498a, 617b, 713a, **729b** — II, 87b, 90b; III, 624b; IV, 357b; V, 497a, 501b, 621b, 718a, **734b**
Lezgi → Lezgh
Liʿān i, 1150b; iv, 689a; v, **730a** — I, 1185a; IV, 717a; V, **735b**
Liʿb → Laʿib
Libān → Lubnān
Libās ii, 206b; v, 6a, 476a, **732a** — II, 213a; V, 6b, 479a, **737b**
Liberal Union → Ḥürriyet we iʾtilāf
Liberia v, **753a** — V, **758b**
Liberté → Āzādī; Djumhūriyya; Ḥurriyya
Libertin(e)s → Mudjdjān
Lībiyā i, 39b, 1071a, 1177a; ii, 94a, 667a, 676a; iii, 385a, 1049a; iv, 262a; v, 696a, **753b**, 1066a; s, 216a — I, 40b, 1103a, 1212a; II, 96a, 684a, 693a; III, 397b, 1075b; IV, 274a; V, 700b, **759b**, 1063b; S, 216a
- demography/démographie s, **216a** — S, **216a**
- inscriptions v, 221b, **754b** — V, 219a, **760b**
- literature/littérature ii, 470b — II, 482b
- university/université ii, 425a; v, 912a — II, 436a; V, 917b
Libn → Labin
Libraries → Khizāna; Kitābkhāna; Maktaba
Libre Arbitre → Ḳadar; Ikhtiyār
Libya/Libye → Lībiyā

Libyan/Libyque i, 1180b, 1185a; v, 694b — I, 1215b, 1220a; V, 699b
Lice → Ḳaml
Licence → Idjāza
Lièvre → Arnab
Life → Ākhira; Dunya; Ḥayāt
Ligue des États arabes → al-Djāmiʿa al-ʿArabiyya
Ligue musulmane → al-Rābita al-Islāmiyya
Liḥyān i, 562b; v, **761b** — I, 580b; V, **767b**
al-Liḥyānī, ʿAlī b. Ḥāzim v, 763a — V, 769a
Liḥyānite → Liḥyān
Liḥya-yi Sherīf v, **761a** — V, **767a**
Līlī b. al-Nuʿmān s, 356b, 357a — S, 356b
Līm, Līmūn → Muḥammadāt
Limassol → Ḳubruṣ
Limbang Valley s, 152b — S, 152b
Limni v, 257b, **763b** — V, 255a, b, **769b**
Linceul → Djanāza
Linen/Lin → Ḳaṭṭān
Linga v, 507b, 674b, **765a** — V, 511a, 679b, **770b**
Lion → al-Asad; Ḥaydar; Minṭaḳat al-Burūdj
Liongo s, 351a, b — S, 351a, b
Lipḳa v, **765b** — V, **771a**
Liptako ii, 942a — II, 964a
Lisān v, 803a, 805a — V, 809a, 811a
Lisān al-ʿArab → Ibn Manẓūr
Lisān al-Dīn Ibn al-Khaṭīb → Ibn al-Khaṭīb
Lisān al-Ḥummara → Ibn Lisān al-Ḥummara
Lisānī iv, 68b — IV, 72a
Lisbon/Lisbonne → al-Ushbūna
Lishbūna i, 1338b — I, 1379a
Liṣṣ v, **767b** — V, **773b**
Līṭānī, Nahr al- iv, 483a — IV, 504a
Literature/Littérature → Adab; ʿArabiyya; Ghazal; Madīḥ; Maḳāma; Marthiya; Taʾrīkh, etc.
Literie → Mafrūshāt
Lithām v, 744a, b, 745a, **769a** — V, 749b, 750a, b, **775a**
Lithography/Lithographie → Maṭbaʿa
Lithomancy/Lithomancie → Ṭarḳ
Lithuania/Lithuanie v, 137b, 140a, 765b — V, 140b, 142b, 771b
Liu (T)Chiai-lien → Liu (T)Chih
Liu (T)Chih v, **770a** — V, **776a**
Livadya v, **772a** — V, **778a**
Liver → Kabid
Livestock → Ghanam
Livno v, **774a** — V, **780a**
Livres → Kitāb
Liwāʾ i, 349a; ii, 507b; iii, 383b, 384b; v, **776a** — I, 359b; II, 520a; III, 396a, 397a; V, **782a**
Līwā → al-Djiwāʾ
Līwān → Īwān
Liwāṭ v, **776b** — V, **782b**
Lixus i, 605a — I, 625a
Liyāḳat ʿAlī Khān iii, 532b; v, **779b** — III, 551a; V, **785b**
Liyāḳat al-Lāh iii, 119b — III, 122a
Liyūn v, **781a** — V, **787b**
Lizzard/Lézard → Ḍabb
Lobbo → Aḥmadu Lobbo; Ba Lobbo
Locust → Djarād
Lōdī i, 756b; ii, 258b, 263b, 264a, 270b, 274b; iii, 442b; iv, 513a; v, **782a**; s, 1b, 313a — I, 779a; II, 265a, 271b, 272a, 279a, 283a; III, 457b; IV, 535a; V, **788b**; S, 1b, 313a
Loe Djirga s, 66a — S, 66b
Logic/Logique → Manṭiḳ
Logone v, 278b — V, 276b
Loja → Lawsha
Loḳmān, Seyyid → Luḳmān b. Sayyid Ḥusayn
Lombardy/Lombardie → al-Ankubarda
Lombok i, 1219b, 1226a; v, **785a** — I, 1250b, 1257b; V, **791b**
Lope b. Musa → Lubb b. Mūsā
Lor, Lorī → Lur, Lurī
Loralai district (Balūčistān) s, 331b — S, 331b
Lorca → Lurḳa
Los Pedroches → Faḥṣ al-Ballūṭ
Lot/Loth → Lūṭ
Lōtōn → Khotan
Loup → Dhiʾb
Louxor → al-Uḳṣur
Love → ʿIshk; Maḥabba
Lowarāʿī ii, 29a — II, 29b
Lōya Djirga i, 232b; ii, 657b — I, 239b; II, 674a
Luarsab I v, 492b, 493a — V, 495b, 496a
Luʿba v, 616a — V, 620a
Lubān v, **786a** — V, **792a**
Lubb b. Muḥammad iv, 713a — IV, 742a
Lubb b. Mūsā b. Mūsā iv, 713a — IV, 741b
Lubka → Lipḳa
Lubnān i, 975b, 1078a, b; ii, 185a, 403b, 443b, 444a, 595a, 661a; iii, 559a; iv, 834b; v, **787a**, 1253a — I, 1006a, 1110b; II, 190b, 414a, 455a, b, 610a, 677b; III, 578b; IV, 867b; V, **793b**, 1244a
- history/histoire iv, 261b — IV, 273b
- industries iii, 211a; v, 791b, 795b — III, 217a; V, 798a, 801b
- institutions ii, 424a; iii, 523a; v, 912a, b, 1051a — II, 435a; III, 541a; V, 917b, 918b, 1047b
- language, literature/langue, littérature i, 575a; ii, 467a — I, 594a; II, 479a
Lubūd v, **798a** — V, **804a**
al-Lubūdī s, 267b, 341b — S, 267b, 341a
Lucena → al-Yussāna
Lucera → Lūshīra
Lucknow → Lakhnaw
Ludd v, **798b** — V, **804b**
Lūdhiāna v, **803a** — V, **809a**
Lūdjāra → Lūshīra
al-Ludjdj i, 1083b — I, 1115b
Lugha iv, 122a, b, 524a; v, **803a** — IV, 127b, 128a, 546b; V, **809a**
Lugha, ʿIlm al- → Lugha
Lughat-nāma → Dehkhudā
al-Lughawī → Abu ʾl-Ṭayyib
Lughz v, 806b — V, 812b
Luhayfa bint Abū Safyān i, 145b — I, 150a
al-Luḥayya v, **807a**; s, 30b — V, **813a**; S, 30b
Luhrāsb iv, 809a — IV, 842a
Luḳaṭa v, **809b** — V, **815b**
al-Lukkām, Djabal v, **810a** — V, **816a**
al-Lukaymī → Asʿad
Lukayz i, 73a — I, 75a
Luḳmān i, 146a, 984a; ii, 112b; iii, 309a; v, **811a** — I, 150a, 1014b; II, 115a; III, 318b; V, **817a**
Luḳmān b. Sayyid Ḥusayn v, **813b** — V, **820a**
Luḳmāndji b. Ḥabīb Allāh v, **814b** — V, **821a**
Lüleburgaz v, **815a** — V, **821a**
Lūlī ii, 40b, 41a; v, **816b** — II, 41b, 42a; V, **822b**
Lulon → Luʾluʾa
Luʾluʾ (pearl/perle) v, **819a**, 969b — V, **825b**, 972b
Luʾluʾ (al-Yaḥyā) i, 1337a; iii, 86b, 1118b — I, 1377a; III, 89a, 1146a
Luʾluʾ, amīr iii, 398a — III, 410b
Luʾluʾ, Badr al-Dīn i, 195b, 1161a; ii, 348b; iii, 961a; iv, 76b; v, **821a** — I, 201a, 1195b; II, 358b; III, 985b; IV, 80b; V, **827a**
Luʾluʾ, Ḥusām al-Dīn i, 784a, 932b; v, 368b — I, 807a, 961a; V, 369b
Luʾluʾ al-Kabīr al-Djarrāḥī iii, 130b; v, **820a**, 923b — III, 133a; V, **826a**, 929a
Luʾluʾa ii, 36a, b, 37b — II, 37a, 38b
Lummasar i, 1359b — I, 1399b

Lune → Hilāl; Ḳamar
Lūnī (river/fleuve) s, 329b — S, 329a
Lur(s) i, 513a, 955b; iii, 1096b, 1097b, 1102b; iv, 5b, 8a, 9a; v, 616b, 817a, **821a**; s, 147b — I, 528b, 985a; III, 1123a, 1124b, 1129b; IV, 6a, 8b, 9b; V, 621a, 823b, **827b**; S, 147b
Lūrā v, 234a — V, 232a
Lūrī v, 816b, 817a — V, 823a
Lūrī → Lūlī
Lurī (language/langue) iii, 1261a; v, 818a, 823a, b — III, 1293b; V, 824b, 829b
Lur-i Buzurg iii, 1097b; v, **826a** — III, 1124b; V, **832b**
Lur-i Kūčik iii, 1106a; v, 821b, 824b, 826a, **828a**, 829b — III, 1133a, b; V, 828a, 830b, 832a, **834a**, 835b
Luristān i, 8a, 732a, 840a; iii, 337a, 1102a; v, 63a, 617a, 817b, 824a, 828a, **829b** — I, 8a, 754a, 863a; II, 347a, 1129a; V, 65a, 621a, 823b, 830b, 834a, **835b**
Lūrḳa v, **832b** — V, **839a**
Lū<u>sh</u>īra iv, 274b — IV, 287a
Lusignan v, 303a — V, 302b
Lustre iv, 1167a — IV, 1199b
Lūṭ v, 421a, 776b, **832b** — V, 423a, 782b, **839a**
Lūṭ b. Yaḥyā → Abū Mi<u>kh</u>naf
Lute → al-ʿŪd
Luṭf (grace/grâce) v, **833b** — V, **839b**
Luṭf → Amān, Mīr
Luṭf ʿAlī Beg Ā<u>dh</u>ar iv, 69b; v, **834a** — IV, 73a; V, **840a**
Luṭf ʿAlī <u>Kh</u>ān iii, 604a — III, 624b
Luṭf ʿAlī <u>Kh</u>ān Zand i, 246b, 1008b; ii, 812a; iv, 391a, b, 476a; v, 156a, 164b, **835a**; s, 336a, 405b — I, 254b, 1039b; II, 831b; IV, 408a, 497a; V, 162a, **841a**; S, 335b, 405b
Luṭf Allāh, Mullā s, 353b — S, 353b
Luṭf Allāh <u>Kh</u>ān s, 76a, b — S, 76b
Luṭfī ii, 1133a; v, **835b** — II, 1160a; V, **841b**
Luṭfī, ʿAbd al-Ma<u>dj</u>īd v, 189b — V, 186b
Luṭfī, Mollā iv, 880a — IV, 912b
Luṭfī, Muṣṭafā → al-Manfalūṭī
Luṭfī Beg → Luṭfī Pa<u>sh</u>a
Luṭfī Efendi i, 286a, 972b, 974a; ii, 714a; iii, 515a, 593b; v, **836b** — I, 295a, 1002b, 1004a; II, 732b; III, 532b, 614a; V, **843a**
Luṭfī Pa<u>sh</u>a v, 268b, **837b** — V, 266b, **844a**
Luṭfī al-Sayyid, Aḥmad v, **838b**, 1092a — V, **845a**, 1089a
Luṭfiyya → <u>Sh</u>ā<u>dh</u>iliyya
Luth → al-ʿŪd
Lūṭī iv, 99b; v, 776b, **839a** — IV, 103b; V, 782b, **846a**
Luwāta → Lawāta
Luxor → al-Uḳṣūr
Luzon s, 152a — S, 152a
Luzūm mā lā yalzam v, **839b**, 931a, 932a — V, **846a**, 935b, 936a
Lydda → Ludd
Lyre → Ḳi<u>th</u>āra

M

Māʾ i, 1029b, 1094-7; ii, 343b; v, **859b**, 1007a, 1108b — I, 1061a, 1127-30; II, 353a; V, **866b**, 1002b, 1104a
Maʿabiyat → al-Mabyāt
Mā al-ʿAynayn al-Ḳalḳamī, <u>Sh</u>ay<u>kh</u> i, 734a; v, **889b**; s, 47b — I, 755b; V, **896a**; S, 48a
Maʿād v, **892b** — V, **899a**
Maʿadd i, 102b, 544b, 549a; iv, 448a, b; v, **894b** — I, 105b, 562a, 566a; IV, 468a, b; V, **901a**
Maʿadd b. ʿAdnān v, 315a, 894b — V, 314b, 901a
Maʿādī → Miʿdān
Maadid s, 144b — S, 144b
Maʿāfir v, **895a** — V, **901a**
al-Maʿāfirī, Abu 'l-Ḥasan ʿAlī v, **895b** — V, **902a**
al-Maʿāfirī, Muḥammad b. <u>Kh</u>ayrūn iv, 825b — IV, 858b
Maʿal<u>th</u>āyā v, **896a** — V, **902b**
Maʿān v, **897a** — V, **903a**
al-Maʿānī i, 784b, 858a; ii, 550a — I, 808a, 882a; II, 563b
Maʿānī ʾl-<u>sh</u>iʿr iii, 110b — III, 113a
al-Maʿānī waʾl-bayān v, **898a** — V, **904a**
Maʿārif v, **902b** — V, **908b**
Maʿarrat Maṣrīn (Miṣrīn) v, **921a** — V, **926b**
Maʿarrat al-Nuʿmān i, 1289a; v, **922a** — I, 1328b; V, **927b**
al-Maʿarrī, Abū ʾl-ʿAlāʾ i, 108a, 131a, 591a, 592b, 1092b, 1290b; ii, 127b; iii, 640b, 686b, 1019b; v, 840a, 922b, 926b, **927a**, 1211a, 1212b; s, 32b, 37b, 119b, 289a — I, 111a, 134b, 610a, 611b, 1125a, 1330a; II, 130b; III, 662a, 708b, 1045b; V, 846b, 928a, 932a, **932b**, 1201a, 1202a; S, 32b, 38a, 119a, 289a
Maʾāṣir ii, 143a — II, 147a
Maʾā<u>th</u>ir al-Umarāʾ v, **935b** — V, **939b**
Maba s, 164a — S, 164a
Maʿbad b. Wahb (singer/chanteur) i, 118a; ii, 428b; iii, 698b; iv, 821b; v, **936b** — I, 121b; II, 439b; III, 720b; IV, 854b; V, **940a**
Maʿbad b. al-ʿAbbās b. ʿAbd al-Muṭṭalib i, 862b — I, 886b
Maʿbad al-<u>Dj</u>uhanī ii, 1026b; iii, 1142a; iv, 370a, 371a, b; v, **935b** — II, 1050a; III, 1170b; IV, 386a, 387b; V, **939b**
Mā baʿd al-ṭabīʿa v, **841a** — V, **848a**
Ma Chʾao-ching → Ma Hua-lung
Ma Chung-ying v, **844b** — V, **856b**
Ma Hu-shan v, 846b — V, 858b
Ma Hua-lung iv, 554b; v, **847a**, 850b — IV, 578b; V, **851a**, 855a
Ma Huan v, **849a** — V, **853b**
Ma Ming-hsin iv, 554b; v, 847b, **850b** — IV, 578a; V, 851b, **854b**
Mā warāʾ al-Nahr i, 8a, 103b, 147b, 454b, 1188a, 1294a, 1312a; ii, 3b, 45a, 587a, 1108a; iv, 175a, 188b; v, **852b**; s, 50b, 97a, b, 122a, 176b, 192b, 228a, 244b, 326b, 340a, 411a — I, 8a, 106b, 152a, 467b, 1223a, 1333b, 1352a; II, 3b, 46a, 601b, 1134a; IV, 182b, 197a; V, **859a**; S, 51a, 96b, 121a, 177b, 194a, 228a, 244b, 326a, 339b, 411a
Ma Yüan-chʾang iv, 554b — IV, 578b
Maʿbar iii, 407a; v, **937a**, 1122a — III, 419b; V, **940b**, 1118b
al-Maʿbarī, <u>Sh</u>ay<u>kh</u> Zayn al-Dīn v, **938a** — V, **942a**
Mābeyn i, 64a; v, **938b** — I, 66a; V, **942b**
Mab<u>kh</u>ara → Mib<u>kh</u>ara
Mablaḳa iv, 747a, b — IV, 777a, b
al-Mabyāt v, 498a — V, 501a
Māčar iv, 350a — IV, 365a
Macassar → Makassar
Macina i, 303a, b; ii, 941b; iii, 39b — I, 312b, 313a; II, 963b; III, 41a
Mad (insane) → Ma<u>dj</u>nūn
Mad Mullah → Muḥammad b. ʿAbd Allāh Ḥassān al-Mahdī
Madagascar v, **939a** — V, **943a**
- language/langue v, 942b, 943b — V, 946b, 947a
al-Madāʾin i, 77a, 810b; iii, 241b; iv, 386a; v, **945a**; s, 118a, 263b — I, 79a, 833b; III, 248b; IV, 402b; V, **948b**; S, 117b, 263a
Madāʾin Ṣāliḥ → al-Hi<u>dj</u>r
al-Madāʾinī, Abu ʾl-Ḥasan i, 758b, 760a; ii, 1097a; iii, 682a, 723a, 1263a; iv, 291a, 927a, v, **946b** — I, 781b,

782b; II, 1123a; III, 704a, 745b, 1296a; IV, 304a, 960a; V, **950b**
Madalī i, 504b — I, 520a
Madali Khān → Muḥammad ʿAlī Khān (Khōkand)
Maʿdān s, 243a — S, 243a
al-Madanī, Aḥmad Tawfīḳ iv, 159b — IV, 166a
al-Madanī, Shaykh Muḥammad i, 808a; iii, 28b; v, 948b, 949a — I, 831a; III, 30a; V, 952b
Madaniyya v, **948b**; s, 371a — V, **952b**; S, 371a
Madār, Shāh→ Badīʿ al-Dīn
Madārī i, 859a — I, 883a
Mādar-i Shāh iv, 1015a, 1016b — IV, 1046-7a, 1048b
al-Madd waʾl-djazr v, **949b** — V, **953b**
Mādda iii, 328b, 329b — III, 338b, 339b
Maddāḥ iii, 368a; iv, 735a; v, **951a** — III, 379b; IV, 765a; V, **954b**
Maḍḍar, Shaykh iii, 206b — III, 212a
Māddiyya ii, 97b — II, 99b
Maʿden ii, 707a — II, 725a
Madghalīs iii, 852a — III, 876a
Mādghīs i, 1349b — I, 1390a
Madḥ → Madīḥ
Madhāb iii, 52a — III, 54a
al-Mādharāʾī iii, 979a; v, 50a, **953a** — III, 1003b; V, 51b, **957a**
Madhav Rāo iii, 316b — III, 326a
Madhhab v, 1129a, 1141b, 1150b — V, 1125a, 1134b, 1141a
Madhḥidj i, 544b, 728a; v, 120b, **953b** — I, 561b, 750a; V, 123a, **957b**
Madḥiyya → Madīḥ
Māḍī v, **954b** — V, **958b**
Madīḥ/Madḥ iv, 714b; v, 931a, **955a** — IV, 743b; V, 935b, **959a**
al-Madjḥidjī, Muḥammed b. al-Ḥasan i, 600b; iii, 791b — I, 620a; III, 815a
Maʾdhūn i, 29a; ii, 97b; iii, 50b — I, 29b; II, 99b; III, 52a
Maʿdīkarib Yaʿfur ii, 244a; v, 118b — II, 251a; V, 121a
Maʿdin ii, 29b, 924a; v, **963b** — II, 29b, 945b; V, **968a**
al-Maʿdin v, **993b** — V, **989a**
Maʿdin Banī Sulaym s, 198b — S, 198b
Maʿdin al-Naḳira s, 198b — S, 198b
al-Madīna i, 45a, 50b, 53a, 110b, 609a; ii, 592b, 854a; iii, 362a, 1067a; v, **994a**; s, 198b, 267b, 335a, 337b — I, 46b, 51b, 54b, 113b, 629a; II, 607b, 874a; III, 373b, 1093b; V, **989a**; S, 198b, 267a, 334b, 337a
- city/ville v, 1000-1007 — V, 996b-1003a
- constitution of/de v, 995b — V, 991a
- history/histoire iii, 896b; iv, 335b; v, 994a — III, 921a; IV, 350a; V, 989b
- population v, 999a, b, 1003a — V, 994b, 995a, 998b
- university/(é) v, 1005b — V, 1001b
Madīna (town centre/centre civil) v, 347b, 348a, 1108a — V, 348b, 1104a
al-Madīna al-Zāhira v, **1007b**, 1239b — V, **1003b**, 1230a
Madīnat Fās ii, 818a; iii, 1031b, 1032a — II, 838a; III, 1057b, 1058a
Madīnat Ibn Hubayra iii, 266a — III, 273b
Madīnat al-Salām i, 894b — I, 921b
Madīnat Sālim ii, 998a; v, **1008a** — II, 1021a; V, **1004a**
Madīnat al-Zahrāʾ i, 84a, b, 202a, 459a, 498a, 950a; ii, 745b, 747b, 957a; iii, 498b; iv, 1165b; v, 510b, **1008b** — I, 86a, b, 208a, 472a, 513a, 979a; II, 764a, 766a, 979a; III, 516a; IV, 1198a; V, 514b, **1004a**
Madīnat Zāwī i, 511b — I, 527a
al-Madīnī → Abū Ayyūb; Muḥammad b. ʿUmar
Maḍīra v, **1010a** — V, **1005b**
al-Madiyya v, **1010a** — V, **1006a**
Madjabra i, 763b — I, 786a
Madjādhīb ii, 944b; iv, 686b — II, 966b; IV, 714b
Madjālis → Madjlis
Madjalla → Medjelle
Madjallat al-Azhar i, 819a, 820b — I, 842b, 844a
Madjānīḳ i, 1057a, 1059a — I, 1089a, 1090b
Madjapahit iii, 1219a, 1221b; s, 201a, 202a — III, 1249b, 1252b; S, 201a, b
Madjar, Madjaristān v, **1010b** — V, **1006b**
al-Madjarra v, **1024b** — V, **1020b**
Madjāz iii, 898b; v, **1025b** — III, 923a; V, **1021b**
Madjbūb iv, 1087a — IV, 1118b
Madjd al-Dawla, Abū Ṭālib Rustam (Būyid(e)) iii, 764b; iv, 100b, 465a; v, **1028a**; s, 118b — III, 787b; IV, 105a, 486a; V, **1024a**; S, 118a
Madjd al-Dīn → Hibat Allāh b. Muḥammad
Madjd al-Dīn b. al-Athīr → Ibn al-Athīr
Madjd al-Dīn al-Baghdādī i, 347a, 764a — I, 357b, 787a
Madjd al-Dīn Isḥāḳ iii, 708a — III, 730a
Madjd al-Mulk al-Balāsānī i, 1052b, 1336b; ii, 333b; v, **1028b** — I, 1084a, 1377a; II, 343a; V, **1024b**
Madjd al-Mulk Sīnakī iv, 787b — IV, 819b
Madjd al-Mulk Yazdī ii, 334a, 607b — II, 343b, 622b
al-Madjdal i, 846a — I, 869b
Madjdhūb v, **1029a** — V, **1025a**
al-Madjdhūb v, **1029a** — V, **1025a**
Madjdhūbī → Madjādhīb
Madjd-i Hamgar s, 235b — S, 235a
al-Madjdjāsī, Muḥammad b. al-Ḥasan s, 126a — S, 125a
Madjdī b. ʿAmr v, 316b — V, 316a
al-Madjdjāwī, ʿAbd al-Ḳādir v, **1029b** — V, **1025b**
Madjdūd b. Masʿūd iii, 168a — III, 171b
Madjghariyya → Madjar
Madjhūl ii, 897a; iii, 26b — II, 918a; III, 27b
Mādjid b. Saʿīd i, 1282b; ii, 129a; v, **1030a**; s, 355b, 356a — I, 1321b; II, 132a; V, **1026a**; S, 355b
Mādjid b. ʿUrayʿir iv, 925b — IV, 958b
Madjīdiyya → Ḥāfiẓiyya
Mādjir (tribe/tribu) s, 387a — S, 387a
al-Madjisṭī → Baṭlamiyūs
Madjkasa Berbers s, 111b — S, 110b
Madjlis i, 891b, 974a, b, 975a, 976a, 979b, 1035b; ii, 87a; iii, 528a, 529a; v, 920a, **1031a** — I, 918a, 1004a, b, 1005b, 1006a, 1010a, 1067a; II, 88b; III, 546a, 547a; V, 925b, **1027a**
Madjlis al-ʿaskudār ii, 324b — II, 334a
Madjlis al-Aʿyān ii, 658b, 659b; iii, 528a; v, 262b, 1035b, 1044a, 1054a — II, 675a, 676a; III, 546b; V, 260a, 1031b, 1040b, 1051a
Madjlis Ḳiyādat al-Thawra s, 6b — S, 6a
Madjlis-niwīs iv, 758a — IV, 788a
Madjlis al-nuwwāb v, 1044a, 1051b, 1054a, 1060b, 1061a, 1064a, 1066b — V, 1040b, 1048a, 1050b, 1057b, 1058a, 1061b, 1063b
Madjlis al-shaʿb v, 1049a, 1059b, 1061b, 1065a — V, 1045b, 1056b, 1058b, 1062a
al-Madjlis al-Sharʿī al-Islāmī al-Aʿlā s, 68a — S, 68b
Madjlis ul-Islam il-Aʿlā Indonesia iii, 1229b — III, 1261b
Madjlis-i Khāṣṣ iii, 553a — III, 572a
Madjlis Ḳuṭub ii, 797b — II, 816b
Madjlis al-Nuẓẓār ii, 647a; iii, 557a — II, 663b; III, 576a
Madjlis-i shūrā ii, 658b, 660a; v, 1042a, 1058a, 1059a, **1082b** — II, 675a, 767b; V, 1038a, 1055a, 1056a, **1080a**
Madjlis Shūrā al-Nuwwāb ii, 647a, 659b — II, 663b, 676a
Madjlis al-umma v, 1044a, 1054a, 1057a, 1061a, 1066b, 1068b — V, 1040b, 1050b, 1054a, 1058a,

1063b, 1066a
Madjlis-i ʿumūmī ii, 643a; v, 1035a, b, 1085b — II, 659a; V, 1031b, 1082b
Madjlis-i wālā v, 1084b, 1085a — V, 1082a
Madjlis-i wükelā ii, 643a — II, 659a
al-Madjlisī, Muḥammad Bāḳir i, 593a; iii, 588b, 1169b; iv, 278a; v, **1086b**, 1089b; s, 134b — I, 612b; III, 608b, 1198b; IV, 290a; V, **1084a**, 1086b; S, 134a
al-Madjlisī, Muḥammad Taḳī → Madjlisī-yi Awwal
Madjlisī-yi Awwal v, 1087a, **1088b** — V, 1084a, **1086a**
Madjmaʿ al-baḥrayn i, 935b, 940b; iv, 903a, b — I, 964a, 969b; IV, 936a, b
al-Madjmaʿ ʿIlmī i, 572b; v, 438a, **1090a**; s, 11b — I, 591a; V, 440b, **1087a**; S, 11a
al-Madjmaʿ al-ʿIlmī al-ʿArabī i, 572a; ii, 290a — I, 591a; II, 298a
al-Madjmaʿ al-ʿIlmī al-Miṣrī → Institut d'Égypte
Madjmaʿ al-Lugha al-ʿArabiyya i, 572b; s, 11b — I, 591a; S, 10b
Madjmaʿ-i Ukhuwwat ii, 434a — II, 445a
Madjnūn ii, 1031a; iii, 273a, 841b; v, **1101a** — II, 1055a; III, 281a, 865b; V, **1097a**
Madjnūn Banī ʿĀmir → Madjnūn Laylā
Madjnūn Laylā v, **1102b** — V, **1098b**
Madjrā iv, 412a, b — IV, 430a, b
Madjrīṭ iv, 533a; v, **1107a** — IV, 556a; V, **1103a**
al-Madjrīṭī, Abu 'l-Ḳāsim Maslama i, 600b, 1101a; iii, 924a, 1072b; v, **1109a** — I, 620a, 1134b; III, 948b, 1099a; V, **1105a**
Mādjūdj → Yādjūdj wa-Mādjūdj
Madjūs (Norsemen/Nordiques) i, 83a, 494a, 864b; ii, 525a; iii, 74b; iv, 115b; v, 503b, 586a, 1013a, **1118a** — I, 85b, 509a, 888b; II, 538a; III, 77a; IV, 120b; V, 506b, 591b, 1008b, **1114b**
Madjūs (Zoroastrians/Zoroastriens) i, 15b, 264a, 626a, 1354b; ii, 638a, 970b, 1035b, 1124a; iv, 43a, 54a, 910a, 1063a; v, 157a, 370b, **1110a**, 1121b — I, 16a, 272b, 647a, 1393b; II, 654b, 993a, 1059b, 1150b; IV, 45b, 56b, 943a, 1094b; V, 156b, 371a, **1105b**, 1118a
al-Madjūsī → ʿAlī b. al-ʿAbbās al-Madjūsī
Madjūsiyān ii, 162b — II, 167b
Madjzūʾ i, 671a — I, 691b
Maḍmūn v, **1121b** — V, **1118b**
Madras i, 979a; ii, 426a; v, **1122a**; s, 47a, 247a — I, 1009a; II, 437a; V, **1118b**; S, 47b, 247a
Madrasa i, 20b, 593a, 899a, 1272a; iii, 1124a, 1227b, 1255b, 1264a; iv, 28a, 167b, 288b, 1025b; v, 255b, 907b, **1123a**, 1200a — I, 21b, 612a, 926a, 1311a; III, 1152a, 1259a, 1288a, 1297a; IV, 29b-30a, 174b, 301a, 1057b; V, 253b, 913a, **1119b**, 1190a
Madraṭān s, 352a — S, 352a
Madrid → Madjrīṭ
Madura ii, 391b; iii, 1213b, 1219a, 1226a; v, **1154b**; s, 202b — II, 402a; III, 1244b, 1249b, 1257b; V, **1144a**; S, 202a
al-Madya → al-Madiyya
Madyan Shuʿayb v, **1155b** — V, **1145b**
Mafākhir i, 892a — I, 918b
Mafākhir al-Barbar iii, 782b; v, **1156b** — III, 805b; V, **1146b**
al-Māfarrūkhī, Mufaḍḍal b. Saʿd v, **1157a** — V, **1147a**
Mafia (island/île) v, **1157b** — V, **1147a**
Mafḥaḳ iii, 327a — III, 337a
Mafḳūd ii, 995b — II, 1018b
Mafraḳ s, 157a — S, 157b
Mafrūshāt v, **1158a** — V, **1148a**
Mafṣūl v, **1159a** — V, **1149a**
Magal s, 182a — S, 182b
Magas iv, 345b, 349b — IV, 360a, 364b
Maggan b. Kāmil b. Djāmiʿ iii, 386b — III, 398b
Magh i, 952a — I, 981a
Maghāfir iii, 64b — III, 67a
Maghāghā (Egypt/Égypte) s, 408a — S, 408b
Maghāgha (tribe/tribu) v, 695a, b, 697a — V, 700a, b, 702a
Maghāʾir Shuʿayb v, 1156a — V, 1146a
Maghāra ii, 14a — II, 14a
Maghāriba v, **1159a** — V, **1149a**
al-Maghāzī iii, 698a; v, 996a, **1161b** — III, 720a; V, 991b, **1151a**
Maghīla iii, 1040b, 1041a; v, **1164a** — III, 1066b, 1067a; V, **1154a**
al-Maghīlī, Muḥammad b. ʿAbd al-Karīm ii, 977b; iii, 276a; iv, 548b, 549b, 550a; v, **1165a** — II, 1000a; III, 284a; IV, 572b, 573b; V, **1155a**
Maghmadās i, 125a; iii, 654a — I, 128b; III, 675a
Maghnāṭīs v, **1166b** — V, **1156a**
Maghnisa i, 1225b; iv, 593b; v, **1169b** — I, 1262a; IV, 617b; V, **1159b**
Maghōsha v, **1171a** — V, **1160b**
Maghrāwa i, 122b, 1246b; ii, 821b; iii, 1041b, 1042a; v, 596a, **1173b** — I, 126a, 1284b; II, 841a; III, 1067a, 1068a; V, 599b, **1163b**
al-Maghrāwī, Sīdī ʿAbd Allāh i, 127a — I, 1161a
al-Maghrib i, 50a, 92a, 162a, 366b, 1231b; ii, 130b 748a; iii, 38a, 66a, 163a, 1041a, 1049b; v, 742b, 1149b, 1150a, 1159a, 1175a, b, **1183b**; s, 215a — I, 51b, 95a, 166b, 377b, 1268a; II, 133b, 766a; III, 39b, 68b, 166b, 1067a, 1075b; V, 748a, 1140b, 1149a, 1165a, b, **1173b**; S, 214b
- administration i, 1148b; ii, 145a, 307b; iii, 561b; iv, 784b — I, 1183a; II, 149a, 316a; III, 581a; IV, 816a
- demography/démographie s, **215a** — S, **214b**
- language, literature/langue, littérature i, 96a, b, 156b, 571b, 578b; iii, 902b; v, 1159a — I, 99a, 161a, 590a, 597b; III, 927a; V, 1149a
- monuments v, 289b — V, 289a
al-Maghrib, al-Mamlaka → Morocco/Maroc
al-Maghribī → ʿAbd al-Ḳādir; Abu ʾl- ʿAbbās; Muḥammad Shīrīn
al-Maghribī, Abu 'l-Ḥasan ʿAlī b. al-Ḥusayn i, 824b; iii, 79a; v, 928a, **1210b** — I, 847b; III, 81b; V, 933b, **1201a**
Maghribī, Aḥmad Khattū → Aḥmad Khattū
al-Maghribī, Banū v, **1210a** — V, **1200b**
al-Maghribī, al-Ḥusayn b. ʿAlī (d./m. 965) v, **1210b** — V, **1200b**
al-Maghribī, al-Ḥusayn b. ʿAlī (d./m. 1017) ii, 483b; iii, 80a, 896b; v, 929b, **1211b** — II, 496a; III, 82a, 920b; V, 934b, **1201a**
Maghumi i, 1259b; iv, 566b — I, 1297b; IV, 589a
Magic/Magie → Siḥr
Magic Square → Wafḳ
Māgiriyyūn iii, 339a — III, 349a
Magnesia/Magnésie → Maghnisa
Magnetism(e) → Maghnāṭīs
Māgres s, 167a — S, 167a
Māh al-Baṣra iv, 13b; v, **1212b** — IV, 14b; V, **1202a**
Māh al-Kūfa → Dīnawar
Māh-Peyker ii, 183b — II, 189b
Maḥa i, 1028b — I, 1060a
Mahābād v, 466a, **1213a** — V, 469a, **1202b**
Mahābat Khān (Mughal) i, 81a, 686a; ii, 180a, 381a; iv, 1018a, b, 1020a; v, 250b, **1214a** — I, 83b, 707a; II, 185b, 391a; IV, 1050a, b, 1052a; V, 248b, **1203b**
Mahābat Khān II (Mughal) v, 1214b — V, 1204a
Mahābat Khān (Shīr) → Muḥammad Mahābat Khān
Maḥabba ii, 55b; iii, 103a; iv, 94b, 119b — II, 56b; III, 105b; IV, 98b, 124b
Maḥabbat Khān (Bareilly) ii, 602a; iii, 61b — II, 617a; III, 64a
Mahābhārata i, 856b — I, 880b

Mahadba s, 144b — S, 144a, b
Mahādila → al-Ahdal
al-Maḥādjir i, 766b — I, 789b
Maḥall i, 317a; v, **1214b** — I, 326b; V, **1204a**
Maḥalla v, **1220b** — V, **1211a**
Maḥalla Daḳalā v, 1221b — V, 1212a
al-Maḥalla al-Kubrā ii, 1009b; v, **1221a** — II, 1033b; V, **1211b**
Maḥalla Sharḳiyūn v, 1221b — V, 1212a
Maḥallat Abū ʿAlī s, 18a — S, 18a
Maḥallātī, Āghā Khān v, **1221b** — V, **1212a**
Maḥalle iv, 229b-231b, 234a, 238a, 239b; v, **1222b** — IV, 239b-241b, 244b, 248b, 250a; V, **1213a**
al-Maḥallī, Djalāl al-Dīn v, **1223a** — V, **1213b**
Maham → Mahīm
Māham iii, 455b — III, 471b
Māham Anaga i, 1136b — I, 1170b
al-Mahāmīd i, 1299a — I, 1339a
Maḥammad b. Abī Bakr s, 223a — S, 223a
Maḥammad al-Ḥādjdj → al-Dilāʾ
al-Māhānī, Abū ʿAbd Allāh ii, 362a; iv, 1182b — II, 372a; IV, 1215b
al-Māhānī, Abū ʿAlī Muḥammad b. ʿĪsā s, 412a, 413b — S, 412a, 413b
Māhānī, Ustādh Muʾmin b. Ḳuṭb al-Dīn s, 139a — S, 138b
Maharashtra s, 246b — S, 246b
Mahari → Kotoko
Maḥārim → Ḥarīm
Maḥasī i, 1029a — I, 1060b
Maḥāsin i, 981b — I, 1012a
al-Maḥāsin wa-ʾl-masāwī v, **1223b** — V, **1214a**
Mahāt v, 651b, **1227a** — V, 655b, **1217b**
Maḥbūb b. al-Raḥīl al-ʿAbdī, Abū Sufyān iii, 651a; v, **1230a** — III, 672a; V, **1220b**
Maḥbūb ʿAlī Khān ii, 84a; iii, 322b — II, 85b; III, 332a, b
Maḥbūba (singer/chanteuse) iv, 821b, 822b — IV, 854b, 855a
Maḥbūbī, Āl-i v, 858a — V, 865a
al-Maḥbūbī, Maḥmūd iii, 163b — III, 167a
al-Maḥbūbiyyūn iii, 659b — III, 680b
Mahd ʿUlyā s, 71a — S, 71b
Mahd-i ʿUlyā iii, 157b — III, 161a
Mahdawīs ii, 500a; iii, 492b; v, **1230b**; s, 222a — II, 512b; III, 509b; V, **1221a**; S, 222a
al-Mahdī ii, 851a; iii, 1167a; iv, 203b, 204a, 278b, 456b, 662a; v, **1230b** — II, 871a; III, 1195b; IV, 212b, 213a, 291a, 477a, 688b; V, **1221a**
Mahdī → al-Djawnpūrī; Ibn Tūmart al-Mahidyya; Sayyid Muḥammad
al-Mahdī (Fāṭimid(e)) → al-Mahdī ʿUbayd Allāh
al-Mahdī, Abū ʿAbd Allāh Muḥammad (ʿAbbāsid(e)) i, 59b, 103b, 107b, 402b, 550b, 710b, 897a; ii, 143b, 159b, 234b, 281b, 305a; iii, 20a, 22a, 232b, 265b, 616a, 749b, 876a, 996a, 1015b; iv, 88b, 645a, 838a, 939b, 940b, 1164a; v, 69b, 1233a, **1238a**; s, 17b, 35a, 48b, 89a, 94a, 199a, 225b, 304b, 326b, 352a — I, 61a, 106b, 110b, 414a, 568a, 732a, 923b; II, 147b, 164b, 241b, 289b, 313b; III, 21a, 23a, 239b, 273a, 636b, 772b, 900a, 1021a, 1041a; IV, 92b, 671b, 871a, 972b, 973b, 1196a; V, 71b, 1223b, **1228b**; S, 17b, 35b, 49a, 89a, 93b, 199a, 225b, 304a, 326a, 352a
al-Mahdī, Muḥammad b. Hishām Abu ʾl-Walīd (Umayyad(e)) i, 84b; ii, 485b; iii, 495b; v, 1107b, **1239a**; s, 153a — I, 86b; II, 498a; III, 512b; V, 1103b, **1230a**; S, 153a
al-Mahdī (Sudanese/Soudanais) → Muḥammad Aḥmad b. ʿAbd Allāh
Mahdī ʿAlī Khān iv, 170b; v, **1240a** — IV, 178a; V, **1230b**
Mahdī Baḥr al-ʿUlūm, Sayyid s, 157b — S, 158a
Mahdī Khān Astarābādī iv, 69b; v, **1240a** — IV, 73a; V, **1231a**
Mahdī Ḳulī Hidāyat v, 24b — V, 25b
Mahdī Ḳulī Khān iv, 573a — IV, 596a
al-Mahdī li-dīn Allāh Aḥmad b. al-Ḥusayn (Zaydī Imām) v, **1241a** — V, **1231b**
al-Mahdī li-Dīn Allāh Aḥmad b. Yaḥyā (Zaydī Imām) v, **1241a** — V, **1232a**
al-Mahdī li-Dīn Allāh Aḥmad b. al-Ḥasan b. al-Ḳāsim (Zaydī Imām) i, 554a; v, **1241b** — I, 571b; V, **1232b**
Mahdī b. Tawālā ii, 874a — II, 894b
Mahdī Ḳuli Sulṭān i, 240a — I, 247b
al-Mahdī ʿUbayd Allāh (Fāṭimid(e)) i, 48a, 104a, 249a, 1175b, 1178b, 1238a; ii, 168b, 453a, b, 850b, 852a, b, 860b, 861b; iii, 123b, 785a; iv, 198a, b, 204a, 458b, 660b; v, 1175a, 1237b, **1242a**, 1246a; s, 236b — I, 49b, 107a, 257a, 1210b, 1213b, 1275b; II, 174a, 464b, 465b, 870b, 872a, b, 880a, 881b; III, 126b, 808b; IV, 207a, 213a, 479a, 687a; V, 1165a, 1228a, **1233a**, 1236b; S, 236b
Mahdid(e)s i, 552b; iii, 125b; v, **1244a** — I, 570a; III, 128b; V, **1235a**
al-Mahdiyya (movement/mouvement Sudan) ii, 63b, 124a; iii, 5a; iv, 952b; v, 267b, **1247b** — II, 64b, 127a; III, 5a; IV, 985a; V, 265b, **1238b**
al-Mahdiyya (town/ville Morocco/Maroc) i, 356a; iii, 500a; v, **1245a**; s, 144b — I, 367a; III, 517a; V, **1236a**; S, 144a
al-Mahdiyya (town/ville Tunisia/Tunisie) i, 163b, 700a, 830a, 1319b; ii, 853a, 862b, 956a; iii, 138b, 470b; iv, 460a; v, 1243a, **1246a**; s, 11a — I, 168a, 721a, 853a, 1359b; II, 873a, 882b, 978a; III, 141a, 486b; IV, 480a; V, 1234a, **1236b**; S, 10b
al-Mahdjar v, **1253a** — V, **1244a**
Maḥdjūr iii, 50a — III, 52a
Maḥfūr iv, 897b — IV, 930b
Maḥfūz iii, 26b — III, 27b
Maḥfūz ʿAlī al-Bārūnī s, 15b — S, 15b
Maḥfūz, Nadjib v, 190b, 191a, b — V, 187b, 188b
Māh-i Mulk Khātūn s, 65a — S, 65b
Māhī Sawār ii, 32a — II, 32b
Mahīm (Maham) v, **1257b** — V, **1248b**
Māhīm v, **1258a** — V, **1249a**
Mahisur, Maysūr iii, 428a; v, 1216a, **1258b** — III, 442a; V, 1206a, **1249a**
- monuments v, 1259b — V, 1250b
Māhiyya i, 513b, 514a, 785a; v, **1261a** — I, 529b, 808a; V, **1252a**

End of volume V/Fin du volume V

Maḥmal iii, 34a — III, 35b
Maḥmashādh iv, 669a — IV, 696a
Maḥmūd (Samarḳand) s, 65a — S, 65b
Maḥmūd, Sayyid (Nīshāpūr) s, 360a — S, 360a
Maḥmūd II (Bengal) ii, 486b — II, 498b
Maḥmūd III (Bengal) iii, 422b — III, 436a
Maḥmūd Shāh I, Nāṣir al-Dīn (Dihlī) i, 1194b, 1300a, 1322b; ii, 260a, 267b, 268a, 274b, 609b, 973a, 1047b; iv, 749b; v, 546a; s, 124a — I, 1229b, 1340a, 1363a; II, 269a, 275b, 276a, 283a, 624b, 995a, 1072a; IV, 779b; V, 551a; S, 123a
Maḥmud II Nāsir al-Dīn Ṭughluḳ (Dihlī) i, 1068b; ii, 218b, 270a, 276b, 498b, 1125a; iii, 417b; iv, 533b, 543a; s, 206b — I, 1101a; II, 225b, 278b, 284b, 511a, 1151b; III, 430b; IV, 557a, 566b; S, 206a
Maḥmud I Begra (Gudjarāt) i, 924a, 1068b, 1200a; ii, 10b, 54a, 597b, 678a, 814b, 1127a; iii, 421b; v, 26b, 1216b — I, 952a, 1101a, 1235b; II, 11a, 55a, 612a, 695a, 834a, 1153b; III, 435b; V, 27a, 1206b
Maḥmud III (Gudjarāt) i, 1135b; ii, 1128b; iv, 901b — I, 1170a; II, 1155a; IV, 934b

Maḥmūd I Khaldji (Malwā) i, 924a, 1200a; ii, 12b, 219a, b, 1125b; iii, 418b, 638b; v, 1a; s, 280a – I, 952a, 1235b; II, 13a, 226a, 1153a; III, 431b, 660a; V, 1a; S, 279b
Maḥmūd II Khaldjī (Malwā) i, 914b; ii, 12b, 1128a; iii, 421b – I, 942b; II, 13a, 1154b; III, 435a
Maḥmūd I (Ottoman) i, 56a, 776a; iv, 900b; v, 643b – I, 58a, 799a; IV, 933a; V, 647b
Maḥmūd II (Ottoman) i, 61a, 399a, 790b, 836b, 948a; ii, 209b, 684a, 714a; iii, 91a, 628b; iv, 295b; v, 19a, 36a, 816a, 903b, 1084b; s, 168a, 211b – I, 63a, 410b, 814a, 859b, 977b; II, 216a, 701b, 732b; III, 93b, 649b; IV, 308b; V, 19b, 37a, 822a, 909b, 1082a; S, 168a, 211b
- reforms/réformes i, 469a, 657a, 778b, 783a, 837b, 838a, 905b, 972b, 1226a, 1304a; ii, 202a, 207a, 339a, 512b, 513b, 519b, 563a, 615a, 641b, 724a, 907b, 1091a; iii, 203b, 384b, 552b, 1153b, 1257b – I, 483a, 678a, 801b, 806a, 861a, b, 933a, 1002b, 1262b, 1344a; II, 208b, 213b, 349a, 525b, 526b, 532b, 577a, 630a, 657b, 742b, 929a, 1116b; III, 209a, 397a, 571b, 1182a, 1290b
Maḥmūd I b. Turkān Khātūn (Saldjūḳ) i, 1051b, 1070b; s, 384a – I, 1083a, 1103a; S, 384a
Maḥmūd II (Saldjūḳ) i, 300a, 353b, 858b; ii, 894a; iii, 195a, 345a, 1118b, 1255b; iv, 29a, 466a; s, 3a – I, 309b, 364a, 882b; II, 914b; III, 200a, 355b, 1146b, 1288b; IV, 31a, 487a; S, 2a
Maḥmūd b. ʿAbd al-Djabbār i, 82b – I, 85a
Maḥmūd b. Abī Saʿīd i, 148a, 852b; iii, 483b; iv, 410a; v, 389a – I, 152b, 876a; III, 500b; IV, 428a; V, 389b
Mahmūd b. Aḥmad al-kwstī of/de Ḳalhāt iv, 500b – IV, 522a
Maḥmūd b. ʿAlī s, 83a – S, 83a
Maḥmūd b. Būrī → Shihāb al-Dīn Maḥmūd
Maḥmūd b. Ghulām Muḥammad Ṭarzī iii, 13b – III, 14a
Maḥmūd b. Ḥamza al-Hamzāwī ii, 182b – II, 188b
Maḥmūd b. al-Malāḥimī s, 393a – S, 393b
Maḥmūd b. Malikshāh → Maḥmud I (Saldjūḳ)
Maḥmūd b. Mīrways i, 229a, b, 1008b; ii, 1001a; iii, 604a, b; iv, 37a, 537a – I, 236a, b, 1039b; II, 1024b; III, 624b, 625a; IV, 39b, 560b
Maḥmūd b. Muḥammad b. Malikshāh → Maḥmūd II (Saldjūḳ)
Maḥmūd b. Nāṣir Raʾīsiyya ii, 29b – II, 30a
Maḥmūd b. Naṣr → Rashīd al-Dawla Maḥmūd
Maḥmūd b. Sebüktigin i, 217b, 226b, 424b, 506b, 662a, 780a, 1020a, 1036b, 1068b, 1130b, 1194a, 1218b, 1300a, 1356a; ii, 119b, 308b, 488b, 597a, 730a, 799a, 809b, 919a, 972b, 1043b, 1049a, 1050b, 1099b, 1123b; iii, 195a, 196b, 197b, 255b, 347b, 415b, 1113b; iv, 24b, 189b, 294b, 410a, 543a, 1066b, 1150b; v, 956b, 1028b; s, 125b, 252b, 253b, 280a, 284b, 305a – I, 223b, 233b, 436b, 522a, 683a, 803a, 1051a, 1068a, 1100b, 1164b, 1229b, 1255a, 1339b, 1395a; II, 122b, 317b, 500b, 612a, 749a, 818a, 828b, 940a, 994b, 1068a, 1073b, 1075a, 1125b, 1150a; III, 199b, 201a, 202b, 263a, 358b, 428b, 1141a; IV, 26a-b, 197b, 307b, 427b, 566b, 1098a, 1182b; V, 960b, 1024b; S, 124b, 252b, 253b, 280a, 284b, 304b
Maḥmūd b. Turghut Oghlu iv, 624b – IV, 649a
Maḥmūd b. Walī s, 227b, 419b – S, 227b, 419b
Maḥmūd b. Zangī, Nūr al-Dīn i, 150a, 197a, 198b, 215a, 446b, 639a, 664b, 791b, 797a, 971a, 1017a, 1025a, 1224a, 1332a, b, 1349a; ii, 64b, 111a, 126a, 283a, 318a, b, 347b, 354b, 856b; iii, 87a, 109b, 208b, 228b, 399a, 504a, 681b, 714a; iv, 482a, 1088a; v, 104a, 924b, 1129a; s, 195a – I, 154a, 202b, 204b, 221b, 459b, 660a, 684b, 815a, 820b, 1001a, 1048b, 1056b, 1260b, 1372b, 1373a, 1389b; II, 66a, 113b, 129a, 291a, 327b, 357b, 364a, 876b; III, 89b, 112a, 214a, 235a, 411b, 521a, 703b, 736b; IV, 503a, 1119a; V, 106a, 930a, 1125a; S, 195a
Maḥmūd Aḥmad i, 735a, 765a, 929b; ii, 124a; v, 267b, 268a, 1250b, 1251a, b – I, 757a, 788a, 958a; II, 127a; V, 265b, 1241a, 1242a
Maḥmūd Ālūsī-zāde → Maḥmūd Shukrī
Maḥmūd ʿAyyād iv, 1153b – IV, 1185b
Maḥmud Barzandjī, Shaykh v, 466b, 467a, b – V, 469b, 470a
Maḥmūd Beg (Ḳarāmān-oghlu) iv, 621b – IV, 646a
Maḥmūd of/de Betl-Kakhab rosso i, 765a – I, 778b
Maḥmūd Bey iii, 636a – III, 657a
Maḥmūd Djalāl al-Dīn iv, 1125b – IV, 1157a
Maḥmūd Gawān i, 199a, 924a, b, 925a, 1200a, 1323a; iii, 15a, 421a, 577a, 1159b; v, 1135a – I, 204b, 952a, b, 953a, 1235b, 1363b; III, 15b, 434b, 597a, 1187b; V, 1130b
Maḥmūd Ghalzai → Maḥmūd b. Mīrways
Maḥmūd Ghazān → Ghazān Khān
Maḥmūd of/de Ghazna → Maḥmūd b. Sebuktigin
Maḥmūd Ghizhduwānī s, 46b – S, 47a
Maḥmūd Ghūrī ii, 752a, 1103a; iv, 917b – II, 770a, 1129a; IV, 950b
Maḥmūd Gokaldāsh i, 628a, 1192a – I, 648b, 1227b
Maḥmūd al-Hamzāwī iii, 156a – III, 159b
Maḥmūd Ḥasan ii, 437a; v, 7a – II, 448b; V, 7b
Maḥmūd Ḳābādū iv, 1153b – IV, 1185b
Maḥmūd Karantao ii, 1003b – II, 1027a
Maḥmūd Kārī i, 1342b; iii, 355b – I, 1382b; III, 366b
Maḥmud II Khān (Ḳarākhānid(e)) iii, 1114b, 1116b; iv, 581b; v, 45b – III, 1142a, 1144a; IV, 604b; V, 47a
Maḥmūd Khān Lōdī, Masnad-i ʿAlī s, 73b – S, 74a
Maḥmūd Khān Māzandarānī Mushīr al-Wizāra s, 23b – S, 24a
Maḥmūd Khān b. Nāṣir i, 1006a – I, 1037a
Maḥmūd Khān Rohillā i, 1206a – I, 1242a
Maḥmūd Kokaltāsh → Maḥmūd Gokaldāsh
Maḥmūd Langāh iii, 633a, 634a – III, 654a, 655a
Maḥmūd al-Malāḥimī s, 25b – S, 25b
Maḥmūd Mukhtār Pasha iv, 284a – IV, 296a
Maḥmūd Nadīm Pasha i, 56b, 285b; iii, 250b, 621a; iv, 681b – I, 58a, 294a; III, 257b, 641b; IV, 709b
Maḥmūd Pasha → al-Falakī; Ḳara Maḥmūd; Ṭayyār
Maḥmūd Pasha Welī ii, 691a, 722b; iv, 230a, 1017a; s, 282b – II, 708b, 741a; IV, 240b, 1049a; S, 282b
Maḥmūd Pasīkhānī iii, 600b – III, 621b
Maḥmūd Riyāḍ s, 240b – S, 241a
Maḥmūd Samarḳandī ii, 678a – II, 695a
Maḥmūd-i Shabistarī iv, 67b – IV, 71a
Maḥmūd Shāh (Bahmanī) i, 923b, 1047a; iii, 15a, 421a, 1159b – I, 951b, 1078b; III, 16a, 434b, 1188a
Maḥmūd Shāh (Özbeg) i, 853a; ii, 30b – I, 876b; II, 31a
Maḥmūd Shāh Durrāni i, 230b; ii, 637b, 839a – I, 237b; II, 635b, 858b
Maḥmūd Shāh Īndjū iii, 1208a – III, 1239a
Maḥmūd Shāh Khaldjī → Maḥmūd I Khaldjī
Maḥmūd Shāh Sharḳī ii, 270b, 499a; iii, 419b – II, 279a, 511b; III, 433a
Maḥmūd Shewket Pasha i, 64a; ii, 15b, 431a, 531a, 682b, 698b; iii, 204a, 595a, 994a; iv, 296b, 297a – I, 65b; II, 15b, 422b, 544a, 699b, 716b; III, 209b, 615b, 1018b; IV, 310a
Maḥmud Shukri al-Alūsī i, 425b, 596b – I, 437a, 616a
Maḥmūd Ṭarabī i, 1295a; v, 858a – I, 1335a; V, 865a
Maḥmūd Ṭarzī s, 65b, 109b – S, 66a, 109a
Maḥmūd Ṭayyār → Ṭayyār Maḥmūd Pasha
Maḥmūd Tughluḳ → Maḥmūd II (Dihlī)

Maḥmūd Urmewī ii, 345b; v, 5a — II, 355a; V, 5a
Maḥmūd Yalavač ii, 2b, 791b; iv, 1020a; v, 38b, 858a — II, 2b, 810b; IV, 1052a; V, 39b, 865a
Maḥmūd Zarkūn i, 280a, 289a — I, 288b, 298a
Maḥmūdabād ii, 1127a, 1129a; iii, 445b — II, 1153b, 1155b; III, 460a
Maḥmūdek Khān iv, 723a, 849a — IV, 752a, 882a
Maḥmūdī (Kurd(e)s) v, 460a — V, 462b
al-Maḥmūdiyya s, 371a — S, 371a
Mahr i, 172b, 174a, 209a — I, 177b, 179a, 215b
Mahra i, 110b, 543b; iii, 9a, 652a; v, 184a; s, 339b — I, 113b, 560b; III, 9b, 673a; V, 181b; S, 339a
Mahrattās → Marāṭhās
Mahrī i, 575a; iii, 176b; s, 339b — I, 593b; III, 180b; S, 339a
Mahriyya iii, 666a, 667b — III, 678b, 689b
Māhrū iv, 758b — IV, 789a
Mahsatī iv, 62a — IV, 65b
Mahsūd(e)s s, 285a — S, 285a
Maḥw iv, 277a — IV, 289a
Maḥyā i, 1040a — I, 1071b
Māʾi Daya Kawr i, 432b — I, 445a
Maimonides, Abraham iv, 305a, 306a, b — IV, 318b, 319b, 320a
Maimonides, Moses → Ibn Maymūn
Maʿīn i, 525a, 548a — I, 540b, 565b
Main, la → Yad
Maʿīn, Banū v, 183b — V, 180b, 181a
Maʿīn al-Din i, 803a — I, 826a
Mainu Kano, Malam iv, 549b — IV, 573b
Majorca/Majorque→ Mayurka
Maḳābir Ḳuraysh → Kāẓimayn
Maḳʿad ii, 114b — II, 117a
Maḳāla ii, 802a — II, 821a
Maḳām iii, 83b — III, 86a
Maḳām Ibrāhīm iv, 317b, 318a, b — IV, 331b, 332a, 333a
Maḳām-i Aʿlā i, 918a — I, 946a
Maḳāma iii, 106b, 221b, 373a; iv, 64a; s, 267a — III, 109a, 228a, 384b; IV, 67a; S, 266b
Maḳāmāt ii, 246a; iii, 899a — II, 253a; III, 923a
Mākān b. Kākī i, 688a, 866a, 867a, 1350a; ii, 928a; iii, 255a, 1157a; iv, 23a; v, 158a; s, 357a — I, 709a, 890a, 891a, 1390b; II, 949b; III, 262b, 1185b; IV, 24b; V, 157b; S, 357a
Makanpur s, 358b — S, 358b
Makarfi, Malam Shuʾaibu iii, 283a — III, 291b
Makāri → Kotoko
Makassar iii, 1219b; v, 1155a; s, 151a, 199b, 201b — III, 1250b; V, 1145a; S, 151a, 199b, 201b
Maḳbūl iii, 26b — III, 27b
Maḳdishū iii, 3a; iv, 885b; v, 131b — III, 3b; IV, 918a; V, 134a
al-Maḳdisī, ʿAbd al-Ghanī iii, 161a, 735a, 752a, 842b — III, 164b, 758a, 775a, 866b
al-Maḳdisī, ʿAbd al-Karīm b. ʿAbd al-Raḥmān iv, 511a — IV, 533a
al-Maḳdisī, Abū ʿAbd Allāh (d./m. 1000) → al-Muḳaddasī
al-Maḳdisī, Abū ʿAbd Allāh (d./m.1343) iii, 763a — III, 786b
al-Maḳdisī, Abū Bakr b. Muḥammad iv, 511a — IV, 533a
al-Maḳdisī, Abū Sulayman Muḥammad iii, 1071b; v, 330a — III, 1098a; V, 330a
al-Maḳdisī, Diyāʾ al-Dīn s, 195b — S, 195b
al-Maḳdisī, Ibrāhim b. ʿAlī iv, 511a — IV, 533a
al-Maḳdisī, Muḥammad b. ʿAlī i, 949b — I, 979a
al-Maḳdisī, Naṣr b. Ibrāhīm s, 326a — S, 325b
al-Makhaḍīb → al-Mukhaḍḍaba
al-Makhāʾī → ʿAlī b. ʿUmar al-Shādhilī
Makhāziniyya iv, 456b — IV, 477a
Makhāridj iii, 598a — III, 618b
al-Makhdūm → Sharīf Awliyā Karīm
Makhdūm Djahāniyān s, 10b — S, 10b
Makhdūm Ḥāmid Gandj Bakhsh ii, 186b — II, 192b
Makhdūm Ḳuli iv, 853b; v, 859b — IV, 886b; V, 866b
Makhdūm al-Mulk → ʿAbd Allāh Sulṭānpūrī
Makhiwal s, 361a — S, 360b
Makhkhan Singh iii, 336a — III, 346a
Makhlad b. Kaydād al-Nukkārī → Abū Yazīd al-Nukkārī
Makhrama, Bā i, 255b; iii, 881a — I, 263b; III, 905a
Mākhūkh, Banū iii, 138a — III, 141a
Makḥūl b. Abī Muslim al-Dimashḳī iv, 356b, 369a — IV, 372a, 385b
Makhzan i, 79b, 288b, 355b, 368b, 369a, 1145b, 1191a; ii, 146a, 326b, 510a, b; v, 48b, 1191a, 1192b, 1193a, 1198b; s, 336b — I, 82a, 297b, 366a, 379b, 380a, 1180a, 1226b; II, 150a, 336b, 522b, 523a; V, 50a, 1181a, 1182b, 1183a, 1188b; S, 336a
Makhzen → Makhzan
Makhzūm, Banū i, 9a, 115b; iii, 3b, 975b; s, 32b — I, 9a, 118b; III, 3b, 1000a; S, 33a
al-Makhzūmī v, 863a — V, 870a
Maʿḳil i, 93b, 211a, 355b, 356a, 374b, 533a; ii, 134a; iii, 256b, 288b, 300b; v, 1196b — I, 95b, 217a, 366b, 385b, 549b; II, 137a; III, 265a, 297b, 310a; V, 1187a
Maʿḳil b. ʿĪsā iv, 718b; s, 122b — IV, 747b; S, 122a
Maʿḳil b. Ḳays al-Riyāḥī v, 19b — V, 20a
Maʿḳil b. Sinān al-Ashdjaʿī iii, 226b, 227a — III, 233b, 234a
al-Makīn b. al-ʿAmīd s, 396a, 400a — S, 396b, 400b
Mākisīn iv, 898a — IV, 930b
Makk i, 1171b; ii, 615a — I, 1206b; II, 630b
Makka i, 12a, 35a, 55a, 77a, 80a, 136a, 151b, 549a, 551b, 552b, 890b, 976a, 1032b, 1232b; ii, 453a, 854a; iii, 33b, 260a, 362a; iv, 318b, 321b, 335b; v, 77a; s, 3b, 106a, 198b, 267b, 278b — I, 12a, 36a, 57a, 79a, 82b, 140a, 155b, 566b, 569a, 570b, 916b, 1006a, 1064a, 1269b; II, 465a, 874a; III, 35a, 267a, 373b; IV, 332b, 335b, 350a; V, 79b; S, 3a, 105a, 198b, 267a, 278b
- literature/littérature i, 826b, 965b; ii, 91b, 590a, 757a, 829a; iii, 760a; v, 850a — I, 849b, 995b; II, 93a, 604b, 775b, 848b; III, 783b; V, 854b
al-Maḳḳarī, Abu ʾl-ʿAbbās Aḥmad i, 157a, 595a; iii, 814a; v, 1159b, 1160b; s, 223a, 381a — I, 161a, 614b; III, 837b; V, 1149b, 1150a; S, 223a, 381b
Makkhourēbi → Maghrāwa
al-Makkī → ʿAbd al-Wahhāb; Abū Ṭālib; Ibn Ḥumayd
Makkī, Banū v, 696a — V, 701a
Makkī b. Kāmil b. Djāmiʿ iv, 337b — IV, 351b
al-Makkiyya al-Fāsiyya → Madaniyya
al-Maklātī, Muḥammad b. Aḥmad iii, 468b — III, 484b
Maḳlūb iii, 26a — III, 27b
Makramat Khān i, 254a — I, 261b
Makramid(e)s i, 552b; ii, 517b; iii, 179b; iv, 201a — I, 570a; II, 530b, III, 183b; IV, 210a
Makrān i, 211b, 1005a; iii, 1121b; iv, 3b; v, 684a; s, 129a, 222a, 332a, b — I, 217b, 1036a; III, 1149a; IV, 4a; V, 689a; S, 128a, 222a, 331b, 332a
Makrand Ray i, 1042b — I, 1074a
Makrānī i, 1005a, 1007a — I, 1036a, 1038a
al-Maḳrīzi, Tāḳī al-Dīn i, 138b, 594b, 595a, 791a, 965b; ii, 107b, 327a, 328a; iii, 268b, 488b, 676a, 679b, 756b; v, 29b, 863a; s, 210b, 273b, 295a, 388b, 396a — I, 142b, 614a, 814b, 995a; II, 110a, 337a, 338a; III, 276a, 505b, 698a, 701a, 779b; V, 23a, 870a; S, 210a, 273a, 294b, 389a, 396b
Maks al-Manāh i, 170a; ii, 146a; iii, 1182b; iv, 134b — I, 174b; II, 150a; III, 1211b; IV, 140b
al-Maḳs s, 120b — S, 120a

Maḳṣūra i, 240a; ii, 115b — I, 24b; II, 118a
Maḳtaba iv, 635a; v, 38a, 43b, 159a, 261a, 338a, 371b, 641b, 890b, 1005a, 1125a, 1212b — IV, 661a; V, 33a, 45a, 158a, 259a, 338b, 372a, b, 646a, 897a, 1000b, 1001a, 1121b, 1202a
Maktabī iv, 1010a; v, 1105a — IV, 1042b; V, 1100b
Maḳtal iii, 374a — III, 386a
Maḳṭūʿ ii, 563b; iii, 25b — II, 577b; III, 27a
Maktūbāt ii, 55b, 56a — II, 56b, 57a
Maktūm b. Baṭī b. Suhayl ii, 619a — II, 634b
Makurra i, 1029a — I, 1060b
al-Maḳwa s, 50a — S, 50b
Māl ii, 148a, 150b; iv, 1034a — II, 152b, 155a; IV, 1066a
Māl al-bayʿa iii, 1201b — III, 1231b
Māl Khātūn i, 348a — I, 358b
Māla ii, 905b — II, 926b
Malabar iv, 547; v, 360a, 937a — IV, 570b; V, 361a, 941a
Malacca i, 979a, b; iii, 1218b, 1219b, 1225b; iv, 467b; s, 199b — I, 1009b, 1010a; III, 1249a, 1250b, 1257a; IV, 488b; S, 199b
Malachite → al-Dahnadj
Malaga → Mālaḳa
Malāḥim ii, 377a — II, 387a
Malak Ṭāʾūs i, 263a — I, 271a
Mālaḳa i, 6a, 43b, 1321a; ii, 747b; iii, 498b, 500a, 681a; s, 381b — I, 6a, 6b, 45a, 1361a; II, 766a; III, 515b, 517a, 703a; S, 382a
Malāmatiyya i, 313a, 794b, 1137a, 1239b, 1245a; ii, 395a, 963b; iii, 132a, 662b, 899a; iv, 46a, 472b, 473a, 1109b; s, 361a — I, 322b, 818a, 1171b, 1277b, 1283a; II, 405b, 985b; III, 134b, 684a, 923b; IV, 49a, 493a, 494a, 1141a; S, 361a
Mālamīr → Īdhadj
Mālān → Mālīn
Malāryā v, 867a — V, 873b
Malay language/Malais i, 41b, 88a, 92a; ii, 27b, 549b; iii, 377a, 1215b, 1216a, 1220a, 1231a, 1234a; iv, 1128a; v, 205a — I, 42b, 90b, 94b; II, 28a, 563b; III, 388b, 1246b, 1247a, 1251a, 1263a, 1266a; IV, 1159b; V, 202b
Malaya/Malaisie i, 41b, 979a; iii, 377a, 385a, 502b, 1214b, 1219b; v, 226a, b, 227a, 228a, b; s, 220b — I, 42b, 1009b; III, 388b, 397b, 520a, 1245a, 1250b; V, 224a, b, 225b, 226a, b; S, 220b
Malays s, 150b — S, 150b
Malāzgird → Mantzikert
Maldives iii, 385a, 407a; iv, 547a, 1085b; v, 587a — III, 397b, 419b; IV, 570b, 1116b; V, 661b
Malfūẓāt ii, 55b; iii, 435b — II, 56b; III, 449b
Malḥam b. Ḥaydar ii, 635b — II, 651b
Malḥam b. Maʿn ii, 635a — II, 651a
Malhar Rāo Holkar iii, 60b — III, 62b
Malḥūn i, 571b; v, 1207a — I, 590a; V, 1197b
Mālī ii, 63a, 94a; iii, 276a, 657a; iv, 313b; s, 218a, 295b — II, 64a, 96a; III, 284a, 678b; IV, 327b; S, 217b, 295a
Māli-Amīr → Īdhadj
al-Malik ii, 858a; iv, 818b; v, 627b — II, 877b; IV, 851a; V, 631b
Malik b. Adham al-Bāhilī iv, 447a — IV, 467a
Mālik b. al-ʿAdjlān i, 771a; iv, 1187b; v, 995a — I, 794a; IV, 1220a; V, 990a
Malik b. ʿAli al-Barānī, Shāh (Djand) s, 245b — S, 245b
Mālik b. ʿAlī al-Ḳaṭanī i, 600a — I, 619b
Mālik b. ʿAlī al-Khuzāʿī s, 122b — S, 122a
Mālik b. ʿAmr al-Ḥimyarī v, 315a — V, 314b
Mālik b. Anas i, 164a, 280a, 338b, 412a, 550b, 588b, 685a, 773b, 957b, 966b, 1244b; ii, 889b; iii, 23b, 24a, 763b, 811a, 817a, 963a; iv, 146a, 257a, 718a; v, 711b, 712a, 731b, 997b; s, 384b — I, 169a, 288b, 349a, 424a, 568a, 607b, 706a, 796b, 987a, 996a, 1282a; II, 910a; III, 25a, 786b, 834a, 840b, 987b; IV, 152a, 268b, 747a; V, 716b, 717a, 736b, 993a; S, 385a
Mālik b. Asmāʾ b. Khāridja iv, 1002b — IV, 1035a
Mālik b. ʿAwf al-Naṣrī ii, 627a; iii, 286a, 578a — II, 643a; III, 294b, 598a
Mālik b. Badr al-Fazārī s, 177b — S, 178b
Malik b. Dīnār i, 1080b — I, 1113a
Mālik b. Fahm, Banū iv, 500b — IV, 522a
Mālik b. al-Ḥārith al-Nakhaʿī → al-Ashtar
Mālik b. Ḥudhayfa b. Badr al-Fazārī s, 178b — S, 179b
Mālik b. Mismaʿ i, 964b; iii, 540a — I, 994a; III, 559a
Mālik b. Rabīʿa b. Riyāḥ al-Hilālī s, 92b — S, 92b
Mālik b. Ṭawḳ i, 751b, 1289b; s, 122b — I, 773b, 1329a; S, 122a
Mālik b. Zuhayr s, 177b — S, 178b
al-Malik al-ʿĀdil → al-ʿĀdil I, II
al-Malik al-Afḍal → al-Afḍal b. Ṣalāḥ al-Dīn
Malik Aḥmad Baḥrī → Aḥmad Niẓām Shāh
Malik Aḥmad Ghāzī → Dānishmend
Malik Aḥmad Pasha v, 461a — V, 463b
Malik Altūniya i, 1194a; ii, 973a — I, 1229b; II, 995a
Malik ʿAnbar i, 81a, 768a, 781b, 1204a; ii, 158b; iii, 15b, 202b, 424a, 426b; iv, 1018a, 1023a — I, 83b, 791a, 804b, 1239b; II, 163b; III, 16a, 208a, 437b, 440b; IV, 1050a, 1055a
Malik Andīl → Fīrūz Shāh, Sayf al-Dīn
Malik ʿArab → ʿArab
Malik Arslān b. Masʿūd → Arslān Shāh b. Masʿūd
Malik Arslan b. Sulaymān ii, 239b — II, 246b
al-Malik al-Ashraf (Ayyubid(e)) → al-Ashraf, al-Malik
Malik Ashraf (Cobanid(e)) i, 325a; ii, 401a; iii, 1208b — I, 335a; II, 411b; III, 1239a
Malik Ashraf Shaʿbān → Shaʿban II
Malik Ayāz ii, 322a, 1127b, 1128a — II, 331b, 1154a, b
al-Malik al-ʿAzīz b. Djalāl → al-ʿAzīz b. Djalāl al-Dawla
al-Malik al-ʿAzīz Ghiyāth al-Dīn iii, 934a — III, 958b
al-Malik al-ʿAzīz ʿUthmān → al-ʿAzīz ʿUthmān (Ayyubid(e))
al-Malik al-ʿAzīz Yūsuf → Yūsuf b. Barsbāy
Malik Bahrām v, 782b — V, 789a
Malik Dīnār (d./m. 1195) → Dīnār, Malik
Malik Dīnār (d./m. 1319) → Ẓafar Khān (Gudjarāt)
Malik Djuwān i, 769a; ii, 134b — I, 792a; II, 138a
Malik Firūz v, 782b, 783a — V, 789a, b
Malik Ghāzī v, 172b — V, 170a
Malik Hifnī Nāṣif → Nāṣif
Malik Kāfūr → Kāfūr Hazārdīnārī
Malik Kālā v, 782b, 783a — V, 789a
al-Malik al-Kāmil I Nāṣir al-Dīn (Ayyūbid(e)) i, 14b, 198a, 665a, 765b, 766a, 798b, 799a, b, 800b, 803a, 804a, 940b; ii, 65b, 126a, 292b, 347b, 911b; iii, 504a, 747a; iv, 200b, **520a**, 818a; v, 331a; s, 197a, 392b, 407b — I, 15a, 203b, 684b, 788b, 789a, 822a, b, 824a, 826a, 828a, 969a; II, 66b, 129a, 300b, 357b, 933a; III, 521a 770a; IV, 209b, **543a**, 850b; V, 331a; S, 197a, 393a, 407b
al-Malik al-Kāmil II (Ayyūbid(e)) iv, **521a** — IV, **544a**
Malik Khurram ii, 405b — II, 416b
Malik Ḳummī i, 1203a — I, 1238b
Malik Maḥmūd Mengüček iv, 871a — IV, 904b
al-Malik al-Manṣūr ʿUmar (Rasūlid(e)) s, 338b — S, 338a
al-Malik al-Masʿūd (Artuḳid(e)) s, 250a — S, 250a
al-Malik al-Masʿūd Yūsuf (Ayyūbid(e)) i, 552b — I, 570b

al-Malik al-Muʾayyad → Abu ʾl-Fidā
al-Malik al-Muʿaẓẓam Sharaf al-Dīn (Ayyūbid(e)) i, 198a, 434b, 780b, 799a, b, 804a, 1124b; ii, 284a; iii, 399b, 747a, 962a, 967a; iv, 520b, 779a, 842a; v, 331a, 925a — I, 203b, 446b, 803b, 822b, 823a, 828a, 1158b; II, 292a; III, 412a, 770a, 991b; IV, 543a, 810b, 875a; V, 331a, 930b
Malik Muḥammad (Dānishmend) → Muḥammad b. Ghāzī
Malik Muḥammad Djāyasī iii, 457a — III, 472b
Malik Muḥammad Nādjī s, 366a — S, 366a
Malik al-Mutakallimīn iv, 789a — IV, 820b
Malik Muẓaffar b. Bahrāmshāh → Malik Ghāzī
al-Malik al-Muẓaffar ʿUmar i, 197b, 798b, 1160b; ii, 347b; iii, 120a, 683b; iv, 614a, 640b — I, 203b, 822a, 1195b; II, 357b; III, 122b, 705a; IV, 638b, 667a
Malik Nāʾib → Kāfūr Hazārdīnārī
al-Malik al-Nāṣir I → Ṣalāh al-Dīn
al-Malik al-Nāṣir II Yūsuf (Ayyūbid(e)) i, 804b; ii, 284a, b, 348a; iii, 87b, 186b, 187b, 399b, 933b, 989b; iv, 521a; s, 197a — I, 828b; II, 292a, b, 357b; III, 90a, 191a, b, 412a, 958a, 1014b; IV, 544a; S, 197a
al-Malik al-Nāṣir . . . → al-Nāṣir . . .
Malik Rādjā Fārūkī ii, 814a; iii, 417a; iv, 1023a — II, 833b; III, 430a; IV, 1055a
al-Malik al-Raḥīm → Khusraw Fīrūz
Malik al-Sādāt Ghāzī → Sayyid Masʿūd
al-Malik al-Saʿīd (Artukid(e)) → Ghāzī I (Artukid(e))
al-Malik al-Saʿīd (Mamlūk(e)) → al-Saʿīd Baraka Khān
al-Malik al-Ṣāliḥ (Samudra-Pasè) i, 742b; iii, 1218b, 1225b — I, 764b; III, 1249a, 1257a
al-Malik al-Ṣāliḥ Ayyūb → al-Ṣāliḥ Nadjm al-Dīn
al-Malik al-Ṣāliḥ Ismāʿīl → al-Ṣāliḥ ʿImād al-Dīn
Malik Sandjas → Alp Khān
Malik Sarwar ii, 270b, 498b, 1084b; iii, 14b, 417a, 419b; iv, 276b, 533b, 907b — II, 278b, 511a, 1110a; III, 15a, 430b, 432b; IV, 288b, 556b, 940b
Malik Shāh → Kh(w)ādja-i Djahān Turk
Malik Shāh I → Malikshāh
Malik Shāh III b. Maḥmūd iv, 1097a — IV, 1128a
Malik Shāh b. Tekish s, 246a — S, 246a
Malik Shīr Khān i, 1194b — I, 1229b
Malik al-shuʿarāʾ iv, 56a — IV, 59a
Mālik al-Ṭāʾī iii, 698b — III, 720b
Malik Tādj al-Dīn s, 105b — S, 105a
Malik al-Tudjdjār ii, 602a, 814b; v, 1258a — II, 616b, 834a; V, 1249a
Malik Yak Lakhī s, 105b — S, 105a
Malik Yāḳūt Sulṭānī iii, 16a — III, 17a
al-Malik al-Ẓāhir Ghāzī → al-Ẓāhir Ghāzī
Mālikāne i, 728a; iv, 1096a — I, 801b; IV, 1127a
al-Mālikī s, 306b — S, 306a
Malikī, Khalīl iii, 529a, b; s, 60b — III, 547b, 548a; S, 61a
Maliki b. Muḥammad ii, 1146b — II, 1173b
Mālikī madhhab i, 249b, 338b, 339a, 494a; ii, 618b, 828b, 859b, 1010a; iii, 6b, 17a, 308b, 350b, 695a; iv, 87a-b, 290a, 341a, 404b; v, 895b; s, 113a — I, 257a, 349a, b, 508b; II, 634a, 848a, 879b, 1033b; III, 6b, 18a, 318a, 361b, 717a; IV, 91a-b, 303a, 355b, 422a; V, 902a; S, 112b
Malikī → Djalālī
Malik-nāma i, 421a — I, 433a
Malikpur i, 1322b; ii, 260a — I, 1363a; II, 269a
Malikshāh i, 243b, 353a, 421a, 465b, 517a, 552a, 639b, 662b, 664a, 731a, 750b, 780b, 870a, 901a, 1051b, 1336b; ii, 282a, 344a, 347b, 384b, 397b, 406a; iii, 86b, 195a, 208b, 471b, 1114b, 1202a; iv, 27a-b, 28a, 101a, 458a, 807b; v, 159b; s, 14b, 73b, 94b, 383b — I, 250b, 363b, 432b, 479b, 532b, 569b, 660a, 683a, b, 753a, 773a, 803b, 894a, 928a, 1083a, b, 1376b; II, 290a, 354a, 357a, 394b, 408a, 417a; III, 89a, 199b, 214a, 488a, 1142a, 1232b; IV, 29a-b, 30a, 105b, 478b, 840a; V, 158b; S, 15a, 74a, 94a, 384a
Malīla i, 356b; iii, 298b; s, 325b — I, 367a; III, 308a; S, 325a
Mālīn i, 952b — I, 981b
Malindi iv, 887a, b, 888b — IV, 920a, b, 921b
Malinké ii, 63a; v, 252b; s, 295b — II, 64a, b; V, 250b; S, 295a
Māliyāt → Māl
Māliyye i, 1090b; ii, 83b — I, 1123a; II, 85a
Malkam Khān, Mīrzā (Nāẓim al-Dawla) ii, 650a; iii, 554b; iv, 72a, 73b, 164a, 397b, 788a; v, 919b, 1086a; s, 23b, 53b, 71b, 108b, 109a, 290b — II, 666a; III, 573b; IV, 76a, 77b, 171a, 415a, 820a; V, 925a, 1083b; S, 24a, 54a, 72a, 108a, b, 290b
Malkoč-oghullarí i, 340b — I, 351a
Malkum Khān, Mīrzā → Malkam Khān
Malla Khān iv, 631b; v, 30a — IV, 656b; V, 31a
Mallāḥ i, 181a; i, 230a — I, 186a; II, 237a
Mallel → Mālī
Malloum, General s, 166b — S, 166b
Mallū Iḳbāl Khān i, 1300a; iii, 417b; iv, 533b; s, 206a — I, 1340a; III, 430b; IV, 557a; S, 206a
Mallū Khān → Ḳādir Shāh
Malta/Malte i, 250b, 936a; ii, 801b; iii, 251b; s, 47b, 55a, 120b — I, 258b, 965a; II, 820b; III, 258b; S, 48a, 55b, 120a
Malthai → Maʿalthāyā
al-Maʿlūf, Fawzī iii, 112a; v, 1257a — III, 114b; V, 1248a
Maʿlūf, Louis iv, 525a — IV, 547b
al-Maʿlūf, Michel v, 1256a — V, 1247a
al-Maʿlūf, Shafīk v, 1256b, 1257a — V, 1247b, 1248a
Mālwā i, 208a, 923b, 924a, 1026a, 1155a; ii, 219a, 276a, 1125a; iii, 421a, b, 446a, 481b, 638a; v, 1216a; s, 105a, 280a, 331b — I, 214b, 951b, 952a, 1057b, 1189b; II, 225b, 284b, 1151b; III, 434b, 435a, 460b, 498a, 659b; V, 1206a; S, 104b, 279b, 331a
Malwiyya (river/rivière) v, 1185a, 1187a — V, 1175a, 1177a
al-Malzūzī → Abū Ḥātim al-Malzūzī
Mama Bonfoh iv, 352a — IV, 367a
Mamadu Djoue ii, 960a, 1132b — II, 982b, 1159a
Mamālīk iv, 36a, 976b, 977b, 1044a — IV, 38b, 1009a, 1010a, 1075a
Maʿmar Abu ʾl-Ashʿath s, 88b — S, 88b
Māmash i, 1217b — I, 1254a
Mamassanī iii, 1102b, 1106b; iv, 9a, 498b; v, 822a, 825a, 829b; s, 147b — III, 1129b, 1134a; IV, 10a, 520a; V, 828a, 831a, 835b; S, 147b
Mamay (Tatar(e)) i, 1107b — I, 1141a
Māmāy Bey iv, 723a — IV, 752a
Mamdūḥ v, 956a, 959b — V, 960a, 963b
Mamikonian i, 636b; ii, 679a — I, 657b; II, 696a
Māmiya al-Rūmī iv, 451b — IV, 471b
Mamlān i, 638a — I, 658b
Mamlūk i, 34a; ii, 506b — I, 34b; II, 519a
Mamlūks i, 33a, 34a, 63a, 182b, 468a, 666b, 786b, 804a, 905b, 910a, 971a, 1119b, 1138a, 1190b, 1288b; ii, 38a, 65b, 284b, 292b, 340a, 348a, 572a, 1043b, 1056b; iii, 120b, 402b; iv, 31b; v, 373b, 739b; s, 205b, 395b — I, 33b, 34b, 65a, 187b, 482a, 687a, 810a, 828b, 932b, 937b, 1001a, 1153a, 1172b, 1225b, 1328a; II, 38b, 66b, 292b, 300b, 350a, 357b, 586b, 1067b, 1081a; III, 123a, 415a; IV, 33b; V, 374b, 744b; S, 205b, 396a
- administration i, 34a, 102a, 435b, 444a, 765a, 816b, 1046a, 1349a; ii, 23b, 102b, 172b, 230a, 301b, 330a, 414a, 421b, 508b; iii, 48a, 346a, 758b, 773b; iv, 210a, 267b; v, 332a, b, 627b, 628a; s, 138a, 393a — I, 34b, 105a, 448a, 456b, 788a, 839b, 1077b, 1389b; II, 24b,

105a, 177b, 236b, 309b, 339b, 424b, 432b, 521a; III, 49b, 356b, 781b, 797a; IV, 219b, 279b; V, 332b, 631b, 632a; S, 137b, 393a
- art, architecture i, 1316b; iv, 430b; v, 218a, 1140b — I, 1358a; IV, 449b; V, 215b, 1133b
- history/histoire i, 1128a; iii, 775b, 813a; iv, 462b — I, 1162a; III, 798b, 836b; IV, 483a
- military/militaire i, 445b, 944b, 945b, 1058b, 1324b; ii, 130a, 444b; iii, 99a, 184a, 472b — I, 458b, 973b, 974b, 1090b, 1365b; II, 135b, 456a; III, 101b, 188a, 489a
al-Mammasī s, 306b — S, 306a
Mamūḳ b. Ibāḳ iv, 849a — IV, 882a
al-Maʾmūn (ʿAbbāsid(e)) i, 18a, 78a, 271a, b, 272b, 279a, 316a, 399b, 400a, 402b, 437a, 844a, 1280a; ii, 235a, 281b, 505b, 726b, 730b, 731a, 911a; iii, 173a, 228a, 231b, 234a, 243b, 618a, 987b, 1148a; iv, 17a, 45b, 645a, b, 939b, 940b; s, 15a, 22b, 26a, 32b, 35a, 88b, 144a, 252b, 263a, 338a, 384b, 408a — I, 18b, 80a, 279b, 280a, 281a, 288a, 325b, 411a, b, 414a, 449b, 867b, 1319a; II, 241b, 289b, 518b, 745a, 749b, 750a, 932b; III, 177a, 235a, 238a, 241a, 250b, 638b, 1012a, 1176b; IV, 18a-b, 48a, 671b, 972b, 973b; S, 15b, 23a, 26b, 33a, 35b, 88b, 144a, 252b, 263a, 337b, 385a, 408a
- reforms/réformes i, 589a, 114a; ii, 198a, 232a, 578a — I, 608a, 1175b; II, 204b, 238b, 592b
al-Maʾmūn (Almohad(e)) → Idrīs al-Maʾmūn
Maʾmūn I Khwarazmshāh ii, 1142a; iv, 1066b — II, 1169a; IV, 1098a
Maʾmūn II Khwarazmshāh i, 1236b; iv, 1066b — I, 1274a; IV, 1098a, b
al-Maʾmūn b. al-Baṭāʾiḥī → al-Baṭāʾiḥī
al-Maʾmūn b. Dhu ʾl-Nūn i, 6b, 986a; ii, 243a, 901a; iv, 665b — I, 6b, 1016b; II, 250a, 922a; IV, 692b
al-Maʾmūn b. Muḥammad al-Shaykh al-Mahdī i, 55b, 56a — I, 57b
Maʾmūnid(e)s iv, 1063b, 1066b — IV, 1095a, 1098a
Maʿmūr Khān, ʿAbd al-Karīm v, 600a — V, 603b
al-Maʿmūra → al-Mahdiyya
Maʿmūrat al-ʿAzīz iv, 1084b — IV, 1115b
Maʿmūriyye Ḳalʿesi i, 481a — I, 495b
Man → Insān
Maʿn, Banū i, 181b, 552a, 767a; ii, 634b, 635a, 749b; iv, 834b; v, 259a, 602a, 792b; s, 49b, 338a — I, 186b, 569b, 789b; II, 650b, 651a, 768a; IV, 867b; V, 257a, 606a; S, 50a, 337b
Maʿn b. Ḥātim iii, 125b — III, 128a
Maʿn b. Ṣumādiḥ iii, 740a — III, 763a
Maʿn b. Zāʾida i, 364a, 964b; iii, 892a; s, 338a, 386b — I, 375a, 994a; III, 916a; S, 337b, 386b
Mān Singh ii, 1144a; iii, 632a — II, 1171a; III, 653a
Maʿnā v, 320b, 321b — V, 320a, b
Manākha iii, 179a, 327a — III, 183a, 337a
Manāḳib v, 1209a — V, 1199b
al-Manāma i, 540a, 941a, b, 942b; s, 42a — I, 556b, 970a, b, 971b; S, 42b
Manār iv, 132b — IV, 138b
Manāra iv, 383b — IV, 400a
Manārat al-ʿAbd iv, 638a, b — IV, 664a, 665a
Manas iii, 116a — III, 118b
Manashshā i, 823b — I,846b
Manāṣīr, Banū i, 371a, 372a — I, 382a, 383a
Manāstir → Monastir
Manāstirli Meḥmed Rifʿat s, 359b — S, 359a
Manāt iii, 540b; iv, 322a; v, 692a, b, 995b — III, 559a; IV, 336a; V, 697a, b, 990b
Manāzil 1, 1225a; iii, 83b; iv, 517a — I, 1261b; III, 86a; IV, 539b
Manāẓir i, 98a — I, 101a
Manbidj i, 119b — I, 123a
al-Manbidjī, Naṣr al-Dīn iii, 952a — III, 976b
Mancus ii, 298b — II, 306b
Manda (island/île) iv, 885b; v, 655a — IV, 918a; V, 659a
Mandaeans → Ṣubba
Mandara ii, 114b — II, 117a
Mandesh ii, 1099b — II, 1125b
Mandīl v, 735a, 749b — V, 740b, 755a
Mandīl, Awlād v, 1180a — V, 1170a
Mandil b. ʿAbd al-Raḥmān v, 1180a — V, 1169b
Mandīl al-amān iii, 188a — iii, 192b
Mandingo ii, 1132a; iii, 275b; s, 295b — II, 1159a; III, 283b; S, 295a
Mandjak al-Nāṣirī iii, 775b, 818a — III, 798b, 841b
Mandjak al-Yūsufī iv, 425b — IV, 446a
Mandjanīḳ i, 658b; ii, 188a; iii, 201b, 469b, 472b, 482a — I, 679b; II, 194a; III, 207a, 486a, 489a, 499a
Māndjhan, Mīr Sayyid iii, 457a — III, 472b
Mandsore s, 331b — S, 331a
Māndū ii, 219a, 276b, 1128a; iii, 421b, 446a, 638a, b; v, 1216a — II, 226a, 285a, 1154b; III, 435a, 461a, 659a; V, 1206a
Mandūr, Muḥammad v, 1257b; s, 58b — V, 1248a; S, 59a
Manfalūṭ s, 40b, 383b — S, 41a, 384a
al-Manfalūṭī, Muṣṭafā Luṭfī i, 597a; iv, 159b; v, 188a — I, 616b; IV, 166b; V, 185b
Manfiyya → Mafia
Manfūḥa i, 628b — I, 649b
Mangat Rai i, 606b — I, 626a
Manghir ii, 118a — II, 121a
Mangishlaḳ s, 168b, 169a, 245b, 280b, 281a — S, 168b, 169a, 245b, 280b, 281a
Mangit Khāns i, 1295b; ii, 44b, 446a; v, 182a, 273b; s, 97a, b, 228a, 281a, 419b, 420a — I, 1335b; II, 45b, 458a; V, 179b, 271b; S, 96b, 97a, 228a, 281a, 420a
al-Manglī, Muhammad → Muḥammad al-Manglī
Mangū→ Möngke
Mangubars → Mengubars
Mangudjak → Mengüček
Mangūr i, 1217b — I, 1254a
Mangūtakīn i, 824b, 1042a; ii, 483b, 855a; iii, 77a, 130a; v, 820a, b, 928a — I, 847b, 1073b; II, 495b, 875a; III, 79b, 133a; V, 826b, 933b
Manhūk i, 671a — I, 692a
Manīʿ iii, 228a — III, 235a
Mānī i, 1212a — I, 1248a
Manīʿ b. Ḥassān iv, 911a — IV, 944a
Māniʿ b. Rabīʿa al-Muraydī i, 553a; ii, 320b, 321a — I, 571a; II, 330a
Manīc (river/rivière) s, 169a — S, 169a
Manichean/Manichéen i, 130a; iii, 885a; iv, 43b, 1025a; v, 853a — I, 134a; III, 909a; IV, 46a, 1057b; V, 859b
Maʿnid(e)s (peace/paix) s, 159a — S, 159a
Maʿnid(e)s → Maʿn, Banū
Manīkpūr s, 203a — S, 202b
Manila s, 152a — S, 152a
Manisa → Maghnisa
Mankalī-Bughā iii, 818a — III, 841b
Mankit → Mangit
Mankubirnī → Djalāl al-Dīn Khwārizmshāh
al-Mannāwī, Aḥmad b. Muḥammad s, 403a — S, 403b
al-Mannūbiyya i, 309a — I, 318b
Mān-rūd v, 821b, 831b — V, 827b, 837b
Mansā Mūsā iii, 275b; iv, 641a — III, 283b; IV, 667b
Manṣabdārī v, 685b, 688b — V, 691a, 694a
Mansārām i, 1166a — I, 1200b
Manshūr ii, 303a, 309a — II, 311b, 317b
al-Manṣūr (ʿAbbāsid(e)) i, 12b, 17a, 23b, 43a, 45b, 59b, 86b, 103b, 123a, 141b, 212b, 402b, 454a, 485a, 952a, 1030a, 1033b, 1080b, 1232b, ii, 178a, 576b; iii, 135b, 266a, 984a; iv, 939a, b, 940b; v, 69b, 326a, 620b,

1160a, 1233a, 1238a; s, 17b, 31b, 267b, 304b, 306b, 384b, 385b, 386b — I, 12b, 17b, 24a, 44a, b, 61a, 89a, 106b, 126b, 145b, 219a, 414a, 467a, 499b, 981b, 1061b, 1065a, 1112b, 1269b, II, 183b, 591a; III, 138a, 273b, 1008b; IV, 972a, b, 973b; V, 71b, 325b, 624b, 1149b, 1223b, 1228b; S, 17b, 31b, 267b, 304b, 306a, 385b, 386a, b
- foundation of/fondation de Baghdād i, 616a, 895a, 896a, 897a — I, 636b, 921b, 922b, 923b
al-Manṣūr (Afṭasid(e)) → Ibn al-Afṭas; ʿAbd Allāh b. Muḥammad b. Maslama
al-Manṣūr (Almohad(e)) → Abū Yūsuf Yaʿḳūb
al-Manṣūr (Fāṭimid(e)) i, 163b, 1238a; ii, 491b, 861b; iv, 460a; v, 1246b; s, 62b, 144b, 236b — I, 168a, 1275b; II, 503b, 881b; IV, 480a; V, 1237b; S, 63a, 144a, 236b
al-Manṣūr (Ḥammādid(e)) → al-Manṣūr b. al-Nāṣir
al-Manṣūr (Marīnid(e)) → Yaʿḳūb al-Manṣūr
al-Manṣūr I b. Nūḥ (Sāmānid(e)) i, 421b, 984b, 1294b; ii, 100a; v, 430a; s, 259a, 265b — I, 433b, 1015a, 1334b; II, 102a; V, 432b; S, 258b, 265a
al-Manṣūr II (Sāmānide(e)) i, 1236a; s, 259a — I, 1274a; S, 258b
al-Manṣūr (Zīrid(e)) s, 62b — S, 63a
al-Manṣūr, Aḥmad (Saʿdid(e)) → Aḥmad al-Manṣūr
Manṣur b. ʿAbdūn ii, 858a; iii, 79a; v, 1211a — II, 878a; III, 81b; V, 1201a
al-Manṣūr b. Abī ʿĀmir i, 75b, 446a, 489b, 494a, 499a, 601b, 628a, 1055a, 1238a, 1338b; ii, 373a, 485b, 542a, 998a; iii, 46a, 74b, 495b, 713a, 743a, 746b; iv, 216b, 712b; v, 133a, 511a, 626a, 781a, b, 1007b, 1008a, 1107b, 1177b; s, 92b, 125a — I, 77b, 459a, 504a, 509a, 514a, 621a, 649a, 1086b, 1275b, 1379a; II, 383a, 498a, 555b, 1021a; III, 48a, 77a, 512b, 735a, 765b, 769b; IV, 226a, 741a; V, 135b, 514b, 630a, 787b, 788a, 1003b, 1004a, 1103b, 1167b; S, 92a, 124a
al-Manṣūr b. Aʾlāʿ al-Nās → al-Manṣūr b. al-Nāṣir
Manṣūr b. ʿAlī b. ʿIrāḳ Djīlānī → Ibn ʿIrāḳ
al-Manṣūr b. Buluggīn i, 824a, 1309a; iii, 137a — I, 847a, 1349b; III, 139b
Manṣūr b. Djumhūr s, 232b — S, 232b
Mansūr b. Dubays i, 684a — I, 705a
Manṣūr b. Ḳarātegīn iv, 100b — IV, 104b
Manṣūr b. Kutlumush i, 1336b — I, 1376b
Manṣūr b. Luʾluʾ iii, 80b, 130b; v, 623b, 820b — III, 83a, 133a; V, 627b, 826b
Manṣūr b. Maymūn iv, 346b, 347a — IV, 361a, 362a
al-Manṣūr b. al-Mutawakkil i, 242b — I, 250a
al-Manṣūr b. al-Nāṣir i, 1205a; iii, 138a, 753a; iv, 479a — I, 1240b; III, 141a, 806b; IV, 501a
Manṣūr b. Naṣr al-Tunbudhī i, 248a; iv, 827b — I, 256a; IV, 860a
al-Manṣūr b. Nūḥ → al-Manṣūr I, II (Samānid(e))
Manṣūr b. Saʿīd v, 453a — V, 455b
al-Manṣūr ʿAbd Allāh b. Ḥamza s, 363b — S, 363a
Manṣūr Ata i, 299a — I, 308a
Manṣūr al-Bahūtī → al-Bahūtī al-Miṣrī
al-Manṣūr biʾllāh ʿAbd Allāh b. Ḥamza v, 1240b; s, 236b — V, 1231b; S, 236a
al-Manṣūr biʾllāh ʿAlī (Imām) s, 30b — S, 30b
al-Manṣūr biʾllāh al-Ḳāsim (Imām) v, 807b, 1241b — V, 813b, 1233a
al-Manṣūr Muḥammad iii, 697b; s, 205b — III, 719b; S, 205a
al-Manṣūr Ṣalāh al-Dīn Muḥammad s, 395b — S, 396a
Mansūr al-Shihābī ii, 444a, 635b — II, 455b, 651b
Manṣūr Ushurma, Shaykh ii, 18a, 88a — II, 18b, 89b
Manṣūr al-Yaman i, 103b, 551b; ii, 852a; iv, 198a, b, 661a; s, 236b — I, 106b, 569a; II, 872a; IV, 206b, 207a, 687b; S, 236b
Manṣūr Zalzal s, 128b — S 127b
al-Manṣūra iii, 470b — III, 487a
al-Manṣūriyya iv, 479a; s, 62b, 236b — IV, 501a; S, 63a, 236b
Manṣūriyya i, 258a — I, 266a
Manṭiḳ i, 92a — I, 94b
al-Manṭiḳī → Abū Sulaymān al-Manṭiḳī
Mantzikert i, 420b, 465b, 510a; v, 539a — I, 432b, 479b, 525b; V, 543b
Manūčihr I b. Yazīd iv, 347a — IV, 361b
Manučihr II b. Faridūn ii, 764a, 798a; iv, 348b, 915a — II, 782b, 817a; IV, 363a, 948a
Manūčihr (Ṭabaristān) v, 662a — V, 667b
Manūčihr b. Ḳābūs iv, 100b, 358a, 465a; s, 235a — IV, 105a, 373b, 486a; S, 235a
Manūčihr Khān i, 833b; iv, 1091b; v, 825b — I, 856b; IV, 1123a; V, 831b
Manūčihrī i, 1301a; iv, 61a; v, 1104a; s,35a — I, 1341a; IV, 64b; V, 1099b; S, 35b
Manzah Bint al-Sulṭān i, 699b, 700a — I, 721a
Mantzikert → Malāzgird
Manzil → Manāzil
Manzil iv, 335b, 338b, 340a; v, 1217a — IV, 350a, 352b, 354b; V, 1207a
Manẓūr ʿAlī Khān ii, 1092b — II, 1118a
Mao (Kānim) s, 165a, b, 166a — S, 165a, b, 166a
Map → Kharīṭa
Māppilla i, 172a; iii, 411b; iv, 547a; v, 587a — I, 176b; III, 424a; IV, 570b; V, 661b
Mār Sābā v, 330a — V, 330a
Marʾa iv, 720a, b; v, 587b, 895b — IV, 749a, b; V, 662a, 902a
- education v, 905a, b, 907a, 909a — V, 911a, 913a, 915a
Marabout → Murābiṭ
Marādjiʿ al-taḳlīd iii, 491a, b — III, 508a, b
Marāfiḳ ii, 325a — II, 335a
Marāgha i, 300a, 301a — I, 309b, 310a
- observatory/observatoire iii, 1125a, 1135b, 1137b — III, 1153a, 1164a, 1165b
Marāghaʾī, Zayn al-ʿĀbidīn iv, 72a, 164b, 789a; s, 109b — IV, 76a, 171b, 821a; S, 108b
al-Marāghī, ʿAbd al-Ḳādir s, 409a — S, 409a
al-Marāghī, Muṣṭafā iv, 159b; v, 429b — IV, 166a; V, 432a
al-Marāghī, Ṣadr al-Dīn iv, 862b — IV, 895b
Mārahrawī → Aḥsan Mārahrawī
Marāʿī iv, 1042a, b — IV, 1073b, 1074a
Maraḳiyya iii, 474b; v, 582a — III, 491a; V, 587a
Marand iii, 1125a; s, 365b — III, 1153a; S, 365a
Marandjīṣa iii, 1040b, 1041a — III, 1066b, 1067a
Marʿash i, 4a, b, 1190b — I, 4a, b, 1225b
Marʿashī i, 237a; v, 663a — I, 244b; V, 668a
Marʿashī, Ḳarwām al-Dīn i, 237a — I, 244b
Marāṣid ii, 143a — II, 147a
Marāthās i, 208b, 230a, 253a, 296a, 400b, 403b, 418a, 625a, 757a, 796b, 808a, 952a, 1170a, 1202b, 1300a, 1330a, 1331a; ii, 99a, 219a, 808b, 1092b, 1130a; iii, 15b, 60b, 202b, 316b, 320a, 424b, 427b; iv, 1023b; v, 1259a; s, 55b, 246b — I, 214b, 237a, 261a, 305a, 412a, 415a, 429b, 645b, 779b, 792b, 831b, 981a, 1205a, 1238b, 1340a, 1371a, 1372a; II, 101a, 225b, 828a, 1118a, 1156b; III, 16b, 63a, 208a, 326a, 330b, 438a, 441b; IV, 1055b; V, 1250a; S, 56a, 246b
Marāziḳa → Ibn Marzūḳ, Muḥammad VI
Marcuella → Marḳwīz
Mardaïtes → Djarādjima
Mardanīsh, Banū s, 80b — S, 80b
al-Mardāwī, ʾAlāʿ al-Dīn iii, 162a, 766b — III, 165a, 789b
Mardāwidj b. Ziyār i, 125b, 688a, b, 866a, 1350a, b,

1354a; ii, 192b, 299b, 454a, 1082a, 1141b; iii, 105b, 195b, 255a, 1157a; iv, 19a, 23a, 100a, 661b; s, 357a — I, 129a, 709a, b, 890a, 1390b, 1391a, 1393b; II, 198b, 307b, 465b, 1107a, 1168b; III, 180a, 200a, 262a, 1185b; IV, 20b, 24b-25a, 104b, 688b; S, 357a
Mārdīn i, 311b, 664a, 665b, 666b; ii, 344b; iii, 1118a; iv, 898a; v, 248a, 457b, 1145a — I, 321b, 684a, 686b, 687a; II, 354a; III, 1146a; IV, 930b; V, 246a, 460a, 1137a
Mardj s, 159a, 160b — S, 159a, 160b
al-Mardj → Barḳa
Mardj Dābiḳ iv, 553a — IV, 577a
Mardj Rāhiṭ i, 5a, 920a, b; ii, 90a, 1106a; iv, 493a — I, 5a, 947b, 949a; II, 91b, 1132a; IV, 514b
Mardjaᶜ-i taḳlīd v, 371b; s, 75b, 76a, 103b, 158a — V, 372b; S, 76a, 103a, 158a
Mardjān i, 903b; iv, 571a — I, 930b; IV, 593b
Mardjān, Amīr i, 938a — I, 967a
Mardjanī i, 1307 — I, 1347b
Mardūd iii, 26b — III, 28a
Margat → Marḳab
Marghinān ii, 792a; v, 29a, b — II, 811a; V, 30a
Marghīnānī → Bahāʾ al-Dīn
al-Marghīnānī, Burhān al-Dīn iii, 163b — III, 167a
Mari → Čeremiss(es)
Mari → Ḳayyim
al-Marᶜī iii, 954b — III, 979a
Mārī Hills s, 331b — S, 331b
Maʾrib i, 102b, 549a, 890b; ii, 785a, 1060b; iii, 223a; v, 811a; s, 336b, 337a — I, 105b, 566a, 916b, II, 804a, 1085b; III, 230a; V, 817a; S, 336b
Mārid iii, 1050a — III, 1076a, b
Marīda iii, 498b, 499b — III, 515b, 516b
al-Māridānī, ᶜAlī iii, 818a — III, 841b
Māridīn s, 36a — S, 36b
al-Māridīnī, Sibṭ iii, 1141a — III, 1169b
Maᶜrifa ii, 358a; iii, 262a, 1133a; iv, 847a — II, 368a; III, 269b, 1161b; IV, 880a
Marîndja → Bahčekent
Marine → Baḥriyya; Safīna
Marīnid(e)s i, 92b, 93a, 122b, 124b, 129b, 155a, 167b, 290b, 367b, 445b, 495b, 1148b, 1176b, 1346b; ii, 146a, 353a, 819a, 822a, 979a, 1095b; iii, 49a, 68a, 386b, 462a, 825b; iv, 116b, 338a, 633b; v, 531a, 626b, 1128a, 1150a, 1190a, 1208a; s, 45b, 103a, 112a, 113b, 318a, 336b — I, 95a, b, 126a, 128a, 133b, 159a, 172b, 299b, 378a, 458a, 510b, 1183a, 1211b, 1387a; II, 150a, 362b, 838b, 841b, 1001b, 1121b; III, 51a, 70b, 399a, 478a, 849b; IV, 121b, 352b, 659b; V, 535a, 630b, 1124a, 1140b, 1180a, 1198b; S, 46a, 102b, 111b, 113a, 317b, 336a
al-Marīsī → Bishr b. Ghiyāth
al-Marīsiyya i, 1242a — I, 1279b
Māristān → Bīmāristān
Māriya iii, 64a — III, 66b
al-Mariyya i, 32a, 489a, 864b; iii, 135a, 498b, 712b; v, 219a; s, 383a — I, 33a, 504a, 888b; III, 137b, 515b, 734b; V, 216b; S, 383b
Māriz s, 129a — S, 128a
Marḳab i, 118b, 1016b; iv, 485a — I, 122a, 1048a; IV, 506a
Markha, Wādī iv, 747a — IV, 777a
Markhassa i, 640b — I, 661a
Markwīz s, 80a — S, 80a
Marmara i, 463a — I, 476b
Marmoucha s, 145a — S, 144b
Maroc I, 18b, 48b, 59b, 81a, 87a, 297b, 366a — 368b, 1089b, 1361b; II, 635a; III, 247a, 258b, 263b, 1064a; IV, 274b; V, **1174a**; S, 102b, 191b, 215a, 223a
- administration I, 176a, 440a, 1007b; II, 423b, 690a, 693a; III, 408a, 581b, 582b, 583a; V, 1069b, **1188b**
- démographie S, 215a
- ethnographie I, 35b, 40a, b, 549b, 1212b; II, 165a; III, 307b; IV, 343b, 346a, b; V, 701b, 1154b, **1186a**, 1198a
- géographie v, **1174a**
- histoire V, 1178a
- institutions II, 436a; III, 543a; V, 922b, 1091a, 1141a
- langues, littérature I, 325a, 597b; II, 481b; III, 829b, 830a, 837b; V, 762b, **1193b**
- monuments v, 1142a, 1143a, 1191b
- religion V, 1189b
Maronites i, 1280b, 1281a; ii, 65b, 467b, 637a, 750a, 795a; iii, 523a; iv, 255a; v, 791a, b, 792a; s, 268b, 269a — I, 1320a; II, 67a, 479b, 653a, 768a, 814a; III, 541a; IV, 266a; V, 797a, b, 798a; S, 268b
Marrakesh/Marrakech → Marrākush
Marrākūsh i, 79a, 251a, 289a; ii, 818b, 819a, b, 1116b; iii, 148b, 462a, 501a, 675a, 975a; iv, 533a; v, 654a, b, 1186b, 1208a; s, 29a, 48a, 103a, 114a, 124b, 389a, 397b, 401b — I, 81a, 258b, 298a; II, 838a, b, 839a, 1142b; III, 152a, 478a, 518a, 697a, 999b; IV, 556a; V, 658b, 1176b, 1198b; S, 29a, 48b, 102b, 113b, 382b, 389b, 398a, 402a
- Djāmiᶜ al-Kutubiyyīn i, 79a, 166a, 1226b — I, 81a, 170b, 1264a
- literature/littérature i, 1224b;iii, 806b — I, 1261a; III, 829b
- monuments i, 56a, 58b, 85a, 161b, 289a, 459a, 499b, 1320b, 1346b, 1347a; v, 1153b — I, 57b, 60a, 87b, 166a, 298a, 472a, 514b, 1361a, 1357a, b; V, 1143b
al-Marrākushī → ᶜAbd al-Wāḥid; al-Ḥasan b. ᶜAlī ᶜUmar; Ibn ᶜAbd al-Malik; Ibn al-Bannāʾ
al-Marrāsh, Francis iii, 591b — III, 612a
Marrīs s, 332a — S, 331b
Marsa Mūsā s, 125a — S, 124a
Marsā Zafran → Maghmadās
Marṣad i, 1141a; iv, 702b — I, 1175b; IV, 731a; V, 354b
al-Marṣafī, Ḥusayn iii, 593b; iv, 1098a — III, 614a; IV, 1129a
Marsūm ii, 303a, b, — II, 311a, b
Martapura s, 151a — S, 151a
Martel, Charles i, 86b, 493a, 988b — I, 89a, 508a, 1019a
Marthiya i, 508b, 584b; ii, 73a; iv, 1027a; v, 611b, 635b, 1033b — I, 524a, 603a; II, 74b; IV, 1059a; V, 615a, 639b, 1029b
Martolos i, 1164a — I, 1198b
Marūčak s, 281a — S, 281a
Maᶜrūf iii, 26b — III, 27b
Maᶜrūf → Ilāhī Bakhsh
Maᶜrūf, Banū i, 1096a — I, 1129a
Mārūn s, 269a — S, 268b
Mārūn, Yūḥannā v, 791a — V, 797b
Marw i, 16a, 18a, 47b, 750a, 1007a, 1067a, 1293b, 1294a; ii, 4b, 43b; iv, 131b; v, 56b, 58b, 293a, 554b, 868b; s, 89a, 195a, 240a, 281a, 326a, 357a — I, 16b, 19a, 49a, 772b, 1038a, 1099a, 1333a, b; II, 4b, 44a; IV, 137a; V, 58b, 60b, 293a, 559b, 874b; S, 88b, 195a, 240a, 281a, 325b, 356b
al-Marw-al-Rūdī → Ḥusayn b. ᶜAlī; Ḥusayn b. Muḥammad
al-Marwa s, 175a — S, 176a
Marwān I (Umayyad(e)) i, 453b, 1242b; ii, 89b, 360b, 415b, 416a, 726a; iii, 65a, 227a, 242b, 270b, 607b, 620b, 932a; iv, 493a, 929b, 938b; v, 74b, 451a; s, 10a, 52b, 230b — I, 466b, 1280a; II, 91a, 370a, 426b, 744b; III, 67b, 233b, 249b, 278b, 628b, 641a, 956b; IV, 514a, 962b, 971b; V, 76b, 453b; S, 9b, 53a, 230b
Marwān II (Umayyad(e)) i, 43a, 53b, 57b, 65b, 100b, 103a, 108b, 354a, 660b, 787b, 835b, 837a, 1244a, 1343b; ii, 130a, 505a, 523b, 958a; iii, 29a, 228a, 229b,

398a, 493b, 651b, 802b, 990b; iv, 344a, b, 370b, 447b, 1174a – I, 44a, 55a, 59b, 67b, 103b, 106a, 111b, 365a, 681a, 811a, 858b, 860b, 1282a, 1383b; II, 133a, 518a, 536b, 980b; III, 30b, 234b, 236b, 410a, 510b, 673a, 826a, 1015a; IV, 358b, 387a, 467a, 1207a
Marwān b. Abī Ḥafṣa ii, 248b; iii, 1202b – II, 255b; III, 1233a
Marwān b. al-Ḥakam → Marwān I
Marwān b. al-Hay<u>th</u>am ii, 234a – II, 241a
Marwān b. Muḥammad → Marwān II
Marwān b. Yazīd b. al-Muhallab s, 41a – S, 41a
Marwānid(e)s i, 13a, 81b, 82b, 95b, 118a, 493b, 1206b; ii, 344a; iii, 676b; iv, 27b; v, 453a; s, 103b – I, 13a, 84a, 84b, 98b, 121b, 508b, 1242b; II, 353b; III, 698a; IV, 29b; V, 455b; S, 103a
Mārwār → <u>Dj</u>ōdhpur
al-Marwarrūdī → <u>Kh</u>ālid al-Marwarrū<u>dh</u>ī
al-Marwazī → Abū Bakr; Abū Saʿīd; Abū Yaḥyā; Ḥaba<u>sh</u> al-Ḥāsib
al-Marwazī, Abu 'l-Abbās iv, 55a – IV, 57b
al-Marwazī, <u>Sh</u>araf al-Dīn Ṭāhir v, 385b, 1011a, b – V, 386b, 1006b, 1007a
Maryam ii, 848a; iii, 1175a, 1206a; iv, 81b, 82a; v, 90a – II, 868a; III, 1204a, 1236b; IV, 85b, 86a; V, 92b
Marzbān v, 661b; s, 298a – V, 667a; S, 297b
Marzubān b. Ba<u>kh</u>tiyār → Ṣamṣam al-Dawla (Būyid(e))
Marzubān b. <u>Dj</u>ustān ii, 191a – II, 197a
Marzubān b. Muḥammad (Musāfirid(e)) i, 190a, 660b, 1041b; ii, 680a; iii, 703a; iv, 345b, 346a, 662b; v, 452a – I, 194b, 681b, 1073a; II, 697a; III, 725b; IV, 360b, 689b; V, 454b
Marzubān b. Rustam b. <u>Sh</u>ahriyār iii, 372b; iv, 506a; v, 1028a – III, 384b; IV, 528a; V, 1024a
Marzubān-nāma iv, 63b, 506b; v, 1028a – IV, 67a; 528a; V, 1024a
al-Marzubānī, Abū ʿUbayd Allāh i, 154b, 758b; iii, 879a; s, 24b, 33a, 400b – I, 158b, 781b; III, 903a; S, 25a, 33a, 401a
al-Marzūḳī i, 154a – I, 158b
Maṣāff iii, 156b – III, 191a
Maṣāffiyya ii, 1080b; iii, 45b – II, 1105b; III, 47b
Masāḥa iv, 1037b, 1038a – IV, 1069a, b
Masāʾil i, 274a, 320a – I, 282b, 330a
Masākira s, 356a – S, 356a
Maṣāla b. Ḥabūs ii, 853a; iii, 1036a – II, 872b; III, 1062a
al-Masʿala al-minbariyya i, 765a – I, 787b
Masʿala al-Suray<u>dj</u>iyya iii, 949b – III, 974a
Masāliḥ i, 761a – I, 784a
Masālik i, 488a – I, 502b
Maṣāmida ii, 623a – II, 638b
Māsar<u>dj</u>uwayh s, 52b – S, 53a
al-Masāwī → al Maḥāsin wa-l-masāwī
Maṣawwaʿ i, 976a; ii, 91a; iv, 687a – I, 1006b; II, 92b; IV, 715a
Mascate → Masḳaṭ
Mas<u>dj</u>id i, 497-500, 608-624, 830a, 1200b; ii, 777b; iii, 1124a; iv, 229b; v, 366a, 1123b, 1124a, b – I, 512-516, 628-645, 853a, 1236a; II, 796a; III, 1152a; IV, 240a; V, 367a, 1120a, b, 1121a
Mas<u>dj</u>id al-Aḳṣā i, 3a, 201a, 610a, 618b; ii, 263a, 911a; iv, 367b, 1169b; v, 298a, 299a, 323b, 325a, 340b, 342b, 343a; s, 205a – I, 3a, 206b, 630b, 637b; II, 271a, 932b; IV, 383b, 1202a; V, 297b, 298b, 322, 324b, 341a, b, 343b, 344a; S, 204b
Mas<u>dj</u>id al-Dibs s, 234b – S, 234b
Mas<u>dj</u>id-i Sulaymān s, 291a – S, 290b
Mas<u>dj</u>umi, Ma<u>sh</u>umi iii, 534a, b, 1230a – III, 553a, 1262a
Masfūt s, 42a – S, 42b
Mā <u>sh</u>āʾ Allāh i, 722b, 1101b; iii, 8b; v, 130b – I, 744b, 1135a; III, 9a; V, 133b
Maṣḥaf-rā<u>sh</u> v, 208b, 209a, b, 210a – V, 206a, b, 207a, b
Ma<u>sh</u>āʾiyya iv, 120b – IV, 126a
Ma<u>sh</u>āriḳa v, 1159a – V, 1149a
Ma<u>sh</u>āwiriyya iv, 456a – IV, 476b
Ma<u>sh</u>āyi<u>kh</u> iv, 167b – IV, 175a
Ma<u>sh</u>āyi<u>kh</u>, Pīr v, 27a – V, 27b
Ma<u>sh</u>dūf iii, 289a – III, 298a
Ma<u>sh</u>had i, 8a, 400b, 1067a; ii, 173b; iv, 7b, 38a; v, 59a, b, 289a, 1149a; s, 53a, 71a, 73a, 75a, b, 139b, 365a, b, 380a, 423b – I, 8a, 412a, 1099a; II, 178b; IV, 8b, 40b; V, 61a, 288b, 1140a; S, 53b, 71b, 73b, 75b, 76a, 139a, 365a, 380a, 423b
- university/université ii, 426a – II, 437a
Ma<u>sh</u>had al-Ḥāʾir s, 94a – S, 93b
Ma<u>sh</u>had al-Ḥusayn iv, 637b, 638a, b – IV, 663b, 664a, b
al-Ma<u>sh</u>ad al-Kāẓimī → Kāẓimayn
al-Ma<u>sh</u>hadān → Karbalāʾ
Ma<u>sh</u>had-i Miṣriyyān ii, 253b – II, 260b
Ma<u>sh</u>hūr iii, 25b – III, 26b
Ma<u>sh</u>īʾa i, 414b – I, 426b
Ma<u>sh</u>rabiyya v, 1153a – V, 1143a
Ma<u>sh</u>riḳ v, 1159a – V, 1149a
Ma<u>sh</u>riḳ al-A<u>dh</u>kār i, 918a – I, 945b
al-Ma<u>sh</u>riḳī, ʿInāyat Allāh iv, 916b – IV, 949b
Ma<u>sh</u>rūʿ ii, 390a – II, 400b
Ma<u>sh</u>ṭūr i, 671a – I, 692a
Ma<u>sh</u>ʾūm ii, 759a – II, 777b
Ma<u>sh</u>wara ii, 641b – II, 658a
Masīḥ i, 301a; iv, 82b – I, 310b; IV, 86b
Masīḥ b. Ḥakam iv, 329a – IV, 343b
Masīḥ al-Dima<u>sh</u>ḳī s, 314a – S, 313b
Masik → al-Ḥāri<u>th</u>, <u>Dj</u>abal
Māsi<u>kh</u>a iv, 796b – IV, 828b
al-Masīla, wādī i, 538b; s, 337a – I, 555a; S, 337a
Māsina → Macina
Maṣīra i, 535b – I, 552a
Maṣḳala b. Hubayra v, 19b – V, 20a
Masḳaṭ i, 536a, 539a, 554b, 942b, 1071b, 1098b, 1282b, 1283a, 1314a; iv, 500b; v, 183b; s, 332b, 355b, 356a – I, 552a, 556a, 572a, 971b, 1103b, 1131b, 1321b, 1354a; IV, 522b; V, 181a; S, 331b, 355b
Mas<u>kh</u> ii, 95b; iii, 305b, 306a; v, 131a – II, 97b; III, 315a, b; V, 134a
Maskin ii, 197a – II, 203a
Maṣlaḥa i, 276a, 276b; ii, 254b; iii, 954a; iv, 257a, b, 258a – I, 284b, 285a; II, 262a; III, 978b; IV, 268a, b, 269b
Maslama, Banū → Afṭasid(e)s
Maslama b. ʿAbd al-Malik i, 12b, 449b, 835b, 837a, 996a, 1033b, 1094b, 1102b, 1187a; ii, 85b, 234a, 236b; iii, 493b, 1255a; iv, 343b, 344a, 843a, 870b, 938b, 973b, 1173b; v, 533a; s, 31b – I, 12b, 462b, 858b, 860a, 1026b, 1065a, 1127a, 1136a, 1222a; II, 87a, 241a, 243b; III, 510b, 1287b; IV, 358a, b, 876a, 904a, 971b, 1005b, 1207a; V, 537a; S, 31b
Maslama b. Mu<u>kh</u>lid al-Anṣārī ii, 327b – II, 337a
Maṣmūda i, 1176a, 1177b, 1178b, 1350a; iii, 69b, 207a, 959a; iv, 730a – I, 1211a, 1212b, 1213b, 1390a; III, 72a, 213a, 984a; IV, 759a
Maṣmu<u>gh</u>ān v, 661b – V, 667a
Masnad-i ʿAlī → Daryā <u>Kh</u>ān Noḥānī
al-Masnāwī, Abū ʿAbd Allāh s, 403b, 404a – S, 404a
Maṣr al-ʿAtīḳa ii, 958a – II, 980a
Masraḥī v, 516b – V, 520a
Masraḥiyya iv, 73b – IV, 77b
Masrūḳ b. Abraha s, 115b – S, 115a
Masruḳān i, 711b; iv, 674a – I, 733a; IV, 701b
Masrūr b. al-Walīd i, 1244a; iii, 990b – I, 1282a; III, 1015a

Massāḥ iv, 1041b — IV, 1073a
Maṣṣālī Ḥādjdj iv, 362b — IV, 378b
Massar i, 1166b; iv, 275a — I, 1201a; IV, 287a
Massassi → Bambara
Massenya i, 910a, b — I, 937b, 938a
al-Māssī → Ibn Hūd
Maṣṣīṣa i, 42b — I, 43b
Massūfa i, 389b — I, 400b
al-Massūfī → Barrāz
Masʿūd I b. Maḥmūd (Ghaznawid(e)) i, 147a, 217b, 278a, 424b, 459a, 1005b, 1130b, 1236b, 1344b, 1356a; ii, 4b, 1049a, 1051a, 1053a, 1083a, 1100a; iii, 167b, 195b, 255b, 345a, 482b, 1201b; iv, 25a, 100b, 1067a; v, 624a; s, 195a, 235a, 245b — I, 151b, 224a, 286b, 436b, 472b, 1036b, 1164b, 1274a, 1385a, 1395a; II, 4b, 1073b, 1075b, 1077b, 1108a, 1125b; III, 171b, 200a, 263a, 355b, 499b, 1232a; IV, 26b, 105a, 1098b; V, 628a; S, 195a, 235a, 245b
Masʿūd II (Ghaznawid(e)) ii, 1051b — II, 1075b
Masʿūd III (Ghaznawid(e)) ii, 1052a, 1100a; s, 21a, b — II, 1076b, 1126a; S, 21a, b
Masʿūd I (Rūm Saldjūḳ) i, 181b, 182b, 466b, 731b; ii, 37b, 110b; iii, 20a, 1255b; v, 253b — I, 186b, 187b, 480b, 753b; II, 38a, 113a; III, 21a, 1288b; V, 251b
Masʿūd II (Rūm Saldjūḳ) i, 703a; iv, 620b, 621a, 817b — I, 724a; IV, 645b, 850a
Masʿūd I (Zangid(e)) iii, 1119a — III, 1147a
Masʿūd, Badr al-Dīn, Khurshīdī v, 828b — V, 834b
Masʿūd b. ʿAmr al-Atakī i, 304a, 810a — I, 313b, 833b
Masʿūd b. Ibrāhīm → Masʿūd III (Ghaznawid(e))
Masʿūd b. Maḥmūd → Masʿūd I (Ghaznawid(e))
Masʿūd b. Mawdūd → Masʿūd II (Ghaznawid(e)); Masʿūd I (Zangid(e))
Masʿūd b. Muḥammad i, 300a, 522b, 684a; ii, 1083a; iii, 196b, 345a, 1110b — I, 309b, 538b, 705a; II, 1108b; III, 201b, 355b, 1137b
Masʿūd b. Saʿd b. Salmān i, 252b; iii, 456b; iv, 61b; s, 333a, b, 334a — I, 260a; III, 472a; IV, 64b; S, 332b, 333a, b
Masʿūd Bakk ii, 55a, 1115a; iii, 429b — II, 56a, 1141a; III, 443b
Masʿūd Beg → Masʿūd Yalavač
Masʿūd Bilālī iii, 197a — III, 201b
Masʿūd Ghāzī → Ghāzī Miyān, Sālār Masʿūd
Masʿūd Shāh, ʿAlāʾ al-Dīn ii, 267b — II, 276a
Masʿūd-Shāh Īndjū iii, 1208a, b; iv, 498b — III, 1239a; IV, 520a
Masʿūd al-Tāhirī al-Djūṭī s, 404a — S, 404a
Masʿūd Yalavač i, 1240b, 1312a; ii, 2b, 3a, 791b; iv, 808b; v, 38b, 858a — I, 1278a, 1352a; II, 2b, 3a, 810b; IV, 841b; V, 39b, 865a
Masʿūdī iii, 1097b — II, 1124b
al-Masʿūdī (poet/poète) iv, 62b — IV, 65b
al-Masʿūdī, Abuʾl-Ḥasan ʿAlī ii, 361a, 591b, 837a, 851b; ii, 579b, 580b, 583b, 865a; iii, 166a, 405b, 739b, 1206b; iv, 345b; v, 950a, 1012a; s, 42b, 56a, 295a — I, 371b, 610b, 860a, 875a; II, 594a, 595a, 598a, 885a; III, 170a, 418a, 762a, 1237a; IV, 360a; V, 954a, 1007b; S, 43a, 56b, 294b
Masʿūd-i Saʿd-i Salmān → Masʿūd b. Saʿd b. Salmān
Maʿṣūm ii, 86b, 88a — II, 88b, 90a
Maʿṣūm, amīr (Mangit) → Dāniyāl(r) Beg
Maʿṣūm ʿAlī Shāh i, 283b; iv, 51a; s, 23b — I, 292a; IV, 53b; S, 24a
Maʿṣūm Beg Ṣafawī iv, 188a — IV, 196b
Maʿṣūm Nāmī i, 962a, 1192b; iii, 245b — I, 991b, 1227b; III, 252b
Maʿṣūm-i pāk i, 1162a — I, 1196b
Masūsa (tribe/tribu) v, 695b — V, 700b
Maṣyāf iv, 200a — IV, 209a
Maṭābikh Kisrā i, 685b — I, 706b
Maṭāf iv, 318a — IV, 332a, b
al-Matamma v, 1251a — V, 1242a
Matan s, 150b — S, 150b
Maṭar (Mawālī) s, 17b — S, 17b
Mataram iii, 1219b, 1221b; v, 1155a, b; s, 150b, 199b, 201a, 202a — III, 1250a, b, 125a, b; V, 1145a; S, 150b, 199b, 201a, b
Maṭbaʿa i, 282a, 289b, 640b, 641a, 906b, 907b, 1071a, 1299b; ii, 464b, 472b, 533a, 589b, 682b; iii, 136, 993b, 997b; iv, 70a-b, 143a, 310a, 311a, 607b; v, 190a, 641b, 1254b — I, 290b, 298b, 661b, 934a, 935a, 1103a, 1339b; II, 476a, 484b, 546a, 604a, 699b; III, 14a, 1018a, 1022b; IV, 74a, 149a, 324a, 325a, 632a; V, 187a, 645b, 1245b
al-Maṭbaʿa al-Kāstiliyya s, 408a — S, 408b
Maṭbaʿa al-Madīna al-Munawwara s, 18a — S, 18b
Maṭbaʿa-i ʿĀmire v, 313b — V, 313b
Matdjar al-Sulṭānī iv, 136a, b — IV, 142a
Mātem gedjeleri i, 1162a — I, 1196b
Mathal ii, 102a; iii, 369b; iv, 248b; v, 424b — II, 104a; III, 381a; IV, 259b; V, 426b
Mathālib i, 892a — I, 918b
Mathāmina i, 195a — I, 200b
Mathānī v, 424a — V, 426b
Mathematics/Mathématiques → ʿIlm al-ḥisāb
Mathnawī i, 436b, 677a; ii, 395a, 396a; iv, 58a, b, 62a-63a, 66b-67a; v, 201b, 650b, 1106a; s, 324a — I, 449a, 698a; II, 405b, 406b; IV, 61a, b, 65b-66b, 70a-b; V, 198b, 654b, 1102a; S, 323b
Mathurā iv, 177b — IV, 186a
Maṭrān, Khalīl → Muṭrān
Maṭrūḥ iii, 26b — III, 28a
Matruh iv, 529a — IV, 552a
Matrūk iii, 26b — III, 28a
Mattā b. Yūnus (Abū Bishr) i, 151b, 631b, 737a, 982b; ii, 779a; iii, 112a, 368a; iv, 252b — I, 156a, 652a, 759a, 1013a; II, 797b; III, 114a, 380a; IV, 263b
al-Māturīdī, Abū Manṣūr i, 124a, 589b; iii, 1145a; iv, 272a; s, 90b — I, 127b, 609a; III, 1173b; IV, 284a; S, 90a
Māturīdī → Ḥanafī-Māturīdī
Māturīdiyya i, 334a, b, 343a, 410b, 411a, b, 413b, 696a; ii, 834a; iii, 330a, 465b; iv, 183b, 365b — I, 344b, 345a, 353b, 422a, 423a, b, 425a, 717a; II, 853b; III, 340a, 482a; IV, 191b, 381b
Maures I, 32b; II, 27a
Mauritania/Mauretanie i, 211a, 1177b; ii, 672a, 676a, 1122a; iii, 231a, 288b, 385a; v, 697a, 1074a; s, 182b, 218a — I, 217a, 1212b; II, 689a, 693a, 1148a; III, 237b, 297b, 397b; V, 702a, 1071b; S, 182b, 217b
Mawāʿiẓ iv, 56a — IV, 59b
Mawāl, mawāliya i, 404a; iii, 289b — I, 415b; III, 298b
Mawālī i, 569a, 569b; ii, 324a, 951a; iii, 719a; iv, 44a-b; v, 925b — I, 587b, 588a; II, 333b, 973a; III, 741b; IV, 47a; V, 931a
al-Māwardī, Abu ʾl-Ḥasan ʿAlī i, 119a, 328b, 435b, 439b, 982b, 1356a; ii, 116a, 131a; iii, 159b, 486a, 766a, 1165a, 1237a; iv, 173a, 457b, 458b, 949b; s, 192a — I, 122b, 338b, 447b, 452a, 1013a, 1395a; II, 118b, 134b; III, 163a, 503a, 789a, 1193b, 1269a; IV, 180b, 477b, 478b, 982a; S, 193a
Mawārith ḥashriyya i, 1144a; ii, 326b, 329a — I, 1178b; II, 336a, 338b
Mawāsh(i) iv, 1042a, b — IV, 1073b, 1074a
Mawāt iii, 1053b; iv, 1036a — III, 1079b; IV, 1067b
Mawḍūʿ iii, 26b — III, 28a
Mawdūd, amīr i, 1332b; ii, 282a — I, 1373a; II, 290a
Mawdūd, Rukn al-Dīn iv, 521a — IV, 543b
Mawdūd b. Masʿūd i, 278a; ii, 5a, 1051b; iv, 815a — I, 286b; II, 5a, 1075b; IV, 848a
Mawdūd b. Zangī i, 1160b; ii, 489b; iii, 961a — I,

1195a; II, 501b; III, 985b
Mawdūdī → Abu ˀl-ˁAlāˀ
Mawḳūf i, 319b; iii, 25b — I, 329a; III, 27a
Mawlā i, 30b, 890b; iii, 388b, 412a, 1152b — I, 31b, 917a; III, 401a, 424b, 1181a
Mawlāˀīs iv, 202b — IV, 211b
Mawlānā v, 627a — V, 631a
Mawlānā Muḥammad ˁAlī i, 302b; v, 7a, b — I, 312a; V, 7a, b
Mawlānā Rūmī → Djalal al-Dīn Rūmī
Mawlawī → Djalāl al-Dīn Rūmī
Mawlawiyya i, 234a, 1161b; ii, 164b, 224a, 226b, 393b; iv, 48a, 65b, 190b; s, 83b, 283a — I, 241a, 1196b; II, 170a, 231a, 233a, 404a; IV, 50b, 68b, 198b; S, 83a, 283a
Mawlāy (Morocco, Maroc) → under the second name/sous le nom suivant
Mawlāy (title/titre) v, 627a — V, 631a
Mawlāy Idrīs (town/ville) v, 1188b — V, 1178b
Mawlid i, 281a, 1004a, 1161a; v, 1200b — I, 289b, 1035a, 1195b; V, 1190b
Mawlūdiyyāt i, 58b — I, 60a
Mawrūr i, 6a — I, 6a
al-Mawrūrī → Djūdī
Mawṣil i, 731b, 732a, 866b, 907a, 975b, 1074a; ii, 90b, 348a, 385a; iii, 127a, 218a, 1256b, 1258a, 1267b; iv, 584b; v, 145b, 437a, 451a, b, 454a, 463b, 821a; s, 36a, b, 37a, 49b, 100a, 192b, 379b — I, 753b, 754a, 890b, 934a, 1005b, 1106b; II, 92a, 358a, 395a; III, 130a, 224b, 1289a, 1290b, 1300b; IV, 608a; V, 148a, 439b, 453b, 454a, 457a, 466a, 827a; S, 36a, b, 37a, 50a, 99b, 193b, 379b
al-Mawṣilī → Isḥāḳ b. Ibrāhīm
Mawsim s, 53a — S, 53b
Mawwāl → Mawāl
al-Maybadhī i, 1052b — I, 1084a
Maydān ii, 954b — II, 976b
al-Maydānī, Aḥmad i, 794a; ii, 590b; iii, 992a; iv, 525b — I, 817b; II, 605a; III, 1016b; IV, 548b
al-Maydī v, 808b — V, 814b
Mayfaˁ i, 538a; s, 337a — I, 555a; S, 337a
Mayhana i, 147a — I, 151b
al-Mayhanī iii, 1243a — III, 1275a
al-Mayhanī, Shaykh Abū Saˁīd s, 154a — S, 154b
Maymad s, 116a — S, 115b
Maymana ii, 608b, 609a — II, 623b, 624a
Maymandī, Manṣūr b. Saˁīd s, 21a — S, 21b
al-Maymandī, Shamsu ˀl-Kufāt i, 278a; iii, 255b, 345a — I, 286b; III, 263a, 355b
Maymūn iii, 574b; v, 132b — III, 594b; V, 135a
Maymūn b. Aḥmad ii, 1082b; iv, 347a — II, 1108a; IV, 361b
Maymūn b. Yiddar ii, 1013b — II, 1037a
Maymūn al-Ḳaddāḥ i, 48a; ii, 851b; v, 1242b — I, 49b; II, 871a; V, 1233a
Maymūna iii, 362b; s, 311a — III, 374a; S, 311a
Maymūndiz i, 1359b; iii, 501b — I, 1399b; III, 519a
Maymūniyya i, 48a — I, 49b
Mayo ii, 464a — II, 475b
Maysara al- ˁAbdī i, 1292b — I, 1332b
Maysara al-Matgharī i, 1175a; v, 1189a — I, 1210a; V, 1179a
Maysir i, 1111b; iv, 263b; v, 108b; s, 394b — I, 1145a; IV, 275a; V, 111a; S, 394b
Maysūn i, 920a — I, 947b
Maysūr i, 163b; iii, 1036b; iv, 459a, b — I, 168a; III, 1062a; IV, 479a, 480a
Maysūr (Mysore) → Mahisūr
Mayta ii, 1069a — II, 1093b
Mayurḳa i, 490a, 1055a; ii, 111b, 1007a; iii, 704b; iv, 1157a; s, 120b, 307a — I, 504b, 1086b; II, 114a, 1030b; III, 727a; IV, 1189a; S, 120a, 307a
al-Mayūrḳī → Abū Bakr
Maywātīs iii, 433b — III, 447b
Mayyāfāriḳīn i, 665a, 679b; ii, 344b; iii, 129b, 900a; iv, 521a; s, 36b, 37a — I, 684b, 700b; II, 354a; III, 132a, 924a; IV, 544a; S, 36b, 37a
Mayyāra al-Akbar → al-Fāsī, Abū ˁAbd Allāh Muḥammad (d./m. 1662)
Mayyūn i, 535b, 539a, 837b — I, 551b, 556a, 860b
Māza, Banū iii, 163a — III, 166b
Mazagan → al-Djadīda
Mazāḳī v, 261a — V, 259a
Maẓālim i, 209a, 387b; ii, 145b, 519b — I, 215b, 398b; II, 149b, 532b
Māzandarān i, 8a, b, 147b, 148a, 237a; ii, 903b; iv, 808a; v, 663a, b, 664a; s, 239b — I, 8a, b, 152a, b, 244a; II, 924b; IV, 840b; V, 668a, 669a, b; S, 239b
al-Māzandarānī, ˁAbd Allāh b. Muḥammad ii, 81a; s, 95b — II, 82b; S, 95a
Māzandarānī, Mullā Muḥammad Ṣūfī i, 840b — I, 864a
Mazandjān v, 456b — V, 459a
Mazang ii, 41a — II, 42a
Mazār-i Sharīf i, 530b, 1001b; s, 94a, 281a — I, 546b, 1032a; S, 93b, 281a
Mazārīˁ, Āl v, 223b; s, 355b — V, 221a; S, 355b
Mazdaean/Mazdéen iv, 11a-12b, 43a — IV, 12a-13b, 45b
Mazdak i, 2b; v, 63b — I, 2b; V, 65a
Mazdakites i, 844a; ii, 228a; v, 63b, 64a, 853a — I, 867a; II, 235a; V, 65b, 66a, 859b
Mazdalī b. Sulankān i, 986a; ii, 1013a — I, 1016b; II, 1036b
Mazhar ii, 620b, 621a — II, 636a, 636b
Maẓhar s, 23b — S, 23b
Maẓhar, Ismāˁīl iv, 125a — IV, 130a
Maẓhar Djān-i Djānān iii, 430b; iv, 507a — III, 444b; IV, 529a
al-Mazimma s, 377b — S, 377b
al-Māzīnī (d./m. 861) iv, 122b, 822a — IV, 127b, 855a
al-Māzinī, ˁAbd al-Ḳādir i, 597b; v, 189a, b — I, 617b; V, 186b
Mazrūˁī iv, 887a, b, 889b — IV, 919b, 920a, 922a
al-Mazrūˁī, Shaykh al-Amīn iv, 890b; s, 248a — IV, 923b; S, 248a
Maˁzūl iv, 375a — IV, 391b
Mazyad, Banū i, 300b, 512a, 684a, 1052b, 1086a, 1096a; iv, 27b; s, 119a, 326a — I, 309b, 527b, 704b, 1084a, 11118b, 1129a; IV, 29b; S, 118b, 325b
al-Māzyār b. Ḳarin i, 52b, 241a; iv, 20b, 207b, 645b, 646a, b; v, 64b; s, 309a — I, 54b, 248b; IV, 22a, 217a, 672a, b, 673a; V, 66b; S, 308b
Mazyata s, 103a — S, 102b
Mbacké, Āl s, 182a — S, 182b
Mbārak al-Mazrūˁī iv, 889b — IV, 922a
Mecca → Makka
Mechanical technology → Ḥiyal
Mechitar i, 640b — I, 661b
Meclis → Madjlis
Mecque, la → Makka
Meddāḥ → Maddāḥ
Médéa → al-Madiyya
Medicine/Médecine → Ṭibb
Medina/Médine → Madīna
Medinaceli → Madīnat Sālim
Medinī Rāy ii, 13a, 1128a; iii, 421b — II, 13a, 1154b; III, 435a
Mediouna s, 144b, 145a — S, 144a, b
Mediterranean Sea/Méditerranée, la → Baḥr al-Rūm
Medjdi i, 733a — I, 755a
Medjelle i, 285a; iii, 164a, 250a, 661a; iv, 168b — I, 294a; III, 167b, 257b, 682a; IV, 175b

Medjelle-i aḥkām-i ʿadliyye ii, 172a, 473b — II, 177b, 485b
Medjīdīyye ii, 28b, 119b — II, 29a, 122b
Medjlis → Madjlis
Medjmūʿa-yi fewāʾid v, 952a — V, 956a
Medjmūʿa-yi fünūn ii, 473b, 532a — II, 485b, 545a
Medrese → Madrasa
Mefkhari → ʿAṭāʾ Bey, Meḥmed
Meguiden s, 328a — S, 327b
Meharza s, 328a — S, 327b
Meḥemmed I Čelebī (Ottoman) i, 299b, 394a, 432a, 468a, 510b, 869b, 988a; ii, 98a, b, 239b, 599a, 611b, 684a, 984b, 990a; iii, 356b, 711b; iv, 623b — I, 309a, 405b, 444a, 482a, 526a, 893b, 1018b;II, 100b, 246b, 614a, 626b, 701a, 1007a, 1013a; III, 368a, 734a; IV, 648a
Meḥemmed II (Ottoman) i, 312b, 468a, 739a, 767b, 777a, 992b, 999a, 1007b, 1061a, 1062a, 1119a, 1163b, 1253a, 1334b; ii, 239b, 291b, 374a, 529a, 612a, 684a, 691a, 839b, 982b, 1140b; iii, 190b, 213a; iv, 140a, 224b, 225a, 576a, 624a, 969a; s, 257a, 283a, 315b — I, 322a, 482a, 760b, 790b, 800a, 1023a, 1029b, 1038b, 1092b, 1094a, 1153a, 1198a, 1290b, 1374b; II, 246b, 299b, 384a, 542a, 627a, 701a, 708b, 859b, 1005a, 1167b; III, 195a, 219a; IV, 146a, 234b, 235a, 599a, 649a, 1001a; S, 257a, 282b, 315a
- administration i, 310b, 470a, 640b, 655b, 1256a, 1265b; ii, 82b, 118b, 211b, 337b, 338a, 687a, 715a, 907a, 1086b; iii, 1181a, 1183a; iv, 225a, 238a, 376a, 560a, 563a, 564b, 900a; v, 850a, 882a — I, 320a, 484a, 661a, 676a, 1294b, 1304b; II, 84a, 121a, 218a, 347b, 704a, 733a, 928a, 1112a; III, 1210a, 1212b; IV, 235a, 248b, 392a, 582b, 585a, 587a, 933a; V, 886a, 888a
- constructions i, 481a, 775b, 836b, 1078a, 1225b, 1251b; ii, 11b, 684b; iv, 225a, b, 226a, 228a-230b — I, 495a, 798b, 860a, 1110a, 1262a, 1289b; II, 11b, 701b; IV, 234b, 235b, 238a-240b
Meḥemmed III (Ottoman) i, 310a, 380b, 956a; ii, 34a, 690a, 880b; iii, 1185a; iv, 900b; v, 19a, 27b — I, 319b, 391b, 985b; II, 34b, 707a, 901a; III, 1214b; IV, 933b; V, 19b, 28a
Meḥemmed IV (Ottoman) i, 1278b; ii, 345b, 684a, b; iii, 983b, 1185a; iv, 590a, b; v, 260a, b, 261b, 272b, 720b; s, 257b — I, 1318a; II, 355a, 701a, b; III, 1008a, 1214b; IV, 613b, 614a, b; V, 258a, b, 259b, 270b, 725b; S, 257b
Meḥemmed V (Ottoman) i, 64a — I, 65b
Meḥemmed VI (Ottoman) i, 734a; ii, 104b; iv, 873a, b, 946b — I, 756a; II, 107a; IV, 906b, 907a, 979b
Meḥmed Agha (Ḳule Aghasî) s, 281b — S, 281b
Meḥemmed, Meḥmed, Mehmet → Muḥammad
Meḥmed Čelebi → Meḥemmed I
Meḥmed Emīn (Yurdakul) s, 47b, 149b — S, 48a, 149b
Meḥmed Farrūkh Pasha s, 234b — S, 234b
Meḥmed Nedjātī s, 171b — S, 171b
Meḥmed Pasha Bîyîklî ii, 345a, b; v, 248b, 457b — II, 355a; V, 246a, 460a
Meḥmed Rashīd s, 296a — S, 296a
Meḥmed Saʿīd Ghālib Pasha iv, 295b — IV, 308b
Meḥmed Shākir Pasha s, 348b — S, 348b
Meḥmed Sherīf s, 63a — S, 63b
Meḥmed Tewfīḳ Efendi, Khodja s, 149b — S, 149b
Meḥmet ʿĀkif Ersoy iv, 169a — IV, 176a
Mehmet Eşref → Eshref, Meḥmed
Mehtar ii, 30b — II, 31a
Mekke, la → Makka
Meknes/Meknès i, 85a, 356a, 1346b; ii, 819b; iii, 973a; v, 1192a; s, 53a, 103a, 350b, 397b, 399b — I, 87b, 366b, 1387a; II, 839b; III, 997b; V, 1182a; S, 53b, 102b, 350b, 398a, 400a
Melek Aḥmed Pasha ii, 718a — II, 736b
Melek Meḥmed Pasha iv, 455b — IV, 476a
Melek Ṭāwūs → ʿIzrāʾīl
Melilla → Malīla
Melilot/Mélilot → Iklīl al-Malik
Melitene i, 1103a, b, 1104a; ii, 110a, b, 238a; iv, 484a — I, 1137a, b; II, 112b, 113a, 245a; IV, 505a
Mellita iv, 650b, 651b — IV, 676b, 678a
Memdūh, ʿAbd al-Halīm iv, 871b — IV, 905a
Memdūḥ Pasha i, 825b — I, 848b
Memduh Şevket Esendal → Esendal
Memek Čelebi iii, 175b — III, 179b
Memi Shāh → Āteshīzāde Memi
Memish Beg ii, 1046a — II, 1070b
Memons i, 172a — I, 176b
Menāḳib iii, 374a — III, 386a
Menangkabau i, 170b, 173b, 174a; iii, 1214b, 1222b, 1225b, 1228a; s, 151a — I, 175a, 178b; III, 1245a, 1253a, 1253b, 1257a, 1259b; S, 151a
Menderes, Adnan ii, 204a, 432b, 596a; iii, 527a — II, 210b, 444a, 611a; III, 545a
Menemendji — oghlu ii, 207a — II, 213b
Mêng-Kuan iv, 554b — IV, 578b
Mengli Girāy i, 293a, 843a, 893a, 1166b; ii, 1112b, 1113a; v, 137a, 138a, 719b — I, 302a, 866b, 920a, 1201b; II, 1139a; V, 140a, b, 724b
Mengubars i, 1336b, 1358a — I, 1377a, 1398a
Mengüček Ghāzī i, 466a, b, 983a; ii, 340a, 711b — I, 480a, 1013b; II, 350a, 729b
Mengüčekid Aḥmad iv, 871a — IV, 904a, b
Mengüčekid(e)s i, 467a, 639a; ii, 340a; iv, 578b — I, 480b, 659b; II, 350a; IV, 602a
Mengūdjid(e)s → Mengüčekid(e)s
Menstruation → Ḥayḍ
Menteshe i, 467b, 988a, 1250b; ii, 204b, 599a; v, 505b, 506a — I, 481b, 1018b, 1288b; II, 211a, 614a; V, 509a, b
Mer d'Azov → Baḥr Māyuṭis
Mer Baltique → Baḥr al-Warank
Mer Caspienne → Baḥr al-Khazar
Mer Méditerranée → Baḥr al-Rūm
Mer Morte → Baḥr Lūt
Mer Noire → Baḥr Bunṭus
Mer Rouge → Baḥr al-Ḳulzum
Merdjān → Mardjān
Merida/Mérida i, 493a, 1319b; ii, 1009a; iii, 74a, 288a — I, 508a, 1360a; II, 1032b; III, 76b, 296b
Merkit ii, 42a, 43a, 571a — II, 43a, 44a, 585b
Mersin i, 476b — I, 490b
Mertola i, 6a; ii, 1009b — I, 6a; II, 1033a
Merzifon iv, 589b; v, 1147a — IV, 613a, b; V, 1138b
Mesdjid → Masdjid
Meshrūṭiyyet ii, 640a — II, 656a
Mesopotamia/Mésopotamie → Irāḳ
Messahalla → Mā shāʾa ʿllāh
Meṣṣālī al-Hādjdj iii, 524b; iv, 785a — III, 542b; IV, 816b
Metalwork/Métallurgie iii, 310b, 1126a; v, 830b, 970a, 985b, 992b — III, 320a, 1154a; V, 836b, 972b, 981a, 988a
Metaphor/métaphore → Istiʿāra
Metaphysics/métaphysique → Mā baʿd al-ṭabīʿa
Mewati s, 124a — S, 123b
Mewḳūfdju ii, 147b — II, 151b
Mewlewiyet iv, 375a — IV, 391b
Mewlūd → Mawlid
Mezere → Maʿmūrat al-ʿAzīz
Mezö-Keresztes iv, 499a; v, 27b; s, 238b — IV, 520b; V, 28b; S, 238b
Mezzomorto → Ḥusayn Pasha
Mgīld, Bānū s, 113b, 145a — S, 113a, 144b
Mibkhara v, 987b — V, 983a
Midād ii, 307a, 311a — II, 315b, 320a

Miʿdān i, 1097a — I, 1130a
Midḥat, Aḥmed → Aḥmad Midḥat
Midḥat Djemāl Kuntay v, 197a — V, 194b
Midḥat Pasha i, 63b, 285b, 286a, 289b, 906b, 907b, 1096a, 1097a, 1304a; ii, 288b, 289a, 468b, 642a, 909a, 935b; iii, 621b, 1257b; iv, 638a, 765b, 876b; v, 904b — I, 65b, 294a, 298a, 934a, 935a, 1129a, 1130a, 1344a; II,296b, 297a, 480b, 658a, 930a, 957b; III, 642a, 1290b; IV, 664b, 796a, 909b; V, 910b
Midianite → Madyan Shuʿayb
Midjmar s, 23b — S, 23b
Miḍrab iv, 1147a — IV, 1179a
Midrār, Banū i, 83a, 1175b; ii, 495a — I, 85b, 1210b; II, 507a
Miftāḥ v, 990a — V, 985a
Miftāḥ al-Ḥikma i, 995b — I, 1026b
Miftāḥ al-ʿUlūm i, 594a, 858a, 982a — I, 613b, 882a, 1012b
Mihir Bhodja Pratīhāra ii, 1122b, 1123a — II, 1148b, 1149a
Mihmāndār iv, 1043a — IV, 1074b
Miḥna i, 811a; ii, 931a; iii, 1148a; v, 426a, 1124a — I, 834a; II, 953a; III, 1176b; V, 428b, 1121a
Mihnī v, 153b — V, 154b
Mihr-i Māh iii, 147b; v, 66b — III, 150b; V, 68b
Mihr al-Nisāʾ → Nūrdjahān
Miḥrāb Khān i, 1006a; v, 102a — I, 1037a; V, 104a, b
Mihradjān → Isfarāyīn
Mihrān iii, 408a; v, 872b — III, 421a; V, 878b
Mihrān Efendi ii, 474b, 475a; iv, 872b — II, 486b, 487a; IV, 906a
Mihrawlī ii, 259a, 266a — II, 266b, 274b
Mihrgān ii, 798b — II, 817a
Mihrishāh Sulṭān iv, 233b — IV, 244a
Mihrumāh Sulṭān iv, 231b — IV, 241b
Mihyār al-Daylamī i, 592b; s, 119b — I, 611b; S, 119a
Mihzam, Banū s, 24b — S, 25a
Mīkāʾīl ii, 363b, 846b — II, 373a, 866a
Mīkāʾīl b. Djaʿfar i, 1306b, 1307b — I, 1346b, 1348a
Miʿkāl s, 234b — S, 234b
al-Mīkālī, Abu 'l-Faḍl s, 343a — S, 343a
Mīḳāt iii, 362b, 1052b — III, 373b, 1079a
Miḳdād b. ʿAmr ii, 846b; iii, 873b — II, 866b; III, 897b
Miḳdād Aḥmed Pasha ii, 207b — II, 214a
Mikhadda v, 1158b — V, 1148b
Mīkhāl-oghullarî i, 340b — I, 351a
al-Mikhlāf al-Sulaymānī ii, 517a; s, 30a — II, 530a; S, 30b
Miḳlama iv, 471b — IV, 492a
Miknās → Meknes, Meknès
Miknāsa i, 1349b — I, 1390a
Miḳyās iii, 572a; v, 91b, 862b — III, 591b; V, 93b, 869b
Milāḥa ii, 583a, 586a; iii, 856b, 627b — II, 597b, 600b; III, 880b, 648a
Mīlānī, Āyat Allāh Muḥammad iv, 165b — IV, 172b
Milas s, 138 a — S, 137b
Miletus iv, 1169a — IV, 1201b
Milḥ v, 250b, 435b, 965a, 967b, 976a, 981b — V, 248b, 438a, 969a
al-Mīlī, Mubārak iv, 157a, 159b — IV, 163b, 166a
Milk (possession) i, 28b, 661a; iv, 1035b — I, 29b, 682a; IV, 1067a
Milk → Laban
Milla ii, 294b; iv, 174a — II, 302b; IV, 181b
Millat → Millet
Mille et Une Nuits → Alf layla wa-layla
Millet (nation) i, 470a; ii, 6b; iii, 1180b; iv, 785b, 790b — I, 484a; II, 6b; III, 1209b; IV, 817a, 822b
Millet (plant(e)) → Djāwars
Millī Kongre ii, 431b — II, 442b
Milliyyat iv, 785b — IV, 817b
Miʿmār-bashî iv, 235a, b — IV, 245b, 246a
Mīmiyya ii, 1094b — II, 1120b
Minā iii, 32b, 36a; s, 33a, 317a, 350a, 357b — III, 34a, 38a; S, 33b, 316b, 350a, 357a
Mīnāʾ al-Aḥmadī s, 50a — S, 50b
Mīna, Ḥannā v, 190b, 191a — V, 188a
al-Mina ii, 1056a — II, 1080b
Mīnāb s, 129a — S, 128a
Mīnāʾī i, 201b; iv, 1167a — I, 207a; IV, 1199b
Minangkabau → Menangkabau
Minbar i, 202b, 776a — I, 208b, 799a
Miñbashî i, 1229a — I, 1265b
Mindanao s, 152a — S, 152a
Mineralogy/Minéralogie → Maʿdin
Minhādj-i Sirādj → al-Djūzdjānī
Miniatures → Taṣwīr
Minḳād, Wādī s, 157a — S, 157b
Mint → Dār al-ḍarb
Mint/Menthe → Fūdhandj
Minṭāsh i, 1050b, 1051a; ii, 239b; iii, 187a — I, 1082b; II, 246a; III, 191a
Minūčihrī → Manūčihrī
Minūfiyya s, 44a — S, 44b
Minurḳa iv, 1157a — IV, 1189a
al-Minyā s, 18a, 408a — S, 18b, 408b
Minyat ʿAfīf s, 44a — S, 44b
Mīnyo, Nahr i, 489a — I, 503b
Mir ʿAbd Allāh Khān iv, 364b — IV, 380b
Mīr Ākhūr → Amīr Ākhūr
Mīr ʿalem i, 1135a — I, 1169a
Mīr ʿAlī Tabrīzī iv, 1124b — IV, 1156a
Mīr Amman → Amān, Mīr
Mīr Babar ʿAlī → Anīs
Mīr bakhshī i, 316b; v, 686a — I, 326b; V, 691b
Mīr-i Buzurg → Marʿashī, Ḳawām al-Dīn
Mīr-i Dāmād → al-Dāmād
Mīr Djumla → Muḥammad Saʿīd
Mīr Khudādād v, 102b — V, 104b
Mīr Lawḥī v, 1088a — V, 1085a
Mīr Maʿsūm → Maʿsūm Nāmī
Mīr Muhannā iv, 1056b — IV, 1087b
Mīr Munnū → Muʿīn al-Mulk b. Ḳamar al-Dīn
Mīr Sāmān i, 316b — I, 326b
Mīr Shams al-Dīn iv, 709a — IV, 737a
Mīr Shīr ʿAli → Afsūs
Mīr Taḳī Mīr ii, 1036b; iii, 119a, 358b, 376a; v, 961b — II, 1060b; III, 121b, 370a, 388a; V, 965b
Mīr Ways i, 218b, 226b, 229a; ii, 1011a; iii, 603b; iv, 537a — I, 224b, 233a, 236a; II, 1024b; III, 624b; IV, 560b
Mīrāb iv, 103b; v, 872b, 874a, b, 881b — IV, 108a; V, 871a, 880a, b, 887b
Miracle → Karāma
Miʿrādj i, 1310b; ii, 448b — I, 1350b; II, 460a
Mīrafāb i, 1171b, 1172a — I, 1206b, 1207a
Mīrak Ḥusayn Yazdī s, 204a — S, 203b
Mīrak Naḳḳāsh i, 1211a, b — I, 1247a, b
Mīram Čelebī iv, 810a — IV, 842b
Mīrān Muḥammad I ii, 815a, 1128b; iii, 422a, 1160a — II, 834a, 1155a; III, 435b, 1188b
Mīrān Muḥammad II ii, 815a; iii, 1161a, b — II, 834b; III, 1189b, 1190a
Mīrān Shāh ʿAlī iii, 626a — III, 646b
Mīrān Shāh Ḥaydar iii, 625b — III,646b
Mīrānīs ii, 185b — II, 191b
Mīrānshāh b. Timūr i, 66b; ii, 733a, b; iii, 600b; iv, 914b, 1029a — I, 68b; II, 751b, 752b; III, 621a; IV, 947b, 1060b
Mirʿāt al-Aḥwāl ii, 466a, 471a — II, 477b, 483a
Mīrāthī, ʿImād al-Dīn iv, 1041a — IV, 1072b

Mirbad i, 1080a, 1086a; s, 172a – I, 1112b, 1118b; S, 173a
Mirbāt iii, 270a – III, 277b
Mirčea ii, 611a – II, 626b
Mīrdās b. Udayya iii, 169a, 648a, 1175b; iv, 1075b – III, 172b, 669b, 1204b; IV, 1107a
Mīrdāsid(e)s i, 442a, 1349a; iii, 86a, 686b; v, 459a – I, 454b, 1389b; III, 88b, 708a; V, 461b
al-Mīrghanī, Ḥasan b. Muḥammad iv, 686b – IV, 715a
al-Mīrghanī, Muḥammad ʿUthmān i, 1029a; s, 278b – I, 1060b; S, 278b
Mīrghāniyya i, 277b; ii, 710a; iii, 6a – I, 286a; II, 729a; III, 6a
Mīrī i, 1147b; ii, 148a – I, 1181b; II, 152b
Mīrī muḳāṭaʿa iv, 1095b, 1096a, b; v, 792b – IV, 1126b, 1127a, b; V, 798b
Mīrī, Shaykh ii, 768a – II, 786b
Mīrī ʿaskerīs i, 1229a – I, 1265b
Mirkh(w)ānd iv, 1020b; s, 46b – IV, 1052b; S, 46b
Mīrmīran i, 1160a – I, 1194b
Mirror/Miroir v, 988a – V, 984a
Mirwāt → Čeh
Mīrzā ii, 19a – II, 19b
Mīrzā ʿAzīz Kōka i, 80b, 507a; ii, 815a – I, 83a, 522a; II, 834b
Mīrzā Buzurg → Ḳāʾim-maḳām-i Farāhāni, ʿIsā
Mirzā Iskandar v, 163b – V, 161b
Mīrzā Khān (Aḥmadnagar) ii, 921b; iii, 626a; s, 327b – II, 943a; III, 647a; S, 327a
Mīrzā Khān (Badakhshān) i, 852b – I, 876b
Mīrzā Meḥemmed Isfendiyār-oghlu iv, 108b – IV, 113b
Mīrzā Muḥammad Khān → Amir Mukarram Lāridjānī
Mīrzā Ṣādiḳ Khān → Amīrī
Mīrzā Ṣāliḥ ii, 649b – II, 665b
Mīrzā Taḳī Khān → Taḳī Khān
Mīrzāyev, ʿAbd al-Ghanī s, 290a – S, 290a
Mīrzās ii, 1129a, b; iii, 422a, 423b – II, 1156a; III, 435b, 437a
Misalla i, 963a – I, 992b
Misʿar b. Fadakī iv, 269a – IV, 281a
Misʿar b. Muhalhil → Abū Dulaf
Miṣbāḥ al-arwāḥ iv, 67b – IV, 71a
Mīshmast iii, 1103a – III, 1130a
Misiṭṭāsa i, 1037a – I, 1068b
Miskawayh, Abū ʿAlī i, 127a, 234b, 326b, 327b, 328a, 328b, 590a, 1353b, 1354a; ii, 80a, 174a; iii, 703b, 955a, 1237a; s, 72b, 119b, 263b, 398b – I, 130b, 241b, 337a, 337b, 338a, 339a, 609a, 1392b, 1393a; II, 81b, 179b; III, 725b, 979b, 1269a; S, 73a, 119a, 263a, 398b
ʿMiskīnʾ → Furūghī
Miskīn ii, 757b – II, 776a
Miskīn, Mullā i, 423b – I, 435b
al-Mislaḥ s, 198b – S, 198b
al-Mismaʿī, ʿAbd Allāh b. Ibrāhīm iii, 1015b; iv, 100a – III, 1041a; IV, 104b
Miṣr i, 13b, 21a, 215b, 396a, 451a, 531b, 638b, 750b, 797b, 800a, 801a, 870a, 1054a, 1107a; ii, 495a, 668a, 853b, 854a, 914a; iii, 4b, 264a, 384b, 395a, 653b, 1259a; v, 556b, 558b, 1060a; s, 120b, 216a – I, 13b, 22a, 222a, 407b, 464a, 547b, 659b, 773a, 821a, 823b, 824b, 894b, 1085b, 1140a; II, 507b, 684b, 873b, 935a; III, 4b, 272a, 397a, 407b, 675a, 1291b; V, 561a, 563b, 1057a; S, 120a, 216a
- administration i, 976a; ii, 148a, 327a, 595a, 647a; iii, 556a, 1154a, 1185b, 1193b; iv, 192b, 193a, 323b, 1033b – I, 1006a; II, 152b, 336b, 610a, 663a; III, 575a, 1182b, 1215a, 1223b; IV, 200b, 201a, b, 337b, 338a, 1065a
- agriculture iii, 625a, 1154a – III, 645b, 1182b
- demography/démographie s, 216a – S, 216a
- education v, 907b, 1091b – V, 913a, 1088b
- ethnography/ethnographie i, 35a, 37b, 39a; iii, 299b; v, 317b – I, 36a, 38b, 40a; III, 309a; V, 317a
- history/histoire i, 138b, 965a; ii, 355b; iii, 675a, 756b, 813a, 894b; v, 121b – I, 142b, 995a; II, 365a; III, 696b, 779b, 836b, 918b; V, 124a
- institutions ii, 126b, 128a, 129b, 132a, 423b; iii, 1068b; iv, 192b – II, 130a, 131a, 133a, 135a, 434b; III, 1095b; IV, 201a
- language, literature/langues, littérature i, 74b, 142a, 568b, 575a; ii, 465a, 466a, 764a; iii, 935a – I, 76b, 146a, 587a, 594a; II, 477a, 478a, 782b; III, 959b
- monuments v, 290a – V, 289b
- statesmen/hommes d'État i, 51b, 58a, 293b, 391b, 1069b; ii, 764a – I, 53a, 60a, 302b, 402b, 1101b; II, 782b
Miṣr Bay iv, 552a – IV, 576a
Miṣr al-fatāt ii, 429a; iii, 518a; s, 5b – II, 440a; III, 535b; S, 4b
Misrāʿ i, 668a – I, 688b
Misrāḳlî → Sulaymān Pasha
Misrāta iii, 1040a; v, 948b – III, 1066a; V, 952b
Miṣṣīṣa ii, 35b – II, 36b
Mistāwa → al-Nukkār
Mithāliyya iv, 507a – IV, 529a
Mithḳāl iii, 10b; iv, 248b – III, 11a; IV, 259b
Mithḳāl, Amīr v, 1141b, 1142a – V, 1134b, 1135a
Mitīdja → Bulayda
Mitwālī s, 268b, 269a – S, 268b
Miyān Gul Djān ii, 317a – II, 326a
Miyān Gul Gul Shāhzāda ii, 317a – II, 326b
Miyān Ḥasan Khān Sūrī ii, 271a – II, 279b
Miyān Mir → Miyāndjī
Miyān Muṣṭafā Gudjarātī ii, 500a – II, 512b
Miyānābād iv, 107b – IV, 112b
Miyāndjī ii, 134b – II, 138a
Mizādj i, 1084a – I, 1116a
Miyāndurūd iv, 645a; s, 298a – IV, 671b; S, 297b
Mizāb iv, 318a – IV, 332a
Mizʿal Khān iv, 1171a – IV, 1204b
Miẓalla iv, 214a, 1147a – IV, 223b, 1178b
Mīzān ii, 358b; iii, 212b, 465b; iv, 600a, 1186a – II, 368b; III, 218b, 482a; IV, 624b, 1219a
Mīzāndji Murād → Murād Bey (d./m. 1914)
Mizhar → Mazhar
Mizwār i, 687b – I, 708b
al-Mizzī, Djamāl al-Dīn iii, 817b, 818a, 952a, 954b – III, 841a, 842a, 976b, 979a
Mleh i, 182b, 639a; ii, 37b – I, 187b, 660a; II, 38a
Moab s, 190b, 191a – S, 191b, 192a
Mobilier → Athāth
Mocha → Mokhā
Modibbo Adama i, 179b, 180a; ii, 9b, 942b – I, 184b; II, 9b, 964a
Modon v, 270b, 271a – V, 268b
Möʾetüken b. Čaghatay i, 1010a; ii, 2a – I, 1041a; II, 2a
Mogadishu → Maḳdishū
Mogador i, 356b; iii, 70a; v, 1192a – I, 367b; III, 72b; V, 1182a
Mogholistān ii, 45a, b, 622a; v, 858a; s, 96b – II, 46a, b, 637b; V, 865a; S, 96a
Mogul → Mughal
Moḥā u Aḥmad al-Ahansalī iii, 167a – III, 170b
Mohács, Battle of/Bataille de s, 171a – S, 171a
Mohair → Tiftik
Mohamman ii, 1145b – II, 1173a
Mohammed Racim (Rāsim) s, 224b – S, 224b
Mohān s, 360a – S, 359b
Moḥand u l-Hādj iv, 363a – IV, 379a
Mohmand s, 237b – S, 237a

Mois Dibra iv, 139b, 140a — IV, 145b, 146a
Moïse → Mūsā
Mokhā i, 932b, 1140b; iv, 449b, 450a; s, 30b — I, 961a, 1175a; IV, 470a; S, 30b
Moḳrānī i, 369b, 1197a; iv, 478b — I, 380b, 1232b; IV, 499b
Moldavia → Boghdān
Molesalam Grasias i, 172a — I, 176b
Mollā → Mawlā
Mollā Khusraw → Khusraw, Mollā
Moluccas iii, 1219a, 1226a
Moluques, les — III, 1250a, 1257b
Mombasa i, 1282a; iv, 886a; v, 655b; s, 248a, 355b — I, 1321b; IV, 918b; V, 659b; S, 248a, 355b
Monastery → Dayr; Khānḳāh
Monastir (Tunisia/Tunisie) i, 1319a — I, 1359b
Monastir, province ii, 563a — II, 577a
Moncef Bey → Munṣif Bey
Monghyr i, 1209b, 1210a — I, 1245b, 1246a
Möngke i, 1105b, 1106a, 1187b, 1240b, 1311b; ii, 3a, 45b; iii, 1121a; iv, 814a; v, 299b, 300a — I, 1139a, 1223a, 1278a, 1352a; II, 3a, 46b; III, 1148b; IV, 847a; V, 299a, b
Möngke-Temür i, 1188b; ii, 812a, 1112a — I, 1223b; II, 831a, 1138a
Mongolia/Mongolie iv, 988b — IV, 1021a
Mongols i, 21a, 121a, 190a, 227a, 329b, 353b, 354b, 508a, 639b, 660b, 786b, 791b, 804b, 872a, 879b, 902b, 1105a, 1240b, 1295a, 1308a; ii, 3b, 38a, 41b, 67b, 194a, 229b, 285b, 344b, 393a, 707b, 746a, 928b, 1142a; iii, 87b, 105b, 177b, 402b, 702b, 1121a; iv, 30a-32a, 48a-b, 349a, 485a, 512a, 562b, 612b, 817a, 921b, 1049b-1051b; v, 58b, 456a, 748b; s, 184a, 246a, 256a, b — I, 21b, 124b, 194b, 233b, 339b, 364b, 365a, 523a, 660a, 681b, 810a, 815a, 828b, 896a, 905a, 929b, 1138b, 1278a, 1335a, 1348a; II, 3b, 38b, 42a, 68b, 200a, 236b, 293b, 354a, 403a, b, 726a, 764b, 950a, 1169a; III, 90a, 108a, 181b, 415a, 724b, 1148b; IV, 32a-34b, 50b-51a, 364a, 506a, 534a, 584b, 637a, 850a, 954b, 1081a-1083a; V, 60b, 458b, 754a; S, 185b, 246a, 255b, 256a
- art iii, 1125b, 1126a, — III, 1153b, 1154a, b
- histories of/histoires des ii, 606b; iii, 114a — II, 621b; III, 116b
- warfare/en guerre ii, 1083b; iii, 183b, 188a, 197b, 472a, 1099b — II, 1108b; III, 188a, 192b, 202b, 488b, 1126b
Monkey → Ḳird
Monnaies → Sikka
Monnaies, l'hôtel des → Dār al-ḍarb
Monopoly/monopole → Inḥiṣār
Montenegro → Kardagh
Moon → Hilāl; Ḳamar
Moors i, 31b; ii, 27a
Mopla → Māpilla
Mora (game/jeu) iv, 114a — IV, 119a
Mora (Greeks/Grecs) ii, 691a, 985a; iii, 91a; iv, 241a; v, 717b — II, 708b, 1007b; III, 93b; IV, 251b; V, 723a
Moravia → Čeh
Mordve i, 1338a — I, 1378a
Morea/Morée ii, 534a; iii, 212a; v, 268b, 270b; s, 149b — II, 547a; III, 217b; V, 266b, 268b; S, 149b
Morikubala Dore ii, 1132a — II, 1158b
Moriscos/Morisques i, 55b, 404b, 496a, 496b, 502a, 1343a; iv, 239a, 673a; v, 504b; s, 81a — I, 57b, 416b, 511a, 511b, 517a, 1383b; IV, 249b, 700b; V, 507b; S, 81a
Morocco i, 18a, 47a, 57b, 78b, 84b, 288b, 355a-357b, 1058a, 1321a; ii, 619b; iii, 240a, 251b, 256b, 1038a; iv, 262b; v, **1184a**; s, 103a, 190b, 215a, 223a
- administration i, 171a, 428a, 917b; ii, 413a, 673b, 676a; iii, 395b, 562a, 563b, 564a; v, 1072a, **1198b**
- demography s, 215a
- ethnography i, 34b, 39a, b, 533b, 1177b; ii, 160a; iii, 298b; iv, 329b, 331b, 332b; v, 696b, 1164b, **1196a**, 1207b
- geography v, 1184a
- history v, **1188a**
- institutions ii, 425b; iii, 525a; v, 917b, 1094a, 1150b
- language, literature i, 315b, 578b; ii, 469b; iii, 806b, 814a; v, 757a, **1203a**
- monuments v, 1152a, 1153b, 1201a
- religion v, 1199a
Moron → Mawrūr
Mosaic/Mosaïque → Fusayfisāʾ
Moscow/Moscow v, 138b — V, 141a
Moses → Mūsā
Moses of Khoren s, 274b — S, 274b
Mosque → Masdjid
Mosquitoes → Baʿūḍ
Mossadegh → Muṣaddiḳ, Muḥammad
Mōṣul → Mawṣil
Moulay Hafid → Ḥāfiẓ, ʿAbd al-
Moulouya → Malwiyya
Mountain goat → Ayyil
Mourre → Mora
Mouse → Faʾr
Moustiques → Baʿūḍ
Mouton → Ghanam
Mozarabs/Mozárabes i, 82b, 491a, 494a, 1339a; v, 367b, 376a; s, 92a, 397b — I, 85a, 506a, 509a, 1379a; V, 368b, 376b; S, 92a, 398a
Mrābṭīn i, 1049b — I, 1081a
Mshattā i, 613b, 615a, 616a; iii, 310a; v, 183a; s, 117a — I, 634b, 635b, 636a; III, 319a; V, 180a; S, 116b
Msila iv, 479a, b; s, 62b — IV, 501a, b; S, 63a
Mʾtir, Banū s, 145a — S, 144b
Muʾaddib v, 568a — V, 572b
Muʿādh b. Djabal i, 460b, 694a, 695a; ii, 372a; iv, 771a; v, 241a — I, 474a, 715a, 716a; II, 382a; IV, 802a; V, 238b
Muʿādh b. al-Nuʿmān i, 771b; iii, 812a — I, 794b; III, 835b
Muʿadhdhin i, 1215a — I, 1251a, b
Muʿadhdhinzāde ʿAlī Pasha iii, 251b; iv, 571b — III, 258b; IV, 594b
Muʿadjdjal i, 172b — I, 177b
al-Muʿāfā b. Zakariyyāʾ i, 154a; iii, 42a, 824b — I, 158b; III, 44a, 848b
Muʿāfī iv, 1045a — IV, 1076b
Muʿāhidūn v, 376a — V, 376b
Muʾallaf i, 1083b — I, 1116a
Muʾallafa Ḳulūbuhum i, 12a, 266b — I, 12a, 274b
Muʿallaḳ iii, 26a — III, 27a
Muʿallaḳāt iii, 136a, 222b, 1178a — III, 138b, 229a, 1207a
Muʿallal iii, 26a — III, 27a
Muʿallim v, 568a — V, 572b
Muʿallim Nādjī → Nādjī
al-Muʿallim al-Thālith → al-Dāmād
Muʿāmalāt i, 277a; iv, 560b — I, 285b; IV, 583a
Muʿammā v, 806b — V, 812b
al-Muʿāmara ii, 79a — II, 80b
Muʿammar, Āl ii, 321a; iii, 678a — II, 330b; III, 700a
Muʿammar b. ʿAbbād al-Sulamī i, 1243a; iii, 1143a; s, 88b, 226a — I, 1281a; III, 1171b; S, 88b, 226a
Muʿammar b. al-Aḥmar iv, 1132b; v, 702a — IV, 1164a; V, 707a
al-Muʿammarī → Abū Manṣūr al-Maʿmarī
al-Muʿammar al-Maghribī → Abu ʾl-Dunyā
Muʿammarūn i, 117a, 519b — I, 120a, 535b
Muʿanʿan iii, 26a — III, 27a
Muʿanṣar b. Ḥammad v, 1179b — V, 1169b
Muʾarridj s, 73b — S, 74a

Muʾarrikh → Kh(w)āndamīr
Muʿaṭṭib ibn Ḳushayr iv, 839b — IV, 872b
Muʿaṭṭila i, 257b, 334a; ii, 388b — I, 265b, 344a; II, 399a
Muʿāwaḍa iv, 286a — IV, 289b, 299a
Muʿāwiya I b. Abī Sufyān (Umayyad(e)) i, 40b, 43b, 85b, 194b, 275b, 710b, 760a, 1137b; ii, 35b, 89b, 116a, 128b, 129b, 280b, 323b, 343b, 456b, 911a, 931a, 1093b; iii, 20a, 241a, b, 391b, 397b, 455a, 545a, 607b, 1163b; iv, 315a, 493a, 734a, 841b, 938a, 973a, 1074b; v, 302a, 324b, 1123a; s, 10a, 88a, 89b, 103b, 133b, 157a, 221b, 230b, 243a, 394a — I, 41b, 44b, 87b, 200b, 284b, 732a, 782b, 1172a; II, 36b, 91a, 118b, 131b, 133a, 288b, 333a, 353b, 468a, 932b, 952b, 1119a; III, 21a, 248a, b, 404a, 410a, 471a, 564a, 628a, 1192a; IV, 329a, 514a, 763b, 874b, 971a, 1005b, 1106a; V, 301b, 324a, 1119b; S, 9b, 87b, 89b, 103a, 133a, 157a, 221b, 230b, 243a, 394b
- conflict with ʿAlī/conflit avec ʿAlī i, 383a, b, 384a, 451b, 549b, 636b, 704b, 1343b; ii, 480b, 625b; iii, 12b, 889b — I, 394a, b, 395a, 464b, 567a, 657a, 725b, 1384a; II, 493a, 641a; III, 13a, 913b
- constructions i, 341a; ii, 353a — I, 351b; II, 363a
Muʿāwiya II (Umayyad(e)) ii, 89b; iii, 270b; iv, 369b — II, 91a; III, 278b; IV, 385b
Muʿāwiya, Banū v, 118b — V, 121a
Muʿāwiya b. al-ʿĀṣ s, 103b — S, 103a
Muʿāwiya b. Bakr al-ʿImlāḳī iv, 820b; s, 246b — IV, 853b; S, 246b
Muʿāwiya b. al-Ḥārith al-Ṣimma ii, 627a — II, 642b
Muʿāwiya b. Hishām i, 1103a; iii, 494b — I, 1136a; III, 511b
Muʿāwiya b. Ḥudaydj iv, 825b, 826a — IV, 858b, 859a
Muʿāwiya b. al-Mughīra s, 103b — S, 103a
Muʿayn, Banū → Maʿīn, Banū
al-Muʿayṭī ii, 111b — II, 114a
al-Muʾayyad → Hishām II
al-Muʾayyad, Shafīḳ iii, 519b — III, 537a
al-Muʾayyad Aḥmad v, 73a — V, 75a
al-Muʾayyad billāh, Aḥmad b. al-Ḥusayn (Imām) s, 13a, 335b — S, 13b, 335a
al-Muʾayyad fi ʾl-Dīn i, 132b, 832b, 1074a; ii, 98a, 169a, 855b, 856a; iii, 905b; iv, 47a; v, 930a — I, 136a, 855b, 1106a; II, 100a, 174a, 875b, 876a; III, 929b; IV, 49b; V, 934b
al-Muʾayyad Muḥammad i, 553b — I, 571b
Muʾayyad al-Mulk i, 1052a, b — I, 1083b, 1084a
al-Muʾayyad Shaykh ii, 24a, 781b; iii, 48a, 99b, 186a, 187a; iv, 431b, 586a, b, 587a, 623b — II, 24b, 800b; III, 50a, 102a, 190b, 191b; IV, 450b, 608b, 609a, b, 648a
Muʾayyadzāde i, 1082b — I, 1115a
Muʾayyid al-Dawla i, 211b, 1350b; ii, 748b; iii, 258a, 671a, 704a; iv, 100b. 358a; s, 13a — I, 218a, 1390b; II, 767a; III, 265b, 692b, 726a; IV, 104b, 373b; S, 13b
Muʾayyid al-Dīn iv, 974b — IV, 1007a
Muʾayyid al-Mulk i, 1036a — I, 1067b
Muʿaẓẓam, (le) Prince → Bahādur Shāh I
al-Muʿaẓẓam Sharaf al-Dīn, al-Malik → al-Malik al-Muʿaẓẓam Sharaf al-Dīn
Mūbad Shāh ii, 74a — II, 75a
Mubāḥ v, 870b, 878b — V, 877a, 884b
Mubāhala i, 265a; ii, 848b, 849b — I, 273a; II, 868b, 869b
Muballigh ii, 276a — II, 284b
Mubāraʾa i, 1027a — I, 1058b
Mubārak, Āl iii, 582b — II, 602b
Mubārak (Āmirid(e)) i, 446b, 985b — I, 459a, 1016a
Mubārak Āl Ṣabbāh ii, 673a; v, 574a, b — II, 690a; V, 578b
Mubārak Khān ʿAbbāsī ii, 186b — II, 192a
Mubārak Khān I Dāwūdpōtrā ii, 185b, 186a — II, 191b, 192a
Mubārak Khān II Dāwūdpōtrā ii, 186a — II, 192a
Mubārak Khān Fārūkī ii, 814b — II, 834a
Mubārak Khān Lūḥānī i, 1136b — I, 1171a
Mubārak Khān Noḥānī s, 203a — S, 202b
Mubārak al-Maghribī al-Bukhārī i, 449a — I, 462a
Mubārak Nāgawri (al-Mahdawī) i, 117a; ii, 870b, — I, 120b; II, 891a
Mubārak Shāh (Badakhshan) i, 852b — I, 876a
Mubārak Shāh II (Farūkī) ii, 815a, 816a; iii, 422a — II, 834b, 835b; III, 435b
Mubārak Shāh I (Khaldjī) i, 444b; ii, 120a, 179b, 258b, 269a, 1084b, 1085b; iii, 416b; iv, 419b, 923b; s, 105b — I, 457b; II, 123a, 185b, 265a, 277b, 1109b, 1110b; III, 429b; IV, 437b, 956b; S, 104b
Mubārak Shāh II (Sayyid) i, 1323a; ii, 270b; iii, 638b; iv, 513a — I, 1363b; II, 278b; III, 659b; IV, 535a
Mubārak Shāh b. Ḳara Hölegü i, 1311b; II, 3a, b — I, 1352a; II, 3a, b
Mubārak Shāh al-Marwarrūdhī s, 285a — S, 284b
Mubārak Shāh Sharḳī iii, 14b, 419b — III, 15a, 432b
Mubārak (Sayyid) b. Sayyid Ibrāhīm (Bayhaḳī) s, 131b — S, 131a
Mubārakābād i, 1323a; ii, 258b — I, 1363b; II, 265a
Mubārakpur ii, 258b, 263b — II, 265a, 271b
Mubāriz al-Dīn Čawlī ii, 693b — II, 711a
Mubāriz al-Dīn Muḥammad ii, 737a, 812a; iii, 56a, 1022a; iv, 498b, 672a; v, 163a, 554a; s, 415a — II, 755b, 831b; III, 58a, 1048a; IV, 520a, 699b; V, 161a, 559a; S, 415a
Mubāriz al-Dīn Muḥammad Bey i, 703a — I, 724b
Mubāriz Khān (Deccan) ii, 99b; iii, 318b, 320a — II, 101b; III, 328a, 330b
Mubāriz Khān (Dihlī) → Muḥammad Shāh V
al-Mubarrad, Abū ʾl-ʿAbbās i, 97b, 125b, 321b, 590a, 1223b; ii, 300a; iii, 930a, 1263b; iv, 122b; v, 948a; s, 25a, 27b, 352a, 389b — I, 100b, 129a, 331b, 609b, 1260a; II, 308a; III, 954b, 1296b; IV, 128a; V, 951b; S, 25a, 27b, 352a, 390a
Mubashshir b. Fātik i, 235b, 236a, 247a; iii, 463b, 906b — I, 243a, b, 255a; III, 480a, 930b
Mubashshir b. Sulaymān iii, 853a — III, 877a
al-Mubayyiḍa iii, 617a; iv, 16b, 45b; v, 64a — III, 637b; IV, 17b, 48a; V, 66a
Mubham iii, 26a — III, 27b
Mūbiḳāt iv, 1107b, 1109a — IV, 1139a, 1140b
Mubīn, Mullā (Farangī Maḥall) s, 292b — S, 292a
Mubtadiʾ i, 1199b — I, 1235a
Mudabbadj iii, 26a — III, 27b
Mudallas iii, 26a — III, 27a
Muḍar iv, 832b, 833b; v, 76b, 77a — IV, 865b, 866b; V, 79a
Muḍāraba → Ḳirād
Muḍāriʿ i, 108a; v, 954b — I, 111a; V, 958b
Muḍarites i, 529b, 544b, 684b; iii, 233a — I, 545b, 562a, 705b; II, 239b
Mudarris iii, 1153b; iv, 634b; v, 568a, 1124b, 1131a — III, 1181b; IV, 660b; V, 572b, 1121a, 1127b
Mudarrisī, Taḳī iv, 73b; v, 200b — IV, 77a; V, 198a
Muḍarriṭ al-Ḥidjāra → Amr b. Hind
al-Mudawwana i, 120b, 249b, 685a; iii, 817a — I, 124a, 257a, 706a; III, 840b
Mudawwar, Djamīl v, 188a — V, 185b
al-Muḍayrib s, 355b — S, 355a
Mudéjar iv, 118a; s, 81a — IV, 123b; S, 80b
Mudhākara v, 1130b — V, 1126b
Mudīriyya ii, 828a — II, 847b
Mudjaddid-i Alf-i Thānī → Aḥmad Sirhindī
Mudjaddidīs i, 297b — I, 307a
Mudjāhid s, 386b — S, 386b
al-Mudjāhid i, 798b — I, 822a

Mudjāhid, Sayyid Muḥammad s, 75a — S, 75b
Mudjāhid al-ʿĀmirī i, 446b; ii, 111b, 112a, 837a; iii, 743b, 773a — I, 459a; II, 114a, 856b; III, 766a, 796b
Mudjāhidīn ii, 140b, 316b; iii, 335b; iv, 196b, 729b — II, 144a, 326a; III, 345b; IV, 205a, 758b
Mudjāhidin-i islām iv, 52a — IV, 55a
Mudjāhidūn i, 1333b; ii, 140b, 316b; iii, 335b, 1068a — I, 1273a; II, 144a, 326a; III, 345b, 1095a
Muʿdjam ii, 585b; iii, 760a, b — II, 660a; III, 783b
Mudjannada i, 490a — I, 504b
Mudjarrad iv, 517b — IV, 540a
Mudjāshiʿ b. Masʿūd al-Sulamī v, 157b — V, 157a
Mudjassima i, 333b, 410b — I, 344a, 422b
Mudjāwir v, 1134a — V, 1129b
Mudjbira → Djabriyya
Mudjdjāʿa b. Siʿr iii, 41a; iv, 534b — III, 43a; IV, 558a
Mudjdjān iv, 1002b, 1003a, 1004a — IV, 1035a, b, 1036b
Müdjerred resmi i, 1169b — I, 1204b
Mudjīb al-Raḥmān v, 1082a — V, 1079b
Mudjīr al-Dīn, Ḳāḍī iv, 958a — IV, 991a
Mudjīr al-Dīn Abak → Abu Saʿīd Abak
Mudjīr al-Dīn Amīrshāh iv, 738a; s, 59a — IV, 767b; S, 59b
Mudjīr-i Baylaḳānī iv, 62a; s, 239b — IV, 65b; S, 240a
Muʿdjiza iv, 615a, b, 616a, b — IV, 639b, 640a, b, 641a
Mudjrā → Madjrā
Mudjtabā Mīrlawḥī → Nawwāb-i Safawī
Mudjtahid iii, 1025b, 1026b; iv, 278a, 1101a; s, 103b — III, 1051b, 1052b; IV, 290b, 1132a; S, 103a
al-Mudlidjī → Abu ʾl-Ḳāsim al-Mudlidjī
Mudradj iii, 26a — III, 27b
Mudṭarib iii, 26a — III, 27b
Mufādana iv, 324a — IV, 338a
Mufaḍḍal s, 38b — S, 39a
al-Mufaḍḍal b. Abī Faḍāʾil s, 388b — S, 389a
al-Mufaḍḍal b. Salama ii, 135b, 807b; s, 177a — II, 139a, 826b; S, 178b
Mufaddal b. Ṣāliḥ s, 233a — S, 232b
al-Mufaḍḍal b. ʿUmar al-Djuʿfī iv, 1132b, 1133a — IV, 1164a, b
al-Mufaḍḍal b. Yazīd b. al-Muhallab s, 41a — S, 41a
al-Mufaḍḍal al-Ḍabbī i, 168b; iii, 136b, 706b, 985a, 1178a; s, 15b, 38b — I, 172a; III, 139a, 729a, 1009b, 1207a; S, 16a, 39a
Mufaḍḍaliyyāt i, 486a — I, 500b
Mufākhara i, 584b, 586b; iv, 77b, 448b; v, 1223b — I, 603a, 605a; IV, 81b, 468b; V, 1214a
al-Mufarradj b. Sallām iv, 275a — IV, 287b
Mufarridj b. Daghfal al-Ṭāʾī i, 824a, b; ii, 482b, 483a, 854b; iii, 77a, 79b, 128b, 841a; iv, 841b; s, 37a — I, 847a, b; II, 495a, b, 874a; III, 79b, 82a, 131a, 864b; IV, 874b; S, 37b
Mufarridj b. al-Djarrāh v, 327b — V, 327b
al-Mufawwaḍ i, 278b — I, 287a
Mufīd v, 1133b — V, 1129a
al-Mufīd, Shaykh iii, 1266a; iv, 182b; s, 56b, 89b — III, 1299a; IV, 190b; S, 57a, 89b
Mufliḥ → Abū Sāliḥ Mufliḥ
Mufrad i, 95a, 1083b — I, 97b, 1116a
al-Muftari → Ḥā-mīm
Muftī i, 276a; ii, 866a, 867a, 879a, 890a — I, 284b; II, 886a, 887a, 899a, 911a
Müftī-zāde (Müftüoghlu) Aḥmed → Aḥmad Ḥikmet
Mughal i, 81a, 117b, 199a, 228b, 229a, b, 238a, 252b, 316a, 768a, 769a, 1069a, 1159a, 1161a, 1168b, 1347b; ii, 120b, 155a, 157a, 265a, 336b, 806a, 815a, 868a, 1084b, 1129b; iii, 199a, 201a, b, 411a, 422b, 424b, 448b; iv, 268b, 563a, 709a, 759b, 1056a; v, 72a, 629b; s, 131b, 167b, 246b, 252b, 253a, 257b, 258b, 280a, 335b — I, 83b, 121a, 204b, 235b, 236a, b, 245a, 260a, 326a, 791a, 792a, 1101a, 1193b, 1195b, 1203a, 1387b; II, 123b, 160a, 162a, 273a, 346a, 825a, 834b, 888a, 1110a, 1156a; III, 204a, 206a, b, 423b, 436b, 438a, 464a; IV, 280b, 585a, 737b, 789b, 1087a; V, 74a, 633b; S, 130b, 167b, 246b, 252b, 257b, 258a, 279b, 335a
- constructions v, 888b, 889a, 1215a, 1216b — V, 895a, b, 1204b, 1206b
Mughalānī Bēgam i, 296a; iii, 1158b — I, 305a; III, 1187a
al-Mughallis, Abū ʿAbd Allāh al-Ḥusayn s, 119b — S, 119a
Mūghān s, 143a — S, 143a
Mughanni ii, 1073a, b — II, 1098a, b
Mughayd, Banū i, 98a — I, 101a
al-Mughīra b. ʿAbd Allāh → al-Uḳayshir al-Asadī
al-Mughīra b. Abī Burda al-Ḳurashī v, 1160a — V, 1149b
al-Mughīra b. Saʿīd i, 141a, 1099a, 1116b; ii, 1094a; iv, 926b; s, 103b, 232b — I, 145a, 1132a, 1150b; II, 1120a; IV, 959b; S, 103a, 232b
al-Mughīra b. Shuʿba i, 111a, 382b, 695a, 714a; iii, 40a, 545a, 1265b; iv, 385a; v, 346b — I, 114b, 393b, 716a, 735b; III, 41b, 564a, 1298a; IV, 402a; V, 347b
Mughīth, Malik iii, 418b, 638b — III, 431b, 660a
Mughīth al-Rūmī i, 493a; v, 510a — I, 508a; V, 513b
al-Mughith ʿUmar iv, 609a — IV, 634a
Mughuliyya iv, 420a — IV, 438a
Muḥāḍara iv, 697a, b — IV, 725a, b
al-Muhadhdhab, al-Ḳāḍī iv, 214b — IV, 224a
Muhadhdhab al-Dīn v, 272a — V, 269b
al-Muhadhdhab b. Mammātī → Ibn Mammātī
Muhadhdhib al-Dawla ʿAlī b. Naṣr s, 118b, 119a — S, 118a, b
Muhādjarat movement/mouvement v, 171a — V, 168b
Muhādjir, Banuʾl- i, 65b; ii, 305a; iv, 478a; s, 82a — I, 67b; II, 313b; IV, 498b; S, 81b
al-Muhādjir b. ʿAbd Allāh al-Kilābī s, 31b — S, 32a
al-Muhādjir b. Abī Umayya i, 110b — I, 113b
Muhādjirūn i, 54b, 515a; iii, 226b, 366b, 874a; v, 995b — I, 56b, 530b; III, 233b, 378b, 898a; V, 991a
Muḥāfiẓ i, 975a, b — I, 1005b, 1006a
Muḥāfiẓ Khān ii, 1127a — II, 1153b
Muḥaḳḳak iv, 1123a, 1125a — IV, 1155a, 1157a
al-Muḥaḳḳiḳ al-Thānī ii, 104a — II, 106a
al-Muḥakkima al-ūlā → Harūrites
al-Muhalhil iii, 1176b, 1178a — III, 1205b, 1207a
Muhalhil b. Muḥammad i, 512b, 513a — I, 528a, b
al-Muhallab b. Abī Ṣufrā i, 55a, 76b, 77a, 304a, 810b, 1242b; iii, 40b; iv, 15a, 752b, 1075b, 1145b; v, 57a; s, 357b — I, 57a, 77a, 79a, 313b, 833b, 1280b; III, 42a; IV, 16a, 783a, 1107b, 1177a; V, 58b; S, 357b
al-Muhallabī → Yazīd b. Ḥātim
al-Muhallabī, al-Ḥasan b. Muḥammad i, 118a, 126b, 1352b; iii, 780a, 854a; s, 13a, 32b, 362a, b — I, 121b, 130b, 1392a; III, 803b, 878a; S, 13a, 32b, 361b, 362a
Muhallabid(e)s i, 158a, 305a; iii, 649b, 981b; s, 352a — I, 162b, 314b; III, 670b, 1006a; S, 352a
Muḥallil v, 109b — V, 112a
Muḥammad, Prophet i, 453a, 514a, 728a, 959a, 1020b, 1021a, 1092b, 1283b; ii, 168a, 227a, 363a, 538b, 593a, 758b, 932a, 1061a; iii, 32a, 33a, 90b, 435a, 800b, 933a, 1231b, 1240b; iv, 316a, 356a, 994b, 996b; v, 75a, 402b, 734a
- beliefs concerning - i, 178a, 187b, 264a, 266a, 267a, 306b, 314b, 333a, 336b, 337a, 349a, 443a, 1310a, b, 1314b; ii, 363b, 376a, 847a, 883b, 950a, 993a, 1005b, 1058b, 1098b; iii, 94b, 256a, 462a, 607a, 1018b; iv, 270a, 319a, 367b, 821a, 1074a; v, 82a

- companions of - i, 114b, 129a, 343b, 881b, 405a, 448b, 514a, 695a, 1077b, 1313a; ii, 728b; iii, 582b, 873b, 1024a; iv, 896b, 927a; v, 406a
- history of iv, 736b; v, 415a, 771a
- life events i, 12a, 53a, 109b, 110a, 115b, 136b, 151a, 152b, 307b, 381b, 442b, 451a, 509b, 549a, 609a, 633b, 771b, 868a, 922a, 1011b; ii, 113b, 372a, 461b, 625a, 725a, 842b, 846b, 873b, 953a, 993b, 1023b; iii, 33a, 64a, 94a, 223a, 240b, 286a, 366b, 539a, 578a, 975b; iv, 320a, b, 771a, 824a, 832b, 898b, 927b, 928b, 1020b, 1103a, 1138b; v, 78b, 79a, 316a, b, 317a, 436b, 995b, 1161b
- relics of - i, 109a, 736a, 1314b; ii, 695b; iv, 367b, 368a; v, 761a
Muḥammad, le Prophète I, 466a, 530a, 750a, 988b, 1051b, 1053a, 1125b, 1322b; II, 173b, 234a, 373a, 552a, 607b, 777a, 953b, 1085b; III, 33b, 34b, 93a, 449a, 824a, 957b, 1263b, 1272b; IV, 330a, b, 371a, 1027a, 1029a; V, 77a, 403b, 739b
- croyances à l'égard de - I, 183a, 193a, 272a, 274a, 275a, 316a, 324b, 343b, 347a, b, 359b, 455b, 1350a, b, 1354b; II, 373b, 386a, 867a, 904a, 972b, 1016a, 1029a, 1083a, 1124b; III, 94b, 295a, 478b, 628a, 1044a; IV, 282a, 333a, 383b, 854a, 1105b; V, 84a, b
- compagnons de - I, 118a, 133a, 354a, 392a, 416b, 461b, 529b, 716a, 1109b, 1353b; II, 747a; III, 603a, 897b, 1050a; IV, 929a, 960a; V, 407a
- évènements de sa vie I, 12a, 55a, 112b, 113a, 118b, 140b, 155b, 157a, 317a, 392b, 455a, 464a, 524b, 566b, 629a, 654b, 794b, 892a, 922a, 1042b; II, 116a, 382a, 473a, 640b, 743b, 862b, 866a, 893b, 975b, 1016b, 1047a; III, 33a, 66b, 94a, 230a, 247b, 294b, 378a, 557b, 598a, 1000a; IV, 334b, 802a, 857a, 865b, 931a, 960b, 961b, 1052b, 1134b, 1170b; V, 80b, 81a, 315b, 316a, b, 438b, 991a, 1151a
- histoire de - IV, 766b; V, 416b, 777a
- reliques de - I, 112a, 758a, 1354b; II, 712b; IV, 383b, 384a; V, 767a
Muḥammad, Sultan of/de Brunei s, 151b — S, 152a
Muḥammad (Bayhaḳī Sayyid) s, 131b — S, 130b
Muḥammad I (ʿAbbādid(e)) i, 5b, 242a; iv, 115b — I, 5b, 249b; IV, 121a
Muḥammad II (ʿAbbādid(e)) → al-Muʿtamid
Muḥammad I (Aghlabid(e)) i, 248b, 250b — I, 256a, 258a
Muḥammad II (Aghlabid(e)) i, 249a, 250b, 1152a — I, 256b, 258a, 1186b
Muḥammad I (ʿAlawid(e)) i, 355b; s, 113b — I, 366b; S, 113a
Muḥammad II (ʿAlawid(e)) i, 355b; v, 1191b — I, 366b; V, 1181b
Muḥammad III (ʿAlawid(e)) i, 47b, 356a, 506b; ii, 116b, 146a, 308a, 367b, 510b, 727a, 820a; iii, 339b, 395b, 966a; iv, 634a, 635b; v, 1192a; s, 40b, 325b, 401a, b — I, 49a, 367a, 521b; II, 119a, 150a, 317a, 377b, 523a, 745b, 839b; III, 349b, 408a, 990b; IV, 660a, 661b; V, 1182a; S, 40b, 325a, 401b, 402a
Muḥammad IV (ʿAlawid(e)) i, 315b, 356b, 357a; ii, 332a, 510b; iii, 562a, 806b; s, 114a, 303a — I, 325a, 367b, 368a; II, 341b, 523a; III, 581b, 830a; S, 113b, 303a
Muḥammad V (ʿAlawid(e)) i, 357b, 358a; ii, 673b, 1116b; iii, 564a; iv, 634b, 635b, 775a; v, 1072a, 1194b — I, 368b, 369a; II, 690a, 1142b; III, 583a; IV, 660b, 661b, 806a; V, 1069b, 1184b
Muḥammad I (Ḥafṣid(e)) → al-Mustanṣir
Muḥammad II (Ḥafṣid(e)) → Abū ʿAṣīda
Muḥammad III (Ḥafṣid(e)) → Abū Darba
Muḥammad IV (Ḥafṣid(e)) → al-Muntaṣir
Muḥammad V (Ḥafṣid(e)) → Abu ʿAbd Allāh Muḥammad V
Muḥammad I (Ḥammūdid(e)) iii, 147b — III, 150b
Muḥammad III (Ḥammūdid(e)) iii, 147b — III, 150b
Muḥammad I (Ismaʿīlī) i, 353b, 1359b; iv, 859b — I, 364a, 1399b; IV, 893a
Muḥammad II (Ismaʿīlī) i, 353b; iv, 205a — I, 364b; IV, 214a
Muḥammad III (Ismaʿīlī) i, 353b; iv, 205b — I, 364b; IV, 214b
Muḥammad I (Ḳarakhānid(e)) iii, 1114a — III, 1141b
Muḥammad II (Ḳarakhānid(e)) iii, 1114b — III, 1142a
Muḥammad I (Ḳarāmānid(e)) → Muḥammad b. Ḳaramān
Muḥammad II (Ḳarāmānid(e)) iv, 623b — IV, 648a, b
Muḥammad IV (Marinid(e)) iii, 832a, 836a — III, 855b, 859b
Muḥammad I (Naṣrid(e)) i, 495b, 1089a; ii, 307b, 1014a, 1015b, 1016b; iii, 826b; s, 381b — I, 510b, 1121b; II, 316b, 1038a, 1039a, 1040a; III, 850a; S, 382a
Muḥammad II (Naṣrid(e)) ii, 1016b — II, 1040b
Muḥammad III (Naṣrid(e)) iii, 833b — III, 857b
Muḥammad IV (Naṣrid(e)) iv, 355b — IV, 370b
Muḥammad V (Naṣrid(e)) i, 1225a; ii, 115a, 1017a; iii, 804a, 835b, 972b — I, 1261b; II, 117b, 1040b; III, 827b, 859b, 997a
Muḥammad VII (Naṣrid(e)) iii, 804a, 972b — III, 827b, 997a
Muḥammad VIII El Pequeño (Naṣrid(e)) s, 399a — S, 399a
Muḥammad IX El Zurdo (Naṣrid(e)) s, 399a — S, 399a
Muḥammad X El Cojo (Naṣrid(e)) s, 399a — S, 399b
Muḥammad XI, Abū ʿAbd Allāh (Boabdil, Naṣrid(e)) i, 501b; s, 399a — I, 516b; S, 399b
Muḥammad XII (Naṣrid(e)) i, 997a — I, 1027b
Muḥammad I-VI (Ottoman) → Meḥemmed I-VI
Muḥammad I b. Malik Shāh (Saldjūḳ) i, 522b, 664a, 684a, 780a, 1052a, 1336b; ii, 975b; iii, 47a, 196a, 197b, 254a, 1097b; iv, 28b, 29a, 101b, 102a; v, 159a, b, 662a; s, 382b — I, 538b, 683b, 705a, 803b, 1083b, 1377a; II, 998a; III, 49a, 201a, 202a, 261a, 1124a; IV, 30b, 31a, 106a, b; V, 158a, b, 667a; S, 383a
Muḥammad II (Saldjūḳ) i, 684a, 865b; iv, 1097a; v, 160b — I, 705a, 890a; IV, 1128a; V, 159a
Muḥammad I (Umayyad(e)) i, 11a, 83a, 85b, 494a, 498a, 957a; iii, 816a; iv, 713a; v, 510b, 1107b — I, 11a, 85a, 88a, 509a, 513a, 956a; III, 839b; IV, 741b; V, 514a, 1103b
Muḥammad II (Umayyad(e)) → al-Mahdī (Umayyad(e))
Muḥammad III (Umayyad(e)) i, 84a — I, 86b
Muḥammad II (Waṭṭāsid(e)) i, 706b — I, 727b
Muḥammad, Āl iii, 49b — III, 51b
Muḥammad, Awlād ii, 876a — II, 896a
Muḥammad b. al-ʿAbbās b. al-Baṣrī → Ṣāḥib al-Rākūba
Muḥammad b. ʿAbd Allāh (Ḥasanid(e)) s, 232b — S, 232b
Muḥammad b. ʿAbd Allāh b. Ẓafar al-Ṣaḳalī → Ibn Ẓafar
Muḥammad b. ʿAbbād → Muḥammad I (ʿAbbādid(e))
Muḥammad b. ʿAbbād i, 1166b — I, 1201b
Muḥammad b. al-ʿAbbās al-Yazīdī iii, 23b — III, 24b
Muḥammad b. ʿAbd Allāh → Muḥammad III (ʿAlawid(e))
Muḥammad b. ʿAbd Allāh (Ḥamāliyya) → al-Sharīf al-Akhḍar
Muḥammad b. ʿAbd Allāh b. ʿAbd al-Ḥakam → Ibn

ʿAbd al-Ḥakam
Muḥammad b. ʿAbd Allāh b. al-Ḥasan → al-Nafs al-Zakiyya
Muḥammad b. ʿAbd Allāh b. Khāzim i, 1293a — I, 1332b
Muḥammad b. ʿAbd Allāh b. al-Muḳaffaʿ i, 631a; iii, 883b — I, 652a; III, 907b
Muḥammad b. ʿAbd Allāh b. Saʿīd al-Yaharī iii, 124a — III, 127a
Muḥammad b. ʿAbd Allāh b. Ziyād → Muḥammad al-Ziyādī
Muḥammad b. ʿAbd Allāh Āl Khalīfa iv, 953b — IV, 986a
Muḥammad b. ʿAbd Allāh al-Birzālī i, 6a, — I, 6a
Muḥammad b. ʿAbd Allāh al-Ghālib → Muḥammad al-Maslūkh
Muḥammad b. ʿAbd Allāh Ḥassān al-Mahdī i, 1172b — I, 1208a
Muḥammad b. ʿAbd Allāh al-Kharūṣī iv, 1085a — IV, 1116a
Muḥammad b. ʿAbd Allāh al-Khudjistānī iii, 254b — III, 261b
Muḥammad b. ʿAbd Allāh al-Sāmarrī iii, 161a — III, 164b
Muḥammad b. ʿAbd Allāh Yumn al-Dawla i, 1310a — I, 1350a
Muḥammad b. ʿAbd al-ʿAziz b. Saʿūd v, 998b — V, 993b, 994a
Muḥammad b. ʿAbd al-Malik b. Ayman i, 600a — I, 619b
Muḥammad b. ʿAbd al-Malik al-Ṭawīl s, 80a — S, 79b
Muḥammad b. ʿAbd al-Malik al-Zayyāt ii, 385b — II, 396a
Muḥammad b. ʿAbd al-Muʿīn b. ʿAwn iii, 263a, 605b — III, 270b, 626a
Muḥammad b. ʿAbd al-Muʾmin i, 79b, 160b; iii, 386b — I, 82a, 165a; III, 399a
Muḥammad b. ʿAbd al-Raḥmān → Muḥammad IV (Alawid(e))
Muḥammad b. ʿAbd al-Ṣamad iv, 381a — IV, 397b
Muḥammad b. ʿAbd al-Wahhāb → Ibn ʿAbd al-Wahhāb
Muḥammad b. Abi ʾl-ʿAbbās iii, 135b — III, 138a
Muḥammad b. Abī ʿĀmir → al-Manṣūr b. Abī ʿĀmir
Muḥammad b. Abī Bakr i, 44a, 109b, 451b; iii, 241a; s, 92b — I, 45b, 112b, 464b; III, 247b; S, 92b
Muḥammad b. Abī Muḥammad Ibn Abi 'l-Zinād s, 380b — S, 380b
Muḥammad b. Abī Rawḥ Luṭf Allāh b. Abī Saʿīd i, 145b — I, 150a
Muḥammad b. Abi ʾl-Sādj i, 145b; ii, 524a, 679b; v, 49a — I, 149b; II, 537a, 696b; V, 50b
Muḥammad b. Abī Tawādjīn al-Kutāmī i, 91b — I, 94a
Muḥammad b. Abī Yūsuf Yaʿḳūb (al-Nāṣir) i, 166a; ii, 819a, 1007b; iii, 1055a; iv, 337b — I, 170b; II, 838b, 1031b; III, 1081a; IV, 352a
Muḥammad b. ʿAffān iii, 652b — III, 673b
Muḥammad b. al-Aghlab → Muḥammad I (Aghlabid(e))
Muḥammad b. Aḥmad → Muḥammad II (Aghlabid(e))
Muḥammad b. Aḥmad, Abu ʾl-Shalaʿlaʿ ii, 851a — II, 871a
Muḥammad b. Aḥmad Abī ʿAwn iii, 683a — III, 704b
Muḥammad b. Aḥmad al-Ḥabūḍī s, 338b — S, 338a
Muḥammad b. Aḥmad al-Ḥuḍīgī ii, 527a — II, 540a
Muḥammad b. Aḥmad Mayyāra i, 428a; iii, 721a — I, 440a; III, 743b
Muḥammad b. Aḥmad (Sharwān-Shāh) iv, 346b — IV, 361a
Muḥammad b. Aḥmad al-Shaybānī iv, 90b — IV, 94b
Muḥammad b. Aḥmad Ṭāhāzāde iii, 88a — III, 90b
Muḥammad b. al-Aḥmar → Muḥammad I (Naṣrid(e))
Muḥammad b. ʿĀʾid i, 98b, 106b, 709b; v, 808b — I, 101a, 109b, 731a; V, 814b
Muḥammad b. ʿAlī b. ʿAbbās i, 15a, 48b, 124b, 381a; ii, 168b; iii, 1265b; iv, 15b, 837a; v, 2a, 3a — I, 15b, 50a, 128b, 392a; II, 173b; III, 1298b; IV, 16b-17a, 870a; V, 2b, 3a
Muḥammad b ʿAlī b. Yūsuf ii, 1007a — II, 1030b
Muḥammad b. ʿAlī al-Baḥrānī iii, 588b — III, 609a
Muḥammad b. ʿAlī al-Bāḳir → Muḥammad b. al-Ḥanafiyya
Muḥammad b. ʿAlī al-Barḳī s, 127a — S, 126b
Muḥammad b. ʿAlī al-Fenārī iv, 244b — IV, 255b
Muḥammad b. ʿAlī al- Hamadānī i, 392b — I, 404a
Muḥammad b. ʿAlī al-Idrīsī → al-Idrīsī, Muḥammad b. ʿAlī
Muḥammad b. ʿAlī al-Riḍā i, 713a — I, 734b
Muḥammad b. ʿAlī al-Shawkānī iv, 142b — IV, 148a
Muḥammad b. ʿAlī Sipāhīzāde i, 119a; ii, 587b — I, 122b; II, 602a
Muḥammad b. ʿĀmir Abū Nuḳṭa al-Rufaydī i, 709a — I, 729b
Muḥammad b. ʿAmmār b. Yāsir i, 448b — I, 461b
Muḥammad b. ʿAnnāz i, 512a; iii, 258b, 571b — I, 528a; III, 266a, 591b
Muḥammad b. al-ʿArabi → Ibn al-ʿArabī
Muḥammad b. al-ʿArabiyya i, 47b — I, 48b
Muḥammad b. ʿArafa i, 357b, 358a; v, 1194b — I, 368b, 369a; V, 1184b
Muḥammad b. ʿĀrif b. Aḥmad ʿAbd al-Ḥaḳḳ s, 313a — S, 312b
Muḥammad b. Arslan → Muḥammad I (Saldjūḳ)
Muḥammad b. al-Ashʿath iii, 715a — III, 737b
Muḥammad b. al-Ashʿath al-Khuzāʿī i, 134b; iii, 654b, 981b, 1040b, 1041b; iv, 827a — I, 138a; III, 675b, 1006a, 1066b, 1067b; IV, 860a
Muḥammad b. ʿAshūr → Ibn ʿĀshūr
Muḥammad b. ʿĀṣim i, 600a — I, 619b
Muḥammad b. ʿAttāb v, 488a — V, 491a
Muḥammad b. ʿĀyid → Muḥammad b. ʾĀʿid
Muḥammad b. ʿAyshūn al-Sharrāṭ iv, 380a — IV, 396b
Muḥammad b. ʿAyyāsh ii, 1014b — II, 1038a
Muḥammad b. Ayyūb al-Bakrī i, 6a, 155b — I, 6a, 159b
Muḥammad b. Azhar i, 1212b — I, 1249a
Muḥammad b. Badr al-Dīn i, 310a — I, 319b
Muḥammad b. al-Baʿīth (Buʿayth) iv, 88b — IV, 92b
Muḥammad b. Balban ii, 268a; s, 67a, 124b — II, 276a; S, 67a, 123b
Muḥammad b. Bānī iii, 326b — III, 336b
Muḥammad b. Barakāt i, 553a, 1032b; ii, 517b — I, 571a, 1064a; II, 530a
Muḥammad b. Buzurg-Ummīd → Muḥammad I (Ismaʿīlī)
Muḥammad b. Dāwūd b. al-Djarrāḥ → Ibn al-Djarrāḥ
Muḥammad b. Dāwūd al-Isfahānī → Ibn Dāwūd
Muḥammad b. al-Djabbār ii, 1009a — II, 1032b
Muḥammad b. Djābir b. ʿAbd Allāh s, 231a — S, 230b
Muḥammad b. Djaʿfar b. Abī Ṭālib s, 92b — S, 92b
Muḥammad b. Djaʿfar al-Azkawī → Ibn Djaʿfar
Muḥammad b. Djaʿfar, al-Dībādj i, 145a, 402b, 551a — I, 149b, 414a, 568b
Muḥammad b. al-Djahm i, 153b, 1036a; iii, 355a — I, 157b, 1067b; III, 366a
Muḥammad b. Djarīr ii, 790b — II, 809b
Muḥammad b. Dushmanziyār → ʾAlāʿ al-Dawla

Muḥammad b. Eretna → Ghiyāth al-Dīn Muḥammad
Muḥammad b. Faḍl Allāh iii, 155b — III, 159a
Muḥammad b. al-Faḍl al-Djardjarāʾī → al-Djardjarāʾī
Muḥammad b. Fakhr al-Dīn Muḥammad iii, 457b — III, 473b
Muḥammad b. Falāḥ iv, 49a — IV, 52a
Muḥammad b. Farīghūn → Abuʾl-Ḥārith
Muḥammad b. Fayṣal b. ʿAbd al-ʿAzīz Āl Suʿūd s, 305b — S, 305b
Muḥammad b. al-Furāt → Ibn al-Furāt, Muḥammad
Muḥammad b. Ghāzī (Dānishmend) ii, 110b; iv, 843a — II, 113a; IV, 876a
Muḥammad b. Ghāzī (Malatya) iv, 506b — IV, 528a
Muḥammad b. Ḥabīb i, 158b; ii, 480a; iii, 820a, 907b; s, 177a — I, 162b; II, 492a; III, 843b, 931b; S, 178a
Muḥammad b. al-Ḥādjdj ii, 1013a; iii, 542b — II, 1036b; III, 561b
Muḥammad b. Hadjdjādj iv, 665b — IV, 692b
Muḥammad b. al-Hadjdjām ii, 1009b — II, 1033a
Muḥammad b. Ḥamad al-Sharḳi ii, 936b — II, 958b
Muḥammad b. Ḥammād b. Isḥāḳ Ibn Dirham s, **385a** — S, **385b**
Muḥammad b. al-Ḥanafiyya i, 15a, 41a, 48b, 55b, 124b, 381a, 402a, 959a, 1116b; ii, 168b, 1026a, 1094b; iii, 608b, 1232b, 1265b; iv, 836b, 1086b; v, 433b, 552a, 1231a, 1235b; s, 48b, 343a, 357b, 401a — I, 15b, 42a, 50a, 57a, 128b, 392a, 412b, 1150a; II, 173b, 1049b, 1120a; III, 629a, 1264a, 1298b; IV, 869b, 1117b; V, 435b, 557a, 1221b, 1226a; S, 49a, 342b, 357b, 401b
Muḥammad b. al-Ḥanash iv, 552b — IV, 576a
Muḥammad b. Ḥanbal i, 272b — I, 280b
Muḥammad b. al-Ḥarsh → Bū Dalī
Muḥammad b. Hārūn iii, 254b — III, 261b
Muḥammad b. Ḥasan → Muḥammad II, III (Ismaʿīlī)
Muḥammad b. Ḥasan (Sayyid Bayhaḳī) s, 131b — S, 131a
Muḥmmad b. Ḥasan b. Idrīs (Dāʿī Muṭlaḳ) s, 358b — S, 358b
Muḥammad b. Ḥasan al-Sarakhsī i, 146a — I, 150a
Muḥammad b. al-Hayṣam iv, 668a — IV, 695b
Muḥammad b. al-Haytham i, 154a — I, 158a
Muḥammad b. Hazzaʿ b. Zaʿal ii, 619a — II, 634b
Muḥammad b. Hindūshāh → Nakhdjawānī
Muḥammad b. Hishām i, 627a — I, 647b
Muḥammad b. Hishām b. ʿAbd al-Djabbār → al-Mahdī (Umayyad(e))
Muḥammad b. Ḥumayd al-Ṭūsī iii, 573a — III, 593a
Muḥammad b. Ḥusām iv, 68a — IV, 71b
Muḥammad b. Ḥusayn (Ḥusaynid(e)) iii, 635b; iv, 828b — III, 657a; IV, 861b
Muḥammad b. Ḥusayn b. al-Astarābādī → Ghiyāth al-Dīn Muḥammad
Muḥammad b. Ibrāhīm b. Ḥadjdjādj iv, 115b — IV, 120b
Muḥammad b. Ibrāhīm b. Ṭabāṭabā → Ibn Ṭabāṭabā
Muḥammad b. Idrīs → Ibn Idrīs
Muḥammad b. Idrīs II i, 1088a; ii, 874a; iii, 1035b — I, 1120a; II, 894a; III, 1061b
Muḥammad b. Ilyās → Abū ʿAlī
Muḥammad b. ʿĪsā (Burghūth) i, 1326b; iii, 1037a; iv, 692b — I, 1367a; III, 1063a; IV, 721a
Muḥammad b. ʿĪsā al-Māhānī → al-Māhānī
Muḥammad b. ʿĪsa al-Ṣufyānī al-Mukhtārī iv, 93b — IV, 97b
Muḥammad b. Isḥāk b. Ghāniya ii, 112a, 1007a — II, 114b, 1030b
Muḥammad b. Isḥāk b. Kundādjīk iv, 90a, 494a — IV, 94a, 515a
Muḥammad b. Isḥāḳ b. Manda → Ibn Manda, Abū ʿAbd Allāh
Muḥammad b. Isḥāḳ b. Miḥmashādh i, 146b; iv, 668b — I, 151a; IV, 695b
Muḥammad b. Ismāʿīl b. Djaʿfar i, 48a; ii, 375a; iii, 123b, 1072a, 1167b; iv, 198a, 203b, 204a, 1133a — I, 49b; II, 385a; III, 126b, 1099a, 1196a; IV, 207a, 212b, 213a, 1164b
Muḥammad b. Ismāʿīl Ibn ʿAbbād iii, 740a — III, 763a
Muḥammad b. Kaʿb al-Ḳuraẓī i, 140a; v, 436a, b — I, 144a; V, 438b, 439a
Muḥammad b. al-Ḳalḳashandī → Ibn Abī Ghudda
Muḥammad b. Ḳalaʾun → al-Nāṣir Muḥammad
Muḥammad b. Ḳara Arslan i, 665a; iii, 507a — I, 684b; III, 524b
Muḥammad b. Ḳaramān i, 467a; ii, 204b, 989a; iv, 620a, b — I, 481a; II, 211a, 1012a; IV, 644b, 645a
Muḥammad b. Ḳārin → al-Māziyār
Muḥammad b. Karrām ii, 1011a; iv, 183b, 667a — II, 1034b; IV, 191b, 694a
Muḥammad b. al-Ḳāsim i, 52b; ii, 485a; iii, 74a — I, 54a; II, 497b; III, 76b
Muḥammad b. al-Ḳāsim b. Hammūd iii, 786a; iv, 115b — III, 809b; IV, 120b
Muḥammad b. Ḳāsim al-Thaḳafī i, 679a, 1005b, 1068b, 1192a; ii, 27a, 154a, 188a, 488a, 1123a; iii, 41a, 323b, 482a; iv, 533b; s, 163a, 243a — I, 699b, 1036b, 1100b, 1227a; II, 27a, 158b, 194a, 500b, 1149a; III, 43a, 333b, 499a; IV, 556b; S, 162a, 243a
Muḥammad b. al-Ḳāsim b. ʿUbayd Allāh iv, 424a — IV, 442a
Muḥammad b. Khalaf b. al-Marzubān iii, 111a, 820a — III, 113b, 843b
Muḥammad b. Khālid i, 1034b, 1035a, 1036a — I, 1066a,b, 1067a
Muḥammad b. Khalīfa b. Salmān iv, 953a, b — IV, 985b, 986a
Muḥammad b. Khalīl iv, 535a — IV, 558a
Muḥammad b. Khalīl Ibn Ghalbūn iv, 617b — IV, 642a
Muḥammad b. al-Khayr Ibn Khazar iii, 1042b; v, 1176a — III, 1086b; V, 1166a
Muḥammad b. al-Khayr b. Muḥammad v, 1176b, 1177a — V, 1166b, 1167a
Muḥammad b. Khazar b. Ḥafṣ v, 1174a — V, 1165a
Muḥammad Ibn Khazar al-Zanātī → Ibn Khazar b. Ṣūlāt
Muḥammad b. Khunays i, 1293a — I, 1332b
Muḥammad b. Lope (Lubb) Ibn Ḳasī iii, 816a; iv, 713a — III, 839b; IV, 741b
Muḥammad b. Maḥammad b. Abī Bakr al-Murābiṭ s, 223b — S, 223b
Muḥammad (al-Mahdī) b. al-Manṣūr s, 31b — S, 31b
Muḥammad b. Maḥmūd → Muḥammad II (Saldjūk)
Muḥammad b. Maḥmūd (Ghaznawīd(e)) ii, 1051a; iii, 1201b — II, 1075b; III, 1232a
Muḥammad b. Maḥmūd, Sultan i, 300b — I, 310a
Muḥammad b. Maḥmūd al-Khwārazmī i, 124a — I, 128a
Muḥammad b. Malikshāh → Muḥammad I (Saldjūk)
Muḥammad b. Maʿn b. Ṣumādiḥ → al-Muʿtaṣim Ibn Ṣumādiḥ
Muḥammad b. Marwān i, 42a, 77a, 100b, 1041a; ii, 523b; iii, 29a — I, 43b, 79b, 103b, 1072b; II, 537a; III, 30b
Muḥammad b. Marzūḳ → Ibn Marzūḳ
Muḥammad b. Maslama al-Anṣārī i, 382b; iv, 315a

— I, 393b; IV, 329a
Muḥammad b. Mas'ūd i, 1132a — I, 1166a
Muḥammad b. al-Mi'mār → Ibn al-Mi'mār
Muḥammad b. Mu'aykil ii, 492b — II, 504b
Muḥammad b. al-Mubāriz ii, 736b — II, 755a
Muḥammad b. al-Mughīra b. Ḥarb s, 352a — S, 352a
Muḥammad b. Muḥammad b. Abi 'l-Luṭf i, 759a — I, 782a
Muḥammad b. Muḥammad b. Zayd i, 149b; iii, 951a — I, 154a; III, 976a
Muḥammad b. Muḥammad Čiwizāde ii, 56b — II, 57b
Muḥammad b. Muḥannā → Nu'ayr
Muḥammad b. Mukaththir iv, 748b — IV, 778b
Muḥammad b. Murtaḍā → Fayḍ-i Kāshānī
Muḥammad b. Mūsā ('Abd al-Wādid(e)) → Abū Zayyān II
Muḥammad b. Mūsa Kudatlī i, 756a — I, 778b
Muḥammad b. Mūsā al-Kh(w)ārizmī → al-Kh(w)ārizmī
Muḥammad b. Musāfir Kangarī ii, 192a — II, 198a
Muḥammad b. Musallam al-Bālisī iv, 641a — IV, 667a
Muḥammad b. al-Musayyab ii, 348b — II, 358a
Muḥammad b. Mushārī ii, 321b — II, 331a
Muḥammad b. al-Mustanīr → Ḳuṭrub
Muḥammad b. al-Muwallad iv, 89a — IV, 93a
Muḥammad b. al-Muẓaffar ii, 401b; iv, 221b — II, 412a; IV, 231a
Muḥammad b. Nūḥ i, 272b — I, 281a
Muḥammad b. al-Nu'mān ii, 374b — II, 385a
Muḥammad b. al-Nu'mān, Ḳāḍī i, 823b; ii, 169b; iii, 76b — I, 846b; II, 174 b; III, 79a
Muḥammad b. Nūr i, 813a, 942a; iii, 652b — I, 836a, 971a; III, 674a
Muḥammad b. Nuṣayr al-Namīrī i, 713a — I, 734b
Muḥammad b. Rā'iḳ → Ibn Rā'iḳ
Muḥamad b. Rashīd → Ibn Rashīd
Muḥammad b. Rushayd iv, 337a, b — IV, 351b, 352a
Muḥammad b. Saba' i, 181b, 1214b, 1215a; iv, 200b; v, 1244b — I, 186b, 1251a; IV, 209a; V, 1235a
Muḥammad b. Sa'd → Ibn Sa'd
Muḥammad b. Sa'd b. Abī Waḳḳās iii, 717a — III, 739b
Muḥammad b. Sa'd al-Awfī iii, 922b — III, 947a
Muḥammad b. Sa'dān s, 177a — S, 178a
Muḥammad b. Saḥnūn → Ibn Saḥnūn
Muḥammad b. Sa'īd i, 554a; ii, 321a; iii, 162a, 678b — I, 571b; II, 330b; III, 165b, 700a
Muḥammad b. Sa'īd b. Hārūn i, 6a; ii, 1009a — I, 6a; II, 1032b
Muḥammad b. Ṣāliḥ s, 279a — S, 278b
Muḥammad b. Sālim al-Ḥifnī iv, 992a — IV, 1024b
Muḥammad b. Ṣāliḥ al-Īfranī iii, 1042a — III, 1068a
Muḥammad b. Ṣa'lūḳ iii, 254b, 255a — III, 261b, 262a
Muḥammad b. Sām → Ghiyāth al-Dīn Muḥammad; Mu'izz al-Dīn Muḥammad
Muḥammad b. Shādān iii, 856b, 857b — III, 880b, 881b
Muḥammad b. Shaddād ii, 680a — II, 697a
Muḥammad b. Shahriyār, Ispahbad s, 356b — S, 356b
Muḥammad b. Shīrkūh iii, 399b — III, 411b
Muḥammad b. Sulaymān (Ḥasanid(e)) i, 551a; iii, 135b, 617a, 682b — I, 568b; III, 138a, 637b, 704b
Muḥammad b. Sulayman (Ḳarakhanid(e)) i, 1294b; iii, 1114b, 1115a — I, 1334a; III, 1142a, b
Muḥammad b. Sulaymān b. 'Abd Allāh iii, 1032a, 1035b — III, 1058a, 1061b
Muḥammad b. Sulaymān al-Kātib ii, 281b; iii, 126a, 345a, 759a — II, 289b; III, 129a, 355b, 782a
Muḥammad b. Sulaymān al-Rūdānī i, 1032b — I, 1064a
Muḥammad b. Sulaymān al-Tanakabunī i, 113a; v, 197b — I, 116a; V, 195a
Muḥammad b. Sūrī ii, 1096b, 1099b — II, 1122b, 1125b
Muḥammad b. Tādjīt al-Maṣmūdī v, 498b — V, 501b
Muḥammad b. Ṭāhir → Ibn al-Ḳaysarānī
Muḥammad b. Ṭāhir (Khurasān) ii, 1082b; iv, 20b, 21a, 667b — II, 1107b; IV, 22a, b, 694b
Muḥammad b. Ṭāhir al-Ahdal i, 255b — I, 263b
Muḥammad b. Takash Khwārazm-Shāh i, 1295a; iv, 30a — I, 1335a; IV, 32a
Muḥammad b. al-Ṭayyib, Sīdī i, 303a, 367b; iv, 383a — I, 312b, 377b; IV, 400a
Muḥammad b. al-Ṭayyib al-'Alamī → al-'Alamī
Muḥammad b. Tekish → Muḥammad b. Takash
Muḥammad b. Thānī ii, 177a; iv, 751b — II, 183a; IV, 782a
Muḥammad b. Tughdj al-Ikhshīd i, 870b; ii, 36b, 281b, 305a, 1080b; iii, 86a, 129a, 768b; iv, 418a, 459a; v, 91b, 327a, 953b; s, 120b — I, 895a; II, 37b, 289b, 313b, 1105b; III, 88a, 131b, 791b; IV, 436b, 479b; V, 94a, 327a, 957b; S, 120a
Muḥammad b. Tughluḳ i, 756b, 855b, 868b, 923b, 1036a, b, 1165b, 1192a, 1199b, 1300a, 1322a, 1329a; ii, 48a, 50a, 51a, 99b, 120a, 154b, 179b, 218b, 220a, 258a, 269b, 276b, 597a, 924b, 1076b, 1084b, 1124b, 1135a; iii, 202b, 416b, 428b, 442a, 453a, 492a; iv, 218b, 514a, 538a, 907b, 923b, 1019a; v, 598a; s, 73b, 105b, 117b, 352b, 409a, b — I, 779a, 879b, 893a, 951a, 1067b, 1068a, 1200b, 1227a, 1235a, 1340a, 1362b, 1369b; II, 49a, 51a, 52a, 101b, 123a, 159b, 185b, 225b, 226b, 264a, 277b, 284b, 612a, 946a, 1101b, 1109b, 1150b, 1162a; III, 207b, 429b, 442b, 456b, 469a, 509a; IV, 228a, 536a, 561b, 940b, 956b, 1051a; V, 601b; S, 74a, 105a, 117a, 352b, 409b
Muḥammad b. Tūmart → Ibn Tūmart
Muḥammad b. 'Ubayd Allāh → Abu 'l-Ma'ālī
Muḥammad b. 'Umar b. Lubāba i, 600a — I, 619b
Muḥammad b. 'Umar al-Aṣamm ii, 100b — II, 102b
Muḥammad b. 'Umar al-Kashshī → al-Kashshī, Abū 'Amr
Muḥammad b. 'Umar al-Madīnī iv, 742a — IV, 772a
Muḥammad b. 'Umar al-Tūnusī → al-Tūnusī
Muḥammad b. 'Uray'ir iv, 925a — IV, 958a
Muḥammad b. 'Uthmān ('Abd al-Wādid) → Abū Zayyān I
Muḥammad b. 'Uthmān al-'Amrī i, 713a — I, 734b
Muḥammad b. Wandarīn v, 230a — V, 227b
Muḥammad b. Wānūdīn ii, 744b — II, 763a
Muḥammad Ibn Warsand b. al-Ḥasan s, 402b — S, 403a
Muḥammad b. Wāsi' i, 959b — I, 989a
Muḥammad b. Wāṣīl al-Tamīmī v, 158a — V, 157b
Muḥammad b. Yaḥyā b. Abī Ṭālib → 'Azafī
Muḥammad b. Yaḥya al-Barmākī ii, 1036a — I, 1067b
Muḥammad b. Yaḥyā al-Dhuhlī i, 1296b — I, 1336b
Muḥammad b. Yaḥyā al-Yaḥṣubī i, 6a; ii, 1009a; v, 586b — I, 6a; II, 1033a; V, 591b
Muḥammad b. Ya'kūb al-Nīsābūrī → al-Aṣamm, Muḥammad
Muḥammad b. Yāḳūt ii, 453b; iii, 46a; iv, 100a, 127a — II, 465a; III, 47b; IV, 104b, 132b
Muḥammad b. Yallas → Ibn Yallas, Muḥammad
Muḥammad b. Yasār iv, 190a — IV, 198a
Muḥammad b. Yasīr iii, 309a — III, 318b
Muḥammad b. Yazīd i, 50a; iii, 587b — I, 51b; III, 607b
Muḥammad b. Yazīd (Sharwān-Shāh) iv, 345b —

IV, 360a
Muḥammad b. Yūsuf → Muḥammad V (Alawīd(e))
Muḥammad b. Yūsuf b. Aḥmad → Muḥammad I (Naṣrid(e))
Muḥammad b. Yūsuf b. Hūd ii, 1014a; iii, 543a; iv, 116a, 254b — II, 1037b; III, 562a; IV, 121b, 265b
Muḥammad b. Yūsuf b. al-Sarrādj → Ibn al-Sarrādj
Muḥammad b. Yūsuf b. Yaʿḳūb → Ibn Dirham, Muḥammad b. Yūsuf b. Yaʿḳūb
Muḥammad b. Yūsuf al-ʿĀmirī → al-ʿĀmirī, Muḥammad b. Yūsuf
Muḥammad b. Zayd (Zaydī) ii, 191b; iii, 245a, 254b; iv, 189a; v, 662a; s, 335a — II, 197b; III, 252a, 261b; IV, 197a; V, 667a; S, 334b
Muḥammad b. Ziyād s, 338a — S, 337b
Muḥammad ʿAbd Allāh al-ʿĀdil s, 389a — S, 389b
Muḥammad ʿAbd al-Ḥayy al-Kattānī iv, 774b — IV, 806a
Muḥammad ʿAbd al-Karīm Ṣābūn ii, 123b — II, 126b
Muḥammad ʿAbd al-Munʿim i, 13b — I, 14a
Muḥammad ʿAbdīlle Ḥassān → Muḥammad b. ʿAbd Allāh Ḥassān
Muḥammad ʿAbduh i, 38b, 327a, 414a, 416a, 597a, 817b; ii, 97a, 417b, 429a, 451b, 465b, 471a, 1065b; III, 59a, 1020a, 1145b, 1149b; iv, 112a, 143b, 144a, 146b, 149b, 151a, 159a, 162b, 321b, 471a, 720b, 856a; v, 187a; s, 64a, 121b, 123a, 244b, 248a, 296a — I, 39b, 337a, 426a, 427b, 616b, 841a; II, 99a, 428a, 440a, 463a, 477a, 483a, 1090b; III, 61b, 1046a, 1174a, 1178a; IV, 117a, 149b, 150a, 152b, 155b, 157b, 165b, 169b, 335b, 491b, 749a, 889b; V, 184b; S, 64b, 121a, 122b, 244b, 248a, 296a
Muḥammad ʿAbid Ḥusayn ii, 205a — II, 211b
Muḥammad Abū Ḥatīm i, 940a — I, 968b
Muḥammad ʿĀdil-Shāh i, 199b, 1202b, 1204a, b — I, 205a, 1238a, 1240a
Muḥammad V ʿĀdil-Shāh → Muḥammad Shāh V
Muḥammad Afḍal Khān → Afḍal Khān Barakzay
Muḥammad al-Afshīn → Muḥammad b. Abi ʾl-Sādj
Muḥammad Aḥmad b. ʿAbd Allāh i, 49b, 50a, 168b, 735a, 765a, 929b, 962a, 1172a; ii, 123b, 828a; iv, 687a, 952b; v, 70a, 267b, 1247b, **1248b** — I, 50b, 51b, 173b, 757a, 788a, 957b, 991b, 1207a; II, 126b, 847b; IV, 715a, 985a; V, 72a, 265b, 1238b, **1239a**
Muḥammad Akbar Ḥusaynī ii, 56a — II, 56b
Muḥammad Akbar Khān i, 231b; ii, 638a; s, 237b — I, 238b; II, 654a; S, 237b
Muḥammad Akmal, Mullā s, 134b — S, 134a
Muḥammad al-ʿAlamī i, 352a — I, 363a
Muḥammad Alfī i, 1288b; iv, 853a — I, 1328a; IV, 886a
Muḥammad ʿAlī (Andjumān) v, 7a; s, 5a, 74a, 247b, 293b, 360a — S, 4a, 74b, 75a, 247b, 293a, 360a
Muḥammad ʿAlī (Mustaʿlī) i, 1254b — I, 1292b
Muḥammad ʿAlī, Prince/le prince iii, 1199b; s, 300a — III, 1230a; S, 299b
Muḥammad ʿAlī b. Muẓaffar al-Dīn → Muḥammad ʿAlī Shāh Ḳādjār
Muḥammad ʿAlī b. Tawfīḳ i, 13b — I, 13b
Muḥammad ʿAlī Bahāʾī i, 915b — I, 943b
Muḥammad ʿAlī Bārfurūshī i, 833b, 847a — I, 856b, 870a
Muḥammad ʿAli Furūghī ii, 952a; v, 1095b, 1096a, b, 1097a — II, 974b; V, 1092b, 1093a, b
Muḥammad ʿAlī Kānpūrī ii, 132b — II, 135b
Muḥammad ʿAlī Khān, Nawwāb i, 625a; iv, 666b — I, 645b; IV, 693b
Muḥammad ʿAlī Khān Ḳāshḳāy iii, 1106b; iv, 706a — III, 1133b; IV, 734b
Muḥammad ʿAli Khān (Khōkand) iv, 631b; v, 30a — IV, 656b; V, 31a
Muḥammad ʿAlī Khān al-Bukhārī → al-Bukhārī
Muḥammad ʿAlī Māhir ii, 1004b — II, 1028a
Muḥammad ʿAlī Mīrzā (Ḳādjār) iv, 392a, b, 394b, 861b; v, 170a — IV, 409a, 411b, 894b; V, 167b
Muḥammad ʿAlī Nāṣiḥ iv, 71b — IV, 75b
Muḥammad ʿAlī Pasha, Khedive i, 13a, 35a, 182b, 404a, 554b, 571b, 755a, 1078b, 1172a, 1288b, 1299a, b; ii, 123b, 128a, 148b, 149a, 288b, 356a, 423b, 465a, 514a, 647a; iii, 218b, 238a, 556a, 999a, 1086b, 1154a, 1193b; iv, 442a, 490a; v, 267a, b, 907b, 1085b, 1248a; s, 30a, b, 38a, 179a, 301b, 379a — I, 13a, 136a, 188a, 415b, 572a, 590b, 777b, 1111a, 1207a, 1328a, 1339a, b; II, 126b, 131a, 152b, 153a, 296b, 365b, 434b, 477a, 526b, 663b; III, 224b, 245a, 575a, 1024a, 1113b, 1182b, 1223b; IV, 462a, 511a; V, 265a, 913a, 1082b, 1238b; S, 30b, 38b, 180a, 301b, 379a
Muḥammad ʿAlī Shāh Ḳādjār ii, 650b, 651b, 652a; iv, 39b, 392a, 398b, 789b; s, 53b, 72a, 91b, 291a, 365b — II, 667a, 668a; IV, 42a, 408b, 415b, 821a; S, 54a, 72a, 91b, 290b, 365a
Muḥammad ʿAlī-i Zandjānī i, 847a — I, 870a
Muḥammad al-ʿĀlim b. Mawlāy Ismāʿīl s, 126a — S, 125a
Muḥammad Amīn i, 1190a — I, 1225a
Muḥammad Amīn (China/la Chine) → Ma Ming-hsin
Muḥammad Amīn, Inak iv, 1065a; v, 24a, s, 420a — IV, 1096b; V, 25a, S, 420a
Muḥammad Amīn Badakhshī i, 1023a — I, 1054b
Muḥammad al-Amīn Bey iv, 262b — IV, 274b
Muḥammad Amīn Bukhārī s, 419b — S, 419b
Muḥammad al-Amīn al-Kānemī → al-Kānemī, Muḥammad al-Amīn
Muḥammad Amīn Khān (d./m. 1518) iv, 849a — IV, 882a
Muḥammad Amīn Khān (d./m. 1855) s, 46a — S, 46b
Muḥammad Amīn al-Kurdī → al-Kurdī
Muḥammad Amīr Pandja Kash ii, 83b — II, 85b
Muḥammad Anūsha iv, 1064b, 1068a — IV, 1096a, 1100a
Muḥammad Anwar Shāh al-Kashmīrī al-Hindī iv, 84b — IV, 88b
Muḥammad ʿĀrif i, 287b; ii, 391b — I, 296a; II, 402a
Muḥammad ʿAshīḳ → ʿAshīḳ, Muḥammad
Muḥammad ʿAyn al-Dawla iii, 1114a — III, 1141b
Muḥammad Aʿẓam b. Awrangzīb i, 913b, 1201b; ii, 216b; iii, 457b — I, 941a, 1237a; II, 223a; III, 473b
Muḥammad Aʿẓam b. Dūst Muḥammad i, 232a; ii, 417a, 638a — I, 239a; II, 428a, 654a
Muḥammad Aʿẓam b. Pāyinda Khān i, 231a; ii, 637b; v, 501b — I, 238a; II, 653b; V, 504b
Muḥammad Badāʾūnī → Shaykh Niẓām al-Dīn Awliyāʾ
Muḥammad al-Badr iv, 745b — IV, 775b
Muḥammad Bahāwal Khān → Bahāwal Khān
Muḥammad Baḥrī Pasha ii, 990b — II, 1013a
Muḥammad Bakhtiyār i, 393b, 1209b; ii, 267b, 297a, 1103a; v, 638a — I, 404b, 1245b; II, 275b, 305a, 1129a; V, 642a
Muḥammad Bāḳī b. ʿĪsā Khān i, 628a — I, 648b
Muḥammad Bāḳī Naḳshbandī → Bāḳī Biʾllāh
Muḥammad al-Bāḳir, Amīr (Imām) iv, 202a; s, 129b, 231a, 232b, 233a — IV, 210b, 211a; S, 128b, 230b, 232b
Muḥammad Bāḳir al-Madjlisī → al-Madjlisī
Muḥammad Bāḳir Shaftī s, 75a — S, 75b
Muḥammad Bāḳir-i Bihbihānī iv, 51a — IV, 53b
Muḥammad al-Balʿamī → al-Balʿamī
Muḥammad al-Baṭāʾihī (Ḳādiriyya) iv, 381a — IV, 397b
Muḥammad al-Baṭāʾihī (Rifāʿiyya) iv, 350a — IV,

365a
Muḥammad Bayram al-Khāmis iv, 1154a — IV, 1186a
Muḥammad Beg (Turcoman) ii, 204b — II, 211a
Muḥammad Beg Aydinoghlu i, 783a; ii, 989a, 1044b — I, 806a, b; II, 1012a, 1069a
Muḥammad Beg Ḳarāmānid(e) → Muḥammad b. Ḳarāmān; Muḥammad II (Ḳarāmānid(e))
Muḥammad Beg Ustādjlū i, 1067a — I, 1099a
Muḥammad Behdjet iv, 195a — IV, 203b
Muḥammad Bey (Ḥusaynid(e)) i, 977a; ii, 638b; iii, 561b, 636a — I, 1007a; II, 654b; III, 581a, 657b
Muḥammad Bey b. Aḥmad Bey Mirzā i, 1208b — I, 1244b
Muḥammad Bey b. Maḥmūd i, 1049a; ii, 161a — I, 1081a; II, 166a
Muḥammad Bey b. Yaḥya i, 1164a, b — I, 1198 b, 1199a
Muḥammad Bey Abu ʾl-Dhahab → Abu ʾl-Dhahab, Muḥammad Bey
Muḥammad Bey Abuʾl-Dhahab → Muḥammad Abuʾl-Dhahab
Muḥammad Bey al-Alfī → Muḥammad Alfī
Muḥammad Bey Khālid → Muḥammad Khālid Zuḳal
Muḥammad Bey Khusraw ii, 123b, 351b; iv, 686b; v, 267a — II, 126b, 361a; IV, 714b; V, 265a
Muḥammad Bey Minnet-oghlu i, 1263b — I, 1302a
Muḥammad al-Bukhārī → al-Bukhārī
Muḥammad al-Bulālī i, 929a — I, 957b
Muḥammad al-Burtuḳālī → Muḥammad II (Waṭṭāsid(e))
Muḥammad Čavush iv, 592b — IV, 616b
Muḥammad Čelebī (Ottoman) → Meḥemmed I
Muḥammad Čelebi b. Burhān al-Dīn i, 1328a — I, 1368b
Muḥammad Čelebi Efendi → Yirmisekiz Čelebi Meḥmed
Muḥammad Čelebi Üsküdarī ii, 442b — II, 454b
Muḥammad Dāʾim ii, 28b — II, 29a
Muḥammad Dāwūd Shāh i, 744a; v, 1079b — I, 766a; V, 1077a
Muḥammad Demirdāsh al-Muḥammadī s, 208a — S, 207b
Muḥammad al-Dībādj → Muḥammad b. Djaʿfar
Muḥammad Djaʿfar Khān → Djaʿfar, Mīr
Muḥammad Djaʿfar Munshī i, 332a — I, 342b
Muḥammad Djamālī ii, 420a — II, 431a
Muḥammad Djān i, 232a — I, 239a
Muḥammad al-Djawād ʿAlī al-Riḍā iii, 1167a; iv, 855a; s, 95a, 127b — III, 1195b; IV, 888a; S, 94a, 126b
Muḥammad Djawād al-Djazāʾirī s, 28a — S, 28b
Muḥammad Djūkī i, 135a, 148a; s, 51a — I, 139a, 152a; S, 51b
Muḥammad Edīb ii, 590a — II, 604b
Muḥammad Efendī Aḳ Kirmānī i, 310b — I, 320a
Muḥammad Efendī Čiwizāde ii, 57a — II, 57b
Muḥammad Emīn b. Hadjdjī Meḥmed i, 295a — I, 304a
Muḥammad Emīn Ḥayātī-zāde iii, 303b — III, 312b
Muḥammad Emīn Pasha iii, 1199a — III, 1229a
Muḥammad-Enweri Kadić i, 1271b — I, 1310b
Muḥammad Eretna → Ghiyāth al-Dīn Muḥammad
Muḥammad Eshref iii, 357b — III, 368b
Muḥammad al-Fāḍil b. Āshūr → Ibn Āshūr, Muḥammad al-Fāḍil
Muḥammad Fāḍil al-Ḳalkamī v, 889b, 890a — V, 896a, b
Muḥammad al-Faḥḥām iv, 165b — IV, 172b
Muḥammad al-Faḳīh → Muḥammad II (Naṣrid(e))
Muḥammad Farīd (d./m. 1919) iii, 515a — III, 533a
Muḥammad Farīd → Abū Ḥadīd
Muḥammad Fasandjus → Abu ʾl-Faradj Muḥammad Fasandjus
Muḥammad Fatḥ Allāh Barakāt iii, 516a — III, 534a
Muḥammad Ferīd → Dāmād Ferīd Pasha
Muḥammad al-Ghālib biʾllāh → Muḥammad I (Naṣrid(e))
Muḥammad al-Ghānī → Muḥammad V (Naṣrid(e))
Muḥammad Ghardjistānī i, 227a — I, 234a
Muḥammad Ghawth ii, 1144a; iii, 430a, 436a — II, 1171a; III, 444a, 450a
Muḥammad Ghuri → Muʿizz al-Dīn Muḥammad b. Sām
Muḥammad Ghūrī → Muḥammad Shāh Ghūrī
Muḥammad Girāy I ii, 1046a, 1113a; iv, 849b — II, 1070b, 1139b; IV, 882b
Muḥammad Girāy II iv, 178b; v, 138b — IV, 185b; V, 141a, b
Muḥammad Girāy III i, 310b; v, 719b — I, 320b; V, 724b
Muḥammad Girāy IV ii, 25a; v, 139b, 719b — II, 25b; V, 142b, 725a
Muḥammad Gīsū Darāz → Gīsū Darāz
Muḥammad Gulandām iii, 56a — III, 58b
Muḥammad al-Ḥabīb Bey iii, 636b — III, 658a
Muḥammad al-Hādī Bey iii, 636b — III, 658a
Muḥammad Ḥāfiẓ Ibrāhīm → Ḥāfiẓ Ibrāhīm
Muḥammad Ḥakīm, Mīrzā i, 316a, 733a, 1122b; iii, 423b; iv, 410b; v, 649b; s, 122a — I, 326a, 755a, 1156b; III, 437b; IV, 428a; V, 653b; S, 121a
Muḥammad Ḥāmid Khān ii, 597b — II, 612b
Muḥammad Ḥasab Allāh ii, 91b — II, 93a
Muḥammad Ḥasan (Zarrīn ḳalam) s, 167b — S, 167b
Muḥammad Ḥasan Gīlānī s, 23b — S, 23b
Muḥammad Ḥasan Khān Ḳādjār i, 701b; iii, 1103a; iv, 389b, 390a, b, 639b — I, 722b; III, 1130a; IV, 406b, 407a, 666a
Muḥammad Ḥasan Khān Ṣāniʿ al-Dawla ii, 433b, 952a; iv, 70b; s, 71b, 75b — II, 445a, 974a; IV, 74b; S, 72a, 76a
Muḥammad Ḥasan Mīrzā i, 262b — I, 270b
Muḥammad Ḥasan Nūrī, Mīrzā s, 23b — S, 23b
Muḥammad Ḥaydar Dughlāt → Ḥaydar Mīrzā
Muḥammad al-Hifnī ii, 167a — II, 172a
Muḥammad al-Hilālī → Muḥammad al-Bulālī
Muḥammad Ḥusayn b. Muḥammad Faḍl ii, 123b, 124b — II, 126b, 127b
Muḥammad Ḥusayn Dūghlāt ii, 622b; iii, 317a — II, 638a; III, 326b
Muḥammad Ḥusayn Khān Develū iv, 390a, b — IV, 406b, 407a
Muḥammad Ḥusayn Khān Nāẓim al-Dawla iv, 104b, 578a — IV, 109b, 601a
Muḥammad Ḥusayn Shahriyār iv, 71b — IV, 75b
Muḥammad Ḥusayn ʿAṭā Khān iii, 376a — III, 388a
Muḥammad al-Ḥusaynī al-Bukhārī s, 10b — S, 10a
Muḥammad Ibrāhīm Dhawḳ → Dhawḳ
Muḥammad al-Idrīsī → al-Idrīsī
Muḥammad Iḳbāl → Iḳbāl, Muḥammad
Muḥammad al-Ilkhān ii, 401a — II, 411b
Muḥammad al-Ikhshīd → Muḥammad b. Ṭughdj
Muḥammad ʿIllīsh ii, 167a — II, 172b
Muḥammad Ilyās iii, 433b — III, 447b
Muḥammad Īndjū iii, 1208b — III, 1239a
Muḥammad ʿĪsā Tarkhān i, 628a, 1192a; iii, 1030a -I, 648b, 1227b; III, 1056a
Muḥammad Isfandiyārī → Nīmā Yūshīdj
Muḥammad Ismāʿīl Khān Nūrī v, 155b, 165a — V, 156a, 162b
Muḥammad Ismāʿīl Shahīd → Ismāʿīl Shahīd

Muḥammad Ḳāḍī s, 51b — S, 52a
Muḥammad al-Ḳāʾim iii, 247a — III, 254a
Muḥammad al-Ḳāʾim bi-Amr Allāh i, 245a — I, 252b
Muḥammad Ḳadrī Pasha iii, 164a — III, 167b
Muḥammad Kāmil Pasha v, 314a — V, 313b
Muḥammad Ḳaramānlî iv, 617b — IV, 642a
Muḥammad Ḳāsim ii, 205a; iii, 431a — II, 211b; III, 445b
Muḥammad Ḳāsim Khān Mīr-i Baḥr i, 253a — I, 261a
Muḥammad Kāzim Khurāsānī s, 54a — S, 54b
Muḥammad Kh(w)adja i, 808b — I, 831b
Muḥammad Khālid Zuḳal ii, 123b, 124a, 827b; v, 1250a — II, 127a, 847b; V, 1240b
Muḥammad Khān (1864) s, 46a — S, 46b
Muḥammad Khān (Ḳarakhānid(e)) → Muḥammad I, II, III; Muḥammad b. Sulaymān
Muḥammad Khān (Turcoman) iv, 389b — IV, 406a
Muḥammad Khān b. Balban s, 124a — S, 123b
Muḥammad Khān Bangash ii, 808a, 1085a — II, 827b, 1110b
Muḥammad Khān Ḳoyunlū iv, 390b — IV, 407b
Muḥammad Khān Madjd al-Mulk Sinakī iv, 397b — IV, 415a
Muḥammad Kh(w)arizmshāh → ʿAlā al-Dīn Muḥammad Kh(w)arizm Shāh
Muḥammad Khodja iii, 605a — III, 625b
Muḥammad Khudābanda i, 7b, 8b; iii, 157b — I, 7b, 8b; III, 161a
Muḥammad Khusraw Pasha ii, 292b — II, 300b
Muḥammad Ḳulī Khān Ḳāshḳāy iv, 706a — IV, 734b
Muḥammad Ḳulī Ḳuṭb Shāh iii, 318b, 319a, 426b; v, 550a, 630a, 961a — III, 328a, 440b; V, 555a, 634a, 965a
Muḥammad Ḳuṭb Shah iii, 427a — III, 440b
Muḥammad Lashkarī → Muḥammad Shāh III (Bahmanī)
Muḥammad al-Liḥyānī → Muḥammad III (Ḥafṣīd(e))
Muḥammad Mahābat Khān I ii, 597b — II, 612b
Muḥammad Mahābat Khān (d./m. 1960) ii, 598a — II, 613a
Muḥammad al-Mahdī (Ḥammūdid(e)) → Muḥammad I (Ḥammūdid(e))
Muḥammad al-Mahdī (Imām) i, 402b; s, 95a — I, 414b; S, 94b
Muḥammad al-Mahdī (Saʿdid(e)) v, 1191a — V, 1181a
Muḥammad al-Mahdī (Sanūsī) ii, 493a; s, 165a — II, 505a; S, 164b
Muḥammad al-Mahdī (Umayyad(e)) → Muḥammad II (Umayyad(e))
Muḥammad Mahdī Khān s, 46b — S, 47a
Muḥammad Mahdī of/de Djawnpūr v, 1230b; s, 222a — V, 1221a; S, 222a
Muḥammad Maḥmūd ii, 934b; iii, 516a, 517a, 518b; s, 18a — II, 956a; III, 534a, b, 536b; S, 18b
Muḥammad al-Makhlūʿ → Muḥammad II (Naṣrid(e))
Muḥammad al-Māmī, Shaykh v, 891b, 892a — V, 898a, b
Muḥammad al-Manglī i, 1154a; ii, 740b — I, 1188a; II, 759a
Muḥammad al-Maslūkh i, 56a, 706b; ii, 367b; iii, 721a — I, 57b, II, 377b; III, 743b
Muḥammad Masʿūd iv, 72b; v, 199a — IV, 76b; V, 196a
Muḥammad Mīrāb, Shīr s, 46a, 97b, 228a — S, 46b, 97a, 228a
Muḥammad Mīrzā → Muḥammad Shāh (Ḳādjār)
Muḥammad Mubārak Khān → Mubārak Khān
Muḥammad Mufīd iii, 490b — III, 507a
Muḥammad Muḥsin iv, 626a — IV, 650b
Muḥammad Muḳīm Khān → Muḳīm Khān
Muḥammad al-Mundhir ii, 1009a — II, 1033a
Muḥammad al-Muntaṣir → Muḥammad b. Idrīs II
Muḥammad Murād Beg → Murād Beg
Muḥammad al-Murtaḍā b. al-Ḥādī s, 335b — S, 335a
Muḥammad Murtadā al-Zabīdī → Murtadā al-Zabīdī
Muḥammad Mūsā Kudatlī ii, 87b — II, 89a
Muḥammad al Mustaʿīn → Muḥammad VII (Naṣrid(e))
Muḥammad al-Mustaḳfī → Muḥammad III (Umayyad(e))
Muḥammad al-Mustaʿlī → Muḥammad III (Ḥammūdid(e))
Muḥammad al-Muʿtamid → al-Muʿtamid
Muḥammad al-Mutawakkil al-Maslūkh → Muḥammad al-Maslūkh
Muḥammad al-Muẓaffar → al-Muẓaffar (Afṭasid(e))
Muḥammad al-Nafs al-Zakiyya → al-Nafs al-Zakiyya
Muḥammad al-Nasawī ii, 962a — II, 984a
Muḥammad al-Nāṣir (Almohad(e)) → Muḥammad b. Abī Yūsuf Yaʿḳūb
Muḥammad al-Nāṣir (Ḥusaynid(e)) iii, 636b — III, 658a
Muḥammad Naẓīm iii, 581a — III, 601b
Muḥammad Nergisi i, 1271a — I, 1310b
Muḥammad Pāʿīzī iii, 114a — III, 116b
Muḥammad Panāh, Mīr iii, 1158a — III, 1186b
Muḥammad Pasha → Meḥmed Pasha Bîyîḳlî; Derwīsh Meḥmed Pasha; Duče Meḥmed Pasha; Kalender-oghlū Meḥmed Pasha; Khāṣṣakī Meḥmed Pasha; Köprülü Meḥmed Pasha; Soḳollu Meḥmed Pasha; Ṣofu Meḥmed Pasha
Muḥammad Pasha Baltadjî i, 269a, 395a, 1004b — I, 277a, 406a, 1035a
Muḥammad Pasha Bushatlî i, 657a; iv, 588b — I, 677b; IV, 612a
Muḥammad Pasha Čerkes i, 174b; v, 33a — I, 179b; V, 34a
Muḥammad Pasha Djalīlī ii, 402a — II, 413a
Muḥammad Pasha Kōra i, 920a — I, 948a
Muḥammad Pasha Lala → Lala Meḥmed Pasha
Muḥammad Pasha Muḥsin-zāde i, 56b, 62b; iii, 158a, 253a — I, 58a, 64b; III, 161b, 260a
Muḥammad Pasha Silāḥdār iv, 437b — IV, 457b
Muḥammad Pasha Sulṭānzāde iii, 623a, 983a — III, 644a, 1007b
Muḥammad Pasha Yegen i, 56b, 292a; ii, 534a; iv, 544a; v, 729a — I, 58a, 301a; II, 547a; IV, 567b; V, 734a
Muḥammad Rabaḍān i, 404b — I, 416b
Muḥammad Radīf Pashā i, 709b — I, 731a
Muḥammad Rafīʿ Bādhil iii, 114b — III, 116b
Muḥammad Raḥīm Khān Atalîk (Khīwa, 1825) i, 1295b; ii, 116a; iv, 610b, 1065a; v, 24a, 29a; s, 46a, 97a, 420a — I, 1335b; II, 118b; IV, 635b, 1096b, 1097a; v, 25a, 30a; S, 46b, 96b, 420a
Muḥammad Raḥīm Khān II, Sayyid (1872) s, 46a, 228b — S, 46b, 228b
Muḥammad Rashād → Meḥemmed V
Muḥammad al-Rashīd → Muḥammad b. Ḥusayn (Ḥusaynid(e))
Muḥammad Rashīd Pasha i, 906b; iii, 628b, 999b; v, 36a, 462a — I, 933b; III, 649b, 1024b; V, 37a, b, 464b
Muḥammad Rashīd Riḍā → Rashīd Riḍā
Muḥammad Rasūl Khān ii, 598a — II, 612b
Muḥammad Raʾūf iii, 622b — III, 643a

Muḥammad Rezā Shāh → Muḥammad Riḍā Shāh Pahlawī
Muḥammad Riḍā' b. Sangīn ʿAlī ii, 29b – II, 30a
Muḥammad Riḍā ʿIshkī iv, 71a – IV, 75a
Muḥammad Riḍā Khān iii, 1106b – III, 1134a
Muḥammad Riḍā Mīrāb b. Er Niyāz Bek → Āgahī
Muḥammad Riḍā al-Shabībī v, 1093b – V, 1090b, 1091a
Muḥammad Riḍā Shāh Pahlawī ii, 653a; iii, 454a; iv, 40b-42b, 165a; v, 721b, 920b, 1042b, 1098a – II, 669b; III, 469b; IV, 43a-45b, 172a; V, 726b, 926a, 1039a, 1094a
Muḥammad Rinānī iv, 104b; v, 834a – IV, 109a; V, 840b
Muḥammad Ṣādīḳ iv, 284b – IV, 297a
Muḥammad al-Ṣādiḳ Bey i, 37a; ii, 638b; iii, 562a, 636b; iv, 1154a – I, 38a; II, 654b; III, 581a, 657b; IV, 1186b
Muḥammad al-Ṣaghīr s, 208b – S, 208a
Muḥammad al-Ṣaghīr b. Yūsuf i, 863a – I, 887a
Muḥammad Saʿīd (Mīr Djumlā) i, 719b, 769a; ii, 216b, 1135a; iii, 318b, 427a; iv, 1020a – I, 741b, 792a; II, 223a, 1162a; III, 328a, 440b; IV, 1052a
Muḥammad al-Saʿīd → Marīnid(e)s
Muḥammad Saʿīd Bābasēl ii, 91b – II, 93b
Muḥammad Sāḳī Mustaʿid Khān i, 954a – I, 983b
Muḥammad Ṣāliḥ Beg (d./m. 1621) iv, 476a – IV, 497a
Muḥammad Ṣāliḥ Efendī i, 973a – I, 1003a
Muḥammad Ṣāliḥ Kańbū iii, 1203b; v, 600b – III, 1234a; V, 604b
Muḥammad Ṣāliḥ Shīrāzī iv, 787a – IV, 818b
Muḥammad Sālim, Ḳāḍī iv, 410b – IV, 428a
Muḥammad al-Sammān i, 92a – I, 94b
Muḥammad Shāh I (Bahmanī) i, 924b, 925b, 1068b; ii, 1119a – I, 952a, 953b, 1101a; II, 1145a
Muḥammad Shāh II (Bahmanī) i, 925b, 1200a; iii, 417b – I, 953b, 1235b; III, 431a
Muḥammad Shāh III Lashkarī (Bahmanī) i, 923b, 1047a, 1200a, 1323a; iii, 1159a; s, 280a – I, 951b, 1078b, 1235b, 1363b; III, 1187b; S, 279b
Muḥammad Shāh I ʿAlā' al-Dīn Khaldjī (Dihlī) i, 444b, 506b, 710a, 1036a, b, 1068b, 1202b, 1322a; ii, 99b, 120a, 154b, 179b, 256b, 260b, 268b, 272b, 405a, 1084b, 1124a; iii, 201a, 416a, 434a, 492a; iv, 218b, 419a, 921a-923b; v, 883b; s, 73b, 105a, 176a, 279b, 325a – I, 457a, 522a, 731b, 1067b, 1068a, 1100b, 1238a, 1362a; II, 101b, 123a, 159b, 185a, 263b, 269a, 276b, 281a, 416a, 1109b, 1150b; III, 206a, 429b, 448a, 509a; IV, 228a, 437a, 954a-956b; V, 890a; S, 74a, 104b, 177b, 279b, 324b
Muḥammad Shāh II (Dihlī) → Muḥammad b. Tughluḳ
Muḥammad Shāh III (Dihlī) iv, 276a – IV, 288b
Muḥammad Shāh IV (Dihlī) ii, 270b; v, 598a, 783a, b – II, 278b; V, 602a, 789b
Muḥammad Shāh V (Dihlī) ii, 271b, 1144a; iii, 423a – II, 279a, 1160b; III, 436b
Muḥammad Shāh Djahān Khān ii, 317a – II, 326b
Muḥammad Shāh Fārūkī → Mīrān Muḥammad I, II
Muḥammad Shāh Gaṇeśa ii, 797b; iii, 419a – II, 816b; III, 432b
Muḥammad Shāh Ghūrī iii, 638b; iv, 1067b – III, 660a; IV, 1099b
Muḥammad Shāh (Gudjarātī) ii, 1125b; iii, 1010a – II, 1153a; III, 1035b
Muḥammad Shāh (Ḳādjār) i, 246b; ii, 812b, 839a; iii, 554a; iv, 38b, 105a, 392a, 393a; s, 71a, 94b, 108b – I, 254a; II, 831b, 858b; III, 573a; IV, 41a, 109b, 408b, 409b; S, 71b, 94a, 108a
Muḥammad Shāh (Kashmīr) s, 324b, 423b – S, 324a, 423b
Muḥammad Shāh (Mughal) i, 229b, 295b, 834a, 1026a, 1042b, 1166a, 1330a; iii, 59b, 320a, 454a; iv, 666a – I, 236b, 305a, 857a, 1057b, 1074b, 1200b, 1371a; III, 62a, 330b, 469b; IV, 693a
Muḥammad Shāh b. Ḥadjdjādj v, 162b, 163a, 554a – V, 160b, 161a, 558b
Muḥammad Shāh b. Ḥasan Shāh (Kashmīr) s, 131b – S, 130b, 131a
Muḥammad Shāh Khusraw ii, 316b, 317a – II, 326a, b
Muḥammad Shāh Özbeg i, 853a – I, 876b
Muḥammad Shāh Sayyid → Muḥammad Shāh IV (Dihlī)
Muḥammad Shāhī imāms iv, 201b, 202a – IV, 210b, 211a
Muḥammad Shākir Efendi iv, 618a – IV, 642b
Muḥammad al-Sharīf → Muḥammad I (Alawid(e))
Muḥammad Sharīf, Khalīfa i, 765a; v, 1249a, 1250a, b, 1251b – I, 788a; V, 1239b, 1240b, 1241b, 1242b
Muḥammad Sharīf b. Iʿtimād al-Dawla iv, 282a – IV, 294b
Muḥammad Sharīf Ḳābil → Ḳābil Khān
Muḥammad Sharīf Khān ii, 316b, 317a – II, 326a
Muḥammad Sharīf Pasha → Sharīf Pasha
Muḥammad Sharīf al-ʿUlamā', Mullā s, 75a – S, 75b
Muḥammad al-Sharīf al-Wadā'ī s, 164b – S, 164b
Muḥammad Sharḳī iii, 419b – III, 433a
Muḥammad al-Shaṭṭī → al-Shaṭṭī, Muḥammad
Muḥammad Shaybānī → Shaybānī Khān
Muḥammad al-Shaybānī → al-Shaybānī
Muḥammad al-Shaykh al-Mahdī i, 245a; iii, 251a – I, 252b; III, 258b
Muḥammad al-Shaykh II al-Ma'mūn i, 605a, 1058a; iii, 810a; s, 29a – I, 624b, 1089b; III, 833a; S, 29a
Muḥammad Shirān i, 393b – I, 404b
Muḥammad Shīrīn Maghribī i, 1301a; iv, 66a – I, 1341a; IV, 69b
Muḥammad al-Ṣūfī, Shaykh s, 353b – S, 353a
Muḥammad Ṣūfī Māzandarānī → Māzandarānī, Mullā Muḥammad Ṣūfī
Muḥammad Ṣughrā i, 1218b – I, 1255a
Muḥammad Sulṭān (1834) iv, 197a – IV, 205b
Muḥammad Sulṭān Bayātī iii, 1101a – III, 1128b
Muḥammad Sulṭān Rūmī i, 1168a – I, 1202b
Muḥammad Ṭāhir → Pīr ʿAlī
Muḥammad Ṭāhir (d. 1677) iv, 286b – IV, 299b
Muḥammad al-Ṭāhir → Ibn ʿĀshūr
Muḥammad Ṭāhir al-Ṣiḳillī al-Ḥusaynī iv, 736a – IV, 766a
Muḥammad al-Taḳī → Muḥammad al-Djawād
Muḥammad Taḳī, Mīrzā v, 169b – V, 167a
Muḥammad Taḳī ʿAlī Ābādī ii, 433b – II, 445a
Muḥammad Taḳī Bahār → Bahār
Muḥammad Taḳī Iṣfahānī, Shaykh → Āḳā Nadjafī
Muḥammad Taḳī Khān, Mīrzā → Taḳī Khān, Mīrzā Muḥammad (Amīr Kabīr)
Muḥammad Taḳī Khān Pisyān s, 110a, 366a – S, 109b, 365b
Muḥammad Taḳī Madjlisī → Madjlisī-yi Awwal
Muḥammad Taḳī Mīr → Mīr Taḳī Mīr
Muḥammad Taḳī Sipihr iv, 70a – IV, 73b
Muḥammad Ṭalʿat → Ṭalʿat, Meḥmed
Muḥammad Tapar i, 353a, 1359b – I, 364a, 1399b
Muḥammad al-Tawdī → Ibn Sūda, Abī ʿAbd Allāh
Muḥammad Tawfīḳ → Tawfīḳ Pasha
Muḥammad Tayrāb ii, 123a; v, 267a – II, 126a; V, 265a
Muḥammad Ṭayyib ii, 205b – II, 212a
Muḥammad al-Ṭayyib al-Anṣārī v, 998b – V, 994a
Muḥammad Tewfīḳ → Tewfīḳ Meḥmed; Čerkes

Meḥmed Tewfīḳ
Muḥammad Tīmūr i, 1019a — I, 1050b
Muḥammad Touré → Askia Muḥammad
Muḥammad Tughluḳ → Muḥammad Shāh II, III (Dihlī)
Muḥammad al-Tūnisī s, 306a — S, 306a
Muḥammad ʿUbayd Allāh b. Hazārmard v, 451b — V, 454a
Muḥammad Ulugh Khān s, 335b — S, 335a
Muḥammad ʿUmar b. ʿAbd al-Raḥmān iii, 13a — II, 14a
Muḥammad ʿUmar al-Tūnusī ii, 137a — II, 141a
Muḥammad ʿUthmān al-Mīrghānī → al-MīrghānīE
Muḥammad Walī Khān ii, 435b, 652b — II, 447a, 668b
Muḥammad Wārith s, 46b — S, 47a
Muḥammad al-Yaḥṣubī → Muḥammad b. Yaḥyā
Muḥammad Yaḥyā, Khʷādja s, 51b — S, 52a
Muḥammad Yūsuf... al-Kāzarūnī i, 1218b — I, 1255a
Muḥammad Ẓāhir Shāh i, 232b — I, 240a
Muḥammad al-Zākī ʿUthmān i, 1172a — I, 1207a
Muḥammad Zamān Khan → Abū Ridjāʾ
Muḥammad Zamān Khān b. Asʿad Khān s, 237b — S, 237b
Muḥammad Zanjina ii, 1003b — II, 1026b
Muḥammad al-Ẓāfir iv, 1154b — IV, 1186b
Muḥammad al-Ziyadī i, 551a; v, 602a — I, 568b; V, 606a
Muḥammadābād ii, 11a, 1127a; s, 325a — II, 11a, 1153b; S, 324b
Muḥammadan Union → Ittiḥād-i Muḥammedī Djemʿiyyeti
Muḥammad-i Khaṭībī s, 333b — S, 333a
Muḥammad-i Waṣīf iv, 55a — IV, 58a
Muḥammad-i Zamān, Mīrzā i, 914b; ii, 322b, 1128b; iii, 422b; iv, 1021a — I, 942b; II, 332a, 1155a; III, 436b; IV, 1053a
Muḥammadī b. Djahangīr v, 829a — V, 835a
Muḥammadiyya (al-Ḳāhira) iii, 992a — III, 1016b
Muḥammadiyya (Indonesia/Indonésie) i, 745b, 746a; iii, 534a, 1229a; s, 151a — I, 768a; III, 552b, 1261a; S, 151a
Muḥammadnagar → Golkondā
Muhammadu Bello ii, 942a, 1145a; iii, 38b, 276b — II, 964a, 1172a; III, 40b, 284b
Muhammadu dan Amu iv, 550b, 551a — IV, 574b
Muḥammadzays → Bārakzays
Muhamman Alwali iv, 549a — IV, 573a
Muhamman Rumfa iv, 549a, 550a — IV, 572b, 573b
Muḥammara iv, 675a, b; v, 66a — IV, 702b, 703a; V, 67b
Muḥammira v, 64a, 65a — V, 66a, 67a
Muhandis-khāne → Muhendiskhāne
Muhannā, Āl iv, 88a — IV, 92a
Muhannā, Banū i, 403a, 1313a — I, 414b, 1353a
Muhannā b. ʿĪsā iii, 952a; iv, 88a — III, 976b; IV, 92a
Muḥanna b. Naṣīr, Mir v, 507a, b — V, 510b
al-Muḥāribī → Ibn ʿAṭiyya
Muḥārish i, 1074b; 1075a — I, 1106b, 1107a
Muḥarraf iii, 26a — III, 27b
al-Muḥarraḳ i, 941a — I, 970a
Muḥarram, Aḥmad iii, 112a — III, 114b
Muḥarriḳ → Amr b. Hind
Muḥarrirān iv, 757b — IV, 787b
Muḥāsaba ii, 81a — II, 82b
Muḥasayn, Āl iv, 1171a — IV, 1204b
al-Muḥāsibī, Ḥārith i, 277a, 326b, 694b, 1245b; ii, 242b, 450b; iii, 83b, 466a, 720a; iv, 212a; s, 392a — I, 285b, 336b, 716a, 1283b; II, 249b, 462a; III, 85b, 482b, 742a; IV, 221b; S, 392b
al-Muḥassin Ibn al-Furāt i, 387a; iii, 702b, 767b — I, 398b; III, 725a, 791a
al-Muḥassin al-Tanūkhī → al-Tanūkhī
Muḥaṣṣiṣ-i mamlakat iv, 475a — IV, 495b
Muḥāwere iv, 602a — IV, 626a
al-Muḥayditha s, 27b — S, 28a
Muḥaysīn iv, 10a — IV, 11a
Muḥdath ii, 96b; iii, 1051b; v, 96b — II, 98b; III, 1077b; V, 99a
Muhendiskhāne i, 63a, ii, 425b; v, 903a, 908a — I, 65a; II, 436b; V, 909b, 914a
Muḥibb Allāh Allāhābādī ii, 54b, 55a, 134b; s, 293a — II, 55b, 56a, 138a; S, 293a
Muḥibb Allāh Bihārī → al-Bihārī
Muḥibb al-Dīn al-Khāṭib iii, 519a; iv, 160a — III, 537a; IV, 166b
al-Muḥibbī i, 68b, 594b — I, 70a, 614a
Mühimme Defteri i, 1090b — I, 1123a
Muḥkam Čand s, 332a — S, 331b
Muhr ii, 121a, 311b, 806a; s, 256b — II, 124a, 320b, 825b; S, 256a
Muhrdār iv, 1104a — IV, 1135b
Muḥrim iii, 1052b, 1053a — III, 1078b, 1079a
Muḥriz b. Khalaf, Sīdī iii, 695a; iv, 341a — III, 717a; IV, 355b
Muḥriz b. Ziyād iii, 386a, b; iv, 827b; v, 59b, 60b — III, 398b, 399a; IV, 860b; V, 61b, 62b
al-Muḥrizā iv, 674b — IV, 702a
Muḥsin, Ḥādjdjī Āḳā s, 342a — S, 341b
Muḥsin Khan Ghazī i, 1123a — I, 1156b
Muḥsin, Mawlā → Fayḍ-i Kāshānī
Muḥsin b. Farīd i, 181b, 767a — I, 186b, 790a
Muḥsin b. al-Ḳāʾid iii, 137b — III, 140a
Muḥsin b. Sālim iii, 294a — III, 303a
Muḥsin Fānī ii, 74a — II, 75a
Muḥsine iii, 998b — III, 1023b
Muḥsin-zāde → ʿAbd Alāh Pasha; Muḥammad Pasha
al-Muhtadī (ʿAbbāsid(e)) iv, 89a; s, 402a — IV, 93a; S, 402b
Muḥtādj ii, 1b; iv, 60b — II, 1b; IV, 64a
Muḥtaram Shāh I ii, 29b — II, 30a
Muḥtaram Shāh II ii, 30a — II, 30b
Muḥtaram Shāh III ii, 30a — II, 30b
Muḥtasham iv, 68a — IV, 71b
Muḥtasib i, 26b, 344b, 477a, 629b, 752a, 898b, 977b; ii, 228b, 519b; iii, 485b, 487a, 490a, 492a; v, 280a, 876a — I, 27b, 355a, 491b, 650a, 774b, 925b, 1008a; II, 235b, 532b; III, 503a, 504a, 507a, 509a; V, 278a, 882a
al-Muḥtasib → Abū ʿAbd Allāh al-Shīʿī
Muḥyi ʾl-Dīn Masʿūd b. Ḳilidj Arslan II i, 510a — I, 525b
Muḥyi ʾl-Dīn Meḥemmed Fenārī-zāde ii, 879b; iv, 333b — II, 900a; IV, 348a
Muḥyi al-Dīn Muḥammad Čiwi-zāde ii, 56b — II, 57b
Muḥyi al-Dīn Shāh Meḥemmed Fenārī-zāde ii, 879b — II, 899b
Muḥyi al-Dīn Yaḥya b. Faḍl Allāh ii, 732a; iii, 758b — II, 750b; III, 781b
Muḥyī-i Gülshenī ii, 1136a — II, 1162b
Muʿīd v, 1133b — V, 1129a
Muʿīn al-Dīn ʿAlī → Ḳāsim-i Anwār
Muʿīn al-Dīn Ḥasan b. Ṣadr al-Dīn i, 766a, b — I, 789a, b
Muʿīn al-Dīn Ḥasan Čishtī → Čishtī
Muʿīn al-Dīn Sulaymān Parvāna iii, 1269a; iv, 619b, 814a, 817a — III, 1302a; IV, 644a, 846b, 850a
Muʿīn al-Dīn Unur (Anar) i, 1332a; ii, 282a; iii, 399a — I, 1372b; II, 290b; III, 411b
Muʿīn al-Fuḳarāʾ → Aḥmad b. Muḥammad

Muʿīn al-Mulk b. Ḳamar al-Dīn i, 295b, 296a; iii, 1158b — I, 304b, 305a; III, 1187a
al-Muʿizz (Mamlūk) → ʿIzz al-Dīn Aybak (Mamlūk)
al-Muʿizz b. Bādīs (Zīrid(e)) i, 533a, 860a, 1023b; iii, 137a, 324b, 385b, 386a, 688a, 695a, 903a, 936a; iv, 199a, 497a, 805a, 827b; v, 59b, 530b, 1182b, 1246b; s, 26b, 62b — I, 549a, 884a, 1055a; III, 140a, 334b, 398a, b, 709b, 717b, 927b, 960b; IV, 207b, 208a, 518b, 837b, 860b; V, 61b, 534b, 1172b, 1237b; S, 27a, 63a
al-Muʿizz b. Muḥammad b. Walmiya iv, 337a — IV, 351b
al-Muʿizz b. Zīrī b. ʿAtiyya v, 1177b, 1178b, 1179a — V, 1167b, 1168b, 1169a
Muʿizz al-Dawla Aḥmad (Būyid(e)) i, 11b, 19b, 20a, 419a, 711b, 866b, 899b, 1047a, 1352a; ii, 178b, 994a, 1082b; iii, 127b, 195b, 1156b, 1157a, 1175b, 1202a; iv, 23a, b, 266a, 855a; s, 13a, b, 36b, 127a, 259a, 362a — I, 11b, 20a, 21a, 431a, 733a, 890b, 926b, 1078b, 1391b; II, 184a, 1017a, 1108a; III, 130a, 200a, 1185a, b, 1204b, 1232b; IV, 25a-b, 278a, 888b; S, 13a, 14a, 36b, 126a, 258b, 361b
Muʿizz al-Dīn al-Kurtī iv, 672a — IV, 699b
al-Muʿizz li-Dīn Allāh (Fāṭimid(e)) i, 592a, 814a, 823a, 1175b; ii, 195a, 329a, 491b, 494b, 495a, 853a, b, 855a, 860a, b, 861b, 963a, 994a, 1099a; iii, 246a, 298b, 785b, 840b, 886a, 1084a; iv, 198b, 662b, 663b; v, 862b; s, 62b, 236b, 252b — I, 611b, 837b, 846a, 1210b; II, 201a, 338b, 503b, 507a, b, 873a, b, 875a, 879b, 880b, 881b, 985a, 1017a, 1125a; III, 253a, 307b, 808b, 864b, 910a, 1111a; IV, 207b, 689b, 690a; V, 869b; S, 63a, 236b, 252b
Muʿizz al-Dīn Ḥusayn ii, 1049b — II, 1074a
Muʿizz al-Dīn Muḥammad b. Sām i, 208b, 217b, 1165b, 1192b, 1194a, 1300a; ii, 119b, 266b, 752a, 922b, 972b, 1049b, 1052b, 1101a, b, 1122b, 1123b; iii, 414b, 433b; iv, 666b, 669a; v, 501a, 782b; s, 242a, 284b, 360a — I, 214b, 224a, 1200b, 1228a, 1229b, 1339b; II, 122b, 274b, 770a, 943b, 994b, 1074a, 1077b, 1127a, b, 1148b, 1150a; III, 428b, 448a; IV, 693b, 696b; V, 504b, 788b; S, 242a, 284b, 359b
Muʿizz al-Dīn Sandjar iii, 603a — III, 623b
Muʿizzī b. Burhānī iv, 61b, 466b; s, 384a — IV, 65a, 487b; S, 384b
Muʿizziyya ii, 1083a — II, 1108b
Muʿizziyya (Sicily/Sicile) → Taormina
Muḳābal iii, 84a; iv, 259a — III, 86b; IV, 271a
Muḳābala (law/loi) iv, 193a — IV, 201a
Muḳaddam iii, 184b — III, 188b
Muḳaddam, Dr. Muḥammad v, 1098a — V, 1094a
Muḳaddam b. Muʿāfā i, 601a; iv, 355a — I, 620b; IV, 370b
al-Muḳaddasī, Muḥammad i, 488a, 570b; ii, 127a, 581a, 582a; iii, 761b, 1078a, 1252b; iv, 45b, 220a, 223a, 1079a, 1088a; v, 328b, 330a; s, 266a, 363a, 392a — I, 502b, 589a; II, 130b, 596a, b; III, 784b, 1104b, 1285a; IV, 48b, 229b, 233a, 1110b, 1119a; V, 328a, 330a; S, 265b, 362b, 392b
Mukaddī iv, 735a — IV, 765a
al-Mukaḥḥal → ʿAmr b. al-Ahtam
Muḳāʿis, Banū iv, 832a — IV, 865a
Muḳali ii, 43a — II, 43b
al-Mukallā i, 182a, 554b; ii, 173b; s, 338b — I, 187a,, 572a; II, 179a; S, 338a
Mukallafa ii, 79b — II, 81a
al-Muḳammiṣ iv, 304a — IV, 317b
al-Muḳannaʿ i, 141b, 1294a; ii, 1107a; iv, 16b; v, 64a, 181b, 855a, 1238b; s, 411a — I, 145b, 1333b; II, 1133a; IV, 17b; V, 66a, 179a, 862a, 1229b; S, 411b
Muḳannī iv, 529b — IV, 552b
Muḳāraḍa → Ḳirād
Muḳarnas i, 1229a; ii, 777b, 864a; iv, 481a — I, 1265b; II, 796a, 884a; IV, 502a
Muḳarrab Khān ii, 973b, 1131b — II, 996a, 1158a
Mukarram b. Yām → al-Karam b. Yām
al-Muḳarram Aḥmad b. ʿAlī al-Ṣulayḥī i, 181b, 552a; iii, 125b — I, 186b, 570a; III, 128a
al-Muḳarrariyya iii, 284a — III, 292b
Mukarrib i, 547b — I, 565a
Mukarzal, Naʿʿūm ii, 471a — II, 483a
Mukarzal, Sallūm ii, 471b — II, 483b
Muḳāsama ii, 158a; iv, 1032a, 1037b, 1038a, 1055b — II, 163a; IV, 1063b, 1069a, b, 1087a
Mukāshafa iv, 696b, 697a, b — IV, 725a, b
Mukāsir ii, 97b — II, 99b
Muḳāṭaʿa i, 642b, 651b, 1080a, 1144b; ii, 33b, 118b, 147b, 188a, 907b; iii, 284a; iv, 225b, 323b, 1038a, 1046a; v, 792a, b — I, 663a, 672a, 1112a, 1179a; II, 34a, 121b, 151b, 193b, 929a; III, 293a; IV, 235b, 337b, 1070a, 1077b; V, 798b
Mukātaba i, 30a; ii, 302b, 328b; iii, 27a — I, 31a; II, 310b, 338a; III, 28b
Muḳātil b. ʿAṭiyya v, 1176b, 1177a, 1178b — V, 1166b, 1167a, 1168b
Muḳātil b. Sulaymān s, 90b — S, 90a
Muḳaṭṭaʿāt iv, 58a — IV, 61a
al-Muḳaṭṭam ii, 288b, 403b, 466b — II, 296b, 414b, 478b
Muḳawḳis i, 1016a; v, 90b — I, 1047a; V, 92b
Muḳayyin iv, 822b — IV, 855b
Mukhā → Mokhā
al-Mukhabbal b. Rabīʿa s, 394b — S, 395a
al-Mukhaḍḍaba iii, 49b — III, 51b
Mukhaḍramūn i, 12a, 140a — I, 12a, 144b
Mukhallafāt i, 1147b, 1148a — I, 1181b, 1182a
Mukhammisa iv, 1132b, 1133a — IV, 1164b
Mukhāriḳ s, 64a — S, 64b
Mukharrim i, 897b, 900a, 901a — I, 924b, 927a, 928a
al-Mukharrimī → Abū Saʿd al-Mubārak
Mukhāṭara iii, 511b — III, 528b
Mukhayrikḳ ii, 844b — II, 864a
Mukhbir al-Salṭana → Mahdī Ḳulī Hidāyat
Mukhtalif iii, 27b — III, 29a
Mukhtār i, 972b, 974a — I, 1002b, 1004b
al-Mukhtar b. Abī ʿUbayd i, 5a, 15a, 41a, 45a, 50b, 55a, 76b, 304a, 850b; ii, 198b, 523b; iii, 236a, 715a, 718a, 987a, 1255a, 1265b; iv, 44b, 836a, b; v, 349b, 350a; s, 357b — I, 5a, 15b, 42a, 46a, 52a, 57a, 78b, 313b, 874a; II, 204b, 536b; III, 243a, 737b, 740b, 1011b, 1287b, 1298b; IV, 47a, 869a, b; V, 350b; S, 357b
al-Mukhtār b. ʿAwf al-Azdī i, 550b; ii, 141a; iii, 651b, 658a; iv, 1076a; s, 337b, 338a — I, 568a; II, 145a; III, 673a, 679b; IV, 1108a; S, 337b
Mukhtār b. Maḥmūd al-Zāhidī iv, 1062b — IV, 1094a
Mukhtar b. ʿUmar Tal i, 297a — I, 306a
al-Mukhtār al-Kabīr, Sīdī v, 393b, 394a — V, 394b
al-Mukhtār al-Ṣaghīr, Sīdī v, 394a — V, 395a
Mukhtar Pasha Tepedelenli i, 398b, 399a — I, 410a, b
al-Mukhtāra i,133b, 389a; ii, 444a — I, 137b, 400a; II, 455b
Mukhtarī s, 416a — S, 416b
Mukhtāriyya v, 393b, 394a — V, 394b, 395a
al-Mukhtārūn v, 50a — V, 51b
Mukhtaṣṣ Khān iv, 276b — IV, 288b
Muḳīm i, 741a — I, 763a
Muḳīm Khān i, 227b, 627b; ii, 1049b; iv, 357a, 536b — I, 234b, 648a; II, 1074a; IV, 372b, 560a
Muḳīm Khān Sārawī v, 663b — V, 669a
Mukram i, 711b — I, 733a
Muḳrānī → Moḳrānī
Mukrī iii, 1102b, 1109a; v, 460b — III, 1129b, 1136b; V, 463a

Mukrianī, Ḥusayn Ḥuznī v, 483b – V, 486b
Muḳrim i, 553b, 942b; iv, 764b – I, 571a, 971b; IV, 795a
Mukrin b. Adjwad s, 234b – S, 234a
Muḳtaᶜ ii, 272b, 273a, 508a; v, 862b – II, 280b, 281a, 520b; V, 869b
al-Muḳtabis i, 82b, 600b – I, 85a, 620a
al-Muḳtadī (ᶜAbbāsid(e)) i, 901a; iv, 458a, 942b; s, 192b, 194a – I, 928a; IV, 478b, 975b; S, 193a, b
al-Muḳtadir (ᶜAbbāsid(e)) i, 19a, 387a, 446a, 688b, 867a, 898a, 899a, 936a; ii, 344b, 383b, 388b, 462a, 1080b; iii, 100b, 126b, 344b, 388a, 619b, 691b, 692a, 739a, 750b, 757b, 767b, 768a, 886b, 892b, 1201b; iv, 214b; v, 132a, 737b; s, 118a, 192a, 199a, 372a, 385b – I, 20a, 398b, 458b, 709b, 891b, 925a, b, 965a; II, 354b, 393a, 399a, 473b, 1105b; III, 103a, 129b, 355a, 400b, 640a, 713b, 714a, 761b, 773b, 780b, 790b, 791a, 910b, 916b, 1232a; IV, 224a; V, 135a, 743a; S, 117a, 193a, 199a, 372a, 386a
al-Muḳtadir b. Hūd → Aḥmad I (Hūdid(e))
al-Muḳtafī (ᶜAbbāsid(e)) i, 11a, 19a, 898a; ii, 461b; iii, 345a, 892b, 1044b; iv, 494a, 940a; s, 118a, 304b – I, 11a, 19b, 924b; II, 473b; III, 355b, 916b, 1070b; IV, 515a, 973a; S, 117b, 304b
al-Muḳtafī bi-Amr Allāh (ᶜAbbāsid(e)) i, 865b; iii, 160b, 197a, 1255b; s, 193b – I, 890a; III, 164a, 201b, 1288b; S, 194a
Muktagīrī s, 280a – S, 280a
al-Muḳtanā, Bahāʾ al-Dīn i, 552a; ii, 632b; iii, 154b – I, 569b; II, 648b; III, 158a
Muktasaba iv, 692b – IV, 720b
al-Muḳtaṭaf ii, 288b, 403b, 428a, 466b – II, 296b, 414a, 439a, 478b
al-Muḳurra iv, 568a – IV, 590a
Mukūs i, 1144a; ii, 142b; iv, 323a, b, 324a – I, 1178b; II, 146b; IV, 337a, b, 338b
al-Mulāᶜī → Abū Nuᶜaym
Mulalhil ii, 1028b – II, 1052b
Mulāṭafa, mulaṭṭifāt ii, 304a – II, 312b
Mulaththamūn v, 652b, 744a, 769b – V, 656b, 749b, 775b
Mūlāy → Mawlāy
Mūlāy ᶜAlī Bū Ghālem iv, 729a – IV, 758a
Mūlāy Būᶜazzā i, 159b – I, 164a
Mulāy Bushᶜīb → Abū Shuᶜayb
al-Mulayda s, 3b – S, 2b
Mulāzimiyya v, 1252a, b – V, 1242b, 1243a, b
Mulham, Nāṣir al-Muslimīn ii, 318a, b – II, 327b
Mulk v, 623a – V, 627a
Mulk Amān ii, 30a – II, 30b
Mülkiyye ii, 425b, 692a; iv, 909a; v, 904a – II, 436b, 709b; IV, 942b; V, 910a
Mullā → Mawlā
Mullā ... → under the following name/sous le nom suivant
Mullā Apāḳ s, 331b – S, 331a
Mullā-bāshī iv, 104a – IV, 108b
Mullāᶜī i, 225b; iii, 1102b – I, 232a; III, 1130a
Mulla Ṣadrā s, 24a, 308a, b – S, 24a, 308a, b
Multān i, 218a, 230b, 628a, 912a; iii, 419b, 433b, 441b, 443b, 633a, b, 634a, 1155b; iv, 199a; v, 26a, 782b, 783a, 885a; s, 10b, 66b, 105a, 284b, 329b, 332a, 423b – I, 224a, 237b, 648b, 939b; III, 433a, 447b, 456a, 458b, 654a, b, 655a, 1184a; IV, 207b; V, 27a, 788b, 789a, 891b; S, 10a, 67a, 104b, 284b, 329a, 331b, 423b
Multān Mall i, 218a – I, 224a
al-Multazam iv, 318a – IV, 332a
Multazim ii, 147b, 148a, b; iii, 1154a – II, 151b, 152a, b; III, 1182b
Mulūk al-ṭawāʾif i, 6a, b, 94b, 130b, 155b, 242a, 495a, 865a, 1320a; ii, 331b; iii, 496a, 640a, 791b – I, 6a, 97a, 134a, 160a, 249b, 510a, 889a, 1360b; II, 341a; III, 513a, 661b, 814b
Mulūya, Wādī s, 113b – S, 113a
Mumahhid al-Dawla i, 1298b; iii, 130b; v, 453a – I, 1338a; III, 133a; V, 455b
Mumayyiz i, 993b – I, 1024a
al-Mumazzaḳ i, 74a – I, 76a
Muʾmin b. Aḥmad i, 1306b, 1307b – I, 1346b, 1348a
Muʾmin b. al-Ḥasan i, 1306b, 1307b – I, 1346b, 1348a
Muʾmin Khān (Gudjarāt) i, 1053a; ii, 1130a; – I, 1084b; II, 1156b
Mūʾmin Khān (poet/poète) iii, 119b; v, 961b – III, 122a; V, 966a
Muʾmina Khatūn iii, 110b – III, 1137b
Muʾminid(e)s i, 78a, 79a, 94b, 121b, 160b – I, 80a, 81a, 97a, 125a, 165a
Mumtaḥin al-Ḍawla s, 109a – S, 108b
Mumtāz Efendi iv, 1126a – IV, 1158a
Mumtāz Khan → Iᶜtibar Khān
Mumtāz Maḥall i, 253b, 686a, 1161a, 1331a; I, 261b, 707a, 1196a, 1371b
Munādjāt iv, 715b – IV, 744b
Munādjaza iv, 324a – IV, 338a, b
al-Munadjdjim, ᶜAlī b. Hārūn s, 362b – S, 362a
Munadjdjim, Banu 'l- i, 1141a; s, 375b – I, 1175b; S, 375b
Munadjdjim Bāshī i, 836a – I, 859a
Munāfara iv, 77b – IV, 81b
Munaffidh i, 1148b; ii, 146a – I, 1183a; II, 150a
Munāfiḳūn i, 53b; v, 996a, b – I, 55a; V, 991b
Munakhkhal b. Djamīl s, 233a – S, 232b
Munāwala iii, 27a – III, 28b
al-Munāwī, ᶜAbd al-Raʾūf iii, 29a – III, 30b
al-Munawwar, Muḥammad b. s, 154a – S, 154b
al-Munayzila s, 234b – S, 234a
Munāẓara iii, 431b; v, 1130b, 1223b – III, 445b; V, 1126b, 1214a
al-Munāzī, Abū Naṣr Aḥmad v, 929b – V, 934b
Mundā iii, 412a – III, 425a
al-Mundhir I (Lakhmid(e)) i, 939a; v, 633a – I, 967b; V, 637a
al-Mundhir III Ibn al-Nuᶜmān (Lakhmid(e)) i, 99a, 115b, 451b, 526b, 527a, 548b; ii, 1021a; iii, 94a, 222a, 462b; v, 633a, 640a – I, 101b, 119a, 464b, 542b, 543a, 566a; II, 1044b; III, 96b, 229a, 479a; V, 637a, 644b
al-Mundhir IV (Lakhmid(e)) v, 633b – V, 637b
al-Mundhir b. al-Ḥārith b. Djabala i, 1249b; ii, 244b, 1021a, b; v, 633b – I, 1287b; II, 251b, 1044b, 1045a; V, 637b
al-Mundhir b. Māʾ al-Samāʾ → al-Mundhir III
al-Mundhir b. Muḥammad i, 49a, 85b; s, 92a, 153a – I, 50b, 88a; S, 92a, 153a
al-Mundhir b. al-Muḳtadir ii, 112a – II, 114b
Mundhir b. Saᶜīd al-Ballūṭī i, 497a, 600a; ii, 744b – I, 512a, 619b; II, 763a
al-Mundhir b. Yaḥyā al-Tudjībī iii, 147a, 743a – III, 150b, 766a
al-Mundhirī, Abū Muḥammad al-Ḳawī s, 194a – S, 195a
al-Mundhirī, Muḥammad b. Djaᶜfar i, 114b, 822a – I, 117b, 845a
Mundji i, 225a – I, 231b
Münedjdjim-bashî ii, 110a; iii, 392b; iv, 1175a; s, 59a – II, 112b; III, 405a; IV, 1208b; S, 59b
Munfaṣil iii, 26a – III, 27a
Mungīr → Monghyr
Münīf s, 83a – S, 83a
Munīf Pasha ii, 473b, 532a, 682b – II, 485b, 545a, 699b
Munᶜim Khān i, 1136b; ii, 183b, 498b, 499b; iv, 1020a; v, 638b – I, 1170b; II, 189a, 511a, 512a; IV,

1052a; V, 642b
Münīrī Belghrādī i, 324b; ii, 968b — I, 334b; II, 990b
Muʾnis → Muḥammad Mīrāb, Shīr
Muʾnis s, 419b, 420a — S, 420a
Muʾnis al-Khādim i, 11a, 19a, 34a, 386b, 387a, 446a; ii, 191b, 325b; iii, 46a, 126b, 619b, 620a; iv, 22b, 423b; v, 1243b — I, 11a, 20a, 34b, 398a, b, 458b; II, 198a, 335b; III, 47b, 129a, 640a, b; IV, 24a, 442a; V, 1234a
Muʾnis b. Yaḥyā al-Mirdāsī iii, 386a; iv, 337a — III, 398b; IV, 351b
Muʾnisa (Kayna) s, 252b — S, 252b
Munkar iii, 26b — III, 27b
Munkar wa-Nakīr i, 187a, 334b; iii, 1231b; iv, 667b — I, 192a, 345a; III, 1263b; IV, 694b
Munshaʾāt al-salāṭīn ii, 128a, 589a, 881a — II, 131a, 603b, 901b
Munshī iv, 757b, 758b, 760a — IV, 787b, 788b, 790a
Munshī al-māmālik iv, 757b, 760a — IV, 787b, 788a, 790a
Munshī Mawlawī → ᶜAbd al-Karīm Munshī
Munṣif Bey iii, 636b — III, 658a
Muntadjab al-Dīn Abu ʾl-Ḥasan ᶜAlī iii, 1151b — III, 1179b
al-Muntafiḳ, Banū i, 270b, 873a, 942a, 11086a, 1087a, 1096a,b; ii, 77a; iii, 1107b, 1257b; v, 81a; s, 119a, 234b — I, 279a, 897a, 971a, 1118b, 1119b, 1129a, b; II, 78b; III, 1134b, 1290a; V, 83a; S, 118b, 234b
Munṭaḳa i, 297a — I, 306b
al-Muntakhab → Abū Zakariyyāʾ Yaḥyā III
Muntakhab al-Dawla iv, 842a — IV, 875a
al-Muntaṣir (Abbāsid(e) i, 402b; ii, 461b, 837b — I, 414a; II, 473b, 857b
al-Muntaṣir (Ḥafṣid(e)) iii, 69a; iv, 416a — III, 71a; IV, 434a
al-Muntaṣir b. Khazrūn v, 1181a, 1182b — V, 1171a, 1172b, 1173a
Muntazah (palace/palais) s, 301a — S, 300b
al-Murābī, Abu ʾl-ᶜAbbās iv, 736a — IV, 766a
Murābiṭ i, 355b, 371b, 389b, 1176b; v, 1191a, b, 1200b, 1201b — I, 366a, b, 382a, 400b, 1211b; V, 1181a, b, 1191a, 1192a
al-Murābiṭūn i, 7a, 78b, 165a, 242b, 251a, 367a, 389a, 495a, 602a, 986a, 1092a, 1176a; ii, 134a, 1007a; iii, 207a, 800a, 959a, 1043a; v, 744a, 1178b, 1189b; s, 27a, 80b — I, 7a, 81a, 170a, 250a, 258b, 378a, 400b, 510a, 621b, 1016b, 1124b, 1211a; II, 137a, 1030b; III, 213a, 823b, 984a, 1069a; V, 749b, 1168b, 1179b; S, 27b, 80b
- administration i, 445b, 1148b; ii, 145b, 230a; v, 626a — I, 458b, 1183a; II, 149b, 237a; V, 630a
- constructions i, 499a, 1320b; ii, 818b, 821b, 1015a; iii, 300b; iv, 633a; v, 1150a I, 514b, 1361a; II, 838a, 841a, 1039a; III, 309b; IV, 659a; V, 1140b
- history/histoire i, 44a, 156b; iii, 932b; v, 653b — I, 45a, 161a; III, 957a; V, 657b
Murād I (Ottoman) i, 322b, 394a, 468a, b, 481a, 510b, 1117b, 1191b, 1263a, 1302b, 1325b; ii, 15b, 210b, 291b, 444b, 684b, 983b; iv, 376a, 623a, 945a; v, 44b, 276a; s, 314b, 331a — I, 332b, 405b, 482a, b, 495a, 526a, 1151b, 1227a, 1301b, 1342b, 1366b; II, 15b, 217a, 299b, 456b, 701b, 1006a; IV, 392a, 648a, 978a; V, 46a, 274a; S, 314b, 329b
Murād II (Ottoman) i, 199a, 468a, 654b, 655b, 992a, 1061a, 1225b, 1248a, 1252b, 1334a; ii, 82b, 98a, 210b, 443a, 599b, 684a,b, 685a, 697a, 703a, 721a, 984b, 990a, 1086a; iv, 139b, 624a, 656a, 968b, 1093a; v, 1170a; s, 274a, 315a — I, 204b, 482a, 675a, 676a, 1023a, 1093a, 1262a, 1286a, 1290b, 1374b; II, 84a, 100b, 217a, 454b, 614b, 701a, b, 702a, 714b, 721a, 739b, 1007b, 1013a, 1111b; IV, 145a, 648b, 682b, 1001a, 1124a; V, 1159b; S, 273b, 314b
Murād III (Ottoman) i, 775b, 1017b, 1208b; ii, 82b, 208a, 442b, 615a, 881a; iv, 638a; v, 27b, 766a, 814b, 1170a; s, 138a — I, 798b, 1049a, 1244b; II, 84a, 214b, 454b, 630b, 901b; IV, 664a; V, 28a, 772a, 820b, 1160a; S, 137b
Murād IV (Ottoman) i, 4a, 310b, 424a, 468b, 475a, 481a, 775b, 826a, 904a; ii, 49a, 119b, 345b, 718a; iii, 91b, 352a, 357a, 626a, 1257a; iv, 451b, 574a, 717a, 728b; v, 18b, 34b, 272b, 493b; s, 49a, b, 94b, 171b, 315b — I, 4b, 320b, 436a, 482b, 489a, 495a, 799a, 849a, 931b; II, 50a, 122a, 355a, 736b; III, 94a, 363a, 368a, 647a, 1290a; IV, 472a, 596b, 745b, 757b; V, 19a, 35b, 270a, 496b; S, 49b, 50a, 94a, 172a, 315a
Murād V (Ottoman) i, 63b; ii, 49a, 642a; iv, 876a, b; S, 63a — I, 65b; II, 50a, 658a; IV, 909a, b; S, 63b
Murād, Banū iii, 223a; v, 954a — III, 229b; V, 958a
Murād, Ḥadjdjī → Shāmil
Murād b. Aḥmad b. Bāyazīd iv, 716b — IV, 745b
Murād b. Dāniyār Beg, Shāh s, 97a — S, 96b
Murād b. Akbar i, 81a; ii, 981b — I, 83a; II, 1003b
Murād b. Djem ii, 530b — II, 543bMurād b. Yaᶜḳūb i, 311b, 312a — I, 321b
Murād Bakhsh i, 768b; ii, 134b; iv, 914b — I, 791b; II, 138a; IV, 947b
Murād Beg i, 853a; ii, 638a; v, 48a; s, 228b — I, 876b; II, 654a; V, 49b; S, 228b
Murād Beg Tardić v, 774b — V, 780b
Murād Bey (d./m. 1801) iii, 992a; iv, 853a; s, 38b — III, 1016b; IV, 886a; S, 38b
Murād Bey (d./m. 1914) ii, 474b; iv, 871b — II, 486b; IV, 905a
Murād Bey Abū Bālā iv, 828a — IV, 861a
Murād Girāy iv, 178b; v, 140a — IV, 185b; V, 142b
Murād Khān b. Ismāᶜīl Pasha i, 920a — I, 948a
Murād Khān (Kashmīr) → Iᶜtiḳād Khān
Murād Pasha (d. 1473) iv, 230a — IV, 240b
Murād Pasha Ḳuyudju i, 267b, 511a, 904a; ii, 635a, 750a; iv, 499a, 970a; s, 239a — I, 275b, 526b, 931a; II, 651a, 768a; IV, 520b, 1002a; S, 239a
Murād Raʾīs v, 504a — V, 507b
Murād Sulṭān i, 1076b — I, 1108b
Murad-suyu ii, 945b, 947a — II, 967a, b, 969a
Murādābād s, 73b, 74a — S, 74a, b
al-Murādī (d./m. 1791) i, 594b; ii, 355b, 839b — I, 614a; II, 365b, 859a
al-Murādī, Muḥammad b. Manṣūr (IXe c./s.) s, 48b — S, 49a
Muradjdjih v, 98a — V, 100b
Murāhiḳ i, 993b — I, 1024a
Murāḳaba ii, 55b — II, 56b
Murakkab i, 1083b — I, 1116a
al-Muraḳḳish al-Aṣghar i, 963b; iv, 998a, b — I, 993a; IV, 1030b, 1031a
Murat Su v, 441b — V, 444a
Murcia/Murcie → Mursiya
Murḍā b. ᶜAlī i, 798a — I, 821b
al-Murdār, Abū Mūsā iii, 1019b, 1266a — III, 1045a, 1299a
Murder → Ḳatl
Murdjān i, 781a — I, 804a
Murdjiʾa i, 123b, 124a, 249b, 276b, 1241b; ii, 833b, 931a, 1022a; iii, 807b, 1142b, 1164a, 1171a; iv, 408a; s, 358a — I, 127a,b, 257b, 285a, 1279b; II, 853a, 952b, 1046a; III, 830b, 1171a, 1192b, 1200a; IV, 425b; S, 357b
Murghāb i, 222b, 313b, 853b; v, 868b, 873b — I, 229a, 323a, 877a; V, 874b, 879b
Murīd ii, 58b, 164b; iii, 84b; iv, 950b, 992b — II, 60a, 169b; III, 86b; IV, 983a, 1025a
Mūrid(e)s ii, 63b — II, 64b
Murīdism/Murīds s, 182a — S, 182a
Murīdism(e) iii, 157a; s, 182a — III, 160b; S, 182a
Murr, Banū s, 5a — S, 4a

Murra, Āl i, 545b, 873b; ii, 176b, 725b, 1023b — I, 563a, 897b; II, 182a, 744a, 1047a
al-Murrī, al-Djunayd iii, 223b — III, 230b
al-Murrī, Ṣāliḥ iv, 734b — IV, 764a
Mursal iii, 26a — III, 27a
Murshid Kulī Khān i, 7b, 786b; ii, 157b, 488b, 810a; iv, 976b — I, 7b, 791b; II, 162b, 500b, 829a; IV, 1009a
Murshidī → ʿAbd al-Raḥmān b. ʿĪsā, Aḥmad
Murshidiyya → Kāzarūniyya
al-Mursī → Yāḳūt
al-Mursī, Abu 'l-ʿAbbās v, 17b; s, 159a — V, 18a; S, 159a
Mursiya i, 6b, 58b, 82b, 489a, 1320a, 1347a; ii, 115a; iii, 706a, 904b; iv, 672b; s, 144b — I, 7a, 60b, 85a, 504a, 1360b, 1387b; II, 117b; III, 728a, 929a; IV, 700a; S, 144a
Murtaḍā (Hind) s, 329b — S, 329a
al-Murtaḍā (Almohad(e)) s, 112a, 389a, b — S, 111a, 389b, 390a
al-Murtaḍā → ʿAbd al-Raḥmān IV (Marwānid(e)); al-Sharīf al-Murtaḍā
Murtaḍa ʿAlī ii, 88a — II, 89b
Murtaḍā b. ʿAlī Marʿashī, Sayyid v, 663a — V, 668a
Murtaḍā Baktāshī ii, 735a,b — II, 754a
Murtaḍā Ḥusayn i, 1219a — I, 1255a
Murtaḍā Ḳulī Khān Shamlu iv, 390b, 391a, 1124b — IV, 407b, 1156a
Murtaḍā Kulī Khān Wākil al-Mulk v, 165a — V, 162b
Murtaḍā Niẓām Shāh I ii, 815a, 921b; iii, 426b, 1161a — II, 834b, 943a; III, 440a, 1189b
Murtaḍā Nizām Shāh II iii, 15b; iv, 1018b — III, 16a; IV, 1050b
Murtaḍā Pasha i, 4b, 236b; v, 34b, 258a, b, 1023a — I, 4b, 244a; V, 35b, 256a, 1018b
Murtaḍā al-Zabīdī i, 596b, 782a; ii, 355b, 927a, 948b; iv, 524b — I, 615b, 805a; II, 365b, 948b, 973a; IV, 547b
Murtadd iv, 408a, 771a, 1076b; v, 179a — IV, 426a, 801b, 1108a; V, 176b
Murtahin iv, 488b — IV, 509b
Mūrthā → Mūtā
Murud s, 246b — S, 246b
Muruwwa ii, 961a — II, 983a
Murwan-Ḳru i, 100b; v, 487b, 488a — I, 103b; V, 490b
Murzūk i, 38a; ii, 876a — I, 39a; II, 896a
Mūsā (Moses/Moïse) ii, 280a, 917b; iii, 231b, 1175a; iv, 293a, 903a, b, 904a; v, 421a, 423b — II, 288b, 939a; III, 238b, 1204a; IV, 306a, 935b, 936b; V, 423a, 425b
Mūsā, Banū i, 84b, 403a; s, 267a, 371b, 372b, 373a, 412b — I, 87a, 414b; S, 266b, 371b, 372a, 373a, 412b
Mūsā, Salāma iv, 125a — IV, 130a
Mūsā I al-Djawn iii, 262b, 984b — III, 270a, 1009a
Mūsā II b. ʿAbd Allāh iii, 262b — III, 270a
Mūsā b. ʿAbd Allāh b. Ḥasan → Mūsā I al-Djawn
Mūsā b. ʿAbd Allāh b. Khāzim i, 48a, 529b; iii, 304a — I, 49a, 546a; III, 313a
Mūsā b. Abi 'l ʿĀfiya ii, 853a, 979a; iii, 1036a; iv, 459a — II, 872b, 1001a; III, 1062a; IV, 479a
Mūsā b. Abī Djābir al-Azkānī iii, 652a — III, 673b
Mūsā b. al-ʿĀzār i, 344b — I, 355a
Mūsā b. Bughā i, 278b, 1287b; ii, 191a; iii, 29a, 245a; iv, 493b, 859a — I, 287a, 1327a; II, 197b; III, 30b, 252a; IV, 515a, 892a
Mūsā b. Djaʿfar → Mūsā al-Ḳāzim
Mūsā b. Fortūn iv, 712b — IV, 741b
Mūsā b. Ḥafṣ iv, 645b — IV, 672a
Mūsā b. Ḥudayr i, 600a — I, 619b
Mūsā b. Ibrāhīm b. Shīrkūh → al-Ashraf Mūsā
Mūsā b. ʿĪsā i, 162b — I, 166b
Mūsā b. Maymūn → Ibn Maymūn
Mūsā b. Mūsā Ibn Ḳasī i, 1012a; iii, 815b; iv, 712b; s, 82a — I, 1043a; III, 839b; IV, 741b; S, 81b
Mūsā b. Nuṣayr i, 58b, 492b, 1079b, 1242b, 1338b; ii, 1009a, 1095b; iii, 271b; iv, 115a, 494b, 665a; v, 1189a; s, 81b, 125a — I, 60b, 507b, 1111b, 1280b, 1378b; II, 1032b, 1121a; III, 279a; IV, 120a, 515b, 692a; V, 1179a; S, 81b, 124a
Mūsā b. Rabīʿa b. Māniʿ al-Muraydī ii, 569a — II, 583b
Mūsā b. Ṭalḥa v, 1231a — V, 1221b
Mūsā b. ʿUḳba v, 1162a, 1163a — V, 1151b, 1152b
Mūsā b. Yaḥyā al-Barmikī i, 1036a — I, 1067b
Mūsā ag Amāstan i, 255a — I, 263a
Mūsā Aydînoghlu i, 783b; ii, 599a — I, 806b; II, 614a
Mūsā Beg (Ḳarāmān-oghlu) iv, 621b, 622a — IV, 646b, 647a
Mūsā Čelebi ii, 291b, 599a, 611b, 684a — II, 299b, 614a, 626b, 701a
Mūsā al-Hādī iv, 858b — IV, 892a
Mūsā Ḥarfūsh ii, 750a; iii, 205b — II, 768a; III, 211a
Mūsā al-Ḳāzim (Imām) i, 108a, 402b, 550b, 850b; ii, 374b, 375a; iii, 233b, 497a, 616b; iv, 855a, b, 1132b; v, 1236a; s, 95a, 383a, 402b — I, 111a, 414a, 414b, 568b, 874a; II, 385a; III, 240b, 514a, 637a; IV, 888a, b, 1164a; V, 1226b; S, 94a, b, 383a, 403a
Mūsā Khān Pūlādī i, 1136b — I, 1171a
Mūsā Rayna s, 423b — S, 423b
Mūsā Shahawāt iv, 190a — IV, 198a
Mūsā Sulaymān iii, 370b — III, 382a
Muṣʿab b. al-Zubayr i, 55a, 76b, 304a, 453b, 810b, 1242b, 1243a, 1349a; ii, 197a; iii, 40a, 715a, 970a, 1255a, 1265b; iv, 494b; v, 731a; s, 357b, 380b — I, 57a, 79a, 313b, 466b, 833b, 1280b, 1389a; II, 203b; III, 41b, 737b, 994b, 1287b, 1298b; IV, 516a; V, 736a; S, 357b, 381a
al-Muṣʿabayn i, 1133a — I, 1167b
Musabbaʿāt ii, 122a,b; v, 267a — II, 125a,b; V, 265a
al-Muṣabbiḥī iii, 81a, 894b — III, 83a, 918b
al-Muṣʿabī → Abā Yazmū
Muṣādara i, 1144a; ii, 152b; iv, 463b — I, 1178b; II, 157a; IV, 484a
Muṣaddiḳ, Muḥammad i, 978b; ii, 653a, 882b; iii, 529b; iv, 41b, 695b, 790a, 1028b; v, 630b, 1042b; s, 60b, 110b, 158a — I, 1009a; II, 669b, 903a; III, 547b, 548a; IV, 44a, 724a, 822a, 1060b; V, 634b, 1039a; S, 61a, 109b, 158a
Musāfirid(e)s i, 98b, 637b, 638a, 1041b; ii, 192a, 680a; iv, 345a, 346a — I, 101b, 658b, 1073a; II,, 198a, 697a; IV, 360a, b
Muṣaḥḥaf iii, 26a — III, 27b
Muṣāḥib Muṣṭafā Pasha i, 96b; ii, 684b — I, 99b; II, 701b
Musāḳāt v, 871b — V, 878a
Musālima i, 491a — I, 505b
Muṣallā i, 482a; v, 1141a, 1147a — I, 496b; V, 1134a, 1138b
Musallamī iv, 1045a — IV, 1076b
Musallim al-Tardjāwī v, 267a, b — V, 265a
Musalmānī i, 952a — I, 981a
Musalmānī Bānglā i, 1167a — I, 1202a
Musalsal iii, 26a; iv, 1124a, 1125b — III, 27a; IV, 1155b, 1157a
Musāmaḥat ii, 303a — II, 311b
Musammat i, 677b; iv, 715a — I, 698a; IV, 743b
Musandam i, 536a; v, 508a — I, 552a; V, 511b
Muṣannifek i, 867b — I, 891b
Musāwāt iii, 530b — III, 549a
al-Mūsawī i, 256a — I, 263b
al-Mūsawī, Sayyid Sharaf al-Dīn → Bulbul Shāh
Mūsawī Shīʿa s, 402b — S, 403a

Mūsāwid(e)s i, 552a; iii, 262b — I, 569b; III, 270a
Musāwir ii, 524a — II, 537a
Muṣawwaʿ → Maṣawwaʿ
al-Musawwida iii, 617a — III, 637b
Musaylima al-Kadhdhāb i, 110b, 964a; ii, 1060a — I, 113b, 993b; II, 1084b
Muscat → Maskaṭ
Müsellem, müsellim i, 1268b; ii, 33a — I, 1307b; II, 33b
Mūsh i, 644a — I, 664b
Mushāʿ i, 661a — I, 682a
Mushabbiha i, 275a, 333b — I, 283b, 343b
Muṣḥaf/maṣḥaf v, 207a — V, 204b
al-Muṣḥafī (d./m. 982) i, 601b, 628a; iii, 346b — I, 621a, 649a; III, 357b
Muṣḥafī, Shaykh Ghulām Hamadānī iii, 358b, 1244a; s, 102a — III, 370a, 1276b; S, 101b
Mushāhada iv, 697a — IV, 725a
Mushārī b. Saʿūd ii, 321b — II, 331a
al-Musharraf b. Muradjdjaʾ v, 330a, 332a — V, 330a, 332a
Musharrif al-Dawla i, 131b; ii, 391a; iv, 378b — I, 135b; II, 401a; IV, 395a
Mushaʿshaʿ i, 1096a; iii, 1256b; iv, 49a; v, 80b — I, 1129a; III, 1289a; IV, 52a; V, 82b
Mushāt iii, 187a — III, 191a
Mushattā v, 183a — V, 180a
Mushidd i, 802a — I, 825a
Mushīr al-Dawla, Djaʿfar Khān iv, 787a, 788a; s, 108b — IV, 818b, 820a; S, 108a
Mushīr Ḥusayn Ḳidwāī s, 4b, 74a — S, 3b, 74b
Müshīr, müshīriyyet i, 1111a; ii, 724a — I, 1144b; II, 742b
Mushk-i ʿĀlam i, 232a — I, 239a
Mushkān → Abū Naṣr Mushkān
Mushrif ii, 146a; iv, 759a — II, 149b; IV, 789a
Mushtāḳ ii, 433b; iv, 69b — II, 444b; IV, 73a
Mushtāḳī s, 1b — S, 1b
al-Mushtarik i, 184b — I, 190a
Mūsī i, 261a — I, 269a
Music → Mūsīḳī
Musical metrics → Īḳāʿ
Mūsīḳī i, 1124a; iii, 974b; v, 477b — I, 1158a; III, 999a; V, 480a
Musique → Mūsīḳī
Muṣliḥ iv, 141a — IV, 147a
Muṣlī Čawush i, 267b — I, 276a
Muṣliḥ al-Dīn Lārī → al-Lārī, Muṣliḥ al-Dīn
Muṣlih al-Dīn Muṣṭafā al-Ḳarāḥiṣārī → Akhtarī
Muslim iv, 171b, 173a, b, 176a, b, 177a; v, 1015a, 1019a — IV, 179a, 180b, 181a, 183b, 184a, b; V, 1010b, 1014b
Muslim b. ʿAḳīl i, 337b; iii, 164b, 608a, 609a, 620b, 715a — I, 348a; III, 168a, 629a,b, 641a, 737b
Muslim b. al-Ḥadjdjādj i, 114b, 1297a; ii, 159a; iii, 24a, 708b, 803a, 909b; s, 232b — I, 117b, 1336b; II, 164a; III, 25b, 731a, 826b, 933b; S, 232b
Muslim b. Ḳuraysh i, 517a, 664a; ii, 282a, 347b, 348b, 384b; iii, 86b, 686b, 790a — I, 532b, 683b; II, 290a, 357a, 358a, 394b; III, 89a, 708b, 813b
Muslim b. ʿUbays i, 810a — I, 833b
Muslim b. ʿUḳba al-Murrī i, 45a, 55a, 76b; ii, 89b, 1023b; iii, 226b, 227a, 620b; v, 997a — I, 46b, 57a, 78b; II, 91a, 1047b; III, 233b, 234a, 641a; V, 992a
Muslim b. al-Walīd i, 10a, 587b, 857b; ii, 248b; iii, 73a, 1264a; iv, 1004b — I, 10a, 606b, 881a; II, 255b; III, 75b, 1297a; IV, 1037a
Muslim Brothers → al-Ikhwān al-Muslimūn
Muslim League → al-Rābiṭa al-Islāmiyya
Muslu Čawush s, 239a — S, 239a
Musnad i, 273b, 275b; iii, 25b — I, 281b, 284a; III, 27a
Mussoorie s, 66a — S, 66a
Mustacaplioğlu, Esat Adil iv, 124b — IV, 129b
al-Mustaḍīʾ (ʿAbbāsid(e)) i, 212b, 273a; iii, 751a; s, 193b — I, 219a, 281b; III, 774a; S, 194b
al-Mustaḍīʾ b. Ismāʿīl i, 47b — I, 48b
Muṣṭafā I (Ottoman) ii, 183b, 713a; iv, 884a; v, 272a — II, 189b, 731b; IV, 917a; V, 270a
Muṣṭafā II (Ottoman) i, 96b, 398a; ii, 684a; iv, 1104b; v, 18b, 262b — I, 99b, 409b; II, 701a; IV, 1136a; V, 19a, 260b
Muṣṭafā III (Ottoman) i, 1004a; ii, 49a; iii, 158a, 269a; iv, 892a — I, 1035a; II, 50a; III, 161b, 277a; IV, 925a
Muṣṭafā IV (Ottoman) iv, 322b — IV, 337a
Muṣṭafā, Prince/le prince i, 244a; ii, 184a — I, 251a; II, 190a
Muṣṭafā b. Ḥādjdjī Ākā Muḥsin, Sayyid s, 342a — S, 341b
Muṣṭafā b. Ismāʿīl ii, 173a — II, 178a
Muṣṭafā b. Muḥammad → Muṣṭafā II (Ottoman)
Muṣṭafā b. Sulaymān Ḳānūnī i, 1301b; ii, 737b, 738a; iii, 147b — I, 1341b; II, 756a,b; III, 150b
Muṣṭafā b. Umūr II ii, 599b — II, 614b
Muṣṭafā Abū Ṭāhir al-Ḥusaynī s, 67a — S, 67b
Muṣṭafā Agha iv, 194a, 590b — IV, 202b, 614b
Muṣṭafā Agha ʿOthmān-oghlu iv, 593a — IV, 617a
Muṣṭafā ʿAlī → ʿAlī, Muṣṭafā b. Aḥmad
Muṣṭafā ʿAṣim s, 328b — S, 328a
Muṣṭafā Bārzānī, Mullā i, 1072a; v, 467a, b, 468a, b, 469a, b, 1213b, 1214a — I, 1104a,b; V, 470a, b, 471a, b, 472a, 1203a, b
Muṣṭafā Behdjet Efendi → Bahdjat Muṣṭafā
Muṣṭafā Bey Čapan-oghlu ii, 207b — II, 214a
Muṣṭafā Čelebi → Bičaḳdji-zāde; Djalālzāde;
Muṣṭafā Dāʿī, Shaykh v, 952a — V, 956a
Muṣṭafā Davidovič ii, 979b, 980a — II, 1002a,b
Muṣṭafā Düzme i, 783b, 899b; ii, 599b, 684a, 697a, 721a; v, 763b — I, 806b, 893b; II, 614a,b, 701a, 714b, 739b; V, 769b
Muṣṭafā Fāḍil Pasha → Fāḍil Pasha
Muṣṭafā Feyḍī iii, 303a — III, 312b
Muṣṭafā ʿIzzet Efendi i, 776a — I, 799a
Muṣṭafā Kabakčî → Kabakčî
Muṣṭafā Kāmil i, 597a; iii, 59a, 515a; iv, 967a — I, 616b; III, 61b, 532b; IV, 999b
Mustafā Kemāl → Atatürk
Muṣṭafā Kemāl Pasha (town/ville) → Kirmāstī
Muṣṭafā Khān i, 1155a — I, 1189b
Muṣṭafā Khaznadār i, 282a; iii, 636a, b; iv, 1153b, 1154a; s, 387a — I, 290b; III, 657b; IV, 1185b, 1186a; S, 387b
Muṣṭafā Khodja iii, 636a — III, 657a
Muṣṭafā al-Marāghī, Shaykh s, 300a — S, 299b
Muṣṭafā Nadjīb Pasha iv, 618a — IV, 643a
Muṣṭafā al-Naḥḥās Pasha ii, 934b; iii, 515b, 516a, 517a; s, 5b, 300a, b — II, 956a; III, 533a, 534a, b; S, 4b, 5a, 299b, 300a
Muṣṭafā Nāʾilī Pasha i, 397a — I, 408b
Muṣṭafā Nūrī Pasha ii, 636b — II, 652b
Mustafa Oğulcuk → Esendal
Muṣṭafā Pasha → Ḳara; Khodja; Köprülüzāde; Muṣāḥib; Soḳollu
Muṣṭafā Pasha (1623) ii, 751a — II, 769a
Muṣṭafā Pasha (1760) i, 1152a — I, 1186a
Muṣṭafā Pāsha Bayraḳdār i, 778b, 1304a; ii, 207a, 512b, 640a, 641b, 713a; iv, 322b — I, 801b, 1344a; II, 213b, 525b, 656a, 657b, 731a; IV, 337a
Muṣṭafā Pasha Bushatlî i, 657a; v, 276b — I, 678a; V, 274b
Muṣṭafā Pasha Ipshir → Ipshir
Muṣṭafā Pasha Isfendiyār-oghlu iv, 108b — IV, 113b

Muṣṭafā Pas͟ha Ḳaplan i, 905a — I, 932a
Muṣṭafā Pas͟ha Lala i, 380a, 468b; iv, 670b; v, 305a, 493a — I, 391a, 482b; IV, 697b; V, 304b, 496a
Muṣṭafā Pas͟ha Ṭūḳān al-Nābulusī s, 20b — S, 20b
Muṣṭafā Rāḳim iv, 1125b — IV, 1157a
Muṣṭafā Res͟hid Pas͟ha → Ras͟hīd " Pas͟ha
Muṣṭafā Riyāḍ Pas͟ha iii, 514b, 515a — III, 532b
Muṣṭafā Ṣafī Efendi v, 18a — V, 19a
Mustafa Yalînkat → Esendal
Muṣṭafā Zühdi s, 171b — S, 171b
Muṣṭafābād ii, 597b, 1127a — II, 612b, 1153b
Mustafīd iii, 25b — III, 26b
al-Mustaʿīn (862-66) (ʿAbbāsid(e)) i, 21b, 145a, 278b, 897b, 1287b; v, 1160a — I, 22a, 149b, 287a, 924b, 1327a; V, 1149b
al-Mustaʿīn (1406-14) (ʿAbbāsid(e)) ii, 781b — II, 800a
al-Mustaʿīn (Hūdid(e)) → Aḥmad II; Sulāyman b. Hūd
al-Mustaʿīn (Umayyad(e)) → Sulaymān al-Mustaʿīn
al-Mustakfī i, 20a, 1352b — I, 21a, 1391b
Mustak͟hirūn iv, 259b — IV, 271a
Mustak͟hridj v, 376a — V, 377a
Muṣṭalaḥāt i, 572a — I, 590b
al-Mustaʿlī Aḥmad i, 215b, 353a, 1254a; ii, 170b, 857a; iv, 200a — I, 221b, 364a, 1292a; II, 175b, 877a; IV, 208b
Mustaʿlī-Ṭayyibī Ismāʿīlīs s, 61b, 62a, 70b, 358b, 407a — S, 62a, b, 71a, 358a, 407a
Muṣṭalik v, 78b — V, 80b
Mustaʾmin i, 429a; ii, 227b, 341b, 565a; iii, 1180a, 1181b, 1182a; v, 179a — I, 441b; II, 234b, 351b, 579a; III, 1209a, 1210b, 1211a; V, 176b
Mustamlī v, 1133b — V, 1129a
al-Mustand͟jid (1160-71) (ʿAbbāsid(e)) i, 212b, 684a; iii, 160b, 730b, 751a; s, 193b — I, 219a, 705a; III, 164a, 753a, 774a; S, 194a
al-Mustand͟jid (1455-79) (ʿAbbāsid(e)) iii, 1198b — III, 1228b
al-Mustanṣir I (ʿAbbāsid(e)) i, 21b; iii, 203b, 219b — I, 22b; III, 209a, 226b
al-Mustanṣir II (ʿAbbāsid(e)) i, 21b; ii, 966a; iv, 944b — I, 22a; II, 988a; IV, 977b
al-Mustanṣir, Abū Yaʿḳūb Yūsuf (Almohad(e)) s, 389a — S, 389b
al-Mustanṣir (Fāṭimid(e)) i, 200b, 215a, 814b, 832b, 869b, 901b, 1073b, 1074b; ii, 169a, 855b, 856a, 857b, 859a, 861b, 958b; iii, 686b; s, 260b, 390a — I, 206a, 221b, 837b, 855b, 894a, 929a, 1105b, 1106b; II, 174b, 875b, 876a, 877b, 878b, 881a, 981a; III, 708a; S, 260a, 390b
al-Mustanṣir (Ḥafṣid(e)) i, 21a, 1152a, 1346b; iii, 66b, 338a, 673a, 705a; iv, 179a — I, 22a, 1186b, 1386b; III, 69a, 348a, 695a, 727a; IV, 186b
al-Mustanṣir (Hūdid(e)) → Aḥmad III
al-Mustanṣir II (Nizarī Imām) iv, 206a; v, 26b — IV, 215a; V, 27b
al-Mustanṣiriyya i, 902a, b, 903a; v, 1127a — I, 929a, b, 930a; V, 1123b
al-Mustars͟hid i, 353b, 522b, 858b, 901a; iii, 345a, 1255b; iv, 29b, 942b; s, 194a — I, 364a, 538b, 882b, 928a; III, 355b, 1288b; IV, 31b, 975b; S, 193b
Mustas͟har al-Dawla Tabrīzī iv, 787b; s, 53b — IV, 819b; S, 54a
al-Mustaʿṣim (ʿAbbāsid(e)) i, 21a, 902b, 919a; s, 199a — I, 21b, 929b, 947a; S, 199a
Mustawdaʿ ii, 851b — II, 871b
Mustawfī ii, 83a, 333b; iv, 977b — II, 84b, 343a; IV, 1010a
Mustawfī, Ḥamd Allāh → Ḥamd Allāh Mustawfī al-Ḳazwīnī
Mustawfī al-mamālik ii, 335a, b — II, 344b, 345a
al-Mustawrid iii, 1265b — III, 1298a
Mustazād i, 677b — I, 698a
al-Mustaẓhir (ʿAbbāsid(e)) i, 659b, 901a; ii, 385a; iii, 351b; s, 194a, b, 326a — I, 680a, 928a; II, 395a; III, 362b; S, 193b, 325b
al-Mustaẓhir biʾllāh → ʿAbd al-Raḥmān V
Muʾta ii, 372b — II, 382b
Mutʿa i, 209a; ii, 551b; s, 133a — I, 215b; II, 565a; S, 132b
Mūtā ii, 190b — II, 196b
al-Muṭāʿ v, 544a — V, 548b
Mutadārik iv, 412b — IV, 430b
al-Muʿtadd → His͟hām III
al-Muʿtaḍid (ʿAbbāsid(e)) i, 11a, 14b, 19a, 249a, 592a, 637a, 896a, 897b, 898a, 964b, 1141a; ii, 128b, 325b, 344b, 524a, 1080a; iii, 344b, 761b, 767b, 818a, 892b, 908a; iv, 21b, 22a, 42b, 90a, b, 189a, 265b, 940b, 49b; s, 117b, 284a — I, 11a, 14b, 19b, 256b, 611b, 658a, 922b, 924b, 994b, 1175b; II, 131b, 335b, 354b, 537a, 1105a; III, 355a, 784b, 790b, 841b, 916b, 932a; IV, 23a, b, 51a, 94a, b, 197b, 277b, 973b, 51a; S, 117a, 284a
al-Muʿtaḍid b. ʿAbbād i, 5b, 155b, 242a, 1040b, 1339a; ii, 389a, 1009a; iii, 496a, 640a, 705b; iv, 115b; v, 586b — I, 6a, 160a, 249b, 1072a, 1379a; II, 399b, 1032b; III, 513a, 661b, 728a; IV, 121a; V, 591b
al-Muṭahhar (mosque/mosquée, Cairo/Caire) s, 244a — S, 244a
al-Muṭahhar b. S͟haraf al-Dīn iv, 201a — IV, 210a
al-Muṭahhar al-Hillī i, 593a — I, 612b
Muṭahhar b. Ṭāhir al-Makdisī v, 65a, 330a — V, 67a, 330a
Muṭahharī, Murtaḍā iv, 166a — IV, 173a
Muṭahharten Bey i, 1119a; iv, 871a — I, 1152b; IV, 904b
Muʿtaḳ i, 30b — I, 31b
Mutaḳābilāt ii, 249a — II, 256a
al-Mutakallimūn i, 266a; ii, 95b, 824b; iv, 469a; v, 238a, b — I, 274a; II, 97b, 843b; IV, 489b; V, 236a, b
Mutakāwis iv, 412b — IV, 430b
al-Mutalammis i, 451b — I, 464b
Muʾtaman al-Dawla Isḥāḳ K͟hān i, 680a — I, 701a
Muʾtaman al-K͟hilāfa iv, 613a — IV, 638a
al-Muʾtaman al-Sād͟jī i, 515b; iii, 730b — I, 531b; III, 753b
al-Muʿtamid (ʿAbbādid(e)) i, 6a, b, 251a, 592b, 601b; ii, 389b, 874a; iii, 677a, 706a, 783a, 853a, 905a, 963a, 973b; iv, 115b, 1007a; s, 1a — I, 6b, 258b, 611b, 621b; II, 399b, 894b; III, 699a, 728a, 806a, 877a, 929a, 987b, 998a; IV, 121a, 1039b; S, 1a
al-Muʿtamid (ʿAbbāsid(e)) i, 18b, 279a, 637a, 897b; ii, 389b; iii, 247a, 839b; s, 16a, 402a — I, 19a, 287b, 658a, 924b; II, 400a; III, 254a, 863a; S, 16b, 402b
al-Muʿtamīd (Zīrid(e)) iv, 117a — IV, 122a
Muʿtamid al-Dawla → Ḳarwās͟h b. al-Muḳallad
Muʿtamid al-Dawla iii, 1105b; v, 646a — III, 1133a; V, 650a
al-Muʾtamin b. Hūd → Yūsof b. Aḥmad al-Muʾtamin
al-Mutanabbī, Abū Ṭayyib i, 119b, 212b, 592a, 601a, 827b, 845b, 1249b; ii, 802b; iii, 338a, 672a, 738b, 743b, 754b, 780a, 807a, 1264a; iv, 418b, 867b, 1069b; v, 927b, 934b; s, 24a, 27b, 32b, 58b, 277b, 361b — I, 123a, 218b, 611b, 620b, 850b, 869a, 1287b; II, 821b; III, 348a, 693b, 761b, 766b, 777b, 803b, 830b, 1297a; IV, 437a, 900b, 1101a; V, 933a, 938b; S, 24b, 27b, 32b, 59a, 277a, 361b
Mutarādif iv, 412b — IV, 430b
Mutarākib iv, 412b — IV, 430b
Muṭarrif b. ʿAbd Allāh al-Marwānī s, 153a — S, 153a

al-Muṭarrif b. al-Mughīra b. Shuʿba iii, 40b — III, 42b
Muṭarrifiyya s, 22b, 236a — S, 22b, 236a
al-Muṭarrizī v, 319a, b, 320b — V, 318a, b, 319b
Mutaṣarrifiyya iv, 794a; v, 1253a, b — IV, 800a; V, 1244a, b
Mutashābih i, 275a, 409a, 412a — I, 283b, 421a, 423b
al-Muʿtaṣim (ʿAbbāsid(e)) (833-842) i, 11b, 16b, 18b, 52b, 153b, 241a, 271a, 273a, 279b, 437b, 449b, 510a, 844a, b, 897b, 1096a, 1287b, 1346a; ii, 235b, 328a, 505b, 730b, 1079b; iii, 618a; iv, 97b, 215a, 646b; s, 106a, 127b, 243a, 384b — I, 12a, 17a, 19a, 54a, 157b, 248b, 279b, 281a, 288a, 449b, 462b, 525b, 867b, 924a, 1129a, 1327a, 1386a; II, 242a, 337b, 518b, 749a, 1104b; III, 639a; IV, 101b, 224b, 673a; S, 105b, 127a, 243a, 385a
al-Muʿtaṣim (ʿAbbāsid(e)) (1242-58) iv, 30b; s, 252b — IV, 32b; S, 252b
al-Muʿtaṣim Ibn Ṣumādiḥ iii, 775b, 934b — III, 799a, 959b
al-Mustaʿṣimī → Yāḳūt
al-Mutawakkil I (ʿAbbāsid(e)) i, 18b, 271b, 273a, 386a, 620b, 637a, 713a, 1287b, 1289b; ii, 130a, 281b, 292b, 324b, 385b, 437b, 837b, 1080a; iii, 579a, 618a, 691a, 824a, 940b; iv, 637b, 940b; v, 1111a; s, 16b, 26a, 35a, 48a, 64a, 94b, 106a, 117b, 199a, 252a, b, 384b, 392a — I, 19a, 279b, 281a, 397b, 640b, 659b, 734b, 1327a, 1329a; II, 133a, 289b, 300a, 334a, 396a, 449a, 857a, 1105a; III, 599a, 639a, 713a, 848a, 965b; IV, 663b, 973b; V, 1107a; S, 16b, 26b, 35b, 49a, 64b, 93b, 105b, 117a, 199a, 252a, b, 385a, 392b
al-Mutawakkil III (ʿAbbāsid(e)) i, 21b; iv, 945b — I, 22b; IV, 978b
al-Mutawakkil (Aftasid(e)) → ʿUmar b. al-Aftas
al-Mutawakkil (Hūdid(e)) → Muḥammad b. Yūsuf b. Hūd
al-Mutawakkil Aḥmad b. Sulaymān iii, 125b; v, 1240b; s, 236a — III, 128b; V, 1231b; S, 236a
al-Mutawakkil Ismāʿīl b. al-Ḳāsim ii, 517b; iii, 688b; v, 1241b — II, 530b; III, 710b; V, 1233a
al-Mutawakkil Yaḥyā b. Muḥammad i, 555a — I, 572b
Mutawallī iii, 1170a — III, 1199a
al-Mutawassiṭ → ʿAbd al-Raḥmān II
Mutawātir iii, 25b; iv, 412b — III, 26b; IV, 430b
Muṭayr i, 545b; ii, 77a; iii, 1065b, 1068a; iv, 680b — I, 563a; II, 78b; III, 1092a, 1094; IV, 708b
Muṭayyabūn v, 581a, b — V, 586a, b
Mutayyam al-Hāshimiyya iv, 821b; s, 116b, 252b — IV, 854b; S, 116a, 252b
Mutazawwidjāt i, 308b — I, 318a
Muʿtazila i, 4b, 59b, 127b, 266a, 271a, 272a, 326a, 454a, 694a, 1002b, 1243a; ii, 365a, 373a, 388a, 449a, 569b; iii, 496b, 658b, 699a, 1142b, 1143a, 1148a, 1150a, 1165b, 1266a; iv, 46a, 366a, 379a, 1162a; s, 12b, 16b, 17a, 23a, 25a, b, 30a, 31b, 56b, 88b, 103a, 225b, 306a, 335b, 343a, b, 344a, 391b, 392a, 393a — I, 5a, 61b, 131a, 274a, 279b, 280a, 336b, 467a, 715a, 1033b, 1281a; II, 375a, 383a, 398b, 461a, 584a; III, 513b, 680a, 721b, 1171a, b, 1176b, 1178a, 1194a, 1298b; IV, 48b, 382a, 395b, 1194a; S, 13a, 17a, 23b, 25b, 30a, 32a, 57a, 88a, b, 102b, 225b, 306a, 335a, 342b, 343b, 344a, 391b, 392b, 393b
- doctrine i, 17b, 128a, 178b, 187b, 204b, 209a, 334a, 410a-415b, 713b, 714a, 1092b; ii, 518a, 618a, 772a, 833b; iii, 171b, 465b, 661a, 672a, 1063a, 1146a; iv, 126b, 172a, 183a, 271b, 408a, 469a; v, 576b, 702a — I, 18b, 131b, 183b, 193a, 210b, 215b, 344b, 422a-427b, 735a, b, 1125a; II, 531a, 633b, 790b, 853a; III, 175b, 481b, 682b, 693b, 1089b, 1174a; IV, 132a, 179b, 190b, 283b, 425b, 490a; V, 581a, 707a
al-Muʿtazz i, 273a, 278b, 897b, 1287b; ii, 36b, 1079b; iv, 89a, 126b; v, 1160a — I, 281b, 287a, 924b, 1327a; II, 37a, 1104b; IV, 93a, 132a; V, 1150a
al-Muthaḳḳib i, 74a — I, 76a
Muthannā iv, 1124b, 1126a — IV, 1156a, 1158a
al-Muthannā b. Ḥāritha i, 111a, 964a; ii, 241a; iii, 194b, 1254b; iv, 13b, 385a — I, 114a, 994a; II, 248a; III, 199b, 1287a; IV, 14a-b, 401b, 402a
Muthbita → Ahl al-ithbāt
al-Muṭīʿ liʾllāh i, 211b, 1352b; iii, 128a — I, 217b, 1391b; III, 130b
Muṭīʿ b. Iyās i, 160a; ii, 1031b; iii, 135b; iv, 1003b — I, 164b; II, 1055b; III, 138b; IV, 1036a
al-Muṭīʿ lillāh s, 36a — S, 36b
al-Muṭīʿa s, 121b — S, 121a
Muṭʿim al-Ṭayr iv, 91b — IV, 95b
Mutiny, Indian/Mutinerie aux Indes i, 822a, 856a, 953b, 1012b, 1300a; iv, 551b; v, 635a; s, 107a — I, 845a, 879b, 982b, 1043b, 1340a; IV, 575a; V, 639a; S, 106b
Muṭrān, Khalīl → Khalīl Muṭrān
al-Muttaḳī s, 386a — S, 386b
al-Muttaḳī (Abbāsid(e)) i, 867a; iii, 127b — I, 891a; III, 130a
al-Muttaḳī al-Hindī i, 593a; ii, 500b; iii, 435a — I, 612a; II, 513a; III, 449a
Muṭṭalib, Banū i, 258a — I, 266a
al-Muṭṭalib b. ʿAbd Manāf i, 80a, 115b; iii, 1093a — I, 82a, 118b; III, 1120a
Muttaṣil iii, 25b — III, 27a
Mütügen → Möeʿtüken
Muwādaʿa iv, 253b — IV, 264b
al-Muwāfaḳa wa ʾl-djamāʿa ii, 78b — II, 80a
al-Muwaffaḳ (ʿAbbāsid(e)) i, 18b, 145a, 278b, 279a, 389a, 898a; ii, 196a, 1080a; iii, 859b, 976b; iv, 189a, 655a, 940b; v, 49a, b; s, 117b, 384b, 385a, 402a — I, 19b, 149b, 287a, b, 400a, 925a; II, 202a, 1105a; III, 883b, 1001a; IV, 197a, b, 681a, 973b; V, 50b, 51a; S, 117a, 385b, 402b
al-Muwaffaḳ, Abū ʿAlī b. Ismāʿīl s, 118b — S, 118a
Muwaffaḳ b. ʿAlī al-Harawī i, 213b, 686a, 1014b; iii, 267a; iv, 1123b — I, 220a, 707a, 1045b; III, 274b; IV, 1155a
Muwaffaḳ al-Dīn b. Ḳudāma → Ibn Ḳudāma
Muwaffaḳ al-Dīn Abu ʾl-Maʿālī Aḥmad iii, 684b, 685a — III, 706b, 707a
Muwaffaḳ al-Dīn Yaʿḳūb s, 391a — S, 391a
al-Muwaḥḥidūn i, 78a, 92b, 122a, 160b, 165a, 367a, 495b, 602a, 1176a, 1205b, 1339b; ii, 112a, 527a, 818b, 1007b, 1009b, 1110b; iii, 207a, 300b, 461b, 771b, 864b, 959b; v, 744b, 1189b, 1199b; s, 103a, 111b, 113b, 153a, 336b — I, 80a, 95a, 125b, 165a, 169b, 378a, 510b, 621b, 1211a, 1241b, 1379b; II, 114b, 540a, 838a, 1031a, 1033a, 1136b; III, 212b, 309b, 478a, 794b, 889a, 984a; V, 750a, 1179b, 1190a; S, 102b, 111a, 113a, 153a, 336a
- administration i, 1148b; ii, 145b, 230a, 307b; iv, 943b; v, 626a — I, 1183a; II, 149b, 237a, 316b; IV, 976b; V, 630a
- constructions i, 1320b; ii, 822a; iii, 499b; iv, 633b — I, 1361a; II, 841bb; III, 516b; IV, 659b
- history/histoire i, 94b; iii, 570a, 924b; iv, 337b; v, 530b — I, 97a; III, 590a, 949a; IV, 352a; V, 534b
Muwalladūn i, 49a, 491a, 494a; iii, 770b — I, 50b, 505b, 508b; III, 794a
al-Muwāṣafa ii, 79a — II, 80b
Muwashshaḥ i, 426b, 595b, 601a, 602a; ii, 1033a, 1074a; iii, 729b, 851b, 855b, 929a — I, 438b, 615a, 620b, 621b; II, 1057a, 1098b; III, 752b, 875b, 879b, 953b
al-Muwayliḥī, Muḥammad i, 597a; iii, 59b — I, 616b; III, 62a
Muwaẓẓaf ii, 158a — II, 163a

Muyāka b. Ḥādjdjī al-Ghassānī iv, 887a — IV, 919b
al-Muẓaffar (Afṭasid(e)) i, 6a, 242a, 1096a; iii, 674a — I, 6a, 249b, 1129a; III, 695b
al-Muẓaffar (Artukid(e)) i, 665a — I, 686a
al-Muẓaffar (Ayyūbid(e)) → al-Malik al-Muẓaffar ʿUmar
Muẓaffar (Balansīya) i, 446b, 985b — I, 459a, 1016a
al-Muẓaffar, ʿAbd al-Malik → ʿAbd al-Malik b. Abī ʿĀmir
al-Muẓaffar, Abu ʾl-Fatḥ ii, 1142b — II, 1169b
al-Muẓaffar b. ʿAlī iii, 1176a — III, 1204b
al-Muẓaffar b. al-Manṣūr → ʿAbd al-Malik b. Abī ʿĀmir
al-Muẓaffar Aḥmad iii, 1198a — III, 1228a
Muẓaffar al-Dīn b. ʿAlī Shīr ii, 989a — II, 1012a
Muẓaffar al-Dīn b. Naṣr Allāh v, 30b — V, 31b
Muẓaffar al-Dīn Gökbüri i, 300b, 1160b, 1161a; iii, 228b; iv, 76a-b; v, 477a — I, 310a, 1195a, b; III, 235a; IV, 80a; V, 479b
Muẓaffar al-Dīn Muḥammad Shāh → Muḥammad Shāh b. Ḥadjdjādj
Muẓaffar al-Dīn Shāh Ḳādjār i, 1088b, 1296a; ii, 310b, 650a, b; iii, 555b; iv, 392a, 393b; s, 72a, 84a — I, 1120b, 1335b; II, 319b, 666b, 667a, 668a; III, 574b; IV, 408b, 410b; S, 72a, 83b
Muẓaffar al-Dīn Yavlaḳ Arslan iv, 738a — IV, 767b
Muẓaffar Djang i, 153a; iii, 320b — I, 157b; III, 331a
Muẓaffar Khān (Shāh) iv, 631b — IV, 656b
Muẓaffar al-Mulk ii, 31a — II, 31b
Muẓaffar Shāh I Gudjarātī i, 506b, 1193a, 1300a, 1329b; ii, 218b, 270b, 276b, 322a, 405b, 597b, 1124b, 1125a; iii, 417a, 638a — I, 522a, 1228b, 1340a, 1370a; II, 225b, 278b, 285a, 331b, 416b, 612a, 1151a, 1151b; III, 430b, 659b
Muẓaffar Shāh II Gudjarātī ii, 322a, 405b, 1128a; iii, 422a, 1010a — II, 331b, 416b, 1154b; III, 435b, 1035b
Muẓaffar Shāh III i, 80b, 156a, 938b; ii, 678a, 815a, 1129a — I, 83a, 161a, 967a; II, 695a, 834b, 1156a
Muẓaffar Shāh Ḥabshī ii, 1084b; iii, 14b, 631b — II, 1110a; III, 15b, 652b
al-Muẓaffar Yūsuf (Rasūlid(e)) s, 338b, 387b, 388a — S, 338a, 388a
Muẓaffarid(e)s i, 3b; ii, 401b; iii, 56a, 57b, 1208b; iv, 32a, 102b, 498b; v, 163b; s, 327a, 335b, 415a — I, 3b; II, 412a; III, 58a, 60a, 1239a; IV, 34b, 107a, 520a; V, 161a; S, 326b, 335a, 415a
Muzaffarnagar s, 126b — S, 125b
al-Muzanī i, 686b — I, 707b
Muzāraʿa ii, 187b, 905b; iv, 1154a; v, 871b — II, 193b, 926b; IV, 1186a; V, 878a
Muzawwir v, 1004a — V, 1000a
Muzayn, (Muzayyin) Banū i, 6a; ii, 1009a — I, 6a; II, 1032b
Muzdalifa iii, 32b, 36a; s, 33a — III, 34a, 37b; S, 33b
Muzdawidj i, 2b, 587a; iv, 58a — I, 2b, 606a; IV, 61a
Muznī, Banū i, 1247a — I, 1284b
Mwengo b. Athumani, Bwana s, 351b — S, 351b
Myrobalanus/myrobolan → Halīladj
Myrt(l)e → Ās
Mysia iv, 627b, 628a — IV, 652b, 653a
Mysore → Mahisūr
Mzāb i, 171b, 687a; ii, 1010a; iii, 96a, 97b, 98b, 656b; s, 15b — I, 176a, 708a; II, 1033b; III, 98b, 100a, 101a, 677b; S, 15b
Mzabites i, 371a; ii, 1010a; iii, 95a, 97a, b, 145a — I, 382a; II, 1033b; III, 97b, 100a, 148a

N

al-Naʿāʾim s, 320b — S, 320a
Nabʿ iv, 797b — IV, 830a
Nabaʾ iii, 369a — III, 381a
Năbal i, 936a — I, 965a
Nabāt i, 213a; ii, 908b, 1038a, 1058b — I, 219a; II, 929b, 1062b, 1083a
Nabataeans/Nabatéens i, 528a, 548a, 563a, 564b, 1096a; ii, 246b, 278b, 1060a; iii, 366a; iv, 995a; v, 762a, 1156a — I, 544a, 565b, 581a, 582b, 1129a; II, 253b, 287a, 1084b; III, 377b; IV, 1027b; V, 768a, 1146a
al-Nabātī → Abu ʾl-ʿAbbās
Nabawiyya ii, 964a — II, 986a
Nabaz iv, 180a — IV, 188a
Nabeul s, 11a, 145a — S, 10b, 144b
Nabhān (Ṭayyiʾ) s, 305a — S, 304b
Nabhān, Wādī iv, 779b — IV, 811a
Nabhānid(e) i, 553b; iv, 885b, 886b — I, 571a; IV, 918b, 919b
Nabī v, 423b — V, 425b
Nabī, Yūsuf s, 83a, 324a — S, 83a, 323b
Nabīdh iv, 996a — IV, 1028b
Nābigha al-Dhubyānī i, 196a, 1149a, 1241b; ii, 1020b; iii, 1261a; s, 178b — I, 202a, 1183b, 1279b; II, 1044b; III, 1294a; S, 179b
al-Nābigha al-Djaʿdī i, 115b; iv, 315b; v, 710a — I, 119a; IV, 329b; V, 715a
al-Nabīt i, 771b — I, 794b
Nābita ii, 386b — II, 397a
Nabl iv, 799a — IV, 831b
Nabtāb i, 440b; ii, 252b — I, 453a, II, 260a
Nabuchodonosor → Bukht-naṣar
Nābulus iv, 834b, 835a — IV, 867b, 868a
al-Nābulusī, Shams al-Dīn v, 9b — V, 10a
al-Nābulusī, ʿUthmān b. Ibrāhīm i, 800b, 801b; ii, 329b; v, 862b — I, 824a, b; II, 339a; V, 869b
Naceur Bey → Muḥammad al-Nāṣir
Nacir Ed Dine → Dinet, Alphonse
Nadhīr Aḥmad iii, 359a; v, 203a — III, 370a; V, 200b
Nadhīr Ḥusayn → Sayyid Nadhīr Ḥusayn
Nadhr iv, 688a; s, 221b — IV, 716b; S, 221b
Nadhr al-Islām i, 1169a — I, 1204a
Nadhr Muḥammad Khān i, 1195b, 1197a — I, 1230b, 1232b
Nadīm iv, 696a, b; v, 1032a — IV, 724b; V, 1028a
Nadīm, ʿAbd Allāh i, 597a; ii, 429a; v, 909b — I, 616b; II, 440a; V, 915a
Nadīm, Aḥmad i, 270a, 1302a; ii, 1000a; iii, 1002b; iv, 574a, 715b; v, 641a, b, 642a; s, 324a — I, 278a, 1341b; II, 1023a; III, 1027b; IV, 597a, 744b; V, 645b, 646a; S, 323b
Naḍīr, Banū i, 53a; ii, 869b; iv, 1139a, 1140b; v, 436a, 996a — I, 55a; II, 889b; IV, 1170b, 1172a; V, 438b, 991b
Nādir Khān ii, 973b — II, 996a
Nādir Shāh Afshār i, 71b, 95a, 190a, 229a, b, 240b, 270a, 291a, 295a, 395b, 431b, 460a, 625b, 701b, 905a, 928a, 970b, 1001b, 1005b, 1008b, 1020a, 1087a, 1217b, 1281b, 1295b, 1330a, 1341b; ii, 88a, 186a, 206a, 265b, 310b, 350b, 1049b, 1114b, 1131b; iii, 106a, 177b, 427b, 485a, 1103a, 1257b; iv, 37b-38a, 50b, 104a, 357a, 389b, 390a, 537a, 638a, 666a, 978a, 1048b; v, 103a, 164a, 312a, 461a, 494a, 643a, 1240a; s, 94b, 97b, 237b, 251b, 259a, 260b, 276a, 281a; s, 336a, 358b, 420a — I, 73b, 98a, 196a, 236a, b, 248a, 278b, 300a, 304b, 407a, 443b, 473a, 646b, 722b, 932b, 956b, 1000a, 1032a, 1036b, 1039b, 1051b, 1119b, 1254a, 1321a, 1335b, 1371a, 1381b; II, 89b, 192a,

212b, 273b, 319b, 360a, 1074a, 1140b, 1158a; III, 108b, 182a, 441b, 502a, 1130a, 1290a; IV, 39b-40b, 53b, 109a, 372b, 406a, b, 560b, 664a, 693a, 1010b, 1080a; V, 105a, 162a, 311b, 464a, 497a, 647a, 1231a; S, 94a, 97a, 237a, 251b, 259a, 260a, 275b, 281a; S, 335b, 358b, 420a
Nādir Shāh Bārakzay ii, 232b, 658b; v, 1079a; v, 1079a — II, 239b, 675a; V, 1076b
Nādira ii, 536b; iii, 369b — II, 550a; III, 381b
al-Naḍīra iii, 51a — III, 53a
Nādira Begam ii, 135a — II, 138b
Nadīr-i Nādirpūr iv, 72a — IV, 75b
Nadjadāt iii, 1167b — III, 1196b
al-Nadjaf i, 385a; iv, 703b; s, 54b, 75b, 76a, 91b, 94a, b, 104a, 119a, 157b, 342a, 380a — I, 396a; IV, 732a; S, 54b, 76a, 91b, 93b, 94a, 103b, 118b, 158a, 341b, 380a
Nadjaf Khān i, 253a, 403a; iv, 666a; v, 283a — I, 261a, 415a; IV, 693a; V, 281a
Nadjaf-Ḳulī (Ḳādjār) s, 290b — S, 290a
Nadjafī, Shaykh Djaʿfar s, 134b, 135a — S, 134a, b
Nadjāḥ s, 22b — S, 22b
Nadjaḥid(e)s i, 552a, 552b; v, 1244a, b — I, 569b, 570a; V, 1235a
Nadjas al-ʿayn v, 8b — V, 8b
al-Nadjāshī i, 482a; iii, 10a, 272b — I, 496b; III, 10b, 280a
al-Nadjāshī, Aḥmad b. ʿAlī iii, 1151b; s, 233a — III, 1179b; S, 233a
al-Nadjāshī (poet/poète d./m. ca. 660) s, 394a, b — S, 394b
Nadjd i, 233a, 539a, 554a; ii, 159b, 320b, 660a; iii, 362b, 1066b, 1067b; iv, 717a, 1143b; s, 3b, 234b, 304b, 318a — I, 240a, 555b, 571b; II, 164b, 330a, 676b; III, 373b, 1093a, 1094a; IV, 746a, 1175b; S, 2b, 234a, 304a, 318a
- dialect i, 573b — I, 592b
Nadjd al-Djāḥ s, 22b — S, 22b
Nadjd b. Muslim iv, 1103b — IV, 1134b
Nadjda b. ʿĀmir al-Ḥanafī i, 55a, 120a, 550a, 810a, 942a; iii, 661a; iv, 764a, 1076a; s, 338a — I, 57a, 123b, 567b, 833a, 971a; III, 682b; IV, 794b, 1107b; S, 337b
al-Nadjdī → ʿAbd Allāh b. Ibrāhīm
al-Nadjdjād, Abū Bakr iii, 159a, 734b — III, 162b, 757b
al-Nadjdjār i, 204b, 1242a; iv, 271b, 692b, 1187b — I, 210b, 1280a; IV, 284a, 720b, 1220a
al-Nadjdjār, ʿAbd al-Wahhāb v, 180b — V, 178a
al-Nadjdjār, Abū Ḥāmid Aḥmad b. Muḥammad s, 343a — S, 342b
Nadjdjāriyya i, 1326a — I, 1367a
Nadjdjārzāda, ʿAbd al-Raḥīm → Ṭālibov
Nadjdiyya i, 77a; s, 338a — I, 79a; S, 337b
Nādjī, Muʿallim ii, 474b; iv, 195b, 874b, 930b — II, 486b; IV, 204a, 908a, 963b
Nadjīb, Muḥammad → Neguib/Néguib
Nadjīb Diyāb s, 28a — S, 28a
Nadjīb Pasha iv, 638a — IV, 664b
Nadjīb Allāh Khān iii, 336a — III, 346a
Nadjīb al-Dawla i, 296a, 1042b, 1206a; iii, 61a, 1158b — I,305a, 1074b, 1242a; III, 63b, 1187a
Nadjīb al-Rīḥānī ii, 39b — II, 40b
Nādjiya, Banū v, 19b — V, 20a
Nadjm al-Dawla Khumārtigin s, 382b — S, 382b
Nadjm al-Dīn Ibn Abī Asrūn iii, 681b, 682a — III, 703b
Nadjm al-Dīn Ayyūb → al-Ṣāliḥ Nadjm al-Dīn
Nadjm al-Dīn Ghāzī → Ghāzī I, II (Artukid(e))
Nadjm al-Dīn Ḳārin → Ḳārin b. Shahriyār Bāwand
Nadjm al-Dīn Kubrā i, 754b; iv, 1064a; s, 423a — I, 777a; IV, 1095b; S, 423b
Nadjm al-Dīn-i Dāya s, 364a, b — S, 364 a, b
Nadjm-i Thānī i, 848a, 1019a — I, 871a, 1050b
Nadjrān i, 151b, 538a, 555a; ii, 127b, 131a, 244b; iii, 223a; s, 335a — I, 155b, 554b, 572b; II, 131a, 134b, 251b; III, 229b; S, 334b
al-Nadjrānī, ʿAlī b. ʿAbd Allāh b. ʿUṭba s, 393a — S, 393b
Nadjwā iii, 81a — III, 83b
al-Naḍr b. al-Ḥārith i, 358b; iii, 370a; s, 91a — I, 369b; III, 382a; S, 90b
Naḍr b. Kināna i, 1021b — I, 1053a
al-Naḍr b. Saʿīd al-Ḥarashī i, 53b; ii, 90a — I, 55b; II, 92a
al-Naḍr b. Shumayl iii, 155a; s, 317b — III, 158b; S, 317b
Nadwat al-ʿUlamāʾ ii, 132b; iii, 433a — II, 135b; III, 447a
Nadwī → Sulaymān Nadwī
Nafādh iv, 412a — IV, 430a
Nafaḳa iii, 1011b — III, 1037a
Nafaḳat al-safar iii, 184a, 186a — III, 188b, 190b
Nafar iv, 9b — IV, 10a
al-Nafāthiyya iii, 659b — III, 680b
Naffātī → Nafāthiyya
Nāfiʿ i, 140a, 718a; iii, 155b, 732b; iv, 269a; v, 127b, 997b — I, 144a, 739b; III, 158b, 755b; IV, 281a; V, 130b, 993a
Nāfiʿ b. ʿAlḳama ii, 1011b — II, 1035a
Nāfiʿ b. al-Azraḳ i, 120a, 810a; iii, 367a, 648b — I, 123b, 833a; III, 378b, 669b
Nāfiʿ b. al-Ḥārith b. Kalada s, 354b — S, 354b
Nāfiʿ b. Kalada s, 354b — S, 354b
Nāfidh, Aḥmed iv, 877b, 878a — IV, 910b
Nafīr i, 1291a, b — I, 1330b, 1331a
Nafīs b. ʿIwaḍ s, 271b — S, 271b
Nafs iv, 487a — IV, 508a
al-Nafs al-Zakiyya i, 45b, 103b, 123a, 402a, b, 550b; ii, 485a, 745a; iii, 256b, 616a; v, 1233a, b — I, 46b, 106b, 126b, 412b, 414a, 568a; II, 497b, 763b; III, 265a, 636b; V, 1223b, 1224a
Nafṭ i, 967a, 1055b, 1056a, 1059a, 1068b; ii, 507a; iii, 470a, 475b — I, 996b, 997a, 1087a, b, 1090b, 1100b; II, 519b; III, 486a, 492a
Nafṭa (Ḳasṭīliya) s, 402b — S, 403a
Nafūd i, 537a, 1312b; ii, 92a — I, 553b, 1352b; II, 93b
Nafūsa i, 1349b; iii, 654a, 655b — I, 1390a; III, 675a, 677a
Nafzāwa i, 1349b; v, 696a, 1181b, 1182a — I, 1390a; V, 701a, 1171b, 1172a
al-Nafzāwī, Muḥammad ii, 552b — II, 566b
Nagar s, 327b — S, 327a
Nagarkōt → Kāṅgrā
Nāgawr iii, 441b; v, 884a; s, 353a, b — III, 455b; V, 890a; S, 353a, b
Naghmī, Naghamī v, 951b — V, 955b
Naghrallā, Banū ʾl- i, 491b — I, 506a
Nagir s, 158b — S, 158b
Nāgōshias i, 1255a — I, 1293a
Nahār → Layl and/et Nahār
Nahāwandī → ʿAbd al-Bāḳī
al-Nahāwandī, Benjamin iv, 604a, b, 606b — IV, 628a, 629a, 630b
Nahḍa iv, 142b, 143b; v, 794b — IV, 148b, 149a; V, 800b
al-Nahḍa (al-Ḳāhira) s, 5b — S, 4b
Nahdat al-ʿUlamāʾ iii, 534a, b, 1229b, 1230b — III, 552b, 553a, 1261a, 1262a
Nahdatul Ulama s, 151a — S, 151a
al-Naḥḥāsīn (al-Ḳāhira) s, 5a — S, 4b
Nahīk Mudjāwid al-Rīḥ iv, 91b — IV, 95b
Nāḥiye iv, 229b, 230a, b — IV, 239b, 240a, b
Nāḥiyy Tūnb iv, 778a, b; s, 417b — IV, 809b, 810a; S, 418a

Nahr i, 52b, 1029b, 1094b; ii, 438a; iv, 133b, 193a; v, 368a, 885a, 886a — I, 54a, 1061a, 1127a; II, 449b; IV, 139a, 201a; V, 369a, 891b, 892a
Nahr Abī Fuṭrus i, 103a — I, 106a
Nahr ʿĪsā ibn ʿAlī → ʿĪsā, Nahr
Nahr Maʿḳil s, 16a — S, 16b
Nahr Tīrā s, 352a — S, 352a
Nahr Yazīd s, 197a — S, 197a
Nahr al-Zuṭṭ s, 243a — S, 243a
al-Nahradjūrī, Abū Aḥmad iii, 1071b — III, 1098a
Nahrawān i, 40b, 384b; iii, 236b; iv, 1075a — I, 41b, 395b; III, 243a; IV, 1106b
- canal system/système de canaux ii, 250a, 343b — II, 257a, 353a
al-Nahrawānī, Abū Ḥakīm iii, 751a — III, 774a
Nahray ben Nissim ii, 988b — II, 1011b
Nahrōī i, 1006a — I, 1037a
Nahrwāla → Anhalwāra
Naḥw iv, 122a; v, 804a — IV, 127b; V, 810a
Naḥwī v, 1133b — V, 1129b
Nāʾib iii, 1153a; iv, 375a — III, 1181a; IV, 391b
Nāʾiba ii, 146a; iv, 456b — II, 150a; IV, 476b
Nāʾik iii, 632b — III, 653b
Naïl, Awlād i, 371b — I, 382b
Nāʾilī i, 1302a; ii, 1000a; s, 324a — I, 1341b; II, 1023a; S, 323b
Naʿīm, Aḥmed s, 83a — S, 83a
Naʿīm, Āl iv, 752a; s, 42a — IV, 782a; S, 42b
Naʿīmā ii, 74a, 543a; iv, 761a — II, 75b, 556b; IV, 791b
Nāʾīnī, Mīrzā Muḥammad Ḥusayn iv, 164b; s, 109b, 342a — IV, 171b; S, 109a, 341b
Najāra, Israel iv, 310a — IV, 324a
Nakad i, 1078a — I, 1110b
Naḳb, naḳaba iii, 473b, 474a — III, 490a, b
Nakhāwila v, 998b, 999b — V, 994a, 995a
Nakhčiwān i, 8a, 191b — I, 8a, 197a
Nakhdjawānī, Muḥammad b. Hindūshāh iii, 284a, 1243a; iv, 526a; v, 872b — III, 293a, 1275a; IV, 548b; V, 878b
Nakhidjevan s, 275a — S, 274b
Nakhkhās i, 32b — I, 33a
Nakhla i, 540a; ii, 1058a; iii, 237b; iv, 995b; v, 595b — I, 557a; II, 1082b; III, 244b; IV, 1028a; V, 599b
Nakhla al-Mudawwar s, 161a — S, 161a
Nakhlī → Ḥāfiẓ Tanīsh
Nakhshab → Ḳarshi
Nakhshabī iv, 69a — IV, 73a
al-Naḳīʿ iv, 1144a — IV, 1175b
Naḳīb iii, 184a; iv, 267a; v, 1131b; s, 208b — III, 188b; IV, 279a; V, 1127b; S, 208a
al-Naḳīb, ʿAbd al-Raḥmān iii, 521a — III, 539a
Naḳīb al-ashrāf iii, 1152b; iv, 103b, 474b; s, 122b, 132b — III, 1181a; IV, 108a, 495b; S, 122a, 132a
Nakīr → Munkar wa-Nakīr
Naḳīr (drink/boisson) iv, 995b — IV, 1028b
Nakiye, Elgün (Khanîm) iv, 933b — IV, 966b
Nakkārī → al-Nukkār
Naḳḳāsh → Ghiyāth al-Dīn
Naḳḳāsh ʿAlī Pasha v, 649b — V, 654a
al-Naḳḳāsh, Mārūn i, 597a — I, 616b
Naḳḳāsh, Muḥammad → Darwīsh Muḥammad
Naḳḳāshkhāne iv, 1169a — IV, 1202a
Naḳsh-i Radjab iv, 220b — IV, 230b
Naḳsh-i Rustam (Shāpūr) ii, 135b; iv, 220b, 221a, b — II, 139a; IV, 230b, 231a
al-Naḳshabandī, ʿAbd al-Haḳḳ v, 1005b — V, 1001a
Naḳshband, Bahāʾ al-Dīn s, 50b — S, 51b
al-Naḳshbandī, Bahāʾ al-Dīn s, 364b — S, 364b
Naḳshbandiyya i, 755b, 782a, 1072a, 1137a, 1295b; ii, 18a, 88a, 91b, 137b, 293a, 296b, 711b, 879a, 1078a; iii, 38a, 432b, 662b; iv, 48b; v, 53b, 475a, 486a, 851a, 859a; s, 50b, 51b, 71a — I, 778a, 805a, 1104a, 1171b, 1335a; II, 18a, 90a, 93a, 141b, 301a, 304b, 730a, 899a, 1103a; III, 39b, 446b, 684a; IV, 51b; V, 55a, 478a, 489a, 855b, 866a; S, 51a, 52a, 72a
Nakūk i, 1072b — I, 1104b
Nakūr v, 1119a; s, 377a — V, 1115b; S, 377a
Nāḳūs i, 188a — I, 193a
Naʿl v, 733a, 735b, 736a, 752b — V, 738a, 740b, 741a, 758a
Naldrug iii, 448a — III, 463a
al-Namalī, Muḥammad b. Ḥassān ii, 552a — II, 566a
Nāmdār Khān b. Ṣalābat Djang s, 280a — S, 280a
Nāmdjīn → Bāḥmīn
Name → Ism
Nāme-i humāyūn i, 1090b — I, 1123a
Nāmiḳ Kemāl → Kemāl, Meḥmed Nāmiḳ
Nāmiḳ Pasha i, 906b — I, 933b
al-Namir i, 545a — I, 562a
Nāmūs ii, 486b — II, 499a
Nānā Ṣāḥib i, 822b; iv, 551b — I, 845b; IV, 575a
Nānak iii, 456b — III, 472b
Nanda → Djām Nanda
Nandjarādj iii, 316b — III, 326a
Nangrahar (Ningrahar) s, 237a, b — S, 237a, b
Naples → Nābal
Napoléon Bonaparte i, 630b; ii, 464b — I, 651a; II, 476b
Nar → Nūr
Nār iii, 78a; iv, 237a — III, 80a; IV, 247b
Nār al-ḥarratayn iv, 928a; v, 1110a, 1111a, 1112a, 1113a, 1115b — IV, 961a; V, 1106a, 1107a, 1108a, 1109a, 1112a
Narāḳī, Mullā Aḥmad s, 75b — S, 75b
Narameikhla, King/roi i, 606a, 1333a — I, 625b, 1272b
Narāyan Singh ii, 47b — II, 48b
Narbonne → Arbūna
Nārbūta Beg (Khān) v, 29a — V, 30a
Nard v, 109a, 110a — V, 111b, 112b
Nargūnd ii, 220a — II, 227a
Nariman Narimanov s, 365a — S, 365a
Nārimān Ṣādiḳ s, 299b — S, 299a
Narkh iii, 489a — III, 506a
Narnāla iii, 1161b — III, 1189b
Narseh iv, 753b — IV, 784a
Narshakhī i, 1294a, b; v, 856b; s, 125b, 326b, 327a — I, 1334a; V, 863b; S, 124b, 326b
Narsingh Ray s, 206b — S, 206a
Narwar s, 10b — S, 10a → Ḥiṣār-i Muḥammad
Nasā i, 320b, 701a — I, 330b, 722a
Nasab iii, 238b; iv, 179b, 495b — III, 245b; IV, 187b, 516b
Nasaf iv, 671b — IV, 699a
Naṣaf iii, 1236b — III, 1268b
al-Nasafī, Abū ʿAbd Allāh i, 125b, 160b, 414b; iv, 198a, 203b, 661b, 662b; v, 167a — I, 129a, 165a, 426a; IV, 206b, 212b, 688b, 689b; V, 164b
al-Nasafī, Abu ʾl-Barakāt iii, 163b — III, 167a
al-Nasafī, Abū Hafs i, 593a; iii, 901b — I, 612a; III, 925b
al-Nasafī, Nadjm al-Dīn i, 333a; iv, 737a — I, 343a; IV, 767a
al-Nasāʾī (d./m. 915) iii, 24a; s, 87b — III, 25b; S, 87b
al-Nasāʾī al-Madlidjī, Aḥmad iv, 509b — IV, 531b
Nasaḳ ii, 156a, 157a, 158a — II, 161a, 162a, b
Naṣārā i, 31b, 264b, 265a, b, 470a, 1020a, 1040b; ii, 229a, b, 230a, 459a, 637a, 859b; iii, 77b, 1206a, b; iv, 43b, 76b, 241a, 243b; v, 141b, 265a, 326b, 330b, 334a, 335b, 793b, 795b, 799a, 1020a — I, 32b, 272b, 273a, b, 484a, 1051b, 1072a; II, 236a, b, 237a, 471a, 653a, 879b; III, 80a, 1236b, 1237a; IV, 46a, 80b, 252a, 254b; V, 144a, 263a, 326a, 330b, 334a, 336a, 799b,

801b, 805a, 1016a
al-Nasawī, Muḥammad b. Aḥmad i, 1354a — I, 1393a
al-Nasawī, Muḥammad b. Manṣūr i, 434a — I, 446a
Nashāshībīs iii, 523b — III, 541b
Nashāshībī, Isʿāf s, 159b — S, 159b
al-Nāshiʾ al-Akbar s, 89b, 225b, 265a — S, 89b, 225b, 264b
Nāshid iv, 422a — IV, 440a
Nāshira al-Yarbūʿī s, 26a — S, 26b
Nashīṭ i, 828a; iii, 878b — I, 851a; III, 902b
Nashḳ iv, 335b — IV, 350a
Nashtakin → al-Darazī
Nashwān b. Saʿīd al-Ḥimyarī i, 564a; iii, 124a; s, 225b, 289b, 339b — I, 582a; III, 127a; S, 225b, 289b, 339a
Nasīʾ iv, 472a — IV, 493a
Nasīb i, 583b, 584a; ii, 1028a, b; iv, 488a, 714a, 715a; v, 930b, 956a — I, 602a, II, 1052a, b; IV, 509a, 742b, 744a; S, 935a, 960a
Nasīb Djanbulāṭ ii, 444a — II, 455b
al-Naṣībī, Abū Isḥāk Ibrāhīm b. ʿAlī s, 13b — S, 13b
Naṣībīn iv, 898a; s, 36a, 37a — IV, 930b; S, 36b, 37a
Nāṣif, Malik Ḥifnī i, 597b; iii, 360a; iv, 720b — I, 617a; III, 371a; IV, 749b
Nāṣīf al-Yāzidjī → al-Yāzidjī
al-Nāṣiḥī, Abū Muḥammad s, 343a — S, 343a
Nāsikh, Shaykh Imām Bakhsh ii, 84b; s, 102a — II, 86a; S, 101b
al-Nāsikh wa ʾl-mansūkh iii, 28a — III, 29b
Nasīm ghlu Aḥmad b. Ḥasan i, 310a — I, 319b
al-Nāṣir (ʿAbbāsid(e)) → al-Nāṣir li-Dīn Allāh
al-Nāṣir (Almohad(e)) → Muḥammad b. Abī Yūsuf Yaʿḳūb
al-Nāṣir (Ayyūbid(e)) → al-Malik al-Nāṣir; al-Nāṣir Dāwūd
al-Nāṣir (Mamlūk) → Ḥasan, Nāṣir al-Dīn; al-Nāṣir Muḥammad
al-Nāṣir (Umayyad(e)) → ʿAbd al-Raḥmān III
Nāṣir, Banū s, 395a — S, 395b
al-Nāṣir, Mawlāy i, 605a — I, 624b
al-Nāṣir b. ʿAlannās (Ḥammādid(e)) i, 1205a; iii, 137b, 386a; iv, 479a; v, 59b — I, 1240b; III, 140b, 398b; IV, 501a; V, 61b
Nāṣir b. Khalīfa al-Bāʿūnī i, 1109a -I, 1142b
Nāṣir b. Mubārak iv, 752a — IV, 782b
Nāṣir b. Murshid i, 554a — I, 571b
al-Nāṣir, Abu ʾl-Saʿādāt Muḥammad i. 1060a — I, 1092a
al-Nāṣir Aḥmad (Rasūlid(e)) → Aḥmad b. Ismāʿīl
Nāṣir al-Dawla (Kirmān) s, 53a — S, 53b
Nāṣir al-Dawla (Labla) v, 586b — V, 591b
Nāṣir al-Dawla b. Sikandar iii, 322a — III, 332a
Nāṣir al-Dawla Badr → Badr b. Ḥsanwayh
Nāṣir al-Dawla al-Ḥasan (Ḥamdānid(e)) i, 119b, 866b, 870b, 1352b; ii, 178b, 524b; iii, 126b, 127a, 346a, 902b; s, 36b, 379b — I, 123a, 890b, 895a, 1391b, 1392a; II, 184a, 537b; III, 129b, 130a, 356b, 926b; S, 36b, 379b
Nāṣir al-Dawla Ḥusayn ii, 856a, 857b, 858b; iii, 129a — II, 876a, 877b, 878b; III, 131b
al-Nāṣir Dāwūd b. al-Muʿaẓẓam i, 766b, 799a, 804a, 912b, 940b; ii, 284a; iii, 989b; iv, 520b, 958b — I, 789b, 822b, 828a, 940a, 969a; II, 292a; III, 1014a; IV, 543a, b, 992a
Nāṣir al-Dīn b. Ḥasan Karlugh i, 227a — I, 234a
Nāṣir al-Dīn b. Musallam iv, 643a — IV, 669b
Naṣīr al-Dīn, Shaykh s, 352b — S, 352b
al-Nāṣir li-Dīn Allāh i, 20a, b, 322b, 1150a; ii, 327a, 964a, 1044a; iii, 109b, 160b, 488b, 1256a; iv, 29b, 749a, 942b; s, 193b, 378b — I, 20b, 21b, 332a, 1184b; II, 336b, 986a, 1068b; III, 112a, 164a, 505a, 1288b; IV, 32a, 779a, 975b; S, 194b, 378b
Nāṣir al-Dīn al-Asad iv, 820b, 821a — IV, 853b, 854a
Nāṣir al-Din Čirāgh → Čirāgh-i Dihlī
Nāṣir al-Dīn Ḳabača (Kubādja) i, 764a, 1192a, 1194a; ii, 267b, 393a, 609a, 1103a; iii, 416a, 1155a; v, 597b; s, 360a — I, 787a, 1227a, 1229b; II, 275b, 403b, 624a, 1129a; III, 429a, 1183b; V, 601b; S, 359b
Nāṣir al-Dīn al-Kaymarī iv, 842b — IV, 875b
Nāṣir al-Din Khaldjī ii, 381a — II, 391b
Nāṣir al-Dīn Maḥmūd s, 266b — S, 266a
Nāṣir al-Dīn Maḥmūd b. Iltutmish → Maḥmūd I (Dihlī)
Nāṣir al-Dīn Maḥmūd Shāh → Maḥmūd I (Bengal)
Nāṣir al-Dīn Muḥammad b. Dhuʾl-Karnayn ii, 111a — II, 113b
Nāṣir al-Dīn Muḥammad b. Khalīl ii, 239b — II, 246a
Nāṣir al-Dīn Muḥammad Shāh (Doʾāb) s, 126b — S, 125b
Nāṣir al-Dīn Muḥammad al-Zurayḳ iii, 155b — III, 159a
Nāṣir al-Dīn Mukram b. ʿAlāʾ s, 326a — S, 325b
Nāṣir al-Dīn Shāh Ḳādjār i, 626b, 833b, 846b, 847a, 916a, 1088b; ii, 152b, 418a, 433b, 649b, 650a; iii, 554a, 1103b; iv, 39a, 72a, 392a, 393a, 696a, 788a, 855b; v, 659a, 919b, 1085b; s, 23b, 41a, 70b, 71a, 94b, 108b, 260b, 290b, 302a — I, 647a, 856b, 870a, 944a, 1120b; II, 157a, 429a, 445a, 666a, b; III, 573a, 1130b; IV, 41b, 76a, 408b, 410a, 724b, 819b, 888b; V, 663b, 925a, 1083a; S, 24a, 41b, 71a, b, 94a, 108a, 260a, 290b, 301b
Nāṣir al-Dīn al-Ṭūsī i, 113a, 326b, 328b, 353b, 393a, 450a, 594a, 721a, 839a, 1198a; ii, 362a, 399b, 607b, 765b, 774a; iii, 24b, 103b, 390a, 726b, 1122a, 1137b, 1151b, 1266a; iv, 48b, 121a, 205b, 976a, 1028a, 1036a; v, 547a; s, 412a, 413a, 414a — I, 116a, 337a, 339a, 364b, 404b, 463a, 613b, 743a, 862a, 1233b; II, 372a, 410a, 622b, 784a, 792b; III, 25b, 106a, 402b, 749a, 1149b, 1165b, 1179b, 1299a; IV, 51a, 126a, 214b, 1008a, 1060a, 1067b; V, 552a; S, 412a, 413a, 414b
Nāṣir Djang (Farrukhābād) → Imdād Ḥusayn Khān
Nāṣir Djang (Ḥaydarābād) iii, 320a, b — III, 331a
al-Nāṣir Faradj → Faradj
Nāṣir al-Ḥakk Abū Muḥammad iv, 19a — IV, 20b
al-Nāṣir Ḥasan → Ḥasan, Nāṣir al-Dīn
al-Nāṣir al-Kabīr → Ḥasan al-Uṭrūsh
Nāṣir Khān II i, 1006a — I, 1037a
Nāṣir Khān Brahūʾī i, 230a, 296a, 1006a, 1010b; iv, 1059b; v, 102a, 580a; s, 222a, 332b — I, 237a, 305b, 1036b, 1037a, 1041b; IV, 1091a; V, 104a, 584b; S, 222a, 331b
Nāṣir Khān Fārūḳī i, 710a, 1329a, 1331a; ii, 814b, 1125a; iii, 419a, 638a — I, 731b, 1369b, 1371b; II, 833b, 1151b; III, 432a, 659b
Nāṣir Khān Ḳashḳāy iv, 706b — IV, 734b
Naṣīr Khān Lārī (18th c./18e s.) v, 673b, 674a — V, 679a
Naṣīr Khān Lārī (19th c./19e s.) v, 674a — V, 679a
Nāṣir Khān Noḥānī s, 203a — S, 202b
Nāṣir-i Khusraw i, 137a, 233b, 450a, 552a, 852a, 1220b; ii, 584b, 861a, 997b; iii, 328b, 1130b; iv, 61b, 63a, 199b; v, 175b, 930a, 956b; s, 108a, 203b, 208a — I, 141b, 240b, 463a, 569b, 876a, 1257a; II, 599a, 881a, 1020b; III, 338b, 1158b; IV, 65a, 66b, 208a; V, 173a, 934b, 960b; S, 107a, 203a, 207b
Nāṣir Mīrzā i, 228a, 852b — I, 234b, 876a
al-Nāṣir Muḥammad b. Ḳalāwūn (Mamlūk) i, 118b, 610b, 779a, 1126b, 1127b, 1128a, 1299b, 1324b; ii, 38a, 68a, 285a, b, 330a; iii, 99a, 189b, 220a, 346b, 744b, 890b, 923b, 952b; iv, 136b, 424b, 430b, 464b, 609a, 834b, 864a, 965b; v, 373b, 595a, 1140b; s, 395b

— I, 122a, 631b, 802a, 1160b, 1162a, 1339b, 1365b; II, 39a, 69b, 293a, b, 339b; III, 101b, 194a, 226b, 357a, 767a, 914b, 947b, 977a; IV, 142a, 443a, 449b, 485a, 634a, 867b, 897a, 998a; V, 374b, 598b, 1134a; S, 396a
Nāṣir al-Mulk (Čitrāl) ii, 31a — II, 31b
Nāṣir al-Mulk (Irān) ii, 652a, b — II, 668b, 669a
al-Nāṣir Ṣalāḥ al-Dīn Yūsuf (Ayyūbid(e)) s, 391a — S, 391b
al-Nāṣirī → Ibn Nāṣir
al-Nāṣirī → Aḥmad al-Nāṣirī al-Salāwī
Nāsir-i Khusraw iv, 61b, 63a, 199b; v, 175b, 930a, 956b; s, 108a, 203b, 208a — IV, 65a, 66b, 208a; V, 173a, 934b, 960b; S, 107a, 203a, 207b
Nāṣiriyya (Caspian region/Région caspienne) s, 363a — S, 363a
Nāṣiriyya (Dimashḳ) s, 197a — S, 197a
Nāṣiriyya (Morocco/Maroc) i, 290a, b; ii, 134a; s, 395a — I, 299a, b; II, 137b; S, 395b
Nāṣiriyya (Yemen/Yémen) iii, 255a — III, 262a
Nāṣirwand v, 603a — V, 607a
Naskh i, 265b, 850b; iii, 898b; iv, 170a; v, 415b — I, 273b, 874b; III, 923a; IV, 177b; V, 417a
Naskh (calligraphie) iv, 1121a, 1123a, b, 1125a, 1127a; v, 221a, 230b — IV, 1152b, 1155a, 1157a, 1158b; V, 218b, 228b
Nasnās v, 133a, b — V, 136a, b
Naṣr I (Ḳarakhānid(e)) i, 1295a; iii, 1114b, 1115a; iv, 217b — I, 1334b; III, 1142a, b; IV, 227a
Naṣr I (Sāmānid(e)) i, 1294a; iv, 21b, 188b; s, 265b — I, 1333b; IV, 23b, 196b, 197a; S, 265a
Naṣr II (Sāmānid(e)) i, 278a, 1294b; ii, 1082b; iii, 254b, 759a, 1156b; iv, 22b; v, 856b; s, 265a, 411a — I, 286b, 1334b; II, 1107b; III, 262a, 782a, 1185a; IV, 24a; V, 863b; S, 264b, 411b
Naṣr b. ʿAbbās b. Abi 'l-Futūḥ i, 9b, 198b; ii, 318a; iv, 514a — I, 9b, 204b; II, 327a; IV, 536b
Naṣr b. Abī Layth → al-Aṣamm, Abū Bakr (Egypt/Égypte)
Naṣr b. Aḥmad → Naṣr I, II (Samānid(e))
Naṣr b. ʿAlī Khan iii, 1113b — III, 1141a
Naṣr b. ʿĀṣim iv, 731b — IV, 761a
Naṣr b. Ibrāhīm (Ilek-Khān) s, 65a — S, 65b
Naṣr b. Maḥmūd iii, 790a — III, 813b
Naṣr b. Marzūḳ s, 88a — S, 87b
Naṣr b. Muḥammad iii, 833b — III, 857b
Naṣr b. Muzāḥim al-Minkarī i, 383b; s, 233a — I, 394b; S, 233a
Naṣr b. Sayyār i, 16a, 206b, 529b, 1293b; ii, 561a; iii, 224a, 471a, 493b, 802b, 988a; iv, 15b, 446b; v, 57a, b, 711a, 854a — I, 16b, 212b, 545b, 1333b; II, 575a; III, 230b, 231a, 487b, 510b, 826a, 1013a; IV, 16b, 466b; V, 59a, 716a, 861a
Naṣr b. Sebüktigin iv, 189b; v, 1126b — IV, 197b; V, 1123a
Naṣr b. Shabath i, 52b; ii, 524a; iii, 950b — I, 54a; II, 537a; III, 975b
Naṣr Āl Madhkūr i, 942b — I, 971b
Naṣr Allāh (Afghānistān) s, 65b, 237b — S, 66a, 237b
Naṣr Allāh, amīr (Bukhārā) i, 1296a; iv, 694b; v, 30a, 46a — I, 1335b; IV, 722b; V, 31a, 47a
Naṣr Allāh b. ʿAbd al-Ḥamīd iii, 372b; iv, 504b — III, 384b; IV, 526a
Naṣr Allāh b. ʿAbd al-Raḥmān i, 232b; iii, 13a — I, 239b; III, 14a
Naṣr Allāh b. al-Djazarī s, 267a — S, 266b
Naṣr Allāh b. Muḥammad iv, 64a — IV, 67b
Naṣr Allāh Iṣfahānī, Mīrzā iv, 164a — IV, 171a
Naṣr Allāh Munshī s, 21b — S, 22a
Naṣr al-Dawla b. Marwān ii, 384a, 484b; iii, 344b; v, 453a — II, 394b, 496b; III, 355a; V, 455b
Naṣr al-Dīn, *makk* i, 1172a — I, 1207a
Naṣr al-Dīn Khodja i, 313a; ii, 591a; iii, 375a; s, 170b — I, 323a; II, 605b; III, 387a; S, 170b
Naṣr Khān → Naṣr I (Ḳarakhanid(e))
Naṣr al-Ḳushūrī iii, 45b, 101a, 886b — III, 47b, 103b, 910b
Naṣr al-Mulk Ḳaragözlū iv, 578a — IV, 601a
Naṣrābādī s, 340b — S, 340a
Naṣrat Shāh ii, 218b — II, 225b
Naṣrid(e)s i, 495b, 500a; ii, 307b, 1015b, 1016b; iii, 499a; v, 625b; s, 112b, 256b, 307a, 398b — I, 510b, 515a; II, 316b, 1039a, 1040a; III, 516a; V, 629b; S, 112a, 256b, 307a, 399a
Nassādjī iv, 1042b — IV, 1074a
Naṣṣār, Nadjīb ii, 468a — II, 480a
Nasser, Colonel → ʿAbd al-Nāṣir, Djamāl
Nastaʿlīḳ iv, 1124a, b, 1126a, 1127a; v, 224a — IV, 1156a, 1157b, 1158b; V, 222a
Naṣūh aḳ Ḥiṣārī i, 310a — I, 319b
Naṣūḥ Pasha i, 268a; ii, 443b, 750a, b; s, 238b — I, 276a; II, 455a 768b, 769a; S, 238b
Naṣūh Pasha ʿOthmān-oghlu i, 395a — I, 406b
Naṣūḥ al-Ṣilāḥī i, 904b — I, 931b
al-Naṣūḥiyya iv, 991b — IV, 1024a
Nāsūt v, 611b, 612a — V, 615b, 616a
Naʿt ii, 302a; iv, 715b — II, 310b; IV, 744b
Naṭanz iii, 1124b — III, 1152b
Naṭanzī, Ḥusayn iv, 525b — IV, 548b
Nathrī, Shaykh Mūsā iv, 72b; v, 198a — IV, 76b; V, 195b
Nāṭiḳ iv, 203a, b — IV, 212b
al-Nāṭiḳ bi'l-Ḥaḳḳ, Abū Ṭālib iii, 832a; s, 13a, 343a — III, 856a; S, 13b, 343a
al-Natīlī → al-Ḥusayn b. Ibrāhīm
National Front (Iran) iv, 41a, b, 42a
National Mahommedan Association i, 443a — I, 455b
Nationalism(e) → Ḳawmiyya
Natron → Bawraḳ
Naṭrūn i, 1068b; v, 965a, 979b; s, 130b — I, 1100b; V, 969b; S, 130a
Naṭṭāḥa → Ibn al-Khāṣīb, Abū ʿAlī
Nāʿūra i, 492a, 1232a; iii, 29b; v, 860b, 861a, 863b, 864a, 969a — I, 507a, 1269a; III, 31a; V, 867b, 868a, 870b, 871a, 972a
Navā'ī, ʿAlī-Shīr i, 292b, 504b, 813b, 1019a, 1082b, 1211b, 1212b; ii, 179a, 421b, 422a, 792a; iii, 177b, 358a, 603a; iv, 66a-b, 1010a, 1020b; v, 835b; s, 83a, 324a — I, 301b, 520a, 837a, 1050a, 1115a, 1247b, 1248b; II, 185a, 432b, 811a; III, 181b, 369a, 624a; IV, 70a, 1042a, 1052b; V, 842a; S, 83a, 323b
Navas de Tolosa, Las iii, 1055a — III, 1081a
Navigation → Milāḥa
Navy → Baḥriyya; Safīna
Nawālī → Naṣūh aḳ Hiṣārī
Nawar ii, 40b — II, 41b
al-Nawawī, Muḥyi al-Dīn iii, 25b, 763a, 779a, 860b, 927a; iv, 1108a; v, 20a; s, 83a, 390b — III, 27a, 786b, 802b, 885a, 951b; IV, 1139b; V, 20b; S, 82b, 391a
Nawbahār i, 1033a — I, 1064b
al-Nawbakhtī, al-Ḥasan b. Mūsā iii, 497b; s, 225b, 393b — III, 514b; S, 225b, 394a
Nawbat iii, 453b — III, 469b
Nawfal, Banū v, 435a — V, 437a
Nawr al-Ward v, 827b — V, 833b
Nawrōdjī, Dādābhā'ī ii, 545b — II, 559a
Nawrūz iv, 8b, 477a — IV, 9b, 479b
Nawrūz, Amīr i, 1130a; ii, 1043a; iv, 878a; v, 554a — I, 1164a; II, 1067b; IV, 910b; V, 559a
Nawrūz Aḥmed Khān i, 46b; iv, 512a — I, 48a; IV, 534a
Nawrūz al-Ḥāfiẓī ii, 781b; iii, 186a — II, 800a; III, 190b

Nawrūznāma iv, 64a — IV, 67b
Naws͟hahr s, 131b — S, 131a
al-Naws͟harī iv, 89a — IV, 93a
Nāwūsiyya ii, 375a — II, 385a
Nawwāb v, 635a — V, 639a
Nawwāb-i Ṣafawī ii, 882b; iii, 529b; iv, 165a — II, 902b; III, 548a; IV, 172b
Nawwāb-Wazīrs (Awadh) s, 74b, 325b — S, 75a, 325a
Nayčari ii, 97a — II, 99a
Nayman ii, 42a; s, 97b, 420a — II, 43a; S, 97a, 420a
Nayrab iv, 724a — IV, 753a
al-Nayrīzī, Abu᾽l-ʿAbbās i, 727a; iii, 1137a; v, 85b; s, 412a, b, 414a — I, 749a; III, 1165b; V, 88a; S, 412a, 413a, 414b
Naysābūr → Nīs͟hāpūr
al-Naysābūrī → al-Nīsābūrī
al-Naysābūrī, al-Ḥasan b. al-Muẓaffar s, 289b — S, 289a
Nayzak iv, 811a — IV, 843b
Naẓar i, 949a — I, 978b
Naẓar Muḥammad K͟hān i, 768b — I, 791b
Nazhūn iii, 850a — III, 874a
Nāẓîm, Dr iv, 284b, 285a — IV, 297a, b
Nāẓim, Nabī-zāde i, 287b; ii, 699b, 700b — I, 296a; II, 717b, 718a
Nazim Hikmet iv, 882b — IV, 915a
Nāẓim Pas͟ha i, 906b; ii, 624a, 698b; iii, 402a; iv, 296b, 297a — I, 934a; II, 639b, 716b; III, 414a; IV, 310a
Nāẓîrzāde iii, 538a — III, 557a
Nazlī (queen/reine) s, 299a — S, 299a
Nazwā i, 1071b; iii, 652b — I, 1103b; III, 673b
al-Naẓẓām i, 128b, 272a, 713b, 737a; ii, 386a, 518b, 569b; iii, 302b, 1143a, 1266a; iv, 183a, 615a; v, 240b, 384a, b, 893b; s, 90b, 226a, 393b — I, 132b, 280a, 735a, 759a; II, 396a, 531b, 584a; III, 312a, 1171b, 1299a; IV, 190b, 640a; V, 238b, 385a, b, 899b; S, 90a, 226a, 394a
NDiassâne s, 182b — S, 182b
Ndjamena s, 166b — S, 166b
Nebuchadnezzar → Buk͟ht-Naṣar
Nečari → Nayčari
Nedīm → Nadīm
Nedjātī i, 292b; ii, 221a; s, 324a — I, 301b; II, 227b; S, 323b
Nedjātī, Muṣṭafā v, 282a — V, 280a
Nedroma v, 379a; s, 144b — V, 379b; S, 144a
Nefes v, 275a — V, 273a
Nefʿī iii, 357a; iv, 715b; s, 282b, 324a — III, 368a; IV, 744a; S, 282b, 323b
Nefṭa ii, 463a, 464a — II, 475a, 476a
Negara Dār ul-Islām iii, 1228b — III, 1260b
Neguib, Muḥammad ii, 648b; s, 6a, b, 7a, 301a — II, 665a; S, 5a, b, 6a, 301a
Negübey → Nīkpāy
Nememcha i, 371b; ii, 464a; s, 144b — I, 382b; II, 476a; S, 144a, b
Nesīmī iii, 600b; s, 324a — III, 621b; S, 323b
Nesin, Aziz iii, 357b; iv, 882b; v, 195a — III, 369a; IV, 915b; V, 192a
Nestorians/Nestoriens ii, 67a, b, 1120a; iii, 886a, 1122a, 1206a; v, 121a, 896b — I, 68b, 1146b; III, 910a, 1149b, 1236b; V, 123b, 902b
Net → Ṣayd
Nevruz, Emīr → Nawruz, Amīr
Nevzāt, Refiḳ iv, 123b — IV, 129a
Newā᾽ī → Navā᾽ī
Newʿī s, 83a — S, 83a
New Saray i, 1188b — I, 1223b
Newʿī-zāde ʿAṭā'ī → ʿAṭā'ī
Newspaper → Djarīda
Newzād, Tewfik iv, 930b — IV, 963b
Nēzak Ṭark͟hān → Nīzak Ṭark͟hān
N᾽gaous → Niḳaws
Niassenes s, 182b — S, 182b
Nicaea/Nicée → Iznīḳ
Nicander s, 59b — S, 60a
Nicephorus Phocas i, 789b; iii, 86a, 120a, 398a, 1084a, b; v, 921b, 923b — I, 813a; III, 88b, 122b, 410b, 1111a, b; V, 927a, 929a
Nicobar islands/Nicobar, îles → Lankabālūs
Nicosia/Nicosie → Lefḳos͟ha
Nidjābat K͟hān iv, 666b, IV, 693b
Niebla → Labla
Nifṭawayh i, 822a — I, 845a
Nigde, Ḳāḍī Aḥmad of/de s, 59a — S, 59b
Niger s, 218a — S, 217b
Nigeria/Nigéria i, 39a, 179a; ii, 10a, 942a; iii, 275a; s, 217a — I, 40a, 184a; II, 10b, 963b; III, 283a; S, 217a
Night → Layl and Nahār
Nightingale → Bulbul
Nigīsa iv, 53b — IV, 56b
Nihāwand i, 16a; iv, 13b, 447a, 653b; v, 1212b, 1213a; s, 297b — I, 16b; IV, 14b, 467a, 680a; V, 1202a, b; S, 297b
Nihḍat-i Āzādī iv, 166a — IV, 173b
Nīk ʿĀlam K͟hān i, 1193a — I, 1228b
Niḳābat al-as͟hrāf ii, 330a — II, 339b
Niḳaws s, 103a — S, 102b
Nīkpāy ii, 3a — II, 3b
Niksar s, 154a — S, 154b
al-Nīl i, 735a, 929a; iii, 71b; iv, 133b, 424b, 442b; v, 862a, 863a, 1249b; s, 413a — I, 757a, 957a; III, 74a; IV, 139a, 443a, 462b; V, 869a, 870a, 1240a, b; S, 413a
Nīlambar i, 719b — I, 741a
Nilometer/Nilomètre → Miḳyās
Nīmā Yūs͟hīdj iv, 71b — IV, 75a
Niʿmat Allāh, Hadjdjī i, 261b — I, 269b
Niʿmat Allāh b. Aḥmad al-Rūmī i, 776b; iv, 526a — I, 799b; IV, 549a
Niʿmat Allāh Harawī s, 1b — S, 1b
Niʿmat Allāh al-Kirmānī i, 925b, 1342a; iv, 49b, 66a, 961b; v, 157a — I, 953b, 1382b; IV, 52a, 69b, 994a; V, 156b
Niʿmat Allāh Walī → Niʿmat Allāh al-Kirmānī
Niʿmatallāhiyya iv, 49b, 51b, 951b; v, 1222a; s, 134b — IV, 52a, 54b, 984a; V, 1212b; S, 134a
Niʿmatīs iv, 99a, 860b — IV, 103b, 893b
Nimr, Banū iv, 834b — IV, 867b
Nimr, Fāris → Fāris Nimr
al-Nimr b. Ḳāsiṭ iv, 493b — IV, 515a
Nimr Muḥammad ii, 351b — II, 361a
Nimrān i, 1239b — I, 1277a
Nimrūd s, 101a — S, 100b
Nimzat s, 182b — S, 182b
Nindru s, 74a — S, 74a
Nioro iii, 289a — III, 298a
Nīrīz i, 954b — I, 984a
Nisā → Nasā
Nīsābūr → Nīs͟hāpūr
al-Nisābūrī → Ismāʿīl b. Muḥammed; al-Ḥākim;
Nīsān, Banū i, 256a; iii, 1197b — I, 264a; III, 1228a
Nisba iv, 180a — IV, 187b
Nis͟hān i, 1170b; ii, 309a — I, 1205b; II, 317b
Nis͟hāndjî iv, 560b, 561a — IV, 583a, b
Nis͟hāndjî, Khodja → Djalālzāde Muṣṭafā Čelebi
Nīs͟hāpūr i, 3b, 452b, 750a; ii, 4b, 43b, 746b; iii, 472a; iv, 669a; v, 58a, 354a, 526b, 1126b; s, 14b, 21a, 32a, 72b, 149a, 204a, 235a, 251a, 253a, 254b, 259b, 299a, 343a, 357a, 359b, 392a — I, 3b, 465b, 772b; II, 4b, 44a, 764b; III, 488b; IV, 696a; V, 60a, 355b, 530b, 1122b; S, 15a, 21a, 32a, 73a, 149a, 203b, 234b, 251a, 253a, 254a, 259a, 298b, 343a, 356b, 359b, 392b
Nis͟hāt ii, 433b — II, 444b

Nishdān iv, 488a — IV, 509a
Nishtār, Sardār ʿAbd al-Rabb iii, 532b — III, 551a
Niṣībīn → Naṣībīn
Nisibis s, 357b — S, 357b
Nisnās → Nasnās
Nissīm ben Yaʿḳob Ibn Shāhīn iv, 306b — IV, 320a, b
Nitra s, 171a — S, 171b
Niyāzi iii, 423a — III, 436b
Niyāzi Bey i, 63b; ii, 698b — I, 65b; II, 716a
Nīzak Ṭarkhān i, 857a, 1001a; iii, 304a; iv, 208a; v, 57a, 541b — I, 881a, 1031b; III, 313a; IV, 217a; V, 58b, 546a
«Niẓām» → ʿImād al-Mulk
Niẓām ʿAlī Khān iii, 320b — III, 331b
Niẓām Burhānpūrī i, 1331a; ii, 837b — I, 1372a; II, 857a
Niẓām al-Dawla b. Marwān v, 453a — V, 455b
Niẓām al-Dīn (amīr-i dād) iv, 818a — IV, 851a
Niẓām al-Dīn, Mullā (Farangī Maḥall) i, 936b; ii, 132a; v, 1135b; s, 292a, b, 293a — I, 965b; II, 135b; V, 1131a; S, 292a, b
Niẓām al-Dīn Aḥmad al-Harawī i, 60b, 856b, 857a; ii, 922a; s, 302a — I, 62b, 880b; II, 943b; S, 301b
Niẓām al-Dīn Awliyā, Shaykh i, 444b, 856a, 1024a, b, 1036b, 1328b; ii, 48a, 50a, 51a, 55a, b, 1076b; iii, 249a; iv, 921b; v, 884b; s, 352b, 353a — I, 457b, 879b, 1055b, 1068a, 1369b; II, 48b, 51a, 52a, 56a, b, 1101a; III, 256a; IV, 954b; V, 891a; S, 352b, 353a
Niẓām al-Dīn Awrangābādī ii, 55a; iv, 507b — II, 56a; IV, 529b
Niẓām al-Dīn Fārūḳī ii, 54b — II, 55b
Niẓām al-Dīn Maḥmūd s, 414b — S, 415a
Niẓām al-Dīn Thānesarī → Thānesarī
Nizām al-Dīn ʿUmar s, 197a — S, 197a
Niẓam Khān (prince) → Sikandar Shāh Lōdī
Niẓām al-Milla → Malik b. ʿAlī al-Barānī
Niẓām al-Mulk (d./m. 1092) i, 353a, 421a, 552a, 593a, 696a, 731a, 1051b, 1130a; ii, 5a, 344a, 384b, 605a, 963b, 1083a; iii, 253b, 347b, 774b, 1088b, 1099a; iv, 25b, 26a, 27b, 807b, 942b, 1073b; v, 387b, 388b, 625a, 1126b, 1127a, 1128b, 1137b; s, 14b, 29b, 30a, 384a — I, 364a, 433a, 569b, 612a, 717a, 753a, 1083a, 1164a; II, 5a, 354a, 394b, 620a, 985b, 1108b; III, 261a, 358a, 797b, 1115b, 1126a; IV, 27b, 28a, 29b, 840a, 975a, 1105a; V, 389a, b, 629a, 1123a, 1125a, 1132a; S, 15a, 29b, 30a, 384a
Niẓām al-Mulk (Dōʾāb) s, 126b — S, 125b
Niẓām al-Mulk b. Abī Saʿḍ al-Djunaydī i, 764a — I, 787a
Nizām al-Mulk Āṣaf Djāh → Āṣaf Djāh I
Niẓām al-Mulk Dakhnī iii, 1159b — III, 1188a
Niẓām Shāh Bahmanī ii, 1127a — II, 1153b
Niẓām-Shāhī i, 303a, 768a, 1170a; ii, 180a; iii, 425a, 426a, 447a, 1161a; s, 246a, 259a — I, 312b, 791a, 1205a; II, 185b; III, 439a, 440a, 462a, 1189b; S, 246b, 259a
Nizāmī, Nizām al-Dīn Abū Muḥammad i, 680a, 1213a; ii, 794a, 966b, 1143a; iii, 114a, 1112a; iv, 62b, 63a, 66b, 92b, 127b, 128a, 1009b; v, 1104a; s, 46b, 415a — I, 701a, 1249a; II, 813a, 988b, 1170a; III, 116b, 1139b; IV, 66a, b, 70a, 97a, 133a, b, 1041b; V, 1100a; S, 47a, 415b
Niẓāmī, Shāh Ḳudrat Allāh s, 293a — S, 293a
Niẓāmī ʿArūḍī Samarḳandī s, 333a, 359b — S, 332b, 359b
Niẓām-i Djadīd ii, 207a, 511b, 512a, b, 713a; iv, 322b; v, 35b, 907b — II, 213b, 524b, 525a, 731a; IV, 337a; V, 36b, 913a
Niẓām-i Wafā iv, 71b — IV, 75b
Niẓāmiyya i, 1051b, 1052b; ii, 1083a — I, 1083a, 1084a; II, 1108b
Niẓāmiyya (Čishtiyya) ii, 55a — II, 56a
Nizāmiyya (Dimashḳ) s, 197a — S, 197a
Niẓāmiyya madrasa (Baghdād) i, 901b, 902a; iv, 458a; v, 1126a, 1127a; s, 4b, 29b, 192a, b, 326a — I, 928b, 929a; IV, 478b; V, 1122b, 1123b; S, 4a, 30a, 193a, b, 325b
Nizāmiyya madrasa (Marw) s, 326a — S, 325b
Niẓāmiyya, Madrasa-yi ʿĀliya (Farangī Maḥall) s, 4b, 292a, 293a — S, 4a, 292a, 293a
Nizamuddin ii, 262b, 263a; iii, 442b — II, 270a, 271a; III, 457a
Nizār b. Maʿadd i, 544b; v, 894b — I, 562a; V, 901a
Nizār b. al-Mustanṣir i, 215b, 353a, 552b; ii, 170b, 857a, 858b; iv, 28a, 200a — I, 222a, 364a, 570a; II, 175b, 877a, 878a; IV, 30a, 208b
Nizārī i, 1233a; iv, 67b — I, 1270a; IV, 71a
Nizārīs i, 20b, 215b, 246a, b, 352b, 353a, 440a, 552b, 659a, 853b, 1052b, 1099b, 1126a, 1233a, 1254a, 1359b; ii, 64b, 98a, 170b, 859b, 882a, 1039a, 1040b; iii, 72a, 254a, 267b, 268a, 544b, 1169a; iv, 47a, 200a, 201b, 202a, b, 944a; v, 25b; s, 95b — I, 21b, 222a, 254a, 363b, 452b, 570a, 680a, 877b, 1084a, 1132b, 1160a, 1270a, 1292a, 1399b; II, 66a, 100a, 176a, 879a, 902b, 1063a, 1065a; III, 74b, 261a, 275b, 563b, 1197b; IV, 50a, 208b, 210a, b, 211a, b, 976b; V, 26b; S, 95a
- doctrine iv, 205a — IV, 214a
Nizhād iv, 785b — IV, 817a
Noah → Nūh
Nogai, Noghay i, 721b, 1000a, 1075b, 1189b, 1287a; ii, 25a, 44b, 89a; iv, 569b; v, 140b, 141a, 314b — I, 743b, 1031a, 1108a, 1224b, 1326b; II, 25b, 45b, 90b; IV, 592a; V, 143a, 144a, 314b
Noghai (Prince/le prince) i, 1107a, 1188b; ii, 44b, 610a; iii, 117a — I, 1140b, 1223b; II, 45b, 625b; III, 119b
Nógrad s, 171a — S, 171a
Noix → Djawz
Nokra ii, 91a — II, 92b
Nom → Ism
Nomadism(e) i, 872-892; iii, 1096a; iv, 263b, 1177b; v, 472b, 648a, 658a, 659a, 1197b — I, 896b-919a; III, 1122b; IV, 275b, 1211a; V, 475b, 652a, 663b, 1187b
Nonhera s, 325a — S, 324b
Noria → Nāʿūra
Nourriture → Ghidhā'; Ṭaʿām
Nové Zámky v, 259b, 260a, 261a; s, 171a — V, 257b, 259a; S, 171b
Nuʿaym → Naʿīm, Āl
Nuʿaym b. Ḥammād ii, 388a — II, 398b
Nuʿayma, Mikhā'īl i, 598a; v, 188b, 189b, 1254b, 1255a, b, 1256b — I, 617b; V, 186a, 187a, 1245b, 1246a, b, 1247b
al-Nuʿaymī, ʿAbd al-Ḳādir ii, 585b; s, 195b — II, 600a; S, 195b
Nuʿayr ii, 614a; iv, 88a — II, 629a; IV, 92a
Nūba i, 966a; ii, 127b, 131a, 940a; iv, 485b; v, 266b; 268a, 521b; s, 19b — I, 996a; II, 131a, 134b, 962a; IV, 506b; V, 264b, 265b, 525a; S, 19b
Nūbār Pasha ii, 696b; iii, 1194b — II, 714a; III, 1224b
Nubāta, Banū i, 665a — I, 686a
Nubāta b. Ḥanẓala al-Kilābī iv, 447a — IV, 467a
Nubia/Nubie → Nūba
al-Nudjabā' i, 95a; v, 995b — I, 97b; V, 991a
Nudjūm iv, 492a; v, 100b, 1024b — IV, 513a; V, 103a, 1020b
Nudjūm, Aḥkām al- i, 1101a; iii, 1063b — I, 1134b; III, 1090b
Nufayʿ b. Masrūḥ → Abū Bakra
Nufayla → Ibn Buḳayla
Nuffār i, 382b, 383a — I, 393b, 394a

Nūḥ i, 177a; iv, 528b; 609b; v, 421a — I, 182a; IV, 551b, 634b; V, 423a
Nūḥ → Djuḥā
Nūḥ b. Asad ii, 791a; iii, 1113b — II, 810a; III, 1140b
Nūḥ I b. Naṣr iv, 22b-23a, 24b; s, 35a — IV, 24b, 26a; S, 35a
Nūḥ II b. Manṣūr i, 985a; ii, 100a, 799a; s, 265b — I, 1015b; II, 102a, 817b; S, 265a
Nuḥās v, 964b, 966a, 967b, 970b, 977b — V, 968b, 970b, 973a, 977a
Nuit → Layl et Nahār
al-Nukabā' → al-Nudjabā'
Nukhayridjan ii, 197b — II, 203b
al-Nukkār i, 195b, 471b, 571a, 770b; ii, 16a, 184b, 459b, 526a, 1042a, 1070a; iii, 95b, 656a, b, 659a, b, 1040a, 1253b; v, 462a, 475b, 644a — I, 201b, 485b, 589b, 793b; II, 16b, 190b, 471a, 539a, 1066a, 1095a; III, 98a, 677a, b, 680a, b, 1066a, 1286a; V, 464b, 478b, 648b
al-Nukkārī → Abū Yazīd
Nuḳḳawī iv, 860b — IV, 893b
al-Nuḳrāshī iii, 1069a; s, 58a — III, 1095b; S, 58b
Nuḳṭawiyya iii, 600b; iv, 50a — III, 621b; IV, 52b
Nukūr s, 103a — S, 102b
Nukuz s, 97b, 420a — S, 97a, 420a
Nūl al-Aḳṣā v, 652a, b, 654a — V, 656a, b, 658a
al-Nuʿmān I (Lakhmid(e)) i, 196b; iv, 1133b; v, 633a — I, 202a; IV, 1165a; V, 637a
al-Nuʿmān II (Lakhmid(e)) v, 633a — V, 637a
al-Nuʿmān III (Lakhmid(e)) i, 73a, 196a, 452a, 728b, 1241a; ii, 241a, 354a; iii, 812a; iv, 1024b; v, 583b, 633b — I, 75a, 202a, 465a, 750a, 1279a; II, 248a, 363b; III, 835b; IV, 1056b; V, 588b, 637b
al-Nuʿmān, Abū Ḥanīfa (Ḳāḍī) ii, 859a, 861b; iii, 308a, 1084b; s, 70b, 402b — II, 879a, 881b; III, 317b, 1111a; S, 71a, 403a
al-Nuʿmān b. ʿAbd al-ʿAzīz iii, 1085a, b — III, 1111b, 1112a
al-Nuʿmān b. Bashīr al-Anṣārī i, 952b, 1078a; iii, 226b, 272b, 398a, 608b; iv, 1187b; v, 922b — I, 982a, 1110a; III, 233a, 280a, 410a, 629a; IV, 1220b; V, 928a
al-Nuʿmān b. Djasr iv, 820a — IV, 852b
al-Nuʿmān b. al-Mundhir → al-Nuʿman III (Lakhmid(e))
al-Nuʿmān b. Mundhir (Ghassānid(e)) ii, 1021a, b — II, 1045a
al-Nuʿman b. Thābit → Abū Hanīfa
al-Nuʿman al-Gharūr v, 634a — V, 638a
Nuʿmān Pasha → Köprülüzāde
Numāyish → Masraḥiyya
Numayr i, 551a — I, 568b
Numayr, Banū ii, 347b; iii, 228a — II, 357a; III, 235a
al-Numayrī, Djaʿfar v, 1065a — V, 1062a
Numidian v, 754b, 755a — V, 760b, 761a
Nūniyya iv, 668a — IV, 695b
Nūr Afzā (garden/jardin) s, 366b — S, 366a
Nūr ʿAlī Shāh i, 261b — I, 269b
Nūr Allāh b. Aḥmad al-Miʿmār iv, 507a — IV, 529a
Nūr Allāh Beg v, 462a — V, 465a
Nūr Allāh Shūshtarī i, 721a; ii, 380b; iii, 434a, 1152a; v, 54b — I, 742b; II, 391a; III, 448a, 1180a; V, 55b
al-Nūr Bey Muḥammad ʿAnḳara i, 1156b; ii, 123b — I, 1191a; II, 126b
Nūr Dawlat Girāy Khān iv, 723b — IV, 752b
Nūr al-dīn (deputy/représentant) iv, 500a — IV, 521b
Nūr al-Dīn (Khōdja dāʿī) → Satgur Nūr
Nūr al-Dīn Maḥmūd → Maḥmūd b. Zangī
Nūr al-Dīn Pasha iv, 873b — IV, 907a
Nūr-Djahān i, 253b, 686a, 1161a; ii, 380b; iv, 282a, 709a, 914b; v, 600b, 601a — I, 261b, 707a, 1196a; II, 390b; IV, 294a, b, 737b, 947b; V, 604b, 605a
Nūr Ḳuṭb-i ʿĀlam i, 1168a; ii, 51b; iii, 1003a — I, 1203a; II, 52b; III, 1028a
Nūr Muḥammad Alīzay i, 295b — I, 305a
Nūr Muḥammad Kalhorā i, 431b, 1192a — I, 443b, 1227b
Nūr Muḥammad Shāh iv, 202b; v, 26b — IV, 211b; V, 27a
al-Nūr al-Muḥammadī iii, 1240a; s, 411b — III, 1272a; S, 411b
Nūr Turk iii, 433b — III, 448a
Nūrbakhsh, Muḥammad i, 392b; iv, 48b; v, 301a; s, 423a — I, 404a; IV, 51b; V, 300b; S, 423b
Nūrbakhshiyya i, 392b; v, 301a, 604b; s, 366b, 423a, b — I, 404a; V, 300b, 608b; S, 366a, 423b
Nūrdjahān ii, 380b; s, 366b — II, 390b; S, 366a
al-Nūrī, Abu 'l-Ḥusayn iii, 1247a; iv, 990b — III, 1279a; IV, 1023a
Nūrī, Mīrzā → Bahāʾ Allāh; Ṣubḥ-i Azal
Nūrī, Shaykh Faḍl Allāh s, 110a — S, 109a
al-Nūrī b. Shaʿlān i, 483a; ii, 492b, 626a — I, 497b; II, 505a, 641b
Nūrī Pasha (Killigil) i, 191b, 1071a; ii, 701b — I, 197a, 1103a, b; II, 719b
Nūrī al-Saʿīd ii, 872b; iii, 521b, 522a; v, 1045a; s, 7a — II, 893a; III, 539b, 540a; V, 1041b; S, 6b
Nūristān i, 223b, 224b; iv, 409a; s, 237a — I, 230a, 231a; IV, 427a; S, 237a
Nūriyya (Cairo/Caire) s, 197a — S, 197a
Nūrzāy ii, 629a — II, 644b
Nuṣayb ii, 1029b — II, 1053a
Nuṣayr b. Ṣāliḥ al-Ibāḍī iii, 655a — III, 676a
Nuṣayriyya i, 134a, 470b, 471b, 688a, 832b, 1082a, 1098b, 1099b; ii, 358b, 994a, 1070b, 1094b; iv, 202a, 1133a; s, 207a, 364b — I, 138a, 484b, 485b, 709a, 856a, 1114b, 1131b, 1132b; II, 368a, 1017a, 1095a, 1120b; IV, 211a, 1164b; S, 206b, 364b
al-Nūshadjān b. Wahrīz s, 354b — S, 354b
Nūshirwān → Anūshi(a)rwān
Nushshāb iv, 799a — IV, 831b
Nūshtagin → Anūshtigin
al-Nushūʾ Abū Shākir s, 396a — S, 396b
Nushūr → Ḳiyāma
Nuṣrat al-Dīn Abū Bakr → Abū Bakr b. Pahlawān Muḥammad
Nuṣrat al-Dīn b. Khāmush i, 301a — I, 310b
Nuṣrat al-Dīn b. Ṣāḥib ʿAṭāʾ i, 243b — I, 250b
Nuṣrat al-Dīn Aḥmad Ibn Hazārasp iii, 337a, b, 1016a; v, 827a — III, 347a, b, 1041b; V, 833a
Nuṣrat al-Dīn Khāṣṣ-bek → Arslan Abīhī
Nuṣrat Khān i, 506b, 1192a; ii, 1124a; iv, 922a — I, 522a, 1227a; II, 1150b; IV, 955a
Nuṣrat Shāh (Bengal(e)) iii, 422b, 632a; v, 638b — III, 436a, 653a; V, 643a
Nuṣrat Shāh (Dihlī) ii, 270a — II, 278b
Nuṣratī iii, 119a — III, 121b
Nut → Djawz
al-Nuwayrī i, 595a, 794a, 1116b; iv, 334a, b, 485b; s, 43a, 128b — I, 614a, 817b, 1150a; IV, 349a, 506b; S, 43a, 128a
Nyitas i, 173a — I, 177b

O

Oath → Ḳasam
Oba v, 472a – V, 475a
Obat iv, 648b – IV, 675a
Obelisk/Obélisque → Misalla
ʿObhadya, ʿObhedel → ʿĪsāwiyya
Oblučica → Isakča
Observatory/observatoire → Marṣad
Océan Atlantique → al-Baḥr al-Muḥīṭ
Océan Indien → Baḥr al-Hind; Baḥr al-Zandj
Ocsónoba → Ukshūnuba
Oczakov → Özi
Oda ii, 1087b, 1088b – II, 1113a, 1114a
Odjaḳ i, 1256a, b, 1277b; ii, 1091a; iv, 167b; s, 409b – I, 1294a, b, 1317a; II, 1116b; IV, 174b; S, 409b
Odjaḳ bayt al-māldjîsî i, 1147b – I, 1182a
Odjaḳlîḳ i, 947b, 1267a – I, 977a, 1305b
Odon → Khotan
Ögedey (Mongol) i, 227a, 1105a, b; ii, 2a, b, 3a, 43a, 44a, 45b, 606a, 928b; iv, 584a, 612b; v, 38b, 858a – I, 233b, 1138b; II, 2a, b, 3a, 44a, 45a, 46b, 621a, 950a; IV, 607b, 637a; V, 39b, 865a
Oghlan → Ghulām(iv)
Oghul Ḳaymish ii, 45b – II, 46b
Oghur iv, 1172a, b – IV, 1205b
Oghurdjik Alp s, 280b – S, 280b
Oghuz → Ghuzz
Oghuz-Khān (Kaghan) ii, 1109a; iii, 115b, 314b; v, 125b – II, 1135a; III, 118a, 324a; V, 128a
Oghuznāme iii, 115a – III, 117a
Oirats ii, 44b; v, 595a – II, 45b; V, 598b
Öküz Meḥmed Pasha ii, 635a; iv, 970b – II, 651a; IV, 1002b
Okyar, ʿAlī Fethi ii, 432a; iv, 297b, 872b – II, 443b; IV, 310b, 906a
ʿÖlah → ʿUlah
Öldjeytu Khān → Uldjaytū Khudābanda
Olive (oil) → Zaytūn
Oman → ʿUmān
Omar Ali Saifuddin, Sultan Sir s, 152a – S, 152a
Omar, Ömer → ʿUmar
Omar Khayam → ʿUmar al-Khayyām
Omdurman i, 50a, 976a; v, 70a, 1249b, 1250b, 1251b – I, 51a, 1006a; V, 72a, 1240b, 1241b, 1242a
Omen → Faʾl
ʿÖmer Ḍiyāʾ al-Dīn s, 83a – S, 83a
Ömer Seyfettin → ʿUmar Seyf al-Dīn
Omo v, 522a, 523b – V, 526a, 527b
Oncle → ʿAmm; Khāl
One thousand and one nights → Alf layla wa-layla
Oneiromancy → Taʿbīr
Ong Khān i, 418b; ii, 42a, 571a, 1112b – I, 430b; II, 42b, 585b, 1138b
Onguents → Khiḍāb
Onirocritique → Taʿbīr
Opec/Opeac s, 241a
O.P.E.P./O.P.A.E.P. s, 241a
Oporto → Burtuḳāl
Opthalmology(ie) → ʿAyn
Or → Dhahab
Oran → Wahrān
Orbay → Ḥüseyin Raʾūf
Orda i, 1105a, 1106b; ii, 44a, 571b – I, 1138b, 1140a; II, 45a, 586a
Orenburg s, 245a – S, 245a
Öreng Timur → Urang Temür
Oreto → Urīt
Orientalistes, Société des s, 224a – S, 224a
Orkhān i, 175a, 318a, 348a, 468a, 468b, 994a, 1187a, 1229a, 1334a; ii, 337b, 443a, 686b, 722a, 982b, 1045a; iii, 212a; iv, 291b, 628a, 969a; v, 248b, 283b – I, 180a, 327b, 358b, 482a, 482b, 1024b, 1222b, 1265b, 1374a; II, 347b, 454b, 704a, 740b, 1005a, 1069a; III, 218a; IV, 304b, 653a, 1001a; V, 246b, 281b
Orkhan Seyfī s, 168a – S, 168a
Orkhan Welī Kanik s, 150a – S, 150a
Orkhon i, 1240a – I, 1277b
Orkîna Khātūn i, 418b; ii, 3a, b – I, 430b; II, 3a, b
Ōrmuṛī i, 225a, 1006b – I, 231b, 1037b
Ōrmuṛs i, 217a, 224a – I, 223b, 230b
Ornithomancy/Ornithomancie → ʿIyāfa, Ṭīra
Oromo → Galla
Orontes/Oronte → al-ʿĀṣī
Orta oyunu iv, 806b – IV, 839a
Ortaḳčî-ḳul ii, 1090b – II, 1116a
Oruč Owasî s, 239a – S, 239a
Orudj b. Timurtash ii, 599b – II, 614b
Örüg-Temür b. Ananda iv, 553b – IV, 577b
Oryx → Mahāt
Ösek → Eszék
Ösh ii, 791b – II, 810a
Osman → ʿUthmān
Osmanov Muḥammad v, 383a – V, 384a
Ossetes/Ossètes i, 354a, 837a, 1000a – I, 365a, 860a, 1031a
Ossetia/Ossétie iv, 349b – IV, 364b
Ossetic/Ossète (language/langue) iv, 351a, b – IV, 365b, 366b
Ostādh → Ustādh
Ostriches, The → al-Naʿāʾim
ʿOtba (ʿOtūb), Banū → ʿUtba, Banū
Otčigin ii, 2b – II, 2b
Otčigin-ājān iv, 499b – IV, 521a
Ötemish iv, 849b – IV, 882b
ʿOthmān I (Ottoman) i, 467b, 1191a; II, 710b, 715b; iv, 375a – I, 481b, 1226a; II, 727b, 734a; IV, 391a
ʿOthmān II (Ottoman) i, 395b, 1253b; ii, 183b, 277a, 713a; iv, 971a – I, 406b, 1291b; II, 189b, 285b, 731b; IV, 1003a, b
ʿOthmān III (Ottoman) i, 395b – I, 407a
ʿOthmān b. al-ʿĀs iv, 220a – IV, 229b
ʿOthmān b. Ertoghrul v, 256a – V, 254a
ʿOthmān Faḍlī iv, 191a – IV, 199b
ʿOthmān Ḥamdi Bey ii, 210a, 694b; iii, 993b – II, 216b, 712a; III, 1018a
ʿOthmān Khodja ii, 700b – II, 718b
ʿOthmān Nūrī → Ergin, Osman
ʿOthmān Pasha al-Kurdjī iii, 325a; v, 925b – III, 335a; V, 931a
ʿOthmān Pasha Özdemir-oghlu i, 697b; ii, 880b, 1046b; v, 249a, 270a – I, 719a; II, 901a, 1070b; V, 247a, 267b
ʿOthmān Pasha al-Ṣādiḳ s, 20b – S, 20b
ʿOthmāniyya → Erganī
ʿOthmānlî ii, 989b – II, 1012b
ʿOthmānlî Ḥürriyet Djemʿiyyeti iv, 284a – IV, 296b
ʿOthmānlî Ikhtilāl Fîrḳasî iii, 393a – III, 405b
ʿOthmānlî Ittiḥād we Teraḳḳī Djemʿiyyeti → Ittiḥād we Teraḳḳī Djemʿiyyeti
ʿOthmānlî Sosyalist Fîrḳasî iv, 123b – IV, 128b
ʿOthmān-zāde Tāʾib s, 83a – S, 83a
Otranto/Otrante i, 293a – I, 302a
Otrār ii, 43a, 778b – II, 44a, 797a
Ottoman Freedom Society → ʿOthmānlî Ḥürriyet Djemʿiyyeti
Ottomans i, 8a, 21b, 190a, 467a-468b, 640a, 767b, 791b, 808b, 942b, 998b, 1060b-1064b, 1119b, 1128b, 1218b, 1250b, 1252a, 1321a; ii, 286b, 345a, 634b, 710b, 1056b; iii, 88a, 1086b, 1183a; iv, 35a, b, 36b, 37b, 1156a; v, 493a, 494a, 716a, 726a, 739b, 974a – I, 8a, 122a, 194b, 481a-482b, 661a, 790b, 815a, 831b,

971b, 1029b, 1092b-1096b, 1153a, 1162b, 1254b, 1288b, 1290a, 1361b; II, 294b, 355a, 650b, 727b, 1081a; III, 90b, 1113a, 1212a; IV, 37b, 38b, 40a, 1188a; V, 496a, 497a, 721a, 731a, 745a, 975b
- administration i, 435b, 1159a, 1225b; ii, 118a, 146b, 230b, 313b-316a, 429b-433a, 562b-565b, 1085b-1091a; iii, 164a, 190b-193b, 211b-215b, 349a, 476a-480b, 489a, 552b, 997a; iv, 268a, 560a, 562b, 678b, 893b, 945b-947a, 1053b, 1094b; v, 249a, 334a, b, 878b, 1035a, 1082b — I, 448a, 1194a, 1262a; II, 121a, 150b, 237a, 323a-325b, 440b-444a, 576b-580a, 1111a-1117a; III, 167b, 195a-198a, 217b-221b, 360a, 492b-497a, 505b, 571b, 1022a; IV, 280a, 582b, 585a, 706b, 926b, 978a-979b, 1085a, 1125a; V, 247a, 334a, b, 884b, 1031b, 1080a
- architecture iv, 236a, 570a; v, 292a, b — IV, 246b, 593a; V, 292a
- education v, 902b — V, 908b
- history/histoire v, 814a — V, 820a
- literature/littérature ii, 587b; iii, 352a; iv, 527a, 877b, 878a, 1153a; v, 28a — II, 602a; III, 363a; IV, 550a, 910b, 1185a; V, 28b
Ouarou Ouari v, 281a — V, 279a
Ouarsenis → Wansharī
Oubangui-Chari s, 165b — S, 165a
Oudh → Awadh
Oued Nīnī iv, 422b — IV, 441a
Oued Saoura s, 328a — S, 327b
El-Oudiane ii, 464a — II, 476a
Oued → Wādī
Oudjda → Wadjda
Ould Dādda, Mukhtār v, 1074b, 1075a — V, 1072a, b
Ouled → Awlād
Ouolof → Djolof
Ourdou → Urdu
Oxus, river/fleuve → Āmū Daryā
Ōy iv, 1150b — IV, 1182b
Oymāḳ v, 243b, 245a — V, 241b, 242b
Oyrat → Kalmuks
Ozan i, 697b — I, 718b
Özbeg b. Pahlawān i, 353b; ii, 393a, 975b; iii, 1112a; s, 378b — I, 364b; II, 403b, 998a; III, 1139a; S, 378b
Özbeg Khān i, 908b, 1107a; v, 136b; s, 203b — I, 936a, 1140b; V, 139a; S, 203a
Özbegistan → Uzbekistan
Özbegs i, 8a, 46b, 47a, 135a, 148a, 224a, 227b, 228b, 406a, 530b, 839b, 847b, 852b, 1001b, 1066b, 1067b, 1107b, 1295b; ii, 44b, 792a; iii, 116b, 177b; iv, 35a, b, 36b, 186b, 1064b; v, 55a, 389a, 859a; s, 46a, 51a, 66a, 97a, b, 168b, 169a, 340a, 419b — I, 8a, 48a, 138b, 152a, 230b, 234b, 235a, 417b, 547a, 862b, 871a, 876b, 1032a, 1098b, 1100a, 1140b, 1335a; II, 45b, 811a; III, 119a, 181b; IV, 37a-b, 38b, 194b, 1096a; V, 56b, 390a, 866a; S, 46b, 51b, 66b, 96b, 97a, 169a, 339b, 419b
Özdemir-oghlī ʿOthmān Pasha → ʿOthmān Pasha
Özdemir Pasha iii, 4b, 11b; iv, 450a; v, 628a — III, 4b, 12a; IV, 470a; V, 632a
Özi iii, 252a; v, 103a — III, 259a; V, 105a, b
Özkänd ii, 791b — II, 810b
Özü i, 1287a — I, 1326b

P

Pādhūspān ii, 74b — II, 76a
Pādhūspānid(e)s → Bādūsbānid(e)s
Pādishāh Khātūn v, 162a, b, 553b — V, 160a, b, 558b
Padris War/Guerre des iii, 1222b — III, 1253b
Pādshāh ii, 806a — II, 825a
Pādshāh Bēgam i, 1161a; ii, 378b — I, 1195b; II, 389a
Paghmān s, 65b — S, 66a
Pahlavī ii, 1142b; iii, 113a, 1136b; iv, 40a — II, 1169b; III, 115b, 1164b; IV, 42b
Pahlavī (language/langue) v, 229a, 660b, 1112a — V, 226b, 666a, 1108a
Pahlavī Foundation → Bunyād-i Pahlavī
Pahlwān Bahādur ii, 30b — II, 31a
Pai Yen-hu v, 848a — V, 852a
Pain, le → Khubz
Pakhtūn → Pashto
Pakistan ii, 29b, 132a, 437a, 545b, 595a, 598a, 668b, 676a, b; iii, 385a, 409b, 440a, 532a, 564b; iv, 1b, 171a, 711a; v, 501a, 599a, 780b, 1081a; s, 220a, 327b, 331b, 332a — II, 30a, 135b, 448b, 559a, 610a, 613a, 685b, 693a, b; III, 397a, 422a, 454a, 550b, 584a; IV, 1b, 178b, 739b; V, 504a, 602b, 786a, 1078b; S, 220a, 327a, 331a, b
Palace/palais → Ḳaṣr
Palam (Dihlī) s, 206b — S, 206a
Palamaū i, 1210a — I, 1246a
Palangka Raya s, 150a — S, 150b
Palembang s, 150b, 200a, 201a — S, 150b, 200a; 201a
Palermo → Balarm
Palestine → Filasṭīn
al-Palimbānī → ʿAbd al-Ṣamad
Palm tree → Nakhla
Palmier → Nakhla
Palmoscopy/Palmomancie → Ikhtilādj
Palmyra/Palmyre → Tadmur
Pambak → Panbuk
Pāmir i, 454b, 853a, b; ii, 997b — I, 467b, 877a; II, 1020b
- language/langue → Ghalča
Pamir Agreement/Accord de i, 87b — I, 90a
Pamplona → Banbalūna
Pāmpūr s, 332a — S, 332a
Pamuk-ova → Aḳ Ḥiṣār
Pan-Islamism(e) iv, 164b; v, 310a — IV, 171b; V, 309b
Panāh ʿAlī Khān iv, 573a — IV, 595b
Panāhī i, 955b — I, 984b
Panbuk v, 557a — V, 561b, 562a
Pānč Pīr i, 868b — I, 892b
Panča (pantja) sīla ii, 663a; iii, 534b, 1230a — II, 679b; III, 553b, 1261b
Pančatantra i, 42a, 1359b; iii, 313b; iv, 503a, 506a — I, 43a, 1399b; III, 323a; IV, 525a, 528a
Pančāyat i, 758a, 978b; v, 1114b, 1115a — I, 780b, 1009a; V, 1111a
Pandačuk s, 333a — S, 332a
Pandārī ii, 156a — II, 160b
Pandj, river/fleuve i, 454b — I, 467b
Pandjāb i, 72a, b, 230a; ii, 426a, 1050b; iii, 443b; v, 886a; s, 21a, 63a, 66b, 203a, 241a, 367a — I, 74b, 237a; II, 437a, 1075a; III, 458a; V, 892a; S, 21a, 63b, 67a, 202b, 241b, 368a
Pandjābī iii, 1b; v, 610a — III, 1b; V, 614a
Pandjdih i, 87b — I, 90a
Pandjhīr, Pandjshīr i, 504a; v, 968b; s, 125b — I, 519a; V, 971b; S, 124b
Pandjpāw ii, 629a — II, 644b
Pāndvā iii, 444a — III, 458b

Pandjwāy iv, 536b – IV, 559b
Pāndū (Čak) s, 167a – S, 167a
Pānīpāt, battle of/bataille de (1526) i, 848a, 1068b; iii, 199b, 200a, 995b; v, 784a; s, 312a, 313a, 325a, 331b – I, 871b, 1101a; III, 204b, 205b, 1020b; V, 790a; S, 312a, 324b, 331a
- (1761) i, 296b, 1053a; iii, 61a – I, 305b, 1084b; III, 63b
Pānipātī, Niẓām al-Dīn s, 308b – S, 308b
Panjgūrī i, 1007a – I, 1038a
Pānka iv, 1160b – IV, 1193a
Pantelleria → Ḳawṣara
Paper money/papier monnaie → Ḳāʾime
Paper/Papier → Kāghad; Ḳirṭās
Papyrus i, 531b; ii, 307a; iv, 742a; v, 173b – I, 547b; II, 315b; IV, 772a; V, 171a
Para ii, 119b; s, 325a – II, 122a; S, 324b
Parāčī i, 224a, 225a; v, 649a – I, 230b, 231b; V, 653a
Paradise/Paradis → Djanna
Parakou ii, 94b – II, 96b
Paramāra ii, 218b – II, 225a
Parasang → Farsakh
Parasramdēv s, 242a – S, 242a
Parchment/Parchemin → Djild; Ḳirṭās; Raḳḳ
Parenté → Ḳarāba
Parfum → Ḳumḳum
Pariyān (river/rivière) v, 868a – V, 874b
Pardadār iii, 48b – III, 50b
Parendā i, 1323b – I, 1364a
Pargana i, 317a; ii, 156b – I, 326b; II, 161a
Parkent → Fārkat
Parliament/Parlement → Madjlis
Parmaḳ ḥisābî i, 677b – I, 698b
Paropamisus (Mountains/Monts) i, 221b; s, 367b – I, 228a; S, 367a
Parrot → Babbaghāʾ
Pārs → Fārs
Pārsī ii, 1124a; v, 1114a, b, 1115a, 1116a, 1117a – II, 1150b; V, 1110b, 1111a, b, 1112b, 1113b
Pārsiwāns i, 224a – I, 230b
Parsiyā → Bīr Sāl
Partai Sarekat Islam Indonesia iii, 1229b, 1230a – III, 1261b, 1262a
Parti politique → Ḥizb
Parti du renouveau → Tedjeddüd Fîrḳasî
Parwān → Farwān
Parwīn-i Iʿtiṣāmī iv, 71b; s, 110a – IV, 75b; S, 109b
Parwīz → Kisrā II
Parwīz (Parwez), Ghulām Aḥmad iv, 171a – IV, 178b
Parwiz b. Djahangīr i, 81a, 1331a; v, 1214a – I, 83b, 1371b; V, 1204a
Paryāb → Faryāb
Pasai, Pasè i, 742b; iii, 1218b; s, 199b – I, 764b; III, 1249b; S, 199b
Pās-i anfas ii, 55b – II, 56b
Pasargadae s, 129a – S, 128b
Pasarofča i, 269b; iii, 1002a; v, 641b – I, 277b; III, 1027a; V, 645b
Pasha i, 368a – I, 379a
Pashaī (language/langue) i, 225a; ii, 138b – I, 231b; II, 142b
Pashaīs i, 224b; iv, 410a; v, 356a, 649a – I, 231a; IV, 427b; V, 357b, 653a
Pasha-Yigit i, 654a, 1118a, b, – I, 674b, 1151b, 1152a
Pashang b. Yūsuf Shāh II v, 827b – V, 833b
Pashmaḳlik iv, 1095a – IV, 1125b
Pashto i, 217a, 220a, b, 1124a; ii, 31b, 101b, 1103b; iii, 1b; iv, 538a, 1102a; v, 72a, 356a; s, 41b – I, 223b, 226b, 227a, 1158a; II, 32a, 103b, 1129b; III, 1b; IV, 561a, 1133a; V, 74b, 357b; S, 41b
Pashtūn v, 72a; s, 367a – V, 74a; S, 368a
Pashtūnistān Movement s, 285b – S, 285a
Pasir s, 151a – S, 151a
Passarovitz → Pasarofča
Pastor → Ghanam
Paswan-oghlu ʿOthmān i, 398b, 778b, 1304a; ii, 971b; iii, 628a – I, 410a, 801b, 1344a; II, 994a; III, 648a
Patan i, 80b, 506b; ii, 1124a; iii, 444b – I, 83a, 522a; II, 1150b; III, 459b
Pate (island/île) iv, 885b, 886a, b; v, 655a, b; s, 351b, 355b – IV, 918b, 919b; V, 659a, 660a; S, 351b, 355b
Paṭhāns i, 216b, 218a, 769a, 864a; iii, 411a; s, 270a, 285a, 329b – I, 223a, 224b, 792a, 888b; III, 423b; S, 270a, 285a, 329a
Patiālā i, 1194b; ii, 488b; s, 66b – I, 1229b; II 501a; S, 67a
Patih Yūnus iii, 1219a – III, 1250a
Patna i, 1018a – I, 1049b
Patrai, Patras → Baliabadra
Pâtre → Ghanam
Patrona Khalīl i, 97a, 270b; iii, 1002b; v, 643a – I, 99b, 278b; III, 1027b; V, 647a
Patta → Pate
Paulus of/de Aigina s, 52a – S, 52b
Pawan (river/rivière) s, 150b – S, 150b
Pāyak iii, 199a; v, 686b – III, 204a; V, 691b
Pāygāh iv, 218a, b – IV, 227b, 228a
Payinda Khan i, 12b, 230b, 231a; ii, 637b – I, 14b, 237b, 238a; II, 653b
Paykand v, 853b – V, 860a, b
Paylāwagh s, 331b – S, 331b
Pʿaytarakan s, 116a – S, 115b
al-Pazdawī, Abū ʾl-Yusr iii, 163b, 164a, 1024a, 1165a – III, 167a, b, 1050a, 1193b
Pāzūkī → Bāzūkiyyūn
Pāzvandoghlu → Paswan-oghlu
Pazyryk s, 136b, 145a, 146a, 148a – S, 136a, 145a, b, 148a
Pearl → Djawhar; Durr; Farīd; Luʾluʾ
Pečeneg i, 607b, 1305b, 1307b; iv, 1175b, 1176b; v, 1011a, 1013b, 1014a, 1015b, 1016b, 1017a, b, 1018a – I, 627a, 1345b, 1348a; IV, 1208b, 1210a; V, 1006b, 1009b, 1011a, 1012b, 1013b, 1014a
Pečewī, Ibrāhīm i, 1286a; s, 171a – I, 1325b; S, 171b
Péché → Khaṭīʾa
Pedroche → Biṭrawsh
Pégon iii, 1234b – III, 1266b
Pekin → Khān Balîḳ
Pèlerinage → Ḥadjdj
Pemuda Pusa i, 745b – I, 768a
Pen (writing implement) → Ḳalam
Penang i, 979b – I, 1009b, 1010a
Penbe v, 558b, 559a – V, 563b, 564a
Penbox → Ḳalamdār
Penče i, 1357b; ii, 314b – I, 1397b; II, 323b
Pendjik ii, 210b, 1087a – II, 217a, 1112b
Penholder → Miḳlama
Péninsule Arabique → ʿArab, Djazīrat al-
Peñon iv, 1156b – IV, 1188b
People → Ḳawm
Pepene i, 1076b – I, 1108b
Pera → Beyoghlu
Pérez, Ivan → Ibrahim Taybilī
Perfume → Ḳumḳum
Pergamon → Bergama
Peri ii, 548a – II, 561b
Perim/Périm → Mayyūm
Periodicals/Périodiques → Djarīda
Perle → Djawhar; Durr; Farīd; Luʾluʿ
Permission → Idhn
Perovsk → Ak Masdjid
Persane (langue) I, 581b, 586b, 831a; II, 317b; III,

426b; V, 194b, 228a, 1091b, 1094a, 1099b
Persatuan Ulama-ulama Seluruh Atjèh i, 745b, 746b, 747b – I, 768a, 769a, 769b
Persepolis iv, 221a, b, 535b – IV, 230b, 231a, 558b
Persia/Perse → Irān
Persian (language) i, 563b, 568a, 807b; ii, 308b; iii, 413a, b; v, 197b, 230b, 1095a, 1098a, 1103b
Persian Gulf → Baḥr Fāris
Persian Tobacco Concession s, 53b, 54b
Pertev Pa<u>sh</u>a iv, 112b – IV, 117b
Pērūz <u>Sh</u>āpūr → al-Anbār
Pe<u>sh</u>āwar i, 223a, 238b, 282b, 970a; ii, 426b; iv, 196b; v, 251a; s, 41a, 237a – I, 229b, 245b, 291a, 1000a; II, 437b; IV, 205a; V, 248b; S, 41b, 237a
Pē<u>sh</u>dādī iv, 12b – IV, 13a
Peshwa s, 246b – S, 246b
Petančić, Feliks (Petancius) s, 185b – S, 186b
Peter the Great i, 268b, 269a, 270a, 394b, 808b; iii, 604a; iv, 1065a
Petroleum/Pétrole
- Gulf/Golfe iv, 752a, 778b, 1057a, 1171b; v, 40b, 573a – IV, 782b, 809b, 1088a, 1205a; V, 41b, 577b
- Irāḳ v, 146a – V, 148b
- Iran iv, 41b, 42b; v, 81a, 831b – IV, 44a, 45a; V, 83a, 837b
- Lībiyā v, 758b, 760b – V, 764b, 766b
Peul → Fulbe
Peuple → Ḳawm
Peyāmī Ṣafā v, 196b – V, 193b
Phalūṛā ii, 31a – II, 31b
Phanariot/Phanariote ii, 688b, 880a – II, 705b, 900a
Pharaoh → Firʿawn
Pharos iv, 132b, 133a – IV, 138b
Philadelphia (Anatolia/Anatolie) → Ala<u>sh</u>ehir
Philippines iii, 1219b – III, 1250b
Philoponus, John/Philopon, Jean → Yaḥyā al-Naḥwī
Philosophy/Philosofie → Ḥāl
Phlebotomist(e) → Faṣṣād
Pidië i, 744a, 745a – I, 766a, 767a
Pierre → Ha<u>dj</u>ar; Karkūr
Pierre le Grand I, 277a, 278b, 406a, 832a; III, 624b; IV, 1096b
Pierre Noire → al-Ḥa<u>dj</u>ar al-aswad
Pierres précieuses → <u>Dj</u>awhar; Durr; Luʾluʾ
Pig → <u>Kh</u>inzīr
Pigeon → Ḥamām
Pīl → Fīl
Pīla<u>kh</u>na s, 331b – S, 331a
Pilgrimage → Ḥa<u>dj</u>d<u>j</u>
Pīlībhīt iii, 60b – III, 63a
Pīl<u>kh</u>āna iv, 218b, 219b – IV, 228a, 229a
Pillars of Hercules → Ḳādis
Pindārī i, 1195b – I, 1230b
Pīr iii, 411b; iv, 202b, 206a – III, 424b; IV, 211b, 215b
Pīr Aḥmad b. Pa<u>sh</u>ang iii, 337a, b; v, 827b – III, 347b; V, 833b
Pīr Aḥmad Beg Ḳarāmān-og<u>h</u>lu iv, 624a, b – IV, 649a
Pīr ʿAlī ii, 486b – II, 498b
Pīr ʿAlī (Kart) → <u>Gh</u>iyā<u>th</u> al-Dīn Pīr ʿAlī
Pīr Budaḳ iv, 586b – IV, 609a, b
Pīr Ḥasan Beg iv, 584b, 586a – IV, 608a, b
Pīr Ḥusayn iii, 1208b – III, 1239a
Pīr Ḥusayn b. Sahat iv, 670a – IV, 697b
Pīr Meḥmed Wehbī <u>Kh</u>ayyāṭ ii, 878b – II, 898b
Pīr Muḥammad b. <u>Dj</u>ihāngīr i, 227a; ii, 1049b; iii, 417a; iv, 536b – I, 234a; II, 1074a; III, 430b; IV, 560a
Pīr Muḥammad <u>Kh</u>ān i, 1155a; ii, 815a; iii, 576a – I, 1189b; II, 834b; III, 596a
Pīr-<u>Sh</u>āh → <u>Gh</u>iyā<u>th</u> al-Dīn
Pīr Tārīk → Bāyazid Anṣārī
Pīr ʿUmar iv, 871a – IV, 904b
Pīrān i, 1217b – I, 1254a
Pirates → <u>Gh</u>uzāt al-baḥr; Kurṣān
Pîremêrd → Tewfīq, Hacî
Pīrī Beg b. Kalb ʿAlī Beg iv, 1045a – IV, 1076b
Pīr-i Kāmil i, 1121b, 1122a – I, 1155b, 1156a
Pīrī Meḥmed Pa<u>sh</u>a i, 293b; ii, 400a; iii, 341b; iv, 232a, 566a – I, 302b; II, 410b; III, 351b; IV, 242a, 588a
Pīrī Pa<u>sh</u>a s, 168b – S, 168b
Pīrī Reʾis i, 936b; ii, 588a, 590a; iv, 882a, 1082b – I, 965b; II, 602b, 604b; IV, 914b, 1113b
Pīrī-zāde Meḥmed Ṣāiʾb i, 286b – I, 295a
Pīrpanthis i, 173a – I, 177b
Pīrūzābād → Firūzābād
Pisar-i Kākū → ʿAlāʾ al-Dawla Muḥammad b. Du<u>sh</u>manziyār
Pī<u>sh</u>āwarī, Adīb iv, 789b – IV, 821b
Pī<u>sh</u>dādid(e)s iv, 809a – IV, 841b
Pī<u>sh</u>īn v, 579b, 580b – V, 584b, 585a
Pi<u>sh</u>kān (cape/cap) s, 332a – S, 331b
Pī<u>sh</u>ka<u>sh</u> ii, 150b, 152b; iii, 347b – II, 155a, 157a; III, 358a
Pī<u>sh</u>kūh iii, 1106a; v, 826a, 829b, 830a, b – III, 1133a; V, 832a, 835b, 836a, 837a
Pī<u>sh</u>pek ii, 67b – II, 68b
Pī<u>sh</u>tāḳ v, 599b, 600a – V, 603b, 604a
Pī<u>sh</u>yān ii, 106b – II, 109a
Pisḳopiye v, 265b – V, 263a
Pithorā Rāy → Prithvī Rā<u>dj</u>
Piyāle Pa<u>sh</u>a ii, 461a; iv, 233a, 571b; v, 304b – II, 473a; IV, 243a, 594b; V, 304a
Piyārē, <u>Sh</u>ay<u>kh</u> s, 313a – S, 312b
Plank/planche → Lawḥ
Plants/Plantes → Nabāt
Plaques → Kā<u>sh</u>ī
Plato/Platon → Aflāṭūn
Plomb → <u>Kh</u>ārṣīnī; Raṣāṣ
Plotinus/Plotin → al-<u>Sh</u>ay<u>kh</u> al-Yūnānī
Plough → Filāḥa; Miḥrā<u>th</u>
Plovdiv → Filibe
Pluie, rites de → Istisḳāʾ
Plume (pour l'écriture) → Ḳalam
Plumes, boîte à → Ḳalamdār
Plumier → Miḳlama
Poem/Poème → Ḳaṣīda
Poison → Aḳūnīṭun
Poitiers → Balāt al-<u>Sh</u>uhadāʾ
Poland (Leh) i, 4a, 1119b; iv, 178b, 179a, 516b, 590b; v, 139b, 140a, b, 260b, **719a**, 766a, b
Pole/pôle → al-Ḳuṭb
Polemon of/de Laodicea → Aflīmūn
Poley → Bulāy
Police → Karakol
Political parties → Ḥizb
Polo iv, 266a – IV, 278a
Pologne (Leh) I, 4b, 1153b; IV, 185b, 186a, 539a, 614b; V, 142b, 143a, 258b, **724a**, 772a, b
Polnyi Wakuf → Aḳ Ḥiṣār
Pomegranate (Blossom) → <u>Dj</u>ullanār
Pomaḳ i, 1000a, 1304a – I, 1030b, 1344a
Pont → <u>Dj</u>isr; Ḳanṭara
Pontianak s, 150a, b, 151a, 199b – S, 150b, 151a, 199b
Popalzāy i, 95b; ii, 629a – I, 98a; II, 645a
Porc → <u>Kh</u>inzīr
Porcupine/Porc-épic → Ḳunfu<u>dh</u>
Porphyry → Furfūriyus
Porsī s, 169a – S, 169a
Port Said s, 7b – S, 7a

Port Sudan/Soudan iv, 687b — IV, 715b
Porte → Bāb; Ḳapï
Porto-Novo ii, 93b, 94a, b; v, 279b — II, 95b, 96a, b; V, 277b
Portugal → Burtuḳāl
Portuguese/Portugais i, 56a, 139a, 199a, 244b, 286b, 506b, 553b, 604b, 689a, 706b, 809b, 914b, 932b, 942b, 945b, 946a, 1038b, 1088a, 1321a; ii, 27b, 322b, 367a, 572a, 586a, 1127b, 1128a; iii, 4b, 11a, 414a, 422a, 585a, 858b; iv, 552b, 886a; v, 360b, 938b, 1158a, 1190b — I, 57b, 143a, 205a, 252b, 295b, 521b, 571a, 624b, 709b, 727b, 832b, 942b, 961a, 971b, 974b, 975b, 1070a, 1131b, 1361b; II, 27b, 332a, 377a, 586b, 600b, 1154a, b; III, 4b, 12a, 427a, 435b, 605b, 882b; IV, 576b, 918b; V, 361b, 942a, 1147b, 1180b
Pot → Ibrīk
Potash/potasse → al-Ḳily
Pōthōhārī v, 611a — V, 614b
Potiphar → Ḳiṭfīr
Pottery/Poterie → Fa<u>kh</u><u>kh</u>ar
Poturnāk ii, 211b — II, 218a
Poudre → Bārūd
Poux → Ḳaml
Pozanti → Bozanti
Prang sabi i, 747a — I, 769a
Pratap Singh i, 426b; iv, 709b — I, 438b; IV, 738a
Pratīhāra ii, 1122b — II, 1148b
Prayāg → Allāhābād
Prayer → Ṣalāt
Precious stones → <u>D</u>jawhar; Durr; Luʾluʾ
Premčand iii, 458b; v, 204a — III, 474b; V, 201b
Prem-gāthā iii, 456b — III, 472b
Prenk Bib Doda i, 652a — I, 673a
Presse → <u>D</u>jarīda
Prester John/Prêtre Jean ii, 42a, 1143b; iv, 581b — II, 42b, 1170b; IV, 605a
Prière → Ṣalāt
Printing → Maṭbaʿa
Prithvī Rā<u>dj</u> i, 217b, 1194a; ii, 50a, 256a, 1122b; iii, 168a — I, 224a, 1229b; II, 51a, 263b, 1148b; III, 171b
Proclus → Buruḳlus
Profit → Kasb
Prostitution → Bi<u>gh</u>āʾ; Liwāṭ
Protection → <u>Kh</u>afāra
Proverb(e)s v, 480b — V, 483b
Prūmīyon iii, 963b — III, 988b
Psalms/Psaumes → al-Zabūr
Ptolemy/Ptolémée → Baṭlamiyūs
Puces → Bur<u>gh</u>ū<u>th</u>
Puit → Ḳanāt
Pul → Fulbe
Pular → Fula
Pulpit → Minbar
Pulūr v, 657b, 659b — V, 663a, 665a
Pulwar iv, 220b, 221b — IV, 230b, 231b
Punč-Bārāmūla s, 423b — S, 423b
Pun<u>dj</u>a ii, 1125a — II, 1151b
Puniāl s, 327b — S, 327a
Punishment → ʿA<u>dh</u>āb al-Ḳabr; Barza<u>kh</u>; ʿIḳāb; Ḳatl
Punjab → Pan<u>dj</u>āb
Purchase → Bayʿ
Pūr Dāʾūd iv, 789b — IV, 821b
Purification → Istin<u>dj</u>āʾ
Purnā (river/rivière) s, 279b — S, 279b
P.U.S.A. → Persatuan Ulama
Pu<u>sh</u>t-i Kūh iii, 1106a; v, 646b, 829b, 830a — III, 1133a; V, 650b, 835b, 836a
Pu<u>sh</u>to → Pa<u>sh</u>to
Pu<u>sh</u>tūn s, 237b — S, 237a
Putiphar → Ḳiṭfīr
Pyramid/Pyramide → Haram
Pythagoras/Pythagore → Fī<u>th</u>ā<u>gh</u>ūras

Q

Qasr → Ḳaṣr
Qassem → Ḳāsim
Qatar → Ḳaṭar
Qena → Ḳunā
Qiltu iii, 1259b — III, 1292a
Qom → Ḳumm
Quedah → Kĕdah
Quetta → Kwaṭṭa
Quiloa → Kilwa
Quilon → Kūlam
Quinsai → <u>Kh</u>ansā
Qwl → Ḳayl

R

Rabāb i, 1124a — I, 1158a
al-Raba<u>dh</u>a iv, 1144a; s, 198b — IV, 1175b; S, 198b
al-Rabaḍiyyūn iii, 1082b — III, 1109b
Rabāḥ b. ʿA<u>dj</u>ala i, 659b — I, 680b
Rabāḥ b. <u>D</u>janbulāt ii, 443b — II, 455b
al-Rabāḥī ii, 575a — II, 589b
Rabāṭ i, 34b, 35a, 79b, 832b, 1225a, 1226b, 1228a, 1320b; iii, 143b, 499a; v, 504b, 1245b; s, 144b, 223b — I, 35b, 81b, 855b, 1261b, 1264a, 1265a, 1361a; III, 146a, 516b; V, 507b, 1236b; S, 144a, 223b
- university/université ii, 425b — II, 436b
Rabb iv, 421b — IV, 439b
Rabbath, Edmund iv, 783a — IV, 814b
Rabeh i, 910b, 1260a; v, 358b — I, 938a, 1298b; V, 359b
al-Rabīʿ b. Dāʾūd i, 157b — I, 162a
al-Rabīʿ b. Ḥabīb al-Baṣrī iii, 651a — III, 672a
al-Rabīʿ b. Yūnus iii, 45b; iv, 1164a — III, 47a; IV, 1196a
Rabīʿ b. Zayd i, 628b — I, 649a
al-Rabīʿ b. Ziyād al-ʿAbsī s, 177b, 178a, b — S, 178b, 179a, b
al-Rabīʿ b. Ziyād al-Ḥāri<u>th</u>ī i, 1313a; iv, 14b, 356b; v, 57a, 157b — I, 1353b; IV, 15b, 372a; V, 58b, 157a
Rabīʿa, Banū i, 1a, 72b, 526b, 529b, 544b, 545b, 964b, 1029a, 1096b, 1158a; v, 537a; s, 122a — I, 1a, 74b, 542b, 545b, 562a, b, 994a, 1060b, 1129b, 1192b; V, 541b; S, 121b
Rabīʿa b. Abī ʿAbd al-Raḥmān ii, 888b, 1067b — II, 909a, 1092b
Rabīʿa b. Ḥāri<u>th</u>a v, 77a — V, 79b
Rabīʿa b. Kaʿb al-Aslamī i, 266b — I, 274b
Rabīʿa b. Muḳaddam i, 520a — I, 535b
Rabīʿa b. Riyāḥ al-Hilālī s, 92b — S, 92b
Rabīʿa b. Rufayʿ ii, 627a — II, 643a
Rābiʿa Ḳuzdārī iv, 61a — IV, 64b
Rabies → al-Kalab
Rābi<u>gh</u> iii, 362b — III, 374a
Rābiḥ (Bornu) → Rabeh
Rābiḥ b. Faḍl Allāh i, 1157a; v, 278b; s, 164b — I, 1191a; V, 276b; S, 164b
al-Rābiṭa al-Islāmiyya ii, 132a, 546a; iii, 532b, 534a, 1204b; iv, 793a — II, 135b, 559b; III, 551a, 552b, 1235a; IV, 825b
al-Rābiṭa al-Ḳalamiyya ii, 364a — II, 374a
al-Rābiṭa al-<u>Sh</u>arḳiyya s, 121b — S, 121a
Rabwah i, 302a — I, 311b

Radawlī → Rudawlī
Raḍḍiya Sulṭāna i, 1194a; ii, 120a, 267b, 973a, 1143b; iii, 14a, 433b,, 1156a — I, 1229b; II, 123a, 276a, 995a, 1170b; III, 15a, 448a, 1184a
Raden Patah iii, 1219a — III, 1250a
Raden Raḥmat → Sunan Ampel
Raden Trenggana iii, 1219b — III, 1250a
Rādhān, Nahr i, 184a — I, 189b
al-Radhāniyya i, 32a; ii, 817a; iii, 1044b; iv, 1088b — I, 33a; II, 836b; III, 1070b; IV, 1119b
al-Rāḍī, al-Sharīf → al-Sharīf al-Rāḍī
al-Rāḍī biʾllāh i, 19a, 866a, b, 1038a, 1298b; ii, 453b; iii, 46a, 127a, 159a, 345a, 346a, 902b; iv, 424a, 940b; s, 386a — I, 20a, 890a, b, 1069b, 1338b; II, 465a; III, 47b, 130a, 162b, 355b, 356b, 926b; IV, 442b, 973b; S, 386a, b
Raḍī al-Dīn al-Hanbalī v, 609b — V, 613a
Rāḍī al-Dīn, shaykh i, 954a — I. 983b
Rādī Kiyā, Sayyid ii, 194a; v, 603b; s, 363b — II, 200a; V, 607a; S, 363a
Radīf iv, 57a; v, 836a — IV, 60b; V, 842a
Raḍiyya Begum → Raḍḍiya Sulṭāna
Radiyya Sulṭān Bēgum (d./m. 1722) iv, 638a — IV, 664a
Radjʿā i, 51a; i, 79a; iv, 457a, 837a; v, 236a, 433b — I, 52b; II, 80a; IV, 477a, 870a; V, 234a, 436a
Radjā b. Ayyūb ii, 198a — II, 204b
Rādjā Aḥmad (Farukī) → Malik Rādjā
Rādjā ʿAlī Khān → ʿĀdil Shāh IV
Rādjā Bhādj → Bhōdja
Rādjā Bīrbal i, 229a; ii, 296b; iii, 457b — I, 236a; II, 304b; III, 473b
Rādjā Chait Singh i, 757a — I, 779b
Rādjā Dāhir i, 1068b; ii, 188a — I, 1100b ; II, 194a
Rādjā Djay Singh I, II → Djay Singh Sawāʾī
Rādjā Gaṇesh iii, 417b, 1003a — III, 430b, 1028a
Rādjā Har Datt i, 1300a — I, 1339b
Rādjā Kans ii, 51b — II, 52b
Rādjā Mān Singh i, 229a, 1210a, 1254a; ii, 296b; s, 333a — I, 236a, 1245b, 1292a; II, 304b; S, 332a
Rādjā Prithiwīrādj s, 325a — S, 324b
Rādjā Rām iii, 424b — III, 438b
Rādjā Shitāb Rāyʾ i, 702a — I, 723b
Rādjā Srī i, 1218b — I, 1255a
Rādjā Suhādeva s, 156a, 366a — S, 156a, 366a
Radjaʿa v, 892b, 894b — V, 899a, 900b
Radjab ʿAlī Beg Surūr, Mīrzā v, 202a — V, 199b
Radjab Dīwān-Begi s, 228b — S, 228b
Radjab Pasha v, 34b — V, 35b
Radjabiyya iii, 35a — III, 36b
al-Radjabiyyūn i, 95a — I, 97b
Radjaurī s, 324b — S, 324a
Radjaz i, 142a, 673b; ii, 246a, 1073a; iv, 80b, 714a — I, 146a, 694a; II, 253a, 1097b; IV, 84b, 742b
al-Radjdjāf v, 1250b, 1251a — V, 1241b, 1242a
Radjdjāla iii, 187a — III, 191a
Rādjī iii, 114b — III, 117a
Rādjpūts i, 208b, 252b, 913b; ii, 271b, 272a, 567a, 597b, 1122a; iii, 202a, 423b; v, 264b; s, 55b, 73b, 126b, 332a, 353b — I, 214b, 260b, 941b; II, 280a, 581a, 612a, 1148b; III, 207b, 437a; V, 262b; S, 56a, 74a, 125b, 331b, 353b
Rādjshāhī ii, 426b — II, 437b
Radloff iii, 116b — III, 119a
Radmān s, 22b — S, 22b
al-Rādūyānī, Muḥammad b. ʿUmar iv, 59b — IV, 62b
Raḍwā i, 536a; v, 433b — I, 552b; V, 436a
al-Raffāʾ iv, 936b — IV, 969b
Raffo i, 282a — I, 290b
Rāfiʿ b. Harthama i, 452b; ii, 191b; iv, 21a, b — I, 465b; II, 197b; IV, 23a
Rāfiʿ b. al-Layth ii, 1b; iii, 233b, 234a, 859b; iv, 16b, 17a, 658b; v, 45a, 711a, 855b — II, 1b; III, 240b, 241a, 859b; IV, 18a, 685a; V, 46b, 716a, 862a, b
Rāfiʿ b. Makkī b. Djāmiʿ iv, 337a, b — IV, 351b, 352a
Rafīʿ al-Daradjāt i, 1026a; ii, 810b — I, 1057b; II, 829b
Rafīʿ al-Dawla i, 914a, 1026a — I, 914b, 1057b
Rafīʿ al-Dīn Nāʾinī s, 23b — S, 23b
Rafīʿ al-Shān i, 914a, 1210a; ii, 379a — I, 941b, 1246a; II, 389b
Rāfiʿ al-Ṭahṭāwī → al-Ṭahṭāwī
al-Rāfiḍiyya iii, 308a; iv, 46b; v, 236a; s, 86a — III, 317b; IV, 49a; V, 234a; S, 86a
al-Rāfiʿī, Muṣṭafā Ṣādiḳ i, 598a; iii, 1018b — I, 617b; III, 1044a
Rafīḳ, Aḥmad → Aḥmad Rafīḳ
Rafīḳ Khān i, 87b — I, 90a
al-Rāfiḳa s, 48b — S, 49a
Rage, la → al-Kalab
al-Rāghib al-Iṣfahānī s, 172a — S, 173a
Rāghib Pasha i, 965b; iii, 157a, 269a — I, 995b; III, 160b, 277a
Raghiwa s, 103a — S, 102b
Ragrāga ii, 623a — II, 638b
Ragusa/Raguse i, 999a, 1266a; iv, 1055a; s, 183b, 184a, b — I, 1030a, 1305a; IV, 1086a; S, 185a, b
Raḥāmina iii, 300b — III, 310a
Raḥba s, 36a — S, 36b
al-Raḥbī iii, 693b — III, 715b
Raḥbiyyān s, 356a — S, 356a
Rāhdār, rāhdārī i, 151b, 156a, 861a — I, 156a, 160b, 885a
Rahdj al-ghār iv, 482b — IV, 503b
Raḥḥāṣiyya ii, 964a — II, 986a
al-Rāhib Anbā Buṭrus → al-Sanā al-Rāhib
Rāhib Ḳuraysh → Abū Bakr b. al-Mughīra al-Makhzūmī
Raḥīl v, 930b — V, 935a
Raḥīm i, 81b, 1084b — I, 84a, 1117a
Raḥīm Bakhsh ii, 187a — II, 193a
Raḥīm Ḳulī Khān s, 46a — S, 46b
Raḥīm Yār Khān → Bahāwal Khān
Rahīna iv, 488a — IV, 509a
Raḥma b. Djābir i, 928a; ii, 108b; iv, 751a, 765a; v, 508a, b — I, 956b; II, 110b; IV, 781b, 795b; V, 511b, 512a
Raḥmān i, 406b, 1084b — I, 418a, 1117a
Raḥmāniyya i, 371a; ii, 224a; iv, 362b, 993b — I, 382a; II, 231a; IV, 378a, 1026a
Raḥmat Allāh, shaykh ii, 54a — II, 55a
Raḥmat Allāh Khān ii, 316b — II, 326a
Raḥmat al-Nisāʾ Nawāb Bāʾī i, 913b — I, 941a
Raḥmī, Hüseyin iv, 284b, 285a, b, 932a; v, 195b — IV, 296b, 297b, 298a, 964b; V, 193a
Rahnamā, Zayn al-ʿĀbidīn iv, 166b — IV, 173b
Raḥraḥān v, 640a, b — V, 644b
Rāhu ii, 502a — II, 514b
al-Rāʿī i, 196a; ii, 245a; s, 24b — I, 201b; II, 252a; S, 24b
Raid → Ghazw
Railway, trans-Iranian iv, 40b
Rainbow → Ḳaws Ḳuzaḥ
Rain-making → Istisḳāʾ
Raʾīs iv, 474b; v, 1131b — IV, 495b; V, 1127b
Raʾīs Ahl Naghd → Adjwad b. Zāmil
Raʾīs al-balad i, 256a, 975b, 976a, 978a — I, 264a, 1006a, b, 1008b
Raʾīs baʿthat al-ḥādjdj i, 443b — I, 456b
Raʾīs Ḥāmid i, 928a — I, 956a
Raʾīs al-Kuttāb → Reʾīs ül-Küttāb
Raʾīsiyya ii, 29b; v, 154a — II, 30a; V, 155a
Raʾiyyet resmi i, 1169b — I, 1204b

Rajāʾ b. Ḥaywa v, 325b — V, 325a
Rajputana iv, 922a — IV, 955a
Raḳam ii, 803a, b — II, 822a, b
Rakāsh, Banū i, 2b — I, 2b
Raḳāshīs iv, 734b — IV, 764a
Rakhīk, Awlād iv, 637b — IV, 664a
al-Raḳīm i, 691a — I, 712a
Rāḳiṣa ii, 1048a — II, 1072b
Raḳḳa (ceramic/céramique) iv, 1167b, 1168a — IV, 1200a, 1201a
al-Raḳḳa i, 11a, 457b, 831b; iii, 1268a; s, 36a, 413b — I, 11a, 472a, 854b; III, 1301a; S, 36b, 414a
Raḳḳāda i, 24a, 250b, 1346a; ii, 955b; iv, 829a, 830b; s, 144a — I, 25a, 258a, 1386b; II, 978a; IV, 862a, 863b; S, 144a
al-Raḳḳī → Aḥmad al-Raḳḳī
al-Raḳḳī → al-Muḳammiṣ
al-Raḳḳī, Sulaymān b. Djarīr s, 130a — S, 129a
Rákoczy, George (II) v, 257b, 258a, b — V, 255b, 256b
Ram (Aries) → Mintaḳat al-Burūdj; Silāḥ
Rām Dās i, 454a — I, 467b
Rām Narăyan ii, 1091b — II, 1117a
Rām Rāy i, 1047a; iii, 626a — I, 1079a; III, 646b
Rama Čandra iv, 922a, b — IV, 955a, b
Ramaḍān i, 265a; iii, 379b — I, 273a; III, 391a
Ramaḍān, Saʿīd iv, 160a — IV, 167a
Ramaḍān-oghlu i, 182b, 183a, 468b, 790a; ii, 38b; iv, 623a — I, 187b, 188a, 482a, 813a; II, 39a; IV, 647b
Rāmadeva, Rādja iv, 419a, b — IV, 437a, b
al-Ramādī i, 601b; v, 744a, 779a — I, 621a; V, 749a, 785b
al-Rāmahurmuzī iii, 27a — III, 28a
Ramal iii, 883a — III, 907a
Rămāyana i, 856b — I, 880b
Rāmčandra s, 366a — S, 366a
Rāmdjird v, 868a — V, 874b
Rāmhurmuz s, 90a — S, 90a
Rāmī Meḥmed Pasha i, 394b; iv, 657b — I, 406a; IV, 684a
Rāmk i, 1217b — I, 1254a
Raml ii, 220b, 761b; iv, 1128b; v, 943a — II, 227b, 780a; IV, 1160a; V, 947a
Ramla, rimāl i, 537a — I, 553b
Ramla i, 618b, 1030a; ii, 483b, 911a; iii, 287b; v, 326a, 328a, 329a, 799b, 800b; s, 20b, 37a — I, 637b, 1061b; II, 495b, 932b; III, 296b; V, 325b, 327b, 329a, 805b, 806b; S, 20b, 37b
al-Ramlī iii, 779a — III, 802b
al-Ramlī, Malik iv, 604a — IV, 628a
Ramm iii, 1096b; v, 450b — III, 1123b; V, 453a
Ramm, Djabal i, 169b — I, 174a
Rāmpūr i, 218a; s, 73b, 292a, b — I, 224b; S, 74a, 292a
Rāṇā Kumbha iii, 418b — III, 431b
Ranbīr Singh iv, 709b — IV, 738a
Rañčī s, 106b — S, 106a
Rançon → Fidāʾ
Rand, Banu 'l- iv, 415b, 416b; v, 1181b — IV, 434a, b; V, 1171b
Randjit-dēv s, 242a — S, 242a
Randjīt Singh i, 230b, 432b, 454b, 1020a, 1347b; ii, 47b, 186b, 929a, 1131a; iii, 336a; iv, 196b, 709b; v, 353b, 599a; s, 242a, 332a — I, 237b, 445a, 467b; 1051b, 1388a; II, 48b, 192b, 950b, 1157b; III, 346a; IV, 205a, 738a; V, 354b, 602b; S, 242a, 331b
Rangīn Maḥal i, 1047a, b — I, 1079a, b
al-Rānīrī, Nūr al-Dīn i, 88a, 742a; iii, 1220a, 1233a, 1234a — I, 91a, 764a; III, 1251a, 1265a, 1266a
Ransom → Fidāʾ
Ranya i, 538a — I, 554b
Rāo Pahāṛ Singh iii, 61b — III, 64a
Raʾs ʿAsīr → Guardafui
Raʾs ʿAyn i, 789a; iv, 898a — I, 812b; IV, 930b
Raʾs al-Djibāl → Musandam
Raʾs al-Khayma i, 928a; iv, 777b; v, 508a, 765a; s, 416b — I, 956b; IV, 808b; V, 511b, 771a; S, 417a
Raʾs al-Khums → Raʾs al-rubʿ
Raʾs māl i, 1112b — I, 1146a
Raʾs al-rubʿ v, 23b — V, 24a
Raʾs al-tīn (palace) s, 301a — S, 300b
Raʾs al-Wādī i, 1171b — I, 1207a
Rasāʾil al- Ḥikma ii, 633a — II, 649a
Raṣāṣ v, 964b, 967a — V, 969a
Rashahr i, 451a — I, 464a
Rashāyida iii, 642a — III, 663b
Rashīd s, 18a — S, 18a
al-Rashīd (Abbāsid(e)) (786-809) → Hārūn al-Rashīd
al-Rāshid (Abbāsid(e)) (1135-36) i, 353b; iii, 1255b — I, 364a; III, 1288b
al-Rashīd (Almohad(e)) → ʿAbd al-Wāḥid II al-Rashīd
Rāshid (Idrīsid(e)) iii, 1031a, 1032a — III, 1057a, b
Rashīd, Āl i, 554b, 1313a; ii, 176b, 492b; iii, 1066a; iv, 717b, 1073a, 1142b; v, 574b; s, 3b, 305a — I, 572b, 1353a; II, 182a, 505a; III, 1092b; IV, 746a, 1104b, 1174a; V, 579a; S, 305a
Rāshid, Banū iv, 481b; s, 145a, 350b — IV, 502b; S, 144b, 350b
al-Rashīd, Mawlāy i, 355b; ii, 510a, 819b, 823a; iv, 729b; v, 1191b; s, 223b, 377b — I, 366b; II, 522b, 839a, 842b; IV, 758b; V, 1181b; S, 223b, 377b
Rashīd b. Ḥumayd s, 42a — S, 42b
Rāshid b. Maṭar al-Ḳāsimī iv, 777b — IV, 809a
Rāshid b. Mughāmis iii, 1257a; iv, 764b; s, 234b — III, 1289b; IV, 795a; S, 234b
Rashīd b. al-Naḍr iii, 757a — III, 780a
Rāshid b. Saʿīd iii, 653b — III, 674b
Rāshid b. Saʿīd al-Maktum s, 418b — S, 418b
Rashīd ʿAlī al-Gaylānī (Kīlānī) iii, 264a, 521b, 522a, b, 1258b; s, 69a — III, 271b, 539b, 540a, b, 1291b; S, 69b
Rashīd al-Dawla Maḥmūd iii, 86a, 790a; v, 924a — III, 88b, 813b; V, 929b
Rashīd al-Dīn Faḍl Allāh Ṭabīb i, 595a, 1011a; ii, 334a, 1043b, 1109b; iii, 57b, 122a, 215b, 1045a, 1089b, 1122b; iv, 31b, 975b, 1035b, 1037a; s, 280b — I, 614b, 1042a; II, 343b, 1067b, 1135b; III, 60a, 124b, 221b, 1071a, 1116a, 1150a; IV, 34a, 1008a, 1067a, 1069a; S, 280b
Rāshid al-Dīn Sinān i, 353b; iv, 206a — I, 364b; IV, 215a
Rashīd al-Dīn Waṭwāṭ iv, 62a, 267b; v, 902b; s, 240a — IV, 65a, 279b; V, 908b; S, 240a
Rāshid Efendi iv, 845a, 874a — IV, 878b, 907b
Rashīd Khān i, 1124a — I, 1158a
Rashīd Muḥammad Pasha → Muḥammad Rashīd Pasha
Rashīd Pasha, Muṣṭafā i, 284b, 309b, 396b, 397b, 505b, 1089b; ii, 693a, 934b; iii, 592a, 993a; v, 36a, b; s, 168a — I, 293a, 319a, 408a, b, 520b, 1122a; II, 710b, 956b; III, 612a, 1017b; V, 37b; S, 168a
Rashīd Riḍā i, 46a, 598a; ii, 170b, 294b, 295b, 451b, 466b; iii, 162b, 520b, 1168b; iv, 142a, b, 143b-149a, 159a, 162b, 775b, 782b, 947a; s, 151a, 248a — I, 47a, 617b; II, 176a, 302b, 303a; 463a, 478b; III, 166a, 538b, 1197b; IV, 148a, 149b-155a, 165b, 169b, 807a, 814a, 979b; S, 151a, 248a
Rāshid Rustum s, 224b — S, 224b
Rashīdī s, 65a — S, 65b
al-Rashīdī, Muḥammad Gūlēd s, 279a — S, 278b
al-Rashīdiyya s, 279a — S, 278b
Rāshidūn iii, 1164a, 1168b; iv, 937b — III, 1193a, 1197b; IV, 970b

Rasht ii, 1111a; iv, 7b, 631a; s, 91b — II, 1137a; IV, 8b, 656b; S, 91b
Rashtī, Ḥabīb Allāh s, 76a — S, 76a
Rāshṭrakūṭa → Balharā
Rashwa iii, 343b — III, 354a
Rāsim, Aḥmad → Aḥmad Răsim
Rasmī → Aḥmad Rasmī
Rass iv, 412a — IV, 430a
al-Rass i, 252a, 634b; v, 397a, 441b; s, 116a, 274b — I, 259b, 655a; V, 398a, 444a; S, 115b, 274b
Raṣṣās i, 762b — I, 785b
Rassid(e)s i, 403a — I, 414b
Rasūl v, 423b — V, 425b
Rasūlid(e)s i, 552b, 553a, 803b; iv, 1188b; v, 895b, 1241a; s, 338a, 387b — I, 570b, 828a; IV, 1221b; V, 901b, 1231b; S, 338a, 388a
Rat → Djuradh
Ratan, Bābā Hādjdjī i, 1194b — I, 1230a
Raṭhors i, 769a; ii, 567a; iv, 93a; s, 55b, 420b — I, 792a; II, 581a; IV, 97a; S, 56a, 421a
Rattle → Nāḳūs
Raʾūf, Muḥammad → Muḥammad Raʾūf
Rauf Bey i, 836b; ii, 6b — I, 859b; I I, 6b
Raʾūf Pasha iii, 4b; v, 36b — III, 5a; V, 37b
Ravi s, 63a — S, 63b
Ravza → Khuldābād
Rawāfiḍ i, 257b, 864a; ii, 605a — I, 265b, 888a; II, 620a
Rāwal Rāy Singh ii, 186a — II, 192a
Rāwalpindi, Treaty of/Traité de s, 66a — S, 66a
Rawān iv, 732b — IV, 762a
Rāwandān i, 239a — I, 246b
al-Rāwandī, Maḥmūd b. Muḥammad iv, 1074a — IV, 1105b
Rāwandiyya i, 15b, 17b; iv, 45b, 837b — I, 15b, 18a; IV, 48a, 870b
Rawḍ al-Ḳirṭās ii, 818a — II, 837b
al-Rawda i, 944b — I, 973b
al-Rawḍa iv, 424b, 430a; s, 120b — IV, 443a, 448b; S, 120a
Rawḍakhwān iv, 50b — IV, 53a
Rawḍat al-ṣafā ii, 922a — II, 943b
Rawḥ b. Ḥātim iii, 655a; v, 69b — III, 676a; V, 71b
Rawḥ b. Zinbāʿ al-Djudhāmī i, 436a, 1242b; ii, 360b, 573b; iii, 270b, 1175b — I, 448b, 1280b; II, 370a, 588a; III, 278b, 1204a
Rawī (rhyme letter/lettre de la rime) iv, 412a, 413a — IV, 430a, 431a
Rāwī (raconteur) i, 566b, 584b; iv, 735a — I, 584b, 603b; IV, 765a
Rāwīnī s, 83a — S, 83a
Rawḳ iii, 99a, 863a, 1090a; iv, 557b — III, 101b, 887a, 1116b; IV, 581b
Rāwnīr s, 83a — S, 83a
al-Rawshan i, 1239b — I, 1277a
Rawshaniyya i, 1123b — I, 1157b
Rawthers v, 582a — V, 587a
Rawwādid(e)s i, 190a, 300a, 638a; iv, 346a — I, 194b, 309b, 658b; IV, 360b
Ray → Rayy
Raʾy i, 276a, 692a, 730a; ii, 182b, 886a; iv, 153b, 948b — I, 284b, 713a, 752b; II, 188a, 906b; IV, 160a, 981b
al-Raʾy al-mushtarak i, 341b — I, 352a
Rāya → Liwāʾ
Rāyčūr iii, 425a, b — III, 438b, 439a
Raydān al-Saḳlabī i, 1042a; iv, 1091b — I, 1073b; IV, 1122b
al-Raydāniyya iii, 184b — III, 189a
Raydūn iii, 31a — III, 32b
Rayḥān, Imād al-Dīn ii, 609b, 1084a — II, 624b, 1109b
Rayḥān, Muʾayyid al-Dīn v, 159a, 160a — V, 158a, b
Rayḥāna v, 436b — V, 439a
al-Rayḥānī, Amīn i, 597a — I, 616b
Rāyin s, 327a — S, 326b
Raymond II of/de Tripoli, Count/Comte s, 204b — S, 204b
Raysūlī i, 1281b — I, 1320b
Rayṭa i, 107b; iv, 1164a — I, 110b; IV, 1196a
Rayy i, 125b, 1356a; ii, 127a, 190a, 191a, 192b, 746a; iii, 219b, 287a; iv, 465b, 1167a; v, 661b, 662a, 1028b, 1137b, 1238a; s, 13a, 15a, 23b, 32a, 33a, 56b, 72b, 118b, 236a, 297b, 309a, 356b, 357a, 416a, 423b — I, 129a, 1395a; II, 130b, 196a, 197b, 198b, 764b; III, 226a, 296a; IV, 486a, 1199b; V, 667a, 1024b, 1132a, 1229a; S, 13b, 15a, 24a, 32a, 33a, 57a, 72b, 118a, 236a, 297b, 309a, 356b, 357a, 416a, 423b
Rayyān b. al-Aslaʿ s, 178b — S, 179b
al-Rayyān b. al-Walīd ii, 917b — II, 939a
Rayyo, Djabal i, 489a — I, 503b
Razbār i, 261a — I, 269a
Razgrad → Hezārghrad
al-Rāzī → Fakhr al-Dīn; Abū Ḥātim; Abū Muhammad; Ḳuṭb al-Dīn
al-Rāzī, Abū ʿAbd Allāh → Fakhr al-Dīn al-Rāzī
al-Rāzī, Abū Bakr Muḥammad i, 112a, 125b, 213b, 235a, 327b, 328a, 344b, 387b, 486a, 589b, 1223b, 1224a, 1340b; ii, 359a, 780b, 1068a; iii, 328b, 944b; iv, 329b, 847a; v, 112a, 167b; s, 14a, 52b, 271b, 314a, 392b — I, 115a, 129a, 220a, 242a, 337b, 338a, 355a, 399a, 500b, 608b, 1260a, b, 1380b; II, 368b, 799b, 1092b; III, 338b, 969a; IV, 344a, 880b; V, 114b, 165a; S, 14b, 53a, 271a, 313b, 393a
al-Rāzī, Aḥmad i, 156b, 381a, 488a, b, 489b, 600b; iii, 771b; iv, 718a — I, 160b, 392a, 502b, 503a, 504a, 620a; III, 795a; IV, 747a
Razīn, Banū s, 80b — S, 80b
Razmak s, 285a — S, 285a
Razmārā, Ḥādjdjī ʿAlī ii, 882b; iv, 41a — II, 903a; IV, 43b-44a
Reading → Ḳirāʾa
Reʿāyā i, 712a, 999b, 1169b, 1266b; iv, 563a, 564a, 565a, 1096a; v, 262a, 880b — I, 733b, 1030a, 1204b, 1305b; IV, 585a, 586b, 587b, 1126b; V, 260a, 886b, 887a
Recitation → Ḳirāʾa
Reconquista i, 494a, 495a, 496a; v, 367b — I, 508b, 510a, 511a; V, 368b
Red Sea → Baḥr al-Ḳulzum
Redjāʾīzāde Maḥmūd Ekrem → Ekrem Bey
Redjeb Agha i, 175a — I, 179b
Redjeb Pasha iii, 252a — III, 259a
Reed → Ḳaṣab
Refet Pasha i, 836b; iv, 636a — I, 859b; IV, 662a
Refīʿ Djewād iv, 873b — IV, 907a
Reform/réforme → Iṣlāh
Register/Registre → Daftar; Sidjill
Rehanina → Raḥāmina
Reʾīs ül-Küttāb i, 433a — I, 445b
Reʾīs al-aṭibbāʾ iii, 340a — III, 350a
Reʾīs al-ʿulamāʾ i, 1274a, b — I, 1313a, b
Reji iv, 930b — IV, 963b
Rēkhtī iii, 1244b — III, 1276b
Reliure → Kitāb
Renewal party → Tedjeddüd Fîrḳasî
Republic/République → Djumhūriyya
République arabe unie → al-Djumhūriyya al-ʿarabiyya al-muttaḥida
Reshād Nūrī Güntekin v, 196b; s, 96a — V, 193b; S, 95b
Reshīd → Rashīd
Resim yazî iv, 1126b — IV, 1158a
Resmī → Aḥmad Rasmī
Resm-i filori ii, 915a — II, 936a

Resm-i ḳismet iv, 735b — IV, 765a
Resurrection → Ḳiyāma
Reth ii, 828a — II, 847b
Retranchement → Burdj
Retreat/Retraite → Khalwa
Rêve → Taʿbīr; al-Ruʾyā
Reverter → al-Ruburtayr
Révolte Arabe I, 47a; II, 297b, 892b; III, 271a, 664b
Révolte indienne → Mutiny/Mutinerie
Rewān i, 8a, 640a, 643a, 644a, 645a, b; s, 365a — I, 8a, 661a, 664a, b, 665b, 666a; S, 365a
Rey Lobo → Ibn Mardanīsh
Reynald iv, 483a, b — IV, 504a
Rezā Shāh → Riḍā Shāh Pahlawī
Rezzā → Muḥammad Riḍā
Rezzou → Ghazw
Rḥa ii, 510b — II, 523b
Rhapsodomancy/Rhapsodomancie → Ḳurʿa
Rhinoceros → Karkaddan
Rhodes i, 293a, 935b, 945b, 1250b; ii, 6a; iv, 1169b; v, 506b; s, 222a — I, 302b, 964b, 974b, 1288b; II, 6a; IV, 1202b; V, 510a; S, 222a
Rhyme → Ḳāfiya
Rhythm → Īḳāʿ
Riʿāyat Shāh → ʿAlāʾ al-Dīn
Ribā i, 693b, 1111b, 1112b; iv, 691b — I, 715a, 1145a, 1146a; IV, 719b
al-Ribāb ii, 71b — II, 72b
al-Ribāb (Ḳayna) s, 247a — S, 247a
Ribāṭ i, 50, 248b, 901b, 1023b; ii, 36a, 539b; iii, 499a; iv, 380b, 434a, 677a, 1026a; v, 856a, 1129b, 1150a — I, 5b, 256a, 929a, 1055a; II, 36b, 553a; III, 516a; IV, 397a, 453a, 705a, 1058a; V, 863a, 1125b, 1140b
Rice → Ruzz
Richard I, Coeur-de-Lion i, 197b, 341a, 662b, 711a; ii, 163a; iii, 474a; iv, 842a; v, 303a — I, 203b, 351b, 683b, 732b; II, 168a; III, 490b; IV, 875a; V, 302a
Ridāʾ (garment/vêtement) iii, 1053a — III, 1079a
Riḍā, Imām s, 75b, 365a — S, 76a, 365a
Riḍā Khān Ḳādjar → Riḍā Shāh Pahlawī
Riḍā Kirmānī, Mīrzā s, 53b — S, 54a
Riḍā Ḳulī Khān iv, 1065a; v, 103a — IV, 1096b; V, 105a
Riḍā Ḳulī Khān (poet/poète) iv, 70a, 526b; s, 46b — IV, 73b, 549b; S, 47a
Riḍā Ḳulī Khān Ḳādjār iv, 391a; v, 312a, 663b — IV, 407b, 408a; V, 311b, 669a
Riḍā Ḳulī Mīrzā iv, 393a; s, 290b — IV, 409b; S, 290a
Riḍā-i ʿAbbāsī i, 1213b — I, 1249b
Riḍā (Rizā) Nūr iii, 595a; iv, 113a, 791b, 872b — III, 615b; IV, 118a, 823b, 906a
Riḍā Shāh Pahlawī i, 5b, 190b, 720b, 978a, b, 1014a; ii, 445b, 514b, 654a, 903a, 1112a; iii, 528b, 1110a, 1193a; iv, 40a, b, 52a, 398b, 789b, 1172a; v, 826a, 920a, 1042b, 1095a, b; s, 84a, 91b, 110a, 207b, 342b — I, 5b, 196a, 742a, 1008b, 1045a; II, 457b, 527b, 670b, 924a, 1138a; III, 547a, 1137a, 1223a; IV, 42b, 43a, 55a, 416a, 821b, 1205a; V, 832b, 925b, 1038b, 1092a; S, 83b, 91b, 109b, 207b, 342a
Ridda i, 110b, 683b, 728a, 964a — I, 113b, 704b, 749b, 993b
Riddles → Bilmedje
Ridf iv, 412a — IV, 430a
Ridjāl iv, 711b — IV, 740a
Ridjāl al-ghayb i, 94b, 772a; ii, 1025b — I, 97b, 795a; II, 1049b
Riḍwān (angel/l'ange) ii, 846a, b — II, 866a, b
Riḍwān (ḥādjib) iii, 836a — III, 859b
Riḍwān b. Muḥammad al-Sāʿātī s, 371b, 372b — S, 371b, 372a
Riḍwān b. Tutush i, 664a, 1052a; ii, 169b, 282a; iii, 86b, 398b; v, 921b, 924a, b — I, 683b, 1083b; II, 175a, 290a; III, 89a, 411a; V, 927a, 929b, 930a
Riḍwān b. Walakhashī i, 939b; ii, 858a, b; iii, 55a; iv, 137a; v, 627b — I, 968a; II, 877b, 878b; III, 57a; IV, 142b; V, 631b
Riḍwān Bannigash (Banegas) s, 399a — S, 399a
Riḍwān Begovič i, 1268b — I, 1307b
Riḍwān Bey ii, 233a; iv, 723a — II, 240a; IV, 752a
Riḍwān Kāhya al-Djulfī iv, 852b — IV, 885b
Rīf i, 749b, 859b; ii, 820b; iii, 499b; v, 1184b, 1185b, 1194a; s, 191a, 377b — I, 771b, 883b; II, 840a; III, 516b; V, 1174b, 1175b, 1184b; S, 192a, 377b
Rifāʿa Bey → al-Taḥtawi
Rifāda i, 9a, 80a — I, 9a, 82b
Rifāʿī i, 281a; ii, 16a, 164b, 1134a; iii, 122b, 291a, 952a — I, 289b; II, 16b, 170a, 1160b; III, 125b, 300a, 976b
Rifat, Oktay iv, 545a — IV, 568b
Rifʿat, Ṣādiḳ → Ṣādiḳ Rifʿat Pasha
al-Rīfī → Aḥmad al-Rīfī
Rīgha, Banū v, 1181a, b — V, 1171a, b
Rīgistān i, 1294b — I, 1334a, b
Rihān ii, 953b — II, 975b
Rīḥān iv, 1123a, 1125a — IV, 1155a, 1157a
al-Rīḥānī, Amīn v, 1254b, 1255b, 1256b — V, 1245b, 1246b, 1247b
Riḥla v, 1159b — V, 1149b
Rikāʿ iv, 1123b, 1126a — IV, 1155b, 1157b
Rikāb → Ibil and/et Dhalūl
Riḳḳa iv, 929a — IV, 962a
Rimāya iv, 795b, 797a — IV, 828a, 829b
Rime → Ḳāfiya
Rimm s, 135b — S, 135b
Rinčana s, 156a — S, 156a
Rinds i, 1005b; s, 332a — I, 1036b; s, 331b
Risāla i, 1042b — I, 1067a
Rīshahr i, 1341a — I, 1381b
Rishīs s, 114b — S, 114a
Riwā iv, 216b — IV, 226a
Riwāḳ ii, 113b, 114a; v, 1134a — II, 116a, b; V, 1129b
Riwāya iii, 369b — III, 381b
Riyāḍ i, 1346b; ii, 115b — I, 1387a; II, 118a
al-Riyāḍ i, 628b, 1231a; ii, 425a, 569b; iv, 1073a; s, 3b — I, 649b, 1267b; II, 435b, 583b; IV, 1104b; S, 2b
Riyāḍ al-Ṣulḥ v, 787b, 794b — V, 793b, 801a
Riyāḥ, Banū i, 161b, 533a; ii, 463b; iii, 66b, 137b, 386a; iv, 337a; v, 48b — I, 166a, 549b; II, 475a; III, 69a, 140b, 398b; IV, 351b; V, 50a
al-Riyāḥī → Abu 'l-Hindī; Maʿḳil b. Ḳays
al-Riyāḥī, Muḥammad b. Yaḥyā i, 600a — I, 619b
Riyāḥiyya iv, 837a — IV, 870a
Riz → Ruzz
Rizā → Riḍā
al-Rizaḳ al-aḥbāsiyya ii, 148b — II, 153a
Rizām b. Sābiḳ iv, 838a — IV, 870b
Rizāmiyya v, 63b — V, 65b
Rizayḳāt Baḳḳāra i, 929a, 962a; ii, 122a, 123b — I, 957b, 991b; II, 125a, 126b
Rize ii, 62a — II, 63b
Rizḳ i, 204b — I, 210b
Rizḳ Allāh Ḥassūn → Ḥassūn
Rizwan → Riḍwān
Robe → Libās
Robe of honour/Robe d'honneur → Khilʿa
Rod (staff) → Ḳaḍīb
Rodent → Faʾr
Roger II, King of Sicily/roi de Sicile i, 79a; ii, 585a, 855a; iii, 1032b; iv, 337b, 651a; v, 1246b — I, 81b; II, 599b, 875a; III, 1058b; IV, 352a, 677b; V, 1237b
Rōh s, 1b — S, 1b
Rohilkhand i, 218a; iv, 749b — I, 224b; IV, 779b
Rohillā i, 253a, 856a, 953b, 1042b, 1206a; iii, 59b, 61b, 427b — I, 261a, 879b, 982b, 1074a, 1242a; III, 62a, 64a, 441b

Rohtak v, 1258a — V, 1248b
Rōhtās ii, 1091b; iii, 449a — II, 1117b; III, 464b
Rome → Rūmiya
Ronda → Runda
Rose → Gul
Roseau → Ḳaṣab
Rosetta s, 120b — S, 120a
Rō<u>sh</u>ān i, 853b, 854a — I, 877a, b
Rō<u>sh</u>ānī i, 225a — I, 231b
Rossignol → Bulbul
Rostom (Kay <u>Kh</u>usraw) v, 493b — V, 496b
Roumanie II, 705a, b
Roumélie → Rūm-eli
Roupéniens → Rubenides
Round City i, 896b, 898a, 899b
Roxalani i, 354a — I, 365a
Roxelana/Roxelane → <u>Kh</u>urrem Sulṭān
Rozagī → Rūzagī
Ṛ<u>sh</u>tuni, Theodoros i, 636a, b — I, 657a, b
al-Ruʾāsī i, 105b; ii, 806b — I, 108b; II, 826a
al-Ruʾaynī al-I<u>sh</u>bīlī ii, 743b; iv, 468a — II, 762a; IV, 489a
al-Rubʿ al-<u>Kh</u>ālī i, 537a, b, 539a, 759b, 1231a — I, 553b, 554a, 555b, 782a, 1268a
Ruʾba b. ʿA<u>dj</u><u>dj</u>ā<u>dj</u> i, 142a, 207b, 1154b; iii, 73a, 573b, 1262a; s, 31b, 286b — I, 146b, 214a, 1188b; III, 75b, 593b, 1294b; S, 31b, 286b
Rubāʿī i, 677a; iv, 58a, 62a; v, 166a — I, 698a; IV, 61a, 65b; V, 163b
Rubayyiʿ b. Zayd ii, 176b — II, 182a
Rubenid(e)s i, 182a, 466a, 639a, 790a — I, 187b, 479b, 660a, 813a
Rubūbiyya i, 71b — I, 73b
al-Ruburtayr i, 78b, 390a — I, 81a, 401b
Rūdakī i, 1216a; iv, 53a, 60b, 63a, 504b, 773b; v, 956a; s, 35a — I, 1252b; IV, 56a, 64a, 66a, 526a, 804b; V, 959b; S, 35b
Rudawlawī, Aḥmad ʿAbd al-Ḥaḳḳ s, 312b, 313a — S, 312b, 313a
Rudawlī ii, 54b; s, 293a, 312b — II, 55b; S, 293a, 312b
Rū<u>dh</u>bār iii, 254a; iv, 859b; v, 149a, b, 247a — III, 261a; IV, 893a; V, 151a, 152a, 245a
Ru<u>dh</u>rawārī → Abū <u>Sh</u>u<u>dj</u>āʿ
Rūd-i <u>Sh</u>ahr s, 97a — S, 96b
Rūdisar → Hawsam
Rudwān → Riḍwān
Rug → Bisāṭ
al-Rūgī → Bū Ḥmāra
Rūḥ iv, 487a — IV, 508a
Rūḥ al-Amīn <u>Kh</u>ān al-ʿU<u>th</u>mānī i, 1219a — I, 1255a
al-Ruhā i, 466a, 639b, 1054a; ii, 63b, 347b — I, 480a, 660a, 1085b; II, 65a, 357a
Rūḥānī → Amīr Rūḥānī
Rūḥānī (b/n. 1896) iv, 71b — IV, 75b
Rūḥī iii, 91b — III, 94a
Rūḥī, <u>Sh</u>ay<u>kh</u> Aḥmad s, 53a — S, 53b
Rūhiyyè <u>Kh</u>ānum i, 916a — I, 943b
al-Ruḳabāʾ → Abdāl
Ruḳayya b. Hā<u>sh</u>im b. ʿAbd Manāf i, 80a — I, 82a
Ruḳayya b. Muḥammad i, 136b; ii, 845a — I, 140b; II, 865a
Ruḳayya Bēgam iii, 456a — III, 471b
Ru<u>kh</u>āma iv, 354a — IV, 369b
al-Ru<u>kh</u>k<u>h</u>a<u>dj</u> i, 86a — I, 88b
Ru<u>kh</u>ṣa i, 823a — I, 846a
Ru<u>kh</u>ṣatī s, 91b — S, 91a
al-Ruḳʿī, al-Ḥā<u>dj</u><u>dj</u> al-<u>Kh</u>ayyāṭ s, 403b, 404a — S, 404a, b
Rukn al-Dawla, Atabeg s, 382b — S, 382b
Rukn al-Dawla Ḥasan (Būyid(e)) i, 211b, 419a, 955a; ii, 178b, 680a, 928a; iii, 258a, 703a, 704a, 1157a; iv, 23a, b, 100b, 859b; v, 452b; s, 36b, 259a — I, 217b, 431a, 984a; II, 184a, 697a, 949b; III, 265a, 725b, 726a, 1185b; IV, 25a, 104b, 892b; V, 455a; S, 37a, 258b
Rukn al-Dawla <u>Kh</u>ān → Iʿtiḳād <u>Kh</u>ān
Rukn al-Dīn b. ʿAbd al-Ḳādir al-<u>Dj</u>īlī iii, 751b — III, 774b
Rukn al-Dīn b. Burāḳ i, 1311b; v, 161b, 162a, 553b — I, 1351b; V, 159b, 160a, 558a
Rukn al-Dīn Aḥmadīlī i, 300b — I, 310a
Rukn al-Dīn ʾAlāʾ al-Dawla → ʿAlāʿ al-Dawla al Simnānī
Rukn al-Dīn Čanda ii, 1077a — II, 1102a
Rukn al-Dīn al-Iṣfahānī ii, 125b — II, 129a
Rukn al-Dīn Kart iv, 672a — IV, 699b
Rukn al-Dīn <u>Kh</u>ur-<u>Sh</u>āh ii, 606a; iv, 201b — II, 621b; IV, 210a
Rukn al-Dīn Kili<u>dj</u> Arslān → Kili<u>dj</u> Arslān IV
Rukn al-Dīn Mawdūd, <u>sh</u>ay<u>kh</u> ii, 54a — II, 55a
Rukn al-Dīn Sām b. Lankar iv, 466b — IV, 487a
Rukn al-Dīn al-Samarḳandī → al-ʿAmīdī
Rukn al-Dīn Sulaymān II i, 431b, 510a; iv, 575b, 816a — I, 444a, 525b; IV, 598b, 849a
Rukn al-Dīn Ṭu<u>gh</u>rïl II → Ṭu<u>gh</u>rïl II, Rukn al-Dīn
Rukn al-Dīn Ṭu<u>gh</u>rïl III → Ṭu<u>gh</u>rïl III b. Arslān Rukn al-Dīn
Rukn al-Dīn Yūsuf → Yūsuf <u>Sh</u>āh II
Rukna iv, 1128a — IV, 1159b
Rūm i, 83a, 468a, 470a, 638b, 639a; ii, 81a; iii, 344b, 1046a, 1089a; iv, 175a, 839a; v, 104a, b — I, 85b, 482a, 484a, 659a, b; II, 82b; III, 354b, 1072b, 1115b; IV, 182b, 817b; V, 106a, b
Rūma → Rūmiya
Rumania ii, 688a, b
Rūmeli i, 97a, 396a, 398a, b, 469a, 697b, 998b, 1160a, 1304b; ii, 83a, 443a, 722a; iv, 232b; v, 261a, 881a; s, 268b — I, 99b, 407a, 409b, 410a, 482b, 719a, 1029a, 1194b, 1344b; II, 85a, 455a, 741a; IV, 242b; V, 258b, 887b; S, 268a
Rumeli Ḥiṣārï i, 1251b, 1318a; iii, 483a — I, 1289b, 1358b; III, 500a
Rumeli Kavag<u>h</u>ï i, 481a, 1252a — I, 495a, 1290a
al-Rūmī → A<u>sh</u>raf; <u>Dj</u>alāl al-Dīn; Ḳusṭūs
Rūmī <u>Kh</u>ān i, 1062a, 1068b; iii, 482a — I, 1094a, 1101a; III, 499a
Rūmiya (Rome) iv, 274b, 275a — IV, 286b, 287a
al-Rumiyya v, 945a, b — V, 949a, b
Rūmlū iii, 1101b — III, 1128b
Rumman, Banū i, 1246b — I, 1284b
al-Rummānī, ʿAlī b. ʿĪsā i, 126b, 858a, 1115b; iii, 1020a; iv, 249a; v, 242b, 426b; s, 13a, 27b, 362b — I, 130a, 881b, 1149a; III, 1045b; IV, 260a; V, 240a, 429a; S, 13b, 27b, 362a
Rūna s, 21a — S, 21a
al-Rūnī → Abu 'l-Fara<u>dj</u> Rūnī
Runda i, 6a, 11b — I, 6a, 11b
al-Rundī → Ibn al-Ḥakīm
Rupenians → Rubenid(e)s
Rupiya (rupee) ii, 121a — II, 123b
Rūpmatī i, 1155a — I, 1189b
Rūs i, 4a, 625b, 738b, 836a; iii, 759a; iv, 346b, 347a, 348b, 1175b, 1176a; v, 1120a, b, 1121b — I, 4a, 646b, 760b, 859a; III, 782b; IV, 361a, b, 363b, 1209a; V, 1116b, 1117a, 1118a
al-Ruṣāfa, Abbāsiyya i, 24a, 1320a — I, 25a, 1360b
al-Ruṣāfa, Ba<u>gh</u>dād i, 897a, b, 898b, 901a, 902b; s, 193b, 386a, 400b — I, 923b, 924b, 925a, 928a, 929b; S, 194b, 386b, 401a
Ruṣāfa, al-Nuʿmān s, 117a — S, 116b
al-Ruṣāfī i, 602a — I, 621b
al-Ruṣāfī, Maʿrūf i, 597b; iii, 1264b — I, 617a; III, 1297b
Rū<u>sh</u>anī → ʿUmar Rū<u>sh</u>anī

Rushayd b. Kāmil b. Djāmiʿ iv, 337a, b — IV, 351b, 352a
Rushayd al-Daḥdāḥ ii, 795b — II, 814b
Rushd i, 993b — I, 1024a
Rushdī Pāshā → ʿAbd al-Raḥmān; Ḥusayn Rushdī Pasha; Shirwānī-zāde
Rüshdiyye i, 285b, 1272a; v, 904a, b, 905a — I, 294a, 1311a; V, 910a, b, 911b
Russians/Russes i, 269a, 722a, 1041a, b, 1128b; ii, 88a, b, 179a, 206a, 476b, 652b, 684b, 792b, 980a, 1135b; iii, 13a, 158a, 348b, 530b, 1186a, 1192a, 1236a; iv, 38b, 39a, b, 185b, 297a, 392b, 569a, 576b, 591b, 630b, 792a, 869b, 1065a; v, 30b, 141a, b, 312b, 459a, 497a — I, 277a, 743b, 1073a, 1162b; II, 89b, 90a, 184b, 212b, 488b, 669a, 701b, 811a, b, 1002a, b, 1162a; III, 13b, 161b, 359a, 549a, 1215b, 1222a, 1268a; IV, 41a, b, 42a, 193b, 310b, 409b, 591b, 599b, 615b, 655b, 824a, 903a, 1096b; V, 31b, 143b, 144a, 312a, 498a, 500a
Russo-Turkish wars (1769-1774) i, 4b, 294b, 948a; iii, 193a, 253a
- (1877-1878) ii, 88b, 613b; iii, 993a
al-Rustāḳ iv, 1085a; s, 355b — IV, 1116a; S, 355b
Rustaḳubādh i, 711b — I, 733a
Rustam b. Maḳṣūd i, 312a; iv, 186b, 387a, b — I, 321b; IV, 194b, 404a, b
Rustam b. Nūr al-Dīn Khurshīdī v, 828a — V, 834b
Rustam (Shāh-nāma) iii, 113a, 114a, 153b; iv, 809a, b, 813a — III, 115b, 116b, 156b; IV, 842a, 846a
Rustam II b. Ardashīr b. Ḥasan → Rustam Bāwand II
Rustam b. Sharwīn s, 309a — S, 309a
Rustam Bāwand I, Shāh Ghāzī v, 662a — V, 667b
Rustam Bāwand II, Shams al-Mulūk i, 1110a; iii, 810a — I, 1143b; III, 833b
Rustam Khān (Ḳaytaḳ) → Rustum Khān
Rustam Khān, Mīr i, 1192b — I, 1227b
Rustam Pasha i, 291b, 1279b; ii, 685a; iii, 147b; iv, 232a; v, 35b, 67a — I, 300b, 1318b; II, 702b; III, 150b; IV, 242a; V, 36b, 69a
Rustamdar iv, 808a; v, 663a, b — IV, 840b; V, 668b
Rustum s, 91a — S, 90b
Rustum, general/général ii, 893b; iii, 195a, 1254b; iv, 385b — II, 914a; III, 199b, 1287a; IV, 402a
Rustum Khān ii, 87b; iv, 846b — II, 89a; IV, 879b
Rustumid(e)s i, 83a, 167a, 445b; ii, 141a, 145b, 852b; iii, 655a, 658b, 924b — I, 85b, 172a, 458b; II, 144b, 149b, 872a; III, 676b, 679b, 949a
Rusudan (queen/reine) v, 490b — V, 493a, b
Rusūkhī, Ismāʿīl s, 83a — S, 83a
Rusūm i, 999b, 1144a; ii, 142b, 146b; iv, 1032a — I, 1030a, 1178b; II, 146b, 150b; IV, 1064a
Rusūm-i sitte ii, 677b — II, 694b
Ruswā, Muḥammad Hādī v, 203b, 1106b — V, 201a, 1102b
Ruṭab iv, 339b — IV, 354a
Ruṭaynā iv, 679b — IV, 707b
Rutbīl → Zunbīl
Ruʾūs Ḳalemi ii, 338b — II, 348b
Ruwalā i, 483a, 873b, 1093b; ii, 492b; iii, 1018a — I, 497a, 897b, 1126a; II, 505a; III, 1043b
Ruwaym iii, 823b — III, 847a
al-Ruʾyā iii, 600a; iv, 259b, 260a — III, 621a; IV, 271b
Ruʾyā-i ṣādiḳa iv, 72b — IV, 76b
Rūyān ii, 74b; iv, 808a; v, 661b; s, 297b — II, 76a; IV, 840b; V, 666b; S, 297a
Rūyānī, Abu 'l-Maḥāsin iv, 859b — IV, 892b
Ruʾyat Allāh i, 411b — I, 423b
Rūyīn-diz i, 300b, 301a — I, 310a
Rūzagī v, 458b, 459a — V, 461b
Rūzbahān b. Windād-Khūrshīd iii, 703a, 1202a — III, 725b, 1232b
Rūzbahān Baḳlī iii, 823a; iv, 851b; v, 53b — III, 847a; IV, 885a; V, 55a
Rūzbihan al-Wazzān al-Miṣrī v, 300b — V, 299b, 300a
Ruzhekī → Ruzāgī
al-Rūznāmadj ii, 78b, 79b, 81a — II, 80a, 81a, 82b
Ruzz ii, 904a, 907a, 1062b; iv, 519b; v, 879b — II, 925a, 928b, 1087a; IV, 542a; V, 885b
Ruzzīk b. Ṭalāʾiʿ i, 197a; ii, 318a; iv, 376a — I, 202b; II, 327a; IV, 392b
Rythme → Īḳāʿ

S

Sāʿa iii, 921a; v, 708b — III, 945b; V, 713b
Saʿāda, Antūn iii, 523a, b; iv, 125a — III, 541b; IV, 130b
Saʿādat b. Muḥammad Girāy II iv, 178b — IV, 185b
Saʿādat ʿAlī Khān i, 757b, 809a; iii, 1244a; v, 637a — I, 780a, 832b; III, 1276b; V, 641a, b
Saʿādat Allāh Khān i, 624b — I, 645b
Saʿādat Girāy Khān I ii, 179a, 1046a, 1113b; iv, 178a — II, 184b, 1070b, 1139b; IV, 185a
Saʿādat Khān Bahādur → Burhān al-Mulk
Saʿādat Khān Burhān al-Mulk → Burhān al-Mulk
Saʿādat Khān Swātī iii, 335b — III, 346a
Saʿādat Yār Khān → Ṣādiḳ Muḥammad Khān III
Saʿādī i, 1049b — I, 1081a
Saadia Gaon → Saʿadyā al-Fayyūmī
Saʿadya al-Fayyūmī i, 343a; ii, 95b; iv, 304a, 305b, 306a, 604a — I, 353b; II, 97b; IV, 317b, 319a, 320a, 628b
al-Saʿātī, Muḥammad s, 371b, 373a, b — S, 371b, 373a, b
Sabaʾ (Yaman) i, 548a, b; iii, 9a; s, 337a — I, 565b, 566a; III, 9b; S, 336b
Ṣabā (zephyr) ii, 1035a — II, 1059a
Ṣabāʾ (poet/poète) iii, 114a; iv, 69b — III, 116b; IV, 73a
Saba (queen of/la reine de) → Bilḳīs
Sabāʾ b. Abī ʾl-Suʿūd i, 1214b; iii, 134a; v, 954a — I, 1251a; III, 136b; V, 958a
Sabaʾ b. Managhfād ii, 1095b — II, 1121b
Sabaʾ al-Aṣghar s, 337b — S, 337a
Sabab i, 671b, 672a; iii, 1129b — I, 692a, b; III, 1157b
Sabaean → al-Ṣābiʾa
Sabah (island/île) s, 150a — S, 150a
Ṣabāh (jeweller/bijoutier) s, 251b — 252a
Ṣabāh, Āl i, 233b, 540a; ii, 176b; v, 573b, 574a — I, 241a, 556b; II 181b; V, 578a, b
Sabāḥ al-Dīn ii, 430b, 474b, 475a; iii, 593a — II, 442a, 487a; III, 613b
Ṣabāh al-Dīn ʿAlī v, 195a, 197a — V, 192a, 194a
Sabahattin (Raḥmī) Eyuboğlu → Eyyūboghlu, Sabāḥ al-Dīn Raḥmī
Sabaʾiyya i, 382b; iii, 1265a; s, 357b — I, 393b; III, 1298a; S, 357b
Sabarta → Isparta
Sabʿat Khawātim v, 222b — V, 220b
Sabʿatayn s, 337a — S, 336b
al-Ṣabbāgh i, 374b — I, 385a
al-Ṣabbāgh, Aḥmad b. Muṣṭafā al-Sikandarānī s, 44a — S, 44b
Sabbagh, Michel s, 153b — S, 153b
Sabéen → al-Ṣābiʾa
al-Ṣābīʾ → Hilāl
al-Ṣābiʾ, Ibrāhīm b. Hilāl s, 398a — S, 398b
al-Ṣābiʾa i, 264a, 527b; iii, 9b, 52a, 166a, 228a, 1075b;

v, 120a, 895a; s, 336b — I, 272a, 543b; III, 10a, 54a, 169b, 170a, 235a, 1102b; V, 122b, 901b; S, 336b
Ṣabīḥ s, 251b — S, 251b
al-Ṣābīʿī, Abū Isḥāḳ Ibrāhīm i, 591b, 955a, 1354a; ii, 305a; iii, 258a, 387b, 671b, 703b, 780a; iv, 756b; s, 4a, 19a — I, 611a, 984b, 1393a; II, 313b; III, 265b, 400a, 693a, 726a, 803b; IV, 786b; S, 3b, 19a
al-Sabīʿī al-Hamdānī s, 400b — S, 401a
Sābiḳ b. Maḥmūd iii, 790a — III, 813b
Sabīl iv, 435b — IV, 455a
Ṣābir → ʿAlī Akbar Ṣābir
Ṣābir (Lombardia) iv, 275b; v, 1244a — IV, 287b; V, 1234b
al-Ṣābir, ʿAlāʾ al-Dīn ʿAlī b. Aḥmad s, 313a — S, 312b
Ṣābiriyya ii, 54a; s, 313a — II, 55a; S, 312b
Sabirs (Central Asia/Asie Centrale) iv, 1172a, b, 1178b — IV, 1205b, 1212a
Sabʿiyya i, 178b — I, 183a
Sabḳ ii, 953a — II, 975a
Sabḳ-i Hindī ii, 999b, 1034a; iv, 60a, 68b-69a — II, 1023a, 1058a; IV, 63a-b, 72b
Sabḳ-i ʿIrāḳī iv, 60a — IV, 63a
Sabḳ-i Khurāsānī iv, 60a — IV, 63a
Sabḳ-i Turkistānī iv, 60a — IV, 63a
Sābla iv, 674a, 675a — IV, 702a, b
Sablān, Djabal i, 625b — I, 646a
Saʿbōnī i, 531a — I, 547a
Sabor i, 1273b, 1274b — I, 1312b, 1313b
Ṣabra-Manṣūriyya ii, 114b, 861b, 863a; iv, 830a, b — II, 117a, 881b, 883a; IV, 862b, 863b
Sabre → Sayf
Sabta i, 83b, 356b; iv, 355b; v, 1192a; s, 111b, 124b, 125a — I, 86a, 367a; IV, 371a; V, 1182a; S, 110b, 124a
al-Sabtī i, 1289a — I, 1328b
al-Sabtī, Abu ʾl-ʿAbbās iii, 893b, 975a — III, 917b, 999b
Sabū, Wādī v, 1185b, 1245a, b — V, 1175b, 1236a
Sabuk i, 507a — I, 522b
Sabuktakīn → Sebuktegin
al-Ṣābūndjī, Ḥusayn iv, 852b — IV, 885b
Sābūr, Dhuʾl-Aktāf → Shāpūr II
Sābūr b. Abī Ṭāhir iv, 664a — IV, 691a
Sābūr b. Ardashīr i, 242a, 899a, 1352b; ii, 127a; s, 119b, 361b — I, 249b, 926a, 1391b; II, 130b; S, 119a, 361b
Sābūr b. Sahl i, 344b, 1224a — I, 355a, 1260b
Sābūr al-Djunūd → Shāpūr I
Ṣabyā s, 278b — S, 278b
Sabzawār s, 41a — S, 41b
al-Sabzawārī, Abū Saʿīd al-Ḥasan iv, 704b — IV, 733a
Sabzawārī, Hādī iv, 50b; s, 41a — IV, 53b; S, 41b
Sabzawārī, Muḥammad Bāḳir s, 308a — S, 308a
Saʿd (Naṣrid(e)) s, 399a — S, 399b
Saʿd, Banū s, 73b — S, 73b
Saʿd b. Abī Waḳḳāṣ i, 140a, 336b, 382b, 445a, 485a, 697a; iii, 260a, 587a, 739b, 874a, 1254b; iv, 385a, b, 775b, 796a; v, 345b, 451a, 945a — I, 144a, 347a, 393b, 458a, 499a, 718a; III, 267b, 607a, 762a, 898a, 1287a; IV, 402a, b, 806b, 828b; V, 346b, 453b, 949a
Saʿd b. ʿĀʾidh al-Ḳaraẓ s, 172a — S, 173a
Saʿd b. al-ʿĀṣ iv, 858b — IV, 891b
Saʿd b. Bakr iii, 94a, 363b — III, 96b, 375a
Saʿd b. Fayṣal b. ʿAbd al-ʿAzīz Āl Suʿūd s, 305b — S, 305b
Saʿd b. Mardanīsh → Ibn Mardanīsh
Saʿd b. Muʿādh i, 514b, 771b; v, 436b — I, 530a, 794b; V, 439a
Saʿd b. Muḥammad → Ḥayṣa Bayṣa
Saʿd b. ʿUbāda i, 514b; v, 996b — I, 530b; V, 992a
Saʿd b. Zangī i, 434a; iv, 1037a, 1041a; v, 161a — I, 446b; IV, 1068b, 1072b; V, 159b
Saʿd b. Zayd Manāt, Banū s, 31a, 178a — S, 31b, 179a
Saʿd b. Zayd Manāt b. Tamīm i, 102a; ii, 71b — I, 104b; II, 72b
Saʿd Allāh Khān (Sartōr Faḳir) ii, 317a — II, 326a
Saʿd Allāh Khān ʿAllāmī al-Tamīmī ii, 47b; iv, 759b — II, 48b; IV, 790a
Saʿd Allāh Khān Rohilla iii, 60a, b — III, 62b, 63a
Saʿd Allāh Lāhorī iii, 634a — III, 655b
Saʿd al-Aysar v, 49a, 50a — V, 50b, 51b
Saʿd Buh s, 182b — S, 182b
Saʿd al-Dawla i, 903a; iii, 1122a; iv, 48a — I, 930a; III, 1150a; IV, 51a
Saʿd al-Dawla Sharīf (Ḥamdānid(e)) i, 119b; iii, 86a, 128a, b, 129b; v, 820a, 923b; s, 37a — I, 123a; III, 88b, 130b, 131a, 132a; V, 826b, 929a; S, 37a
Saʿd al-Dawla al-Ṭawāshī → al-Ṭawāshī
Saʿd al-Dīn (d./m. 1599) → Khodja Efendi
Saʿd al-Dīn (Ethiopia/Éthiopie) i, 176b, 763b — I, 181b, 786b
Saʿd al-Dīn Hammūʾī s, 235b — S, 235a
Saʿd al-Dīn Khiḍr i, 766b — I, 789b
Saʿd al-Dīn Muḥammad al-Kāshgharī ii, 421b — II, 432b
Saʿd al-Dīn Taftazānī → al-Taftazānī
Saʿd al-Dīn-i Warāwīni (Varāminī) iv, 506b — IV, 528b
Saʿd Zaghlūl ii, 417b, 423a, 467a, 934a; iii, 59a, 516a; iv, 197b, 856a; v, 910a; s, 58a — II, 428a, 434a, 478b, 956a; III, 61b, 533b; IV, 206a, 889b; V, 915b; S, 58b
Ṣaʿda (Yaman) s, 22a, 236a, 335a, 407a — S, 22b, 236a, 334b, 407a
Saʿdābād i, 232b; v, 642a — I, 240a; V, 646a
Ṣadaf v, 819b — V, 825b
al-Ṣadafī → Abū ʿAlī al-Ṣadafī
Ṣadaḳa i, 1048a, 1142a, 1144a; iii, 350a; iv, 1151b; v, 424b — I, 1080a, 1176b, 1178b; III, 361a; IV, 1183b; V, 426b
Ṣadaḳa b. Abi ʾl-Ḳāsim Shirāzī iii, 373a; iv, 63b — III, 385a; IV, 67a
Ṣadaḳa b. Manṣūr i, 684a; iii, 197b, 389b, 774b; iv, 27b, 29a, 911b — I, 705a; III, 202a, 402a, 797b; IV, 29b, 31a, 944b
Saʿdān v, 132b — V, 135a
Saʿdaniyya iii, 291a — III, 300a
al-Sadārā → Sudayrī
Sadāshiv Bhāu i, 296a — I, 305b
Sādāt iv, 859a — IV, 892a
al-Sādāt, Anwar v, 1062a; s, 5b, 6a, 306a — V, 1059a; S, 4b, 5a, 305b
Sādāt-i Marʿashī iv, 48b — IV, 51a
Saddayn iv, 342a — IV, 356a
Sadd i, 929a — I, 957a
Sadekov s, 365b — S, 365b
Saʿdī i, 241b, 680a, 780a, 1301a, 1345b; ii, 1034a, 1035a, b; iii, 93b, 373a, 573a; iv, 65b, 67b; s, 46b, 415a — I, 249a, 701a, 803a, 1341a, 1385b; II, 1058a, 1059a, b; III, 96a, 385a, 592b; IV, 69a, 71a; S, 47a, 415a
al-Saʿdī (Tinbuktū) i, 595a — I, 614b
Saʿdī b. Abi ʾl-Shawk i, 513a — I, 528b
Saʿdī Čelebi iii, 90a; iv, 333b — III, 92b; IV, 348a
Saʿdid(e)s i, 55b, 56a, 58b, 93a, 245a, 288b, 355a, 403a, 496b, 689a, 1058a, 1149a; ii, 134a, 146a, 164b, 181b, 510a, 819b, 823a; iii, 70a, 251b, 257a, 426a, 1047a; v, 627a, 1191a, b; s, 28b, 29a, 223b, 336b — I, 57b, 60a, 96a, 252b, 297b, 366a, 414b, 511b, 710a, 1089b, 1183a; II, 137a, 150a, 170a, 187a, 522b, 839a, 842a; III, 72b, 258b, 264a, 478b, 1073a; V, 631a, 1181a, b; S, 29a, 223b, 336a
Ṣādîḳ, Colonel iii, 595a — III, 615b
Ṣādik, G.M. iv, 711a — IV, 739b
Ṣādiḳ Beg iv, 593b — IV, 617b
Ṣādiḳ Ḥalwāʾī, Mawlānā s, 122a — S, 121a

Ṣādiḳ Hidayāt → Hidayāt
Ṣādik Khān Shakākī i, 1030b; ii, 838b; iii, 1109a — I, 1062a; II, 858a; III, 1136b
Ṣādiḳ Khān Zand i, 1087a; iv, 104b; v, 674a — I, 1119b; IV, 109a; V, 679a
Ṣādiḳ Muḥammad Khān I (Dāwūdpotrā) ii, 185b, 186a — II, 191b, 192a
Ṣādiḳ Muḥammad Khān II ii, 186b — II, 192b
Ṣādiḳ Muḥammad Khān III ii, 186b — II, 192b
Ṣadiḳ Muḥammad Khān IV ii, 187a — II, 193a
Ṣādiḳ Muḥammad Khān V ii, 187a — II, 193a
Ṣādiḳ Muṭṭalibī i, 432b — I, 445a
Ṣādiḳ Rifʿat Pasha iii, 552a, 591a — III, 571a, 611a
Ṣādiḳī College v, 915a — V, 920b
Sādin iv, 421b — IV, 439b
Ṣādirāt ii, 152a; iv, 1041a, 1042a — II, 156b; IV, 1072b, 1073a, b
Sadjʿ i, 591a, 594a, 673b; ii, 307a; iii, 1242b; v, 420a, 839b — I, 610a, 613b, 694b; II, 315b; III, 1274b; V, 422a, 846a
Sadjāh iv, 463b — IV, 484b
Sadjāḥī i, 110b, 247b, 451a; iii, 169a, 224b — I, 113b, 255a, 463b; III, 172b, 231b
al-Sadjāwandī, Sirādj al-Dīn iii, 163b — III, 167a
Sadjdjād Ḥusayn iii, 359a — III, 370a
Sadjdjāda iv, 950a — IV, 982b
Sādjid(e)s i, 145a, 190a, 637a, 660b; ii, 679b; iv, 22a, b; v, 489a — I, 149b, 194b, 658a, 681b; II, 696b; IV, 23b, 24a; V, 491b
Sādjīyya i, 866a; ii, 1080b — I, 890b; II, 1105b
Sadjsin v, 1016a, b — V, 1011b, 1012a
Sadō i, 95a, 229a — I, 98a, 236a
Sadōzays i, 229a, 230a, 295a — I, 236a, 237a, 304b
Ṣadr (official/foncionnaire) iv, 33a, 34b, 50a; v, 858a — IV, 35b, 37a, 53a; V, 865a
Ṣadr (Ḳumm) s, 157b — S, 158a
Ṣadr al-Dīn, Pīr iv, 202b — IV, 211b
Ṣadr al-Dīn → Rinčana
Ṣadr al-Dīn al-Ardabīlī s, 382b — S, 383a
Saḍr al-Dīn Azurda → Āzurda, Saḍr al-Dīn
Ṣadr al-Dīn (Kashmīr) iv, 708a — IV, 736b
Ṣadr al-Dīn al-Ḳūnawī iii, 708a, b, 710b, 1269a — III, 730b, 731a, 733a, 1302a
Ṣadr al-Dīn Mūsā, Shaykh iv, 721a — IV, 750a
Ṣadr al-Dīn Shīrāzī → al-Shīrāzī, Ṣadr al-Dīn
Ṣadr al-Sharīʿa al-Thānī iii, 163b — III, 167a
Ṣadr al-Ṣudūr i, 316b, 1327b — I, 326b, 1368a
Ṣadrā Shīrāzī → al-Shīrāzī, Ṣadr al-Dīn
Sadrāta i, 1246b; v, 697b — I, 1284b; V, 702b
al-Sadrātī → ʿĀṣim
Ṣadr-i Aʿẓam i, 1091a; ii, 333a, 335b; iii, 554a, 555a; iv, 393b; v, 631a — I, 1123b; II, 343a, 345a; III, 573a, 574a; IV, 410b; V, 635a
Ṣadūk, Shaykh-i → Ibn Bābawayh
Saʿdullāh Pasha iii, 592b — III, 613a
Saʿdūn, Banū i, 1096b — I, 1129b
Saʿdūn, Shaykh iii, 1191a — III, 1221a
Saʿdūn b. Muḥammad Āl Ghurayr ii, 321a; iv, 925a — II, 330b; IV, 958a
Saʿdūn al-Surunbāḳī i, 85b — I, 88a
Ṣafā ii, 71a; s, 175a — II, 72b; S, 176a
Ṣafāʾ Khān iv, 849b — IV, 882b
al-Ṣafadī, Khalīl b. Aybak i, 594b; ii, 285b; iv, 863b; v, 609a; s, 48b, 381a, 388a, b, 400a — I, 614a; II, 293b; IV, 896b; V, 613a; S, 49a, 381b, 388b, 389a, 400b
Ṣafadī, Muṭāʿ v, 191a — V, 188a
Ṣafarov, ʿAlī Ḳulī s, 71b — S, 72a
Ṣafātene/Ṣafāite i, 562b — I, 580b
Ṣafawid(e)s i, 190a, 311b, 1066a-1068b, 1120a; ii, 7b, 598b; iii, 177b, 220a, 315b, 1100a; iv, 34a-37b, 49a, 68b, 103a-104a, 118b, 130b, 186a, b, 187a, 387b, 537a, 670b; v, 33b, 34a, 59a, 379a, 603b, 749a; s, 51b, 71a, 139a, 227b, 257a, 308a, 327a — I, 194b, 321a, 452a, 1098a-1100b, 1154a; II, 7b, 613b; III, 181b, 226b, 325a, 1127a; IV, 36b-40a, 51b, 72a, b, 107b-108b, 123b, 136a-b, 194a, b, 195a, 404a, 560a, 697b; V, 34b, 35a, 60b, 380a, 607b, 754b; S, 52a, 71b, 138b, 227b, 256b, 308a, 326b
- administration i, 36a, 240a, 1088a, 1159a, 1346a; ii, 150a, b, 162b, 311b, 334a, 967a, 1083b; iii, 47b, 198b, 490b, 1257a; iv, 474b, 757b, 860b, 951b, 976b, 1048b, 1052b, 1092b; v, 244a, 630a, 869a — I, 37a, 247b, 1120b, 1193b, 1386b; II, 154b, 155a, b, 167b, 320b, 344a, 989a, 1108b; III, 49b, 203a, 507b, 1289b; IV, 495b, 788a, 893b, 984a, 1009a, 1080a, 1084a, 1123b; V, 242a, 634a, 875b
Ṣafawiyya (order/ordre) s, 382b, 383a — S, 383a
Safdar ʿAlī b. Ghazan Khān iii, 581a — III, 601b
Ṣafdar ʿAlī b. Saʿādat Allāh i, 625a — I, 645b
Ṣafdar Djang i, 757a; ii, 808b, 870a; iii, 60a, b, 1158b, 1163a — I, 779b; II, 827b, 890b; III, 62a, 63a, 1186b, 1191b
Ṣaff iv, 334b — IV, 349a
al-Saffāḥ → Abū 'l-ʿAbbās al-Saffāḥ
Ṣaffārid(e)s i, 18b, 23b, 226b, 439b, 452b, 1354b; ii, 191b, 962b, 1082b; iii, 346a; iv, 20b-21b, 188b, 208b; s, 113a — I, 19b, 24a, 233b, 452a, 465b, 1393b; II, 197b, 984b, 1107b; III, 356b; IV, 22a-23a, 197a, 218a; S, 112b
Ṣafī I Shāh (Ṣafawid(e)) i, 228b; ii, 104a, 335a; iii, 220b, 348b, 1190a; iv, 977a; v, 1089b; s, 63a, 83b, 276a — I, 235b; II, 106b, 345a; III, 227a, 359b, 1220a; IV, 1009b; V, 1086b; S, 63b, 83a, 275b
Ṣafī II (Sulaymān) (Ṣafawid(e)) iv, 1092b; v, 1087a — IV, 1123b; V, 1084b
Safi (Morocco/Maroc) i, 85a, 687b; s, 29a, 401b — I, 87b, 708b; S, 29a, 402a
Safi (tribe/tribu) s, 237b — S, 237a
Ṣafī b. Ḥusayn-i Wāʿiẓ-i Kāshifī iv, 69a — IV, 73a
Ṣafī ʿAlī Shāh ii, 434a; iv, 52a — II, 445a; IV, 54b
Ṣafī Amīr al-Muʾminīn → Bahāʾ al-Dawla Fīrūz
Ṣafī al-Dīn ʿAbd Allāh b. Shukr iii, 863a — III, 887a
Ṣafī al-Dīn ʿAbd al-Muʾmin ii, 1074a — II, 1098b
Ṣafī al-Dīn al-Ardabīlī i, 625b, 1197b; ii, 967a; s, 139a, 382b — I, 646b, 1233a; II, 989a; S, 138b, 383a
Ṣafī al-Dīn al-Ḥillī i, 595b, 666b, 858a, 982b; ii, 1033a; iii, 852a, 1264b; iv, 1006a — I, 614b, 687a, 882a, 1013a; II, 1057a; III, 876a, 1297b; IV, 1038b
Ṣafī Ḳuli Khān i, 229b, 904a — I, 236a, 931b
Ṣafiābād i, 701b — I, 722b
Safīd Kūh i, 222a; s, 237b — I, 228b; S, 237a
Safīd-pūsh iv, 409b — IV, 427a
Safīd-Rūd ii, 189b; iv, 6b; v, 602b, 866a; s, 356b, 363a — II, 195b; IV, 7a; V, 606b, 872b; S, 356a, 362b
Safīna iv, 1085b — IV, 1117a
Ṣafīnāz Dhu 'l-Fiḳār s, 299b — S, 299a
Ṣafīpur s, 293a — S, 293a
Safīrs ii, 1026a — II, 1050a
Ṣafiyat al-Nīsāʾ iv, 93a — IV, 97a
Ṣafiyya (wife of/femme de Muḥammad) i, 55b, 1022a; ii, 275a; iv, 1140a; v, 619b — I, 57a, 1053b; II, 283a; IV, 1171b; V, 623b
Ṣafiyye Sulṭān Baffa i, 267b; iv, 233b, 900b — I, 275b; IV, 243b, 933b
Ṣafḳa i, 1112a — I, 1146a
Ṣafr v, 970b — V, 973b
Safvet-bey Bašagić i, 1271b — I, 1311a
Ṣafwān b. al-Muʿaṭṭal al-Sulamī i, 307b; iii, 272a; iv, 870b — I, 317a; III, 280a; IV, 904a
Ṣafwān b. Umayya i, 115b, 151a — I, 119a, 155b
Ṣafwān al-Anṣarī i, 1080b — I, 1113a
Ṣafwat al-Mulk iii, 399a — III, 411b
Sagartians v, 448b — V, 451a

Sagbāns ii, 512b — II, 525b
Sag͟h G͟harībler → G͟hurabāʾ
al-Sag͟hānī, ʿAbd al-Muʾmin b. al-Ḥusayn iv, 504a — IV, 526a
al-Ṣag͟hānī, Raḍī al-Dīn Ḥasan i, 856a; iii, 435a, 1155b — I, 879b; III, 449a, 1183b
Ṣag͟hāniyān → Čag͟hāniyān
Ṣag͟hīr v, 615a, b — V, 619a, b
Sag͟hrouchen, Aīt s, 145a — S, 144b
Saguiet-el-Hamra s, 294a — S, 294a
Sagi i, 741a — I, 763a
Ṣaḥāba iv, 149a, 899b, 1163b; v, 406a — IV, 155a, 932a, 1195b; V, 407a
Saḥabī iv, 68b — IV, 72a
Sāhād͟jī (Marāṭha) s, 246b — S, 246b
Sahara → al-Ṣahrāʾ
Sahāranpūr district s, 312b — S, 312b
al-Sahbāʾ i, 538b — I, 555a
al-Ṣahbāʾ → Umm Ḥabīb
al-Ṣāḥib b. ʿAbbād → Ibn ʿAbbād
Ṣāḥib ʿĀdil ii, 736b — II, 755a
Ṣāḥib al-as͟hg͟hāl ii, 145b, 146a — II, 149b, 150a
Ṣāḥib ʿAṭāʾ Fak͟hr al-Dīn ʿAlī i, 243b, 313a; ii, 81a; iv, 620a, b, 817a — I, 250b, 323a; II, 82b; IV, 644b, 645a, 850a
Ṣāḥib al-dīwān i, 1143a; ii, 334a, 607a — I, 1177b; II, 343b, 622a
Ṣāḥib al-D͟jawāhir, S͟hayk͟h Muḥammad Ḥasan s, 75b — S, 76a
Ṣāḥib Fak͟hk͟h → al-Ḥusayn b. ʿAlī
Ṣāḥib al-Fuṣūl, S͟hayk͟h Muḥammad Ḥusayn s, 75b — S, 76a
Ṣāḥib Girāy K͟hān I i, 1075b; ii, 25a, 1113a; iv, 178a, 849b; v, 138a — I, 1108a; II, 25b, 1139a; IV, 185a, 882b; V, 140b
Ṣāḥib al-Ḥamrāʾ i, 829a — I, 852a
Ṣāḥib al-ḥimār → Abū Yazīd al-Nukkārī
Ṣāḥib al-K͟habar iv, 895b — IV, 928b
Ṣāḥib K͟hān ii, 12b, 1128a — II, 13a, 1154b
Ṣāḥib-Ḳirān-nāma iii, 114b, 153b — III, 116b, 157a
Ṣāḥib Mirbāt i, 829a — I, 852a
Ṣāḥib al-Nāḳa → Yaḥyā b. Zikrawayh
Ṣāḥib al-naẓar fi 'l-maẓālim i, 439a — I, 451b
Ṣāḥib al-Rākūba iv, 1005b — IV, 1038a
Ṣāḥib al-S͟hāma → Ḥusayn b. Zikrawayh
Ṣāḥib-ṭaraf iv, 209a — IV, 218b
Ṣāḥib al-zamān iv, 456b — IV, 477a
Ṣāḥib al-Zand͟j → ʿAlī b. Muḥammad al-Zand͟jī
Ṣaḥīḥ i, 791a, 1297a; ii, 389b; iii, 25a — I, 814b, 1336b; II, 400a; III, 26b
al-Sāḥil i, 539b; ii, 619a, 936b; iv, 778a — I, 556b; II, 634b, 958b; IV, 809b
Sahl b. Abān iii, 856b, 857b — III, 880b, 881b
Sahl b. Bis͟hr i, 1100b, 1102a — I, 1133b, 1135a
Sahl b. Hārūn i, 1141a; iii, 309a, 1263a — I, 1175b; III, 318b, 1296a
Sahl b. Maṣlīaḥ iv, 605a — IV, 629b
Sahl b. Muḥammad al-Ṣuʿlukī i, 686b — I, 707b
Sahl b. Sunbāṭ i, 660b, 844b; iv, 344b — I, 681b, 867b; IV, 359b
Sahl al-Dīn al-Kūhī ii, 362a — II, 372a
Sahl al-Tustarī i, 1039a; iii, 100a, 159a — I, 1070b; III, 102b, 162b
Sahl al-Warrāḳ s, 306b — S, 306b
Sahl-i Sumbatian → Sahl b. Sunbāṭ
al-Sahlagī i, 162b — I, 167a
Sahlān b. Musāfir iii, 258a — III, 265a
Sahm → Ashām
Sahm-i imām iv, 165b — IV, 172b
Saḥnūn b. Saʿīd i, 249b, 250b, 685a; iii, 681a, 817a; v, 503b — I, 257b, 258a, 706a; III, 703a, 840b; V, 507a
Saho iii, 6a; v, 522a — III, 6b; V, 525b
al-Ṣaḥrāʾ i, 307a, 748b, 770a, 1177b, 1231b; iii, 288b; v, 653a, 755b, 757b, 890a, 1187b; s, 328a — I, 316b, 771a, 793a, 1212b, 1268a; III, 297b; V, 657a, 761a, 763a, 896b, 1177b; S, 327b
al-Ṣaḥṣāḥ b. D͟jandaba ii, 234a, 237b — II, 241a, 244b
Sahsārām iii, 449a — III, 464a
Saḥūr v, 372b — V, 373b
Ṣāʾib iv, 69a — IV, 72b
al-Sāʾib b. Abi 'l-Sāʾib iv, 898b — IV, 931a
al-Sāʾib b. Bis͟hr → al-Kalbī, al-Sāʾib
Sāʾib K͟hāt͟hir i, 828a; ii, 428b, 878b — I, 851a; II, 439b, 902b
Ṣāʿid, Āl-i s, 239b — S, 239a
Ṣāʿid (Mawālī) s, 17a — S, 17b
Saʿīd, Banū s, 382a — S, 382b
Saʿīd b. ʿAbd al-Raḥmān b. al-Ḥakam s, 10a — S, 9b
Saʿīd b. Abī ʿArūba s, 386b — S, 386b
Saʿīd b. Aḥmad, Imām i, 1281b — I, 1321a
Saʿīd b. ʿAmr al-Ḥaras͟hī i, 864a, 1134a; iii, 493b, 802b; v, 45a, 854a — I, 888a, 1168b; III, 510b, 825b; V, 46b, 860b
Saʿīd b. al-ʿĀṣ i, 695b, 704a; ii, 1141b; v, 56b, 499b; s, 103b, 298a — I, 716b, 725b; II, 1168b; V, 58a, 502b; S, 103a, 297b
Saʿīd b. Asad b. Mūsa b. Ibrāhīm s, 88a — S, 88a
Saʿīd b. Bā Ḥmād s, 114a — S, 113b
Saʿīd b. Bahdal ii, 90a — II, 92a
Saʿīd b. Barakāt i, 1032b — I, 1064b
Saʿīd b. Bas͟hīr iv, 748b — IV, 778b
Saʿīd b. al-D͟jubayr iv, 926a — IV, 959a
Saʿīd b. Hibat Allāh i, 111b; iii, 754a — I, 114b; III, 777a
Saʿīd b. Ḥumayd s, 25a, 284b, 352a — S, 25a, 284b, 352a
Saʿīd b. al-Ḥusayn al-Anṣarī iv, 712b — IV, 741b
Saʿīd b. ʿĪsā, S͟hayk͟h ii, 173b — II, 179a
Saʿīd b. K͟halfān al-K͟halīlī iv, 1085a; s, 355b, 356a — IV, 1116a; S, 355b
Saʿīd b. K͟hazrūn b. Fulful v, 1180b — V, 1170b
Saʿīd b. Ḳays al-Hamdānī iii, 123b, 241b — III, 126a, 248a
Sāʿid b. Mak͟hlad → Ibn Mak͟hlad, Sāʿid
Saʿīd b. Masʿūd I i, 424b — I, 436b
Saʿīd b. Masʿūd al-Hud͟halī iii, 950a — III, 975a
Ṣāʿid b. Muḥammad al-Ustuwāʿī i, 146b — I, 151a
Saʿīd b. Muk͟hallad v, 621a — V, 625a
Saʿīd b. al-Musayyab al-Mak͟hzūmī ii, 888a; iii, 948a; v, 1124a, 1231b; s, **311b** — II, 908b; III, 972b; V, 1120b, 1222a; S, **311b**
Saʿīd b. Muslat i, 709b — I, 729b
Saʿīd b. Sabandād s, 352a — S, 352a
Saʿīd b. Sulṭān, Sayyid i, 37b, 554b; iv, 887b; v, 183b; s, 355b — I, 38b, 572a; IV, 920a; V, 181a; S, 355b
Saʿīd b. Taymūr i, 1071b; iii, 1005a — I, 1103b; III, 1030a
Saʿīd b. ʿUt͟hmān v, 181a, 551a — V, 178b, 556a
Saʿīd b. Yūsuf al-Ahansalī iii, 167a — III, 170b
Ṣāʿid al-Andalusī i, 235b; ii, 951b — I, 243a; II, 973b
Saʿīd Ata i, 299a — I, 308a
Said Atba i, 371b — I, 382b
Ṣāʿid al-Bag͟hdādī i, 601b; iii, 713a — I, 621a; III, 735b
al-Saʿīd Baraka K͟hān i, 1234a; ii, 285a; iii, 679a; iv, 484b — I, 1270b; II, 293a; III, 701a; IV, 505b
Saʿīd al-Dawla Saʿīd iii, 130a; v, 928a — III, 133a; V, 933b
Saʿīd D͟janbulāṭ ii, 444a; iii, 991b — II, 455b; III, 1016b
Saʿīd al-Fayyūmī iv, 111b — IV, 116b
Saʿīd al-Ḥabs͟hī iii, 16a — III, 16b

Saʿīd Ḥalīm Pasha ii, 698b, 699a — II, 716b
Saʿīd Imām-zāde iii, 269a — III, 277a
Saʿīd Khān i, 852b; iii, 317a — I, 876b; III, 326b
al-Saʿīd al Muʿtaḍid (Almohad(e)) v, 48b — V, 50a
Saʿīd Pasha (1822-1863) ii, 149b, 423b; iii, 1193b, 1194a; iv, 192a, 442a; v, 908b; s, 379a — II, 153b, 434b; III, 1223b, 1224a; IV, 200a, 462a; V, 914b; S, 379b
Saʿīd Pasha (-1912) ii, 643b; iii, 595a — II, 659b; III, 615b
Saʿīd Pasha Küčük → Küčük Saʿīd Pasha
Saʿīd Pasha Yirmisekiz iii, 997b — III, 1022b
Saʿīd al-Suʿadā iv, 433a — IV, 452a
Saʿīd al-Yaḥṣubī al-Maṭarī iv, 115a — IV, 120b
Sāʿida b. Djuʾayya i, 115a — I, 118a
Ṣaʿīdī s, 9b — S, 9a
Saʿīdī, Āl ii, 167b — II, 173a
Sāʿidī, Ghulām Ḥusayn v, 200b — V, 198a
Saʿīdov, Hārūn v, 618b — V, 622b
Saʿīdpūr s, 325a — S, 324b
Saifa Arʾad iii, 3b — III, 4a
Saifawa i, 1259b; s, 164a — I, 1297b; S, 163b
Sainteté → Ḳadāsa
Saʾis iv, 215b — IV, 255a
Sāʾis s, 113b — S, 113a
Saḳa v, 882b — V, 889a
Saka (language/langue) v, 37a, b — V, 38b, 39a
Saka (tribe/tribu) v, 375b — V, 376b
Saḳal v, 761a, 768a — V, 767a, 774a
Saḳal-ī Sherīf → Liḥya-yi Sherīf
Ṣaḳāliba i, 32a, 76a, 490b, 909b; iv, 344a, 1088b; v, 1120b; s, 297b — I, 33a, 78a, 505b, 937a; IV, 359a, 1119b; V, 1117a; S, 297a
Sakan b. Saʿīd i, 600b — I, 620a
Saḳar, Banū v, 582a — V, 587a
Sakarya (river/rivière) v, 880b — V, 887a
al-Saḳaṭī i, 32b, 157a; iii, 486b, 681a — I, 33b, 161b; III, 503b, 703a
al-Sakhāwī → ʿAlam al-Dīn al-Sakhāwī
al-Sakhāwī i, 594b, 595a, 1109b, 1110a, 1309a; iii, 746a, 777b, 814b; iv, 509a; v, 54a — I, 614a, 614b, 1142b, 1143a, 1349a; III, 769a, 801a, 838a; IV, 531b; V, 55b
Ṣakhr → Abū Sufyān
Ṣakhr (demon/démon) ii, 106b — II, 109a
Ṣakhr, Banū i, 528b; iv, 335a — I, 544b; IV, 349b
Sāḳī-nāma iv, 59a — IV, 62a
Saḳīm iii, 25a — III, 26b
Sāḳiya i, 492a; v, 861a, b, 884b, 930b — I, 507a; V, 868a, b, 891a, 954b
Sāḳiyat al-Ḥamrā i, 1176b; v, 890a, 892a — I, 1211b; V, 896b, 898b
Saḳīz i, 268b; iii, 210b, 252b, 629b; v, 557a; s, 281b — I, 276b; III, 216b, 259b, 650b; V, 562a; S, 281b
Saḳīzlī Aḥmad Asʿad iv, 966b — IV, 998b
Saḳīzlī Edhem Pasha → Ibrāhīm Edhem Pasha
Saḳīzlī Ohannes Pasha ii, 473b — II, 485b
al-Ṣakk ii, 79a, 382b — II, 80b, 393a
Saḳḳā → Saḳa
al-Saḳḳāʾ → Ibrāhīm b. ʿAlī b. Ḥasan
al-Sakkākī, Abū Bakr i, 594a, 858a, 982a, 1116a; iv, 251b, 864a; v, 898a, 899b, 900b, 902b, 1026a — I, 613b, 882a, 1012b, 1149b; IV, 262b, 897b; V, 904a, 906a, 907a, 908b, 1021b
Sakkākiyya iii, 660a — III, 681a
al-Saḳlāwiyya, Nahr i, 485b — I, 499b
Ṣaḳr b. Muḥammad b. Sālim al-Kasīmī iv, 778b — IV, 810a
Ṣaḳr b. Rāshid al-Kāsimī iv, 778a — IV, 809a
Saḳr b. Sulṭān i, 1314a — I, 1354b
Sakrūdj s, 269a — S, 268b
Sakūn v, 119b — V, 122a, b
Saḳy i, 491b — I, 506b
Sāla i, 780b — I, 804a
Ṣalābat Djang ii, 180a; iii, 320b; iv, 1023b; s, 280a — II, 185b; III, 331a, b; IV, 1055b; S, 280a
Saladin → Ṣalāḥ al-Dīn Yūsuf
Salādjiḳa v, 154a — V, 155a
Salaf i, 1112b — I, 1146a
Salafī ii, 412a — II, 423a
Salafiyya i, 272b, 416b, 425b; ii, 295a; iii, 701a, 727b, 1145b; iv, 142b, 145b-160b passim; v, 595b, 597a; s, 63b — I, 280b, 428b, 437b; II, 303a; III, 723a, 750a, 1174a; IV, 148b, 151b-167b passim; V, 599a, 601a; S, 64a
Ṣalāḥ i, 352b — I, 363a
Salāḥ Bey i, 1247a — I, 1285a
Ṣalāḥ al-Dīn b. Mubārak al-Bukhārī iv, 298b — IV, 312a
Ṣalāḥ al-Dīn Abū Fāṭima Khātun s, 83b — S, 83a
Ṣalāḥ al-Dīn Khudā Bakhsh v, 44a — V, 45a
Ṣalāḥ al-Dīn Yūsuf b. Ayyūb (Saladin) i, 96b, 150a, 197b, 353b, 517a, 552b, 662b, 665a, 711a, 797a, 814b, 832a, 932b, 971a, 989b, 1016b, 1138a, 1140a, 1358a; ii, 64b, 127a, 144a, 163a, 283b, 292b, 344b, 353b, 461b, 501b, 556a, 856b, 959a, 1056a; iii, 87a, 99a, 120a, 208b, 228b, 399b, 474a, 510b, 693b, 751b, 933b, 934a, 1157b, 1158a, 1201a; iv, 137a, 376b, 429b, 613a, 640b, 877b, 899b, 944a; v, 92a, 330b, 455a, 800b, 924b, 1127b; S, 121a, 123b, 154a, 205a — I, 99a, 154a, 202b, 364b, 532b, 570a, 683b, 684b, 732b, 820b, 837b, 855b, 961a, 1001a, 1020a, 1048a, 1172a, 1174b, 1398a; II, 66a, 130a, 148a, 168a, 291b, 300b, 354a, 363a, 473a, 514a, 570a, 876b, 981a, 1081a; III, 89b, 101b, 122b, 214b, 235a, 411b, 490b, 528a, 715b, 774a, 958b, 1186a, b, 1231b; IV, 142b, 392b, 448b, 638a, 667a, 910b, 932b, 977a; V, 94a, b, 330b, 457b, 806b, 930a, 1123b; S, 120b, 123a, 154b, 205a
Ṣalāḥ al-Dīn Zarkūb ii, 394b, 397a — II, 405a, 407b
Ṣalāḥ Raʾīs i, 1247a — I, 1285a
Salāla s, 337a — S, 336b
Salam iv, 326a; v, 559a — IV, 340a; V, 564a
Salama, Banū → Tudjībid
Salāma, Būlus iii, 112a — III, 114b
Salama b. ʿĀṣim i, 10b; ii, 807a — I, 10b; II, 826a
Salāma b. al-Ḥārith i, 527a; v, 118b — I, 543a; V, 121a
Salama b. Kuhayl s, 129b — S, 129a
Salāma b. Saʿīd iii, 653b — III, 675a
Salāma b. Ẓarib iv, 832b — IV, 865a
Salāma al-Khayr v, 526a — V, 530a
Salāmāt s, 166a — S, 166a
Salāmat ʿAlī → Dabīr
Salāmat Allāh s, 293b — S, 293b
Salāmgāh iii, 1170a — III, 1199a
Salāmī ii, 156a — II, 160b
al-Salāmī, Muḥammad iii, 821a — III, 844b
Salāmish, al-ʿĀdil iv, 484b — IV, 505b
al-Salāmiyya iv, 202a; s, 93b, 101a — IV, 211a; S, 93a, 100b
Salār i, 1126b, 1139a, 1325a; iii, 952a — I, 1160b, 1173b, 1365b; III, 976b
Salar (tribe/tribu) iv, 553b, 554b; v, 850b, 851a — IV, 577b, 578b; V, 855a
Sālār al-Dawla ii, 652b; iv, 393b; v, 171a, 466a, 826a — II, 669a; IV, 410b; V, 168b, 468b, 832a
Sālār al-Dawla (Ḳādjār) iv, 393b — IV, 410a
Sālār al-Dīn, Shaykh s, 114a — S, 113b
Salar Djang ii, 158b; iii, 322b — II, 163b; III, 332a
Sālār Khalīl v, 230a — V, 228a
Sālār Masʿūd Ghāzī → Ghāzī Miyān
Ṣalāt i, 188a; ii, 593b, 617a; iii, 1057a; iv, 321a, 771b; v, 74a, b, 75a, 82a, b, 395a, 424b, 709a — I, 193b; II, 608a, 632b; III, 1083a; IV, 335a, 802b; V, 76a, b, 77a,

84b, 85a, 396a, 426b, 714a
Ṣalāt al-ʿīd iii, 1007a — III, 1032b
Ṣalāt al-ʿishāʾ i, 733b — I, 755b
al-Ṣalatān i, 74a — I, 76a
Ṣalāt-i Maʿkūsa s, 313a — S, 313a
Saldjūḳ b. Duḳāḳ s, 245a — S, 245a
Saldjūḳs i, 20b, 98b, 236b, 465b, 510a, 639a, 661b, 799b, 900b, 1001a, 1336b, 1356a; ii, 4a, 344a, 855b, 1051a, 1108a; iii, 471b, 891b, 1255b; iv, 18b, 20a, 25a-29b, 208b, 294b, 347a, 1067a; v, 58a, 159b, 623a, 739a, 748a; s, 29b, 59a, 119a, 146a, 149a, 154a, b, 168b, 192a, 195a, 205a, 245b, 279a, 326a, 378a — I, 21a, 101b, 244a, 479a, 525b, 659b, 682b, 822b, 927b, 1032a, 1376b, 1395a; II, 4a, 353b, 875b, 1075b, 1134a; III, 488a, 915b, 1288a; IV, 20a, 21b, 27a-32a, 218a, 307b, 362a, 1098b; V, 60a, 158b, 627a, 744b, 753b; S, 29b, 59b, 118b, 146a, 149a, 154a, b, 168b, 193a, 195a, 205a, 245b, 279a, 325b, 378b
- administration i, 256a, 318a, 340a, 420a, 434a, 439b, 731a, 1045b, 1159a; ii, 80b, 229b, 506a, 1083a; iii, 47a, 1088b, 1098b; iv, 267a, b, 807a, 975a; v, 159a — I, 264a, 327b, 350b, 431b, 446a, 452a, 753a, 1077b, 1193b; II, 82b, 236b, 519a, 1108a; III, 49a, 1115b, 1125b; IV, 279a, b, 839b, 1007b; V, 158a
- art, architecture v, 217b, 1144b — V, 215a, 1137a
- literature/littérature i, 570b; iii, 1158a — I, 589a; III, 1186b
- of/de Rūm i, 215a, 346a, 466b, 467b, 477a, 510a, 702b, 843b, 1107a, 1159b, 1190b; ii, 13b, 344b, 444b, 712a, 989a; iii, 215b, 737b; iv, 294b, 464b, 813b; v, 103b, 104a, 271b — I, 221b, 356b, 480a, 481b, 491a, 525b, 724a, 866b, 1140a, 1194a, 1225b; II, 13b, 354a, 456a, 730b, 1012a; III, 221b, 760a; IV, 307b, 485a, 846a; V, 106a, b, 269b
Saldjūḳshāh (Salghūrid(e)) i, 1358a; iv, 498a — I, 1398b; IV, 519b
Salé → Shāla
Sale, Contract of → Bayʿ
Salghîr → Salur, Banū
Salghūrid(e)s ii, 812a; iii, 337a, 1099b; iv, 29b — II, 831a; III, 347a, 1126b; IV, 31b
Salifu bi Hama ii, 942a — II, 964a
Ṣāliḥ ii, 462a; iii,25b — II, 474a; III, 26b
Ṣālīḥ (prophet(e)) v, 124b, 421a — V, 127b, 423a
Ṣāliḥ (rāwī) i, 154a, 274b — I, 158a, 282b
Ṣāliḥ, Banū i, 14b, 403a, 526a — I, 15a, 414b, 542a
Ṣāliḥ b. ʿAbd al-Ḳuddūs i, 128a; ii, 1072a; iv, 1004a — I, 131b; II, 1097a; IV, 1036b
Ṣāliḥ b. Aḥmad b. Ḥanbal i, 273b; iii, 158b — I, 281b; III, 162a
Salīḥ b. ʿAlī s, 355b — S, 355b
Ṣāliḥ b. ʿAlī b. ʿAbd Allāh i, 108b; iii, 398a; iv, 375b — I, 111b; III, 410b; IV, 392a
Ṣāliḥ b. Ḥusayn Djibil i, 762b — I, 785b
Ṣāliḥ b. Kuthayr iii, 659a — III, 680b
Ṣāliḥ b. Mirdās ii, 484a; iii, 86a, 130b, 398b; v, 921b, 929a, 933a — II, 496a; III, 88b, 133b, 411a; V, 927a, 934a, 937a
Ṣāliḥ b. Rashīd iii, 234a, 618a — III, 241a, 638b
Ṣāliḥ b. Ṭarīf i, 1044a, b, 1178b, 1186a; v, 1199b — I, 1076a, 1213b, 1221a; V, 1190a
Ṣāliḥ b. Yaḥyā i, 946b; v, 791b — I, 976a; V, 797b
al-Ṣāliḥ Ayyūb → al-Ṣāliḥ Nadjm al-Dīn
Ṣāliḥ Bey (Ḳāsimī) iv, 723a — IV, 752a
Ṣāliḥ Bey (Algeria/Algérie) iii, 300a; v, 531b, 532a — III, 309a; V, 536a
Ṣāliḥ Čelebi → Djalālzāde
al-Ṣāliḥ ʿImād al-Dīn Ismāʿīl (Ayyūbid(e)) i, 711a, 766b, 799a, 804a; ii, 284a; iii, 989b; iv, 483b; s, 255b — I, 732b, 789b, 822b, 828a; II, 292a; III, 1014a; IV, 504b; S, 255a
al-Ṣāliḥ ʿImād al-Dīn Ismāʿīl (Mamlūk(e)) s, 255b — S, 255a
al-Ṣāliḥ Ismāʿīl (Zangid(e)) i, 1358a; ii, 283b; iii, 87a — I, 1398a; II, 291b; III, 89b
al-Ṣāliḥ Nadjm al-Dīn i, 198b, 711a, 766a, b, 801a, 802b, 804a, 912b, 944b, 1124b; ii, 284a, 347b; iii, 184b, 875b, 967a, 989b; iv, 430a, b, 521a; v, 628a, 922a — I, 204a, 732b, 789a, b, 824b, 826a, 828a, 940a, 973b, 1158b; II, 292a, 357b; III, 188b, 899b, 991b, 1014a; IV, 448b, 449a, 543b; V, 632a, 927b
Ṣāliḥ Reʾīs v, 506b — V, 510a
al-Ṣāliḥ Ṣalāḥ al-Dīn Hadjdjī → Hadjdjī II
al-Ṣāliḥ Ṣalāḥ al-Dīn Ṣāliḥ iii, 239b — III, 246b
Ṣāliḥ Ṣidḳī Ef. Hadžihusejnović i, 1271b — I, 1310b
Ṣāliḥ al-Yamanī ii, 87b — II, 89a
al-Ṣāliḥa i, 165a — I, 169b
Ṣāliḥī, Muḥammad b. Muslim iv, 1163a; v, 806a — IV, 1195a; V, 811b
al-Ṣāliḥiyya (Egypt/Égypte) iii, 184b — III, 188b
al-Ṣāliḥiyya (order/ordre) s, 279a — S, 278b
Ṣāliḥiyya (regiment/régiment) i, 1325a — I, 1365b
al-Ṣāliḥiyya (Syria/Syrie) iv, 532b; s, 20b — IV, 555b; S, 20b
Ṣāliḥiyya (Zaydī) iii, 244a — III, 251a
Sālik v, 1029a — V, 1025a
Sālim, mawlā iv, 755b — IV, 785b
Sālim, Shaykh al-Asad i, 684a — I, 705a
Salīm b. ʿAbd Allāh, Jumbe v, 278a — V, 276a
Sālim b. ʿAbdallāh i, 277b — I, 286a
Sālim b. Abī Ḥafṣa s, 129b — S, 129a
Sālim b. Aḥmad al-Nafrawī s, 44a — S, 44b
Salīm b. Akbar → Djahāngīr
Sālim b. Ghalbūn i, 250b — I, 258a
Sālim b. Idrīs al-Ḥabūḍī s, 338b — S, 338a
Sālim b. Ḳāsim iv, 749a — IV, 779a
Sālim b. Mālik ii, 354b — II, 364a
Sālim b. Mubārak Āl Ṣabāḥ iii, 1066a; iv, 680b; v, 574b — III, 1092b; IV, 708b; V, 579b
Sālim b. Sulṭān i, 1282a — I, 1321a
Sālim b. Thuwaynī s, 355b — S, 355b
Salīm Bābān i, 291a, 1217b — I, 300a, 1254a
Salīm al-Bishrī s, 132b — S, 132a
Salīm Čishtī, Shaykh ii, 379b, 840a, b — II, 390a, 860a
Salīm Fāris ii, 801a; iii, 593a — II, 820a; III, 613b
Salīm Ḳabūdān i, 929a — I, 957b
Sālim al-Kharūsī i, 1283a — I, 1321b
Sālim al-Maghribī i, 280b — I, 289a
Salīm al-Naḳḳāsh iv, 112a — IV, 117a
Salīm Shāh → Islām Shāh Sūrī
Sālim al-Tūmī i, 678a; ii, 520a — I, 699a; II, 533a
Salīma, Banū iv, 500b; s, 131a — IV, 522a; S, 130b
Salīma Sulṭān Bēgam i, 1136a, b; ii, 380a — I, 1170b, 1171a; II, 390b
al-Sālimī iii, 935a — III, 959b
al-Sālimī → ʿAbd Allāh b. Ḥumayyid
Sālimiyya i, 153a; iii, 269b, 570b — I, 157a; III, 277b, 590b
Salimu, al-Ḥādjdj → Karamba
Ṣalkhad i, 780b; iii, 293a — I, 804a; III, 302a
Sallām, Āl i, 95b — I, 98a
Sallāma al-Zarḳāʾ ii, 428b; iii, 2b, 682a; iv, 821b — II, 439b; III, 2b, 704a; IV, 854b
al-Sallāmī s, 326b — S, 326a
Sallār, Prince/le prince i, 688b — I, 709b
Sallārid(e)s ii, 680a — II, 697a
Salm b. Ḳutayba iv, 493b — IV, 514b
Salm b. Ziyād i, 5a, 47b; v, 853b; s, 26a — I, 5a, 49a; V, 860a; S, 26a
Salm al-Khāsir i, 1081b — I, 1114a
Salmā → Adjaʾ wa-Salmā
Salma bint ʿAmr i, 80a; iii, 260a — I, 82a; III, 267b
Salma b. Saʿd → Salāma b. Saʿīd

Salmān, Shaykh ii, 181a; iv, 314b, 675a — II, 187a; IV, 328b, 702b
Salmān b. Ḥamad i, 944a; iv, 954a — I, 973b; IV, 986b
Salmān b. Rabīʿa al-Bāhilī i, 635b, 636a, 660a, 921b, 1041a; iv, 343b — I, 656b, 681a, 949b, 1072b; IV, 358a
Salmān al-Fārisī i, 114a, 258a, 922b; ii, 846a, b, 847a, 850a, 1094b; iii, 470b; v, 430a, 945b, 946a — I, 117a, 266a, 950a; II, 866a, b, 867a, 870a, 1120b; III, 487a; V, 432b, 949a, b
Salmān, Masʿūd-i Saʿd-i s, 21a — S, 21b
Salmān Pāk → Salmān al-Fārisī
Salmān Sāwadjī i, 300a, 764b; ii, 439b; iv, 66a, 67a — I, 309a, 787b; II, 451a; IV, 69b, 70b
Salmon b. Jeroham → Sulaymān b. Ruhaym
Sālnāme i, 75a, 975a — I, 77a, 1005b
Salomon → Sulaymān
Salonika s, 63a, 296b — S, 63b, 296a
Salpêtre → Naṭrūn
Salt → Milḥ
al-Ṣalt b. Mālik i, 140b, 141b; iii, 748b, 757a — I, 145a, b; III, 771b, 780a
Saltes → Shalṭīsh
Saltpetre → Naṭrūn
Saltuḳ-oghlu i, 639a; ii, 712a; iv, 578b, 670a — I, 659b; II, 730b; IV, 602a, 697a
Saltūḳid(e)s → Saltuḳ-oghlu
Salūḳī iv, 491a — IV, 512a
Salūḳiyyīn ii, 352a, 1122b — II, 361b, 1148b
Salur, Banū v, 582a; s, 146b, 280b, 281a — V, 587a; S, 146b, 280b
Salur Ḳazan s, 280b — S, 280b
Sālyāne ii, 83a, 723a — II, 85a, 741b
Sām Mīrzā i, 228b; iv, 68b — I, 235a; IV, 72a
Samāʿ ii, 55b, 224a; iii, 27a; s, 313a — II, 56b, 231a; III, 28b; S, 313a
Samā' al-Dawla iii, 331a — III, 341a
al-Samā' al-dunyā i, 89b — I, 92a
fi'l-Samā' wa 'l-ʿĀlam i, 349b — I, 360b
Samāḥa, Masʿūd v, 1255b — V, 1246b
Samandar ii, 86a; iv, 1173a — II, 87b; IV, 1206b
al-Samʿānī, ʿAbd al-Karīm b. Muḥammad Tādj al-Dīn i, 146b, 594b; iii, 327b, 756a; s, 195a, 246a, 304a, 326a, b — I, 151a, 614a; III, 337b, 779a; S, 195a, 246a, 304a, 325b, 326a
Sāmānid(e)s i, 33a, 125b, 278a, 421b, 434a, 439b, 570b, 662a, 688a, 1001a, 1294a, 1344b, 1354b; ii, 192b, 253b, 748b, 791a, 1050b, 1082b; iii, 46b, 1113b, 1116a; iv, 18b, 21b-22b, 60b, 188b, 189a, 266b, 1066a; v, 622b, 856a, b; s, 21b, 35a, 72b, 149a, 204a, 245a, 356b, 411a — I, 33b, 129a, 286b, 433a, 446a, 452a, 589a, 682b, 709a, 1032a, 1333b, 1384b, 1393b; II, 198b, 261a, 767a, 810a, 1075a, 1107b; III, 48a, 1141a, 1143b; IV, 20a, 23a-24a, 63b-64a, 197a, 278b, 1097b; V, 626b, 862b, 863a; S, 21b, 35a, 73a, 149a, 203b, 245a, 356a, 411a
Sāmānkhudāt i, 685a — I, 706a
Samar iii, 369b — III, 381b
Samara → Kuybishev
Samarinda s, 150a, 151a — S, 150b, 151a
Samarḳand i, 32a, 46b, 135a, 147b, 148a, 848a; ii, 43a, 61b, 746a; iii, 711b, 799a, 1137b; iv, 33a; v, 541b, 551a, 853b, 1149a; s, 50b, 97a, 125b, 340a — I, 33a, 48a, 139a, 151b, 152a, 871a; II, 44a, 62b, 764b; III, 734a, 822b, 1166a; IV, 35b; V, 545b, 556a, 860b, 1140a; S, 51a, 96b, 124b, 339b
al-Samarḳandī → ʿAbd al-Razzāḳ; Abu 'l-Layth; al-Hāfiẓ
al-Samarḳandī, ʿAlā' al-Dīn iv, 690a — IV, 718a
Samarḳandī', Badr al-Dīn v, 301a — V, 300a
Sāmarrā' i, 18b, 211b, 897b; ii, 745b; iii, 1255a; iv, 215a, 384a, 653b, 1166a; v, 293a; s, 94a, 95a, 106a, 251a, 256a, b, 342a — I, 19a, 218a, 924b; II, 764a; III, 1288a; IV, 224b, 400b, 679b, 1198a; V, 292b; S, 93b, 94a, b, 105b, 251a, 255b, 256a, 341b
- dams/barrages ii, 948a; iii, 1251a — II, 969b; III, 1283b
- great mosque/la grande mosquée i, 620a, b, 622b, 830a, 1228a, 1315b; iii, 287a — I, 639b, 640b, 643a, 853b, 1264b, 1356a; III, 295b
- monuments i, 457b, 1346a; ii, 114a; iii, 1267b — I, 472a, 1386a; II, 116b; III, 1300b
al-Sāmarrī → Muḥammad b. ʿAbd Allāh
al-Samaṭrānī → Shams al-Dīn
al-Samaw'al iii, 1177a — III, 1206a
Samaw'al b. ʿĀdiyā' i, 565a; iv, 303a — I, 583a; IV, 316b
Samaw'al b. Yaḥyā al-Maghribī i, 520b, 690a; ii, 238a, 552b; iv, 600a — I, 536b, 711a; II, 245a, 566a; IV, 624a
Sambas s, 150a, b, 151a — S, 150b, 151a
Sambāṭ I i, 507a, 637a; ii, 679b — I, 522b, 658a; II, 696b
Sambāṭ II i, 507b, 637b, 638a — I, 522b, 658b
Sambhādjī (Marātha) i, 769b; iv, 1023b; s, 246b — I, 792b; IV, 1055b; S, 246b
Sambhal iv, 749b; s, 73b, 331b — IV, 779b; S, 74a, 331a
al-Samḥ b. Mālik al-Khawlānī i, 608b; iii, 587b; v, 510a; s, 81b — I, 628a; III, 608a; V, 514a; S, 81b
al-Samhūdī s, 234b, 304b, 350a — S, 234a, 304a, 350a
Sāmī al-Bārūdī iii, 59a — III, 61b
Sāmī Bey → Shams al-Dīn Sāmī
Sāmī Pasha ii, 637b — II, 653b
Samʿiyyāt i, 343a; iii, 1147b; iv, 469b — I, 353b; III, 1175b; IV, 490a
Samlis ii, 770b — II, 789a
Sammā i, 627b; iii, 419b — I, 648b; III, 433a
Sammād → Kannās
al-Ṣammān i, 536b; ii, 92a — I, 553a; II, 93b
al-Sammāniyya iv, 991b, 993a — IV, 1024b, 1026a
Sammūra iii, 842a — III, 865b
Samn i, 541a; ii, 1057b — I, 558a; II, 1082a
Sāmogaṛh iii, 202a, b — III, 207b
Samori Touré i, 297a; ii, 63a, 1003b, 1132b; v, 253a — I, 306b; II, 64a, 1027a, 1159b; V, 251a
Sampit s, 150b — S, 150b
al-Ṣamṣām, Ḥasan i, 986b; iii, 788a; iv, 497a — I, 1017a; III, 811a; IV, 518b
Ṣamṣām al-Dawla iii, 1193a — III, 1223a
Ṣamṣām al-Dawla Khān i, 241b, 808a; iii, 320b; iv, 914b — I, 249a, 831a; III, 331b; IV, 947a
Ṣamṣām al-Dawla Marzubān (Būyid(e)) i, 1351a; ii, 749a; iii, 128b, 244b; iv, 220a; v, 452b; s, 4a, 118a, 119b, 398a — I, 1396a; II, 767b; III, 131b, 251b; IV, 230a; V, 455b; S, 3b, 117b, 119a, 398b
al-Ṣamṣāma i, 453a — I, 466a
Samsī i, 525a — I, 541a
Sāmsūn i, 476b; ii, 20b, 446b; iv, 575b — I, 490b; II, 20b, 458a; IV, 598b
Samudra, Pangeran s, 150b — S, 150b
Samuel b. Moses al-Maghribī iv, 306b, 605b — IV, 320b, 630a
Samuel b. Nagrēlla i, 130b; ii, 1012b, 1016b — I, 134a; II, 1036b, 1040a
Samurzakan i, 101a — I, 104a
Ṣanʿā' i, 102b, 440b, 551a, 554b; ii, 1096a; iii, 125a; v, 808b; s, 22a, b, 61b, 62a, 115b, 236a, 335a, 337b, 338a, 387b — I, 105b, 453b, 568b, 572b; II, 1121b; III, 128a; V, 814b; S, 22b, 62a, b, 115a, 236a, 334b, 337a, 338a, 388a
Ṣanāʿ (near/près de Ṣanʿā') s, 236a — S, 236a
Sanā' al-Mulk al-Ḥusayn i, 440a — I, 452b

al-Sanā al-Rāhib s, 396a — S, 396b
Sanābira iv, 664b — IV, 691a
al-Sanādjiḳ iii, 186b — III, 191a
al-Ṣanāfīrī iii, 776a — III, 799b
Sanāʾī i, 764b, 1019a; iv, 57b, 61b, 63a; s, 240a, 334a, 416b — I, 787b, 1050b; IV, 61a, 65a, 66b; S, 240a, 333b, 416b
al-Ṣanam iv, 384a — IV, 401a
Sanandadj s, 136b, 145b — S, 136a, 145a
al-Ṣanʿānī, Ḥanash b. ʿAbd Allāh s, 81b — S, 81b
Ṣanāriyya iv, 345a; v, 487b, 488a — IV, 359b; V, 490b, 491a
Ṣanʿatīzāda, ʿAbd al-Ḥusayn iv, 72b; v, 198a — IV, 76b; V, 195b
al-Ṣanawbarī iv, 55b — IV, 58b
Sanbar b. al-Ḥasan iv, 664a — IV, 691a
Sanbāt → Sambāṭ
Sancho Garcia i, 75b, 76a — I, 78a
Sancho Gimeno → Jimeno
Sanchuelo → ʿAbd al-Raḥmān b. ʿAbī ʿĀmir
Sandābil i, 116a — I, 119b
Ṣandal iv, 459a — IV, 479b
Sandgrouse → Ḳaṭā
Sandjaḳ i, 468b, 469a, 652a, 655b, 1263b, 1264a; ii, 722b, 723b; iv, 563b, 1094b; v, 776a — I, 482b, 483a, 672b, 676a, 1302a, b; II, 741a, 742a; IV, 586a, 1125b; V, 782a
Sandjaḳdār i, 1135a — I, 1169a
Sandjaḳ-i Sherif v, 19a — V, 19b
Sandjan v, 1113a, b — V, 1109b
Sandjar (Saldjūḳ) i, 94b, 283a, 353b, 504a, 524a, 662a, 687a, 750a, 940a, 1001b, 1052a, 1132a; ii, 81a, 382a, 893b, 1052a, 1100a, 1101a, 1109a, 1143b; iii, 196a, b, 336b, 345a, 1099a, b, 1114b; iv, 18b, 29a, b, 217b, 466a, 581b, 1067a, 1186a; v, 58b, 439a, 454a; s, 65a, 245b, 279a, 326a, 333b — I, 97a, 291b, 364a, 519a, 540a, 683a, 708a, 772b, 968b, 1032a, 1083b, 1084a, 1166a; II, 82b, 392b, 914b, 1076b, 1126a, 1127a, 1135a, 1170b; III, 200b, 201b, 346b, 355b, 1126a, b, 1142a; IV, 20a, 31a, b, 227a, 487a, 604b, 1099a, 1219a; V, 60a, 441b, 456b; S, 65b, 245b, 279a, 325b, 333b
Sandjar Abū Shudjāʿī i, 1138a, 1324b — I, 1172b, 1365b
Ṣandūḳ iv, 227b — IV, 237b
Ṣanf ii, 8b; iii, 1209a — II, 8b; III, 1239b
Sang-i Maghribī i, 1068b — I, 1100b
Sangat Singh i, 432b — I, 445a
Sangīn ʿAlī I ii, 29b — II, 30a
Sangīn ʿAlī II ii, 30a — II, 30a
Sanglēčī i, 225a — I, 231b
Sanglier → Khinzīr
Sāngrām, Mahārānā ii, 1128a; iii, 1010a — II, 1154b; III, 1035b
Ṣanhādja i, 699a, 700a, 762a, 1174b, 1175b, 1309a, 1319b, 1350a; ii, 115a, 873b, 1121b; iv, 199a, 479b; v, 652b, 653a, 769b, 1177b, 1204a, b; s, 113b — I, 720b, 721a, 785a, 1209b, 1210b, 1349b, 1359b, 1390a; II, 117b, 894a, 1148a; IV, 208a, 501b; V, 656b, 657a, 775b, 1167b, 1194b, 1195a; S, 113a
al-Ṣanhādjī, Abu 'l-Gharīb → Ibn Shaddād, ʿAbd al-ʿAzīz
Ṣanhādjiyyūn iii, 339a — III, 349a
Ṣāniʿ i, 898b; iv, 819a — I, 925b; IV, 852a
Ṣāniʿ al-Dawla → Muḥammad Ḥasan Khān
al-Sāniḥ iv, 290b — Iv, 303b
Sanīn Ḥusayn ii, 124a — II, 127a
Sāniya i, 492a — I, 507a
Saniyya Lands s, 179a — S, 180a
Ṣannādj al-ʿArab → Ibn Muḥriz
Saʿnōnī i, 531a — I, 547a
Sansār Čand iv, 543b — IV, 567a
Sanskrit/Sanscrit iii, 412b, 1136a, 1215b, 1216a; v, 540a — III, 425b, 1164a, 1246a, 1247a; V, 544a
Santa Cruz i, 245a — I, 252b
Santa Maria de Alarcos → al-Arak
Santa Maria de Algarve → Shantamariyat al-gharb
Santa Maria del Puerto i, 1320a — I, 1360b
Santa Maura → Levkas
Santarem → Shantarīn
Santaver → Shantabariyya
Santiago (Andalus) → Shant Yāḳub
Sanua, James/Jacques → Abū Naḍḍāra
Sanūb → Sinob
al-Sanūsī, al-Mahdī b. Muḥammad v, 352b — V, 353a
al-Sanūsī, Muḥammad b. ʿAlī ii, 224a, 378a, 492b; iv, 952b; v, 760a; s, 164b, 278b — II, 231a, 388a, 505a; IV, 985a; V, 766a; S, 164b, 278b
al-Sanūsī, Muḥammad b. Yūsuf i, 333a, 334a, 593a, 696a, 867b, 1019b; iii, 780a; s, 403a, b — I, 343a, 344a, 612a, 717b, 891b, 1051a; III, 803a; S, 403a, b
Sanusi, Sir Muhammadu iv, 550a — IV, 573b
Sanūsiyya i, 136a, 277b, 763a, 1049b, 1071a, 1258b, 1260b; ii, 161b, 165a, 224a, 378a; iv, 541b, 777a, 952a, 954b; v, 352a, 760a; s, 164b — I, 140a, 286a, 786a, 1081a, 1103a, 1296b, 1298b; II, 166b, 170a, 231a, 388a; IV, 564b, 808b, 984b, 986b; V, 353a, 766a; S, 164b
Saphadin → al-ʿĀdil I
Sar-i Pul-i Dhuhāb → Ḥulwān (Irān)
Sāra (singer/chanteuse) iv, 821a — IV, 854a
Sara (tribe/tribu) s, 163b, 165b, 166a, b — S, 163b, 165a, 166a, b
Sāra b. Aḥmad al-Sudayrī s, 3b — S, 2b
Sarāb i, 8a — I, 8a
Saraceni v, 1014b, 1019a — V, 1010b, 1015a
Sarāfīl, Sarāfīn → Isrāfīl
Saragossa/Saragosse → Saraḳusṭa
Sarajevo i, 1263a, b, 1265b, 1266b, 1267a, b, 1268a, b, 1270b, 1273a; v, 32a — I, 1301b, 1302a, 1304a, 1305a, 1306a, 1307a, b, 1309b, 1312a; V, 33a
Sarakata i, 741a, b — I, 763a, b
Sarakhs i, 47b; v, 293b; s, 195a — I, 49a; V, 293a, b; S, 195a
al-Sarakhsī, ʿAbd al-Raḥmān ii, 752a — II, 770a
al-Sarakhsī, Aḥmad i, 339a, 590a, 1003b; ii, 578b — I, 349b, 609a, 1034a; II, 593a
al-Sarakhsī, Shams al-Aʾimma iii, 163a, b, 1024a; v, 130a — III, 166b, 167a, 1050a; V, 133a
Sarāḳūdj iii, 186a — III, 190b
Saraḳusṭa i, 82a, 390a, 493a, 495b; iii, 542a, b, 728a, 1093a; v, 219a; s, 81b, 82a, 383a — I, 84b, 401a, 508a, 510a; III, 560b, 561a, 750b, 1064b; V, 216b; S, 81b, 383b
- monuments i, 497b, 499a — I, 512b, 514a
Sarāna iv, 1042b — IV, 1074a
Sarandīb → Ceylon
Sarandjām i, 260b, 262a — I, 268b, 270a
Sārang Khān v, 31b — V, 32b
al-Sarāt i, 536a, 707b; iii, 362a — I, 552b, 729a; III, 373a
Sarawak s, 150a, 151a, 152a — S, 150a, 151a, 152a
Sarāy i, 904b, 906a — I, 932a, 933a
Saray (Astrakhān) i, 1106a, b, 1108a; iv, 349b, 350a; s, 203b — I, 1139b, 1141a; IV, 364b, 365a; S, 203a
Sarāy-aghasî ii, 1088a, 1089a; iv, 571a — II, 1113b, 1114b; IV, 593b
Saray Bosna s, 354a — S, 354a
Saray Ovasî → Sarajevo
Sarbadārid(e)s iii, 968b, 1123a; iv, 32a, 48b; v, 59a — III, 993a, 1150b; IV, 34b, 51a; V, 60b
Sarbandī iv, 10b — IV, 11b
Sarbuland Khān i, 1053a, 1330a — I, 1084b, 1370b

Sarčam iii, 1125a — III, 1153a
Sardāb ii, 114a — II, 116b
Sardār Muḥammad Hāshim Khān i, 232b — I, 240a
Sardār Muḥammad Ibrāhīm iv, 711a — IV, 739b
Sardinia/Sardaigne i, 86b; s, 120b — I, 89a; S, 120a
Sar-djahān i, 98b — I, 101b
Sardjīs Rāsaʿnī i, 213a — I, 219b
Sardjūn iv, 755a — IV, 785b
Sardsir → Kîshlaḳ
Sarekat Islam iii, 534a, 1223b, 1229a — III, 552b, 1254b, 1261a
Ṣarf iv, 326a — IV, 340a
Sarfrāz Khān i, 400b; ii, 371a — I, 412a; II, 381a
Sarghitmish iii, 239b, 699a; iv, 424a — III, 246b, 721a; IV, 442b
Sarghūn II v, 68a, b — V, 70a, b
Sārī (Ḳumān) v, 373a — V, 374a
Sārī (Ṭabaristān) s, 309a — S, 308b
Ṣarî ʿAbd Allāh iii, 711a — III, 733b
al-Sarī al-Aḳṣam iv, 1132b — IV, 1164a
Ṣarî Beyoghlî Muṣṭafā iv, 593a — IV, 617a
Sarî Demir Tash Pashā iv, 623a — IV, 648a
Sarî Kenʿān Pasha → Kenʿān Pasha
Sarî Muṣṭafa Pasha iv, 969b — IV, 1001b
Sarī al-Saḳaṭī i, 1245b — I, 1283b
Ṣarî Ṣalṭîḳ i, 299a, 838b, 842b, 843a, 993a, 998b, 1031b; ii, 610b, 612a; iii, 115a; iv, 628a, 885a — I, 308a, 862a, 865b, 866b, 1023b, 1029b, 1063a; II, 625b, 627a; III, 117a; IV, 653a, 917b
Ṣarīfa i, 1097a — I, 1130a
al-Ṣarīfīnī s, 195a — S, 193a
Sarighshin iv, 1178a — IV, 1211a, b
Sarîḳ (tribe/tribu) s, 143b, 146b, 281a — S, 143a, 146b, 281a
Sarikat → Shirka
Ṣārim al-Dīn Ḳaymaz Kāfūrī iv, 483b — IV, 504b
Sar-i-mūsh iv, 811a — IV, 843b
Sarīr ii, 86a; iv, 343a, 346a — II, 87b; IV, 357b, 361a
Sāriya s, 298a, 356b, 357a — S, 297b, 356b, 357a
Sarkan Bashkurt i, 1075b — I, 1107b
Sarkārs i, 316b; iii, 320b — I, 326b; III, 331b
Sarkash iv, 53b — IV, 56b
Sarkel → Sharkil
Sarkhad s, 391a — S, 391b
Sarkhāstān iv, 646b, 647a — IV, 673a, b
Sarkhēdj iii, 445a, b — III, 460a, b
Sarkīs, Khalīl ii, 467b — II, 479a
Sarmad ii, 134b; iii, 492b — II, 138a; III, 509b
Sarmast, Saččal v, 611a — V, 615a
Ṣarmis → Čeremiss(es)
Sārōē → Sārūya
al-Sarrādj → Abū Muḥammad Djaʿfar al-Sarrādj
Sarrādj, ʿAbd al-Ḥamīd s, 8a — S, 7a
al-Sarrādj, Abū ʿAlī → Ibn al-Sarrādj, Abū ʿAlī
al-Sarrādj, Abū Naṣr iii, 546b, 589a — III, 565b, 609b
al-Sarrādj, Banū → Ibn al-Sarrādj
al-Sarrādj, Yaḥyā iii, 670b — III, 692b
Ṣarrāfs i, 898b — I, 925b
Sarrasins → Saraceni
Ṣarrūf, Yaʿḳūb i, 597a — I, 616b
Sarshār, Ratan Nāth iii, 359a, 376a; v, 202b — III, 370a, 388a; V, 200a
Sar-shumārī iv, 1042b — IV, 1074a
Sartak i, 1106a, 1187b — I, 1139a, 1223a
Sart(e)s v, 30a, 273b — V, 31a, 271b
Ṣaru Ṣaltuḳ → Ṣarî Ṣaltîḳ
Sarudja (Sarîdja) iii, 317b — III, 327b
Ṣarudja Pasha ii, 985b — II, 1008a
Saruḳ s, 142b — S, 142a
Ṣarukhān i, 467b, 654a; v, 505b, 506a — I, 481b, 674b; V, 509a, b
Ṣārūkhān-oghullarî v, 1169b — V, 1159b
Sarūkhānī → Gulshanī
Sarūr iii, 376a — III, 388a
Sārūya ii, 74b — II, 76a
Sarvistān s, 327a — S, 326b
Sarwār Khān s, 329b — S, 329a
Sasa Beg i, 783a — I, 806b
Ṣaʿṣaʿa i, 382b — I, 393b
Sasak v, 785a, b — V, 791b, 792a
Sāsān iv, 809b — IV, 842b
Sāsān, Banū s, 250a — S, 250a
Sāsānid(e)s i, 66a, 226a, 938b, 1041a, 1094a; ii, 77b, 190a, 951a; iii, 50b, 113a, 177a, 304a, 470b, 884a; iv, 13a-b, 219b, 850b; v, 56b, 184b, 634a, 831a, 1110a; s, 116a, 251a, 297b — I, 67b, 232b, 967b, 1072b, 1126b; II, 79a, 196a, 973a; III, 52b, 115b, 181a, 313a, 487a, 908a; IV, 14a-b, 229b, 883b; V, 58a, 182a, 638a, 837a, 1106a; S, 115a, 251a, 297a
- art, architecture ii, 742b, 743a — II, 761a, b
Sasî Buḳa (Özbeg) s, 246a — S, 246a
Ṣāṣūn v, 459a — V, 461b
Satgur Nūr iv, 202b; v, 26a — IV, 211b; V, 26b
Sātī-Beg ii, 68a, b, 401a — II, 69a, b, 411b
Sāṭiʿ al-Huṣrī ii, 1117b; v, 905b — II, 1143b; V, 910b
Saṭīḥ b. Rabīʿa iii, 739b — III, 762a
Satire → Hidjāʾ
Satpanth iv, 206a — IV, 215a
Sat-panthīs i, 173a; iii, 1163a; iv, 202b — I, 177b; III, 1191b; IV, 211b
Satr iv, 205b — IV, 214b
Sattār Khān s, 365b — S, 365a
Satuḳ Bughra Khān → ʿAbd al-Karīm Khān
Saturdjî Meḥmed Pasha v, 27b — V, 28b
Saturiḳ iii, 1125a — III, 1153a
Satyadharmas i, 173a — I, 177b
Satyapīr iii, 422b — III, 436a
Saʿūd, Āl i, 98b, 554b, 942b, 1313a; ii, 176b, 320b, 573a; iii, 363b; iv, 717b, 765a, 778a, 953a, 1072b; v, 574b, 575a; s, 30a — I, 101b, 572a, 971b, 1353a; II, 182a, 330a, 587a; III, 375a; IV, 746a, 795b, 809b, 985b, 1104b; V, 579a, b; S, 30b
Saʿūd b. ʿAbd al-ʿAzīz (1803-14) ii, 321a; iv, 765a, 925b — II, 330b; IV, 795b, 958b
Saʿūd b. ʿAbd al-ʿAzīz (1953-64) i, 555a, 958a; ii, 660b — I, 572b, 987b; II, 677a
Saʿūd b. ʿAzzān b. Ḳays s, 356a — S, 356a
Saʿūd b. Fayṣal (1860) ii, 176b; iv, 1073a — II, 182a; IV, 1104b
Saʿūd b. Fayṣal b. ʿAbd al-ʿAzīz Āl Suʿūd s, 305b — S, 305b
Saʿūd al-Kabīr iv, 1073a — IV, 1104b
Saʿūdi Arabia i, 39a, b, 534a, 539a, 1314a; ii, 557b, 660a; iii, 363a; s, 417b
- institutions ii, 425a; v, 1056b
Saul/Saül → Ṭālūt
Sauterelle → Djarād
Sava ii, 746a — II, 764b
Savak iv, 41b — IV, 44a
Sarak (Savaz) ii, 70a — II, 71a
Sāwa v, 868b — V, 875a
Sawād i, 382b; ii, 577a; iv, 1140b; v, 345b, 347b; s, 59a — I, 393b; II, 591b; IV, 1172b; V, 346b, 348b; S, 59b
Ṣawāfī i, 1144a; iv, 972b, 973a — I, 1178b; IV, 1005a
Sawāʿī → Djay Singh
Sawākin i, 782b, 1158a, 1172a; iv, 643a, 687a; v, 1249b, 1251a — I, 806a, 1192b, 1207a; IV, 669b, 715a; V, 1240a, 1241b
Sawār, amīr v, 124b, 125b, 922a — V, 127a, 128a, 927b
Sawda s, 172a — S, 173a
al-Sawdāʾ i, 535b — I, 551b
Sawdā, Mīrzā Rafīʿ i, 241b; iii, 119a, 358b; iv, 716b;

v, 959a, b, 961a; s, 109b, 358b — I, 249a; III, 121b, 369b; IV, 745a; V, 963a, b, 965a; S, 109a, 358b
Sawda bint Zamʿa i, 307b — I, 317a
Sawdān i, 1166b; iv, 275b — I, 1201a; IV, 287b
Sāwdj-Bulāḳ v, 1213a — V, 1202b
al-Sāwī, Djamāl al-Dīn iv, 473a, b — IV, 494a
Ṣawlat al-Dawla Khān iv, 706b — IV, 734b
Ṣawlat Djang ii, 1091b — II, 1117a
al-Ṣawmaʿī → Aḥmad b. Abi 'l-Ḳāsim
Sāwra (valley/vallée de) s, 28b — S, 29a
Sawra b. Ḥurr al-Tamīmī ii, 600b — II, 615b
Sawrān s, 245a, b — S, 245a, b
Sawrāshtra ii, 1123b, 1130b — II, 1149b, 1157b
Sawsanī, Abū Sahl iii, 256a — III, 263a
Sāwtegin, ʿImād al-Dīn i, 660b; ii, 1082b; iii, 471b; iv, 348a; s, 383b — I, 681b; II, 1107b; III, 488a; IV, 363a; S, 384a
Sāwudjbulāgh s, 73a — S, 73b
Sawwār b. ʿAbd Allāh s, 113a — S, 112b
Sawwār b. Ḥamdūn ii, 1012b — II, 1036a
Saʿy iii, 35a, 36b; iv, 185a — III, 37a, 38a; IV, 193a
Sayābidja i, 761b — I, 784b
Sayd → Sayyid
Ṣaydā iii, 474b; iv, 483a, 484a; s, 49a, 120b, 268a — III, 491a; IV, 504a, b; S, 49b, 120a, 267b
Sayf (sword/épée) ii, 1122a; iv, 502b; v, 972b, 973a — II, 1148b; IV, 524a; V, 974b, 975a
Sayf b. Dhī Yazan i, 102a; ii, 1096a; iv, 566b; s, 115b, 164a — I, 105a; II, 1122a; IV, 589a; S, 115a, 163b
Sayf b. Sulṭān I v, 507a — V, 510b
Sayf b. Sulṭān II i, 1281b — I, 1321a
Sayf b. ʿUmar i, 51a, 629a; iv, 385a; v, 324a — I, 52b, 650a; IV, 401b; V, 323b
Sayf b. Zāmil b. Djabr s, 234a — S, 234a
Sayf ʿAlī Beg i, 1135a — I, 1169b
Sayf ʿAyn al-Mulk iii, 1161a — III, 1189b
Sayf al-Dawla Aḥmad b. Hūd → Aḥmad III (Hūdid(e))
Sayf al-Dawla ʿAlī (Ḥamdānid(e)) i, 118a, 119b, 329a, 517a, 679b, 789b, 791b, 845b; ii, 36b, 178b, 344a, 693b; iii, 20a, 86a, 127a, b, 129a, b, 398a, 404b, 507a, 824b, 900a; v, 124b, 525a, 923b; s, 12b, 36a, 37b, 361b, 362a — I, 121b, 123a, 339b, 532b, 700b, 813a, 815a, 869a; II, 37b, 184a, 353b, 710b; III, 21a, 88a, 129b, 130a, 131b, 132a, 410b, 416b, 524a, 848b, 924a; V, 127a, 529a, 929a; S, 13a, 36b, 38a, 361a, b
Sayf al-Dawla Maḥmūd ii, 1052a; s, 21a, 24a — II, 1076b; S, 21a, 24a
Sayf al-Dawla Ṣadaḳa s, 326a — S, 325b
Sayf al-Dīn → al-ʿĀdil I
Sayf al-Dīn Fīrūz → Fīrūz Shāh (Bengal(e))
Sayf al-Dīn Ghāzī → Ghāzī I, II (Zangid(e))
Sayf al-Dīn ʿImād al-Dīn Farāmurz s, 416a — S, 416b
Sayf al-Dīn al-Malik al-Nāṣirī ii, 126a — II, 129a
Sayf al-Dīn Muḥammad ii, 1101a, 1103a — II, 1127a, 1129b
Sayf al-Dīn Sūrī i, 940a; ii, 382a, 1100a — I, 968b; II, 392b, 1126a
Sayf al-Islām Badr ii, 674b — II, 691b
Sayf al-Mulūk s, 335b — S, 335b
Sayf al-Raḥmān ii, 31a — II, 31b
Sayfī i, 323a; v, 314b — I, 333a; V, 314a
Saygun, Adnan iii, 1094b — III, 1121a
al-Sayḥ i, 233a — I, 240b
Ṣayhad (desert/désert) s, 337a — S, 336b
Sayḥān i, 184a; ii, 35a, 502b — I, 189a; II, 36a, 515b
Sayḥūn → Sīr Daryā
Sayhūt s, 337a — S, 337a
Sāyin Bulāt iv, 723b — IV, 752b
Sayl i, 538a — I, 554b
Sayl al-layl i, 554a — I, 571b
al-Ṣaymarī, Abū 'l-ʿAnbas ii, 552a — II, 566a
Sayrām ii, 39a, 45b — II, 39b, 46a
Sayʾūn s, 337b, 338b — S, 337a, 338b
Ṣayyād iv, 10b — IV, 11b
Sayyāḥ, Ḥādjdj s, 109b — S, 108b
Sayyiʾa iv, 1106b — IV, 1138a
Sayyid i, 1022b; ii, 687b; iii, 411a; v, 627a — I, 1054a; II, 705a; III, 423b; V, 631a
Sayyid ʿAbd al-ʿAẓīm Mīrzā → Aghā-bakhsh
Sayyid Abū Bakr iii, 1218b — III, 1249b
Sayyid Āghā Ḥasan → Amānat
Sayyid Aḥmad b. ʿAbd al-Raḥmān iv, 780a — IV, 811b
Sayyid Aḥmad Brēlwī → Aḥmad Brēlwī
Sayyid Aḥmad Khān → Aḥmad Khān, Sir Sayyid
Sayyid Aḥmad Shāh, Mīrzā v, 164a — V, 162a
Sayyid Akbar i, 238b; iv, 1143a — I, 246a; IV, 1174b
Sayyid ʿAlī Dūghlāt ii, 622a — II, 637b
Sayyid ʿAlī Khān ii, 47b — II, 48a
Sayyid ʿAlī Muḥammad → Bāb
Sayyid al-Awwal i, 606b — I, 626a
Sayyid ʿAẓīm i, 193b — I, 199b
Sayyid Baṭṭāl i, 1102b — I, 1136a
Sayyid Burhān Khān iv, 724a — IV, 753a
Sayyid Ḍiyāʾ s, 84a — S, 83b
Sayyid Dūst Muḥammad b. Sayyid Ḳuṭb al-Dīn s, 325a — S, 324b
Sayyid Ḥasan Beg iv, 201b — IV, 210b
al-Sayyid al-Ḥimyarī i, 431b; ii, 136a; iii, 882a; iv, 836b; v, 552b — I, 443b; II, 139b; III, 906a; IV, 869b; V, 557a
Sayyid Isḥāḳ ii, 733a — II, 751b
Sayyid Kāẓim Rashtī i, 304b, 833a — I, 314a, 856a
Sayyid Khān ii, 973b — II, 995b
Sayyid Ḳuṭb al-Dīn b. Sayyid Masʿūd s, 325a — S, 324b
Sayyid Maḥmūd Djawnpūrī ii, 500a — II, 512b
Sayyid Masʿūd s, 325a — S, 324b
Sayyid Muḥammad, Mīr s, 340a — S, 339b
Sayyid Muḥammad, Mīrzā s, 23b, 74a — S, 23b, 74a
Sayyid Muḥammad b. ʿAlī → al-Idrīsī
Sayyid Muḥammad b. Sayyid ʿAlāʾ al-Dīn ii, 967b — II, 989b
Sayyid Muḥammad b. Sayyid ʿAlī al-Hamdānī iv, 708b — IV, 736b
Sayyid Muḥammad Buzurg-Sawār i, 262a; ii, 194a — I, 270a; II, 200b
Sayyid Muḥammad Djawnpūrī → al-Djawnpūrī
Sayyid Muḥammad Khān (Awadh) ii, 1046a — II, 1070a
Sayyid Muḥammad Khān (Dihlī) s, 247a — S, 247a
Sayyid Muḥammad Mīrzā Dughlāt ii, 622b — II, 638a
Sayyid Murād iv, 1158a — IV, 1190a
al-Sayyid Murtaḍā i, 266a,b — I, 274b
Sayyid Nadhīr Ḥusayn i, 259b — I, 267b
Sayyid Nūḥ ii, 588b — II, 603a
Sayyid al-Tābiʿīn → Saʿīd b. al-Musayyab
Sayyid Ṭālib al-Rifāʿī al-Naḳīb iii, 520a — III, 538a
Sayyid Yaḥyā b. Sayyid Ḳuṭb al-Dīn s, 325a — S, 324b
al-Sayyida → ʿĀʾisha al-Mannūbiyya
Sayyida Ḥurra bint Aḥmad i, 181b, 552a; ii, 856a; iii, 134a; iv, 200b — I, 186b, 570a; II, 876a; III, 136b; IV, 209a
Sayyida Umm Fakhr al-Dawla iv, 465a; v, 1028a, b — IV, 486a; V, 1024a
Sayyidī Abū Saʿīd i, 863b — I, 887b
Sāz s, 91b — S, 91a
Sbaʿa i, 483a — I, 497b
Sbuk → Subuk
Scanderbeg → Iskender Beg

Scapular → Khirḳa; Ṣūf
Scenites i, 527b
Schnitzer, Carl → Emīn Pasha
Scorpion → ʿAḳrab
Scribe, Secretary/Secrétaire → Dabīr; Kātib; Yazîdjî
Script → Khaṭṭ
Sculpture v, 14a-b — V, 14b
Scutari → Üsküdār
Seʿadya → Saʿīd
Seal → Khātam
Seat → Kursī
Sebastopol/Sébastopol i, 12b — I, 13a
Sebeos (bishop/l'évêque) i, 635b, 636b — I, 656b, 657b
Sebḥa ii, 877b — II, 897b
Sebkha ii, 463a — II, 474b
Sebou (river/rivière) → Sabū, Wādī
Sebüktegin i, 11b, 142b, 226b, 421b, 424b, 899b, 1348b; ii, 799a, 978a, 1049a, 1050b; iii, 46b, 197a, 415b; iv, 24b, 208b, 917b; v, 622b, 649a; s, 284b — I, 11b, 147a, 233b, 433b, 436b, 926b, 1388b; II, 818a, 1000b, 1073a, 1075a; III, 48b, 202a, 428b; IV, 26a, 218a, 950b; V, 626b, 653a; S, 284b
Secret History of the Mongols ii, 41a, 43b, 571a
Secretary/Secrétaire → Kātib
Secunderabad → Sikandarābād
Sedrata ii, 115a — II, 117b
Sefāretnāme ii, 590a; iii, 590a — II, 604b; III, 610a
Sefawa iv, 566b — IV, 589a
Sefer-beg i, 101a — I, 104a
Sefer Ghāzī (Agha) iv, 178b, 630a — IV, 185b, 655a
Seferli odasî ii, 1088b — II, 1114a
Sefrou s, 191a — S, 192a
Segu, Segou i, 297a; iii, 39a — I, 306a; III, 41a
Segura → Shaḳūra
Şehir i, 974b — I, 1005a
Sekbān iii, 317b — III, 327b
Sekkīn ii, 511a — II, 524a
Sekou Ouattara v, 252b — V, 250b
Sekou Touré ii, 1133a — II, 1159b
Seku Hamadu → Aḥmadu
Sel, le → Milḥ
Selāmlîk ii, 114b — II, 117a
Selčuk → Aya Solūk
Seldjen-oghlu iii, 1199a — III, 1229a
Seldjuḳs/Seldjuḳides → Saldjūḳ
Selīm I (Ottoman) i, 21b, 182b, 310b, 329b, 362a, 396a, 441a, 468a, 475a, 477a, 553b, 1032b, 1120b, 1207b, 1208a, 1234a; ii, 7b, 38b, 72b, 240a, 286a,b, 291b, 340a, 373b, 374a, 400a, 420b, 634b, 684a, 722b, 968a, 1042a; iii, 213b, 216a, 341b, 708b, 1183b; iv, 376a, 553a, 716b, 868b, 880a, 899b, 900a, 945b, 1156a; v, 269b; s, 274a — I, 22b, 187b, 320b, 340a, 373a, 407b, 453b, 482a, 489a, 491a, 571a, 1064a, 1154a,b, 1243b, 1244a, 1271a; II, 7b, 39a, 73b, 246b, 294a,b, 299b, 350a, 384a, 410b, 431a, 650b, 701a, 741a, 1066b; III, 219b, 222a, 351b, 730b, 1212b; IV, 392b, 576b, 745b, 902a, 912b, 932b, 933a, 978b, 1188a; V, 267b; S, 273b
Selīm II (Ottoman) i, 152a, 329b, 380a, 775b; ii, 25a, 82b, 737b; iii, 1183b; v, 67a, 138b, 814a — I, 156a, 340a, 391a, 798b; II, 25b, 84a, 756a; III, 1213a; V, 69a, 141a, 820b
Selīm III (Ottoman) i, 63a, 790b, 948a, 1064b, 1165a, 1171b, 1252a, 1268a, 1278a; ii, 12a, 83b, 206b, 339a, 511b, 512a, 684a, 694a, 697a, 712b, 999a; iii, 384b, 627b; iv, 168a, 322b, 589a, 900b; v, 725a — I, 65a, 814a, 977a, 1096b, 1199b, 1206b, 1290a, 1307a, 1317b; II, 12a, 85a, 213a, 349a, 524b, 525a, 701a, 711b, 715a, 731a, 1022a; III, 397a, 647b; IV, 175b, 337a, 612b, 933a; V, 730a
Selīm Girāy I i, 4b, 893b; ii, 990b, 1047a; iv, 569a; v, 140a — I, 4b, 920a; II, 1013a, 1071b; IV, 591b; V, 142b, 143a
Selīm Girāy III v, 141a — V, 143b
Selīm Meḥmed Pasha v, 36a — V, 37a
Selīm Pasha ii, 636a — II, 652b
Selmān Reʾīs iv, 552b — IV, 576b
Semarang s, 201a — S, 201a
Semaun s, 151b — S, 152a
Sembat Bagratuni iv, 90a — IV, 94a
Semirečye ii, 43a; iii, 1120a; v, 858b — II, 43b; III, 1148a; V, 865b
Semitic/Sémitique i, 561b — I, 579b
Şemo, Ereb v, 484a — V, 487a
Sened-i Ittifāḳ ii, 640a,b — II, 656a,b
Senegal ii, 94a, 567a; s, 179a, 218a — II, 95b, 581b; S, 180b, 218a → Dakar
Senekʿerim i, 638a — I, 658b
Sennār i, 35a — I, 36a
Senneh s, 136b, 142b, 145a — S, 136a, 142a, 145a
Senoufo ii, 63a; v, 252b — II, 64b; V, 250b
Sepoy → Sipāhī
Sepoy Mutiny (1857) s, 325b — S, 325a
Serajévo → Sarajevo
Serʿasker i, 838a; ii, 513a; iii, 552b — I, 861b; II, 525b; III, 571b
Serbest Firka s, 47b — S, 48a
Serbest(iyyet) iii, 589b — III, 610a
Serbia/Serbie i, 1163b, 1165a; v, 276a — I, 1198b, 1199b; V, 274a
Seringapatam → Shrīrangapaṭṭanam
Serḳīn, Awlād v, 596a, b — V, 600a
Serment → Ḳasam
Sermon → Khuṭba
Sermonnaire → Ḳāṣṣ
Serpent → Ḥayya
Serres (Siroz) s, 330a — S, 329b
Servant/Serviteur → Khādim
Setif s, 145a — S, 144b
Sevan → Gökče-Tengiz
Sevdalinka i, 1271a — I, 1310a
Severus/Sévère → Ibn al-Muḳaffaʿ
Sèves, Colonel → Sulaymān Pasha
Seville/Séville → Ishbīliya
Sevin Beg → Khān-zāda Bēgum
Sevindj b. Būrī iii, 120a — III, 122b
Sex/Sexe → Djins
Sextant → al-Suds al-Fakhrī
Seydī Aḥmed Pasha v, 258b — V, 256b
Seydī ʿAlī Pasha v, 764a — V, 770a
Seyf el-Dīn, Ömer v, 194b — V, 191b
Seyhan → Sayḥān
Seyyid → Sayyid
Sezāʾī Ḥasan Dede ii, 686a — II, 703b
Sezāʾī, Sāmī Pasha-zāde v, 194a, 195a — V, 191b, 192b
Şfar, Bashīr iv, 159b — IV, 166b
Sfax v, 220b — V, 218a-b
Sgrafiatto iv, 1166b — IV, 1199a
Shaʿanba v, 361b, 362a — V, 362b, 363a
Shaʿb i, 535a; iv, 334a, 746a, 819a — I, 551b; IV, 348b, 776a, 851b
Shab-i barāt i, 1027b — I, 1059a
Shab-niwīs iv, 759a — IV, 789a
Shaba iv, 749b — IV, 780a
Shabāb → Ibn Khayyāt al-ʿUṣfurī
Shabāb, Shabbāba ii, 1028a — II, 1052a
Shabah v, 971a — V, 973b
Shabah ʿamd iv, 768b, 769b — IV, 799b, 800b
Shabak i, 990a; iv, 187b — I, 1020b; IV, 196a
Shaʿbān I, al-Kāmil (Mamlūk) iii, 48a; v, 1141a — III, 50a; V, 1134a

Shaʿbān II, al-Ashraf Nāṣir al-Dīn (Mamlūk) i, 790a, 1050b; ii, 970a; iii, 346b; s, 395b — I, 813a, 1082a; II, 992a; III, 357a; S, 396a
al-Shābandar, ʿAbd al-Raḥmān iii, 522b — III, 540b
al-Shaʿbāniyya i, 426b; iv, 991b, 992a — I, 439a; IV, 1024a, b
Shabānkāra iii, 1097a; v, 161a, 450b, 454a, 671a; s, 326a, 382b — III, 1124a; V, 159b, 453a, 456b, 676a; S, 325b, 383a
Shabānkārihī, Muḥammad i, 1131a — I, 1165b
Shabb v, 965a, 967b, 978b, 981a — V, 969b
al-Shābb al-Ẓarīf → Ibn al-ʿAfīf
al-Shabbās iv, 663b — IV, 690b
Shabbaz → Kāth
Shabbetai Ṣebi ii, 615b, 987a — II, 631a, 1009b
al-Shābbī, ʿAbu ʾl-Ḳāsim i, 598b — I, 618a
Shābbiyya iii, 69b; iv, 828a — III, 71b; IV, 861a
Shabbūr i, 1291b — I, 1331a
al-Shaʿbī s, 232b — S, 232b
Shabīb b. Badjara iii, 887a, 889a — III, 911a, 912b
Shabīb b. Yazīd al-Shaybānī i, 77a, 693b; iii, 40b, 203b, 649b, 715b, 1168a; iv, 369b, 1075b — I, 79a, 714b; III, 42b, 209a, 670b, 737b, 1196b; IV, 385b, 1107b
Shabīb al-Nadjrānī iv, 369b — IV, 385b
Shabībiyya iv, 369b — IV, 385b
Shābīn Ḳarā Ḥiṣār iv, 578b — IV, 601b
Shabistarī, Maḥmūd-i v, 605a — V, 609a
Shabistarī, Mudjtahid iv, 166b — IV, 173b
Shaʿbiyya → al-Nukkār
Shābkhāne iv, 579a — IV, 602b
Shabrīṭ b. al-Ṭawīl, Banū s, 82a — S, 81b
al-Shābushtī ii, 127a, 195a — II, 130a, 201a
Shabwa iii, 52a,b; s, 336b, 337a, b — III, 54a,b; S, 336b, 337a
Shādagān ii, 181a — II, 187a
Shadd i, 802a — I, 825a
Shaddād iv, 215b — IV, 225a
Shaddād Abū ʿAntara s, 178a — S, 179a
Shaddād b. ʿĀd i, 181a; iii, 173b, 1270b — I, 186a; III, 177b, 1303b
Shaddād b. ʿAmr i, 44b — I, 46a
Shaddādid(e)s i, 420b, 421a, 507b, 639a, 660b, 796b; iv, 345a, 347a, b, 670a; v, 452a, 489a — I, 432b, 433a, 523a, 659b, 681b, 820a; IV, 360a, 361b, 362a, 697b; V, 454b, 492a
Shādgeldī → Hadjdjī Shādgeldī
Shādhdh iii, 25b, 26b — III, 27a,b
Shādhī iii, 115a — III, 117b
Shādhī Ayyūb → Ayyūb b. Shādhī
al-Shādhilī, Abu ʾl-Ḥasan ʿAlī i, 1b, 91b, 309a, 1019b; iii, 513b, 722b; iv, 449b; s, 350b — I, 1b, 94a, 318b, 1050b; III, 531a, 745a; IV, 469b; S, 350b
al-Shādhiliyya i, 70b, 371a, 596b, 679b, 966a, 1260b; ii, 160a, 224a,b; iii, 339b, 535b, 670b; iv, 992b; v, 948b; s, 18a, 44a, 93a, 208b, 223a, 244a, 278b, 408a, 411a — I, 72b, 382a, 615b, 700a, 996a, 1298b; II, 165a, 231a,b; III, 349b, 554b, 692b; IV, 1025a; V, 952b; S, 18b, 44b, 93a, 208a, 223a, 244a, 278b, 408b, 411b
Shadirwān iv, 481a; v, 1146a — IV, 502a; V, 1137b
Shadjāʿat Khān iv, 93a — IV, 97a
Shadjarat al-Durr i, 732a, 766a — I, 754a, 789a
al-Shadjdjār i, 704a — I, 725a
Shadow play → Ḳaragöz; Khayāl al-ẓill
Shādūf iv, 629a; v, 861a, 863b — IV, 654a; V, 868a, 870b
Shafāʿa i, 334b, 958b; ii, 306b — I, 345a, 988a; II, 315a
Shafak v, 709a — V, 714a
Shafiʿ Māzandarānī, Mīrzā s, 336a, 406b — S, 335b, 406a
Shafīʿa iv, 1124b — IV, 1156a
al-Shāfiʿī i, 123b, 155a, 259a, 272b, 551a, 588b, 773a, 1130b, 1199a, 1242a; ii, 102b, 889b; iii, 24a, 63b, 162b, 674b, 1024a; iv, 256a, 425a, 430a, 896a; v, 240a, 731b, 1131a, 1142a — I, 127a, 159a, 267a, 281a, 568b, 607b, 796a, 1164b, 1234b, 1280a; II, 104b, 910a; III, 25a, 66a, 166a, 696a, 1049b; IV, 267b, 443b, 449a, 928b; V, 237b, 736b, 1127a, 1135a
Shafiʿiyya i, 150b, 338a, 339a; ii, 559a; iii, 6b, 17a, 512b, 687b; iv, 46a, 47b, 172b, 269b; v, 109b — I, 155a, 349a, b; II, 573a; III, 6b, 17b, 530a, 709b; IV, 48b, 50a, 180a, 281b; V, 112a
Shāfil i, 446a — I, 459a
Shafshawān i, 55b — I, 57b
Shaftī, Sayyid Muḥammad Bāḳir s, 75b, 135a — S, 76a, 134b
Shāgirds iii, 217b — III, 224a
Shāh v, 630a, b — V, 634a, b
Shāh ʿAbbās → ʿAbbās I, Shāh
Shāh ʿAbd al-ʿAẓīm ii, 650b — II, 667a
Shāh ʿAbd al-ʿAzīz i, 282a, 827b; iii, 431a; iv, 196a, 625b — I, 291a, 850a; III, 445a; IV, 204b, 650b
Shāh ʿAbd al-Ḳādir i, 282b, 827b; iii, 431a; v, 803a — I, 291a, 850a; III, 445a; V, 809a
Shāh ʿAbd al-Laṭīf → Bhitāʾī
Shāh ʿAbd al-Raḥīm al-ʿUmarī i, 1023a; ii, 254a; v, 1135b — I, 1054b; II, 261b; V, 1131a
Shāh Abu ʾl-Ḳāsim Sulṭān → Bēglār
Shāh Afḍal ii, 30a — II, 30b
Shāh Afdal II ii, 30a — II, 30b
Shāh ʿĀlam i, 1329b; ii, 121b — I, 1370a; II, 124a
Shāh ʿĀlam I → Bahādur Shāh I
Shāh ʿĀlam II i, 813b; ii, 186a, 808b, 1092b; iii, 428a — I, 836b; II, 192a, 827b, 1118a; III, 441b
Shāh ʿĀlam Khān iii, 59b — III, 62a
Shāh ʿAlī Khān iv, 723b, 849b — IV, 752b, 882b
Shāh-i Arman i, 300a, 329a, 639a, 666a — I, 309b, 339b, 659b, 686b
Shāh Beg Arghūn i, 227b, 228a, 627b, 961b, 1192a; iii, 420a, 632b; iv, 535a, 536b — I, 234b, 235a, 648a, 991b, 1227b; III, 433b, 654a; IV, 558a, 560a
Shāh Dawla ii, 1131b — II, 1158a
Shāh Djahān I (Mughal) i, 60b, 66a, 81a, 199b, 208a, 228b, 252b, 253a, 686b, 710a, 856a, 1161a, 1200a, 1324a, 1329b, 1331a, 1347b; ii, 99b, 121a, 157b, 162a, 180a, 446a, 598b; iii, 424a, 450a, 492b, 1204a; iv, 507a, 543a, 914b, 1018a, b; v, 74a, 598a, 600a, 688a, 1135b, 1214a; s, 63a, 142b, 167b, 258a, b, 313b, 366b, 420b — I, 62b, 68a, 83b, 205a, 214b, 235b, 260b, 261a, 707b, 731b, 879b, 1196a, 1235b, 1364b, 1370b, 1371b, 1387b; II, 101b, 124a, 162a, 167a, 185b, 458a, 613b; III, 438a, 465b, 509b, 1234b; IV, 529a, 566b, 947b, 1050a, b; V, 76a, 602a, 603b, 693a, 1131a, 1203b; S, 63b, 142a, 167b, 258a, 313a, 366b, 421a
Shāh Djahān II → Rafīʿ al-Dawla
Shāh Djahān b. Suyurghatmīsh v, 163a, 554a — V, 161a, 558b
Shāh Dūst → Fatḥ Khān
Shāh Fāḍil ii, 30a — II, 30b
Shāh Fakhr al-Dīn ii, 55a, 56a; iii, 436a, 1158b — II, 56a, 57a; III, 450a, 1187a
Shāh Fulādī peak/sommet i, 221b — I, 228a
Shāh Ghāzī Rustam I iv, 266a — IV, 278a
Shāh Ḥātim Dihlawī iii, 119a — III, 121b
Shāh Ḥusayn Abbāsī v, 829a — V, 835a
Shāh Ḥusayn Khān i, 1219a — I, 1255b
Shāh-i Djangal Bash ii, 205a — II, 211b
Shāh Ibrāhīm i, 262b — I, 270b
Shāh Ismāʿīl I, II, III Ṣafawid(e) → Ismāʿīl I, II, III
Shāh Ismāʿīl Ghāzī ii, 297a — II, 305a
Shāh Ḳāsim b. Muḥammad Nūr Bakhsh s, 423b — S, 423b

Shāh Khāmūsh iv, 202b — IV, 211b
Shāh Ḳulī Ḳadjār iv, 389a — IV, 404b
Shāh Ḳulī Sulṭān iv, 476a — IV, 496b
Shāh Kābulī i, 1201a — I, 1237a
Shāh Ḳādirī, Mullā ii, 134b, 378b — II, 138a, 389a
Shāh Kalīm Allāh ii, 55a; iii, 432b — II, 56a; III, 446b
Shāh Ḳāsim Huwaʾllāhī i, 1201a — I, 1237a
Shāh Katōr → Muḥtaram Shāh II
Shāh Madār → Badīʿ al-Dīn
Shāh Maḥmūd ii, 401b — II, 412a
Shāh Mālang iv, 202b — IV, 211b
Shāh Malik ii, 4b, 1108a; iv, 1067a — II, 4b, 1134a; IV, 1098b
Shāh-i Mashhad v, 1147b, 1148a — V, 1139a
Shāh Meḥmed b. Ḳarā Yūsuf iv, 586b, 587b — IV, 609a, 611a
Shāh Mīnā v, 634b, 636a — V, 639a, 640a
Shāh Mīr (Mīrzā) → Shams al-Dīn Shāh Mīrzā
Shāh Mīrs s, 167b — S, 167b
Shāh Muḥammad ʿAlī v, 24b — V, 25a
Shāh Muẓaffar i, 1211b — I, 1247b
Shāh Naṣīr ii, 221b — II, 228b
Shāh Nawāz I v, 493b — V, 496b
Shāh Nawāz Khān → Gurgīn Khān
Shāh Nawāz Khān → Ṣamṣām al-Dawla Khān
Shāh Nawāz Khān (Chitral) ii, 30a — II, 30b
Shāh-Nawāz Khān Awrangābādī v, 935b — V, 939b
Shāh Nawāz Khān (Iridj) → Iridj Shāhnawāz Khān
Shāh Niʿmat Allāh Fārsī s, 156a — S, 156a
Shāh Niyaẓ Aḥmad ii, 55a — II, 56a
Shāh Niẓām al-Dīn i, 853a — I,876b
Shāh Nizār iv, 201b — IV, 210b
Shāh Nūr Muḥammad ii, 55a — II, 56a
Shāh Raḍī al-Dīn i, 852b; iv, 202b — I, 876b; IV, 211b
Shāh Rafīʿ al-Dīn i, 69a; iii, 430b, 431a; iv, 196a — I, 70b; III, 444b, 445a; IV, 204b
Shāh Rukh I ii, 45a, 792a; iv, 1020a — II, 46a, 811a; IV, 1052a
Shāh Rukh (Čaghatayid(e)) → Shahrukh b. Timūr
Shāh Rustam v, 829a — V, 835a
Shāh Ṣafī I → Ṣafī I Shāh
Shāh Shudjāʿ (Afghānistān) → Shudjāʿ al-Mulk Durrānī
Shāh Shudjāʿ (Bengal(e)) i, 229a, 606a, 768b, 769a, 1333a; ii, 216b, 813b — I, 236a, 625b, 791b, 792a, 1272b; II, 223a, 832b
Shāh Shudjāʿ (Irān) ii, 401b; iii, 56a; iv, 498b; v, 827b, 828b; s, 415a — II, 412a; III, 58a; IV, 520a; V, 833b, 835a; S, 415a
Shāh Sulaymān ii, 56a — II, 57a
Shāh Sulṭān Nuḥammad Badakhshī i, 852b — I, 876a
Shāh Walī Allāh al-Dihlawī → al-Dihlawī
Shāh Walī Khān i, 232b — I, 239b
Shāhābād ii, 1120a; s, 313a — II, 1146a; S, 312b
Shahāda i, 332b, 407b; iii, 269b — I, 342b, 419a; III, 277a
Shāhanshāh v, 622a — V, 626a, b
Shahawāt i, 1245b — I, 1283b
Shāh-bandar i, 1013a; s, 199b, 200a — I, 1044a; S, 200a
Shahbanderzāde → Ḥilmī, Aḥmed
Shāh-budaḳ ii, 239b — II, 246b
Shahbāz Girāy ii, 25b, 1114a — II, 26a, 1140a
Shāhbāz Ḳalandar iv, 474a — IV, 494b
Shāhdiz iii, 725b; iv, 200a — III, 748a; IV, 208b
Shāhdjahān Bēgam i, 1196a, 1197a — I, 1231a, b, 1232b
Shāhdjahānābād i, 253a; ii, 258a, 259a; iii, 450b; v, 889a — I, 260b; II, 266a; III, 466a; V, 895b
Shāhdjahānpūr s, 292b — S, 292a
Shāhdjī Bhōnsla i, 769a, 1202b — I, 792a, 1238a
Shāhgarh → Kanawdj
al-Shaḥḥām, Abū Yaʿḳūb Yūsuf i, 128b; ii, 569b; iv, 1163a; s, 226b — I, 132b, II, 584a; IV, 1195a; S, 226b
Shāh-i Zinda (Timūrid) s, 154b — S, 154b
Shāhid iv, 354a — IV, 369b
Shahīd Balkhī s, 35a — S, 35b
Shahīd Muḥammad Pasha iv, 970a — IV, 1002a
Shāhidbāzī v, 166a — V, 163b
Shāhīn s, 109b — S, 109a
Shāhīn, Banū i, 1096a — I, 1129a
Shāhīn, Lala → Lala Shāhīn
Shāhīn, Mawlānā iv, 309a, b — IV, 323a, b
Shāhīn Girāy i, 310b — I, 320b
Shāhīn Girāy Khān i, 63a; ii, 447a; v, 141a, b — I, 64b; II, 458b; V, 143b, 144a
Shāhīn Pasha i, 653b; ii, 1086a; iv, 1093a — I, 674b; II, 1111b; IV, 1124a
Shāhnāma ii, 100a, 106b, 918a, 920a; iii, 111b, 112b, 113b; iv, 128a; v, 951a — II, 102a, 109a, 939b, 941a; III, 114a, 115a, 116a; IV, 133b; V, 955a
Shahr b. Bādhām i, 728a; s, 116a — I, 750a; S, 115b
Shahr-angīz → Shahr-āshūb
Shahr-āshūb iv, 59a — IV, 62a
Shahrān iv, 994a — IV, 1026b
al-Shahrastānī i, 129a, 130a, 151b, 234b, 247a, 450a, 483b, 1340b; ii, 96b, 764b, 767a, 930a; iii, 328b, 496b; iv, 847a; s, 25b, 43b, 343b, 345a — I, 132b, 133b, 156a, 242a, 255a, 463a, 498a, 1380b; II, 98b, 783a, 785b, 951b; III, 339a, 513b; IV, 880a, b; S, 26a, 44a, 343b, 344b
al-Shahrastānī, Muʿīn al-Dīn iii, 600a — III, 620b
Shahrazād i, 361a, 362a, b — I, 372a, 373a
al-Shahrazūrī, Shams al-Dīn i, 236a; iv, 121a — I, 243a; IV, 126a
al-Shahrazūrī, Taḳī 'l-Dīn iv, 1108a — IV, 1139b
al-Shahrazūrī (wazīr) iii, 1157b — III, 1186a
Shahrbarāz iv, 342b — IV, 357a
Shahrdārī i, 978b — I, 1009a
Shahr-i Bābak v, 152a, b — V, 154a
Shahr-i Bilḳīs iv, 107b — IV, 112b
Shahr-i Khān v, 30a — V, 30b
Shahr-i Naw i, 952b — I, 981b
Shahr-i Sabz → Kash; Kish
Shāhrikī iv, 10b — IV, 11b
Shahristān i, 320b; iv, 98b; s, 406b — I, 330b; IV, 103a; S, 406b
Shahrīyār I (Bāwandid(e)) i, 871b, 1110a; ii, 919b; iv, 645b; s, 356b — I, 896a, 1143b; II, 940b; IV, 672a; S, 356b
Shahriyār b. Dārā s, 309a — S, 309a
Shahriyār b. Djahāngīr i, 686b; ii, 381a; iv, 1018a — I, 707b; II, 391a; IV, 1050b
Shahrizūr i, 16a, 261a; v, 33b, 34a, 144b, 145b, 455b — I, 16b, 269a; V, 34b, 35a, 147a, 148a, 458a
Shahr-kent → Djand
Shāh-Rūd (river/rivière) v, 656b; s, 149a — V, 660b; S, 149a
Shāhrukh, Mīrzā i, 230a, b, 246b, 295b; v, 59a; s, 43b — I, 237a, b, 254b, 305a; V, 61a; S, 44a
Shāhrukh b. Timūr i, 66b, 90b, 227a, 1001b, 1054a, 1133b; ii, 6a, 270b; iii, 57b, 58a, 114a, 346b, 778a; iv, 33a, b, 34a, 102b, 586b, 587a, b, 642b, 721b, 945a, 1040b; v, 858b; s, 49a, 84a — I, 68b, 93b, 234a, 1032a, 1086a, 1168a; II, 6a, 278b; III, 60a, b, 116b, 357a, 801b; IV, 35b, 36a, 107a, 609a, b, 611a, 669a, 750b, 978a, 1072a; V, 865b; S, 49b, 84a
Shāhrukh Bī v, 29a; s, 97b — V, 30a; S, 97a
Shāhrukhī ii, 120b — II, 123b
Shāhrukhiyya i, 148a, 1011a; s, 51a — I, 152a, 1042a; S, 51b
Shahrwīn b. Rustam Bāwand i, 871b; s, 356b — I,

896a; S, 356b
Shāh-sewan i, 7b; ii, 1083b — I, 8a; II, 1108b
Shāhsivan iii, 1102a, 1108b, 1109a, 1110a; iv, 9b, 858b — III, 1129a, 1136a, b, 1137a; IV, 10b, 891b
Shāhsuwār i, 182b; ii, 38b, 239b; iii, 186b; iv, 462b — I, 187b; II, 39a, 246b; III, 190b; IV, 483a, b
Shāhū i, 913b; ii, 219a; iv, 1023b — I, 941b; II, 225b; IV, 1055b
Shāhwardī b. Muḥammadī v, 829a, b — V, 835b
Shāhzada ii, 1084b — II, 1110a
Shāhzāda → Miyān Gul Gul Shāhzāda
Shāzāda Aḥmad v, 823a — V, 829a
Shaᶜīb i, 538a — I, 554b
Shāʾiḳiyya (tribe/tribu) s, 278b — S, 278b
Shāᶜir iv, 1109b — IV, 1141a
Shāʾista Khān iv, 177b — IV, 186a
Shaḳāḳī iii, 1102b, 1109a — III, 1129b, 1136b
Shakānī iii, 1097b — III, 1124b
Shaker Beklū i, 1157a — I, 1191b
Shaḳḥab iii, 189a — III, 193b
Shakhbūṭ b. Dhiyāb i, 166b — I, 171a
Shakhbūṭ b. Sulṭān i, 166b; iv, 778b — I, 171a; IV, 809b
Shakhṣ i, 409b, 785a — I, 421a, 808a
Shakīb Arslān → Arslān
Shaḳīf ᶜArnūn → Ḳalᶜat al-Shaḳīf
Shākir, Banū s, 413b, 414a — S, 414a
Shākir Pasha v, 462b — V, 465b
Shaḳīshaḳiyya s, 197a — S, 197a
Shakkāf s, 111b, 112a — S, 111a
Shakkī iv, 350a — IV, 365a
Shakla ii, 1075b — II, 1100b
Shākmīn i, 1284a — I, 1323a
Shaḳoloz i, 1062b — I, 1094b
Shakshāk ii, 621a — II, 636b
Shāḳshāḳī Ibrāhīm Pasha i, 268a — I, 276a
Shaḳūra i, 7a — I, 7a
Shaḳyā b. ᶜAbd al-Wāḥid al-Miknāsī i, 82a, 634a — I, 84b, 654b
Shāl, Shālkot → Kwaṫṫa
Shāla i, 85a, 780b, 1224b; iii, 500a, 1043a; v, 290a, 504a, b; s, 63b, 145a, 397b — I, 87b, 804a, 1261b; III, 517a, 1069a; V, 289a, 507b; S, 64a, 144b, 398a
al-Shalawbīn iii, 338a — III, 348a
Shālīmār i, 1347b, 1348a; s, 63a — I, 1388a, b; S, 63b
al-Shalmaghānī ii, 218a, 1094b; iii, 101a, 683a — II, 225a, 1120b; III, 103b, 704b
Shalṭīsh i, 6a, 155b — fI, 6a, 160a
Shaltūt, Maḥmūd iv, 159b; s, 158a — IV, 166a; S, 158a
al-Shalūbīnī ii, 528b — II, 541b
Shālūs iii, 254b; s, 356b — III, 261b; S, 356a
Sham s, 331b — S, 331b
Shām Bayadî i, 1117a — I, 1150b
Shamākhī ii, 87b; iii, 604a; iv, 350a — II, 89b; III, 625a; IV, 365a
Shamāl i, 537b — I, 554a
Shamāmūn iv, 485b — IV, 506b
Shamanism iv, 1173b
Shāmāt s, 327a — S, 326b
Shambhadjī s, 55b — S, 56a
Shamᶜdānīzāde iv, 761a — IV, 791b
Shamdīnān i, 427a — I, 439a
Shamᶜī i, 1208b, 1345b — I, 1244b, 1386a
al-Shāmī, Abū Bakr s, 194a — S, 193b
al-Shāmī, Ibrāhīm b. Sulaymān i, 83a — I, 85b
Shāmī, Nizāmuddīn iii, 57b, 58a — III, 60a, b
Shāmil i, 755b, 756a; ii, 18a, 87b, 88b; iii, 157a; iv, 631a; v, 618a — I, 778a, 778b; II, 18b, 89a, 90a; III, 160b; IV, 656a; V, 622a
Shamir b. Dhi ʾl-Djawshan iii, 609b, 610b; iv, 836a — III, 630b, 631a; IV, 869a
Shamīrān → Tārom
Shamkh, Banū s, 37b — S, 37b
Shāmkhāl ii, 87a; v, 382a, b, 618a — II, 88b; V, 383a, b, 622a
Shāmlū i, 1159b; iii, 1100a, 1109b; iv, 577b; v, 243b — I, 1194a; III, 1127a, 1136b; IV, 601a; V, 241b
Shāmlū-Ustadjlū iii, 157b — III, 161a
al-Shammākh i, 1154b; s, 304b — I, 1188b; S, 304b
al-Shammākhī i, 121a, 125a, 167a, 1186a, 1287b; iii, 656b, 927b — I, 124b, 128b, 171b, 1221a, 1327a; III, 678a, 952a
al-Shammākhī, Abū Sākin ᶜĀmir i, 1053b — I, 1085a
Shammār i, 528b, 873b; ii, 77a, 492b; iii, 180a, 326b, 1065b, 1253b; v, 348a; s, 101b — I, 544b, 897b; II, 78b, 505a; III, 184a, 336b, 1092a, 1286a; V, 349a; S, 101a
Shammar Yuharᶜish i, 548b; iii, 10a — I, 566a; III, 10b
Shammāsiyya i, 897b, 899b — I, 924b, 926a
Shampa → Ṣanf
Shams Badrān s, 8b, 9a — S, 8a, b
Shams al-Dawla Abū Ṭāhir (Būyid(e)) i, 512b, 1354a; iii, 671b; v, 1028a; s, 118b — I, 528a, 1393a; III, 693a; V, 1024a; S, 118a
Shams al-Dawla Sulaymān i, 664b — I, 684a
Shams al-Dīn (Bahmanī) i, 1200a — I, 1235b
Shams al-Dīn b. Taman Djāndār iv, 108b — IV, 113a
Shams al-Dīn (Ḳarāmān-oghlu) iv, 622b — IV, 647a
Shams al-Dīn Khān ii, 83b — II, 85a
Shams al-Dīn Kurt I (Kart) iii, 177b; iv, 672a — III, 181b; IV, 699b
Shams al-Dīn II Kurt (Kart) iv, 536b, 672a — IV, 560a, 699b
Shams al-Dīn, Pīr iv, 202b; v, 26a — IV, 211b; V, 26b
Shams al-Dīn Abū Rādjāʾ ii, 597b — II, 612a
Shams al-Dīn Īletmish → Īltutmish
Shams al-Dīn ᶜIrāḳī, Mīr s, 353b, 366b — S, 353b, 366a
Shams al-Dīn Māhūnī iii, 633a, 634a — III, 654a, 655b
Shams al-Dīn Muḥ. b. Ḳays al-Rāzī → Shams-i Ḳays
Shams al-Dīn Muḥammad al-Babāwī ii, 330b — II, 340a
Shams al-Dīn Muḥammad al-Dimashḳī i, 775a, 1327b — I, 798a, 1368b
Shams al-Dīn Muḥammad Ghūrī ii, 1101a — II, 1127a
Shams al-Dīn Muḥammad Tabrīzī → Shams-i Tabrīzī
Shams al-Dīn al-Samarḳandī s, 413a — S, 413b
Shams al-Dīn al-Samaṭrānī i, 742a; iii, 1220a, 1233a — I, 764a; III, 1251a, 1265a
Shams al-Dīn Sāmī Bey Frasherī i, 298b; ii, 474a; v, 195a — I, 307b; II, 486a; V, 192b
Shams al-Dīn Shāh Mīrzā Swātī iv, 708a; s, 167a — IV, 736b; S, 167a
Shams al-Dīn Sulṭānpūrī (Pandjāb) s, 3a — S, 2a
Shams al-Maᶜālī → Ḳābūs b. Wushmagīr
Shams al-Mulk b. Niẓām al-Mulk i, 522b, 902a — I, 538b, 929a
Shams al-Mulk Naṣr → Naṣr I (Ḳarakhanid(e))
Shams al-Muluk → Dukak; Ismāᶜīl; Rustam etc.
Shams-i Fakhrī → Fakhrī Shams al-Dīn Muḥammad
Shams-i Ḳays i, 982b; iv, 59b, 64b, 714a; v, 1027a; s, 21b — I, 1013a; IV, 62b, 68a, 743a; V, 1022b; S, 22a
Shamsī Khān v, 33b — V, 34b
Shams-i Munshī → Nakhdjawānī, Muḥammad
Shamsī Pasha iv, 108b — IV, 113b
Shams-i Tabrīzī ii, 394a; v, 26a — II, 404b; V, 26b
Shamsān i, 98b — I, 101a

Shamshān i, 180b — I, 185b
Shamshīr b. Azar s, 327b — S, 327a
Shamshīr Bahādur i, 1012b — I, 1043b
Shamsīyān iv, 473b — IV, 494b
Shamsiyya ii, 1070b; iv, 203a, 473b, 991b; v, 26a — II, 1095a; IV, 212a, 494b, 1024a; V, 27a
al-Shanāwī, Aḥmad i, 829b — I, 852b
Shanbal i, 829a — I, 852a
Shandī ii, 351b — II, 361a
Shandjwilo, Shandjūl → ʿAbd al-Raḥmān b.Abī ʿAmīr
Shandūr ii, 29a — II, 29b
al-Shanfarā iv, 744b, 919a; s, 176a — IV, 774b, 952a; S, 177a
Shānīzāde ʿAtāʾ Allāh Efendi ii, 713a; iii, 590a; v, 1083b — II, 731a; III, 610b; V, 1081a
Shanḳīr s, 295a — S, 294b
Shann i, 73a, 74a — I, 75a, 76a
Shans adāsi → Ada Ḳalʿe
Shansabanī ii, 1099a, 1100a, 1101a — II, 1125a, b, 1127a
Shant Yāḳub i, 494b — I, 509a
Shantabariyya ii, 243a; iii, 299a — II, 250a; III, 308a
al-Shantamarī, al-Aʿlam i, 521b, 601a; iii, 111a, 807a, 963a — I, 537b, 620b; III, 113b, 830b, 987b
Shantamariyat al-Gharb i, 6a — I, 6a
Shantarīn i, 161b, 1338b — I, 166a, 1379a
Shanūʾa i, 812a — I, 835a
Shāpūr (town/ville) iv, 850b — IV, 883b
Shāpūr I i, 484b, 516b, 788b; ii, 1119b; iii, 50b; iv, 675b; v, 573b — I, 499a, 532a, 812a; II, 1146a; III, 52b; IV, 703b; V, 578a
Shāpūr II i, 225b, 484b, 548b; iii, 303b; v, 640a — I, 232b, 499a, 566a; III, 312b; V, 644a
Shāpūr b. Shahriyār Bāwand iv, 645b — IV, 672a
Shāpūr-Kh(w)āst v, 831b — V, 837b
al-Sharaf i, 7a, 135b; iv, 115a — I, 7a, 139b; IV, 120a
Sharaf al-Dawla (ʿUḳaylid(e)) iii, 228a — III, 235a
Sharaf al-Dawla Shīrzīl i, 1354a; iii, 244b; s, 118a, 398a — I, 1393a; III, 251b; S, 117b, 398b
Sharaf al-Dīn, Mawlānā s, 353a — S, 353a
Sharaf al-Dīn Abū Tawwāma ii, 216a — II, 223a
Sharaf al-Dīn Husām al-Dīn al-Bulghārī i, 1307b — I, 1347b
Sharaf al-Dīn ʿĪsā → al-Muʿaẓẓam ʿĪsā
Sharaf al-Dīn Saʿd Allāh i, 322b, 346b, 510b — I, 332b, 357a, 526a
Sharaf al-Dīn Shufurwa iv, 62a — IV, 65b
Sharaf al-Dīn Yaḥyā Manerī i, 868b — I, 893a
Sharaf Khān → Bidlīsī
Sharaf Khwādja, Shaykh s, 280b — S, 280b
Sharaf al-Maʿālī i, 440a — I, 452b
Sharaf al-Mulk, Ṣadr i, 301a; s, 359b — I, 310a; S, 359b
Sharaf nāma iv, 127b, 128a, b — IV, 133a, b, 134a
al-Sharafa s, 335a — S, 334b
al-Sharafī, ʿAlī b. Aḥmad iv, 1082a — IV, 1113b
Sharīfī, Mīrzā Makhdūm iv, 860b — IV, 893b
al-Sharafī, Muḥammad b. ʿAlī iv, 1082b — IV, 1113b
Sharafshāh b. Djaʿfarī iv, 859b — IV, 892b
Sharāḥīl Dhū Yazan ii, 244b — II, 251b
al-Shaʿrānī, ʿAbd al-Wahhāb i, 596a; iii, 901a; v, 1237a — I, 615b; III, 925b; V, 1227b
Sharar, ʿAbd al-Halīm v, 203b — V, 201a
Sharāra, ʿAbd al-Laṭīf iv, 783a — IV, 814b
al-Sharārāt i, 546a, 873a; iii, 642a — I, 563b, 897a; III, 663a
al-Sharāt ii, 535a — II, 548b
Shārdja s, 42a — S, 42b
Shārekī → Shāhrikī
Sharḥ i, 816b — I, 840a
Shari (river/rivière) s, 164b — S, 164a
Sharīʿa i, 152a, 170a, 173b, 260b, 353b, 1099b, 1142b, 1143a; ii, 146b, 660a, b, 668a; iii, 76a, 164a, 662b; iv, 156b, 556b, 559a; v, 860a, 870b — I, 156b, 174b, 178a, 268b, 364b, 1132b, 1177a, b; II, 150b, 676b, 677a, 685a; III, 78b, 167b, 684a; IV, 163a, 580b; V, 867a, 876b
Shariat Act 1937 i, 172a, b — I, 176b, 177b
Sharīʿat Allāh i, 952a; ii, 783b; iv, 625b — I, 981a; II, 802b; IV, 650b
Sharīʿatī, Muḥammad Taḳī iv, 166a — IV, 173b
Sharīf v, 23b — V, 24a
Sharīf (Makka) i, 552a — I, 569b
Sharīf (Morocco/Maroc) → Shurafāʾ
al-Sharīf, Mawlāy → Muḥammad I (ʿAlawid(e))
Sharīf Aḥmad (Abū ʿArīsh) s, 30b — S, 30b
al-Sharīf al-Akhḍar iii, 107a, 289a — III, 109b, 298a
Sharīf Awliyā Karīm al-Makhdūm iii, 1218b — III, 1249b
al-Sharīf al-Idrīsī → al-Idrīsī
al-Sharīf al-Murtaḍā i, 130a, 154b, 1352a; ii, 127b; iii, 1266a; iv, 182b; v, 363a; s, 23a, 25b, 56b, 95a — I, 133b, 158b, 1391b; II, 130b; III, 1299a; IV, 190b; V, 364a; S, 23b, 25b, 57a, 94b
Sharīf Pasha i, 1070a; iii, 515a — I, 1102a; III, 532b
Sharīf Pasha Ṣabrī s, 300a — S, 299b
al-Sharīf al-Rāḍī i, 592b, 1352a; iii, 244b, 463a, 780b, 1266a; iv, 277b; s, 23a, 95a — I, 611b, 1391b; III, 251b, 479a, 804a, 1299a; IV, 290a; S, 23b, 94b
al-Sharīf al-Tilimsānī iii, 670b — III, 692a
Sharifīs iv, 51b — IV, 54b
Shāriḥ al-Manārzāde ii, 751a — II, 769b
Sharīk b. Shaykh al-Mahrī i, 1294a; iv, 16a — I, 1333b; IV, 17b
Sharīk al-ʿAbsī ii, 525b — II, 538b
Sharika ii, 436b — II, 448a
al-Shāriḳa i, 166b, 928b; ii, 619a, 936b; iv, 777b; s, 42a, 416b, 418a — I, 171a, 956b; II, 634b, 958b; IV, 808b; S, 42b, 417a, 418a
al-Sharīshī i, 602a; iii, 221b — I, 622a; III, 228a
Shāriya iv, 821b — IV, 854b
Sharḳ al-Andalus i, 82b — I, 85a
Sharḳāt s, 101b — S, 100b
al-Sharḳāwī, ʿAbd Allāh i, 819b — I, 842b
Sharḳāwiyya s, 40b — S, 41a
Sharkhā i, 176b; iii, 3b — I, 181a; III, 3b
Sharḳīs i, 756b; iii, 632a; iv, 533b, 534a; s, 203a, 325a — I, 779a; III, 653a; IV, 557a; S, 202b, 324b
Sharkil iv, 1175a, 1176a, 1178a — IV, 1208b, 1209b, 1211b
Sharḳīshla s, 91b — S, 91a
al-Sharḳiyya i, 901b, 1011a; s, 385b — I, 928b, 1042a; S, 386a
Sharm i, 535b — I, 552a
Sharm al-Shaykh s, 8b — S, 8a
al-Shārrāt i, 487a, 489a — I, 501b, 503b
Sharshal iv, 1156a; s, 145a — IV, 1188a, b; S, 144b
Sharūr iv, 186b — IV, 194b
Sharvashidze i, 101a; v, 496a — I, 103b; V, 499a
Sharwān → Shirwān
Sharwīn (Djabal) iv, 645b, 646b; s, 298a — IV, 672a, 673a; S, 297b
Shāsh (Tashkent) → Čāč
Shāsha i, 1098a — I, 1131a
al-Shāshī → ʿAbd Allāh b. Maḥmūd; Abū Bakr
al-Shāṭibī, Abū Isḥāḳ iv, 149b — IV, 155b
al-Shāṭibī, Abu 'l-Ḳāsim iv, 736b — IV, 766b
al-Shātibī, Muḥammad b. Sulaymān iv, 137a — IV, 143a
Shāṭir Beg Muḥammad i, 840b — I, 864a
Shaṭnīl s, 135b, 136a — S, 135b
Shatrandj ii, 955a, 1038b, 1359a, b; iii, 775a; v, 110a, 478b — II, 977a, 1062b, 1399a, b; III, 798a; V, 112b,

481a
Shaṭṭ al-Amaya (Aʿmā) iv, 674a, b – IV, 702a, b
Shaṭṭ al-ʿArab i, 5a, 133b, 1086b, 1087b; ii, 175b; iii, 1251b; iv, 6a, 674b, 675a; v, 65b, 66a – I, 5a, 137b, 1119a, 1120a; II, 181a; III, 1284a; IV, 6b, 702a, b; V, 67b, 68a
Shaṭṭ Bamishīr (Behemshīr) iv, 674b, 675a – IV, 702a, b
Shaṭṭ al-Ḳadīmī iv, 674a – IV, 702a
Shaṭṭ Ḳobān (Goban) → Shaṭṭ al-Amaya
al-Shaṭṭanawfī i, 70a, 596a; iii, 160b – I, 72a, 615b; III, 164a
Shaṭṭāriyya i, 88a, 1284a; iii, 1233b – I, 90b, 1323b; III, 1265b
al-Shaṭṭī, Muḥammad Djamīl ii, 182b; iii, 161b – II, 188b; III, 165a
Shāʾul, Anwar v, 189b – V, 186b
Shawādhdh v, 128a – V, 130b
Shāwar i, 197a, 797a; ii, 318a, b, 856b, 858b, 959a; iv, 376a – I, 202b, 820b; II, 327b, 876b, 878b, 981a; IV, 392b
al-Shawāribī iv, 514b – IV, 536b
Shawdhab iii, 650a – III, 671b
Shāwiya i, 371a, 372a, 770a; ii, 117a – I, 382a, 383a, 793a; II, 119b
Shawḳal ii, 86b, 87a – II, 88a, b
al-Shawkānī → Muḥammad b. ʿAlī al-Shawkānī
Shawḳat ʿAlī s, 5a, 74a, b, 293b, 360a – S, 4a, 74b, 293a, 360a
Shawkat Bukhārī i, 1301b – I, 1341a
Shawkat Djang ii, 371b, 1091b – II, 381b, 1117a
Shawḳī, Aḥmad i, 597b, 598a; iv, 856a; s, 34a, 57b – I, 617a, 618a; IV, 889b; S, 34b, 58a
Shawḳī Efendī i, 916a, 917b – I, 943b, 945b
al-Shawwāf, ʿAbd al-Wahhāb iv, 719a – IV, 748a
Shayba, Banū iv, 317a, b, 318a, 320b – IV, 331b, 332a, 334b
Shaybān, Banū iii, 1103a; iv, 88b-90b; v, 362b; s, 15b – III, 1130a; IV, 92b-94b; V, 363b; S, 16a
Shaybān b. Djoči ii, 44b, 67b – II, 45b, 68b
Shaybān al-Ṣaghīr iii, 988b; iv, 447a – III, 1013a; IV, 467a
al-Shaybānī (d./m. 1890) iv, 70a – IV, 73b
al-Shaybānī → al-Daḥḥāk b. Ḳays; ʿĪsā b. al-Shaykh; Yazīd b. Mazyad
al-Shaybānī, Abū ʿAbd Allāh Muḥammad i, 123a, 124a, 164b, 588b; iii, 162b, 512b; iv, 377a, 691a – I, 126b, 127b, 169a, 607b; III, 166a, 529b; IV, 393b, 719a
al-Shaybānī, Abu 'l-Ḳāsim Hibat Allāh s, 193a – S, 194a
Shaybānī Khān i, 135b, 227b, 228a, 627b, 847b, 849a, 1001b, 1019a, 1211b, 1295b; ii, 44b; iii, 198a, 1101a; iv, 1036b; v, 54b, 55a, 59a, 859a; s, 51b – I, 139a, 234b, 648a, 871a, 872a, 1032a, 1050b, 1247b, 1335a; II, 45b; III, 203a, 1128a; IV, 1068a; V, 56a, b, 60b, 866a; S, 52a
Shaybānid(e)s i, 8a, 46b, 120b, 121a, 228b, 637a, 690a, 963b, 964b, 1110b; ii, 44b, 72a, 792a; iv, 9b, 1064b; v, 859a, b; s, 96b, 227b, 340a, b – I, 8a, 47b, 124a, 125a, 235a, 658a, 711a, 993b, 994a, 1144a; II, 45b, 73a, 811a; IV, 10a, 1096a; V, 866a, b; S, 96a, 227b, 339b, 340a
Shayfta, Muṣṭafā Khān iii, 93b – III, 96a
Shāyista Khān i, 606a, 769a; ii, 32a, 216b – I, 626a, 792a; II, 32b, 223a
Shāyḳa i, 1062b – I, 1094b
Shaykh iii, 411a, 721a; iv, 335a, 678a; v, 1131a, 1133a – III, 423b, 743b; IV, 349b, 706a; V, 1127a, 1129a
Shaykh (Mamlūk) → al-Muʾayyad Shaykh
Shaykh b. ʿAbd Allāh b. Shaykh (1) i, 781a – I, 804b
Shaykh b. ʿAbd Allāh b. Shaykh (2) i, 781b – I, 804b
Shaykh ʿAbd Allāh (Kashmīr) iv, 710a, b – IV, 738b, 739a
Shaykh ʿAbduh i, 1070a; v, 188a – I, 1102a; V, 185b
Shaykh Aḥmad i, 310b – I, 320b
Shaykh al-Aḳl i, 1078b – I, 1110b
Shaykh ʿAlī b. Uways ii, 401b; iv, 584b – II, 412a; IV, 608a
Shaykh ʿAlī Khān Zand iv, 390b – IV, 407a
Shaykh al-Andalus i, 496a – I, 511a
Shaykh al-Bakrī i, 966a; ii, 165a, 181b – I, 995b; II, 170a, 187a
Shaykh Ghālib → Ghālib Dede, Shaykh
Shaykh Ibrāhīm (Sharwan-Shāh) iv, 350a, 586b – IV, 364b, 609a
Shaykh al-Islām i, 837b; ii, 420b, 867a, b; iii, 250a, 552b, 1152a; iv, 168a, 573b; v, 1083b – I, 861a; II, 431a, 887a, b; III, 257a, 571b, 1180b; IV, 175b, 596b; V, 1080b
Shaykh al-Islām Yaḥyā iii, 1200b; s, 324a – III, 1230b; S, 323b
al-Shaykh al-Kabīr → Ibn Khafīf
al-Shaykh al-Kāmil iv, 93b – IV, 97b
Shaykh Maḥmūd i, 262b – I, 271a
Shaykh Manṣūr ii, 25b – II, 26a
Shaykh al-mashāyikh i, 966a; iii, 206a – I, 995b; III, 211b
Shaykh Muʾayyad i, 1328a – I, 1368b
Shaykh Mūsā Barāhima ii, 166b – II, 171b
Shaykh Rifāʿa → al-Taḥtāwī
al-Shaykh Saʿīd i, 837b – I, 860b
Shaykh Saʿīd Nakshbandī v, 463b, 464b – V, 466b, 467b
al-Shaykh al-Ṣāliḥ → ʿAbd Allāh al-Shaykh
al-Shaykh al-Shīrāzī → Ibn Khafif
Shaykh Saʿūd iv, 638a – IV, 664b
Shaykh al-Ṭayyib al-Madjdhūb ii, 122b; iv, 687a – II, 125b; IV, 715a
al-Shaykh al-Yūnānī i, 234b; ii, 765a; iii, 942b – I, 241b; II, 783b; III, 967b
Shaykh Yūnus → Küčik Khān Djangalī
Shaykh Ẓāhir i, 341b – I, 352a
Shaykh Zayn i, 849a, b – I, 872b, 873a
Shaykha → Shīkha
Shaykhā (Khokar) v, 31b – V, 32b
Shaykhī (sect/secte) i, 304b, 850b; iv, 51a, 854a, b; s, 305a – I, 314a, 874a; IV, 54a, 887b; S, 305a
Shaykhī (poets/poètes) ii, 990a; iii, 43b – II, 1013a; III, 45a
Shaykhiyya-Djūriyya iv, 48b – IV, 51a
Shaykhū al-ʿUmarī → Ibn Faḍl Allāh al-ʿUmarī
Shaykhūn al-ʿUmarī i, 444a; iii, 239b – I, 456b; III, 246b
Shayḳiyya ii, 351a, 615b, 944b – II, 360b, 630b, 966b
al-Shayṭān i, 177a; iii, 668b, 1050a; iv, 643b – I, 181b; III, 690a, 1076a; IV, 670a
Shayṭān Ibrāhīm Pasha i, 1284b – I, 1324a
Shayṭan al-Ṭāḳ → Muḥammad b. al-Nuʿmān
al-Shayzarī, ʿAbd al-Raḥmān i, 800b; ii, 482a; iii, 486b – I, 823b; II, 494a; III, 503b
al-Shayzārī, Abu 'l-Ḥasan ʿAlī iii, 761a – III, 784b
Sheba, Queen of → Bilḳīs
Shebīn Ḳarā Ḥiṣār → Shābīn Ḳarā Ḥiṣār
Sheep → Ghanam
Shefḳatī, ʿAlī iv, 681b – IV, 709b
Shehīd ʿAlī Pasha iv, 1093b – IV, 1124b
Shehir Ketkhudasî i, 974a – I, 1004b
Shehremānet i, 972b, 974b, 975a – I, 1003a, 1004b, 1005b
Shehremīni i, 972b, 974a – I, 1002b, 1004a
Shehrīzāde Aḥmed b. Müdhehhib ii, 589b – II, 604a
Shehu i, 1260a, b – I, 1298a, b, 1299a

Shekib Efendi ii, 636b — II, 652b
Sheikh → Shaykh
Shensi v, 848a, b — V, 852a, b
Shepherd → Čūpān
Shepherd, the (astronomy) s, 321a
Shēr Aḥmad Khān iv, 711a — IV, 739b
Shēr Shāh Sūr → Shīr Shāh Sūrī
Shēr Singh → Shīr Singh
Sherāga ii, 510a, b — II, 522b, 523b
Sherāḳa i, 371b — I, 382b
Sherārda ii, 510a — II, 523a
Sherefli Ḳočhisar v, 247b — V, 245b
Śḥerí → Djibbālī
Sherley, Anthony and/et Robert i, 8b, 1066a, 1067a, b; ii, 16b; iii, 214a, 348a, 1190a; iv, 861a — I, 8b, 1098a, 1099a, b; II, 17a; III, 220a, 358b, 1219b; IV, 894a
Shērs ii, 1010b — II, 1034a
Shērzăd b. Masʿūd ii, 1052a; s, 21a — II, 1076b; S, 21b
Shesh Bolūḳī Reshkūlī s, 148a — S, 148a
Shetiyya iv, 401b — IV, 419a
Sheykhī iii, 356b — III, 367b
Shīʿa i, 15a, 16b, 20a, 51a, 124b, 130a, 149b, 224a, 347a, 382a, 399b, 402a, 589b, 713a, 794b, 832b, 941b, 1040a, 1120a, 1162a, 1198a, 1254a; iii, 411b, 434a, 1265a; iv, 34b, 46b, 277b, 855a; v, 1033a; s, 342a, 367b, 402a, b, 423b — I, 15b, 17a, 21a, 52b, 128a, 134a, 153b, 231a, 357b, 392b, 411a, 412b, 608b, 734b, 818a, 855b, 970b, 1071b, 1154a, 1196b, 1233b, 1292a; III, 424b, 448a, 1298a; IV, 37a, 49a, 289b, 290a, 888a; V, 1029b; S, 341b, 367b, 402b, 424a
- doctrine i, 188a, 258a, 334a, 339b, 402a, 1026b, 1098b, 1113b, 1352a; ii, 374b, 539a, 834a; iii, 78b, 242b, 544b, 664a, 1130a; iv, 19a, 278b, 698a; v, 1235b; s, 305a — I, 193b. 266a, 344b, 350a, 412b, 1058a, 1131b, 1147a, 1391a, b; II, 384b, 552a, 853b; III, 81a, 249b, 563b, 685b, 1158a; IV, 20b, 290b, 726a; V, 1226a; S, 305a
Shiʿb Djabala s, 177a, 178a — S, 178a, 179a
Shibām s, 337b, 338a, 407a — S, 337a, b, 407a
Shiban s, 96b — S, 96a
Shibān → Shaybān
Shībānī Khān → Shaybānī Khān
al-Shiblī i, 758b, 759a — I, 781a, b
al-Shiblī (d./m. 1080) → Ibn Shibl
al-Shiblī, Abū Bakr i, 387b; iv, 990a — I, 399a; IV, 1023a
Shiblī al-Aṭrash ii, 637a — II, 653b
Shiblī al-Mallāṭ s, 159b — S, 159b
Shiblī Nuʿmānī ii, 132b, 489a; iii, 433a; v, 960a, 1136a; s, 106a, b, 293a — II, 135b, 501a; III, 447a; V, 964a, 1131a; S, 105b, 292b
al-Shidyāḳ → Fāris; Asʿad
Shidyāma i, 84b — I, 87a
Shield → Turs
al-Shifāʾī iv, 69a — IV, 72b
Shigaley → Shāh ʿAlī
Shihāb al-Dīn, Pīr v, 26a — V, 27a
Shihāb al-Dīn b. ʿAlāʾ al-Dīn, Sayyid iii, 155b — III, 159a
Shihāb-al-Dīn Aḥmad b. Faḍl Allāh → Ibn Faḍl Allāh
Shihāb al-Dīn Dawlatābādī → Dawlatābādī
Shihāb Mahmrā s, 66b — S, 67a
Shihāb al-Dīn Maḥmūd b. Būrī i, 1332a; ii, 282a; iii, 399a — I, 1372b; II, 290b; III, 411b
Shihāb al-Dīn Maḥmūd b. Ḳarādja iii, 120a — III, 122b
Shihāb al-Dīn Mālik ii, 354b — II, 364a
Shihāb al-Dīn Muḥammad Ghūrī → Muʿizz al-Dīn Muḥammad b. Sām
Shihāb al-Dīn Shāhīn Pasha → Shāhīn Pasha
Shihāb al-Dīn Shīrāshāmak iii, 420a; iv, 708a — III, 433b; IV, 736b
Shihāb al-Dīn ʿUmar → ʿUmar Shāh
al-Shihābī (d./m. 1800) iv, 69b — IV, 73a
al-Shihābī → ʿAbd al-Khāliḳ; Aḥmad; Ḥaydar; Manṣūr
Shihābid(e)s i, 1078a; ii, 634b, 635a; iv, 834b; v, 259a; s, 268a, b, 269a — I, 1110b; II, 650b, 651a; IV, 867b; V, 257a; S, 268a, b
Shiḥna ii, 162a; iii, 1099a; iv, 209a — II, 167a; III, 1126a; IV, 218b
al-Shiḥr i, 554b; iv, 901b; v, 656a, 786a, b; s, 337b, 338a, b — I, 572a; IV, 934b; V, 660a, 792b; S, 337b, 338a
Shiism → Shīʿa
Shiḳāḳ i, 1031a — I, 1062b
Shikār aghalarî ii, 6a — II, 6a
Shikārpūr ii, 185b, 186a — II, 191b, 192a
Shikasta taʿlīḳ (nastaʿlīḳ) iv, 1124b, 1126a, 1128a — IV, 1156a, 1157b, 1159b
Shīkha iv, 823b — IV, 856b
Shiḳḳa Banāriya → al-Kāf
Shiḳḳdār ii, 273a, 868a — II, 281a, 888a
Shilb i, 6a, 165b, 862a, 1339a; ii, 1009a; iii, 816b — I, 6a, 170a, 886b, 1379a; II, 1032b; III, 840a
al-Shilbī → Ibn al-Imām
al-Shillī, Muḥammad b. Abū Bakr i, 828b — I, 851b
Shilluk ii, 828a, 944a — II, 847b, 966a
Shiṇa s, 158b — S, 158b
Shināsī, Ibrāhīm i, 61b, 294a, 298a, 973a; ii, 466a, 473b, 682a; iii, 591b; iv, 875b — I, 63b, 303a, 307b, 1003a; II, 478a, 485b, 699a; III, 612a; IV, 908b
Shinḳīṭ i, 211a, 733b — I, 217a, 755b
al-Shinḳīṭī, Aḥmad b. ʿAmīn v, 892a; s, 123a — V, 898b; S, 122b
Shinwārīs i, 238a; s, 66b, 237b — I, 245b; S, 67a, 237a
Ship → Baḥriyya; Safīna
Shīr Afdal ii, 30b, 317a — II, 31a, 326a
Shīr Afkan → ʿAlī Ḳulī Khān Istadjlū
Shīr ʿAlī Khān i, 87a, 231b, 232a, 796b; ii, 417a, 638a; iv, 537b — I, 89b, 239a, 819b; II, 428a, 654a; IV, 561a
Shīr ʿAlī Khān (Khōkand) v, 30a — V, 31a
Shīr Khăn (Bengal(e)) i, 1254a — I, 1292a
Shīr Khān Bābī ii, 597b — II, 612b
Shīr Shāh Sūrī i, 218a, 228b, 252b, 316a, 1015a, 1135b, 1155a, 1209b, 1218b, 1323b; ii, 13a, 121a, 154b, 155b, 259a, 271a, 272b, 498b, 973a, 1122b, 1144a; iii, 199b, 201b, 422b, 423a, 449a, 575b; iv, 276b, 1127b; v, 598a, 687b; s, 1b, 3a, 176b, 203a, 312a, 325a — I, 224b, 235b, 260b, 326a, 1046b, 1169b, 1189b, 1245b, 1255a, 1364b; II, 13a, 123b, 159b., 160a, 266a, 279a, 281a, 511a, 995b, 1149a, 1171a; III, 205a, 206b, 436a, b, 464a, 595b; IV, 288b, 1159a; V, 602a, 693a; S, 1b, 2b, 177b, 203a, 312a, 324b
Shīr Singh ii, 140b; iii, 336a; iv, 196b — II, 144a; III, 346a; IV, 205a
Shīrāshāmak → Shihāb al-Dīn Shīrăshāmak
Shīrawayh → Abū Shudjāʿ
Shīrāz i, 36a, 132a, 1341b; ii, 812a; iii, 55b, 1208b; iv, 7b, 220a; v, 835a; s, 38a, 118b, 119b, 142b, 147b, 291a, 302a, 305a, 336a — I, 37a, 136a, 1382a; II, 831b; III, 58a, 1239a; IV, 8b, 229b; V, 841a, b; S, 38a, 117b, 118a, 119a, 142a, 147b, 290b, 301b, 305a, 335b
- institutions i, 212b; ii, 426a — I, 218b; II, 437a
- monuments i, 127a; iii, 1124b — I, 131a; III, 1152b
al-Shīrāzī → al-ʿAbbās b. al-Ḥusayn; Ḳuṭb al-Dīn
al-Shīrāzī, Abū ʿAbd Allāh iv, 1074a — IV, 1105b
al-Shīrāzī, Abu ʾl-Faradj iii, 161a, 766b — III, 164b, 789b
al-Shīrăzī, Abuʾl-Ḥasan ii, 649b; iv, 787a; v, 61a — II, 666a; IV, 819a; V, 63a

al-Shīrāzī, Abū Isḥāḳ iii, 899a; s, 29b, 192a — III, 923a; S, 30a, 193a
Shīrāzī, Banū v, 380b, 381a — V, 381b, 382a
Shīrāzī, Mīrzā Ṣāliḥ s, 108a, 290b — S, 107b, 290a
Shīrāzī, Muḥammad Ḥasan s, 76a, 77a — S, 76a, 77a
al-Shīrāzī, Muḥammad b. lyās i, 344b — I, 355a
al-Shīrāzī, Ṣadr al-Dīn (Ṣadrā) i, 596a; ii, 104a, 774a; iii, 103b, 664a, 1130b; iv, 50b, 121a, 509a; v, 605a; s, 305a — I, 615b; II, 106b, 792b; III, 106a, 685b, 1158b; IV, 53b, 126b, 531a; V, 609a; S, 305a
al-Shirbīnī i, 571b, 595b — I, 590a, 615a
Shīrgīr → Anūshtigin Shīrgīr
Shīrī → ʿAlī Beg Hersek-zāde
Shīrīn ii, 793b; iv, 730b — II, 812b; IV, 759b
Shirin Begī ii, 1113b; iv, 630a — II, 1139b; IV, 654b
Shirk i, 70a, 333a — I, 72a, 343b
Shirka i, 170a — I, 175a
Shīrkūh I, Asad al-Dīn i, 197a, 197b, 797a; ii, 318b, 856b, 858a; iii, 399a, 862b; iv, 210a — I, 202b, 203a, 820b; II, 328a, 876b, 878a; III, 411b, 886b; IV, 219b
Shīrkūh II, Asad al-Dīn iii, 399b — III, 412a
Shīrpūr i, 1254a — I, 1292a
Shīrwān i, 8a, 191b, 406a, 958a; ii, 86a, 193a; iii, 211a; iv, 343a, 344b, 346a-350a; v, 296a, 458b; s, 139b, 143a, 326a, 333b — I, 8a, 197a, 417b, 987b; II, 87b, 199a; III, 216b; IV, 357b, 359a, 361a-365a; V, 287b, 461a; S, 139a, 142b, 143a, 325b, 333a
Shirwān (river/rivière) → Diyālā
Shīrwān Shāhs i, 835b, 967b; ii, 1082b; iv, 345a, b, 348a, 350a — I, 859a, 997a; II, 1108a; IV, 360a, 363a, 365a
Shirwānī-zāde Rüshdü Pasha i, 285a; iii, 621a — I, 294a; III, 642a
Shīrzādiyān iv, 860a — IV, 893a
Shishaklī, Adīb al- ii, 662a; v, 1048a — II, 678b; V, 1044b, 1045a
Shishman i, 1118b, 1302b, 1303a; ii, 611a — I, 1152a, 1342b, 1343a; II, 626a
Shishmanid(e)s i, 1302b — I, 1342b
Shīth b. Ādam i, 178a, 247a — I, 183a, 255a
Shīth b. Bahrām ii, 1099b — II, 1125a
Shīth b. Ibrāhīm al-Ḳifṭī iii, 780a — III, 803a
Shīthānī ii, 1100a, 1101a — II, 1125b, 1127a
Shitrandj → Shatrandj
Shiw Prasād iii, 458a — III, 474a
Shīwādjī i, 769a, 1202b; ii, 99b, 602a, 1129b; iii, 15b, 202b, 424b, 427a; iv, 1023a — I, 792a, 1238a; II, 101b, 616b, 1156b; III, 16b, 208a, 438a, 440b; IV, 1055b
Shīz v, 1110a, 1112a — V, 1106a, 1108a
Shkarawa i, 1189b, 1190a — I, 1224b, 1225a
Shlūḥ i, 433b; ii, 116b — I, 446a; II, 119a
Shoa i, 763b; ii, 10a, b; iii, 3b; iv, 540b — I, 786b; II, 10a, b; III, 3b; IV, 564a
Shoes → Naʿl
Shoghi → Shawḳī
Shōlāpūr iii, 426a, 1160a, 1161a — III, 439b, 1188b, 1189b
Shor Bazaar s, 66b — S, 67a
Shorfā → Sharīf; Shurafāʾ
Shrīrangapattanam v, 1259a, 1260a, b — V, 1250a, 1251a, b
Shrārda i, 84b — I, 87a
Shrīnagar → Srīnagar
Shrīrangapattanam iii, 451a — III, 466b
Shriwardhan s, 246b — S, 246b
Shu → Ču
Shūʿ i, 1010b — I, 1041b
Shuʿāʿ al-Salṭana ii, 652b; iv, 393b — II, 669a; IV, 410b
Shuʿayb i, 680b; v, 421a, 1156a, b — I, 701b; V, 423a, 1146a
Shuʿayb b. al-Ḥabḥāb al-Azdī i, 104b — I, 107b
Shuʿayb b. Mahdam iii, 53a — III, 55a
al-Shuʿayba s, 50a — S, 51a
Shuʿaybiyyūn iii, 339a — III, 349a
Shuʿba b. ʿAyyāsh i, 105b; iii, 63a; s, 18a, 232b — I, 108b; III, 65b; S, 18a, 232b
Shuʿba b. al-Hadjdjādj i, 445b — I, 458b
Shubha ii, 831b; iii, 21b — II, 851b; III, 21b
Shubrā ii, 105b — II, 107b
Shubrāwī, Shaykh ʿAbd Allāh i, 819b, 1152a — I, 842b, 1186a
Shubruma b. al-Ṭufayl iii, 938a — III, 963a
Shudjāʿ b. Shāh Djahān iii, 634b; s, 258b — III, 656a; S, 258a
Shudjāʿ al-Dawla i, 680a, 702a, 757a, 1042b, 1357b; ii, 870b; iii, 61a, b, 1158b, 1244a; v, 637a — I, 701a, 723b, 779b, 1074b, 1397b; II, 890b; III, 63b, 64a, 1187a, 1276a; V, 641a
Shudjāʿ al-Dīn Khurshīd v, 828a — V, 834a
Shudjāʿ al-Dīn Sulaymān Pasha iv, 108b — IV, 113a-b
Shudjāʿ Khān i, 1155a — I, 1189b
Shudjāʿ al-Mulk b. ʿAmān al-Mulk ii, 30b — II, 31a
Shudjāʿ al-Mulk Bukhārī iii, 634a — III, 655b
Shudjāʿ al-Mulk Durrānī i, 72b, 230b, 231a, b; ii, 186b, 638a, 1001a; iv, 537b; v, 102a; s, 270a — I, 74b, 237b, 238a, b; II, 192b, 654a, 1024b; IV, 561a; V, 104a, b; S, 270a
Shudjāʿ al-Salṭana → Ḥasan ʿAlī Mīrzā
Shūf ii, 749b; s, 159a — II, 768a; S, 159a
Shufʿa i, 172b; v, 878b — I, 177a; V, 884b
Shughnān i, 851b, 853b, 854a; iv, 202b — I, 875a, 877b; IV, 211b
Shughnī i, 225a — I, 231b
Shughr ii, 556a — II, 570a
al-Shuhadāʾ ii, 744b — II, 763a
Shuhaym, Banū s, 356a — S, 356a
Shükr Allāh Efendī v, 19a — V, 19b
Shukrī, ʿAbd al-Raḥmān s, 58a — S, 58a
Shukrī al-Khūrī → al-Khūrī
Shukrī al-Ḳuwwatlī ii, 290a — II, 298a
Shukriyya iv, 686a, b, 687a — IV, 714a, b, 715a
Shükrü, Midḥat iv, 284b — IV, 296b
Shükrü Bey iii, 1199a — III, 1229b
Shükūfe ii, 908b — II, 929b
Shūl v, 826b — V, 832b
Shuʿla iv, 69b — IV, 73a
Shulayr, Djabal i, 489a — I, 503b
Shūlistān iv, 498a; v, 824a, 829b — IV, 519b; V, 830b, 835b
Shulūḥ i, 1350a — I, 1390a
Shūmān → Ḥiṣār
Shumaṭiyya i, 509a — I, 524b
al-Shumayn al-Ḥillī iii, 111a, 221b — III, 113b, 228a
Shumayyil, Shiblī iv, 125a — IV, 130a
Shumla i, 239b, 513b — I, 247a, 529a
al-Shūnīzī → Kāẓimayn
Shūrā i, 84b; ii, 866a; v, 1084a — I, 87a; II, 886a; V, 1081b
Shūrā-yi dewlet i, 56b, 285a; ii, 641b, 692a — I, 58b, 293b; II, 657b, 709b
Shurafāʾ i, 355a, b, 368b, 371b, 403a; iii, 1037a; v, 1187b, 1191a, b, 1200a, 1201b — I, 366a, b, 379b, 382a, 414b; III, 1062b; V, 1177b, 1181a, b, 1190a, 1192a
Shuraḥbīl b. al-Ḥārith i, 527a; v, 118b — I, 543a; V, 121a
Shuraḥbīl b. Ḥasana i, 111a, 341a, 1139a, 1149a; ii, 498a; iii, 397b, 569a; iv, 927b; v, 119b — I, 114a, 351b, 1173b, 1183b; II, 510b; III, 410a, 589a; IV, 960b; V, 122a
Shuraḥbīl b. al-Simṭ i, 1343b; iii, 168b — I, 1384a;

III, 172b
Shurāt iii, 648a; iv, 1075b — III, 669b; IV, 1106b
Shurṭa ii, 505a, 507a, 510a; iii, 487b; iv, 373b — II, 517b, 520a, 522b; III, 504b; IV, 390a
Shūsha iv, 573a; s, 47a — IV, 595b; S, 47b
Shushānī → Shwāshna
Shushtar i, 695a, 711b; ii, 350b; iv, 674a, 675b; v, 451b, 867a — I, 716b, 733a; II, 360b; IV, 701b, 703a, b; V, 454a, 873b
al-Shūshtarī, ʿAbd al-Laṭīf Mūsawī Djazāʾirī s, 108a, 290a — S, 107b, 289b
al-Shushtarī, Abu ʾl-Ḥasan ʿAlī i, 501b; iii, 921b; iv, 1006b; s, 264a — I, 516b; III, 946a; IV, 1039a; S, 263b
al-Shushtarī Sayyid → Nūr Allāh
al-Shushtarī, Sayyid Niʿmat Allāh al-Djazāʾirī s, 57a — S, 57b
Shustar → Shushtar
Shuʿūb iv, 334a — IV, 348b
Shuʿūbiyya i, 16b, 158a, 206b, 276a, 1080b; ii, 729a, 951b; iii, 353b, 773b, 846a, 885a; iv, 16a, 54b, 190a, 786a; s, 17b, 404b — I, 17a, 162b, 212b, 284b, 1113a; II, 748a, 973b; III, 364b, 796b, 870a, 909a; IV, 17a, 57b, 198a, 817b; S, 18a, 405a
Shuʿurī Ḥasan Efendī iv, 526b — IV, 549a
Shuwa i, 1259b; s, 164a — I, 1297b; S, 164a
Shwăshna ii, 877a — II, 897a
Sī Aḥmad al-Bakkăy iii, 39a — III, 40b
Sialkōt (district) s, 241b — S, 241b
Ṣibā iv, 488b — IV, 509b
Sibāʿ b. ʿAbd al-ʿUzzā al-Khuzāʿī iv, 896b — IV, 929a
Sibāʿ b. Nuʿmān iv, 16a — IV, 17b
al-Sibāʿī, Muṣṭafā iii, 1069b, 1070a; iv, 160a — III, 1096b, 1097a; IV, 167a
Sibāʿī, Yūsuf v, 190a — V, 187b
Sibāḳ → Sabḳ
Sībawayh(ī) i, 321b, 588b; ii, 896a; iii, 204b. 205a, 1162a; iv, 122b, 255a, 399b; v, 174b, 803b; s, 22b — I, 331b, 607b; II, 916b; III, 210a, b, 1190b; IV, 127b, 266b, 417a; V, 172a, 809b; S, 23a
Sībāy iii, 400a; iv, 552a, b, 553a — III, 412b; IV, 576a, b
Sībī s, 270b — S, 270a
Sibir ii, 45a — II, 46a
Sibṭ → Ibn al-Djawzī; Ibn al-Taʿāwīdhī; al-Māridīnī
Sichi-berg i, 808b — I, 831b
Sicily/Sicile → Ṣiḳilliyya
al-Sīd i, 986a; ii, 526b; iii, 542b, 770b; s, 81a — I, 1016b; II, 539b; III, 561b, 794a; S, 80b
Sidama iii, 6a — III, 6b
Sidamo v, 524b — V, 527b
Siddi Lebbe ii, 28a — II, 28a
Ṣiddīḳ Ḥasan Khān i, 259b, 827b, 1196a; s, 293a — I, 267b, 850b, 1231b; S, 292b
al-Siddīḳī → al-Fīrūzābādī
Sīdī Abu 'l-Hasan ʿAlī b. Ḥamdush s, 350b — S, 350b
Sīdī Aḥmad (Banū ʿAbbās) iv, 478a, b — IV, 499a, b
Sīdī Aḥmad b. ʿAlī iv, 350a — IV, 365a
Sīdī Aḥmad u-Mūsā → Ḥmad u-Mūsā
Sīdī Aḥmad b. Yūsuf → Aḥmad b. Yūsuf
Sīdī Aḥmad Dghughī → Sīdī Abu 'l-Ḥasan ʿAlī b. Ḥamdush
Sīdī ʿAlī → Sīdī Abu 'l-Ḥasan ʿAlī b. Ḥamdush
Sīdī ʿAlī b. Khlef b. Ghālib → Mūlāy ʿAlī Bū Ghālem
Sīdī ʿAlī Arulatī iv, 349b — IV, 364b
Sidī Badr → Muẓaffar Shāh Ḥabshī
Sīdī Bel-ʿAbbās iv, 729a — IV, 758a
Sīdī Ben Aḥmed iv, 729a — IV, 758a
Sīdī Ben ʿAmmār → Ibn ʿAmmār, Abuʾl-ʿAbbās
Sīdī Ben ʿArūs → Ibn ʿArūs
Sīdī Ben Slīmān → al-Djazūlī
Sīdī Berridjāl → Ibn Barradjăn
Sīdī Bou Said → Sayyidī Abū Saʿīd
Sīdī Bū ʿAzzā → Abū Yaʿzā
Sīdī Bū Madyan → Abū Madyan
Sīdī Bū ʿUthmān s, 48a — S, 48b
Sīdī Bū Yaʿḳūb → Abū Yaʿḳūb Yūsuf al-Bādisī
Sīdī Būshta (Abu 'l-Shitāʾ) s, 405b — S, 405b
Sīdī 'l-Ḥādjdj v, 596a — V, 600a
Sīdī Ḥammū i, 1186a — I, 1221a
Sīdī Khalīl → Khalīl b. Isḥāḳ al-Djundī
Sīdī Maḥrez → Muḥriz b. Khalaf
Sīdī Muḥammad b. ʿAbd Allāh → Muḥammad III (ʿAlawid(e))
Sīdī Muḥammad ʿAbd Allāh (Ḥamāliyya) → al-Sharīf al-Akhḍar
Sīdī Muḥammad b. al-Mukhtār v, 394a — V, 395a
Sīdī Muḥammad b. al-Ṭayyib → Muḥammad b. al-Ṭayyib
Sīdī Muḥammad al-ʿAyyăshī ii, 367b — II, 377b
Sīdī Muwallih iv, 921a — IV, 953b
Sīdī (ʿAlī) Reʾīs ii, 588b, 589b; iii, 856b — II, 603a, 604a; III, 880b
Sīdī ʿUḳba → ʿUḳba b. Nāfiʿ
Sīdī Yāḳūt (Ḥabshī) s, 246a — S, 246b
Sidjādī, ʿAlāʾ al-Dīn v, 481b — V, 484b
Sidjdjīn iii, 1132b — III, 1161a
Sidjill i, 9b, 1090a; ii, 79a, 302b, 308b — I, 9b, 1123b; II, 80b, 310b, 317b
Sidjilmāssa ii, 885a; iii, 149a, 256b; v, 1175a, 1177a, 1178a; s, 28b, 29a, 295b, 370a, 389b — II, 905b; III, 152b, 263b; V, 1165a, 1167a, 1168a; S, 29a, 295a, 370a, 389b
al-Sidjilmāssī → al-Lamaṭī
Sidjistān → Sīstān
al-Sidjistānī → Abū Bakr; Abū Dāʿūd; Abū Ḥātim
al-Sidjzī → Abū Yaʿḳūb; Aḥmad; Amīr Ḥasan
Ṣidḳ iv, 487b — IV, 508b
Ṣidḳī → Bakr Ṣidḳī; al-Zahāwī
Ṣidḳī, Muḥammad iv, 148b; v, 191a — IV, 154b; V, 188a
Sidon → Ṣaydā
Sidona → Shadūna
Sidrāy b. Wazīr i, 1339a; ii, 1009a; iii, 816b — I, 1379b; II, 1033a; III, 840a
al-Sidrī s, 35b — S, 35b
Sīduh → Ibn Sīda
Siège → Kursī
Siege/Siège → Ḥiṣār
Sierra Leone s, 217b — S, 217a
Sīf al-Naṣr ii, 876a — II, 896b
Sīf ʿUmāra s, 222b, 223a — S, 222b, 223a
Ṣifa iv, 182a — IV, 190a
Ṣifāt i, 333b, 410b; ii, 550b — I, 344a, 422b; II, 564a
Ṣifātiyya i, 334a — I, 344a
Ṣiffīn i, 40b, 51b, 304a, 383b, 448b, 451b, 697a; iii, 12b; v, 936a; s, 89b, 230b — I, 41b, 53b, 313b, 394b, 461b, 464b, 718a; III, 13a; V, 939b; S, 89b, 230b
Sïghnāḳ s, 245a, 246a — S, 245a, 246a
Sigismund, John/Jean ii, 703b, 704a — II, 721b, 722a
Sihālī s, 292a — S, 291b
Sihām al-Mulk s, 365a — S, 365a
Siḥr i, 1084b; iv, 770a; v, 100b — I, 1117a; IV, 801a; V, 102b
Ṣihrīdj → Ḳanāt
Sikandar → Iskandar
Sikandar (Gudjarāt) ii, 1128b — II, 1155a
Sikandar b. Sulṭān Fatḥ Shāh s, 324b — S, 324a
Sikandar ʿĀdil-Shāh i, 199b, 769b, 1202b — I, 205a, 792b, 1238a
Sikandar Bēgam i, 1195b, 1197a — I, 1231a, 1232b
Sikandar But-shikan b. Ḳuṭb al-Dīn iii, 420a; iv,

708a, b; s, 131b — III, 433b; IV, 736b, 737a; S, 130b
Sikandar Djāh iii, 322a — III, 332a
Sikandar Shāh Lōdī i, 252b, 914b, 1323a; ii, 12b, 155a, 205a, 271a, 421a, 498b, 1048a, 1114a; iii, 420b, 439a, 453b, 492a, 631b, 632a; v, 784a, b, 1135a; s, 10b, 73b, 203a, 312a, 313a, b — I, 260b, 942a, 1363b; II, 13a, 160a, 211b, 279a, 431b, 511a, 1072b, 1171a; III, 434a, 453b, 469a, 509a, 653a, 653b; V, 790a, b, 1130b; S, 10a, 74a, 202b, 312a, b, 313a
Sikandar Shāh I (Bengal(e)) i, 719b — I, 741a
Sikandar Shāh Sūr i, 316a, 1135b; ii, 271b; iii, 423b, 576a — I, 326a, 1170a; II, 279b; III, 437a, 596a
Sikandara iv, 131b — IV, 137b
Sikandarābād iii, 318b — III, 328b
Siḳāya i, 9a, 80a — I, 9a, 82b
Sikh i, 72a, 230a, b, 231a, 282b, 296a, b, 454a, 913b, 970b, 1020a; ii, 28b, 637b, 929a, 973b; iii, 63a, 225b, 245b, 335b, 336a, 435b; iv, 666a, 709b; v, 597b, 598b; s, 242a, 332a — I, 74b, 237a, b, 238b, 291a, 305a, 467b, 941b, 1000b, 1051b; II, 29a, 654a, 950b, 996a; III, 65b, 232b, 252b, 345b, 346a, 450a; IV, 693a, 738a; V, 601a, 602a, b; S, 242a, 331b
Ṣiḳilliyya i, 86a, b, 248b, 250a, 935b; ii, 130b, 853a; iii, 220a, 299a, 657b, 788a; iv, 274b, 275b, 459b, 496a, b, 805a; v, 697a, 1243b; s, 120b, 303a — I, 88b, 89a, 256a, 258a, 964b; II, 133b, 873a; III, 226b, 308a, 679a, 811a; IV, 286b, 287b, 479b, 517b, 837b; V, 702a, 1234b; S, 120a, 303a
Sikka ii, 117b; iii, 256a, 384a; iv, 190b, 220a, 467a, 945a, 1177b; v, 965b, 966a — II, 120a; III, 263b, 396b; IV, 199a, 230a, 487b, 977b, 1211a; V, 969b, 970a
al-Sikkīn ii, 858b — II, 878a
al-Sikkīt ii, 300a; iii, 940b — II, 308a; III, 965a
al-Ṣiḳlabī, ʿAbd al-Raḥmān iv, 672b — IV, 700a
Sīkūl iv, 213a — IV, 222b
Ṣila iv, 412a, 413b — IV, 430a, 431b
al-Silafī, Ḥāfiẓ iv, 137a — IV, 142b
Silāḥ i, 1055b; ii, 506b; v, 973a — I, 1087b; II, 519b; V, 975a
Silāḥdār ʿAlī Pasha → ʿAlī Pasha Silāḥdār
Silāḥdār Dāmād ʿAlī Pasha → ʿAlī Pasha Dāmād
Ṣilāḥdār Ḥusayn Pasha i, 905a — I, 932a
Siʿlāt ii, 1078b — II, 1103b
Sile s, 136a — S, 135b
Silhādī i, 914b — I, 942b
Silifke iii, 1007a — III, 1032a
Silistre i, 4b; ii, 611b; iii, 253a; iv, 878a — I, 4b; II, 626b; III, 260a; IV, 910b
Silivri Kapîsî iv, 232b — IV, 243a
Siliwan → Mayyāfāriḳīn
Silk → Ḥarīr
Silm, Āl i, 759b — I, 782b
Silsila ii, 50b, 164b; v, 617a — II, 51a, 169b; V, 621a, b
Silsilat al-Dhahab s, 173a — S, 173b
Silver → Fiḍḍa
Silves → Shilb
Simāṭ iv, 957a, b — IV, 990b
Sīmāvī, Sedād ii, 475a, b — II, 487b
Sīmāw s, 359b — S, 359a
al-Sīmāwī → Abu 'l-Ḳāsim Muḥammad al-ʿIrāḳī
Simdjūr, Banū i, 1354b — I, 1393b
Sīmdjūr al-Dawātī s, 357a — S, 357a
Simferopol i, 312a — I, 322a
Simḥah Isaac b. Moses iv, 606a — IV, 630a
Ṣīmḳo → Ismāʿīl Agha Ṣīmḳo
Simnān s, 73a, 309b — S, 73b, 309a
Simnānī → ʿAlāʾ al-Dawla; Tāʾūs
al-Simnānī, Abu 'l-Ḥasan Aḥmad s, 194a — S, 193b
Simplicius → Samlis
Simsār ii, 103a; iii, 213a — II, 105a; III, 219a
al-Simṭ b. al-Aswad v, 119b — V, 122a
Sīmurgh i, 509a, 753a; ii, 106b, 1099b, 1138a; iii, 112b; iv, 402a — I, 524b, 775b; II, 109a, 1125b, 1165a; III, 115a; IV, 419b
Sīmyāʾ iv, 264b — IV, 276b
Sin → Khaṭṭʾa
Sīn iii, 1125a — III, 1153a
al-Ṣīn i, 91a, 390b, 927b; ii, 42b, 45b, 477b, 583a, 1076a; iii, 653b, 1115b; iv, 553a; v, 364a, 770a, 854b — I, 93b, 402a, 956a; II, 43b, 46b, 490a, 597b, 1101a; III, 674b, 1143a; IV, 577a; V, 365a, 776a, 861a
- porcelain(e) iv, 1168b, 1169a, 1170a; v, 857a — IV, 1201b, 1202a, 1203a; V, 864a
Ṣinā (language/langue) ii, 139a — II, 142b
Sinād iv, 412b — IV, 430b
Sinān (architect(e)) i, 511a, 768a, 843b, 1256b; ii, 685b, 686a, 705b; iii, 144b; iv, 232a, b, 233a, 1017a, 1158a; v, 67a, 815b, 837b, 882a — I, 526b, 791a, 866b, 1295a; II, 702b, 703a, 723b; III, 147a; IV, 242a, 243a, 1049a, 1190a; V, 69a, 821b, 844a, 888b
Sinān (d./m. 685) iv, 534b; s, 131a — IV, 558a; S, 130b
Sinān, Rāshid al-Dīn → Rāshid al-Din Sinān
Sinān b. Sulaymān ii, 484a — II, 496a
Sinān b. Thābit i, 387b, 867a, 899a — I, 399a, 891a, 925b
Sinān Beg i, 654b — I, 675b
Sinān Pasha → Čighālazāde; Khodja
Sinān Pasha Dāmād i, 292b; ii, 985b; iv, 230b — I, 301b; II, 1008a; IV, 240b
Sinān Pasha Khādim ii, 1042a; iii, 341b; iv, 1093a — II, 1066b; III, 351b, 352a; IV, 1124a
Sinān Pashazāde Meḥmed Pasha iv, 594b — IV, 618b
Sinbādnāma iii, 313b, 373a — III, 323a, 384b
Sind i, 43b, 228a, 229b, 230b, 246b, 627b, 962a, 1194b; ii, 74a, 153b, 185a; iii, 323b, 404b, 415a, 419b, 448b; iv, 199b, 202b, 597b, 793a, 1160a; s, 252a — I, 44b, 235a, 236b, 237b, 254a, 648b, 991b, 1230a; II, 75a, 158b, 191a; III, 333b, 417a, 428b, 433a, 463b; IV, 208a, 211b, 621b, 825b, 1192a; S, 252a
Sind (river/rivière) s, 366b — S, 366a
Ṣindābur ii, 1127b — II, 1154a
Sindbād i, 2b, 204a, 359a, 362b, 955a; iv, 16a; v, 64a, 69a — I, 2b, 210a, 370a, 373b, 984b; IV, 17b; V, 65b, 71a
Sindhī i, 1007b; ii, 101b — I, 1038b; II, 103b
Sindhia ii, 1144a — II, 1171a
Sindhind i, 11a; iii, 1137a — I, 11b; III, 1165a
Sindhiyā, Mahādjī ii, 1092b — II, 1118a
al-Sindī → Abū ʿAṭāʾ; Abū ʿAlī; Abū Maʿshar
Sindī, Banū i, 1246b — I, 1284b
al-Sindī b. Shāhak iii, 990a — III, 1014b
Sindjār iii, 1268a; s, 381a, 413b — III, 1301a; S, 381b, 414a
Sindjas, Banū v, 1179a, b, 1181a, b, 1182a — V, 1169a, b, 1171a, b, 1172a
Sinet → Khitān
Ṣinf i, 477a; ii, 967a; iii, 217b; iv, 894a — I, 491b; II, 989a; III, 223b; IV, 927a
Singapur i, 979a; ii, 426b; s, 220b — I, 1009b; II, 437b; S, 220b
Singe, le → Ḳird
Singer → ʿĀlima; Ghināʾ; Ḳayna; Mughannī
Singing → Ghināʾ; Khayāl
Ṣinhādja i, 79a, 84a, 355b, 356a, b, 367a; ii, 623a — I, 81b, 86b, 366b, 367a, 378a; II, 638b
Sīnimā → Cinema/Cinématographe
Sinkāt iv, 686b, 687a — IV, 714b, 715a
Singkawang s, 151a — S, 151b
Sinkiang ii, 43a; v, 846a, b — II, 43b; V, 857b, 858a
Sinlessness → ʿIṣma
Sinn i, 1217b — I, 1254a

al-Sinnabra s, 117a — S, 116b
Sinnār ii, 943b; v, 267a — II, 965b; V, 265a
Sinob, Sīnūb, Sinope i, 476b; iv, 575b, 577a, 813b; v, 505b — I, 490b; IV, 598b, 600a, 846b; V, 509a
Sionisme II, 934a, b
Sipāhī i, 1264b, 1265a, 1268b; iii, 191a, b, 192b; iv, 565a, 1095b — I, 1303a, b, 1307b; III, 195b, 196a, 197b; IV, 587b, 1126b
Sipāhī Meḥmed v, 775a — V, 781a
Sipāhī og͟hlanlarî i, 102a, 1004a — I, 105a, 1034b
Sipahsālār → Ispahsālār
Sipahsālār, Mīrzā Ḥusayn K͟hān s, 109a — S, 108a
Sipihr S͟hukōh ii, 134b II, 138a
Sīr b. Abī Bakr i, 7a, 242b; ii, 1013a; iv, 116a — I, 7b, 250a; II, 1036b; IV, 121a
Ṣīr Banī Yās i, 535b — I, 552a
Sir Daryā i, 135a, 607a; ii, 778a, 790a, 791a; v, 30b, 45a, 46a; s, 244b, 245a, b — I, 139a, 627a; II, 797a, 809a, 810a; V, 31b, 46b, 47a; S, 244b, 245a, b
Sir Sayyid → Aḥmad K͟hān
Sīra iii, 369b, 374a; v, 1161b, 1163b — III, 381a, 386a; V, 1151b, 1153a
Sirād͟j ʿAfīf, S͟hams al-Dīn s, 105b — S, 105a
Sirād͟j al-Dawla Mīrzā Maḥmūd i, 400b; ii, 7a, 371a, 1091b — I, 412a; II, 7a, 381b, 1117a
Sirād͟j al-Dīn → Ak͟hī Sirād͟j
Sīrāf i, 550b, 552a, 927b, 1355a; ii, 130b; iv, 500b, 1085b; v, 670b; s, 118a — I, 568a, 569b, 956a, 1394a; II, 134a; IV, 522a, 1116b; V, 676a; S, 117b
al-Sīrāfī, Abū Saʿīd i, 97b, 126b; ii, 896b; s, 362b — I, 100b, 130a; II, 917a; S, 362a
Sirāikī v, 610b, 611a — V, 614b, 615a
Sirāj v, 986b — V, 982b
Sīrat al-Amīr Ḥamza iii, 153b, 376a, 1207a — III, 156b, 387b, 1237b
Sirat ʿAntar → ʿAntar
Sīrat Banī Hilāl iii, 387a — III, 399b
Sīrat al-Baṭṭāl → D͟hu ʾl-Himma
Sirdāb v, 12b — V, 11b
Sīrd͟jān v, 150a, 151a, 152a, b; s, 327a — V, 152a, b, 154a; S, 326b
Sirhind i, 1194a; s, 126b, 313a — I, 1229a; S, 125b, 312b
Sirhīndī, Yaḥyā s, 105a — S, 104b
Siri s, 206b — S, 206a
Sīrī i, 1322a; ii, 256b, 269a; iii, 481b; iv, 921b — I, 1362a; II, 263b, 277a; III, 498a; IV, 954b
Sirius s, 320b — S, 320a
Sirkap s, 259b — S, 259b
Sirr al-Asrār i, 1155b; ii, 916b; iii, 30a, 464a — I, 1190a; II, 938a; III, 32a, 480b
Sirrī Pas͟ha i, 907b — I, 935a
Sīs i, 8a; ii, 36a, 38a; v, 283b — I, 8a; II, 36b, 38b; V, 282a
Sīstān i, 5a, 43b, 86a, 147b, 211b, 222b, 223a, 452b, 1344a; ii, 5a, 49b, 903b; iv, 4b, 19a-b, 54a, b, 55a; v, 57a, 390a, 868a; s, 21a, 26a, 326b — I, 5a, 44b, 88b, 152a, 217b, 229a, b, 230a, 465b, 1384b; II, 5a, 50b, 924b; IV, 5a, 20b, 57a, b, 58a; V, 58b, 391a, 874b; S, 21a, 26a, 326a
Sīstānī → Farruk͟hī-i Sīstānī
Sitāra iii, 360a; iv, 823b — III, 371b; IV, 856b
Sitt K͟hātūn ii, 895a — II, 916a
Sitt al-Mulk ii, 484a, 855b, 857a; iii, 80b; iv, 944a — II, 496a, 875a, 877a; III, 83a; Iv, 976b
Sitt al-Tud͟jd͟jār iv, 136a — IV, 142a
Siu (battle of/bataille de) s, 355b — S, 355b
Sīvāsiyya iv, 991b — IV, 1024a
Sivrialan s, 91b — S, 91a
Siwā iv, 272b, 273a — IV, 284b, 285a
Sīwād͟jī (Marātha) i, 199b; s, 246b — I, 205a; S, 246b
Siwāl s, 353b — S, 353b
Sīwās i, 511a; iv, 1167b; v, 248a; s, 146a, 274a — I, 526b; IV, 1200a; V, 246a; S, 146a, 273b
Siyāhčas͟hm iv, 661b — IV, 688b
Siyāh-pūs͟h iv, 409b, 410b — IV, 427a, 428b
Siyāḳa(t) ii, 128a, 332b, 952a; iv, 1124a, 1125b — II, 131a, 342a, 974a; IV, 1155b, 1157a
al-Siyālkōtī, ʿAbd al-Ḥākim i, 297b, 1022b — I, 307a, 1054a
Ṣiyām v, 424b — V, 426b
Siyar v, 1162b — V, 1152b
Siyar al-mas͟hāyik͟h v, 697b — V, 702b
Siyar al-mulūk iii, 113b — III, 116a
Siyārwardiyya iv, 342b — IV, 357a
Siyāsa I, 170a — I, 174b
al-Siyāsa i, 597b; ii, 467a — I, 617a; II, 478b
Siyāsa s͟harʿiyya i, 276b — I, 285a
Siyāwus͟h, ʿAlāʾ al-Dīn i, 703a; iv, 620a, b; v, 274b — I, 724a; IV, 645a; V, 272b
Siyāwus͟h b. Kay Kāʾūs iv, 813b, 815b, 1061b — IV, 846a, 848b, 1092b
Siyāwus͟h Pas͟ha i, 380b, 1284b; iv, 193b — I, 391b, 1324a; IV, 202a
Siyer → Sīra
Sjahrir ii, 664a, b — II, 681a
Skandelion → Iskandaruna
Skanderbeg → Iskender Beg
Skārdū i, 1004b — I, 1035b
Skénites I, 543b
Sḳīfa ii, 115b — II, 118a
Sklēros s, 37a — S, 37a
Skopje → Üsküb
Slander → Ḳad͟hf
Slaughterer → D͟jazzār
Slave, slavery → ʿAbd; G͟hulām; Kayna; K͟hādim; Mamlūk
Slave trade s, 164b — S, 164b
Slavs → Saḳāliba
Slēmān, Awlād ii, 876a — II, 896b
Slīmān → Sulaymān
Sliman ben Ibrahim s, 224a, b — S, 224a, b
Slovakia → Čeh
Smacid(e)s i, 733b, 734a — I, 755b
Smala i, 67b — I, 69b
Ṣmara v, 890a, b — V, 896b, 897a
Smbat → Sambāṭ
Smyrna/Smyrne → Izmir
Snake → Ḥayya
Snouck Hurgronje ii, 497a; iii, 1223a, 1228b, 1234b — II, 509b; III, 1254a, 1260a, 1266b
Soaïtou Mamadou v, 279b — V, 277b
Sōba i, 425b; iv, 892b — I, 437b; IV, 925b
Socialism → Is͟htirākiyya
Society/Société → D͟jamʿiyya
Société ottomane de la liberté → ʿOt͟hmanlî Ḥürriyet D͟jemʿiyyeti
Socotra → Suḳuṭra
Socrates/Socrate → Suḳrāṭ
Soda Rād͟jpūts i, 431a — I, 443b
Sodom(e) v, 833a — V, 839a
Sodomy/Sodomie → Liwāṭ
Ṣoffs i, 1179b — I, 1214b
Ṣofu Muḥammad Pas͟ha iii, 983b — III, 1008a
Sogguen ii, 1095b — II, 1121b
Sog͟hd, Sog͟hdian/Sog͟hdien ii, 67a, 790b; iii, 1060b; v, 181a, 541b, 542a, 852b, 854a; s, 64a, 65a, 176b — II, 68a, 80b; III, 1087a; V, 178b, 546a, b, 859a, 860b; S, 64b, 65a, 177b
Sögüd͟juk i, 63a — I, 65a
Sōhāg ii, 1114b — II, 1140b
Sohrān, amīr i, 1031a — I, 1062b
Sohrān, Banū v, 460b — V, 463a
Soie → Ḥarīr

Sokna ii, 575b — II, 590a
Ṣoḳollî-zade Ḥasan Pasha iv, 594b, 901a — IV, 618b, 933b
Ṣoḳollu Muḥammad Pasha i, 291b, 1018a, 1264b; ii, 56b, 103b, 704a, 881a; iii, 995a; v, 815b — I, 300b, 1049a, 1303a; II, 57b, 105b, 722a, 901b; III, 1019b; V, 821b
Ṣoḳollu Muṣṭafā Pasha i, 1285b, 1286a; ii, 880b; v, 775a — I, 1324b, 1325b; II, 901a; V, 781a
Sokolović → Ṣoḳollu
Sokoto ii, 1145a; iii, 277a; iv, 549b — II, 1172b; III, 285a; IV, 573a, b
Sol Gharībler → Ghurabāʾ
Solakzāde iii, 249a — III, 256a
Soldaïa → Sudak
Solitude → Khalwa
Solomon → Sulaymān
Somālī i, 176b, 553a, 1038a, 1172b; ii, 113b, 535b; iii, 4a, 5b; v, 522a, 524a — I, 181a, 571a, 1069b, 1207b; II, 116a, 549a; III, 4a, 6a; V, 525b, 527b
Somba ii, 94a — II, 96a
Sōmnāth ii, 597a, 598a, 1123b, 1125a — II, 612a, b, 1150a, 1151a
Sonargaon i, 868b; ii, 216a, 751b — I, 893a; II, 223a, 770a
Sonde, îles → Sunda
Songhai, Songhoy i, 1259b; ii, 94a, 252a, 977a; iii, 1038b; iv, 549a, 754b — I, 1298a; II, 96a, 259a, 999b; III, 1064b; IV, 572b, 784b
Soninké iii, 288b; iv, 314a — III, 297b; IV, 328a
Sonni Ali ii, 252a, 977a — II, 259a, 999b
Sōpūr iv, 707b — IV, 736a
Soraya → Thurayya
Sori ii, 942b — II, 964a
Soudan → Sūdān
Souf s, 145a — S, 144b
Soufi → Ṣūfī
Soufre → al-Kibrīt
Souk → Sūḳ
Soul → Nafs
Souris → Faʾr
Sousse → Sūsa
Soy iii, 374a — III, 385b
Soyinadji (Soyin Ḥadjī) s, 168b, 169a — S, 169a
Spahi → Sipāhī
Spahpat → Ispahbadh
Spain → al-Andalus
Sphere/Sphère → Falak; al-Kura
Sphinx i, 125b — I, 129b
Spices → Afāwīh
Spider → ʿAnkabūt
Split i, 1267a; v, 774b; s, 186a — I, 1306a; V, 780b; S, 187b
Spy → Djāsūs
Sri Lanka → Ceylon
Srīnagar iii, 448a; iv, 707b; s, 114a, 131b, 156a, 332a, 333a, 353b, 366a, b, 423b — III, 463b; IV, 735b; S, 113b, 131a, 156a, 332a, 353b, 366a, 423b
Stable → Iṣṭabl
Stars → Nudjūm
Steel → Fūlādh
Stephanos → Iṣṭifan b. Basīl
Štip → Ishtib
Stone → Ḥadjar; Karkūr
Story-teller → Ḳāṣṣ; Maddāḥ; Rāwā
Stribant i, 172a — I, 177a
Su aghasî v, 881b — V, 888a
Su kemeri iv, 424b, 438a; v, 726b, 727b, 882a — IV, 443a, 457b; V, 731b, 732b, 888a, b
Su-Lu i, 684b; iii, 493b — I, 705b; III, 510b
Su-ssu-shi-san v, 851b — V, 855b, 856a
Su yoldjularî v, 882a, b — V, 888a, b, 889a
Suakin → Sawākin
Suʿāt i, 1045b — I, 1077b
Ṣūbadār ii, 337a — II, 346b
Ṣūba i, 316b — I, 326b
Ṣubashi Tigin iii, 47a — III, 49a
Subayʿ i, 628b; v, 62b — I, 649b; V, 64a
Ṣubba i, 1096a; iii, 1254a — I, 1129a; III, 1286b
Sübetey i, 836a; ii, 43a; iv, 107b; v, 311b — I, 859a; II, 44a; IV, 112a; V, 311b
Subḥa i, 714b — I, 736a
Subḥān-Ḳulī Khān s, 419b — S, 419b
Ṣubḥī, Muṣṭafā iv, 124a — IV, 129a
Ṣubḥ-i Azal → Yaḥyā Nūrī, Mīrzā
Ṣubḥ-i Ṣādik ii, 187a — II, 193a
al-Subkī, Bahā al-Dīn Aḥmad ii, 107b; iv, 863b — II, 110a; IV, 897a
al-Subkī, Maḥmūd Khaṭṭāb s, 244b — S, 244b
al-Subkī, Tādj al-Dīn ʿAbd al-Wahhāb i, 593a, 594b, 1308b; ii, 215a; iii, 818a, 954b — I, 612b, 614a, 1348b; II, 221b; III, 841b, 979a
al-Subkī, Taḳī al-Dīn ʿAlī ii, 215a, 926a; iii, 822a, 954b — II, 221b, 947b; III, 845b, 979a
al-Subkī Taḳī al-dīn Muḥammad iii, 711a — III, 733a
al-Subkiyyūn s, 244b — S, 244b
al-Subūʿī, al-Subūʿī b. Muḥammad iv, 828b — IV, 861b
Subuk i, 637b; ii, 679b — I, 658a; II, 696b
Subuktigîn → Sebuktegin
Subutāi → Sübetey
Suchow iv, 553b, 554a; v, 848a — IV, 577a, 578a; V, 852a
Sucre → Sukkar
Sucre, canne à → Ḳaṣab al-Sukkar
Suʿdā, Sūdābeh iv, 813a — IV, 846a
Sudak iv, 575b, 576a — IV, 598b
Sūdān i, 49a, 279b, 289a, 297a, 1058a; ii, 121b; iii, 657b; iv, 262a; v, 70a, 1248a, b; s, 217b — I, 50b, 51a, 288b, 297b, 306a, 1089b; II, 124b; III, 678b; IV, 274a; V, 72a, 1238b, 1239a; S, 217b
- administration i, 976a, 1156b; ii, 595a, 668a; iii, 385a; v, 1063b — I, 1006a, 1191a; II, 610a, 684b; III, 397b; V, 1061a
- ethnography/ethnographie i, 1a, 37b, 39a, 1058a; ii, 767b, 1110b; iii, 300a; v, 317b, 318b — I, 1a, 35b, 40a, 1089b; II, 786a, 1136b; III, 309b; V, 317a, 318a
- institutions ii, 425a; iii, 523b — II, 436a; III, 541b
- language, literature/langue, littérature i, 575b; ii, 467a; iii, 949a — II, 594a; II, 479a; III, 973b
Sudayr i, 748a; ii, 175b — I, 770a; II, 181a
Sudayrī ii, 175b — II, 181a
Sūdī, Aḥmad i, 310a, 1271a, 1345b; iii, 56b — I, 319b, 1310b, 1386a; III, 58b
al-Sūdī, Aḥmad b. ʿAbd Allāh b. Sālim ii, 730a — II, 748b
Sudjān Rāʾe i, 241b — I, 249a
al-Suds al-fakhrī v, 46b — V, 47b, 48a
Suez → Suways
Ṣūf v, 798a — V, 804a
Ṣufayna s, 198b — S, 198b
Ṣuff v, 759b — V, 765b
Ṣuffa i, 266a; iv, 287a, 1147b — I, 274a; IV, 299b, 1179a
Ṣūfī, ṣūfism i, 60a, 69a, 70b, 89a, 92a, 96a, 138b, 142b, 146a, 195a, 234b, 266b, 280a, 283a, 297b, 298b, 346b, 352a, 392b, 441a, 515b, 592b, 701b, 765b, 794b, 829a, 951a, 960b, 1088b, 1239b, 1244a; ii, 166b, 220b, 242b, 422b, 1041a; iii, 75b, 83b, 662a, 707b, 752a, 763b; iv, 35a, 46a-b, 47b, 49a, 51b, 64b-65a, 114a, 183b, 467a, 554b, 616a, 1074a; v, 333a, 698b, 1235b — I, 62a, 71a, 72b, 91b, 94b, 98b, 143a, 147a, 150b, 201a, 242a, 275a, 289a, 291b, 306b, 308a, 357a, 363a, 403b, 453b,

531a, 612a, 723a, 788b, 817b, 852a, 980a, 990a, 1121a, 1277a, 1282a; II, 172a, 227b, 249b, 433b, 1065a; III, 78a, 86a, 683b, 729b, 775a, 787a; IV, 37b, 49a, 50a-b, 52a, 54b, 68a-b, 119a, 191b, 488a, 578a, 641a, 1105b; V, 333b, 703b, 1226a
al-Ṣūfī → ᶜAbd al-Raḥmān al-Ṣūfī
Ṣūfid(e)s iv, 1064a — IV, 1095b
Ṣūfīgarī v, 244a — V, 242a
Ṣufriyya iii, 648a, 654b, 657b, 1040b, 1175a — III, 669b, 675b, 679a, 1066b, 1204a
Suftadja ii, 382b; iii, 283b — II, 393a; III, 292a
Sufyān, Banū v, 48b — V, 50a
Sufyān b. al-Abrad al-Kalbī i, 686b, 810b; ii, 809a; iii, 716b; iv, 753a — I, 707b, 834a; II, 828b; III, 739a; IV, 783b
Sufyān b. Khālid al-Liḥyānī v, 763a — V, 769a
Sufyān b. Muᶜāwiya al-Muhallabī iii, 883b — III, 907b
Sufyān b. ᶜUyayna i, 272b, 827a, 960b; s, 386b — I, 281a, 850a, 990a; S, 386b
Sufyān al-Thawrī ii, 538b, 889b; iii, 155a, 687b, 843a; s, 232b, 384b — II, 552a, 910a; III, 158b, 709a, 867a; S, 232b, 385a
Sufyān al-Yamanī i, 829a — I, 852a
al-Sufyānī i, 17a; ii, 281b; iv, 457a, 494a; v, 1232a; s, 103b — I, 17b; II, 289b; IV, 477a, 515a; V, 1222b; S, 103a
Sugar → Sukkar
Sugar cane → Ḳaṣab al-Sukkar
Sughd → Soghd
Sughdāḳ iv, 817b — IV, 850b
al-Sughdī → Abū Ḥafṣ Sughdī
Sughnāk → Suḳnāḳ
Sughundjak Noyan iv, 1046b — IV, 1078a
Sūhādj → Sōhāg
Ṣuḥār i, 563b, 1098a, 1281b; iv, 500b; s, 234b — I, 581b, 1131a, 1321a; IV, 522a; S, 234b
Ṣuḥār al-ᶜAbdī iii, 650a — III, 671a
Ṣuhayb iii, 587a — III, 607a
Suhayl b. ᶜAmr i, 115b, 151a — I, 119a, 155b
al-Suhaylī s, 382a — S, 382b
Suḥaym b. Wathīl al-Riyāḥī ii, 998b — II, 1021b
Ṣuḥbatiyya i, 195b — I, 201b
Suhrāb Khān Tālpūr iv, 1160a — IV, 1192a
Suhrawardī, Ḥusayn Shahīd iii, 533a, b — III, 552a
al-Suhrawardī, Abū Ḥafṣ ᶜUmar (d./m. 1234) i, 347a, 596a; ii, 55a, 964b, 966b; iv, 516a, 990b; s, 313a, 353a, 380a, 414b, 415b — I, 357b, 615a; II, 56a, 986b, 988b; IV, 538a, 1023a; S, 312b, 353a, 380b, 415a, b
al-Suhrawardī, Shihāb al-Dīn Yaḥyā (d./m. 1191) i, 234b, 351b, 416b, 595b, 803a; ii, 774a; iii, 1131b; iv, 64a, 119b, 120b, 943a; s, 41a, 67a — I, 242a, 362b, 428a, 615a, 826a; II, 792b; III, 1160a; IV, 67b, 125a, b, 975b; S, 41b, 67b
Suhrawardiyya i, 912a; ii, 421a; iii, 823a; iv, 48a, 1026b; s, 10b, 156a, 312a, 353a — I, 939b; II, 431b; III, 847a; IV, 50b, 1058b; S, 10a, 156a, 312a, 353a
al-Suhūl i, 628b — I, 649b
Suicide → Intiḥār
Sūḳ i, 898b; ii, 959a, 962a; iii, 486b; iv, 136a; v, 665b — I, 925a; II, 981a, 984a; III, 503b; IV, 141b; V, 671a
al-Sūḳ (Sahara) → Tādemekket
Sūḳ al-Ahwāz → al-Ahwāz
Sūḳ al-ᶜAṭṭārīn s, 422b — S, 422b
Sūḳ al-Gharb (Bairūt) s, 162a — S, 162a
Sūḳ Ḥamza iv, 479a, b — IV, 501a, b
Sūḳ Kutāma iv, 729b — IV, 758b
Sūḳ al-Thalāthāʾ i, 899b, 900a; s, 381a — I, 926b, 927a; S, 381a
Sukadana s, 150b, 201a — S, 150b, 201a
Sukarno ii, 663a, 664a, 665a, 666a; iii, 534a — II, 679b, 680b, 682a, 683a; III, 552b
Sukayna bint al-Ḥusayn i, 305a; ii, 1011b — I, 314b; II, 1035a
Sukhf ii, 552a; iii, 354b, 780b — II, 565b; III, 365b, 804a
Sūkhrā iv, 644a — IV, 670b
Sūkhrāniyyān → Ḳārinid(e)s
Sukhum i, 100b, 101a, b — I, 103b, 104a
Sukkar i, 305b; ii, 904a, 1062b, 1064b; iv, 682b — I, 315a; II, 925a, 1087a, 1089a; IV, 710b
al-Sukkarī, Abū Saᶜīd i, 107a, 154b, 158b, 331a, 718b; ii, 245b; iii, 820a; v, 768a; s, 37b, 394b — I, 110a, 158b, 162b, 341b, 740a; II, 252b; III, 843b; V, 774a; S, 37b, 395a
al-Sukkarī, Aḥmad s, 371a — S, 371a
Sukkūt i, 1028b — I, 1060a
Suḳmān b. Artuḳ al-Ḳuṭbī i, 300a, 329a, 639a, 664a, 983a, 1052a; iii, 507a, 1118a; v, 454a — I, 309b, 339b, 659b, 684a, 1013b, 1084a; III, 524a, 1145b; V, 456b
Suḳmān II iii, 1119a — III, 1147a
Sukmāniyya iv, 483b — IV, 504b
Suḳnāḳ Tigin i, 418b — I, 430b
Suḳrāṭ i, 235b; s, 154b — I, 243a; S, 155a
al-Suktānī → ᶜĪsā al-Suktānī
Süktür i, 1010b — I, 1042a Sukūn iii, 169b, 173a — III, 173b, 176b
Sükūtī, Isḥāḳ → Isḥāḳ Sükūtī
Suḳuṭrā i, 535b; iii, 270a, 652a; v, 184a — I, 551b; III, 277b, 673a; V, 181b
al-Ṣulaba i, 546a, 873a, b — I, 563b, 897a, 898a
al-Sulāmī → Abu ʾl-Aᶜwar; Yazīd b. Usayd
al-Sulāmī, Abū ᶜAbd al-Raḥmān i, 146a, 266b; s, 343a — I, 150b, 274b; S, 343a
al-Sulāmī, Djamāl al-Islām iii, 714a — III, 736a
Sulawesi → Celebes/Célèbes
Ṣulayb iii, 642a — III, 663a
al-Ṣulayḥī, ᶜAlī b. Muḥammad iv, 199b, 664a; s, 22a, 62a — IV, 208a, 691a; S, 22b, 62b
Ṣulayḥid(e)s i, 552a; ii, 170b, 856a; iii, 125a, 259b; iv, 199b; s, 62a, 236a, 338a, 407a — I, 569b; II, 175b, 876a; III, 128a, 266b; IV, 208a; S, 62b, 236a, 337b, 407b
Sulayk b. Sulaka iv, 1106b — IV, 1138a
Sulaym, Banū i, 12a, 108a, 374b, 532b, 533a, 544b, 1049a, 1232b, 1240b; ii, 234a, 235a, 741a; iii, 66b; iv, 1144a; v, 760a; s, 199a — I, 12a, 111a, 385b, 548b, 549a, 562a, 1081a, 1269a, 1278b; II, 240b, 242a, 759b; III, 69a; IV, 1175b; V, 766a; S, 199a
Sulaymā bint ᶜAṣar al-ᶜUḳaylī s, 394a — S, 394b
Sulaymān, Awlād i, 1258b — I, 1296b
Sulaymān, Banū v, 927a — V, 932b
Sulaymān, Ḳānūnī i, 152a, 293a, 398a, 406a, 432a, 468b, 553b, 557b, 842b, 956a, 1117b, 1128b, 1163b, 1250b, 1253b; ii, 612a, 715b; iii, 147b; iv, 638a, 1157a; v, 630b; s, 94b, 95a, 154a, 238a, 274a, 315b — I, 156a, 302a, 409b, 417b, 444a, 482b, 571a, 575b, 866a, 985b, 1151a, 1162b, 1198b, 1288b, 1291b; II, 627a, 734a; III, 150b; IV, 664a, 1189b; V, 635a; S, 94a, b, 154b, 238a, 273b, 315b
- administration i, 712a, 469a, 1266a; ii, 103b, 118b, 287a, 907a; iii, 213b, 1183a; iv, 565a, b, 900a; v, 882a — I, 733b, 483a, 1304b; II, 105b, 121a, 295a, 928b; III, 220a, 1212b; IV, 587b, 933a; V, 888b
- constructions i, 768a, 1134a, 1166b, 1225b; ii, 12a, 345b; iv, 232a; v, 333b — I, 791a, 1168b, 1201b, 1262a; II, 12a, 355a; IV, 242a, b; V, 334a
- literature/littérature ii, 400a, 588b, 869a; iv, 574a — II, 410b, 603a, 889a; IV, 596b
Sulaymān, King/le roi i, 686a; iii, 236b, 541b; iv, 221a; v, 423b — I, 707a; III, 243b, 560b; IV, 230b, 231a; V, 425b
Sulaymān, Mawlāy i, 315a, 356b; ii, 117a, 160b, 308a, 510b, 820a, 885b; iv, 634a; v, 1192a; s, 113b, 114a,

132a, 390b, 401b — I, 325a, 367b; II, 119b, 165b, 317a, 523a, 839b, 905b; IV, 660a; V, 1182b; S, 113a, b, 131b, 391a, 402a
Sulaymān, Shaykh (Kaʿb) → Salmān, Shaykh
Sulaymān I (Ottoman) → Sulaymān, Ḳānūnī
Sulaymān II (Ottoman) v, 262a — V, 260a
Sulaymān I (Ṣafawid(e)) → Ṣafī II
Sulaymān II, Shāh (Ṣafawid(e)) iv, 390a; s, 276a — IV, 406b; S, 275b
Sulaymān (traveller/voyageur) ii, 583b, 1123b — II, 598a, 1150a
Sulaymān b. ʿAbd al-Malik (Umayyad(e)) i, 50a, 58a, b, 77b, 124b, 305a, 1030a; ii, 72b, 327b, 911a; iii, 42a, 85b, 155a; v, 533a, 799b, 1231a; s, 311b — I, 51b, 60a, b, 80a, 128a, 314b, 1061b; II, 73b, 337b, 932b; III, 43b, 88a, 158b; V, 537a, 805b, 1221b; S, 311b
Sulaymān b. ʿAbd al-Raḥmān I ii, 1009a; iii, 74a, 495a; iv, 254b, 672b — II, 1032b; III, 76b, 512a; IV, 265b, 700a
Sulaymān b. ʿAbd al-Wahhāb iii, 678b — III, 700b
Sulaymān b. Aḥmad (Brunei) s, 152a — S, 152a
Sulaymān b. ʿAlī al-Absī i, 43a, 105a, 1080b; iii, 883a; iv, 495a; s, 352a — I, 44b, 108a, 1112b; III, 907b; IV, 516a; S, 352a
Sulaymān b. Čaghrī Beg Dāʾūd i, 420a; ii, 5a; iii, 1201a; iv, 27a — I, 432a; II, 5a; III, 1231b; IV, 29a
Sulaymān b. Dāʾūd b. al-ʿĀḍid iv, 200b — IV, 209b
Sulaymān b. Dāwud iii, 836a; iv, 1104b — III, 860a; IV, 1135b
Sulaymān b. Djaʿfar b. Fallāḥ i, 1042a; ii, 483b; iii, 77a — I, 1073b; II, 495b; III, 79b
Sulaymān b. Djarīr al-Raḳḳī i, 851a; s, 225b, 392a — I, 875a; S, 225b, 392b
Sulaymān b. Ghāzī iii, 507b — III, 524b
Sulaymān b. al-Ḥakam → Sulaymān al-Mustaʿīn
Sulaymān b. al-Ḥasan al-Hindī iv, 201a — IV, 210a
Sulaymān b. al-Ḥasan b. Makhlad → Ibn Makhlad, Sulaymān b. al-Ḥasan
Sulaymān b. Ḥassān → Ibn Djuldjul
Sulaymān b. Hishām I i, 1103a; ii, 90b; iii, 398a, 990b; s, 183a — I, 1136a; II, 92a; III, 410a, 1015a; S, 184b
Sulaymān b. Hūd al-Mustaʿīn ii, 243a; iii, 496a, 542a; iv, 478a — II, 250a; III, 513a, 561a; IV, 499a
Sulaymān b. Kathīr al-Khuzāʿī i, 15b, 16a, 103b, 141a, 1293a; iii, 988a; v, 3a — I, 16a, 106b, 145a, 1332b; III, 1012b; V, 3a
Sulaymān b. Ḳilīdj Arslan II → Rukn al-Dīn Sulaymān II
Sulaymān b. Ḳutlumish i, 182b, 346a, 465b, 517a, 909b, 1336b; ii, 354b; iii, 86b, 195b, 208b; iv, 291b; v, 103b — I, 187b, 356b, 479b, 532b, 937b, 1376b; II, 364b; III, 89a, 200b, 214a; IV, 304b; V, 105b
Sulaymān b. al-Mundhir ii, 112a — II, 114b
Sulaymān b. Mūsā II iii, 262b — III, 270a
Sulaymān b. Ruhaym iv, 305b, 605a — IV, 319a, b, 629a
Sulaymān b. Shihāb s, 81b — S, 81b
Sulaymān b. Ṣurad al-Khuzāʿī ii, 196b, 523b; iii, 608a, 620b; iv, 637b — II, 202b, 536b; III, 629a, 641a; IV, 663b
Sulaymān b. Ṭarf i, 709a, 737b; ii, 517a — I, 729b, 759b; II, 529b
Sulaymān b. ʿUfayṣān iv, 1072b — IV, 1104b
Sulaymān b. Wahb al-Kātib s, 402a — S, 402b
Sulaymān b. Yaʿḳūb b. Aflaḥ iii, 660a — III, 681a
Sulaymān b. Yasār al-Ḥilālī s, **311a** — S, **311a**
Sulaymān b. al-Zubayr Raḥma i, 929b, 1157a; ii, 123b — I, 957b, 1191a; II, 126b
Sulaymān ʿAskerī ii, 699b — II, 717a
Sulaymān al-Balansī → Sulaymān b. ʿAbd al-Raḥmān I
Sulaymān Beg Bābān i, 845a — I, 868a
Sulaymān Beg Bālṭa-oghlū → Bālṭa-oghlū
Sulaymān Beg Ḳarāmān-oghlu iv, 622b — IV, 647a, b
Sulaymān Bek b. Muhammad iv, 506b — IV, 528b
Sulaymān Bey Ashraf-oghlu i, 703a; iv, 620b, 621a — I, 724a; IV, 645b
Sulaymān Bey Čapen-oghlu ii, 207b — II, 214a
Sulaymān Bey Isfendiyār-oghlu iv, 108b — IV, 113b
Sulaymān Čelebi (Ḳadiʿasker) i, 312b; ii, 98a; iii, 132a — I, 322b; II, 100b; III, 134b
Sulaymān Čelebi b. Bayazid i, 394a, 654a; ii, 98a, 159a, 599a, 611b, 684a, 984b; iii, 1183a — I, 405b, 674b; II, 100b, 164a, 614a, 626b, 701a, 1007a; III, 1212b
Sulaymān Djāndārid(e) i, 1117b, 1118a — I, 1151b
Sulaymān al-Ḥarīrī al-Tūnisī s, 40a — S, 40b
Sulaymān Kāhya v, 532a — V, 536a
Sulaymān Kararanī i, 316a; ii, 183a — I, 326a; II, 189a
Sulaymān Khān al-Thānī → Bihrūz Khān
Sulaymān al-Mahrī ii, 586a; iii, 856b; iv, 97a, 1082b, 1083a; v, 941a, b — II, 600b; III, 880b; IV, 101a, 1114a; V, 945a, b
Sulaymān Mīrzā iii, 528a, b — III, 546b, 547a
Sulaymān Mīrzā-Khān i, 228b, 852b, 1123b — I, 235a, 876b, 1157b
Sulaymān Mountains ii, 205b, s, 329b, 331b — S, 329a, 331b
Sulaymān al-Mustaʿīn ii, 243a, 516a, 1012a; iii, 147a, 495b, 1043b; v, 1239b — II, 250a, 528b, 1035b; III, 150a, 512b, 1069b; V, 1230b
Sulaymān Nadwī ii, 132b; iii, 435a, 1174a — II, 136a; III, 449a, 1203a
Sulaymān al-Naḥwī al-Ḥalabī ii, 795a — II, 814a
Sulaymān Pasha → Kücük Sulaymān Pasha
Sulaymān Pasha (1316-59) i, 510b; ii, 683b, 983b — I, 526a; II, 700b, 1006a
Sulaymān Pasha (1804-19) i, 1078b; ii, 635b — I, 1110b; II, 652a
Sulaymān Pasha (1838-1932) iv, 791a — IV, 822b
Sulaymān Pasha (Joseph Sève) ii, 514a; iii, 999b, 1000a; iv, 428a; v, 907b, 908a — II, 526b; III, 1024b, 1025a; IV, 447a; V, 913b, 914a
Sulaymān Pāsha Babān i, 845a — I, 868b
Sulaymān Pasha Büyük i, 62b, 905b, 1087a; ii, 184b; iii, 1257b — I, 64b, 932b, 1119b; II, 190a; III, 1290a
Sulaymān Pasha Isfendiyār-oghlu iv, 738a — IV, 768a
Sulaymān Pasha Khādim → Khādim Sülaymān Pasha
Sulaymān Pasha Misrāḳlī i, 199a, 905a, 1087a — I, 204b, 932b, 1119b
Sulaymān Shafīḳ Kamālī Pasha i, 98b, 709b — I, 101a, 731a
Sulaymān Shāh (Ottoman) ii, 354b — II, 364a
Sulaymān Shāh (Saldjūḳ) iii, 1110b — III, 1137b
Sulaymān Shāh Germiyān-oghlu i, 299b; ii, 98a, 989b; v, 359b, 539a — I, 309a; II, 100b; V, 360b, 543b
Sulaymān Shukōh b. Dara i, 768b; ii, 134b — I, 791b; II, 138a
Sulaymān Shukōh b. Shāh ʿĀlam ii, 602a; iii, 1095a — II, 617a; III, 1122a
Sulaymān Solong ii, 122b — II, 125b
Sulaymān al-Tādjir s, 56a — S, 56b
Sulaymānān iv, 674b — IV, 702b
al-Sulaymānī iii, 799a — III, 822b
Sulaymānī Kurds v, 459b — V, 462a
Sulaymānid(e)s (Makka) i, 403a; ii, 517a — I, 414b; II, 530a
Sulaymānid(e)s (Yemen) i, 403a, 709a; ii, 517a; v,

1244b – I, 414b, 729b; II, 530a; V, 1235a
Sulaymānis (Hind) i, 552b, 1255a; ii, 98a; iv, 201a – I, 570a, 1293a; II, 100a; IV, 210a
Sulaymāniyya v, 467b – V, 470a, b
Sulaymāniyye (Istanbul) iv, 232a – IV, 242b
Sulaymannāme ii, 921a – II, 942b
Sulaymān-shāh b. Parčam Īwāʿī i, 919a – I, 947a
Sulaymanu iv, 549a – IV, 573a
Sülemish iv, 621a – IV, 646a
Süleyman → Sulaymān
Süleymān Efendi → ʿIzzī Süleymān Efendi
Ṣulḥ i, 1143b; ii, 131a; iv, 14b – I, 1178a; II, 134b; IV, 15b
Ṣulḥ-i-ḳull i, 117b, 317a – I, 120b, 327b
al-Ṣūlī, Abū Bakr i, 10a, 144b, 154a, 590a, 867a; iii, 466b, 893a, 908b; s, 24b, 35b, 37b, 118a, 386a – I, 10a, 148b, 158b, 609b, 891a; III, 483a, 917a, 932b; S, 25a, 35b, 38a, 117a, 386a
Sūlī b. Ḳaradja ii, 239b – II, 246a
Sullam s, 396b – S, 396b
Sulphur → al-Kibrīt
Sulṭān iv, 942a, b; v, 628a – IV, 975a, b; V, 632a
Sulṭān b. Aḥmad (Bū Saʿīd) i, 1282a; v, 183b; s, 332b – I, 1321a; V, 180b; S, 331b
Sulṭān b. Bidjād Āl Ḥumayd ii, 354a; iii, 1065b, 1066b, 1067b – II, 363b; III, 1092a, 1093b, 1094a
Sulṭān b. Ḥāmid al-Ḳaysī iv, 925a – IV, 958a
Sulṭān b. Muḥammad b. Ṣaḳr iv, 778b – IV, 810a
Sulṭān b. Ṣaḳr i, 928a; ii, 619a; iv, 778a – I, 956b; II, 634b; IV, 809a, b
Sulṭān b. Salāmah iv, 752a – IV, 782b
Sulṭān I b. Sayf v, 507a – V, 510b
Sulṭān II b. Sayf v, 507a – V, 510b
Sulṭān b. Thumāl iv, 911a – IV, 944a
Sulṭān Ādam Gakkhaṙ ii, 973a; iii, 576a ; II, 995b; III, 596a
Sultan Agung ii, 390b; iii, 1221b; s, 201a, b – II, 400b; III, 1252b; S, 201a, b
Sultan Aḥmad (Djalāyīrid(e)) → Aḥmad b. Uways
Sulṭān Aḥmad Khān Avar i, 755b – I, 778a
Sulṭān Aḥmad Mīrzā i, 227b, 847b – I, 234b, 870b
Sulṭān ʿAlī Gunābādī i, 841a – I, 864b
Sulṭān ʿAlī Kātib i, 1212a, b – I, 1248a, b
Sulṭān ʿAlī Oghlu → Sulṭān Galiev
Sulṭān ʿAlī Sadōzay i, 231a – I, 238a
Sulṭān al-Aṭrash ii, 290a, 637b – II, 297b, 653b
Sulṭān Bāyazid Dūrī iv, 1127b – IV, 1159a
Sulṭān al-Dawla Abū Shudjāʿ i, 131b; ii, 391a; iv, 378b; s, 119a, b – I, 135b; II, 401a; IV, 395a; S, 118b, 119a
Sulṭān Djahān Bēgam i, 1195b, 1196a, 1197a – I, 1231a, b, 1232b
Sulṭān Galiev iii, 532a; iv, 792b – III, 550b; IV, 824b
Sulṭān Ghāzī Shāh Čak → Ghāzī Khān Čak
al-Sulṭān al-Ḥanafī s, 18b – S, 18b
Sulṭān al-ḥarāfish iii, 206a – III, 211b
Sulṭān Ḥasan Mīrzā Nayyir al-Dawla s, 23b – S, 24a
Sulṭān Ḥusayn Bayḳara → Ḥusayn Bayḳara
Sulṭān Ḥusayn Lingāh → Ḥusayn Shāh Langāh I
Sulṭān Ḥusayn Mīrzā → Ḥusayn I (Ṣafawid(e))
Sulṭān Isḥāḳ → Sulṭān Ṣohāk
Sulṭān Ismāʿīl Shāh (Čak) s, 324b – S, 324a
Sulṭān Khalīl b. Uzun Ḥasan iv, 267b – IV, 279b
Sulṭān Khātun i, 1117b; v, 679b – I, 1151b; V, 684b
Sulṭān Ḳulī → Ḳulī Ḳuṭb al-Mulk
Sulṭān Maḥmūd Māhīsawār i, 1168a – I, 1202b
Sulṭān Muḥammad Khān (Bārakzay) i, 231a; ii, 637b – I, 238b; II, 654a
Sulṭān Muḥammad Khān Ḳashḳāy iv, 706a – IV, 734b
Sulṭān Muḥammad Shāh → Agha Khān III
Sulṭān Naṣīr al-Dīn Ghāzī Čak → Ghāzī Khān Čak
Sulṭān Sandjar (Tīmūrīd(e)) i, 147b – I, 152a
Sulṭān Ṣārang ii, 973a – II, 995b
Sulṭān Shāh (Khʷārazmshāh) ii, 253a, 1101b; iv, 583a, 1067b – II, 260b, 1127b; IV, 606b, 1099a
Sulṭān-Shāh (Saldjūḳ) iii, 86b, 87a; v, 159b – III, 89a; V, 158b
Sulṭān Shāh Lōdī v, 782b, 783a – V, 789a
Sulṭān Shāhzāda → Bārbak Shāh Ḥabshi
Sulṭān Ṣohāk i, 260b, 261b, 262a, b – I, 269a, 269b, 270a, b
Sulṭān Uways b. Idgü v, 163b – V, 161b
Sultan-üyügi i, 468b – 482b
Sulṭān Ways Mīrzā i, 852b – I, 876a
Sulṭān Yaʿḳūb (Aḳ-Ḳoyunlu) → Yaʿḳūb b. Uzun Ḥasan
Sulṭāna bint Aḥmad al-Sudayrī s, 305b – S, 305b
Sulṭānābād s, 73a – S, 73b
Sulṭān-i Walad i, 147a; ii, 394a; iv, 67a; s, 49b, 83b – I, 151b; II, 404b; IV, 71a; S, 50a, 83a
Sulṭāniyya i, 261a; iii, 1124b; iv, 1167b; v, 294a; s, 83b – I, 269a; III, 1152b; IV, 1200b; V, 293b; S, 83b
Sultansky, Mordecai iv, 606a – IV, 630b
Sulṭānzāde Isḥāḳ Bey iv, 112b – IV, 117b
Sulṭānzāde Muḥammad Pasha → Muḥammad Pasha Sulṭānzāde
Sulu iii, 1218b; s, 151b, 152a – III, 1249b; S, 152a
Suluk iii, 1234b – III, 1266b
Ṣuʿlūk v, 768a; s, 37a – V, 774a; S, 37b
Sumak s, 136a – S, 135b
Sumaniyya i, 15b, 17b, 953a, 1031a, 1092b, 1284a, 1333b; ii, 972b; iii, 335b, 1122a; iv, 43b, 356a, 512b; v, 37b, 853a – I, 16a, 18a, 982a, 1062b, 1125a, 1273a, 1323a; II, 994b; III, 345b, 1150a; IV, 46a, 371b, 534b; V, 38b, 859b
Sumatra iii, 1213a, b, 1214b, 1215b, 1218a, 1219a, 1225b; v, 226a, b; 227b, 228a, b – III, 1243b, 1244b, 1245a, 1246a, 1249a, 1250a, 1257a; V, 223b, 224a, 225a, 226a, b
al-Ṣumayl b. Ḥātim al-Kilābī i, 135a; iii, 602a; iv, 494b; s, 81b, 82a – I, 138b; III, 622b; IV, 515b, 516a; S, 81b
Sumayr iii, 41b – III, 43a
Sumayya s, 354b – S, 354b
Sumbawa i, 1219b, 1226a – I, 1250b, 1257b
Sumer iv, 276b – IV, 288b
al-Summān → al-Ṣammān
Summaya bint Khubāṭ s, 354b – S, 354b
al-Sumnānī, Abū Djaʿfar iii, 544a, 1146b – III, 563a, 1174b
Sūmra Rādjpūts i, 431a – I, 443b
Sūnām s, 66b – S, 67a
Sunan Ampel iii, 1219a – III, 1249b
Sunan Bonang iii, 1218b, 1219a – III, 1249b
Sunan Giri iii, 1218b, 1219a; v, 1155a – III, 1249b; V, 1144b
Sunaq-qurghan s, 245a – S, 245a
Sunbādh → Sindbād
al-Sunbāṭī, Aḥmad b. ʿAbd al-Ḥaḳḳ iv, 451a – IV, 471a
al-Sünbüliyya iv, 991b, 992a – Iv, 1024a, b
Sūndā, islands/îles iii, 1213a, 1226a; v, 785a – III, 1243b, 1257b; V, 791b
Sun-dial → Tawḳīt
Sungur Bey Shamsī Pasha → Shams al-Dīn b. Taman
Sunḳur ii, 812a; iii, 1097b; v, 826b – II, 831a; III, 1124b; V, 832b
Sunḳur al-Ashḳar ii, 285a; iii, 403a, 832b; iv, 88a, 485a; v, 594b – II, 293a; III, 415a, 856b; IV, 92a, 506a; V, 598b
Sunna i, 175b, 258b, 275b, 325b, 773a, 1039b, 1199a; ii, 859a, 888b; iii, 953b, 994b; iv, 142a-b, 147b, 148a

— I, 180a, 266b, 284a, 335b, 796a, 1071a, 1234b; II, 879a, 909b; III, 978a, 1019b; IV, 148a-b, 153b, 154a
Sunnetdji v, 21a — V, 21b
Sunnī i, 1254a; ii, 64b, 283a, 290a, 859b, 931b; iii, 87a, 411b, 1168b — I, 1292b; II, 65b, 291a, 298a, 879a, 953a; III, 89b, 424b, 1197a
Ṣūr → Tyre/Tyr
Sūr, Afghān i, 228b; iii, 423a; s, 1b — I, 235b; III, 436b; S, 1b
Sūr Dās iii, 457a — III, 473a
Sūra v, 409b — V, 411a
Ṣūra i, 1084a — I, 1116a
Ṣūra Maʾmūniyya i, 1003b; ii, 578b — I, 1034a; II, 593a
Surabaya s, 150b, 202b — S, 150b, 202a
Surādik iv, 1147a — IV, 1178b
Sūradj Kund ii, 255b — II, 263a
Sūradj Mal Djāt i, 1193a; ii, 488b; iii, 1158b — I, 1228a; II, 501a; III, 1187a
Surāḳa b. ʿAmr i, 921b; iv, 342b — I, 949a; IV, 357a
Surat v, 1114a, b — V, 1110b
Sūrat Singh s, 361a — S, 360b
Ṣuraym ii, 71b — II, 73a
Surgeon → Djarrāḥ
Sūrghān Shīra ii, 67b — II, 69a
Sürgün iv, 225a, 238a, 239a; v, 305b — IV, 235a, 248b, 249b; V, 305a
Surḥūbiyya → Djarūdiyya
Surkhāb i, 512b, 513a — I, 528a, b
Surkhāb b. ʿAnnāz i, 513b; v, 824b, 828a — I, 529a; V, 830b, 834a
Surkhāb b. Badr i, 513a; v, 454a — I, 529a; V, 456b
Surkhāb b. Bāw iv, 644b — IV, 671a
Surkhāb Beg i, 406a — I, 418a
Ṣurkhābiyya iv, 1086b — IV, 1118a
Surkhay Khān → Čulāḳ-Sūrkhay
Sūrkhāy-Mīrzā ii, 87a — II, 89a
Sürmeli ʿAlī Pasha → ʿAlī Pasha Sürmeli
Ṣurna s, 136a — S, 135b
Ṣurra i, 483b; iv, 1133b — I, 497b; IV, 1165a
Ṣurrat al-Ḥaramayn iv, 1133b — IV, 1165a
Surrender to God → Islām
Surūr al-Fātikī v, 1244b — V, 1235a
Surūrī, Muḥammad i, 380a; iv, 526a — 391a; IV, 549a
Surūsh iv, 70a — IV, 73b
Sūrya i, 4b, 17a, 19a, 46a, 103a, 111a, 145a, 279a, 383b; ii, 595a, 661a, b, 676a, 854a; iii, 85a, 184a, 233a, 263b, 521a, 522b, 559a, 560b, 1254b; iv, 206a — I, 4b, 17b, 19b, 47b, 106a, 114a, 149b, 287b, 394b; II, 610a, 677b, 678a, 693a, 874a; III, 87a, 188a, 239b, 271a, 539a, 540b, 578a, 580a, 1287a; IV, 215a
- art, architecture i, 609b, 1226a; v, 291a, b — I, 629a, 1262b; V, 290b
- demography/démographie s, 212a — S, 212b
- ethnography/ethnographie v, 440a, 469b, 1253b — V, 442b, 472b, 1244b
- history/histoire iv, 261b; v, 438a — IV, 273b; V, 440b
- institutions ii, 125b, 424a; iii, 99b, 521a; v, 912a, b, 1046b, 1090b — II, 128b, 435a; III, 102a, 538b; V, 918a, 1043a, 1088a
- language, literature/langue, littérature i, 568b, 575a; ii, 468a — I, 586b, 594a; II, 479b
- products/produits iii, 211a, 218b — III, 217a, 225a
Sūryānūs ii, 770b — II, 789a
Sūs i, 86a, 245a; ii, 527a; v, 1178b, 1187b; s, 29a, 40a, 47b, 133b, 336b, 402b — I, 88b, 252b; II, 540a; V, 1168b, 1177b; S, 29b, 40b, 48a, 133a, 336a, 403a
Sūsa i, 248b, 620a, 1319a; ii, 130a; iii, 499b; iv, 654a; v, 830a — I, 256a, 640a, 1359b; II, 133b; III, 517a; IV, 680b; V, 836b
Sūsan iv, 675b — IV, 703a
Sūsandjird v, 498b — V, 502a
Sūsū i, 762b — I, 785a
Sūsūn iv, 1042b — IV, 1074a
Sūtānuti ii, 7a — II, 7a
Sutaylī iv, 584a — IV, 607b
Sutledj v, 885b — V, 891b
Sütlüdje iv, 233a; s, 168b — IV, 243a; S, 168b
Sutūda, Manūčihr s, 376a — S, 376a
Suṭūḥiyya i, 280b — I, 289a
Suʿūd → Saʿūd
Suwāʿ iii, 540b — III, 559a
Suwār i, 1305b, 1306b; v, 686a — I, 1345b, 1346b; V, 691a
Suwayd b. al-Khadhdhāk i, 74a — I, 76a
Suwayd b. Muḳarrin i, 1247a; iv, 207b, 644a; v, 378a; s, 297b — I, 1285a; IV, 217a, 670b; V, 378b; S, 297b
Suwayd al-Haranī s, 366b — S, 366b
Suwaydān iv, 751b — IV, 781b
Suwaydī, Banū v, 459a — V, 461b
Suwayf, Banū s, 371a — S, 371a
Sūways i, 13a, 315a, 554b; iv, 206b; v, 368b; s, 6b — I, 13a, 324b, 572b; IV, 215b; V, 369b; S, 5b
Sūyāb ii, 67a — II, 68a
Sūyūmbigi, Princess(e) iv, 850a — IV, 883a
Suyūrghāls ii, 150b, 152a; iv, 1043b — II, 155a, 156b; IV, 1075a
Suyūrghatmish b. Ḳuṭb al-Dīn v, 162a, b, 553b, 554a — V, 160a, b, 558b, 559a
Suyūrsāt ii, 152a; iv, 1043a — II, 157a; IV, 1074b
al-Suyūṭī, Djalāl al-Dīn i, 27a, 72a, 429a, 594b, 595a, 721a, 729a, 759a, 1110a, 1198a, 1309a; ii, 826b; iii, 90a, 435a, 697a, 711a, 957b; iv, 550a, 863b; v, 419b, 1223a, 1235a; s, 352b, 388a — I, 28a, 74a, 441a, 614a, b, 742b, 751a, 782a, 1143a, 1233b, 1349a; II, 846b; III, 92b, 449a, 719a, 733a, 982a; IV, 574a, 897a; V, 421b, 1213b, 1225b; S, 352b, 388b
Sūzanī iii, 355b; iv, 62a; s, 65a — III, 366b; IV, 65a; S, 65a
Sūzmanī v, 818a — V, 824a, b
Svatopluk → Čeh
Swahili ii, 59a, 129a; iv, 886b, 888b; v, 177a, 205b, 223a, 655b, 962b — II, 60a, 132a; IV, 919a, 921a; V, 174a, 203a, 221a, 659b, 967b
Swāt i, 864a; v, 356a — I, 888b; V, 357b
Sweeper → Kannās
Swimon I v, 493a — V, 495b, 496a
Sword → Sayf
Sy, el-Hadji Abdoul Aziz s, 182a — S, 182a
Sy, el-Hadji Malick s, 182a — S, 182a
Sylla → Fodié; Yaʿḳūba
Synagogue → Kanīsa
Syracuse i, 250b — I, 258a
Syria, Greater s, 212b — S, 212b
Syria/Syrie → Sūrya
Syriac, Syriaque iv, 671b — IV, 699a
Syrianus → Sūryānūs
Szécsény s, 171a — S, 171a
Szigetrar ii, 881b — II, 902a

T

Taʾabbaṭa Sharran i, 130b; ii, 1079a; iii, 540b — I, 134b; I, 1104a; III, 559a
Taʿaddī ii, 105a — II, 107a
Taʿāʾisha i, 49b; ii, 122a, 124a; v, 1250a, b — I, 50b; II, 125a, 127a; V, 1241a, b
Taʿalluḳ ii, 158b — II, 163a
Taʿāsīf → ʿAlam al-Dīn Ḳayṣar

Taʿāzīr i, 29b – I, 30b
Taba i, 64b – I, 66b
Ṭābaʿ iv, 1105b – IV, 1137a
Tabac → Tūtūn
Tabaddul iii, 170b – III, 174a
al-Tabaḳa al-Khāmisa i, 1060a – I, 1092a
Ṭabaḳ al-manāṭiḳ iv, 703a – IV, 731a
Ṭabakāt i, 106a, b, 274b; ii, 922a – I, 109a, b, 282b; II, 943b
Tabārakallāh i, 1032a; v, 425b – I, 1063b; V, 427b
al-Ṭabarānī, Abu 'l-Ḳāsim i, 273b; iii, 159a, 864a; s, 400b – I, 282a; III, 162b, 888a; S, 401a
Tabardār i, 1004a – I, 1034b
Ṭabarī (language/langue) i, 872a – I, 896a
al-Ṭabarī, Abu ʾl-Ṭayyib i, 459a, 773a, 1039b; ii, 412a; iii, 302a; s, 192a – I, 472b, 796a, 1071a; II, 422b; III, 311a; S, 193a
al-Ṭabarī, Aḥmad b. ʿAbd Allāh iv, 797a – IV, 829a
al-Ṭabarī, ʿAlī b. Rabban i, 213b, 265b; iii, 378a; v, 701b; s, 314a – I, 220a, 273b; III, 389b; V, 706b; S, 313b
al-Ṭabarī, Muḥammad b. Djarīr i, 51a, 140a, 459a, 567b, 591a, 628a, 760a, 984b; ii, 133a, 215a, 793a, 1111b; iii, 57b, 608a, 1062a, 1206b; v, 1130b – I, 52b, 144a, 472b, 585b, 610b, 649a, 782b, 1015a; II, 136b, 222a, 812a, 1138a; III, 60a, 628b, 1088b, 1237a; V, 1126b
Ṭabarīs s, 335a – S, 335a
Ṭabaristān i, 40a, 52b, 688a, 760a, 871b, 1110a, 1350a; iii, 233b, 245a, 810a; iv, 644a, b; v, 68b, 69b, 661a; s, 13a, 235a, 297b, 298a, 299a, 356b, 357a, 363a, b – I, 41b, 54a, 709a, 782b, 896a, 1143a, 1390b; III, 240a, 252a, 833b; IV, 670b, 671a; V, 70b, 71b, 666b; S, 13b, 235a, 297a, b, 298b, 356a, 357a, 362b, 363a
Tabarka v, 50b, 51b – V, 52a, 53a
Ṭabarsarān ii, 85b, 87b, 89a; iv, 343a, 345b – II, 87a, 89a, 90b; IV, 357b, 360a
Ṭabarsī → Ḥusayn Nūrī
al-Ṭabarsī i, 326a – I, 336a
Ṭabas i, 1052b; v, 354b; 868b – I, 1084a; V, 356a, 875a
Ṭabāṭabāʾī, ʿAlīm Allāh ii, 1092a – II, 1117b
Ṭabāṭabāʾī, Āyatullāh Muḥsin Ḥakīm s, 104a – S, 103b
Ṭabāṭabāʾī, Ḍiyāʾ al-Dīn i, 978a; iii, 529a; v, 310b – I, 1008b; III, 547b; V, 310a
Ṭabāṭabāʾī, Muḥammad Ḥusayn iv, 166a, b – IV, 173a, b
Ṭabāṭabāʾī, Sayyid Ṣādiḳ iv, 164a – IV, 171a
Ṭabīʿiyyūn ii, 96a – II, 98a
Ṭābīnān v, 686a, b, 689a – V, 691b, 694a
Taʿbīr ii, 300b; iii, 772a, 948a; iv, 1074a; s, 295a – II, 309a; III, 795b, 972b; IV, 1105b; S, 294b
Tabissa/Tébessa i, 163a – I, 167b
Ṭābiʿūn i, 276a; iv, 149a – I, 284b; IV, 155b
Ṭabl ii, 621a – II, 636b
Table, tablet(te) → Lawḥ
Tablīgh iv, 166b – IV, 174a
Tabriʾa i, 1026b – I, 1058b
Tabrīz i, 190b, 325a; ii, 8a, 435b; iii, 157b, 212b; iv, 7b, 33a, 392a; s, 73a, 110a, 135a, 138b, 139a, b, 140a, 142a, 208a, 275a, 289a, 365b – I, 196a, 335a; II, 8a, 447a; III, 161a, 218a; IV, 8a, 35b, 409a; S, 73b, 109a, 134b, 138a, b, 139a, b, 142a, 208a, 274b, 289a, 365a
- institutions ii, 426a, 1043a – II, 437a, 1067b
- monuments i, 1124a, 1125a; iv, 702a – III, 1152a, 1153a; IV, 730a
al-Tabrīzī → al-Tibrīzī
Tabrīzī, Aḥmad iii, 114a – III, 116b
Tabrīzī, Fakhr al-Dīn ʿAlī → Ṣāḥib ʿAtāʾ
al-Tabrīzī, Muḥammad Ḥusayn → Burhān
Tabrīzī, Radjab ʿAlī s, 308a – S, 308a
Tabṣīrat al-ʿawāmm ii, 74a – II, 75a
Tabūk i, 9a; s, 351b – I, 9a; S, 351b
Tabula Smaragdina i, 995a – I, 1025b
Ṭābūr i, 1062b – I, 1094a
Tabūshkān iii, 224a – III, 230b
Tābūt v, 864a – V, 871a
Ṭābya i, 1226b – I, 1264a
Tacapas → Ḳābis
Tadbīr i, 30a, b – I, 31a
Taddart i, 372a – I, 383a
Tādemmeket, Tādmekka iii, 657a – III, 678b
Tadhkira ii, 80a, 179a, 304a; v, 193a – II, 81b, 185a, 312b; V, 190b
Tadhkirat al-mulūk iv, 758a – IV, 788a
Tādj v, 634a, 748a, 749a – V, 638a, 753b, 754b
Tādj al-ʿAdjam i, 440a – I, 452b
Tādj al-Dawla → Tutush
Tādj al-Dawla (Labla) ii, 1009a; v, 586b – II, 1033a; V, 591b
Tādj al-Dīn → Abū Muḥammad ʿAbd Allāh b. ʿUmar; Altîntash; Firūz Shāh (Bahmānī); al-Subkī; Yîldîz
Tādj al-Dīn, Mawlanā s, 352b – S, 352b
Tādj al-Dīn, Pīr v, 26b – V, 27a
Tādj al-Dīn Abū Bakr s, 66b – S, 67a
Tādj al-Dīn Ḥusayn b. Fakhr al-Dīn ʿAlī i, 243b – I, 250b
Tādj al-Dīn Mukhtaṣ iv, 76b – IV, 80b
Tādj al-Dīn Muʿtazz iv, 738a – IV, 767b
Tādj Khātūn bint Muḥammad Bayhaḳī s, 131b – S, 130b
Tādj Maḥall i, 253b; ii, 47b, 287a; iii, 450b – I, 261b; II, 48b, 296a; III, 466a
Tādj al-Mulk i, 1051b; iii, 774b – I, 1083a; III, 797b
Tādj al-Mulk (Dihlī) v, 6a – V, 6a
Tādj al-Mulūk Būrī i, 1017a, 1332a, b; ii, 282a; iii, 120a – I, 1048b, 1372b, 1373a; II, 290a; III, 122b
Tadjammul Ḥusayn Khān ii, 809a – II, 828a
Tadjārib al-ʿām i, 135b – I, 139b
Tādjīk i, 224a, 530b, 853b, 854a, 857a, 1010a; iv, 310a, b, 313b; v, 244b, 614b, 857b, 858a; s, 98a, 237b, 367b – I, 230b, 547a, 877b, 881a, 1041a; IV, 324a, b, 327b; V, 242b, 618b, 864b; S, 97a, 237a, 367a
Tādjīkistān i, 531a – I, 547a
Tādjiyya Madrasa s, 384a – S, 384b
Tādjnāma iii, 884a – III, 908a
Tadjnīs i, 730b, 1348b – I, 752b, 1389a
Tadjrīda iii, 184b – III, 188b
al-Tadjrīshī, al-Amīr Muṣṭafā iv, 856b – IV, 890a
Tādlā s, 132a, 223a – S, 131b, 223a
Tadmait s, 328a – S, 327b
Taḍmīn iv, 57a, 413a – IV, 60a, 431a
Tadmur i, 563a; s, 117a – I, 581a; S, 116b
Tafaḍḍul Ḥusayn Khān ii, 809a – II, 828a
Tafāwut-i ʿamal ii, 152b, 153a – II, 157b, 158a
Ṭaff iv, 384b – IV, 401a
Tāfīlālet i, 355b; iii, 256b; v, 1187b; s, 223b, 370a – I, 366b; III, 263b; V, 1177b; S, 223b, 370a
Tafna i, 67b – I, 69a
Tafsīr i, 40a, 60b, 274b, 410a; ii, 363a; iii, 172a, 434b; iv, 147a, 984b – I, 41a, 62b, 283a, 422a; II, 373a; III, 175b, 449a; IV, 153a, 1017a
Tāfta iii, 216b – III, 223a
al-Taftazānī, Saʿd al-Dīn i, 342b, 858a, 982b, 1019b, 1116a, 1345b; ii, 174a, 602b, 774b; iii, 163b, 711a, 1168a; iv, 414b – I, 353a, 882a, 1013a, 1051a, 1149b, 1386a; II, 179b, 617b, 793a; III, 167a, 733b, 1197a; IV, 432b
Tafwīḍ i, 304b, 411a, 412a; ii, 303a – I, 314a, 423a, 423b; II, 311a
Tagdaoust → Awdaghust
Tagh Boyu → Akhāl Tekke

Taghā → Tughā
Taghāliba ii, 175b, 176a — II, 181a, b
Taghazzul iv, 715b — IV, 744a
Ṭaghī ii, 1124b — II, 1151a
Taghlib, Banū i, 526b, 527a, 528a, 545a, 963a, 1240b, 1241a; iii, 222b, 1254a; iv, 1143b; v, 362a; s, 178a — I, 542b, 543a, 544a, 562a, 993a, 1278b; III, 229a, 1287a; IV, 1175b; V, 363a; S, 179a
Taghlib b. Wāʾil ii, 176a — II, 181b
Taghrībirdī al-Bashbughāwī ii, 781a, b, 782a — II, 800a, b
Taghrībirdī al-Ẓāhirī ii, 286a — II, 294a
Tagore, Rabindranath s, 162a — S, 162a
Tagus/Tage → Wādī Tadjū
Ṭāhā Ḥusayn i, 331b, 565b, 598a, 890a; iv, 195a, 906b; v, 189a, b, 1092a; s, 58a — I, 342a, 584a, 617b, 916a; IV, 203b, 939b; V, 186b, 187a, 1089a; S, 58b
Taḥaddī iii, 1019a — III, 1044b
Taḥāluf i, 1151a — I, 1185b
Taḥammus iii, 577b — III, 597b
Tahamtan, Ḳuṭb al-Dīn i, 942b; iii, 585a; iv, 764b — I, 971b; III, 605a; IV, 795a
al-Tahanawī, Muḥammad ʿAlī i, 595a; iii, 170b, 1238b, 1241b — I, 614a; III, 174a, 1270b, 1273b
Taḥannuf iii, 165b, 166a — III, 169a, b
Ṭahār, Ṭahāra iv, 372b; v, 20b — IV, 389a; V, 21a
Tāhart i, 1175b; iii, 654b, 655a, 657a; v, 696b, 1164b — I, 1210b; III, 676a, 678a; V, 701b, 1154a
al-Ṭaḥāwī, ʿAbd al-Djalīl i, 123b, 310a; iii, 163a; s, 156a, 310b — I, 127a, 319b; III, 166b; S, 156b, 310b
Tahawwur Khān s, 420b — S, 420b
Taḥayyur iv, 95a — IV, 99a
Taḥdjīr iii, 1054a — III, 1080a
Ṭāhir I → Ṭāhir b. al-Ḥusayn
Ṭāhir II iv, 20b — IV, 22a
al-Ṭāhir, ʿAlī Nāṣūḥ v, 412b — V, 413b
Ṭāhir b. Abū Ṭayyib iii, 107a — III, 109b
Ṭāhir b. Aḥmad b. Bābashād iii, 733a, 761a — III, 755b, 784a
Ṭāhir b. Hilāl b. Badr i, 512b; iii, 258b — I, 528a; III, 266a
Ṭāhir b. al-Ḥusayn i, 18a, 52b, 271b, 437b, 751b, 897b; ii, 524a; iii, 231b, 694b; iv, 17a, 20a, b, 645a; v, 621a; s, 15a — I, 19a, 54a, 280a, 450a, 773b, 924a; II, 537a; III, 238a, 716b; IV, 18a, b, 22a, 671b; V, 625a; S, 15a
Ṭāhir b. Ḥusayn al-Ahdal, Sayyid i, 255b — I, 263b
Ṭāhir b. Khalaf iii, 502a; s, 118b — III, 519b; S, 118a
Ṭāhir b. Muḥammad al-Isfarāʾinī iv, 107b — IV, 112a
Ṭāhir b. Zayn al-ʿAbidīn s, 95a — S, 94b
Ṭāhir al-Balkhī iv, 797a, 800b — IV, 829b, 833a
Ṭāhir Efendi iv, 882b — IV, 915a
al-Ṭāhir al-Ḥaddād iv, 720b — IV, 749b
Ṭāhir al-Ḥusaynī s, 67a — S, 67b
Ṭāhir Ḥusaynī Dakkanī iv, 202a — IV, 210b
Ṭāhir Pasha i, 1269a; v, 35b — I, 1308a; V, 36b
Ṭāhir Selām i, 630a — I, 651a
Ṭāhira → Ḳurrat al-ʿAyn
Ṭāhirid(e)s i, 52b, 439b, 440b, 441a, 553a, 1008b, 1342b; ii, 253b, 505b, 1081b; iii, 245a, 746a; iv, 18b, 20a, b, 646a; v, 57b; s, 338b — I, 54a, 452a, 453b, 571a, 1039b, 1383a; II, 261a, 518b, 1107a; III, 252a, 769a; IV, 20a, 21b-22a, 672b; V, 59a, b; S, 338a
Ṭahmāsibī, Khalīl ii, 882b; s, 158a — II, 903a; S, 158b
Ṭahmāsp I, Shāh (Ṣafawid(e)) i, 228b, 291a, 329b, 406a, 967b, 1066b, 1068a, 1135b, 1208b, 1211a, b; ii, 310b, 334b; iii, 214a, 253b, 575b, 1101a, 1189b, 1191a, 1257a; iv, 35a, b, 102b, 103a, 188a, 537a, 610a; v, 244b, 492b; s, 43b, 140a, 383a — I, 235a, 300a, 340a, 417b, 997a, 1098b, 1100a, 1170a, 1244b, 1247a, b; II, 319b, 344a; III, 220a, 260b, 595b, 1128a, 1219b, 1220b, 1289b; IV, 37b, 38a, 107b, 196a, 560a, 634b; V, 242b, 495b; S, 44a, 139b, 383b
Ṭahmāsp II, Shāh (Ṣafawid(e)) i, 395b; iii, 604b, 1002b; iv, 37a, 389b, 390a; v, 663b — I, 407a; III, 625a, 1027b; IV, 39b, 406a, b; V, 669a
Ṭahmāsp Khān iv, 860b — IV, 893b
Ṭahmāsp Ḳulī Khān → Nādir Shāh
Ṭahmāsp Mīrzā i, 8b; ii, 1083b; iii, 157b; iv, 861a — I, 8b; II, 1108b; III, 161a; IV, 894a
Ṭahmūrath, King/le roi i, 459a; v, 494b — I, 472a; V, 497b
Taḥrīḍ i, 1089b — I, 1121b
Taḥrīf iv, 147a — IV, 153a
Taḥrīr i, 654a; ii, 32b, 695b; iv, 558b; v, 1023b — I, 674b; II, 33b, 713a; V, 1019a
Taḥsīn Efendī (Pasha) i, 61b, 64a; iii, 1199a — I, 63a, 66a; III, 1229a
al-Tahṭāwī Rāfiʿ i, 571b, 596b, 755a; ii, 641b, 801a; iii, 590b; iv, 1155a; v, 907b, 908a, b, 909a — I, 590b, 616a, 777b; II, 658a, 820a; III, 610b; IV, 1187a; V, 913b, 914a, b
Tahūda iv, 827a — IV, 860a
Taḥwīf iii, 289b — III, 298b
Taḥwīl ii, 338b — II, 348b
al-Ṭāʾī → Abū Tammām; Dāwūd; Djundab b. Khāridja; Ḥātim
al-Ṭāʾiʿ li-ʾllāh (ʿAbbāsid(e)) i, 212a, 955a, 1352b; ii, 195a; iii, 345a; s, 23a, 118b — I, 218b, 984a, 1391b; II, 201b; III, 355a; S, 23b, 118a
Taičiʿut ii, 41b — II, 42b
al-Ṭāʾif i, 9a, 55a, 609a; iii, 363a; v, 434b, 692b; s, 3b, 133b, 134a, 152a, 318a, 354a, b — I, 9a, 57a, 629a; III, 374b; V, 436b, 697b; S, 3a, 133a, b, 152a, 318a, 354a, b
Ṭāʾifa i, 5b, 7b, 490b, 499a — I, 5b, 6b, 7b, 505a, 514a
Ṭāʾifat al-ruʾasā i, 368a — I, 379a
Ṭāʾifat al-salaf iv, 142a — IV, 148a
Tailor, tailleur → Khayyāt
Tāʾir v, 184b — V, 181b
al-Ṭāʾir → Nudjūm
Taʿizz s, 338b — S, 338a
Ṭāḳ iii, 501b, 502a; v, 69b — III, 518b, 519b; V, 71b
al-Ṭāḳā → Kasala
Taḳaddum v, 97b — V, 99b
Taḳalī v, 267a — V, 264b
Taḳālīd ḥukmiyya ii, 303b — II, 312a
Takārina, takārīr i, 546b; ii, 767b — I, 564a; II, 786a
Takash → Tekish
Taḳbīl i, 1255a; iv, 940b — I, 1293a; IV, 973b
Takbīr ii, 846b — II, 866a
Takfīr i, 276b, 811a — I, 285a, 834a
Takhalluṣ iv, 57b-58a, 181a — IV, 61a, 189a
Takhmīs v, 963a — V, 967a
Takhṣīṣ iv, 256a — IV, 267b
Takht Singh, Mahārādjā ii, 567a — II, 581b
Takhta-bashi̊ iii, 1153a — III, 1181b
Takhtabosh ii, 114b — II, 117a
Takhtadji̊s i, 518a; ii, 695a — I, 533b; II, 712b
Takhtaḳalʿe iv, 228a — IV, 238a
Takht-i Djamshīd iv, 220b — IV, 230b
Takht-i Fūlād (Iṣfahān) s, 308a — S, 308a
Takht-i Rustam iv, 221b — IV, 231b
Takht-i Sulaymān iii, 1125a; iv, 1166a, 1167b — III, 1153a; IV, 1198a, 1200a
Taḳī Arānī s, 110a — S, 109b
Ṭāḳ-i Bustān v, 169a — V, 166b
Taḳī Bāfḳī, Shaykh Muḥammad s, 342b — S, 342a
Tajī al-Dīn b. Maʿrūf v, 27b; s, 372a — V, 28b; S, 371b
Taḳī al-Dīn al-Futūḥī → Ibn al-Nadjdjār
Taḳī al-Dīn ʿIrāḳī s, 415b — S, 415b
Taḳī Kāshī s, 415a, 415b — S, 415a, 416b
Taḳī al-Dīn ʿUmar → al-Malik al-Muẓaffar ʿUmar

Taḳī Khān, Mīrzā (Amīr Kabīr) i, 833b; ii, 649b; iii, 554b, 1105b, 1107a; iv, 70b, 394a, 395b, 396b, 398a, 787a, b, 1043a; v, 919a; S, **70b** – I, 856b; II, 666a; III, 573b, 1132b, 1134a; IV, 74a, 411a, 412b, 413b, 415a, 819a, 1074b; V, 924b; S, **71a**
Taḳī Shīrāzī, Mīrzā Muḥammad s, 342a – S, 341b
Takirwan iv, 826a – IV, 859a
Taḳiyya i, 402a, 811a, 1099a; v, 375a; s, 230b – I, 414a, 834a, 1132a, b; V, 375b; S, 230b
Taḳīzāda, Sayyid Ḥasan v, 1097b; s, 365b – V, 1093b; S, 365b
Takkalūs v, 245a – V, 242b
Taḳlā, Bishāra and/et Sālīm ii, 466b; iv, 967a – II, 478a; IV, 999a
Takla b. Hazārasp iii, 337a, b – 347a, b
Taḳlīd i, 1039a; II, 182b, 303a, 890a; iii, 1026b, 1173b; iv, 152a – I, 1070b; II, 188b, 311a, 910b; III, 1052b, 1202b; IV, 158a
Taklīf i, 272a – I, 280b
Takrīt iii, 1252b, 1268a; iv, 289a; s, 36b – III, 1285a, 1301a; IV, 302a; S, 37a
al-Takrītī, ʿAbd al-Laṭīf b. Rushayd iv, 137a – IV, 143a
Taḳrīẓ ii, 304a – II, 312b
Takrūr iii, 657a – III, 678b
Takshīf iv, 678a – IV, 705b
Takūdār → Aḥmad Takūdār
Taḳwā i, 1235b; iii, 1051a – I, 1273a; III, 1077b
Taḳwīm-i Weḳāʾiʿ i, 285a; ii, 465b; v, 313b – I, 293b; II, 477a; V, 313b
Takwīn iii, 664b – III, 686a, b
Ṭalab al-ʿilm ii, 125b – II, 128b
Ṭalaba iii, 97b, 98a, b; v, 1134a – III, 100a, b, 101a; V, 1129b
Tālabānī, Shaykh Riḍā v, 147a – V, 149b
Ṭalāʾiʿ b. Ruzzīk i, 9b, 196b; ii, 318a, 855b, 856b, 858a; iv, 429a, 944a; v, 514b; s, 115b – I, 9b, 202b; II, 327a, 875b, 876b, 878a; IV, 448a, 976b; V, 518a; S, 115a
Ṭalāḳ i, 27b, 28b, 172b, 173b, 174a, 177a, 178a, 179a; ii, 836b; iii, 19a, 949b, 952b; iv, 286a, 689a – I, 28b, 177a, 178a, 179a; II, 856a; III, 19b, 974b, 977b; IV, 298b, 717a
Ṭālaḳān ii, 43b – II, 44a
Ṭalāl, King/le roi iii, 264b – III, 272a
Ṭalāl b. ʿAbd al-Azīz ii, 660b; iv, 1142b – II, 677a; IV, 1174a
Talas iv, 188b – IV, 197a
Ṭalʿat, Meḥmed → Ṭalʿat Pashā Ḥarb
Ṭalʿat Pashā Ḥarb ii, 431a, b, 497b, 698b, 699a, b; iii, 360a, 622b; iv, 284b, 285a, b, 636a, 720b; v, 1003b; s, 98a, 296b – II, 442a, 443a, 510a, 716a, b, 717b; III, 371a, 643b; IV, 296b, 297b, 298a, 662a, 749b; V, 999b; S, 97b, 296a
Ṭalbiya iii, 37a; v, 582a – III, 38b; V, 587a
Ṭaldjiʾa iii, 394a, 1113a – III, 406b, 1140a
Ṭalḥa b. Ṭāhir i, 52b, 272a; iv, 20b – I, 54a, 280a; IV, 22a
Ṭalḥa b. ʿUbayd Allāh al-Taymī i, 43b, 110a, 308a, 381b, 382a, 383a; ii, 414b, 415b; iii, 1165b; iv, 316a; v, 316a; s, 89b – I, 44b, 112b, 317b, 392b, 393a, 394a; II, 425a, 426b; III, 1194a; IV, 330a; V, 316a; S, 89b
Ṭalḥa b. Yaḥyā s, 113b – S, 113a
Ṭalḥa al-Naḍrī al-Laythī i, 266b – I, 274b
Ṭalḥa al-Ṭalaḥāt s, 26a – S, 26a
Ṭālib → Ṭalaba
Ṭālib b. Abī Ṭālib i, 152b – I, 157a
Ṭālib b. Aḥmad i, 1306b, 1307b – I, 1346b, 1348a
Ṭālib al-Ḥaḳḳ i, 550b; ii, 592b; iii, 651b, 658a; iv, 1076a; v, 1230a; s, 337b, 338a – I, 568a; II, 607a; III, 672b, 679b; IV, 1108a; V, 1220b; S, 337b
Ṭalibid(e)s → ʿAlid(e)s
Ṭālibiyya s, 401a – S, 401a
Ṭālibov, Mīrzā ʿAbd al-Raḥīm iv, 72a, 164b, 789a; s, 109b – IV, 76a, 171b, 821a; S, 108b
Ṭālibzada → Ṭālibov
Taʿliḳ → Ṭalāḳ
Taʿlīḳ iv, 1124a, b, 1125b – IV, 1155b, 1156a, 1157b
Taʿlīḳa v, 1130b – V, 1127a
Ṭāliḳa i, 558a – I, 576a
Ṭāliḳānī, Maḥmūd iv, 166a – IV, 173b
Taʿlīm iii, 254a; iv, 205a – III, 261a; IV, 214a
Tālish s, 143a – S, 143a
Tall, el-Hadji Omar s, 182a – S, 182b
Tall, el-Hadji Seydou Nourou s, 182a – S, 182b
al-Tallaʿfarī v, 110a – V, 112a
al-Tallaʿukbarī, Hārūn b. Mūsā s, 400b – S, 401a
Talmīḥ iii, 1091b – III, 1118a
Tālpūrs i, 230b; ii, 168a; iii, 323b; iv, 1160a – I, 237b; II, 191b; III, 333b; IV, 1192a
Ṭaluḳdār i, 758a – I, 780b
Ṭālūt i, 404b – I, 416a
Tam i, 1190a – I, 1225a
Ṭamaʿ ii, 79a – II, 80b
Tāmaghilt → Maghīla
Tamahaḳḳ iii, 1038b – III, 1064b
Taman Siswa i, 746a – I, 768a
Tamanrasset i, 255a – I, 263a
Tamar, Georgian queen/reine v, 490a – V, 493a
Tāmasnā ii, 623a – II, 638b
Tamattuʿ iii, 35a, 36b, 53b – III, 37a, 38a, 55b
Tamazight (dialect(e)) s, 113b – S, 113a
Tambour → Darabukka, Ṭabl, Tunbur
Tambourine/Tambourin → Duff
Tamerlane → Tīmūr Lang
Tamgha i, 861b; ii, 147a, 310a; iii, 489b; iv, 31a, 1050a – I, 885b; II, 151a, 319a; III, 506b; IV, 33a, 1081b
Tāmgrūt i, 290b; s, 395a – I, 299b; S, 395b
al-Tamgrūtī → Abu ʾl Ḥasan al-Tamgrūtī
Ṭāmī b. Shuʿayb al-Rufaydī ii, 518a – II, 530b
Tamil ii, 28a; v, 582a – II, 28b; V, 587a
Tamīm, Banū i, 47b, 304a, 343b, 528b, 529b, 545a, 963b, 1247b, 1293a; ii, 70a, 181a, 353b, 480b; iii, 49a, 295a, 1254a; iv, 717a, 832b; v, 346a; s, 177a, 243a – I, 49a, 313b, 354a, 544b, 545b, 562a, 993a, 1285b, 1332b; II, 71a, 187a, 363b, 493a; III, 51a, 304a, 1287a; IV, 746a, 865b; V, 347a; S, 178a, 243a
Tamīm b. Bulugin b. Bādīs i, 43b – I, 45a
Tamīm b. al-Muʿizz (Fāṭimid(e)) ii, 852b, 857a, 861b; iii, 903b – II, 872b, 877a, 881b; III, 927b
Tamīm b. al-Muʿizz b. Bādīs iii, 137b, 138a, 386a, b; v, 60a – III, 140b, 398b; V, 62a
Tamīm b. Naṣr b. Sayyār iv, 447a – IV, 467a
Tamīm b. Yūsuf b. Tāshufīn i, 389b, 390a; ii, 516a, 901b, 1013a; s, 397b – I, 401a; II, 528b, 922b, 1036b; S, 398a
Tamīm b. Zīrī → Abu 'l-Kamāl
Tamīm al-Dārī i, 405a; ii, 306b, 486b; iv, 734a, 956a – I, 416b; II, 315a, 498b; IV, 763b, 989b
al-Tamīmī, Abu 'l-Ḥasan v, 10a – V, 10b
al-Tamīmī, Abū Khuzayma s, 309a – S, 309a
Tamīmīs s, 305a – S, 305a
Tamīsha s, 298a, 356b, 357a – S, 298a, 356b, 357a
Tamkīn iii, 84b – III, 87a
Tammām, Abū Ghālib → Ibn ʿAlḳama
Tammām b. ʿĀmir → Ibn ʿAlḳama
Tammām al Tamīmī iii, 982a – III, 1006b
Tamthīl iv, 249a, 250a – IV, 260a, b
Tamyīz iii, 959b – III, 984a
Tānā Shāh → Abū ʾl-Ḥasan Ḳuṭb Shāh
al-Tanakabunī → Muḥammad b. Sulaymān
Tanas i, 678b – I, 699a
al-Tanasī s, 403b – S, 403b
Tanāsukh ii, 136b; iv, 45a – II, 140a; IV, 48a

Tanawlī iii, 336a — III, 346a
Ṭanbal i, 847b — I, 871a
Tancred/Tancrède i, 215a; ii, 37a; v, 330a, 590b — I, 221b; II, 37b; V, 330a, 594b
Ṭandja i, 85a, 356a, 706b; s, 112a — I, 87a, 367a, 727b; S, 111b
Tandja Bāliya iii, 500a — III, 517a
Tanfīdha ii, 308a — II, 317a
T'ang v, 38a — V, 39a
Tanganyika → Tanzania
Tanger → Ṭandja
Tanghiz → Tankiz
Tangier → Ṭandja
Tangistān s, 336a — S, 335b
Tangut ii, 2a, 42b, 43b; iii, 115b; iv, 553b — II, 2a, 43b, 44b; III, 118a; IV, 577b
Tanḥūm ben Yōsēf ha-Yerushalmī iv, 306a — IV, 319b
Tanibak, Sayf al-Dīn ii, 285b — II, 293b
Tank s, 329b — S, 329a
Tanka ii, 119b, 120a; v, 785a — II, 122b, 123a; V, 791a
Tankiz i, 119a, 1138a, 1214a; ii, 285b, 354b; iii, 952b; iv, 960a — I, 122a, 1172b, 1250b; II, 293b, 364a; III, 977a; IV, 992b
Tankizbughā, amīr iv, 432b — IV, 451b
Tanner/Tanneur → Dabbāgh
Tanpinar, Aḥmed Ḥamdī v, 195a — V, 192a
Tānsen ii, 1144a; iii, 453b — II, 1171a; III, 469b
Ṭanṭā i, 281a, 404a; ii, 1009b; iv, 367b; s, 40b — I, 289b, 415b; II, 1033b; IV, 384a; S, 41a
Tanūkh, Āl i, 528a; ii, 634b, 751a; iii, 85b; iv, 289a; s, 284a — I, 544a; II, 650b, 769b; III, 88a; IV, 302a; S, 284a
al-Tanūkhī, ʿAbd Allāh ii, 633a — II, 649a
al-Tanūkhī, Abū ʿAlī al-Muḥassin i, 176a, 764a, 1249b; iii, 373a, 1263b; iv, 703a; v, 768b; s, 32b, 361a, 398a — I, 180b, 787a, 1287b; III, 385a, 1296b; IV, 731b; V, 774b; S, 32b, 361a, 398b
al-Tanūkhī, Abu 'l-Ḳāsim s, 361a — S, 361a
Tanwīn iv, 413a, b — IV, 431b
Ṭanyūs Shāhīn ii, 595a; iii, 591b — II, 609b; III, 612a
Tanzania i, 39a; iv, 890a; s, 248b — I, 40a; IV, 923a; S, 248b
Tanzīh i, 410b, 415b — I, 422b, 427b
Tanzīl i, 1099a — I, 1132a
Tanẓīmāt i, 13a, 37a, 56b, 286a, 318a, 397a, 469a, 652a, 657a, 693a, 972b, 1090b, 1304a; ii, 33b, 682b, 936a; iii, 285a, 592b, 1188a; iv, 168a, 560b; v, 36b, 631a, 904a, 1084b — I, 13a, 38a, 58b, 294b, 328a, 408b, 483a, 673a, 678a, 714a, 1002b, 1123a, 1344a; II, 34a, 699b, 957b; III, 293b, 613a, 1217b; IV, 175b, 583a; V, 37b, 635a, 910a, 1081b
Taormina iv, 496b — IV, 518a
Taoudenni i, 809a — I, 832a
Tapanta i, 1189b, 1190a — I, 1224b, 1225a
Tapis → Bisāṭ
Tappa Ḥiṣār ii, 107a — II, 109b
Tāptī river/rivière iv, 1022b; s, 279b — IV, 1054b; S, 279b
Tapu i, 1090b; ii, 147a — I, 1123a; II, 151a
Tar → Ḳaṭrān
Ṭār ii, 621a — II, 636b
Ṭarab iv, 823a — IV, 856a
Taraba i, 1299a; v, 62b — I, 1339a; V, 64a
Ṭarabay iii, 325a; v, 594a — III, 335a; V, 597b, 598a
Ṭarābulus al-gharb i, 1317a; v, 759b, 760b, 1183a; s, 1a, 163b — I, 1358a; V, 765a, b, 766b, 1173a; S, 1a, 163b
Ṭarābulus al-shām i, 125a, 448a, 946b; iii, 474b; iv, 485a; v, 591a — I, 128b, 461a, 976a; III, 491b; IV, 506a; V, 595a
al-Ṭarābulusī al-Raffāʾ iii, 821b — III, 845a
Tarabzun i, 468b, 476b, 645a; v, 712b; s, 328b — I, 482a, 490b, 665b; V, 717b; S, 328a
Ṭaradiyyāt I, 587a, 1154b; iii, 309a — I, 606b, 1189a; III, 318b
Ṭarafa i, 451b; ii, 1028b; iii, 666b; iv, 998b — I, 464b; II, 1052a; III, 688a; IV, 1031a
al-Ṭarāʾifī, Aḥmad b. ʿAbdūs iv, 668a — IV, 695b
Ṭarāʾifiyya iv, 668a — IV, 695b
Tārā Khān s, 327b — S, 327a
Tarāna i, 677a — I, 698a
Tarannum iv, 413b — IV, 431b
Taranto/Tarante iv, 275b — IV, 287b
Tarassul iv, 1124a — IV, 1156a
Tardī Beg i, 1135b, 1136a — I, 1170a
Tardjīʿ-band i, 677b; iii, 273b; iv, 715a — I, 698a; III, 281b; IV, 743b
Ṭarfid(e)s i, 709a — I, 729b
Ṭarghī ii, 268b; iv, 921b — II, 277a; IV, 954b
Tari Taghāʿī iii, 968b — III, 993a
al-Taʾrīdj ii, 78b — II, 80a
Ṭarīf i, 493a, 1044a — I, 507b, 1075b
Ṭarīf, Āl (Yemen) s, 335a — S, 334b
Ṭarīfa → Djazīrat Ṭarīf
Ṭarīfiyya (Ibāḍī) iii, 659a — III, 680b
Ṭāriḳ b. Suwayd al-Ḥaḍramī iv, 995b — IV, 1028a
Ṭāriḳ b. Ziyād i, 50a, 493a, 985b, 1175a; ii, 352b, 524b, 786a; iii, 298b; iv, 665a; s, 92a — I, 51b, 507b, 1016a, 1210a; II, 362b, 537b, 805a; III, 307b; IV, 692a; S, 91b
al-Ṭarīḳ al-Sharḳi iii, 362b — III, 374a
al-Ṭarīḳ al-Sulṭānī iii, 362b — III, 373b, 374a
Ṭarīḳa ii, 164a, 224a; iv, 47b, 167b, 168a; v, 1200a — II, 169a, 231a; IV, 50b, 174b, 175a, b; V, 1190b
Taʾrīkh ii, 307a, 315a; iii, 468a, 838b — II, 315b, 324a; III, 484a, 862b
Taʾrīkh al-Bāb i, 836a; iv, 346a — I, 859a; IV, 360b
Taʾrīkh al-Hind al-Gharbī iii, 1045b — III, 1071b
Taʾrīkh al-Islām ii, 215a, b — II, 222a, b
Taʾrīkh al-Mustabṣir iii, 881a — III, 905a
Taʾrīkh al-Sūdān ii, 251b, 252a — II, 259a
Tāʾrīkh-i Djalālī → Djalālī
Taʾrīkh-i Ilāhī → Ilāhī Era
Taʾrīkh-i ʿOthmānī Endjümeni i, 505b, 1089b; ii, 475a — I, 520b, 1122a; II, 487a
Tarīm s, 337b, 338a, 339a, 420b — S, 337a, 337b, 338b, 420b
Tarīn iii, 335b, 336a — III, 345b, 346a
Tariverdiov → Ḥaydar Khān ʿAmū Ughlī
Tarkanrī i, 864a — I, 888b
Tarkhān iv, 1045a — IV, 1076b
Tarkhān, Ras, al-Kh(w)arizmī iv, 1174a — IV, 1207b
Ṭarkhān Nīzak → Nīzak Ṭarkhān
Tarkhāniyyāt ii, 303b — II, 311b
Ṭarkī (Tārkhū) ii, 86a, 87a — II, 87b, 89a
Tarkīb-band i, 677b — I, 698a
Tarma ii, 114a — II, 116b
Tarmashīrīn i, 418b; ii, 4a, 45a, 922b; v, 598a — I, 430b; II, 4a, 46a, 944a; V, 601b
Tārom ii, 192a — II, 198a
Taroudannt/Tārūdānt s, 48a, 402b — S, 48b, 403a
Ṭarsūs i, 183a; ii, 35b, 36b, 129b; s, 120b — I, 188a; II, 36b, 37a, 133a; S, 120a
Ṭarsūsī → Abū Ṭāhir
Tartar → Tatar
Tarṭūs i, 825a ; I, 848a
Tārūt iv, 763b — IV, 794a
Tarwiya iii, 32b — III, 34a
Taṣawwuf i, 142b, 326a, 416a, 717a, 957a; ii, 165a, 223b, 450a, 1025b; iii, 75b, 103b, 262a, 697a; iv, 508a,

950a — I, 146b, 336b, 427b, 738b, 986b; II, 170a, 230b, 462a, 1049b; III, 78a, 105b, 269b, 719a; IV, 530a, 982b
Taṣdīḳ i, 1242a; iv, 279a — I, 1279b; IV, 291b
Tāsh Farrāsh iii, 1097b; III, 1124b
Tāsh Mangū iv, 1047a — IV, 1078b
Tashbīb ii, 1028b; iii, 1006a; iv, 714b; v, 958b — II, 1052a; III, 1031a; IV, 743b; V, 962b
Tashbīh i, 410b, 414b; iii, 160a; iv, 249b — I, 422b, 426b; III, 163b; IV, 260b
Tashelḥit i, 1186a — I, 1221a
Tāshfīn b. ʿAlī b. Yūsuf i, 78b, 390b; ii, 100b, 744b, 1013b; iii, 850b; iv, 290a — I, 81a, 401b; II, 102b, 763a, 1037a; III, 874b; IV, 303a
Tāshfīn b. Tināmer i, 699b — I, 720b
Taṣḥīḥa iv, 268b — IV, 280b
Taʿshīra iii, 294a — III, 303b
Tāshkent i, 46b, 47a; ii, 45b; iii, 224a; v, 30a, b, 399b; s, 50b, 51a, 98a, 228b, 245a, b, 411a — I, 48a; II, 46a; III, 230b; V, 31a, b, 400b; S, 51a, b, 97a, 228b, 245a, b, 411a
Tāshköprü-zāde i, 89a, 594b, 698a, 732b; iii, 164a, 467b; iv, 704b; s, 381b, 383b — I, 91b, 614a, 719b, 745b; III, 167b, 483b; IV, 733a; S, 381b, 384a
Tashkun Oghullarî i, 1159b — I, 1194a
Tashlama iii, 358a — III, 369a
Tashlîdjalî Yaḥyā ii, 937a; iv, 1137b — II, 959a; IV, 1169a
Tashmūt b. Hūlāgū iv, 521a — IV, 544a
Tashnaksutyun i, 641b — I, 662a
Ṭashöz v, 763b — V, 769b
Tashrīf v, 6a, b — V, 6b, 7a
Tashrīḥ ii, 482a — II, 494a
Tashrīḳ iii, 33a — III, 34b
Ṭashtamur al-ʿAlāʾī ii, 24a, 1112a — II, 25a, 1138a
Tāshufīn → Tāshfīn
Ṭasinī v, 460a — V, 463a
Taṣʿīr ii, 151a, 153a; iv, 1039b — II, 155b, 158a; IV, 1071a
Taʾsīs iv, 412a — IV, 430a
Taṣrīʿ iv, 413b — IV, 431b
Taṣrīf iv, 122a, b — IV, 127b
Ṭassūdj i, 3a; iii, 1252a — I, 3b; III, 1284b
Ṭasūdjī, ʿAbd al-Laṭīf iv, 72a — IV, 76a
Taṣwīr iii, 1127a; iv, 981a — III, 1155a; IV, 1013b
Tāt ii, 89a; iv, 313b; v, 604b — II, 90b; IV, 327b; V, 608b
Tātār Khān b. Muẓaffar ii, 1125a — II, 1151b
Tatār Khān (Lāhawr) ii, 973a; iii, 570a — II, 995b; III, 589b
Tatar Khān Lūdī s, 242a — S, 242a
Tātār Khān Sarang Khānī ii, 1144a; iii, 455b; s, 331b — II, 1171a; III, 471b; S, 331a
Tatar(e)s i, 32b, 269a, 721b, 722a, 808b, 893b, 1028a, 1106b, 1107a, 1108a, 1188b, 1287a, 1297a, 1302b; ii, 41b, 42b, 68b, 70a, 610b, 995b; iii, 403a; iv, 179a, 280b, 848a, 850a; s, 171b — I, 33b, 277a, 743b, 831b, 920a, 1059b, 1139b, 1140b, 1141a, 1223b, 1326b, 1337a, 1342b; II, 42a, b, 43a, 69b, 71b, 625b, 1018b; III, 415b; IV, 186a, 293a, 881a, 883a; S, 171b
- Ḳazan i, 1188b, 1307b; ii, 366a, 980a — I, 1224a, 1347b; II, 376a, 1002b
- Krîm i, 722a, 893b, 894a, 983b, 1000a, 1252a, 1286b; ii, 24b, 88a, 612b; iii, 531b; iv, 500a, 630a, b, 849b; v, 136a, 137b, 139a, b, 720a, **765b** — I, 743b, 920a, b, 1014b, 1031a, 1290a, 1326a; II, 25b, 89b, 627b; III, 550a; IV, 521b, 655a, b, 882b; V, 139a, 140a, 141b, 142b, 725a, **771b**
Taṭbīḳ ii, 254b — II, 261b
Tathlīth i, 538a — I, 554b
Tātī iv, 858b — IV, 891b
Taʿṭīl i, 411a, 414b; v, 576b — I, 422b, 426b; V, 581a
Tatmīn → Taḍmīn
Ṭaṭr, Sayf al-Dīn i, 1053b; iii, 186a; s, 39a — I, 1085b
al-Tattawī → ʿAbd al-Rashīd al-Tattawī
Ṭāʾūḳ → Daḳūḳāʾ
Ṭāʿūn iii, 240a — III, 246b
Taurus → Toros
Ṭāʾūs b. Kaysān i, 1245a; v, 1131b; s, 232b — I, 1283a; V, 1222a; S, 232b
Ṭāʾūs Sīmnānī, Ḳuṭb al-Dīn i, 91a, 148a — I, 93b, 152b
Tavī s, 241b — S, 242a
Ṭavīla iv, 219a — IV, 228b
Tavium ii, 62b — II, 63b
Tavus, Jacob b. Joseph iv, 308b — IV, 322b
Tawābiʿ i, 1144a ; I, 1178b
Tawābil ii, 1063a — II, 1088a
Tawaddud i, 364a — I, 375a
Tawadjdjuh iii, 170b — III, 174a
Ṭawāf iii, 35a, 36b; iv, 318a, 321a — III, 37a, 38a; IV, 332a, b, 335a
Tawaffā iv, 84a — IV, 88a
Ṭawāʾif i, 44a — I, 45a
Tawakkul i, 1245a — I, 1283a
Tawakkul Khān iv, 512a; v, 135a — IV, 534a; V, 138a
Tawallud i, 128b, 413b, 1243b — I, 132a, 425b, 1281a
Tawallulī, Farīdūn iv, 72a — IV, 75b
Ṭawārīḳ i, 36b, 39b, 170b, 210b, 254b, 307a, 371a, b, 433b, 809a, 1179b, 1221b, 1259b; ii, 368b, 509b, 740a, 977b, 1022b; iii, 726a, 1038b, 1195b; iv, 777a, 1150a; v, 221b, 754b, 759b, 769b; s, 164b — I, 37a, 40b, 175a, 217a, 262b, 316b, 382a, b, 446a, 832a, 1214b, 1258a, 1297b; II, 378b, 522a, 758b, 1000a, 1046a; III, 749a, 1064a, 1225b; IV, 808a, 1181b; V, 219a, 760b, 765b, 775b; S, 164b
Tawārīkh-i Ḳosṭanṭiniyya i, 776b — I, 799b
al-Ṭawāshī, Saʿd al-Dawla i, 440a — I, 452b
Ṭawāshin i, 33a; iv, 1088a — I, 34a; IV, 1119b
Tawāt → Tuwāt
Tawba iv, 1108a, b — IV, 1139b, 1140a
Tawba b. al-Ḥumayyir iv, 912a; v, 710a — IV, 945a; V, 715a
Tawātur ii, 171b; iii, 1023b — II, 177a; III, 1049b
Tawāyiha iii, 643a — III, 664b
Ṭawb i, 1226b — I, 1264a
Ṭawf i, 687a — I, 708a
al-Ṭawfi, Nadjm al-Dīn iii, 700a; iv, 258a, b — III, 722a; IV, 269b, 270a
Tawfīḳ i, 413b — I, 425b
Tawfīḳ, Sulaymān iv, 857a — IV, 890a
Tawfīḳ Aḥmad s, 224b — S, 224b
Tawfīḳ Pasha, Khedive i, 13b, 142a, 815a, 1069b; ii, 181b, 514a, 647b; iii, 557a; v, 94a; s, 40a, 408b — I, 13b, 146a, 838b, 1102a; II, 187b, 527a, 663b; III, 576b; V, 96b; S, 40a, 408b
Tawfīḳ Rifʿat Pasha v, 1092a — V, 1089a
Tawḥīd i, 78a, 79a, 389b, 390a, 407b, 409b, 410a, 414b, 415b; ii, 225a; iii, 262a, 1143b; iv, 156a, 715b — I, 80a, 81a, 400b, 401b, 419a, 421b, 422a, 426b, 427b; II, 232a; III, 269b, 1172a; IV, 162b, 744b
al-Tawḥīdī → Abū Ḥayyān al-Tawḥīdī
Ṭawīl → Ibrāhīm Pasha Ṭawīl
Taʾwīl i, 412a, 672b, 1039b, 1098b, 1099a; iv, 147a — I, 423b, 693a, 1071a, 1131b, 1132a; IV, 153a
Ṭawīl v, 684a — V, 689a
Ṭawīl, Banu 'l- s, 80b — S, 80b
Ṭawīl Khālīl (Djalālī) s, 238b — S, 238b
Ṭawīla v, 737b — V, 742b
Tawḳīʿ ii, 303a, b, 311b; iv, 1123b, 1125a — II, 311a, b, 312a, 320b; IV, 1155b, 1157a
al-Tawḳīʿ ʿalā- 'l-ḳiṣaṣ ii, 303b, 304b, 305b, 306a — II, 312a, 313a, 314a, b
Tawḳīʿāt ii, 328b — II, 338a

Tawliyat, Abu 'l-Faḍl s, 158a — S, 158a
al-Tawrāt i, 264a; iii, 579a — I, 272a; III, 599a
Tawrīḳ i, 560a — I, 576b
al-Tawrīzī, Nūr al-Dīn ʿAlī iv, 642b — IV, 669a
Ṭāwūs → Ṭā'ūs
Tawwābūn iii, 1265b — III, 1298b
al-Tawwātī, Aḥmad al-Tihāmī s, 44a — S, 44b
Tawzīʿ ii, 145b — II, 149b
Tawzīhi i, 172a — I, 177a
Tax → Bādj; Ḍarība; Djahbadh; Kharādj
Taxila s, 259b — S, 259b
al-Ṭayālisī iii, 24a — III, 25a
Ṭaybarṣ, ʿAlā' al-Dīn i, 814b; iii, 228b — I, 838a; III, 235b
Ṭaybughā al-Ashrafī al-Yūnānī iv, 797a — IV, 829b
Ṭayfūr iv, 811a — IV, 843b
Ṭayfūr b. ʿĪsā → Abū Yazīd al-Bisṭāmī
Ṭayfūr al-Dīn i, 859a — I, 882b
Ṭayfūrid(e)s i, 862a — I, 886b
Taymā' i, 547b, 1231a; s, 117a — I, 565a, 1267b; S, 116b
Taymallāt b. Thaʿlaba i, 963b — I, 993b
Taymannīs i, 224b; ii, 5b; s, 367b — I, 231a; II, 5b; S, 367a
al-Taymī → Abū Ḥanīfa al-Nuʿmān
Taymūr, Maḥmūd i, 597b, 598a, b; v, 187b, 189a, b, 192a — I, 617a, b, 618a; V, 184b, 186a, 187a, 189a
Taymūr, Muḥammad i, 597b, 598a; v, 189a — I, 617a, b; V, 186a
Taymūr, Sayyid i, 1283a — I, 1322a
Taymūr Mīrzā iv, 393a; s, 290b — IV, 409b; S, 290a
Taymūrī i, 224b; ii, 5b; iii, 1107b — I, 231a; II, 5b; III, 1135a
al-Taymūriyya → ʿĀ'isha
Tayrāb → Muḥammad Tayrāb
Ṭayy i, 683a — I, 704a
Tayyār al-Furāt → al-Ḳaʿkaʿ b. Maʿbad
Ṭayyār Maḥmūd Pasha ii, 207b; iv, 322b — II, 214a; IV, 337a
Ṭayyār Pasha-zāde Aḥmed Pasha v, 258a — V, 256a
Ṭayyārāt ii, 147a — II, 151a
al-Tayyāriyya → al-Djanāḥiyya
Ṭayyi' i, 528a, b, 544b, 563b, 1241a; ii, 482b; v, 348a; s, 37b, 304b — I, 544a, b, 561b, 581b, 1279a; II, 495a; V, 349a; S, 37b, 304a, b
Ṭayyi', Djabala i, 203a; ii, 482b — I, 209a; II, 495a
al-Ṭayyib, Mawlāy s, 404a — S, 404b
al-Ṭayyib b. al-Āmir i, 440a; ii, 170b, 858b; iii, 1168b; iv, 200a — I, 452b; II, 175b, 878b; III, 1197b; IV, 209a
Ṭayyibdjī, Badr al-Dīn iii, 1204a — III, 1234b
Ṭayyibī iii, 1107a — III, 1134a
Ṭayyibiyya i, 371a; ii, 98a; iii, 71b, 134a, 1168b; iv, 200b, 201a, 204a, b; v, 166b; s, 44a, 61b — I, 382a; II, 100a; III, 74a, 136b, 1197b; IV, 209a, b, 210a, 213a, b; V, 164b; S, 44b, 62a
Ṭayyibshāh → Djalāl al-Dīn Ṭayyibshāh
Ṭāz, amīr iii, 239b — III, 246b
Tāzā i, 355b; iii, 499a; s, 63b, 377b — I, 366b; III, 516a; S, 64a, 377b
Tazerwalt iii, 535b — III, 554a, b
Taʿzīr ii, 519a — II, 532a
Taʿziya ii, 848b; iv, 50b, 73b, 857a; v, 636b — II, 868a; IV, 53a, 77b, 890a; V, 640b
Tchad → Čad
Tea → Čay
Teba s, 152b — S, 153a
Tebessa s, 144b, 145a, 387a — S, 144a, b, 387b
Tebou ii, 875a, 876a, 877a; v, 760a — II, 895b, 896b, 897b; V, 766a
Technology, Mechanical/Technologie mécanique → Ḥiyal
Teda i, 1221b, 1258a; ii, 368b; iv, 541a; v, 352a; s, 163b, 164b, 165a, 166a — I, 1258a, 1296a; II, 378b; IV, 564a; V, 353a; S, 163b, 164b, 165a, 166a
Tedhkiredjī i, 625a, 314a — I, 646a, 323a
Tedjeddüd Fîrkasî iv, 285b — IV, 298a
Te'elkhunu i, 525b — I, 541a
Tegüder → Aḥmad Takūdār
Tehran/Teheran → Tihrān
Tʿeimuraz → Tahmūrath
Teke-oghlu i, 517b — I, 533a
Tekerleme iv, 602a — IV, 626a
Tekfur i, 1333b — I, 1374a
Tekīn v, 329b — V, 329b
Tekine Mirza iii, 44a — III, 46a
Tekish, ʿAlā' al-Dīn ii, 253a, 606a, 1101b; iii, 1111b; iv, 29b, 102a, 583a, 1067b; s, 245b — II, 260b, 621a, 1127b; III, 1139a; IV, 32a, 106b, 606b, 1099a; S, 245b
Tekish b. Alp Arslan iv, 27b — IV, 29b
Tekke i, 467b; ii, 695a; v, 269b — I, 481b; II, 712b; V, 267a
Tekke (Türkmen) s, 143b, 145a, 146b, 147a, 281a — S, 143a, 145a, 146b, 147a, 281a
Tekkelū iii, 1105a — III, 1132b
Teknedji-zāde Ibrāhīm Efendi i, 776a — I, 799a
Teleorman → Deli-Orman
Tell Abū Sēfe iv, 556a — IV, 580a
Tell ʿAdjāba → ʿArbān
Tell al-Aḥmar → Tell Abū Sēfe
Tell Espīd iv, 498b — IV, 520a
Tell el-Kheleyife i, 558b — I, 576a
Telugu v, 648a — V, 652a
Temesvár i, 291b; v, 1023a — I, 300b; V, 1019a
Temirboghā → Timurbugha
Templars/Templiers → Dāwiyya and/et Isbitāriyya
Temple → Kanīsa
Temüdjin → Činghiz Khān
Temürtash → Timurtash
Tenedos → Bozdja-ada
Ténès → Tanas
Tenggarong s, 151a — S, 151a
Tengku Abdul Rahman s, 152a — S, 152a
Tenovajib iii, 289a — III, 298a
Tent(e) → Bayt; Khayma
Tenure of land/Tenure des terres ii, 900b, 907a — II, 921b, 928a
Tepedelenli ʿAlī Pasha → ʿAlī Pasha Tepedelenli
Teraḳḳīperver Djumhūriyyet Fîrkasî ii, 432a, 596a; iv, 854a, 934b; s, 41b — II, 433b, 610b; IV, 887a, 967b; S, 42a
Terdjümān ii, 476b, 980a — II, 488b, 1002b
Terdjümān-i Aḥwāl ii, 466a, 473b — II, 478a, 485b
Terdjüme Odasî iii, 553b — III, 572b
Terek i, 1076b — I, 1108b
Terken Khātūn → Turkān Khātūn
Ternate s, 199b — S, 199b
Terres → Khāliṣa
Terter I i, 1302b — I, 1342a
Terter II i, 1302b — I, 1342a
Teshrīfātdji ii, 338b — II, 348b
Teuku Muḥammad Ḥasan i, 745a, 746a, 746b — I, 767a, 768b
Teuku Njaʿ Arif i, 745a, 746a, 746b — I, 767a, 768b, 769a
Teuku Panglima Pōlém Muḥammad Dāwūd i, 744a, 746a — I, 766a, 768b
Teungku i, 740b — I, 762b
Teungku Andjōng i, 742a — I, 764b
Teungku di-Kuala → ʿAbd al-Ra'ūf al-Sinkilī
Teungku Muḥammad Dāwūd Bevereu'éh i, 746a, 747a — I, 768b, 769b

Teutonic Knights → Dāwiyya and/et Isbitāriyya
Tewfîq, Hacî v, 482b – V, 485b
Tewfik Bey → Ebüzziya Tevfik
Tewfīk Fikret i, 287b; ii, 440a, 474b, 475a; iii, 357b; iv, 169a, 195b, 931a; s, 98a, 149b – I, 296a; II, 451b, 486b, 487a; III, 368b; IV, 176a, 204a, 964a; S, 97b, 150a
Tewfīḳ Meḥmed ii, 474a – II, 486b
Tewḳīʿ i, 1170b – I, 1205b
Textiles → Ḳumāsh
Teyran, Feqiyê v, 482a – V, 485a
al-Thaʿālibī, Abū Manṣūr i, 321b, 590a, 591a, 845b, 952b, 1348b; ii, 133b, 918b; iii, 114a, 1157b; iv, 54b, 1066b; v, 619a, 1226b; s, 119b – I, 331b, 609b, 610a, 869a, 981b, 1389a; II, 136b, 940a; III, 116a, 1186a; IV, 57b, 1098a; V, 623a, 1216b; S, 119a
al-Thaʿālibī, al-Shaykh v, 1161a – V, 1151a
al-Thaʿālibī, Sīdī ʿAbd al-Raḥmān ii, 520a – II, 533a
Thabāba b. Salāma al-Djudhāmī iv, 494b – IV, 516a
Thābit, Banū → ʿAmmār, Banū
Thābit b. Ḳays iii, 403b – III, 416a
Thābit b. Ḳurra i, 235b, 589b, 1100b, 1101a; iii, 166a, 228a, 1135a, 1136b, 1138b; iv, 110b, 629a, 804b, 1078b; s, 59b, 271b, 411b, 412a, 414a – I, 242b, 608b, 1113b, 1134a; III, 169b, 235a, 1163b, 1165a, 1167a; IV, 115b, 654a, 836b, 1110a; S, 60a, 271a, 412a, 414a
Thābit b. Sinān i, 1223b, 1353b; iii, 387b, 388a – I, 1260a, 1392b; III, 400a, b
Thābit al-Ḥaddād, Abu 'l-Miḳdād s, 129b – S, 129a
Thabraca → Tabarka
Thaddarth iv, 359a, 361b – IV, 375a, 377b
Thaghr al-Aʿlā s, 80b – S, 80b
al-Thaghrī, Abū Saʿīd Yūsuf i, 1289a – I, 1328b
Thailand v, 227a – V, 224b
al-Thāʾir fi ʾllāh → Abu 'l-Faḍl Djaʿfar
Thāʾirid(e)s s, 363a – S, 363a
Thajmāʿth ii, 413a – II, 423b
al Thaḳafī → ʿĪsā b. ʿUmar; Ismāʿīl b. ʿAlī b. ʿUthmān; Muḥammad b. Ḳāsim; Yusūf b. ʿUmar
Thaḳīf i, 145a, 544b; iii, 286a, 363b; v, 520b – I, 149a, 562a; III, 294b, 375a; V, 524a
Thala s, 387a – S, 387a
Thaʿlab i, 321b, 485b, 590a, 718b, 971b; ii, 245b, 806b, 1093b; iii, 758a, 820b; iv, 249a; v, 320a, 351a, 607b, 1033a; s, 15b, 25a, 388a, 389b – I, 331b, 500a, 609b, 740a, 1001b; II, 252b, 826a, 1119a; III, 781a, 844a; IV, 260a; V, 319a, 351b, 611b, 1029a; S, 16a, 25a, 388b, 390a
Thaʿlaba i, 962b; ii, 71b – I, 992b; II, 73a
Thaʿlaba b. Salāma al-ʿĀmilī i, 134b; ii, 1009a; iii, 602a – I, 138b; II, 1032b; III, 622b
al-Thaʿlabī, Abū Isḥāḳ Aḥmad v, 180b – V, 178a
Al-Thaʿlabī al-Nīshābūrī, Aḥmad b. Muḥammad s, 90b – S, 90a
al-Thaʿlabiyya s, 198b – S, 198b
Thālnēr iii, 446b – III, 461b
Thamādi → al-Djarādatānⁱ
Thamal, amīr i, 449b – I, 462b
al-Thamara iii, 746a – III, 768b
Thāmir iv, 314b – IV, 328b
Thamūd i, 145a, 169b, 548a; iii, 366a, 1270a; v, 763a – I, 149a, 174a, 565a; III, 377b, 1303a; V, 769a
Thamūdic/Thamudéen i, 562b, 564b – I, 580b, 582b
Thanāʾ Allāh iii, 431b – III, 445b
Thānēsarī, Djalāl al-Dīn Muḥammad b. Maḥmūd s, 313a – S, 312b
Thānesarī, Niẓām al-Dīn ii, 55a – II, 56a
Thānī, Āl i, 539b; ii, 177b; iv, 751b – I, 556b; II, 183a; IV, 782a
Thannuris s, 229b – S, 229b
Thaʾr ii, 340b; iii, 388b – II, 350b; III, 401a
al-Tharwānī, Muḥammad b. ʿAbd al-Raḥmān iv, 1003a – IV, 1035a
Tharwat ʿUkāsha s, 6a – S, 5a
Thasos → Ṭashöz
Thatta i, 80b; iii, 448b, 633a – I, 83a; III, 463b, 654a
Thawāb ii, 518a – II, 531a
Thawāba b. Salāma i, 135a; iii, 602a – I, 138b; III, 622b
Thawr b. Yazīd v, 329b – V, 329b
al-Thawrī → Sufyān
Thawriyya iv, 46a – IV, 48b
Thé, le → Čay
Théâtre d'ombre → Ḳaragöz; Khayāl al-Ẓill
Theodosia, Théodosie → Kefe
Theology/Théologie → ʿIlm al-Kalām; Kalām
Theophrastus/Théophraste i, 736b, 737b; s, 59b – I, 758b, 759a; S, 60a
Therwet-i Fünūn i, 287a; ii, 439b, 440a, 474b, 692b, 877b; iii, 261a; iv, 931a; v, 194b, 195b – I, 296a; II, 451a, b, 486b, 710a, 898a; III, 268a; IV, 964a; V, 191b, 192b
Thief → Liṣṣ
Thimāl b. Ṣāliḥ b. Mirdās iii, 686b, 740b; v, 924a – III, 708a, 763b; V, 929b
Thopia i, 653b, 654b – I, 674b, 675b
Thoros I, II ii, 37a, b – II, 38a
Throne → Kursī
Thughūr i, 465b, 761a, b, 789b; ii, 36a, 503a; s, 120a – I, 479a, 783b, 784a, 813a; II, 36b, 37a, 515b; S, 119b
Thuluth iv, 1123b, 1125a, 1127b; v, 218a – IV, 1155a, 1157a, 1159a; V, 215b
Thumāl, amir iv, 911a – IV, 944a
Thumāma b. Ashras i, 271b; ii, 386a; iii, 1266a; s, 48b, 89a – I, 280a; II, 396a; III, 1299a; S, 49a, 88b
Thumāma b. Uthāl i, 964a; iii, 167a – I, 993b; III, 170b
Thurayya ii, 1011b – II, 1035a
al-Thurayyā i, 898a – I, 924b
Thurayyā bint Maḥmūd Ṭarzī s, 65b – S, 66a
Thuwaynī b. Saʿīd i, 1282b; v, 1030b – I, 1321b; V, 1026a, b
Ṭibb ii, 1120a – II, 1146b
Ṭibbiyye-i ʿadliyye-i Shāhāne ii, 996b – II, 1019b
Tibesti s, 163b, 165a, 166a – S, 163b, 165a, 166a
Tibet i, 71a – I, 73a
Ṭībī i, 942b – I, 971b
al-Tibrīzī, Abū Zakariyyāʾ Yaḥyā i, 69a, 154b, 593a, 794a; iii, 111a; v, 930a – I, 71a, 159a, 612a, 817a; III, 113b; V, 934b
al-Tibrīzī, Ibn Khalaf → Burhān
Tibrīzī, Shams al-Dīn → Shams-i Tabrīzī
al-Tidjānī, Aḥmad i, 297a; ii, 941b; iii, 107b; iv, 550b – I, 306a; II, 963b; III, 110a; IV, 574b
al-Tidjānī, Muḥammad i, 207a; ii, 552b; iv, 339b – I, 213b; II, 566b; IV, 354a
Tidjāniyya i, 297a, 315b, 371a, 1009a, 1260b; ii, 10a, 63a, 94b, 432b, 975a, 1004a; iii, 38b, 107a, 289a, 646b; iv, 549b; v, 287b; s, 165a, 182a, 371a, 387a – I, 306a, 325a, 382a, 1040a, 1298b; II, 10a, 64b, 96b, 444a, 997b, 1027a; III, 40a, 109b, 298a, 667b; IV, 573b; V, 286a; S, 165a, 182a, 371a, 387b
Tidjīn-Rūd s, 309b – S, 309a
Tidore s, 199b – S, 199b
Tʾien Wu v, 851b – V, 856a
al-Tifāshī, Aḥmad b. Yūsuf i, 419b, 1220b; ii, 93b; iv, 881b – I, 431a, 1257a; II, 95a; IV, 914a
Tifinagh i, 1185a; v, 221b, 222a, 754b-757b – I, 1220a; V, 219a, b, 760a-763a
Ṭiflī Aḥmed Čelebi v, 952a – V, 955b
Tiflīs i, 644a; iv, 346b, 349a, 391b; v, 487a-489b, 493a,

495a, 497a; s, 47a, 275a — I, 664b; IV, 361a, 364a, 408a; V, 490a-492b, 496a, 498a, 500a; S, 47b, 274b
Tiflīsī, Abu 'l-Faḍl Ḥubaysh iv, 525b — IV, 548b
al-Tiflīsī, Abū ʿImrān iv, 604a — IV, 628a
Tiftik i, 511a; s, 318a — I, 526b; S, 318a
al-Ṭighnarī ii, 901b — II, 922b
Tighremt i, 1321b — I, 1361b
Tigīnābād iv, 536b — IV, 537a
Tigre (Tigrinya) ii, 709b; iii, 6a, 7b — II, 729a; III, 6a, 7b
Tigris/Tigre(fleuve) → Didjla
Tihāma i, 536b, 539a; ii, 1025a; v, 808a, 809a, 1244a, b; s, 22b, 236a, 335a — I, 553a, 555b; II, 1048b; V, 814a, 815a, 1235a; S, 22b, 236a, 334b
Tihbat-i khurd → Baltistān
Ṭihrān i, 978a, 1088b; iv, 7b, 391a; v, 876a; s, 23b, 41a, 73a, 142a, 291a, 423a — I, 1008b, 1121a; IV, 8a, 408a; V, 882a; S, 23b, 41b, 73b, 142a, 290b, 423b
- University/Université ii, 426a — II, 437a
Ṭihrānī, Djalāl al-Dīn s, 376a — S, 376a
Ṭihrānī, Mīrzā Ḥusayn Khalīlī s, 95b — S, 95a
Tikla b. Hazārasp v, 826b — V, 832b
Ṭilāʾ iv, 995b, 996b — IV, 1028a, 1029a
Tīla (mosque/mosquée) s, 292a — S, 292a
Tilangānī, Khān-i Djahān iv, 907b — IV, 940b
Tiles → Kāshī
Tilimsān i, 92a, 93a, 122b, 124b, 155a, 168a, 367a, 678b; ii, 173a, 1008a; iii, 251a, 339b, 470a, 1041a, 1042b; v, 518a, 1175a, 1179a; s, 29a, 145a, 376b, 403a — I, 95a, b, 126a, 128a, 159a, 172b, 378a, 699a; II, 178a, 1032a; III, 258b, 349b, 486b, 1067a, 1068b; V, 521b, 1165a, 1169a; S, 29a, 144b, 376b, 403a
- literature/littérature iii, 832a, 865b — III, 855b, 889b
- monuments i, 499b; iii, 144a; v, 290a, 1151b — I, 514b; III, 145b; V, 289a, b, 1141b
al-Tilimsānī → al-Sharīf
al-Tilimsānī, ʿAfīf al-Dīn i, 596a — I, 615b
Tīmār i, 652b, 654a, 655b, 656b, 999b, 1147b, 1264a, 1266b; ii, 32b, 33b, 82a, 147a, b; iii, 284b, 1089a; iv, 1094b; v, 249a, 880b, 881a; s, 238b — I, 673a, 674b, 675a, 676a, 677b, 1030a, 1182a, 1302b, 1305a; II, 33a, 34a, 83b, 151a, b; III, 293a, 1116a; IV, 1125a; V, 247a, 886b, 887a; S, 238a
Timbuctu → Tinbuktū
Timimoun s, 328a, b — S, 327b, 328a
Timm s, 135b — S, 135b
Timnaʿ i, 1132b; iv, 746b, 747a — I, 1167a; IV, 776b, 777a
Tīmūr Lang i, 66b, 227a, 237a, 244a, 311b, 468a, 470a, 530b, 721b, 852b, 903b, 999a, 1046a, 1051a, 1107b, 1119a; ii, 45a, 86b, 120b, 204b, 239b, 270a, 285b, 697a, 781b, 990a; iii, 187b, 189b, 198a, 199b, 417a, 827b, 1100b; iv, 32b-33a, 102b, 349b, 410a, 586a, 670a, 871a, 1104b; v, 182a, 457a, 491b, 858b; s, 49a, 94b, 242a, 327a — I, 68b, 234a, 244b, 251a, 321a, 482a, 484a, 546b, 743a, 876a, 930b, 1029b, 1077b, 1082b, 1141a, 1152b; II, 46a, 88a, 123b, 211a, 246a, 278b, 293b, 714b, 800b, 1012b; III, 192a, 194a, 202b, 204b, 430b, 851b, 1127b; IV, 34b-35b, 107a, 364b, 428a, 608b, 697b, 904b, 1136a; V, 179b, 459b, 494a, 865b; S, 49b, 94a, 242a, 326b
- literature/littérature ii, 591b; iii, 58a, 274a, 711b — II, 606a; III, 60a, 281b, 734a
Tīmūr Shāh Durrānī (Abdālī) i, 230a, b, 296a, 970b; ii, 186a, 628b, 952a; iii, 1158b — I, 237a, b, 305a, 1000a; II, 192a, 644b, 974a; III, 1187a
Timurbugha iv, 462b — IV, 483a
Tīmūrid(e)s i, 135a, 147b, 227a, b, 1001b; ii, 45b, 309a, 334a, 792a; iii, 483b, 1256b; i, 227b; iv, 33a, 66a, 350a; v, 59a, 824b; s, 71a, 138b, 227b, 256a, b, 313a — I, 139a, 151b, 234a, 1032a; II, 46a, 317b, 343b, 810b; III, 500b, 1289a; I, 234a; IV, 35a, b, 69b, 364b; V, 60b, 830b; S, 71b, 138a, 227b, 255b, 256a, 313a
- history of iv, 914b; s, 96b — IV, 947a; S, 96a
Tīmurtash, Ḳara i, 738b, 1159b, 1302b; ii, 722a — I, 760b, 1194b, 1342b; II, 741a
Tīmurtash b. Čūbān i, 468a, 703a; ii, 68a, 706a; iv, 622a — I, 481b, 724b; II, 69b, 724a; IV, 646b
Tīmurtash b. Īlghāzī i, 664b — I, 684a
Tin → Ḳalʿī
Tinbuktū i, 35a, 280a; ii, 252a; v, 394a; s, 29a, 295b — I, 35b, 288b; II, 259b; V, 395a; S, 29a, 295a
Tindi i, 504a — I, 519b
Tinerkouk s, 328b — S, 328a
Tingiz s, 195b — S, 195b
Tīnmāl, Tinmallal i, 459a; iii, 207b, 959a — I, 472a; III, 213a, 984a
Tinnīn s, 191a — S, 192b
Tinnīs ii, 72b — II, 74a
Tippu Tip iv, 750a, b; v, 176b — IV, 780a, b; V, 174a
Tipū Mastān Awliyā i, 625a — I, 645b
Tipū Sulṭān i, 625a, 1015b; ii, 220a; iii, 119b, 316b, 322a; iv, 547b; v, 648a, 884b, 886a, 1259a, 1260a, b — I, 645b, 1047a; II, 227a; III, 122a, 326b, 331b; IV, 571a; V, 652b, 890b, 892a, 1250a, 1251a, b
Ṭīra ii, 758b, 759b, 760a, 1097a; iv, 290b — II, 777a, b, 778b, 1123a; IV, 303b
Tirāh i, 238a, b — I, 245b, 246a
Tirāhi i, 237b — I, 245a
Tirān, Straits of/Détroits de s, 8b — S, 8a
Ṭirāz i, 501a; ii, 301b, 302a; iii, 218a, 219a; v, 498b, 736b, 857a; s, 144a, 341a — I, 516a; II, 310a; III, 224b, 225b; V, 502a, 741b, 864a; S, 144a, 340b
al-Ṭirāz iii, 863a — III, 887a
Tirfa iv, 97a — IV, 101a
Tirhān v, 617a, b — V, 621a, b
Tirhut s, 409a — S, 409b
Ṭirimmāḥ ii, 1011a — II, 1034b
Tirmidh ii, 1a, 4b, 43a — II, 1a, 4b, 44a
al-Tirmidhī, Abū ʿĪsā i, 114b; iii, 24a, 25a, 27b, 707a; s, 232b — I, 117b; III, 25b, 26a, 29a, 729b; S, 232b
Ṭirs ii, 540b — II, 553b
Tīryākī Ḥasan Pasha i, 267b; iv, 546b, 878a — I, 275b; IV, 570a, 910b
Tisserand → Ḥāʾik
Ṭiṭarī, Ṭiṭerī i, 368a, 699b — I, 379a, 721a
Tivaouane s, 182a — S, 182a
Tiyek s, 171b, 172a — S, 172a, b
Tiyūl ii, 150b, 152a, 153a; v, 244b — II, 155a, 156b, 158a; V, 242a
Tiyūywīn s, 402b — S, 403a
Tīzī n'Maʿshū s, 48a — S, 48b
Tizi Ouzou iv, 359b — IV, 375a, b
Tiznīt s, 47b, 48a — S, 48a, b
Tlemcen → Tilimsān
Tobacco → Tūtūn
Tobacco Régie Concession s, 71b, 77a, 104a — S, 72a, 77a, 103b
Tobiah b. Moses iv, 605b — IV, 629b
Tobīrčiḳoghlū Ḳayib Khān → Ḳayib Khān
Todar Mall ii, 156a, 183b; iii, 457b — II, 161a, 189a; III, 473b
Togan, Zekī Welīdī i, 1077a; ii, 700b — I, 1109a; II, 718b
Togha, Toghan → Tugha, Tughan
Toghluk → Tughluk
Toghril → Tughril
Toghuzghuz i, 1240a — I, 1278a
Togo iv, 351b — IV, 367a
Tokar → Tūkar
Tokat iii, 212b; v, 557b — III, 218b; V, 562b
Tokhtamīsh Khān i, 1107b; ii, 44a, b, 86b, 1112a — I, 1141a; II, 45a, b, 88a, 1138b

Tokhtu Khān ii, 610b — II, 625b
Toḳmaḳ ii, 67b — II, 68b
Tokolors → Tukulors
Toḳtamish Girāy ii, 1047a, 1113b; iv, 1064a; v, 765b — II, 1071a, 1139b; IV, 1095b; V, 771b
Toḳtoʾa ii, 42b — II, 43b
Tökü sh i, 664a — I, 683b
Toledo/Tolède → Tulaytula
Tolobey i, 808b — I, 831b
Toluy i, 227a, 1105a; ii, 43b, 45b; iv, 542b — I, 233b, 1138b; II, 44a, 46b; IV, 566a
Tomb/tombeau → Ḳabr; Ḳubba
Tombalabaye, François s, 166a, b — S, 166a, b
Tombouctou → Tinbuktū
Tonguç, Ismail Hakki v, 281b, 282a, b — V, 280a, b
Tonk i, 444a, 1195b — I, 457a, 1230b
Ṭoñuzlu → Deñizli
Ṭop ʿArabadjîlarî i, 1061b — I, 1093b
Topal Meḥmed Pasha v, 257b, 764a — V, 255a, 770a
Topal ʿOthmān Pasha (1) i, 292a; v, 144b, 461b, 494a — I, 301a; V, 147a, 464a, 497a
Ṭopal ʿOthmān Pasha (2) i, 1268b, 1272a — I, 1307b, 1311a
Topčîbashî, ʿAlī Merdān s, 47a — S, 47b
Ṭopdjular i, 1061b — I, 1093b
Ṭopḳapî Sarāyî i, 836b, 1091a; ii, 694b, 996b; iv, 231b, 232b, 233a, 368a; v, 67a, b, 274a — I, 860a, 1123b; II, 712a, 1019b; IV, 241b, 243a, b, 384a; V, 69a, b, 272a
Ṭopkhāne i, 1061b; ii, 129b, 513a; iv, 233a; s, 314b, 315b — I, 1093b; II, 132b, 525b; IV, 243a; S, 314a, 315b
Ṭopraḳ Kalʿe → Athūr
Torah → al-Tawrāt
Töregene ii, 45b — II, 46b
Torghud → Turghud
Torī Khēl s, 285a — S, 285a
Torlaḳ Hū Kemāl i, 869b — I, 893b
Toros i, 463a; ii, 35a — I, 476b; II, 36a
Tortum s, 308a — S, 307b
Tosḳ i, 650a, 651a — I, 670a, 671b
Touareg → Ṭawārīḳ
Touareg (language/langue) i, 792a, 1180b, 1182a, b, 1183a, b, 1185a — I, 815b, 1216a, b, 1217a, b, 1218a, b, 1220a
Touat → Tuwāt
Touba s, 182a — S, 182a
Tour → Burdj
Tower → Burdj
Town → Ḳarya
Town Crier → Dallāl
Tozeur ii, 463a, 464a — II, 475a, 476a
Trabzon → Tarabzun
Trabzonlu Hüseyn Rüshdī Pasha ii, 200a — II, 206b
Tradition/Tradition → Ḥadīth
Trahgām s, 167a — S, 167a
Tralleis → Aydîn
Transcaucasia/Transcaucasie iv, 349a, b; v, 440a, 495b, 496b — IV, 364a; V, 442b, 498b, 499b
Transjordan/Transjordanie → al-Urdunn
Transoxania/Transoxiane → Mā warāʾ al-Nahr
Transylvania/Transylvanie → Erdel
Trāra i, 372a; v, 379a — I, 383a; V, 379b
Travnik i, 1270b — I, 1309b
Treasury → Bayt al-Māl; Khazīne
Trebizond/Trébizonde → Tarabzun
Trésor, Maison de - → Bayt al-Māl; Khazīne
Trestenik-oghlu Ismāʿīl → Ismāʿīl Bey (Serez)
Tribe/tribu → Ḳabīla
Trigonometry/Trigonométrie → ʿIlm al-Handasa
Tripoli (Lībīya) → Ṭarābulus al-gharb
Tripolis → Ṭarābulus al-shām
Tripolitania/Tripolitaine i, 134b, 139a, 1071a; ii, 595a; iii, 296b, 654b, 655a, 1040a; iv, 617a, 919b; v, 758a, b, 759b, 760a, 1182a — I, 138a, 143a, 1103b; II, 609b; III, 305b, 675b, 676b, 1066a; IV, 641b, 952b; V, 763b, 764a, 765a, 766a, 1172a
Troki iv, 608a, b — IV, 632b, 633a
Trône → Kursī
Trucial Coast → al-Sāḥil
Trucial States → al-Imārāt al-ʿArabiyya al-Muttaḥida
Trumpet → Būḳ
Truna Jaya v, 1155a, b — V, 1145a
Tskhum → Sukhum
Tualtae i, 354a — I, 365a
Tuʿām → al-Buraymī
Tuanku Maḥmūd i, 745b — I, 767b
Tuanku Radja Keumala i, 745a — I, 767b
Tuāreg → Ṭawārīḳ
Ṭūb v, 585b — V, 590b
Tubal b. Lamak ii, 620a — II, 635b
Tuban s, 201b — S, 201b
Tubbaʿ iii, 882a — III, 906b
Tuberon, Ludovik Crijević s, 185b — S, 186b
Ṭubna i, 125a, 1246b; iii, 1041b — I, 128b, 1284b; III, 1067b
Tūbū i, 1258a — I, 1296a
Tūbū → Teda
Tūda iii, 529a, b, 530a — III, 547a, b, 548a
Tudeh party/parti iv, 40b-41a, 41b, 790a; s, 60b — IV, 43a-b, 44a, 822a; S, 61a
Tudela → Tuṭīla
Tudjībīd(e)s iii, 816a; iv, 478a, 713a; v, 119b, 120a, 683a; s, 80b, 82a — III, 839b; IV, 499a, 741b; V, 122a, b, 688a; S, 80a, 81b
Tūdjīn, Banū i, 122b, 167b — I, 125a, 172b
Tudmīr b. ʿAbdūs i, 58b; iii, 706a; iv, 672b; s, 81b — I, 60b; III, 728a; IV, 700a; S, 81b
Tuer → Ḳatl
Tufāl Khān Dakhnī ii, 815a; iii, 425a, 1161a — I, 834b; III, 439a, 1189b
Tufang i, 1066a, 1068a, b — I, 1098a, 1100a, 1101a
Tufangčī i, 8a, 1068a, 1256b — I, 8a, 1100a, 1294b
Tufangčī-āḳāsī iv, 36b — IV, 39a
Ṭufayl b. ʿAwf al-Ghanawī i, 115b, 772a; ii, 1005a — I, 119a, 795a; II, 1028b
Tūfīḳ iv, 359a — IV, 375a
Tūgh iii, 191b; v, 766b — III, 196a; V, 772b
Ṭughā Tīmūr ii, 3b, 44a, 401a; v, 663a — II, 3b, 45a, 411b; V, 668a
Tughalčin iii, 417b — III, 431a
Tūghān b. Ayāz ii, 322a — II, 331b
Tughān Arslān ii, 680b, 764b — II, 697b, 783a
Tughan Khān i, 987a — I, 1017b
Ṭughānshāh b. Alp Arslan i, 827a; ii, 552a — I, 850a; II, 566a
Ṭughdj b. Djuff ii, 281b; iv, 493b — II, 289b; IV, 515a
Tughluḳ v, 688b — V, 693b
Tughluḳ, Malik → Ghīyath al-Dīn Tughluḳ I
Tughluḳ Shah → Ghiyāth al-Dīn Tughluḳ
Tughluḳ Temür ii, 45a, 622a; iv, 32b — II, 46a, 637b; IV, 34b
Tughluḳābād i, 1322a; ii, 257b, 262a; iii, 441b, 481b; v, 888a, 1215a — I, 1362b; II, 263b, 265a, 269b; III, 456a, 498a; V, 894b, 1204b
Tughluḳid(e)s v, 884a; s, 206b — V, 890a; S, 206a
Ṭughrā ii, 310a, 311b, 314b, 804a, b; iv, 796b, 1104b; v, 232b — II, 319a, 320b, 323b, 823a, b; IV, 829a, 1136a; V, 230b
al-Ṭughrāʾī, Abū Ismāʿīl al-Ḥusayn s, 326b — S, 326a
al-Ṭughrāʾī, Ḥusayn b. ʿAlī i, 206b; iii, 1264b; v,

112a, 114a — I, 212b; III, 1297a; V, 114b, 116b
Ṭughrïl I (Ṭughrïlbeg) (Saldjūḳ) i, 20b, 132a, 420a, 512b, 513a, 627a, 839b, 900b, 1073b, 1074b, 1075a, 1336b, 1356a; ii, 4b, 5a, 192b, 348b, 680b, 855b, 856a, 1051a, 1108b; iii, 159b, 344b, 345b, 471b, 891b, 1098b; iv, 25a, 26b-27a, 101a, 347b, 457b, 458a, 465b, 942a; v, 388a, b, 623a; s, 14b, 29b, 192a, 195a — I, 21a, 136a, 432a, 528b, 647b, 863a, 927b, 1105b, 1106b, 1107a, 1376b, 1395a; II, 4b, 5a, 199a, 358a, 697b, 875b, 876a, 1075b, 1134b; III, 163a, 355a, 356a, 488a, 915b, 1125b; IV, 26b, 28b-29a, 105a, 362b, 478a, b, 486b, 975a; V, 389a, b, 627a; S, 15a, 29b, 193a, 195a
Ṭughrïl II, Rukn al-Dīn (Saldjūḳ) s, 416a — S, 416b
Ṭughrïl III b. Arslān, Rukn al-Dīn (Saldjūḳ) i, 20b; ii, 894a; iii, 1111a, b; iv, 948b, 1067b; s, 378b, 416a — I, 21b; II, 915a; III, 1138b, 1139a; IV, 981a, 1099b; S, 378b, 416b
Ṭughrïl b. Muḥammad (Malik) i, 300b; iii, 196b; iv, 860a — I, 309b; III, 201b; IV, 893a
Ṭughrïl-Arslan i, 983a; ii, 110b — I, 1013b; II, 113a
Ṭughrïl Birār i, 1130b; ii, 1052a — I, 1165a; II, 1076a
Ṭughrïl Khān (governor/gouverneur Bengal) s, 124a — S, 123b
Ṭughrïl Khān (Ḳarakhānid(e)) i, 987a — I, 1017b
Ṭughrïl Khān (Kereyt) → Ong Khān
Ṭughrïl-tigin b. Ekinči s, 279a — S, 279a
Ṭughshāda i, 1293b — I, 1333b
Ṭughtakin, Ẓahīr al-Dīn i, 664a, 731b, 1332a, 1337a; ii, 282a, 353b, 458a; iii, 120a, 398b, 503b, 1118b; iv, 200a — I, 684a, 753b, 1372b, 1377a; II, 290a, 363a, 469b; III, 122b, 411a, 521a, 1146a; IV, 208b
Tuḥfat al-Aḥbāb i, 214b — I, 221a
Tukal Bogha ii, 610b — II, 625b
Ṭūḳān iv, 834b — IV, 867b
Tūkar iv, 680b, 687a — IV, 714b, 715a
Tukarōʿī iii, 202b — III, 208a
Ṭukhāristān s, 125a — S, 124a
Tukhāristān i, 852a — I, 875b
al-Tukhāwī, Muḥammad Aḥmad s, 371a — S, 371a
al-Tukhāwiyya s, 371a — S, 371a
Ṭūkhī, ʿAbd Allāh v, 190a — V, 187b
Tukhum v, 618a — V, 622a
Tukulors i, 297a; ii, 941b, 970a — I, 306a; II, 963a, b, 992a
Tūlak s, 66b — S, 67a
Tūlakī, Malik Ḍiyā al-Dīn i, 1194a — I, 1229b
al-Tūlawī → Buṭrus
Ṭulayḥa b. Khuwaylid al-Asadī i, 110b, 683b, 1358b; iv, 385b, 858b — I, 113b, 704b, 1398b; IV, 402b, 891b
Tulaytula i, 6b, 7a, 82b, 83a, 242b, 493a; iii, 12a, 74a, 702a; s, 23a — I, 6b, 7a, 85a, 86a, 250a, 508a; III, 12b, 76b, 724a; S, 23a
Ṭulb iii, 185b — III, 190a
Tulip/Tulipe → Lāle
Tulsī Dās iii, 457a — III, 473a
Tulumbadjï i, 270a; iv, 234b, 237b — I, 278a; IV, 245a, 248a
Ṭūlūnids i, 14b, 18b, 278a, 435b, 439b, 1346a; ii, 36b, 281b; s, 120b — I, 15a, 19b, 287a, 448a, 452a, 1386b; II, 37a, 289b; S, 120a
Tulūy → Toluy
Tūmān, Amīr iv, 578a — IV, 601a
Ṭūmān Bay, al-ʿĀdil iv, 552a — IV, 575b
Tūmān Bay, al-Ashraf i, 779a; ii, 172b, 1042a; iii, 188a, 813a; iv, 552a, 553a — I, 802b; II, 178a, 1066b; III, 192b, 836b; IV, 576a, 577a
Ṭūmār iv, 742a; v, 873b — IV, 772a; V, 879b
Tūmārī i, 260b — I, 268b
Tumenggung, Pangeran s, 150b — S, 150b
Tūn v, 355a — V, 356a
Tūnb-i Buzurḳ iv, 778a, b; s, 417b — IV, 809b, 810a; S, 418a
al-Tunbudhī → Manṣūr b. Naṣr al-Tunbudhī
Tunceli ii, 208a; v, 465a — II, 214b; V, 468a
Tundjur i, 1258a; ii, 122a; iv, 541a; s, 164a — I, 1296a; II, 125a; IV, 564b; S, 164a
Tunganistan v, 846b — V, 858b
Tunggang Parangan, Tuan s, 151a — S, 151a
Tūnis i, 86b, 163b, 248b, 281b, 1225a; ii, 130a, 189b, 1008b; iii, 94b, 145a, 605a; v, 1127b, 1151a; s, 133b, 145a — I, 89a, 168a, 256b, 290a, 1261b; II, 133b, 195b, 1032a; III, 97a, 148a, 625b; V, 1124a, 1141b; S, 133a, 144b
- great mosque/grande mosquée, la i, 950a, 1228a — I, 979a, 1264b
Tunisia/Tunisie i, 18a, 19a, 34b, 35a, 37a, 79a, 171a, 977a, 1177a, 1321a; ii, 413a, 526a, 595a, 638b, 676a, 748a; iii, 297a, 384b, 395b, 561b, 563a, b, 605a, 635b, 683b, 684a, 927b; iv, 175a, 262b, 403a, 824b, 954b, 1157a; v, 59b, 696a, 915a, 1067b; s, 11a, 215b, 254b — I, 18b, 20a, 35b, 36a, 38a, 81b, 176a, 1007a, 1212a, 1361b; II, 424a, 539a, 610a, 654b, 693a, 766b; III, 306b, 397a, 408a, 581a, 582b, 583a, 625b, 657a, 705b, 952a; IV, 182b, 274a, 420b, 857b, 986b, 1189a; V, 61b, 701a, 920b, 1065a; S, 10b, 215b, 254a
- demography/démographie s, 215b — S, 215b
- institutions ii, 425a, 436a; iii, 524a — II, 436a, 447b; III, 542a
- language, literature/langue, littérature ii, 470a — II, 482a
- population v, 1181b — V, 1171b
Tūnk iv, 213a — IV, 222b
Tūnkath s, 411a — S, 411a
al-Tūnusī → Khayr al-Dīn
al-Tūnusī, Muḥammad b. ʿUmar ii, 122b, 827b — II, 125b, 847a
Tūpčiyān i, 1066a, 1068a, b, 1069a — I, 1098a, 1100a, 1101a
Tura Khāns i, 135a, 1075b — I, 139a, 1108a
Turaba → Taraba
Ṭurābāy ii, 912a — II, 933b
Tūrān i, 236a; v, 314b — I, 243b; V, 314a
Tūrān-čar s, 299a — S, 298b
Tūrān Shāh II b. Tughrïl v, 160a, b — V, 158b, 159a
Tūrānshāh of/de Hurmuz i, 942b — I, 971b
Tūrānshāh b. Ayyūb i, 181b, 552b, 709a; iii, 125b; v, 895b, 1244b; s, 338a — I, 186b, 570b, 729b; III, 128b; V, 901b, 1235a, b; S, 337b
Tūrān-Shāh b. al-Ṣāliḥ b. al-Malik al-Kāmil, al-Malik al-Muʿaẓẓam → al-Malik al-Muʿ-aẓẓam Sharaf al-Dīn
al-Ṭurayf ii, 320b, 321a — II, 330a, b
Turayḥīb b. Bandar b. Shuḳayr iv, 680b, 681a — IV, 708b
Türba iv, 352b; v, 214b, 289a, 1139b, 1140a — IV, 367b; V, 212a, 288a, 1133a, b
Turban v, 734b, 738a, 749a, 751a — V, 739b, 743b, 754b, 756b
Turbat-i Shaykh-i Djām i, 283a; iii, 1125a; s, 41a, 367b — I, 292a; III, 1152b; S, 41b, 367a
Turcoman → Türkmen
Turcs I, 19a, 20b, 21a, 32a, 33b, 57b, 96a, 172b, 179b, 188b, 378a, 920a, 518b; II, 615b, 1003a, 1133a; IV, 698b
Ṭurfa Āl al-Shaykh s, 305b — S, 305b
Turfān ii, 45b; iv, 529a; s, 136b — II, 46b; IV, 552a; S, 136a
Türgesh i, 684b; iii, 224a; iv, 583b; v, 854a, b, 855b — I, 705b; III, 230b; IV, 607b; V, 860b, 861a, 862a
Tūrghūd ʿAlī Pasha ii, 459b, 461a; iii, 69b; iv, 416a, 656b, 828a; v, 504a, 1247a — II, 471b, 473a; III, 72a; IV, 434a, 683a, 861a; V, 507b, 1237b
Turghut Oghlu Ḥasan Beg iv, 624a — IV, 648b

Tūrī, Banū v, 501b — V, 504b
al-Ṭūrī, Muḥammad b. ʿAlī iii, 901b — III, 925b
Turīsha s, 299a — S, 298b
Türk Odjaghî (Odjaklarî) ii, 431a, 432a; iv, 791a, 933b; s, 47b — II, 442a, 443b; IV, 823a, 966b; S, 48a
Turk b. Yāfit iv, 914b — IV, 947b
Turkān Khātūn i, 1051b, 1070b; iv, 28b, 30a, 101b; v, 162a, 553b, 554a; s, 384a — I, 1083a, 1103a; IV, 30b, 32a, 106a; V, 160a, 558b, 559a; S, 384a
Turkče Bilmez i, 709b; v, 391a, 808a — I, 731a; V, 392a, 814a
Türkčülük v, 264a — V, 261b
Türkes, Alparslan iv, 791b — IV, 823b
Turkey i, 13b, 37b, 39a, 62b, 74b, 238b, 281b, 462a, 734a, 871a, 972b; ii, 594b, 595a, 640a, 966b; iii, 213b; iv, 1b, 790b; v, 464b, 505a; s, 214a
- demography s, 214a
- education v, 906a, 1099b
- ethnography v, 439b, 750b
- institutions i, 972b, 1225b; ii, 425b, 429b, 708b; iii, 526a; iv, 167b; v, 1037b
- languages, literature ii, 473b; iii, 373b, 1115b; iv, 699b, 715a, 853b; v, 193a, 223b, 538a, 1100a, 1101a
Turkhān Sulṭān iv, 233b; v, 273a; s, 257b — IV, 243b; V, 270b; S, 257b
Ṭurkhān-oghlu ʿÖmer Beg v, 772a — V, 778a, b
Turkhān-oghullarî i, 340b — I, 351a
Turkī b. ʿAbd Allāh i, 554b; ii, 176b, 321b; iv, 765a, 953a, 1073a — I, 572a; II, 182a, 331a; IV, 795b, 985b, 1104b
Turkī b. Fayṣal b. ʿAbd al-ʿAzīz Āl Suʿūd s, 305b — S, 305b
Turkī b. Saʿīd i, 1283a; v, 183b, 1030b; s, 356a — I, 1321b; V, 181a, 1026a; S, 355b
Turkish bath → Ḥammām
Turkistān i, 36a, 72b, 147b, 223b; ii, 477a; iv, 175a; 792a; v, 858a, 859a; s, 51b, 66a, 125a, 143b, 240a — I, 37a, 74b, 152a, 230a; II, 489a; IV, 182b, 824b; V, 865a, 866a; S, 52a, 66b, 124a, 143a, 240a
Türkiye Büyük Millet Meclisi v, 1037b, 1040a — V, 1034a, 1036a
Türkiye Işçi Partisi iv, 124b — IV, 130a
Türkiye Işči ve Čiftči Sosyalist Fîrkasî iv, 123b, 124a — IV, 129a
Türkiye Komünist Partisi iv, 124a — IV, 129a
Türkiye Sosyalist Fîrḳasî iv, 123b, 124b — IV, 129a, b
Türkmen i, 4a, 120b, 224a, 311a, 340a, 420b, 460a, 467a, 470b, 639a, 665b, 666b, 700b, 750b, 843b, 1133b; ii, 1108b, 1117a; iii, 1098b, 1108a, 1110a, 1256b; iv, 10a, 25b, 28b, 1065a; v, 24a, 104a, 145b; s, 49a, 75b, 143b, 146b, 147a, 168b, 280b — I, 4a, 124a, 231a, 320b, 350b, 432b, 473a, 481a, 484b, 659b, 686a, 687a, 722a, 773a, 866b, 1168a; II, 1134b, 1143a; III, 1125a, 1135a, 1137a, 1289b; IV, 10b, 27a, 30b, 1096b; V, 25a, 106b, 148a; S, 49b, 76a, 143a, 146a, 147a, 168b, 280b
Turkomančay ii, 152a; iii, 1191b; iv, 38b, 394b; v, 495b — II, 156b; III, 1221b; IV, 41a, 411b; V, 498b
Turkomānī, Shaykh Süleymān v, 173a — V, 170b
Turks i, 18b, 19b, 20b, 31b, 33a, 55b, 93a, 168a, 174b, 183b, 367b, 893b, 505b; ii, 601a, 980b, 1107a; iv, 671a
Turquie I, 14a, 38b, 40a, 64b, 77a, 246a, 290b, 475b, 756a, 895a, 1002b; II, 609a, b, 656a, 988b; III, 219b; IV, 1b, 822b; V, 467b, 508b; S, 213b
- démographie s, 213b
- éducation V, 911b, 1095a
- ethnographie V, 442a, 756a
- institutions I, 1002b, 1262a; II, 436b, 440b, 708b; III, 544a; IV, 174b; V, 1034a
- langues, littérature II, 485b; III, 385b, 1143a; IV, 727b, 744a, 886b; V, 190a, 221b, 542b, 1096a, 1101a
Turquoise → Fīrūzadj
Turshīz s, 149a — S, 149a
al-Ṭurṭūshī i, 594a, 602a; iv, 136b; v, 1160b — I, 613a, 621b; IV, 142a; V, 1150a
Ṭuruf, Banū iii, 1107b — III, 1134b
Ṭūs v, 293b; s, 14b, 357a — V, 293b; S, 15a, 356b
Tushtarī, Shams al-Dīn Muḥammad i, 703b — I, 725a
al-Ṭūsī → ʿAlī b. ʿAbd Allāh; Naṣīr al-Dīn
al-Ṭūsī, Abū Djaʿfar, Shaykh iv, 711b; s, 56b, 233a — IV, 740b; S, 57a, 233a
al-Ṭūsī, al-Muẓaffar i, 727a — I, 748b
al-Ṭūsī Ḳāniʿī, Aḥmad b. Maḥmūd iv, 504b, 1081a — IV, 526b, 1112a
Tustar → Shustar
al-Tustarī → Ḥasan b. Ibrāhīm
Ṭūsūn b. Muḥammad ʿAlī iii, 362b, 999a; v, 997b — III, 374a, 1024a; V, 993a
Tuṭīla iii, 816a; s, 80a, 81a, 82a — III, 839b; S, 80a, b, 81b
al-Tuṭīlī, al-Aʿmā → al-Aʿmā al-Tuṭīlī
Ṭūṭī-nāma iii, 373a, 376b, 377a; v, 205a — III, 384b, 388a, 389a; V, 202b
Tūtiyā v, 965a, 967b, 970b — V, 969a, 973a
Tūtūn ii, 904b, 909b, 1070a; iv, 39b — II, 925b, 931a, 1094b; IV, 41b
Tütünsüz Aḥmed Beg → Aḥmad Riḍwān
Tutush, Tādj al-Dawla i, 314a, 466a, 517a, 664a, 731a, 751a, 971a, 1051b, 1332a, 1349a; ii, 282a, 347b, 1039a; iii, 86b, 1118a; iv, 27b, 28b; v, 328a, 437a, 924a — I, 324a, 479b, 532b, 683b, 753b, 773a, 1001a, 1083a, 1372b, 1389b; II, 290a, 357a, 1063a; III, 89a, 1145b; IV, 29b, 30b; V, 328a, 439b, 929b
Ṭuwāna i, 11b, 12b — I, 12a, 13a
Tuwāt i, 210b; v, 1165a, b; s, 328a — I, 216b; V, 1155a, b; S, 327b
Ṭuwayḳ i, 536b, 628b, 747b — I, 553a, 649b, 770a
Ṭuways ii, 620b, 1073b; iii, 878b; s, 183a — II, 636a, 1098b; III, 902b; S, 184b
Tuyūl iv, 1044a, 1045b — IV, 1075a, 1076b
Tuz Gölü i, 464b — I, 478a
Tūzar iv, 740a — IV, 769b
Tūzīn, Banū s, 113b — S, 113a
Tūzūn iii, 127b — III, 130a
Twelvers → Ithnā-ʿashariyya
Tyana/Tyane → Ṭuwāna
Tyawka Khān v, 135a — V, 138a
Tyre/Tyr i, 215b; ii, 129b; v, 789a; s, 120b — I, 222a; II, 133a; V, 796a; S, 120a
Tzachas → Čaka

U

U Nu i, 1333b; v, 431a — I, 1273a; V, 433a
U.S.S.R./U.R.S.S. ii, 427a, 476a, 595a — II, 438a, 488b, 609b
ʿUbāda, Banū iv, 911b — IV, 944b
ʿUbāda b. Ṣāmit v, 324b, 590a — V, 324a, 594a
ʿUbayd b. Maʿālī iv, 430a — IV, 449a
ʿUbayd b. Sharya → Ibn Sharya
ʿUbayd Abū Ziyād s, 355a — S, 354b
ʿUbayd Allāh, Shaykh v, 462b; s, 71a — V, 465a; S, 72a
ʿUbayd Allāh b. ʿAbbās i, 41a; iii, 241a, 242a, 617a — I, 42a; III, 248a, 249a, 637b
ʿUbayd Allāh b. ʿAbd Allāh al-Hudhalī s, **311b** — S, **311a**
ʿUbayd Allāh b. Abī Bakra iv, 356b — IV, 372a
ʿUbayd Allāh b. Abī Ṭāhir iii, 693a; iv, 21a — III,

715a; IV, 22b
ʿUbayd Allāh b. Arṭāh i, 399b — I, 411a
ʿUbayd Allāh b. al-Ḥabḥāb i, 439a, 1157b; ii, 328a; iii, 494a — I, 451b, 1192a; II, 337b; III, 511a
ʿUbayd Allāh b. Maḥmūd Shībānī i, 1295b — I, 1335a
ʿUbayd Allāh b. al-Māḥūz i, 810b — I, 833b
ʿUbayd Allāh b. Nabhān ii, 188a — II, 194a
ʿUbayd Allāh b. Samura iii, 717a, b — III, 739b, 740a
ʿUbayd Allāh b. Sulaymān b. Wahb iii, 750a, 892b, 955b; iv, 90b — III, 773a, 916b, 980a; IV, 94b
ʿUbayd Allāh b. ʿUmar iii, 65a, 587a — III, 67b, 607a
ʿUbayd Allāh b. Yaḥyā → Ibn Khākān, ʿUbayd Allāh
ʿUbayd Allāh b. Ziyād i, 3b, 76b, 304a, 337b, 1086a, 1293b; ii, 89b, 759b, 788a; iii, 164b, 226b, 270b, 588a, 608b, 609a, 715a, 882a, 987a, 1254b; iv, 1186b; v, 853b — I, 4a, 78b, 313b, 348a, 1118a, 1333a; II, 91b, 778a, 807a; III, 168a, 233b, 278b, 608a, 629a, b, 737b, 906a, 1011b, 1287b; IV, 1219a; V, 860a
ʿUbayd Allāh Aḥrār, Kh(w)ādja → Aḥrār, Khʷādja ʿUbayd Allāh
ʿUbayd Allāh Khān Özbeg (d./m. 1540) i, 228b, 1067b; iii, 388a; v, 55a; s, 51b, 340a — I, 235b, 1100a; III, 400b; V, 56b; S, 52a, 339b
ʿUbayd Allāh Khān Özbeg (d./m. 1711) v, 273b; s, 97a, 419b — V, 271b; S, 96b, 419b
ʿUbayd Allāh al-Mahdī → al-Mahdī ʿUbayd Allāh
ʿUbayd Allāh Sindhī s, 360a — S, 360a
ʿUbayd al-Ḥarfūsh (Ḥurayfīsh) iii, 206a — III, 212a
ʿUbayd-i Zākāni iii, 355b, 373a, 1208b; iv, 66a, 67b — III, 366b, 385a, 1239a; IV, 69b, 71a
ʿUbayda b. al-Djarrāh ii, 353a; iv, 365a — II, 363a; IV, 381a
ʿUbaydid(e)s iii, 782b; s, 306b — III, 805b; S, 306a
Ubayy b. Kaʿb i, 104b; iv, 1112b; v, 127b, 406a, 407b; s, 227a — I, 107b; IV, 1144b; V, 130a, 407b, 408b; S, 227a
al-Ubayyiḍ v, 267b, 1249b — V, 265a, b, 1240a
al-ʿUbbād i, 137b; iii, 866a; s, 403a — I, 141b; III, 890a; S, 403a
al-ʿUbbādī, Abū ʿAbd Allāh Muḥammad s, 403a — S, 403b
ʿUbey s, 161a — S, 160b
al-Ubrūḳ ii, 340b — II, 350a
Ubulla i, 43b, 1085a; ii, 143a; iii, 1252b — I, 44b, 1117b; II, 147a; III, 1285a
Uččh iii, 443b, 633a; v, 26a, b; s, 10b, 66b — III, 458b, 654a; V, 27a; S, 10a, 67a
Uclés → Uklīdj
ʿŪd v, 646b — V, 650b
ʿŪda, ʿAbd al-Ḳādir iii, 1069b — III, 1096a
ʿUdār ii, 1078b — II, 1103b
Udāya i, 47a; ii, 510b, 820a — I, 48b; II, 523a, 839b
ʿUdhra, Banū ii, 427b, 1031b; v, 317b, 497b — II, 438b, 1055b; V, 317a, 500b
ʿUdhrī ii, 1031a — II, 1055a
al-ʿUdhrī, Aḥmad b. ʿUmar i, 157a; iii, 991b; s, 80a, 92a — I, 161a; III, 1016a; S, 80a, 91b
Udhruḥ → Adhruḥ
Udj ii, 611a, 613a, 1044b — II, 626b, 628a, 1068b
Udj-beyi i, 1118a; ii, 1044b — I, 1152a; II, 1068b
Udjak i, 1217b — I, 1254a
ʿUdjayf b. ʿAnbasa i, 11b — I, 12a
ʿUdjayr b. ʿAbd Allāh al-Salūlī iv, 1002b — IV, 1035a
Udjdjayn ii, 577a; iii, 1155b; v, 297a; s, 105a — II, 591b; III, 1184a; V, 296b; S, 104b
ʿUdjma → ʿAdjam
al-ʿUdjmān i, 545b, 873b; iii, 238b, 1065b — I, 563a, 897b; III, 245a, 1092a
ʿUdūl → ʿAdl
ʿUdwat al-Andalus iii, 1032a — III, 1058a
Uftāde, Muḥyī al-Dīn ii, 542b, 543a; iii, 538b — I, 556a; III, 557a
Uggʷag → Wadjdjādj
Ughānān v, 163a — V, 161a
Ughurlu Muḥammad iv, 588a — IV, 611b
Uguday → Ögedey
Uḥaymir → Aḥmar
ʿUhda ii, 149a — II, 153a
Uhdjiyya v, 807a — V, 812b
Uḥud s, 230a, 351b — S, 230a, 351b
Uigur i, 1240a; iii, 115b, 116a — I, 1278a; III, 118a
Ujiji ii, 58b — II, 59b
ʿUkāsha → ʿUkkāsha
Ukawafi s, 351a — S, 351a
Ukaydir b. ʿAbd al-Malik al-Sakūnī ii, 625a; v, 119b — II, 640b; V, 122a
ʿUḳayl, Banū i, 421a, 442a, 512a, 942a, 1073a, 1356a; ii, 348b; iii, 129a; iv, 27b, 764a, b, 911a; s, 37a, 119a — I, 433a, 454b, 527b, 971a, 1105b, 1395a; II, 358a,; III, 131b; IV, 29b, 794b, 795a, 944a; S, 37b, 118b
ʿUḳayl al-ʿUkbarī i, 116a — I, 119b
al-Uḳayshir al-Asadī iv, 1002b — IV, 1035a
al-Uḳayṣir ii, 1024a — II, 1047b
ʿUkāẓ i, 343a; iii, 760b — I, 353b; III, 783b
ʿUḳba ii, 234b, 235a, 236a — II, 241b, 242a, b
ʿUḳba b. Abī Muʿayṭ i, 115b, 136b; ii, 842b — I, 118b, 140b; II, 862a
ʿUḳba b. al-Ashʿath i, 150b — I, 154b
ʿUḳba b. al-Ḥadjdjādj al-Salūlī i, 76a, 1011b, 1079b — I, 78a, 1043a, 1111b
Uḳba b. Nāfiʿ i, 248b, 367a, 532b, 770a, 1175a, 1221b, 1259b; ii, 575a, 875b, 992a; iii, 667b; iv, 415b, 567a, 739b, 777a, 826a, b, 827a; v, 393a, 518a, 1189a; s, 81b — I, 256a, 377b, 548b, 793a, 1210a, 1258a, 1297b; II, 589b, 896a, 1014b; III, 689a; IV, 433b, 589b, 769b, 808b, 859a, b, 860a; V, 393b, 521b, 1179a; S, 81b
ʿUḳba b. Ruʾba i, 1080b — I, 1113a
ʿUḳba b. Salm i, 45b, 1080b — I, 46b, 1112b
ʿUkbānī, Āl s, 403a — S, 403a
al-ʿUḳbānī, al-Ḳāsim b. Saʿīd iv, 477a; s, 403a — IV, 498a; S, 403b
al-ʿUkbarī → Ibn Baṭṭa
al-Ukbarī, Ismāʿīl iv, 604a — IV, 628a
al-ʿUkbarī, Mīshawayh iv, 604a — IV, 628a
al-ʿUḳbī, Ṭayyib iv, 159b — IV, 166a
Ukhayḍir i, 618a, 831b, 1226b, 1315b; ii, 114a; iii, 1267b; iv, 88b, 384b; s, 115b — I, 637a, 855a, 1264a, 1356a; II, 116b; III, 1300b; IV, 92b, 401a; S, 114b
Ukhayḍir, Banū i, 403a, 551a; iii, 262b — I, 414b, 568b; III, 270a
Ukiyānūs → al-Baḥr al-Muḥīṭ
ʿUḳḳāl → ʿĀḳil
ʿUkkāsha b. ʿAbd al-Ṣamad iv, 1004a — IV, 1036b
ʿUkkāsha b. Ayyūb al-Fazārī iii, 169b; iv, 336b, 826a — III, 173a; IV, 351a, 859a
ʿUkkāz, Bu i, 1247a — I, 1285a
al-ʿUklī, Abu 'l-Wadjīh s, 85b — S, 85a
Uḳlīdish iv, 596a, 600a, 1182a; v, 123a — IV, 620a, 624b, 1215b; V, 126a
al-Uḳlidīsī, Aḥmad b. Ibrāhīm iii, 1139b — III, 1168a
Uklīdj i, 390a — I, 401a
Ukraine v, 260b — V, 258b
Ukshūnuba i, 1339a; ii, 1009a — I, 1379a; II, 1032b
Uḳṣūṣa v, 185b, 187b — V, 183a, 185a
ʿUḳūba i, 186b — I, 192a
ʿUḳūbāt i, 29a — I, 29b
ʿUḳūl mufāriḳa i, 342b — I, 353a
al-ʿUlā v, 497b, 761b — V, 501a, 767b
Ūlād Slīmān iv, 540b, 541a — IV, 564a, b
Ulagh → Ulugh
Ulaghči Khān i, 1187b — I, 1223a
ʿUlah ii, 167b — II, 173a

Ulaḳ v, 838a — V, 844b
ʿUlamāʾ i, 117a, b, 270a, 593a, 742a, 744a, 745b, 838a; iii, 1133b, 1152a, 1153b; iv, 160b, 164b, 167b-168b, 398a, 794b; v, 642b, 1084a — I, 120b, 121a, 278a, 612a, 764b, 766a, 768a, 861a; III, 1161b, 1180b, 1182a; IV, 167a, 171b, 174b-175b, 415a, 826b; V, 646b, 1081b
Ulama Medžlis i, 1274b — I, 1313b, 1314a
al-ʿUlaymī, Mudjīr al-Dīn iii, 161b, 954b; v, 322b — III, 165a, 979a; V, 321b
Ulays, Banu ʾl- iv, 494a — IV, 515a
ʿUlayyān, Āl i, 1312b — I, 1353a
Uldjaytū Khudābanda i, 162a, 347a, 903a, 1031b; ii, 14b, 194a, 1111b; iii, 57b, 390a, 952b, 1122b, 1124b, 1127a; iv, 32a, 48b; v, 554b, 630a; s, 83b — I, 166b, 357b, 930a, 1063a; II, 15a, 200a, 1137b; III, 60a, 402b, 977a, 1150b, 1152b, 1155a; IV, 34a, 51a; V, 559a, 634a; S, 83b
Ulèëbalangs i, 741a, 742a, 744a, 744b, 745b, 747a — I, 763a, 764b, 766a, 766b, 768a, 769b
Ulema/Uléma → ʿUlamāʾ
al-ʿUlthī, Isḥāḳ b. Aḥmad iii, 161a — III, 164b
Ūlū ʾl-amr iv, 153a, 154a, 156b — IV, 159b, 160b, 163a
ʿUlūdj ʿAlī iii, 94b; v, 726b — III, 97a; V, 731b
Ulugh Beg b. Abī Saʿīd iv, 357a — IV, 372b
Ulugh Beg b. Shāh Rukh i, 227b, 393a, 1295b; ii, 399a, 586b; iii, 1137b; iv, 584a, 702b; v, 858b — I, 234a, 404b, 1335a; II, 409b, 601a; III, 1166a; IV, 607b, 731a; V, 865b
Ulugh Bilge Iḳbāl Khān i, 767a — I, 790a
Ulugh Khān iii, 16a — III, 16b
Ulugh Khān, Almas Beg i, 506b, 1193a; ii, 597a, 1124a; iv, 922a — I, 522a, 1228b; II, 612a, 1150b; IV, 955a
al-Ulugh-Khānī, al-Āṣafī i, 561b, 595a; s, 335b — I, 579a, 614b; S, 335a
Ulugh Khān-i Aʿẓam i, 217b; ii, 609b — I, 224a; II, 624b
Ulugh Muḥammad i, 1252b, 1308a; ii, 44b; iii, 44a; iv, 849a — I, 1290b, 1348b; II, 45a; III, 46a; IV, 882a
Ulugh Noyon i, 1010b — I, 1042a
ʿUlyā Ḥaḍrat s, 65b — S, 66a
ʿUlyāʾiyya i, 1082a, 1096a — I, 1114b, 1129a
Umāma bint Abi ʾl-ʿĀs i, 400b — I, 412a
ʿUmān i, 73a, 110b, 132a, 140b, 141b, 211b, 535a, 539b, 545a, 551b, 552a, 555a, 811b, 928a, 1013b, 1281b, 1283a, 1354b; ii, 592b; iii, 652a; iv, 500b, 777b, 807b, 1130b; v, 507a, 1059a; s, 42a, 118b, 178a, 222b, 234b, 332a, b, 338a, 355a, 417a — I, 75a, 113b, 136a, 145a, b, 217b, 551b, 556a, 562a, 569a, b, 572b, 834b, 956a, 1044b, 1321a, b, 1393b; II, 607a; III, 673a; IV, 522a, 809a, 840a, 1162a; V, 510b, 1055b; S, 42b, 118a, 178a, 223a, 234a, 331b, 332a, b, 337b, 355a, 417b
ʿUmar (Timūrid(e)) iv, 586a — IV, 609a
ʿUmar II b. ʿAbd al-ʿAzīz(Umayyad(e)) i, 53b, 117a, 181b, 257b, 305a, 435a, 729b, 966b; ii, 36a, 72b, 198a, 227b, 304b, 327b, 480a, 561a, 622b, 726a; iii, 228a, 428b, 650a, 674b; iv, 369b, 742a, 939a, 997a; v, 53a, 590b, 923a, 1124a, 1231b; s, 41a, 52b, 311b, 358a — I, 55a, 120b, 186b, 265b, 314b, 447b, 751b, 996a; II, 36b, 73b, 204b, 234b, 313a, 337b, 492a, 575a, 638a, 145a; III, 234b, 442b, 671a, 696a; IV, 386a, 772a, 972a, 1029b; V, 54b, 594a, 928b, 1120b, 1222a; S, 41a, 53a, 311a, 358a
ʿUmar I b. al-Khaṭṭāb i, 9a, 12a, 52a, 104b, 110a, 129a, 145b, 158b, 188a, 337b, 343b, 381b, 382a, 445a, 545b, 549b, 687a, 718a, 729a, 738a, 932a, 1085a, 1141a, b, 1143b, 1215b, 1343b; ii, 77b, 159b, 190b, 232a, 304b, 323b, 360a, 454b, 725b, 842b, 888b, 1006a, 1056a; iii, 64a, 65a, 586b; iv, 14a, 270b, 316b, 320b, 365a, 386a, 927b, 928b, 937b, 995b, 1140b, 1142a; v, 324a; s, 48b, 89b, 129b, 130a, 198b, 343a — I, 9a, 12a, 53b, 107b, 113a, 133a, 150a, 163a, 193b, 348a, 354a, 392b, 393a, 458a, 562b, 567a, 707b, 739b, 751a, 760a, 960b, 1117b, 1175b, 1176a, 1178a, 1251b, 1384a; II, 79a, 164b, 196b, 239a, 313a, 333a, 370a, 466a, b, 744b, 862a, 909b, 1029b, 1080b; III, 66b, 67b, 606b; IV, 15a, 282b, 330b, 335a, 381a, 403a, 960b, 961b, 970b, 1028a, 1172b, 1173b; V, 323b; S, 49a, 89a, 129a, 198b, 343a
ʿUmar, Banū iii, 299b — III, 309a
ʿUmar b. ʿAbd al-ʿAzīz → ʿUmar II (Umayyad(e))
ʿUmar b. ʿAbd al-Muʾmin i, 160b — I, 165a
ʿUmar b. Abī Bakr ii, 1004a — II, 1027b
ʿUmar b. Abī Rabīʿa i, 10b, 305a, 566a; ii, 427b, 428b, 1011b, 1029b, 1030b; iii, 682a; iv, 488b, 1008b, s, 10a — I, 10b, 314b, 584a; II, 438b, 439b, 1035a, 1053a, 1054b; III, 704a; IV, 509b, 1040b; S, 9b
ʿUmar b. Abi ʾl-Ṣalt iv, 207b; v, 541a — IV, 217a; V, 545b
ʿUmar b. ʿAlī (Rasūlid(e)) i, 553a; v, 1241a — I, 570b; V, 1231b
ʿUmar b. Bāyazīd Anṣārī i, 1123a, b — I, 1157a, b
ʿUmar b. al-Fāriḍ → Ibn al-Fāriḍ
ʿUmar b. Ḥafṣ (Hazārmard(e)) i, 125a — I, 128b
ʿUmar b. Ḥafṣ al-Ballūṭī → Abū Ḥafs ʿUmar al-Ballūṭī
ʿUmar b. Ḥafṣūn i, 83b, 494a, 997a, 1150a, 1300b, 1343a; ii, 516a, 915b, 1012b; iii, 785a, 842a; iv, 254b, 534a; v, 376b, 1243b; s, 152b — I, 86a, 509a, 1027b, 1184a, b, 1340a, 1383b; II, 528b, 937a, 1036a; III, 808b, 865b; IV, 265b, 557b; V, 377a, 1234a; S, 152b
ʿUmar b. Hāniʾ al-ʿAnsī iv, 370a — IV, 386a
ʿUmar b. al-Ḥubāb al-Sulamī iv, 870b — IV, 904a
ʿUmar b. Idrīs II ii, 874a; iii, 1035b — II, 894a; III, 1061b
ʿUmar b. Īmkaten iii, 654a — III, 675a
ʿUmar b. Ismāʿīl al-Hawwārī iii, 299b — III, 309a
ʿUmar b. al-Ḳāsim al-Nashshār i, 105b — I, 108b
ʿUmar b. al-Khaṭṭāb → ʿUmar I (Umayyad(e))
ʿUmar b. Muḥammad al-Kanemī i, 1260a; v, 357b, 358a — I, 1298a; V, 359a
ʿUmar b. al-Nuʿmān i, 361b, 363a; ii, 238a — I, 372b, 374a; II, 245a
ʿUmar b. Ramaḍān al-Thalātī i, 121b — I, 125a
ʿUmar b. Riyāḥ s, 129b — S, 129a
ʿUmar b. Rubayʿān → Ibn Rubayʿān
ʿUmar b. Saʿd b. Abī Waḳḳāṣ iii, 588a, 609b, 611a; iv, 836a — III, 608a, 630a, 632a; IV, 869a
ʿUmar b. Shabba i, 158b; v, 607b; s, 38b — I, 163a; V, 611b; S, 39a
ʿUmar b. Sulaymān al-Shayẓamī → ʿUmar al-Sayyāf
ʿUmar b. ʿUbayd Allāh b. Maʿmar i, 120a, 810a, 1242b — I, 123b, 833b, 1280b
ʿUmar b. Yūsuf b. Rasūl iii, 267a — III, 274b
ʿUmar Agha Ḳara ʿOthmān-oghlu iv, 593a, b — IV, 617a, b
ʿUmar Efendi i, 1271b; ii, 20a — I, 1310b; II, 20a
ʿUmar Fākhūrī s, 224b — S, 224b
ʿUmar Fatḥī s, 301a — S, 300b
ʿUmar Khān b. Nārbūta v, 29b — V, 30a, b
ʿUmar Khān Avar i, 755b — I, 778a
ʿUmar Khān Kāsī ii, 54b; s, 313a — II, 55b; S, 312b
ʿUmar Khān Sarwānī → ʿAbbās Sarwānī
ʿUmar al-Khayyām i, 113a, 839a, 841a, 1132a; ii, 362a, 397b, 533b; iii, 1139a; iv, 54a, 62a, 64a; s, 35a, 235b, 412a, 413a, b, 414a — I, 116a, 862b, 864a, 1166a; II, 371b, 408b, 546b; III, 1167a; IV, 57a, 65b, 67b; S, 35a, 235b, 412a, 413a, b, 414b
ʿUmar al-Mukhtār v, 758a — V, 764a
ʿUmar al-Mutawakkil i, 242b; iii, 680b, 813b — I, 250a; III, 702a, 837a

ʿUmar Nasuhī Bilmen → Bilmen
ʿUmar Pas͟ha (1678) i, 905a — I, 932a
ʿUmar Pas͟ha (1764) i, 199a, 905a — I, 204b, 932b
ʿUmar Pas͟ha Latas i, 1268b — I, 1307b
ʿUmar al-Rūs͟hanī ii, 1136b, 1137a, b; iv, 991b; s, 208a — II, 1163a, 1164a, b; IV, 1024a; S, 208a
ʿUmar al-Sayyāf ii, 527b — II, 540b
ʿUmar Seyf al-Dīn ii, 440a; iii, 357b; iv, 636b; s, 55a, 98b, 282a — II, 451b; III, 368b; IV, 662b; S, 55b, 98a, 282a
ʿUmar Shāh, S͟hihāb al-Dīn ii, 269a; iv, 419b, 923b — II, 277b; IV, 437b, 956b
ʿUmar al-Shayk͟h ii, 1003b — II, 1026b
ʿUmar S͟hayk͟h Ibn Tīmūr i, 148a, 847b; ii, 792a — I, 152b, 870b; II, 810b
ʿUmar Tal → al-Ḥād͟jd͟j ʿUmar
ʿUmar al-Ẓāhir → Ẓāhir al-ʿUmar
ʿUmāra, Banū s, 222b — S, 222b
ʿUmāra b.ʿAlī al-Ḥakamī i, 197a, 552b, 593b — I, 202b, 570a, 613a
ʿUmāra b. ʿAmr i, 113b — I, 116b
Umarāʾ al-ulus i, 1159b — I, 1194a
ʿUmāra al-Yamanī ii, 861b; iii, 814b; v, 1244a — II, 881b; III, 838b; V, 1235a
al-ʿUmarī iii, 616a, 617a — III, 636b, 637b
al-ʿUmarī, ʿAbd al-Raḥmān i, 1158a — I, 1192b
al-ʿUmarī, Aḥmad → Ibn Faḍl Allāh
al-ʿUmariyya i, 1009a; iii, 659b — I, 1040a; III, 681a
Umaru Bakatara ii, 1146b — II, 1173b
Umaru Salaga iv, 550b — IV, 574a
ʿUmayr b. Bayān al-ʿId͟jlī iv, 1132b — IV, 1164a
ʿUmayr b. Ḥubāb al-Sulamī ii, 1023b; iii, 819b; iv, 493a, 1186b — II, 1047b; III, 843a; IV, 514b, 1219a
Umayya b. ʿAbd Allāh b. K͟hālid i, 148b, 1293a — I, 153a, 1333a
Umayya b. Abi 'l-Ṣalt i, 44b, 418a, 565a, 584b; iii, 165b, 541b, 975b, 1206a; v, 180b; s, 247a — I, 46a, 429b, 583a, 603b; III, 169a, 560a, 1000a, 1236b; V, 178a; S, 247a
Umayya b. K͟halaf i, 1215a — I, 1251a
Umayyad(e)s i, 16a, 43a, 45a, 49a, 51b, 55b, 76a, 103a, 439b, 550a, 920a; ii, 360a; iv, 15b-16a; v, 736a; s, 103b, 116b, 396b — I, 16b, 44a, 46b, 50b, 53a, 57a, 78b, 106a, 452a, 567b, 947b; II, 370a; IV, 16b-17a; V, 741b; S, 102b, 116a, 397a
- administration ii, 304b, 323b; iv, 755b, 938a — II, 313a, 333a; IV, 785b, 971a
- constructions i, 609b, 612b; ii, 280b, 821b; v, 10b-16b, 17a, 216b, 325b — I, 629b, 632b; II, 288b, 841a; V, 11a-17a, 17b, 214a, 325a, b
- literature/littérature i, 118a, 760a — I, 121b, 782b
Umbay Ïnaḳ s, 420a — S, 420a
ʿUmdat al-mulk iv, 758b — IV, 789a
Umīdī iv, 68b — IV, 72a
Umm ʿĀṣim i, 58b — I, 60b
Umm al-Banīn i, 400b; ii, 1023b — I, 412a; II, 1047a
Umm Dubaykarāt i, 50a — I, 51b
Umm al-Faḍl i, 713a — I, 734b
Umm G͟harayāt i, 418a — I, 430a
Umm Ḥabīb i, 400b — I, 412a
Umm Ḥabība i, 151a; iv, 927b — I, 155b; IV, 960b
Umm al-Ḥasan Fāṭima bint al-Ḥasan s, 334b — S, 334b
Umm al-Ḳaywayn s, 416b — S, 417a
Umm al-Kitāb i, 89b; ii, 849a; iv, 203a — I, 92a; II, 869a; IV, 212a
Umm Kult͟hūm bint ʿAlī i, 109b, 136b, 308b; ii, 843a; iii, 889a; s, 13b — I, 112b, 140b, 318a; II, 863a; III, 913a; S, 14a
Umm Mūsā iv, 637b; s, 94a — IV, 663b; S, 93b
Umm Rūmān bint ʿĀmir i, 109b, 110a, 307b — I, 112b, 113a, 317a
Umm Salāma i, 258a, 308a; ii, 846a; iii, 64a, 612b; iv, 927a; s, 230b — I, 266a, 317b; II, 866a; III, 66b, 633b; IV, 960a; S, 230b
Umm S͟harīḳ bint ʿAṣar al-ʿUḳaylī s, 394a — S, 394b
Umm Walad i, 28a, 75b; iv, 253a; iv, 253a — I, 29a, 78a; IV, 264a
Umm Zaynab iii, 954b — III, 979a
Umma ii, 411a; iv, 785b, 1154b — II, 422a; IV, 817a, 1186b
Umma K͟hān Avar i, 755b; ii, 87b — I, 778a; II, 89a
ʿUmmāl → ʿĀmil
Ummarār i, 1158b, 1239b — I, 1193a, 1277b
ʿUmra ii, 304a; iii, 35a, 1052b — II, 312b; III, 36b, 1078b
ʿUmrā iii, 351a — III, 362a
ʿUmrā K͟hān ii, 30b, 317a — II, 31a, 326a
al-ʿUmud i, 95a, 772a — I, 97b, 795a
Ümür I Aydînog͟hlu i, 346a, 653b, 783a, 1302b; ii, 683b, 983b; iii, 115a, 1086a; v, 505b, 506a; s, 330a — I, 356b, 674a, 806b, 1342b; II, 700b, 1006a; III, 117b, 1113a; V, 509a; S, 329b
Ümür II Aydînog͟hlu i, 783b; ii, 599a — I, 806b; II, 614a
Ümür Beg/Pas͟ha → Ümür I Aydînog͟hlu
Ümür Beg Timūrtāshog͟hlu v, 250a — V, 248a
Umūr-i ḥisbī iii, 491a, b — III, 508a, b
ʿUnāza (ʿUnayza) i, 534a, 1312b; iv, 717a — I, 550a, 1352b; IV, 746a
Uncle → ʿAmm; K͟hāl
Union arabe → al-Ittiḥād al-ʿarabī
Union of Arab Banks/Union des Banques Arabes s, 241a — S, 241a
Union of Chambers of Arab Commerce, Industry and Agriculture/Union des Chambres de Commerce, d'Industrie et d'Agriculture s, 241a — S, 241a
Union islamique → Ittiḥād-i Muḥammedī D͟jemʿiyyeti
Union Socialiste Arabe S, 7b, 8b
United Arab Emirates → al-Imārāt al-ʿArabiyya al-Muttaḥida
United Arab Republic → al-D͟jumhūriyya al-ʿarabiyya al-muttaḥida
Universities/Universités → D͟jāmiʿa
Unḳaliyyīn, Unḳūriyya → Mad͟jar
Ūnsa, King/le roi ii, 944a, b — II, 965b, 966a
ʿUnṣur iii, 329b — III, 339b
ʿUnṣurī iv, 61a, 62b; s, 21b — IV, 64b, 66a; S, 22a
Unūd͟jūr iii, 129a; iv, 418a, b — III, 132a; IV, 436b
ʿUnwān ii, 314b — II, 324a
Upanis͟had(e)s ii, 135a; iii, 436b — II, 138a; III, 450b
Ūparkōt ii, 597b, 598a — II, 612b, 613a
Ura Tübe v, 29b, 30a; s, 228a — V, 30b, 31a; S, 228a
ʿUrābī Pas͟ha i, 141b, 142a, 815a, 1070a; ii, 28a, 417b, 514b; iii, 514a, 515a; s, 132b, 408b, 411b — I, 146a, 838b, 1102a; II, 28a, 428b, 527a; III, 531b, 532b; S, 132a, 408b, 411b
ʿUrāʿir, Day of/Journée de s, 178a — S, 179a
Urang Temür ii, 1112a; iv, 868a — II, 1138a; IV, 901b
ʿUrayʿir, Banū iv, 925a, b — IV, 958a, b
Uraz Muḥammad K͟hān iv, 724a — IV, 753a
al-Urbus i, 104a, 163a, 250b; iv, 403a — I, 107a, 168a, 258b; IV, 420b
Urdu i, 430b, 505b, 807b, 827b; ii, 101a, 490b, 797a, 1036a; iii, 1b, 93b, 119a, 358b, 375b, 413a, 460b, 536b, 1057a, 1244b; iv, 716b; v, 201a, 635b, 958a, 1106a; s, 247a, 358b — I, 442b, 521a, 830b, 850b; II, 103b, 503a, 815b, 1060a; III, 1b, 96a, 121b, 369b, 387b, 426a, 477a, 555a, 1083b, 1276b; IV, 745a; V, 198b, 639b, 962a, 1102a; S, 247a, 358b
Urdumāniyyūn i, 83a, 494a; v, 1119b — I, 85b, 509a;

V, 1116a
Urdunn i, 39a, 46a, 534a, 975b; ii, 662b; iii, 264a, 560a, b; iv, 262a; v, 337b, 912a, 1053b; s, 251b — I, 40a, 47a, b, 550a, 1005b; II, 679a; III, 272a, 579b, 580a; IV, 273b; V, 338a, 917b, 1050b; S, 251b
- west bank/rive occidentale v, 1054b, 1055a — V, 1051a, 1052a
ʿUrf i, 170a; ii, 146b, 890b, 1087a; iv, 560b — I, 174b; II, 150b, 911a, 1112b; IV, 583a
Urfa v, 453a — V, 455b
ʿUrfī i, 680a; ii, 794b, 878a; iv, 69a; v, 958a — I, 701a; II, 813a, 898b; IV, 72b; V, 962a
Urganč, Urgandj → Gurgandj
Urīṭ iv, 482b — IV, 503b
al-Urmawī, Ṣafī al-Dīn s, 408b, 409a — S, 409a
Urmiyā → Irmiyā
Urmiya, Lake/Lac i, 191a; iii, 569b — I, 196b; III, 589a
ʿUrr ʿAdan → ʿAdan
ʿUrūḳ al-Rumayla ii, 92a — II, 93b, 94a
Urumchi v, 846a, b — V, 858a
Urus Khān ii, 44a — II, 45a
Urus Mīrzā i, 1075b — I, 1108a
Uruzgān s, 367a — S, 367b
ʿUrwa b. Masʿūd iv, 839a — IV, 872a
ʿUrwa b. Udayya iii, 169a — III, 172b
ʿUrwa b. al-Ward al-ʿAbsī i, 518b; ii, 1072b; iii, 941a — I, 534a; II, 1097a; III, 965b
ʿUrwa b. al-Zubayr i, 867b; iii, 24a; iv, 189b; v, 997b; s, **311a** — I, 892a; III, 25a; IV, 198a; V, 993a; S, **311a**
ʿUrwa al-Raḥḥāl ii, 883b; iii, 285b; v, 101b — II, 904a; III, 294b; V, 103b
al-ʿUrwa al-wuthḳā ii, 429a — II, 440b
Uşak s, 137b — S, 137a
al-Usāma i, 682b — I, 703b
Usāma b. Munḳidh i, 9b, 570b, 593b, 665b, 680b, 1153b; ii, 64b, 318a, 739a, 740b, 1037a, 1065b; iii, 809a; iv, 514a; v, 9a, 330b; s, 205a, 362a — I, 9b, 589b, 613a, 686a, 701b, 1188a; II, 65b, 327a, 757b, 759a, 1061b, 1090b; III, 832b; IV, 536b; V, 9b, 330b; S, 204b, 362a
Usāma b. Zayd i, 110b, 382b; ii, 327b; v, 1161b — I, 113b, 393b; II, 337b; V, 1151a
Usayd b. Ḥuḍayr i, 514b — I, 530b
Usays s, 117a, 229a — S, 116a, 229a
ʿUṣfūr al-Azdī iv, 796b — IV, 828b
ʿUṣfūrid(e)s i, 553a, 942b; iv, 764b — I, 570b, 971b; IV, 795a
Ushāḳī-zāde iv, 930a — IV, 963a
al-Ushbūna i, 1338b — I, 1379a
Ushmūm i, 126a — I, 129b
al-Ushnāndānī, Abū ʿUthmān iii, 757a — III, 780a
ʿUshr i, 656a, b, 1142a, 1144a; ii, 142b, 146b, 154a; iv, 1037a; v, 872a — I, 677a, 1176b, 1178b; II, 146a, 150b, 158b; IV, 1069a; V, 878a
Ushrūsana i, 241a; s, 406b — I, 248b; S, 406b
Uskāf Banī Djunayd iii, 1267a — III, 1300a
Üsküb i, 698a, 1263a — I, 719b, 1301b
Üsküdār iii, 216b, 220a, 623a; iv, 233a, 244a, 720a, 1017a; v, 273a; s, 315a — III, 223a, 226b, 644a; IV, 243a, 255a, 749a, 1049a; V, 271a; S, 315a
Uslūdj b. al-Ḥasan ii, 860a; iii, 840b — II, 879b; III, 864b
Usman dan Fodio → ʿUthmān b. Fūdī
Ūsmī ii, 87a, 88a, 141b; iv, 846b — II, 88b, 90a, 145b; IV, 879b
Ustādh i, 898b; v, 1131a — I, 925b; V, 1127a
al-Ustādh al-aʿẓam i, 829a — I, 852a
Ustādh-Hurmuz iii, 244b — III, 251b
Ustādhdār i, 33a, 801b — I, 34a, 825a
Ustadhsīs iii, 177b; iv, 16b; v, 1111b — III, 181b; IV, 17b; V, 1107b
Ustādjlū (tribe/tribu) iii, 1101b, 1105a — III, 1128b, 1132b
Ustān v, 398a — V, 399a
Ustolnī Belghrād → Istōnī (Istolnī) Belghrād
Usṭūl s, 120a — S, 119b
Usṭūra iii, 369a — III, 381a
Uṣūl i, 170a, 671a, b, 1053b, 1144a; ii, 78b, 182b, 889b; iii, 182a, 550a — I, 174b, 691b, 692b, 1085a, 1178b; II, 80a, 188b, 910a; III, 186a, 569a
Uṣūl al-dīn i, 92a; ii, 295b; iv, 278b — I, 94b; II, 303b; IV, 290b
Uṣūl al-khamsa s, 225b — S, 225b
Uṣūlī s, 83a — S, 83a
Uṣūlīs iv, 50a; s, 103b — IV, 53a; S, 103a
Uṣūliyya s, 56b, 95b — S, 57a, 95a
Usuman iv, 550a — IV, 574a
Usuoghullarî s, 282b — S, 282a
Uswān v, 514b, 887a; s, 7a, 8b, 35b, 36a, 57b — V, 518a, 893a; S, 6b, 8a, 36a, 58a
al-Uswārī, Abū ʿAlī iv, 734b — IV, 764a
al-Uswārī, Mūsā b. Sayyār iv, 734b — IV, 764a
Ūsya iii, 1154b — III, 1183a
ʿUṭārid b. Ḥādjib iii, 49a — III, 51a
ʿUṭārid b. Muḥammad i, 87a — I, 89b
ʿUtayba i, 545b, 1247b; ii, 354a; iii, 1065b — I, 563a, 1285b; II, 363b; III, 1092a
ʿUtayba b. Abū Lahab i, 136b — I, 140b
ʿUtayba b. al-Ḥārith i, 1247b — I, 1285b
ʿUṭayf b. Niʿma iv, 493b — IV, 515a
ʿUtba i, 107b; iv, 1164b — I, 110b; IV, 1196b
ʿUtba (ʿUtūb), Banū i, 482b — I, 497a
ʿUtba b. Abū Lahab i, 136b — I, 140b
ʿUtba b. Farḳad al-Sulamī v, 896b — V, 903a
ʿUtba b. Ghazwān i, 1085a; iii, 583a; v, 80b; s, 354b — I, 1117b; III, 603a; V, 82b; S, 354b
ʿUtba b. Ḳays b. Zuhayr al-ʿAbsī s, 177b — S, 178b
al-ʿUtbī (d./m. 869) i, 600a — I, 619b
al-ʿUtbī (d./m. 1035) i, 591b — I, 611a
al-ʿUtbī, Abu 'l-Ḥusayn (Samānid(e)) s, 72b, 265b — S, 73a, 265b
ʿUthmān I, II, III (Ottoman) → ʿOthmān I, II, III
ʿUthmān II Abū Saʿīd iii, 909a; s, 112b — III, 933b; S, 112a
ʿUthmān, Abū ʿUmar i, 1152b; ii, 540a; iii, 69a — I, 1186b; II, 553b; III, 71b
ʿUthmān, Sayyid iii, 457a — III, 473a
ʿUthmān b. ʿAbd Allāh b. Bishr iii, 103a — III, 105b
ʿUthmān b. Abi 'l-ʿĀṣ i, 695b; ii, 811b, 823b; iv, 14b — I, 716b; II, 831a, 843a; IV, 15b
ʿUthmān b. Abī Bakr → ʿUthmān Digna
ʿUthmān b. Abī Yūsuf → ʿUthmān II (Marīnid(e))
ʿUthmān b. ʿAffān i, 43b, 51b, 52a, 92b, 93a, 114b, 195a, 308a, 336b, 381b, 382a, 451b, 549b, 704a, 957b; ii, 414a, 1023b; iii, 240b, 272a, 539a, 583a, 587a, 1163b; iv, 937b; v, 405a, 996b; s, 10a, 89b, 129b, 130a, 131a, 198b, 221b, 230b, 304b, 343a — I, 44b, 53a, 53b, 95b, 118a, 200b, 317b, 347a, 392b, 393a, 464b, 567a, 725b, 987a; II, 425a, 1047a; III, 247b, 279b, 558a, 603a, 607a, 1192a; IV, 970b; V, 406b, 992a; S, 9b, 89b, 129a, 130a, 198b, 221b, 230b, 304b, 343a
ʿUthmān b. Aḥmad → ʿUthmān b. Muʿammar
ʿUthmān b. Čaḳmaḳ ii, 6b; iii, 1198a — II, 6b; III, 1228b
ʿUthmān b. Fūdī i, 179b, 303a; ii, 941b, 942a, 1003b, 1144b; iii, 276b; iv, 549b; v, 394b, 1166a — I, 184b, 312b; II, 963b, 1027a, 1172a; III, 284b; IV, 573b; V, 395b, 1155b
ʿUthmān b. Ḥayyān i, 113a — I, 116b
ʿUthmān b. Ḥunayf ii, 415a; iii, 583a — II, 425b; III, 603a
ʿUthmān b. Ḳaṭan iii, 715b — III, 738a
ʿUthmān b. Maẓʿūn i, 957b; ii, 1060a; iii, 1017b; iv,

1089a — I, 987a; II, 1084b; III, 1043a; IV, 1120b
ʿUthmān b. Muʿammar ii, 321a; iii, 678a; iv, 925a — II, 330b; III, 700a; IV, 958a
ʿUthmān b. Saʿīd i, 713a; iii, 247a — I, 734b; III, 254a
ʿUthmān b. Ṭalḥa iii, 975b; iv, 320b — III, 1000a; IV, 334b
ʿUthmān b. al-Walīd II iii, 990b — III, 1015a
ʿUthmān Ādam v, 267b, 1250b — V, 265b, 1241a
ʿUthmān Āghā Mustaḥfiẓān iv, 438a — IV, 457b
ʿUthmān ʿAlī Khān ii, 99b; iii, 323a — II, 101b; III, 332b
ʿUthmān al-Battī v, 731a — V, 736a
ʿUthmān Bey al-Bardīsī ii, 292b; iv, 853a — II, 300b; IV, 886a
ʿUthmān Bey Dhuʾl-Faḳār iv, 852a, b — IV, 885b
ʿUthmān Dāy i, 496a, b; ii, 161a; iv, 338b — I, 511a; II, 166a; IV, 352b
ʿUthmān Digna (Diḳna) i, 49b, 1158b, 1239b; iv, 687a; v, 1249b, 1250a, 1251a — I, 51a, 1193a, 1277b; IV, 715a; V, 1240a, 1241a, b
ʿUthmān al-Djāzānī ii, 517b — II, 530b
ʿUthmān dan Fodio → ʿUthmān b. Fūdī
ʿUthmān al-Ḥaddād v, 51a — V, 52b
ʿUthmān Katkhudā al-Kazdughlī i, 815a — I, 838a
ʿUthmān Khān (Djālor) ii, 1127a — II, 1153b
ʿUthmān Khān b. Ibrāhīm iii, 1115a; iv, 583a, 1067b, 1068a — III, 1142b; IV, 607a, 1099b
ʿUthmān-i Marandī → Shāhbāz Ḳalandar
ʿUthmān al-Muḍāʾifī iii, 363b — III, 375a
ʿUthmān al-Nābalusī → al-Nābalūsī
ʿUthmān Pasha → ʿOthmān Pasha
ʿUthmān Shaykh al-Dīn v, 1250b, 1251b, 1252a — V, 1241b, 1242b, 1242b
ʿUthmān al-Zandjīlī i, 181b; s, 338a — I, 186b; S, 337b
ʿUthmānid(e)s iv, 89b — IV, 93b
ʿUthmānzāde iv, 505a — IV, 527a
ʿUthmānzay s, 285a — S, 285a
al-ʿUṭrūsh → Ḥasan al-Uṭrūsh
Utsmi → Ūsmī
Uttar Pradesh s, 74a, 325a, 360a — S, 74b, 324b, 359b
al-ʿUtūb iv, 751a — IV, 781a
Uwāl iv, 664a, b — IV, 690b, 691a
Uwaym b. Lāwudh (Lud) iii, 1270a — III, 1303a
ʿUwaymir b. Ḥārith v, 730b — V, 736a
ʿUways → Aʿyāṣ
Uways I b. Ḥasan Buzurg i, 325a, 720a, 1096a; ii, 401a, 733b; iv, 584b — I, 335a, 741b, 1129a; II, 411b, 752a; IV, 608a
Uways b. Muḥammad b. Baykarā i, 148a — I, 152a
al-ʿUyayna i, 628b; ii, 321a; iii, 677b, 678a — I, 649b; II, 330b; III, 699a, 700a
ʿUyayna b. Ḥiṣn al-Fazārī i, 690a, 1077b, 1358b; ii, 873b, 1023a; v, 79b — I, 711a, 1110a, 1398b; II, 893b, 1047a; V, 81b
Uyghur ii, 2b, 311a, 315b, 840a, 1106b; iii, 217a, 1116a; iv, 699b; v, 846a, b; s, 97b, 419a, 420a — II, 2b, 320a, 324b, 859b, 1133a; III, 223b, 1143a; IV, 727b, 728a; V, 858a; S, 97a, 419b, 420a
Uyrat → Kalmuks
ʿUyūn Mūsā i, 788a — I, 811b
ʿUyūnid(e)s i, 73b, 552a, 553a, 942a; iii, 238a; iv, 764b — I, 76a, 570a, b, 971a; III, 245a; IV, 795a
Uyvar s, 171a — S, 171b
Ūzār → Ong Khān
ʿUzayr i, 265a; s, 33b — I, 273a; S, 33b
al-ʿUẓayyim ʾal-ʿAḍaym
ʿUzayyiz b. Fayṣal iii, 1067b, 1068a — III, 1094b
Uzbek → Özbeg
Uzbekistān i, 531a — I, 547a
Uzuk ii, 806a — II, 825b
Uzun Ḥasan i, 148b, 244a, 293a, 311b, 340a, 393a, 468b, 861b, 1067a, 1234a, 1252b; ii, 150a, 151a, 174a, 598b, 839b, 1136a; iii, 212b, 315b, 1101a; iv, 34a, 463a, 474a, 562b, 588a, 871a, 945a, 1048a; v, 492a; s, 208a — I, 152b, 251a, 302a, 321a, 350b, 404b, 482a, 885b, 1099a, 1270b, 1290b; II, 154b, 155b, 179b, 613b, 859b, 1163a; III, 218b, 325a, 1128a; IV, 36b, 483b, 495a, 585a, 611b, 904b, 978a, 1079b; V, 495a; S, 208a
Uzun Khalīl i, 1257a — I, 1295a
al-ʿUzzā iv, 321b; v, 692a, b — IV, 336a; V, 697a, b

V

Vahrām → Bahrām
Vakf-Mearif i, 1274b — I, 1313b
Vakhtang (d. 1676) → Shāh Nawāz I
Vakhtang (d. 1724) v, 493b, 494a — V, 496b
Valachie → Eflāḳ
Valencia/Valence → Balansiya
Valenia → Bāniyās
Vālide Djāmiʿi → Yeni Djāmiʿ
Valona → Awlonya
Van (lake/lac) i, 627a, 634b, 637b, 638a, 644a, 1207a; ii, 34a; v, 441a, 442a, b; s, 130b — I, 647b, 655b, 658a, 658b, 664b, 1242b; II, 34b; V, 443b, 444b; S, 129b
Van Ḳaraḥiṣārî iv, 580b — IV, 604a
Van Kulu ii, 497a — II, 509a
Vannerie → Ḥalfāʾ
Varvar ʿAlī Pasha iii, 318a, 983b; v, 257a — III, 327b, 1008a; V, 254b
Vasak i, 939b — I, 968a
Vaspurakan i, 637b, 638a — I, 658a, 658b
Vasvár, treaty of/traité de v, 259b — V, 257b
Vautour → Humā
Vāv i, 1024a — I, 1055b
Vayu iv, 11b — IV, 12b
Veda iii, 112b; iv, 206a — III, 115a; IV, 215b
Végétaux → Nabāt
Veil → Ḥidjāb; Lithām
Velez/Vélez → Bālish
Venetians/Vénitiens iv, 225a, 228a; v, 257b, 260a, 270b, 304a, 727b — IV, 235a, 238a; V, 255a, 258a, 268b, 303a, b, 732b
Venice/Venise i, 269a, 654a, 654b, 1008a, 1120a; iii, 214a, 1086a, 1182b, 1183a, 1184a — I, 277b, 674b, 675a, 1039a, 1153b; III, 220b, 1113a, 1212a, b, 1213a
Vente → Bayʿ
Vente, Contrat de → Bayʿ
Ventilation Shaft → Bādgīr
Ventouseur → Faṣṣād; Ḥadjdjām
Vernāg s, 366b — S, 366a, b
Verne s, 136a — S, 135b
Verrerie → Zudjādj
Vérria → Karaferye
Vertu → Faḍīla
Vêtements → Libās
Veterinary/Vétérinaire → Bayṭār
Vezīr Köprü v, 256a — V, 254a
Vidin iii, 628a, 629b — III, 648a, 650b
Vīdjāyanagara i, 199b; ii, 981a; iii, 147b, 417a, b, 421a, 425a, 426a, 1160b; v, 549b, 938a, 1258b — I, 205a; II, 1003b; III, 151a, 430b, 431a, 434b, 438b, 440a, 1189a; V, 554b, 942a, 1249b
Vidyāpati i, 1168a — I, 1203a
Vie, la → Ākhira; Dunyā; Ḥayāt
Vienna/Vienne → Viyana
Vietnam ii, 9a; iii, 1208b — II, 9a; III, 1239b
Vigne → Karm
Vikings → Madjūs (Norsemen)

Vikram → Bikrami
Vilayet → Wilāyāt
Vilches → Bildj
Village → Ḳarya
Ville → Ḳarya
Ville Ronde I, 923a, 924b, 926b
Vin → Khamr
Vine → Karm
Vishtāsp → Bishtāsb
Viyana i, 294b, 1157b, 1285b; iv, 591b — I, 303b, 1191b, 1325a; IV, 615b
Vizier → Wazīr
Vloras i, 767b — I, 790b
Vocabulista i, 501b — I, 517a
Voile → Ḥidjāb; Lithām
Voleur → Liṣṣ
Volga → Itil (river/rivière)
Voyage → Safar
Voyvoda i, 1253a; iv, 1095b — I, 1291a; IV, 1126b
Vrančić, Antun (Verantius) s, 185b — S, 186b
Vulture → Humā

W

Waḍʿ v, 805b — V, 811b
Wabdha i, 161a — I, 165b
Wadāʾi (Wādāy) i, 98a, 910b, 1260a; ii, 123a, b, 124a; v, 357b; s, 164a, b, 165b, 166a — I, 100b, 938a, 1298a, b; II, 126a, b, 127b; V, 359a; S, 164a, b, 165b, 166a
al-Waḍḍāḥ s, 272b — S, 272a
Waddān ii, 575a, b — II, 589b, 590a
Wadhārī s, 176b — S, 177b
Wādī i, 538a — I, 554b
Wādī Abū Ḍabʿa s, 173b — S, 174b
Wādī ʾl-Abyaḍ v, 1156a — V, 1145b
Wādīʿ ʿAḳl s, 159b — S, 159b
Wādī ʿAllāḳī → al-ʿAllāḳī
Wādi(y)Ānā i, 489a — I, 503b
Wādī ʿAraba → ʿAraba
Wādī Arīgha → Wādī Rīgh
Wādī Āsh s, 399a — S, 399a
Wādī Damā s, 356a — S, 356a
Wādi ʾl-Dawāsir i, 337a, 341a, 538a; ii, 177a — I, 347b, 351a, 554b; II, 182b
Wādī Duwayro i, 489a — I, 503b
Wādī Ḥaḍramawt i, 538a; iii, 51b, 52a — I, 555a; III, 53b
Wādī Hadjar i, 538a — I, 555a
Wāsī al-Ḥamd → Ḥamḍ, Wādī al-
Wādī Ḥanīfa i, 538b, 628b; ii, 92a — I, 555a, 649b; II, 94a
Wādī Ibro → Ibruh
al-Wādī ʾl-Kabīr i, 487b, 489a; iv, 116a — I, 502a, 503b; IV, 121a
Wādī al-Ḳilt s, 173b — S, 174b
Wādī ʾl-Ḳurā v, 317b, 497b — V, 317a, 500b
Wādī ʾl-Makhāzin i, 288b, 1058a; iii, 721a; v, 48b — I, 297b, 1098b; III, 743b; V, 50a
Wādī ʾl-Raml v, 530a — V, 534a
Wādī Rīgh v, 1181b — V, 1171b
Wādī al-Rumah i, 538a, 1097b — I, 554b, 1130b
Wādī al-Sadīr → Wādī Tūmīlāt
Wādī Shaḳūra i, 489a — I, 503b
Wādī al-Sirḥān i, 538a — I, 554b
Wādī Tadghat s, 132a — S, 132a
Wādī Tadjū i, 489a — I, 503b
Wādī Tūmīlāt i, 14b — I, 14b
Wādī Wargha s, 103a — S, 102b
Wāḍiḥ i, 1044b; iii, 495b, 791a — I, 1076a; III, 512b, 814b
al-Wādiyāshī, Muḥammad b. Djābir ii, 744a — II, 762b
Wadjda i, 357b, 1281b; v, 1177a, 1187a — I, 368a, 1320b; V, 1167a, 1177a
Wadjdī, Farīd i, 598a; iv, 159b, 720b — I, 617b; IV, 166a, 749b
Wadjdjādj s, 27a — S, 27a
Wadjh al- Ḳamar i, 280b — I, 289a
Wadjhī, Mullā ii, 865b; iii, 375b — II, 885b; III, 387b
Wādjib ii, 790a — II, 809a
Wādjid ʿAlī Shāh i, 757b; ii, 7b, 73a; v, 635a — I, 780a; II, 7b, 74b; V, 639a
Wadjīh al-Dīn i, 764b — I, 787b
al-Wādjikā → Abū Aḥmad ʿAbd al-Salām
Wafd ii, 467a, 934a; iii, 516a, 1069a; iv, 197b, 261a; s, 5b, 58a, 300b — II, 478b, 956a; III, 533b, 1095b; IV, 206a, 272b; S, 4b, 58b, 300a
Wāfidiyya i, 946b, 1324b — I, 975b, 1365b
Wafīk Pasha → Aḥmad Wafīk Pasha
Wafḳ ii, 370a; v, 222b — II, 380a; V, 220a
Wagon → Araba
Wahb b. Baḳiyya i, 949a — I, 978a
Wahb b. al-Munabbih ii, 363b; iii, 14a, 370a, 538a; iv, 212a, 369a; v, 811b; s, 88a, 116a — II, 373b; III, 14b, 382a, 556b; IV, 221b, 385b; V, 817b; S, 87b, 115b
Wahbiyya ii, 459b, 460a; iii, 659a — II, 471a, 472a; III, 680a
Waḥdat al-shuhūd i, 416a; iii, 102a — I, 428a; III, 104b
Waḥdat al-wudjūd i, 60b, 416b, 596a, 1137a; ii, 50a, 55a, 226a, 1137b; iii, 102b, 697a, 701b; iv, 992a — I, 62a, 428a, 615a, 1171b; II, 51a, 56a, 233a, 1164a; III, 104b, 719a, 723b; IV, 1024b
Waḥdetī → Derwīsh Wāḥdetī
Wahhābiyya i, 38b, 98b, 106b, 166b, 233b, 277a, 528b, 554a, 628b, 748a, 1282a; ii, 10a, 63b, 254b, 517b, 572b, 625b, 783b; iii, 162b, 238a, 291b, 431a, 433a, 606a, 677b, 954b, 999a, 1064b; iv, 626a, 778a, 1073a; v, 62b, 507b, 808a, 997b, 998b; s, 3b, 30b, 94b, 244b, 355b — I, 39b, 101a, 109b, 171a, 241a, 286a, 544b, 571b, 649b, 770b, 1321a; II, 10a, 64b, 262a, 530b, 587a, 641b, 802b; III, 166a, 245a, 300b, 445a, 447a, 627a, 699a, 979b, 1024a, 1091a; IV, 651a, 809a, 1104b; V, 64b, 511a, 814a, 993a, 994a; S, 2b, 30b, 94a, 244a, 355b
- doctrine i, 188b, 259b, 416b, 714b, 1199b; iii, 679a; iv, 142b — I, 194a, 267b, 428b, 736a, 1235a; III, 700b; IV, 148b
- literature/littérature i, 796b; ii, 91b; iii, 773a — I, 820a; II, 93a; III, 796a
Wahhās b. Ghānim v, 1244b — V, 1235a
Waḥīd → Yaḥyā-i Dārābī
Waḥīd-i Dastgardī iv, 71b — IV, 75b
Wāḥidī ii, 222b — II, 229b
al-Wāḥidī iv, 472b, 473b; v, 415b — IV, 493b, 494b; V, 417a
Wāḥidiyya iv, 668a — IV, 695b
Wahm i, 112a; iii, 509b — I, 115a; III, 527a
Wahrān i, 270b; ii, 160b, 173a; s, 376b — I, 279a; II, 165b, 178a; S, 376b
Wahrīz ii, 190b, 193a; s, 115b — II, 196b, 199a; S, 115a
Wahriz Boēs (Bōya) i, 102a, 102b; ii, 190a — I, 105a, 105b; II, 196a
Waḥshī iv, 68b — IV, 72b
Wahsūdān b. Djustān ii, 191a; iii, 245a; v, 602b — II, 197a; III, 252a; V, 606b
Wahsūdān b. Mamlān iv, 347b, 453b — IV, 362b, 456a
Wahsūdān b. Muḥammad iv, 662b — IV, 689b
Wahsūdānid(e)s ii, 192a; iv, 773a — II, 198a; IV,

804a
Waḥy iii, 1119b — III, 1147a
Wā'il i, 920b — I, 949a
Wā'il b. Ḥadjr s, 337b — S, 337a
Wā'iẓ iii,1153b — III, 1182a
Wā'iẓ b. Isḥāḳ, 'Ubayd Allāh v, 1106a, b — V, 1102a, b
al-Waḳā'i' al-Miṣriyya ii, 465a — II, 477a
Wakāla → Wikāla
Waḳ'anuwīs i, 317a; ii, 338b — I, 326b; II, 348b
Waḳash s, 236a — S, 236a
Waḳ'at al-Shi'b ii, 600b — II, 615b
Waḳf i, 56b, 152a, 170a, 173a, 661a, 760b, 1090a, 1091a, 1146a, 1148b; ii, 144a, 148b, 151a, 304a, 335a; iii, 175a; iv, 229b, 978a, 1036a; v, 333b, 876a, 879a, 1128b — I, 58b, 156b, 175a, 178a, 682a, 783b, 1122b, 1123b, 1180b, 1182b; II, 147b, 153a, 155b, 312a, 344b; III, 179a; IV, 240a, 1010b, 1067b; V, 334a, 882a, 885a, 1125a
Wakhān i, 223b — I, 230a
Wakhī i, 225a; ii, 31b — I, 231b; II, 32a
Wakhsh v, 75b; s, 125a — V, 77b; S, 124b
Wakī' i, 693b, 694a; s, 386b — I, 714b, 715a; S, 386b
Wāḳi' b. al-Djarrāḥ i, 272b — I, 281a
Wāḳi'a nuwīs → Waḳ'anuwīs
Wāḳid b. Djunaydib s, 177b — S, 178b
al-Wāḳidī i, 140a; ii, 159a, 922bl; v, 1161b; s, 263a — I, 144a; II, 164a, 946b; V, 1151a; S, 263a
Wāḳīf, Mollā Panāh i, 193b; ii, 217a — I, 199a; II, 223b
Wāḳifiyya i, 275a; v, 1236a — I, 283b; V, 1226b
Wakīl ii, 333a, 334b; iv, 532a — II, 342b, 344a; IV, 555a
Wakīl al-Dawla, 'Abd al-Raḥīm v, 171a — V, 168b
Wakīl-i Khāṣṣ iv, 217b — IV, 227a
Wakīl-i nafs-i nafīs-i humāyūn iv, 35b — IV, 38a
Waḳḳās, Sayyid v, 771a — V, 777b
al-Waḳḳashī i,149a — I, 153b
Waḳt iii, 84a — III, 86b
Wāḳ-wāḳ v, 939b, 940a — V, 943b, 944a
Walā' i, 30b, 490b, 681a; iii, 388b — I, 31b, 505b, 702a; III, 401a
Wālādjāh Muḥammad 'Alī Khān i, 937a — I, 965b
Wālādjāhī mosque/mosquée (Madras) s, 292b, 293a — S, 292a, 293a
Walasma' i, 763b; iii, 3b, 4a, 176a — I, 786b; III, 3b, 4a, 180a
Walata ii, 1002b — II, 1026a
Walba i, 6a, 155b — I, 6a, 160a
Wald 'Alī i, 483a — I, 497b
Wald Sulaymān (Bishr) i, 483a — I, 497b
Wālī i, 439b, 468b, 626b, 906b, 1160a; ii, 22b, 165a, 272b; v, 80b — I, 452a, 482b, 647a, 934a, 1194b; II, 23a, 170a, 280b; V, 82b
Walī i, 173b, 174a — I, 178b, 179a
Walī (saint) i, 371b; iv, 615a; v, 1200b — I, 382a; IV, 639b; V, 1191a
Walī Allāh (Farangī Maḥall) s, 292b — S, 292a
Walī, Amīr ii, 401b — II, 412a
Walī, Shaykh i, 1284b — I, 1323b
Walī al-dam iv, 689b — IV, 717b
Walī al-Dawla ii, 178a — II, 184a
Walī al-Dīn i, 893a; iii, 24b — I, 919b; III, 25b
Walī al-Dīn Efendī iii, 158a — III, 161b
Walī al-Dīn Yakan iii, 593b — III, 614a
Walī Khān Bakash iii, 1106b; iv, 498b — III, 1134a; IV, 520a
Walī Mīrzā iv, 393a — IV, 409b
Walī Muḥammad Khān ii, 638a — II, 654a
Wāliba b. al-Ḥubāb i, 107b, 143b; iv, 1003b — I, 110b, 147b; IV, 1036a
al-Walīd I (Umayyad(e)) i, 45a, 58a, b, 77b, 196a, 305a, 381a, 493a, 610b, 612a, 761b, 787b, 1223a; ii, 198a, 280b, 304b, 788b, 956a, 957a; iii, 41a, 42a, 85b; iv, 712b, 742a, 973a; s, 10a, 229a, 243a, 273a, b, 311a, b — I, 46a, 60a, 60b, 80a, 201b, 392a, 508a, 631b, 632a, 784b, 811a, 1259b; II, 204a, 289a, 313a, 807a, 978a, 979a; III, 43a, b, 88a; IV, 741a, 772a, 1005b; S, 9b, 229a, 243a, 273a, 310b, 311b
al-Walīd II (Umayyad(e)) i, 12b, 57b, 587a, 613a, 952b; ii, 198a; iii, 136a, 494b, 878a; iv, 1003a; v, 936b; s, 117a, 243a — I, 12b, 59a, 606a, 633a, 982a; II, 204b; III, 139a, 511b, 902a; IV, 1035b; V, 940b; S, 116b, 243a
al-Walīd b. 'Abd al-Malik → al-Walīd I
Walīd b. Hishām ii, 858b; iii, 78b, 79b; iv, 567b — II, 878a; III, 81a, 82a; IV, 590a
al-Walīd b. al-Mughīra i, 115b; iii, 1017b — I, 118b; III, 1043a
al-Walīd b. Ṭarīf ii, 524a; iii, 233b — II, 537a; III, 240a
al-Walīd b. 'Uḳba i, 382a; iii, 874a — I, 393a; III, 898a
al-Walīd b. 'Utba b. Abī Sufyān iii, 607b, 608a — III, 628b
Walīd b. Yazīd i, 196b; ii, 427b — I, 202a; II, 439a
al-Walīd b. Yazīd → al-Walīd II
al-Walīd al-'Abdī iii, 648b — III, 669b
al-Walīd al-Ḳurayshī, Āl s, 62a — S, 62b
Walīdād Khān i, 1300a — I, 1340a
Wālide Sulṭān Bezm-i 'Alem i, 74b, 1226a; iv, 720a; v, 257a, 261b — I, 77a, 1262b; IV, 749a; V, 255a, 259a
Wālide Sulṭān Ṣafiyye → Ṣafiyye Sulṭān Baffa
Walikota i, 981a — I, 1011b
Walīla (Volubilis) iii, 1031b, 1032a; s, 103a — III, 1057a, 1058a; S, 102b
Walīma iii, 210a — III, 215b
Wallachian → Eflāḳ
Wallāda bint al-Mustakfī i, 601b; iii, 681b, 973b — I, 621b; III, 703a, 998b
Walnut → Djawz
Wāmiḳ wa-'Adhrā i, 1301a — I, 1341a
Wanč i, 853b, 854a — I, 877a, b
Wandād-Hurmuzd, amīr iv, 645a — IV, 671b
Wandād-Safān iv, 645a — IV, 671b
Wangara iv, 548b, 773b — IV, 572a, 804b
al-Wānī, Muḥammad b. Muṣṭafā i, 310a — I, 319b
Wansharī i, 371a, 372a; s, 103a — I, 382a, 383a; S, 102b
al-Wansharīshī i, 1341a; s, 27a, 403a — I, 1381b; S, 27b, 403b
al-Wansharīsī → Bashīr
Wānūdīn b. Khazrūn b. Khazar v, 1178a, b — V, 1168a, b
Wanzamār, Banū v, 1174a, b, 1179a, 1180b — V, 1164a, b, 1169a, 1170b
Wanzammār b. 'Arīf ii, 979a — 1001b
Wara i, 98a; s, 164a — I, 100b; S, 164a
Warād, Banū s, 350b — S, 350b
Waraīn, Banū s, 145a — S, 144b
Waraḳ i, 589a — I, 608a
Waraḳa b. Nawfal iii, 1206a; iv, 898b — III, 1236b; IV, 931b
Warangal v, 1216b — V, 1206b
Ward, Banu 'l- i, 1023b; iii, 386b — I, 1055a; III, 398b
al-Ward al-Lakhmī i, 1023b — I, 1055a
Warda → al-Djarādatān[i]
Wardak s, 367a — S, 367b
Wardān iii, 887a, 889a — III, 911a, 913a
al-Wardī, Zayn al-Dīn 'Umar iv, 864b — IV, 898a
Wardjlān → Wargla
al-Wardjlānī → Abū Zakariyyā' al-Wardjlānī
Wargla iii, 656b, 657b, 1041a; s, 15b — III, 677b,

678b, 1067a; S, 15b
al-Wārith b. Kaʿb al-Kharūṣī iii, 652b; iv, 1085a — III, 673b; IV, 1116a
Warḳāʾ al-Nakhaʿī iv, 495a — IV, 516a
Wārkū, Banū iii, 1040b — III, 1066b
Warrā, Banū v, 1178b, 1179a — V, 1168b
al-Warrāḳ, Abū ʿĪsā → Abū ʿĪsā al-Warrāḳ
al-Warrāḳ, Muḥammad b. Yūsuf i, 156b — I, 161a
Warrū b. Saʿīd v, 1182a, b — V, 1172a, b
Warsifān, Banū v, 1179a, b, 1183a — V, 1169a, b, 1173a
al-Warthīlānī ii, 161a; s, 403a — II, 166a; S, 403a
Warwar ʿAlī Pasha → Varvar ʿAlī
Waryāghal, Banū s, 377a — S, 377a
Warzamār, Banū → Wanzamār, Banū
Washer of Clothes/of the dead → Ghassāl
Washing → Ghusl
Washka i, 1057b — I, 1089a
Washmgīr b. Ziyār iii, 255a; iv, 23a, 100a, b — III, 262b; IV, 25a, 104b
al-Washshāʿ ii, 1032b; iii, 1263b; iv, 822b; v, 737a — II, 1056a; III, 1296b; IV, 855b; V, 742b
Wāsiʿ Alīsī iv, 505a — IV, 527a
Waṣīf i, 271b, 273a, 789b; ii, 26b — I, 279b, 281b, 813a; ii, 27a
Wasīf b. Ṣuwārtigin s, 304b — S, 304b
Wāṣifī s, 46b — S, 47a
Wāṣil b. ʿAṭāʾ i, 127b, 454a, 1080b; ii, 833b; iii, 985a, 1025b, 1142b; iv, 142a; s, 225b, 227a — I, 131b, 467a, 1113a; II, 853a; III, 1009b, 1051b, 1171a; IV, 148a; S, 225b, 227a
Wasīn, Banū → Wisyān, Banū
Wāsiṭ i, 77a, 103a, 132a, 867a, 949a, 1094b; ii, 248a, 319b; iii, 41a, 1252b, 1255a, 1267a; iv, 724b; s, 41a, 118a, 119a, 126b, 193a, 243a, 385a — I, 79b, 106a, 135b, 891a, 978a, 1127a; II, 255a, 328b; III, 42b, 1285a, 1287b, 1300a; IV, 753b; S, 41b, 117b, 118b, 125b, 193b, 243a, 385b
Wāsiṭa ii, 857b — II, 877b
al-Wāsiṭī, Abū Bakr v, 332a — V, 332a
al-Wāsiṭī, Abu ʾl-Fatḥ ii, 166b — II, 171b
al-Wāsiṭī, Abu ʾl-Ḳāsim ʿAlī b. Muḥammad s, 13b — S, 13b
al-Wāsiṭī, Aḥmad b. Ibrāhīm iii, 954b — III, 979a
al-Wāsiṭī, Aḥmad b. Muḥammad v, 49a; s, 1a — V, 50b; S, 1a
Waṣiyya ii, 302a, 304a; iii, 27b; iv, 944a — II, 310b, 312b; III, 28b; IV, 976b
Waṣl iv, 412a, 413a — IV, 430a, 431a
Waṣṣāf iv, 67b — IV, 71b
Wasūṭ iv, 1147a — IV, 1178b
Waṭan i, 64a; iv, 785b, 790b — I, 66a; IV, 817a, 822b
Waṭaniyya iv, 784b, 785a — IV, 816a, b
Water → Māʾ
Water-clocks → Ḥiyal
Water-wheel → Nāʿūra; Ṣāḳiya
al-Wāthiḳ (ʿAbbāsid(e)) i, 10b, 18b, 271a, 551a, 1298b; ii, 188b, 198a, 236a; iii, 618a; iv, 138a; s, 33a, 106a, 199a — I, 10b, 19a, 279b, 568b, 1338a; II, 194b, 204b, 243a; III, 639a; IV, 143b; S, 33a, 105b, 199a
al-Wāthiḳ (Almohad(e)) → Abū Dabbūs
al-Wāthiḳ (Ḥafṣid(e)) iii, 67a — III, 69a
Wathīḳa i, 296a, 313a, 478a, 624b, 1089b, 1269b; ii, 77b, 128a, 304b — I, 305b, 322a, 492b, 645a, 1122a, 1308b; II, 79a, 131a, 312b
Wāthila b. al-Asḳaʿ i, 266b — I, 274b
Waththāb iii, 228a — III, 235a
Watid i, 670b, 671b, 674b — I, 691b, 692b, 695a
Waṭṭār, Ṭāhir al- v, 190a, 191a — V, 187b, 188a
Waṭṭāsid(e))s i, 706a, 1057b; ii, 463a, 510a, 819b; iv, 94a; v, 1190b, 1200a — I, 727b, 1089b; II, 475a, 522b, 839a; IV, 98a; V, 1180b, 1190a
al-Waṭwāṭ → Djamāl al-Dīn
Wāwazgīt, Aīt i, 161b; s, 144b — I, 166a; S, 144b
Ways Khān iv, 512a — IV, 534a
Ways Khān Zand v, 664a — V, 669a
Wāziʿ, Āl i, 1299a — I, 1339a
Waẓīfa iv, 1055b — IV, 1087a
Wazīr i, 19b, 801b, 1034a; ii, 330a, 333a, 334b, 857b; iii, 45b; iv, 103b, 941b, 1105a; s, 246a — I, 20a, 824b, 1065b; II, 339b, 342b, 344b, 877b; III, 47a; IV, 108a, 974b, 1136b; S, 246b
Wazīr al-Dawla, Nawāb iv, 197a — IV, 205b
Wazīr Khān (Lāhawr) i, 914a; ii, 47b; v, 600a — I, 941b; II, 48b; V, 604a
Wazīr Khān Harawī i, 80b — I, 83a
Wazīr Muḥammad Khān i, 1195b — I, 1230b
Wazīr Singh ii, 797b — II, 816b
Wazīrābād v, 888a — V, 894b
Wazīrīstān s, 285a, 329b — S, 285a, 329a
Wazzān i, 687b; s, 404a — I, 708b; S, 404b
al-Wazzānī, Muḥammad Ḥasan iii, 525a, b; s, 10a — III, 543a, b; S, 9b
Weapons → Silāḥ
Weasel → Ibn ʿIrs
Weaver → Ḥāʾik
Weaving → Nasdj
Wedjīhī Pasha ii, 636b — II, 652b
Wehbī → Pīr Meḥmed
Welfare → Khayr
Welī Maḥmūd → Maḥmūd Pasha Welī
Welī Pasha i, 175a, 398b, 399a — I, 179b, 410a, 410b
Well → Ḳanāt
Wenceslaus → Čeh
Werčikwār s, 158b — S, 158b
Wheat → Ḳamḥ
Whēbyōt s, 339b — S, 339b
White Horde i, 1106b; ii, 44a, b
Widādī i, 193b — I, 199a
Widjaʾ iv, 1088a, 1089b — IV, 1119a, 1120b
Widjāda iii, 27b — III, 28b
al-Widyān i, 538b — I, 555a
Wikāla ii, 148b; iv, 435a, b, 840b, 1015b — II, 152b; IV, 454b, 873b, 1047b
Wiḳār al-Mulk s, 74a — S, 74b
Wilāya i, 1027b — I, 1059b
Wilāyāt ii, 302b — II, 311a
Wilāyāt belediyye ḳānūnu i, 974a, 975b — I, 1004b, 1005b
Wilāyāt-i sitte i, 640b — I, 661a
Wilāyet → Eyālet
Wine → Khamr
Wīrān, Ḥāfiẓ Ghulām ii, 222a — II, 228b
Wird ii, 224a; iv, 94b; s, 93a — II, 231a; IV, 99a; S, 93a
Wīs u-Rāmīn ii, 1142b — II, 1169b
Wiṣāl, Kučak ii, 433b; IV, 69b — II, 445a; IV, 73b
Wīsū i, 1305a, 1306a — I, 1345b, 1346b
Wisyān, Banū iii, 1041a — III, 1066b
al-Wisyānī, Abū Mūsā iii, 657a — III, 678b
Witu Sultanate iv, 889a, b — IV, 921b, 922a
Wizāra → Wazīr
Wizr b. Djābir Asad al-Rahīṣ i, 519a — I, 534b
Wolf → Dhiʾb
Wolof → Djolof
Woman → Marʾa
Wood → Khashab
Wool → Ṣūf
Worm wood → Afsantīn
Writing → Khaṭṭ
Wu Ma v, 844b — V, 856b
Wudjūd Allāh i, 410a — I, 422a
Wuḍūʾ iv, 264b — IV, 276b
Wuhayb b. ʿAbd Manāf i, 438b — I, 450b

Wuḳūf iii, 32a, 35b — III, 33b, 37a
Wurukasha, lake/lac iv, 400b — IV, 418a
Wushmgīr → Washmgīr
Wuthūḳ al-Dawla v, 24b — V, 25b

X

Xanî, Ehmedê v, 482a — V, 485a

Y

Yaʿāḳīb iii, 1004b — III, 1030a
Yaʿāriba imamate s, 355a — S, 355a
Yabdar s, 402b — S, 403a
Yabghu i, 420a, 661b, 852a; ii, 1107b; iv, 658b; s, 244b, 245a — I, 432a, 682b, 875b; II, 1133b; IV, 685a; S, 244b, 245a
Yaʿburī iii, 134a — III, 137a
Yacoub → Yaʿḳūb
Yad iv, 1009a — IV, 1041b
Yaddar, Banū ii, 527a — II, 540a
Yaddū b. Yaʿlā iii, 1042b, 1043b; v, 1177a — III, 1068b, 1069b; V, 1167a
Yādgār Muḥammad (Tīmūrid(e)) i, 148b — I, 152b
Yādgar Nāṣir Mīrzā iii, 633a — III, 654a
Yādigār Muḥammad Khān iv, 849b — IV, 882b
Yāfaʿ ii, 675b; s, 20b — II, 692a; S, 21a
Yāfiʿī iv, 745b; s, 338b — IV, 775b; S, 338a
al-Yāfiʿī ʿAbd Allāh i, 255b; ii, 392a — I, 263b; II, 402b
Yafran iii, 1039b, 1040a — III, 1065b, 1066a
Yaʿfur → Yuʿfir
Yaʿfūr ii, 624a; iii, 393b — II, 639b; III, 406a
Yaʿfūrid(e)s i, 551a, b — I, 568b, 569a
Yaghî-basan b. Ghāzī b. Dānishmand ii, 110b; s, 154a — II, 113a; S, 154b
Yaghî-bastî iii, 1208b — III, 1239a
Yāghîsiyān i, 517a; v, 921b, 924a — I, 532b; V, 927a, 929b
Yāghistān ii, 140a — II, 143b
Yaghlîkčî Emīr iv, 193b — IV, 202a
Yaghmā Djandaḳī iii, 355b; iv, 69b — III, 366b; IV, 73b
Yaghmāʾī, Ḥabīb-i iv, 71b — IV, 75b
Yaghmurāsan b. Zayyan i, 92b; iii, 866a; v, 1180a — I, 95a; III, 890a; V, 1170a
al-Yaghmūrī, Shihāb al-Dīn iv, 960a — IV, 992b
Yaghūth iii, 223a — III, 229b
al-Yaḥīrī, Yaḥyā b. al-Ḥusayn s, 236a — S, 236a
Yaḥmad, Āl iv, 1084b — IV, 1116a
Yahūd i, 264b, 265a, b, 491b, 546b, 565a, 1020-22, 1178a; ii, 85b, 145b, 229a, 230a, 563b, 620a, 725b, 835b, 859b, 912b, 913a, 1010a; iii, 80a, 147b, 324b, 326a; iv, 8a, 43b, 98b, 99a, 133b, 239a, 241b, 299a-313b, 603b, 824a, 1138a-1142a, 1174b; v, 326b, 334a, b, 337a, 436a, 668b, 994b — I, 272b, 273a, b, 506a, 563b, 583a, 1051-53, 1213a; II, 87a, 149b, 236a, 237a, 577b, 635b, 744b, 855a, 879b, 934a, b, 1033b; III, 80a, 150b, 334b, 336a; IV, 8b, 46a, 103a, 139a, b, 249b, 252b, 312b-327b, 627b, 857a, 1170a-1173b, 1208a; V, 326a, 334a, b, 337b, 438b, 673b, 990a
Yahūdī, Yūsuf iv, 310a — IV, 324a
Yahūdiyya iv, 98b, 106a — IV, 103a, 110b
Yaḥyā, Imām → Yaḥyā Maḥmūd al-Mutawakkil
Yaḥyā I (Ḥammūdid(e)) i, 5b; iii, 147a — I, 5b; III, 150b
Yaḥyā I (Idrīsid(e)) iii, 1035b; iv, 632a — III, 1061b; IV, 657b
Yaḥyā II (Idrīsid(e)) iii, 1035b — III, 1061b
Yaḥyā III (Idrīsid(e)) iii, 1036a — III, 1062a
Yaḥyā IV (Idrīsid(e)) iii, 1036a; s, 132a — III, 1062a; S, 131b
Yaḥyā b. ʿAbd Allāh (al-Daylamī) i, 271b, 402b, 1034b; ii, 191a; iii, 233b, 616a, 617a; s, 130a — I, 280a, 414a, 1066a; II, 197a; III, 240a, 637a, b; S, 129a
Yaḥyā b. ʿAbd Allāh b. Saʿīd al-Ḥaḥī s, 29a — S, 29b
Yaḥya b. ʿAbd al-Malik b. Makkī iv, 338a — IV, 352b
Yaḥyā b. Abī Bakr b. Yūsuf b. Tāshufīn i, 389b; iii, 728a — I, 401a; III, 751a
Yaḥyā b. Abī Ḥāshid b. al-Ḍaḥḥāk s, 22a — S, 22b
Yaḥyā b. Abī Manṣūr iii, 8b, 1136b — III, 9a, 1165a
Yaḥyā b. Abī Ṭālib ʿAbd Allāh → ʿAzafī
Yaḥyā b. Abī Yaḥyā, Shams al-Dīn s, 236a — S, 236a
Yaḥyā b. Ādam iv, 1141b — IV, 1173a
Yaḥyā b. ʿAdī i, 126b, 130a, 151b, 234b, 235a, 328a, 631b, 737a; ii, 779a; iii, 895b, 980a; v, 121a; s, 25a, 398b — I, 130b, 134a, 156a, 241b, 242a, 338b, 652a, 759a; II, 797b; III, 919b, 1004b; V, 123b; S, 25b, 398b
Yaḥyā b. Aktham i, 271a, 273a; iii, 879a — I, 279b, 281b; III, 903b
Yaḥyā b. ʿAlī b. Abī Ṭālib s, 92b — S, 92b
Yaḥyā b. ʿAlī b. Ghāniya i, 390a; ii, 1007a — I, 401b; II, 1030b
Yaḥyā b. ʿAlī b. Ḥammūd → Yaḥyā I (Ḥammūdid(e))
Yaḥya b. ʿAlī b. al-Munadjdjim iv, 111a — IV, 116a
Yaḥyā b. al-ʿAzīz iii, 138b; iv, 479b — III, 141a; IV, 501a
Yaḥyā b. al-Biṭrīḳ i, 235a, 589b, 736b; iii, 311b — I, 242a, 608b, 758b; III, 321a
Yaḥyā b. Ghāniya i, 165b; ii, 463b, 575a, 1007b; iii, 66b, 1039a; iv, 337b, 614b, 828a — I, 170a; II, 475a, 589b, 1031a; III, 69a, 1064b; IV, 352a, 639a, 860b
Yaḥyā b. Ḥamdūn i, 1088a — I, 1120b
Yaḥyā b. Ḥamza al-ʿAlawī iv, 252a; v, 901a — IV, 263a; V, 907a
Yaḥyā b. al-Ḥārith al-Dhimārī iii, 704b — III, 726b
Yaḥyā b. Harthama iv, 100a — IV, 104a
Yaḥyā b. al-Ḥasan b. Djaʿfar s, 401a — S, 401b
Yaḥyā b. Hubayra → Ibn Hubayra, Yaḥyā
Yaḥyā b. al-Ḥusayn → Yaḥyā al-Hādī
Yaḥyā b. Ibrāhīm al-Gudālī ii, 1121b; v, 653b; s, 27a — II, 1148a; V, 657b; S, 27a
Yaḥyā b. Idrīs → Yaḥyā IV (Idrīsid(e))
Yaḥyā b. al-Ḳāsim → Yaḥyā III (Idrīsid(e))
Yaḥyā b. Khaldūn → Ibn Khaldūn, Yaḥyā
Yaḥyā b. Khālid al-Barmakī i, 936a, 1033a, 1034a, b, 1223a; ii, 79b, 305a; iii, 232b, 989a; iv, 16b, 119a, 1164a; v, 1238b; s, 48b, 225b, 393b — I, 964b, 1065a, b, 1066a, 1259b; II, 81a, 313b; III, 239b, 1014a; IV, 18a, 124a, 1196a; V, 1229b; S, 49a, 225b, 394a
Yaḥya b. Maḥmūd al-Gudjarātī iv, 507a — IV, 529a
Yaḥyā b. Manda s, 193a — S, 194a
Yaḥyā b. Muʿādh i, 844a — I, 867b
Yaḥyā b. Muḥammad → Yaḥyā I (Idrīsid(e))
Yaḥyā b. Muḥammad Ḥamīd al-Dīn iv, 745b — IV, 775b
Yaḥyā b. al-Mundhir iii, 743a — III, 766a
Yaḥyā b. Ṣaʿīd → al-Antākī
Yaḥyā b. Ṣaʿīd iii, 24b — III, 26a
Yaḥyā b. Ṣāʿid (d./m. 318/930) s, 400b — S, 401a
Yaḥyā b. Sallām al-Baṣrī iv, 829b — IV, 862b
Yaḥyā b. al-Samīna i, 600a — I, 619b
Yaḥyā b. al-Shāṭir iii, 228a — III, 235a
Yaḥyā b. Taʿfūft i, 689a — I, 710a
Yaḥyā b. Tamīm i, 149a — I, 153b
Yaḥyā b. ʿUmar iii, 486a — III, 503a

Yaḥyā b. ʿUmar (Almoravid(e)) ii, 1002b, 1122a; iii, 288b; v, 653b, 654a, b — II, 1025b, 1148a; III, 297b; V, 657b, 658b
Yaḥyā b. ʿUmar al Ṭālibī ii, 485a; iii, 908a, 1022b — II, 497b; III, 932a, 1048b
Yaḥyā b. Wasīnū ii, 1013a — II, 1036b
Yaḥyā b. Yaḥyā → Yaḥyā II (Idrīsid(e))
Yaḥyā b. Yaḥyā (Malīkī) iv, 87a — IV, 91a
Yaḥyā b. Yaʿmur iv, 731b — IV, 761a
Yaḥyā b. Zakariyyāʾ ii, 279b, 281a; iii, 613b, 1175a, 1206a; iv, 724a, 912b; v, 421a — II, 287b, 289a; III, 634b, 1204a, 1236b; IV, 753a, 945b; V, 423a
Yaḥyā b. Zayd b. ʿAlī i, 402b; ii, 608b, 1139b; iii, 1265b; iv, 446b; v, 3a, 230a — I, 414a; II, 623b, 1166b; III, 1298b; IV, 466a; V, 3a, 228a
Yaḥyā b. Zikrawayh ii, 850b; iv, 493b, 660b — II, 870a; IV, 515a, 687a
Yaḥyā b. Ziyād al-Ḥarithī iv, 1003b — IV, 1036a
Yaḥyā al-Aṭrash ii, 637b — II, 653b
Yaḥyā al-Barmākī → Yaḥyā b. Khālid
Yaḥyā Efendī iv, 505a — IV, 527a
Yaḥyā al-Hādī ila 'l-ḥaḳḳ iv, 944b — IV, 977a
Yaḥyā-i Dārābī i, 847a — I, 870a
Yaḥyā al-Ghazāl → al-Ghazāl
Yaḥyā al-Ḳādir i, 446b, 986a; ii, 243a; s, 23a — I, 459a, 1016b; II, 250a; S, 23b
Yaḥyā al-Kātib iii, 1243a — III, 1275a
Yaḥyā Kemāl Beyatlî v, 195a; s, 167b, 324b — V, 192a; S, 168a, 324a
Yaḥyā Khān iv, 177b; v, 1081b — IV, 186a; V, 1079a
Yaḥyā al-Laythī i, 83a — I, 85b
Yaḥyā al-Maghribī → Abū Zakariyyāʾ al Maghribī
Yaḥyā Maḥmūd al-Mutawakkil v, 809a — V, 815a
Yaḥyā al-Naḥwī ii, 771b, 780b — II, 790a, 799b
Yaḥyā Nūrī, Mīrzā i, 809a, 833b, 847a, 911b; iv, 51b, 696a; s, 53b — I, 832a, 856b, 870b, 939a; IV, 54b, 724a; S, 53b
Yaḥyā Pāsha-zāde Küčük Bālī Beg iv, 657a — IV, 683b
Yaḥyā-i Shirwanī ii, 1136b; iv, 991a, 992b; s, 208a — II, 1163a; IV, 1024a, 1025b; s, 208a
Yakhshî Khān (Beg) iv, 621b, 622a, b — IV, 646a, b, 647a
Yakhshī Khān b. Ḳarasî iv, 628a — IV, 653a
Yakhshī b. Tīmurtash i, 1303a; ii, 611a — I, 1342b; II, 626a
Yaktan iv, 448a — IV, 468a
Yaḳṭīn b. Mūsā s, 199a — S, 199a
Yaʿḳūb iii, 980a — III, 1004b
Yaʿḳūb I (Germiyān-oghlu) i, 346a, 510b; ii, 989a, b — I, 356b, 526a; II, 1012a
Yaʿḳūb II (Germiyān-oghlu) i, 1118a; ii, 990a — I, 1151b; II, 1012b
Yaʿḳūb, Abū Yūsuf → Abū Yūsuf Yaʿḳūb
Yaʿḳūb b. ʿAlī Shīr → Yaʿḳūb I (Germiyān-oghlu)
Yaʿḳūb b. Dāʾūd → Abū ʿAbd Allāh Yaʿḳūb b. Dāʾūd
Yaʿḳūb b. Isḥāḳ b. al-Ward iv, 275b, 459b — IV, 287b, 479b
Yaʿḳūb b. Killis → Ibn Killis
Yaʿḳūb b. Layth al-Ṣaffār i, 145a, 452b, 1001a, 1008b, 1009b, 1294a, 1344b; ii, 196a, 553b, 812a, 978a, 1048b, 1082b, 1120a; iii, 195b, 245a; iv, 20b, 21a, b, 356b, 673a, 917b; v, 58a, 158a, 451b; s, 125b, 127a — I, 149b, 465b, 1032a, 1039b, 1041a, 1333b, 1384b; II, 202a, 567b, 831a, 1000b, 1073a, 1107b, 1146a; III, 200b, 252a; IV, 22a, b, 23a, 372a, 700b, 950b; V, 59b, 157b, 454a; S, 124b, 126a
Yaʿḳūb b. Muḥammad al-Taʿāʾishī i, 49b; v, 1250b, 1251b, 1252b — I, 51a; V, 1241b, 1242a, 1243a
Yaʿḳūb b. Nuʿmān al-Bulghārī i, 1307b — I, 1347b
Yaʿḳūb b. Sulaymān → Yaʿḳūb II (Germiyān-oghlu)
Yaʿḳūb b. Sulṭān Shāh iv, 1159a — IV, 1191a
Yaʿḳūb b. Ṭāriḳ iii, 1136a — III, 1164b
Yaʿḳūb b. Uzun Ḥasan i, 293a, 311b, 1019a, 1067a; ii, 884a, 1136b, iii, 316a; iv, 1048b; v, 54a, 243b, 492b — I, 302a, 321a, 1050a, 1099a; II, 905a, 1163a; III, 325b; IV, 1080a; V, 55b, 241b, 495a
Yaʿḳub Beg (Kāshghar) i, 314a, 733b; iii, 1120b; v, 30b, 364a; s, 98a — I, 323b, 751a; III, 1148a; V, 31b, 365a; S, 97b
Yaʿḳūb al-Dibsī ii, 795a — II, 814a
Yaʿḳūb Efendi ii, 203b — II, 209b
Yaʿḳūb Ḥanna, Muʿallim v, 93b, 94a — V, 96a
Yaʿḳūb Ḳadrī ʿOthmān-oghlu iv, 593b; v, 196a — IV, 617b; V, 193b
Yaʿḳūb Khān Barakhzay i, 87b, 232a, 796b — I, 90a, 239a, 819b
Yaʿḳūb al-Manṣūr (Almohad(e)) → Abū Yūsuf Yaʿḳūb al-Manṣūr
Yaʿḳūb Pasha iii, 340a — III, 350a
Yaʿḳūb Pasha Ḳara ʿOthmān-oghlu iv, 593b — IV, 617b
Yaʿḳūb Ṣarfī, Shaykh iv, 709a; s, 167b — IV, 737b; S, 167b
Yaʿḳūb Shāh (Kashmīr) iv, 709a — IV, 737b
Yaʿḳūb Shāh Čak b. Yūsuf Shāh s, 132a, 167a — S, 131a, 167b
Yaʿḳūb Čarkhī s, 50b — S, 51b
Yaʿḳūb al-Tammār s, 25a — S, 25a
Yakūba Sylla ii, 63b; iii, 107b, 180a — II, 64b; III, 110a, b
al-Yaʿḳūbī, Aḥmad i, 591b; ii, 579b, 580a; iii, 1077b, 1206b — I, 610b; II, 594a, b; III, 1104a, 1237a
Yaʿḳūbiyya v, 121a, 896b — V, 123b, 902b
Yakun, Walī al-Dīn i, 597a — I, 616b
Yāḳūt i, 1046b; iii, 46a, 197a, 1157a — I, 1078a; III, 47b, 202a, 1185b
Yāḳūt the Abyssinian/l'Abyssin i, 1194a — I, 1229b
Yāḳūt al-Ḥamawī i, 456b, 488a, 571a, 594b, 712b; ii, 585b; iii, 724a, 840a; iv, 131b, 132a, 223b; v, 1012a, 1019a, b; s, 195a — I, 470a, 502b, 589b, 614a, 734a; II, 600a; III, 746b, 864a; IV, 137a, b, 233a; V, 1008a, 1015a, b; S, 195a
Yāḳūt Khān iii, 15b — III, 16b
Yāḳūt al-Mawṣilī ii, 496b — II, 509a
Yāḳūt al-Mursī i, 1070a — I, 1102b
Yāḳūt al-Mustaʿṣimī iii, 736b; iv, 1122b — III, 759b; IV, 1154b
Yāḳūtī b. Caghrî ii, 5a — II, 5a
Yaʿlā b. Muḥammad al-Ifranī ii, 494b; iii, 1042a — II, 507a; III, 1068a
Yaʿlā b. Muḥammad b. al-Khayr v, 1179a — V, 1169a
Yaʿlā b. Munya iv, 1134b — IV, 1166b
Yalangtush Biy s, 97a — S, 96b
Yalbugha, Aḥmad s, 409a — S, 409b
Yalçin → Ḥusayn Djāhid
Yālī ii, 1119b — II, 1145b
Yaltakīn i, 824b — I, 847b
Yām i, 545b; ii, 517b; iii, 179b, 259b, 327b; iv, 201a; s, 387b — I, 563a; II, 530b; III, 183b, 266b, 337b; IV, 210a; S, 388a
Yām b. Nūḥ iv, 528b — IV, 551b
Yamak iv, 322b — IV, 337a
al-Yamāma i, 110b; ii, 126b, 569a; iv, 1072b; s, 32a, 178a — I, 113b; II, 129b, 583b; IV, 1104a; S, 32b, 179a
al-Yamāmī, Muḥammad b. ʿAbd al-Waḥīd iv, 89b — IV, 93b
Yaman i, 98b, 102a, 110b, 441a, 535a, 539a, 543b, 549a, 551b, 728a, 803b; ii, 660b; iii, 294a, 651b; iv, 198a, 199b, 448a, 519a, 745b, 834a, b, 902a; v, 807a, 895a, 1059a,; s, 3b, 8b, 22a, 32b, 115b, 318a, 335a,

343b — I, 101a, 105a, 113b, 453b, 551b, 556a, 560b, 566b, 569a, 749b, 826b; II, 677a; III, 303a, 672b; IV, 206b, 208a, 467b, 541b, 775a, 867a, b, 934b; V, 813a, 901a, 1056a; S, 3a, 8a, 22b, 32b, 115a, 317b, 334b, 343a
- ethnography/ethnographie i, 39b, 194b; v, 346a, 953b — I, 40b, 200b; V, 347a, 957b
- literature/littérature ii, 441a; iii, 124b, 688b, 746b; iv, 1188b — II, 452b; III, 127a, 710b, 769b; IV, 1221a
- South/Sud v, 1059b — V, 1056b
Yamanī ii, 635a; iii, 233a; s, 338a — II, 651a; III, 239b; S, 338a
Yaᶜmar (Ḥazn) b. Zāʾida b. Laḳīṭ → Abū Nukhayla
Yāmid s, 61b — S, 62a
Yamīn ii, 304a; iv, 687b, 688b — II, 312b; IV, 715b, 716b
Yamlūl, Banū ii, 463b; iv, 739b — II, 475a; IV, 769b
Yamūt iii, 1108a — III, 1135a
Yanāltegīn i, 1130a — I, 1164a
Yanbuᶜ iv, 748b; s, 383b — IV, 778b; S, 384a
Yang Dipertuan Agung s, 152a — S, 152a
Yanidj Beg ii, 984a — II, 1006b
Yānis i, 939a; ii, 858a; iii, 54b — I, 968a; II, 878a; III, 56b
Yānis al-Mutaᶜarrab ii, 234b, 237a — II, 241b, 244a
Yanko b. Dobrotič ii, 611a, 971b — II, 626a, 993b
Yannaḳo b. Yanniḳo iv, 713a — IV, 741b
Yanosh → Sigismund, John
Yanova v, 258a, 259a — V, 255b, 257a
Yanya i, 398b — I, 410a
Yār Beg i, 853a — I, 876b
Yār Muḥammad Khān i, 231b, 282b, 1195a; ii, 185b, 186a; iv, 523b — I, 238b, 291a, 1230b; II, 191b, 192a; IV, 546b
Yarbay iv, 461b — IV, 482b
Yardjūkh i, 278b — I, 287a
Yarī Beg i, 1068a — I, 1100a
Yārī Mudhahhib i, 1211b, 1212a — I, 1247b, 1248a
Yārkand i, 46b; s, 98a — I, 48a; S, 97b
Yārkandī Turks s, 327b — S, 327a
Yarligh ii, 303b, 309a — II, 312a, 318a
Yaᶜrubid(e)s i, 554a, 1282a — I, 571b, 1321a
Yārūkh ii, 483b — II, 496a
Yās, Banū i, 166a; ii, 557b, 618b, 619a; iv, 751b, 752a; v, 508b; s, 419a — I, 171a; II, 571b, 634a, b; IV, 781b, 782b; V, 512a; S, 419a
Yasa ii, 2a; iii, 48a; iv, 559b, 562b — II, 2a; III, 49b; IV, 582a, 584b
Yasaḳčï iv, 808b — IV, 841a
Yasaḳnāme iv, 562a — IV, 584b
Yasārīzāde Muṣṭafā ᶜIzzet iv, 1126a — IV, 1157b
Yasawī → Aḥmad Yasawī
Yasawiyya i, 299a; iii, 1115a; iv, 48a — I, 308a; III, 1142b; IV, 50b
Yashbak al-Shaᶜbānī ii, 781b; iv, 210a — II, 800a; IV, 219b
Yashīr i, 700a — I, 721a
Yashkurī (Kaskar) s, 354b — S, 354b
Yasht iii, 112b — III, 115a
Yasî i, 147b, 299a; v, 859a — I, 152a, 308a; V, 866a
Yāsidj v, 9a — V, 9b
Yāsīn al-Hāshimi iii, 521b — III, 539a, b
Yāsīn valley/vallée de ii, 30b; s, 158b, 327b — II, 31a; S, 158b, 327a
Yāsir ᶜArafat s, 9a — S, 8b
Yaṣlitan → Īslitan
Yathrib i, 429a; iv, 824a, 835b; v, 436a, 994b — I, 441a; IV, 857a, 868b; V, 438b, 989b
Yāṭib s, 407b — S, 407b
al-Yatīma (pearl/perle) s, 253a — S, 252b
Yavlaḳ Arslan → Muẓaffar al-Dīn Yavlaḳ
Yawa ii, 147a — II, 151a
Yawm al-djumᶜa ii, 592b, 593b — II, 607b, 608a
Yaxartes → Sīr Daryā
Yaya i, 348a; ii, 33a, 444b — I, 358b; II, 33b, 456b
Yazbak ii, 444a — II, 455b
Yayče v, 32a — V, 33a
Yaylak v, 182b — V, 180a
Yazanīs iv, 541a — IV, 564a
Yazd i, 3b; iii, 216a, 502a; iv, 7b, 465b, 466a, b; v, 152a, 171a, 871a, 1115b, 1116a, 1148b; s, 54b, 61a, 73a, 115a, 139b, 342a, 386a — I, 3b; III, 222a, 519a; IV, 8b, 486a, b, 487a, b; V, 154a, 168b, 877b, 1112a, b, 1139b; S, 55a, 61b, 73b, 114b, 139a, 341b, 386b
Yazdān iii, 584a — III, 604a
Yazdī → Madjd al-Mulk
Yazdī, Sharaf al-Dīn s, 46b — S, 47a
Yazdigird II v, 144b — V, 147a
Yazdigird III iii, 571b, 586a; iv, 13b, 14b, 207b, 385a, b, 386a; v, 56b; s, 298a, 312a — III, 591b, 606b; IV, 14b, 15b, 216b, 402a, b; V, 58a; S, 297b, 311b
Yazīd I b. Muᶜāwiya (Umayyad(e)) i, 5a, 40a, 45a, 50a, 54a, 55a, 109a, 453b, 550a, 920a, 1029b, 1152a; ii, 89b, 198a, 280b, 541a, 739b; iii, 226a, 227a, 270b, 607b, 620b, 645b, 976a; iv, 938b; v, 132a, 997a; s, 10a, 26a, 230b, 231b — I, 5a, 41b, 46b, 51b, 56a, b, 112a, 466b, 567b, 947b, 1061a, 1186b; II, 91a, 204a, 289a, 554a, 758a; III, 233a, 234a, 278a, 628b, 641a, 666b, 1000b; IV, 971b; V, 134b, 992a; S, 9b, 26a, 230b, 231b
Yazīd II (Umayyad(e)) i, 50a, 305a, 1149a; ii, 228b, 726b, 788b; iii, 2b, 42a, 650a, 802a; iv, 75b-76a; v, 590b; s, 10a, 52a, 243a — I, 51b, 314b, 1183b; II, 235b, 745a, 807a; III, 2b, 43b, 671b, 825b; IV, 79b; V, 594a; S, 9b, 52b, 243a
Yazīd III (Umayyad(e)) i, 53b, 57a; iii, 224a, 990b; iv, 370b — I, 55a, 59a; III, 230b, 1015a; IV, 386b
Yazīd, Banū iv, 345a — IV, 359b
al-Yazīd, Mawlāy → al-Yazīd b. Muḥammad b. ᶜAbd Allāh
Yazīd b. ᶜAbd al-Malik → Yazīd II
Yazīd b. Abī Anīsa iv, 1076b — IV, 1108b
Yazīd b. Abī Ḥabīb v, 1124a — V, 1120b
Yazīd b. Abī Muslim i, 50a; ii, 145b; iii, 42a — I, 51b, II, 149b; III, 43b
Yazīd b. Abī Sufyān i, 111a, 151b, 447a, 460b, 997b; ii, 280a, b, 535a, 911a — I, 114a, 155b, 460a, 474a, 1028b; II, 288b, 548b, 932b
Yazīd b. Aḥmad iv, 346b — IV, 361a
Yazīd b. Ḥammād b. Zayd s, 384b — S, 385a
Yazīd b. Hārūn s, 89a — S, 88b
Yazīd b. Ḥātim al-Muhallabī i, 18a, 125a; iii, 233a, 654b, 785a, 876a; iv, 336b, 827a, 829a — I, 18b, 128b; III, 240a, 676a, 808a, 900a; IV, 351a, 860a, 862a
Yazīd b. Ilyās iii, 1032a — III, 1058a
Yazīd b. Maysara i, 959b — I, 989a
Yazīd b. Mazyad al-Shaybānī i, 149b; iii, 233b, 234a; iv, 645a — I, 153b; III, 240a, 241a; IV, 671b
Yazīd b. Miḳsam Ibn Dabba iv, 1003a — IV, 1035b
Yazīd b. Mufarrigh iv, 54b — IV, 57b
Yazīd b. al-Muhallab i, 12b, 77a, 550a, 720a; ii, 809a, 1141b; iii, 41a, 42a, 177a, 649b, 650a, 717b, 1255a; iv, 15a-b, 644b, 926b, 1098b; v, 157b; s, 41a, 299a, 350a — I, 13a, 79b, 567b, 742a; II, 828b, 1168b; III, 42b, 43b, 181b, 670b, 671a, 740a, 1287b; IV, 16b, 671a, 959b, 1129a; V, 157a; S, 41a, 298b, 350a
al-Yazīd b. Muḥammad b. ᶜAbd Allāh, Mawlāy i, 356b; ii, 510b, 835b; v, 1192a; s, 401b — I, 367b; II, 523a, 855a; V, 1182b; S, 402a
Yazīd b. ᶜUmar b. Hubayra → Ibn Hubayra, Yazīd
Yazīd b. Usayd al-Sulamī i, 837a; iv, 344b, 578b, 1174a — I, 860b; IV, 359a, 602a, 1207b
Yazīd b. al-Walīd → Yazīd III
Yazīd b. Yazīd b. al-Muhallab s, 41a — S, 41a
Yazīd b. Zurayᶜ iii, 838b — III, 862a

Yazīd al-Rāḍī iii, 748a — III, 771a
al-Yazīdī → Muḥammad b. al-ʿAbbās
al-Yazīdī, Yaḥyā ii, 293a; v, 174b — II, 301a; V, 172a
Yazīdī, Yazīdiyya → al-Nukkār
Yazīdīs (Shārwān) → Yazīd, Banū
Yazīdiyya (Sharwān) iv, 347a, 348a — IV, 362a, 363a
Yazīdiyya (sub-sect) iii, 660a; iv, 1076b; v, 208b, 210b — III, 681a; IV, 1108b; V, 206a, 208a
al-Yāzidjī, Ibrāhīm i, 572a, 596b; ii, 428a; iv, 967a — I, 590b, 616a; II, 439a; IV, 999a
al-Yāzidjī, Nāṣīf i, 596b; ii, 428b; s, 40a, 159b, 161a, b — I, 616a; II, 440a; S, 40a, 159b, 160b, 161a
Yazîdjî-oghlu Aḥmed → Bīdjān, Aḥmed
Yazîdjî-oghlu ʿAlī i, 21b, 419b; ii, 81a; iii, 738a; iv, 813a — I, 22b, 431b; II, 82b; III, 760b, 761a; IV, 845b
Yazîdjî-oghlu Meḥmed i, 1202a; ii, 985b; iii, 43b, 711a — I, 1237b; II, 1008a; III, 45a, 733b
al-Yāzūrī i, 533a, 1074a, b; ii, 495b, 856a, 858a, 860b; iii, 385b; v, 623b — I, 549a, 1106a, b; II, 507b, 876a, 878a, 880b; III, 398a; V, 627b
Yedigey → Edigü
Yedikule iv, 225a, 233a — IV, 234b, 243b
Yefet ben Eli → Japheth b. Eli
Yefremoy, Filipp v, 29a — V, 30a
Yegen Meḥmed Pasha → Muḥammad Pasha Yegen
Yegen ʿOthmān Pasha iv, 194a — IV, 202a, b
Yeh-lü Ta-shih iv, 581a, b, 583a — IV, 604b, 605a, 606b
Yemen/Yémen → Yaman
Yengikent → Djand
Yenibaghče iv, 232b — IV, 243a
Yeni-Čeri i, 4a, 36a, 199a, 206b, 268b, 270b, 293b, 904a, 1061a, b, 1119a, 1120b, 1147b, 1162b, 1165a, 1256a, b, 1268a, 1277b; ii, 16a, 33b, 184b, 189b, 210b, 212a, 287a, 374a, 443a, 512b, 532b, 684a, 687a, 880b, 1086a, 1089b, 1135a; iii, 88a, 192a, b, 341b, 552b, 628b, 636a; iv, 237b, 242b, 867b; v, 32b, 275b, 359b, 642b, 643a; s, 269b — I, 4a, 36b, 204b, 213a, 276b, 278b, 302b, 931a, 1093a, b, 1153a, 1154b, 1182a, 1197a, 1199b, 1294a, b, 1307a, 1317a; II, 16b, 34a, 190b, 195b, 217a, 218b, 295a, 384a, 454b, 525a, 545b, 701a, 704b, 901a, 1111a, 1115a, 1161b; III, 90b, 197a, 351b, 571b, 649b, 657a; IV, 248a, 253a, b, 901a; V, 34a, 273b, 360b, 647a, b; S, 269a
Yeničeri Aghasî i, 658b, 687a, 838a, 1256a; ii, 34a, 212b, 723b; iv, 232a — I, 679a, 708a, 861b, 1294b; II, 34b, 219a, 742a; IV, 242b
Yeni Il i, 241a — I, 248b
Yeni Djāmiʿ iv, 233b — IV, 243b
Yeñi Ḳale iv, 892a; v, 140a, 141a — IV, 925a; V, 143a, b
Yeni Kapî iv, 233a — IV, 243b
Yeni Odalar iv, 228b, 229b — IV, 238b, 239b
Yeni Othmanlîlar i, 13b, 37b, 61b, 63b, 64a, 210a, 641b, 657a, 974b; ii, 430b, 642a, 643b, 728a, 876a; iii, 553b, 592a; iv, 872a — I, 13b, 38b, 63b, 65b, 216a, 662a, 678a, 1004b; II, 441b, 658a, 659b, 746b, 896b; III, 572b, 612a; IV, 905b
Yeñishehirli ʿAwnī s, 324b — S, 324a
Yeprim Khān iv, 862b — IV, 895b
Yĕrāḳā, Afdah, Shabbethai iv, 607b — IV, 632a
Yesḥaḳ iii, 4a — III, 4a
Yeshbek iv, 463a — IV, 483b
Yeshbum i, 767a — I, 789b, 790a
Yeşil Hisar iv, 580a — IV, 603b
Yesü Möngke ii, 3a, b — II, 3a, b
Yesügei ii, 41b — II, 42a
Yesün-Toʾa i, 1311b — I, 1352a
Yetīm ʿAli Čelebi iv, 1158b — IV, 1190b
Yidghā ii, 31b — II, 32a
Yigit i, 322b — I, 332b
Yigit Pasha i, 1263a; v, 276b — I, 1301b; V, 274b
Yîlanlî-oghlu ii, 207b — II, 214a
Yilbughā → Ylbughā
Yîldîz, Tādj al-Dīn i, 64a, 393b, 855b; ii, 120a, 267a, 1049b, 1101b, 1103a; iii, 1155a; v, 501a, 546a; s, 360a — I, 66a, 404b, 879b; II, 122b, 275b, 1074a, 1127b, 1129a; III, 1183b; V, 504b, 551a; S, 359b
Yîltuwar i, 1305b — I, 1345b
Yima → Djamshīd
Yimāk → Kipčak
Yināl → Ināl
Yintān b. ʿUmar iii, 959a — III, 983b
Yirmisekiz Čelebi Meḥmed iii, 997b, 1002a; v, 641b, 642a — III, 1022b, 1027b; V, 645b, 646a
Ylbughā Nāṣirī i, 1050b; ii, 285b, 286a — I, 1082b; II, 293b, 294a
Ylbughā al-Sālimī iv, 437b — IV, 457a
Ylbughā ʿUmarī i, 1050b; iii, 239b — I, 1082a; III, 246b
Yoga i, 434b, 1031b — I, 447a, 1063a
Yoḳlama iv, 268a — IV, 280a
Yol parasî i, 475b — I, 489b
Yola i, 180a; ii, 942b — I, 185a; II, 964a
Yomut Türkmen iv, 1065a; v, 24a; s, 143b, 146b, 281a — IV, 1096b; V, 24b; S, 143a, 146b, 281a
Yoruba iii, 646a — III, 667a
Yōsēf ben Abraham → Yūsuf al-Baṣīr
Yotḳan v, 37a — V, 38a
Young Turks → Yeni Othmanlîlar
Youssi, Aīt s, 145a — S, 144b
Yücel, Ḥasan ʿAlī iii, 1199b, 1200b; v, 281b, 282a, b; s, 42a, 283b — III, 1230a, 1231a; V, 280a, b; S, 42a, 283b
Yūdāsaf → Bilawhar wa-Yūdāsaf
Yūdghān iv, 96a, b, 603b — IV, 100a, b, 628a
Yugoslavia/Yougoslavie i, 1275a; iv, 574a, b; v, 32a, 277a — I, 1314b; IV, 597a; V, 33a, 275a
Yuḥannā b. Haylān ii, 778b — II, 797b
Yuḥannā b. Sarābiyūn i, 213b; s, 271b — I, 219b; S, 271a
Yuḥannā b. Yaʿḳūb b. Abkār iv, 130b — IV, 136a
Yuḥannā al-Kaṣīr v, 368a — V, 369a
Yük iii, 212b — III, 218b
Yukhārībāsh iv, 387b, 389b, 390b — IV, 404a, 406a, 407a
Yuknakī → Aḥmad Yuknakī
Yulbars Khān v, 846a — V, 858a
Yuldash-oghlu Fazyl → Fāḍil Yuldash
Yulūḳ Arslān iii, 1119b — III, 1147a
Yumgān iv, 199b — IV, 208a
Yumugul-oghlu → Togan, Z.V.
Yund Adalarî i, 792a — I, 815b
al-Yūnīnī, Ḳuṭb al-Dīn iii, 752b; s, 400a — III, 775b; S, 400b
al-Yūnīnī, Sharaf al-Dīn iii, 861b — III, 885b
Yünnan v, 869a — V, 875a
Yūnus, Ḳapudān iii, 1176b — III, 1205a
Yūnus, Shaykh ii, 181b; iv, 428a — II, 187b; IV, 446b
Yūnus b. ʿAbd al-Raḥmān iii, 497b — III, 514b
Yūnus b. ʿAlī Bey iii, 605a, 635b — III, 625b, 657a
Yūnus b. Ḥabīb i, 105b, 158a — I, 108b, 162b
Yūnus b. Ilyās → Yūnus b. al-Yasaʿ
Yūnus b. al-Yasaʿ i, 1044a; v, 1160b — I, 1076a; V, 1150a
Yūnus al-Aṣṭurlābī s, 267a, 372a — S, 266b, 372a
Yūnus al-Dawādār iv, 425b — IV, 446a
Yūnus Emre iii, 1094a; iv, 812a; v, 264a, 677a, 681b; s, 283a — III, 1121a; IV, 844b; V, 262a, 682a, 686b; S, 282b
Yūnus al-Kātib s, 183a — S, 184b
Yūnus Khān i, 148a; ii, 45b, 622a — I, 152a; II, 46a,

637b
Yūnus Maʿn ii, 443b, 750b — II, 455b, 769a
Yūnus Nādī ii, 475b; iii, 1117a — II, 487b; III, 1144b
Yūnus Pasha ii, 1042a — II, 1066b
Yuʿfir, Āl s, 335a — S, 334b
Yūra i, 1305a, 1306a — I, 1345b, 1346b
Yüregir-oghlu Ramaḍān i, 182b; ii, 38b — I, 187b; II, 39a
Yurt iv, 1150b; v, 659a — IV, 1182a; V, 663b
Yürük i, 470b, 651b, 1302b; ii, 40b, 612b; iv, 563a — I, 484b, 672a, 1342b; II, 41b, 627b; IV, 585b
Yūshaʿ v, 926b — V, 931b
al-Yūsī s, 28b, 223a — S, 29a, 223a
al-Yussāna i, 491b — I, 506a
Yūsuf i, 1229b; ii, 873a; v, 193b, 233b, 423b — I, 1266b; II, 893a; V, 190b, 231b, 425b
Yūsuf I (Almohad(e)) → Abū Yaʿḳūb Yūsuf
Yūsuf I (Naṣrid(e)) i, 1339b; ii, 115a, 1017a; iii, 835b; v, 1128a, 1149b — I, 1379b; II, 117b, 1040b; III, 859b; V, 1124b, 1140b
Yūsuf II (Naṣrid(e)) iii, 972b — III, 997a
Yūsuf III (Naṣrid(e)) ii, 353a — II, 362b
Yūsuf IV (Naṣrid(e)) s, 399a — S, 399b
Yūsuf V (Naṣrid(e)) s, 399a — S, 399b
Yūsuf I (Rasūlid(e)) i, 553a; v, 1241a — I, 570b; V, 1231b
Yūsuf, Abū Yaʿḳūb → Abū Yaʿḳūb Yūsuf
Yūsuf, Mawlāy i, 357b; ii, 160a; iv, 634b; s, 48a — I, 368b; II, 165a; IV, 660b; S, 48a
Yūsuf b. al-Abbār iv, 338a — IV, 352b
Yūsuf b. ʿAbd al-Hādī iii, 486b, 842b — III, 503b, 866b
Yūsuf b. ʿAbd al-Muʾmin → Abū Yaʿḳūb Yūsuf
Yūsuf b. ʿAbd al-Raḥmān al-Fihrī i, 82a, 493b, 608b, 1079b; iv, 494b; v, 510b; s, 81b — I, 84b, 508b, 628a, 1111b; IV, 515b; V, 514a; S, 81b
Yūsuf b. ʿAbd Allāh → Abu ʾl-Futūḥ Yūsuf
Yūsuf b. ʿAbd al-Wahhāb s, 11a — S, 10b
Yūsuf b. Abū ʾl-Sādj i, 205a, 387a, 507a, 642b; ii, 191b, 453a, 679b; iii, 126b, 236a, 619b; iv, 22b — I, 211a, 398a, 522b, 663b; II, 198a, 465a, 696b; III, 129b, 243a, 640b; IV, 24a
Yūsuf b. Abī Saʿīd Muḥammad ii, 679a — II, 696a
Yūsuf b. Aḥmad → Yūsuf al-Muʾtamin
Yūsuf b. ʿAlī Küčük i, 1160b — I, 1195a
Yūsuf b. Bābak i, 153b — I, 158a
Yūsuf b. Barsbāy ii, 6a — II, 6a
Yūsuf b. Djihānshāh iv, 588a — IV, 611b
Yūsuf b. Ḥasdāy i, 1091b — I, 1124a
Yūsuf b. Ibrāhīm, Sulṭān ii, 124a — II, 127a
Yūsuf b. Ibrāhīm al-Dāya iii, 745b — III, 768a, b
Yūsuf b. Ḳādis iii, 1055b — III, 1082a
Yūsuf b. Kaʾus i, 637a — I, 658a
Yūsuf b. Khalīl iv, 244b — IV, 255b
Yūsuf b. Nagralla i, 130b — I, 134a
Yūsuf b. Nūḥ iv, 605a — IV, 629b
Yūsuf b. Saʿīd al-Ahansalī iii, 167a — III, 170b
Yūsuf b. al-Sarrādj → Ibn al-Sarrādj
Yūsuf b. al-Sarrādj (wazīr) → Ibn al-Sarrādj
Yūsuf b. Sulaymān (Gharnāṭa) ii, 1014a — II, 1037b
Yūsuf b. Sulaymān (dāʿī muṭlaḳ) s, 358b — S, 358b
Yūsuf b. Tāshufīn i, 7a, 43b, 251a, 389b, 495a, 1148b, 1176a; ii, 525a, 818b, 821b, 874a, 1013a; iii, 138a, 542b, 771a, 904b, 977a; iv, 672b, 943a; v, 654b, 655a, 1178a, 1179a, 1189b — I, 7a, 45a, 258b, 401a, 510a, 1183a, 1211a; II, 538a, 838a, 841a, 894b, 1036b; III, 141a, 561b, 794a, 929a, 1001b; IV, 700a, 976a; V, 658b, 659a, 1168a, 1169a, 1179b
Yūsuf b. ʿUmar → Yūsuf I (Rasūlid(e))
Yūsuf b. ʿUmar al-Thaḳafī iii, 493b; iv, 926a, 927a; v, 374b; s, 127a, 232b, 251b — III, 510b; IV, 959a, 960a; V, 375a; S, 126b, 232b, 251b
Yūsuf b. Uzun Ḥasan → Ḳarā Yūsuf
Yūsuf b. Yaʿḳūb (Imāmī) s, 233a — S, 232b
Yūsuf (Sanūsī) s, 165a — S, 164b
Yūsuf ʿĀdil Shāh i, 199a, 1202b; ii, 922b, 1084b; iii, 15a, 1159b — I, 204b, 1238a; II, 944a, 1110a; III, 16a, 1187b, 1188a
Yūsuf Agha iii, 623a, 983a, 1086a — III, 644a, 1007b, 1113a
Yūsuf Akčura s, 47b — S, 48a
Yūsuf ʿAlī Khān i, 827b; ii, 83b — I, 850b; II, 85a
Yūsuf Asʿar → Dhū Nuwās
Yūsuf al-Athīr s, 159b, 161a, b — S, 159b, 160b, 161a
Yūsuf al-Badīʿī s, 362a — S, 361b
Yūsuf al-Barm iv, 16b; v, 855a — IV, 17b; V, 862a
Yūsuf al-Baṣīr iv, 305a, 306b, 605a — IV, 319a, 320b, 629b
Yūsuf Beg i, 354b — I, 365b
Yūsuf al-Bitrūdjī ii, 1009a; v, 586b — II, 1033a; V, 591b
Yūsuf Buluggīn → Buluggīn b. Zīrī
Yūsuf Ḍiyāʾ s, 168a — S, 168a
Yūsuf Ḍiyā Pasha ii, 202a — II, 208a
Yūsuf al-Fihrī → Yūsuf b. ʿAbd al-Raḥmān
Yūsuf Hamadhānī i, 299a, 515b; ii, 1078a — I, 308a, 531b; II, 1103a
Yūsuf Ḥubaysh ii, 801a — II, 819b
Yūsuf Kadîr Khān → Kadîr Khān
Yūsuf Kāmil Pasha iii, 1199a — III, 1229a
Yūsuf Ḳaramanlî ii, 161b; iv, 617b, 618a — II, 166b; IV, 642b
Yūsuf Khān Čak s, 366b — S, 366a
Yūsuf Khān Mustashār al-Dawla iv, 164a, 397b; s, 71b, 109a — IV, 171a, 415a; S, 72a, 108a
Yūsuf Khān Riḍwī iv, 709a; s, 132a, 167b — IV, 737b; S, 131a, 167b
Yūsuf Khāṣṣ Ḥādjib i, 299a, 987a; iii, 1114a, 1116a; iv, 699a; v, 538a — I, 308b, 1017b; III, 1141b, 1143a; IV, 727a; V, 542b
Yūsuf Khayl, Tatār Khān s, 203a — S, 202b
Yūsuf Ḳurayshī, Shaykh iii, 633b, 634a — III, 654b, 655a
Yūsuf Mukhliṣ Pasha i, 992b — I, 1023b
Yūsuf al-Muʿtamin i, 7a; iii, 542b, 706a — I, 7a; III, 561b, 728a
Yūsuf al-Muẓaffar v, 683a — V, 688a
Yūsuf Pasha (d./m. 1646) → Yūsuf Agha
Yūsuf Pasha (d./m. 1838) → Yūsuf Ḳaramānlî
Yūsuf Pasha ii, 635b — II, 652a
Yūsuf Pasha Khodja → Khodja Yūsuf Pasha
Yūsuf Pasha Sayf-oghlu ii, 443b, 635a, 749b, 750b — II, 455a, 651a, 768a, 769a
Yūsuf Shāh i, 1168a — I, 1203a
Yūsuf Shāh I b. Alp Arghūn v, 826b — V, 833a
Yūsuf Shāh II v, 827a — V, 833b
Yūsuf Shāh Čak (Kashmīr) iv, 709a; s, 131b, 132a, 167a, 332b — IV, 737b; S, 131a, 167a, 332a
Yūsuf Shihāb i, 1078a; ii, 444a, 635b; s, 268b — I, 1110b; II, 455b, 651b; S, 268a
Yūsuf Sinān ii, 203b — II, 210a
Yūsuf al-Thaḳafī s, 354b — S, 354b
Yūsuf Wahbī ii, 39b — II, 40a
Yūsuf u Zalīkhā (Zulaykhā) iv, 62b; s, 65a — IV, 66a; S, 65b
Yūsufzays i, 218b, 220a, 229a, 229b, 769a, 864b; iv, 1102a — I, 224b, 226a, 236a, 792a, 888b; IV, 1133a
Yu-tʾien → Khotan
Yüz (tribe/tribu) s, 46a — S, 46b
Yüz Āsaf i, 1217a — I, 1253b
Yüzellilikler s, 149b — S, 149b

Z

Zaʿāʾir i, 84b — I, 87a
Zāb iii, 982a; v, 1180b; s, 103a — III, 1006b; V, 1170b; S, 102b
Zāb (river/rivière) i, 16a, 43a, 424a, 426b; ii, 249b; iv, 1186b; v, 442a — I, 16b, 44a, 436a, 439a; II, 256b; IV, 1219a; V, 444b
al-Zabādī, Abu ʾl-Ḥasan al-Manālī s, 404a — S, 404a
Zabān-i ḥāl iv, 58b — IV, 61b
al-Zabbāʾ i, 450b, 548b; iv, 556b — I, 463b, 566a; IV, 580b
Zabbāl → Kannās
Zabbān b. Sayyār al-Fazārī i, 690a; iii, 23a — I, 711a; III, 24b
Zabibē i, 525a — I, 541a
Zabīd ii, 91a, 996a; iii, 746a; iv, 1188b; v, 1244a, b; s, 30b, 289a, 338a — II, 92b, 1019a; III, 769a; IV, 1221b; V, 1235a; S, 30b, 289a, 337b
al-Zabīdī → Murtaḍā al-Zabīdī
Zabīta → Ḍābiṭ
Zābita Khān → Ḍābiṭa Khān
Zabtiyye → Ḍabṭiyya
Zābulistān i, 86a, 147b, 226b; ii, 1048b; iii, 304a, 715b; iv, 356b; v, 1166b; s, 125b, 263a — I, 88b, 152a, 233b; II, 1073a; III, 313a, 738a; IV, 372a; V, 1156b; S, 124b, 263a
Zabuls/Zabols i, 226a — I, 232b
al-Zabūr i, 264a — I, 272a
Ẓabya (Ḳayna) s, 247a — S, 247a
Zād al-Rākib ii, 785a; iv, 1143b — II, 804a; IV, 1175b
Zādawaih i, 451b — I, 464b
Zadjal i, 501b, 574b, 595b, 602a; ii, 1033a; iii, 849b, 851a; v, 1207a — I, 516b, 593a, 615a, 621b; II, 1057a; III, 873b, 875a; V, 1197b
al-Zadjdjādj, Abū Isḥāḳ iii, 838a; iv, 181b — III, 861b; IV, 189b
al-Zadjdjādjī, Abu ʾl-Ḳāsim iii, 597a, 838a, 1128a — III, 617b, 861b, 1156a
Zadjr i, 659b; ii, 760a; iv, 290b — I, 680b; II, 778b; IV, 303b
Zafadola → Aḥmad III (Hūdid(e))
Ẓafār → Ẓufār
Ẓafar ʿAlī Khān iii, 359a; s, 247b — III, 370a; S, 247b
Ẓafar Djang → Tadjammul Ḥusayn Khān
Ẓafar Khān (Bahmanī) → ʿAlāʾ al-Dīn Ḥasan Bahman
Ẓafar Khān (Gudjarāt) (d./m. 1319) ii, 1124a — II, 1150b
Ẓafar Khān (Gudjarāt (d./m. 1376) ii, 1124b — II, 1151a
Ẓafar Khān (Kashmīr) iv, 709a — IV, 737b
Zafarabad ii, 498b, 499b — II, 510b, 512a
al-Zaʿfarānī, Mūsā → al-Tiflīsī, Abū ʿImrān
Zaʿfarānlū iii, 1104a, 1108a; v, 312a — III, 1131a, 1135a; V, 311b
Zafīr → Ḍafīr
al-Zāfir i, 9a, 198b; iii, 868a — I, 9b, 204a; III, 892b
Zāfir b. Sulaymān iv, 289b — IV, 302b
Zafrullah Khān i, 302a — I, 311b
Zaganos Pasha iv, 969a — IV, 1001a
al-Zaghall → Muḥammad XII (Naṣrid(e))
Zaghārī (dog/chien) iv, 491a — IV, 512a
Zaghāwa s, 190a, b — S, 191a, b
Zaghlūl → Saʿd Zaghlūl
Zaghra s, 330a — S, 329b
Zagros iii, 1253a; iv, 1a, 2b, 5a-b, 8a; v, 865b; s, 147b — III, 1285b; IV, 1a, 2b, 5b-6a, 8b; V, 872a; S, 147b
al-Zahāwī, Djamīl Ṣidḳī i, 597b; iii, 1264b; iv, 145a, 720b — I, 617a; III, 1297b; IV, 151a, 749b
Zāhid al-ʿUlamāʾ al-Fāriḳī i, 1224a — I, 1260b
Zāhidī iv, 41b — IV, 44a
Ẓahīr ii, 302b, 306a, 308a — II, 310b, 314b, 317a
Ẓāhir i, 1039a, 1099a; iv, 203a — I, 1070b, 1132a; IV, 212a
al-Ẓāhir (Mamlūk title/titre mamlūk) → under following name/sous le nom suivant
al-Ẓāhir (ʿAbbāsid(e)) i, 198a, 227a — I, 203b, 234a
al-Ẓāhir (Fāṭimid(e)) ii, 855a, b, 856a, 859a; iv, 514a — II, 874b, 875a, b, 878b; IV, 536b
Ẓahīr al-Dīn Marʿashī s, 363b — S, 363a
Ẓahīr-i Fāryābī iv, 62a; s, 108a, 239b — IV, 65a; S, 107a, 240a
al-Ẓāhir, al- Malik → al-Ẓāhir Ghāzī
Ẓahīr al-Dawla, ʿAlī Khān ii, 434a — II, 445a
al-Ẓāhir Ghāzī, al-Malik (Ayyūbid(e)) i, 197b, 798b, 803a, 989b, 996a, 1316b; ii, 37b, 353b, 556b; iii, 87b, 178a, 208b, 399b, 693b, 863a; iv, 482a; v, 924b — I, 203b, 822a, 826a, 1020a, 1026b, 1356b; II, 38b, 363a, 570a; III, 89b, 182a, 214b, 412a, 715b, 887a; IV, 503a; V, 930a
Ẓāhir Hamdān (region) s, 22a — S, 22b
Ẓāhir al-ʿUmar i, 63a, 391b; ii, 534a, 635b, 912a; iii, 325a, 992a; s, 20b, 268a, b, 269a — I, 65a, 403a; II, 547a, 651b, 933b; III, 335a, 1016b; S, 20b, 268a, b
al-Ẓāhira i, 1098a; iii, 1004b — I, 1131a; III, 1029b
al-Ẓāhirī → ʿAbd Allāh b. Ḳāsim; Ibn Dāwūd; Ibn Ḥazm, ʿAlī
Ẓāhiriyya i, 414a, 1325a; ii, 182b, 890a; iii, 308a, 744b, 790b, 1149a; iv, 46a; v, 73a; s, 386a, 396b — I, 425b, 1365b; II, 188a, 910b; III, 317a, 767b, 814a, 1177b; IV, 48b; V, 75a; S, 386b, 397a
al-Ẓāhiriyya madrasa ii, 286a, 290a — II, 294a, 298a
al-Ẓahr s, 50a — S, 50b
Ẓahrān i, 73a, 811b; ii, 108b; iii, 363b — I, 75a, 835a; II, 111a; III, 375a
al-Zahrāwī, Abu ʾl-Ḳāsim i, 214a, 600b; ii, 482a, 901a; s, 271b, 272a — I, 220b, 620a; II, 494a, 922a; S, 271b
al-Zaʿīm, Ḥusnī ii, 662a; v, 1047b — II, 678b; V, 1044a
Zāʾir v, 1004a — V, 1000a
Zaïre iv, 749b — IV, 780a
al-Zaʿīrī, Muḥammad b. Mubārik s, 28b — S, 29a
Zakandar v, 969a — V, 972a
Zākānī → ʿUbayd-i Zākānī
Zakʿarid(e)s i, 507b, 508a — I, 523a
Zakariyāʾ s, 402b — S, 403a
Zakariyyāʾ b. Mammatī → Ibn Mammātī, Muhadhdhab
Zakāriyyāʾ al-Anṣārī iii, 779a — III, 802a
Zakariyya Khān v, 598b — V, 602b
Zakariyyā Muḥyī al-Dīn s, 5b, 6a — S, 4b, 5a
Zakariyyāzāde Yaḥyāʾ Efendi iv, 884a — IV, 917a
Zakāt i, 968b, 1099b, 1142a, 1144a, 1146a; ii, 142b, 154a; iv, 485b, 1151b, 1152b; v, 424b, 1252a — I, 998b, 1132b, 1176b, 1178b, 1180b; II, 146a, 158b; IV, 506b, 1183b, 1185a; V, 426b, 1243a
al-Zaḳāzīḳ s, 262b — S, 262a
Zakhūr Rāhib, Raphaël Anṭūn iii, 1245a — III, 1277b
Zakī, Aḥmad → Abū Shādī
Zaki al-Dīn Muḥammad al-Birzālī i, 1238a — I, 1276a
al-Zākī Ṭamal ii, 828a — II, 847b
Zakka Khēls i, 238a, b — I, 245b, 246a
al-Zaḳḳāḳ, ʿAlī i, 428a; iii, 948b — I, 440a; III, 973a
Zakrī → Ibn Zakrī
al-Zallāḳa i, 7a, 43b, 242b; v, 1189b — I, 7a, 45a, 250a; V, 1179b
Zallīdj ii, 748a — II, 766a
Zām iv, 96b — IV, 101a
al-Zamakhsharī, Maḥmūd i, 120a, 412a, 594a, 709a,

1129a; ii, 896a, 1079a; iii, 249a, 302a, 368b, 968a; iv, 524b, 525a, b, 527a, 615a; s, 343a — I, 123b, 424a, 613a, 729b, 1163a; II, 917a, 1104a; III, 256a, 311a, 380b, 992b; IV, 547a, b, 548b, 550a, 640a; S, 343a
Zamān Shāh Durrānī i, 72b, 230b; ii, 838b; iii, 1158b; iv, 391b; v, 599a — I, 74b, 237b; II, 858b; III, 1187a; IV, 408b; V, 602b
Zamāna Beg → Mahābat Khān
Zamān-i Yazdī i, 1301a — I, 1341a
Zamāniyya s, 325a — S, 324b
Zāmil b. Djabr ii, 176a — II, 181b
Zamīn Dāwar i, 86a; ii, 1100b — I, 88b; II, 1126b
Zamīndārī ii, 158b, 784b; v, 686b — II, 163b, 803a; V, 691b
Zamindāwar iv, 536a, b; v, 691a — IV, 559b; V, 695b
Zamora → Sammūra
Zammāra ii, 1027b — II, 1051b
Zammūr iii, 1043b — III, 1069a
Zammūr, Banū iv, 78a — IV, 82a
Zamorins iv, 547a — IV, 570b, 571a
Zamzam iv, 91b, 185a, 318a, 321a — IV, 95b, 193a, 332b, 335a
Zanādiḳa ii, 96a, 770b — II, 98a, 789a
Zanāfidj i, 1157b — I, 1192a
Ẓanāga → Ṣanhādja
Zanāna iii, 148a — III, 151a
Zanāra v, 695a, 697a — V, 700a, 702a
Zanāta i, 92a, 367a, 533a, 699b, 762b, 860a, 1174b, 1175b, 1177b, 1309a; ii, 818b, 821a, 852b; iii, 137b, 138a, 654a, 1036a, 1039a; v, 1174a, b, 1179a, 1182b; s, 328b — I, 95a, 378a, 549b, 720b, 785a, 884a, 1209b, 1210b, 1212b, 1349b; II, 838a, 840b, 872b; III, 140b, 141a, 675a, 1062a, 1065a; V, 1164a, b, 1169a, 1172b; S, 328a
al-Zanātī, Abū ʿAbd Allāh Muḥammad iv, 1129b — IV, 1161a
Zand iii, 1102b; iv, 38a; v, 461b, 617a, 663b; s, 405b — III, 1129b; IV, 40b; V, 464a, 621a, 669a; S, 405b
Žanda Pīl → Aḥmad-i Djām
Zandādj (Zandāk), Banū v, 1181a — V, 1171a
Zandaḳa → Zindīḳ
Zanda-rūd → Zāyanda-rūd
Zandaward s, 354b — S, 354b
Zandī s, 71a — S, 71b
Zandj i, 18b, 23b, 33b, 36a, 73b, 133b, 388b, 551a, 921a, 937b, 1086a, 1096a; iii, 880a; iv, 567a; v, 940b, 941b; s, 49a — I, 19a, 24a, 34a, 37a, 76a, 137b, 400a, 569a, 949a, 966b, 1118b, 1129a; III, 904a; IV, 589b; V, 944a, 945a; S, 49b
Zandj, sea of/mer des → Baḥr al-Zandj
Zandjān s, 71a — S, 72a
al-Zandjānī, Abu ʾl-Ḥasan ʿAlī iii, 1071b — III, 1098a
al-Zandj → ʿAlī b. Muḥammad
Zandjibār i, 36a, 554b, 1043b, 1282a, b; iv, 887b, 888a, 889a; v, 106b, 1030a; s, 351b — I, 37a, 572a, 1075a, 1321a, b; IV, 920a, b, 921b; V, 109a, 1026a; S, 351b
Zangana iii, 1109a; v, 169b, 461a — III, 1136a; V, 167a, 463b
Zangī, Mullā i, 1121b — I, 1155a
Zangids/Zankides i, 665b, 1161a; ii, 282b; s, 205a — I, 686a, 1195b; II, 290b; S, 205a
Zankī (Zangi) i, 314a, b, 426b, 466b, 664b, 797a, 971a, 1160b, 1332a, 1358a; ii, 64b, 347b, 348b, 354b, 489a, 1082a; iii, 87a, 120a, 228b, 399a; v, 332a, 454a, b, 922a, 924b — I, 324a, 439a, 480a, 684b, 820a, 1001a, 1195a, 1373a, 1398a; II, 66a, 357b, 358a, 364a, 501b, 1107b; III, 89b, 122b, 235a, 411a; V, 332a, 457a, 927b, 930a
Zanzibar → Zandjibār
Zar v, 676a — V, 681a
Zarāfa iii, 346b, 666a — III, 357a, 687b
Zarafshān (river, fleuve) iii, 483a; v, 247a; s, 97a — III, 500a; V, 245a; S, 96b
Zarah iii, 150a — III, 153b
Zarandj v, 151a, 868a — V, 153a, 874b
al-Zarānīḳ i, 1140b — I, 1175a
Zarhūn s, 103a, 350b — S, 102b, 350b
Zarībiyya iv, 668a — IV, 695b
Ẓarīf ii, 1032a — II, 1056a
Zarīr(-ān) iii, 113a — III, 115b
Zarḳaʾ al-Yamāma iii, 455a; v, 777b — III, 470b; V, 783b
al-Zarkalī i, 600b, 725b, 726a, 727a; ii, 243b; iii, 1137a — I, 620a, 747b, 748a, b; II, 250b; III, 1165b
al-Zarḳawī, Aḥmad Mūsā s, 153a — S, 153b
Zarmihr iv, 644a; s, 298a — IV, 670b; S, 297b
Zarrūk, Aḥmad b. Aḥmad al-Fāsī s, 404b — S, 404b
Zarrūḳ, Aḥmad b. Muḥammad al-Fāsī s, 44a, 403a — S, 44b, 403b
Zarrūḳī iv, 380a — IV, 396b
Zarūd s, 198b — S, 198b
Zarwāl, Banū i, 84b — I, 87a
Zattallī → Djaʿfar
al-Ẓawāhir i, 1313b, 1314a — I, 1354a
al-Zawāwī → Ibn Muʿṭī
al-Zawāwī, ʿAlī iii, 720a — III, 742b
Zāwī b. Zīrī i, 84a; ii, 1012a; iii, 1110a — I, 86b; II, 1035b; III, 1137b
Zawīla ii, 875b; iii, 657b; iv, 567a — II, 896a; III, 678b; IV, 589b
Zāwiya i, 139a, 290b, 1225a; iv, 380b, 383a, 433a; v, 1129b, 1201b, 1208b; s, 223a — I, 143a, 299b, 1261b; IV, 397a, 399b, 452a; V, 1126a, 1191b, 1199a; S, 223a
al-Zawzān iv, 910a; v, 450b — IV, 943a; V, 453a
al-Zawzanī, Abū ʿAbd-Allāh iv, 910a; s, 289b — IV, 943a; S, 289b
Zawzanī, Aṣīl al-Dīn s, 363a — S, 362b
Zawzanī, Ḥusayn iv, 525b — IV, 548b
Zāyanda-rūd iv, 98a, 674a; v, 869a, 872b, 873b, 874a; s, 275a — IV, 102b, 701b; V, 875b, 878b, 879b, 880a; S, 275a
al-Zayānī → al-Zayyānī
Zayānid(e)s → ʿAbd al-Wādid(e)s
Zayd b. ʿAlī b. Ḥusayn i, 402b; ii, 889a; iii, 493b, 617b, 1265b; iv, 371b, 446b, 1086b, 1161a; v, 3a; s, 19a, 48b, 127a, 130a, 401a — I, 414a; II, 910a; III, 510b, 638a, 1298b; IV, 387b, 466a, 1117b, 1193a; V, 3a; S, 19a, 49a, 126b, 129a, 401b
Zayd b. ʿAmr b. Nufayl ii, 1060a; iii, 1206a — II, 1084b; III, 1236b
Zayd b. al-Djabal al-Ṭāʾī iv, 858b — IV, 891b
Zayd b. Ḥamād i, 565a — I, 583a
Zayd b. Ḥāritha i, 25a, 50b, 109b; ii, 275a, 372a, 573b, 842b, 873b; iv, 492b, 898b — I, 25b, 52a, 112b; II, 283b, 382a, 588a, 862a, 893b; IV, 514a, 931b
Zayd b. ʿĪsā s, 48b — S, 49a
Zayd b. Khalīfa i, 928b — I, 956b
Zayd b. al-Khaṭṭāb i, 1241b; ii, 569b — I, 1279b; II, 583b
Zayd b. Rifāʿa i, 127a; iii, 1071b — I, 130b; III, 1098b
Zayd b. Thābit ii, 540b, 886b; iii, 65a; v, 404b, 405a — II, 554a, 907a; III, 67b; V, 406a, b
Zayd b. Zāmil iv, 1072b — IV, 1104b
Zayd al-Khayl al-Ṭāʿī ii, 1005a; iii, 812a; iv, 832b; s, 304b — II, 1028b; III, 835b; IV, 865b; S, 304a
Zayd al-Khayr → Zayd al-Khayl al-Ṭāʾī
Zaydān, Djirdjī i, 597a; ii, 466b; v, 188a; s, 161a, 263a — I, 616b; II, 478a; V, 185b; S, 161a, 262b
Zaydān, Mawlāy iii, 256b — III, 265a
Zaydān al-Nāṣir, Mawlāy i, 280a; iv, 970b; v, 1191b; s, 29a — I, 288b; IV, 1002b, 1003a; V, 1181b; S, 29a
Zaydāni → Saʿdid

Zaydiyya i, 48b, 106b, 402b, 403a, 551b, 552a, 553b, 554a, 1350a, b; ii, 218a, 1111b; iii, 125b, 254a, 688b, 984b; iv, 44a, 46b, 944b; v, 1240b; s, 13a, b, 19a, 25b, 32a, 48a, b, 129b, 334b, 338a, 343a, 356b, 363a, 401a — I, 50a, 109b, 414a, b, 569a, b, 571a, b, 1390b, 1391a; II, 224b, 1137b; III, 128b, 261b, 710b, 1009a; IV, 47a, 49a-b, 977a; V, 1231b; S, 13a, 14a, 19a, 26a, 32b, 48b, 49a, 128b, 334b, 338a, 342b, 356a, 363a, 401a
- doctrine i, 445b, 1113b; iii, 486b, 1166a, 1265b; iv, 183a, 944b; v, 1237b; s, 236a — I, 458b, 1147a; III, 503b, 1194b, 1298b; IV, 190b, 977a; V, 1228a; S, 236a
Zāyid b. Khalīfa i, 166b; iv, 778a — I, 171a; IV, 809b
Zāyid al-Malṭūm ii, 175b, 176a — II, 181a
Zāyid b. Sulṭān al-Nihayyān, Shaykh s, 418b — S, 418b
Ẓaylaʿ i, 176b, 763b; iii, 3a, 5b — I, 181a, 786b; III, 3b, 5b
al-Zaylaʿī iii, 163b — III, 167a
Zayn al-ʿĀbidīn (Kashmīr) iii, 420a, 453a; iv, 707a, 708b; s, 131b, 167a — III, 433b, 469a; IV, 735b, 736b; S, 130b, 167a
Zayn al-ʿĀbidīn b. Ismaʿīl i, 47b — I, 48b
Zayn al-ʿĀbidīn ʿAlī b. al-Ḥusayn iii, 227b, 610a, b, 611b; iv, 277b, 638b; s, 95a, 231b, 401a — III, 234a, 630b, 631b, 632a; IV, 289b, 664b; S, 94b, 231b, 401b
Zayn al-ʿĀbidīn al-Kuntī v, 394a — V, 395a
Zayn al-ʿĀbidīn Pasha iv, 194a — IV, 202b
Zayn al-ʿAbidīn Sharīf iv, 1123a — IV, 1155a
Zayn al-Aṣnām i, 359a ; I, 370a
Zayn al-Dīn ʿAbd al-Salām Kamūyī s, 414b — S, 415a
Zayn al-Dīn Barakāt → Barakāt b. Mūsā
Zayn al-Dīn, Shaykh iii, 588b — III, 608b
Zaynab, queen of/reine de Palmyra → al-Zabbāʾ
Zaynab bint ʿAbd Allāh iii, 616a — III, 636b
Zaynab bint ʿAlī ii, 843a; iii, 609b — II, 863a; III, 630b
Zaynab bint Djaḥsh i, 44b — I, 45b
Zaynab bint Isḥāḳ v, 1178b — V, 1168b
Zaynab bint Maẓʿūn iii, 63b, 1017b — III, 66a, 1043a
Zaynab bint Ṭahmāsp iv, 977a — IV, 1009a
Zaynab al-Nafzāwiyya i, 251a, 389b; v, 654b, 655a — I, 258b, 401a; V, 658b, 659a
Zaynābād i, 1331a — I, 1371b
al-Zaynabī, Abu ʾl-Ḳāsim s, 193a — S, 194a
al-Zaynabī, ʿAlī b. Ṭarrād iii, 327b — III, 337b
Zaynal Khān v, 33b — V, 34b
Zaytūn ii, 1063a — II, 1087b
Zaytūna s, 334a — S, 334a
Zayyān b. Mardanīsh iv, 673a — IV, 700b
al-Zayyānī, Abu ʾl-Ḳāsim i, 315b, 593b; ii, 874b; iii, 806a; s, 401b — I, 325a, 613a; II, 895a; III, 829b; S, 402a
Zayyānid(e)s → Zayānid(e)s
al-Zayyāt, AbūṬālib iii, 963b — III, 988a
Zāzā ii, 193a, 1139b — II, 199a, 1166b
Zeʿāmet i, 1266b — I, 1305a, b
Zēbākī i, 225a — I, 231b
Zehrā Khanïm ii, 980a — II, 1002b
Zeila → Ẓaylaʿ
Zekī Welīdī → Togan, Zekī
Zemmūr i, 84b, 171b; s, 144b — I, 87a, 176a; S, 144b
Zenāga (Morocco/Maroc) ii, 885a — II, 905b
Zenāga → Ṣanhādja
Zenāta → Zanāta
Zenghī b. Bursuḳ i, 1336b — I, 1377a
Zengi ʿImād al-Dīn → Zankī
Zenkid(e)s → Zangid(e)s
Zenobia → al-Zabbāʾ
Zenta iii, 193b — III, 198a
Zerdabi, Ḥasan Bey Melikov ii, 476b — II, 488b
Zerzāya iii, 139a — III, 142a
Žha → Djuḥā
Zhana ii, 25a — II, 25b
Zhōb (river/rivière) s, 329b — S, 329a
Zhukotin i, 1305b — I, 1345b
Zhūpīn iii, 197a — III, 202a
Zia ul-Haqq v, 1082a — V, 1079b
Zibel → Djabala
al-Zibriḳān b. Badr i, 343b; iii, 641a; iv, 832b — I, 354a; III, 662b; IV, 865b
Zīdj i, 393a, 1141a; ii, 504a, 578b, 584b, 586b; iii, 8b, 928b, 969b, 1136a, b, 1137b; iv, 517b; v, 47a — I, 404b, 1175b; II, 516b, 593a, 599a, 601a; III, 9a, 953a, 994a, 1164a, 1165a, 1166a; IV, 540a; V, 48a
Zigana mountains/monts i, 462b — I, 476a
Ẓihāfāt i, 671b, 672a — I, 692a, b
Ẓihār iv, 688a — IV, 716b
Zikrawayh b. Mihrawayh i, 96a; iv, 198b, 660b, 661a; v, 1242b — I, 98b; IV, 207a, 687a, b; V, 1233b
Ẓill al-Sulṭān, Mīrzā Masʿūd iv, 105a, 392a, 393b, 979a; s, 53a, 54b, 302a — IV, 109b, 110a, 408b, 410b, 1011b; S, 53b, 55a, 301b
Zimān ii, 324a, 325a — II, 334a, b
Zimma i, 87b — I, 90a
Zināʾ i, 29b, 910b; ii, 551a; iii, 20b — I, 30a, 938a; II, 564b; III, 21b
Zindīḳ i, 11b, 17b, 127b; ii, 228a, 236b; iv, 16b, 771b, 1003b; v, 1238b — I, 11b, 18b, 131a; II, 235a, 243b; IV, 17b, 802b, 1035b; V, 1229a
Zindj i, 145a, 278b, 279a — I, 149b, 287b
Zindjibar Ḳalʿesi iv, 580b — IV, 603b
Zionism ii, 912b, 913a
Zirāʿa ii, 899a — II, 920a
Zīrak ii, 629a; s, 105b — II, 644b; S, 105a
Zīrbādh (island/île) s, 223a — S, 223a
Zīrī b. ʿAṭiyya i, 860a; iii, 819a, 1043a; v, 1176b, 1177a, b — I, 884a; III, 842b, 1069a; V, 1166b, 1167a, b
Zīrī b. Manād i, 699a, 1309a; ii, 495a; iv, 459a; v, 1176a — I, 720b, 1349b; II, 507b; IV, 479b; V, 1166a
Zīrid(e)s i, 6a, 9a, 43b, 491b, 533a, 699b, 863a, 986b, 1148b, 1175b, 1204b, 1309a, 1341a; ii, 145b, 747b, 1012a, b, 1015a; iii, 137a, 138b, 324b, 386a; iv, 337a, 651a; v, 503b, 1182a, b — I, 6b, 9b, 45a, 506a, 549a, 720b, 887a, 1017a, 1183a, 1210b, 1240b, 1349a, 1381b; II, 149b, 766a, 1035b, 1036a, 1038b; III, 139b, 141b, 334b, 398b; IV, 351b, 677b; V, 507a, 1172a, b
Zirih → Zarah
Zirīhgarān ii, 85b, 86b; iv, 343a; v, 285b — II, 87a, 88a; IV, 357b; V, 284a
Ziryāb i, 83a, 600b; ii, 1072a; v, 743b — I, 85b, 620b; II, 1096b; V, 749a
Ziwar Pasha → Aḥmad Ziwar Pasha
Ẓiyā Gökalp → Gökalp
Ẓiyā Pasha i, 62a, 630a; ii, 466a, 474a, 682b, 878a; iii, 357a, 1188a; iv, 196a, 877a; s, 324b — I, 651a; II, 478a, 486a, 699a, 898b; III, 368b, 1218a; IV, 204b, 910a; S, 324a
Ziyād b. ʿAbd Allāh b. ʿAdjlān al-Hamdānī s, 400b — S, 401a
Ziyād b. Abī Sufyān i, 3b, 86a, 195a, 1085b; iv, 14a, b, 491b; v, 346b — I, 4a, 88b, 200b, 1117b, 1118a; IV, 15a, 16a, 512b; V, 347b
Ziyād b. Abīhi i, 107a, 111b, 385a, 1313b, 1343b; ii, 232a, 323b, 480b, 788a; iii, 40b, 42a, 224b, 545a, 782a, 1254b, 1265b; iv, 222a, 755a; v, 1111a; s, 26a, 133b, 157a — I, 110a, 114b, 396a, 1353b, 1384a; II, 238b, 333a, 493a, 807a; III, 42a, 44a, 231b, 564a, 805b, 1287b, 1298a; IV, 232a, 785b; V, 1107a; S, 26a, 133a, 157a
Ziyād b. Khalfūn iv, 829b — IV, 862b
Ziyād b. Khaṣafa v, 19b — V, 20a

Ziyād b. Labīd al-Anṣarī s, 337b — S, 337a
Ziyād b. Ṣāliḥ i, 103b, 1294a; iv, 16a; v, 854b, 855a — I, 106b, 1333b; IV, 17b; V, 861a, b
Ziyād b. Sumayya s, 354b — S, 354b
Ziyād al-Aʿdjam i, 74a — I, 76a
Ziyādat Allāh I b. Ibrāhīm i, 248a, 250a, 619b; iv, 822a, 827b, 829b — I, 256a, 258a, 639a; IV, 855a, 860a, 862b
Ziyādat Allāh II b. Muḥammad i, 250b — I, 258a
Ziyādat Allāh III b. ʿAbd Allāh i, 104a, 249a, 250b — I, 107a, 257a, 258b
Ziyādāt al-thiḳāt iii, 26a — III, 27a
Ziyādid(e)s i, 551a, 551b, 552a, 932a; v, 895b; s, 338a — I, 568b, 569a, 569b, 960b; V, 901b; S, 337a
Ziyādoghlu iv, 389a — IV, 404b
Ziyaeddin Fahri Findikoğlu → Fîndîḳoghlu
Ziyāra ii, 585b; iii, 953a; iv, 352a; v, 1201a — II, 600a; III, 977b; IV, 367b; V, 1191b
Ziyāratnāma s, 95a — S, 94b
Ziyārid(e)s i, 1354b; ii, 192b; iv, 358a; s, 235a, 363a — I, 1393b; II, 198b; IV, 373b; S, 235a, 363a
Zlā, Banū iv, 828b — IV, 861b
Zlīṭen (Zalīṭan) s, 93a — S, 92b
Zmāla ii, 173a — II, 178a
Zog, King/le roi i, 657b; v, 285a — I, 678b; V, 283b
Zolota ii, 119b — II, 122a
Zoology/Zoologie → Ḥayawān
Zōrāwar Singh i, 1004b — I, 1035b
Zoroaster iv, 12b; v, 1112b — IV, 13b; V, 1109a
Zoroastrians/Zoroastriens → Madjūs
Zorṭalbī ii, 597b, 598a — II, 612b
Zoṭṭ → Zuṭṭ
Zouaves → Zwāwa
Zouila → Zawīla
Zraḳī, Banū v, 459b — V, 462a
Zubāla, Ḳaṣr s, 198b, 199b — S, 198b, 199b
al-Zubāra ii, 177b; iv, 751a, 752a, 953b — II, 183a; IV, 781b, 782a, 986a
Zubayd, Banū i, 1096b — I, 1129b
Zubayda Khātūn bint Djaʿfar i, 107b, 505b, 897a, 909b, 1233a; iv, 653a, 694b; s, 198b, 199a — I, 111a, 568a, 924a, 937b, 1269b; IV, 679b, 723a; S, 198b, 199a
al-Zubaydī al-Ishbīlī i, 501b; iv, 501a; v, 606a, 608a; s, 306a, 388a — I, 516b; IV, 522b; V, 610a, 612a; S, 306a, 388b
al-Zubayr b. ʿAbd al-Muṭṭalib iii, 389b; s, 37a — III, 401b; S, 37b
al-Zubayr b. al-ʿAwwām i, 1a, 43b, 109b, 152b, 308a, 381b, 382a, 383a, 451a, 482a, 713b, 738a; ii, 414b, 415b; iii, 209b, 1165b; iv, 521b; s, 44b, 89b, 267b — I, 1a, 44b, 112b, 157a, 317b, 392b, 393a, 394a, 464a, 496b, 735b, 760a; II, 425a, 426b; III, 215b, 1194a; IV, 544a; S, 44b, 89b, 267a
al-Zubayr b. Bakkār i, 793b; ii, 1029b; iii, 757a, 820a, 878a — I, 816b; II, 1053a; III, 780a, 843b, 902a
Zubayr b. al-Māhūẓ i, 810b — I, 833b
Zubayr Pasha s, 164b — S, 164b
Zubayr Rāghī i, 852b — I, 876a
al-Zubayr Raḥma Manṣūr i, 49b, 929a, 962a, 1156b; ii, 123b; v, 1248b — I, 51a, 957b, 991b, 1191a; II, 126b; V, 1239a
al-Zubayrī i, 591a — I, 610b
Zubayrid(e)s i, 1086a — I, 1118a
Zubdat al-Mulk → ʿUthmān Khān
Zudjādj iv, 135a; v, 107a, 397b — IV, 141a; V, 109b, 398b
Ẓufār i, 76b, 539b, 872b; v, 71a; s, 22a, 234b, 338b, 339b — I, 79a, 556a, 896b; V, 73a; S, 22b, 234b, 338a, 339a
Zufar b. al Ḥārith al-Kilābī i, 76b; ii, 523b, 1023b; iii, 1175b; iv, 493a, 655a; v, 541a — I, 78b; II, 536b, 1047b; III, 1204a; IV, 514b, 681a; V, 545b
Zufar b. al-Hudhayl i, 124a; iii, 163a; iv, 269b — I, 127b; III, 166a; IV, 281b
Zughārī → Zaghārī
Zughba i, 374a; iii, 137b, 386a; v, 1179a — I, 385a; III, 140b, 398b; V, 1169a
Zuhab iv, 978b; v, 170a — IV, 1011a; V, 167b
Zuhāb, treaty of/traité de iii, 1257a — III, 1290a
Zuḥal s, 153b — S, 153b
Zuhara s, 153b — S, 153b
Zuhayr (ʿĀmirid(e)) i, 1310a — I, 1350a
Zuhayr b. Abī Sulmā ii, 1023a; iii, 641a; iv, 744b; s, 304b — II, 1047a; III, 662a; IV, 774b; S, 304a
Zuhayr b. Djadhīma al-ʿAbsī ii, 1023a; iii, 285b; s, 177a — II, 1046b; III, 294b; S, 178a
Zuhayr b. Djanāb al-Kalbī ii, 1024a; iv, 421a, 492b — II, 1047b; IV, 439b, 513b
Zuhayr b. al-Ḳayn al-Badjalī iii, 608b, 610a — III, 629b, 631a
Zuhayr al-Balawī ii, 160b; iii, 271a; iv, 403a; v, 518a, b — II, 165b; III, 279a; IV, 420b; V, 522a
Zühdī Pasha ii, 682b — II, 699b
Zuhra b. Kilāb, Banū iv, 896b; s, 81b — IV, 929b; S, 81b
Zuhra Bēgam i, 296a — I, 305a
al-Zuhrī, Muḥammad b. Abī Bakr ii, 585a; iv, 383b, 1078a — II, 599b; IV, 400b, 1110a
al-Zuhrī, Muḥammad b. Muslim ii, 888b; iii, 24a, 494b; v, 731a; s, 310b, 311a, b, 358a, 386b — II, 909a; III, 25a, 511b; V, 736a; S, 310a, b, 311a, 358a, 386b
al-Ẓuhūr iii, 658a — III, 679a
Ẓuhūri i, 1203a; iv, 69a — I, 1238b; IV, 73a
Zūiya i, 763b — I, 786a
Zūḳ Mīkhāʾīl s, 33b — S, 33b
al-Zuḳur i, 535b — I, 551b
Zulālī iv, 69a — IV, 72b
Zülālī Ḥasan Efendi v, 642b, 643b — V, 646b, 647b
Zulātī, Abu ʾl-Ḥasan i, 780a — I, 803b
Zuldjū iv, 708a — IV, 736a
Ẓulla → Ṣuffa
Zunbīl ii, 1048b; iii, 715b, 716a, 717b; iv, 356b, 536a; v, 541b; s, 125b — II, 1073a; III, 738a, b, 739b; IV, 372a, 559a; V, 546a; S, 124b
Zunnār ii, 228a; iii, 77b — II, 235a; III, 80a
Zurʿa b. ʿĪsā b. Nasṭūrus ii, 858a — II, 878a
Zurʿa b. Tibbān Asʿad → Dhū Nuwās
Zurayʿid(e)s i, 181b, 552a, 1214b; iii, 125b, 134a; iv, 200b; v, 602a, 895b, 954b, 1244b; s, 236a, 338a — I, 186b, 570a, 1251a; III, 128b, 136b; IV, 209a; V, 606a, 901b, 958a, 1235a; S, 236a, 337b
Zurayḳ, Cōstī (Ḳusṭanṭīn) iv, 783a — IV, 814b
Zūrkhāna ii, 433a; iv, 8b — II, 444b; IV, 9b
Zurna ii, 1027b — II, 1051b
Zurvān iv, 12b — IV, 13b
Zuṭṭ i, 761b, 789b, 1005b, 1086a, 1094b, 1095a, 1096a, 1292b; ii, 36a, 40b, 456b; iii, 488a; iv, 534b, 1024b; v, 817b; s, 163a, 243a — I, 784b, 813a, 1036a, 1118b, 1127a, 1128a, b, 1332a; II, 36b, 41b, 468b; III, 500a; IV, 557b, 1057a; V, 823b; S, 163a, 243a → Djaṭ
Zwāwa iv, 362a — IV, 378a

For Reference

Not to be taken from this room